THEORIES OF
POLITICAL PROCESSES

THEORIES OF POLITICAL PROCESSES

A Bibliographic Guide to the Journal Literature, 1965–1995

Compiled by
GREGORY G. BRUNK

Bibliographies and Indexes in Law and Political Science,
Number 27

GREENWOOD PRESS
Westport, Connecticut • London

Library of Congress Cataloging-in-Publication Data

Brunk, Gregory G.
    Theories of political processes : a bibliographic guide to the
journal literature, 1965–1995 / compiled by Gregory G. Brunk.
        p.   cm.—(Bibliographies and indexes in law and political
science, ISSN 0742–6909 ; no. 27)
    Includes bibliographical references (p.) and indexes.
    ISBN 0–313–30259–6 (alk. paper)
    1. Political science literature—Bibliography.   I. Title.
II. Series.
Z7161.A2B76   1997
[JA71]
016.320'01—dc21   96–52498

British Library Cataloguing in Publication Data is available.

Library of Congress Catalog Card Number: 96–52498
ISBN: 0–313–30259–6
ISSN: 0742–6909

First published in 1997

Greenwood Press, 88 Post Road West, Westport, CT 06881
An imprint of Greenwood Publishing Group, Inc.

Printed in the United States of America

The paper used in this book complies with the
Permanent Paper Standard issued by the National
Information Standards Organization (Z39.48–1984).

10 9 8 7 6 5 4 3 2 1

CONTENTS

Introduction	vii	Ethics	42
Journal Specializations	ix	Altruism	44
Journal Abbreviations	xvii	Cooperation	44
Attitudes and Beliefs	1	Human Rights	45
Belief Systems and Ideology	2	Justice	46
Foreign Policy Attitudes	5	Norms	47
Surveys	6	Public Ethics	47
Values	7	Tolerance	49
Citizen Participation	8	International Relations	50
Direct Democracy	9	Alliances	53
Turnout	10	Arms Races	54
Voting Behavior	11	Foreign Aid	55
Domestic Conflict	15	International Conflict	55
Coups d'Etat	16	Military Deterrence	56
Revolution	17	Military Establishments	57
Riots and Social Movements	18	Nuclear Weapons	59
Strikes and Unions	19	War	59
Terrorism	20	World Systems	63
Dynamic Processes	22	Legal and Criminal Studies	64
Catastrophes	23	Constitutions	65
Chaos	23	Crime and Punishment	66
Complexity	24	Deterrence	69
Economic Cycles	25	Gun Control	69
Socio-Political Cycles	26	Homicide and Death Penalty	69
Economic Policy	27	Judicial Politics	70
Domestic Economic Policy	28	Policing	72
Employment	29	Subcultures of Violence	72
Growth and Industrial Policy	30	Legislatures and Executives	73
Income and Savings	34	Cabinets	74
Inflation	35	Chief Executives	74
Regulation	36	Committees	76
Taxes	38	Constituencies	77
Trade and Tariffs	40	Leaders and Careers	78

Legislative Behavior   79
Legislative Parties   81
Margins and Turnover   82
Roll Call Voting   83
Vote Trading and Pork   84
Minority Politics   86
Affirmative Action   86
Discrimination   87
Election of Minorities   88
Gender and Politics   89
Racial and Ethnic Politics   92
Organizational Behavior   95
Administration   96
Bureaucratic Behavior   97
Crisis Decision Making   98
Government Size   99
Organizational Ecology   100
Voluntary Associations   101
Policy Analysis   102
Approaches   103
Biopolitics   104
Evaluation and Utilization   105
Innovation and Diffusion   106
Political Communication   108
Agenda Setting   109
Media Effects   110
News Coverage   110
Political Campaigns   111
Political Economy   112
Budgets   113
Economics and Elections   114
Interest Groups   117
International Debt   119
Political Business Cycle   119
Public and Private Goods   120
Rent Seeking   122
Political Geography   123
Contagion and Neighborhoods   124
Location and Migration   125
Political Culture and Region   126
Political Parties   129
Campaign Finance   130
Conventions and Nominations   130
General Elections   131
Identification   133

Interparty Competition   134
Machines and Corruption   134
Party Systems   136
Realignments   137
Political Systems   138
Communism   139
Democracy   139
Federalism   140
Imperialism   141
Military Regimes   142
Political Development   142
Socialism   143
Religion and Politics   144
Churches   144
Economics and Society   145
Policy Concerns   145
Political Participation   146
Social Choice   147
Coalitions   149
Collective Action   150
Electoral Systems   150
Fuzzy Logic   152
Game Theory and Simulations   153
Impossibility Theorems   154
Median Voter   155
Paradoxes   155
Power   156
Rationality   156
Risk and Uncertainty   157
Spatial Models   158
Strategic Manipulation   159
Social Policy   160
Abortion   160
Demography and Health   161
Education   162
Poverty   164
State and Local   164
Welfare   167
Technology and Resources   169
Agriculture and Rural Areas   169
Environment and Resources   170
Science and Technology   171
Miscellaneous   173
Author Index   179
Subject Index   215

INTRODUCTION

Not only has there been a tremendous increase in the number of political science journals since the middle 1960s, but similar increases have occurred in all the other social sciences, as well. Consequently, the problem of keeping track of the literature has greatly multiplied because the journals of many disciplines now routinely publish papers of major theoretical importance for students of politics and public policy.

Ironically, a number of detrimental consequences have resulted from this seemingly positive explosion of scholarly writings. For one, the literature on politics and policy is highly balkanized. This has contributed to the "sects and cults" characteristic of political science in which the members of each specialized group know the contours of their own literature very well, but are largely ignorant of writings in other subfields. Also, it has become so difficult to keep abreast of the important advances in more than a few subfields that there is the real possibility of totally missing an important theoretical development because it has not yet penetrated your particular areas of interest.

This current situation is most unfortunate since similar sorts of theoretical models are used by many different disciplines, but because of our myopia, political scientists often have overlooked important theoretical advances made by others since at first glance they do not appear to be directly relevant to our own, highly specialized research. So another annoying result of the inability to easily access all the theoretical literature is that researchers in widely scattered fields repeatedly have stumbled upon the same theoretical problems without realizing what they viewed as new already had been discussed in a separate scholarly literature.

While two decades ago professors commonly handed out mimeographed listings of relevant journal literature to their graduate classes, many of us now find even this effort is no longer practical. The overwhelming volume of literature must be a particular nightmare to Ph.D. candidates, who are expected to demonstrate some knowledge of its contours on their exams. How can they hope to gain more than a superficial overview of the scholarly writings without a general guide to the literature? This is mirrored among faculty since only a few of us are willing to teach the "scope of the discipline" course as most of us only grasp a small part of contemporary political science, and cannot be sure our understanding accurately reflects the major theoretical trends.

Such problems are exacerbated further by the fact that relatively few general reviews have been published about many specific topics, and those that have been published can be very difficult to locate. Today most of us are on our own in trying to trace a particular topic of theoretical interest. Even with the availability of computer data bases, you still have to know something about what has been published in order to search for it, and many of the important theoretical papers on politics and policy are not listed in any obvious sources, and certainly not in any single source. Eventually we may master one or two fields in detail, but all of us have problems in trying to explore a new area of research. If we get lucky, we will find a particularly relevant article. If we are not lucky, we will never find it. Still worse, given the dispersion and the volume of the journal literature, most of the time we have no way of knowing if we have discovered all the writings of theoretical important for our research.

Faced with this situation, the possibility of anyone mastering the general landscape of contemporary social science has seemed remote, and we consider ourselves lucky if we can find the material that has been published in our own areas of specialization. This is unfortunate as major intellectual advances often occur when techniques and ideas are borrowed from disciplines that at first seem to have little to do with one's traditional interests.

What political scientists have needed for a long time is a general guide to the theoretical journal literature on politics and policy. Such a guide should point to the major papers published in the empirical subdisciplines; the theoretically interesting problems that are being discussed by contemporary scholars; the review articles and symposium issues providing overviews of the research published in specialized areas; and the unique, interesting papers that deal with topics so unusual that only one or two authors have addressed them.

The purpose of this work is to provide such a reference, and in producing it I have tried to cast my theoretical net very broadly. I not only included articles dealing directly with empirical theories of politics and policy, but searched the literatures of many disciplines for models and theories that have potential applicability for the study of politics. While individual citations are only provided for the important English language papers, all the important symposium issues that I have identified are listed, no matter what the usual language of the journal.

Over a decade ago I started searching bibliographies to identify interesting papers appearing to offer theoretical insights into politics. In the summers I went to various university libraries and spent a week or so in their periodical reading rooms searching for the potentially interesting papers. This also gave me time to review journals of various other disciplines. If I saw a paper of particular interest to my current research, I photocopied it. If it was potentially important for my future work, I made a note about its contents, and included the citation in an ever expanding bibliography.

On reflecting about a decade's work, I realized that I had examined over 250,000 article titles, and had reviewed contents of at least 10,000 of them. (In putting together a general bibliography it helps if you can speed read!) From this large mass of articles I distilled a listing of about two percent of all the papers published on politics and policy, having discovered that only about this proportion is particularly useful from a theoretical standpoint. Most of the other papers are descriptive, historical or other types of writings that are not helpful in any direct way to the theory building process.

To ensure that the most complete coverage was given to all types of important theoretical journal literature on politics, I then contacted numerous other political scientists, told them about this project, and asked if they would contribute. Specifically, I asked if they could review the material in their areas of specialization and provide me with lists of the following sorts of articles:

Papers of major theoretical importance.
Papers addressing issues not discussed elsewhere.
Papers offering empirical tests of theories.
Papers providing broad reviews of the literature.
Papers from non-political science journals that
    provide major insights into politics or policy.

The class reading lists, research bibliographies and general reviews that they provided me were used as a means to cross-check my citations and to ensure that the most important works in each subfield are listed. Their input was particularly important since my initial methodology had a major flaw: it is not always possible to identify the most important papers in a subfield from titles. If the title of an article outside of my areas of specialization did not appear to be particularly interesting, I did not physically search it out and review it. By consulting with specialists I have tried to correct this omission by including the papers commonly cited by researchers in all the various theoretical subfields of political science and public policy. Hopefully, the end result contains most of the important and interesting papers that have been published.

After all the various citations were collected, I discovered that many important papers on politics do not have just a narrow scope. Instead, they often are cited by scholars in quite different areas of specialization. So rather than always following the traditional subfield boundaries, many of the categories used in this reference are thematic.

These represent the major problems addressed in contemporary research, and were determined *after* all the citations were gathered, rather than defined in an *a priori*, and somewhat arbitrary fashion. When a reasonable number of interesting papers was identified on a particular topic, it was given a separate category in this reference. Other important papers are in a miscellaneous section, and all of them can be accessed using the subject and author indexes.

As my major emphasis is on theoretical contributions and tests of theories, traditional approaches are only included if a new framework is discussed in a traditional format. Accordingly, studies in comparative politics dealing with theoretically important issues are listed, but just historical accounts are not. As another example of this rule, an extensive listing is included of articles that test the proposals of such contemporary theorists as John Rawls, whose *Theory of Justice* has major importance for empirical research, but the purely historical and philosophical discussions common in many political theory articles are not cited.

The majority of the political science papers that are published each year are descriptive, rather than empirical tests or theoretical expositions. By adopting a criterion of theoretical importance, this allowed me to produce a bibliography of contemporary scholarship that is a manageable length, whereas a comprehensive listing of all the papers published on politics and public policy would cite perhaps half a million articles and run to dozens of volumes.

To produce the successive drafts of this work I went to various university libraries and physically scanned most of the papers published over the last thirty years in all the major political science journals and those of many other disciplines. I then examined all the article titles in a quarter century of *ABC Polsci*, the last decade of *The Journal of Economic Literature*, and innumerable bibliographies, including those in the APSA's *Political Science: The State of the Discipline*. This amounted to scanning well over 250,000 article titles, many of them having been published in obscure journals from the standpoint of political science. I then attempted to trace and verify the actual contents of the most potentially interesting of these articles in order to ensure they would be of use to theoretically mined students of politics and public policy.

Finally, I contacted other political scientists, and a few scholars in related disciplines, and asked if they had access to any other useful material for this project. Many of them responded by sending me the bibliographies they had collected for their specialized fields. This information was used to verify the citations already collected and supplemented my listings. Without such help this effort would not have been nearly as successful. In particular, I would like to thank Joel Aberbach, James David Barber, Stephen Bennett, Steven Brams, Jeff Cohen, Stephen Craig, Robert Darcy, Paul Diehl, Robert Golembiewski, Kennith Hunter, Gary King, Vincent Mahler, Don Maletz, Cliff Morgan, Samuel Patterson, Fred Shelley, Steve Sloan, and Howard Tamashiro, who provided extensive materials used in producing this reference.

JOURNAL SPECIALIZATIONS

African and Asian Politics

Africa
Africa Report
Africa Today
African Studies
African Studies Review
African Urban Studies
Asian Affairs
Asian Survey
Asian Thought and Society
Australian Journal of Political Science
Australian Journal of Politics and History
Australian Outlook
Australian Quarterly
Cahiers d'Etudes Africaines
Canadian Journal of African Studies
Chinese Economic Studies
Europe-Asia Studies
Geneve-Afrique
India Quarterly
Indian Journal of Political Science
Indian Journal of Politics
Indian Political Science Review
International Journal of Middle Eastern Studies
Journal of Arab Affairs
Journal of Asian and African Studies
Journal of Asian Studies
Journal of Japanese Studies
Journal of Modern African Studies
Journal of Palestine Studies
Journal of Southeast Asian Studies
Journal of Southern African Studies
Journal of the Japanese and International Economies
Melbourne Journal of Politics
Middle East Journal
Middle Eastern Studies
Modern Asian Studies
Modern China
Pacific Affairs
Pakistan Horizon
Political Science (New Zealand)
Politikon (South Africa)
Rural Africa
Southeast Asian Journal of Social Science
South East Asian Review

Cliometrics (Quantitative History)

American Historical Review
Comparative Studies in Society and History

Cycles
Economic History Review
Explorations in Economic History
Historical Methods
Historical Social Research
International Review of Social History
Journal of Economic History
Journal of European Economic History
Journal of Historical Geography
Journal of Interdisciplinary History
Journal of Psychohistory
Journal of Social History
Social Science History
Scandinavian Economic History Review

Communication Studies

Central States Speech Journal
Communication
Communication Monographs
Communication Quarterly
Communication Research
Communication Yearbook
Critical Studies in Mass Communication
Discourse and Society
European Journal of Communication
Human Communication Research
Journal of Broadcasting and Electronic Media
Journal of Communications
Journalism Quarterly
Mass Communication Research
Media, Culture and Society
Newspaper Research Journal
Nordicom Review of Nordic Mass Communication
    Research
Political Communication
Southern Speech Communication Journal
Speech Monographs

Comparative Politics (General)

Canadian Review of Studies in Nationalism
Communist and Post-Communist Studies
Comparative Economic Studies
Comparative Political Studies
Comparative Politics
Comparative Social Research
Economic Development and Cultural Change
European Journal of Political Research
Government and Opposition

International Journal of Comparative Sociology
International Migration Review
International Political Science Review
International Review of Law and Economics
Journal of Area Studies
Journal of Common Market Studies
Journal of Commonwealth and Comparative Politics
Journal of Communist Studies
Journal of Comparative Economics
Journal of Comparative Revolutions
Journal of Economic Development
Journal of International and Comparative Politics
New York University Journal of International Law
    and Politics
Plural Societies
Problems of Communism
Revue Internationale de Droit Compare
Rivista Internazionale di Scienze Economiche e
    Commerciali
Studies in Comparative Communism
Third World Quarterly
Universal Human Rights

Conflict and Peace Studies

Conflict
Conflict Quarterly
Conflict Management and Peace Science
Cooperation and Conflict
International Journal of Group Tensions
International Journal on World Peace
Journal of Conflict Resolution
Journal of Interpersonal Violence
Journal of Peace Research
SAIS Review
Simulation and Gaming
Papers of the Peace Research Society
Peace and Change
Peace Research
Peace Research Reviews
Studies in Conflict and Terrorism
Terrorism

Demography and Health Policy

Demography
Human Resources Development Quarterly
Inquiry
International Migration
Journal of Health and Human Resources Administration
Journal of Health Economics
Journal of Health Politics, Policy and Law
Journal of Human Resources
Journal of Population Economics
Journal of Safety Research
Journal of Studies on Alcohol
Population and Development Review
Population and Environment
Population Research and Policy Review
Population Studies

Development Studies

Canadian Journal of Development Studies
Development and Change
Developing Economics
Economic Development and Cultural Change
Economic Development Quarterly
International Development
International Trade and Economic Development
Journal of Developing Areas
Journal of Development Economics

Journal of Development Studies
Journal of Economic Development
Manchester School of Economics and Social Studies
Problems of Economic Transition
Studies in Comparative International Development
World Development

Economics and Business

Acta Oeconomica
American Economic Review
American Journal of Economics
American Journal of Economics and Sociology
Antitrust Bulletin
Atlantic Economic Journal
Australian Economic Papers
Australian Economic Review
Bell Journal of Economic and Management Science
British Review of Economic Issues
Brookings Papers on Economic Activity
Bulletin of Economic Research
Business Economics
Business History Review
Cahiers Economiques de Bruxelles
Cambridge Journal of Economics
Canadian Journal of Economics
Computational Economics
Contemporary Economic Policy
Developing Economics
Eastern Economic Journal
Eastern European Economics
Econometrica
Economica
Economic and Social Review
Economic Inquiry
Economic Journal
Economic Notes
Economic Policy: A European Forum
Economic Record
Economic Review (Keizai Kenkyu)
Economics and Industrial Democracy
Economics and Policy
Economics and Politics
Economics Letters
Economics of Planning
Economie Appliquee
Economies et Societes
Empirical Economics
European Economic Review
European Journal of Law and Economics
European Journal of Political Economy
Federal Reserve Bank of Atlanta Economic Review
Federal Reserve Bank of Minneapolis Quarterly Review
Federal Reserve Bank of Richmond Economic Review
Federal Reserve Bank of San Francisco Economic
    Review
Federal Reserve Bank of St. Louis Review
Federal Reserve Bank of New York Economic Policy
    Review
Fiscal Studies
German Economic Review
Harvard Economic Review
History of Political Economy
Indian Economic Journal
Information Economics and Policy
Interamerican Economic Affairs
International Economic Review
International Economic Journal
International Journal of Social Economics
International Monetary Fund Staff Papers
International Review of Applied Economics
International Review of Law and Economics
Jahrbucher fur Nationalokonomie und Statistik
Journal of Advertising
Journal of Advertising Research
Journal of Banking and Finance

Journal of Behavioral Decision-Making
Journal of Behavioral Economics
Journal of Business
Journal of Business Ethics
Journal of Consumer Affairs
Journal of Comparative Economics
Journal of Cultural Economics
Journal of Development Economics
Journal of Econometrics
Journal of Economic Behavior and Organization
Journal of Economic Issues
Journal of Economic Literature
Journal of Economic Perspectives
Journal of Economic Studies
Journal of Economic Surveys
Journal of Economic Theory
Journal of Economics
Journal of Economics and Business
Journal of Futures Markets
Journal of Industrial Economics
Journal of Industrial Relations
Journal of Institutional and Theoretical Economics
Journal of Interdisciplinary Economics
Journal of International Economics
Journal of International Money and Finance
Journal of Land Economics
Journal of Law and Economics
Journal of Macroeconomics
Journal of Managerial and Decision Economics
Journal of Mathematical Economics
Journal of Monetary Economics
Journal of Money, Credit and Banking
Journal of Political Economy
Journal of Post Keynesian Economics
Journal of Public Economics
Journal of Quantitative Economics
Journal of Regulatory Economics
Journal of Research in Islamic Economics
Journal of Socio-Economics
Journal of Studies in Economics and Econometrics
Journal of the American Statistical Association
Journal of the Japanese and International Economics
Journal of Transport Economics and Policy
Journal of Transportation
Keio Economic Studies
Kredit und Kapital
Kykos
Labour Economics
Logistics and Transportation Review
Macroeconomic Annual
Managerial and Decision Economics
Mathematical Social Sciences
Metroeconomica
Natural Resources Journal
New England Economic Review
OECD Economic Studies
Oxford Bulletin of Economics and Statistics
Oxford Economic Papers
Oxford Review of Economic Policy
Problems of Economics
Quarterly Journal of Business and Economics
Quarterly Journal of Economics
Quarterly Review of Economics and Business
Quarterly Review of Economics and Finance
Rand Journal of Economics
Recherches Economiques de Louvain
Review of Applied Economics
Review of Black Political Economy
Review of Business and Economic Research
Review of Economic Studies
Review of Economics and Statistics
Review of Income and Wealth
Review of Political Economy
Review of Social Economy
Revista Espanola de Economia
Revue d'Economie Politique
Revue Economique
Ricerche Economiche

Rivista Internazionale di Scienze Economiche e
   Commerciali
Scandinavian Journal of Economics
Scottish Journal of Political Economy
Singapore Economic Review
Social and Economic Studies
Social Indicators Research
Southern Economic Journal
Statistical Journal
Studies in Economic Analysis
Weltwirtschaftliches Archiv
World Bank Economic Review
World Bank Research Quarterly
Yorkshire Bulletin of Economics and Social Research
Zeitschrift fur Nationalokonomie

Education Policy

American Education Research Journal
American Journal of Education
Applied Measurement in Education
British Journal of Educational Psychology
Comparative Education Review
Economics of Education Review
Education and Urban Society
Educational and Psychological Measurement
Educational Evaluation and Policy Analysis
Journal of Education Finance
Journal of Education Measurement
Oxford Review of Education
Research in Higher Education
Research in Science and Technology Education
Review of Higher Education
Sociology of Education

European Politics

Acta Politica (Netherlands)
Annaire Suisse de Science Politique (Switzerland)
British Journal of Political Science
Canadian-American Slavic Studies
East European Politics and Societies
East European Quarterly
Eastern European Economics
Est-Ovest (Italy)
Europa-Archiv (Germany)
Europe-Asia Studies
European Politics
Internasjonal Politikk (Norway)
Osterreichisches Jahrbuch fur Internationale
   Politik (Austria)
Osteuropa-Wirtschaft
Osteurope
Politico (Italy)
Politiikka (Finland)
Politique Etrangere (France)
Politische Vierteljahresschrift (Germany)
Post-Soviet Affairs
Recherche Sociale (France)
Res Publica (Belgium)
Revue d'Etudes Comparative Est-Ouest (France)
Revue Francaise de Science Politique (France)
Rivista de Estudios Politicos (Spain)
Rivista Italiana di Scienza Politica (Italy)
Revue Internationale de Droit Compare (France)
Scandinavian Political Studies
Schweizerische Zeitschrift fur Volkswirtschaft
   und Statistik (Switzerland)
Slavic Review
Southeastern Europe
Soviet Economy
Soviet Studies
Soviet Union
Statsvetenskaplig Tidskrift (Sweden)

Studies in Comparative Communism
Studies in Soviet Thought
Die Verwaltung (Germany)
West European Politics
Zeitschrift fur Politik (Germany)

Geography

Annals of Regional Science
Annals of the American Association of Geographers
Applied Geography
Area
Canadian Geographer
Canadian Journal of Regional Science
Economic Geography
Ecumene
Environment and Planning A
Environment and Planning B
Environment and Planning C
Environment and Planning D
Geoforum
Geographical Analysis
Geographical Journal
Geographical Perspectives
Geographical Review
Geography
Historical Geography
International Regional Science Review
Journal of Historical Geography
Journal of Land Economics
Journal of Regional Science
Location Science
Political Geography
Professional Geographer
Progress in Human Geography
Regional Science and Urban Economics
Socio-Spatial Dynamics
Transactions of the Institute of British Geographers

International Relations

Australian Journal of International Affairs
Chronique de Politique Etrangere
Diplomacy and Statecraft
Etudes Internationales
Fletcher Forum of World Affairs
Foreign Affairs
Foreign Policy
Foreign Service Journal
International Affairs
International Conciliation
International Interactions
International Organization
International Relations
International Studies
International Studies Journal
International Studies Notes
International Studies Quarterly
Jerusalem Journal of International Relations
Journal of International Affairs
Journal of International and Comparative Politics
Millennium: Journal of International Studies
NATO Review
Orbis
Review of International Studies
Rivista di Studi Politici Internazionali
SAIS Review
Stanford Journal of International Studies
World Affairs
World Economy
World Policy Journal
World Politics

Latin American Politics

Bulletin of Latin American Research
Caribbean Quarterly
Caribbean Studies
Cepal Review
Cuban Studies
Foro Internacional (Mexico)
Journal of Interamerican Studies and World Affairs
Journal of Latin American Studies
Latin American Perspectives
Latin American Research Review
Rivista Brasileira de Estudos Politicos (Brazil)
Rivista Mexicana de Ciencias Politicas y Sociales

Legal and Criminal Studies

American Journal of Comparative Law
American Journal of Jurisprudence
American Journal of Legal History
Boston College International and Comparative Law
    Review
Columbia Journal of Law and Social Problems
Columbia Law Review
Contemporary Crises
Corrective and Social Psychiatry Journal
Crime and Delinquency
Crime and Social Justice
Crime, Law and Social Change
Criminal Justice and Behavior
Criminal Justice Policy Review
Criminology
FBI Law Enforcement Journal
George Washington Law Review
Harvard Journal of Law and Public Policy
Hofstra Law Review
International and Comparative Law Quarterly
International Criminal Police Review
International Journal of Crime and Penology
Journal of Correctional Education
Journal of Criminal Law and Criminology
Journal of Interpersonal Violence
Journal of Law and Economics
Journal of Law and Politics
Journal of Law and Society
Journal of Law, Economics and Organization
Journal of Legal Studies
Journal of Legislation
Journal of Police Science and Administration
Journal of Quantitative Criminology
Journal of Research in Crime and Delinquency
Justice Quarterly
Justice System Review
Law and Contemporary Problems
Law and Human Behavior
Law and Policy Quarterly
Law and Society
Law and Society Review
Law and Transition Quarterly
Police Journal
Prison Decisions
Research in Law and Policy Studies
Response to Family Violence
Rutgers Law Review
Scandinavian Studies in Criminology
Social Justice Review
Stanford Journal of International Law
Stanford Law Review
Texas Law Review
University of Chicago Law Review
University of Pennsylvania Law Review
Villanova Law Review
Wisconsin Law Review
Yale Journal of Law and Humanities
Yale Law Journal

Legislative and Executive Studies

Campaigns and Elections
Congress and the Presidency
Journal of Constitutional and Parliamentary Studies
Legislative Studies Quarterly
Parliamentarian
Parliamentary Affairs
Parliaments, Estates and Representation
Presidential Studies Quarterly

Methodology and Applied Mathematics

American Journal of Political Science
American Statistician
Annales d'Economie et de Statistique
Annals of Economic and Social Measurement
Biometrics
Control and Cybernetics
Cybernetics and Systems
Econometric Reviews
Econometric Theory
Econometrica
Economic Thought and Methodology
Fuzzy Sets and Systems
International Journal of Forecasting
International Statistical Review
Journal for Studies in Economics and Econometrics
Journal of Applied Econometrics
Journal of Bifurcations and Chaos
Journal of Business and Economic Statistics
Journal of Econometrics
Journal of Economic Dynamics and Control
Journal of the American Statistical Association
Journal of the Royal Statistical Society
Mathematical and Computer Modeling
Mathematical Systems Theory
Mathematics of Operations Research
Political Analysis
Political Methodology
Problems of Complex Control Systems
Psychometrika
Review of Economics and Statistics
Simulation: Systems Analysis, Modelling, Simulation
Sociological Methodology
Sociological Methods and Research
System Dynamics Review
Technometrics

Psychology

American Behavioral Scientist
American Psychologist
British Journal of Mathematical and Statistical
    Psychology
Cognitive Psychology
Group and Organization Studies
Journal of Applied Behavioral Research
Journal of Applied Psychology
Journal of Applied Social Psychology
Journal of Community Psychology
Journal of Cross-Cultural Psychology
Journal of Economic Psychology
Journal of Experimental and Social Psychology
Journal of Experimental Psychology
Journal of Mathematical Psychology
Journal of Personal and Social Psychology
Journal of Psychohistory
Journal of Social and Biological Structures
Personality and Social Psychology Bulletin
Political Psychology
Psychological Bulletin
Psychological Review

Small Group Behavior
Social Behavior and Personality
Social Cognition
Social Psychology Quarterly

Public Administration

Academy of Management Journal
Academy of Management Review
Administration
Administration and Policy Journal
Administration and Politics
Administration and Social Work
Administration and Society
Administrative Science Quarterly
Advanced Management Journal
American Review of Public Administration
Annals of Public Administration
British Journal of Industrial Relations
Bureaucrat
California Management Review
Canadian Public Administration
Economic Analysis and Workers' Management
Group and Organization Studies
Harvard Business Review
Industrial and Labor Relations Review
Industrial Relations
International Journal of Organizational Analysis
International Journal of Public Administration
International Labour Review
International Review of Administrative Sciences
Journal of Labor Economics
Journal of Labor Research
Journal of Law, Economics and Organization
Journal of Management
Journal of Management Issues
Journal of Management Science and Policy Analysis
Journal of Policy Analysis and Management
Journal of Public Administration Theory and Research
Journal of the Academy of Management
Korean Journal of Public Administration
Labor History
Labour
Management Review
Management Science
Midwest Review of Public Administration
Organization Development Journal
Organizational Behavior and Human Decision Processes
Organizational Behavior and Human Performance
Personnel Administration
Philippine Journal of Public Administration
Public Administration
Public Administration and Development
Public Administration Review
Public Personnel Management
Public Productivity and Management Review
Public Sector
Research in Organizational Behavior
Review of Industrial Organization
Review of Public Personnel Administration
Social Service Review
Southern Review of Public Administration
Training and Development Journal

Public Finance

Finance Quarterly
Financial Analyst Journal
Financial Review
Finanzarchiv
Government Finance Review
Journal of Finance
Journal of Labor Economics
Journal of Public Economics

National Tax Journal
Public Budgeting and Finance
Public Budgeting and Financial Management
Public Finance

Public Opinion

Campaigns and Elections
Electoral Studies
International Journal of Public Opinion Research
Public Opinion
Public Opinion Quarterly

Public Policy (General)

Alternatives: A Journal of World Policy
Applied Economics
Basic and Applied Social Research
Canadian Public Policy
Carnegie-Rochester Conference Series on Public
    Policy
Cato Journal
Comparative Policy Issues
Contemporary Policy Issues
Decision Sciences
Economics of Planning
Evaluation
Evaluation and Program Planning
Evaluation Quarterly
Evaluation Review
Governance
Government and Policy
Growth and Change
Harvard Journal of Law and Public Policy
International Journal of Sociology and Social Policy
Journal of Applied Behavioral Sciences
Journal of Policy Analysis and Management
Journal of Policy History
Journal of Policy Modeling
Journal of Public Policy
Journal of Risk and Insurance
Journal of Risk and Uncertainty
Journal of Social Policy
Journal of the American Planning Association
Knowledge and Policy
Knowledge: Creation, Diffusion, Utilization
Knowledge in Society
Law and Contemporary Problems
Law and Policy Quarterly
New Left Review
Operations Research
Philosophy and Public Affairs
Planning and Administration
Policy and Politics
Policy Analysis
Policy Review
Policy Sciences
Policy Studies Journal
Policy Studies Review
Public Policy
Quality and Quantity
Regulation
Review of Radical Political Economics
Review of Social Economy
Risk Analysis
Social Theory and Practice
Socio-Economic Planning Sciences
Social Policy
World Policy Review
Yale Journal on Regulation

Regional, State and Local Studies

African Urban Studies
Annals of Regional Science
Canadian Journal of Regional Science
Comparative Urban and Community Research
Comparative Urban Research
Current Municipal Problems
International Journal of Urban and Regional Research
International Regional Science Review
Journal of Peasant Studies
Journal of Regional Science
Journal of State Government
Journal of Urban Affairs
Journal of Urban Economics
Journal of Urban History
Papers of the Regional Science Association
Peasant Studies Newsletter
Policy and Politics
Public Affairs
Public Management
Publius
Regional and Federal Studies
Regional Politics and Policy
Regional Science and Urban Economics
Regional Science Perspectives
Regional Studies
Review of Regional Studies
Rural Africa
Rural Sociology
Spectrum: The Journal of State Government
State Government
State and Local Government Review
Urban Affairs Quarterly
Urban and Social Change Review
Urban Ecology
Urban Geography
Urban Studies

Religious Studies

Journal of Church and State
Journal of Psychology and Theology
Journal for the Scientific Study of Religion
Review of Religious Research
Science of Religion
Social Compass
Sociological Analysis

Resources, Science and Technology

American Journal of Agricultural Economics
British Journal for the History of Science
British Journal for the Philosophy of Science
Bulletin of Science, Technology and Society
Bulletin of the Atomic Scientists
Energy Economics
Energy Journal
Environmental Forum
Environmental Impact Assessment Review
European Review of Agricultural Economics
Historia Mathematica
Historia Scientiarum
Inquiry
Isis
Issues in Science and Technology
Journal of Agricultural and Applied Economics
Journal of Energy and Development
Journal of Environmental Economics and Management
Journal of Environmental Education
Journal of Environmental Systems
Journal of the History of the Behavioral Sciences
Methodology and Science

National Resources Journal
Osiris
Philosophy of Science
Philosophy of the Social Sciences
Politics and the Life Sciences
Research in Science and Technology Education
Research Policy
Resource Management and Optimization
Resources and Energy Economics
Resources Policy
Review of Marketing and Agricultural Economics
Revue d'Histoire des Sciences
Science Exploration
Science and Society
Science in Context
Science of Science
Science, Technology, Human Values
Scientific American
Scientometrics
Social Studies of Science
Sociologica Ruralis
Studies in History and Philosophy of Science
Technology and Culture
Technology Forecasting and Social Change
Technology in Society
Western Journal of Agricultural Economics

Social Choice

American Economic Review
American Political Science Review
Analyse und Kritik
Behavioral Science
Constitutional Political Economy
Economia delle Scelte Pubbliche
Economics and Philosophy
Games and Economic Behavior
International Journal of Game Theory
Journal of Mathematical Sociology
Journal of Public Finance and Public Choice
Journal of Theoretical Politics
Mathematical Modelling
Public Choice
Rationality and Society
Social Choice and Welfare
Theory and Decision

Sociology

Acta Sociologica
American Behavioral Scientist
American Journal of Economics and Sociology
American Sociological Review
Annual Review of Sociology
Behavior Science Research
Behavioral Science
Black Sociologist
British Journal of Sociology
California Sociologist
Development and Change
Environment and Behavior
Ethnic and Racial Studies
Ethnic Groups
Group and Organization Studies
International Journal of Comparative Sociology
International Journal of Political Education
International Journal of Sociology
International Journal of Sociology and Social Policy
International Review of Modern Sociology
International Social Science Journal
Journal of Applied Behavioral Science
Journal of Behavioral Economics
Journal of Human Relations
Journal of Mathematical Sociology

Journal of Social Issues
Mid-American Review of Sociology
Multivariate Behavioral Research
Pacific Sociological Review
Proceedings of the American Philosophical Society
Quality and Quantity
Review of Black Political Economy
Revue Francaise de Sociologie
Rural Sociology
Social Forces
Social Indicators Research
Social Networks
Social Problems
Social Research
Social Science
Social Science Information
Social Science Journal
Social Science Research
Sociological Focus
Sociological Inquiry
Sociological Methods and Research
Sociological Perspectives
Sociological Quarterly
Sociological Spectrum
Sociologische Gids
Sociology
Sociology and Social Research
Sociology of Education
Soviet Sociology
Theory and Research
Youth and Society

Strategic Studies

Armed Forces and Society
Arms Control
Coexistence
Comparative Security Policy
Comparative Strategy
Contemporary Security Policy
Defense Analysis
International Security
Journal of Strategic Studies
JPMS: Journal of Political and Military Sociology
Military Affairs
NATO Review
Naval War College Review
Parameters: US Army War College Quarterly
Royal United Services Institute for Defense
    Studies Journal
Strategic Review

Specialty Journals

Amerasia Journal
American Quarterly
Aztlan (Chicano Studies)
Civilizations
Climate Change
Comparative Frontier Studies
Corruption and Reform
Cuban Studies
Cycles (a Journal Publishing Cyclical Data)
Disasters
Empirical Studies of the Arts
Ethics
Experimental Studies of Politics
Futures (Forecasting)
General Systems Yearbook
Hispanic Behavioral Science Review
Hispanic Journal of Behavioral Sciences
Human Ecology
Human Rights Quarterly
International Migration Review

Journal of American Ethnic History
Journal of American Studies
Journal of Black Studies
Journal of Consumer Research
Journal of Contemporary History
Journal of Democracy
Journal of Environmental Education
Journal of Ethnic Studies
Journal of Libertarian Studies
Journal of Negro History

Micropolitics
Perspectives on Political Science
Plural Societies
Political Anthropology
Review of Public Data Use
Signs: Journal of Women in Culture and Society
Simulation and Gaming
Southern Studies
Women and Politics

JOURNAL ABBREVIATIONS

AAAG	Annals of the Association of American Geographers		CAPCS	Communist and Post-Communist Studies
AAS	Administration and Society		CAR	Corruption and Reform
ABS	American Behavioral Scientist		CC	Contemporary Crises
AC	Arms Control		CE	Computational Economics
AE	Applied Economics		CEA	Cahiers d'Etudes Africaines
AEJ	Atlantic Economic Journal		CEP	Contemporary Economic Policy
AER	American Economic Review		CES	Comparative Economic Studies
AES	Annales d'Economie et de Statistique		CJ	Cato Journal
AFAS	Armed Forces and Society		CJAS	Canadian Journal of African Studies
AFSR	African Studies Review		CJDS	Canadian Journal of Development Studies
AHS	American Historical Review		CJE	Cambridge Journal of Economics
AJAE	American Journal of Agricultural Economics		CJPS	Canadian Journal of Political Science
AJCL	American Journal of Comparative Law		CJPST	Canadian Journal of Political and Social Theory
AJEAS	American Journal of Economics and Sociology		CLASC	Crime, Law and Social Change
AJJ	American Journal of Jurisprudence		CLR	California Law Review
AJLH	American Journal of Legal History		CMAPS	Conflict Management and Peace Science
AJPS	American Journal of Political Science		CMR	California Management Review
AJS	American Journal of Sociology		COMM	Communication Monographs
AMASJ	Amerasia Journal		COMQ	Communication Quarterly
ANNALS	Annals of the American Academy of Political and Social Sciences		COMR	Communication Research
			COMY	Communication Yearbook
ANRS	Annual Review of Sociology		CORLR	Cornell Law Review
AO	Acta Oeconomica		CP	Comparative Politics
AP	Acta Politica		CPA	Canadian Public Administration
APQ	American Politics Quarterly		CPI	Contemporary Policy Issues
APSR	American Political Science Review		CPS	Comparative Political Studies
AQ	Asia Quarterly		CRCSPP	Carnegie-Rochester Conference Series on Public Policy
ARP	Annual Review of Psychology			
ARPA	American Review of Public Administration		CRSN	Canadian Review of Studies in Nationalism
ARS	Annals of Regional Science		CSMC	Critical Studies in Mass Communication
AS	Acta Sociologica		CSR	Comparative Social Research
ASQ	Administrative Science Quarterly		CSSH	Comparative Studies in Society and History
ASR	American Sociological Review		CSSJ	Central States Speech Journal
ASSP	Annuaire Suisse de Science Politique		CUR	Comparative Urban Research
ASUR	Asian Survey		DAC	Development and Change
AT	Africa Today		EAP	Economics and Politics
ATAS	Asian Thought and Society		EAPHIL	Economics and Philosophy
AUSER	Australian Economic Review		EARS	Ethnic and Racial Studies
AUSJPS	Australian Journal of Political Science		EAS	Europe-Asia Studies
AUSQ	Australian Quarterly		EASR	Economic and Social Review
BE	Business Economics		EAUS	Education and Urban Society
BER	Bulletin of Economic Research		ECONR	Economic Record
BJEMS	Bell Journal of Economic and Management Science		EDACC	Economic Development and Cultural Change
			EDQ	Economic Development Quarterly
BJIR	British Journal of Industrial Relations		EE	Empirical Economics
BJPS	British Journal of Political Science		EEH	Explorations in Economic History
BJS	British Journal of Sociology		EEJ	Eastern Economic Journal
BPEA	Brookings Papers on Economic Activity		EEPS	East European Politics and Societies
BS	Behavioral Science		EER	European Economic Review
BSR	Behavior Science Research		EG	Economic Geography
CAC	Cooperation and Conflict		EI	Economic Inquiry
CANJE	Canadian Journal of Economics		EINT	Etudes Internationales
CAP	Congress and the Presidency		EJ	Economic Journal

EJPE	European Journal of Political Economy		ISSJ	International Social Science Journal
EJPR	European Journal of Political Research		JAAS	Journal of Asian and African Studies
EL	Economics Letters		JABS	Journal of Applied Behavioral Science
ELR	Emory Law Review		JAE	Journal of Applied Econometrics
EN	Economic Notes		JAPA	Journal of the American Planning
EOER	Economics of Education Review			Association
EPA	Environment and Planning A		JAS	Journal of Area Studies
EPC	Environment and Planning C		JASA	Journal of the American Statistical
ER	Econometric Reviews			Association
ES	Electoral Studies		JASIAS	Journal of Asian Studies
ESOP	Experimental Study of Politics		JBAES	Journal of Business and Economic Statistics
ET	Econometric Theory		JBEM	Journal of Broadcasting and Electronic
FA	Foreign Affairs			Media
FFWA	Fletcher Forum of World Affairs		JBS	Journal of Black Studies
FRBA	Federal Reserve Bank of Atlanta Economic		JCACP	Journal of Commonwealth and Comparative
	Review			Politics
FRBM	Federal Reserve Bank of Minneapolis		JCCP	Journal of Cross-Cultural Psychology
	Quarterly Review		JCE	Journal of Comparative Economics
FRBNY	Federal Reserve Bank of New York Economic		JCH	Journal of Contemporary History
	Policy Review		JCLAC	Journal of Criminal Law and Criminology
FRBS	Federal Reserve Bank San Francisco Economic		JCMS	Journal of Common Market Studies
	Review		JCON	Journal of Consumer Research
FRBSTL	Federal Reserve Bank of St. Louis Review		JCR	Journal of Conflict Resolution
FS	Fiscal Studies		JCS	Journal of Communist Studies
FUZZY	Fuzzy Sets and Systems		JDA	Journal of Developing Areas
GAC	Growth and Change		JDE	Journal of Development Economics
GAEB	Games and Economic Behavior		JDS	Journal of Development Studies
GAO	Government and Opposition		JEAB	Journal of Economics and Business
GF	Governmental Finance		JEBAO	Journal of Economic Behavior and
GFR	Government Finance Review			Organization
GSY	General Systems Yearbook		JEDAC	Journal of Economic Dynamics and Control
HCR	Human Communication Research		JEE	Journal of Economic Education
HILJ	Harvard International Law Journal		JEEH	Journal of European Economic History
HJBR	Hispanic Journal of Behavioral Sciences		JEEM	Journal of Environmental Economics and
HJLPP	Harvard Journal of Law and Public Policy			Management
HLR	Harvard Law Review		JEH	Journal of Economic History
HPE	History of Political Economy		JEI	Journal of Economic Issues
HR	Human Relations		JEL	Journal of Economic Literature
HRQ	Human Rights Quarterly		JEP	Journal of Economic Perspectives
IA	International Affairs		JEPSY	Journal of Economic Psychology
IACLQ	International and Comparative Law Quarterly		JES	Journal of Economic Surveys
IAS	Issues and Studies		JESTUD	Journal of Economic Studies
IC	International Conciliation		JET	Journal of Economic Theory
IEJ	Indian Economic Journal		JFM	Journal of Futures Markets
IER	International Economic Review		JHR	Journal of Human Relations
II	International Interactions		JHRES	Journal of Human Resources
IJ	International Journal		JIA	Journal of International Affairs
IJCS	International Journal of Comparative		JIAS	Journal of Interamerican Studies and World
	Sociology			Affairs
IJF	International Journal of Forecasting		JIDH	Journal of Interdisciplinary History
IJGT	International Journal of Game Theory		JIE	Journal of International Economics
IJPA	Indian Journal of Public Administration		JIMF	Journal of International Money and Finance
IJPE	International Journal of Political		JITE	Journal of Institutional and Theoretical
	Education			Economics
IJPOR	International Journal of Public Opinion		JJAIE	Journal of the Japanese and International
	Research			Economics
IJPS	Indian Journal of Political Science		JJIR	Jerusalem Journal of International
IJSE	International Journal of Social Economics			Relations
IJURR	International Journal of Urban and Regional		JLAS	Journal of Law and Society
	Research		JLATAS	Journal of Latin American Studies
ILRR	Industrial and Labor Relations Review		JLR	Journal of Labor Research
IMFSP	International Monetary Fund Staff Papers		JLS	Journal of Legal Studies
IMR	International Migration Review		JMAFS	Journal of Modern African Studies
INDREL	Industrial Relations		JMATHE	Journal of Mathematical Economics
INTEJ	International Economic Journal		JMCB	Journal of Money, Credit and Banking
IO	International Organization		JME	Journal of Monetary Economics
IP	Internasjonal Politikk		JMS	Journal of Mathematical Sociology
IPSR	International Political Science Review		JNS	Jahrbucher fur Nationalokonomie und
IR	International Relations			Statistik
IRAE	International Review of Applied Economics		JOC	Journal of Communications
IRAS	International Review of Administrative		JOD	Journal of Democracy
	Sciences		JOE	Journal of Econometrics
IRLE	International Review of Law and Economics		JOL	Journal of Legislation
IRMS	International Review of Modern Sociology		JOLAP	Journal of Law and Politics
IRSR	International Regional Science Review		JOLAS	Journal of Latin American Studies
IS	International Security		JOLE	Journal of Law and Economics
ISN	International Studies Notes		JOLEAO	Journal of Law, Economics and Organizations
ISQ	International Studies Quarterly		JOM	Journal of Macroeconomics

JOP	Journal of Politics	PALS	Politics and the Life Sciences
JOPS	Journal of Peace Science	PANAL	Political Analysis
JORAU	Journal of Risk and Uncertainty	PAP	Policy and Politics
JOTEAP	Journal of Transport Economics and Policy	PAPA	Philosophy and Public Affairs
JPAAM	Journal of Policy Analysis and Management	PAPS	Proceedings American Philosophical Society
JPALS	Journal of Palestine Studies	PAPSC	Proceedings of the Academy of Political Science
JPART	Journal of Public Administration Research and Theory	PAR	Public Administration Review
JPE	Journal of Political Economy	PARLA	Parliamentary Affairs
JPHIL	Journal of Philosophy	PAS	Politics and Society
JPKE	Journal of Post Keynesian Economics	PB	Political Behavior
JPM	Journal of Policy Modeling	PBA	Political Behavior Annual
JPMS	Journal of Political and Military Sociology	PBAF	Public Budgeting and Finance
JPOPE	Journal of Population Economics	PC	Public Choice
JPP	Journal of Public Policy	PE	Politique Etrangere
JPR	Journal of Peace Research	PF	Public Finance
JPS	Journal of Political Science	PFQ	Public Finance Quarterly
JPSP	Journal of Personality and Social Psychology	PG	Political Geography
		PGEO	Professional Geographer
JPUBE	Journal of Public Economics	PI	Public Interest
JQ	Journalism Quarterly	PIHG	Progress in Human Geography
JQE	Journal of Quantitative Economics	PLS	Plural Societies
JRE	Journal of Regulatory Economics	PM	Political Methodology
JRS	Journal of Regional Science	POLAN	Policy Analysis
JRSS	Journal of the Royal Statistical Society	POLCOM	Political Communication
JSAF	Journal of Southern African Studies	POLST	Political Studies
JSBS	Journal of Social and Biological Structures	POPS	Perspectives on Political Science
JSE	Journal of Socio-Economics	POQ	Public Opinion Quarterly
JSEAS	Journal of Southeast Asian Studies	POS	Philosophy of Science
JSEE	Journal of Studies in Economics and Econometrics	PP	Political Psychology
		PPM	Public Personnel Management
JSG	Journal of State Government	PPRS	Papers of the Peace Research Society
JSI	Journal of Social Issues	PQ	Political Quarterly
JSP	Journal of Social Policy	PR	Psychological Review
JSPES	Journal of Social, Political and Economic Studies	PRAPR	Population Research and Policy Review
		PRP	Peace Research Papers
JSSR	Journal for the Scientific Study of Religion	PRQ	Political Research Quarterly
		PRR	Peace Research Reviews
JTP	Journal of Theoretical Politics	PS	PS: Political Science and Politics
JUE	Journal of Urban Economics	PSCI	Policy Sciences
JUH	Journal of Urban History	PSCQ	Political Science Quarterly
KON	Konjunkturpolitik	PSJ	Policy Studies Journal
LACP	Law and Contemporary Problems	PSNZ	Political Science (New Zealand)
LAP	Law and Policy	PSQ	Presidential Studies Quarterly
LAPER	Latin American Perspectives	PSR	Policy Studies Review
LARR	Latin American Research Review	PSYB	Psychological Bulletin
LASR	Law and Society Review	PT	Political Theory
LATR	Logistics and Transportation Review	PUBP	Public Policy
LE	Land Economics	QAQ	Quality and Quantity
LSQ	Legislative Studies Quarterly	QJBE	Quarterly Journal of Business and Economics
MAS	Modern Asian Studies	QJE	Quarterly Journal of Economics
MBR	Multivariate Behavioral Research	QJS	Quarterly Journal of Speech
MC	Modern China	QRB	Quarterly Review of Biology
MCM	Mathematical and Computer Modeling	QREF	Quarterly Review of Economics and Finance
MF	Municipal Finance	RAS	Rationality and Society
MJPS	Midwest Journal of Political Science	RBPE	Review of Black Political Economy
MLR	Michigan Law Review	RE	Ricerche Economiche
MRPA	Midwest Review of Public Administration	REAS	Review of Economics and Statistics
MS	Management Science	RECEO	Revue d'Etudes Comparatives Est-Ouest
MSESS	Manchester School of Economics and Social Studies	REGS	Regional Studies
		REL	Recherches Economiques de Louvain
MSS	Mathematical Social Sciences	RES	Review of Economic Studies
MSSR	Munich Social Science Review	RESTAT	Review of Economic Statistics
NCR	National Civic Review	RFAD	Revue Francaise d'Administration Publique
NEER	New England Economic Review	RFSP	Revue Francaise de Science Politique
NLR	Northwestern Law Review	RIO	Review of Industrial Organization
NPSR	National Political Science Review	RIS	Review of International Studies
NRJ	Natural Resources Journal	RISEC	Rivista Internazionale di Scienze Economiche e Commerciali
NTJ	National Tax Journal		
NYUJ	New York University Journal of International Law and Politics	RIW	Review of Income and Wealth
		RJE	Rand Journal of Economics
OBES	Oxford Bulletin of Economics and Statistics	RMCPS	Revista Mexicana de Ciencias Politicas y Sociales
OECD	OECD Economic Studies		
OEP	Oxford Economic Papers	ROP	Review of Politics
PA	Public Administration	ROSE	Review of Social Economy
PAAD	Public Administration and Development	RP	Res Publica
PACSR	Pacific Sociological Review	RPAP	Regional Politics and Policy
PADR	Population and Development Review	RPPA	Review of Public Personnel Administration

RRPE	Review of Radical Political Economics
RRR	Review of Religious Research
RRS	Review of Regional Studies
RS	Recherche Sociale
RSP	Regional Science Perspectives
RSUE	Regional Science and Urban Economics
SA	Scientific American
SAES	Social and Economic Studies
SAG	Simulation and Gaming
SALGR	State and Local Government Review
SAS	Science and Society
SASR	Sociology and Social Research
SB	Social Behavior
SC	Social Cognition
SCAW	Social Choice and Welfare
SCC	Studies in Comparative Communism
SDR	System Dynamics Review
SE	Science Exploration
SEHR	Scandinavian Economic History Review
SEJ	Southern Economic Journal
SEPS	Socio-Economic Planning Sciences
SF	Social Forces
SG	State Government
SI	Sociological Inquiry
SICID	Studies in Comparative International Development
SIR	Social Indicators Research
SJE	Scandinavian Journal of Economics
SJIL	Stanford Journal of International Law
SJIS	Stanford Journal of International Studies
SJPE	Scottish Journal of Political Economy
SLR	Stanford Law Review
SM	Sociological Methodology
SMAR	Sociological Methods and Research
SOCP	Social Problems
SOCSER	Social Service Review
SP	Sociological Perspectives
SPAP	Social Philosophy and Policy
SPQ	Social Psychology Quarterly
SPS	Scandinavian Political Studies
SQ	Sociological Quarterly
SR	Social Research
SS	Soviet Studies
SSH	Social Science History
SSI	Social Science Information
SSJ	Social Science Journal
SSQ	Social Science Quarterly
SSR	Social Science Research
SSS	Social Studies of Science
ST	Statsvetenskaplig Tidskrift
STAP	Social Theory and Practice
TAD	Theory and Decision
TFASC	Technological Forecasting and Social Change
TIBG	Transactions of the Institute of British Geographers
TLR	Texas Law Review
TPS	Teaching Political Science
TWQ	Third World Quarterly

UAQ	Urban Affairs Quarterly
UASCR	Urban and Social Change Review
UCLR	University of Chicago Law Review
UHR	Universal Human Rights
UPLR	University of Pennsylvania Law Review
US	Urban Studies
VLR	Virginia Law Review
WA	World Affairs
WAMQ	William and Mary Quarterly
WAP	Women and Politics
WBER	World Bank Economic Review
WD	World Development
WE	World Economy
WEP	West European Politics
WELTA	Weltwirtschaftliches Archiv
WP	World Politics
WPQ	Western Political Quarterly
WQ	Washington Quarterly
YLJ	Yale Law Journal
ZN	Zeitschrift fur Nationalokonomie
ZS	Zeitschrift fur die gesamte Staatswissenchaft

Some Notes about the Listings

Quite a few journals have made very minor changes in their titles over time (e. g. Political Geography used to be Political Geography Quarterly). When such changes have been only minor, the same abbreviation has been used to represent the journal in all the years of its publication.

In referring to journal issues, 3/4 means that the issues 3 and 4 were published as one, while 3-4 indicates a subject was first addressed in issue 3 and the discussion was continued in issue 4.

If a paper was written by four or more authors, it is listed under the first author and et al. The other author's names are not given.

Some long titles have been shortened by deleting parenthetical remarks and unnecessary phrases.

Commonly encountered abbreviations been standardized to a single format (e. g., UK and US).

About forty percent of journals only present the initials of authors, rather than their full names. Because of this, all citations have been standardized in the same manner by only presenting first and middle initials of authors.

So far as could be determined, all papers by the same author have been listed with similar and standardized initials, no matter how the author's name was presented in the journals.

ATTITUDES AND BELIEFS

1 Ajzen, A.; Fishbein, M. 1977. Attitude-Behavior Relations. PSYB 84: 888-918.
2 Anderson, J. J. 1985. A Theory for Attitude and Behavior Applied to an Election Study. BS 30: 219-229.
3 Brady, H. E.; Ansolabehere, S. 1989. Nature of Utility Functions in Mass Publics. APSR 83: 143-164.
4 Brady, H. E.; Sniderman, P. M. 1985. Attitude Attribution: A Group Basis for Political Reasoning. APSR 79: 1061-1078.
5 Brody, R. A.; Shapiro, C. R. 1989. The Rally Phenomenon in Public Opinion. PBA 2: 77-102.
6 -. 1989. Policy Failure and Public Support: The Iran-Contra Affair and Assessments of President Reagan. PB 11: 353-369.
7 Brown, C.; MacKuen, M. B. 1987. Political Context and Attitude Change. APSR 81: 471-490.
8 Bullock, D. 1994. In Search of Rational Government: What Political Preference Function Studies Measure and Assume. AJAE 76: 347-361.
9 Burnham, W. D. 1965. Changing Shape of the American Political Universe. APSR 59: 7-28.
10 Converse, P. E. 1966. Status of Nonattitudes. APSR 68: 650-660.
11 -. 1975. Some Mass-Elite Contrasts in Perception of Political Spaces. SSI 14: 49-83.
12 Dekker, P.; Ester, P. 1995. Political Attitudes in a Generational Perspective. AP 30: 57-74.
13 Delli Carpini, M. X.; Keeter, S. 1991. Stability and Change in the Public's Knowledge of Politics. POQ 55: 583-612.
14 DiPalma, G.; McClosky, H. 1970. Personality and Conformity: The Learning of Political Attitudes. APSR 64: 1054-1073.
15 Dugan, W. E.; Taggart, W. A. 1995. Changing Shape of the American Political Universe Revisited. JOP 57: 469-482.
16 Gilljam, M.; Granberg, D. 1995. Intense Minorities and the Pattern of Public Opinion. IJPOR 7: 199-210.
17 Glynn, C. J. 1989. Perceptions of Others' Opinions as a Component of Public Opinion. SSR 18: 53-69.
18 Green, D. P. 1992. Price Elasticity of Mass Preferences. APSR 867: 128-148.
19 Guilford, J. 1980. Cognitive Styles. Educational and Psychological Measurement 40: 715-735.
20 Hastie, R.; Park, B. 1986. Relationship between Memory and Judgement Depends on Whether the Task is Memory Based or On Line. PR 93: 258-268.
21 Helbing, D. 1992. Mathematical Model for Attitude Formation Pair Interactions. BS 37: 190-214.
22 Huckfeldt, R. R., et al. 1995. Political Environments, Cohesive Social Groups, and the Communication of Public Opinion. AJPS 39: 1025-1054.
23 Iyengar, S. 1989. How Citizens Think about National Issues: Matter of Responsibility. AJPS 33: 878-900.
24 Jarlov, C.; Teogby, L. 1979. Political Involvement and Development of Political Attitudes. SPS 2: 121-140.
25 Jennings, M. K.; Niemi, R. G. 1978. Persistence of Political Orientations. BJPS 8: 333-363.
26 Jones, R. C.; Zannaras, G. 1982. Belief Change and Its Determinants in a Regional Setting. ARS 16: 37-50.
27 Judd, C. M., et al. 1981. Political Involvement and Attitude Structure in US. ASR 46: 660-669.
28 Kabeer, N. 1994. Structure of Revealed Preference: Race, Community and Female Labor Supply in the London Clothing Industry. DAC 25: 307-332.
29 Kahle, L. R.; Klingel, D. M.; Kukla, R. A. 1981. A Longitudinal Study of Adolescents' Attitude-Behavior Consistency. POQ 45: 402-414.
30 Kaw, M. 1990. Choosing Sides: Testing a Political Proximity Model. AJPS 34: 441-470.
31 Kenny, C. B. 1994. Microenvironment of Attitude Change. JOP 56: 715-728.
32 Kiecolt, K. J. 1987. Age and Political Sophistication. JPMS 15: 47-60.
33 Knoke, D. 1979. Stratification and Dimensions of American Political Orientations. AJPS 23: 772-791.
34 Krosnick, J. A. 1990. Government Policy and Citizen Passion: Issue Publics in Contemporary America. PB 12: 59-92.
35 -. 1991. Stability of Political Preferences: Comparisons of Symbolic and Nonsymbolic Attitudes. AJPS 35: 547-576.
36 Lau, R. R. 1985. Two Explanations for Negativity Effects in Political Behavior. AJPS 29: 119-140.
37 Luskin, R. C. 1987. Measuring Political Sophistication. AJPS 31: 856-899.
38 -. 1990. Explaining Political Sophistication. PB 12: 331-361.
39 MacKuen, M. B.; Brown, C. 1987. Political Context and Attitude Change. APSR 81: 471-490.
40 Marcus, G. E. 1988. The Structure of Emotional Response: 1984 Presidential Candidates. APSR 83: 737-762.
41 Margolis, M. 1977. From Confusion to Confusion: Issues and the American Voter, 1956-1972. APSR 71: 31-43.
42 Margolis, M.; Mauser, G. A. 1989. Public Opinion as a Dependent Variable. POLCOM 6: 87-108.

43 Markus, G. B. 1988. Stability and Change in Political Attitudes. PB 8: 21-44.

44 Marwell, G.; Aiken, M. T.; Demerath, N. J. 1987. Persistence of Political Attitudes among 1960s Civil Rights Activists. POQ 51: 359-375.

45 McCombs, M. E.; Xhu, J. H. 1995. Capacity, Diversity and Volatility of the Public Agenda: Trends from 1954 to 1994. POQ 59: 495-525.

46 Milburn, M. A., et al. 1995. Childhood Punishment, Denial and Political Attitudes. PP 16: 447-478.

47 Milburn, M. A.; Judd, C. M. 1981. Interpreting New Methods in Attitude Structure Research. ASR 46: 675-677.

48 Mutz, D. C. 1992. Impersonal Influence: Effects of Representations of Public Opinion on Political Attitudes. PB 14: 89-122.

49 Nadeau, R.; Niemi, R. G.; Amato, R. 1995. Emotions, Issue Importance, and Political Learning. AJPS 39: 558-574.

50 Nathan, J. A.; Remy, R. C. 1976. Political Structure and Attitudes. APQ 4: 423-440.

51 Neuman, W. R. 1981. Differentiation and Integration: Two Dimensions of Political Thinking. AJS 86: 1236-1268.

52 Niemi, R. G.; Hedges, R. B.; Jennings, M. K. 1977. Similarity of Husbands and Wives Political Views. APQ 5: 133-148.

53 Nisbett, R. E.; Wilson, T. D. 1977. Telling More than We Can Know: Verbal Reports on Mental Processes. PR 84: 231-257.

54 Noelle-Neumann, E. 1979. Public Opinion and Classic Tradition. POQ 41: 113-158.

55 Norpoth, H.; Lodge, M. 1985. Difference between Attitudes and Nonattitudes in the Mass Public. AJPS 29: 291-307.

56 Nowak, A.; Szamrej, J.; Latane, B. 1970. From Private Attitudes to Public Opinion. PR 97: 362-376.

57 Ottati, V. C.; Steenbergen, M. R.; Riggle, E. D. 1992. The Cognitive and Affective Components of Political Attitudes: Determinants of Candidate Evaluations. PB 14: 423-442.

58 Parker, S. L. 1995. Toward an Understanding of Rally Effects: Public Opinion in the Persian Gulf War. POQ 59: 526-546.

59 Pierce, J. C.; Rose, D. D. 1974. Non-Attitudes and American Public Opinion. APSR 68: 626-649.

60 Pizza, T.; Sniderman, P. M.; Tetlock, P. E. 1990. Analysis of Dynamics of Political Reasoning. PANAL 1: 99-120.

61 Putnam, R. D.; Leonardi, R.; Nanetti, R. Y. 1979. Attitude Stability among Italian Elites. AJPS 23: 463-494.

62 Rabinowitz, G.; Macdonald, S. E. 1989. A Directional Theory of Issue Voting. APSR 83: 93-122.

63 RePass, D. 1971. Issue Saliency and Party Choice. APSR 65: 389-400.

64 -. 1976. Political Methodologies in Disarray: Issues and American Voters, 1956-1968. APSR 70: 814-831.

65 Rosenberg, S. W. 1988. Structure of Political Thinking. AJEAS 32: 539-566.

66 Sahr, R. C. 1984. Levels of Political-Economic Information and Support of Reaganomics among University Students. PSQ 14: 361-380.

67 Schoultz, L. 1978. Political Normlessness in Comparative Perspective. JOP 40: 82-111.

68 Schubert, G. 1983. Structure of Attention. JSBS 6: 65-80.

69 Schulman, H.; Johnson, M. P. 1976. Attitudes and Behavior. ANRS 2: 161-207.

70 Sears, D. O.; Lau, R. R. 1983. Inducing Apparently Self-Interested Political Preferences. AJPS 27: 223-252.

71 Sigelman, L.; Konda, T. M. 1983. Understanding Opinion Dynamics: Subjective Powerlessness. SSQ 64: 119-126.

72 Sigelman, L.; Thomas, D. 1984. Opinion Leadership and Crystallization of Nonattitudes. Polity 16: 484-493.

73 Sniderman, P. M., et al. 1986. Reasoning Chains: Causal Models of Policy Reasoning in Mass Publics. BJPS 16: 405-430.

74 Social Science Quarterly. 1970. Papers on Political Attitudes. SSQ 51 (3).

75 Strickland, D. A.; Johnston, R. E. 1970 Issue Elasticity. JPE 78: 1069-1092.

76 Taylor, D. G. 1984. Procedures for Evaluating Trends in Public Opinion. POQ 44: 86-100.

77 Thomas, L.; Heise, D. R. 1995. Mining Error Variance and Hitting Pay-Dirt: Discovering Systematic Variation in Social Sentiments. SQ 36: 425-439.

78 Tourangeau, R.; Rasinski, K. A. 1988. Cognitive Processes Underlying Context Effects in Attitude Measurement. Psychological Bulletin 103: 299-314.

79 Tversky, A.; Thaler, R. H. 1990. Anomalies: Preference Reversals. JEP 4 (4): 201-211.

80 Tyler, T. R.; Rasinski, K. A.; McGraw, K. M. 1985. Influence of Perceived Injustice on the Endorsement of Political Leaders. Journal of Applied Social Psychology 15: 700-725.

81 Vedlitz, A. 1984. Impact of College Education on Political Attitudes and Behaviors: The Self Selection Hypothesis. SSQ 64: 145-153.

82 Wanta, W.; King, P.; McCombs, M. E. 1995. A Comparison of Factors Influencing Issue Diversity. IJPOR 7: 353-365.

83 Watts, M. W.; Sumi, D. 1979. Studies in the Physiological Component of Aggression Related Social Attitudes. AJPS 23: 528-558.

84 Wayman, F. W.; Stockton, R. R. 1983. Structure and Stability of Political Attitudes. POQ 47: 329-346.

Belief Systems and Ideology

85 Akerlof, G. A. 1983. Loyalty Filters. AER 73: 54-63.

86 Allen, R. L.; Dawson, M. C.; Brown, R. E. 1989. A Schema Based Approach to Modeling an African-American Racial Belief System. APSR 83: 421-441.

87 American Behavioral Scientist. 1973. Papers on Varieties of Political Conservatism. ABS 17 (2).

88 American Journal of Political Science. 1978 Papers on Whether Attitude Constraint Has Increased. AJPS 22: 227-269.

89 Axelrod, R. 1973. Schema Theory: An Information Processing Model of Perception and Cognition. APSR 67: 1248-1266.

90 Barton, A. H. 1995. Asking Why about Social Problems: Ideology and Causal Models in the Public Mind. IJPOR 7: 299-327.

91 Barton, A. H.; Parsons, R. W. 1977. Measuring Belief System Structure. POQ 41: 159-180.

92 Bennett, S. E. 1995. Americans' Knowledge of Ideology. APQ 23: 259-278.

93 Bennett, S. E., et al. 1979. Education and Mass Belief Systems. PB 1: 53-72.

94 Bennett, W. L. 1977. The Growth of Knowledge in Mass Belief Studies. AJPS 21: 465-500.

95 Berry, W. D.; Freeman, J. R.; Job, B. L. 1983. Using Markov Models to Analyze Perceptual Frameworks. PM 9: 249-284.

96 Brint, S. 1984. New Class and Cumulative Trend Explanations of the Liberal Political Attitudes of Professionals. AJS 90: 31-71.

97 Brown, S. R. 1970. Consistency and the Persistence of Ideology. POQ 34: 60-68.

98 Carley, K.; Palmquist, M. 1992. Extracting, Representing and Analyzing Mental Models. SF 70: 601-636.

99   Carlsnaes, W. 1981. Can Perceptions Be Ideological? CAC 16: 183-188.

100 Carson, R.; Oppenheimer, J. A. 1984. A Method of Estimating Personal Ideology of Political Representatives. APSR 78: 163-178.

101 Cassel, C. A. 1984. Issues in Measurement: Levels of Conceptualization Index of Ideological Sophistication. AJPS 28: 418-432.

102 Castles, F. G.; Mair, P. 1984. Left-Right Political Scales: Expert Judgments. EJPR 12: 73-88.

103 Chafetz, J. S.; Ebaugh, H. R. F. 1983. Growing Conservatism in the US? SP 26: 275-298.

104 Cobb, R. W. 1973. The Belief Systems Perspective. JOP 35: 121-153.

105 Comparative Studies in Society and History. 1991. Papers on Belief Systems and Political Behavior. CSSH 33 (1).

106 Congleton, R. D. 1991. Ideological Conviction and Persuasion in the Rent-Seeking Society. JPUBE 44: 65-86.

107 Conover, P. J.; Feldman, S. 1981. Origins and Meanings of Liberal-Conservative Self-Identifications. AJPS 25: 617-645.

108 -. 1981. Self-Identifications. AJPS 25: 617-645.

109 -. 1984. How People Organize the Political World. AJPS 29: 95-126.

110 Converse, P. E. 1969. Of Time and Partisan Stability. CPS 2: 139-171.

111 Coughlin, R. M. 1979. Social Policy and Ideology. CSR 2: 3-40.

112 Dalton, R. J. 1987. Generational Change in Elite Politics Beliefs: Growth of Ideological Polarization. JOP 49: 976-997.

113 Dawson, P. A. 1979. Formation and Structure of Political Belief Systems. PB 1: 99-122.

114 Denver, D.; Hands, G. 1989. Issues, Principles, or Ideology? How Young Voters Decide. ES 9: 19-36.

115 Devine, J. A. 1989. Paradigms as Ideologies: Liberal vs. Marxian Economics. ROSE 47: 293-312.

116 Dougan, W. R.; Munger, M. C. 1989. Rationality of Ideology. JOLE 32: 119-142.

117 Eckhardt, W. 1971. Conservatism, East and West. JCCP 2: 109-128.

118 Entman, R. M. 1983. Impact of Ideology on Legislative Behavior and Public Policy in the States. JOP 45: 160-182.

119 Feldman, S. 1983. Economic Individualism and Mass Belief Systems. APQ 11: 3-29.

120 -. 1988. Structure and Consistency in Public Opinion: Core Beliefs and Values. AJPS 32: 416-440.

121 Feldman, S.; Conover, P. J. 1984. Structure of Issue Positions: Beyond Liberal-Conservative Constraint. Micropolitics 3: 281-308.

122 Field, J. O.; Anderson, R. E. 1969. Ideology in the Public's Conceptualization of 1964 Election. POQ 33: 380-398.

123 Fiske, S.; Lerter, M. 1983. Novice and Expert: Knowledge-Based Strategies in Public Cognition. Journal of Experimental and Social Psychology 19: 381-400.

124 Fiske, S.; Linville, D. 1980. What Does Scheme Concept Buy Us? Personality and Social Psychology Bulletin 6: 543-555.

125 Fleishman, J. A. 1986. Types of Political Attitude Structure: Results of a Cluster Analysis. POQ 50: 371-388.

126 -. 1988. Attitude Organization in General Public: A Bidimensional Structure. SF 67: 159-184.

127 Form, W. H.; Rythina, J. 1969. Ideological Beliefs on Distribution of Power. ASR 34: 19-30.

128 Gans, H. J. 1993. Varieties of American Ideological Spectra. SR 60: 513-530.

129 Gick, M.; Holyoak, K. 1983. Schema Induction and Analogical Transfer. Cognition Psychology 15: 1-38.

130 Glazer, A.; Grofman, B. 1989. Why Representatives Are Ideologists Though Voters Are Not. PC 61: 29-40.

131 Granberg, D.; Brown, T. A. 1992. Perception of Ideological Distance. WPQ 45: 727-750.

132 Green, D. P. 1988. On the Dimensionality of Public Sentiment toward Partisan and Ideological Groups. AJPS 32: 758-780.

133 Greenfield, L. 1988. Professional Ideologies and Patterns of Gatekeeping: Evaluation and Judgment within Two Art Worlds. SF 66: 903-925.

134 Grube, J. W.; Mayton, D. M.; Ball-Rokeach, S. J. 1994. Inducing Change in Values, Attitudes, and Behaviors: Belief System Theory and the Method of Value Self-Confrontation. JSI 50: 153-174.

135 Hagner, P. R.; Pierce, J. C. 1982. Correlative Characteristics of Levels of Conceptualization in the American Public. JOP 44: 779-809.

136 Haltom, W. 1990. Liberal-Conservative Continua: Comparison of Measures. WPQ 43: 387-402.

137 Hamill, R.; Lodge, M.; Blake, F. 1985. Breadth, Depth and Utility of Class, Partisan and Ideological Schemata. AJPS 29: 850-870.

138 Hayduck, L. A., et al. 1995. Attitudes, Ideology and the Factor Model. PP 16: 479-507.

139 Heath, A.; Evans, G.; Martin, J. 1994. Measurement of Core Beliefs and Values: Development of Balanced Socialist / Laisse Faire and Libertarian / Authoritarian Scales. BJPS 24: 115-131.

140 Herrera, R. 1992. Understanding of Ideological Labels by Political Elites. WPQ 45: 1021-1036.

141 Herzon, F. D. 1980. Ideology, Constraint and Public Opinion: Lawyers. AJPS 24: 233-258.

142 Himmelstrand, U. 1982. Ideology, Science and Policy Impact. ISSJ 34: 503-534.

143 Hinich, M. J.; Munger, M. C. 1992. A Spatial Theory of Ideology. JTP 4: 5-30.

144 Hobrook-Provow, T. M.; Poe, S. C. 1987. Measuring State Political Ideology. APQ 15: 399-416.

145 Holm, J. D.; Robinson, J. P. 1978. Ideological Identification and the American Voter. POQ 42: 235-246.

146 Howell, S. E. 1985. Ideological Identification and Candidate Choice. PB 7: 325-334.

147 Huber, J. D. 1989. Values and Partisanship in Left-Right Orientations: Measuring Ideology. EJPR 17: 599-621.

148 Inglehart, R. 1985. Aggregate Stability and Individual Level Flux in Mass Belief Systems: Level of Analysis Paradox. APSR 79: 97-116.

149 Jacoby, W. G. 1986. Levels of Conceptualization and Reliance on Liberal-Conservative Continuum. JOP 48: 423-432.

150 -. 1988. Sources of Liberal-Conservative Thinking: Education and Conceptualization. PB 10: 316-332.

151 -. 1991. Ideological Identification and Issue Attitudes. AJPS 35: 178-205.

152 -. 1995. Structure of Ideological Thinking in the American Electorate. AJPS 39: 314-335.

153 Jennings, M. K. 1984. Intergenerational Transfer of Political Ideologies. EJPR 12: 261-276.

154 -. 1992. Ideological Thinking among Mass Publics and Political Elites. POQ 56: 419-441.

155 Judd, C. M.; Milburn, M. A. 1980. Structure of Attitude Systems in the General Public. ASR 45: 627-646.

156 Kazin, M. 1992. New Histories of US Conservatism in the Twentieth Century. AHR 97: 136-155.

157 Kitschelt, H.; Hellemans, S. 1990. Left-Right Semantics and the New Politics Cleavage. CPS 23: 210-238.

158 Knight, K. 1985. Ideology in the 1980 Election: Ideological Sophistication Does Matter. JOP 47: 828-853.

159 Kritzer, H. M. 1978. Ideology and American Political Elites. POQ 42: 484-502.

160 Kuklinski, J. H.; Luskin, R. C.; Bolland, J. M. 1991. Where Is Schema? Going beyond the S Word in Political Psychology. APSR 85: 1341-1357.

161 Lambert, R. D. 1983. Question Design, Response Set and the Measurement of Left-Right Thinking in Survey Research. CJPS 16: 135-144.

162 Lanternari, V. 1980. Ethnocentrism and Ideology. EARS 3: 52-66.

163 Larrain, J. 1984. Three Different Concepts of Ideology? CJPST 8: 151-161.

164 Lawrence, D. G. 1994. Ideological Extremity, Issue Distance and Defection. PRQ 47: 397-422.

165 Levitin, T. E.; Miller, W. E. 1979. Ideological Interpretations of Presidential Elections. APSR 73: 751-771.

166 Listhaug, O.; MacDonald, S. E.; Rabinowitz, G. 1994. Ideology and Party Support in Comparative Perspective. EJPR 25: 111-150.

167 Lodge, M.; Hamill, R. 1986. Partisan Schema for Political Information Processing. APSR 80: 505-519.

168 Lodge, M.; McGraw, K. M.; Conover, P. J. 1991. Where Is the Schema? APSR 85: 1358-1380.

169 Luttbeg, N. R. 1968. Structure of Beliefs among Leaders and the Public. POQ 32: 398-409.

170 Luttbeg, N. R.; Gant, M. M. 1985. The Failure of a Liberal-Conservative Ideology as a Cognitive Structure. POQ 49: 80-93.

171 Lyons, W. E.; Scheb, J. M. 1992. Ideology and Candidate Evaluation in the 1984 and 1988 Presidential Elections. JOP 54: 573-584.

172 MacGaffey, W. 1984. African Ideology and Belief. AFSR 24: 139-226.

173 Marcus, G. E.; Tabb, D. H.; Sullivan, J. L. 1974. Application of Individual Differences Scaling to Measurement of Political Ideologies. AJPS 18: 405-420.

174 McDermott, M. 1994. Race and Class Interactions in the Formation of Political Ideology. SQ 35: 347-366.

175 McGee, M. C. 1980. The Ideograph: A Link between Rhetoric and Ideology. QJS 60: 1-16.

176 Merelman, R. M. 1969. Development of Political Ideology. APSR 63: 750-767.

177 Middendorp, C. P. 1993. Authoritarianism: Personality and Ideology. EJPR 24: 211-228.

178 Milbrath, L. W. 1984. How Our Belief Systems Can Affect Poll Results. ANNALS 472: 35-49.

179 Miller, A. H.; Hesli, V. L.; Reisinger, W. H. 1995. Comparing Citizen and Elite Belief Systems in Post-Soviet Russia. POQ 59: 1-40.

180 Miller, A. H.; Listhaug, O. 1993. Ideology and Political Alienation. SPS 16: 167-192.

181 Miller, A. H.; Miller, W. E. 1976. Ideology in the 1972 Election. APSR 70: 832-849.

182 Miller, A. H.; Wattenberg, M. P.; Malanchuk, O. 1986. Schematic Assessments of Presidential Candidates. APSR 80: 521-540.

183 Modern China. 1987. Papers on the Folk Ideologies of China. MC 13 (3).

184 Mondak, J. J. 1993. Public Opinion and Heuristic Processing of Source Clues. PB 15: 167-192.

185 Mueller, C. M.; Judd, C. M. 1981. Belief Constraint and Belief Consensus: Analysis of Social Movement Ideologies. SF 60: 182-187.

186 Mullins, W. A. 1972. On the Concept of Ideology in Political Science. APSR 66: 498-510.

187 Nie, N. H.; Andersen, K. 1974. Mass Belief Systems Revisited: Political Change and Attitude Structure. JOP 36: 540-591.

188 Niemi, R. G., et al. 1985. Testing the Converse Model with New Electorates. CPS 18: 300-323.

189 Ornstein, M. D.; Stevenson, H. M. 1984. Ideology and Public Policy in Canada. BJPS 14: 313-344.

190 Ottati, V. C.; Fishbein, M.; Middlestadt, S. E. 1988. Determinants of Voters Beliefs about Candidate Stands on Issues: Role of Evaluative Bias Heuristics. JPSP 55: 517-529.

191 Palfrey, T. R.; Poole, K. T. 1987. Relationship between Information, Ideology and Voting Behavior. AJPS 31: 511-530.

192 Pierce, J. C. 1975. Relationship between Linkage Salience and Linkage Organization in Mass Belief Systems. POQ 39: 102-110.

193 Pierce, J. C.; Hanger, P. R. 1983. Levels of Conceptualization and Political Belief Consistency. Micropolitics 2: 311-348.

194 Public Choice. 1993. Papers on Representation and Ideology in American Politics. PC 76 (1/2).

195 Putnam, R. D. 1971. Studying Elite Political Culture: Ideology. APSR 65: 651-681.

196 Quigley, F. 1995. Social Welfare and Ideological Attitudes of US Nonvoters: National Voter Registration Act of 1993. JPMS 23: 213-230.

197 Robinson, J. P.; Fleishman, J. A. 1984. Ideological Trends in American Public Opinion. ANNALS 471: 50-60.

198 Roemer, J. E. 1994. Strategic Role of Party Ideology When Voters Are Uncertain about How the Economy Works. APSR 88: 327-335.

199 Rosenberg, S. W. 1987. Reason and Ideology: Interpreting People's Understanding of American Politics. Polity 20: 114-144.

200 Sabatier, P. A.; Hunter, S. 1989. Incorporation of Causal Perceptions into Models of Elite Belief Systems. WPQ 42: 229-262.

201 Sartori, G. 1969. Politics, Ideology and Belief Systems. APSR 63: 398-411.

202 Searing, D. D.; Schwartz, J. J.; Lind, A. E. 1973. Political Socialization and Belief Systems. APSR 67: 415-432.

203 Smith, E. R. A. N. 1980. Levels of Conceptualization: False Measures of Ideological Sophistication. APSR 74: 685-696.

204 Smith, T. W. 1990. Liberal and Conservative Trends since World War II. POQ 54: 479-507.

205 Steed, R. P.; Boykin, M. L. 1982. Development of Political Belief Systems: Comparison of Leaders and Non-Leaders. JPS 9: 96-109.

206 Stimson, J. A. 1975. Belief Systems: Constraint, Complexity and 1972 Election. AJPS 19: 393-417.

207 Sullivan, J. L., et al. 1978. Ideological Constraint in the Mass Public. AJPS 22: 233-249.

208 -. 1979. Stability of Mass Belief Systems. AJPS 23: 176-186.

209 Sullivan, J. L.; Piereson, J. E.; Marcus, G. E. 1978. Ideological Constraint in the Mass Public. AJPS 22: 233-249.

210 Szalay, L. B.; Kelly, R. M. 1982. Political Ideology and Subjective Culture. APSR 76: 585-602.

211 Tetlock, P. E. 1983. Cognitive Style and Political Ideology. JPSP 45: 118-126.

212 -. 1984. Cognitive Style and Political Belief Systems in the British House of Commons. JPSP 46: 365-375.

213 -. 1986. A Value Pluralism Model of Ideological Reasoning. JPASP 50: 819-827.

214 Thomas, D. B. 1979. Psychodynamics, Symbolism and Socialization: Object Relations Perspectives on Personality, Ideology and Political Perception. PB 1: 243-268.

215 Veerman, T. J. 1981. Belief Publics or Elites? Models for Danish Belief System. SPS 4: 109-126.

216 Wagner, J. 1990. Rational Constraint in Mass Belief Systems: Role of Developmental Moral Stages. PP 11: 147-172.

217 Walker, S. G. 1983. Motivational Foundations of Belief Systems. ISQ 27: 179-201.

218 -. 1990. Evolution of Operational Code Analysis. PP 11: 403-418.

219 Walker, S. G. Murphy, T. G. 1981. Utility of the Operational Code in Forecasting. PP 3: 24-60.

220 Williams, R. H.; Williams, S. A. 1987. Level of Identification as Predictor of Attitude Change. SAG 18: 471-487.

221 Wray, J. H. 1979. Comment on Interpretation of Early Research into Belief Systems. JPS 7: 1173-1184.

222 Wright, G. C.; Erikson, R. S.; McIver, J. P. 1985. Measuring State Partisanship and Ideology with Survey Data. JOP 47: 469-489.

223 Wyckoff, M. L. 1987. Issues in Measuring Ideological Sophistication. PB 9: 193-224.

224 -. 1987. Measures of Attitudinal Consistency as Indicators of Ideological Sophistication. JOP 49: 148-168.

Foreign Policy Attitudes

225 Bardes, B. A.; Oldendick, R. W. 1978. Beyond Internationalism: Multiple Dimensions in Foreign Policy Attitudes. SSQ 59: 497-508.

226 Bennett, S. E. 1974. Attitude Structures and Foreign Policy Opinions. SSQ 55: 732-742.

227 Blum, D. W. 1993. Soviet Foreign Policy Belief System. ISQ 37: 373-394.

228 Bohman, G. M.; Shapiro, M.; Trumble, T. 1979 The October War: Changes in Cognitive Orientation toward the Middle East Conflict. ISQ 23: 3-46.

229 Brody, R. A.; Verba, S. 1972. Hawk or Dove: The Search for an Explanation of Vietnam Policy Preferences. AP 7: 285-322.

230 Caspary, W. R. 1968. US Public Opinion during the Onset of the Cold War. PPRS 9: 25-46.

231 -. 1970. Mood Theory: A Study of Public Opinion and Foreign Policy. APSR 64: 536-547.

232 Chap, S. 1979. Rationality, Bureaucratic Politics and Belief System: Explaining the Chinese Policy Debate. JPR 16: 333-348.

233 Chittick, W. O.; Billingsley, K. R. 1989. Structure of Elite Foreign Policy Beliefs. WPQ 42: 201-224.

234 Chittick, W. O.; Billingsley, K. R.; Travis, R. 1990. Persistence and Change in Elite and Mass Attitudes toward Foreign Policy. PP 11: 385-402.

235 -. 1995. A Three-Dimensional Model of American Foreign Policy Beliefs. ISQ 39: 313-332.

236 Cutler, N. E. 1970. Generational Succession as a Source of Foreign Policy Attitudes. JPR 1: 33-48.

237 D'Agostino, B. 1995. Self-Images of Hawks and Doves: A Control Systems Model of Militarism. PP 16: 259-296.

238 Dent, D. W.; McWilliams, W. C. 1986. What College Students Think about the International Role of the US. ISN 12: 48-55.

239 Freeman, G.; Adams, P. 1983. Ideology and Analysis in Security Policymaking. JSP 12: 75-96.

240 Gannon, K. 1994. Case-Based, Model-Based and Explanation-Based Styles of Reasoning in Foreign Policy. ISQ 38: 61-90.

241 Glad, B. 1983. Black and White Thinking: Reagan's Approach to Foreign Policy. PP 4: 33-76.

242 Gourevitch, P. A. 1978. Second Image Reversed: International Sources of Domestic Politics. IO 32: 881-913.

243 Hahn, H. 1970. Correlates of Public Sentiments about War: Local Referenda on the Vietnam Issue. APSR 64: 1186-1198.

244 Hakvoort, I.; Oppenheimer, L. 1993. Children and Adolescents' Conceptions of Peace, War and Strategies to Attain Peace. JPR 30: 65-78.

245 Hallenberg, J. 1994. Public Opinion, Elections and Foreign Policy: US Foreign Policy toward the Soviet Union. CAC 29: 149-184.

246 Herrmann, D. 1985. American Perceptions of Soviet Foreign Policy. PP 6: 375-411.

247 Herrmann, R. K.; Fischerkeller, M. P. 1995. Beyond the Enemy Image and Spiral Model: Cognitive-Strategic Research after the Cold War. IO 49: 415-450.

248 Hinckley, R. H. 1988. Public Attitudes toward Key Foreign Policy Events. JCR 32: 295-318.

249 Holsti, O. R. 1970. Operational Code Approach to Study of Political Leaders: John Foster Dulles. CJPS 3: 123-147.

250 -. 1992. Public Opinion and Foreign Policy: Challenges to the Almond-Lippmann Consensus. ISQ 36: 439-466.

251 Holsti, O. R.; Rosenau, J. N. 1979. Vietnam, Consensus and Belief Systems of American Leaders. WP 32: 1-56.

252 -. 1980. Impact of Generation on Post-Vietnam Foreign Policy Beliefs. POQ 44: 1-22.

253 -. 1986. Consensus Lost, Consensus Regained. ISQ 30: 375-409.

254 -. 1986. Foreign Policy Beliefs of American Leaders. ISQ 30: 473-484.

255 -. 1988. The Domestic and Foreign Policy Beliefs of American Leaders. JCR 32: 248-294.

256 -. 1990. Emerging US Consensus on Foreign Policy. Orbis 34: 579-595.

257 -. 1990. Structure of Foreign Policy Attitudes among American Leaders. JOP 52: 94-125.

258 -. 1993. Structure of Foreign Policy Beliefs among American Opinion Makers after the Cold War. Vol 22: 235-278.

259 Hurwitz, J.; Peffley, M. 1987. How Are Foreign Policy Attitudes Structured? Hierarchical Model. APSR 81: 1099-1120.

260 -. 1990. Public Images of the Soviet Union. JOP 52: 3-28.

261 Hurwitz, J.; Peffley, M.; Seligson, M. A. 1993. Foreign Policy Belief Systems in Comparative Perspective: US and Costa Rica. ISQ 37: 245-270.

262 Jentleson, B. W. 1992. The Pretty Prudent Public: Post Post-Vietnam American Opinion on the Use of Military Force. ISQ 36: 49-74.

263 Journal of Social Issues. 1989. Papers on Image of the Enemy: US Views of the Soviet Union. JSI 45 (2).

264 Kanwisher, N. 1989. Cognitive Heuristics and American Security Policy. JCR 33: 652-675.

265 Kaplowitz, N. 1990. National Self-Images, Perceptions of Enemies and Conflict Strategies. PP 39-82.

266 Kegley, C. W. 1986. Assumptions and Dilemmas in the Study of Americans' Foreign Policy Beliefs. ISQ 30: 447-471.

267 Kirkpatrick, S. A.; Regens, J. L. 1977. Military Experience and Foreign Policy Belief Systems. JPMS 6: 29-47.

268 Krosnick, J. A.; Telhami, S. 1995. Public Attitudes toward Israel: Attentive and Issue Publics. ISQ 39: 535 ff.

269 Lagon, M. P. 1994. Realignment of American Elite Beliefs after the Cold War. POPS 23: 89-95.

270 Larson, D. W. 1988. Problems of Content Analysis in Foreign Policy Research: Cold War Belief Systems. ISQ 32: 241-255.

271 -. 1994. Role of Belief Systems and Schemas in Foreign Policy Decision Making. PP 15: 17-34.

272 Lau, R. R.; Brown, T. A.; Sears, D. O. 1978. Self-Interest and Civilians' Attitudes toward the Vietnam War. POQ 42: 464-483.

273 Lockerbie, B.; Borrelli, S. A. 1990. Question Wording and Public Support for Contra Aid. POQ 54: 195-208.

274 Maggiotto, M. A.; Wittkopf, E. R. 1981. American Public Attitudes toward Foreign Policy. ISQ 25: 601-631.

275 McCormick, J. M.; Black, M. 1983. Ideolo Senate Voting on the Panama Canal Treatie 8: 45-64.

276 Modigliani, A. 1972. Hawks and Doves: Isolationism and Political Distrust: Public Opinion on Military Policy. APSR 66: 960-978.

277 Mueller, J. E. 1971. Trends in Popular Support for Wars in Korea and Vietnam. APSR 65: 358-375.

278 -. 1979. Public Expectations of War during the Cold War. AJPS 23: 301-329.

279 Oldendick, R. W.; Bardes, B. A. 1981. Belief Structures and Foreign Policy: Comparing Dimensions of Elite and Mass Opinions. SSQ 62: 432-442.

280 Oneal, J. R.; Bryan, A. L. 1995. Rally Round the Flag Effect in US Foreign Policy Crises. PB 17: 379-402.

281 Peffley, M.; Hurwitz, J. 1985. A Hierarchical Model of Attitude Constraint. AJPS 29: 871-890.

282 -. 1992. International Events and Foreign Policy Beliefs: Public Responses to Changing Soviet-US Relations. AJPS 36: 431-461.

283 -. 1993. Models of Attitude Constraint in Foreign Affairs. PB 15: 61-90.

284 Powlick, P. J. 1991. Attitudinal Bases for Responsiveness to Public Opinion among American Foreign Policy Officials. JCR 35: 611-641.

285 -. 1995. Sources of Public Opinion for American Foreign Policy Officials. ISQ 39: 427-452.

286 Risse-Kappen, T. 1991. Public Opinion, Domestic Structure and Foreign Policy in Liberal Democracies. WP 43: 479-512.

287 Russett, B. 1990. Doves, Hawks and US Public Opinion. PSCQ 105: 515-538.

288 Schneider, W. 1974. Public Opinion: Beginning of Ideology. Foreign Policy 17: 88-120.

289 Schuman, H.; Rieger, C. 1992. Historical Analogies, Generational Effects and Attitudes toward War. ASR 57: 315-326.

290 Secrest, D.; Brunk, G. G.; Tamashiro, H. 1991. Moral Justifications for Resort to War with Nicaragua. WPQ 44: 541-559.

291 -. 1991. American Elite Views on Conduct of War. JPMS 19: 195-215.

292 -. 1991. Investigation of Normative Discourse on War: Donagan-Aquinas Thesis. JPR 28: 393-406.

293 Shamir, M.; Arian, A. 1994. Competing Values and Policy Choices: Israeli Public Opinion on Foreign and Security Affairs. BJPS 24: 249-272.

294 Sniderman, P. M.; Citrin, J. 1971. Psychological Sources of Political Beliefs: Self Esteem and Isolationist Attitudes. APSR 65: 401-417.

295 Stuart, D.; Starr, H. 1982. Inherent Bad Faith Model Reconsidered: Dulles, Kennedy and Kissinger. PP 3: 1-33.

296 Suedfeld, P.; Tetlock, P. E.; Ramirez, C. 1977. War, Peace and Integrative Complexity. JCR 21: 427-442.

297 Taber, C. S. 1992. An Expert System Model of US Foreign Policy Belief Systems. APSR 86: 888-904.

298 Tamashiro, H.; Secrest, D.; Brunk, G. G. 1989. Underlying Structure of Ethical Beliefs toward War. JPR 26: 139-152.

299 Tetlock, P. E. 1986. Cognitive Perceptions of Foreign Policy. PBA 1: 147-180.

300 Walker, S. G. 1977. Interface between Beliefs and Behavior: Henry Kissenger's Operational Code and the Vietnam War. JCR 21: 129-168.

301 White, S.; Kryshtanovskaya, O. 1993. Public Attitudes to the KGB. EAS 45: 169-190.

302 Wilcox, C.; Ferrara, J.; Allsop, D. 1993. Group Differences in Early Support for Military Action in the Gulf. APQ 21: 343-359.

303 Wittkopf, E. R. 1981. Structure of Foreign Policy Attitudes. SSQ 62: 108-123.

304 -. 1987. Elites and Masses: Attitudes toward America's World Role. ISQ 31: 131-159.

305 Wittkopf, E. R.; Maggiotto, M. A. 1983. Elites and Masses: A Comparative Analysis of Attitudes toward America's World Role. JOP 45: 303-334.

306 -. 1983. Two Faces of Internationalism. SSQ 64: 288-304.

307 -. 1986. Foreign Policy Beliefs of the American People. ISQ 30: 425-444.

308 Wittkopf, E. R.; McCormick, J. M. 1990. Cold War Consensus: Did It Exist? Polity 22: 627-654.

Surveys

309 Abramson, P. R. 1990. Decline of Over Time Comparability in the National Election Studies. POQ 54: 177-190.

310 Achen, C. H. 1975. Mass Political Attitudes and the Survey Response. APSR 69: 1218-1223.

311 American Behavioral Scientist. 1993. Papers on Improving Organizational Surveys. ABS 36 (4).

312 Annals. 1984. Papers on Polling. ANNALS 472.

313 Balch, G. I. 1974. Multiple Indicators in Survey Research: Political Efficacy. PM 1: 1-43.

314 Bishop, G. F.; Oldendick, R. W.; Tuckfarber, A. J. 1982. Political Information Processing: Question Order and Context Effects. PB 4: 177-200.

315 Converse, P. E.; Markus, G. B. 1979. Plus ca Change... The New CPS Election Study Panel. APSR 73: 32-49.

316 Dran, E. M.; Hildreth, A. 1995. What the Public Thinks about How We Know What It Is Thinking. IJPOR 7: 129-144.

317 Edwards, J. E.; Thomas, M. D. 1993. The Organizational Survey Process. ABS 36: 419-442.

318 Erikson, R. S. 1979. SRC Panel Data and Mass Political Attitudes. BJPS 9: 89-114.

319 Erikson, R. S.; Sigelman, L. 1995. Poll-Based Forecasts of Midterm Congressional Election Outcomes: Do Pollsters Get It Right? POQ 59: 589-605.

320 Feldman, S. 1990. Measuring Issue Preferences: Response Instability. PANAL 1: 25-60.

321 Fields, J. M.; Schulman, H. 1976. Public Beliefs about Beliefs of the Public. POQ 40: 427-448.

322 Gelman, A.; King, G. 1993. Why Are American Presidential Election Campaign Polls So Variable When Votes Are So Predictable? BJPS 23: 409-452.

323 Goyder, J. 1986. Surveys on Surveys. POQ 50: 27-41.

324 Granberg, D.; Holmberg, S. 1992. The Hawthorne Effect in Election Studies: Impact of Survey Participation on Voting. BJPS 22: 240-247.

325 Groves, R. M. 1987. Research on Survey Data Quality. POQ 51 Winter Supplement: S156-S172.

326 Jackson, J. E. 1983. Systematic Beliefs of the Mass Public: Estimating Policy Preferences with Survey Data. JOP 45: 840-865.

327 Kuechler, M. 1987. The Utility of Surveys for Cross National Research. SSR 16: 229-244.

328 Kulba, R. A. 1982. Monitoring Social Change via Survey Replication: Replication Study of Social Roles and Mental Health. JSI 38: 17-28.

329 Marcus, G. E. 1988. Democratic Theories and the Study of Public Opinion. Polity 21: 25-44.

330 Rosenfeld, P.; Booth-Kewley, S.; Edwards, J. E. 1993. Computer Administered Surveys in Organizational Settings. ABS 36: 485-511.

331 Rusk, J. G. 1982. Michigan Election Studies. Micropolitics 2: 87-110.

332 Schleifer, S. 1986. Trends in Attitudes toward and Participation in Survey Research. POQ 50: 17-26

333 Schuman, H.; Kalton, G.; Ludwig, J. 1983. Context and Contiguity in Survey Questionnaires. POQ 17: 112-120.

334 Smith, T. W. 1987. The Art of Asking Questions. POQ 51 (Winter Supplement): S95-S108.

335 Squire, P. 1988. Why the 1936 Literary Digest Poll Failed. POQ 52: 125-134.

336 van der Veen, R. J.; Pellikaan, H. 1994. Motives, Preferences and Choices: A Framework for Testing Their Consistency in Survey Research. AP 29: 411-452.

337 Zaller, J.; Feldman, S. 1992. A Simple Theory of the Survey Response: Answering Questions vs. Revealing Preferences. AJPS 36: 579-616.

Values

338 Abramson, P. R.; Inglehart, R. 1987. Generation-al Replacement and Future of Post-Materialist Values. JOP 49: 231-241.

339 Andersen, K. 1993. The Role of Ethical / Value Issues in Campaigns: Family Values. ABS 37: 302-307.

340 Arts, W.; Hermkens, P.; van Wijck, P. 1995. Anomie, Distributive Injustice, and Dissatisfaction with Material Well-Being in Eastern Europe. IJCS 36: 1-16.

341 Baer, D.; Grabb, E.; Johnson, W. A. 1990. Values of Canadians and Americans. SF 68: 693-713.

342 Brooks, C.; Manza, J. 1994. Do Changing Values Explain the New Politics? A Critical Assessment of the Postmaterialist Thesis. SQ 35: 541-570.

343 Clarke, H. D.; Dutt, N. 1991. Measuring Value Change in Western Industrial Countries: Impact of Unemployment. APSR 85: 905-920.

344 Clarke, H. D.; Dutt, N.; Kornberg, A. 1993. Political Economy of Attitudes toward Polity and Society in Western European Democracies. JOP 55: 998-1021.

345 Comparative Political Studies. 1985. Papers on Materialism, Postmaterialism and Changing Values. CPS 17 (4).

346 Conover, P. J.; Feldman, S. 1984. Group Identification, Values and Nature of Political Beliefs. APQ 12: 151-175.

347 Cook, T. E. 1985. Bear Market in Political Socialization and Cost of Misunderstood Theories. APSR 79: 1079-1084.

348 de la Garza, R. O.; Vaughn, D. 1984. Political Socialization of Elites. SSQ 65: 290-307.

349 Delli Carpini, M. X.; Sigelman, L. 1986. Do Yuppies Matter? Competing Explanations of Their Political Distinctiveness. POQ 50: 502-518.

350 Dennis, J. 1987. Groups and Political Behavior: Legitimation, Deprivation and Competing Values. PB 9: 323-372.

351 Eisner, M. 1990. Long Term Dynamics of Political Values in International Perspective. EJPR 18: 605-622.

352 Ester, P.; Vinken, H. 1993. Yuppies in Cross-National Perspective: A Yuppie Value System. PP 14: 667-698.

353 Feldman, S. 1988. Structure and Consistency in Public Opinion: Core Beliefs and Values. AJPS 32: 416-440.

354 Flanagan, S. C. 1979. Value Change and Partisan Change in Japan: Silent Revolution Revisited. CP 11: 253-278.

355 -. 1982. Changing Values in Advanced Industrial Society: Inglehart's Silent Revolution from the Perspective of Japanese Findings. CPS 14: 403-444.

356 -. 1987. Changing Values in Industrial Societies Revisited. APSR 81: 1303-1319.

357 Fliegal, F. C. 1970. A Comparative Analysis of the Impact of Traditional Values. Rural Sociology 41: 431-451.

358 Futuribles. 1995. Papers on the Evolution of European Values. Vol 200.

359 Garramone, G. M.; Atkins, C. K. 1986. Mass Communication and Political Socialization. POQ 50: 76-86.

360 Guy, M. E. 1984. Measuring Conflicting Political Values. PM 10: 125-142.

361 Hammond, J. 1986. Yuppies. POQ 50: 487-501.

362 Hedley, R. A. 1980. Work Values: Convergence and Cultural Diversity Theses. IJCS 21: 100-108.

363 Hoge, D. R.; Hoge, J. L. 1992. Return of the Fifties? Value Trends at University of Michigan. SQ 33: 611-624.

364 Huber, J. D.; Powell, G. B. 1994. Congruence between Citizens and Policymakers in Two Visions of Liberal Democracy. WP 46: 291-326.

365 Inglehart, R. 1971. Silent Revolution in Europe: Intergenerational Change in Post-Industrial Societies. APSR 65: 991-1017.

366 -. 1981. Post-Materialism in an Environment of Insecurity. APSR 75: 880-900.

367 -. 1995. Changing Values, Economic Development and Political Chance. ISSJ 47: 379-404.

368 Inglehart, R.; Abramson, P. R. 1994. Economic Security and Value Change. APSR 88: 336-354.

369 International Political Science Review. 1987. Papers on Political Socialization. IPSR 8 (3).

370 Jennings, M. K. 1987. Aging of the American Protest Generation. APSR 81: 367-382.

371 Jennings, M. K.; Niemi, R. G. 1968. Transmission of Political Values from Parent to Child. APSR 62: 168-184.

372 Journal of Economic Psychology. 1990. Papers on the Child Economic Socialization. JEPSY 11 (4).

373 Journal of Social Issues. 1994. Papers on Human Values and Social Issues. JSI 50 (4).

374 Kallos, N.; Trasnea, O. 1982. Political Values: Status and Social Function. IPSR 3: 182-189.

375 Knutsen, O. 1995. Value Orientations, Political Conflicts and Left-Right Identification. EJPR 28: 63-94.

376 Landsburg, S. E. 1981. Taste Change in the UK, 1900-1955. JPE 89: 92-104.

377 Leiser, D.; Sevon, G.; Levy, D. 1990. Children's Economic Socialization. JEPSY 11: 591-614.

378 Lindsay, P.; Know, W. E. 1984. Continuity and Change in World Values among Young Adults. AJS 89: 918-931.

379 Marsh, A. 1975. Silent Revolution, Value Priorities and Quality of Life in Britain. APSR 69: 1-30.

380 McAllister, I.; Studlar, D. T. 1991. Bandwagon, Underdog or Projection: Opinion Polls and Electoral Choice in Britain. JOP 53: 720-741

381 Meulemann, H. 1983. Value Change in West Germany 1950-1980. SSI 22: 777-800.

382 Namenwirth, J. Z. 1973. Wheels of Time and the Interdependence of Value Change in America. JIDH 4: 649-683.

383 Peterson, S. A.; Somit, A. 1982. Cognitive Development and Childhood Political Socialization. ABS 25: 313-334.

384 Policy Studies Journal. 1980. Papers on Social Values and Public Policy. PSJ 9 (4).

385 Review of Radical Political Economics. 1989. Papers on Theories of Value. RRPE 21 (1/2).

386 Rohrschneider, R. 1994. Influence of Institutions on Political Elites' Democratic Values in Germany. APSR 88: 927-944.

387 Sasaki, M.; Suzuki, T. 1990. Trend and Cross National Study of General Social Attitudes. IJCS 31: 193-205.

388 Schwartz, S. H. 1994. Are There Universal Aspects in Structure and Contents of Human Values? JSI 50: 19-46.

389 Shamir, M.; Shamir, J. 1995. Competing Values in Public Opinion. PB 17: 107-133.

390 Tourangeau, R.; Rasinski, K. A.; Bradburn, N. 1991. Measuring Happiness in Surveys. POQ 55: 255-266.

391 Waldron, J. 1989. Particular Values and Critical Morality. CLR 77: 561-589.

392 Zaller, J. 1991. Information, Values and Opinion. APSR 85: 1215-1238.

CITIZEN PARTICIPATION

1 Aberbach, J. D. 1969. Alienation and Political Behavior. APSR 63: 86-99.

2 Abowtiz, D. A. 1990. Sociopolitical Participation and the Significance of Social Context. SSQ 71: 543-566.

3 Acock, A.; Clarke, H. D.; Stewart, M. C. 1985. A Covariance Structure Analysis of Political Efficacy. JOP 47: 1062-1084.

4 Beck, P. A.; Jennings, M. K. 1979. Political Periods and Political Participation. APSR 73: 737-750.

5 -. 1982. Pathways to Participation. APSR 76: 94-108.

6 Becquart-Leclercq, J. 1980. Local Political Recruitment in France and the US: Mayors. EJPR 8: 407-422.

7 Bell, R. 1969. The Determinants of Psychological Involvement in Politics. MJPS 13: 237-253.

8 Brady, H. E.; Verba, S.; Schlozman, K. L. 1995. Beyond SES: A Resource Model of Political Participation. APSR 89: 271-294.

9 Cable, S.; Walsh, E. J.; Warland, R. H. 1988. Differential Paths to Political Activism: Mobilization Processes after the Three Mile Island Accident. SF 66: 951-969.

10 Citrin, J. 1974. Political Relevance of Trust in Government. APSR 68: 973-988.

11 -. 1987. Political Alienation as a Social Indicator. SIR 4: 381-419.

12 Citrin, J., et al. 1975. Personal and Political Sources of Political Alienation. BJPS 5: 1-31.

13 Conge, P. J. 1988. Concept of Political Participation. CP 20: 241-249.

14 Conover, P. J. 1983. Mobilization of the New Right. WPQ 36: 632-649.

15 Conover, P. J.; Crewe, I.; Searing, D. D. 1991. The Nature of Citizenship. JOP 53: 800-832.

16 Coulter, P. B. 1992. Redefining Citizen Contacting of Governmental Officials. UAQ 28: 297-316.

17 Craig, S. C.; Maggiotto, M. A. 1981. Political Discontent and Political Action. JOP 43: 514-522.

18 -. 1982. Measuring Political Efficacy. PM 8: 85-109.

19 Dahl, R. 1994. A Demographic Dilemma: System Effectiveness vs. Citizen Participation. PSQ 109: 23-34.

20 Denters, B.; Geurts, P. 1993. Aspects of Political Alienation. AP 28: 445 ff.

21 Dominguez, J. I. 1974. Political Participation and the Social Mobilization Hypothesis: Chile, Mexico, Venezuela and Cuba, 1800-1825. JIDH 5: 237-266.

22 Erber, R.; Lau, R. R. 1990. Political Cynicism Revisited: Information Processing Reconciliation of Policy Based and Incumbency Based Interpretations of Changes in Trust in Government. AJPS 34: 236-253.

23 Feldman, S. 1983. Measurement and Meaning of Trust in Government. PM 9: 341-354.

24 Fenifter, A. W. 1970. Dimensions of Political Alienation. APSR 64: 389-410.

25 Finkel, S. E. 1985. Reciprocal Effects of Participation and Political Efficacy. AJPS 29: 891-913.

26 Finkel, S. E.; Miller, E. N.; Opp, K. D. 1989. Personal Influence, Collective Rationality and Mass Political Action. APSR 83: 885-904.

27 Fraser, J. 1970. The Mistrustful-Efficacious Hypothesis and Political Participation. JOP 32: 444-449.

28 Hessenius, C. 1991. Explaining Who Writes to Congressmen. PG 10: 149-161.

29 Hirlinger, M. W. 1992. Citizen Initiated Contacting of Local Government Officials. JOP 54: 553-564.

30 Iyengar, S. 1980. Subjective Political Efficacy as a Measure of Diffuse Support. POQ 44: 249-256.

31 Jankowski, T. B.; Strate, J. M. 1995. Modes of Participation over the Adult Life Cycle. PB 17: 89-106.

32 Journal of Applied Behavioral Science. 1981. Papers on Citizen Participation in Public Policy. JABS 17 (4).

33 Journal of Theoretical Politics. 1991. Papers on Political Entry. JTP 3 (2).

34 Judd, C. M.; Krosnick, J. A.; Milburn, M. A. 1981. Political Involvement and Attitude Structure. ASR 46: 660-669.

35 Krampen, G. 1991 Political Participation in an Action Theory Model. PP 12: 1-26.

36 Latin American Perspectives. 1993. Papers on Popular Participation in Latin America. LAPER 6 (3) and 1993 20 (4).

37 Marcus, G. E.; MacKuen, M. B. 1993. Anxiety, Enthusiasm and the Vote: Emotional Underpinnings of Learning and Involvement during Presidential Campaigns. APSR 87: 672-685.

38 Marquette, J. F. 1974. Social Change and Political Mobilization in the US. APSR 68: 1058-1074.

39 McVeigh, R. 1995. Social Structure, Political Institutions and Mobilization Potential. SF 74: 461-486.

40 Miller, A. H. 1974. Political Issues and Trust in Government, 1964-1970. APSR 68: 951-972.

41 Miller, A. H.; Gurin, P.; Gurin, G. 1981. Group Consciousness and Political Participation. AJPS 25: 494-511.

42 Mirande, A. M. 1973. Social Mobility and Participation: Dissociative and Socialization Hypotheses. SQ 14: 19-31.

43 Modern China. 1980. Papers on Popular Movements and the Political Economy of China. MC 6 (1-3).

44 Moon, D.; Serra, G.; West, J. P. 1993. Citizen Contacts with Bureaucratic and Legislative Officials. PRQ 46: 931-941.

45 Muller, E. N.; Jukam, T. O. 1983. Discontent and Aggressive Political Participation. BJPS 13: 159-180.

46 Nachmias, D. 1974. Modes and Types of Political Alienation. BJS 254: 478-493.

47 National Civic Review. 1995. Papers on Citizen Participation. NCR 84 (1).

48 Nie, N. H.; Powell, G. B.; Prewitt, K. 1969. Social Structure and Political Participation. APSR 63: 361-378, 808-832.

49 Niemi, R. G.; Craig, S. C.; Mattein, F. 1991. Measuring Internal Political Efficacy in the 1988 National Election Study. APSR 85: 1407-1416.

50 Opp, K. D., Burrow-Auffarth, K.; Heinrichs, U. 1981. Conditions for Conventional and Unconventional Political Participation. EJPR 9: 147-168.

51 Perloff, R. M. 1984. Political Involvement: A Process-Oriented Reformulation. CSMC 1: 146-160.

52 Planning and Administration. 1981. Papers on European Citizen Participation. Vol 8 (2).

53 Political Science. 1982. Papers on Political Commitment. PSNZ 34 (2).

54 Res Publica. 1993. Papers on Belgium Political Participation. RP 35 (2).

55 Rosenberg, S. W. 1985. Sociology, Psychology and Political Behavior: Political Socialization. JOP 47: 715-731.

56 Rusk, J. G. 1976. Political Participation in America. APSR 70: 583-591.

57 Sabucedo, J. M.; Arce, C. C. 1991. Types of Political Participation. EJPR 20: 93-106.

58 Scaff, L. A. 1975. Two Concepts of Political Participation. WPQ 28: 447-462.

59 Schneider, S. K.; Ingraham, P. 1984. The Impact of Political Participation on Policy Adoption and Expansion. CP 17: 107-122.

60 Seligson, M. A. 1980. Trust, Efficacy and Modes of Political Participation. BJPS 10: 75-98.

61 Sigel, R. S. 1975. Psychological Antecedents and Political Involvement: Locus-of-Control. SSQ 56: 315-323.

62 Sigelman, L.; Feldman, S. 1983. Efficacy, Mistrust and Political Mobilization. CPS 16: 118-143.

63 Sproule-Jones, M.; Hart, K. D. 1973. A Public Choice Model of Political Participation. CJPS 6: 175-194.

64 Thomas, J. C. 1982. Citizen Initiated Contacts with Government Agencies. AJPS 26: 504-522.

65 Trilling, R. J.; Lindquist, D. P. 1975. Effective Support. CPS 7: 395-429.

66 Umez, B. N. 1993. Has Social Mobilization Caused Political Instability in Africa? Granger Causality Test. RBPE 22: 33-54.

67 Van den Broek, A. 1994. Political Involvement in the Netherlands. AP 29: 173-198.

68 Vedlitz, A. 1984. The Impact of College Education on Political Participation Hypothesis. SSQ 64: 145-153.

69 Verba, S., et al. 1993. Citizen Activity: Who Participates? What Do They Say? APSR 87: 303-318.

70 Waterman, H. 1981. Collective Political Activity in Comparative and Historical Perspective. WP 33: 554-589.

71 Winkler, J. D.; Hester, P. G.; Kopala, P. S. 1974. Collective Protest and Legitimacy of Authority. JCR 18: 37-54.

72 Wolfsfeld, G. 1985. Political Efficacy and Political Action: A Change in Focus Using Data from Israel. SSQ 66: 617-628.

73 Woshinsky, D. H.; Payne, J. L. 1972. Incentives for Political Participation. WP 24: 518-546.

74 Zuckerman, A. S.; West, D. M. 1985. Political Bases of Citizen Contacting. APSR 79: 117-131.

Direct Democracy

75 Annuaire Suisse de Science Politique. 1987. Papers on Direct Democracy in Switzerland. ASSP 27, and 1991 31.

76 Archer, J. C.; Reynolds, D. R. 1976. Locational Logrolling and Citizen Support of Municipal Bond Proposals. PC 17: 21-39.

77 Atkeson, L. R.; Partin, R. W. 1995. Economic and Referendum Voting: A Comparison of Gubernatorial and Senatorial Elections. APSR 89: 99-107.

78 Barnum, D. T.; Helburn, I. B. 1982. Influencing the Electorate: Experience with Referenda on Public Employee Bargaining. ILLR 35: 330-342.

79 Bohnet, I.; Frey, B. S. 1994. Direct Democracy Rules: Role of Discussion. Kyklos 47: 341-354.

80 Bowler, S.; Donovan, T. 1994. Information and Opinion Change on Ballot Propositions. PB 16: 411-436.

81 Bradbury, K. L. 1991. Can Local Governments Give Citizens What They Want? Referendum Outcomes in Massachusetts. NEER 1991 (May): 3-22.

82 Brodsky, D. M.; Thompson, E. 1993. Ethos, Public Choice and Referendum Voting. SSQ 74: 286-299.

83 Brokaw, A. J.; Gale, J. R.; Metz, T. E. 1990. The Effect of Tax Price on Voter Choice in Local School Referenda. NTJ 43: 53-60.

84 Campbell, B. C. 1977. Did Democracy Work? Prohibition in Late Nineteenth Century Iowa. JIDH 8: 87-116.

85 Franklin, M. N.; van der Eijk, C.; Marsh, M. 1995. Referendum Outcomes and Trust in Government. WEP 18: 101-117.

86 Frey, B. S. 1992. Efficiency and Democratic Political Organization: The Case for Referendum. JPP 12: 209-222.

87 Hersch, P. L.; McDougall, G. S. 1988. Voting for Sin in Kansas. PC 57: 127-145.

88 LeDuc, L.; Pammett, J. H. 1995. Referendum Voting: Attitudes in the 1992 Canadian Constitutional Referendum. CJPS 28: 3-34.

89 Lupia, A. 1994. Effect of Information on Voting Behavior and Electoral Outcomes: Direct Legislation. PC 78: 65-86.

90 Magleby, D. B. 1988. Taking the Initiative: Direct Legislation and Direct Democracy. PS 21: 600-611.

91 Matsusaka, J. G. 1992. Economics of Direct Legislation. QJE 107: 541-571.

92 McConnell, K. E. 1990. Models for Referendum Data. JEEM 18: 19-34.

93 Morel, L. 1993. Party Attitudes towards Referendums in Western Europe. WEP 16: 225-244.

94 Mueller, J. E. 1969. Voting on Propositions: Ballot Patterns and Historical Trends in California. APSR 63: 1197-1212.

95 Pierce, R.; Valen, H.; Listhaug, O. 1983. Referendum Voting Behavior: Membership in the European Community. AJPS 27: 43-63.

96 Romer, T.; Rosenthal, H.; Munley, V. G. 1992. Economic Incentives and Political Institutions: School Budget Referenda. JPUBE 49: 1-33.

97 Ross, R. S. 1985. In Search of Theory in School Finance Elections. WPQ 38: 502-509.

98 Santerre, R. E. 1986. Representative vs. Direct Democracy: A Tiebout Test of Relative Performance. PC 48: 55-63.

99 Schoolmaster, F. A. 1984. Water-Related Constitutional Amendment Voting Patterns in Texas. SSQ 65: 1147-1156.

100 Schroeder, L. D.; Sjoquist, D. L. 1978. The Rational Voter: Analysis of Atlanta Referenda on Rapid Transit. PC 33: 27-44.

101 Sharp, E. B. 1987. Voting on Citywide Propositions. UAQ 23: 233-248.

102 Svensson, P. 1984. Class, Party and Ideology: A Danish Case Study of Electoral Behavior in Referendums. SPS 7: 175-196.

Turnout

103 Abramson, P. R.; Aldrich, J. H. 1982. Decline of Electoral Participation in America. APSR 76: 502-521.

104 Aldrich, J. H. 1993. Rational Choice and Turnout. AJPS 37: 246-290.

105 American Politics Quarterly. 1981. Papers on Turnout. APQ 9 (2).

106 Ashenfeld, O.; Kelley, S. 1965. Determinants of Participation in Presidential Elections. JOEL 18: 695-733.

107 Bauer, J. R. 1990. Patterns of Voter Participation in the American States. SSQ 71: 824-834.

108 Bennett, S. E.; Resnick, D. 1990. Implications of Nonvoting for Democracy. AJPS 34: 771-802.

109 Berch, N. 1993. Another Look at Closeness and Turnout: Canadian National Elections. PRQ 46: 421-432.

110 Boyd, R. W. 1981. Decline in US Vote Turnout: Structural Explanations. APQ 9: 133-159.

111 Brunk, G. G. 1980. Impact of Rational Participation Models on Voting Attitudes. PC 35: 549-564.

112 Capron, H.; Kruseman, J. L. 1988. Is Political Rivalry an Incentive to Vote? PC 56: 31-44.

113 Cassel, C. A.; Luskin, R. C. 1988. Simple Explanations of Turnout Decline. APSR 82: 1321-1332.

114 Cohen, J. E. 1982. Change in Electoral Calendars and Turnout Decline. APQ 10: 246-254.

115 Colomer, J. M. 1991. Benefits and Costs of Voting. ES 10: 313-325.

116 Cox, G. W. 1988. Closeness and Turnout. JOP 50: 768-775.

117 Crepaz, M. 1990. Impact of Party Polarization and Postmaterialism on Voter Turnout. EJPR 18: 183-205.

118 Erikson, R. S. 1995. State Turnout and Presidential Voting. APQ 23: 387-396.

119 Fenton, J. 1979. Turnout and the Two-Party Vote. JOP 41: 229-234.

120 Ferejohn, J. A.; Fiorina, M. P. 1974. The Paradox of Not Voting. APSR 68: 525-537.

121 -. 1975. Closeness Counts Only in Horseshoes and Dancing. APSR 69: 620-625.

122 Filer, J. E.; Kenny, L. W. 1980. Voter Turnout and the Benefits of Voting. PC 25: 575-586.

123 Hartwig, F. 1981. Rationality and Voting. JPS 9: 1-16.

124 Hinich, M. J. 1981. Voting as an Act of Contribution. PC 36: 135-140.

125 Hinich, M. J.; Ordeshook, P. C. 1969. Abstentions and Equilibrium in the Electoral Process. PC 7: 81-106.

126 Hirczy, W. 1994. Impact of Mandatory Voting Laws on Turnout. ES 13: 65-76.

127 Jaarsma, B.; Schram, A. J. H. C.; Van Winden, F. 1986. The Voting Participation of Public Bureaucrats. PC 48: 183-187.

128 Jackman, R. W. 1987. Political Institutions and Voter Turnout in the Industrialized Democracies. APSR 81: 405-424.

129 Jackman, R. W. 1995. Clarifying the Relationship between Education and Turnout. APQ 23: 279-299.

130 Jackman, R. W.; Miller, R. A. 1995. Voter Turnout in the Industrial Democracies. CPS 27: 467-492.

131 Jackson, J. E. 1983. Election Night Reporting and Voter Turnout. AJPS 27: 615-635.

132 Johnson, G. W. 1971. Political Correlates of Voter Participation. APSR 65: 768-776.

133 Kennamer, J. D. 1987. How Media Use during a Campaign Affects the Intent to Vote. JQ 64: 291-300.

134 Kenney, P. J.; Rice, T. W. 1989. An Examination of the Minimax Hypothesis. APQ 17: 153-162.

135 Kirchgassner, G.; Schimmelpfennig, J. 1992. Closeness Counts If It Matters for Electoral Victory. PC 73: 283-300.

136 Klinkner, P. A. 1993. Relationship between Judicial Activism and Voter Turnout. Polity 25: 633-646.

137 Knack, S. 1993. The Voter Participation Effects of Selecting Jurors from Registration Lists. JOLE 36: 99-114.

138 -. 1994. Does Rain Help the Republicans? Theory and Evidence on Turnout and Vote. PC 79: 187-209.

139 Matsusaka, J. G. 1993. Election Closeness and Voter Turnout: California Ballot Propositions. PC 76: 313-334.

140 -. 1995. Explaining Voter Turnout Patterns: An Information Theory. PC 84: 91-118.

141 Merrifield, J. 1993. Institutional and Political Factors that Influence Voter Turnout. PC 77: 657-667.

142 Miller, W. E. 1992. Explaining Declining Turnout. PB 14: 1-43.

143 Mitchell, G. E.; Wlezien, C. 1995. Impact of Legal Constraints on Voter Registration, Turnout and the Composition of the American Electorate. PB 17: 179-202.

144 Moon, D. 1992. The Determinants of Turnout in Presidential Elections. PB 14: 123-140.

145 Morton, R. B. 1991. Groups in Rational Turnout Models. AJPS 35: 758-776.

146 Nagler, J. 1991. Effect of Registration Laws and Education on Voter Turnout. APSR 85: 1393-1406.

147 Niemi, R. G.; Barkan, J. D. 1987. Age and Turnout in New Electorates and Peasant Societies. APSR 81: 583-588.

148 Norrander, B.; Grofman, B. 1988. Rational Choice Model of Citizen Participation in High and Low Commitment Electoral Activities. PC 57: 187-192.

149 Nownes, A. J. 1992. Primaries, General Elections and Voter Turnout: Multinominal Logit Model of the Decision to Vote. APQ 20: 205-226.

150 Olsen, M. E. 1972. Social Participation and Voter Turnout. APSR 37: 317-333.

151 Overbye, E. 1995. Making a Case for the Rational, Self-Regarding, Ethical Voter and Solving the Paradox of Not Voting. EJPR 27: 369-396.

152 Owen, G.; Grofman, B. 1984. To Vote or Not to Vote: The Paradox of Nonvoting. PC 42: 311-325.

153 Pacek, A. C.; Radcliff, B. 1995. Turnout and Vote for Left of Center Parties. BJPS 25: 137-143.

154 Palfrey, T. R.; Rosenthal, H. 1985. Voter Participation and Strategic Uncertainty. APSR 79: 50-61.

155 Petrocik, J. R. 1981. Voter Turnout and Electoral Oscillation. APQ 9: 161-180.

156 -. 1991. Algorithm for Estimating Turnout as a Guide to Predicting Elections. POQ 55: 643-647.

157 Powell, G. B. 1986. American Voting Turnout in Comparative Perspective. APSR 80: 17-44.

158 PS. 1984. Should You Brush Your Teeth on November 6? Rational Perspective. PS 17: 571-576.

159 Radcliff, B. 1992. The Welfare State, Turnout and the Economy. APSR 86: 444-456.

160 -. 1994. Turnout and the Democratic Vote. APQ 22: 259-276.

161 Ragsdale, L.; Rusk, J. G. 1993. Who Are Nonvoters? AJPS 37: 721-746.

162 Rhine, S. L. 1995. Registration Reform and Turnout Change in the American States. APQ 23: 409-426.

163 Rosenstone, S. J. 1982. Economic Adversity and Voter Turnout. AJPS 26: 25-46.

164 Rosenstone, S. J.; Wolfinger, R. E. 1978. Effect of Registration Laws on Voter Turnout. APSR 72: 22-45.

165 Rubinfeld, D. L.; Thomas, R. 1980. The Economics of Voter Turnout in Local School Elections. PC 35: 315-332.

166 Salkever, S. G. 1980. Who Knows Whether It's Rational to Vote? Ethics 90: 203-217.

167 Schlozman, K. L.; Verba, S.; Brady, H. E. 1995. Participation's Not a Paradox. BJPS 25: 1-36.

168 Schram, A. J. H. C.; Van Winden, F. 1991. Why People Vote: Free Riding and the Production and Consumption of Social Pressure. JEPSY 12: 575-620.

169 Schwartz, T. 1987. Your Vote Counts on Account of the Way It is Counted: An Institutional Solution to the Paradox of Voting. PC 54: 101-122.

170 Shaffer, S. D. 1981. A Multivariate Explanation of Decreasing Turnout in Presidential Elections. AJPS 25: 68-95.

171 Shortridge, R. M. 1980. Democracy's Golden Age? Voter Turnout in the Midwest, 1840-1872. SSQ 60: 617-629.

172 Sigelman, L., et al. 1985. Voting and Not-Voting. APSR 20: 749-765.

173 Silberman, J. I.; Durden, G. C. 1975. The Rational Behavior Theory of Voter Participation. PC 23: 101-108.

174 Sinnott, R.; Whelan, B. J. 1992. Turnout in Second Order Elections: European Parliament Elections. EASR 23: 147-166.

175 Southwell, P. L. 1995. Alienation and Nonvoting in the Presidential Elections. JPMS 23: 99-118.

176 Straits, B. C. 1990. Social Context of Voter Turnout. POQ 54: 64-73.

177 Stubbings, R. G.; Carmines, E. G. 1991 Is It Rational to Vote? Polity 23: 629-640.

178 Thompson, F. 1982. Closeness Counts in Horseshoes and Dancing... and Elections. PC 38: 305-316.

179 Tideman, T. N. 1985. Remorse, Elation and the Paradox of Voting. PC 45: 103-106.

180 Tollison, R. D.; Willett, T. D. 1973. Some Simple Economics of Voting and Not Voting. PC 26: 59-71.

181 Tuckel, P. S.; Maisel, R. 1994. Voter Turnout among European Immigrants. JIDH 24: 407-430.

182 Tullock, G. 1992. Is There a Paradox of Voting? JTP 4: 225-230.

183 Uhlaner, C. J. 1989. Rational Turnout: The Neglected Role of Groups. AJPS 33: 390-422.

184 Weisberg, H. F.; Grofman, B. 1981. Candidate Evaluations and Turnout. APQ 9: 197-220.

Voting Behavior

185 Abramowitz, A. I. 1980. A Comparison of Voting for US Senator and Representative. APSR 74: 633-640.

186 -. 1995. The End of the Democratic Era? PRQ 48: 873-890.

187 Agnew, J. A. 1994. National vs. Contextual: The Controversy over Measuring Electoral Change in Italy Using Goodman Flow-of-Vote Estimates. PG 13: 245-254.

188 Aldrich, J. H.; Alvarez, R. M. 1994. Issues and the Presidential Primary Voter. PB 16: 289-318.

189 Aleskerov, F. T. 1985. Collective Decision Making Using Voting Procedures. Problems of Complex Control Systems 2: 357-366.

190 -. 1986. Hierarchical Voting.Information Science 39: 41-86.

191 Alvarez, R. M.; Schousen, M. M. 1993. Policy Moderation or Conflicting Expectations? Testing Intentional Models of Split-Ticket Voting. APQ 21: 410-438.

192 American Politics Quarterly. 1975. Papers on American Electoral Behavior. APQ 3 (3).

193 Ando, H. 1969. Voting Patterns in the Philippines Presidential and Senatorial Elections. MJPS 13: 567-586.

194 Ansolabehere, S., et al. 1994. Does Attack Advertising Demobilize the Electorate? APSR 88: 829-838.

195 Ascher, W.; Tarrow, S. 1975. The Stability of Communist Electorates. AJPS 19: 475-500.

196 Austen-Smith, D. 1989. Sincere Voting in Models of Legislative Elections. SCAW 6: 287-299.

197 Axelrod, R. 1972. An Analysis of Electoral Coalitions, 1952-1968. APSR 66: 11-20.

198 Bean, C. S. 1990. The Personal Vote in Australian Federal Elections. POLST 38: 253-268.

199 Bean, C. S.; Mughan, A. 1989. Leadership Effects in Parliamentary Elections in Australia and Britain. APSR 83: 1165-1179.

200 Beck, P. A., et al. 1992. Patterns and Sources of Ticket Splitting in Subpresidential Voting. APSR 86: 916-928.

201 Black, J. H. 1980. The Probability Choice Perspective in Voter Decision Making Models. PC 35: 565-574.

202 Blais, A., et al. 1995. Do People Vote on the Basis of Minimax Regret? PRQ 48: 827-836.

203 Books, J. W.; Reynolds, J. A. B. 1975. Class Voting in Great Britain and US. CPS 8: 360-375.

204 Brody, R. A.; Page, B. I. 1972. The Assessment of Policy Voting. APSR 66: 450-458.

205 Brody, R. A.; Sniderman, P. M. 1977. Relevance of Personal Concerns for Voting. BJPS 7: 337-360

206 Brown, R. D.; Carmines, E. G. 1995. Materialists, Postmaterialists, and Criteria for Political Choice in US Presidential Elections. JOP 57: 483-494.

207 Calvert, R. L.; Ferejohn, J. A. 1983. Coattail Voting in Recent Presidential Elections. APSR 77: 407-419.

208 Campbell, J. E. 1986. Predicting Seat Gains from Presidential Coattails. AJPS 30: 165-183.

209 Carmines, E. G.; Stimson, J. A. 1980. Two Faces of Issue Voting. APSR 74: 78-91.

210 Cassel, C. A. 1978. Class Bases of Southern Politics among Whites. SSQ 58: 700-707.

211 Comparative Political Studies. 1969. Papers on Social Structure, Party Systems and Voting Behavior. CPS 2 (1).

212 Conover, P. J.; Feldman, S. 1989. Candidate Perception in an Ambiguous World: Campaigns, Cues and Inference Processes. AJPS 33: 912-940.

213 Coughlin, P. J. 1988. Expectations about Voter Choices. PC 44: 49-59.

214 -. 1990. Majority Rule and Election Models. JES 4: 157-188.

215 Cox, G. W.; McCubbins, M. D.; Sullivan, T. 1984. Policy Choice as an Electoral Investment. SCAW 1: 231-242.

216 Cox, G. W.; Morgenstern, S. 1995. Incumbency Advantage in Multimember Districts. LSQ 20: 329-350.

217 Croley, S. P. 1994. Imperfect Information and the Electoral Connection. PRQ 47: 509-523.

218 Dasgupta, S.; Williams, K. C. 1995. Search Behavior of Asymmetrically Informed Voters. EAP 7: 21-41.

219 De Boef, S.; Stimson, J. A. 1995. The Dynamic Structure of Congressional Elections. JOP 57: 630-648.

220 De Graaf, N. D.; Nieuwbeerta, P.; Heath, A. 1995. Class Mobility and Political Preferences. AJS 100: 997-1027.

221 Denzau, A. T.; Parks, R. P. 1983. Existence of Voting-Market Equilibria. JET 30: 243-265.

222 Dubois, P. L. 1980. Public Participation in Trial Court Elections. LAP 2: 137-160.

223 Edwards, G. C. 1979. The Impact of Presidential Coattails on Outcomes of Congressional Elections. APQ 7: 94-108.

224 Electoral Studies. 1990. Papers on Eastern European Elections. ES 9 (4).

225 Enelow, J. M.; Hinich, M. J. 1983. Voting One Issue at a Time: The Question of Voter Forecasts. APSR 77: 435-445.

226 European Journal of Political Research. 1980. Papers on Eastern Europe's First Elections. EJPR 8 (1).

227 -. 1991. Papers on the Micro and Macro Analysis of Elections. EJPR 19 (4).

228 -. 1994. Papers on the Intellectual History of Election Studies. EJPR 25 (3).

229 Faith, R. L.; Buchanan, J. M. 1981. Toward a Theory of Yes-No Voting. PC 37: 231-245.

230 Feld, S. L.; Grofman, B. 1988. Majority Rule Outcomes and the Structural Debate in One Issue at a Time Decision Making. PC 59: 239-252.

231 Ferejohn, J. A.; McKelvey, R. D.; Packel, E. 1984. Limiting Distributions for Continuous State Markov Voting Models. SCAW 1: 45-67.

232 Fishburn, P. C. 1980. Deducing Majority Candidates from Election Data. SSR 9: 216-224.

233 Fishburn, P. C.; Gehrlein, W. V. 1977. Towards a Theory of Elections with Probabilistic Preferences. Econometrica 45: 1907-1924.

234 Fleitas, D. 1971. Bandwagon and Underdog Effects in Minimal Information Elections. APSR 65: 434-438.

235 Flemming, G. N. 1995. Presidential Coattails in Open-Seat Elections. LSQ 20: 197-212.

236 Fowler, L. L. 1980. Candidate Perceptions of Electoral Outcomes. APQ 8: 483-494.

237 Franklin, M. N.; Mughan, A. 1978. The Decline of Class Voting in Britain. APSR 72: 523-534.

238 Gant, M. M.; Davis, D. F. 1984. Mental Economy and Voter Rationality: Informed Citizen Problem in Voting Research. JOP 46: 132-153.

239 Gehrlein, W. V.; Fishburn, P. C. 1978. The Effects of Abstentions on Election Outcomes. PC 33: 69-82.

240 Goldberg, A. S. 1966. Discerning a Causal Pattern among Data on Voting Behavior. APSR 60: 913-922.

241 Gopoian, J. D.; Hadjiharalambous, S. 1994. Late-Deciding Voters in Presidential Elections. PB 16: 55-78.

242 Greene, J. P. 1993. Presidential Election Forecasting Models and the 1992 Election. PS 17-20.

243 Hartwig, F.; Jenkins, W. R.; Temchin, E. M. 1980. Variability in Electoral Behavior. AJPS 24: 553-558.

244 Hernstein, J. A. 1981. A Cognitive Process Analysis of Decision Making in Voting. JPSP 40: 843-861.

245 Hinckley, B.; Hofstetter, C. R.; Kessel, J. H. 1974. Information and the Vote. APQ 2: 131-153.

246 Holbrook, T. M. 1993. Institutional Strength and Gubernatorial Elections. APQ 21: 261-271.

247 Hurley, P. A.; Hill, K. Q. 1980. Issue Voting in Congressional Elections. APQ 8: 425-448.

248 International Political Science Review. 1981. Papers on Experimentatal Elections. IPSR 2 (4).

249 Irwin, G.; Meeter, D. A. 1969. Building Voter Transition Models from Aggregate Data. MJPS 13: 545-566.

250 Jackman, R. W. 1975. Elections and the Democratic Class Struggle. WP 39: 123-146.

251 Jackson, J. E. 1975. Issues, Party Choices and Presidential Votes. AJPS 19: 161-185.

252 Jewell, M. E. 1994. State Legislative Elections: What We Know and Don't Know. APQ 22: 483-509.

253 Johnston, R. J.; Hay, A. M. 1983. Voter Transition Probability Estimates: An Entropy Maximizing Approach. EJPR 11: 81-92.

254 Johnston, R. J.; Pattie, C. J. 1992. The End of Thatcherism and Changing Voting Patterns in Great Britain. EPA 24: 1491-1505.

255 Kaase, M. 1994. Is There Personalization in Politics? Candidates and Voting Behavior in Germany. IPSR 15: 211-230.

256 Kelley, J.; McAllister, I. 1985. Social Context and Electoral Behavior in Britain. AJPS 29: 564-586.

257 Kelley, R. C. 1985. Independent Voting Behavior and Its Effects on Rational Social Choice. WPQ 38: 377-387.

258 Kelley, S.; Mirer, T. 1975. The Simple Act of Voting. APSR 68: 572-591.

259 Kirchgassner, G.; Wolters, J. 1987. Influence of Poll Results on Election Outcomes. MSS 13: 165-175.

260 Knoke, D. 1974. Causal Synthesis of Sociological and Psychological Models of US Voting Behavior. SF 53: 92-101.

261 Knoke, D.; Kyriazis, N. 1977. Persistence of the Black Belt Vote: A Test of Key's Hypothesis. SSQ 57: 899-906.

262 Laponce, J. A. 1980. Voting for X: Of Men, Women, Religion and Politics: Use of an Election Experiment for Comparative Analysis of Conservative Behavior. SSI 19: 955-970.

263 -. 1981. Use of in Vitro and Laboratory Experiments in Study of Elections. IPSR 2: 385-406.

264 Ledyard, J. 1984. The Pure Theory of Large Two-Candidate Elections. PC 44: 7-41.

265 Lewis-Beck, M. S.; Rice, T. W. 1982. Presidential Popularity and Presidential Vote. PCQ 46: 534-537.

266 Li, R. 1976. A Dynamic Comparative Analysis of Presidential and House Elections. AJPS 20: 671-691.

267 Lodge, M.; McGraw, K. M.; Stroh, P. 1989. An Impression Driven Model of Candidate Evaluation. APSR 83: 399-419.

268 Lodge, M.; Stroh, P.; Wahlke, J. C. 1990. Black Box Models of Candidate Evaluation. PB 12: 5-18.

269 Maas, C. F.; Van Doorn, L. J.; Saris, W. E. 1991. Smallest Distance Hypothesis and Explanation of the Vote Reconsidered. AP 26: 65-84.

270 MacDonald, S. E.; Rabinowitz, G.; Listhaug, O. 1995. Political Sophistication and Models of Issue Voting. BJPS 25: 453-484.

271 Markus, G. B.; Converse, P. E. 1979. A Dynamic Simultaneous Equation Model of Candidate Choice. APSR 73: 1055-1070.

272 McCormick, R. E.; McKenzie, R. B. 1979. The Cost of Voting: Its Fiscal Impact on Government. PC 34: 271-284.

273 McCraw, D. J. 1992. The Electoral Cycle in New Zealand. JCACP 30: 243-255.

274 McCubbins, M. D.; Schwartz, T. 1988. Congress, the Courts and Public Policy: Consequences of the One Man, One Vote Rule. AJPS 32: 388-415.

275 McCurley, C.; Mondak, J. J. 1995. The Influence of Incumbents' Competence and Integrity in US House Elections. AJPS 39: 864-885.

276 McDonagh, E. L. 1992. Representative Democracy and State Building in the Progressive Era. APSR 86: 938-950.

277 Meier, K. J. 1980. Rationality and Voting: A Downsian Analysis. WPQ 33: 38-49.

278 Miller, A. H.; Wattenberg, M. P. 1985. Throwing the Rascals Out. APSR 79: 359-372.

279 Minns, D. R. 1984. Voting as an Influential Behavior: Child and Adolescent Beliefs. APQ 12: 285-304.

280 Mondak, J. J. 1990. Determinants of Coattail Voting. PB 12: 265-288.

281 -. 1995. Competence, Integrity and the Electoral Success of Congressional Incumbents. JOP 57: 1043-1069.

282 Moon, D. 1990. Information Effects on the Determinants of Electoral Choice. APQ 18: 3-24.

283 Morton, R. B.; Schmidt, A. B. 1994. Retrospective Voting and Political Mobility. AJPS 38: 999-1024.

284 Nadeau, R.; Niemi, R. G.; Amato, T. 1994. Expectations and Preferences in British General Elections. APSR 88: 371-383.

285 Neeler, M. C. 1977. Closeness of Elections in Latin America. LARR 12: 115-122.

286 Norrander, B. 1993. Nomination Choice, Caucus and Primary Outcomes. AJPS 37: 343-364.

287 Page, B. I. 1977. Elections and Social Choice: The State of the Evidence. AJPS 21: 639-668.

288 Page, B. I.; Jones, C. C. 1979. Reciprocal Effects of Policy Preferences, Party Loyalties and Vote. APSR 73: 1071-1089.

289 Pammett, J. H. 1988. A Framework for the Comparative Analysis of Elections across Time and Space. ES 7: 125-142.

290 Piereson, J. E. 1975. Presidential Popularity and Midterm Voting at Different Electoral Levels. AJPS 19: 683-694.

291 Powell, L. W. 1989. Analyzing Misinformation: Perception of Congressional Candidates' Ideologies. AJPS 33: 272-293.

292 Przeworski, A. 1975. The Institutionalization of Voting Patterns or Is Mobilization the Source of Decay. APSR 69: 49-67.

293 Rabinowitz, G.; Macdonald, S. E. 1989. A Directional Theory of Issue Voting. APSR 83: 93-122.

294 Rabinowitz, G.; Prothro, J. W.; Jacoby, W. G. 1982. Salience as a Factor in Impact of Issues on Candidate Evaluation. JOP 44: 41-63.

295 Rahn, W. M.; Aldrich, J. H.; Borgida, E. 1994. Individual and Contextual Variations in Political Candidate Appraisal. APSR 88: 193-199.

296 Rahn, W. M.; Krosnick, J. A.; Breuning, M. 1994. Rationalization and Derivation Processes in Survey Studies of Political Candidate Evaluation. AJPS 38: 582-600.

297 Rasinski, K. A.; Tyler, T. R. 1988. Fairness and Vote Choice in the 1984 Presidential Election. APQ 16: 5-24.

298 Ray, D. 1982. Sources of Voting Cues in Three States. JOP 44: 1074-1087.

299 Reed, W. R. 1994. A Retrospective Voting Model with Heterogeneous Politicians. EAP 6: 39-58.

300 Regens, J. L.; Gaddie, R. E.; Lockerbie, B. 1995. Electoral Consequence of Voting to Declare War. JCR 39: 168-182.

301 Revue Francaise de Science Politique. 1993. Papers on the Act of Voting. RFSP 43 (1).

302 Richardson, B. M. 1977. Stability and Change in Japanese Voting Behavior. JASIAS 36: 675-694.

303 -. 1988. Constituency Candidates vs. Parties in Japanese Voting Behavior. APSR 82: 695-718.

304 Riggle, E. D. 1992. Cognitive Strategies and Candidate Evaluations. APQ 20: 227-246.

305 Riker, W. H.; Ordeshook, P. C. 1968. A Theory of the Calculus of Voting. APSR 62: 25-42.

306 Rivers, D. 1988. Heterogeneity in Models of Electoral Choice. AJPS 32: 737-757.

307 Roemer, J. E. 1994. A Theory of Policy Differentiation in Single Issue Electoral Politics. SCAW 11: 355-380.

308 Romer, T.; Rosenthal, H. 1984. Voting Models and Empirical Evidence. American Scientist 72: 465-473.

309 Romero, D. W. 1989. The Changing American Voter Revisited: Candidate Evaluations in Presidential Elections. APQ 17: 409-421.

310 Rose, R. 1982. From Simple Determinism to Interactive Models of Voting. CPS 15: 145-169.

311 Rosenberg, S. W., et al. 1986. Image and the Vote: Effect of Candidate Presentation. AJPS 30: 108-127.

312 Rosenberg, S. W.; McCafferty, P. 1987. Image and the Vote: Manipulating Voters' Preferences. POQ 51: 31-47.

313 Salisbury, B. R. 1983. Evaluating Voting Behavior: An Experimental Examination. WPQ 36: 88-97.

314 Schram, A. J. H. C. 1992. Testing Economic Theories of Voting Behaviour Using Micro-Data. AE 24: 419-428.

315 Sears, D. O., et al. 1980. Self-Interest vs. Symbolic Politics in Policy Attitudes and Presidential Voting. APSR 74: 670-684.

316 Shabman, L.; Stephenson, K. 1994. A Critique of the Self-Interested Voter Model. JEI 28: 1173-1186.

317 Shively, W. P. 1992. From Differential Abstention to Conversion: A Change in Electoral Change. AJPS 36: 309-330.

318 Snider, G. A. 1979. Assessing the Candidate Preference Function. AJPS 23: 732-754.

319 Social Science Quarterly. 1981. Papers on Voter Participation and Public Opinion. SSQ 62 (3).

320 Songer, D. R. 1981. Voter Knowledge of Congressional Issue Positions. SSQ 62: 424-431.

321 Stokes, D. E. 1966. Some Dynamic Elements of Contests for the Presidency. APSR 60: 19-28.

322 Strom, G. S. 1982. Models of Voting Behavior. Micropolitics 2: 257-278.

323 Struthers, J.; Young, A. 1989. Economics of Voting: Theories and Evidence. JESTUD 16: 1-43.

324 Sudman, S. 1983. Do Exit Polls Influence Voting Behavior? POQ 50: 331-339.

325 Svoboda, C. J. 1995. Retrospective Voting in Gubernatorial Elections. PRQ 48: 135-150.

326 Swank, D. H. 1995. Rational Voters in a Partisanship Model. SCAW 12: 13-27.

327 Tether, P. 1994. The Overseas Vote in British Politics. PARLA 47: 73-93.

328 Theilmann, J.; Wilhite, A. 1995. Congressional Turnover: Negating the Incumbency Advantage. SSQ 76: 594-606.

329 Thorson, G. R.; Stambough, S. J. 1995. Anti-Incumbency and the 1992 Elections: Presidential Coattails. JOP 57: 210-220.

330 Tuckel, P. S.; Tejera, F. 1983. Changing Patterns in American Voting Behavior, 1914-1980. POQ 47: 230-246.

331 Tullock, G. 1981. Why so Much Stability? PC 37: 189-202.

332 Turner, A. W. 1993. Postauthoritarian Elections: Testing Expectations about First Elections. CPS 26: 330-349.

333 Upton, G. J. G.; Sarlvik, B. 1981. A Loyalty-Distance Model of Voting Change. JRSA 144: 247-259.

334 Utter, G. H. 1988. Voting, Political Obligation and Political Education. TPS 15: 113-121.

335 Vanderleeuw, J. M.; Utter, G. H. 1993. Voter Roll-Off and the Electoral Context. SSQ 74: 664-673.

336 Van Deth, J. W. 1986. Political Science as a No Risk Policy: The American Voter and Contemporary Voting Research. AP 21: 185-199.

337 Visser, M. 1994. An Analysis of Balance Theory to Electoral Behavior. PP 15: 699-712.

338 Wattenberg, M. P. 1995. Role of Vice Presidential Candidate Ratings in Presidential Voting Behavior. APQ 23: 504-514.

339 Wattier, M. J. 1983. Ideological Voting in the 1980 Republican Presidential Primaries. JOP 45: 1016-1026.

340 Weakliem, D. L. 1993. Class Consciousness and Political Change: Voting and Political Attitudes in the British Working Class. ASR 58: 382-397.

341 -. 1995. Two Models of Class Voting. BJPS 25: 254-270.

342 Weisberg, H. F.; Rusk, J. G. 1970. Dimensions of Candidate Evaluation. APSR 64: 1167-1185.

343 Weiss, H. J. 1988. Is Vote Selling Desirable? PC 59: 55-65.

344 Wright, G. C. 1976. Community Structure and Voting in the South. POQ 40: 200-215.

345 -. 1978. Candidate's Policy Position and Voting in US House Elections. LSQ 3: 445-464.

346 -. 1989. Level of Analysis Effects of Explanations of Voting: Senate Elections. BJPS 19: 381-398.

347 -. 1993. Errors in Measuring Vote Choice in National Election Studies. AJPS 37: 291-316.

348 Wright, G. C.; Berkman, M. B. 1986. Candidates and Policy in US Senate Elections. APSR 80: 567-588.

349 Zelle, C. 1995. Social Dealignment vs. Political Frustration: Contrasting Explanations of the Floating Vote. EJPR 27: 319-345.

350 Zipp, J. F. 1985. Perceived Representativeness and Voting: An Assessment of Impact of Choices vs. Echoes. APSR 79: 50-61.

351 Zuckerman, A. S.; Lichbach, M. I. 1977. Stability and Change in European Electorates. WP 29: 523-551.

352 Zuckerman, A. S.; Valentino, N. A.; Zuckerman, E. W. 1994. A Structural Theory of Vote Choice: Social and Political Networks and Electoral Flows. JOP 56: 1008-1033.

353 Zupan, M. A. 1990. Test of a Simple Economic Explanation for Existence and Nature of Ticket Splitting. EL 33: 21-27.

354 -. 1991. An Economic Explanation for the Existence and Nature of Political Ticket Splitting. JOLE 34: 343-369.

DOMESTIC CONFLICT

1 Afatooni, A.; Allen, M. P. 1991. Government Sanctions and Collective Political Protest in Periphery and Semipheriphery. JPMS 19: 29-46.
2 American Behavioral Scientist. 1972. Papers on Conflict Models. ABS 15 (6).
3 Banks, A. S. 1972. Patterns of Domestic Conflict. JCR 16: 41-50.
4 -. 1980. Hypergames: Conflict. Futures 12: 489-519.
5 Bennett, P. G. 1991. Modelling Complex Conflicts. RIS 17: 349-364.
6 Brockett, C. D. 1992. Measuring Political Violence and Land Inequality in Central America. APSR 86: 169-176.
7 Chalmers, D. A.; Robinson, C. H. 1982. Why Power Contenders Choose Liberalization. ISQ 26: 3-36.
8 Comparative Political Studies. 1982. Papers on Political Cleavage. CPS 15 (2).
9 Comparative Studies in Society and History. 1982. Papers on Social Conflict in Popular Culture. CSSH 24 (2).
10 Cooper, M. N. 1975. Plural Societies and Conflict. International Journal of Group Tensions 4: 408-430.
11 Corning, P. A.; Corning, C. H. 1972. General Theory of Violent Aggression. SSI 11: 7-35.
12 Denton, F. H., Phillips, W. 1968. Some Patterns in the History of Violence. JCR 12: 182-195.
13 Deudney, D. H. 1995. The Philadelphia System: Sovereignty, Arms Control, and Balance of Power in the American States-Union, c. 1787-1861. IO 49: 191-228.
14 Deutsch, M.. 1994. Constructive Conflict Resolution. JSI 50: 13-32.
15 Dixon, W. J.; Moon, B. E. 1989. Domestic Political Conflict and Basic Needs Outcomes. CPS 22: 178-198.
16 Druckman, D. 1994. Determinants of Compromising Behavior in Negotiation. JCR 38: 507-556.
17 Druckman, D.; Broome, B. J. 1991. Value Differences and Conflict Resolution. JCR 35: 571-593.
18 Druckman, D.; Broome, B. J.; Korper, S. H. 1988. Value Differences and Conflict Resolution. JCR 32: 389-510.
19 Ember, C. R.; Ember, M. 1994. War, Socialization and Interpersonal Violence. JCR 38: 620-646.
20 Etudes Internationales. 1979. Papers on Conflict. Vol 10 (1).
21 Feierabend, I. K.; Feierabend, R. L. 1966. Aggressive Behaviors within Polities. JCR 10: 249-271.
22 Feierabend, R. L.; Feierabend, I. K.; Sleet, D. A. 1973. Need Achievement, Coerciveness of Government and Unrest. JCCP 4: 314-325.
23 Fisher, R. J. 1994. Generic Principles for Resolving Intergroup Conflict. JSI 50: 47-66.
24 Flanigan, W. H.; Fogelman, E. 1970. Patterns of Political Violence. CP 3: 1-20.
25 Foff, R. W. 1988. Dealing with Conflict: Creative, Peaceful Methods of Resolving Conflict. PRR 11: 1-38.
26 Geller, D. S. 1987. Impact of Political Structure on Patterns of Internal Disorder. AJPS 31: 217-235.
27 Giles, M. W.; Evans, A. S. 1985. External Threat, Perceived Threat and Group Identity. SSQ 66: 50-66.
28 Greenawalt, R. K. 1983. Violence: Legal Justification and Moral Appraisal. ELR 32: 437-498.
29 Grofman, B.; Muller, E. N. 1973. Relative Gratification and Potential for Political Violence: The V Curve Hypothesis. APSR 67: 514-529.
30 Gupta, D. K. 1987. Economic Behavior and Analysis of Violent Collective Actions. Journal of Behavioral Economics 16: 33-44.
31 Gupta, D. K.; Singh, H.; Sprague, T. 1993. Government Coercion of Dissidents. JCR 37: 301-339.
32 Gurr, T. R. 1973. Civil Conflict. CPS 6: 135-16.
33 Gurr, T. R.; Lichbach, M. I. 1986. Forecasting Internal Conflict. CPS 19: 3-38.
34 Hampton, A. 1995. Limitations of the Prescriptive Dimensions of Lijphart's Consensus Model: Maori within New Zealand. PSNZ 47: 215 ff.
35 Hazelwood, L. A. 1973. Concept and Measurement Stability in the Study of Conflict Behavior within Nations. CPS 6: 171-195.
36 Hoover, D.; Kowalewski, D. 1992. Dynamic Models of Dissent and Repression. JCR 36: 150-182.
37 International Social Science Journal. 1971. Papers on Aggression. ISSJ 23 (1).
38 -. 1978. Papers on Violence. ISSJ 30 (4) and 1992 44 (2).
39 Jehn, K. A. 1995. The Benefits and Detriments of Intragroup Conflict. ASQ 40: 256-282.
40 Journal of Social Issues. 1972. Papers on Collective Violence and Civil Conflict. JSI 28 (1).
41 -. 1977. Papers on Social Conflict. JSI 33 (1), 1985 41 (2).
42 -. 1994. Papers on Conflict Management. JSI 50 (1).
43 Karklins, R.; Petersen, R. 1993. Decision Calculus of Protesters and Regimes. JOP 55: 588-614.
44 Karmeshu, J. V. P.; Mahajan, A. K. 1990. Dynamic Model of Domestic Political Conflict Process. JCR 34: 252-269.
45 Landau, S. F. 1984. Trends in Violence and Aggression. IJCS 25: 133-158.

46 LaTour, S., et al. 1976. Preferences for Modes of Conflict Resolution. JCR 20: 319-346.

47 Leatherman, J.; Vayrynen, R. 1995. Conflict Theory and Conflict Resolution. CAC 30: 53-82.

48 Levy, S. G. 1969. Assassination Levels, Motivation and Attitudes. PPRS 14: 47-82.

49 -. 1993. Some Thoughts on the Study of Intergroup Conflict. CMAPS 13: 1-28.

50 Lichbach, M. I. 1989. An Evaluation of Does Economic Inequality Breed Political Conflict Studies. WP 41: 431-470.

51 Lind, E. A., et al. 1980. Procedure and Outcome Effects on Reactions to Adjudicated Resolutions of Conflicts of Interest. JPASP 39: 643-653.

52 Lineham, W. J. 1976. Models for the Measurement of Political Instability. PM 3: 441-486.

53 Midlarsky, M. I. 1988. Patterned Inequality and the Onset of Mass Political Violence. APSR 82: 491-510.

54 Morgan, T. C.; Bickers, K. N. 1992. Domestic Discontent and External Use of Force. JCR 36: 25-52.

55 Mukonoweshuro, E. G. 1991. Containing Political Instability in a Polyethnic Society: Mauritius. EARS 14: 199-224.

56 Muller, E. N. 1985. Income Inequality, Regime Repressiveness and Political Violence. ASR 50: 47-61.

57 Muller, E. N., et al. 1989. Land Inequality and Political Violence. APSR 83: 577-595.

58 Muller, E. N.; Jukam, T. O.; Seligson, M. A. 1982. Diffuse Political Support and Anti-System Political Behavior. AJPS 26: 240-264.

59 Muller, E. N.; Weede, E. 1990. Cross-National Variation in Political Violence. JCR 34: 624-251.

60 Nielsen, K. 1981. On Justifying Violence. Inquiry 24: 21-74.

61 Parnes, A. H. 1973. Economic Determinants of Political Unrest. JCR 17: 271-296.

62 Peace Research Reviews. 1973. Papers on the Cost of Aggression. PRR 5 (1).

63 Peterson, S. A. 1981. Psychophysiological Arousal as a Predictor of Student Protest. JPS 8: 108-113.

64 Pitcher, B. L.; Hamblin, R. L.; Miller, J. L. L. 1978. Diffusion of Collective Violence. ASR 43: 23-35.

65 Policy Studies Journal. 1987. Papers on Alternative Dispute Resolution. PSJ 16 (3).

66 Rasler, K. A. 1986. War, Accommodation and Violence in the US. APSR 80: 921-945.

67 Reychler, L. 1979. Effectiveness of a Pacifist Strategy in Conflict Resolution. JCR 23: 228-260.

68 Rosenbaum, H. J.; Sederberg, P. C. 1975. Vigilantism: An Analysis of Establishment Violence. CP 6: 541-570.

69 Ross, M. H. 1986. A Cross-Cultural Theory of Political Conflict and Violence. PP 7: 427-471.

70 Rouhana, N. M.; Fiske, S. T. 1995. Perception of Power, Threat and Conflict Intensity in Asymmetric Intergroup Conflict. JCR 39: 49-81.

71 Rubin, J. Z. 1994. Models of Conflict Management. JSI 50: 33-46.

72 Rummel, R. J. 1966. Dimensions of Conflict within Nations. JCR 10: 65-73.

73 -. 1984. Libertarianism, Violence within States and the Polarity Principle. CP 16: 443-462.

74 -. 1985. Libertarian Propositions on Violence within and between Nations. JCR 29: 419-455.

75 Sampson, R. J. 1984. Group Size, Heterogeneity and Intergroup Conflict. SF 62: 618-639.

76 Sayles, M. L. 1984. Relative Deprivation and Collective Protest. SI 54: 449-465.

77 Schneider, P. R.; Schneider, A. L. 1971. Social Mobilization, Political Institutions and Political Violence. CPS 4: 69-90.

78 Scolnick, J. 1975. An Appraisal of Studies of Linkages between Domestic and International Conflict. CPS 6: 485-509.

79 Shernock, S. K. 1984. Continuous Violent Conflict as a System of Authority. SI 54: 301-329.

80 Sigel, R. S. 1979. Students' Comprehension of Democracy and Its Application to Conflict Situations. IJPE 2: 47-66.

81 Sigelman, L.; Simpson, M. E. 1977. Cross National Test of the Linkage between Economic Inequality and Political Violence. JCR 21: 105-128.

82 Simowitz, R.; Price, B. L. 1990. The Expected Utility Theory of Conflict. APSR 84: 439-460.

83 Smith, C. G.; Teitler, R. J.; Boren, L. C. 1979. Personality Concomitants of Attitudes toward the Use of Violence for Settlement of Disputes. SI 49: 45-54.

84 Snyder, D.; Tilly, C. 1972. Hardship and Collective Violence in France. ASR 37: 520-532.

85 Social Research. 1981. Papers on Violence. SR 48 (1).

86 Sociological Quarterly. 1971. Papers on Violence. SQ 12 (3).

87 Stein, A. A. 1976. Conflict and Cohesion. JCR 20: 143-172.

88 Sternberg, R. J.; Soriano, L. J. 1984. Styles of Conflict Resolution. JPSP 47: 115-126.

89 Sullivan, L. K. 1975. Economic Correlates of Political Violence. SJIS 9: 298-318.

90 Svalastoga, K. 1978. Differential Rates of Change and Violence. AS 21: 23-34.

91 Tanter, R. 1966. Dimensions of Conflict Behavior within and between Nations. JCR 10: 41-64.

92 Thomas, D. B.; Craig, R. B. 1973. Student Dissent in Latin America. LARR 8: 71-96.

93 Thomas, R. E.; Thomas, C. B. 1977. The Political System and Aggression. Anthropologica 19: 133-152.

94 Townshend, C. 1987. The Necessity of Political Violence. CSSH 29: 314-319.

95 Vernon, R.; LeSelva, S. V. 1984. Justifying Violence. CJPS 17: 3-24.

96 Vuchinich, S.; Teachman, J. 1993. Influences on the Duration of Wars, Strikes, Riots and Arguments. JCR 37: 544-568.

97 Welch, S. 1976. Crowding and Political Activity. Polity 9: 40-62.

98 Welch, S.; Booth, A. 1975. Crowding and Civil Disorder. CPS 8: 58-74.

99 -. 1975. Crowding as a Factor in Political Aggression. SSI 13: 151-162.

100 Welton, G.; Pruitt, D. G.; McGillicuddy, N. B. 1988. The Role of Caucusing in Community Mediation. JCR 32: 181-202.

101 White, R. R. 1993. On Measuring Political Violence: Northern Ireland. ASR 58: 575-585.

102 Williams, K. R.; Timberlake, M. 1984. Structured Inequality, Conflict, Control: Threat Hypothesis. SF 63: 414-432.

103 Wolf-Dieter, E., et al. 1979. External and Internal Conflict Behavior among Nations. JCR 23: 715-742.

104 Worchel, P.; Hester, P. G.; Kopala, P. S. 1975. Collective Protest and Legitimacy of Authority. JCR 18: 37-54.

105 World Affairs. 1983. Papers on Subnational Conflict. WA 146 (3).

Coups d'Etat

106 Cohen, Y. 1991. The Heresthetics of Coup Making. CPS 24: 344-364.

107 Dean, W. 1970. Latin American Golpes and Economic Fluctuations. SSQ 51: 70-80.

108 Jackman, R. W. 1978. Predictability of Coups d'Etat. APSR 72: 1262-1275.

109 Jackman, R. W., et al. 1986. Explaining African Coups d'Etat. APSR 88: 225-250.

110 Johnson, T. H.; Slater, R. O.; McGowan, P. J. 1984. Explaining African Military Coups d'Etat. APSR 78: 622-640.

111 Kowalewski, D. 1991. Periphery Praetorianism in Cliometric Perspective. IJCS 32: 289-303.

112 Li, R. P. Y.; Thompson, W. R. 1975. The Coup Contagion Hypothesis. JCR 19: 63-88.

113 Londregan, J.; Poole, K. T. 1990. Poverty, the Coup Trap and the Seizure of Executive Power. WP 42: 151-183.

114 Mbaku, J. M. 1994. Military Coups as Rent Seeking Behavior. JPMS 22: 241-284.

115 McGowan, P. J.; Johnson, T. H. 1984. African Military Coups d'Etat and Underdevelopment. JMAFS 22: 633-666.

116 Mendeloff, D. 1994. Explaining Russian Military Quiescence: The Paradox of Disintegration and the Myth of a Military Coup. CAPCS 27: 225-246.

117 O'Kane, R. H. T. 1981. A Probabilistic Approach to the Causes of Coups d'Etat. BJPS 11: 287-308.

118 -. 1983. Toward an Examination of the General Causes of Coups d'Etat. EJPR 11: 27-44.

119 -. 1993. Coups d'Etat in Africa: A Political Economy Approach. JPR 30: 251-270.

120 Raack, R. C. 1970. When Plans Fail: Small Group Behavior and Decision Making in the Conspiracy of 1808 in Germany. JCR 14: 3-20.

121 Rowe, E. T. 1975. Aid and Coups d'Etat. ISQ 8: 239-255.

122 Thompson, W. R. 1975. Regime Vulnerability and the Military Coup. CP 7: 459-488.

123 -. 1976. Organizational Cohesion and Military Coup Outcomes. CPS 9: 255-276.

124 Zimmermann, E. 1979. Toward a Causal Model of Military Coups d'Etat. AFAS 5: 387-413.

Revolution

125 American Behavioral Scientist. 1977. Papers on Revolution and Counter-Revolution. ABS 20 (4).

126 Artigiani, R. 1987. Revolution and Evolution: Applying Prigogine's Dissipate Structures Model. JSBS 10: 249-264.

127 Barkey, K. 1991. Rebellious Alliances: The State and Peasant Unrest in Early Seventeenth Century France and the Ottoman Empire. ASR 56: 699-715.

128 Bowen, D. R. 1977. Guerrilla War in Western Missouri: Extenstions of the Relative Deprivation Hypothesis. CSSH 19: 30-51.

129 Brocheux, P. 1983. Moral Economy or Political Economy? The Peasants Are Always Rational. JASIAS 42: 791-804.

130 Buechler, S. M. 1995. New Social Movement Theories. SQ 36: 441-465.

131 Campbell, L. G. 1973. Historiography of the Peruvian Guerrilla Movement. LARR 8: 45-70.

132 -. 1979. Some Recent Research on Andean Peasant Revolts: 1750-1820. LARR 14: 3-50.

133 Clark, E. 1976. Revolutionary Ritual: Thought Reform and the Show Trial. SCC 9: 226-243.

134 Comparative Economic Studies. 1987. Papers on Trotsky's The Revolution Betrayed. CES 29 (3).

135 Comparative Politics. 1973. Papers on Revolution. CP 5 (3) and 8 (3).

136 Comparative Studies in Society and History. 1986. Papers on Revolution. CSSH 28 (3) and 1990 32 (3).

137 -. 1987. Papers on Peasant Rebellions. CSSH 29 (3).

138 Dix, R. H. 1984. Why Revolutions Succeed and Fail. Policy 16: 423-446.

139 Dunn, J. 1982. Understanding Revolution. Ethics 92: 299-315.

140 Eckstein, S. 1986. Impact of the Cuban Revolution: Comparative Perspective. CSSH 28: 502-534.

141 Feierabend, I. K.; Feierabend, R. L.; Nesvold, B. A. 1973. The Comparative Study of Revolution and Violence. CP 5: 393-424.

142 Fowler-Salamini, H. 1993. The Boom in Regional Studies of the Mexican Revolution. LARR 28: 175-190.

143 Francisco, R. A. 1993. Theories of Protest and the Revolutions of 1989. AJPS 37: 663-680.

144 Francois, M. E. 1975. Revolts in Late Medieval and Early Modern Europe: A Spiral Model. JIDH 5: 19-44.

145 Goldstone, J. A. 1980. Theories of Revolution. WP 32: 425-453.

146 Greene, J. P. 1973. Social Origins of the American Revolution. PSQ 88: 1-22.

147 Grossman, H. I. 1991. A General Equilibrium Model of Insurrections. AER 81: 912-921.

148 Gurr, T. R. 1970. Sources of Rebellion in Western Societies. ANNALS 391: 128-144.

149 -. 1993. Why Minorities Rebel. IPSR 14: 161-202.

150 Hechter, M. 1992. Dynamics of Secession. AS 35: 267-284.

151 Herrick, P. B.; Robins, R. S. 1976. Varieties of Latin American Revolutions and Rebellions. JDA 10: 317-336.

152 International Journal. 1973. Papers on Revolution. IJ 28 (3).

153 International Political Science Review. 1989. Papers on the Historical Framework of Revolutions. IPSR 10 (2).

154 Jenkins, J. C. 1982. Why Do Peasants Rebel? Structural and Historical Theories of Peasant Rebellion. AJS 88: 487-514.

155 Kautsky, J. H. 1981. The Question of Peasant Revolts in Traditional Empires. SICID 16: 3-35.

156 Kershaw, G. 1991. The Mau Mau from Below. CJAF 25: 274-299.

157 Kowalewski, D. 1991. Core Intervention and Periphery Revolution. AJS 97: 70-95.

158 Laffey, E. S. 1976. In the Wake of the Taipings: Some Patterns of Local Revolt in Kwangsi Province. MAS 10: 65-82.

159 Landsberger, H. A. 1973. The Problem of Peasant Wars. CSSH 15: 378-388.

160 Latin American Perspectives. 1981. Papers on the Nicaraguan and Central American Revolutions. LAPER 8 (2), 1983 10 (1), 1984 12 (2), 1985 13 (3), 1986 14 (1), and 1988 16 (3).

161 Law, D. 1986. Revolutions Compared: Russia and China. CSSH 28: 545-551.

162 Lewis-Beck, M. S. 1979. Some Economic Effects of Revolution: Models, Measurement and the Cuban Evidence. AJS 84: 1127-1149.

163 Lichbach, M. I. 1994. What Makes Rational Peasants Revolutionary? WP 46: 383-418.

164 Lindstrom, R.; Moore, W. H. 1995. Why Minorities Rebel Revised. JPMS 23: 167-190.

165 Lipsky, W. E. 1976. Comparative Approaches to the Study of Revolution. ROP 38: 494-509.

166 MacHardy, K. J. 1992. The Rise of Absolutism and Noble Rebellion in Early Modern Habsburg Austria. CSSH 34: 407-438.

167 Markoff, J.; Shapiro, G. 1985. Consensus and Conflict at the Outset of the Revolution: France in 1789. AJS 91: 28-53.

168 Mate, M. 1992. Economic and Social Roots of Medieval Popular Rebellion. Economic History Review 45: 661-679.

169 Mazlish, B. 1970. The French Revolution in Comparative Perspective. PSQ 85: 240-258.

170 McCrary, P.; Miller, C.; Baum, D. 1978. Class and Party in the Secession Crisis: Voting Behavior in the Deep South. JIDH 8: 429-458.

171 McDonogh, G. W. 1987. Other People's Nations: An Interactive Model of Nationalist Movements. CRSN 14: 297-326.

172 Mitchell, E. J. 1969. Some Econometrics of the Huk Rebellion. APSR 63: 1159-1171.
173 Modern China. 1983. Papers on Peasant Rebellions in China. MC 9 (3).
174 Muller, E. N.; Dietz, H. A.; Finkel, S. E. 1991. Discontent and the Expected Utility of Rebellion: Peru. APSR 85: 1261-1282.
175 Muller, E. N.; Opp, K. D. 1986. Rational Choice and Rebellious Collective Action. APSR 80: 471-487.
176 Outram, D. 1992. Revolution and Repression. CSSH 34: 58-67.
177 Paust, J. J. 1983. The Human Right to Participate in Armed Revolution. ELR 32: 545-582.
178 Popper, F. J. 1971. Internal War as a Stimulant of Political Development. CPS 3: 413-424.
179 Ramsey, R. W. 1973. Critical Bibliography on La Violencia in Colombia. LARR 8: 3-44.
180 Raymond, G. A.; Kegley, C. W. 1987. Long Cycles and Internationalized Civil War. JOP 49: 481-499.
181 Roemer, J. E. 1985. Rationalizing Revolutionary Ideology. Econometrica 53: 85-108.
182 Russell, C. A.; Miller, J. A.; Hildner, R. E. 1975. The Urban Guerrilla in Latin America. LARR 9: 37-80.
183 Scott, J. C. 1977. Peasant Revolution. CP 9: 231-248.
184 Shapiro, H. 1984. Impact of the Aptheker Thesis: American Negro Slave Revolts. SAS 48: 52-73.
185 Skocpol, T. 1982. What Makes Peasants Revolutionary? CP 14: 351-375.
186 Studies in Comparative Communism. 1977. Papers on Trotsky and Trotskyism. SCC 10 (1/2).
187 Suedfeld, P.; Rank, A. D. 1971. Revolutionary Leaders. JPSP 34: 169-178.
188 Tanter, R.; Midlarsky, M. I. 1967. A Theory of Revolution. JCR 11: 264-280.
189 Thaxton, R. 1975. Some Critical Comments on Peasant Revolts and Revolutionary Politics in China. JASIAS 33: 279-288.
190 Wakeman, F. 1977. Rebellion and Revolution: The Study of Popular Movements in Chinese History. JASIAS 36: 201-238.
191 Walt, S. M. 1992. Revolution and War. WP 44: 321-368.
192 Wickham-Crowley, T. P. 1991. Qualitative Comparative Approach to Latin American Revolutions. IJCS 32: 82-109.
193 Zagorin, P. 1973. Theories of Revolution in Contemporary Historiography. PSQ 88: 23-52.

Riots and Social Movements

194 American Behavioral Scientist. 1973. Papers on Urban Riots. ABS 16 (3).
195 -. 1982. Papers on Group Protest and Public Policy. ABS 26 (3).
196 -. 1995. Papers on Social Advocacy. ABS 38 (4).
197 Anderson, L.; Seligson, M. A. 1994. Reformism and Radicalism among Peasants. AJPS 38: 944-972.
198 Annals. 1969. Papers on Protest. ANNALS 382, 1971 (391), and 1993 (528).
199 -. 1970. Papers on Collective Violence. ANNALS 391.
200 Betts, R. K.; Huntington, S. P. 1985. Dead Dictators and Rioting Mobs: Does the Demise of Authoritarian Rulers Lead to Political Instability? IA 10: 112-146.
201 Bohstedt, J.; Williams, D. E. 1988. The Diffusion of Riots: Devonshire. JIDH 19: 1-24.
202 Breton, A.; Breton, R. 1969. An Economic Theory of Social Movements. AER 59: 198-205.
203 Carter, G. L. 1987. Local Police Force Size and the Severity of the 1960s Black Rioting. JCR 31: 601-614.
204 Chai, S.K. 1993. Organizational Economics Theory of Anti-Government Violence. CP 26: 99-110.
205 Chung, P. 1978. On the Behavior of a Totalitarian Regime toward Dissidents. PC 33: 75-84.
206 Cole, J. R. I. 1989. Rethinking Colonial Empires: Afro-Asian Riots and European Expansion. CSSH 31: 106-133.
207 Comparative Studies in Society and History 1975. Papers on Political Mobilization in Latin America. CSSH 17 (4).
208 Craig, S. C. 1980. Mobilization of Political Discontent. PB 2: 189-209.
209 David, H. 1983. Statist Ideology, National Political Control of Education and Youth Protests. JCR 27: 563-589.
210 Everett, K. D. 1992. Professionalization and Protest: Changes in the Social Movement Sector. SF 70: 957-976.
211 Feeny, D. 1983. The Moral or the Rational Peasant? Competing Hypotheses of Collective Action. JASIAS 42: 769-790.
212 Feinberg, W. E.; Johnson, N. R. 1988. Outside Agitators and Crowds. SF 67: 398-423.
213 Francisco, R. A. 1995. The Relationship between Coercion and Protest. JCR 39: 263-282.
214 Frey, R. S.; Dietz, T.; Kalof, L. 1992. Characteristics of Successful American Protest Groups. AJS 98: 368-387.
215 Greenberg, C. 1992. Politics of Disorder: Reexamining Harlem's Riots of 1935 and 1943. JUH 18: 395-441.
216 Gurr, T. R.; Duvall, R. 1973. Civil Conflict in the 1960s. CPS 6: 135-170.
217 Hellman, J. A. 1983. The Role of Ideology in Peasant Politics: Mobilization and Demobilization. JIAS 25: 3-30.
218 Jennings, E. T. 1980. Urban Riots and Growth of State Welfare Expenditures. PSJ 9: 34-39.
219 Journal of Asian Studies. 1983. Papers on Rational Approaches and Moral Approaches to Peasant Strategies. JASIAS 42 (4).
220 Kelley, J.; Evans, M. D. R. 1995. Class and Class Conflict in Six Western Nations. ASR 60: 157-178.
221 Koopmans, R. 1993. Dynamics of Protest Waves. ASR 58: 637-659.
222 Kowalewski, D. 1993. Ballots and Bullets: Election Riots in the Periphery. JDS 29: 518-540.
223 Latin American Perspectives. 1993. Papers on Mexico's Political Economy, Social Movements and Migration. LAPER 20 (3).
224 -. 1994. Papers on Latin American Social Movements. LAPER 21 (2-3).
225 Lehmann, D. 1973. Generalizing about Peasant Movements. JDS 9: 323-331.
226 Lewis-Beck, M. S.; Lockerbie, B. 1989. Economics, Votes and Protests: Western European Cases. CPS 22: 155-177.
227 Lichbach, M. I. 1985. Protest in America: Univariate Arima Models of the Postwar Era. WPQ 38: 388-412.
228 Lieske, J. A. 1978. Conditions of Racial Violence in American Cities. APSR 72: 1324-1340.
229 -. 1979. A Critique of the J Curve Theory and Black Urban Riots. PM 6: 29-74.
230 Lipsky, M. 1968. Protest as a Political Resource. APSR 62: 1144-1158.
231 Lord, P. P. 1972. Latin American Peasant Movements. EDACC 20: 743-749.
232 McPhail, C. 1971. Civil Disorder Participation. ASR 36: 1058-1073.
233 -. 1994. Individual and Collective Violence in Riots. SQ 35: 1-32.
234 Meyer, D. S. 1993. Protest Cycles and Political Process: US Peace Movements. PRQ 46: 451-480.
235 Midlarsky, M. I. 1978. Analyzing Diffusion and Contagion Effects: Urban Disorders of the 1960s. APSR 72: 996-1008.

236 -. 1988. Rulers and Ruled: Patterned Inequality and Onset of Mass Political Violence. APSR 82: 491-509.

237 Millennium. 1994. Papers on Social Movements. Vol 23 (3).

238 Miller, A. H.; Bolce, L. H.; Halligan, M. 1977. The J Curve and Black Urban Riots: Progressive Relative Deprivation Theory. APSR 71: 964-982.

239 Oegema, D.; Klandermans, B. 1994. Why Social Movement Sympathizers Don't Participate: Erosion and Nonconversion of Support. ASR 59: 703-722.

240 Paige, J. M. 1971. Political Orientation and Riot Participation. ASR 36: 810-820.

241 Peterson, S. A. 1981. Psychological Arousal as a Predictor of Student Protests. JSBS 2: 65-72

242 Proceedings. 1968. Papers on Urban Riots. PAPSC 29 (1).

243 Rohrschneider, R. 1990. Roots of Public Opinion toward New Social Movements. AJPS 34: 1-30.

244 Schaedel, R. P. 1976. Peasant Movements. JIAS 18: 505-515.

245 Seegers, A. 1992 Theories of Revolution. Politikon 19: 5-28.

246 Social Research 1985. Papers on Social Movements. SR 52 (4).

247 Social Science Quarterly. 1968. Papers on the US Riot Commission Report. SSQ 49 (3).

248 -. 1970. Papers on Urban Riots. SSQ 51: 329-388.

249 Spilerman, S. 1970. Causes of Racial Disturbances. APSR 35: 627-649.

250 Sussman, G.; Stell, B. S. 1991. The Support for Protest Methods and Political Strategies among Peace Movement Activists. WPQ 44: 519-540.

251 Tarrow, S. 1993. Modular Collective Action and the Rise of Social Movements. PAS 21: 69-90.

252 Thomas, D. B., et al. 1984. Moral Reasoning and Political Obligations: Cognitive Development Correlations of Orientations to Law and Civil Disobedience. IJPE 6: 223-244.

253 Thompson, J. L. P. 1989. Deprivation and Political Violence in Northern Ireland. JCR 33: 676-699.

254 Tilly, C. 1973. Does Modernization Breed Revolution? CP 5: 425-447.

255 Wang, T. Y. 1995. Dependency, World System Position and Political Violence in Developing Countries. JPMS 23: 25-42.

256 Wang, T. Y., et al. 1993. Inequality and Political Violence Revisited. APSR 87: 979-993.

257 Woods, R. 1983. Individuals in the Rioting Crowd. JIDH 17: 1-24.

258 Zald, M.; Berger, M. A. 1978. Social Movements in Organizations: Coup d'Etat, Insurgency and Mass Movements. AJS 83: 823-861.

Strikes and Unions

259 Annals. 1984. Papers on Unionism. ANNALS 473.

260 Beck, E. M. 1980. Labor Unionism and Radical Income Inequality. AJS 85: 791-814.

261 Belman, D. L.; Voos, P. B. 1993. Wage Effects of Increased Union Coverage. ILRR 46: 368-380.

262 Bennett, J. T.; Delaney, J. T. 1993. Research on Unions. JLR 14: 95-110.

263 Black, J. M.; Bulkley, G. 1989. Do Trade Unions Reduce Job Opportunities of Non-Members? EJ 99: 177-186.

264 Bronars, S. G.; Deere, D. R.; Tracy, J. S. 1994. The Effects of Unions on Firm Behavior. INDREL 33: 426-451.

265 Card, D. 1990. Strikes and Bargaining. AER 80: 410-415.

266 Carruth, A.; Schnabel, C. 1990. Empirical Modelling of Trade Union Growth in Germany: Traditional vs. Cointegration and Error Correction Model. WELTA 126: 326-346.

267 Cebula, R. J. 1983. Right to Work Laws and Geographic Differences in Living Costs: Analysis on Effects of Union Shop Ban. AJEAS 42: 329-340.

268 Clark, A.; Oswald, A. 1993. Trade Union Utility Functions: A Survey of Union Leaders. INDREL 32: 391-411.

269 Clark, G. L.; Johnston, K. 1987. The Geography of US Union Elections. Series of articles in EPA from 19 (1) to 19 (6).

270 Cohn, S.; Eaton, A. 1989. Historical Limits on Neoclassical Strike Theories. ILRR 42: 649-662.

271 Conell, C.; Cohn, S. 1995. Environmental Variation and Diffusion in French Coal Mining Strikes. AJS 101: 366-403.

272 Creedy, J.; McDonald, I. M. 1991. Models of Trade Union Behaviour. ECONR 67 (Dec): 649-659.

273 Delaney, J. T.; Fiorito, J.; Masters, M. F. 1988. Effects of Union Organization and Environmental Characteristics on Union Political Activity. AJPS 32: 616-642.

274 Demsetz, R. S. 1993. Voting Behavior in Union Representation Elections. ILRR 47: 99-113.

275 Detken, C.; Gartner, M. 1992. Governments, Trade Unions and the Macroeconomy: The Political Business Cycle. PC 73: 37-54.

276 Dickerson, A. P. 1994. Cyclicality of British Strike Frequency. OBES 56: 285-303.

277 Druckman, D., et al. 1976. Cultural Differences in Bargaining Behavior. JCR 20: 413-452.

278 Education and Urban Society. 1979. Papers on Collective Bargaining in Public Education. EAUS 11 (2).

279 Farber, H. S. 1978. Bargaining Theory, Wage Outcomes and the Occurrence of Strikes. AER 68: 262-271.

280 Fisher, T. C. G. 1991. The Adverse Selection Model of Strikes. CANJE 24: 499-516.

281 Florkowski, F.; Schuster, M. 1987. Predicting the Decisions to Vote and Support Unions in Certification Elections. JLR 8: 191-207.

282 Franzosi, R. 1989. One Hundred Years of Strike Statistics. ILRR 42: 348-362.

283 Friedman, G. 1988. Strike Success and Union Ideology. JEH 48: 1-25.

284 Furnham, A. 1984. The Protestant Work Ethic, Voting Behavior, and Attitudes to the Trade Unions. POLST 32: 420-436.

285 Garson, G. D. 1970. Collective Violence Reexamined: US Labor Violence. Politics 5: 129-147.

286 Glazer, A. 1992. An Expressive Voting Theory of Strikes. EI 30: 733-741.

287 Godard, J. 1992. Strikes as Collective Voice. ILRR 46: 161-175.

288 Golden, M. 1993. Dynamics of Trade Unionism and National Economic Performance. APSR 87: 439-454.

289 Griffin, L. J., et al. 1991. Qualitative Comparative Analysis of Trade Union Growth and Decline. IJCS 32: 110-136.

290 Groot, W.; van den Berg, A. 1994. Why Union Density Has Declined. EJPE 10: 749-764.

291 Hancke, B. 1993. Trade Union Membership in Europe. BJIR 31: 593-613.

292 Harrison, A.; Stewart, M. B. 1989. Cyclical Fluctuations in Strike Durations. AER 79: 827-841.

293 -. 1993. Strike Duration and Strike Size. CANJE 26: 830-849.

294 -. 1994. Is Strike Behavior Cyclical? Journal of Labor Economics 12: 524-553.

295 Hedstrom, P. 1994. The Spatial Diffusion of Swedish Trade Unions. AJS 99: 1157-1179.

296 Hibbs, D. A. 1976. Industrial Conflict in Advanced Industrial Societies. APSR 70: 1033-1058.

297 -. 1978. The Political Economy of Long Run Trends in Strike Activity. BJPS 8: 153-176.

298 Hirsch, W. Z.; Green, J. M. 1988. Anti-Strike Laws and Their Effects on Work Stoppages by Public School Teachers. JUE 24: 331-351.

299 Hundley, G. 1988. Taxation and Strikes. BJIR 26: 57-61.
300 Industrial and Labor Relations Review. 1971. Papers on the Effects of Unions. ILRR 24 (2).
301 -. 1982. Papers on the Determinants of Strikes. ILRR 35 (4).
302 -. 1995. Papers on Union Decline in Britain. ILRR 48: 389-419.
303 Ingham, M.; Ingham, H. 1992. Strikes and Deindustrialization in the European Community. IRAE 6: 93-113.
304 Isaac, W. L.; Griffin, L. J. 1989. Ahistoricism in Time Series Analyses of Historical Processes: Critique, Redirection and Illustrations from US Labor History. ASR 54: 873-890.
305 Jarrell, S. B.; Stanley, T. D. 1990. A Meta-Analysis of the Union-Nonunion Wage Gap. ILRR 44: 54-67.
306 Jas, R. 1988. Impact of Trade Unions on Productivity. IJPA 34: 1060-1072.
307 Jones, E. B. 1992. Private Sector Union Decline and Structural Employment Change. JLR 13: 257-272.
308 Journal of Area Studies. 1986. Papers on Unions in Crisis. JAS 13 (Spring).
309 Journal of Communist Studies. 1993. Papers on Unions in Eastern Europe. JCS 9 (4).
310 Katz, H. C. 1993. Decentralization of Collective Bargaining. ILRR 47: 3-22.
311 Lewis, P.; Murphy, L. 1991. A Theory of Trade Union Membership Retention. BJIR 29: 277-292.
312 Marks, G. 1989. Variations in Union Political Activity. CP 22: 83-104.
313 Mason, B.; Bain, P. 1993. Determinants of Trade Union Membership in Britain. ILRR 46: 332-351.
314 McClendon, J. A.; Klass, B. 1993. Determinants of Strike-Related Militancy. ILRR 46: 560-573.
315 McClendon, J. A.; Kriesky, J.; Eaton, A. 1995. Member Support for Union Mergers: An Analysis of an Affiliation Referendum. JLR 16: 9-23.
316 McConnell, S. 1990. Cyclical Fluctuations in Strike Activity. ILRR 44: 130-143.
317 Meador, M.; Walters, S. J. K. 1994. Unions and Productivity: Academe. Journal of Labor Research 15: 373-386.
318 Misra, J.; Hicks, A. 1994. Catholicism and Unionization in Affluent Postwar Democracies. ASR 59: 304-326.
319 Mixon, F. G.; Ressler, R. W. 1993. Union Influence and Right-to-Work Laws Passage. AJEAS 52: 183-192.
320 Moore, W. J., et al. 1995. Political Influence of Unions and Corporations on COPE Votes in a Representative Democracy. JLR 16: 203-221.
321 Moore, W. J.; Newman, R. J. 1988. Analysis of Postwar Decline in American Trade Union Membership. JLR 9: 111-125.
322 Mulvey, G. C. 1994. Labour Economics: A Review. British Review of Economic Issues 16: 111-116.
323 O'Brien, K. M. 1994. Impact of Union Political Activities on Public Sector Pay, Employment and Budgets. INDREL 33: 297-321.
324 Paldam, M.; Pedersen, P. J. 1982. The Macroeconomic Strike Model. ILRR 35: 504-521.
325 Perry, J. S.; Levine, C. H. 1976. An Interorganizational Analysis of Power, Conflict and Settlements in Public Service Collective Bargaining. APSR 70: 1185-1201.
326 Proceedings. 1970. Papers on Unionism of Municipal Employees. PAPSC 30 (2).
327 Reshef, Y. 1993 Employees, Unions and Technological Changes. JLR 14: 111-129.
328 Review of Public Personnel Administration. 1993. Papers on Public Sector Labor Relations. RPPA 13 (3).
329 Reynolds, M. O. 1980. The New Rationale for Unionism. Journal of Social and Political Studies 5: 259-269.
330 Rose, D. C. 1994. Firm Diversification and Strike Duration. INDREL 33: 482-491.
331 Sanders, D. 1978. Away from a General Model of Mass Political Violence: Evaluating Hibbs. QAQ 12: 103-130.
332 Sapsford, D.; Turnbull, P. J. 1994. Strikes and Industrial Conflict in Britain's Docks: Balloons or Icebergs? OBES 56: 249-265.
333 Schmidt, D. E. 1993. Public Opinion and Media Coverage of Labor Unions. JLR 14: 151-164.
334 Scott, C.; Simpson, J.; Oswald, S. L. 1993. An Empirical Analysis of Union Election Outcomes. JLR 14: 355-365.
335 Shorter, E.; Tilly, C. 1971. The Shape of Strikes in France, 1830-1960. CSSH 13: 60-86.
336 Skeels, J. W.; McGrath, P.; Arshanapalli, G. 1988. The Importance of Strike Size in Strike Research. ILRR 41: 582-591.
337 Social Policy. 1994. Papers on Unionism. Vol 25 (2).
338 Stanford Law Review. 1986. Papers on the National Labor Relations Act. SLR 38 (4).
339 Stephens, G. 1995. Remodeling Collective Violence: James Tong's Rational Choice Model and the Great Strikes of 1877. PRQ 48: 345-370.
340 Stephens, J. D.; Wallerstein, M. B. 1991. Industrial Concentration, Country Size and Trade Union Membership. APSR 85: 941-954.
341 Turnbull, P. J. 1988. Economic Theory of Trade Union Behaviour. BJIR 26: 99-118.
342 Vroman, S. B. 1989. A Longitudinal Analysis of Strike Behavior in US Manufacturing. AER 79: 816-826.
343 Waddington, J. 1993. Trade Union Membership Concentration. BJIR 31: 433-457.
344 Wallerstein, M. B. 1989. Union Organization in Advanced Industrial Democracies. APSR 83: 481-501.
345 Waters, M. S., et al. 1994. The Relationship between Public Sector Bargaining Legislation and Unionization. JLR 15: 355-372.
346 Western, B. 1995. Union Decline in Eighteen Advanced Capitalist Countries. ASR 60: 179-201.
347 West European Politics. 1980. Papers on Western European Trade Unions and Politics. WEP 3 (1).

Terrorism

348 Annals. 1982. Papers on Terrorism. ANNALS 463.
349 Bassiouni, M. C. 1981. Terrorism, Law Enforcement and the Mass Media. JCLAC 72: 1-51.
350 Bell, J. B. 1972. Assassination in International Politics. ISQ 1: 59-82.
351 -. 1977. Analysis of Political Violence. WP 29: 476-488.
352 Beres, L. R. 1975. Guerrillas, Terrorists and Polarity. WPQ 74: 624-636.
353 Comparative Studies in Society and History. 1990. Papers on Terrorism. CSSH 32: 201-281.
354 Delli Carpini, M. X.; Williams, B. A. 1987. Television and Terrorism. WPQ 40: 45-64
355 Enders, W.; Sandler, T. 1993. The Effectiveness of Anti-Terrorism Policies. APSR 87: 829-844.
356 George, D. 1988. Distinguishing Classical Tyrannicide from Modern Terrorism. ROP 50: 390-419.
357 Hamilton, L. C.; Hamilton, J. D. 1983. Dynamics of Terrorism. ISQ 27: 39-54.
358 Hocking, J. 1984. Orthodox Theories of Terrorism: The Concept of Democratic Consensus. Politics 19: 103-110.
359 Human Rights Quarterly 1983. Papers on Terrorism. HRQ 5 (2).
360 International Conciliation. 1971. Papers on Air Hijacking. IC 585 (Nov).
361 Journal of International Affairs. 1978. Papers on Terrorism. JIA 32 (1).

362 Journal of Political Science. 1986. Papers on Terrorism. JPS 14 (1/2).

363 Kirk, R. M. 1983. Political Terrorism and Size of Government: A Positive Institutional Analysis of Violent Political Activity. PC 40: 41-52.

364 Laqueur, W. 1977. Interpretations of Terrorism. JCH 12: 1-42.

365 Maranto, R. 1986. The Rational Terrorist: Toward a New Theory of Terrorism. JPS 14: 16-24.

366 Mason, T. D.; Krane, D. A. 1989. Political Economy of Death Squads: A Theory of the Impact of State Sanctioned Terror. ISQ 33: 175-198.

367 Midlarsky, M. I., et al. 1980. Why Violence Spreads: Contagion of International Terrorism. ISQ 24: 262-306.

368 Moss, R. 1973. International Terrorism and Western Societies. IJ 28: 418-430.

369 Orbis. 1984. Papers on Terrorism. Vol 28 (1) and 1985 29 (3).

370 Overgaard, P. B. 1994. Scale of Terrorist Attacks as a Signal of Resources. JCR 38: 452-478.

371 Pisano, V. S. 1979. A Survey of Terrorism of the Left in Italy. Terrorism 2: 171-212.

372 Politique Etrangere. 1986. Papers on Terrorism. PE 51 (4).

373 Price, H. E 1977. The Strategy and Tactics of Revolutionary Terrorism. CSSH 19: 52-66.

374 Rapoport, D. C. 1988. Messianic Sanctions for Terror. CP 20: 195-214.

375 Raub, W.; Keren, G. 1993. Hostages as a Commitment Device. JEBAO 21: 43-67.

376 Ross, J. I. 1993. Structural Causes of Oppositional Political Terrorism. JPR 30: 317-330.

377 Stanford Journal of International Studies. 1977. Papers on Terrorism. SJIS 12 (Spring).

378 World Affairs. 1983. Papers on Terrorism. WA 146 (1).

DYNAMIC PROCESSES

1 Aguirre, B. E.; Quarantelli, E. L.; Mendoza, J. L. 1988. The Collective Behavior of Fads. ASR 53: 569-584.

2 Badalamenti, A. F.; Langs, R. J. 1991. An Empirical Investigation of Human Dyadic Systems in the Time and Frequency Domains. BS 36: 100-114.

3 Banerjee, A. V. 1992. A Simple Model of Herd Behavior. QJE 107: 797-817.

4 Berndsen, R.; Daniels, H. 1994. Causal Reasoning and Explanation in Dynamic Economic Systems. JEDAC 18: 251-271.

5 Beyerchen, A. 1992. Clausewitz, Nonlinearity and the Unpredictability of War. IA 17: 59-90.

6 Bikhchandani, S.; Hirshleifer, D.; Welch, I. 1992. A Theory of Fads, Fashion, Custom and Cultural Change as Informational Cascades. JPE 100: 992-1026.

7 Brams, S. J.; Garriga-Pico, J. E. 1975. Bandwagons in Coalition Formation: The Two-Thirds Rule. ABS 18: 472-496.

8 Brown, C. 1993. Nonlinear Transformations in a Landslide: Johnson and Goldwater in 1964. AJPS 37: 582-609.

9 Carleson, L. 1991. Stochastic Behavior of Deterministic Systems. JEBAO 16 (1/2).

10 Cass, D.; Shell, K. 1983. Do Sunspots Matter? JPE 91: 193-227.

11 Cochrane, J. H. 1994. Shocks. CRCSPP 41: 295-364.

12 Craine, R. 1993. Rational Bubbles. JEDAC 17: 829-846.

13 De Greene, K. B. 1990. Turbulent Field Environment of Sociotechnical Systems. BS 35: 49-59.

14 -. 1994. The Challenge to Policymaking of Large-Scale Systems Evolution, Instability and Structural Change. JTP 6: 161-188.

15 Donaldson, R. G. 1992. Sources of Panics. JME 30: 277-305.

16 Eisenstadt, S. N. 1985. Civilization Formations and Political Dynamics. SPS 8: 231-252.

17 Ekelund, R. B.; Thornton, M.; De Lorme, C. 1993. The Anatomy of Financial Panics. RISEC 40: 915-930.

18 Glance, N. S.; Huberman, B. A. 1994. Dynamics of Social Dilemmas. SA 270 (3): 76-81.

19 Granger, C. W. J. 1991. Developments in the Nonlinear Analysis of Economic Systems. SJE 93: 263-276.

20 -. 1993. Strategies for Modelling Nonlinear Time-Series Relationships. ECONR 69: 233-238.

21 Grin, F. 1992. Towards a Threshold Theory of Minority Language Survival. Kyklos 45: 69-97.

22 Henshel, R. L.; Johnston, W. 1987. The Emergence of Bandwagon Effects. SQ 28: 493-512.

23 Hogan, K. C.; Melvin, M. T. 1994. Sources of Meteor Showers and Heat Waves in the Foreign Exchange Market. JIE 37: 239-247.

24 Hoover, D.; Kowalewski, D. 1992. Dynamic Models of Dissent and Repression. JCR 36: 150-182.

25 Jarsulic, M. 1993. A Nonlinear Model of the Pure Growth Cycle. JEBAO 22: 133-151.

26 Journal of Applied Econometrics. 1992. Papers on Nonlinear Dynamics. JAE 7 (Dec Special Issue).

27 Khalil, E. L. 1995. Nonlinear Thermodynamics and Social Science Modeling. AJEAS 54: 423-438.

28 Kiel, L. D. 1993. Nonlinear Dynamical Analysis: Assessing Systems Concepts in a Government Agency. PAR 53: 143-153.

29 Kiel, L. D.; Elliott, E. 1992. Budgets as Dynamic Systems: Change, Variation, Time and Budgetary Heuristics. JPART 2: 139-156.

30 Kling, J. L. 1987. Predicting the Turning Points of Business and Economic Time Series. Journal of Business 60: 201-238.

31 Kramer, G. H. 1977. A Dynamical Model of Political Equilibrium. JET 16: 310-334.

32 Lux, T. 1994. Herd Behavior, Bubbles and Crashes. EJ 105: 881-896.

33 Mills, T. C. 1991. Nonlinear Time Series Models in Economics. JES 5: 215-242.

34 Nadeau, R.; Cloutier, E.; Guuay, J. H. 1993. New Evidence about the Existence of a Bandwagon Effect in the Opinion Formation Process. IPSR 14: 203-213.

35 Saari, D. G. 1991. Erratic Behavior in Economic Models. JEBAO 16: 3-35.

36 Schofield, N. J. 1978. Instability of Simple Dynamic Games. RES 45: 575-594.

37 Singer, B.; Spilerman, S. 1976. The Representation of Social Processes by Markov Models. AJS 82: 1-54.

38 Staffin, P. D. 1977. The Bandwagon Curve. AJPS 21: 695-708.

39 Tu, P. N. V.; Wilman, E. A. 1992. A Generalized Predator-Prey Model. JEEM 23: 123-138.

40 Uhlig, R. 1994. What Macroeconomists Should Know about Unit Roots. ET 10: 645-671.

41 Van Geert, P. 1991. A Dynamic Systems Model of Cognitive and Language Growth. PR 98: 3-53.

42 Wolfson, M.; Puri, A.; Martelli, M. 1992. Nonlinear Dynamics of International Conflict. JCR 36: 119-149.

43 Zaslavskii, A. I. 1992. Technical Progress in Dynamic Economic Models. Matekon 28: 5-20.

Catastrophes

44 Adelman, I.; Hihn, J. 1982. Politics in Latin America: Catastrophe Theory Model. JCR 26: 592-620.

45 Baack, D.; Cullen, J. B. 1994. Decentralization in Growth and Decline: Catastrophe Theory Approach. BS 39: 213-228.

46 Behavioral Science. 1978. Papers on Catastrophe Theory. BS 23 (5).

47 Berryman, A. A.; Stenseth, N. C. 1984. Behavioral Catastrophes in Biological Systems. BS 29: 127-137.

48 Bigelow, J. 1982. A Catastrophe Model of Organizational Change. BS 27: 26-42.

49 Bove, F. J. 1981. Trend Surface Analysis and the Lowland Classic Maya Collapse. American Antiquary 46: 93-112.

50 Bulow, J.; Klemperer, P. 1994. Rational Frenzies and Crashes. JPE 102: 1-24.

51 Canadian Journal of Political and Social Theory. 1989. Papers on Crash Theory. CJPST 13 (3).

52 Cobb, L. 1981. Parameter Estimation for the Cusp Catastrophe Model. BS 26: 75-78.

53 Dockens, W. S. 1979. Induction-Catastrophe Theory: Behavioral Ecological Approach to Cognition. BS 24: 94-111.

54 Fararo, T. J. 1984. Catastrophe Analysis of the Simon-Homans Model. BS 29: 212-216.

55 Guastello, S. J. 1981. Catastrophe Modeling of Equity in Organizations. BS 26: 63-74.

56 -. 1984. Catastrophe Theory Evaluation of a Policy to Control Job Absence. BS 29: 263-269.

57 -. 1984. Cusp and Butterfly Catastrophe Modeling of Two Opponent Process Models: Drug Addiction and Work Performance. BS 29: 258-262.

58 -. 1985. Color Matching throughout the Work Week: Application of the Swallowtail Difference Equation. BS 30: 213-218.

59 -. 1985. Euler Buckling in a Wheelbarrow Obstacle Course: A Catastrophe with Complex Lag. BS 30: 204-213.

60 Holt, R. T.; Job, B. L.; Markus, L. 1978. Catastrophe Theory and War. JCR 22: 171-208.

61 McCain, R. A. 1981. Cultivation of Taste, Catastrophe Theory and the Demand for Works of Art. AER Proc 71: 332-334.

62 Murphy, H. S. K. 1981. A Preliminary Empirical Test of a Cusp Catastrophe Model in the Social Scinces. BS 26: 153-162.

63 Murphy, J. W. 1991. Catastrophe Theory. AJEAS 50: 143-147.

64 Pol, E. 1993. Theoretical Economics and Catastrophe Theory. Australian Economic Papers 32: 258-271.

65 Rummel, R. J. 1987. A Catastrophe Theory Model of the Conflict Helix. BS 32: 241-266.

66 Smirnov, A. D.; Ershov, E. B. 1992. Perestroika: A Catastrophic Change in Economic Reform Policy. JCR 36: 415-453.

67 Stewart, J. N.; Peregoy, P. L. 1983. Catastrophe Theory Modeling in Psychology. PSYB 94: 336-362.

68 Sussmann, H. J.; Zahler, R. S. 1978. A Critique of Applied Catastrophe Theory in the Behavioral Sciences. BS 23: 383-389.

69 Vendrik, M. C. M. 1993. Habits, Hysteresis and Catastrophes in Labor Supply. JEBAO 20: 353-372.

70 Zeeman, E. C. 1976. Catastrophe Theory. SA 24: 65-83.

Chaos

71 Aczel, A. D.; Josephy, N. H. 1991. Chaotic Behavior of Foreign Exchange Rates. American Economist 35 (Fall): 16-24.

72 Albin, P. S. 1987. Microeconomic Foundations of Cyclical Irregularities or Chaos. MSS 13: 185-214.

73 Baker, P. L. 1993. Chaos, Order and Sociological Theory. SI 63: 123-149.

74 Baumol, W. J.; Benhabib, J. 1989. Chaos: Significance, Mechanism and Economic Applications. JEL 27: 77-105.

75 Baumol, W. J.; Quandt, R. E. 1995. Chaos Models and Implications for Forecasting. EEJ 11: 3-15.

76 Benhabib, J.; Day, R. H. 1981. Rational Choice and Erratic Behavior. RES 48: 459-472.

77 Brown, C. 1994. Politics and Environment: Nonlinear Instabilities Dominate. APSR 88: 292-303.

78 Bullard, J. B.; Butler, A. 1993. Nonlinearity and Chaos in Economic Models. EJ 103: 849-867.

79 Butler, A. 1990. A Methodological Approach to Chaos: Are Economists Missing the Point? FRBSTL 72 (March): 36-48.

80 Chen, P. 1988. Evidence of Economic Chaos. SDR 4: 88-108.

81 Craig, S. G., et al. 1991. Chaos Theory and Microeconomics. RESTAT 73: 208-215.

82 Dechert, W. D.; Gencay, R. 1992. The Lyapunov Exponents as a Nonparametric Diagnostic for Stability Analysis. JAE 7 (Dec Special Issue): S41-S60.

83 DeCoster, G. P.; Labys, W. C.; Mitchell, D. W. 1992. Evidence of Chaos in Commodity Futures Prices. JFM 12: 291-229.

84 DeCoster, G. P.; Mitchell, D. W. 1992. Dynamic Implications of Chaotic Monetary Policy. JOM 14: 267-287.

85 Dendrinos, D. S. 1991. Quasi-Periodicity and Chaos in Spatial Population Dynamics. Socio-Spatial Dynamics 2: 31-60.

86 Frank, M. Z.; Geneay, R.; Stengos, T. 1988. International Chaos? EER 32: 1569-1584.

87 Frank, M. Z.; Stengos, T. 1988. Chaotic Dynamics in Economic Time Series. JES 2: 103-133.

88 -. 1989. Measuring the Strangeness of Gold and Silver Rates of Return. RES 56: 553-567.

89 Gilmore, C. G. 1993. A New Test for Chaos. JEBAO 22: 209-237.

90 Gordon, T. J. 1991. Forecasting a Chaotic Time Series Using Regression. Technological Forecast Society 39: 337-348.

91 Gordon, T. J.; Greenspan, D. 1988. Chaos and Fractals: New Tools for Technological and Social Forecasting. TFASC 34: 1-25.

92 Gregerson, H.; Sailer, L. 1993. Chaos Theory and Implications for Social Science. HR 46: 777-802.

93 Hansson, P. A. 1991. Chaos: Implications for Forecasting. Futures 23: 50-58.

94 Huckfeldt, R. R. 1990. Structure, Indeterminacy and Chaos. JTP 2: 413-433.

95 Jaditz, T.; Sayers, C. 1993. Is Chaos Generic in Economic Data? International Journal of Bifurcations and Chaos 3: 745-755.

96 Johnson, R. A. 1991. The Loss of Stability and Emergence of Chaos. JEBAO 16: 93-113.

97 Journal of Economic Behavior and Organization. 1991. Papers Dynamic Economic Systems and Chaos. JEBAO 16 (1/2).

98 Kaizouji, T. 1994. Multiple Equilibria and Chaotic Tatonnement. JEBAO 24: 357-362.

99 Keenan, D. C.; O'Brien, M. J. 1993. Competition, Collusion and Chaos. JEDAC 17: 327-353.

100 Kelsey, D. 1988. Economics of Chaos or the Chaos of Economics. OEP 40: 1-31.

101 King, J. B. 1989. Confronting Chaos. Journal of Business Ethics 8 (Jan): 39-50.

102 Larrain, M. 1991. Testing Chaos and Nonlinearities in T Bill Rates. Financial Analysist Journal 47 (Sept): 51-62.

103 Larsen, E. R., et al. 1993. Devil's Staircase and Chaos from Macroeconomic Model Interaction. JEDAC 17: 759-769.

104 Liu, T.; Granger, C. W. J.; Heller, W. P. 1992. Using the Correlation Exponent to Decide whether an Economic Series is Chaotic. JAE (Dec Special Issue): S25-S39.

105 Lorenz, H. W. 1987. Goodwin's Nonlinear Accelerator and Chaotic Motion. ZN 47: 413-418.

106 -. 1987. Strange Attractors in a Multisector Business Cycle Model. JEBAO 8: 397-411.

107 Loye, D.; Eisler, R. 1987. Chaos and Transformation: Implications of Nonequilibrium Theory for Social Science and Society. BS 42: 53-65.

108 Majumdar, M.; Mitra, T. 1994. Robust Chaos in Dynamic Optimization Models. RE 48: 225-240.

109 Marks, G. 1992. Rational Sources of Chaos in Democratic Transition. ABS 35: 397-421.

110 May, R. M. 1983. Thresholds and Breakpoints in Ecosystems with a Multiplicity of Stable States. Nature 269: 471-477.

111 -. 1989. Chaos and the Dynamics of Biological Populations. Proceedings of the Royal Society of London A 413: 27-44.

112 McCaffrey, D., et al. 1992. Estimating the Lyapunov Exponent of a Chaotic System with Nonparametric Regression. JASA 87: 682-695.

113 Medio, A. 1991. Continuous-Time Models of Chaos in Economics. JEBAO 16: 115-131.

114 Mirowski, P. 1989. 'Tis a Pity Econometrics Isn't an Empirical Endeavor: Mandelbrot, Chaos and the Noah and Joseph Effects. RE 43: 76-99.

115 -. 1990. From Mandelbrot to Chaos in Economic Theory. SEJ 57: 289-307.

116 Modis, T.; Debecker, A. 1992. Chaoslike States Can Be Expected before and after Logistic Growth. TFASC 41: 111-120.

117 Mosekilde, E.; Aracil, J.; Allen, P. M. 1988. Instabilities and Chaos in Nonlinear Dynamical Systems. SDR 4: 14-55.

118 Nijkamp, P.; Reggiani, A. 1991. Chaos Theory and Spatial Dynamics. JOTEAP 25: 81-96.

119 -. 1995. Non-Linear Evolution of Dynamic Spatial Systems: The Relevance of Chaos and Ecologically Based Models. RSUE 25: 183-210.

120 Nishimura, K.; Yano, M. 1995. Nonlinear Dynamics and Chaos in Optimal Growth. Econometrica 63: 981-1001.

121 Nusse, H. E.; Hommes, C. H. 1990. Resolution of Chaos with Application to a Modified Samuelson Model. JEDAC 14: 1-19.

122 Packard, N., et al. 1980. Geometry from a Time Series. Physical Review Letters 45: 712-716.

123 Richards, D. 1990. Is Strategic Decision Making Chaotic? BS 35: 219-232.

124 -. 1992. A Chaotic Model of Power Concentration in the International System. ISQ 37: 55-72.

125 -. 1992. Spatial Correlation Test for Chaotic Dynamics. AJPS 36: 1047-1069.

126 Roskamp, K. W. 1994. Chaos to Antichaos and Back to Chaos: The Possibility of a Cycle. Kredit und Kapital 27: 1-10.

127 Rosser, J. B. 1990. Chaos Theory and the New Keynesian Economics. MSESS 58: 265-291.

128 Saari, D. G. 1984. The Ultimate Chaos Resulting from Weighted Voting Systems. Advances in Applied Mathematics 5: 286-304.

129 Saperstein, A. M. 1984. Chaos: A Model for the Outbreak of War. Nature 309 (May 24): 303-305.

130 Smith, R. D. 1995. The Inapplicability Principle: What Chaos Means for Social Science. BS 40: 22-40.

131 Sternman, J. D. 1989. Deterministic Chaos in an Experimental Economic System. JEBAO 12: 1-28.

132 Van Witteloostuijn, A.; Van Lier, A. 1990. Chaotic Patterns in Cournot Competition. Metroeconomica 41: 161-185.

133 Vree, J. K. 1991. Chaos in Europe: Inquiry into Nature of Social Systems and Methodology of the Behavioral Sciences. AP 26: 25-64.

134 Wallace, R. 1993. Recurrent Collapse of the Fire Service in New York City: Failure of Paramilitary Systems as a Phase Change. EP 25: 233-244.

135 White, R. W. 1990. Transient Chaotic Behaviour in a Hierarchical Economic System. EP 22: 1309-1321.

136 Willey, T. 1992. Testing for Nonlinear Dependence in Daily Stock Indices. JEAB 44:63-76.

137 Young, T. R. 1991. Chaos and Social Change: Metaphysics of the Postmodern. SSJ 28: 289-305.

138 -. 1992. Chaos Theory and Human Agency. Humanity and Society 16: 441-460.

Complexity

139 Abrahamson, M. 1969. Correlates of Political Complexity. ASR 34: 690-701.

140 Bak, P.; Chen, K. 1989. Self-Organized Criticality. SA 264 (Jan): 46-53.

141 Behavioral Science. 1980. Papers on Systems Analysis. BS 25 (5).

142 -. 1983. Papers on Methodologies for Investigating Social Systems. BS 28 (2).

143 Carneiro, R. L. 1987. Evolution of Complexity and Human Societies and Its Mathematical Expression. IJCS 28: 111-128.

144 Couclelis, H. 1988. Of Mice and Men: What Rodent Populations Teach Us about Complex Spatial Dynamics. EP 20: 99-109.

145 Day, R. H. 1992. Complex Economic Dynamics: Generic in Theory, Elusive in Data. JAE 7 (Dec Special Issue): S9-S23.

146 De Greene, K. B. 1991. Rigidity and Fragility of Large Sociotechnical Systems. BS 36: 64-79.

147 Duong, D. V.; Reilly, K. D. 1995. A System of IAC Neural Networks as the Basis for Self-Organization in a Sociological Dynamical System Simulation. BS 40: 275-303.

148 Fogel, R. W. 1992. Problems in Modeling Complex Dynamic Interactions: The Political Realignment of the 1850s. EAP 4: 215-254.

149 Forrester, J. W. 1987. Nonlinearity in High-Order Social Systems. European Journal of Operational Research 30: 104-109.

150 Futures. 1994. Papers on Complexity. Vol 26 (6).

151 George, D. A. R. 1990. Chaos and Complexity in Economics. JES 4: 397-404.

152 Horgan, J. 1995. From Complexity to Perplexity. SA 272 (6): 104-109.

153 Knopoff, L. 1993. Self-Organization and the Development of Pattern. PAPS 137: 339-349.

154 Landes, D. S. 1994. What Room for Accident in History? Explaining Big Changes by Small Events. EHR 47: 637-656.

155 Latane, B.; Nowak, A.; Liu, J. H. 1994. Measuring Emergent Social Phenomena: Dynamism, Polarization and Clustering as Order Parameters of Social Systems. BS 39: 1-24.

156 Lohmann, S. 1994. Dynamics of Information Cascades: Monday Demonstrations in Leipzig. WP 47 (1): 42-101.

157 Lung, Y. 1988. Complexity and Spatial Dynamics Modeling: From Catastrophe Theory to Self Organizing Process. ARS 22 (2): 81-111.

158 Radzicki, M. J. 1990. Institutional Dynamics, Deterministic Chaos and Self-Organizing Systems. JEI 24: 57-102.

159 Ray, R. D.; Delprato, D. J. 1989. Behavioral Systems Analysis. BS 34: 81-127.

160 Robinson, J. B. 1991. Modelling the Interactions between Human and Natural Systems. ISSJ 43: 629-648.

161 Ruzavin, G. 1994. Self-Organization and Organization of the Economy and the Search for a New Paradigm in Economic Science. Problems of Economic Transition 37 (6): 67-81.

162 Stephens, J. 1969. Logic of Functional and Systems Analyses in Political Science. MJPS 13: 367-394.

163 Tainter, J. A. 1995. Sustainability of Complex Societies. Futures 27: 397-407.

164 Witt, U. 1986. How Can Complex Economical Behavior Be Investigated? The Ignorant Monopolist Revisited. BS 31: 173-188.

Economic Cycles

165 Alesina, A. 1989. Politics and Business Cycles in Industrial Democracies. Economic Policy: A European Forum 8 (April): 55-98.

166 Amos, O. M. 1989. A Reevaluation of Long Cycle Theories: Development as the Satisfaction of Hierarchical Needs. SSQ 70: 341-355.

167 Amos, O. M.; Currier, K. M. 1989. Foundations of a Hierarchical Theory of the Long Wave Phenomenon. SEJ 56: 142-156.

168 Amos, O. M.; Price, E. O. 1991. Induced Socio-Economic Behavior in Long Waves: Recurrence of Normal and Revolutionary Economic Science. REL 57: 61-75.

169 Backus, D. K.; Kehoe, P. J.; Kydland, F. E. 1993. International Business Cycles. FRBM 17 (Fall): 14-29.

170 Barr, H. 1970. Long Waves: Bibliography. Review 2: 675-718.

171 Barsky, R. B.; Miron, J. A. 1989. The Seasonal Cycle and the Business Cycle. JPE 97: 503-534.

172 Bergman, M.; Jonung, L. 1993. The Business Cycle Has Not Been Dampened: Sweden and the US. SEHR 41: 18-36.

173 Berry, B. J. L.; Kim, H.; Kim, H. M. 1993. Are Long Waves Driven by Techno-Economic Transformations? TFASC 44: 111-135.

174 Brignoli, H. P. 1980. The Economic Cycle in Latin American Agricultural Export Economies. LARR 15: 3-34.

175 Burnside, C.; Eichenbaum, M.; Rebelo, S. 1993. Labor Hoarding and the Business Cycle. JPE 101: 245-273.

176 Canova, F. 1994. Were Financial Crises Predictable? JMCB 26: 102-124.

177 Canova, F.; Ghysels, E. 1994. Changes in Seasonal Patterns: Are They Cyclical? JEDAC 18: 1143-1171.

178 Cattell, R. B. 1982. Inflation and Business Cycles from the Standpoint of Psychology and Sociobiology. JSPES 7: 35-54.

179 Clark, J. A.; Freeman, C.; Soete, L. 1981. Long Waves, Inventions and Innovations. Futures 13: 308-322.

180 Cochrane, J. H. 1988. How Big is the Random Walk in GNP? JPE 96: 893-920.

181 Coombs, R. W. 1981. Innovation, Automation and the Long Wave Theory. Futures 13: 360-370.

182 Craig, L. A.; Fisher, D. 1992. Integration of the European Business Cycle. EEH 29: 144-168.

183 Day, R. H. 1982. Irregular Growth Cycles. AER 72: 406-414.

184 De Greene, K. B. 1988. Long Wave Cycles of Sociotechnical Change and Innovation: Macropsychological Perspective. Journal of Occupational Psychology 61: 7-23.

185 -. 1993. Will There be a Fifth Kondratiev Cycle? Systems Research 10: 41-56.

186 Delbeke, J. 1981. Recent Long Wave Theories. Futures 13: 246-257.

187 Economies et Societes. 1993. Papers on Economic Long Waves. Vol 27 (7/8).

188 Elliott, D. 1986. Technology and the Future: Kondratieff Cycles. Journal of Interdisciplinary Economics 1: 189-204.

189 Falk, B. 1986. Further Evidence on the Asymmetric Behavior of Economic Time Series over the Business Cycle. JPE 94: 1096-1109.

190 Fels, R. 1977. What Causes Business Cycles? SSQ 58: 88-95.

191 Fender, J. 1991. Recent Books on Business Cycles. JES 5: 359-374.

192 Fukao, K.; Otaki, M. 1993. Accumulation of Human Capital and the Business Cycle. JPE 101: 73-99.

193 Futures. 1981. Papers on Technical Innovation and Long Waves in World Development. Vol 13 (4).

194 Glismann, H. H. 1987. Theories and Observations on Long Waves of Economics. EJPR 15: 223-240.

195 Gulalp, H. 1989. Stages and Long-Cycles of Capitalist Development. RRPE 21 (4): 83-92.

196 Ickes, B. W. 1986. Cyclical Fluctuations in Centrally Planned Economies. SS 38: 36-52.

197 -. 1990. Do Socialist Countries Suffer a Common Business Cycle? REAS 72: 397-405.

198 Ifo-Studien. 1988. Papers on Business Cycle Theory. Vol 34 (2/3).

199 Irsigler, F.; Metz, R. 1984. Statistical Evidence of Long Waves. SSI 23: 381-410.

200 Journal of Economic Perspectives. 1990. Papers on Sunspots and Speculative Bubbles. JEP 4 (2).

201 Journal of Economic Theory. 1986. Papers on Economic Cycles. JET 40 (1).

202 Kaskarelis, I. A. 1992. Are There Real or Monetary Business Cycles in the United Kingdom Economy? RISEC 39: 49-67.

203 Kogane, Y. 1988. Long Waves of Economic Growth. Futures 20: 532-548.

204 Lai, K. S.; Pauly, P. 1992. Random Walk or Bandwagon: Some Evidence from Foreign Exchanges. AE 24: 693-700.

205 Larson, C. W. 1989. Business Cycles in Centrally Planned Economies. Coexistence 26: 161-178.

206 Lembcke, J. 1992. Why Fifty Years? Working Class Formation and Long Economic Cycles. SAS 55: 417-445.

207 Lindenberg, M. 1990. World Economic Cycles and Central American Political Instability. WP 42: 391-421.

208 Lloyd-Jones, R. 1990. The First Kondratieff: The Long Wave and the British Industrial Revolution. JIDH 20: 581-606.

209 Long, J. B.; Plosser, C. I. 1983. Real Business Cycles. JPE 91: 39-69.

210 Mandel, E. 1981. Explaining Long Waves of Capitalist Development. Futures 13: 332-338.

211 Manuelli, R.; Sargent, T. J. 1988. Models of Business Cycles. JME 22: 523-542.

212 Moore, G. H. 1977. Business Cycles. SSQ 58: 96-103.

213 Morrison, C. C. 1994. The Macrodynamics of Business Cycles: A Review. AEJ 22: 86-90.

214 Nefci, S. N. 1984. Are Economic Time Series Asymmetric over the Business Cycle? JPE 92: 307-328.

215 Nijkamp, P. 1982. Long Waves or Catastrophes in Regional Development. SEPS 16: 261-272.

216 Norton, B. 1988. Epochs and Essences: A Review of Marxist Long-Wave and Stagnation Theories. CJE 12: 203-224.

217 Roberts, J. M. 1993. Sources of Business Cycles: A Monetarist Interpretation. IER 34: 923-934.

218 Romer, C. D. 1994. Remeasuring Business Cycles. JEH 54: 573-609.

219 Rosenberg, N.; Frischtak, C. K. 1984. Technological Innovation and Long Waves. CJE 8: 7-24.

220 Sachs, J. 1980. The Changing Cyclical Behavior of Wages and Prices. AER 70: 78-90.

221 Sargent, T. J. 1981. Interpreting Economic Time Series. JPE 89: 213-243.

222 Sims, C. A. 1980. Comparison of Interwar and Postwar Business Cycles: Monetarism Reconsidered. AER 70: 250-259.

223 Solomou, S. 1986. Innovation Clusters and Kondratieff Long Waves in Economic Growth, CJE 10: 101-112.

224 Sternman, J. D. 1985. An Integrated Theory of the Economic Long Wave. Futures 17: 104-131.

225 Tarascio, V. J. 1988. Kondratieff's Theory of Long Cycles. AEJ 16: 1-10.

226 Thompson, W. R. 1992. Systematic Leadership and Growth Waves in the Long Run. ISQ 36: 25-48.

227 Turner, P. M. 1993. A Structural Vector Autoregression Model of the UK Business Cycle. SJPE 40: 143-164.

228 van Roon, G. 1981. Historians and Long Waves. Futures 13: 383-388.

229 Vishwakarma, K. P. 1994. Recognizing Business Cycle Turning Points by Means of a Neural Network. CE 3: 175-185.

230 Wallerstein, I. 1984. Economic Cycles and Socialist Policies. Futures 16: 579-585.

231 Windolf, P.; Haas, J. 1993. Higher Education and the Business Cycle. IJCS 34: 167-191.

232 Zarnowitz, V. 1985. Recent Works on Business Cycles in Historical Perspective. JEL 23: 523-580.

233 -. 1990. A Guide to What Is Known about Business Cycles. BE 25 (3): 5-13.

Socio-Political Cycles

234 Alesina, A.; Rosenthal, H. 1989. Partisan Cycles in Congressional Elections and the Macroeconomy. APSR 83: 373-398.

235 Alesina, A.; Roubini, N. 1992. Political Cycles in OECD Economies. RES 59: 663-688.

236 Beck, N. 1991. The Illusion of Cycles in International Relations. ISQ 35: 455-480.

237 Beck, P. A. 1979. The Electoral Cycle and Patterns of American Politics. BJPS 9: 129-156.

238 Brody, A. 1994. Old Hungarian Prints or Does the 200 Year Cycle Exist? AO 46: 163-181.

239 Burklin, W. P. 1987. Why Study Political Cycles? EJPR 15: 131-144.

240 Byers, J. D. 1991. Is Political Popularity a Random Walk? AE 23: 967-973.

241 Bystryn, M. N. 1981. Variation in Artistic Cycles. SQ 22: 120-132.

242 Chu, C. Y. C.; Lee, R. D. 1994. Famine, Revolt and the Dynastic Cycle: Population Dynamics in Historic China. JPOPE 7: 351-378.

243 Cottrell, A. 1994. Hayek's Early Cycle Theory Reexamined. CJE 18: 197-212.

244 Eisner, M. 1987. Cycles of Political Control: The Canton of Zurich. EJPR 15: 167-184.

245 -. 1990. Long Term Dynamics of Political Values in International Perspective. EJPR 18: 605-622.

246 Elazar, D. J. 1978. The Generational Rhythm of American Politics. APQ 6: 55-94.

247 European Journal of Political Research 1987. Papers on Cycles in Politics. EJPR 15 (2).

248 Feld, S. L.; Grofman, B. 1992. Who's Afraid of the Big Bad Cycle? Evidence from Thirty-Six Elections. JTP 4: 231-237.

249 Fenton, J. 1982. Cycle Theory and Political Realignment in the US. POLST 30: 426-431.

250 Frank, A. G.; Gills, B. K. 1993. World System Economic Cycles and Hegemonial Shift: 100 BC to 1500 AD. JEEH 22: 155-183.

251 Gartner, M. 1994. The Quest for Political Cycles in OECD Countries. EJPE 10: 427-440.

252 Gaubatz, K. T. 1991. Election Cycles and War. JCR 35: 212-244.

253 Goldstein, J. S. 1985. Kondratieff Waves as War Cycles. ISQ 29: 411-444.

254 -. 1987. Long Waves in War, Production, Prices and Wages. JCR 31: 573-600.

255 -. 1991. The Possibility of Cycles in International Relations. ISQ 35: 477-480.

256 Keenes, E. 1993. History and International Relations: Long Cycles in World Politics. CJPS 26: 145-156.

257 Kegley, C. W.; Raymond, G. A. 1989. The Long Cycle of Global War and the Transformation of Alliance Norms. JPR 26: 265-284.

258 Kolodziej, E. A. 1979. Living with the Long Cycle Today: New Assumptions to Guide Military Force. PSJ 8: 17-27.

259 Ley, R. D. 1993. Long Wave Rhythms in Economic Development and Political Behavior. AEJ 21 (2): 78-84.

260 Li, R. P. Y. 1976. A Dynamic Comparative Analysis of Presidential and House Elections. AJPS 20: 671-692.

261 Lohmann, S. 1993. Electoral Cycles and International Policy Cooperation. EER 37: 1373-1391.

262 Marchetti, C. 1986. The Fifty Year Pulsation in Human Affairs: Analysis of Some Physical Indicators. Futures 18: 376-388.

263 Modelski, G. 1978. The Long Cycle of Global Politics and the Nation-State. CSSH 20: 214-235.

264 -. 1979. Long Cycles and US Strategic Policy. PSJ 8: 10-16.

265 -. 1983. Long Cycles of World Leadership: Annotated Bibliography. ISN 10: 1-5.

266 Mohler, P. P. 1987. Cycles of Value Change. EJPR 15: 155-166.

267 Mushaben, J. M. 1985. Cycles of Peace Protest in West Germany. WEP 8: 24-40.

268 Piccigallo, P. R. 1987. Cyclical Trends in US Politics. SP 18: 54-60.

269 Rasler, K. A.; Thompson, W. R. 1983. Global Wars, Public Debts and the Long Cycle. WP 35: 489-516.

270 Resnick, D.; Thomas, N. C. 1990. Cycling through American Politics. Polity 23: 1-22.

271 Roemer, J. E. 1995. Political Cycles. EAP 7: 1-20.

272 Rosecrance, R. 1987. Long Cycle Theory and International Relations. IO 41: 283-301.

273 Sayrs, L. W. 1993. The Long Cycle of International Relations: A Markov Specification. ISQ 37: 215-237.

274 Sellers, C. G. 1965. The Equilibrium Cycle in Two-Party Politics. POQ 30: 16-38.

275 Siklos, P. L. 1987. Cyclical Fluctuations in US Monetary Policy and Output. JSEE 11: 69-94.

276 Spiezio, K. E. 1993. Power Cycle Theory and State Involvement in Militarized Interstate Disputes. CMAPS 13: 87-100.

277 Tarascio, V. J. 1989. Economic and War Cycles. HPE 21: 91-101.

278 Thompson, W. R.; Zuk, L. G. 1982. War, Inflation and the Kondratieff Long Waves. JCR 26: 621-644.

279 Usher, D. 1989. The Dynastic Cycle and the Stationary State. AER 79: 1031-1044.

280 Van der Eijk, C. 1987. Testing Theories of Electoral Cycles: Netherlands. EJPR 15: 253-270.

281 Van der Eijk, C.; Weber, R. P. 1987. Notes on the Empirical Analysis of Cyclical Processes. EJPR 15: 271-280.

282 Van Winden, F.; Schram, A. J. H. C.; Groot, F. 1987. The Interaction between Economics and Politics: Modelling Cycles. EJPR 15: 185-202.

283 Weber, R. P. 1987. Cycles in the Third World. EJPR 15: 145-154.

284 Wolfson, M.; Puri, A.; Martelli, M. 1992. Nonlinear Dynamics of International Conflict. JCR 36: 119-149.

285 Zeira, J. 1994. Information Cycles. RES 61: 31-44.

ECONOMIC POLICY

1 Alchian, A. A.; Demsetz, H. 1973. The Property Rights Paradigm. JEH 33: 16-27.
2 Alesina, A. 1988. Macroeconomics and Politics. Macroeconomic Annual 3: 13-52.
3 Amariglio, J.; Callari, A.; Cullenberg, S. 1989. Analytical Marxism. ROSE 47: 415-432.
4 Anderson, M. A.; Goldsmith, A. H. 1994. Economic and Psychological Theories of Forecast Bias and Learning. EEJ 20: 413-427.
5 Annals. 1991. Papers on Foreign Investment in the US. ANNALS 516.
6 Bhattacharya, D. K. 1990. Econometric Method of Estimating the Hidden Economy: United Kingdom. EJ 100: 703-717.
7 Blackford, M. G. 1991. Small Business in America: A Historiographic Survey. Business History Review 65: 1-26.
8 Bloch, P. C. 1986. Politico-Economic Behavior of Authoritarian Governments. PC 51: 117-128.
9 Brennan, T. J. 1992. Refusing to Cooperate with Competitors: A Theory of Boycotts. JOLE 35: 247-264.
10 Brooks, C. 1994. Class Consciousness and Politics in Comparative Perspective. SSR 23: 167-195.
11 Burgelman, R. A. 1994. Fading Memories: A Process Theory of Strategic Business Exit in Dynamic Environments. ASQ 39: 24-56.
12 Cahiers d'Etudes Africaines. 1991. Papers on Anthropology and Capitalism. Vol 31 (4).
13 Collins, D. G. 1992. The Measurement of Temperature in Economic Systems Considered as Thermodynamic Models. Energy Economics 14: 73-78.
14 Crystal, J. 1994. Politics of Capital Flight: Exit and Exchange Rates in Latin America. RIS 20: 131-148.
15 Davis, L.; Legler, J. 1966. The Government in the American Economy. JEH 26: 514-535.
16 Deeg, R. 1995. Institutional Transfer, Social Learning and Economic Policy in Eastern Europe. WEP 18: 38-63.
17 Devine, J. A. 1985. State and State Expenditures: Determinants of Social Investment and Social Consumption Spending in the Postwar US. ASR 50: 150-165.
18 Econometric Reviews. 1994. Papers on Artificial Neural Networks for Economic Series. ER 13 (1).
19 Feldman, A. M.; Weiman, D. 1979. Envy, Wealth and Class Hierarchies. JPUBE 11: 81-91.
20 Ferris, J. M. (17: 7513). Interrelationships among Public Spending Preferences. PC 45: 139-154.
21 Gillespie, S. 1990. Are Economic Statistics Overproduced? PC 67: 227-242.
22 Goidel, R. K.; Langley, R. E. 1995. Media Coverage of the Economy and Aggregate Economic Evaluations. PRQ 48: 313-328.
23 Gramlich, E. M.; Rubinfeld, D. L. 1982. Voting on Public Spending. JPAAM 1: 516-537.
24 Hollingsworth, J. R.; Hanneman, R. A. 1982. Working Class Power and the Political Economy of Western Capitalist Societies. CSR 5: 61-80.
25 Hout, M.; Brooks, C.; Manza, J. 1995. Democratic Class Struggle in the US. ASR 60: 805-828.
26 International Social Science Journal. 1980. Papers on Tourism. ISSJ 32 (1).
27 Ioannidis, C.; Thompson, R. S. 1986. Political Opinion Polls and the Stock Market. Managerial and Decision Economics 7: 267-271.
28 Journal of Law and Economics. 1989. Papers on Empirical Approaches to Market Power. JOLE 32 (2 Pt 2).
29 Journal of Public Policy. 1988. Papers on Monetary Cooperation and Domestic Politics. JPP 8 (3/4).
30 Journal of Social Issues. 1989. Papers on Managing the Economy. JSI 45 (1).
31 Lanning, S. G. 1987. Costs of Maintaining a Cartel. Journal of Industrial Economics 36: 157-174.
32 Law and Contemporary Problems. 1987. Papers on Bankruptcy. LACP 50 (2).
33 Lawson, C. 1994. Theory of State Owned Enterprises in Market Economies. JES 8: 283-309.
34 Lindbeck, A. 1976. Stabilization Policy in Open Economies with Endogenous Politicians. AER 66: 1-19.
35 Lucas, R. E. 1990. Supply-Side Economics. OEP 42: 293-316.
36 Martin, A. 1977. Political Constraints and Economic Strategies in Advanced Industrial Societies. CPS 10: 323-354.
37 McNiel, D. W.; Yu, S. S. 1989. Blue Laws: Impact on Regional Retail Activity. PRAPR 8: 267-278.
38 Muller, E. N. 1982. Graphs and Anonymous Social Welfare Functions. IER 23: 609-622.
39 Nell, E. 1983. On the Conception of the State in Macroeconomic Theory. SR 50: 401-428.
40 North, D. C. 1991. Institutions, Ideology and Economic Performance. CJ 11: 477-488.
41 Plott, C. R. 1972. Ethics, Social Choice and the Theory of Economic Policy. JMS 2: 181-208.
42 Policy Sciences. 1994. Papers on International Capital Mobility. PSCI 27 (4).
43 Policy Studies Journal. 1985. Papers on Small Business and Public Policy. PSJ 13 (4).
44 Policy Studies Review. 1983. Papers on the Economic Revitalization of America. PSR 2 (4).

45 Regional Science and Urban Economics. 1992. Papers on Transportation. RSUE 22 (1).

46 Riker, W. H.; Sened, I. 1991. A Political Theory of the Origin of Property Rights. AJPS 35: 951-969.

47 Rothstein, P. 1994. Learning the Preferences of Governments and Voters from Proposed Spending and Aggregated Votes. JPUBE 54: 361-389.

48 Ruland, L. J.; Viaene, J. M. 1993. The Political Choice of the Exchange Rate Regime. EAP 5: 271-284.

49 Saeed, K. 1990. Government Support for Economic Agendas in Developing Countries. WD 18: 785-801.

50 Salamon, L. M.; Siegfried, J. J. 1977. Economic Power and Political Influence: Impact of Industry Structure on Public Policy. APSR 71: 1026-1043.

51 Scandinavian Political Studies. 1989. Papers on the Politics of Economic Flexibility. SPS 12 (4).

52 Shiller, R. J.; Boycko, M.; Korobov, V. 1992. Hunting for Homo Sovieticus: Situational vs. Attitudinal Factors in Economic Behavior. BPEA 1992 (1): 127-181.

53 Sims, C. A. 1980. Macroeconomics and Reality. Econometrica 48: 1-48.

54 Stanford Journal of International Law. 1981. Papers on Foreign Investment in the United States. SJIL 17 (1).

55 Turner, F. C.; Elordi, C. A. 1995. Economic Values and Role of Government in Latin America. ISSJ 47: 473-488.

56 van Ark, B.; Pilat, D. 1993. Productivity Levels in Germany, Japan and the US: Differences and Causes. BPEA 1993: 1-48.

57 Whaples, R. 1995. Where Is There Consensus among American Economic Historians? JEH 55: 139-154.

58 Zald, M. 1985. Political Change, Citizenship Rights and the Welfare State. ANNALS 479: 48-66.

Domestic Economic Policy

59 Alvarez, R. M.; Garrett, G.; Lange, P. 1991. Government Partisanship, Labor Organization and Macroeconomic Performance. APSR 85: 539-556.

60 Annals. 1984. Papers on Deindustrialization. ANNALS 475.

61 Arce, M.; Arce, D. G. 1994. Fiscal Policy and the Theory of Conflict Management. MSESS 62: 425-437.

62 Attaran, M.; Zwick, M. 1987. Entropy and Other Measures of Industrial Diversification. QJBE 26: 17-34.

63 Baily, M. N. 1981. The Productivity Growth Slowdown and Capital Accumulation. AER Proceedings 71: 326-331.

64 Batemarco, R. 1986. The Laffer Curve. JSPES 11: 413-429.

65 Beck, N. 1984. Domestic Political Sources of American Monetary Policy. JOP 46: 787-815.

66 Bishop, J. H. 1989. Is the Test Score Decline Responsible for the Productivity Growth Decline? AER 79: 178-197.

67 Boadway, R.; Marchand, M. 1995. Use of Public Expenditures for Redistributive Purposes. OEP 47: 45-59.

68 Bowles, P.; White, G. 1994. Central Bank Independence: A Political Economy Approach. JDS 31: 235-264.

69 Brenner, M. J. 1991. Gauging Decline. Polity 24: 107-128.

70 Brierly, A. B. 1990. Economic Development Authorities: The Organizational Response to Economic Decline. PSJ 18: 999-1014.

71 Brittan, S. 1978. How British Is the British Sickness? JOLE 21: 245-269.

72 Buchanan, J. M.; Lee, D. R. 1982 Politics, Time and the Laffer Curve. JPE 90: 816-819.

73 Burdekin, R. C. K. 1987. Cross-Country Evidence on the Relationship between Central Banks and Governments. JOM 9: 391-405.

74 Cato Journal. 1983 Papers on Monetary Reform. CJ 3 (1), 1986 5 (3), 1990 10 (2), and 1993 12 (1), 12 (3).

75 -. 1988. Papers on Financial Services. CJ 7 (3).

76 Chappell, H. W.; Havrilesky, T. M.; McGregory, R. R. 1993. Partisan Monetary Policies: Presidential Influence through the Power of Appointment. QJE 108: 185-218.

77 Chappell, H. W.; Keech, W. R. 1983. Welfare Consequences of a Six-Year Presidential Term Evaluated in the Context of a Model of the US Economy. APSR 77: 75-91.

78 Conover, P. J.; Feldman, S.; Knight, K. 1987. Personal and Political Underpinnings of Economic Forecasts. AJPS 31: 559-583.

79 Cowart, A. T. 1978. The Economic Policies of European Governments. BJPS 8: 285-312, 425-439.

80 Cunningham, S. R.; Vilasuso, J. 1994. Is Keynesian Demand Management Policy Still Viable? JPKE 17: 187-210.

81 de Haan, J.; van 't Hag, G. J. 1995. Variation in Central Bank Independence across Countries. PC 85: 335-352.

82 DeLeon, R. E. 1973. Politics, Economic Surplus and Redistribution in the American States. AJPS 17: 781-797.

83 Ederington, L. H. 1985. Classification Models and Bond Ratings. Financial Review 20 (4): 237-262.

84 Ervasti, H.; Kangas, O. E. 1995. Class Bases of Universal Social Policy: Pension Policy Attitudes. EJPR 27: 347-368.

85 Ferber, R.; Hirsch, W. Z. 1987. Social Experimentation and Economic Policy. JEL 16: 1379-1414.

86 Frey, B. S.; Eichenberger, R. 1994. The Political Economy of Stabilization Programmes in Developing Countries. EJPE 10: 169-190.

87 Frieden, J. A. 1991. Invested Interests: Politics of National Economic Policies in a World of Global Finance. IO 45: 425-451.

88 Friedman, M. 1970. A Theoretical Framework for Monetary Analysis. JPE 78: 193-238.

89 Futures. 1993. Papers on Industrialization. Vol 25 (6).

90 Garrett, G. 1995. Capital Mobility, Trade and the Domestic Politics of Economic Reform. IO 49: 657-688.

91 Garten, J. E. 1987. Is American Decline Inevitable. World Policy Journal 5: 151-174.

92 Gibson, H. E.; Tsakalotos, E. 1994. The Scope and Limits of Financial Liberalization in Developing Countries. JDS 30: 578-628.

93 Gilligan, M. J.; Garrett, G. 1995. The Politics of Public Aid to Private Industry: Policy Networks. CPS 28: 3-61.

94 Goldfeld, S. M.; Quandt, R. E. 1992. Effects of Bailouts, Taxes and Risk-Aversion on Enterprise. JCE 16: 150-167.

95 Goodman, J. B. 1991. The Politics of Central Bank Independence. CP 23: 329-349.

96 Havrilesky, T. M. 1994. Outside Influences on Monetary Policy. CEP 12: 46-51.

97 -. 1994. Political Economy of Monetary Policy. EJPE 10: 111-134.

98 Havrilesky, T. M.; Sapp, R.; Schweitzer, R. 1975. Tests of the Federal Reserve's Reactions to the State of the Economy. SSQ 55: 835-852.

99 Hoggart, K. 1994. Political Parties and District Council Economic Policies. US 31: 59-77.

100 Hoover, K. D.; Perez, S. J. 1994. Post Hoc Ergo Propter Once More: Does Monetary Policy Matter? JME 47-73.

101 International Regional Science Review. 1994. Papers on Regional Policy. IRSR 16 (1/2).

102 International Review of Administrative Sciences. 1991 Papers on Economic Integration. IRAS 57 (4)

103 Jankowski, R.; Wlezien, C. 1993. Substitutability and the Politics of Macroeconomic Policy. JOP 55: 1060-1080.

104 Journal of Economic Perspectives. 1988. Papers on Productivity Growth Slowdown. JEP 2 (4).

105 Journal of Political Economy. 1972. Papers of Milton Friedman's Monetary Theory. JPE 80: 837-950.

106 Karras, G. 1994. Government Spending and Private Consumption. JMCB 26: 9-22.

107 Kau, J. B.; Link, A. N. 1983. The Impact of Labor Unions on the Passage of Economic Legislation. JLR 2: 133-145.

108 Kau, J. B.; Rubin, P. H. 1978. Voting on Minimum Wages. JPE 86: 337-342.

109 Keman, H. 1984. Politics, Policies and Consequences: A Cross National Analysis of Public Policy. EJPR 12: 147-170.

110 King, A. 1973. Ideas, Institutions and the Policies of Governments. BJPS 3: 291-313.

111 Krause, G. A. 1994. Federal Reserve Policy Decision Making: Political and Bureaucratic Influences. AJPS 38: 124-144.

112 Landau, D. 1990. The Pattern of Economic Policies in LDCs. CJ 10: 573-601.

113 Leathers, C. G. 1989. Veblen's Theories of Government Failure. AJEAS 48: 293-306.

114 Lee, D. R. 1989. Special Interest Inefficiency: A Case for or against Government Spending Limits? SSQ 70: 765-771.

115 Lowery, D. 1987. Electoral Stress and Revenue Structures in the States: Searching for Fiscal Illusion. APQ 15: 5-46.

116 Martin, P. 1994. Monetary Policy and Country Size. JIMF 13: 573-586.

117 Matthews, R. C. O. 1993. Political and Economic Causes of the Economic Slowdown. SJPE 40: 129-142.

118 McMillin, W. D.; Smyth, D. J. 1994. A Multivariate Time Series Analysis of the US Aggregate Production Function. EE 19: 659-673.

119 Munnell, A. H. 1990. Why Has Productivity Growth Declined? Productivity and Public Investment. NEER 1990 (Jan): 3-22.

120 Nelson, R. R.; Wright, G. 1992. The Rise and Fall of American Technological Leadership. JEL 30: 1931-1964.

121 Nilsson, E. A. 1994. Empirical Evidence that Social Relations of Production Matter: Antebellum South. CJE 18: 259-277.

122 Owens, J. E. 1995. Good Public Policy Voting in the US Congress: An Explanation of Financial Institutions Politics. POLST 43: 66-91.

123 Policy and Politics. 1988. Papers on Local Economic Policy. PAP 16 (3).

124 Political Quarterly. 1993. Papers on Industrial Relations. PQ 64 (1).

125 Political Psychology. 1995. Papers on Political Economy and Political Psychology. PP 16 (1).

126 Prebisch, R. 1969. Commercial Policy in the Underdeveloped Countries. AER 59: 251-273.

127 Public Opinion Quarterly. 1986. Papers on the Crisis of Confidence. POQ 50 (1).

128 Radice, H. 1975. The National Economy: A Myth? Capital and Class 22: 111-140.

129 Rahn, R. W. 1989. Private Money. CJ 9: 353-366.

130 Richter, S. G. 1989. Climbing Down from the Hill: Decline of America and the National Crisis in Economic Policymaking. PS 22: 600-605.

131 Rowthorn, R. E. 1992. Productivity and American Leadership. RIW 38: 475-496.

132 Santiago, C. E. 1989. The Dynamics of Minimum Wage Policy in Economic Development. EDACC 38: 1-30.

133 Schroeder, G. E. 1988. Property Rights Issues in Economic Reforms in Socialist Countries. SCC 21: 175-188.

134 Scully, G. W.; Slottje, D. J. 1991. Ranking Economic Liberty across Countries. PC 70: 121-152

135 Stigler, G. J. 1975. The Goals of Economic Policy. JOLE 18: 283-293.

136 Swank, D. H. 1988. The Political Economy of Government Domestic Expenditure in Affluence Democracies. APSR 32: 1120-1150.

137 Uslaner, E. M.; Weber, R. E. 1975. The Politics of Redistribution. APQ 3: 130-170.

138 Van Hoose, D. D. 1992. The Political Economy of American Monetary Policy. AEJ 20: 73-80.

139 Vogel, D.; Nadel, M. V. 1977. Who Is a Consumer? An Analysis of the Politics of Consumer Conflict. APQ 5: 27-56.

140 Waller, C. J. 1992. A Bargaining Model of Partisan Appointments to the Central Bank. JME 29: 411-428.

141 Warman, F.; Thirlwall, A.P. 1994 Interest Rates, Saving, Investment and Growth in Mexico: Financial Liberalization Hypothesis. JDS 30: 629-649.

142 Weingast, B. R., et al. 1981. Political Economy of Benefits and Costs: A Neoclassical Approach to Distribution Politics. JPE 89: 642-664.

143 West, D. M. 1988. Activists and Economic Policy Making in Congress. APSR 32: 662-680.

144 Whitehead, L. 1990. Political Explanations of Macroeconomic Management. WD 18: 1133-1146.

145 Wilkins, M. 1991. Foreign Investment in the US Economy before 1914. ANNALS 516: 9-21.

146 Williamson, J. G. 1991. Productivity and American Leadership. JEL 29: 51-68.

147 Wlezien, C. 1995. Dynamics of Preferences for Spending. AJPS 39: 981-1000.

148 Wolf, T. A. 1991. Lessons of Limited Market Oriented Reform. JEP 5: 45-58.

149 Wolff, E. N. 1986. Productivity Slowdown and the Fall of the US Rate of Profit. RRPE 18: 87-109.

150 Woolley, J. T. 1994. Politics of Monetary Policy. JPP 14: 57-85.

151 Woolley, J. T.; LeLoup, L. T. 1989. Adequacy of the Electoral Motive in Explaining Legislative Attention to Monetary Policy. CP 22: 63-82.

152 Yale Law Journal. 1993. Papers on Economic Competitiveness. YLJ 102 (7).

153 Zivot, E.; Andrews, D. W. K. 1992. Further Evidence on the Great Crash, the Oil-Price Shock and the Unit-Root Hypothesis. JBAES 10: 251-270.

Employment

154 Administration. 1987. Papers on Unemployment. Vol 35 (3).

155 Ahluwalia, M. S. 1976. Unequality, Poverty and Development. JDE 3: 307-342.

156 Alt, J. E. 1985. Political Parties, World Demand and Unemployment. APSR 79: 1016-1040.

157 Annals. 1987. Papers on Unemployment. ANNALS 492.

158 Atkinson, A. B.; Micklewright, J. 1991. Unemployment Compensation and Labor Market Transitions. JEL 29: 1679-1727.

159 Bean, C. R. 1994. European Employment. JEL 32: 573-619.

160 Blank, R. M. 1995. Changes in Inequality and Unemployment. JPOPE 8: 1-21.

161 Boyne, G. A. 1988. Politics, Unemployment and Local Economic Policies. US 25: 474-486.

162 Communist and Post-Communist Studies. 1995. Papers on Blue Collar Workers in Post-Communist Transitions. CAPCS 28 (1).

163 Cross, R. 1993. On the Foundations of Hysteresis in Economic Systems. EAPHIL 9: 53-74.

164 Cross, R.; Hutchinson, J.; Yeoward, S. 1990. The Natural Rate vs. the Hysteresis Hypothesis. WELTA 126: 156-164.

165 Cuddington, J. T. 1980. Simultaneous Equation Tests of the Natural Rate. JPE 88: 539-549.

166 Cusack, T. R.; Notermans, T.; Rein, M. 1989. Political-Economic Aspects of Public Employment. EJPR 22: 471-500.

167 Development. 1995. Papers on Unemployment. Vol 1995 (3).

168 Dreze, J.; Bean, C. R. 1990. European Unemployment: Lessons from a Multicountry Econometric Study. SJE 92: 135-165.

169 Empirical Economics. 1990. Papers on Unemployment and Hysteresis. EE 15 (2).

170 Grimes, P. W.; Ray, M. A. 1988. Right-to-Work Legislation and Employment Growth: A Shift-Share Analysis. RSP 18: 78-93.

171 Hadjimatheou, G. 1986. Why Has Britain Not Had Full Employment since the Early 1970s? JPKE 8: 859-870.

172 Heywood, J. S.; Mohtadi, H. 1995. The Racial Composition of Unemployment: The Role of Unions. MSESS 63: 175-195.

173 Hudson, J. 1994. Granger Causality, Rational Expectations and Aversion to Unemployment and Inflation. PC 80: 9-22.

174 Industrial and Labor Relations Review. 1992. Papers on Minimum Wage Research. ILRR 46 (1).

175 Jha, R. 1990. Hysteresis and the Natural Rate of Unemployment. Indian Economic Review 25: 241-258.

176 Journal of Public Policy. 1983. Papers on Industrial Policies in OECD Countries. JPP 3 (1).

177 Juhn, C.; Murphy, K. M.; Topel, R. H. 1991. Why Has the Natural Rate of Unemployment Increased? BPEA 1991 (2): 75-126.

178 Kerbo, H. R.; Shaffer, R. A. 1986. Unemployment and Protest in the US. SF 64: 1046-1056.

179 Koch, J. W. 1991. Explanations of Group Economic Outcomes. APQ 19: 211-228.

180 Kposowa, A. J. 1995. Impact of Immigration on Unemployment and Earnings among Racial Minorities in the US. EARS 18: 605-628.

181 Maddison, A. 1987. Growth and Slowdown in Advanced Capitalist Economies. JEL 25: 649-698.

182 Marcotte, D. E. 1995. Declining Job Stability. JPAAM 14: 590-598.

183 Mitchell, W. F. 1993. Testing for Unit Roots and Persistence in OECD Unemployment Rates. AE 25: 1489-1501.

184 Myatt, A.; Sephton, P. 1990. Unemployment in OECD Countries: An Empirical Test of the Wage Gap Hypothesis. AE 22: 881-890.

185 Nickell, S. J. 1987. A Historical Perspective on Unemployment. JPE 95: 857-869.

186 Piore, M. J. 1987. Historical Perspectives and Unemployment. JEL 25: 1834-1887.

187 Policy Studies Journal. 1979. Papers on Employment Policy. PSJ 8 (3).

188 Political Quarterly 1981. Papers on Unemployment. PQ 52 (1).

189 Politics and Society. 1991. Papers on Labor. PAS 19 (4).

190 Setterfield, M. 1993. A Model of Institutional Hysteresis. JEI 27: 755-774.

191 Social Research 1987. Papers on Unemployment. SR 54 (2).

192 Solow, R. M. 1980. On Theories of Unemployment. AER 70: 1-11.

193 Staber, U. 1993. Worker Cooperatives and the Business Cycle: An Answer to Unemployment. AJEAS 52: 129-144.

194 Taheri, J. 1995. Persistence of High Unemployment in the OECD Countries. JPKE 17: 481-502.

195 Vedder, R.; Gallaway, L. E. 1994. American Unemployment in Historical Perspective. JLR 15: 1-17.

196 West, C. T. 1994. The Problem of Unemployment in the US: Sixty Years of National and State Policy Initiatives. IRSR 16: 17-47.

Growth and Industrial Policy

197 Abrams, B. A.; Lewis, K. A. 1995. Cultural and Institutional Determinants of Economic Growth. PC 83: 273-290.

198 Ades, A. 1995. Economic Development with Endogenous Political Participation. EAP 7: 93-117.

199 Alam, M. S. 1994. Colonialism, Decolonialisation and Growth Rates. CJE 18: 235-257.

200 Albala-Bertrand, J. M. 1993. Natural Disaster Situations and Growth: A Macroeconomic Model for Sudden Disaster Impacts. WD 21: 1417-1434.

201 Alesina, A.; Perotti, R. 1994. The Political Economy of Growth. WBER 8: 351-371.

202 Allen, M. P.; Sanglier, M. 1978. Dynamic Models of Urban Growth. JSBS 1: 265-280, 2: 269-278.

203 Alschuler, L. R. 1973. A Sociological Theory of Latin American Underdevelopment. CPS 6: 41-61.

204 -. 1976. Satellization and Stagnation in Latin America. ISQ 20: 39-82.

205 Ambrosius, M. M. 1989. Effectiveness of State Economic Development Policies. WPQ 42: 283-300.

206 -. 1989. Role of Occupational Interests in State Economic Development Policy. WPQ 42: 53-68.

207 Anglin, R. 1990. Diminishing Utility: Citizen Preferences for Local Growth. UAQ 25: 684-696.

208 Annals of Regional Science. 1995. Papers on Spatial Economic Development. ARS 29 (2).

209 Azam, J. P. 1994. Democracy and Development. PC 80: 293-306.

210 Baganha, M. I. 1994. Growth and Stagnation. JUH 20: 541-547.

211 Banks, A. S. 1975. Industrialization and Development. EDACC 22: 320-337.

212 Barlow, R. 1994. Population Growth and Economic Growth. PADR 20: 153-166.

213 Barro, R. J.; Lee, J. W. 1994. The Sources of Economic Growth. CRCSPP 40 (June): 1-46.

214 Baum, D. N.; Lin, S. A. Y. 1993. The Differential Effects on Economic Growth of Government Expenditures on Education, Welfare and Defense. Journal of Economic Development 18: 175-185.

215 Berman, D. R.; Martin, L. L. 1992. New Approach to Economic Development: Innovativeness in the States. PSJ 20: 10-21.

216 Bingham, R. D.; Bowen, W. M. 1994. Performance of State Economic Development Programs. PSJ 22: 501-513.

217 Bradshaw, Y. W. 1985. Dependent Development in Black Africa. ASR 50: 195-206.

218 Bradshaw, Y. W.; Tshandu, Z. 1990. Foreign Capital Penetration, State Intervention and the Development of Sub-Saharan Africa. ISQ 34: 229-251.

219 Bresnahan, T. F.; Trajtenberg, M. 1995. General Purpose Technologies: Engines of Growth? JOE 65: 83-108.

220 Brierly, A. B.; Feiock, R. C. 1993. Accounting for State Economic Growth: A Production Function Approach. PRQ 46: 657-670.

221 Bruchey, S. 1992. The Sources of the Economic Development of the US. ISSJ 44: 531-548.

222 Buhr, W. 1995. Regional Economic Growth by Policy Induced Capital Flows. ARS 29: 17-40.

223 Canto, V. A.; Webb, R. I. 1987. Effect of State Fiscal Policy on State Economic Performance. SEJ 54: 186-202.

224 Caporaso, J. A. 1981. Industrialization in the Periphery: Evolving Global Division of Labor. ISQ 25: 347-384.

225 Carlino, G. A.; Mills, E. S. 1987. Determinants of County Growth. JRS 27: 39-54.

226 Carritte, J.; Williamson, J. G. 1995. An Analysis of the Impact of Public Pension Spending on Economic Growth in the Affluent Democracies. IJCS 36: 82-95.

227 Carroll, J. J.; Wasylenko, M. 1994. Do State Business Climates Still Matter? NTJ 47: 19-37.

228 Cato Journal. 1987. Papers on Development Economics. CJ 7 (1).

229 Chakravarty, S. 1987. The State of Development Economics. MSESS 55: 125-143.

230 Chase-Dunn, C. 1975. Effects of International Economic Dependence on Development and Inequality. ASR 40: 720-738.

231 Chen, C. H. 1993. Causality between Defense Spending and Economic Growth: China. JESTUD 20: 37-43.

232 Chenery, H. B.; Taylor, L. 1968. Development Patterns among Countries and over Time. REAS 50: 391-416.

233 Chinn, D. L. 1982. Growth, Equity and Gini Coefficients: Taiwan. EDACC 30: 871-886.

234 Chowdhury, A. R. 1991. A Causal Analysis of Defense Spending and Economic Growth. JCR 35: 80-97.

235 Christensen, J. G. 1993. Corporatism, Administrative Regimes and the Mis-Management of Public Funds. SPS 16: 201-226.

236 Clarke, S. E. 1995. Institutional Logics and Local Economic Development. IJURR 19: 513-533.

237 Clingermayer, J. C.; Feiock, R. C. 1990. Adoption of Economic Development Policies by Cities. PSJ 18: 539-552.

238 -. 1994. Campaigns, Careerism and Constituencies: Contacting Council Members about Economic Development Policy. APQ 22: 453-468.

239 Cohn, S. 1982. Michael Hechter's Theory of Regional Underdevelopment: Victorian Railways. ASR 47: 477-488.

240 Collier, R. B.; Collier, D. 1979. Inducements vs. Constraints: Disaggregating Corporatism. APSR 73: 967-986.

241 Columbia Journal of Law and Social Problems. 1983. Papers on Economic Development. Vol 17 (3/4).

242 Comparative Political Studies. 1977. Papers on Corporatism and Policy Making in Western Europe. CPS 10 (1).

243 Courant, P. N. 1994. How Would You Know a Good Economic Development Policy if You Tripped over One? NTJ 32: 49-67.

244 Delacroix, J.; Ragin, C. C. 1981. Structural Blockage: A Cross National Study of Economic Dependency, State Efficacy and Underdevelopment. AJS 86: 1311-1347.

245 Dellaportas, G. 1983. Classification of Nations Developed and Less Developed. AJEAS 42: 153-166.

246 Development. 1988. Papers on Development. Vol 1988 (2/3) and Vol 1989 (2-3).

247 Diamant, A. 1981. Bureaucracy and Public Policy in Neo-Corporatist Settings. CP 14: 101-124.

248 Dorfman, R. 1991. Economic Development from the Beginning to Rostow. JEL 29: 573-591.

249 Dos Santos, T. 1970. Structure of Dependence. AER 60: 231-236.

250 Dowrick, S.; Nguyen, D. T. 1989. OECD Comparative Economic Growth: Catch-Up and Convergence. AER 79: 1010-1030.

251 Duncan, A. K. 1986. Vertical Trading and Uneven Development. Journal of Development Economics 20: 339-359.

252 Durant, R. F.; Thomas, L. W.; Haynes, D. 1993. Politics of Growth Management Reform in the States. PSR 12: 30-54.

253 Durden, G. C.; Elledge, B. 1993. Effect of Government Size on Economic Growth. RRS 23: 183-190.

254 Dye, T. R. 1980. Taxing, Spending and Economic Growth in American States. JOP 42: 1085-1109.

255 Eckstein, Z.; Zilcha, I. 1994. Effects of Compulsory Schooling on Growth, Income Distribution and Welfare. JPUBE 54: 339-350.

256 Eisinger, P. 1990. Do the American States Do Industrial Policy? BJPS 20: 509-536.

257 Evans, P.; Timberlake, M. 1980. Dependence, Inequality and the Growth of Tertiary. ASR 45: 531-552.

258 Fagerberg, J. 1994. Technology and International Differences in Growth Rates. JEL 32: 1147-1175.

259 Feiock, R. C. 1991. Effects of Economic Development Policy on Local Economic Growth. AJPS 35: 643-655.

260 -. 1994. Political Economy of Growth Management. APQ 22: 208-220.

261 Finance and Development. 1993. Papers on Sustainable Development. Vol 30 (4).

262 Firebaugh, G. 1983. Scale Economy or Scale Entropy? Country Size and the Rate of Economic Growth. ASR 48: 257-268.

263 Firebaugh, G.; Beck, F. D. 1994. Does Economic Growth Benefit the Masses? Growth, Dependence and Welfare in the Third World. ASR 59: 631-653.

264 Fleischmann, A.; Feagin, J. R. 1987. Politics of Growth Oriented Urban Alliances. UAQ 23: 207-232.

265 Fong, G. R. 1990. State Strength, Industry Structure and Industrial Policy. CP 22: 273-296.

266 Fowler, P. C.; Richards, D. G. 1995. Relationship between the Size of the Public Enterprise Sector and Economic Growth. IJSE 22: 11-23.

267 Friedland, R.; Sanders, J. 1985. Public Economy and Economic Growth in Western Market Economies. ASR 50: 421-437.

268 Furobotin, E. G. 1989. Group Behavior and Economic Growth. SSQ 70: 759-762.

269 Futures 1988. Papers on Sustainable Development. Vol 20 (6).

270 Gobalet, J. G.; Diamond, L. J. 1979. Effects of Investment Dependence on Economic Growth: Internal Structural Characteristics and Periods in World Economy. ISQ 23: 412-444.

271 Goel, R. K.; Ram, R. 1994. Research and Development Expenditures and Economic Growth. EDACC 42: 403-411.

272 Goetz, E. G. 1994. Expanding Possibilities in Local Development Policy. PRQ 47: 85-110.

273 Grady, D. O. 1987. State Economic Development Incentives: Why Do States Compete? SALGR 19: 86-94.

274 Grant, D. S.; Wallace, M. 1994. The Political Economy of Manufacturing Growth and Decline across the American States. SF 73: 33-64.

275 Gray, V.; Lowery, D. 1990. Corporatist Foundations of State Industrial Policy. SSQ 71: 3-24.

276 Green, G. P.; Fleischmann, A. 1989. Analyzing Local Strategies for Promoting Economic Development. PSJ 17: 557-573.

277 Grier, K. B.; Tullock, G. 1989. An Empirical Analysis of Cross-National Economic Growth. JME 24: 259-276.

278 Grossman, P. J. 1988. Government and Economic Growth: Nonlinear Relationship. PC 56: 193-200.

279 Gulati, U. C. 1992. Foundation of Rapid Economic Growth: The Four Tigers. AJEAS 51: 161-172.

280 Gupta, D. K. Political Psychology and Neoclassical Theory of Economic Growth. PP 8: 637-666.

281 Hammergren, L. A. 1977. Corporatism in Latin American Politics. CP 9: 443-462.

282 Hansen, S. B. 1989. Targeting in Economic Development. Publius 19: 47-62.

283 Hansson, P.; Henrekson, M. 1994. A New Framework for Testing the Effect of Government Spending on Growth and Productivity. PC 81: 381-401.

284 -. 1994. What Makes a Country Socially Capable of Catching Up? WELTA 130: 760-783.

285 Harding, A. 1994. Urban Regimes and Growth Machines. UAQ 29: 356-382.

286 Hare, P. G. 1989. Economic Development in Eastern Europe. OEP 41: 672-697.

287 Helliwell, J. F. 1994. Empirical Linkages between Democracy and Economic Growth. BJPS 24:
225-248.

288 Hendrick, R. M.; Garand, J. C. 1991. Variation
in State Economic Growth. JOP 53: 1093-1110.

289 Hicks, A. 1988. Social Democratic Corporatism
and Economic Growth. JOP 50: 677-704.

290 Hicks, A.; Patterson, W. D. 1989. Robustness of
the Left Corporatist Model of Economic Growth.
JOP 51: 662-675.

291 Higgott, R. 1978. Competing Theoretical Perspectives on Development and Underdevelopment.
Politics 13: 26-41.

292 Hirschman, A. O. 1968. Political Economy of
Import Substituting Industrialization in Latin
America. QJE 82: 2-32.

293 Hollingsworth, J. R. 1982. The Political-Struc-
tural Basis for Economic Performance. ANNALS
459: 28-45.

294 Hooks, G.; Bloomquist, L. E. 1992. The Legacy of
World War II for Regional Growth and Decline:
Cumulative Effects of Wartime Investments on US
Manufacturing. SF 71: 303-338.

295 Humphrey, C. R.; Erickson, R. A.; Ottensmeyer,
E. J. 1988. Industrial Development Groups:
Organizational Resources and the Prospects for
Effecting Growth in Local Economies. GAC 19: 1-
21.

296 Hyde, M.; Hudson, W. E.; Carroll, J. J. 1988.
Business and State Economic Development. WPQ 41:
181-192.

297 Ike, N. 1973. Economic Growth and Intergenerational Change in Japan. APSR 67: 1194-1203.

298 Industrial Organization. 1984. Papers on the
Political Consequences of Industrial Change. IO
38 (1).

299 Inhaber, H. 1977. Scientists and Economic
Growth. SSS 7: 517-524.

300 International Political Science Review. 1983.
Papers on Interest Intermediation toward Corpor-
atisms. IPSR 4 (2).

301 International Social Science Journal. 1989.
Papers on Economic Growth Policy. ISSJ 41 (2).

302 -. 1995. Papers on Measuring and Evaluating
Development. ISSJ 47 (1).

303 Isserman, A. M. 1994. State Economic Development
Policy and Practice in the US. IRSR 16: 49-100.

304 Jackman, R. W. 1980. A Note on the Measurement
of Growth Rates in Cross National Research. AJS
86: 604-617.

305 -. 1982. Dependence on Foreign Investment and
Economic Growth in the Third World. WP 34: 175-
196.

306 -. 1987. The Politics of Economic Growth in
Industrial Democracies. JOP 49: 242-256.

307 -. 1989. The Politics of Economic Growth, Again.
JOP 51: 646-661.

308 Johnson, T. G. 1994. Dimensions of Regional
Economic Development Theory. RRS 24: 119-126.

309 Jones, B. D. 1990. Public Policies and Economic
Growth in the American States. JOP 52: 219-233.

310 Jones, C. I. 1995. R and D Based Models of
Economic Growth. JPE 103: 759-784.

311 Journal of Commonwealth and Comparative Politics. 1984. Papers on State Enterprises. JCACP
22 (1).

312 Journal of Interamerican Studies and World
Affairs. 1980. Papers on Public Enterprise in
Latin America. JIAS 22 (4).

313 Journal of Peace Research. 1975. Papers on
Underdevelopment. JPR 12 (4).

314 Journal of Political Economy. 1990. Papers on
the Problems of Development. JPE 98 (5 Pt 2).

315 Kaufman, R. R.; Geller, D. P.; Chernotsky, H.
1975. A Test of the Theory of Dependency. CP 7:
303-330.

316 Khalaf, N. G. 1979. Country Size and Economic
Growth and Development. JDS 16: 67-72.

317 King, R. G.; Rebelo, S. 1990. Public Policy and
Economic Growth: Neoclassical Explanations. JPE
98: S126-S150.

318 Koester, R. B.; Kormenci, R. C. 1989. Taxation,
Aggregate Activity and Economic Growth. EI 27:
367-386.

319 Krugman, P. R. 1995. Cycles of Conventional
Wisdom on Economic Development. IA 71: 717-332.

320 Kugler, J.; Arbetman, M. 1989. Exploring the
Phoenix Factor with the Collective Goods Perspective. JCR 33: 84-112.

321 Kusi, N. K. 1994. Economic Growth and Defense
Spending in Developing Countries. JCR 38: 152-
159.

322 La Civita, C. J.; Frederiksen, P. C. 1991.
Defense Spending and Economic Growth. JDE 35:
117-126.

323 Landau, D. 1986. Government and Economic Growth
in Less Developed Countries. EDACC 35: 35-75.

324 Lane, F. C. 1976. Economic Growth in Wallerstein's Social Systems. CSSH 18: 517-532.

325 Lane, J. E.; Ersson, S. 1988. Correlates of
Development. ISSJ 40: 271-284.

326 Lange, P.; Garrett, G. 1985. The Politics of
Growth. JOP 47: 792-826.

327 -. 1987. Politics of Growth Reconsidered. JOP
49: 257-274.

328 Lau, L. J., et al. 1993. Education and Economic
Growth: Brazil. JDE 41: 45-70.

329 Leftwich, A. 1994. Governance, the State and the
Politics of Development. DAC 25: 363-386.

330 -. 1995. Bringing Politics Back In: Towards a
Model of the Development State. JDS 31: 400-427.

331 Lim, D. 1994. Explaining Growth Performances of
Asian Developing Economies. EDACC 42: 829-844.

332 Lin, S. A. Y. 1994. Government Spending and
Economic Growth. AE 26: 83-94.

333 London, B.; Ross, R.J.S. 1995. Political Sociology of Foreign Direct Investment: Global Capitalism and Capital Mobility. IJCS 36: 198-218.

334 Looney, R. E. 1989. Impact of Arms Production on
Income Distribution and Growth in Third World.
EDACC 38: 145-153.

335 -. 1993. Government Expenditures and Third World
Economic Growth: Impact of Defense Expenditures.
CJDS 14: 23-42.

336 Mahon, J. E. 1992. Was Latin America Too Rich to
Prosper? Structural and Political Obstacles to
Export-Led Industrial Growth. JDS 28: 241-263.

337 Mamalakis, M. J. 1971. Theory of Sectoral Clashes and Coalitions Revisited. LARR 6: 89-126.

338 Marin, D. 1992. Is the Export-Led Growth Hypothesis Valid for Industrialized Countries? REAS
74: 678-688.

339 Marlin, M. R. 1990. Effectiveness of Economic
Development Subsidies. EDQ 4: 15-22.

340 Martin, R.; Fardmanesh, M. 1990. Fiscal Variables and Growth. PC 64: 239-251.

341 Mbaku, J. M. 1994. The Political Economy of
Development. SICID 29: 3-22.

342 McGinnis, H. 1994. Determining the Impact of
Economic Factors on Local Government Growth
Policy. US 31: 233-246.

343 McGowan, P. J.; Smith, D. L. 1978. Economic
Dependency in Black Africa. IO 32: 179-236.

344 McLennan, B. N.; Cantor, R. D. 1973. Political
Parties and Economic Development in Developing
States. AQ 2: 177-192.

345 McNair, E. S., et al. 1995. Growth and Defense:
Pooled Estimates for the NATO Alliance. SEJ 61:
846-860.

346 Mehay, S. L.; Solnick, L. M. 1990. Defense
Spending and State Economic Growth. JRS 30: 477-
487.

347 Meyer, P. B. 1991. Local Economic Development:
What Difference Does It Make? PSR 10: 172-180.

348 Milner, C.; Westaway, T. 1993. Country Size and Medium Term Growth Process. WD 21: 203-212.

349 Mintz, A.; Stevenson, R. T. 1995. Defense Expenditures, Economic Growth, and the Peace Dividend. JCR 39: 283-305.

350 Mullen, J. K.; Williams, M. 1994. Marginal Tax Rates and State Economic Growth. RSUE 24: 687-705.

351 Murray, A. 1994. Roles of the Public and Private Sectors in Promoting Economic Development in Developing Countries. Administration 42: 233-245.

352 Newman, B. A.; Thomson, R. J. 1989. Economic Growth and Social Development. WD 17: 461-472.

353 Ofer, G. 1987. Soviet Economic Growth. JEL 25: 1767-1783.

354 Olivera, J. H. G. 1976. The Supply of Statistics and Choice of Economic Policies in Developing Countries. ISSJ 28: 493-502.

355 Onis, Z. 1995. Limits of Neoliberalism: Toward a Reformulation of Development Theory. JEI 29: 97-119.

356 Otani, I.; Willanueva, D. 1990. Long-Term Growth in Developing Countries and Its Determinants. WD 18: 769-783.

357 Panitch, L. 1980. Recent Theorizations of Corporatism. BJS 31: 159-187.

358 Pedan, E. A.; Bradley, M. D. 1989. Government Size, Productivity and Economic Growth. PC 61: 229-246.

359 Phillips, J. M.; Goss, E. P. 1995. Effect of State and Local Taxes on Economic Development. SEJ 62: 320-333.

360 Podrecca, E. 1993. Recent Growth Theories. RISEC 40: 411-422.

361 Policy Studies Journal. 1989. Papers on Economic Development. PSJ 17 (3).

362 Przeworski, A.; Limongi, F. 1993. Political Regimes and Economic Growth. JEP 7 (3): 51-69.

363 Public Administration and Development. 1991. Papers on Development Bottlenecks. PAAD 11 (3).

364 Pugno, M. 1995. On Competing Theories of Economic Growth. IRAE 9: 249-274.

365 Quinn, D. P.; Shapiro, R. Y. 1991. Economic Growth Strategies: Effects of Ideological Partisanship on Interest Rates and Business Taxation in the US. AJPS 35: 656-685.

366 Ram, R. 1987. Exports and Economic Growth in Developing Countries. EDACC 36: 51-72.

367 Rasler, K. A.; Thompson, W. R. 1985. War and Economic Growth of Major Powers. AJPS 29: 513-538.

368 Ray, J. L.; Webster, T. B. L. 1978. Dependence and Economic Growth in Latin America. ISQ 22: 409-434.

369 Reese, L. A. 1993. Categories of Local Economic Development Techniques. PSJ 21: 492-513.

370 -. 1993. Decision Rules in Local Economic Development. UAQ 28: 501-513.

371 Sachs, J. 1995. Quantitative and Qualitative Measurement of Development. ISSJ 47: 1-10.

372 Schneider, M. 1992. Undermining the Growth Machine: The Missing Link between Local Economic Development and Fiscal Payoffs. JOP 54: 214-230.

373 Reynolds, L. G. 1983. Spread of Economic Growth to the Third World. JEL 21: 941-980.

374 Rittenberg, L. 1989. The Problem of Identifying the Engines of Economic Growth. SICID 24: 51-61.

375 Rubinson, R. B. 1977. Dependence, Government Revenue and Economic Growth. SICID 12 (Summer): 3-28.

376 Scheide, J. 1993. Does Economic Growth Depend on External Capital? AE 25: 369-377.

377 Scholing, E.; Timmermann, V. 1988. Why LDC Growth Rates Differ. WD 16: 1271-1294.

378 Scully, G. W. 1989. Size of the State, Economic Growth and the Efficient Utilization of National Resources. PC 63: 149-164.

379 Seierstad, S. 1969. Determinants for Economic Growth. JPR 2: 113-122.

380 Sharp, E. B.; Elkins, D. J. 1991. Politics of Economic Development and Policy. EDQ 5: 126-139.

381 Sheehey, E. J. 1993. The Effect of Government Size on Economic Growth. EEJ 19: 321-328.

382 Sirowy, L.; Inkeles, A. 1990. Effects of Democracy on Economic Growth and Inequality. SICID 25: 126-157.

383 Snyder, D.; Kick, E. L. 1979. Structural Position in the World System and Economic Growth. AJS 84: 1096-1126.

384 Spindler, C. J.; Forrester, J. P. 1993. Economic Development Policy: Explaining Policy Preferences among Competing Models. UAQ 29: 28-3.

385 Stephan, G. E. 1971. Variation in Country Size: A Theory of Segmental Growth. ASR 36: 451-460.

386 Stepick, A. 1978. Urbanization, Regional Development and Inequality in Latin America. CUR 6: 59-68.

387 Stern, N. 1989. Economics of Development. EJ 99: 597-685.

388 Storm, K. 1989. Party Competition and the Politics of Economic Openness and Growth. EJPR 17: 1-16.

389 Story, D. 1980. Time Series Analysis of Industrial Growth in Latin America. SSQ 61: 293-307.

390 Stout, D. K. 1980. The Impact of Technology on Economic Growth in the 1980s. Daedalus 109: 159-168.

391 Sullivan, G. 1983. Uneven Development and National Income Inequality in Third World Countries: Effects of External Economic Dependence. SP 26: 201-231.

392 Szymanski, A. 1976. Dependence, Exploitation and Development. JPMS 4: 53-65.

393 Taira, K. 1989. Development, Growth and the Long Run. EDACC 37: 425-433.

394 Talele, C. J. 1993. Myrdal's Theory of Cumulative Causation in Development Economics. IEJ 40: 74-82.

395 Tornell, A.; Velasco, A. 1992. The Tragedy of the Commons and Economic Growth: Why Does Capital Flow from Poor to Rich Countries? JPE 100: 1208-1231.

396 Torres, J. F. 1973. Concentration of Political Power and Levels of Economic Development in Latin American Countries. JDA 7: 397-410.

397 Van Raemdonck, D.; Diehl, P. F. 1989. After the Shooting Stops: Insights on Post-War Economic Growth. JPR 26: 249-264.

398 Vogel, R.; Swanson, B. E. 1989. The Growth Machine vs. the Antigrowth Coalition. UAQ 25: 63-85.

399 Walberg, H. J. 1983. Scientific Literacy and Economic Productivity in International Perspective. Daedalus 112: 1-28.

400 Ward, M. D.; Davis, D. R.; Lofdahl, C. L. 1995. Defense and Growth in Japan and the US. ISQ 39: 27-50.

401 Weede, E. 1983. Military Participation Ratios, Human Capital Formation and Economic Growth. JPMS 11: 11-20.

402 -. 1986. Sectoral Reallocation, Distributional Coalitions and the Welfare State as Determinants of Growth Rates in Industrial Democracies. EJPR 14: 501-519.

403 Weede, E.; Tiefenbach, H. 1981. Three Dependency Explanations of Economic Growth. EJPR 9: 391-406.

404 Wolkoff, M. J. 1990. New Directions in the Analysis of Economic Development Policy. EDQ 4: 334-341.

405 -. 1992. Is Economic Development Decision Making Rational? UAQ 27: 340-355.

406 Woo, W. T. 1990. The Art of Economic Development: Markets, Politics and Externalites. IO 44: 403-429.

407 World Development. 1986. Papers on the Methodological Foundations of Development Economics. WD 14 (2).
408 -. 1987. Papers on Non-Governmental Development Organizations. WD 15 (Autumn Special Issue).
409 -. 1989. Papers on Institutions in Development. WD 17 (9).
410 -. 1989. Papers on Parallel Markets. WD 17 (12).

Income and Savings

411 Abraham, K. G. 1995. Real Wages and the Business Cycle. JEL 33: 1215-1264.
412 Allision, P. D. 1978. Measures of Inequality. ASR 43:865-880.
413 Alperovich, G. 1995. The Relationship between Income Inequality and City Size. US 32: 853-862.
414 Annals. 1973. Papers on Income Inequality. ANNALS 409.
415 Batra, R.; Beladi, H. 1994. A General Equilibrium Analysis of Regulation and Income Distribution. EJPE 10: 625-638.
416 Bell, D.; Rimmer, R.; Rimmer, S. 1994. Earnings Inequality in Great Britain. RIW 40: 287-302.
417 Belman, D. L.; Heywood, J. S. 1995. State and Local Government Wage Differentials. JLR 16: 187-201.
418 Bertola, G. 1994. Theories of Savings and Economic Growth. RE 48: 257-277.
419 Bishop, J. A.; Formby, J. P.; Smith, W. J. 1991. International Comparisons of Income Inequality. Economica 58: 461-477.
420 Blank, R. M.; Card, D. 1993. Poverty, Income Distribution and Growth. BPEA 2: 285-325.
421 Bollen, K. A.; Jackman, R. W. 1985. Political Democracy and the Size Distribution of Income. ASR 50: 438-457.
422 Bornschier, V.; Ballmer-Cao, T. H. 1979. Income Inequality. ASR 44: 487-506.
423 Bound, J.; Johnson, G. 1995. What Are the Causes of Rising Wage Inequity in US? FRBNY 1: 9-17.
424 Bovenberg, A. L. 1989. Tax Policy and National Saving in the US. NTJ 42: 123-138.
425 Boyd, R. L. 1988. Government Involvement in the Economy and the Distribution of Income. PRAPR 7: 223-238.
426 Brauer, D. A.; Hickok, S. 1995. Explaining the Growing Inequality in Wages across Skill Levels. FRBNY 1: 61-75.
427 Brenner, R.; Dagenais, M. G.; Montmarquette, C. 1994. An Overlooked Explanation of the Declining Saving Rate. EE 19: 629-637.
428 Breyer, F. 1994. Political Economy of Intergenerational Redistribution. EJPE 10: 61-84.
429 Brown, G. K. 1982. Effect of the Minimum Wage on Employment and Unemployment. JEL 20: 487-528.
430 Carroll, C. D.; Rhee, B. K.; Rhee, C. 1994. Are There Cultural Effects on Savings? QJE 109: 685-699.
431 Carroll, C. D.; Weil, D. N. 1994. Saving and Growth. CRCSPP 40 (June): 133-192.
432 Carson, C. S. 1987. GNP: An Overview. Survey of Current Business 67 (July): 103-126.
433 Chan, S. 1989. Income Distribution and War Trauma. WPQ 42: 263-282.
434 Chang, R. 1994. Income Inequality and Economic Growth. FRBA 79: 1-10.
435 Christiano, L. J.; Eichenbaum, M. 1990. Unit Roots and Real GNP. CRCSPP 32: 7-61.
436 Clarke, G. R. G. 1995. More Evidence on Income Distribution and Growth. JDE 47: 403-427.
437 Comparative Political Studies. 1981. Papers on the Comparative Analysis of Social Inequities. CPS 13 (4).
438 Creedy, J. 1994. Statics and Dynamics of Income Distribution. AUSER 108: 51-71.
439 Crenshaw, E. M.; Amenn, A. 1993. Dimensions of Social Inequality in the Third World. PRAPR 12: 297-313.
440 -. 1994. Distribution of Income across National Populations. SSR 23: 1-22.
441 Cromwell, J. 1977. Size Distribution of Income. RIW 23: 291-308.
442 Danziger, S.; Haveman, R.; Plotnick, R. D. 1981. How Income Transfer Programs Affect Work, Savings and Income Distribution. JEL 19: 975-1028.
443 Development. 1985. Papers on Affluence. Vol 1985 (2).
444 Devine, J. A. 1983. Fiscal Policy and Class Income Inequality: Distributional Consequences of Government Revenues and Expenditures in the US. ASR 48: 606-622.
445 Devine, J. A.; Canak, W. L. 1986. Redistribution in a Bifurcated Welfare State: Quintile Shares and the US Case. SOCP 33: 391-406.
446 Doshi, K. 1994. Determinants of the Saving Rate. CEP 12: 37-45.
447 Dryzek, J. S. 1978. Politics, Economics and Inequality. EJPR 6: 399-410.
448 Easterlin, R. A. 1995. Will Raising the Incomes of All Increase the Happiness of All? JEBAO 27: 35-47.
449 Ericksen, E. P. 1988. Estimating the Concentration of Wealth in America. POQ 52: 243-253.
450 Fan, C. C.; Casetti, E. 1994. Spatial and Temporal Dynamics of US Regional Income Inequality. ARS 28: 177-198.
451 Felix, D. 1983. Income Distribution and the Quality of Life in Latin America. LARR 18: 3-34.
452 Fields, G. S. 1994. Data for Measuring Poverty and Inequality Changes in the Developing Countries. JDE 44: 87-102.
453 Friedland, R.; Sanders, J. 1986. Private and Social Wage Expansion in Advanced Market Economies. TAD 15: 193-222.
454 Gagliani, G. 1987. Income Inequality and Economic Development. ANRS 13: 313-334.
455 Goodman, A.; Webb, S. 1994. The Changing Distribution of Income in the UK. FS 15: 29-62.
456 Grasso, P. G.; Sharkansky, I. 1980. Economic Development and the Distribution of Income in the States. SSQ 61: 446-457.
457 Green, F.; Henley, A.; Tsakalotos, E. 1994. Income Inequality in Corportist and Liberal Economies. IRAE 8: 303-331.
458 Hagen, E.; Hawrylyshyn, O. 1969. Analysis of World Income and Growth. EDACC 18 (2): 1-96.
459 Hatton, T. J.; Williamson, J. G. 1991. What Explains Wage Gaps between Farm and City? EDACC 40: 267-294.
460 Henry, R. M. 1989. Inequality in Plural Societies. SAES 38 (2): 69-110.
461 Hewitt, C. 1977. The Effect of Political Democracy and Social Democracy on Equality. APSR 42: 450-464.
462 Hibbs, D. A.; Dennis, C. 1988. Income Distribution in the US. APSR 82: 467-490.
463 Hoover, G. A. 1989. Intranational Inequality: A Cross National Dataset. SF 67: 1008-1026.
464 Hubbard, R. G.; Skinner, J.; Zeldes, S. P. 1994. Precautionary Motives in Explaining Individual and Aggregate Saving. CRCSPP 40: 59-125.
465 Jackman, R. W. 1980. Socialist Parties and Income Inequality in Western Industrial Societies. JOP 42: 135-149.
466 Journal of Development Studies. 1978. Papers on Income Distribution. JDS 14 (3).
467 Kanbur, R.; Haddad, L. 1994. Are Better Off Households More Unequal or Less Unequal? OEP 46: 445-458.
468 Kanbur, S. M. 1979. Risk Taking and the Personal Distribution of Income. JPE 87: 769-797.
469 Lawrence, R. Z.; Slaughter, M. J. 1993. International Trade and Wages. BPEA 1993: 161-210.

470 Levy, F.; Murnane, R. J. 1992. US Earning Levels and Earnings Inequality. JEL 30: 1333-1381.

471 Lindert, P. H. 1986. Unequal English Wealth since 1670. JPE 94: 1127-1162.

472 Looney, R. E. 1989. Impact of Arms Production on Income Distribution and Growth in Third World. EDACC 38: 145-154.

473 Mahler, V. A. 1989. Income Distribution within Nations. CPS 22: 3-32.

474 Maital, S.; Maital, S. L. 1994. A Behavioral Theory of the Decline of Saving in the West. JSE 23: 1-32.

475 McGranahan, D. A. 1980. Spatial Structure of Income Distribution in Rural Regions. ASR 45: 313-324.

476 Muller, E. N. 1988. Democracy, Economic Development and Income Inequality. ASR 53: 50-68.

477 -. 1989. Distribution of Income in Advanced Capitalist Societies. EJPR 17: 267-400.

478 Musgrove, P. 1980. Income Distribution and the Aggregate Consumption Function. JPE 88: 504-525.

479 Nagel, J. 1975. Inequality and Discontent. WP 26: 453-472.

480 Nielsen, F. 1994. Income Inequality and Industrial Development. ASR 59: 654-677.

481 Nielsen, F.; Alderson, A. S. 1995. Income Inequality, Development and Dualism. ASR 69: 674-701.

482 Oshima, H. T. 1994. The Impact of Technological Transformation on Historical Trends in Income Distribution. Developing Economies 32: 237-255.

483 Panning, W. H. 1983. Inequality, Social Comparison and Relative Deprivation. APSR 77: 323-329.

484 Park, W. G.; Brat, D. A. 1995. A Global Kuznuts Curve? Kyklos 48: 105-131.

485 Parker, R. N.; Fenwick, R. 1983. Pareto Curve and Its Utility for Open Ended Income Distributions in Survey Research. SF 61: 872-885.

486 Paukert, F. 1973. Income Distribution at Different Levels of Development. International Labour Review 108: 97-126.

487 Raj, B.; Slottje, D. J. 1994. Trend Behavior of Alternative Income Inequality Measures in the US and the Structural Break. JBAES 12: 479-487.

488 Roberti, P. 1975. Income Distribution. EJ 84: 629-638.

489 Rossana, R. J.; Seater, J. J. 1992. Aggregation, Unit Roots and the Time Series Structure on Manufacturing Real Wages. IER 33: 159-179.

490 Rubinson, R. B. 1976. The World Economy and the Distribution of Income within States. ASR 41: 638-659.

491 Rubinson, R. B.; Quinlan, D. 1977. Democracy and Social Inequality. ASR 42: 611-623.

492 Ruiz-Castillo, J. 1995. Income Distribution and Social Welfare. Investigaciones Economicas 19: 3-34.

493 Russett, B., et al. 1994. Did Americans' Expectations of Nuclear War Reduce Their Savings? ISQ 38: 587-604.

494 Russett, B.; Slemrod, J. 1993. Diminished Expectations of Nuclear War and Personal Savings. AER 83: 1022-1033.

495 Saltz, I. S. 1995. Income Distribution in the Third World. AJEAS 54: 15-32.

496 Santiago, C. E. 1989. The Dynamics of Minimum Wage Policy in Economic Development. EDACC 38: 1-30.

497 Saunders, P. 1994. Capitalism, Socialism and Income Distribution. RIW 40: 351-357.

498 Singh, B.; Bahni, B. S. 1986. Patterns and Directions of Causality between Government Expenditure and National Income. JQE 2: 291-308.

499 Slemrod, J. 1986. Saving and the Fear of Nuclear War. JCR 30: 403-419.

500 -. 1990. Fear of Nuclear War and Intercountry Differences in the Rate of Savings. EI 28: 647-657.

501 Smith, R. S. 1990. Factors Affecting Saving, Policy Tools, and Tax Reform. IMFSP 37: 1-70.

502 Smolensky, E., et al. 1994. Growth, Inequality and Poverty. RIW 40: 217-222.

503 Sprout, R. V. A.; Weaver, J. H. 1992. International Distribution of Income. Kyklos 45: 237-258.

504 Stack, S. 1978. The Effect of Direct Government Involvement in the Economy on Income Inequality. ASR 43: 880-888.

505 -. 1978. The Effects of Political Participation and Socialist Party Strength on Income Inequality. ASR 44: 168-171.

506 Stack, S.; Neubeck, K. J. 1978. Education and Income Inequality. IRMS 8: 159-166.

507 Stack, S.; Zimmerman, D. 1982. Effect of World Economy on Income Inequality. SQ 23: 345-359.

508 Stewart, D. B.; Venieris, Y. P. 1985. Sociopolitical Instability and the Behavior of Savings in Less-Developed Countries. REAS 67: 557-563.

509 Stigler, G. J. 1970. Director's Law of Public Income Distribution. JOLE 13: 1-10.

510 Tauchen, G. E. 1981. Evidence on Cross-Sector Effects of the Minimum Wage. JPE 89: 529-547.

511 Theil, H.; Seale, J. L. 1994. Geographical Distribution of World Income. De Economist 142: 387-419.

512 Thomas, D. R. 1994. Estimation of Gini Coefficients in Selected OECS Countries. SAES 43: 71-93.

513 Uri, N. D.; Mixon, J. W. 1980. Economic Analysis of the Determinants of Minimum Wage Voting Behavior. JOLE 23: 167-178.

514 Weede, E. 1980. Beyond Misspecification in Sociological Analyses of Income Inequality. ASR 45: 497-501.

515 -. 1982. Effects of Democracy and Social Strength on the Size of Distribution of Income. IJCS 23: 151-165.

516 -. 1990. Democracy, Party Government and Rent Seeking as Determinants of Distributional Inequality in Industrial Societies. EJPR 18: 515-533.

517 Weede, E.; Tiefenbach, H. 1981. Some Recent Explanations of Income Equality. ISQ 25: 255-282.

518 Weeks, J. 1970. Uncertainty, Risk, Wealth and Income Distribution in Peasant Agriculture. JDS 7: 28-36.

519 Weil, F. D. 1989. The Sources and Structure of Legitimation in Western Democracies. ASR 54: 682-706.

520 Wittman, D. 1989. Pressure Group Size and the Politics of Income Redistribution. SCAW 6: 225-286.

521 Wolff, E. N. 1994. Trends in Household Wealth in the US. RIW 40: 143-174.

522 World Development. 1978. Papers on Cost-Benefit Analyses and Income Distribution in Developing Countries. WD 6 (2).

523 Wright, C. L. 1978. Income Inequality and Economic Growth. JDA 13: 49-66.

524 Zajac, E. J.; Westphal, J. D. 1995. Accounting for the Explanations of CEO Compensation. ASQ 40: 283-308.

525 Zandvakili, S. 1994. Income Distribution and Redistribution through Taxation. EE 19: 473-491.

526 Zegeye, A. A. 1994. Estimating Savings and Growth Functions in Developing Economies. INTEJ 8: 89-105.

Inflation

527 Abuzadah, S., Yousefi, M. 1986. Political Parties, Deficits and the Rate of Inflation. JSPES 11: 393-412.

528 Burns, T. R.; Baumgartner, T.; Deville, P. 1984. Inflation, Politics and Social Change. IJCS 25: 73-90.

529 Darrat, A. F. 1988. Does Inflation Inhibit or Promote Growth? QJBE 27: 113-134.

530 Edwards, S. 1994. Political Economy of Inflation and Stabilization in Developing Countries. EDACC 42: 235-266.

531 Edwards, S.; Tabellini, G. 1991. Explaining Fiscal Policies and Inflation in Developing Countries. JIMF 10 (March): S16-S48.

532 Fischer, B. 1990. Causes and Consequences of Inflationary Politics in Latin American Countries. KON 36: 43-62.

533 Gordon, R. J. 1975. The Demand for and the Supply of Inflation. JOLE 18: 807-836.

534 Green, S. L. 1987. Theories of Inflation. JME 20: 169-175.

535 Hanson, J. A. 1980. The Short Run Relation between Growth and Inflation in Latin America. AER 70: 972-989.

536 Hill, J. K.; Smith, S. L. 1985. The Political Timing of Errors in Inflation Forecasts. PC 46: 215-220.

537 Hogan, T. D. 1988. The Effects of Growth on Local Inflation Rates. ARS 22: 70-80.

538 Hula, D. G. 1991. The Phillips Curve and the Natural Rate of Inflation. PSCI 24: 357-366.

539 Paldam, M. 1994. The Political Economy of Stopping High Inflation. EJPE 10: 135-169.

540 Payne, J. L. 1979. Inflation, Unemployment and Left Wing Political Parties. APSR 73: 181-185.

541 Proceedings. 1979. Papers on Inflation. PAPSC 33 (3).

542 Renshaw, E. F.; Trahan, E. 1991. A Note on the Electorate's Most Preferred Inflation Rate. PC 70: 95-97.

543 Smyth, D. J.; Dua, P. 1989. The Public's Indifference Map between Inflation and Unemployment. PC 60: 71-86.

544 Stronge, W. B.; Schultz, R. R. 1981. Metropolitan Inflation in the US. ARS 15: 53-65.

545 Whitehead, L. 1979. The Political Causes of Inflation. POLST 27: 564-577.

546 World Development 1987. Papers on the Resurgence of Inflation in Latin America. WD 15 (8).

Regulation

547 Aivazian, V. A.; Callen, J. L. 1981. The Coase Theorem and the Empty Core. JOLE 24: 175-181.

548 Amarcher, R., et al. 1985. The Behavior of Regulatory Activity over the Business Cycle. EI 23: 7-19.

549 American Behavioral Scientist. 1975. Papers on the Regulatory Process. ABS 19 (1).

550 Anderson, S.; Glazer, A. 1984. Public Opinion and Regulatory Behavior. PC 43: 187-194.

551 Annals. 1972. Papers on Government as Regulator. ANNALS 400.

552 Azqueta, D. 1993. Coase Theorem and Environmental Economics. Revista Espanola de Economia 10: 59-71.

553 Bagnoli, M.; McKee, M. 1991. Controlling the Game: Political Sponsors and Bureaus. JOLEAO 7: 229-247.

554 Bailey, E. E. 1986. Price and Productivity Change Following Deregulation. EJ 96: 1-17.

555 Baldwin, G. R.; Veljanovski, C. G. 1984. Regulation by Cost-Benefit Analysis. PA 62: 51-70.

556 Bartrip, P. W. J.; Fenn, P. T. 1988. Factory Fatalities and Regulation in Britain. EEH 25: 60-74.

557 Batra, R.; Beladi, H. 1993. Regulation and the Theory of Tax Incidence. PF 48: 329-449.

558 Bennett, R. W.; Loucks, C. 1993. Politics and the Rescue of Insolvent Savings and Loans before 1989. PC 76: 175-188.

559 Bordo, M. D.; Schwartz, A. J. 1995. The Performance and Stability of Banking Systems under Self-Regulation. CJ 14: 452-492.

560 Brown, A. 1985. The Regulatory Policy Cycle and Airline Deregulation Movement. SSQ 66: 552-563.

561 Brown, A.; Cave, M. 1992. Economics of Television Regulation. ECONR 68: 377-394.

562 Cahan, S. F.; Kaempfer, W. H. 1992. Industry Income and Congressional Regulatory Legislation: Interest Group vs. Median Voter. EI 30: 47-56.

563 Calvert, R. L.; McCubbins, M. D.; Weingast, B. R. 1989. Theory of Political Control and Agency Discretion. AJPS 33: 588-611.

564 Canon, B. C. 1969. Voting Behavior on the FCC. MJPS 13: 587-612.

565 Canterbery, E. R.; Marvasti, A. 1992. The Coase Theorem as a Negative Externality. JEI 26: 1179-1189.

566 Cato Journal. 1993. Papers on Financial Deregulation in the Global Economy. CJ 13 (2-3).

567 Caudill, S. B.; Im, B. G.; Kaserman, D. L. 1993. Modeling Regulatory Behavior. JRE 5: 251-262.

568 Cohen, J. E. 1986. Dynamics of the Revolving Door on the FCC. AJPS 30: 689-708.

569 Coulter, P. B. 1972. Democratic Political Development: A Systematic Model Based on Regulative Policy. DAC 3: 25-61.

570 Cropper, M. L., et al. 1992. Determinants of Pesticide Regulation: EPA Decision Making. JPE 100: 175-197.

571 Coughlin, C. C. 1985. Domestic Content Legislation: House Voting and the Economic Theory of Regulation. EI 23: 347-448.

572 DeSerpa, A. C. 1994. Pigou and Coase: A Mathematical Reconciliation. JPUBE 54: 267-286.

573 DeYoung, R. 1994. Do Regulators Read the Literature? Bank Merger Regulations. SEJ 61: 69-84.

574 DiMento, J. F. 1989. Can Social Science Explain Organization Noncompliance with Environmental Law? JSI 45: 109-132.

575 Economic Inquiry. 1992. Papers on Antitrust. EI 30 (2).

576 Elkin, S. L. 1985. Regulation as a Political Question. PSCI 18: 95-108.

577 Erfle, S.; McMillan, H.; Grofman, B. 1989. Testing the Regulatory Threat Hypothesis: Media Coverage of the Energy Crisis and Petroleum Pricing. APQ 17: 132-152.

578 European Journal of Political Research 1989. Papers on European Deregulation. EJPR 17 (2).

579 -. 1991. Papers on Transnational Regulation. Vol 19 (2/3).

580 Flowers, M. R.; Stroup, R. L. 1979. Coupon Rationing and Rent-Seeking Bureaucrats. PC 34: 473-479.

581 Formby, J. P.; Mishra, B.; and Thistle, P. D. 1995. Public Utility Regulation and Bond Ratings. PC 84: 119-136.

582 Garvie, D.; Keeler, A. 1994. Incomplete Enforcement with Endogenous Regulatory Choice. JPUBE 55: 141-162.

583 Gilbert, R. J.; Newbery, D. M. 1994. Dynamic Efficiency of Regulatory Constitutions. RJE 25: 538-554.

584 Gilligan, T. W.; Marshall, W.; Weingast, B. R. 1989. Regulation and the Theory of Legislative Choice: Interstate Commerce Act. JOLE 32: 35-62.

585 Graddy, E. 1991. Toward a General Theory of Occupational Regulation. SSQ 72: 676-695.

586 Harrington, S. E.; Doerpinghaus, H. I. 1993. The Economics and Politics of Automobile Insurance Rate Classification. Journal of Risk and Insurance 60: 59-84.

587 Harrington, W. 1982. Understanding Regulatory Decision Making. PSJ 11: 44-54.

588 Harrison, G. W., et al. 1987. Coasian Solutions to Externality Problem in Experimental Markets. EJ 97: 388-402.

589 Harrison, G. W.; McKee, M. 1985. Experimental Evaluation of Coase Theorem. JOLE 28: 653-670.

590 Hedge, D. M. 1993. A Spatial Model of Regulation. APQ 21: 387-409.

591 Hedge, D. M.; Scicchitano, M. J. 1994. Regulating in Space and Time: Regulatory Federalism. JOP 56: 134-153.

592 Hoffman, E.; Spitzer, M. L. 1982. Coase Theorem: Experimental Tests. JOLE 25: 73-98.

593 -. 1986. Experimental Tests of the Coase Theorem with Large Bargaining Groups. JLS 15: 149-171.

594 Hyldtoft, O. 1994. Modern Theories of Regulation. SEHR 42: 29-53.

595 International Review of Administrative Sciences. 1995. Papers on Regulation and Deregulation. IRAS 61 (2).

596 Jordan, J. L. 1994. A Market Approach to Banking Regulation. CJ 13: 315-332.

597 Journal of Law and Economics. 1981. Papers on Consumer Protection Legislation. JOLE 24 (3).

598 -. 1985. Papers on Antitrust Policy. JOLE 28 (2).

599 Journal of Policy Analysis and Management. 1986. Papers on Deregulation and Regulatory Reform. JPAAM 5 (3).

600 Journal of Social Issues. 1991. Papers on Consumer Protection. JSI 47 (1).

601 Jung, C., et al. 1995. Coase Theorem in a Rent-Seeking Society. IRLE 15: 259-268.

602 Kaserman, D. L.; Mayo, J. W.; Pacey, P. L. 1993. The Political Economy of Deregulation: Long Distance Phone Rates. JRE 5: 49-63.

603 Krause, G. A. 1994. Examining the Consequences of Deregulation in the Banking Industry. APQ 22: 221-243.

604 Krol, R.; Svorny, S. 1994. Regulation and Economic Performance. CJ 14: 55-64.

605 Laffont, J. J.; Tirole, J. 1990. The Politics of Government Decision Making: Regulatory Institutions. JOLEAO 6: 1-31.

606 -. 1991. Politics of Government Decision Making: The Theory of Regulatory Capture. QJE 106: 1089-1127.

607 Law and Contemporary Problems. 1979. Papers on Regulation and Innovation. LACP 43 (1).

608 -. 1981. Papers on Deregulation. LACP 44 (1).

609 -. 1983. Papers on Chemical Industry Regulation. LACP 46 (3).

610 -. 1986. Papers on Regulation of Work. LACP 49 (4).

611 -. 1987. Papers on Economic Regulation. LACP 50: 117-250.

612 -. 1994. Papers on Political Economy of Administrative Procedures and Regulations. LACP 57 (1/2).

613 Law and Policy. 1983. Papers on Regulation and Bureaucratic Behavior. LAP 5 (1).

614 -. 1989. Papers on Regulation in Great Britain and the Netherlands. LAP 11 (1).

615 -. 1991. Papers on Financial Market Regulation. LAP 13 (4).

616 -. 1993. Papers on Business Regulation Responses. LAP 15 (3).

617 Leland, H. E. 1979. Quacks, Lemons and Licensing: A Theory of Minimum Quality Standards. JPE 87: 1328-1346.

618 Lewis-Beck, M. S. 1979. Maintaining Economic Competition: Causes and Consequences of Antitrust. JOP 41: 169-191.

619 Lewis-Beck, M. S.; Alford, J. R. 1980. Can Government Regulate Safety? APSR 74: 745-756.

620 Litz, R. A. 1995. Self-Inflicted Capture: Self-Deception in Enforcement. AAS 26: 419-433.

621 Logistics and Transportation Review. 1986. Papers on Airline Deregulation. LATR 22 (4).

622 Makkai, T.; Braithwaite, J. 1993. The Limits of the Economic Analysis of Regulation. LAP 15: 271-292.

623 McCubbins, M. D. 1985. The Legislative Design of Regulatory Structure. AJPS 29: 721-748.

624 McKenzie, R. B.; Macaulay, H. M. 1980. A Bureaucratic Theory of Regulation. PC 35: 297-313.

625 Michaelis, P. 1994. Regulate Us, Please! On Strategic Lobbying in a Cournot-Nash Oligopoly. JITE 150: 693-709.

626 Michaels, R.; Kalish, L. 1981. The Incentives of Regulators: Banking. PC 36: 187-192.

627 Miller, E. S. 1994. Economic Regulation and the Social Contract: The Social Control of Telecommunications. JEI 28: 799-818.

628 Minnesota Law Review. 1983. Papers on the New Deal's Legacy. Vol 68 (2).

629 Mishan, E. J. 1971. The Postwar Literature on Externalities. JEL 9: 1-28.

630 Moe, T. M. 1982. Regulatory Performance and Presidential Administration. AJPS 26: 197-224.

631 -. 1985. Control and Feedback in Economic Regulation: NLRB. APSR 79: 1094-1116.

632 Moore, M. 1992. Rules or Politics? An Empirical Analysis of ITC Anti-Dumping Decisions. EI 30: 449-466.

633 Moses, L. N.; Savage, L. 1990. Aviation Deregulation and Safety: Theory and Evidence. JOTEAP 24: 171-188.

634 Mulford, C. L. 1978. Implications of Compliance Theory for Policymakers. IJCS 19: 47-62.

635 Natural Resources Journal. 1973. Papers on the Coase Theorem. NRJ 13 (4) and 14 (1).

636 -. 1987. Papers on Natural Gas Regulation. NRJ 27 (4).

637 Nelson, J. C. 1987. Politics and Economics in Transport Regulation and Deregulation: The ICC's Role. LATR 23: 5-32.

638 Noel, A. 1987. Accumulation, Regulation and Social Change: French Political Economy. IO 41: 161-198.

639 Nowell, C.; Tschirhart, J. T. 1993. Testing Theories of Regulatory Behavior. RIO 8: 653-668.

640 Olson, M. K. 1994. Political Influence and Regulatory Policy: 1984 Drug Legislation. EI 32: 363-382.

641 Peltzman, S. 1976. Toward a More General Theory of Regulation. JOLE 19: 211-248.

642 Perry, C. S. 1982. Government Regulation of Coal Mine Safety? Effects of Spending under Strong and Weak Law. APQ 10: 303-314.

643 Plott, C. R. 1983. Externalities and Corrective Policies in Experimental Markets. EJ 93: 106-127.

644 Policy Studies Journal. 1975. Papers on Regulatory Policy. PSJ 4 (1) and 11 (3).

645 Posner, R. A. 1970. A Statistical Analysis of Antitrust Enforcement. JOLE 13: 365-429.

646 -. 1975. Theories of Economic Regulation. BJEMS 5: 335-358.

647 Raines, J. P.; Leathers, C. G. 1995. Veblen's Theory of Institutional Change: Explanation of the Deregulation of Japanese Financial Markets. AJEAS 54: 357-372.

648 Rasmusen, E. B.; Zupan, M. A. 1991. Extending the Economic Theory of Regulation to Form of Policy. PC 72: 167-191.

649 Ringquist, E. J. 1993. Does Regulation Matter? Evaluating the Effects of State Air Pollution Control. JOP 55: 1022-1045.

650 Rowland, C. K.; Marz, R. 1982. Gresham's Law: The Regulatory Analogy. PSR 1: 572-580.

651 Rubin, P. H. 1991. Economics of Regulating Deception. CJ 10: 667-690.

652 Salant, D. J. 1995. Behind the Revolving Door: A New View of Public Utility Regulation. RJE 26: 362-377.

653 Sanders, E. 1986. Industrial Concentration, Sectional Competition and Antitrust Policies in America. Studies in American Political Development 1: 142-214.

654 Scholz, J. T. 1984. Cooperation, Deterrence and the Ecology of Regulatory Enforcement. LASR 18: 179-224.

655 Schulstad, P. 1994. Optimal Regulation and Country Size. CANJE 27: 967-981.

656 Skalaban, A. 1993. Policy Cooperation among the States: Interstate Banking Reform. AJPS 37: 415-428.

657 Skolnick, J. H. 1979. The Dilemmas of Regulating Casino Gambling. JSI 35: 129-143.

658 Spiller, P. T. 1990. Politicians, Interest Groups and Regulators: A Multiple-Principals Agency Theory of Regulation, or Let Them Be Bribed. JOLE 33: 65-101.

659 Steuenberg, B. 1992. Congress, Bureaucracy and Regulatory Policy-Making. JOLEAO 8: 673-694.

660 Stigler, G. J. 1971. The Theory of Economic Regulation. BJEMS 2: 3-51.

661 Teske, P. 1991. Interests and Institutions in State Regulation. AJPS 35: 139-154.

662 Teske, P.; Best, S.; Mintrom, M. 1994. Economic Theory of Regulation and Trucking Deregulations. PC 79: 247-256.

663 Thies, C. F. 1986. Role of Knowledge in Direct Voting on Milk Price Decontrol. PC 49: 191-194.

664 Ulen, T. S. 1980. Market for Regulation: Interstate Commerce Commission. AER 70: 306-310.

665 von der Fehr, N. H. M.; Kuhn, K. U. 1995. Coase vs. Pacman: Who Eats Whom in the Durable Goods Monopoly? JPE 103: 785-812.

666 Vickers, J. 1991. Government Regulatory Policy. Oxford Review of Economic Policy 7: 13-30.

667 Weingast, B. R. 1981. Regulation, Reregulation and Deregulation. LACP 44: 148-177.

668 Weingast, B. R.; Moran, M. J. 1983. Bureaucratic Discretion or Congressional Control? Regulatory Policymaking by the Federal Trade Commission. JPE 91: 765-800.

669 White, L. J. 1993. A Cautionary Tale of Deregulation Gone Awry: S&L Debacle. SEJ 59: 496-514.

670 Whitfield, K.; Marginson, P.; Brown, W. 1994. Workplace Industrial Relations under Different Regulatory Systems. British Journal of Industrial Relations 32: 319-338.

671 Williams, B. A.; Matheny, A. R. 1984. Testing Theories of Social Regulation: Hazardous Waste Regulation in the US States. JOP 46: 428-458.

672 Winston, C. 1993. Economic Regulation. JEL 31: 1263-1289.

673 Winston, C.; Crandall, R. W. 1994. Explaining Regulatory Policy. BPEA 1994: 1-31.

674 Wood, B. D. 1992. Modeling Federal Implementation as a System: The Clean Air Case. APSR 36: 40-67.

675 Woolley, J. T. 1993. Conflict among Regulators and the Hypothesis of Congressional Dominance. JOP 55: 92-114.

676 Yale Law Journal. 1983. Papers on the Legacy of the New Deal and the Administrative State. YLJ 92 (7-8).

677 Ye, M. H.; Yezer, A.M.J. 1994. Collective Choice of Price Caps and Freight Absorption: A Spatial Approach to Regulation. RSUE 24: 185-206.

Taxes

678 Aiyagari, S. R.; Peled, D. 1995. Social Insurance and Taxation under Sequential Majority and Utilitarian Regimes. JEDAC 19: 1511-1528.

679 Allen, M. P.; Campbell, J. L. 1994. State Revenue Extraction from Different Income Groups: Tax Progressivity in the US. ASR 59: 169-186.

680 Alm, J.; Beck, W. 1993. Tax Amnesties and Compliance in the Long Run. NTJ 46: 53-60.

681 Alm, J.; McClelland, G. H.; Schulze, W. D. 1992. Why Do People Pay Taxes? JPUBE 48: 21-38.

682 Alm, J.; Sanchez, I.; de Juan, A. 1995. Economic and Noneconomic Factors in Tax Compliance. Kyklos 48: 1-18.

683 American Journal of Economics and Sociology. 1972. Papers on the Property Tax. AJEAS 31 (2).

684 American Politics Quarterly. 1991. Papers on Tax Reform. APQ 19 (4).

685 Anderson, J. E.; Wassmer, R. W. 1995. Municipal Behavior in Granting Property Tax Abatements. RSUE 25: 739-758.

686 Anderson, W.; Wallace, M. S.; Warner, J. T. 1986. Government Spending and Taxation: What Causes What? SEJ 52: 630-639.

687 Archer, J. C. 1983. The Geography of Federal Fiscal Policies in the US. Government and Policy 1: 377-400.

688 Arlen, J.; Weiss, D. M. 1995. A Political Theory of Corporate Taxation. YLJ 105: 325-392.

689 Athanassakos, A. 1990. General Fund Financing vs. Earmarked Taxes. PC 66: 261-278.

690 Bates, R. H.; Lien, D. H. D. 1985. A Note on Taxation, Development and Representative Government. PAS 14: 53-70.

691 Beck, P. A.; Dye, T. R. 1982. The Sources of Public Opinion on Taxes. JOP 44: 172-182.

692 Berry, F. S.; Berry, W. D. 1992. Tax Innovation in the States: Capitalizing on Political Opportunity. AJPS 36: 715-742.

693 Birch, T. D. 1988. Justice and Taxation: An Appraisal of Normative Tax Theory. SSQ 69: 1005-1013.

694 Blackley, P. R. 1990. Asymmetric Causality between Federal Spending and Tax Changes. PC 66: 1-13.

695 Boadway, R.; Marchand, M.; Pestieau, P. 1994. Towards a Theory of the Direct-Indirect Tax Mix. JPUBE 55: 71-88.

696 Boadway, R.; Wildasin, D. E. 1994. Taxation and Savings: A Survey. FS 15 (3): 19-63.

697 Bowler, S.; Donovan, T. 1995. Popular Responsiveness to Taxation. PRQ 48: 79-100.

698 Brennan, G. 1985. Taxation and Policy Change: A Median Voter Model for Australia. AUSER 71 (Spring): 20-33.

699 Bretschneider, S. I.; Gorr, W. 1992. Economic, Organizational and Political Influences on Biases in Forecasting State Sales Tax Receipts. IJF 7: 457-466.

700 Bucovetsky, S. 1991. Choosing Tax Rates and Public Expenditure Levels Using Majority Rule. JPUBE 46: 113-131.

701 Burgess, R.; Stern, N. 1993. Taxation and Development. JEL 31: 762-830.

702 Button, J. 1992. A Sign of Generational Conflict: Impact of Florida's Aging Voters on Local School and Tax Referenda. SSQ 73: 786-797.

703 Cameron, S. 1989. An Empirical Analysis of the Determinants of Cigarette Tax Rates. Economia delle Scelte Pubbliche 7: 45-54.

704 Campbell, J. L.; Allen, M. P. 1994. The Political Economy of Revenue Extraction in the Modern State: US Income Taxes. SF 72: 643-670.

705 Cato Journal. 1985. Papers on Tax Reform. CJ 5 (2).

706 Citrin, J.; Green, D. P. 1985. Policy and Opinion in California after Prop 13. NTJ 38: 15-35.

707 Codrington, H. 1989. Country Size and Taxation in Developing Countries. JDS 25: 508-520.

708 Courant, P. N.; Gramlich, E. M.; Rubinfeld, D. L. 1980. Why Voters Support Tax Limitation Amendments. NTJ 33: 1-20.

709 Cowell, F. A.; Gordon, J. P. F. 1988. Unwillingness to Pay: Tax Evasion and Public Good Provision. JPUBE 36: 305-321.

710 Craig, E.; Heins, A. J. 1980. The Effect of Tax Elasticity on Government Spending. PC 35: 267-276.

711 Creedy, J.; Francois, P. 1992. Higher Education and Progressive Taxation. JESTUD 19: 17-30.

712 de Haan, J.; Sturm, J. E. 1994. Political and Institutional Determinants of Fiscal Policy in the European Community. PC 80: 157-172.

713 deHaven-Smith, L. 1985. Ideology and the Tax Revolt: Florida's Amendment 1. POQ 49: 300-309.

714 Dye, T. R.; Feiock, R. C. 1995. State Income Tax Adoption and Economic Growth. SSQ 76: 648-654.

715 Eismeier, T. J. 1983. Votes and Taxes: Political Economy of the American Governorship. Polity 15: 368-379.

716 Etzioni, A. 1986. Tax Evasion and Perceptions of Tax Fairness. JABS 22: 177-186.

717 Fisher, R. C. 1985. Taxes and Expenditures in the US: Public Opinion Surveys and Incidence Analysis. EI 23: 525-550.

718 Formuzis, P.; Puri, A. 1980. Inflation, Progressivity and State Income Tax Revenues. PSJ 9: 19-25.

719 Furuta, S. 1990. Economic and Electoral Effects of Japanese Tax Reform. Keio Economic Studies 27: 61-75

720 Gibson, J. G. 1994. Voter Reaction to Tax Change: The Poll Tax. AE 26: 877-884.

721 Goetz, M. L. 1980. Normative Bases of Tax Reform: Constitutional Perspective. PSJ 9: 48-52.

722 Guesnerie, R.; Jerison, M. 1991. Taxation as a Social Choice Problem: The Scope of the Laffer Argument. JPUBE 44: 37-63.

723 Hale, D. 1985. Evolution of the Property Tax: Public Finance and Political Theory. JOP 47: 382-404.

724 Hanssen, J. I.; Pettersen, P. A. 1995. Conservative Mobilization and Fiscal Policies. SPS 18: 231-264.

725 Havrilesky, T. M. 1987. A Partisanship Model of Fiscal and Monetary Regimes. JMCB 19: 308-325.

726 Hawthorne, M. R.; Jackson, J. E. 1987. Individual Political Economy of Federal Tax Policy. APSR 81: 757-774.

727 Helms, L. J. 1985. Effect of State and Local Taxes on Economic Growth. REAS 67: 574-582.

728 Heyndels, B.; Smolders, C. 1995. Tax Complexity and Fiscal Illusion. PC 85: 127-142.

729 Hibbing, J. R. 1983. Washington on Seventy-Five Dollars a Day: Members of Congress Voting on Their Own Tax Break. LSQ 8: 219-230.

730 Hibbs, D. A.; Madsen, H. J. 1981. Public Reactions to Growth of Taxation and Government Expenditure. WP 33: 413-435.

731 Hoggart, K. 1986. Property Tax Resources and Political Party Control in England. US 23: 33-46.

732 Hunter, W. C. 1992. Cheating the Government: The Economics of Evasion. FRBA 77: 35-41.

733 Hunter, W. J.; Nelson, M. A. 1989. Interest Group Demand for Taxation. PC 62: 41-62.

734 Jorgenson, D. W.; Yun, K. Y. 1990. Tax Reform and US Economic Growth. JPE 98: S151-S193.

735 Journal of Economic Psychology. 1992. Papers on Economic and Psychological Perspectives on Taxation. JEPSY 13 (4).

736 Journal of Policy Analysis and Management. 1993. Papers on State and Local Taxation. JPAAM 12 (1).

737 Journal of Political Economy. 1978. Papers on Taxation. JPE 86 (2 pt 2).

738 Journal of Public Policy. 1985. Papers on Taxation. JPP 5 (3).

739 Karren, T. 1985. Determinants of Taxation in Britain. JPP 5: 365-386.

740 Katz, C. J.; Mahler, V. A.; Franz, M. G. 1983. The Impact of Taxes on Growth and Distribution. APSR 77: 871-886.

741 King, R. F. 1983. From Redistribution to Hegemonic Logic: The Transformation of American Tax Politics. PAS 12: 1-52.

742 Kone, S. L.; Winters, R. F. 1993. Taxes and Voting: Electoral Retribution in the American States. JOP 55: 22-40.

743 Kristensen, O. P. 1986. Tax Structure and Public Spending: Or How the Electorate is Deceived into Paying for Bigger Public Spending than It Really Wants. SPS 9: 317-336.

744 Kushner, J. 1992. The Effects of Urban Growth on Municipal Taxes. CPA 35: 94-102.

745 Law and Contemporary Problems. 1985. Papers on Tax Legislation in the Reagan Era. LACP 48 (4).

746 -. 1987. Papers on Exactions for Municipal Funds. LACP 50 (1).

747 Levin, M. A. 1978. Urban Politics and Political Economy: Property Tax. PSCI 9: 237-245.

748 Lindsey, L. B. 1987. Individual Taxpayer Response to Tax Cuts with Implications for Revenue Maximizing Tax Rates. JPUBE 33: 173-206.

749 Lotz, J. R.; Morse, E. R. 1970. A Theory of Tax Level Determinants for Developing Countries. EDACC 18: 328-341.

750 Lowery, D. 1982. Interpreting the Tax Revolt. SALGR 14: 110-116.

751 Lowery, D.; Sigelman, L. 1981. Understanding the Tax Revolt. APSR 75: 963-974.

752 Marhuenda, F.; Ortuno-Ortin, I. 1995. Popular Support for Progressive Taxation. EL 48: 319-324.

753 Mariotti, S. 1978. Economic Analysis of Voting on Michigan's Tax and Expenditure Limitation Amendment. PC 33: 15-26.

754 Mason, R.; Calvin, L. D. 1984. Public Confidence and Admitted Tax Evasion. NTJ 37: 489-496.

755 McCleary, W. 1991. Earmarking of Government Revenue. World Bank Research Observer 6: 84-104.

756 McGraw, K. M.; Scholz, J. T. 1991. Appeals to Civic Virtue vs. Attention to Self-Interest: Effects on Tax Compliance. LASR 25: 471-498.

757 McGuire, T. J. 1986. Interstate Tax Differentials, Tax Competition and Tax Policy. NTJ 39: 367-373.

758 Merrifield, J. 1994. The Factors that Influence the Level of Underground Government. PFQ 22: 462-482.

759 Merriman, D. 1994. Do Cigarette Excise Tax Rates Maximize Revenue? EI 32: 419-428.

760 Mikesell, J. L. 1986. The Path of the Tax Revolt: Statewide Expenditure and Tax Control Referenda since Proposition 13. SALGR 18: 5-12.

761 Miner, R. E. 1975. Property Taxes, Services and the Calculating Voter. PFQ 74: 139-153.

762 Mofidi, A.; Stone, J. A. 1990. Do State and Local Taxes Affect Economic Growth? REAS 72: 686-691.

763 Morgan, D. R. 1994. Tax Equality in the American States. SSQ 75: 510-523.

764 Natural Resources Journal 1982. Papers on the Taxation of Natural Resources. NRJ 22 (3).

765 Pack, J. R. 1988. Congress and Fiscal Policy. PC 58: 101-122.

766 Persson, T.; Tabellini, G. 1994. Representative Democracy and Capital Taxation. JPUBE 55: 53-70.

767 Phares, D. 1985. State and Local Tax Burdens across the Fifty States. GAC 16 (2): 34-42.

768 Pogue, T. F.; Sgontz, L. G. 1989. Taxing to Control Social Costs: Alcohol. AER 79: 235-243.

769 Policy Studies Journal. 1980. Papers on Taxing and Spending Policy. PSJ 9 (1).

770 Political Quarterly. 1971. Papers on Taxation. PQ 42 (1).

771 Preston, A.; Ichniowski, C. 1991. A National Perspective on the Local Property Tax Revolt. NTJ 44: 123-145.

772 Proceedings. 1983. Papers on Property Taxes. PAPSC 35 (1).

773 Public Interest. 1978. Papers on Taxation. PI 50 (Winter).
774 Reckers, P. M. J.; Sanders, D. L.; Roark, S. J. 1994. The Influence of Ethical Attitudes on Taxpayer Compliance. NTJ 47: 825-836.
775 Revue d'Etudes Comparatives Est-Ouest. 1989. Papers on World Tax Systems. RECEO 20 (2).
776 Roberts, M. L.; Hite, P. A.; Bradley, C. F. 1994. Understanding Attitudes toward Progressive Taxation. POQ 58: 165-190.
777 Rodriguez, F. 1993. Tax Reforms in Latin America. SEJ 42: 1-23.
778 Scott, W. J.; Grasmick, H. G.; Eckert, C. M. 1981. Dimensions of Tax Revolt. APQ 9: 71-88.
779 Shapiro, P.; Sonstelie, J. 1982. Did Proposition 13 Slay Leviathan? AER 72: 184-190.
780 Sigelman, L.; Lowery, D.; Smith, R. E. 1983. The Tax Revolt. WPQ 36: 30-51.
781 Simon, D. O. 1984. Immigrants, Taxes and Welfare in the US. PADR 10: 55-70.
782 Stack, S. 1978. Political Organization and the Degree of Tax Progressiveness. IRMS 8: 113-126.
783 Starrett, D. A. 1980. Taxation and the Provision of Local Public Goods. AER 70: 380-392.
784 Thurman, Q. C.; St. John, C.; Riggs, L. 1984. Neutralization and Tax Evasion: How Effective Would a Moral Appeal Be in Improving Compliance to Tax Laws? LAP 6: 309-328.
785 Toye, J. F. J. 1976. Economic Theories of Politics and Public Finance. BJPS 6: 433-448.
786 Van Furstenberg, G. M.; Green, R. J.; Jeong, J. H. 1985. Have Taxes Led Government Expenditures? JPP 5: 321-348.
787 Van Velthoven, B. C. J.; Van Winden, F. 1991. A Positive Model of Tax Reform. PC 72: 61-86.
788 Vedder, R. 1990. Tiebout, Taxes and Economic Growth. CJ 10: 91-108.
789 Verdier, J. M. 1988. The President, Congress and Tax Reform. ANNALS 499: 114-123.
790 Wang, S. W. 1991. The Relation between Firm Size and Effective Tax Rates: A Test of Firms' Political Success. Accounting Review 66: 158-169.
791 Yaniv, G. 1994. Tax Evasion and the Income Tax Rate. PF 49: 107-112.

Trade and Tariffs

792 Ahmed, S. 1987. Government Spending, Balance of Trade and the Terms of Trade in British History. JME 20: 195-220.
793 Amelung, T. 1989. Determinents of Protection in Developing Countries: Interest Group Approach. Kyklos 42: 515-532.
794 Annals. 1991. Papers on Japan's External Economic Relations. ANNALS 513.
795 -. 1993. Papers on Western Free Trade. ANNALS 526.
796 Baldwin, R. 1988. Evaluating Strategic Trade Policies. Aussenwirtschaft 43: 207-230.
797 -. 1989. The Political Economy of Trade Policy. JEP 3 (4): 119-135.
798 Baldwin, R.; Clarke, R. N. 1987. Game Modeling Multilateral Trade Negotiations. JPM 9: 257-284.
799 Barbone, L. 1988. Import Barriers. OECD 11: 155-168.
800 Bhagwati, J. N.; Srinivasan, T. N. 1980. Revenue Seeking: A Generalization of the Theory of Tariffs. JPE 88: 1069-1087.
801 Brander, J. A.; Spencer, B. J. 1981. Tariffs and the Extraction of Foreign Monopoly Rents under Potential Entry. Canadian Journal of Economics 14: 371-389.
802 -. 1985. Export Subsidies and International Market Share Rivalry. JIE 18: 83-100.
803 Cato Journal. 1983. Papers on Protectionism. CJ 3 (3).

804 -. 1988. Papers on Deficits and Trade. CJ 8 (2).
805 Christerson, B. 1994. An Analysis of Trade Flows Using the Gravity Model. IRSR 17: 151-166.
806 Conybeare, J. A. C. 1983. Tariff Protection in Developed and Developing Countries. IO 37: 441-467.
807 -. 1985. Trade Wars: A Comparative Study of Anglo-Hanse, Franco-Italian and Hawley-Smoot Conflicts. WP 38: 147-172.
808 -. 1991. Voting for Protection: An Electoral Model of Tariff Policy. IO 45: 57-81.
809 Deardorff, A. V. 1987. Why Do Governments Prefer Nontarrif Barriers? CRCSPP 26: 191-216.
810 Dixon, W. J.; Moon, B. E. 1993. Political Similarity and American Foreign Trade Patterns. PRQ 46: 5-26.
811 Donovan, J. 1994. Selected Finance and Trade Reference Books on Latin America. FRBA 79 (1): 28-34.
812 Easton, S. T.; Gibson, W. A.; Reed, C. G. 1988. Tariffs and Growth. EEH 25: 147-163.
813 Eaton, J.; Grossman, G. M. 1986. Optimal Trade and Industrial Policy under Oligopoly. QJE 101: 383-406.
814 Economic Development and Cultural Change 1986. Papers on Latin American Trade. EDACC 34 (3).
815 Edwards, S. 1993. Openness, Trade Liberalization and Growth in Developing Countries. JEL 31: 1358-1393.
816 Frey, B. S. 1984. Public Choice View of International Political Economy. IO 38: 199-223.
817 Gasiorek, M.; Smith, A.; Venables, A. J. 1989. Tariffs, Subsidies and Retaliation. EER 33: 480-489.
818 Gill, S.; Law, D. 1989. Global Hegemony and the Structural Power of Capital. ISQ 33: 475-499.
819 Gilpin, R. 1971. The Politics of Transnational Economic Relations. IO 25: 398-419.
820 Goldstein, J. 1988. Ideas, Institutions and American Trade Policy. IO 42: 179-217.
821 Gowa, J. 1989. Bipolarity, Multipolarity and Free Trade. APSR 83: 1245-1256.
822 Grant, R. 1993. Trading Blocs or Trading Blows? Macroeconomic Geography of US and Japanese Trade Policies. EPA 25: 273-291.
823 Hansen, J. M. 1990. Taxation and the Political Economy of the Tariff. IO 44: 527-551.
824 Harvard International Law Journal. 1993. Papers on the North American Free Trade Agreement. HILJ 34 (2).
825 Hook, S. W. 1994. Self-Interest and Foreign Economic Policy. ISN 19: 36-36.
826 Iida, K. 1993. Leadership, Hegemony and the International Economy. ISQ 37: 459-489.
827 Ikenberry, G. J. 1989. Manufacturing Consensus: Institutionalization of American Private Interest in the Tokyo Trade Round. CP 21: 289-309.
828 International Journal. 1986. Papers on the North American Political Economy. IJ 42 (1).
829 -. 1994. Papers on World Trade Regimes. IJ 49 (3).
830 International Organization. 1988. Papers on American Foreign Economic Policy. IO 42 (1).
831 Irwin, D. A. 1994. Political Economy of Free Trade: Voting in the British General Election of 1906. JOLE 37: 75-108.
832 Journal of Development Studies. 1984. Papers on Open Economies. JDS 21 (1).
833 Kaempfer, W. H.; Lowenberg, A. D. 1986. A Model of the Political Economy of International Investment Sanctions: South Africa. Kyklos 39: 377-396.
834 Kitson, M.; Solomou, S. 1989. Macroeconomics of Protectionism. CJE 13: 155-169.
835 Komura, C. 1990. Policy Options toward a Trade Balance: Japan. JJAIE 4: 24-35.
836 Krasner, S. D. 1976. State Power and the Structure of International Trade. WP 28: 317-347.

837 Krugman, P. R. 1987. Is Free Trade Passe? JEP 1: 131-144.

838 Lake, D. A. 1991. Power and the Third World: A Realist Political Economy of North-South Relations. ISQ 31: 217-234.

839 Lawson, C. W. 1975. An Empirical Analysis of the Structure and Stability of Communist Foreign Trade. SS 26: 224-238.

840 Livingston, S. 1992. Knowledge Hierarchies and the Politics of Ideas in American International Commodity Policy. JPP 12: 223-242.

841 Lohmann, S.; O'Halloran, S. 1994. Divided Government and US Trade Policy. IO 48: 595-632.

842 Lothian, J. R. 1991. Political Factors in International Economics. JIMF 10 (March Special Issue): S4-S15.

843 Mansfield, E. D.; Busch, M. L. 1995. Political Economy of Nontariff Barriers. IO 49: 723-750.

844 Markusen, J. R.; Venables, A. J. 1988. Trade Policy with Increasing Returns and Imperfect Competition. JIE 24: 299-316.

845 Mayer, W.; Li, J. 1994. Interest Groups, Electoral Competition and Probabilistic Voting for Trade Policies. EAP 6: 59-77.

846 Mayer, W.; Riezman, R. 1990. Voter Preferences for Trade Policy Instruments. EAP 2: 259-273.

847 McKeown, T. J. 1984. Firms and Tariff Regime Change: Explaining the Demand for Protection. WP 36: 215-233.

848 Midford, P. 1993. International Trade and Domestic Politics: Improving on Rogowski's Model of Political Alignments. IO 47: 535-564.

849 Milner, H.; Yoffie, D. B. 1989. Between Free Trade and Protectionism: Strategic Trade Policy and a Theory of Corporate Trade Demands. IO 43: 238-272.

850 New York University Journal. 1987. Papers on Trade Sanctions. NYUJ 19 (4).

851 -. 1993. Papers on the Morality of Protectionism. NYUJ 25 (2).

852 Norton, D. A. G. 1988. On the Economic Theory of Smuggling. Economica 55 (Feb): 107-118.

853 Oguledo, V. I.; MacPhee, C. R. 1994. Gravity Models: Reformulation and Application to Discriminatory Trade Arrangements. AE 26: 107-120.

854 Patibandla, M. 1994. New Theories of International Trade. IEJ 41: 62-78.

855 Pollins, B. M. 1989. Conflict, Cooperation and Commerce: The Effect of International Political Interactions on Bilateral Trade Flows. AJPS 33: 737-761.

856 -. 1989. Does Trade Still Follow the Flag? A Model of International Diplomacy and Commerce. APSR 83: 465-480.

857 Proceedings. 1990. Papers on Trade. PAPSC 37 (4).

858 Ray, E. J. 1981. Determinants of Tariff and Nontariff Trade Restrictions in the US. JPE 89: 105-121.

859 Richardson, J. D. 1989. Empirical Research on Trade Liberalization with Imperfect Competition. OECD 12: 7-50.

860 Rogowski, R. 1987. Trade and the Variety of Democratic Institutions. IO 41: 203-223.

861 Rozanski, J.; Yeats, A. 1994. On the (In)Accuracy of Economic Observations: Trends in the Reliability of International Trade Statistics. JDE 44: 103-130.

862 Sayrs, L. W. 1990. Expected Utility and Peace Science: Trade and Conflict. CMAPS 11: 17-44.

863 Stahl, D. O.; Turunen-Red, A. H. 1995. Tariff Games: Cooperation with Random Variation in Political Regimes. EJPE 11: 215-238.

864 Stegemann, K. 1989. Policy Rivalry among Industrial States: What Can We Learn from Models of Strategic Trade Policy? IO 43: 73-100.

865 Steiber, S. R. 1979. The World System and World Trade. SQ 20: 23-36.

866 Taagepera, R.; Hayes, J. P. 1977. Why the Trade / GNP Ratio Decreases with Country Size. SSR 6: 108-132.

867 Thompson, W. R.; Vescera, L. 1992. Growth Waves, Systemic Openness and Protectionism. IO 46: 493-532.

868 Verdier, D. 1993. Politics of Trade Preference Formation: US from the Civil War to New Deal. PAS 21: 365-392.

869 Wells, G.; Evans, L. 1989. Time Series Estimates of Tariff Incidence. AE 21: 1191-1202.

870 Winters, L. A. 1987. Britain in Europe: A Survey of Quantitative Trade Studies. JCMS 25: 315-335.

871 World Economy. 1992. Papers on Modeling North American Free Trade. WE 15 (1) and 1994 17 (1).

872 -. 1992. Papers on the Political Economy of International Market Access. Vol 15 (6).

ETHICS

1 Abbott, A. 1983. Professional Ethics. AJS 88: 855-885.
2 Arendt, H. 1984. Thinking and Moral Considerations. SR 51: 7-38.
3 Arnhart, L. 1995. The New Darwinian Naturalism in Political Theory. APSR 89: 389-400.
4 Bendor, J. 1987. In Good Times and Bad: Reciprocity in an Uncertain World. AJPS 31: 531-558.
5 Benn, S. I. 1984. Persons and Values: Reason in Conflict and Moral Disagreement. Ethics 95: 20-37.
6 Beyleveld, D.; Brownsword, R. 1983. Law as a Moral Judgment vs. Law as the Rules of the Powerful. AJJ 28: 79-117.
7 Binmore, K. 1989. Social Contract I: Harsanyi and Rawls. EJ 99 (Sup): 84-102.
8 Blum, L. 1988. Gilligan and Kohlberg: Implications for Moral Theory. Ethics 98: 472-491.
9 Bonacich, E. 1987. A Social Evaluation of Ethics of Immigrant Entrepreneurship. SP 30: 446-466.
10 Brams, S. J. 1977. Deception in 2 X 2 Games. JOPS 2: 171-204.
11 Brilmayer, L. 1991. The Odd Advantage of Reliable Enemies. HILJ 32: 331-338.
12 Brown, S. R. 1984. Subjective Communicability of Meta Ethics. PM 10: 465-478.
13 Chatterjee, B. B. 1974. An Appropriate Game Model for Gandhian Satyagraha. JPR 11: 21-30.
14 Choudhury, M. A. 1994. Ethics and Economics: A View from Ecological Economics. IJSE 22: 40-60.
15 Coburn, R. C. 1982. Morality, Truth and Relativism. Ethics 92: 661-669.
16 Coleman, J. L. 1980. Legal Duties and Moral Argument. STAP 5: 377-408.
17 Cullity, G. 1995. Moral Free Riding. PAPA 24: 3-34.
18 Dagger, R. 1985. Rights, Boundaries and the Bonds of Community: Moral Parochialism. APSR 79: 436-447.
19 Doppelt, G. 1984. Conflicting Social Paradigms of Human Freedom and Justification. Inquiry 27: 51-106.
20 Douglas, M. 1983. Morality and Culture. Ethics 93: 786-791.
21 Dupre, L.; O'Neill, W. 1989. Social Structures and Structural Ethics. ROP 51: 327-344.
22 Ethics. 1982. Papers on Moral Development. Vol 92 (3).
23 -. 1986. Papers on Derek Parfit. Vol 96 (4).
24 -. 1986. Papers on Metaethics. Vol 96 (3).
25 -. 1987. Papers on Gauthier's Morals by Agreement. Vol 97: 715-775.
26 -. 1991. Papers on Impartial Ethical Theory. Vol 101 (4).
27 -. 1991. Papers on Moral Responsibility. Vol 101 (2).
28 -. 1992. Papers on Pluralism and Ethical Theory. Vol 102 (4).
29 -. 1995. Papers on Empathy and Ethics. Vol 105 (4).
30 Fishkin, J.; Keniston, K.; MacKinnon, C. 1973. Moral Reasoning and Political Ideology. JPSP 27: 109-119.
31 Forkosch, M. D. 1979. Economist as Moralist. AJEAS 38: 357-370.
32 Gibbs, J. 1977. Kohlberg's Stages of Moral Judgment. Harvard Education Review 47: 43-61.
33 Goodin, R. E. 1980. Making Moral Incentive Pay. PSCI 12: 131-146.
34 Hagafors, R.; Brehmer, B. 1983. Does Having to Justify One's Decisions Change the Nature of the Judgement Process. Organizational Behavior and Human Performance 32: 223-232.
35 Halman, L. 1995. Is There a Moral Decline? A Cross-National Inquiry into Morality. ISSJ 47: 419-440.
36 Hamilton, V. L.; Sanders, J. 1983. Universals in Judging Wrongdoing. ASR 48: 199-210.
37 Hargrove, E. C. 1985. The Role of Rules in Ethical Decision Making. Inquiry 28: 3-42.
38 Harsanyi, J. C. 1975. Can the Maximin Principle Serve as a Basis for Morality? A Critique of John Rawls. APSR 69: 594-606.
39 -. 1985. Does Reason Tell Us What Moral Code to Follow and, Indeed, to Follow Any Moral Code at All? Ethics 96: 42-55.
40 -. 1995. Prudential Values and a Rule Utilitarian Theory of Morality. SCAW 12: 319-333.
41 Hausman, D. M. 1989. Are Markets Morally Free Zones? PAPA 18: 317-333.
42 Hausman, D. M.; McPherson, M. S. 1993. Taking Ethics Seriously: Economics and Moral Philosophy. JEL 31: 671-731.
43 Himmelfard, G. 1994. A De-Moralized Society: The British-American Experience. PI 117: 57-80.
44 Hitchcock, J. 1981. Church, State and Moral Values: The Limits of American Pluralism. LACP 44: 3-22.
45 Howard, R.E. 1983. The Full Belly Thesis: Should Economic Rights Take Priority over Civil and Political Rights: Africa. HRQ 5: 467-490.
46 Howe, E.; Kaufman, J. L. 1981. Ethics and Professional Practice in Planning and Policy Preferences. PSJ 9: 585-594.
47 Hurka, T. 1983. Value and Population Size. Ethics 93: 496-507.
48 Isaac, J. 1994. The Politics of Morality in the United Kingdom. PARLA 47: 175-189.

49 Jones, W. T. 1984. Public Roles, Private Roles and Differential Moral Assessments of Role Performance. Ethics 94: 603-620.

50 Journal of Human Relations. 1973. Papers on Moving Toward a Science of Values. JHR 21 (1).

51 Journal of Social Issues. 1990. Papers on Moral Exclusion and Injustice. Vol 46 (1).

52 Kahneman, D.; Knetsch, J. L.; Thaler, R. H. 1986. Fairness as a Constraint on Profit Seeking. AER 76: 728-741.

53 Kalleberg, A. L.; Preston, L. M. 1984. Liberal Paradox: Self-Interest and Respect for Political Principles. Polity 17: 360-386.

54 Kaun, D. E. 1994. Lying as Standard Operating Procedure: Deception in the Weapons Testing Process. JSE 23: 229-254.

55 Kekes, J. 1985. Human Nature and Moral Theories. Inquiry 28: 231-246.

56 Klitgaard, R. E. 1971. Gandhi's Non-Violence as a Tactic. JPR 9: 143-154.

57 Klosko, G. 1990. The Moral Force of Political Obligations. APSR 84: 1235-1250.

58 Kocis, R. A. 1983. Toward a Coherent Theory of Human Moral Development. POLST 31: 370-393.

59 Kollock, P. 1994. Emergence of Exchange Structures: An Experimental Study of Uncertainty, Commitment and Trust. AJS 100: 313-345.

60 Kraus, J. S.; Coleman, J. L. 1987. Morality and Theory of Rational Choice. Ethics 97: 715-749.

61 Kress, K. J. 1984. Legal Reasoning and Coherence Theories: Dworkin's Rights Thesis. CLR 72: 369-402.

62 Malnes, R. 1992. Philosophical Argument and Political Practice: The Methodology of Normative Theory. SPS 15: 117-134.

63 Mapel, D. R. 1990. Prudence and the Plurality of Value in International Ethics. JOP 52: 433-456.

64 Martin, M. W. 1981. Rights and the Meta Ethics of Professional Morality. Ethics 91: 619-625.

65 McGuire, M. C. 1985. The Calculus of Moral Obligation. Ethics 95: 199-223.

66 McKenzie, R. B. 1977. Economic Dimensions of Ethical Behavior. Ethics 87: 208-221.

67 Mendola, J. 1987. Gauthier's Morals by Agreement and Two Kinds of Rationality. Ethics 97: 765-775.

68 Miller, D. 1988. The Ethical Significance of Nationality. Ethics 98: 647-662.

69 Miller, G. J.; Oppenheimer, J. A. 1982. Universalism in Experimental Committees. APSR 76: 561-574.

70 Moreh, J. 1994. Game Theory and Common-Sense Morality. SSI 33: 93-116.

71 Munro, J. 1982. Religion, Age, Sex and Moral Issues. Political Science 34: 214-220.

72 Musser, S. J.; Orke, E. A. 1992. Ethical Value Systems. JABS 28: 348-362.

73 Nagel, T. 1987. Moral Conflict and Political Legitimacy. PAPA 16: 215-240.

74 Nelson, A. 1988. Economic Rationality and Morality. PAPA 17: 149-166.

75 O'Connor, R. E. 1974. Political Activism and Moral Reasoning. BJPS 4: 53-78.

76 Oppenheimer, J. A. 1985. Public Choice and Three Ethical Properties of Politics. PC 45: 241-256.

77 Ostrom, V. 1984. The Meaning of Value Terms. ABS 28: 249-262.

78 Plott, C. R. 1972. Ethics, Social Choice Theory and Theory of Economic Policy. JMS 2: 181-208.

79 Pogge, T. W. 1990. Effects of Prevalent Moral Conceptions. SR 57: 649-664.

80 Pollock, J. L. 1986. A Theory of Moral Reasoning. Ethics 96: 506-523.

81 Railton, P. 1984. Alienation, Consequentialism and Demands of Morality. PAPA 13: 134-171.

82 Reilly, B. J.; Kyj, M. J. 1994. Meta-Ethical Reasoning Applied to Economics and Business Principles. AJEAS 53: 147-162.

83 -. 1994. The Moral Community: Additional Dimension to Individualistic Rationalism. IJSE 21 (7): 3-14.

84 Rhode, D. L. 1984. Moral Character as a Professional Credential. YLJ 94: 491-603.

85 Rosenblum, N. L. 1984. Moral Membership in a Postliberal State. WP 36: 581-596.

86 Science and Society. 1984. Papers on the Theory of Value. SAS 48 (4).

87 Segerston, P. S. 1990. Moral Efficiency: A New Criterion for Social Choice. SCAW 7: 109-129.

88 Sen, A. K. 1982. Rights and Agency. PPA 11: 3-39.

89 -. 1983. Liberty and Social Choice. JPHIL 80: 5-28.

90 Shapiro, D. L. 1991. Effects of Explanations on Negative Reactions to Deceit. ASQ 36: 614-630.

91 Shrader-Frechette, K. 1987. Parfit and Mistakes in Moral Mathematics. Ethics 98: 50-60.

92 Sjoberg, G.; Vaughan, T. R.; Sjoberg, A. F. 1984. Morals and Applied Behavioral Research. JABS 20: 311-322.

93 Smith, M. B. E. 1980. Rights, Right Answers and Constructive Model of Morality. STAP 5: 409-426.

94 Sniderman, P. M.; Brody, R. A. 1977 Coping: The Ethic of Self-Reliance. AJPS 21: 501-522.

95 Social Theory and Practice. 1991. Papers on Virtue Ethics. STAP 17 (2).

96 Sociological Inquiry. 1978. Papers on Universalism. SI 48 (3/4).

97 Stephens, W. N. 1972. A Cross-Cultural Study of Modesty. Behavior Science Notes 7: 1-28.

98 Strasnick, S. 1976. Social Choice and Derivation of Rawls' Difference Principle. JPHIL 73: 85-99.

99 -. 1979. Moral Structures and Axiomatic Theory. TAD 11: 195-206.

100 Sugden, R. 1985. Liberty, Preference and Choice. EAPHIL 1: 213-229.

101 Sylvia, R. D.; Mustafa, H.; Hamilton, H. 1981. Political Value Judgments of Children: Moral Development Theory. Polity 13: 383-409.

102 Terrell, T. P. 1984. Flatlaw: Legal Reasoning and Development of Fundamental Normative Principles. CLR 72: 288-342.

103 Thigpen, R. B.; Downing, L. A. 1982. Rawls, Nozick and the De-Politicizing of Political Theory. JPS 9: 70-80.

104 Trainer, F. E. 1977. Kohlberg's Contributions to the Study of Moral Development. Journal for the Theory of Social Behavior 7: 41-63.

105 Tsujimoto, R.N.; Nardi, P. M. 1978. A Comparison of Kohlberg's and Hogan's Theories of Moral Development. SPQ 41: 235-245.

106 Tyler, T. R. 1990. Social Psychology of Authority: Why Do People Obey an Order to Harm Others? LASR 24: 1089-1102.

107 Vanberg, V.; Congleton, R. D. 1992. Rationality, Morality and Exit. APSR 86: 418-431.

108 Van Dyke, V. 1982. Collective Entities and Moral Rights: Problems in Liberal Democratic Thought. JOP 44: 21-40.

109 Van Ijzendoorn, M. H. 1983. Moral and Political Education. IJPE 6: 25-42.

110 Victor, B.; Cullen, J. B. 1988. Organizational Bases of Ethical Work Climates. ASQ 33: 101-125.

111 Wilson, J. Q. 1985. Rediscovery of Character: Private Virtue and Public Policy. PI 81: 3-16.

112 -. 1995. Capitalism and Morality. PI 121: 42-60.

113 Wilson, R. W. 1979. Ideology, Hierarchy and Moral Behavior. IAS 15: 29-39.

114 -. 1981. Political Socialization and Moral Development. WP 33: 153-177.

115 Woodrum, E. 1988. Determinants of Moral Attitudes. JSSR 27: 553-573.

116 Wren, T. E. 1982. Social Learning Theory, Self-Regulation and Morality. Ethics 92: 409-424.

117 Zielonka, J. 1986. Strengths and Weaknesses of Nonviolent Action. Orbis 30: 91-110.

Altruism

118 Bergstrom, T. C. 1995. Evolution of Altruistic Ethical Rules for Siblings. AER 85: 58-81.

119 Boehm, C. 1979. Some Problems with Altruism in the Search for Moral Universals. BS 24: 15-24.

120 Coate, S.. 1995. Altruism, Samaritan's Dilemma and Government Transfer Policy. AER 85: 46-57.

121 Corfman, K. P.; Lehmann, D. R. 1993. The Importance of Others' Welfare in Bargaining Outcomes. JCON 20: 124-137.

122 Frohlich, N. 1974. Self-Interest or Altruism, What Difference? JCR 18: 55-73.

123 Frohlich, N.; Oppenheimer, J. A. 1984. Beyond Economic Man: Altruism, Egalitarianism and Difference Maximizing. JCR 28: 3-24.

124 Haltiwanger, J.; Waldman, M. 1993. Role of Altruism in Economic Interaction. JEBAO 21: 1-15.

125 Harvey, J. W.; McCrohan, K. F. 1988. Voluntary Compliance and the Effectiveness of Public and Non-Profit Institutions: American Philanthropy and Taxation. JEPSY 9: 369-386.

126 Hayashi, F. 1995. Is the Japanese Extended Family Altruistically Linked? A Test Based on Engel Curves. JPE 103: 661-674.

127 Helms, M. M.; Keilany, Z. 1991. Beyond Self-Interest: A Reexamination of Neoclassical Economics in Group Settings. JEBAO 15: 187-200.

128 Helsley, R. W.; O'Sullivan, A. 1994. Altruistic Voting and Campaign Contributions. JPUBE 55: 107-119.

129 Hijiya, J. A. 1980. Four Ways of Looking at a Philanthropist: Robert Weeks de Forest. PAPS 124: 404-418.

130 Hudson, J.; Jones, P. R. 1994. The Importance of the Ethical Voter: An Estimate of Altruism. EJPE 10: 499-510.

131 Khalil, E. L. 1990. Beyond Self-Interest and Altruism. EAPHIL 6: 255-273.

132 Krebs, D. 1982. Psychological Approaches to Altruism: An Evaluation. Ethics 92: 447-458.

133 Kurz, M. 1978. Altruism as an Outcome of Social Integration. AER 68: 216-222.

134 Monroe, K. R. 1991. Explaining Differences between Rational Actors and Altruists through Cognitive Frameworks. JOP 53: 394-433.

135 -. 1994. Altruism and Social Theory. AJPS 38: 861-893.

136 Orbell, J. M.; Dawes, R. M. 1991. A Cognitive Miser Theory of the Cooperators' Advantage. APSR 85: 515-530.

137 Orbell, J. M.; Schwartz-Shea, P.; Simmons, R. T. 1984. Do Cooperators Exit more Readily than Defectors? APSR 78: 147-162.

138 Roberts, R. D. 1984. A Positive Model of Private Charity and Public Transfers. JPE 92: 136-148.

139 Rushton, J. P. 1982. Altruism and Society: A Social Learning Perspective. Ethics 92: 425-446.

140 Schofield, N. J. 1985. Anarchy, Altruism and Cooperation. SCAW 2: 207-219.

141 Sesardic, N. 1995. Recent Work on Human Altruism and Evolution. Ethics 106: 128-157.

142 Smith, V. H.; Kehoe, M. R.; Cremer, M. E. 1995. Private Provision of Public Goods: Altruism and Voluntary Giving. JPUBE 58: 107-126.

143 Stark, O. 1984. Bargaining, Altruism and Demographic Phenomena. PADR 10: 679-692.

144 -. 1985. On Private Charity and Altruism. PC 46: 325-332.

145 Thagard, P.; Nisbett, R. E. 1983. Rationality and Charity. POS 50: 250-267.

146 Trivers, R. 1971. Evolution of Reciprocal Altruism. QRB 46 (March): 35-57.

147 Van de Kragt, A. J. C.; Dawes, R. M.; Orbell, J. M. 1988. Are People Who Cooperate Rational Altruists? PC 1988: 233-248.

Cooperation

148 Alcock, J. E. 1974. Cooperation, Competition and the Effects of Time Pressure. JCR 18: 171-197.

149 Andreoni, J. 1995. The Effects of Positive and Negative Framing on Cooperation. QJE 110: 1-21.

150 Andreoni, J.; Miller, J. H. 1993. Rational Cooperation in the Finitiely Repeated Prisoner's Dilemma. EJ 103: 570-585.

151 Axelrod, R. 1981. Emergence of Cooperation among Egoists. APSR 75: 306-318.

152 Axelrod, R.; Dion, D. 1988. Further Evolution of Cooperation. Science 242: 1385-1390.

153 Axelrod, R.; Keohane, R. O. 1985. Achieving Cooperation under Anarchy. WP 38: 226-254.

154 Bartholdi, J. J.; Butler, C. A.; Trick, M. A. 1986. More on the Evolution of Cooperation. JCR 30: 129-140.

155 Bendor, J. 1993. Uncertainty and the Evolution of Cooperation. JCR 37: 709-734.

156 Bendor, J.; Kramer, R. M.; Stout, S. 1991. When in Doubt... Cooperation in Noisy Prisoner's Dilemma. JCR 35: 691-719.

157 Bonin, J. P.; Jones, D. C.; Putterman, L. 1993. Theoretical and Empirical Studies of Producer Cooperatives. JEL 31: 1290-1320.

158 Busch, M. L.; Reinhardt, E. R. 1993. Nice Strategies in a World of Relative Gains: Cooperation under Anarchy. JCR 37: 427-445.

159 Butler, S.; Skipper, J. K. 1981. Working for Tips: An Examination of Trust and Reciprocity in a Secondary Relationship. SQ 22: 15-28.

160 Chase, I. 1980. Cooperative and Noncooperative Behavior in Animals. American Naturalist 115: 827-857.

161 Chatman, J. A.; Barsade, S. G. 1995. Personality, Organizational Culture and Cooperation. AAS 40: 423-443.

162 Chong, D. 1992. Reputation and Cooperative Behavior. SSI 31: 683-710.

163 Dayton, E. 1979. Utility Maximizers and Cooperative Undertakings. Ethics 90: 130-140.

164 Frohlich, N.; Oppenheimer, J. A. 1970. I Get by with a Little Help from My Friends. WP 23: 104-121.

165 Grieco, J. M. 1988. Anarchy and the Limits of Cooperation: A Realist Critique of the Newest Liberal Institutionalism. IO 42: 485-502.

166 Haas, E. B. 1980. Why Collaborate? Issue Linkage and International Regimes. WP 32: 357-405.

167 Hardin, R. 1971. Collective Action as an Agreeable N Prisoners' Dilemma. BS 16: 472-479.

168 Harrington, J. E. 1995. Cooperation in a One-Shot Prisoners' Dilemma. GAEB 8: 364-377.

169 Hirschleifer, J.; Coll, J. C. M. 1988. What Strategies Can Support the Evolutionary Emergence of Cooperation? JCR 32: 367-401.

170 Hirschleifer, J.; Rasmusen, E. B. 1989. Cooperation in a Repeated Prisoners' Dilemma with Ostracism. JEBAO 12: 97-106.

171 Hollander, H. 1990. A Social Exchange Approach to Voluntary Cooperation. AER 80: 1157-1167.

172 Hovi, J. 1989. Evolution of Cooperation: The Importance of Discrimination. CAC 24: 55-68.

173 International Journal. 1992. Papers on Choosing to Cooperate: How States Avoid Loss. IJ 47 (2).

174 Jervis, R. 1978. Cooperation under the Security Dilemma. WP 30: 167-186.

175 -. 1988. Realism, Game Theory and Cooperation. WP 40: 317-349.

176 Kondo, T. 1990. Some Notes on Rational Behavior, Normative Behavior, Moral Behavior and Cooperation. JCR 34: 495-530.

177 Kreps, D. M., et al. 1982. Rational Cooperation in the Finitely Repeated Prisoners' Dilemma. JET 27: 280-312.

178 McGinnis, M. D. 1986. Issue Linkage in Evolution of International Cooperation. JCR 30: 141-170.

179 Milner, H. 1992. International Theories of Cooperation among Nations. WP 44: 466-496.

180 Moldovanu, B.; Winter, E. 1994. Core Implementation and Increasing Returns to Scale for Cooperation. JMATHE 23: 533-548.

181 Morikawa, T.; Orbell, J. M.; Runde, A. S. 1995. The Advantage of Being Moderately Cooperative. APSR 89: 601-611.

182 Morrow, J. D. 1994. Modeling the Forms of International Cooperation: Distribution vs. Information. IO 48: 387-424.

183 Neyman, A. 1985. Bounded Complexity Justifies Cooperation in the Finitely Repeated Prisoners' Dilemma. EL 19: 227-230.

184 Oye, K. A. 1985. Explaining Cooperation under Anarchy. WP 38: 1-24.

185 Pahre, R. 1994. Multilateral Cooperation in an Iterated Prisoner's Dilemma. JCR 38: 326-352.

186 Patchen, M. 1970. Models of Cooperation and Conflict. JCR 14: 389-408.

187 Schmitt, D. R. 1981. Performance under Cooperation or Competition. ABS 24: 649-680.

188 Schneider, G.; Cederman, L. E. 1994. Change of Tide in Political Cooperation: A Limited Information Model of European Integration. IO 48: 633-662.

189 Schuessler, R. 1990. Threshold Effects and the Decline of Cooperation. JCR 34: 476-495.

190 Sexton, R. J.; Wilson, B. M.; Wann, J. J. 1989. Some Tests of the Economic Theory of Cooperatives: Cotton Ginning. Western Journal of Agricultural Economics 14: 56-66.

191 Snidal, D. 1985. Coordination vs. Prisoners' Dilemma: Implications for International Cooperation and Regimes. APSR 79: 923-942.

192 -. 1991. Relative Gains and the Pattern of International Cooperation. APSR 85: 701-726.

193 Stein, A. A. 1982. Coordination and Collaboration: Regimes in Anarchic World. IO 36: 299-324.

194 Trick, M. A. 1986. More on the Evolution of Cooperation. JCR 30: 129-140.

195 Van de Kragt, A. J. C.; Dawes, R. M.; Orbell, J. M. 1988. Are People Who Cooperate Rational Altruists? PC 1988: 233-248.

196 Vries, M. S. 1990. Interdependence, Cooperation and Conflict. JPR 27: 429-444.

197 Wagner, R. H. 1983. The Theory of Games and the Problem of International Cooperation. APSR 77: 330-346.

198 Watson, J. 1994. Cooperation in the Infinitely Repeated Prisoners' Dilemma with Pertubations. GAEB 7: 260-285.

Human Rights

199 Annals. 1989. Papers on Human Rights. ANNALS 506.

200 Banks, D. L. 1986. Analysis of Human Rights Data over Time. HRQ 8: 654-680.

201 Bollen, K. A. 1986. Political Rights and Political Liberties in Nations: An Evaluation of Human Rights Measures. HRQ 8: 567-591.

202 Bouandel, Y. 1993. Quantitative Approaches to the Comparative Study of Human Rights: Charles Humana. Coexistence 30: 145-164.

203 Cingranelli, D. L.; Wright, K. N. 1986. Measurement of Cross National Variations of Due Process. PSJ 15: 97-109.

204 Crenshaw, E. M. 1995. Influence of Modernity and Proto-Modernity on Political and Civil Rights. ASR 60: 702-718.

205 Davenport, C. 1995. Multi-Dimensional Threat Perception and State Repression. AJPS 39: 683-713.

206 Donnelly, J. 1982. Human Rights and Human Dignity: Analytic Critique of Non-Western Conceptions of Human Rights. APSR 76: 303-316.

207 -. 1984. Human Rights, Humanitarian Intervention and American Foreign Policy. JIA 37: 311-328.

208 Donnelly, J.; Howard, R. E. 1988. Assessing National Human Rights Performance. HRQ 10: 214-248.

209 Ethics. 1981. Papers on Rights. Ethics 92 (1).

210 Fraser, E. E. 1994. Reconciling Conceptual and Measurement Problems in the Comparative Study of Human Rights. IJCS 35: 1-18.

211 Goldstein, R. J. 1968. Political Repression in Modern American History: A Bibliography. Labor History 32: 503-550.

212 -. 1986. Limitations of Using Quantitative Data in Studying Human Rights Abuses. HRQ 8: 607-627.

213 Harff, B. 1987. Empathy for Victims of Massive Human Rights Violations and Support for Government Intervention. PP 8: 1-20.

214 Haslett, D. W. 1980. General Theory of Rights. STAP 5: 427-460.

215 Hewlett, S. A. 1979. Human Rights and Economic Realities. PSCQ 94: 453-474.

216 Hinchman, L. P. 1984. Origins of Human Rights: A Hegelian Perspective. WPQ 37: 7-31.

217 Huaraka, T. 1988. Effects of Military Coups d'Etat and Regimes on Human Rights in Africa. Archiv des Volkerrechts 26: 49-66.

218 Human Rights Quarterly. 1981. Papers on International Human Rights Organizations. HRQ 3 (1).

219 -. 1986. Papers on Statistical Issues in Human Rights. HRQ 8 (4).

220 Innes de Neufville, J. 1986. Human Rights Reporting as Policy Tool: Examination of the State Department Country Reports. HRQ 8: 681-709.

221 Inquiry. 1971. Papers on Rights and Politics. Vol 14 (3).

222 International Studies Quarterly. 1979. Papers on International Perspectives on Human Rights. ISQ 23 (2).

223 Journal of Applied Behavioral Science. 1984. Papers on Ethics, Values and Human Rights. JABS 20 (4).

224 Journal of International Affairs. 1982. Papers on Indigenous Peoples' Human Rights. JIA 36 (1).

225 Journal of Social Issues 1975. Papers on Civil Liberties. JSI 31 (2).

226 Kowalewski, D.; Hoover, D. 1994. Dissent and Repression in the World System. IJCS 35: 161-187.

227 Kukathas, C. 1992. Are There Any Cultural Rights? PT 20: 105-139.

228 Kymlicka, W. 1992. Rights of Minority Cultures. PT 20: 140-146.

229 Law and Contemporary Problems. 1979. Papers on Human Rights and Dissent. LACP 42 (2).

230 Luban, D. 1980. Just War and Human Rights. PAPA 9: 160-181.

231 McNitt, A. D. 1986. Measuring Human Rights: Problems and Possibilities. PSJ 15: 71-83.

232 Mitchell, N. J.; McCormick, J. M. 1988. Economic and Political Explanations of Human Rights Violations. WP 40: 476-498.

233 Moon, B. E.; Dixon, W. J. 1985. Politics, the State and Basic Human Needs. AJPS 29: 661-694.

234 Oppenheim, F. E. 1995. Social Freedom and Its Parameters. JTP 7: 403-420.

235 Park, H. S. 1987. Correlates of Human Rights. HRQ 9: 405-413.

236 Paust, J. J. 1983. Authority: From a Human Rights Perspective. AJJ 28: 64-78.

237 Poe, S. C.; Tate, C.N. 1994. Repression of Human Rights to Personal Integrity in the 1980s. APSR 88: 853-872.

238 Policy Studies Journal. 1976. Papers on Civil Liberties Policy. PSJ 4 (2).

239 -. 1986. Papers on Human Rights. PSJ 15 (1).

240 Political Studies. 1995. Papers on Human Rights and Political Theory. POLST 43 (Special Issue).
241 Proceedings American Philosophical Society. 1991. Papers on US Human Rights. PAPS 135 (1).
242 Regan, P. M. 1995. Systemic Study of the Causes of Political Repression. AUSJPS 30: 137-145.
243 Rose, R. 1995. Freedom as a Fundamental Value. ISSJ 47: 457-472.
244 Social Research. 1971. Papers on Human Rights. SR 38 (2).
245 Stohl, M., et al. 1986. State Violation of Human Rights. HRQ 8: 592-606.
246 Universal Human Rights. 1979. Papers on Human Rights UHR 1 (1-4).

Justice

247 Amdur, R. 1977. Rawls' Theory of Justice. WP 29: 438-461.
248 American Behavioral Scientist. 1991. Papers on Justice. ABS 34 (3).
249 American Political Science Review. 1975. Papers on Rawls's Theory of Justice. APSR 69: 588-674.
250 Arad, S.; Carnevale, P. J. 1994. Partisanship Effects in Judgments of Fairness and Trust in the Palestine-Israeli Conflict. JCR 38: 423-451.
251 Armour, L. 1994. Is Economic Justice Possible? IJSE 21: 32-58.
252 Arrow, K. J. 1973. Ordinalist-Utilitarian Notes on Rawls' Theory of Justice. JPHIL 70: 245-263.
253 -. 1978. Nozick's Entitlement Theory of Justice. Philosophia 7: 265-280.
254 Barry, B. 1995. John Rawls and the Search for Stability. Ethics 105: 874-915.
255 Bayer, R. C. 1990. The Empirical Application of Justice Theories. ISSJ 43: 565-576.
256 Blanchard, W. 1986. Evaluating Social Equity: What Does Fairness Mean? PSJ 15: 29-57.
257 Bond, D.; Park, J. C. 1991. An Empirical Test of Rawls's Theory of Justice. SAG 22: 443-462.
258 Borglin, A. 1982. States and Persons: The Interpretation of Some Fundamental Concepts in the Theory of Justice as Fairness. JPUBE 18: 85-104.
259 Brook, R. 1987. Justice and the Golden Rule: A Commentary on Some Recent Work of Lawrence Kohlberg. Ethics 97: 363-373.
260 Burton, S. J. 1982. A Logical Positivist Analyses on Equality and Rules. YLJ 91: 1136-1166.
261 Casper, J. D.; Tyler, T. R.; Fisher, B. 1988. Procedural Justice in Felony Cases. LASR 22: 483-507.
262 Choptiany, L. 1973. A Critique of John Rawls's Principles of Justice. Ethics 83: 146-150.
263 Clark, B.; Gintis, H. 1978. Rawlsian Justice and Economic Systems. PAPA 7: 302-325.
264 Coexistence. 1986. Papers on Justice and Law. Vol 23 (1/2).
265 Cohn, T. 1983. Social Justice and Social Political Education. IJPE 6: 1-24.
266 Copeland, M. A. 1982. Justice and the Foundations of Economic Thought. AJEAS 41: 97-100.
267 De Meur, G.; Hubaut, X. 1986. Fair Models of Political Fairness. EJPR 14: 237-252.
268 Dworkin, R. 1981. What Is Equity. PAPA 10: 185-246, 283-345.
269 Ellis, R. 1992. Rival Visions of Equality in American Political Culture. ROP 54: 253-280.
270 -. 1993. Quantifying Distributive Justice: Environmental and Risk-Related Public Policy. PSCI 26: 99-123.
271 Ethics. 1989. Papers on Rawls' Theory of Justice. Vol 99 (4).
272 -. 1992. Papers on Markets and Equality. Vol 102 (3).
273 Feather, N. T. 1994. Human Values and Their Relation to Justice. JSI 50: 129-152.
274 Fried, C. 1983. Distributive Justice. SPAP 1: 45-59.
275 Frohlich, N.; Oppenheimer, J. A. 1990. Choosing Justice in Experimental Democracies. APSR 84: 461-477.
276 Frohlich, N.; Oppenheimer, J. A.; Eavey, C. L. 1987. Choices of Principles of Distributive Justice. AJPS 31: 606-636.
277 -. 1987. Laboratory Results on Rawls's Distributive Justice. BJPS 17: 1-22.
278 Gartrell, C. D. 1985. Relational and Distributional Models of Collective Justice Sentiments. SF 64: 64-83.
279 Gauthier, D. P. 1978. Social Choice and Distributive Justice. Philosophia 7: 239-253.
280 Gibbard, A. F. 1979. Disparate Goods and Rawls' Difference Principle: A Social Choice Treatment. TAD 11: 267-288.
281 Goff, E. L. 1983. Justice as Fairness: The Practice of Social Science in a Rawlsian Model. SR 50: 81-97.
282 Green, P. 1985. Equality since Rawls: Objective Philosophers, Subjective Citizens and Rational Choice. JOP 47: 972-997.
283 Hamilton, V. L.; Rytina, S. 1980. Social Consensus on Norms of Justice: Should the Punishment Fit the Crime? AJS 85: 1117-1144.
284 Harsanyi, J. C. 1985. Rule Utilitarianism, Equality and Justice. SPAP 2: 115-127.
285 Heath, W. C. 1988. Von Neumann-Morgenstern Decision Markets and Harsanyi's Theory of Justice. AJEAS 47: 355-362.
286 Howe, R. E.; Roemer, J. E. 1981. Rawlsian Justice as the Core of a Game. AER 71: 880-895.
287 International Political Science Review. 1994. Papers on Biology and Justice. IPSR 15 (4).
288 International Social Science Journal. 1990. Papers on Rawls' Theory of Justice. ISSJ 42 (2).
289 Jasso, G. 1994. Assessing Individual and Group Differences in the Sense of Justice: Framework and Application to Gender Differences in the Justice of Earnings. SSR 23: 368-406.
290 Jones, P. 1995. Two Conceptions of Liberalism, Two Conceptions of Justice. BJPS 25: 515-550.
291 Journal of Law and Society. 1988. Papers on Democracy and Social Justice. JLAS 15 (1).
292 Journal of Social Issues. 1975. Papers on the Justice Motive in Social Behavior. JSI 31 (3).
293 -. 1990. Papers on Moral Exclusion and Injustice. JSI 46 (1).
294 Laden, A. 1991. Games, Fairness and Rawls' Theory of Justice. PAPA 20: 189-222.
295 Lane, R. E. 1986. Market Justice, Political Justice. APSR 80: 383-403.
296 Lissowski, G.; Swistak, P. 1995. Choosing the Best Social Order: New Principles of Justice and Normative Dimensions of Choice. APSR 89: 74-98.
297 Lissowski, G.; Tyszka, T.; Okrasa, W. 1991. Principles of Distributive Justice. JCR 35: 98-119.
298 Miller, J. G.; Bersoff, D. M. 1992. Culture and Moral Judgment: How Are Conflicts between Justice and Interpersonal Responsibilities Resolved? JPSP 62: 541-554.
299 Neal, P. 1990. Justice as Fairness: Political or Metaphysical? PT 18: 24-50.
300 Opotow, S. 1990. Moral Exclusion and Injustice. JSI 46: 1-20.
301 Rabin, M. 1993. Incorporating Fairness into Game Theory and Economics. AER 83: 1281-1302.
302 Rasinski, K. A. 1987. Value Differences Underlying Public Views about Social Justice. JPASP 53: 201-211.
303 -. 1988. Economic Justice, Political Behavior and American Political Values. Social Justice Review 2: 61-79.
304 Rawls, J. 1985. Justice as Fairness: Political Not Metaphysical. PAPA 14: 223-251.

305 Reynolds, D. R.; Shelley, F. M. 1985. Procedural Justice and Local Democracy. PG 4: 267-288.

306 Ricoeur, P. 1990. On John Rawls' A Theory of Justice: Is a Procedural Theory of Justice Possible? ISSJ 42: 553-564.

307 Rothstein, B. 1992. Social Justice and State Capacity. PAS 20: 101-126.

308 Samuels, W. J. 1981. Maximization of Wealth as Justice: Posnerian Law and Economics as Policy Analysis. TLR 59: 147-172.

309 Sen, A. K. 1985. Social Choice and Justice. JEL 33: 1764-1806.

310 Social Theory and Practice. 1974. Papers on Rawls' Theory of Justice. STAP 3 (1).

311 Soltan, K. E. 1982. Empirical Studies of Distributive Justice. Ethics 92: 673-691.

312 Stolte, J. F. 1987. The Formation of Justice Norms. ASR 52: 774-784.

313 Suzumura, K. 1981. On the Possibility of Fair Collective Choice Rules. IER 22: 351-364.

314 -. 1982. Equity, Efficiency and Rights in Social Choice. MSS 3: 131-155.

315 Svensson, L. G. 1989. Fairness, the Veil of Ignorance and Social Choice. SCAW 6: 1-17.

316 Thibaut, J., et al. 1974. Procedural Justice as Fairness. SLR 26: 1271-1289.

317 Tyler, T. R. 1988. What Is Procedural Justice? Criteria Used by Citizens to Assess the Fairness of Legal Procedures. LASR 22: 103-136.

318 Warr, M. 1981. Which Norms of Justice? AJS 87: 433-437.

319 Webster, M.; Smith, L. R. F. 1978. Justice and Revolutionary Coalitions. AJS 84: 267-292.

320 Wittman, D. 1979. A Diagrammatic Exposition of Justice. TAD 11: 207-237.

321 Young, I. M. 1992. Recent Theories of Justice. STAP 18: 63-80.

322 Zuckert, M. 1981. Justice Deserted: Critique of Rawls' A Theory of Justice. Polity 13: 466-483.

Norms

323 Allison, P. D. 1992. The Cultural Evolution of Beneficent Norms. SR 71: 279-302.

324 Arce, D. G. 1994. Stability Criteria for Social Norms with Application to the Prisoner's Dilemma. JCR 28: 749-765.

325 Asher, H. B. 1973. The Learning of Legislative Norms. APSR 67: 499-513.

326 Axelrod, R. 1986. An Evolutionary Approach to Norms. APSR 80: 1095-1112.

327 Bernick, E. L.; Wiggins, C. W. 1983. Legislative Norms in Eleven States. LSQ 8: 191-200.

328 Bettenhausen, K.; Murnighan, J. K. 1985. Emergence of Norms in Competitive Decision Making Groups. ASQ 30: 3783).

329 Binmore, K.; Samuelson, L. 1994. An Economists's Perspective on the Evolution of Norms. JITE 150: 45-63.

330 Congress and the Presidency. 1988. Papers on Congressional Norms. CAP 15 (2).

331 Crowe, E. W. 1983. Consensus and Structure in Legislative Norms: Party Discipline in the House of Commons. JOP 45: 907-931.

332 Ethics. 1990. Papers on Norms in Social Theory. Vol 100 (4).

333 Fiore, W.; Brunk, G. G.; Meyer, C. K. 1992. Norms of Professional Behavior in Highly Specialized Organizations. AAS 24: 81-99.

334 George, A. L. 1986. US-Soviet Global Rivalry: Norms of Competition. JPR 23: 247-262.

335 Gibbard, A. F. 1985. Moral Judgment and the Acceptance of Norms. Ethics 96: 5-21.

336 Hebert, F. T.; McLemore, L. E. 1973. Character and Structure in Legislative Norms. AJPS 17: 506-527.

337 Heckathorn, D. D. 1988. Collective Sanctions and the Creation of Prisoner's Dilemma Norms. AJS 94: 535-562.

338 Heldrich, A. 1983. The Deluge of Norms. Boston College International and Comparative Law Review 6: 377-390.

339 Huang, P. H.; Wu, H. M. 1994. More Order without More Law: A Theory of Social Norms and Organizational Cultures. JOLEAO 10: 390-406.

340 International Political Science Review. 1982. Papers on Norms and Values. IPSR 3 (2).

341 Kaufmann, P. J.; Sterm, L. W. 1988. Rational Exchange Norms: Perceptions of Unfairness and Retained Hostility in Commercial Litigation. JCR 32: 534-552.

342 Kegley, C. W.; Raymond, G. A. 1986. Normative Constraints on the Use of Force Short of War. JPR 23: 213-228.

343 Loewenberg, G.; Mans, T. C. 1988. Individual and Structural Influences on the Perception of Legislative Norms. AJPS 32: 155-177.

344 Onuf, N. G., Peterson, V. S. 1984. Thrasymmachos Revisited: On the Relevance of Norms and the Study of Law for International Relations. JIA 37: 343-356.

345 Panning, W. H. 1982. Rational Choice and Congressional Norms. WPQ 35: 193-203.

346 Rohde, D. W. 1988. Studying Congressional Norms. CAP 15: 139-146.

347 Roth, B. M. 1979. Competing Norms of Distribution in Coalition Games. JCR 23: 513-537.

348 Schneider, S. K. 1992. Governmental Response to Disasters: The Conflict between Bureaucratic Procedures and Emergent Norms. PAR 52: 135-145.

349 Schneier, E. V. 1988. Norms and Folkways in Congress: How Much Has Actually Changed? CAP 15: 117-138.

350 Singer, J. D. 1986. Normative Constraints on Hostility between States. JPR 23: 209-212.

351 Steiner, J.; Lehnen, R. G. 1974. Political Status and Norms of Decision Making. CPS 7: 84-106.

352 Thompson, K. W. 1987. From Illusions to Norms in International Relations. Society 25: 15-20.

353 Tunkin, G. I., et al. 1987. Role of Resolutions of International Organizations in Creating Norms of International Law. Coexistence 24: 5-47.

354 Walker, T. G.; Epstein, L.; Dixon, W. J. 1988. On the Mysterious Demise of Consensual Norms in the US Supreme Court. JOP 50: 371-389.

355 Ward, M. D.; Rajmaira, S. 1992. Reciprocity and Norms in US-Soviet Foreign Policy. JCR 36: 342-368.

356 Weingast, B. R. 1979. A Rational Choice Perspective on Congressional Norms. AJPS 23: 245-262.

357 Wlarwe, J. 1989. Wage Bargaining and Social Norms. AS 32: 113-136.

Public Ethics

358 American Behavioral Scientist. 1984. Papers on Lies, Secrets and Social Control. ABS 27 (4).

359 Amy, D. J. 1984. Why Policy Analysis and Ethics Are Incompatible. JPAM 3: 573-596.

360 Annals. 1995. Papers on Ethics in Public Service. ANNALS 537.

361 Becker, W. E. 1979. Professional Behavior Given a Stochastic Reward Structure. AER 69: 1010-1017.

362 Bell, R. 1985. Professional Values and Organizational Decision Making. AAS 17: 21-60.

363 Cava, A.; West, J.; Berman, E. M. 1995. Ethical Decision Making in Business and Government: Formal and Informal Strategies. Spectrum 68 (2): 28-36.

364 Donabedian, B. 1995. Self-Regulation and the Enforcement of Professional Codes. PC 85: 107-118.

365 Booth, W. J. 1994. On the Idea of the Moral Economy. APSR 88: 653-667.

366 Bowman, J. S. 1990. Ethics in Government: A National Survey of Public Administrators. PAR 50: 345-353.

367 Brady, F. N. 1981. Ethical Theory for the Public Administrator. ARPA 15: 119-126.

368 Brown, D. J. 1985. Business Ethics: Is Small Better? PSJ 13: 766-775.

369 Brown, J. G. 1989. Corporations' Incentives to Ethical Action. Bureaucrat 18: 43-44.

370 Brumbeck, G. B. 1991. Institutionalizing Ethics in Government. PPM 20: 353-366.

371 Brunk, G. G.; Secrest, D.; Tamashiro, H. 1990. Military Views of Morality and War. ISQ 34: 83-109.

372 Bureaucrat. 1975. Papers on Ethics in Government. Vol 4 (1).

373 Burtt, S. 1990. The Good Citizen's Psyche: The Psychology of Civic Virtue. Polity 23: 23-38.

374 California Law Review. 1989. Papers on Community and Moral Reasoning. CLR 77 (3).

375 Callahan, P. 1994. Taking International Ethics Seriously. JOP 56: 261-266.

376 Canadian Public Administration. 1991. Papers on Ethics in Government and Business. CPA 34 (1).

377 Carment, D. 1994. The Ethical Dimension in World Politics. TWQ 15: 551-582.

378 Ciulla, J. B. 1991. Why Is Business Talking about Ethics? CMR 34: 67-86.

379 Corruption and Reform. 1989. Papers on the Iran-Contra Affair. CAR 3 (2).

380 -. 1989. Papers on Political Scandals. CAR 3 (3).

381 Dwivedi, O. P. 1987. Moral Dimensions of Statecraft. CJPS 20: 699-710.

382 Feldman, D. 1987. Ethical Analysis in Public Policymaking. PSJ 15: 441-460.

383 Fischer, F. 1983. Ethical Discourse in Public Administration. AAS 15: 5-42.

384 Fishkin, J. 1979. Moral Principles and Public Policy. Daedalus 108: 55-68.

385 Goerner, E. A. 1983. The Political Ethics of the Rule of Law vs. the Political Ethics of the Rule of the Virtuous. ROP 45: 553-575.

386 Goldman, A. I. 1993. Ethics and Cognitive Science. Ethics 103: 337-360.

387 Golembiewski, R. T. 1993. Ethical Overlays in Public Management. Korean Journal of Public Administration 2: 67-92.

388 Goodin, R. E. 1989. The Political Impact of Moral Values. JPP 9: 241-260.

389 Gordon, J. W. 1986. Principled Organizational Dissent. Research in Organizational Behavior 8: 1-52.

390 Gross, M. L. 1994. The Collective Dimensions of Political Morality. POLST 42: 40-61.

391 Grumet, B. R. 1992. Critique of Ethics Laws. PPM 21: 313-322.

392 Gunn, E. M. 1981. Ethics and Public Service: Annotated Bibliography. PPM 10: 172-178.

393 Gutmann, A.; Thompson, D.F. 1990. Moral Conflict and Political Consensus. Ethics 101: 64-88.

394 Hanekom, S. X.; Bain, E. G. 1991. Moral Foundations for Public Service: Selected Indicators. SAIPA 26 (March): 36-47.

395 Hejka-Ekins, A. 1988. Teaching Ethics in Public Administration. PAR 48: 885-891

396 International Journal. 1988. Papers on Ethics and International Politics. IJ 43: 336-340.

397 International Political Science Review. 1988. Papers on Bureaucratic Morality. IPSR 9 (3).

398 Jackson, M. W. 1978. Ethics and Politics. IJPE 1: 347-358.

399 Janowitz, M. 1980. Observations on the Sociology of Citizenship: Obligations and Rights. SF 59: 1-24.

400 Johnson, M. 1991. Right and Wrong in British Politics: Fits of Morality in Comparative Perspective. Polity 24: 1-26.

401 Jos, P. H.; Tomkins, M. E.; Hays, S. W. 1989. In Praise of Difficult People. PAR 49: 552-561.

402 Journal of State Government. 1989. Papers on Ethics in Government. JSG 62 (5).

403 Kennen, G. F. 1985. Morality and Foreign Policy. FA 64: 205-218.

404 Kidder, R. L.; Hostetler, J. A. 1990. Managing Ideologies: Harmony as Ideology in Amish and Japanese Societies. LASR 24: 895-922.

405 Kloppenberg, J. T. 1987. The Virtues of Liberalism: Christianity, Republicanism and Ethics in Early American Political Discourse. Journal of American History 74: 9-33.

406 Klosko, G. 1990. The Moral Force of Political Obligations. APSR 84: 1235-1250.

407 Kreml, W. P.; Kegley, C. W. 1990. Restoring Ethics to Theory Building in International Relations. Alternatives 15: 155-176.

408 Kymlicka, W.; Norman, W. 1994. A Survey of Recent Work on Citizenship Theory. Ethics 104: 352-381.

409 Long, N. E. 1988. Public Administration, Ethics and Epistemology. ARPA 18: 111-118.

410 -. 1993. Ethics and Efficacy of Resignation in Public Administration. AAS 25: 3-11.

411 McConnell, M. W. 1989. The Role of Democratic Politics in Transforming Moral Convictions into Law. YLJ 98: 1501-1543.

412 McMahon, C. 1995. Political Theory of Organizations and Business Ethics. PAPA 24: 292-313.

413 McSwain, C. J.; White, O. F. 1987. The Case for Lying, Cheating and Stealing: Personal Development as Ethical Guidance for Managers. AAS 18: 411-432.

414 Menzel, D. C. 1992. Ethics, Attitudes and Behaviors in Local Governments. SALGR 24: 94-102.

415 Miceli, M. P.; Near, J. P.; Schwenk, C. R. 1991. Who Blows the Whistle and Why? ILRR 45: 113-130.

416 Miceli, M. P.; Roach, B. L.; Near, J. P. 1988. The Motivation of Anonymous Whistle Blowers. POQ 17: 281-296.

417 Monroe, K. R.; Epperson, C. 1994. Choice, Identity and a Cognitive-Perceptual Theory of Ethical Political Behavior. PP 15: 201-226.

418 Murphy, P. R. 1983. Moralities, Rule Choice and the Universal Legislator. SR 50: 757-802.

419 Murphy, P. R.; Smith, J. E.; Daley, J. M. 1991. Ethical Behavior of US General Freight Carriers. LATR 27: 55-72.

420 Nardin, T. 1989. The Problem of Relativism in International Ethics. Millennium 18: 149-162.

421 Neckel, S. 1989. Power and Legitimacy in Political Scandals. CAR 4: 147-158.

422 Newman, J. O. 1984. Between Legal Realism and Neutral Principles: Legitimacy of Institutional Values. CLR 72: 200-216.

423 Obler, J. 1986. Moral Duty and the Welfare State. WPQ 39: 213-235.

424 Owen, D. 1982. The Moral Basis of Politics. AUSQ 54: 346-361.

425 Perry, J. S.; Wise, L. R. 1990. Motivational Bases of Public Service. PAR 50: 367-373.

426 Public Personnel Management. 1981. Papers on Ethics in Government. PPM 10 (1).

427 Richardson, W. D.; Nigro, L. G. 1991. Constitution and Administrative Ethics. AAS 23: 275-287.

428 Robinson, W. P. 1993. Lying in the Public Domain. ABS 36: 359-382.

429 Rohr, J. A. 1988. Bureaucratic Morality in the US. IPSR 9: 167-178.

430 Rossum, R. A. 1984. Government and Ethics: The Constitutional Foundation. TPS 11: 100-105.

431 Schelling, T. C. 1981. Economic Reasoning and the Ethics of Policy. PI 63: 37-61.

432 Schwartz, M. 1991. Politics as Moral Causes. CSR 4: 65-90.

433 Social Research. 1974. Papers on Citizenship. SR 41 (4).

434 Spectrum. 1993. Papers on the Politics of Ethics. Vol 66 (1).

435 Stewart, D. W. 1991. Theoretical Foundations of Ethics in Administration. AAS 23: 357-373.

436 Stoker, L. 1992. Interests and Ethics in Politics. APSR 86: 369-380.

437 Texas Law Review. 1981. Papers on Ethical Codes and the Legal Profession. TLR 59 (4).

438 Thomas, D., et al. 1983. Moral Reasoning and Political Obligation: Cognitive Development Correlates. IJPE 6: 223-244.

439 Thompson, D. F. 1980. Moral Responsibility of Public Officials. APSR 74: 905-916.

440 -. 1985. Possibility of Administrative Ethics. PAR 45: 555-561.

441 Thompson, K. W. 1980. Ethics of Major American Foreign Policies. BJPS 6: 111-124.

442 -. 1984. The Ethical Dimensions of Diplomacy. ROP 46: 367-357.

443 Vogel, D. 1992. Globalization of Business Ethics: Why America Remains Distinctive. CMR 35 (Fall): 30-49.

444 Weigel, G. 1987. Exorcising Wilson's Ghost: Morality and Foreign Policy. WQ 10: 31-44.

445 Wilson, J. Q. 1985. Rediscovery of Character: Private Virtue and Public Policy. PI 81: 3-16.

446 Wilson, R. W. 1983. Moral Development and Political Change. WP 36: 53-75.

447 Winter, J. A. 1970. On the Mixing of Morality and Politics: A Test of the Weberian Hypothesis. SF 49: 36-40.

448 Wolfe, A. 1989. Market, State and Society as Codes of Moral Obligation. AS 32: 221-236.

449 Wood, M.; Hughes, M. 1984. The Moral Basis of Moral Reform: Status Discontent vs. Culture and Socialization Explanations of Anti-Pornography Social Movement. ASR 49: 86-99.

Tolerance

450 Alozie, N. O. 1995. The Political Tolerance Hypotheses and White Opposition to a Martin Luther King Holiday in Arizona. SSJ 32: 1-16.

451 Beatty, K. M.; Walter, B. O. 1984. Religious Preference and Practice: Political Tolerance. POQ 48: 318-329.

452 Bobo, L.; Licari, F. 1989. Education and Political Tolerance: Testing the Effects of Cognitive Sophistication and Target Group Affect. POQ 53: 285-308.

453 Davis, D. W. 1995. Exploring Black Political Intolerance. PB 17: 1-22.

454 Deutsch, M. 1990. Psychological Roots of Moral Exclusion. JSI 46: 21-25.

455 Ferrar, J. W. 1976. The Dimensions of Tolerance. PSR 19: 63-81.

456 Gassholt, O.; Togeby, L. 1995. Interethnic Tolerance, Education and Political Orientation. PB 17: 265-286.

457 Gibson, J. L. 1987. Homosexuals and the Ku Klux Klan: A Contextual Analysis of Political Tolerance. WPQ 40: 427-448.

458 -. 1988. Political Intolerance and Political Repression during the McCarthy Red Scare. APSR 82: 511-529.

459 -. 1989. Policy Consequences of Political Intolerance: Political Repression during the Vietnam War Era. JOP 51: 13-35.

460 -. 1992. Alternative Measures of Political Tolerance. AJPS 36: 560-577.

461 -. 1992. The Political Consequences of Intolerance: Cultural Conformity and Political Freedom. APSR 86: 338-356.

462 Gibson, J. L.; Duch, R. M. 1991. Elite Theory and Political Intolerance in Western Europe. PB 13: 191-212.

463 -. 1993. Political Intolerance in the USSR. CPS 26: 286-329.

464 Golebiowska, E. A. 1995. Individual Value Priorities, Education and Political Tolerance. PB 17: 23-48.

465 Government and Opposition. 1971. Papers on Tolerance. GAO 6 (2).

466 Green, D. P.; Waxman, L. M. 1987. Direct Threat and Political Tolerance: The Tolerance of Blacks toward Racism. POQ 51: 149-165.

467 Jackman, M. R. 1977. Prejudice, Tolerance and Attitudes toward Ethnic Groups. SSR 6: 145-169.

468 -. 1978. General and Applied Tolerance: Does Education Increase Commitment to Racial Integration? AJPS 22: 302-324.

469 Kautz, S. 1993. Liberalism and Toleration. AJPS 37: 610-632.

470 Kuklinski, J. H., et al. 1991. Cognitive and Affective Bases of Political Tolerance Judgements. AJPS 35: 1-27.

471 Margolis, M.; Haque, K. E. 1981. Applied Tolerance or Fear of Government? AJPS 25: 241-255.

472 McClosky, H.; Brill, A. 1984. Influences on Tolerance: Understanding the Rights and Claims of Others. Micropolitics 3: 253-280.

473 Mueller, J. E. 1988. Trends in Political Tolerance. POQ 52: 1-25.

474 Shamir, M. 1991. Political Intolerance among Masses and Elites in Israel: A Reexamination of the Elitist Theory of Democracy. JOP 53: 1018-1043.

475 Sniderman, P. M., et al. 1989. Principled Tolerance and the US Mass Public. BJPS 19: 25-46.

476 Steiber, S. R. 1980. The Influence of the Religious Factor on Civil and Sacred Tolerance. SF 58: 811-832.

477 Sullivan, J. L., et al. 1979. The Development of Political Tolerance. IJPE 2: 115-140.

478 -. 1981. Sources of Political Tolerance. APSR 75: 92-106.

479 -. 1984. Political Intolerance and Structure of Mass Attitudes. CPS 17: 319-350.

480 -. 1993. Why Politicians Are More Tolerant: Selective Recruitment and Socialization among Political Elites. BJPS 23: 51-76.

481 Sullivan, J. L.; Piereson, J. E.; Marcus, G. E. 1979. An Alternative Conceptualization of Political Tolerance. APSR 73: 781-794.

482 Williams, J. A.; Nunn, C. Z.; St. Peter, L. 1976. Origins of Tolerance. SF 55: 394-418.

483 Wilson, T. C. 1985. Urbanism and Tolerance. ASR 50: 117-123.

484 -. 1994. Trends in Tolerance toward Rightist and Leftist Groups. POQ 58: 539-556.

INTERNATIONAL RELATIONS

1 Agnew, J. A. 1983. Political Geography of American Foreign Policy. PG 2: 151-166.
2 Alker, H. R. 1966. The Long Road to International Relations Theory. WP 18: 623-655.
3 Alt, J. E.; Calvert, R. L.; Humes, B. D. 1988. Reputation and Hegemonic Stability: Game Theoretic Analysis. APSR 82: 445-466.
4 Anderson, P. A.; Thorson, S. J. 1982. Artificial Intelligence Based Simulations of Foreign Policy Decision Making. BS 27: 176-193.
5 Annals. 1970. Papers on Political Intelligence. ANNALS 388.
6 -. 1971. Papers on IR Propaganda. ANNALS 398.
7 -. 1989. Papers on Peace Studies. ANNALS 504.
8 -. 1995. Papers on IR Negotiation. ANNALS 542.
9 Anton, J. J.; Yao, D. A. 1990. Measuring the Effectiveness of Competition in Defense Procurement. JPAAM 9: 60-79.
10 Archibugi, D. 1993. Reform of the UN and Cosmopolitan Democracy. JPR 30: 301-316.
11 Art, R. 1972. Bureaucratic Politics and American Foreign Policy. PSCI 4: 467-490.
12 Ashley, R. K. 1987. Geopolitics of Geopolitical Space: Toward a Critical Social Theory of International Politics. Alternatives 12: 403-434.
13 Axelrod, R. 1977. Argumentation in Foreign Policy Settings. JCR 21: 727-755.
14 Baldwin, D. A. 1979. Power Analysis in World Politics. WP 31: 161-194.
15 Benjamin, R. W.; Edinger, L. 1971. Conditions for Military Control over Foreign Policy Decisions in Major States. JCR 15: 5-32.
16 Bennett, P. G. 1995. Modelling Decisions in International Relations: Game Theory and Beyond. ISQ 39: 19-52.
17 Bercovitch, J.; Langley, J. 1993. Nature of the Dispute and the Effectiveness of International Mediation. JCR 37: 670-691.
18 Boettcher, W. A. 1995. Prospect Theory in International Relations. JCR 39: 561-583.
19 Bonham, G. M.; Shapiro, M. J.; Nozicka, G. J. 1976. Cognitive Process Model of Foreign Policy Decision Making. SAG 7: 123-152.
20 Buzan, B. 1984. Economic Structure and International Security. IO 38: 597-624.
21 Carlsnaes, W. 1993. On Analyzing the Dynamics of Foreign Policy Change. CAC 28: 5-30.
22 Coexistence 1984. Papers on Images and Tensions in International Relations. Vol 21 (3).
23 Cooperation and Conflict. 1981. Papers on Forecasts in Foreign Policy. CAC 16 (1).
24 Cox, R. 1983. Gramsci, Hegemony and International Relations Theory. Millenium 10: 126-155.
25 -. 1994. Rethinking the End of the Cold War. RIS 20: 187-200.
26 Crumm, E. M. 1995. Value of Economic Incentives in International Politics. JPR 32: 313-330.
27 De Dreu, C. K. W. 1995. Coercive Power and Concession Making in Bilateral Negotiation. JCR 39: 646-670.
28 Development. 1989. Papers on Multilateralism. Vol 1989 (4).
29 -. 1991. Papers on International Cooperation. Vol 1991 (2).
30 Dixon, W. J. 1994. Democracy and the Peaceful Settlement of International Conflict. APSR 88: 14-32.
31 Doxey, M. 1972. International Sanctions: A Framework for Analysis with Reference to the UN and Southern Africa. IO 26: 525-550.
32 Doyle, M. W. 1986. Liberalism and World Politics. APSR 80: 1151-1169.
33 Druckman, D.; Harris, R. 1990. Alternative Models of Responsiveness in International Negotiation. JSR 34: 234-251.
34 East, M. A. 1973. Size and Foreign Policy Behavior. WP 25: 556-576.
35 Edelstein, M. 1990. What Price Cold War? Military Spending and Private Investment in the US. CJE 14: 421-437.
36 Eriksen, T. H.; Neumann, I. B. 1993. International Relations as a Cultural System. CAC 28: 233-264.
37 Etheredge, L. S. 1978. Personality Effects on American Foreign Policy: A Test of Interpersonal Generalization Theory. APSR 72: 434-451.
38 Etudes Internationales. 1989. Papers on Strategic Studies. EINT 20 (3).
39 Fischhoff, B. 1983 Strategic Policy Preferences: Decision Theory Perspective. JSI 39: 133-160.
40 Frost, M. 1994. The Role of Normative Theory in International Relations. Millennium 23: 109-118.
41 Futures. 1994. Papers on the End of Strategy. Vol 26 (4).
42 Gaddis, J. L. 1992. International Relations Theory and the End of the Cold War. IS 17 (3): 5-58.
43 Gallhofer, I.N.; Saris, W. E.; Vogt, R. 1994. From Individual Preferences to Group Decisions in Foreign Policy Decision Making. EJPR 25: 151-170.
44 Galtung, J. 1967. On the Effects of International Economic Sanctions with Examples for Rhodesia. WP 19: 378-416.
45 Goldstein, J. S. 1995. Great Power Cooperation under Conditions of Limited Reciprocity. ISQ 39: 453-478.

46 Goldstein, J. S.; Freeman, J. R. 1991 US-Soviet-Chinese Relations: Routine, Reciprocity, or Rational Expectations? APSR 85: 17-35.

47 Grunberg, I. 1990. Exploring the Myth of Hegemonic Stability. IO 44: 431-477.

48 Haas, M. 1987. The Comparative Study of Foreign Policy. ISN 13: 69-74.

49 Halliday, F. 1995. International Relations and Its Discontent. IA 71: 733-746.

50 Harriott, H. H. 1993. The Dilemmas of Democracy and Foreign Policy. JPR 30: 219-226.

51 Henrikson, A. K. 1980. Geographical Mental Maps of American Foreign Policy Makers. IPSR 1: 495-530.

52 Hermann, M. G. 1980. Explaining Foreign Policy Behavior Using the Personality Characteristics of Political Leaders. ISQ 24: 3-46.

53 Hill, K. A. 1993. Domestic Sources of Foreign Policymaking: South Africa. ISQ 37: 195-214.

54 Holsti, K. J. 1971. International Relations Theory, 1945-1970. CJPS 4: 165-177.

55 Hutchings, K. 1992. The Possibility of Judgement: Moralizing and Theorizing in International Relations. RIS 18: 51-62.

56 International Affairs of Great Britain. 1986. Papers on the Study of International Relations. Vol 62 (2).

57 International Journal. 1970. Papers on the United Nations. IJ 25 (2).

58 -. 1971. Papers on Strategic Studies. IJ 26 (4).

59 -. 1975. Papers on Diplomatic Method. IJ 30 (1).

60 -. 1977. Papers on Foreign Affairs Images. IJ 32 (3).

61 -. 1977. Papers on Prediction in Foreign Policy. IJ 32 (4).

62 -. 1980. Papers on Superpower Diplomacy. IJ 35 (3).

63 -. 1986. Papers on the Foreign Policy of Federal States. IJ 41 (3).

64 -. 1989. Papers on International Prenegotiation. IJ 44 (2).

65 -. 1990. Papers on Multilateralism. IJ 45 (4).

66 -. 1991. Papers on Regional Powers. IJ 46 (3).

67 -. 1992. Papers on New Isolationism. IJ 48 (1).

68 -. 1995. Papers on Peacekeeping. IJ 50 (2).

69 International Organization. 1977. Papers on the Foreign Economic Policies of Advanced Industrial Societies. IO 31 (4).

70 -. 1984. Papers on the New Realism. Vol 38 (2).

71 -. 1986. Papers on International Disturbances. IO 40 (2).

72 -. 1986. Papers on International Organization. IO 40 (4).

73 -. 1992. Papers on International Policy Coordination. IO 46 (1).

74 -. 1994. Papers the on End of the Cold War. IO 48 (2).

75 International Political Science Review. 1982. Papers on Mathematical Theory in International Relations. IPSR 3 (4).

76 -. 1990. Papers on Global Policy Studies. IPSR 11 (3).

77 -. 1978. Papers on Territoriality Politics. ISSJ 30 (1).

78 International Security. 1995. Papers on Strategic Culture. IS 19 (4).

79 International Social Science Journal. 1995. Papers on Organizing International Relations. ISSJ 47 (2).

80 International Studies. 1981. Papers on Non-Alignment. Vol 20 (1/2).

81 International Studies Notes. 1981. Papers on Intelligence and Counterintelligence. ISN 8 (3/4).

82 -. 1984. Papers on Secretaries of State. ISSJ 11 (1).

83 -. 1986. Papers on International Studies. ISN 12 (2) and 1991 16/17 (3/1).

84 -. 1987. Papers on Comparative Foreign Policy. ISN 13 (2).

85 -. 1993. Papers on Teaching International Relations. ISN 18 (3).

86 International Studies Quarterly. 1977. Papers on International Politics and Security. ISQ 21 (4).

87 -. 1990. Papers on International Studies. ISQ 34 (3).

88 Intriligator, M. D. 1982. Research on Conflict Theory. JCR 26: 307-327.

89 Isard, W. 1979. A Definition of Peace Science. JOPS 4: 1-47, 97-132.

90 Jerusalem Journal. 1987. Papers on Ideology in International Relations. JJIR 9 (1).

91 Journal of Conflict Resolution. 1972. Papers on Peace Research. JCR 16 (4).

92 -. 1991. Papers on Democracy and Foreign Policy. JCR 35 (2).

93 Journal of International Affairs. 1990. Papers on Theory and Value in International Relations. JIA 44 (1).

94 Journal of Peace Research. 1969. Papers on Peace Research in History. JPR 1969 (4).

95 -. 1981. Papers on Theories of Peace. JPR 18 (2).

96 -. 1986. Papers on Peace Movements. JPR 23 (2).

97 -. 1991. Papers on International Mediation. JPR 28 (1).

98 Journal of Social Issues. 1988. Papers on Psychology and the Promotion of Peace. JSI 44 (2).

99 Kacowicz, A. M. 1995. Explaining Zones of Peace: Democracies as Satisfied Powers? JPR 32: 265-276.

100 Kapstein, E. B. 1995. Is Realism Dead? The Domestic Sources of International Politics. IO 49: 751-774.

101 Keenes, E. 1988. Paradigms of International Relations: Bringing Politics Back In. IJ 44: 41-67.

102 Kegley, C. W. 1994. How Did the Cold War Die? ISQ 38 (April Sup): 11-42.

103 Keohane, R. O.; Nye, J. S. 1987. Power and Interdependence Revisited. IO 41: 725-753.

104 Kleiboer, M.; 't Hart, P. 1995. Multiple Perspectives on Timing of International Mediation. CAC 30: 307-348.

105 Kubalkova, V. 1992. Post-Cold War Geopolitics of Knowledge: International Studies in the Former Soviet Bloc. SCC 25: 405-418.

106 Kugler, J.; Arbetman, M. 1989. Exploring the Phoenix Factor with the Collective Goods Perspective. JCR 33: 84-112.

107 Kugler, J.; Domke, W. 1986. Comparing the Strength of Nations. CPS 19: 39-69.

108 Lepgold, J.; McKeown, T. 1995. Is American Foreign Policy Exceptional? PSCQ 110: 369-384.

109 Levy, J. S. 1994. Learning and Foreign Policy. IO 48: 279-312.

110 Lijphart, A. 1974. The Theoretical Revolution in International Relations. ISQ 18: 41-74.

111 Little, R. 1991. International Relations and the Methodological Turn. POLST 39: 463-478.

112 Maoz, Z. 1983. A Behavioral Model of Dispute Escalation. IR 10: 373-399.

113 -. 1983. Resolve, Capabilities and the Outcome of Interstate Disputes. JCR 27: 195-229.

114 Marlin-Bennett, R.; Roberts, J. C. 1993. Using Events Data to Identify International Processes. ISN 18: 1-8.

115 Martin, L. L. 1992. Interests, Power and Multilateralism. IO 46: 765-792.

116 McCormick, J. M.; Black, M. 1983. Ideology and Senate Voting on the Panama Canal Treaties. LSQ 8: 45-63.

117 McCormick, J. M.; Wittkopf, E. R. 1990. Bipartisanship, Partisanship and Ideology in Congressional-Executive Foreign Policy Relations. JOP 52: 1077-1100.

118 Millennium. 1987. Papers on the Study of International Relations. Vol 16 (2).

119 —. 1988. Papers on Philosophical Traditions in International Relations. Vol 17 (2).

120 —. 1993. Papers on Culture in International Relations. Vol 22 (3).

121 Miller, B. 1992. Explaining Great Power Cooperation in Conflict Management. WP 45: 1-46.

122 Miner, H. 1991. The Assumption of Anarchy in International Relations Theory. ISQ 17: 67-85.

123 Modelski, G. 1970. The World's Foreign Ministers. JCR 14: 135-176.

124 Moore, D. W. 1974. Foreign Policy and Empirical Democratic Theory. APSR 68: 1192-1197.

125 Morrow, J. D. 1988. Social Choice and System Structure in World Politics. WP 41: 45-97.

126 Neufeld, M. 1995. Critical Intervention: New Directions in International Relations Theory. IJ 51: 148 ff.

127 New York University Journal. Papers on Nationalism. NYUJ 26 (3).

128 Niou, E. M. S.; Ordeshook, P. C. 1991. Realism vs. Neoliberalism. AJPS 35: 481-511.

129 Nollkaemper, A. 1992. On the Effectiveness of International Rules. AP 27: 49-70.

130 Nye, J. S.; Lynn-Jones, S. M. 1988. International Security Studies. IS 12 (Spring): 5-27).

131 Orbis. 1983. Papers on Intelligence and Crisis Forecasting. Vol 26 (4).

132 —. 1988. Papers on Foreign Policy Instiitutions. Vol 32 (2).

133 Orme-Johnson, D. W., et al. 1988. The International Peace Project in the Middle East: Effects of Maharishi Technology of the Unified Field. JCR 32: 776-812.

134 Oseth, J. M. 1984. Intelligence and Low Intensity Conflict. Naval War College Review (Nov/Dec): 19-36.

135 Ostrom, C. W. 1977. Evaluating Alternative Foreign Policy Decision Making Models: Arms Race and Organizational Politics. JCR 21: 235-266.

136 Ougaard, M. 1988. Dimensions of Hegemony. CAC 23: 197-214.

137 Peace Research Reviews. 1969. Papers on Simulation in International Relations. PRR 3 (6).

138 —. 1972. Papers on Peace Research. PRR 4 (4).

139 —. 1975. Papers on National Patterns in International Organizations. PRR 6 (4-6).

140 —. 1978. Papers on Empirical Studies of the United Nations. PRR 7 (4-5).

141 —. 1984. Papers on Peace Research. PRR 9 (6).

142 —. 1988. Papers on Municipal Peace Actions. PRR 11 (2).

143 Policy Studies Journal. 1974. Papers on Foreign Policy. PSJ 3 (2).

144 —. 1979. Papers on Security Policy Modeling. PSJ 8 (1).

145 Political Psychology. 1991. Papers on Judgment in International Politics. PP 13 (3).

146 Powell, R. 1991. Absolute and Relative Gains in International Relations Theory. APSR 80: 1151-1169.

147 —. 1994. Anarchy in International Relations Theory: Neorealist-Neoliberal Debate. IO 48: 313-344.

148 Price, R. 1995. A Genealogy of the Chemical Weapons Taboo. IO 49: 73-104.

149 PS. 1985. Papers on International Economic Sanctions. Vol 18 (4).

150 Publius. 1984. Papers on Federated States and International Relations. Vol 14 (4).

151 Putnam, R. D. 1988. Diplomacy and Domestic Politics: Two Level Games. IO 42: 427-460.

152 Quandt, W. B. 1986. The Electoral Cycle and the Conduct of Foreign Policy. PSCQ 101: 825-838.

153 Raphael, T. D. 1982. Integrative Complexity Theory and Forecasting International Crises: Berlin. JCR 26: 423-450.

154 Rasler, K. A.; Thompson, W. R.; Chester, K. M. 1980. Foreign Policy Makers, Personality Attributes and Interviews. ISQ 24: 47-74.

155 Richardson, J. L. 1994. The State of International Relations Theory. AUSJPS 29: 179 ff.

156 Ripley, B. 1993. Psychology, Foreign Policy and International Relations Theory. PP 14: 403-416.

157 Risse-Kappen, T. 1994 Ideas Do Not Free Float Freely: Transnational Coalitions, Domestic Structures and the End of the Cold War. IO 48: 185-214.

158 Rogowski, R. 1983. Structure, Growth and Power: Three Rationalist Accounts. IO 37: 713-738.

159 Rosenberg, J. 1994 International Relations Theory and Classic Social Analysis. Millennium 23: 109-118.

160 Rothstein, R. L. 1988. Epitaph for a Monument to a Failed Protest? A North-South Retrospective. IO 42: 725-748.

161 Ruggie, J. G. 1992. Multilateralism. IO 46: 561-598.

162 Rummel, R. J. 1969. Forecasting International Relations. Technological Forecasting 1: 197-216.

163 —. 1969. Indicators of Cross-National and International Patterns. APSR 63: 127-147.

164 —. 1969. Some Empirical Findings of Nations and Their Behavior. WP 21: 226-241.

165 —. 1995. Democracy, Power, Genocide and Mass Murder. JCR 39: 3-26.

166 Russell, G. 1988. The Ethics of Statescraft. JOP 50: 503-517.

167 Russett, B.; Sullivan, J. D. 1971. Collective Goods and International Organization. IO 29: 845-865.

168 Schmiegelow, H. 1989. Idealism and Realism in US Foreign Policy. Aussenpolitik 40: 15-29.

169 Schrodt, P. A. 1990. A Methodological Critique of a Test of the Effects of the Maharishi Technology of the Unified Field. JCR 34: 745-755.

170 Schroeder, P. W. 1977. Quantitative Studies in the Balance of Power. JCR 21: 3-22.

171 Shapiro, R. Y.; Page, B. I. 1988. Foreign Policy and the Rational Public. JCR 32: 211-247.

172 Shaw, T. M. 1994. The South in the New World (Dis)order: Political Economy of Third World Foreign Policy in the 1990s. TWQ 15: 17-30.

173 Shepard, G. H. 1988. Personality Effects on American Foreign Policy: Interpersonal Generalization Theory. ISQ 32: 91-123.

174 Shofield, N. J. 1972. A Typological Model of International Relations. PPRS 18: 93-112.

175 Singer, J. D. 1976. An Assessment of Peace Research. IS 1: 118-137.

176 —. 1986. Normative Constraints on Hostility between States. JPR 23: 209-212.

177 Singer, J. D.; Wallace, M. D. 1970. Intergovernmental Organizations and the Preservation of Peace. IO 24: 520-547.

178 Small, M. 1976. Application of Quantitative International Politics to Diplomatic History. Historian 38: 281-304.

179 Smith, S. 1983. Foreign Policy Analysis: British and American Orientations and Methodologies. POLST 31: 556-565.

180 —. 1983. The Study of International Relations: Geographical and Methodological Divisions. ISN 10: 8-10.

181 —. 1987. Paradigm Dominance in International Relations. Millennium 16: 189-206.

182 Snidal, D. 1985. Game Theory of International Politics. WP 38: 25-57.

183 —. 1991. Relative Gains and International Cooperation. APSR 85: 1303-1320.

184 Snyder, G. H. 1971. Prisoner's Dilemma and Chicken Models in International Politics. ISQ 15: 66-103.

185 Social Research. 1975. Papers on Peace. SR 42 (1).

186 -. 1981. Papers on Hans Morgenthau. SR 48 (4).

187 Sofer, S. 1987. International Relations and the Invisibility of Ideology. Millennium 16: 489-520.

188 Soroos, M. S. 1977. Behavior between Nations. PRR 57: 1-107.

189 Spector, B. I. 1995. Creativity Heuristics for Impasse Resolution: Reframing Intractable Negotiations. ANNALS 542: 81-99.

190 Stoll, R. J. 1987. System and State in International Politics: A Computer Simulation of Balancing in an Anarchic World. ISQ 31: 387-402.

191 Teaching Political Science. 1987. Papers on Teaching about Security Studies. TPS 14 (3).

192 Tetlock, P. E. 1981. Personality and Isolationism: A Content Analysis of Senatorial Speeches. JPASP 41: 737-743.

193 -. 1985. Integrative Complexity of American and Soviet Foreign Policy Rhetoric. JPASP 49: 1565-1585.

194 -. 1988. Monitoring the Integrative Complexity of American and Soviet Policy Statements. JSI 44: 101-131.

195 Third World Quarterly. 1995. Papers on Nongovernmental Organizations, the United Nations and Global Governance. TWQ 16 (3).

196 Tollison, R. D.; Willett, T. D. 1979. An Economic Theory of Mutually Advantageous Issue Linkage in International Negotiations. IO 33: 425-450.

197 Troden, S. G. 1985. International Relations Theory. Political Science Review 24: 73-85.

198 Trubowitz, P. 1992. Sectionalism and American Foreign Policy. ISQ 36: 173-190.

199 Tsebelis, G. 1990. Are Sanctions Effective? A Game-Theoretic Approach. JCR 34: 3-28.

200 Vaubel, R. 1986. A Public Choice Approach to International Organization. PC 51: 39-57.

201 Vertzberger, Y. Y. I. 1986. Foreign Policy Decisionmakers as Practical-Intuitive Historians: Applied History and Its Shortcomings. ISQ 30: 223-247.

202 Verweij, M. 1995. Cultural Theory and Study of International Relations. Millennium 24: 87-112.

203 Wagner, R. H. 1993. What Was Bipolarity? IO 47: 77-106.

204 Walker, S. G. 1981. The Correspondence between Foreign Policy Rhetoric and Behavior: Role Theory and Exchange Behavior. BS 26: 272-280.

205 Wallace, M. D.; Singer, J. D. 1970. International Organization and the Global System. IO 24: 239-287.

206 Walt, S. M. 1991. Renaissance of Security Studies. ISQ 35: 211-239.

207 Ward, M. D.; House, L. L. 1988. A Theory of the Behavioral Power of Nations. JCR 32: 3-36.

208 Weingast, B. R. 1995. A Rational Choice Perspective on the Role of Ideas: Shared Belief Systems and State Sovereignty in International Cooperation. PAS 23: 449-464.

209 Wendt, A. 1991 Bridging the Theory-Meta Theory Gap in International Relations. RIS 17: 383-392.

210 -. 1994. Collective Identity Formation and the International State. APSR 88: 384-398.

211 Wright, M. 1987. An Anatomy of International Thought. RIS 13: 221-228.

212 Yaffe, M. D. 1994. Realism in Retreat? The New World Order and the Return of the Individual to International Relations Studies. POPS 23: 79-88.

213 Yost, D. S. 1994. Political Philosophy and the Theory of International Relations. IA 70: 263-290.

214 Yunker, J. A. 1989. An Economic Model of the East-West Confrontation. CMAPS 10: 1-20.

215 Zelikow, P. 1994. Foreign Policy Engineering. IS 18: 143-171.

216 Zinnes, D. A. 1980. Three Puzzles in Search of a Researcher. ISQ 24: 315-342.

Alliances

217 American Behavioral Scientist. 1995. Papers on Negotiation and Global Security. ABS 38 (6).

218 Boix, C.; Alt, J. E. 1990. Partisan Voting in the Spanish 1986 NATO Referendum: An Ecological Analysis. ES 10: 18-32.

219 Bueno de Mesquita, B.; Scarborough, G. I. 1988. Threat and Alliance Behavior. II 14: 85-93.

220 Conybeare, J. A. C.; Murdock, J. C.; Sandler, T. 1994. Alternative Collective Goods Models of Military Alliances. EI 32: 525-542.

221 Conybeare, J. A. C.; Sandler, T. 1990. The Triple Entente and the Triple Alliance: A Collective Goods Approach. APSR 84: 1197-1206.

222 David, S. R. 1991. Explaining Third World Alignment. WP 40: 233-256.

223 Etudes Internationales. 1992. Papers on Calling into Question Alliances. EINT 23 (1).

224 -. 1995. Papers on Multilateralism and Regional Security. EI 26 (4).

225 Faber, J.; Weaver, R. 1984. Participation in Conferences, Treaties, and Warfare in the European System. JCR 28: 522-534.

226 Goldstein, A. 1995. Discounting the Free Ride: Alliances and Security in the Postwar World. IO 49: 39-72.

227 Gulati, R. 1995. Social Structure and Alliance Formation Patterns. ASQ 40: 619-652.

228 Iusi Scarborough, G.; Bueno de Mesquita, B. 1988. Threat and Alignment Behavior. II 14: 85-93.

229 Journal of Applied Behavioral Science. 1991. Papers on Collaborative Alliances. JABS 27 (1).

230 Journal of International Affairs. 1989. Papers on US Alliance Management. JIA 43 (1).

231 Levy, J. S.; Barnett, M. 1992. Alliance Formation, Domestic Political Economy and Third World Security. JJIR 14:19-40.

232 Li, R. P. Y.; Thompson, W. R. 1978. The Stochastic Process of Alliance Formation Behavior. APSR 72: 1288-1303.

233 Lieshout, R. H. 1992. Theory of Games and Formation of Defensive Alliances. AP 27: 111-132.

234 Maoz, Z. 1995. National Preferences, International Structures, and Balance-of-Power Politics. JTP 7: 369-394.

235 McGinnis, M. D. 1990. A Rational Model of Regional Rivalry. ISQ 34: 111-135.

236 McGowan, P. J.; Rood, R. M. 1975. Alliance Behavior in Balance of Power Systems: Applying a Poisson Model to Nineteenth Century Europe. APSR 69: 859-870.

237 Morrow, J. D. 1991. Alliances and Asymmetry: An Alternative to the Capability Aggregation Model of Alliances. AJPS 35: 904-933.

238 -. 1993. Arms vs. Allies: Tradeoffs in the Search for Security. IO 47: 207-234.

239 Murdock, J. C.; Sandler, T. 1982. A Theoretical and Empirical Analysis of NATO. JCR 26: 237-263.

240 Niou, E. M. S.; Ordeshook, P. C. 1994. Alliances in Anarchic International Systems. ISQ 38: 167-192.

241 Olson, M.; Zeckhauserk, R. 1966. An Economic Theory of Alliances. REAS 48: 266-279.

242 Oneal, J. R. 1990. The Theory of Collective Action: NATO Defense Burdens. JCR 34: 426-448.

243 Oneal, J. R.; Elrod, M. A. 1989. NATO Burden Sharing and Forces of Change. ISQ 33: 435-456.

244 Oppenheimer, J. A. 1979. Collective Goods and Alliances. JCR 23: 387-407.

245 Oren, I. 1990. War Proneness of Alliances. JCR 34: 208-233.

246 Rothgeb, J. M. 1982. Contagion at the Sub-War Stage: Siding in the Cold War. CMAPS 6: 39-58.

247 Sandler, T. 1993. The Economic Theory of Alliances. JCR 37: 446-484.

248 Saperstein, A. M. 1992. Alliance Building vs. Independent Action: Non-Linear Modeling Approach to International Stability. JCR 36: 518-545.

249 Singer, J. D. 1966. National Alliance Commitments and War Involvement. PPRS 5: 109-140.

250 -. 1966. Formal Alliances. JPR 3: 1-32.

251 Singer, J. D.; Bueno de Mesquita, B. 1973. Alliances, Capabilities and War. Political Science Annual 4: 237-280.

252 Siverson, R. M.; Emmons, J. 1991. Democratic Political Systems and Alliance Choices. JCR 35: 285-306.

253 Siverson, R. M.; Tennefoss, M. R. 1984. Power, Alliance and the Escalation of International Conflict. APSR 78: 1057-1069.

254 Smith, A. 1995. Alliance Formation and War. ISQ 39: 405-426.

255 Sorokin, G. L. 1994. Alliance Formation and General Deterrence: A Game Theoretic Model of Israel. JCR 38: 298-325.

256 Synder, G. H. 1984. The Security Dilemma in Alliance Politics. WP 36: 461-495.

257 Thies, W. 1989. Crises and the Study of Alliance Politics. AFAS 15: 349-369.

258 Weber, S.; Wiesmeth, H. 1991. Economic Models of NATO. JPUBE 46: 181-187.

Arms Races

259 Anderton, C. H. 1985. Bibliography of Arms Race Models and Related Subjects. CMAPS 8: 99-122.

260 -. 1989. Arms Race Modeling. JCR 33: 346-367.

261 -. 1990. Teaching Arms Race Concepts. JEE 21: 148-166.

262 Annals. 1994. Papers on the Arms Trade. ANNALS 535.

263 Brams, S. J.; Davis, M. D.; Straffin, P.D. 1979. Geometry of the Arms Race. ISQ 23: 567-588.

264 Bueno de Mesquita, B.; Lalman, D. 1988. Arms Races and the Opportunity for Peace. Synthese 76: 263-283.

265 Chadwick, R. W. 1986. Richardson Processes and Arms Transfers. JPR 23: 309-328.

266 Contemporary Security Policy. 1994. Papers on Arms Control. Vol 15 (3), and 1995 16 (3).

267 -. 1995. Papers on Middle Eastern Arms Control. Vol 16 (1).

268 Coram, B. T. 1994. Problem of Predictability: Unstable Systems, Traffic Dividers and Arms Races. POLST 42: 5-14.

269 Correa, H.; Kim, J. W. 1992. A Causal Analysis of the Defense Expenditures of the USA and the USSR. JPR 29: 161-174.

270 Daedalus. 1975. Papers on Arms and Arms Control. Vol 104 (3) and 1985 114 (1-2).

271 Diehl, P. F. 1983. Arms Races and Escalation. JPR 20: 205-212.

272 -. 1985. Armaments without War. JCR 22: 249-259.

273 -. 1985. Arms Races to War. SQ 26: 331-349.

274 -. 1985. Contiguity and Military Escalation in Major Power Rivalries. JOP 47: 1203-1211.

275 Diehl, P. F.; Kingston, J. 1987. Messenger or Message? Military Buildups and the Initiation of Conflict. JOP 49: 801-813.

276 Dixon, W. J.; Smith, D. L. 1992. Arms Control and the Evolution of Superpower Relations. SSQ 73: 876-889.

277 Donaghy, K. P. 1995. Arms Race Dynamics and Economic Stability. CMAPS 14: 49-76.

278 Downs, G. W.; Rocke, D. M.; Siverson, R. M. 1985. Arms Races and Cooperation. WP 38: 118-146.

279 Economic Appliquee. 1993. Papers on the Economics of Disarmament. Vol 46 (2).

280 Fischer, D. 1984. Weapons Technology and the Intensity of Arms Races. CMAPS 8: 49-70.

281 Gillespie, J. V., et al. 1977. An Optimal Control Model of Arms Races. APSR 71: 226-244.

282 Gillespie, J. V.; Zinnes, D. A.; Rubison, R. M. 1978. Accumulation in Arms Race Models: A Geometric Lag Perspective. CPS 10: 475-496.

283 Hamblin, R. L., et al. 1977. Arms Races. ASR 42: 338-354.

284 Hill, W. W. 1992. Deterministic Quasi-Periodic Behavior in an Arms Race Model. CMAPS 12: 79-98.

285 Hirao, Y. 1994. Quality vs. Quantity in Arms Races. SEJ 61: 96-103.

286 Hollist, W. L. 1977. Alternative Explanations of Competitive Arms Processes. AJPS 21: 313-340.

287 -. 1977. An Analysis of Arms Processes in the US and Soviet Union. ISQ 21: 503-528.

288 Hunter, J. E. 1980. Mathematical Models of a Three Nation Arms Race. JCR 24: 241-252.

289 International Security. 1978. Papers on Stability and Strategic Arms Control. IS 3 (1).

290 -. 1985. Papers on Star Wars. IS 10 (1).

291 International Social Science Journal. 1976. Papers on the Cycle of Armament. ISSJ 28 (2).

292 Intriligator, M. D.; Brito, D. L. 1984. Can Arms Races Lead to War? JCR 28: 63-84.

293 Isard, W.; Anderton, C. H. 1985. Arms Race Models: A Summary. CMAPS 8: 27-98.

294 Jones, P. 1988. Costs of Disarmament Treaties. AC 9: 280-291.

295 Journal of Conflict Resolution. 1994. Papers on Arm Races, Alliances and Cooperation. JCR 38 (2).

296 Journal of International Affairs. 1986. Papers on the Arms Trade. JIA 40 (1).

297 Kinsella, D. 1994. Arms Transfers and Third World Rivalries during the Cold War. AJPS 38: 557-581.

298 Koubi, V. 1993. International Tensions and Arms Control Agreements. AJPS 37: 148-164.

299 Kugler, J.; Organski, A. F. K.; Fox, D. J. 1974. Deterrence and the Arms Race. IS 4: 105-138.

300 Lambelet, J. C. 1973. Towards a Dynamic Two-Theater Model of the East-West Arms Race. JOPS 4: 1-37.

301 -. 1986. Formal Analysis of Arms Races. CMAPS 9: 1-18.

302 Lambelet, J. C.; Luterbacher, U.; Allan, P. 1979. Dynamics of Arms Races. JOPS 4: 49-66.

303 Levine, P.; Smith, R. 1995. Arms Trade and Arms Control. EJ 105: 471-484.

304 Lichbach, M. I. 1990. When Is an Arms Rivalry a Prisoner's Dilemma? Richardson's Models and 2x2 Games. JCR 34: 29-56.

305 Lucier, C. 1979. Changes in the Value of Arms Race Parameters. JCR 23: 17-39.

306 Luterbacher, U. 1975. Arms Race Models. EJPR 3: 199-217.

307 Majeski, S. J. 1984. Arms Races as International Prisoner's Dilemma Games. MSS 7: 253-266.

308 -. 1985. Expectations and Arms Races. AJPS 29: 217-245.

309 -. 1986. Technological Innovation and Cooperation in Arms Races. ISQ 30: 175-192.

310 Majeski, S. J.; Jones, D. L. 1981. Arms Race Modeling. JCR 25: 259-288.

311 McGinnis, M. D. 1991. Richardson, Rationality and Restrictive Models of Arms Races. JCR 35: 443-473.

312 Melese, F.; Michel, P. 1991. Reversing the Arms Race: A Differential Game Model. SEJ 57: 1133-1143.

313 Moll, K. D.; Luebbert, G. M. 1980. Arms Race and Military Expenditure Models. JCR 24: 153-185.

314 Morrow, J. D. 1989. Effects of Arms Races on the Occurrence of War. JCR 33: 500-529.

315 -. 1991. Electoral and Congressional Incentives and Arms Control. JCR 35: 245-265.

316 Orbis. 1984. Papers on the Strategic Defense Initiative. Vol 28 (2).

317 -. 1985. Papers on Arms Control. Vol 29 (2).

318 Oren, I. 1994. Indo-Pakistani Arms Competition. JCR 38: 185-214.

319 Ostrom, C. W.; Marra, R. F. 1986. US Defense Spending and the Soviet Estimate. APSR 80: 819-842.

320 Pepper, D.; Jenkins, A. 1984. Reversing the Nuclear Arms Race: Geopolitical Bases for Pessimism. PGEO 36: 419-427.

321 Plous, S. 1988. Modeling the Nuclear Arms Race as a Perceptual Dilemma. PAPA 17: 44-53.

322 Rattinger, H. 1976. Econometrics and Arms Races. EJPR 4: 421-439.

323 Saperstein, A. M.; Mayer-Kress, G. 1988. A Nonlinear Dynamical Model of the Impact of SDI on the Arms Race. JCR 32: 636-670.

324 Saris, W. E.; Middendorf, C. 1980. Arms Races. BJPS 10: 121-128.

325 Shapely, D. 1980. Arms Control as a Regulator of Military Technology. Daedalus 109: 145-158.

326 Sherwin, R. G.; Laurance, E. J. 1979. Arms Transfers and Military Capacity. ISQ 23: 360-389.

327 Simaan, M.; Cruz, J. B. 1975. Formulation of Richardson's Model of Arms Race from a Different Game Viewpoint. RES 42: 67-77.

328 Sislin, J. 1994. Arms as Influence. JCR 38: 665-689.

329 Smith, T. C. 1980. Arms Race Instability and War. JCR 24: 253-284.

330 Stoll, R. J. 1982. Use of Richardson Equations to Estimate Parameters of a Dyadic Arms Acquisition Process. AJPS 26: 77-89.

331 Strategic Review. 1994. Papers on Arms Control and Nuclear Testing. Vol 22 (4).

332 Taber, C. S. 1993. National Arms Acquisition as a Rational Competitive Process. SAG 24: 413-428.

333 Ungar, S. 1990. Moral Panics, Military Industrial Complex and the Arms Race. SQ 31: 165-186.

334 Vayrynen, R. 1983. Economic Fluctuations, Technological Innovations and the Arms Race in a Historical Perspective. CAC 18: 135-160.

335 Wallace, M. D. 1979. Role of Arms Races in the Escalation of Disputes into War. JCR 23: 3-16.

336 -. 1982. Armaments and Escalation. ISQ 26: 37-56.

337 Wallace, M. D.; Wilson, J. M. 1978. Non-Linear Arms Race Models. JPR 15: 175-192.

338 Ward, M. D. 1984. Differential Paths to Parity. APSR 78: 297-317.

339 Wayman, F. W. 1985. Arms Control and Strategic Arms Voting in the US Senate. JCR 29: 225-252.

340 Weede, E. 1980. Arms Races and Escalation. JCR 24: 285-288.

341 Williams, J. T.; McGinnis, M. D. 1988. Sophisticated Reaction in the US-Soviet Arms Race. AJPS 32: 698-695.

342 Wittman, D. 1989. Arms Control Verification and Other Games Involving Imperfect Detection. APSR 83: 923-948.

343 Wolfson, M.; Shabahang, H. 1991. Economic Causation in the Breakdown of Military Equilibrium. JCR 35: 43-67.

Foreign Aid

344 Abrams, B. A.; Lewis, K. A. 1993. Human Rights and US Foreign Aid. PC 77: 815-821.

345 Auerbach, K. D. 1976. The Distribution of Multilateral Assistance. SSQ 57: 644-659.

346 Bornschier, V.; Chase-Dunn, C.; Rubinson, R. B. 1978. Effect of Foreign Investment and Aid on Economic Growth and Inequality. AJS 84: 651-683.

347 Davenport, M. 1970. The Allocation of Foreign Aid. Yorkshire Bulletin of Economics and Social Research 22: 26-42.

348 Khan, H. A.; Hoshino, E. 1992. Impact of Foreign Aid on the Fiscal Behavior. WD 20: 1481-1488.

349 Lebovic, J. H. 1988. National Interests and US Foreign Aid. JPR 25: 115-136.

350 McKinlay, R. D. 1979. A Foreign Policy Model and Interpretation of the Distribution of Official Bilateral Economic Aid. CPS 11: 411-464.

351 McKinlay, R. D.; Little, R. 1977. Foreign Policy Model of US Bilateral Aid. WP 30: 58-86.

352 -. 1978. A Foreign Policy Model of the Distribution of British Bilateral Aid. BJPS 8: 313-332.

353 Mosley, P. 1985. Political Economy of Foreign Aid: A Model of the Market for a Public Good. EDACC 33: 373-394.

354 Murshed, S. M.; Sen, S. 1995. Aid Conditionality and Military Expenditure Reduction in Developing Countries: Models of Asymmetric Information. EJ 105: 498-509.

355 Noel, A.; Therien, J. P. 1995. From Domestic to International Justice: Welfare State and Foreign Aid. IO 49: 523-554.

356 Palda, F. 1993. Can Repressive Regimes Be Moderated through Foreign Aid? PC 77: 535-550.

357 Poe, S. C.; Meernik, J. 1995. US Military Aid in the 1980s. JPR 32: 399-412.

358 Regan, P. M. 1995. US Economic Aid and Political Repression. PRQ 48: 613-628.

359 Sexton, E. A.; Decker, T.N. 1992. US Foreign Aid: Is It for Friends, Development, or Politics? JSPES 17: 303-316.

360 Snyder, D. 1990. Foreign Aid and Domestic Savings. EDACC 39: 175-181.

361 Sylvan, D. A. 1976. Consequences of Sharp Military Assistance Increases for International Conflict and Cooperation. JCR 20: 609-636.

362 Tsoutsoplides, C. 1991. The Determinants of the Geographical Allocation of Economic Community Aid to the Developing Countries. AE 23: 647-658.

363 White, H. 1992. The Macroeconomic Impact of Development Aid. JDS 28: 163-240.

International Conflict

364 Annals. 1991. Papers on Regional Conflicts. ANNALS 518.

365 Atlantic Community Quarterly. 1975. Papers on the Concept of Detente. Vol 13 (3).

366 British Journal of International Studies. 1980. Papers on Appeasement. Vol 6 (3).

367 Bueno de Mesquita, B.; Lalman, D. 1988. Empirical Support for Systemic and Dyadic Explanations of International Conflict. WP 41: 1-20.

368 Cannizzo, C. A. 1979. Quantitative International Conflict Studies. AFAS 5: 111-121.

369 Carlson, L. J. 1995. A Theory of Escalation and International Conflict. JCR 39: 511-534.

370 Carment, D. 1995. NATO and the International Politics of Ethnic Conflict. Comparative Security Policy 16: 347-379.

371 Cerny, P. G. 1993. Plurilateralism: Structural Differentiation and Functional Conflict in the Post Cold War World Order. Millennium 22: 27-52.

372 Critchley, W. H. 1979. Strategic Thinking over the Long Cycle. PSJ 8: 28-36.

373 Cusack, T. R.; Eberwein, W. D. 1982. Prelude to War: Incidence, Escalation and Intervention in International Disputes. II 9: 9-28.

374 Diehl, P. F.; Kingston, J. 1987. Military Buildups and the Initiation of Conflict. JOP 49: 801-813.

375 Doty, R. M. 1994. Laboratory Tests of a Motivational-Perceptual Model of Conflict Escalation. JCR 38: 719-748.

376 Faber, J. 1987. Measuring Cooperation, Conflict and the Social Network of Nations. JCR 31: 438-464.

377 Faini, R.; Annez, P.; Taylor, L. 1984. Defense Spending, Economic Structure and Growth. EDACC 32: 487-498.

378 Fearon, J. D. 1994. Domestic Political Audiences and the Escalation of International Disputes. APSR 88: 577-592.

379 Fletcher Forum. 1994. Papers on Peacekeeping. FFWA 18 (1).

380 Fraser, N. M.; Powell, C. A.; Benjamin, C. M. 1987. New Methods of Applying Game Theory to International Conflict. ISN 13: 9-18.

381 Gaddis, J. L. 1987. Expanding the Data Base: The Enrichment of Security Studies. IS 12: 3-22.

382 Gasiorowski, M. J. 1986. Economic Interdependence and International Conflict. ISQ 30: 23-28.

383 Goertz, G.; Diehl, P. F. 1991. Empirical Importance of Enduring Rivalries. II 18: 1-11.

384 -. 1993. Enduring Rivalries: Theoretical Constructs and Empirical Patterns. ISQ 37: 147-171.

385 -. 1995. Initiation and Termination of Enduring Rivalries: Political Shocks. AJPS 39: 30-52.

386 Gowa, J. 1995. Democratic States and International Disputes. IO 49: 511-522.

387 Groom, A. J. R. 1988. Paradigms in Conflict: Strategist, Conflict Researcher and Peace Researcher. RIS 14: 97-116.

388 Hensel, P. R. 1994. Recurrent Militarized Disputes in Latin America. JPR 31: 281-298.

389 Hensel, P. R.; Diehl, P. F. 1994. Nonmilitarized Response in Interstate Disputes. JCR 39: 479-506.

390 Hoole, F. W.; Huang, C. 1992. Political Economy of Global Conflict. JOP 54: 834-858.

391 International Journal. 1985. Papers on Managing Conflict. IJ 40 (4), 1990 45 (2).

392 International Security. 1983. Papers on Non-Nuclear Strategies. IS 8 (3).

393 -. 1990. Papers on Security Paradigms. IS 14 (4).

394 International Social Science Journal. 1986. Papers on Collective Violence and Security. ISSJ 38 (4).

395 -. 1991. Papers on International Conflict. ISSJ 43 (1).

396 Journal of Conflict Resolution. 1982. Papers on Conflict and International Security. JCR 26 (2).

397 Journal of International Affairs. 1993. Papers on Conflict Resolution. JIA 46 (2).

398 Journal of Peace Research. 1984. Papers on Alternative Defense. JPR 21 (2).

399 Kanwisher, N. 1989. Cognitive Heuristics and American Security Policy. JCR 33: 652-675.

400 Katz, N. H. 1989. Conflict Resolution and Peace Studies. ANNALS 504: 14-21.

401 Kegley, C. W.; Hermann, M. G. 1995. Political Psychology of Peace through Democratization. CAC 30: 5-30.

402 Kende, I. 1989. The History of Peace: Concept and Organizations from the Late Middle Ages. JPR 26: 233-248.

403 Kugler, J. 1984. Terror without Deterrence. JCR 28: 470-506.

404 Lalman, D. 1988. Conflict Resolution and Peace. AJPS 32: 590-615.

405 Lumsden, M. 1973. The Cyprus Conflict as a Prisoner's Dilemma Game. JCR 17: 7-32.

406 Majeski, S. J.; Fricks, S. 1995. Conflict and Cooperation in International Relations. JCR 39: 622-645.

407 Maluwa, T. 1989. Peaceful Settlement of Disputes among African States. IACLQ 38: 299-320.

408 Maoz, Z.; Abdolali, N. 1989. Regime Types and International Conflict. JCR 33: 3-36.

409 McGinnis, M. D.; Williams, J. T. 1989. Change and Stability in Superpower Rivalry. APSR 83: 1101-1123.

410 Melko, M. 1992. Long Term Factors Underlying Peace. JPR 29: 99-114.

411 Morrow, J. D. 1986. A Spatial Model of International Conflict. APSR 80: 1131-1150.

412 Nelson, D. N. 1989. Dimensions of Military Commitments in Eastern Europe and the USSR. AC 10: 275-288.

413 Nincic, M. 1982. Understanding International Conflict: Some Theoretical Gaps. JPR 19: 49-60.

414 Niou, E. M. S.; Ordeshook, P. C. 1990. Stability in Anarchic International Systems. APSR 84: 1207-1234.

415 North, R. C.; Choucri, N. 1983. Economic and Political Factors in International Conflict and Integration. ISQ 27: 443-462.

416 Peace Research Reviews. 1971. Papers on Conflict Management. PRR 4 (2).

417 -. 1988. Papers on Conflict Reduction. PRR 11 (1).

418 Review of International Studies. 1989. Papers on the Balance of Power. RIS 15 (2).

419 Richter, J. G. 1992. Perpetuating the Cold War: Domestic Sources of International Patterns. PSCQ 107: 271-302.

420 Risse-Kappen, T. 1991. Did Peace through Strength End the Cold War? IO 16: 162-188.

421 Russett, B. 1990. Doves, Hawks and US Public Opinion. PSCQ 105: 515-538.

422 Sakurai, M. M. 1990. Modeling Strategic Threats: A Competitive Test of the Harsanyi Function H(S) and Characteristic Function v(S). JCR 34: 74-91.

423 Schahczenski, J. J. 1991. Explaining Relative Peace: Major Power Order. JPR 28: 295-310.

424 Simowitz, R.; Price, B. L. 1986. Progress in the Study of International Conflict. JPR 23: 29-40.

425 Sinclair, M. R. 1980. Model for the Evaluation of Strategic Significance. Politikon 7: 63 ff.

426 Skinner, R. A.; Kegley, C. W. 1978. Correlates of International Alignment. JPS 5: 97-108.

427 Stoll, R. J. 1984. Bloc Concentration and Dispute Escalation. SSQ 65: 48-59.

428 Wagner, R. H. 1986. The Theory of Games and the Balance of Power. WP 38: 546-576.

429 Weede, E. 1976. Overwhelming Preponderance as a Pacifying Condition among Contagious Asian Dyads. JCR 20: 395-412.

430 Wilkenfeld, J. 1968. Domestic and Foreign Conflict Behavior of Nations. JPR 5: 56-69.

431 -. 1969. Some Further Findings Regarding the Domestic and Foreign Conflict Behavior of Nations. JPR 6: 147-156.

432 Williams, J. T.; McGinnis, M. D. 1992. Dimension of Superpower Rivalry: A Dynamic Factor Analysis. JCR 36: 86-118.

Military Deterrence

433 Achen, C. H.; Snidal, D. 1989. Rational Deterrence Theory and Comparative Case Studies. WP 41: 143-169.

434 Armed Forces and Society. 1980. Papers on Combat Readiness as a Deterrent Strategy. AFAS 6 (2).

435 George, A. L.; Smoke, R. 1989. Deterrence and Foreign Policy. WP 41: 170-182.

436 Harvey, F. 1995. Rational Deterrence Theory Revisited. CJPS 28: 403-436.

437 Homer-Dixon, T. F.; Karapin, R. S. 1989. Graphical Argument Analysis: A New Approach to Understanding Arguments Applied to a Debate about the Window of Vulnerability. ISQ 33: 389-410.

438 Huth, P.; Gelpi, C.; Bennett, D. S. 1993. Escalation of Great Power Militarized Disputes: Testing Rational Deterrence Theory and Structural Realism. APSR 87: 609-623.

439 Huth, P.; Russett, B. 1984. What Makes Deterrence Work? WP 36: 496-526.

440 -. 1988. Deterrence Failure and Crisis Escalation. ISQ 32: 29-46.

441 -. 1990. Testing Deterrence Theory. WP 42: 466-501.

442 Jervis, R. 1979. Deterrence Theory. WP 31: 289-324.

443 -. 1982. Deterrence and Perception. IS 7: 3-30.

444 -. 1982. Security Regimes. IO 36: 357-378.

445 -. 1989. Rational Deterrence Theory. WP 41: 208-224.

446 Kilgour, D. M.; Zagare, F. C. 1991. Credibility, Uncertainty and Deterrence. AJPS 35: 305-334.

447 Kosterman, R.; Feshbach, S. 1989. Toward a Measure of Patriotic and National Attitudes. PP 10: 257-274.

448 Kugler, J.; Zagare, F. C. 1990. The Long Term Stability of Deterrence. II 15: 255-278.

449 Langlois, J. P. 1989. Modeling Deterrence and International Crises. JCR 33: 67-83.

450 Lebow, R.N.; Stein, J. G. 1990. Deterrence: Elusive Dependent Variable. WP 42: 336-369.

451 Nalebuff, B. 1991. Rational Deterrence in an Imperfect World. WP 43: 313-335.

452 Peace Research Reviews. 1969. Papers on Deterrence Theory. PRR 3 (1).

453 Rhodes, R. 1995. Constructing Peace and War: An Analysis of the Power of Ideas to Shape American Military Power. Millennium 24: 53-86.

454 Schiff, R. L. 1995. Civil-Military Relations Reconsidered: A Theory of Concordance. AFAS 22: 7-24.

455 Steinbrunner, J. 1976. Beyond Rational Deterrence. WP 28: 223-245.

456 Wagner, R. H. 1982. Deterrence and Bargaining. JCR 26: 329-358.

457 -. 1992. Rationality and Misperception in Deterrence Theory. JTP 42: 115-141.

458 Weede, E. 1983. Extended Deterrence by Superpower Alliance. JCR 27: 231-255.

459 World Politics 1989. Papers on Deterrence. WP 41 (1).

460 Zagare, F. C. 1990. Rationality and Deterrence. WP 42: 238-260.

Military Establishments

461 Adams, J., et al. 1980. Personality Characteristics of Male and Female Leaders at the US Military Academy. JPMS 8: 99-106.

462 Alternatives. 1984. Papers on Militarization. Vol 10 (1).

463 Annals. 1973. Papers on the Military and US Society. ANNALS 406.

464 -. 1989. Papers on Universities and the Military. ANNALS 502.

465 -. 1991. Papers on US Defense Policy. ANNALS 517.

466 Armed Forces and Society. 1979. Papers on Military Manpower and the Market Place. AFAS 5 (2).

467 -. 1987. Papers on the Constitution and US National Defense. AFAS 14 (1).

468 Art, R. 1980. To What Ends Military Power? IS 4: 3-14.

469 Avant, D. D. 1993. Institutional Sources of Military Doctrine: Hegemons in Peripheral Wars. ISQ 37: 409-430.

470 Bachman, J. G.; Sigelman, L.; Diamond, G. 1987. Self-Selection, Socialization and Distinctive Military Values. AFAS 13: 169-188.

471 Bartels, L. M. 1994. American Public's Defense Spending Preferences. POQ 58: 479-508.

472 Bearman, P. S. 1991. Desertion as Localism: Army Unit Solidarity and Group Norms in the Civil War. SF 70: 321-342.

473 Beenstock, M. 1993. International Patterns in Military Spending. EDACC 41: 633-650.

474 Blechman, B. M. 1991. The Congressional Role in US Military Policy. PSCQ 106: 17-32.

475 Bredow, W. V. 1981. Asymmetric Images of the Enemy: Political Education in the Armed Forces of the Two German States. JPMS 9: 31-42.

476 Druckman, D. 1994. Nationalism, Patriotism and Group Loyalty. ISQ 38: 43-68.

477 Burk, J. 1989. National Attachments and the Decline of the Mass Armed Force. JPMS 17: 65-82.

478 -. 1992. Morris Janowitz and Origins of Sociological Research on Armed Forces and Society. AFAS 19: 167-186.

479 Butler, J. S.; Johnson, M. A. 1992. Demographic Characteristics of Americans and Attitudes toward Military Issues. JPMS 19: 273-291.

480 Carter, H. 1977. Military Organization as a Response to Residence and Size of Population. BSR 12: 271-290.

481 Cobb, S. 1976. Defense Spending and Defense Voting in the House: The Military Industrial Complex Thesis. AJS 82: 163-182.

482 Cockerham, W. C.; Cohen, L. E. 1979. Attitudes of the US Army Paratroopers toward Participation in the Quelling of Civil Disturbances. JPMS 7: 257-270.

483 -. 1980. Obedience to Orders: Issues of Morality and Legality in Combat among US Army Paratroopers. SF 58: 1272-1288.

484 -. 1981. Volunteering for Foreign Combat Missions. PACSR 24: 329-354.

485 Conybeare, J. A. C. 1994 Arms vs. Alliances: The Capital Structure of Military Enterprise. JCR 38: 215-235.

486 Cooke, T. W.; Quester, A. O. 1992. What Characterizes Successful Enlistees in the All Volunteer Force. SSQ 73: 238-252.

487 Cooperation and Conflict. 1992. Papers on Defense Spending after the Cold War. CAC 27 (4).

488 Crump, J. R. 1989. The Spatial Distribution of Military Spending in the US. GAC 20 (3): 50-62.

489 Cuzan, A. G. 1986. Fiscal Policy, the Military and Political Stability in Iberoamerica. BS 31: 226-238.

490 Diehl, P. F.; Goertz, G. 1985. Trends in Military Allocations since 1816. AFAS 12: 134-144.

491 Fleisher, R. 1985. Economic Benefit, Ideology and Senate Voting on the B-1 Bomber. APQ 13: 200-211.

492 Fullington, M. G. 1983. Impact of the Military on the Physical Quality of Life in Latin America. JPS 11: 40-51.

493 Goertzel, T. 1987. Public Opinion Concerning Military Spending in the US. JPMS 15: 61-72.

494 Hahm, S. D.; Kamlet, M. S.; Mowery, D. C. 1992. Defense Spending under the Gramm-Rudman-Hollings Act. PAR 52: 8-15.

495 Hartley, T.; Russett, B. 1992. Public Opinion and the Common Defense: Who Governs Military Spending in the US? APSR 86: 905-915.

496 Hewitt, D. 1992. Military Expenditures Worldwide: Determinants and Trends. JPP 12: 105-152.

497 Hosek, J. R.; Antel, J.; Peterson, C. E. 1989. Who Stays, Who Leaves? Attrition among First-Term Enlistees. AFAS 15: 389-410.

498 Hossein-Zadeh, E. 1993. Persian Gulf War in the Context of the Debate over the Political Economy of US Militarism. CJE 17: 245-256.

499 International Political Science Review. 1981. Papers on Civil Military Relations. IPSR 2 (3).

500 International Security. 1985. Papers on the US Military Decline and the Decade of Neglect Controversy. IS 10 (2).

501 -. 1986. Papers on the Naval Strategy Controversy. IS 11 (2).

502 Jennings, M. K.; Markus, G. B. 1977. The Effect of Military Service on Political Attitudes. APSR 71: 131-147.

503 Journal of Asian and African Studies. 1977. Papers on the Warrior Tradition in Modern Africa. JAAS 12 (1-4).

504 -. 1991. Papers on Civil Military Interaction in Asia and Africa. JAAS 26 (1/2).

505 Journal of Interamerican Studies and World Affairs. 1972. Papers on Latin American Military Governments. Vol 14 (4).

506 Journal of Social Issues. 1975. Papers on Soldiers after Vietnam. JSI 31 (4).

507 Kammler, H. 1985. Towards a Comparative Political Economy of Defense. EJPR 13: 311-326.

508 Kinnard, D. 1975. Vietnam Reconsidered: An Attitudinal Survey of US Army General Officers. POQ 39: 445-456.

509 Krell, G. 1981. Capitalism and Armaments: Business Cycles and Defense Spending in the US. JPR 18: 221-240.

510 Kriesberg, L.; Murray, H.; Klein, R. A. 1982. Elites and Increased Public Support for US Military Spending. JPMS 10: 275-298.

511 Langbein, L. I. 1995. Shirking and Ideology: Defense in the Senate. CAP 22: 35-56.

512 Langton, K. P. 1984. The Influence of Military Service on Social Consciousness and Protest Behavior: Peruvian Mine Workers. CPS 16: 479-504.

513 Latin American Perspectives. 1985. Papers on the Military in Latin America. LAPER 12 (4).

514 Lebovic, J. H. 1994. The Services and the US Defense Budget. APSR 88: 839-852.

515 Lee, D.; Stekler, H. O. 1987. Modeling High Levels of Defense Expenditures. JPM 9: 437-453.

516 Lemarchand, R. 1976. African Armies in Historical and Contemporary Perspectives. JPMS 4: 261-276.

517 Lindsay, J. M. 1990. Parochialism, Policy and Constituency Constraints: Congressional Voting on Strategic Weapons Systems. AJPS 34: 936-960.

518 Lippert, E.; Schneider, P.; Zoll, R. 1978. The Influence of Military Service on Political and Social Attitudes. IJPE 1: 225-240.

519 Looney, R. E. 1988. The Political Economy of Third World Military Expenditures: Impact of Regime Type on the Defense Allocations Process. JPMS 16: 21-30.

520 Looney, R. E.; Winterford, D. 1993. Environmental Consequences of Third World Military Expenditures and Arms Production: Latin American Case. RISEC 40: 769-786.

521 Luckham, A. R. 1971. A Comparative Typology of Civil Military Relations. GAO 6: 5-35.

522 Majeski, S. J. 1983. Mathematical Models of the US Military Expenditure Decision Making Process. AJPS 27: 485-514.

523 Maneval, H.; Kim, C. K.; Sewing-Thunich, F. 1993. Military Expenditures, National Product and Investment in the Federal Republic of Germany. JNS 211: 1-21.

524 Marks, E. 1983. The Vietnam Generation of Professional American Military Officers. Conflict 5: 37-56.

525 Meeker, B. F.; Segal, D. R. 1987. Soldiers' Perceptions of Conflict Intensity: Effects of Doctrine and Experience. JPMS 15: 105-115.

526 Mintz, A. 1989. Guns vs. Butter. APSR 83: 1285-1293.

527 Mintz, A.; Hicks, A. 1984. Military Keynesianism in the US: Military Expenditures. AJS 90: 411-417.

528 Nincic, M.; Cusack, T. R. 1979. Political Economy of US Military Spending. JPR 16: 101-115.

529 Orbis. 1982. Papers on Navies in Foreign Policy. Vol 26 (3).

530 Ostrom, C. W. 1978. A Reactive Linkage Model of the US Defense Expenditure Policy Making Process. APSR 22: 941-957.

531 Pacific Sociological Review. 1973. Papers on Military Sociology. PACSR 16 (2).

532 Pion-Berlin, D. 1995. Armed Forces and Politics. LARR 30: 147-162.

533 Plural Societies. 1978. Papers on Contributions of the Army in Israel to National Integration. Vol 9 (2/3).

534 Policy Sciences. 1992. Papers on Military Defense Acquisition. PSCI 25 (1).

535 Political Science Quarterly. 1986. Papers on Providing for the Common Defense. PSQ 101 (5).

536 Posen, B. R. 1993. Nationalism, the Mass Army and Military Power. IS 18: 80-124.

537 Regan, P. M. 1994. War Toys, War Movies and the Militarization of the US. JPR 31: 45-58.

538 Rosh, R. M. 1988. Third World Militarization. JCR 32: 671-698.

539 Ross, T. W. 1994. Raising an Army: A Positive Theory of Military Recruitment. JOLE 37: 109-132.

540 Ruhl, J. M. 1982. Social Mobilization, Military Tradition and Current Patterns of Civil Military Relations in Latin America. WPQ 35: 574-586.

541 Rundquist, B. S. 1978. On Testing a Military Industrial Complex Theory. APQ 6: 29-54.

542 Rundquist, B. S.; Griffith, D. E. 1976. A Test of the Distributive Theory of Military Policy Making. WPQ 29: 620-626.

543 Russett, B. 1969. Who Pays for Defense? APSR 63: 412-426.

544 -. 1982. Defense Expenditures and National Well Being. APSR 76: 767-777.

545 Segal, D. R.; Meeker, B. F. 1985. Peacekeeping, Warfighting and Change among Combat Soldiers on Constabulary Duty. JPMS 13: 167-182.

546 Sigmund, P. E. 1993. Approaches to the Study of the Military in Latin America. CP 26: 111-122.

547 Skhelsbaek, K. 1979. Militarism, Its Dimensions and Corollaries. JPR 16: 213-230.

548 Smith, R. P. 1980. Military Expenditure and Investment in OECD Countries. JCE 4: 19-32.

549 Social Science Quarterly. 1992. Papers on the Military and American Society. SSQ 73 (2).

550 Society. 1975. Papers on the Military. Vol 12 (4).

551 Starr, H., et al. 1984. The Relationship between Defense Spending and Inflation. JCR 28: 103-122.

552 Stern, P. 1995. Why Do People Sacrifice for Their Nations? PP 16: 217-236.

553 Stevens, G.; Rosa, F. M.; Gardner, S. 1994. Military Academies as Instruments of Value Change. AFAS 20: 473-484.

554 Studies in Comparative Communism. 1978. Papers on Civil Military Relations in Communist Countries. SCC 11 (3).

555 Terrell, L. M. 1971. Societal Stress, Political Instability and Levels of Military Effort. JCR 15: 329-346.

556 Ward, M. D.; Davis, D. R. 1992. Sizing Up the Peace Dividend: Economic Growth and Military Spending. APSR 86: 748-758.

557 Welch, C. E. 1992. Military Disengagement from Politics: Paradigms, Processes or Random Events. AFAS 18: 323-342.

558 Westbrook, S. D. 1980. Sociopolitical Alienation and Military Efficiency. AFAS 6: 170-189.

559 Wiberg, H. 1983. Measuring Military Expenditures. CAC 18: 161-178.

560 Wiles, P. 1986. Whatever Happened to the Merchants of Death? Normal Supply vs. Catastrophic Demand. Millennium 15: 295-310.

561 Wilson, S. 1980. For a Socio-Historical Approach to the Study of Western Military Culture. AFAS 6: 527-552.

562 Zuk, L. G.; Thompson, W. R. 1982. The Post-Coup Military Spending Question. APSR 76: 60-74.

563 Zuk, L. G.; Woodbury, N. R. 1986. US Defense Spending, Electoral Cycles and Soviet-American Relations. JCR 30: 445-468.

Nuclear Weapons

564 Annals. 1983. Papers on Nuclear Disarmament. ANNALS 469.

565 Arms Control. 1993. Papers on Nuclear Arms Control. AC 14 (1).

566 Benford, R. D. 1993. Frame Disputes within the Nuclear Disarmament Movement. SF 71: 677-702.

567 Beukel, E. 1992. A Fundamental Attribution Error in the Cold War: American Perceptions of Soviet Union as a Nuclear Superpower. AC 13: 396-420.

568 Bueno de Mesquita, B.; Riker, W. H. 1982. Assessing the Merits of Selective Nuclear Deterrence. JCR 26: 283-306.

569 Christie, D. J.; Hanley, C. P. 1994. Some Psychological Effects of Nuclear War Education on Adolescents. PP 15: 177-200.

570 Churchill, R. P. 1983. Nuclear Arms as a Philosophical and Moral Issue. ANNALS 469: 46-57.

571 Cioffi-Revilla, C. A. 1983. A Probability Model of Credibility: Strategic Nuclear Deterrence Systems. JCR 27: 73-108.

572 Dyer, P. W. 1980. Moral Dimensions of Tactical Nuclear Weapons in Europe. Parameters 10: 44-50.

573 Ethics. 1985. Papers on the Ethics and Nuclear Deterrence. Vol 95 (3).

574 Frank, J. D.; Rivard, J. C. 1986. Antinuclear Admirals. PP 7: 23-52.

575 Geller, D. S. 1990. Nuclear Weapons, Deterrence and Crisis Escalation. JCR 34: 291-310.

576 Gwartney-Gibbs, P. A.; Lach, D. H. 1991. Sex Differences in Nuclear War Attitudes. JPR 28: 161-174.

577 Hart, S. 1987. Christian Faith and Nuclear Weapons. JSSR 26: 38-62.

578 Harvey, F.; James, P. 1992. Nuclear Deterrence Theory. CMAPS 12: 17-45.

579 Hogan, J. M.; Smith, T. J. 1991. Public Opinion and the Nuclear Freeze. POQ 55: 534-569.

580 International Conciliation. 1969. Papers on Nuclear Safeguards and the International Atomic Energy Agency. IC 572.

581 -. 1970. Papers on Nuclear Proliferation. IC 578 (May).

582 International Organization. 1981. Papers on Nuclear Proliferation. IO 35 (1).

583 Jervis, R. 1988. Political Effects of Nuclear Weapons. IS 13: 80-90.

584 Journal of Social Issues. 1983. Papers on Images of Nuclear War. JSI 39 (1).

585 Lackey, D. P. 1982. Missiles and Morals: A Utilitarian Look at Nuclear Deterrence. PAPA 11.

586 Larsen, K. S. 1988. Attitudes toward Nuclear Disarmament. JPR 25: 265-271.

587 McCormick, J. M. 1985. Congressional Voting on the Nuclear Freeze Resolutions. APQ 13: 122-134.

588 Meyer, D. S. 1993. Peace Protest and Policy: Explaining the Rise and Decline of Antinuclear Movements. PSJ 21: 35-55.

589 Nalebuff, B. 1986. Brinksmanship and Nuclear Deterrence: The Neutrality of Escalation. CMAPS 9: 19-30.

590 Newlin, J. R. 1983. The Protestant Churches and the Nuclear Freeze. FFWA 7: 355-364.

591 Nye, J. S. 1987. Nuclear Learning and US-Soviet Security Regimes. IO 41: 371-402.

592 Overby, L. M. 1991. Assessing Constituency Influence: Congressional Voting on the Nuclear Freeze. LSQ 16: 297-312.

593 Peace Research Papers. 1982. Papers on Approaches to a Nuclear Free Policy. PRP 9 (2-3).

594 Peace Research Reviews. 1984. Papers on Accidental Nuclear War. PRR 9 (4-5).

595 Plous, S. 1993. Nuclear Arms Race: Prisoner's Dilemma or Perceptual Dilemma? JPR 30: 163-180.

596 Political Psychology. 1988. Papers on Nuclear War Attitudes. PP 9 (1).

597 Powell, R. 1987. Nuclear Brinksmanship with Two Sided Incomplete Information. APSR 82: 155-178.

598 -. 1989. Nuclear Deterrence and the Strategy of Limited Retaliation. APSR 83: 503-520.

599 Rosen, S. 1977. A Stable System of Mutual Nuclear Deterrence in the Arab-Israeli Conflict. APSR 71: 1367-1383.

600 Russett, B. 1984. Ethical Dilemmas of Nuclear Deterrence. IS 8: 36-54.

601 Sagan, S. C. 1994. Perils of Proliferation: Organization Theory, Deterrence Theory and the Spread of Nuclear Weapons. IS 18: 66-107.

602 Schneider, B. R. 1994. Nuclear Proliferation and Counter-Proliferation. ISQ 38: 209-234.

603 Sociological Quarterly 1985. Papers on the Sociology of the Nuclear Threat. SQ 26 (3).

604 Solingen, E. 1994. Political Economy of Nuclear Restraint. IO 19: 126-169.

605 Tetlock, P. E.; McGuire, C. B.; Mitchell, G. 1991. Psychological Perspectives on Nuclear Deterrence. ARP 42: 239-276.

606 Wagner, R. H. 1991. Nuclear Deterrence, Counterforce Strategies and the Incentive to Strike First. APSR 85: 727-750.

607 World Politics. 1989. Papers on the Rational Deterrence Debate. WP 41 (2).

608 Yost, D. S. 1990. The Delegitimization of Nuclear Deterrence? AFAS 16: 487-508.

War

609 Anderson, C. W.; Nesvold, B. A. 1972. Skinnerian Analysis of Conflict Behavior. ABS 15: 883-910.

610 Anderson, G. M., et al. 1992. Economic Interpretation of Medieval Crusades. JEEH 21: 339-363.

611 Annals. 1970. Papers on How Wars End. ANNALS 392.

612 -. 1995. Papers on Small Wars. ANNALS 541.

613 Barzilai, G.; Inbar, E. 1992. Do Wars Have an Impact? Israeli Public Opinion after the Gulf War. JJIR 14: 48-64.

614 Beer, F. A., et al. 1987. War Cues and Foreign Policy Acts. APSR 81: 701-716.

615 Benjamin, J. 1991. Rhetoric and the Performance Act of Declaring War. PSQ 21: 73-84.

616 Brawley, M. R. 1993. Regime Types, Markets and War: The Importance of Pervasive Rents. CPS 26: 178-197.

617 Bremer, S. A. 1992. Dangerous Dyads: Conditions Affecting the Likelihood of Interstate War. JCR 36: 309-341.

618 -. 1993. Advancing the Scientific Study of War. II 19: 1-26.

619 Bremer, S. A.; Singer, J. D.; Luterbacher, U. 1973. Population Density and War Proneness. CPS 6: 329-348.

620 Bueno de Mesquita, B. 1978. Systemic Polarization and the Occurrence and Duration of War. JCR 22: 241-267.

621 -. 1980. An Expected Utility Theory of International Conflict. APSR 74: 917-931.

622 -. 1981. Risk, Power Distributions and the Liklihood of War. ISQ 25: 541-568.

623 -. 1983. Costs of War: Rational Expectations Approach. APSR 77: 347-357.

624 -. 1984. A Critique of a Critique of The War Trap. JCR 28: 341-360.

625 -. 1985. The War Trap Revisited: A Revised Expected Utility Model. APSR 79: 156-177.

626 -. 1987. Conceptualizing War. JCR 31: 370-382.

627 -. 1988. Contribution of Expected Utility Theory to the Study of International Conflict. JIDH 18: 629-652.

628 Bueno de Mesquita, B.; Atfeld, M. 1979. Choosing Sides in War. JCR 23: 87-112.

629 Bueno de Mesquita, B.; Lalman, D. 1986. Reason and War. APSR 80: 1113-1130.

630 -. 1988. Empirical Support for Systemic and Dyadic Explanations of International Conflict. WP 41: 1-20.

631 -. 1990. Domestic Opposition and Foreign War. APSR 84: 747-766.

632 Bueno de Mesquita, B.; Siverson, R. M. 1995. War and Survival of Political Leaders: Regime Types and Political Accountability. APSR 89: 841-855.

633 Burnstein, P.; Freudenburg, W. R. 1977. Ending the Vietnam War: Components of Change in Senate Voting on Vietnam War Bills. AJS 82: 991-1006.

634 Cannizzo, C. A. 1978. Capability Distribution and Major Power War Experience. Orbis 21: 947-957.

635 Cannon, M. W. 1992. Development of the American Theory of Limited War. AFAS 19: 71-104.

636 Caspary, W. R. 1993. New Psychoanalytic Perspectives on the Causes of War. PP 14: 417-446.

637 Cioffi-Revilla, C. A. 1991. Long Range Analysis of War. JIDH 4: 603-624.

638 Claude, I. L. 1980. Just Wars. PSCQ 95: 83-96.

639 Conybeare, J. A. C. 1992. Weak Cycles, Length and Magnitude of War: Duration Dependence in International Conflict. CMAPS 12: 99-116.

640 Conybeare, J. A. C.; Sandler, T. 1993. State-Sponsored Violence as a Tragedy of the Commons: England's Privateering Wars. PC 77: 879-897.

641 Cotton, T. Y. C. 1986. War and American Democracy: Electoral Costs. JCR 30: 616-635.

642 Davis, W. W.; Duncan, G. T.; Siverson, R. M. 1978. The Dynamics of Warfare. AJPS 22: 772-792.

643 Denton, T. 1995. War: Long Range Time Series by Conditioning. IJCS 36: 36-60.

644 DeRouen, K. R. 1995. Politics, the Economy and the Use of Force. JCR 39: 671-695.

645 Dessler, D. 1991. Beyond Correlations: Toward a Causal Theory of War. ISQ 35: 337-355.

646 Diehl, P. F. 1992. Correlates of War Project: A Bibliographical Essay. ISN 17: 21-33.

647 Diehl, P. F.; Goertz, G. 1988. Territorial Change and Militarized Conflict. JCR 32: 103-122.

648 Doran, C. F. 1983. War and Power Dynamics: Economic Underpinnings. ISQ 27: 419-442.

649 Doran, C. F.; Parsons, W. 1980. War and the Cycle of Relative Power. APSR 74: 947-965.

650 Draper, G. I. A. D. 1992. Humanitarianism in the Modern Law of Armed Conflict. IR 11: 239-252.

651 Eden, L. 1993. The End of US Cold War History. IS 18: 174-207.

652 Eberwein, W. D. 1981. The Quantitative Study of International Conflict. JPR 18: 19-38.

653 Etudes Internationales 1992. Papers on International Law and Armed Conflicts. EINT 23 (4).

654 Faber, J.; Houweling, H. W.; Siccama, J. G. 1984. The Diffusion of War. JPR 21: 277-288.

655 Farley, J. E. 1994. Twentieth Century Wars: Some Short Term Effects on Intergroup Relations in the US. SI 64: 214-237.

656 Fearon, J. D. 1995. Rationalist Explanations for War. IO 49: 379-414.

657 Finn, J. 1988. Just War and Matters of Statescraft. WQ 11: 103-114.

658 Fletcher Forum of World Affairs. 1995. Papers on Military Intervention Alternatives. FFWA 19 (2).

659 Franck, T. M. 1983. The Strategic Role of Legal Principles in the Falklands War. American Journal of International Law 77: 109-123.

660 Geller, D. S. 1988. Power System Membership and Patterns of War. IPSR 9: 365-379.

661 -. 1992. Capability Concentration, Power Transition and War. II 17: 269-284.

662 -. 1993. Power Differentials and War in Rival Dyads. ISQ 37: 173-193.

663 Gilpin, R. 1988. Theory of Hegemonic War. JIDH 18: 591-614.

664 Gochman, C. S.; Leng, R. J. 1981. Realpolitik and the Road to War. ISQ 27: 97-120.

665 -. 1988. Militarized Disputes, Incidents and Crises. II 14: 157-163.

666 Gochman, C. S.; Maoz, Z. 1984. Militarized Interstate Disputes. JCR 28: 585-616.

667 Grabendorff, W. 1982. Interstate Conflict Behavior and Regional Potential for Conflict in Latin America. JIAS 24: 267-294.

668 Greenwood, C. 1987. The Concept of War in International Law. IACLQ 36: 283-306.

669 -. 1993. Is There a Right of Humanitarian Intervention? World Today 49 (2): 34-40.

670 Guilmartin, J. F. 1988. Ideology and Conflict: Wars of the Ottoman Empire. JIDH 18: 721-748.

671 Gurr, T. R.; Bishop, V. F. 1976. Violent Nations and Others. JCR 20: 79-110.

672 Hagan, J. D. 1994. Domestic Political Systems and War Proneness. ISQ 38: 183-208.

673 Halliday, F. 1994. The Gulf War and the Study of International Relations. RIS 20: 109-130.

674 Harrison, B. T. 1991. The Impact of Public Opposition on American Foreign Policy with Vietnam. Conflict 11: 41-52.

675 Hipel, K. W.; Wang, M.; Fraser, N. M. 1988. Hypergame Analysis of the Falkland-Malvinas Conflict. ISQ 32: 335-358.

676 Hoffman, S. 1981. States and the Morality of War. PT 9: 149-172.

677 Hooks, G.; McLauchlan, G. 1992. Reevaluating Theories of US War Making. SSQ 73: 437-456.

678 Hopf, T. 1991. Polarity, the Offense-Defense Balance and War. APSR 85: 475-494.

679 Houweling, H. W.; Kune, J. B. 1984. Do Outbreaks of War Follow a Poisson Process? JCR 28: 51-62.

680 Houweling, H. W.; Siccama, J. G. 1985. Epidemiology of War. JCR 29: 641-664.

681 -. 1991. Power Transitions and Critical Points as Predictors of Great Power War. JCR 35: 642-658.

682 -. 1991. Power Transitions as a Cause of War. JCR 32: 87-102.

683 -. 1992. Escalation to World War: The Power Transition Hypothesis as an Alternative to Systemic Theories. AP 27: 93-110.

684 Huntington, S. P. 1993. Clash of Civilizations? FA 72 (Summer): 22-49.

685 Hussein, S. M.; Bueno de Mesquita, B.; Lalman, D. 1987. Modeling War and Peace. APSR 81: 221-232.

686 International Affairs. 1993. Papers on Humanitarian War, Peacekeeping and the UN. IA 69 (3).

687 International Interactions. 1990. Papers on Theories of War. II 16 (3).

688 -. 1993. Papers on Democracy and War. II 18 (3).

689 -. 1993. Papers on the Scientific Study of War. II 19 (1/2).

690 International Journal. 1993. Papers on Humanitarian Intervention. IJ 48 (4).

691 International Studies Quarterly. 1983. Papers on Economic Foundations of War. ISQ 27 (4).

692 -. 1987. Papers on Human Evolution and War. ISQ 31 (1).

693 James, P. 1995. Structural Realism and the Causes of War. ISQ 39: 181-208.

694 Johnson, J. T. 1985. Threats, Values and Defense: Does Defense of Values by Armed Force Remain Moral Possibility? Parameters 15: 13-29.

695 Journal of Interdisciplinary History. 1988. Papers on the Origin and Prevention of Major Wars. JIDH 18 (4).

696 Journal of Peace Research 1981. Papers on the Causes of War. JPS 18 (1).

697 -. 1987. Papers on the Humanitarian Law of Armed Conflict. JPR 24 (3).

698 -. 1994. Papers on Humanitarian Intervention. JPR 31 (2).

699 Journal of Social Issues. 1969. Papers on Racism, War and the Conception of Evil. JSI 25 (1).

700 -. 1993. Papers on Psychological Research on the Persian Gulf War. JSI 49 (4).

701 Kilgour, D. M. 1991. Domestic Political Structure and War: A Game Theoretic Approach. JCR 35: 266-284.

702 Kim, W. 1989. Power, Alliance and Major Wars. JCR 33: 231-254.

703 -. 1991. Alliance Transitions and Great Power War. AJPS 35: 833-850.

704 -. 1992. Power Transitions and Great Power War. WP 45:153-172.

705 Kim, W.; Bueno de Mesquita, B. 1995. How Perceptions Influence the Risk of War. ISQ 39: 51-66.

706 Kim, W.; Morrow, J. D. 1992. When Do Power Shifts Lead to War. AJPS 36: 896-922.

707 Kirby, A. M.; Ward, M. D. 1987. Spatial Analysis of Peace and War. CPS 20: 293-313.

708 Kiser, E.; Drass, K. A.; Brustein, W. 1995. Ruler Autonomy and War in Early Modern Western Europe. ISQ 39: 109-138.

709 Klingberg, F. L. 1966. Predicting the Termination of War. JCR 10: 129-171.

710 Kober, A. 1995. Military Decision in War. AFAS 22: 65-82.

711 Kocs, S. A. 1995. Territorial Disputes and Interstate War. JOP 57: 159-175.

712 Kuper, L. 1981. Theories of Genocide. EARS 4: 320-333.

713 Lake, D. A. 1992. Powerful Pacifists: Democratic States and War. APSR 80: 1151-1169.

714 Lee, J. R.; Milstein, J. S. 1973. A Political Economy of the Vietnam War. PPRS 21: 41-63.

715 Leng, R. J.; Gochman, C. S. 1982. Dangerous Disputes: A Study of Conflict Behavior and War. AJPS 26: 664-687.

716 Leng, R. J.; Singer, J. D. 1988. Militarized Interactive Crises. ISQ 32: 155-173.

717 Levy, J. S. 1981. Alliance Formation and War Behavior: The Great Powers. JCR 25: 581-614.

718 -. 1982. Contagion of Great Power War Behavior. AJPS 26: 562-582.

719 -. 1982. Historical Trends in Great Power War. ISQ 26: 278-301.

720 -. 1985. Theories of General War. WP 37: 344-374.

721 -. 1988. Domestic Politics and War. JIDH 18: 653-674.

722 Levy, J. S.; Morgan, T. C. 1984. Frequency and Seriousness of War. JCR 28: 731-749.

723 -. 1986. The War Weariness Hypothesis. AJPS 30: 26-49.

724 Licklider, R. 1995. Consequences of Negotiated Settlements in Civil Wars. APSR 89: 681-690.

725 Lovell, G. W.; Lutz, C. H. 1994. Conquest and Population: Maya Demography in Historical Perspective. LARR 29: 133-140.

726 Luterbacher, U. 1984. Last Words about War. JCR 28: 165-182.

727 Majeski, S. J.; Sylan, D. J. 1984. Simple Choices and Complex Calculations: A Critique of The War Trap. JCR 28: 316-340.

728 Mansfield, E. D. 1988. Distribution of Wars over Time. WP 41: 21-45.

729 -. 1992. Concentration of Capabilities and the Onset of War. JCR 36: 3-24.

730 Mansfield, E. D.; Snyder, J. 1995. Democratization and the Danger of War. IS 20: 5-38.

731 Maoz, Z. 1983. Resolve, Capacities and the Outcome of International Disputes. JCR 27: 195-229.

732 -. 1984. Peace by Empire? Conflict Outcomes and International Stability, 1816-1976. JPR 21: 227-242.

733 -. 1989. Joining the Club of Nations: Political Development and International Conflict. ISQ 33: 199-231.

734 -. 1989. Power, Capabilities and Paradoxical Conflict Outcome. WP 41: 239-266.

735 Maoz, Z.; Abdolali, N. 1989. Regime Types and International Conflict. JCR 33: 3-36.

736 Maoz, Z.; Russett, B. 1993. Normative and Structural Causes of Democratic Peace. APSR 87: 624-638.

737 Maxwell, M. 1992. The Gulf War and Political Science. PS 25: 693-695.

738 Midlarsky, M. I. 1974. Power, Uncertainty and the Onset of International Violence. JCR 18: 395-431.

739 -. 1990. A Hierarchical Equilibrium Theory of Systemic War. ISQ 30: 77-105.

740 Mintz, A.; Geva, N. 1993. Why Don't Democracies Fight Each Other? JCR 37: 484-503.

741 Mitchell, C. R.; Nicholson, M. 1983. Rational Models and the Ending of Wars. JCR 27: 495-510.

742 Modelski, G.; Morgan, P. M. 1985. Understanding Global War. JCR 29: 391-417.

743 Morgan, T. C.; Campbell, S. H. 1991. Domestic Structure, Decisional Constraints and War: So Why Kant Democracies Fight? JCR 35: 187-211.

744 Morrow, J. D. 1985. A Continuous Outcome Expected Utility Theory of War. JCR 29: 473-502.

745 -. 1986. A Spatial Model of International Conflict. APSR 80: 1131-1150.

746 Morrow, J. D.; Price, B. L.; Simowitz, R. 1991. Conceptual Problems in Theorizing about International Conflict. APSR 85: 923-940.

747 Most, B. A.; Starr, H. 1980. Diffusion, Reinforcement, Geopolitics and the Spread of War. APSR 74: 932-946.

748 -. 1982. Case Selection, Conceptualizations and Basic Logic in Study of War. AJPS 26: 834-856.

749 -. 1983. Conceptualizing War. JCR 27: 137-159.

750 Moul, W. B. 1988. Balances of Power and the Escalation to War of Serious Disputes among the European Great Powers. AJPS 32: 241-275.

751 -. 1994. Predicting the Severity of Great Power War from Its Extent: Statistical Illusions. JCR 38: 160-169.

752 Muhammad, M. E. 1987. Different Conceptions of Jihad and Its Relevance to Islamic Movements. JJIR 9: 45-71.

753 Muncaster, R. G.; Zinnes, D. A. 1982. A Model of Inter-Nation Hostility Dynamics and War. CMAPS 6: 19-38.

754 Nardin, T. 1984. Moral Basis of the Law of War. JIA 37: 295-310.

755 Nicholson, M. 1987. Conceptual Bases of The War Trap. JCR 31: 346-369.

756 Niou, E. M. S.; Ordeshook, P. C. 1987. Preventive War and the Balance of Power: A Game Theoretic Approach. JCR 31: 387-419.

757 O'Loughlin, J. 1986. Spatial Models of International Conflicts: War Behavior. AAAG 76: 63-80.

758 -. 1988. Is There a Geography of International Conflicts? PG 7: 85-91.

759 Organski, A. F. K.; Kugler, J. 1978. Predicting Outcomes of International Wars. CPS 11: 141-180.

760 Page, B. I.; Brody, R. A. 1972. Policy Voting and Electoral Process: The Vietnam War Issue. APSR 66: 679-995.

761 Papers of the Peace Research Society 1969. Papers on the Vietnam War. PPRS 10 (June).

762 Patraeus, D. H. 1989. Military Influence and the Post-Vietnam Use of Force. AFAS 15: 489-506.

763 Paul, T. V. 1995. Time Pressure and War Initiation. CJPS 28: 255-276.

764 Peace Research Reviews. 1969. Papers on War. PRR 3 (5), 1974 5 (4).

765 -. 1979. Papers on Surprise Attacks. PRR 8 (4).

766 Pearson, F. S. 1974. Foreign Military Interventions and Domestic Disputes. ISQ 18: 259-290.

767 -. 1974. Geographic Proximity and Foreign Military Intervention. JCR 18: 432-460.

768 Rasler, K. A.; Thompson, W. R. 1983. Global Wars, Public Debts and the Long Cycle. WP 35: 489-516.

769 -. 1985. Government Expenditures, Tax Revenues and Global Wars. APSR 79: 491-507.

770 Ray, J. L.; Vural, A. 1986. Power Disputes and Paradoxical Conflict Outcomes. II 12: 315-342.

771 Regens, J. L.; Gaddie, R. K.; Lockerbie, B. 1995. Electoral Consequences of Voting to Declare War. JCR 39: 168-182.

772 Reiter, D. 1995. Preemptive Wars almost Never Happen. IS 20: 5-34.

773 Russett, B. 1995. Processes of Dyadic Choice for War and Peace. WP 47: 268-282.

774 Russett, B.; Antholis, W. 1992. Do Democracies Fight Each Other? The Peloponnesian War. JPR 29: 415-434.

775 Samuel, S. G. W. 1990. To Attack or Not to Attack. JCR 34: 531-552.

776 Sandler, S. 1978. Impact of Protracted Peripheral Wars on the American Domestic System. JJIR 3: 27-59.

777 Saperstein, A. M. 1992. Are Democracies More or Less Prone to War? A Dynamical Model Approach. MCM 16: 213-221.

778 Schampel, J. H. 1993. Change in Material Capabilities and the Onset of War: Dyadic Approach. ISQ 37: 395-408.

779 Schulman, H. 1972. Two Sources of Antiwar Sentiment in America. MJPS 78: 513-536.

780 Schweller, R. L. 1992. Democratic Structure and Preventive War: Are Democracies More Pacific? WP 44: 235-269.

781 Shultz, R. H. 1979. Coercive Force and Military Strategy: Deterrence Logic and Cost-Benefit Model of Counterinsurgency Warfare. WPQ 32: 444-466.

782 Sigelman, L.; Conover, P. J. 1981. Knowledge and Opinions about Iranian Crisis. POQ 45: 477-491.

783 Singer, J. D. 1981. Accounting for International War. JPR 18: 1-18.

784 -. 1982. Confrontational Behavior and Escalation to War. JPR 19: 37-48.

785 Singer, J. D.; Small, M. 1974. Foreign Policy Indicators: Predictors of War in History and the State of the World Message. PSCI 5: 271-296.

786 Siverson, R. M.; King, J. 1980. Attributes of National Alliance Membership and War Participation. AJPS 24: 1-15.

787 Siverson, R. M.; Staff, H. 1990. Opportunity, Willingness and the Diffusion of War. APSR 84: 47-67.

788 Siverson, R. M.; Sullivan, M. 1983. Distribution of Power and the Onset of War. JCR 27: 473-494.

789 Siverson, R. M.; Tennefoss, M. R. 1984. Interstate Conflicts: 1815-1965. II 9: 147-178.

790 -. 1984. Power, Alliance and Escalation of International Conflict. APSR 78: 1057-1069.

791 Small, M.; Singer, J. D. 1970. Patterns of International Warfare. ANNALS 391: 145-155.

792 -. 1976. War Proneness of Democratic Regimes. JJIR 1: 50-68.

793 Society. 1983. Papers on the Vietnam War. Vol 21 (1).

794 Sofer, S. 1985. Time and the Conduct of War. JJIR 7: 64-86.

795 Somerville, J. 1981. Patriotism and War. Ethics 91: 568-578.

796 Starr, H. 1992. Democracy and War: Choice, Learning and Security Communities. JPR 29: 207-214.

797 -. 1992. Why Don't Democracies Fight One Another? Evaluating the Theory Findings Feedback Loop. JJIR 14: 41-59.

798 Starr, H.; Most, B. A. 1978. A Return Journey: Richardson, Frontiers and Wars. JCR 22: 441-468.

799 -. 1983. Contagion and Border Effects on Contemporary African Conflict. CPS 16: 92-117.

800 -. 1985. Forms and Processes of War Diffusion: Contagion in African Conflict. CPS 18: 206-228.

801 Stein, A. A. 1976. Conflict and Cohesion. JCR 20: 143-172.

802 Stoll, R. J. 1984. Impact of Major Power War Involvement on Major Power Dispute Involvement. CMAPS 7: 71-82.

803 Suganami, H. 1990. Bringing Order to the Causes of War Debate. Millennnium 19 (1): 19-35.

804 Teaching Political Science. Papers on Vietnam. TPS 12 (4).

805 Terrell, L. M. 1972. Patterns of International Involvement and International Violence. ISQ 16: 167-186.

806 Thompson, W. R. 1982. Phases of the Business Cycle and the Outbreak of War. ISQ 26: 301-311.

807 -. 1983. Uneven Economic Growth, Systemic Challenges and Global Wars. ISQ 27: 341-355.

808 -. 1986. Polarity, the Long Cycle and Global Power Warfare. JCR 30: 587-615.

809 Thompson, W. R.; Duval, R. D.; Dia, A. 1980. Wars, Alliances and Military Expenditures: Two Pendulum Hypotheses. JCR 23: 629-654.

810 Thompson, W. R.; Rasler, K. A. 1988. War and Systematic Capacity Reconcentration. JCR 32: 335-366.

811 Thompson, W. R.; Rasler, K. A.; Li, R. P. Y. 1980. Systemic Interaction Opportunities and War Behavior. II 7: 57-85.

812 Van Evera, S. 1984. Cult of the Offensive and the Origins of the First World War. IS 9 (Summer): 58-108.

813 -. 1994. Hypotheses on Nationalism and War. IS 18: 5-39.

814 Vasquez, J. A. 1987. Steps to War: Toward a Scientific Explanation of Correlates of War Findings. WP 40: 108-145.

815 Vayrynen, R. 1983. Economic Cycles, Power Transitionss, Political Management and Wars between Major Powers. ISQ 27: 389-418.

816 Voevodsky, J. 1969. Quantitative Behavior of Warring Nations. Journal of Psychology 72: 262-292.

817 Volgy, T. J.; Mayhall, S. 1995. Status Inconsistency and Internal War: Exploring the Effects of Systemic Change. ISQ 29: 67-84.

818 Wagner, R. H. 1984. War and Expected Utility Theory. WP 36: 407-423.

819 -. 1994. Peace, War and the Balance of Power. APSR 88: 593-607.

820 Wallace, M. D. 1981. The Para Bellum Hypothesis Revisited. JCR 18: 91-96.

821 Wallensteen, P.; Axell, K. 1993. Armed Conflict at the End of the Cold War. JPR 30: 331-346.

822 Wallensteen, P.; Sollenberg, M. 1995. After the Cold War: Emerging Patterns of Armed Conflict. JPR 32: 345-360.

823 Waltz, K. N. 1988. Origins of War in Neorealist Theory. JIDH 18: 615-628.

824 Wang, K.; Ray, J. L. 1994. The Fate of Initiators of Interstate Wars Involving Great Powers since 1495. ISQ 38: 139-154.

825 Wayman, F. W. 1984. Bipolarity and War: The Role of Capacity Concentration and Alliance Patterns among Major Powers. JPR 21: 24-42.

826 Wayman, F. W.; Singer, J. D.; Goertz, G. 1983. Capabilities, Allocations and Success in Militarized Disputes and Wars. ISQ 27: 497-515.

827 Weart, S. R. 1994. Peace among Democratic and Oligarchic Republics. JPR 31: 299-316.

828 Weede, E. 1984. Democracy and War Involvement. JCR 28: 649-664.

829 -. 1992. Some Simple Calculations on Democracy and War Involvement. JPR 29: 377-384.

830 Wilcox, C.; Ferrara, J.; Allsop, D. 1993. Group Differences in Support for Action in the Gulf: Gender, Generation, Ethnicity. APQ 21: 343-359.

831 Wittman, D. 1979. How a War Ends: A Rational Model Approach. JCR 23: 743-763.

832 Wu, S. 1990. To Attack or Not to Attack. JCR 34: 531-552.

833 Zagare, F. C.; Kilgour, D. M. 1993. Modeling Massive Retaliation. CMAPS 13: 61-86.

World Systems

834 Alexandroff, A.; Rosecrance, R.; Stein, A. A. 1977. History, Quantitative Analysis and the Balance of Power. JCR 21: 35-74.

835 Brown, C. 1988. Ethics of Coexistence: International Theory of Coexistence. RIS 14: 213-222.

836 Buzan, B.; Little, R. 1994. The Idea of International System. IPSR 15: 231-256.

837 Chase-Dunn, C.; Hall, T. D. 1993. Comparing World-Systems. SF 71: 851-886.

838 -. 1994. Historical Evolution of World Systems. SI 64: 257-280.

839 Chirot, D.; Hall, T. D. 1982. World System Theory. ANRS 8: 81-106.

840 Cusack, T. R.; Zimmer, U. 1989. Realpolitik and Multistate System Endurance. JOP 51: 247-285.

841 Daedalus. 1995. Papers on the Quest for World Order. Vol 124 (3).

842 Etudes Internationales. 1986. Papers on Latin America in the World System. EINT 17 (2).

843 Goldgeier, J. M.; McFaul, M. 1992. Core and Periphery in the Post-Cold War Era. IO 46: 467-491.

844 Gurr, T. R. 1994. Peoples against State: Ethnopolitical Conflict and the Changing World System. ISQ 38: 347-378.

845 Healy, B.; Stein, A. A. 1973. Balance of Power in International History. JCR 17: 33-61.

846 Heintz, P. 1976. The Change of Parameters of the International System 1870-1970. JCR 20: 173-184.

847 Holloway, S. K.; Tomlinson, R. 1995. The New World Order and General Assembly: Bloc Realignment at the UN in the Post-Cold War World. CJPS 28: 227-254.

848 Holm, H. H.; Sorensen, G. 1993. A New World Order. CAC 28: 265-302.

849 Hout, W. 1992. Centers and Peripheries: An Assessment of the Contribution of Dependency and World Systems Theories to the Study of International Relations. AP 27: 71-92.

850 International Organization. 1978. Papers on Dependency in the Global System. IO 32 (1).

851 Keohane, R. O. 1990. Multilateralism: An Agenda for Research. IJ 45: 731-764.

852 Kugler, J.; Organski, A. F. K. 1987. The End of Hegemony: Says Who? II 15: 113-128.

853 MacLaughlin, J. 1994. Geopolitics and Geoculture in World Systems Theorizing. SICID 28: 62-69.

854 Marshall, J. R. 1981. Political Integration and the Effect of War on Suicide. SF 59: 771-785.

855 Midlarsky, M. I. 1981. Equilibria in the Nineteenth-Century Balance of Power Systems. AJPS 25: 270-296.

856 -. 1983. Absence of Memory in Nineteenth Century Alliance System: Queuing Theory and Bivariate Probability Distributions. AJPS 27: 762-784.

857 Ostrom, C. W.; Aldrich, J. H. 1978. Relationship between Size and Stability in the Major Power International System. AJPS 22: 743-771.

858 Ray, J. L.; Singer, J. D. 1973. Measuring Concentration of Power in the International System. SMAR 1: 403-437.

859 Russett, B. 1968. Is There a Long-Run Trend toward Concentration in the International System? CPS 1: 103-122.

860 -. 1985. The Mysterious Case of Vanishing Hegemony. IO 39: 207-231.

861 Sharpe, L. J. 1989. Fragmentation and Territoriality in the European State System. IPSR 10: 223-238.

862 Skocpol, T. 1977. Wallerstein's World Capitalist System. AJS 82: 1075-1089.

863 Snidal, D. 1985. Limits of Hegemonic Stability Theory. IO 39: 579-614.

864 Stoll, R. J. 1984. Bloc Concentrations and the Balance of Power. JCR 28: 25-50.

865 Todd, J. E. 1971. Law Making Behavior of States in the United Nations as a Function of Location within Formal World Regions. ISQ 15: 297-315.

866 Van Ham, P. 1992. Hegemonic Stability Theory and Regimes in the Study of International Relations. AP 27: 29-48.

867 Volgy, T. J.; Imwalle, L. E. 1995. Hegemonic and Bipolar Perspectives on the New World Order. AJPS 39: 819-834.

868 Wallace, M. D. 1975. Clusters of Nations in the Global System, 1865-1964. JCR 19: 67-110.

869 Wallerstein, I. 1976. A World System Perspective on Social Sciences. BJS 27: 343-352.

870 -. 1993. The World System after the Cold War. JPR 30: 1-6.

871 Wellhofer, E. S. 1989. Core and Periphery: Territorial Dimensions in Politics. US 26: 340-355.

872 Young, O. R. 1982. Regime Dynamics: Rise and Fall of International Regimes. IO 36: 277-298.

873 Zinnes, D. A. 1967. An Analytic Study of Balance of Power Theories. JPR 4: 270-288.

LEGAL AND CRIMINAL STUDIES

1 Abel, R. L. 1980. Redirecting Social Studies of Law. LASR 14: 805-829.

2 Arnold, B. L.; Hagan, J. 1992. Careers of Misconduct: The Structure of Prosecuted Professional Deviance among Lawyers. ASR 57: 771-780.

3 Atkins, B. M. 1991. Party Capacity Theory as an Explanation for Intervention Behavior in the English Court of Appeal. AJPS 35: 881-903.

4 Bailey, M. J.; Rubin, P. H. 1994. A Positive Theory of Legal Change. IRLE 1994: 467-477.

5 Baum, L.; Canon, B. C. 1981. Patterns of Adoption of Tort Law Innovations. APSR 75: 975-987.

6 Bobbitt, P. 1989. Is Law Politics? SLR 41: 1233-1312.

7 Brigham, J. 1990. Consequences of Survey Research for Constitutional Practice. ROP 52: 582-603.

8 Burke, W. L. 1993. A History of the Opening Statement. AJLH 37: 25-64.

9 Campbell, T. J. 1984. Regression Analysis in Title VII Cases: Minimum Standards, Comparable Worth and Other Issues Where Law and Statistics Meet. SLR 36: 1299-1324.

10 Carro, J. L.; Brann, A. R. 1982. Use of Legislative Histories by the US Supreme Court: Statistical Analysis. JOL 9: 282-303.

11 Chapman, B. 1982. Individual Rights and Collective Rationality: Some Implications for Economic Analysis of Law. Hofstra Law Review 10: 455-481.

12 Chiorazzi, M. 1983. Statistics in Litigation: A Selective Bibliography. LACP 46: 297-303.

13 Chung, T. Y. 1993. Efficiency of Comparative Negligence. JLS 22: 395-404.

14 Coase, R. H. (13: 1978). Economics and Contiguous Disciplines. JLS 7: 201-212.

15 Coleman, J. L. 1984. Economics and the Law: A Critical Review of the Foundations of the Economic Approach to Law. Ethics 94: 649-680.

16 Columbia Journal of Transnational Law. 1985. Papers on Marxism and the Law. Vol 23 (2).

17 Columbia Law Review. 1985. Papers on the Law and Economics. Vol 85 (5).

18 -. 1987. Papers on Kantian Legal Theory. Vol 87 (3).

19 Cooter, R. D.; Rubinfeld, D. L. 1989. Economic Analysis of Legal Disputes and Their Resolution. JEL 27: 1067-1097.

20 Cornell Law Review. 1981. Papers on Legal Theory. CORLR 66 (5).

21 Cross, F. B. 1992. An Empirical Evaluation of the Effect of Lawyers on the US Economy and Political System. TLR 70: 645-684.

22 Driessen, P. A. 1983. The Wedding of Social Science and the Courts. SSQ 64: 476-493.

23 Dyer, J. A. 1976. Do Lawyers Make a Difference? Voting on No Fault Insurance. JOP 38: 452-456.

24 Epstein, L. 1994. Exploring the Participation of Organized Interests in State Court Litigation. PRQ 47: 335-352.

25 Freudenburg, W. R.; Jones, T. R. 1991. Attitudes and Stress in Presence of Technological Risk: The Supreme Court Hypothesis. SF 69: 1143-1168.

26 Galanter, M. 1974. Why the Haves Come out Ahead: Speculations on the Limits of Legal Change. LASR 9: 95-160.

27 Glick, H. 1991. Innovation and Re-Invention of State Policy Making: Living Will Laws. JOP 53: 835-850.

28 Grady, M. F. 1988. Why Are People Negligent? Technology, Nondurable Precautions and the Medical Malpractice Explosion. NLR 82: 293-334.

29 Harvard Law Review. 1971. Papers on the Debate over Mathematics in the Law of Evidence. HLR 84 (8): 1801-1821.

30 Houston, R. A.; Prest, W. A. 1995. The Mortality of English Barristers. JIDH 26: 233-250.

31 Ignagni, J.; Meernik, J. 1994. Explaining Congressional Attempts to Reverse Supreme Court Decisions. PRQ 47: 353-372.

32 International Journal. 1985. Papers on International Law. IJ 40 (3).

33 International Political Science Review. 1992. Papers on Courts, Justices and Political Change. IPSR 13 (3).

34 -. 1994. Papers on Judicialization of Politics. IPSR 15 (2).

35 Journal of State Government. 1988. Papers on State Attorneys General. JSG 61 (3).

36 Kagan, R. A.; Rosen, R. 1985. Social Significance of the Large Law Firm. SLR 1985: 399-446.

37 Kocs, S. A. 1994. Explaining the Strategic Behavior of States: International Law as System Structure. ISQ 38: 535-556.

38 Landes, W. M.; Posner, R. A. 1993. Influence of Economics on Law. JOLE 36: 385-424.

39 Law and Contemporary Problems. 1978. Papers on Social Science and the Law. LACP 42 (4).

40 -. 1983. Papers on Statistical Inference in Litigation. LACP 46 (4).

41 -. 1984. Papers on Law Enforcement Discretion. LACP 47 (4).

42 -. 1987. Papers on Economists on the Bench. LACP 50 (4).

43 -. 1988. Papers on Empirical Studies of Civil Procedure. LACP 51 (3-4).

44 -. 1988. Papers on Vice. LACP 51 (1).

45 -. 1989. Papers on Contract Law Economics. LACP 52 (1).

46 Law and Society Review. 1975. Papers on Law and Society in American History. LASR 10 (1-2).

47 -. 1978. Papers on the Sociology of Law. LASR 12 (4).

48 -. 1979. Papers on Plea Bargaining. LASR 13 (2).

49 -. 1982. Papers on Psychology and the Law. LASR 17 (1).

50 -. 1988. Papers on Ideology and the Law. LASR 22 (4).

51 -. 1990. Papers on Trial Courts. LASR 24 (2).

52 -. 1992. Papers on Legal Culture. LASR 26 (1).

53 -. 1994. Papers on Community and Identity in Sociolegal Studies. LASR 28 (5).

54 Lidz, V. 1979. Law as Index, Phenomenon and Element: Sociology of Law. SI 49: 5-26.

55 Macaulay, S. 1984. Law and Behavioral Sciences. LAP 6: 149-188.

56 MacCoun, R. J.; Tyler, T. R. 1988. Bias of Citizens' Perceptions of the Criminal Jury. Law and Human Behavior 12: 333-352.

57 McGarrell, E. F. 1989. Ideological Bases and Functions of Contemporary Juvenile Law Reform: New York State. CC 13: 163-187.

58 McGuire, K. T. 1993. Lawyers and the US Supreme Court: The Washington Community and Legal Ethics. AJPS 37: 365-390.

59 -. 1995. Repeat Players in the Supreme Court: Experienced Lawyers in Litigation Success. JOP 57: 187-196.

60 Moore, M. 1969. The Need for a Theory of Legal Theories. CORLR 69: 988-1047.

61 Myers, M. A. 1980. Predicting the Behavior of Law. LASR 14: 835-858.

62 Nash, A. E. K. 1983. Radical Interpretations of American Law. MLR 81: 274-345.

63 Newman, J. O. 1984. Between Legal Realism and Neutral Principles: Legitimacy of Institutional Values. CLR 72: 200-216.

64 Norpoth, H., et al. 1994. Popular Influence on Supreme Court Decisions. APSR 88: 711-724.

65 Pashigian, B. P. 1977. Determinants of the Demand and Supply of Lawyers. JOLE 20: 53-86.

66 Perspectives on Political Science. 1992. Papers on Courts and the Judicial Process. POPS 21 (3).

67 Public Administration. 1986. Papers on Judicial Review. PA 64 (2).

68 Review of Politics. 1992. Papers on Public Law. ROP 54 (3).

69 Revue Internationale de Droit Compare. 1978. Papers on Comparative Study of Supreme Courts. Vol 30 (1).

70 Rhodes, W. M. 1976. Economics of Criminal Courts. JLS 5: 311-340.

71 Rizzo, M. J. 1985. Rules vs. Cost-Benefit Analysis in the Common Law. CJ 4: 865-896.

72 Roper, R. T. 1979. Jury Size: Impact on Verdict's Correctness. APQ 7: 438-452.

73 Rosen, S. 1992. The Market for Lawyers. JOLE 35: 215-246.

74 Saks, M. J.; Kidd, R. F. 1980. Human Information Processing and Adjudication: Trial by Heuristics. LASR 15: 123-160.

75 Salzberger, E. M. 1993. Positive Analysis of the Doctrine of Separation of Powers, or Why Do We Have an Independent Judiciary? IRLE 13: 349-379.

76 Sarat, A.; Grossman, J. B. 1975. Courts and Conflict Resolution: Problems in the Mobilization of Adjudication. APSR 69: 1200-1217.

77 Scheppele, K.; Waldron, J. 1991. Contractarian Methods in Political and Legal Evaluation. Yale Journal of Law and Humanities 3: 195-230.

78 Schmalbeck, R. 1986. The Trouble with Statistical Evidence. LACP 49: 221-236.

79 Segal, J. A. 1985. Measuring Change on the Supreme Court: Models. AJPS 29: 461-479.

80 Sheehan, R. S. 1992. Federal Agencies and the Supreme Court: Litigation Outcomes. APQ 20: 478-500.

81 Silbey, S.; Sarat, A. 1987. Critical Traditions in Law and Society Research. LASR 21: 165-174.

82 Smolla, R. A. 1982. Reemergence of the Right-Privilege Distinction in Constitutional Law: The Price of Protesting Too Much. SLR 35: 69-120.

83 Songer, D. R.; Cameron, C. M.; Segal, J. A. 1995. An Empirical Test of the Rational Actor Theory of Litigation. JOP 57: 1119-1129.

84 Songer, D. R.; Segal, J. A.; Cameron, C. M. 1994. Principal Agent Model of Supreme Court-Circuit Court Interactions. AJPS 38: 673-696.

85 Spohn, C.; Gruhl, J.; Welch, S. 1981. The Effect of Race on Sentencing. LASR 16: 71-88.

86 Stanford Law Review. 1985. Papers on the Law Firm as a Social Institution. SLR 37 (2).

87 Stearns, M. L. 1994. The Misguided Renaissance of Social Choice. YLJ 103: 1219-1293.

88 Trubek, D. M. 1984. Critical Legal Studies and Empiricism. SLR 36: 575-622.

89 Tushnet, M. 1991. Critical Legal Studies: A Political History. YLJ 100: 1515-1544.

90 University of Chicago Law Review. 1970. Papers on Product Liability: Economic Analysis and the Law. UCLR 38 (1).

91 -. 1974. Papers on Social Science and the Law. UCLR 41 (2).

92 Waldron, J. 1990. Criticizing Economic Analysis of Law. YLJ 99: 1441-1471.

93 White, M. J. 1991. Economic vs. Sociological Approaches to Legal Research: Bankruptcy. LASR 25: 685-709.

94 Yale Law Journal. 1989. Papers on Popular Legal Culture. YLJ 98 (8).

Constitutions

95 Acker, J. R. 1989. Social Science in Supreme Court Criminal Cases. LAP 12: 1-24.

96 Andjiga, N. G.; Moulen, J. 1988. Binary Games in Constitutional Form and Collective Choice. MSS 16L 189-201.

97 Annals. 1988. Papers on State Constitutions. ANNALS 496.

98 Aranson, P. H. 1987. Procedural and Substantive Constitutional Protection of Economic Liberties. CJ 7: 345-376.

99 Backhaus, J. 1978. Constitutional Guarantees and Distribution of Power and Wealth. PC 33: 45-64.

100 Buchanan, J. M. 1987. Justification in the Compound Republic: The Calculus of Consent in Retrospect. CJ 7: 305-312.

101 -. 1994. Lagged Implementation as an Element in Constitutional Strategy. EJPE 10: 11-26.

102 Buchanan, J. M.; Vanberg, V. 1989. A Theory of Leadership and Deference in Constitutional Construction. PC 61: 15-28.

103 Carroll, J. J.; English, A. 1991. Traditions of State Constitution Making. SALGR 23: 103-109.

104 Cato Journal. 1987. Papers on the Constitution. CJ 7 (2).

105 Chicago-Kent Law Review. 1990. Papers on Classical Philosophy and the American Constitutional Order. Vol 66 (1).

106 Clinton, R. L. 1994. Game Theory, Legal History and the Origins of Judicial Review: A Revisionist Analysis of Marbury vs. Madison. AJPS 38: 285-302.

107 Colantuono, M. G. 1987. Revision of American State Constitutions. CLR 75: 1473-1512.

108 Cooter, R. D.; Drexl, J. 1994. Logic of Power in the Emerging European Constitution: Game Theory and the Division of Powers. IRLE 14: 307-326.

109 Cornell, S.; Kalt, J. P. 1995. Where Does Economic Development Really Come From? Constitutional Rule among the Contemporary Sioux and Apache. EI 33: 402-426.

110 Cornwell, E.; Goodman, J. S.; Swanson, W. R. 1970. State Constitutional Conventions. MJPS 14: 105-130.

111 Denzau, A. T. 1985. Constitution Change and Agenda Control. PC 47: 183-217.

112 Dunn, C. W. 1976. Comparative Partisan and Group Voting Behavior in Constitutional Conventions. APQ 4: 115-120.

113 Dye, T. R. 1987. The Politics of Constitutional Choice. CJ 7: 337-344.

114 Eichberger, J.; Pethig, R. 1994. Constitutional Choice of Rules. EJPE 10: 311-338.

115 Elazar, D. J. 1982. Principles and Traditions Underlying American State Constitutions. Publius 12: 11-26.

116 Eschet-Schwarz, A. 1989. Semi-Direct Democracy in Shaping Swiss Federalism: Revision of the Constitution. Publius 19: 79-106.

117 Gely, R.; Spiller, P. T. 1992. Political Economy of Supreme Court Constitutional Decisions: Roosevelt's Court-Packing Plan. IRLE 12: 45-67.

118 Grafstein, R. 1981. The Problem of Choosing Your Alternatives: A Revision of the Public Choice Theory of Constitutions. SSQ 62: 199-212.

119 Fink, E. C. 1995. Institutional Change as a Sophisticated Strategy: The Bill of Rights as a Political Solution. JTP 7: 477-510.

120 Hardin, R. 1988. Constitutional Political Economy: Agreement on Rules. BJPS 18: 513-530.

121 Hayes, M. N. 1990. Sovereign Immunity in an Economic Theory of Government Behavior. LAP 12: 283-316.

122 Jillson, C. C.; Anderson, T. 1978. Voting Bloc Analysis in the Constitutional Convention: Implications for an Interpretation of the Connecticut Compromise. WPQ 31: 535-547.

123 Journal of Commonwealth and Comparative Politics. 1988. Papers on Constitutions and Development of National Identity. JCACP 26 (2).

124 Kafoglis, M. Z.; Cebula, R. J. 1981. The Buchanan-Tullock Model. PC 35: 179-186.

125 Komesar, N. K. 1984. Taking Institutions Seriously: Introduction to a Strategy for Constitutional Analysis. UCLR 51: 329-365.

126 Law and Contemporary Problems. 1993 Papers on Elected Branch Influences in Constitutional Decisionmaking. LACP 56 (4).

127 Lutz, D. S. 1982. The Purposes of American State Constitutions. Publius 12: 27-44.

128 -. 1994. Toward a Theory of Constitutional Amendment. APSR 88: 355-370.

129 Markovits, I. 1982. Law and Order: Constitutionalism and Legality in Eastern Europe. SLR 34: 513-614.

130 Maser, S. M. 1985. Demographic Factors Affecting Constitutional Decisions: Municipal Charters. PC 47: 121-167.

131 McGuire, R. A. 1988. Constitution Making: A Rational Choice Model of the Federal Convention of 1787. AJPS 32: 483-522.

132 McGuire, R. A.; Ohsfeldt, R. L. 1986. An Economic Model of Voting Behavior over Specific Issues at the Constitutional Convention of 1787. JEH 46: 79-111.

133 -. 1989. Self-Interest, Agency Theory and Political Voting Behavior: Ratification of the US Constitution. AER 79: 219-234.

134 Miller, G. J.; Hammond, T. H. 1987. The Core of the Constitution. APSR 81: 1156-1174.

135 Minford, P. 1995. Time-Inconsistency, Democracy and Optimal Contingent Rules. OEP 47: 195-210.

136 Mitchell, W. C. 1989. The Calculus of Consent: Enduring Contributions to Public Choice and Political Science. PC 60: 201-210.

137 Murphy, P. 1983. Moralities, Rule Choice and the Universal Legislator. SR 50: 757-802.

138 Nice, D. C. 1988. Interest Groups and State Constitutions. SALGR 20: 21-27.

139 Northwestern University Law Review. 1989. Papers on Republican Thinking in Modern Constitutional Theory. NLR 84 (1).

140 Ostrom, V. 1987. Buchanan and the Constitutional Bases of Political Decision Making. PS 20: 242-245.

141 Presidential Studies Quarterly. 1992. Papers on the Bill of Rights and Republican Government. PSQ 22 (1).

142 Press, C. 1982. Assessing the Implications of State Constitutional Change. Publius 12: 99-112.

143 PS. 1991. Papers on Divided Government and Constitutional Reform. Vol 24: 634-657.

144 Publius. 1980. Papers on Constitutionalism. Publius 10 (4).

145 -. 1982. Papers on the Articles of Confederation. Publius 12 (4).

146 Rae, D. W. 1969. Decision Rules and Individual Values in Constitutional Choice. APSR 63: 40-56.

147 Richardson, L. E.; Scheb, J. M. 1993. Divided Government and the Supreme Court: Judicial Behavior in Civil Rights and Liberties Cases. APQ 21: 458-472.

148 Riker, W. H. 1984. Heresthetics of Constitution Making: The Presidency in 1787. APSR 78: 1-16.

149 Sabetti, F. 1982. The Making of Italy as an Experiment in Constitutional Choice. Publius 12: 65-84.

150 Schweizer, U. 1990. The Calculus of Consent: A Game-Theoretic Perspective. JITE 146: 28-54.

151 Sinclair, B. D. 1994. House Special Rules and the Institutional Design Controversy. LSQ 19: 477-494.

152 Stroup, R. L. 1987. Reflections on Freedom, Fairness, and the Constitution. CJ 7: 403-410.

153 Teaching Political Science. 1985. Papers on Teaching about Constitutional Law. TPS 13 (1), and 1986 14 (1).

154 Texas Law Review. 1985. Papers on the Emergence of State Constitutional Law. TLR 63 (6/7).

155 Thompson, P.; Boyd, S. R. 1994. The Use of the Item Veto in Texas. SALGR 26: 38-45.

156 Umbeck, J. 1977. A Theory of Contract Choice and the California Gold Rush. JOLE 20: 421-437.

157 Watson, W. G. 1982. Economics of Constitution Making. LACP 45: 87-108.

158 Whicker, M. L.; Strickland, R. A. 1990. Constitutional Amendments, the Ratification Process and Public Opinion: A Computer Simulation. SAG 21: 115-132.

159 Zusman, P. 1992. Constitutional Selection of Collective-Choice Rules in a Cooperative Enterprise. JEBAO 17: 353-362.

Crime and Punishment

160 American Behavioral Scientist. 1983. Papers on Crime Control Policy. ABS 27 (1).

161 American Journal of Sociology. 1987. Papers on Criminology. AJS 92 (4).

162 Annals. 1976. Papers on US Crime and Justice. ANNALS 423.

163 -. 1985. Papers on Prison Crowding. ANNALS 478.

164 -. 1987. Papers on Neighborhood, Family and Employment Strategies to Prevent Crime. ANNALS 494.

165 -. 1993. Papers on White Collar Crime. ANNALS 525.

166 -. 1995. Papers on Reactions to Crime. ANNALS 539.

167 Barlow, D. E.; Barlow, M. H.; Chircios, T. G. 1993. Long Economic Cycles and the Criminal Justice System in the US. CLASC 19: 143-170.

168 Barnett, A.; Blumstein, A.; Farrington, D. P. 1987. Probabilistic Models of Youthful Criminal Careers. Criminology 25: 83-107.

169 -. 1989. Prospective Test of a Criminal Career Model. Criminology 27: 373-388.

170 Bennett, R. R. 1991. Development and Crime. SQ 32: 343-364.

171 Blair, D. W.; Mabry, R. H. 1980. Regional Crime Growth: Shift-Share Technique. GAC 11: 48-51.

172 Block, C. R.; Block, R. L. 1984. Crime Definition, Crime Measurement and Victim Surveys. JSI 40: 137-160.

173 Block, R. L. 1981. Victim-Offender Dynamics in Violent Crime. JCLAC 72: 743-761.

174 Blumstein, A.; Cohen, J.; Rosenfeld, R. 1991. Trend and Deviation in Crime Rates. Criminology 29: 237-264.

175 Blumstein, A.; Moritra, S. 1979. The Time Series of the Imprisonment Rate. JCLAC 70: 376-390.

176 Bordley, R. F. 1982. Public Perceptions of Crime: Derivation of Warr's Power Function from the Bayesian Odds Relations. SF 61: 134-143.

177 Braithwaite, J. 1981. The Myth of Social Class and Criminality Reconsidered. ASR 45: 36-57.

178 -. 1993. Crime and the Average America. LASR 27: 215-232.

179 Britt, C. L. 1994. Crime and Unemployment among Youths in the US. AJEAS 53: 99-110.

180 Brown, D. W.; McDougal, S. L. 1977. Noncompliance with Law: A Utility Analysis of City Crime Rates. SSQ 58: 195-214.

181 Bursik, R. J.; Grasmick, H. G. 1993. Economic Deprivation and Neighborhood Crime Rates. LASR 27: 263-284.

182 Caldeira, G. A.; Cowart, A. T. 1980. Budgets, Institutions and Change: Criminal Justice Policy. AJPS 24: 413-438.

183 Cantor, D.; Land, K. C. 1985. Unemployment and Crime Rates in the Post-World War II US. ASR 50: 317-332.

184 Chilton, R. 1980. Criminal Statistics in the US. JCLAC 71: 56-87.

185 Clarke, S. H.; Freeman, J. L.; Koch, G. G. 1976. Bail Risk. JLS 5: 341-286.

186 Cloninger, D. O.; Marchesini, R. 1995. Crime Betas: A Portfolio Measure of Criminal Activity. SSQ 76: 634-647.

187 Cloninger, D. O.; Sartorius, L. C. 1979. Crime Rates, Clearance Rates and Enforcement Effort. AJEAS 38: 389-402.

188 Cohen, L. E.; Cantor, D. 1981. Residential Burglary in the US. Journal of Research in Crime and Delinquency 18: 113-127.

189 Cohen, L. E.; Felson, M. 1979. Social Change and Crime Rate Trends. ASR 44: 588-607.

190 Cohen, L. E.; Felson, M.; Land, K. C. 1980. Property Crime Rates in the US. AJS 86: 90-118.

191 Cohen, L. E.; Kluegel, J. S.; Land, K. C. 1981. Social Inequality and Predatory Criminal Victimization. ASR 46: 505-524.

192 Cohen, L. E.; Lichbach, M. I. 1982. Alternative Measures of Crime. SQ 23: 253-266.

193 Cohen, L. E.; Machalek, R. 1988. A General Theory of Expropriative Crime: An Evolutionary Ecological Approach. AJS 94: 465-501.

194 Collins, J. J.; Cox, B.; Langan, P. A. 1986. Job Activities and Personal Victimization. SSR 16: 345-360.

195 Contemporary Crises. 1989. Papers on Punishment. CC 13 (4).

196 Cornwell, C.; Trumbull, W. N. 1994. Estimating the Economic Model of Crime. REAS 76: 360-366.

197 De Haan, W. 1987. The Coming Out of Critical Criminology. JLAS 14: 321-333.

198 Dick, A. R. 1995. When Does Organized Crime Pay? A Transaction Cost Analysis. IRLE 15: 25-45.

199 Ellis, R. D. 1987. General Assistance Payments and Crime Rates in the US. PSR 7: 291-303.

200 Felson, R. B. 1992. Explanations of the Relationship between Stress, Interpersonal Aggression and Violence. SQ 33:1-16.

201 Fisher, S. 1987. Economic Development and Crime: They May Be an Adaptation to Industrialism in Social Revolutions. AJEAS 46: 17-34.

202 Fitch, J. S. 1985. The Garrison State: Trends in Expectation of Violence. JPR 22: 31-46.

203 Flanagan, T. J.; Cohen, D.; Brennan, P. G. 1993. Crime Control Ideology among New York State Legislators. LSQ 18: 411-422.

204 Franke, H. 1994. Violent Crime in the Netherlands. CLASC 21: 73-98.

205 Friedman, J.; Hakim, S.; Weinblatt, J. 1989. Casino Gambling as a Growth Pole Strategy and Its Effect on Crime. JRS 29: 615-623.

206 Garofalo, J. 1981. Fear of Crime. JCLAC 72: 839-857.

207 Gove, W.; Hughes, M.; Geerken, M. 1985. Are Uniform Crime Reports a Valid Indictor of the Index Crimes. Criminology 23: 451-501.

208 Graff, H. J. 1977. Crime and Punishment in the Nineteenth Century. JIDH 7: 477-492.

209 Gyimah-Brempong, K. 1986. Empirical Models of Criminal Behavior: How Significant is Race? RBPE 15: 27-43.

210 Hashimoto, M. 1987. The Minimum Wage Law and Youth Crimes. JOLE 30: 443-464.

211 Hauber, A. R.; Toornvliet, L. G.; Willemse, H. M. 1988. Perceived Seriousness of White Collar Crime and Conventional Crime. CAR 3: 41-64.

212 Herrup, C. 1985. Crime, Law and Society. CSSH 27: 159-170.

213 Hindus, M. S. 1977. Contours of Crime and Justice in Massachusetts and South Carolina, 1767-1878. AJLH 21: 212-237.

214 Hirschi, T.; Gottfredson, M. 1983. Age and the Explanation of Crime. AJS 89: 552-584.

215 Howsen, R. M.; Jarrell, S. B. 1987. Economic Factors Influence Criminal Behavior but Cannot Fully Explain the Syndrome. AJEAS 46: 432-444.

216 Hunt, L. H. 1981. Some Advantages of Social Control. PC 36: 3-16.

217 Ichniowski, C.; Preston, A. 1989. Persistence of Organized Crime in New York City Construction: An Economic Perspective. ILRR 42: 549-565.

218 Jarrell, S. B.; Howsen, R. M. 1990. Transient Crowding and Crime. AJEAS 49: 483-494.

219 Journal of Criminal Law and Criminology. 1987. Papers on Stranger Violence. JCLAC 78 (2).

220 -. 1991. Papers on Juvenile Delinquency. JCLAC 82 (1).

221 Journal of Social Issues. 1983. Papers on Victimization. JSI 39 (2), 1984 40 (1).

222 -. 1987. Papers on Covert Crime Facilitation. JSI 43 (3).

223 Journal of State Government. 1989. Papers on Prison Crowding. JSG 62 (2).

224 Kidd, R. F.; Chayet, E. F. 1981. Why Do Victims Fail to Report? The Psychology of Criminal Victimization. JSI 40: 39-50.

225 Kleck, G. 1987. America's Foreign Wars and the Legitimization of Domestic Violence. SI 57: 237-250.

226 Krohn, M. D. 1976. Inequality, Unemployment and Crime. SQ 17: 303-313.

227 -. 1978. A Durkheimian Analysis of International Crime Rates. SF 57: 654-670.

228 Law and Society Review. 1978. Papers on Criminal Justice. LASR 12 (3).

229 -. 1993. Papers on Crime, Class and Community. LASR 27 (2).

230 Leavitt, G. C. 1992. General Evolution and Rukeheim's Hypothesis of Crime Frequency. SQ 33: 241-264.

231 Liska, A. E.; Bellair, P. E. 1995. Violent Crime Rates and Racial Composition. AJS 101: 578-610.

232 Liska, A. E.; Chamblin, M. B.; Reed, M. D. 1985. Testing the Economic Production and Conflict Models of Crime Control. SF 64: 119-138.

233 Liska, A. E.; Lawrence, J. J.; Benseon, M. 1981. Perspectives on the Legal Order: Social Control. AJS 87: 413-426.

234 Liu, Y. W.; Bee, R. H. 1983. Modeling Criminal Activity in an Area in Economic Decline: Local Economic Conditions Are a Major Factor in Local Property Crimes. AJEAS 42: 385-392.

235 Lodhi, A. Q.; Tilly, C. 1973. Urbanization, Crime and Collective Violence in 19th Century France. AJS 79: 296-318.

236 Logan, J. R.; Messner, S. F. 1987. Racial Residential Segregation and Suburban Violent Crime. SSQ 68: 510-527.

237 Lynch, J. P. 1987. Routine Activities and Victimization at Work. Journal of Quantitative Criminology 3: 283-300.

238 Lynch, M. J.; Groves, W. B.; Lizotte, A. 1994. Rate of Surplus Value and Crime: Marxist Economic Theory and Criminology. CLASC 21: 15-48.

239 Marshall, I. H. 1995. Intra-Individual Variability in Crime and Its Relation to Local Life Circumstances. ASR 60: 655-673.

240 Masumura, W. T. 1977. Law and Violence. Journal of Anthropological Research 33: 388-399.

241 Maxim, P. S. 1985. Cohort Size and Juvenile Delinquency: A Test of the Easterlin Hypothesis. SF 63: 661-681.

242 McClain, P. D. 1992. Reconceptualizing Urban Violence: Policy Analytic Approach NPSR 3: 9-24.

243 Messerschmidt, J. 1981. Marginalization, Reproduction and Assaults against Teachers: Ideological Social Control. CC 5: 83-102.

244 Messner, S. F.; Blau, J. R. 1987. Routine Leisure Activities and Rates of Crime. SF 65: 1035-1052.

245 Miethe, T. D.; Hughes, M.; McDowall, D. 1991. Social Change and Crime Rates. SF 70: 165-186.

246 Miethe, T. D.; McDowall, D. 1993. Contextual Effects in Models of Criminal Victimization. SF 71: 741-760.

247 Mikesell, J. L.; Pirog-Good, M. A. 1990. State Lotteries and Crime. AJEAS 49: 7-19.

248 Myers, S. L. 1980. Why Are Crimes Underreported? What Is the Crime Rate? Does It Really Matter? SSQ 61: 23-43.

249 -. 1984. Do Better Wages Reduce Crime? AJEAS 43: 191-196.

250 Myers, S. L.; Sabol, W. J. 1987. Business Cycles and Racial Disparities in Punishment. CPI 5 (4): 46-58.

251 Naroff, J. L.; Hellman, D.; Skinner, D. 1980. The Boston Experience: Estimates of the Impact of Crime on Property Values. GAC 11: 24-30.

252 Needleman, M. L.; Needleman, C. 1979. Organizational Crime. SQ 20: 517-528.

253 Nelson, J. F. 1980. Multiple Victimization in American Cities. AJS 85: 870-891.

254 -. 1984. Modeling Individual and Aggregate Victimization Rates. SSR 13: 352-372.

255 Neumann, W. L.; Berger, R. J. 1988. Competing Perspectives on Gross National Crime. SQ 29: 281-314.

256 Norstrom, T. 1988. Theft, Criminality and Economic Growth. SSR 17: 48-65.

257 O'Malley, P. 1985. The Illegal Sector of Capital: Organizing Crime. CC 9: 81-92.

258 Opp, K. D. 1989. Economics of Crime and Sociology of Deviant Behavior. Kyklos 42: 405-430.

259 Pearson, G. 1978. Goths and Vandals: Crime in History. CC 2: 119-140.

260 Policy Studies Journal. 1975. Papers on Crime and Criminal Justice Policy. PSJ 3 (1).

261 Policy Studies Review. 1982. Papers on Corrections Policy. PSR 2 (2), 1987 7 (3).

262 Pyle, D.; Deadman, D. 1994. Crime and Unemployment in Scotland. SJPE 41: 314-324.

263 Rahav, G.; Jaamdar, S. 1982. Development and Crime: A Cross National Study. DAC 13: 447-462.

264 Reiss, A. J. 1981. Public Safety: Marshaling Crime Statistics. ANNALS 453: 222-236.

265 Robinson, P. H. 1994. A Functional Analysis of Criminal Law. NLR 88: 857-913.

266 Ruback, R. B.; Greenberg, M. S.; Westcott, D. R. 1984. Social Influence and Crime Victim Decision Making. JSI 40: 51-76.

267 Sack, F. 1995. Socio-Political Change and Crime. CLASC 24: 49-64.

268 Sah, R. K. 1991. Social Osmosis and Patterns of Crime. JPE 99: 1272-1295.

269 Shavell, S. 1993. Economic Analysis of Threats and Their Illegality: Blackmail, Extortion and Robbery. UPLR 141: 1877-1904.

270 Sheley, J. F. 1983. Critical Elements of Criminal Behavior. SQ 24: 509-526.

271 Shotland, R. L.; Goodstein, L. I. 1984. The Role of Bystanders in Crime Control. JSI 40: 9-26.

272 Simpson, S. S. 1987. Cycles of Illegality: Antitrust Violations in Corporate America. SF 65: 943-963.

273 Singer, S. I. 1981. Homogeneous Victim-Offender Populations. JCLAC 72: 779-788.

274 Skogan, W. G. 1977. The Changing Distribution of Big City Crime. UAQ 13: 33-48.

275 Smith, M. D. 1986. Era of Increased Violence: Age, Period, or Cohort Effect? SQ 27: 329-352.

276 Smith, M. D.; Devine, J. A.; Sheley, J. F. 1992. Crime and Unemployment. SP 35: 551-572.

277 Social Science Quarterly. 1981. Papers on Crime. SSQ 62 (4), and 1984 65: 681-734.

278 South, S. J.; Messner, S. F. 1987. Sex Ratio and Women's Involvement in Crime. SQ 28: 171-188.

279 Sparks, R. F. 1981. Multiple Victimization: Evidence, Theory and Future Research. JCLAC 72: 762-778.

280 Steffensmeier, D. J.; Rosenthal, A. S.; Shehan, C. 1980. World War II and Its Effects on the Sex Differential in Arrests. SQ 21: 403-416.

281 Steffensmeier, D. J.; Streifel, C.; Shihadeh, E. S. 1992. Cohort Size and Arrest Rates over the Life Course: The Easterlin Hypothesis Reconsidered. ASR 57: 306-314.

282 Steffensmeier, D. J., et al. 1989. Age and the Distribution of Crime. AJS 94: 803-831.

283 Tanton, J.; Lutton, W. 1993. Immigration and Rising Criminality in the US. JSPES 18: 217-234.

284 Taylor, I. 1981. Crime Waves in Post-War Britain. CC 5: 43-62.

285 Taylor, R. B.; Hale, M. 1986. Testing Alternative Models of Fear of Crime. JCLAC 77: 151-189.

286 Thornberry, T. P.; Farnworth, M. 1982. Social Correlates of Criminal Involvement. ASR 47: 505-517.

287 Tittle, C. R. 1983. Social Class and Criminal Behavior. SF 62: 334-358.

288 Toch, H. 1980. Toward an Interdisciplinary Approach to Criminal Violence. JCLAC 71: 646-653.

289 Trumbull, W. N. 1989. Estimations of the Economic Model of Crime. SEJ 56: 423-439.

290 Van Duyne, P.C. 1993. Organized Crime and Business Crime Enterprises. CLASC 19: 103-142.

291 Vila, B. J.; Cohen, L. E. 1993. Crime as Strategy: Testing an Evolutionary Ecological Theory of Expropriative Crime. AJS 98: 873-912.

292 Viren, M. 1994. A Test of the Economics of Crime Model. IRLE 14: 363-370.

293 Wang, Y. 1993. Urban Crimes in Mainland China: A Social Ecological Approach. IAS 29: 101-117.

294 Warr, M. 1992. Altruistic Fear of Victimization in Households. SSQ 73: 723-736.

295 Watts, M. W. 1977. Anti-Heteroxy and the Punishment of Deviance: A Cognitive Approach to Law and Order Attitudes. WPQ 30: 93-103.

296 Weiner, N. A.; Pasta, S. 1984. Bibliography of Bibliographies on Criminal Violence. JCLAC 75: 1300-1320.

297 Wellford, C. F. 1975. Crime and the Dimensions of Nations. International Journal of Crime and Penology 2: 1-10.
298 Wolf, P. 1971. Crime and Development. Scandinavian Studies in Criminology 3: 107-120.
299 Wolpin, K. L. 1978. An Economic Analysis of Crime and Punishment. JPE 86: 815-840.
300 Women and Politics. 1984. Papers on Criminal Justice Politics and Women. WAP 4 (3).

Deterrence

301 Adelstein, R. P. 1979. Informational Paradox and the Pricing of Crime: Capital Sentencing Standards in Economic Perspective. JCLAC 70: 281-298.
302 Andreoni, J. 1995. Criminal Deterrence in the Reduced Form. EI 33: 476-483.
303 Benson, B. L.; Kim, I.; Rasmussen, D. W. 1994. Estimating Deterrence Effects: A Public Choice Perspective on the Economics of Crime Literature. SEJ 61: 161-168.
304 Berk, R. A.; Rauma, D.; Messinger, S. L.; Cooley, T. F. 1981. A Test of the Stability of Punishment Hypothesis. ASR 46: 805-828.
305 Bianco, W. T.; Ordeshook, P. C.; Tsebelis, G. 1990. Crime and Punishment: Are One Shot, Two Person Games Enough? APSR 84: 569-586.
306 Bordo, M. D.; Landau, D. 1980. Supply and Demand for Protection: a Positive Theory of Democratic Government. ST 5: 335-348.
307 Burnovski, M.; Safra, Z. 1994. Deterrence Effects of Sequential Punishment Policies. IRLE 14: 341-350.
308 Ehrlich, I. 1981. On the Usefulness of Controlling Individuals: Rehabilitation, Incapacitation and Deterrence. AER 71: 307-322.
309 Ekland-Olson, S.; Lieb, J.; Zurcher, L. 1984. The Paradoxical Impact of Criminal Sanctions. LASR 18: 159-178.
310 Engel, D. M. 1984. Deterrence and Subjective Probabilities of Arrest. LASR 18: 583-604.
311 Goldman, A. H. 1979. The Paradox of Punishment. PAPA 9: 42-58.
312 Grasmick, H. G.; Bursik, R. J. 1990. Conscience, Significant Others and Rational Choice: The Deterrence Model. LASR 24: 837-862.
313 Grasmick, H. G.; Green, D. E. 1980. Legal Punishment, Social Disapproval and Internalization as Inhibitors of Illegal Behavior. JCLAC 71: 325-335.
314 -. 1981. Deterrence and the Morally Committed. SQ 22: 1-14.
315 Grasmick, H. G.; Jacobs, D.; McCollom, C. B. 1983. Social Class and Social Control: Application to Deterrence Theory. SF 62: 359-374.
316 Green, P. A.; Allen, H. D. 1981. The Severity of Societal Response to Crime. LASR 16: 181-206.
317 Greenberg, D.; Kellser, R. C.; Logan, C. H. 1979. A Panel Model of Crime Rates and Arrest Rates. ASR 44: 843-850.
318 Grogger, J. 1991. Certainty vs. Severity of Punishment. EI 29: 297-309.
319 Hagan, J. 1980. Legislation of Crime and Delinquency. LASR 14: 603-628.
320 Hampton, J. 1984. The Moral Education Theory of Punishment. PAPA 13: 208-238.
321 Hynes, E. 1985. Socialization Values and Punishment Behavior: Kokn's Thesis. SP 28: 217-240.
322 Journal of Social Issues. 1987. Papers on Moving Beyound Deterrence. JSI 43 (4).
323 Kohfeld, C. W.; Sprague, J. 1990. Demography, Police Behavior and Deterrence. Criminology 28: 111-136.
324 Leung, S. F. 1991. How to Make the Fine Fit the Corporate Crime? Optimal Punishment Theories. JPUBE 45: 243-256.

325 Lichbach, M. I. 1987. Deterrence or Escalation? The Puzzle of Aggregate Studies of Repression and Dissent. JCR 31: 266-297.
326 Logan, C. H. 1975. Arrest Rate and Deterrence. SSQ 56: 376-389.
327 Mookherjee, D.; Png, I. P. L. 1994. Marginal Deterrence in the Enforcement of Law. JPE 102: 1039-1066.
328 Nagel, J. 1982. Relationship between Crime and Incarceration. PSR 2: 193-200.
329 Nagin, D. 1979. Impact of Determinant Sentencing Legislation on Prison Population and Sentence Length. PUBP 27: 69-98.
330 Nash, J. 1991. To Make the Punishment Fit the Crime: A Multi-Period Optimal Deterrence Model. IRLE 11: 101-110.
331 Paternoster, R. 1988. Examining a Three Wave Deterrence Models. JCLAC 79: 135-179.
332 -. 1989. Decisions to Participate in and Desist from Four Types of Common Delinquency. LASR 23: 7-40.
333 Piliavin, I., et al. 1986. Crime, Deterrence and Rational Choice. ASR 51: 101-119.
334 Ray, J. 1982. Prison Sentences and Public Opinion. AUSQ 54: 435-447.
335 Skogh, G.; Stuart, C. 1982. An Economic Analysis of Crime Rates, Punishment and the Social Consequences of Crime. PC 38: 171-180.
336 Taggart, W. A.; Winn, R. G. 1993. Imprisonment in the American States. SSQ 74: 736-749.
337 Tsebelis, G. 1993. Penalty and Crime. JTP 5: 349-374.
338 Warr, M.; Meier, R. F.; Erickson, M. L. 1983. Norms, Theories of Punishment and Publicly Preferred Penalties for Crimes. SQ 24: 75-92.

Gun Control

339 Annals. 1981. Papers on Gun Control. ANNALS 455.
340 Bankston, W. B.; Thompson, C. Y. 1989. Carrying Firearms for Protection. SI 59: 75-87.
341 Journal of Criminal Law and Criminology. 1995. Papers on Guns and Violence. JCLAC 86 (1).
342 Law and Contemporary Problems. 1986. Papers on Gun Control. LACP 49 (1).
343 Law and Policy Quarterly. 1983. Papers on Gun Control. LAP 5 (3).
344 Leff, C. S.; Leff, M. H. 1981. The Politics of Inefficient Federal Firearms Legislation. ANNALS 455: 48-62.
345 Luckenbill, D. F. 1984. Character Coercion, Instrumental Coercion and Gun Control. JABS 20: 181-192.
346 Mauser, G. A.; Kopel, D. B. 1992. Why Media Polls on Gun Control Are Often Unreliable. POLCOM 9: 69-92.
347 McDowall, D. 1991. Firearm Availability and Homicide Rates in Detroit. SF 69: 1085-1102.
348 McDowall, D.; Loftin, C. 1983. Collective Security and the Demand for Legal Handguns. AJS 88: 1146-1161.
349 Pierce, G. L.; Bowers, W. J. 1981. The Bartley-Fox Gun Law's Short Term Impact on Crime in Boston. ANNALS 455: 120-137.
350 Taylor, R. B. 1995. A Game Theoretic Model of Gun Control. IRLE 15: 269-288.
351 Tonso, W. R. 1983. Social Science and Stagecraft in the Debate over Gun Control. LAP 5: 325-344.

Homicide and Death Penalty

352 Acker, J. R. 1993. The Supreme Court, Empirical Research Evidence and Capital Punishment Decisions. LASR 27: 65-88.

353 Archer, D.; Gartner, R. 1976. Comparative Homicide Rates. ASR 41: 937-963.

354 Archer, D.; Gartner, R.; Beittel, M. 1983. Homicide and Death Penalty. JCLAC 74: 991-1013.

355 Bailey, W. C.; Peterson, R. D. 1989. Murder and Capital Punishment: A Time Series Analysis of Execution Publicity. ASR 54: 722-743.

356 -. 1994. Murder, Capital Punishment and Deterrence: Police Killings. JSI 50: 53-74.

357 Baron, L.; Straus, M. A. 1988. Cultural and Economic Sources of Homicide. SQ 29: 371-390.

358 Cameron, S. 1993. The Demand for Capital Punishment. IRLE 13: 47-59.

359 -. 1994. Review of Econometric Evidence on the Effects of Capital Punishment. JSE 23: 197-214.

360 Chesnais, J. C. 1992. Homicide and Suicide through the Ages. ISSJ 44: 217-234.

361 Cover, J. P.; Thistle, P. D. 1988. Time Series, Homicide and Deterrent Effect of Capital Punishment. SEJ 54: 615-622.

362 Diamond, S. S.; Casper, J. D. 1994. Empirical Evidence and the Death Penalty. JSI 50: 177-197.

363 Eckberg, D. L. 1995. Estimates of Early Twentieth-Century Homicide Rates. Demography 32: 1-16.

364 Gartner, R. 1990. Victims of Homicide. ASR 55: 92-106.

365 Hansmann, H. B.; Quigley, J. M. 1982. Population Heterogeneity and the Sociogenesis of Homicide. SF 61: 206-224.

366 Harries, K. 1995. A Geography of Execution in the US. PG 14: 473-495.

367 Hoenack, S. A.; Weiler, W. C. 1980. A Structural Model of Murder Behavior and the Criminal Justice System. AER 70: 327-341

368 Jang, S. J.; Messner, S. F.; South, S. J. 1991. Predictors of Interracial Homicide Victimization for Asian Americans. SP 34: 1-20.

369 Journal of Criminal Law and Criminology. 1983. Papers on the Death Penalty. JCLAC 74 (3).

370 Journal of Social Issues. 1994. Papers on the Death Penalty. JSI 50 (2).

371 Kobbervig, W.; Inverarity, J.; Lauderdale, P. 1982. Deterrence and the Death Penalty. AJS 88: 161-172.

372 Law and Society Review. 1993. Papers on the Death Penalty. LASR 27 (1).

373 Marche, G. W. 1994. The Production of Homicide Solutions. AJEAS 53: 385-402.

374 McFarland, S. G. 1983. Is Capital Punishment a Short Term Deterrent to Homicide? JCLAC 74: 1014-1032.

375 McManus, W. S. 1985. Estimates of the Deterrent Effect of Capital Punishment: The Importance of the Researcher's Prior Beliefs. JPE 93: 417-425.

376 Messner, S. F. 1983. Regional Differences in the Economic Correlates of the Urban Homicide Rate. Criminology 21: 477-488.

377 Mitchell, M.; Sidanius, J. 1995. Social Hierarchy and the Death Penalty: A Social Dominance Perspective. PP 16: 591-619.

378 Nice, D. C. 1992. States and the Death Penalty. WPQ 45: 1037-1048.

379 Peterson, R. D.; Krivo, L. J. 1993. Racial Segregation and Black Urban Homicide. SF 71: 1001-1027.

380 Phillips, D. P. 1980. The Deterrent Effect of Capital Punishment. AJS 86: 139-148.

381 Smith, M. D.; Parker, R. N. 1980. Type of Homicide and Variation in Regional Rates. SF 59: 136-147.

382 Stack, S. 1990. Execution Publicity and Homicide in South Carolina. SQ 31: 599-612.

383 Tygart, C. E. 1994. Respondents' Free Will View of Criminal Behavior and Support for Capital Punishment. IJPOR 6: 371-374.

384 Tyler, T. R.; Weber, R. 1982. Support for the Death Penalty. LASR 17: 21-46.

385 Unnithan, N. P.; Whitt, H. P. 1992. Inequality, Economic Development and Lethal Violence: Analysis of Suicide and Homicide. IJCS 33: 182-196.

386 Whitt, H. P.; Gordon, L. C.; Hofley, J. R. 1972. Religion, Economic Development and Lethal Aggression. ASR 37: 193-201.

387 Wilkinson, K. P. 1984. Homicide and Rurality. SF 63: 445-452.

Judicial Politics

388 Adamany, D. 1973. Legitimacy, Realigning Elections and the Supreme Court. Wisconsin Law Review 1973: 790-846.

389 Annals. 1982. Papers on the American Judiciary. ANNALS 462.

390 Ashenfelter, O.; Eisenberg, T.; Schwab, S. J. 1995. Influence of Judicial Background on Case Outcomes. JLS 24: 257-281.

391 Atkins, B. M. 1973. Judicial Behavior and Tendencies toward Conformity in a Three Member Small Group: Dissent Behavior on the US Courts of Appeals. SSQ 54: 41-53.

392 Baum, L. 1977. Policy Goals in Judicial Gatekeeping: Proximity Model of Discretionary Jurisdiction. AJPS 21: 13-35.

393 -. 1989. Comparing the Policy Positions of the Supreme Court Justices from Different Periods. WPQ 42: 509-521.

394 -. 1993. Case Selection and Decisionmaking in the US Supreme Court. LASR 27: 443-459.

395 Bowen, T.; Scheb, J. M. 1993. Reassessing the Freshman Effect: Voting Bloc Alignment of New Justices on the US Supreme Court. PB 15: 1-14.

396 Brace, P.; Hall, M. G. 1993. Integrated Models of Judicial Dissent. JOP 55: 914-935.

397 -. 1995. Studying Courts Comparatively. PRQ 48: 5-30.

398 Brenner, S. 1980. Fluidity on the US Supreme Court. AJPS 24: 526-535.

399 Brenner, S.; Arrington, T. S. 1980. Some Effects of Ideology and Threat upon the Size of Opinion Coalitions on the Supreme Court. JPS 8: 49-58.

400 Brereton, D.; Casper, J. D. 1981. Does It Pay to Plead Guilty? Differential Sentencing and the Functioning of Criminal Courts. LASR 16: 45-70.

401 Brown, D. W.; Stover, R. V. 1977. Court Directives and Compliance: A Utility Approach. APQ 5: 465-480.

402 Caldeira, G. A. 1985. The Transmission of Legal Precedent: State Supreme Courts. APSR 79: 178-193.

403 -. 1986. Dynamics of Public Confidence in the Supreme Court. APSR 80: 1209-1248.

404 Caldeira, G. A.; Gibson, J. L. 1992. Etiology of Public Support for the Supreme Court. AJPS 36: 635-664.

405 -. 1995. Legitimacy of the Court of Justice in the European Union: Models of Institutional Support. APSR 89: 356-376.

406 Caldeira, G. A.; Wright, J. R. 1988. Organized Interests and Agenda Setting in the Supreme Court. APSR 82: 1109-1129.

407 -. 1990. Amici Curiae before the Supreme Court. JOP 52: 782-806.

408 Canon, B. C. 1977. Testing the Effectiveness of Civil Liberties Policies at the State and Federal Levels: The Exclusionary Rule. APQ 5: 57-82.

409 -. 1992. The Supreme Court as a Cheerleader in Politico-Moral Disputes. JOP 54: 937-956.

410 Cohen, M. A. 1992. Motives of Judges: Evidence from Antitrust Sentencing. IRLE 12: 13-30.

411 Cook, B. B. 1977. Public Opinion and Federal Judicial Policy. AJPS 21: 567-600.

412 -. 1993. Measuring the Significance of US Supreme Court Decisions. JOP 55: 1127-1139.

413 Daniels, W. J. 1978. The Geographical Factor in Appointments to the US Supreme Court. WPQ 31: 226-237.

414 Dometrius, N.; Sigelman, L. 1988. Modeling the Impact of Supreme Court Decisions: Nygant vs. Board. JOP 50: 131-149.

415 Epstein, L.; Walker, T. G.; Dixon, W. J. 1989. The Supreme Court and Criminal Justice Disputes. AJPS 33: 825-837.

416 Feldman, D. 1988. Judicial Review: A Way of Controlling Government? PA 66: 21-34.

417 Funston, R. 1975. The Supreme Court and Critical Elections. APSR 69: 795-811.

418 Gely, R.; Spiller, P. T. 1990. A Rational Choice Theory of Supreme Court Statutory Decisions with Applications to the State Farm and Grove City Cases. JOLEAO 6: 263-300.

419 Gibson, J. L. 1978. Judges' Role Orientations, Attitudes and Decisions. APSR 72: 911-924.

420 -. 1980. Environmental Constraints on Behavior of Judges: A Model of Judicial Decision Making. LASR 14: 343-370.

421 -. 1981. Personality and Elite Political Behavior: Self Esteem on Judicial Decision Making. JOP 43: 104-127.

422 -. 1983. From Simplicity to Complexity: Development of Theory of Judicial Behavior. PB 5: 7-49.

423 Glick, H. 1992. Judicial Innovation and Policy Re-Invention: State Supreme Courts and the Right to Die. WPQ 45: 71-92.

424 Goldman, S. 1975. Voting Behavior on the US Courts of Appeal Revisited. APSR 69: 491-506.

425 Goldman, S.; Jahnige, T. P. 1971. Systems Analysis and Judicial Systems. Polity 3: 336-357.

426 Griffin, K. N.; Horan, M. J. 1982. Judicial Retention Elections. SSJ 19: 93-102.

427 Gruhl, J. 1982. Patterns of Compliance with US Supreme Court Rulings: Libel in Federal Courts of Appeals and State Supreme Courts. Publius 12: 109-130.

428 Haas, K. C. 1982. The Comparative Study of State and Federal Judicial Behavior Revisited. JOP 44: 721-746.

429 Hagle, T. M. 1993. Strategic Retirements: A Political Model of Turnover on the Supreme Court. PB 15: 25-48.

430 Hall, M. G. 1992. Electoral Politics and Strategic Voting in State Supreme Courts. JOP 54: 427-446.

431 -. 1995. Justices as Representatives: Elections and Judicial Politics in the American States. APQ 23: 485-503.

432 Hall, M. G.; Brace, P. 1989. Order in the Courts: A Neo-Institutional Approach to Judicial Consensus. WPQ 42: 391-407.

433 Handberg, R.; Tate, C.N. 1991. Time Binding and Theory Building in Personal Attribute Models of Supreme Court Voting Behavior. AJPS 35: 460-480.

434 Harris, P. 1985. Ecology and Culture in the Communication of Precedent among State Supreme Courts. LASR 19: 449-486.

435 Harvard Journal. 1994. Papers on Judicial Decision Making. HJLPP 17 (1).

436 Hodder-Williams, R. 1992. Six Notions of Political and the US Supreme Court. BJPS 22: 1-20.

437 Hoekstra, V. J. 1995. Supreme Court and Opinion Change: An Experimental Study of the Court's Ability to Change Opinion. APQ 23: 109-129.

438 Johnson, W. 1977. Judicial Decisions and Organizational Change. AAS 11: 27-51.

439 Johnston, R. E. 1973. Statistics on Chief Justice Opinion Writing. WPQ 26: 453-460.

440 Journal of International Affairs. 1984. Papers on Politics of International Law. Vol 37 (2).

441 Kagan, R. A., et al. 1977. The Business of State Supreme Courts. SLR 30: 121-156.

442 King, G. 1987. Presidential Appointments to the Supreme Court. APQ 15: 373-386.

443 Kritzer, H. M. 1978. Correlates of the Behavior of Federal District Judges. JOP 40: 25-58.

444 Kuklinski, J. H.; Stanga, J. E. 1979. Political Participation and Governmental Responsiveness: Behavior of California Supreme Courts. APSR 73: 1090-1099.

445 Landes, W. M.; Posner, R. A. 1975. The Independent Judiciary in an Interest Group Perspective. JOLE 18: 875-905.

446 Levin, M. A. 1972. Urban Politics and Judicial Behavior. JLS 1: 193-221.

447 Link, M. W. 1995. Tracking Public Mood in the Supreme Court. PRQ 48: 61-78.

448 McDowell, G. L. 1982. Were the Anti-Federalists Right? Judicial Activism and the Problem of Consolidated Government. Publius 12: 99-108.

449 Mishler, W.; Sheehan, R. S. 1993. The Supreme Court as a Countermajoritarian Institution? Impact of Public Opinion on Supreme Court Decisions. APSR 87: 87-101.

450 Mondak, J. J. 1992. Institutional Legitimacy, Political Legitimacy and the Supreme Court. APQ 20: 457-477.

451 McMurray, C. D.; Parsons, M. B. 1965. Public Attitudes toward the Representational Role of Legislators and Judges. MJPS 9: 167-185.

452 Nelson, W. E. 1974. Impact of the Antislavery Movement upon Styles of Judicial Reasoning. HLR 87: 513-566.

453 Northwestern University Law Review. 1993. Papers on Judicial Review. NLR 88 (1).

454 O'Connor, K.; Epstein, L. 1981. Amicus Curiae Participation in US Supreme Court Litigation. LASR 16: 311-320.

455 Overby, L. M., et al. 1992. Courting Constituents? Analysis of the Senate Confirmation Votes on Justice Clarence Thomas. APSR 86: 997-1006.

456 PS. 1992. Papers on Politics, Values and the Clarence Thomas Nomination. Vol 25 (3).

457 Robertson, D. 1982. Judicial Ideology in the House of Lords: A Jurimetric Analysis. BJPS 12: 1-26.

458 Rohde, D. W. 1972. Policy Goals and Opinion Coalitions in the Supreme Court. APSR 66: 208-244.

459 Schubert, G. 1977. Political Culture and Judicial Ideology. CPS 9: 363-408.

460 Segal, J. A.; Cameron, C. M.; Cover, A. D. 1992. Spatial Model of Roll Call Voting: Senators, Constituents, Presidents and Interest Groups in Supreme Court Confirmations. AJPS 36: 96-121.

461 Segal, J. A.; Cover, A. D. 1989. Ideological Values and the Votes of US Supreme Court Judges. APSR 83: 557-564.

462 Segal, J. A., et al 1995. Ideological Values and the Votes of US Supreme Court Justices Revisited. JOP 57: 812-823.

463 Shapiro, M. 1965. Stability and Change in Judicial Decision Making. Law and Transition Quarterly 2: 134-157.

464 -. 1990. Interest Groups and Supreme Court Appointments. NLR 84: 935-961.

465 Songer, D. R. 1988. Alternative Approaches to the Study of Judicial Impact: Miranda in State Courts. APQ 16: 425-444.

466 Songer, D. R.; Sheehan, R. S. 1993. Interest Group Success in the Courts: Amicus Participation in the Supreme Court. PRQ 46: 339-334.

467 Hodson, T., et al. 1995. Leaders and Limits: Changing Patterns of State Legislative Leadership under Term Limits. Spectrum 68 (3): 6-15.

468 Tanenhaus, J.; Murphy, W. F. 1981. Patterns of Public Support for the Supreme Court. JOP 43: 24-39.

469 Tate, C.N. 1981. Personal Attribute Models of the Voting Behavior of US Supreme Court Justices: Liberalism in Civil Liberties and Economic Decisions. APSR 75: 355-367.

470 Ulmer, S. S. 1978. Selecting Cases for Supreme Court Review: Underdog Model. APSR 72: 902-910.

471 -. 1982. Supreme Court Appointments as a Poisson Distribution. AJPS 26: 113-116.

472 Volcansek, M. L. 1981. An Exploration of the Judicial Election Process. WPQ 34: 572-577.

473 Weber, R. E. 1995. Redistricting and the Courts: Judicial Activism in the 1990s. APQ 23: 204-228.

474 West European Politics. 1992. Papers on Judicial Politics and Policy Making in Western Europe. WEP 15 (3).

475 Wheeler, S., et al. 1987. Winning and Losing in State Supreme Courts. LASR 21: 403-447.

476 Zuk, G.; Gryski, G. S.; Barrow, D. J. 1993. Partisan Transformation of the Federal Judiciary. APQ 21: 439-457.

Policing

477 American Behavioral Scientist. 1970. Papers on Policing. ABS 13 (5/6).

478 Annals. 1980. Papers on the Police and Violence. ANNALS 452.

479 Baker, M. H., et al. 1983. The Impact of a Crime Wave: Perceptions. LASR 17: 319-336.

480 Benson, P. R. 1981. Political Alienation and Public Satisfaction with Police Services. PACSR 24: 45-64.

481 Brent, E. E.; Sykes, R. E. 1979. A Mathematical Model of Symbolic Interaction between Police and Suspects. BS 24: 388-402.

482 -. 1980. Interactive Bases of Police-Suspect Confrontation. SAG 11: 347-363.

483 Britt, D. W.; Tittle, C. R. 1975. Crime Rates and Police Behavior. SF 54: 441-451.

484 Brown, M. C.; Warner, B. D. 1992. Immigrants, Urban Politics and Policing in 1900. ASR 57: 293-305.

485 Cloninger, D. O. 1991. Lethal Police Response as a Crime Deterrent. AJEAS 50: 59-70.

486 Coulter, P. B. 1972. National Socioeconomic Development and Democracy: The Political Role of the Police. IJCS 13: 55-62.

487 Crime, Law and Social Change. 1992. Papers on Covert Policing. CLASC 18 (1/2).

488 Friedman, J.; Hakim, S.; Spiegel, U. 1989. Short and Long Run Effects of Police Outlays on Crime. AJEAS 48: 177-192.

489 Gianakis, G. A. 1994. Appraising the Performance of Street-Level Bureaucrats: Police. ARPA 24: 299-316.

490 Henderson, T. A. 1975. Effects of Community Complexity on Sheriff Departments APSR 69: 107-132.

491 Heyman, P. B. 1990. Two Models of National Attitudes toward International Cooperation in Law Enforcement. HILJ 31: 99-107.

492 Hunt, R.; Magenau, J. 1983. Value Dilemmas in Law Enforcement. LAP 5: 455-477.

493 Jacob, H.; Rich, M. J. 1980. The Effects of the Police on Crime. LASR 15: 109-122.

494 Jacobs, D. 1979. Inequality and Police Strength: Conflict Theory and Coercive Control. ASR 44: 913-924.

495 Lasley, J. R. 1994. Ethnicity, Gender and Police-Community Attitudes. SSQ 75: 85-97.

496 Lindgren, J. 1981. Organizational and Other Constraints on Controlling the Use of Deadly Force by Police. ANNALS 455: 110-119.

497 Loftin, C.; McDowall, D. 1982. Police, Crime and Economic Theory. ASR 47: 393-401.

498 Marenin, O. 1982. Parking Tickets and Class Repression: The Concept of Policing in Critical Theories of Criminal Justice. CC 6: 241-266.

499 Messner, S. F. 1983. Regional and Racial Effects on the Urban Homicide Rate: Subculture of Violence. AJS 88: 997-1007.

500 Morgan, D. R.; Swanson, C. 1976. Analyzing Police Policies: Environment, Politics, and Crime. UAQ 11: 489-510.

501 Policy Studies Journal. 1978. Papers on Law Enforcement. PSJ 7 (Special Issue).

502 Political Quarterly. 1992. Papers on Police, Prosecutions and Prisons. PQ 63 (1).

503 Poole, E. D.; Regoli, R. M. 1980. Race, Institutional Rule Breaking and Disciplinary Response: Discretionary Decision Making in Prison. LASR 41: 931-646.

504 Reuter, P. 1984. Police Regulation of Illegal Gambling. ANNALS 474: 36-47.

505 Rodgers, H. R.; Taylor, G. 1971. Policeman as an Agent of Regime Legitimation. MJPS 15: 72-86.

506 Sheley, J. F.; Hanlon, J. J. 1978. Unintended Effects of Police Decisions to Actively Enforce Laws. CC 2: 265-276.

507 Social Science Quarterly 1975. Papers on Law Enforcement and Social Control. SSQ 56 (3).

508 Sullivan, P. S.; Dunham, R. G.; Alpert, G. P. 1987. Attitude Structures of Ethnic and Age Groups Concerning Police. JCLAC 78: 177-193.

509 Tyler, T. R. 1984. Influence of Citizen Satisfaction with Police Behavior upon Support for Increases in Police Authority. LAP 6: 329-338.

510 Tyler, T. R.; Folger, R. 1980. Distributional and Procedural Aspects of Satisfaction with Citizen-Police Encounters. Basic and Applied Social Psychology 1: 281-292.

Subcultures of Violence

511 Austin, R. L. 1980. Adolescent Subcultures of Violence. SQ 21: 545-562.

512 Ball-Rokeach, S. J. 1973. Values and Violence: Subculture of Violence Thesis. ASR 38: 736-749.

513 Dixon, C. F.; McCall, P. L. 1989. Region and Violent Attitudes. AJLH 33: 174-177.

514 Ellison, C. G. 1991. The Southern Subculture of Violence Thesis. SF 69: 1223-1240.

515 Ellison, C. G.; McCall, P. L. 1989. Region and Violent Attitudes Reconsidered. AJLH 33: 174-182.

516 Erlanger, H. S. 1975. Is There a Subculture of Violence in the South? JCLAC 66: 483-490.

517 Felson, R. B., et al. 1994. Subculture of Violence and Delinquency. SF 73: 155-174.

518 Hartnagel, T. F. 1980. Subculture of Violence: Further Evidence. PACSR 23: 217-242.

519 Matsueda, R. L., et al. 1992. Prestige of Criminal and Conventional Occupations: A Subcultural Model of Criminal Activity. ASR 57: 752-770.

520 McCall, P. L.; Land, K. C.; Cohen, L. E. 1992. Violent Criminal Behavior: Is There a General Influence of the South? SSR 21: 286-310.

521 Messner, S. F. 1983. Regional and Racial Effects on the Urban Homicide Rate: Subculture of Violence. AJS 88: 997-1007.

522 Reed, J. S. 1971. A Contribution to the Study of Southern Violence. PSQ 86: 429-434.

523 Spectrum. 1993. Papers on Alienated America: Racial Division and Youth Violence. Spectrum 66 (3).

LEGISLATURES AND EXECUTIVES

1 Adams, J. D.; Kenny, L. W. 1986. Optimal Tenure of Elected Public Officials. JOLE 29: 303-328.

2 Annals. 1988. Papers on Conflict between Congress and the President. ANNALS 499.

3 Baumgartner, F. R. 1987. Parliament's Capacity to Expand Political Controversy in France. LSQ 12: 33-54.

4 Berrington, H. 1989. When Does Personality Make a Difference? Lord Cherwell and the Area Bombing of Germany. IPSR 10: 9-34.

5 Born, R. 1994. Split-Ticket Voters, Divided Government and Fiorina's Policy Balancing Model. LSQ 19: 95-130.

6 Boynton, G. R.; Loewenberg, G. 1973. Development of Public Support for Parliament in Germany. BJPS 3: 169-189.

7 Brennan, G.; Hamlin, A. 1992. Bicameralism and Majoritarian Equilibrium. PC 74: 169-179.

8 Coates, D. 1995. Electoral Support and Capture of Legislators. RJE 26: 502-518.

9 Conkin, J. G. 1973. Elite Studies: The Mexican Presidency. JOLAS 5: 233-246.

10 Diermeier, D. 1995. Commitment, Deference, and Legislative Institutions. APSR 89: 344-355.

11 Edinger, L.; Searing, D. D. 1967. Social Background in Elite Analysis. APSR 61: 428-445.

12 European Journal of Political Research. 1978. Papers on European Political Elites. EJPR 6 (1).

13 -. 1993. Papers on Party Leaders. EJPR 24 (3).

14 Ferejohn, J. A.; Fiorina, M. P.; Packel, E. W. 1980. Nonequilibrium Solutions for Legislative Systems. BS 25: 140-148.

15 Fiorina, M. P. 1994. Divided Government in the American States: Byproduct of Legislative Professionalism? APSR 88: 304-316.

16 George, A. L. 1969. Operational Code: Neglected Approach to the Study of Political Leaders and Decision Making. ISQ 13: 190-222.

17 Gilligan, T. W.; Matsusaka, J. G. 1995. Deviations from Constituent Interests: The Role of Legislative Structure and Political Parties in the States. EI 33: 383-401.

18 Grofman, B.; Griffin, R.; Berry, G. 1995. House Members Who Become Senators. LSQ 20: 513-530.

19 Guiton, M. V.; Marvick, E. W. 1989. Family Experience and Political Leadership: The Absent Father Hypothesis. IPSR 10: 63-72.

20 Holbrook, T. M. 1994. Behavioral Consequences of Vice-Presidential Debates. APQ 22: 469-482.

21 Holcombe, R. G.; Sobel, R. S. 1995. Empirical Evidence on the Publicness of State Legislative Activities. PC 83: 47-58.

22 International Political Science Review. 1988. Papers on Political Leadership. IPSR 9 (1-2).

23 Journal of Applied Behavioral Science. 1982 Papers on Styles of Leadership. JABS 18 (3).

24 -. 1990. Papers on Leadership. JABS 26 (4).

25 Journal of Political and Military Sociology. 1986. Papers on Elites and Ruling Classes. JPMS 14 (1).

26 Journal of State Government. 1987. Papers on Leadership. JSG 60 (6).

27 Laband, D. N.; Lentz, B. F. 1985. Favorite Sons: Intergenerational Wealth Transfers among Politicians. EI 23: 395-414.

28 Lane, D.; Ross, C. 1994. Social Background and Political Allegiance of the Political Elite of the Supreme Soviet of USSR. EAS 46: 437-464.

29 Masters, R. D.; Sullivan, D. G. 1989. Nonverbal Displays and Political Leadership in France. PB 11: 121-153.

30 McGraw, K. M.; Timpone, R.; Bruck, G. 1993. Justifying Controversial Political Decisions: Home Style in the Laboratory. PB 15: 289-308.

31 McKay, D. 1994. Recent Research on Divided Government in the US. BJPS 24: 517-534.

32 Meszaros, J. W. 1977. Popular Evaluation of German Chancellors: The Chancellor Effect. BJPS 7: 493-510.

33 Mezey, M. L. 1985. President and Congress. LSQ 10: 519-536.

34 -. 1994. New Perspectives on Parliamentary Systems. LSQ 19: 429-441.

35 Mishler, W.; Hildreth, A. 1984. Legislatures and Political Stability. JOP 46: 25-59.

36 Moe, T. M.; Caldwell, M. 1994. The Institutional Foundations of Democratic Government: Comparison of Presidential and Parliamentary Systems. JITE 150: 171-195.

37 Morris-Jones, W. H. 1983. The Politics of Political Science: Comparative Legislative Studies. POLST 31: 1-24.

38 Mueller, D. C. 1978. Voting by Veto. JPUBE 10: 57-76.

39 National Civic Review. 1995. Papers on the New Paradigm of Leadership. NCR 84 (3).

40 Nurmi, H. 1978. On Economic Theories of Political Institutions. MSSR 1: 7-24.

41 Page, B. I. 1976. The Theory of Political Ambiguity. APSR 70: 742-752.

42 Parker, S. L.; Parker, G. R. 1993. Why Do We Trust Our Congressman? JOP 55: 442-453.

43 Pearson, W. M.; Sanders, L. T. 1981. State Executives' Attitudes toward Some Authoritarian Values. SALGR 13.

44 Peterson, P. E.; Greene, J. P. 1994. Why Executive-Legislative Conflict is Dwindling. BJPS 24: 33-56.

45 Presidential Studies Quarterly. 1992 Papers on Selecting the President, Congress and the Court. PSQ 22 (1).

46 Proceedings. 1975. Papers on Congress against the President. PAPSC 32 (1).

47 Robins, R. S.; Dorn, R. M. 1993. Stress and Political Leadership. PALS 12: 3-18.

48 Schneider, M.; Teske, P. 1992. Toward a Theory of the Political Entrepreneur. APSR 86: 737-747.

49 Searing, D. D. 1969. Comparative Study of Elite Socialization. CPS 1: 471-500.

50 Shachar, R. 1993. Forgetfulness and the Political Cycle. EAP 5: 15-25.

51 Sigelman, L.; Sigelman, C. K.; Walkosz, B. J. 1990. The Public and the Paradox of Leadership. AJPS 36: 366-385.

52 Simon, D. M. 1989. Presidents, Governors and Electoral Accountability. JOP 51: 286-304.

53 Soldatos, G. T. 1994. The Electoral Cycle: A Survey. Revue d'Economie Politique 104: 571-587.

54 Starrels, J. M. 1976. Comparative and Elite Politics. WP 29: 130-142.

55 Studies in Comparative Communism. 1976. Papers on Leadership and Political Succession. SCC 9 (1/2), and 1983 16 (3).

56 Sullivan, D. G.; Masters, R. D. 1988. Happy Warriors: Leaders' Facial Displays, Viewers' Emotions and Political Support. AJPS 32: 345-368.

57 Turett, J. S. 1971. Vulnerability of American Governors, 1900-1969. MJPS 15: 108-132.

58 Wallace, M. D.; Suedfeld, P.; Thachuk, K. 1993. Political Rhetoric of Leaders under Stress in the Gulf Crisis. JCR 37: 94-107.

59 Weber, R. P. 1982. The Long Term Dynamics of Societal Problem Solving: A Content Analysis of Speeches from the Throne. EJPR 10: 387-406.

60 Welsh, W. A. 1970. Methodological Problems in the Study of Political Leadership in Latin America. LARR 5: 3-34.

61 Wirl, F. 1991. The Political Economics of Wackersdorf: Why Do Politicians Stick to Their Past Decisions? PC 70: 343-350.

Cabinets

62 American Political Science Review. 1988. Papers on Cabinet Stability. APSR 82: 923-941.

63 Baron, D. P. 1993. Government Formation and Endogenous Parties. APSR 87: 34-47.

64 Best, J. J. 1981. Presidential Cabinet Appointments. PSQ 11: 62-66.

65 Browne, E. C.; Frendreis, J. P.; Gleiber, D. W. 1984. An Events Approach to the Problems of Cabinet Stability. CPS 17: 167-197.

66 -. 1986. Cabinet Dissolution: Exponential Model of Duration and Stability. AJPS 30: 628-650.

67 Casstevens, T. W. 1990. Probability Models of Turnover and Tenure of Commonwealth Prime Ministers. IJPS 51: 338-347.

68 Casstevens, T. W.; Casstevens, H. T. 1989. The Circulation of Elites. AJPS 33: 294-318.

69 Cioffi-Revilla, C. A. 1984. Political Reliability of Italian Governments: Exponential Survival Model. APSR 78: 318-337.

70 Cohen, J. E.1986. Tenure of Appointive Political Executives: American Cabinet. AJPS 30: 507-516.

71 Comparative Political Studies. 1984. Papers on Cabinet Coalitions. CPS 17 (2).

72 Damgaard, E. 1994. The Termination of Danish Government Coalitions. SPS 17: 193-212.

73 Elgie, R. A.; Maor, M. 1992. Survival of Minority Governments: France. WEP 15: 57-74.

74 European Journal of Poliical Research. 1988. Papers on Western European Cabinet Structure. EJPR 16 (2).

75 -. 1993. Party Government in Twenty Democracies. EJPR 24: 1-120.

76 Green, E. J. 1993. Emergence of Parliamentary Government: Role of Private Information. FRBM 17 (Winter): 2-16.

77 Grofman, B. 1989. Comparative Analysis of Coalition Formation and Duration: Distinguishing between Country and within Country Effects. BJPS 19: 291-302.

78 Grofman, B.; van Roozendaal, P. 1994. Toward a Theoretical Explanation of Premature Cabinet Termination. EJPR 26: 155-170.

79 International Political Science Review. 1981. Papers on the Selection of Cabinet Officials and Political Executives. IPSR 2: 211-234.

80 Iversen, T. 1994. Political Leadership and Representation in West European Democracies. AJPS 38: 45-74.

81 King, G., et al. 1990. A Unified Model of Cabinet Dissolution in Parliamentary Democracies. AJPS 34: 846-871.

82 Laver, M.; Shepsle, K. A. 1990. Coalitions and Cabinet Government. APSR 84: 873-890.

83 Lijphart, A. 1984. Measures of Cabinet Durability. CPS 17: 265-279.

84 Lupia, A.; Strom, K. 1995. Coalition Termination and the Strategic Timing of Parliamentary Elections. APSR 89: 648-668.

85 Martin, J. M. 1988. Frameworks for Cabinet Studies. PSQ 18: 793-814.

86 Narud, H. M. 1995. Coalition Termination in Norway. SPS 18: 1-24.

87 Politics. 1982. Papers on Premier's Departments of the Australian States. Vol 17 (1).

88 Robertson, J. D. 1983. Inflation, Unemployment and Government Collapse. CPS 15: 425-444.

89 -. 1983. Political Economy and Durability of European Coalition Cabinets: A Game Theoretic Perspective. JOP 45: 932-957.

90 -. 1984. Toward a Political-Economic Accounting of the Endurance of Cabinet Administrations. AJPS 28: 693-709.

91 Sanders, D.; Herman, V. 1977. The Stability and Survival of Governments. AP 12: 346-377.

92 Schofield, N. J.; Laver, M. 1985. Bargaining Theory and Portfolio Payoffs in European Coalition Governments. BJPS 15: 143-164.

93 Strom, K., et al 1988. Contending Models of Cabinet Stability. APSR 82: 923-942.

94 Strom, K.; Budge, I.; Laver, M. 1994. Constraints on Cabinet Formation. AJPS 38: 303-335.

95 Thompson, C. R. 1994. The Cabinet Member as Policy Entrepreneur. AAS 25: 395-409.

96 Van Roozendaal, P. 1992. The Effect of Dominant and Central Parties on Cabinet Composition and Durability. LSQ 17: 5-36.

97 Warwick, P. 1979. The Durability of Coalition Governments in Parliamentary Democracies. CPS 11: 465-498.

98 -. 1992. Economic Trends and Government Survival in West European Parliamentary Democracies. APSR 86: 875-887.

99 Warwick, P.; Easton, S. T. 1992. The Cabinet Stability Controversy. AJPS 36: 122-146.

100 Wright, J. R.; Goldberg, A. S. 1985. Risk and Uncertainty as Factors in the Durability of Political Coalitions. APSR 79: 704-718.

Chief Executives

101 Aldrich, J. H.; Sullivan, J. L.; Borgida, E. 1989. Foreign Affairs and Issue Voting: Do Presidential Candidates Waltz before a Blind Audience? APSR 83: 123-142.

102 American Politics Quarterly. 1975. Papers on Watergate. APQ 3 (4).

103 Anderson, D. G. 1988. Power, Rhetoric and the State: A Theory of Presidential Legitimacy. ROP 50: 198-214.

104 Bartels, L. M. 1987. Candidate Choice and the Dynamics of the Presidential Nominating Process. AJPS 31: 1-30.

105 Bennett, W. L. 1981. Assessing Presidential Character: Degradation Rituals in Political Campaigns. QJS 67: 310-321.

106 Berrington, H. 1974. The Fiery Chariot: British Prime Ministers and the Search for Love. BJPS 4: 345-370.

107 Bond, J. R.; Fleisher, R. 1980. Limits of Presidential Popularity as a Source of Influence in the House. LSQ 5: 69-78.

108 Boor, M. 1981. Effects of Presidential Elections on Suicide and Other Causes of Death. ASR 46: 616-618.

109 Brace, P.; Hinckley, B. 1991. The Structure of Presidential Approval. JOP 53: 993-1017.

110 -. 1993. Presidential Activities from Truman through Reagan. JOP 55: 382-398.

111 Browne, S. D., et al. 1988. In the Eye of the Beholder: Leader Images in Canada. CJPS 21: 729-755.

112 Burke, J. P.; Greenstein, F. I. 1989. Presidential Personality and National Security Leadership: Vietnam Decision Making. IPSR 10: 73-92.

113 Callaghan, K. J.; Virtanen, S. 1993. Revised Models of the Rally Phenomenon. JOP 55: 756-764.

114 Citrin, J.; Green, D. P. 1986. Presidential Leadership and the Resurgence of Trust in Government. BJPS 16: 431-454.

115 Cohen, J. E. 1980. Presidential Personality and Political Behavior. PSQ 10: 588-599.

116 Collier, K.; Sullivan, T. 1995. New Evidence Undercutting the Linkage of Approval with Presidential Support and Influence. JOP 57: 197-209.

117 Covington, C. R. 1988. Building Presidential Coalitions among Cross Pressured Members of Congress. WPQ 41: 47-62.

118 Dixon, W. J.; Gaarder, S. M. 1992. Presidential Succession and the Cold War: Soviet-American Relations. JOP 54: 156-178.

119 Donley, R. E.; Winter, D. G. 1970. Measuring Motives of Public Officials at a Distance: Presidents. BS 15: 227-236.

120 Dunleavy, G. W., et al. 1993. Leaders, Politics and Institutional Change: The Decline of Prime Ministerial Accountability in the House of Commons. BJPS 23: 267-298.

121 Dunn, C. W. 1984. The Theological Dimensions of Presidential Leadership. PSQ 14: 61-72.

122 Edwards, G. C. 1976. Presidential Influence in the House: Prestige as a Source of Power. APSR 70: 101-113.

123 Edwards, G. C.; Mitchell, W.; Welch, R. 1995. Explaining Presidential Approval: Issue Salience. AJPS 39: 108-134.

124 Elkin, S. L. 1991. Contempt of Congress: The Iran-Contra Affair and the American Constitution. CAP 18: 1-16.

125 Fairbanks, J. D. 1982. Religious Dimensions of Presidential Leadership. PSQ 12: 260-267.

126 George, A. L. 1974. Assessing Presidential Character. WP 26: 234-282.

127 Glass, D. P. 1985. Evaluating Presidential Candidates: Who Focuses on Their Personal Attributes. POQ 49: 517-534.

128 Grier, K. B.; McDonald, M.; Tollison, R. D. 1995. Electoral Politics and the Executive Veto. EI 33: 427-440.

129 Gustafson, M. 1970. The Religious Role of the President. MJPS 14: 708-722.

130 Hager, G. L.; Sullivan, T. 1994. President Centered and Presidency Centered Explanations of Public Activity. AJPS 38: 1079-1103.

131 Hahn, D. F. 1987. The Media and the Presidency. COMQ 35: 254-266.

132 Haight, T.; Brody, R. A. 1977. Mass Media and Presidential Popularity: Broadcasting and News in the Nixon Administration. COMR 4: 41-60.

133 Hinich, M. J.; Ordeshook, P. C. 1974. The Electoral College: A Spatial Analysis. PM 1: 1-29.

134 Holmes, J. E.; Elder, R. E. 1989. The Best and Worst Presidents: Reasons for Perceived Performance. PSQ 19: 529-558.

135 House, R. J.; Spangler, W. D.; Woycke, J. 1991. Personality and Charisma in the US Presidency: A Psychological Theory of Leader Effectiveness. ASQ 36: 364-396.

136 Hurwitz, J.; Peffley, M. 1986. The Means and Ends of Foreign Policy as Determinants of Presidential Support. AJPS 31: 236-258.

137 Kenney, P. J.; Rice, T. W. 1988. Contextual Determinants of Presidential Greatness. PSQ 18: 161-168.

138 Kerbel, M. R. 1993. The Role of Persuasion in Exercise of Presidential Power. PSQ 23: 347-361.

139 Kiewiet, D. R.; McCubbins, M. D. 1988. Presidential Influence on Congressional Appropriation Decisions. AJPS 32: 713-736.

140 Kinder, D. R., et al. 1980. Presidential Prototypes. PB 2: 315-337.

141 Krosnick, J. A.; Kinder, D. R. 1990. Altering the Foundations of Popular Support for the President through Priming. APSR 84: 497-512.

142 Krukones, M. G. 1980. Predicting Presidential Performance through Political Campaigns. PSQ 10: 527-543.

143 Lanoue, D. J.; Headrick, B. 1994. Prime Ministers, Parties and Public: Dynamics of Government Popularity in Great Britain. POQ 58: 191-209.

144 Law and Contemporary Problems. 1970. Papers on the Institutionalized Presidency. LACP 35 (3).

145 -. 1976. Papers on Presidential Power. LACP 40 (2-3).

146 Lee, J. R. 1975. Presidential Vetoes. JOP 37: 522-546.

147 -. 1977. Rallying Round the Flag: Foreign Policy Events and Presidential Popularity. PSQ 7: 252-256.

148 Lian, B.; Oneal, J. R. 1993. Presidents, the Use of Military Force and Public Opinion. JCR 37: 277-300.

149 Light, P. C. 1981. The President's Agenda: Notes on the Timing of Domestic Choice. PSQ 10: 67-82.

150 Lindsay, J. M.; Sayrs, L. W.; Steger, W. P. 1992. Determinants of Presidential Foreign Policy Choice. APQ 20: 3-25.

151 Lindsay, J. M.; Steger, W. P. 1993. Two Presidencies in Future Research. CAP 20: 103-118.

152 Lockerbie, B.; Borelli, S. A. 1989. Perceptions of Presidential Skill and Success in Congress. BJPS 19: 97-106.

153 Marra, R. F.; Ostrom, C. W.; Simon, D. M. 1990. Foreign Policy and Presidential Popularity. JCR 34: 588-623.

154 Meleskie, M. F.; Hipel, K. W.; Fraser, N. M. 1982. The Watergate Tapes Conflict: A Metagame Analysis. PM 8 (4).

155 Mondak, J. J. 1993. Presidential Coattails and Open Seats: The District Level Impact of Heuristic Processing. APQ 21: 307-319.

156 Mueller, J. E. 1970. Presidential Popularity from Truman to Johnson. APSR 64: 18-34.

157 Mueller, K. J. 1985. Explaining Variation and Change in Gubernatorial Powers. WPQ 38: 424-431.

158 Newman, J.; Taylor, A. 1994. Family Training for Political Leadership: Birth Order of US State Governors and Australian Prime Ministers. PP 15: 435-442.

159 Nice, D. C. 1992. Peak Presidential Approval from Franklin Roosevelt to Ronald Reagan. PSQ 22: 119-126.

160 Nincic, M.; Hinckley, B. 1991. Foreign Policy and the Evaluation of Presidential Candidates. JCR 35: 333-355.

161 Norpoth, H. 1984. Economic Politics and the Cycle of Presidential Popularity. PB 6: 253-273.

162 Ostrom, C. W.; Job, B. L. 1986. The President and Political Use of Force. APSR 80: 541-566.

163 Ostrom, C. W.; Simon, D. M. 1985. A Dynamic Model of Presidential Popularity. APSR 79: 334-358.

164 -. 1988. The President's Public. AJPS 32: 1098-1119.

165 Political Psychology. 1994. Papers on Political Psychology and Alexander L. George. PP 15 (1).

166 Presidential Studies Quarterly. 1986. Papers on Leadership and National Security. PSQ 16 (3).

167 -. 1986. Papers on the Media and the President. PSQ 16 (1).

168 -. 1987. Papers on the Origins of the Presidency. PSQ 17 (2).

169 -. 1993. Papers on Presidential Persuasion. PSQ 23 (2).

170 -. 1993. Papers on the Managerial, Political and Spiritual President. PSQ 23 (4).

171 -. 1993. Papers on the Two Presidents. PSQ 23 (2).

172 -. 1994. Papers on the Domestic and Foreign Policy Objectives of Presidents. PSQ 24 (1).

173 Public Administration Review. 1970. Papers on US Governors. PAR 30 (1).

174 Ragsdale, L. 1991. Strong Feelings: Emotional Responses to Presidents. PB 13: 33-66.

175 Riggs, F. W. 1988. Survival of Presidentialism in America. IPSR 9: 247-278.

176 Ringelstein, A. C. 1985. Presidential Vetoes. CAP 12: 43-56.

177 Rohde, D. W.; Simon, D. M. 1985. Presidential Vetoes and Congressional Response. AJPS 29: 397-427.

178 Rourke, F.; Grossman, M. 1976. The Media and the Presidency: Exchange Analysis. PSQ 91: 455-470.

179 Shaffer, W. R. 1980. A Discriminant Function Analysis of Position Taking: Carter vs. Kennedy. PSQ 10: 451-468.

180 Shields, T. G.; Huang, C. 1995. Presidential Vetoes: An Event Count Model. PRQ 48: 559-572.

181 Sigelman, L. 1979. The Dynamics of Presidential Support. PSQ 9: 206-216.

182 Sigelman, L.; Conover, P. J. 1981. Dynamics of Presidential Support during International Conflict Situations: The Iranian Hostage Crisis. PB 3: 303-318.

183 Sigelman, L.; Knight, K. 1983. Why Does Presidential Popularity Decline? Test of the Expectation-Disillusion Theory. POQ 47: 310-324.

184 Sigelman, L.; Sigelman, C. K. 1981. Shattered Expectations: Public Responses to Out-of-Character Presidential Action. PB 8: 262-286.

185 Simon, D. M.; Ostrom, C. W. 1989. The Impact of Televised Speeches and Foreign Travel on Presidential Approval. POQ 53: 58-82.

186 Simonton, D. K. 1991. Predicting Presidential Greatness. PSQ 21: 301-306.

187 Smith, C. A.; Smith, K. B. 1985. Presidential Values and Recurrent Priorities: Addresses to the Nation. PSQ 15: 743-753.

188 Somit, A., et al. 1994. Birth Order and British Prime Ministers. POLST 42: 120-127.

189 Spitzer, R. J. 1983. How Policies Frame Congressional Responses to the President's Legislative Program. PSQ 13: 556-575.

190 State Government. 1982. Papers on Governors. SG 55 (3).

191 Stimson, J. A. 1976. Public Support for American Presidents. POQ 40: 1-21.

192 Stoker, L. 1993. Judging Presidential Character: The Demise of Gary Hart. PB 15: 193-223.

193 Sullivan, T. 1990. Bargaining with the President: A Simple Game. APSR 84: 1167-1196.

194 -. 1991. Bank Account Presidency: Temporal Path of Presidential Influence. AJPS 35: 686-737.

195 Tatalovich, R.; Gitelson, A. R. 1990. Political Party Linkages to Presidential Popularity: Assessing the Coalition of Minorities Thesis. JOP 52: 234-242.

196 Thomas, D.; Baas, L. A. 1982. Presidential Identification and Mass-Public Compliance with Official Policy: The Carter Energy Program. PSJ 10: 448-464.

197 Tyler, T. R. 1982. Personalization in Attributing Responsibility for Problems to the President. PB 4: 379-399.

198 Wanat, J. 1982. Dynamics of Presidential Popularity Shifts. APQ 10: 181-196.

199 Windt, T. O. 1984. Presidential Rhetoric: Definition of a Field of Study. CSSJ 35: 24-34.

200 Zeidenstein, H. G. 1983. Varying Relationships between Presidents' Popularity and Their Legislative Success. PSQ 13: 530-550.

201 Zupan, M. A. 1992. Measuring the Ideological Preferences of US Presidents. PC 73: 351-361.

Committees

202 Aldrich, J. H. 1994. Model of a Legislature with Two Parties and a Committee System. LSQ 19: 313-340.

203 Annals. 1974. Papers on the Congressional Committee System. ANNALS 411.

204 Bach, S. 1986. Representatives and Committees on the Floor: Amendments to Appropriations Bills. CAP 13: 41-53.

205 Basehart, H. H. 1980. The Effect of Membership Stability on Continuity and Experience in State Legislative Communities. LSQ 5: 55-68.

206 Bendor, J.; Moe, T. M. 1980. Agenda Control, Committee Capture and the Dynamics of Institutional Politics. APSR 80: 1187-1207.

207 Black, D. 1991. Arrow's Work and the Normative Theory of Committees. JTP 3: 259-276.

208 Bond, J. R. 1979. Oiling the Tax Committees in Congress: The Subgovernment Theory, the Overrepresentation Hypothesis and the Oil Depletion Allowance. AJPS 23: 651-664.

209 Boynton, G. R. 1989. The Senate Agriculture Committee Produces a Homeostat. PSCI 22: 51-80.

210 Bullock, C. S. 1973. Committee Transfers in the US House. JOP 35: 85-120.

211 Cameron, C. M.; Rosendorff, B. P. 1993. A Signaling Theory of Congressional Oversight. GAEB 5: 44-70.

212 Coker, D. C.; Crain, W. M. 1994. Legislative Committees as Loyalty-Generating Institutions. PC 81: 195-221.

213 Collie, M. P.; Roberts, B. E. 1992. Choice and Committee Chairs in the Senate. JOP 54: 231-245.

214 Cooper, J. 1971. Study of Congressional Committees. Polity 4: 123-133.

215 Davidson, R. H. 1989. Multiple Referral of Legislation in the US Senate. LSQ 14: 375-392.

216 Davidson, R. H.; Oleszek, W. J.; Kephart, T. 1988. One Bill, Many Committees: Multiple Referrals. LSQ 13: 3-28.

217 Davis, M. L. 1990. Why Is There a Seniority System? To Solve Agency Problem. PC 66: 37-50.

218 Denzau, A. T. 1983. Gatekeeping and Monopoly Power of Committees: Analysis of Sincere and Sophisticated Behavior. AJPS 27: 740-761.

219 Dodd, L. C. 1972. Committee Integration. JOP 34: 1135-1171.

220 Dodd, L. C.; Pierce, J. C. 1975. Roll Call Measurement of Committee Integration. Polity 7: 386-401.

221 Endersby, J. W. 1993. Rules of Method and Rules of Conduct: Procedure and Committee Behavior. JOP 55: 218-236.

222 Eulau, H.; McCluggage, V. 1984. Standing Committees in Legislatures. LSQ 9: 195-270.

223 Feig, D. G. 1979. Stability of Congressional Committees: A Formal Analysis. PM 6: 311-342.

224 Feld, S. L.; Grofman, B. 1986. On the Possibility of Faithfully Representative Committees. APSR 80: 863-879.

225 Francis, W. L. 1982. Legislative Committee Systems, Optimal Committee Size and the Costs of Decision Making. JOP 44: 822-833.

226 Freeman, P. K.; Hedlund, R. D. 1993. Functions of Committee Change in State Legislatures. PRQ 46: 911-930.

227 Gamm, G.; Shepsle, K. A. 1989. Emergence of Legislative Institutions: Standing Committees. LSQ 14: 39-66.

228 Gilligan, T. W.; Krehbiel, K. 1990. Organization of Information Committees by Rational Legislature. AJPS 34: 531-564.

229 Groseclose, T. 1994. Testing Committee Composition Hypotheses for the US Congress. JOP 56: 440-458.

230 Haeberle, S. H. 1978. Institutionalization of the Subcommittee in the US House. JOP 40: 1054-1065.

231 Hall, R. L. 1987. Participation and Purpose in Committee Decision Making. APSR 81: 105-128.

232 Hall, R. L.; Evans, C. L. 1990. Power of Subcommittees. JOP 52: 335-355.

233 Hall, R. L.; Grofman, B. 1990. The Committee Assignment Process and the Conditional Nature of Committee Bias. APSR 84: 1149-1166.

234 Hall, R. L.; Wayman, F. W. 1990. Moneyed Interests and the Mobilization of Bias in Congressional Committees. APSR 84: 797-820.

235 Hamm, K. E. 1980. State Legislative Committee Decisions. LSQ 5: 31-54.

236 -. 1982. Consistency between Committee and Floor Voting in US State Legislatures. LSQ 7: 473-490.

237 Hamm, K. E.; Hedlund, R. D. 1990. Accounting for Change in the Number of State Legislative Committee Positions. LSQ 15: 201-226.

238 Hamm, K. E.; Moncrief, G. F. 1982. The Effects of Structural Change in Legislative Committee Systems on Their Performance in the US States. LSQ 7: 383-400.

239 Hinckley, B. 1975. Policy Content, Committee Membership and Behavior. AJPS 19: 543-558.

240 Hoffman, E.; Packel, E. W. 1982. A Stochastic Model of Committee Voting with Exogenous Costs. BS 27: 43-56.

241 Jorgerst, M. A. 1991. Backbenchers and Select Committees in the British House of Commons. EJPR 20: 21-38.

242 King, D. C. 1994. The Nature of Congressional Committee Jurisdictions. APSR 88: 48-62.

243 Kline, H. F. 1977. Committee Membership Turnover in Colombian National Congress. LSQ 2: 29-44.

244 Krehbiel, K. 1986. Sophisticated and Myopic Behavior in Legislative Committees. AJPS 30: 542-561.

245 -. 1990. Are Congressional Committees Composed of Preference Outliers? APSR 84: 149-164.

246 Krehbiel, K.; Rivers, D. 1988. Analysis of Committee Power: An Application to Minimum Wage. AJPS 32: 1151-1174.

247 Krehbiel, K.; Shepsle, K. A.; Weingast, B. R. 1987. Why Are Congressional Committees Powerful? APSR 81: 929-948.

248 Laing, J. D.; Slotnik, B. 1991. When Anyone Can Veto: A Laboratory Study of Committees Governed by Unanimous Rule. BS 36: 179-195.

249 Londregan, J.; Snyder, J. M. 1994. Comparing Committee and Floor Preferences. LSQ 19: 233-266.

250 Maltzman, F.; Smith, S. S. 1994. Principals, Goals, Dimensionality and Congressional Committees. LSQ 19: 457-476.

251 McKelvey, R. D.; Ordeshook, P. C. 1984. An Experimental Study of the Effects of Procedural Rules on Committee Behavior. JOP 46: 182-223.

252 Miller, G. J.; Hammond, T. H. 1990. Committees and the Core of the Constitution. PC 66: 201-228.

253 Niemi, R. G.; Bjurulf, B. H.; Vlevis, G. 1983. The Power of the Chairman. PC 40: 293-305.

254 Nordin, J. A. 1969. Normalized Vote Margins of Committee Voting. RISEC 16: 529-549.

255 Parker, G. R.; Parker, S. L. 1979. Factions in Committees: US House. APSR 73: 85-102.

256 Payne, J. L. 1982. Rise of Lone Wolf Questioning in House Committee Hearings. Polity 14: 626-640.

257 Perkins, L. P. 1980. Influence of Members Goals on Committee Behavior: House Judicial Committee. LSQ 5: 373-392.

258 Price, D. E. 1978. Policy Making in Senate Committees: Environmental Factors. APSR 72: 548-574.

259 Ray, B. A. 1981. Military Committee Membership in the House and Defense Department Outlays. WPQ 34: 222-234.

260 Rundquist, B. S.; Strom, G. S. 1987. Bill Construction in Legislative Committees. LSQ 12: 97-114.

261 Salant, S. W.; Goodstein, E. 1990. Predicting Committee Behavior in Majority Rule Voting Experiments. RJE 21: 293-313.

262 Shepsle, K. A. 1975. Congressional Committee Assignments: An Optimization Model with Institutional Constraints. PC 22: 55-78.

263 Shepsle, K. A.; Weingast, B. R. 1987. Institutional Foundations of Committee Power. APSR 81: 85-104.

264 Sinclair, B. D. 1986. Senate Styles and Decision Making. JOP 48: 877-908.

265 -. 1988. Distribution of Committee Positions in the US Senate: Explaining Institutional Change. AJPS 32: 276-301.

266 Smith, S. S. 1988. Essay on Sequence, Position, Goals and Committee Power. LSQ 13: 151-176.

267 Snyder, J. M. 1992. Committee Power, Structure Induced Equilibria and Roll Call Votes. AJPS 36: 1-30.

268 Songer, D. R. 1988. Committee vs. Floor Decision Making. LSQ 13: 375-392.

269 Vogler, D. J. 1981. Ad Hoc Committees in the House and Purposive Models of Representative Behavior. Polity 14: 89-109.

270 Weingast, B. R. 1989. Floor Behavior in the US Congress: Committee Power under the Open Rule. APSR 83: 795-816.

271 Westefield, L. P. 1974. Majority Party Leadership and the Committee System in the House. APSR 68: 1593-1604.

272 Whiteman, D. 1983. Committee Size in the House. APQ 11: 49-70.

273 Wilkerson, J. 1991. Analyzing Committee Power. AJPS 35: 624-642.

274 Wilson, R. K. 1986. What Was It Worth To Be on a Committee in the House 1889-1913? LSQ 11: 47-64.

275 Wright, J. R. 1990. Contributions, Lobbying and Committee Voting in the House. APSR 84: 417-438.

Constituencies

276 Bartels, L. M. 1991. Constituency Opinion and Congressional Policy Making: The Reagan Defense Buildup. APSR 85: 457-474.

277 Bogart, W. T.; Van Doren, P. M. 1993. Do Legislators Vote Their Constituents' Wallets? And How Would We Know If They Did? SEJ 60: 357-375.

278 Boynton, G. R.; Hedlund, R. D.; Patterson, S. C. 1969. Missing Links in Legislative Politics: Attentive Publics. JOP 31: 700-721.

279 Cain, B. E.; Ferejohn, J. A.; Fiorina, M. P. 1984. Constituency Service Basis of the Personal Vote for US Representatives and British Members of Parliament. APSR 78: 110-125.

280 Carter, R. G. 1989. Senate Defense Budgeting: Impacts of Ideology, Party and Constituency on Decision to Support President. APQ 17: 332-347.

281 Cnudde, C. F.; McCrone, D. J. 1966. Linkage between Constituency Attitudes and Congressional Voting Behavior. APSR 60: 66-72.

282 Denzau, A. T.; Riker, W. H.; Shepsle, K. A. 1985. Farquharson and Fenno: Sophisticated Voting and Home Style. APSR 79: 1117-1134.

283 Erikson, R. S. 1978. Constituency Opinion and Congressional Behavior: Reexamination of Miller-Stokes Representation Data. AJPS 22: 511-535.

284 Erikson, R. S.; Wright, G. C. 1980. Policy Representation of Constituency Interests. PB 1: 91-106.

285 Fenno, R. F. 1977. House Members in Their Constituencies. APSR 71: 883-918.

286 Fiorina, M. P. 1973. Electoral Margins, Constituency Influence and Policy Moderation. APQ 1: 479-498.

287 Glazer, A.; Robbins, M. 1985. Congressional Responsiveness to Constituency Change. AJPS 29: 259-273.

288 Grier, K. B.; Munger, M. C. 1991. Committee Assignments, Constituent Preferences and Campaign Contributions. EI 29: 24-43.

289 Hedlund, R. D.; Friesema, H. P. 1972. Representatives' Perceptions of Constituency Opinion. JOP 34: 730-752.

290 Herrick, R.; Thomas, S. 1993. Split Delegations in the US Senate. SSI 30: 69-82.

291 Higgs, R. 1989. Do Legislators' Votes Reflect Constituency Preference? A Simple Way to Evaluate the Senate. PC 63: 175-181.

292 Hill, K. Q.; Hurley, P. A. 1979. Mass Participation, Electoral Competitiveness and Issue-Attitude Agreement between Congressmen and Their Constituents. BJPS 9: 507-511.

293 Jewell, M. E. 1988. Legislators and Their Districts. LSQ 13: 403-412.

294 Kenski, H. C.; Kenski, M. C. 1980. Partisanship, Ideology and Constituency Differences on Environmental Issues in the House. PSJ 9: 325-335.

295 King, G. 1991. Constituency Service and Incumbency Advantage. BJPS 21: 119-128.

296 Kuklinski, J. H. 1979. Representative-Constituency Linkages. LSQ 4: 121-140.

297 Lasher, E. L; Kelman, S.; Kane, T. J. 1993. Policy Views, Constituency Pressure and Congressional Action on Flag Burning. PC 75: 79-102.

298 McAllister, I. 1991. Party Elites, Voters and Political Attitudes: Explanations for Mass-Elite Differences. CJPS 24: 237-268.

299 McArthur, J.; Marks, S. V. 1988. Constituent Interest vs. Legislator Ideology: Role of Political Opportunity Cost. EI 26: 461-470.

300 McDonagh, E. L. 1989. Issues and Constituencies in the Progressive Era: House Roll Call Voting on the Nineteenth Amendment. JOP 51: 119-136.

301 -. 1993. Constituency Influence on House Roll Call Votes in Progressive Era. LSQ 18: 185-210.

302 Overby, L. M. 1991. Assessing Constituency Influence: Congressional Voting on the Nuclear Freeze. LSQ 16: 297-312.

303 Richardson, L. E.; Freeman, P. K. 1995. Gender Differences in Constituency Service among State Legislators. PRQ 48: 169-180.

304 Ripley, R. B., et al. 1992. Constituents' Evaluations of US House Members. APQ 20: 442-456.

305 Schwartz, J. E. 1975. Impact of Constituency on British Conservative MPs. CPS 8: 75-89.

306 Serra, G. 1994. Impact of Congressional Casework on Incumbent Evaluation. APQ 22: 403-420.

307 Shapiro, C. R., et al. 1990. Linking Constituency Opinion and Senate Voting Scores. LSQ 15: 599-622.

308 Stone, W. J. 1979. Measuring Constituency-Representative Linkages. LSQ 4: 623-639.

309 Uslaner, E. M.; Wever, R. E. 1979. State Legislators' Opinions and Perceptions of Constituency Attitudes. LSQ 4: 563-586.

310 Yiannakis, D. E. 1981. The Grateful Electorate: Casework and Congressional Elections. AJPS 25: 568-580.

311 Zupan, M. A. 1989. The Extent to which Political Representatives' Voting Behavior Reflects Constitutents' Preferences. EL 30: 291-295.

Leaders and Careers

312 Abramson, P. R.; Aldrich, J. H.; Rohde, D. W. 1987. Progressive Ambition among US Senators. JOP 49: 3-35.

313 Ainsworth, S.; Flathman, M. 1995. Unanimous Consent Agreements as Leadership Tools. LSQ 20: 177-196.

314 Bean, C. S. 1993. Electoral Influence of Party Leader Images in Australia and New Zealand. CPS 26: 111-132.

315 Calvert, R. L. 1987. Reputation and Legislative Leadership. PC 55: 81-119.

316 Camron, D. T. 1989. Institutionalization of Leadership in the US Congress. LSQ 14: 415-433.

317 Clucas, R. A. 1994. Effect of Campaign Contributions on the Power of the California Assembly Speaker. LSQ 19: 417-428.

318 Coates, D.; Munger, M. C. 1995. A Categorical Analysis of Career Patterns in the House of Representatives. PC 83: 95-112.

319 Cooper, J.; Brady, D. W. 1981. Institutional Context and Leadership Style: The House from Cannon to Rayburn. APSR 75: 411-425.

320 Cooper, J.; West, W. 1981. Voluntary Retirement, Incumbency and Modern House. PSCQ 96: 279-300.

321 DeGregorio, C. 1988. Professionals in the US Congress: Working Styles. LSQ 13: 459-476.

322 Dunleavy, P.; Jones, G. W.; O'Leary, B. 1990. Prime Ministers and the Commons: Patterns of Behavior. PA 68: 123-140.

323 Francis, W. L.; Baker, J. R. 1985. Why Do State Legislators Vacate Their Seats? LSQ 11: 119-126.

324 Frantzich, S. E. 1978. Opting Out: Retirement from the House. APQ 6: 251-274.

325 Frendreis, J. P.; Gleiber, D. W.; Browne, E. C. 1986. Study of Cabinet Dissolutions in Parliamentary Democracies. LSQ 11: 619-628.

326 Graham, J. Q. 1982. Legislative Careers in the French Chamber and US House, 1871-1940. LSQ 7: 37-56.

327 Gross, D. A. 1984. Changing Patterns of Voting Agreement among Senatorial Leadership. WPQ 37: 120-142.

328 Hall, R. L.; Van Houweling, R. P. 1995. Avarice and Ambition in Congress: Representatives' Decisions to Run or Retire. APSR 89: 121-136.

329 Herrick, R.; Moore, M. K. 1993. Political Ambition's Effect on Legislative Behavior: Schlesinger's Typology Reconsidered. JOP 55: 765-776.

330 Herrick, R.; Moore, M. K.; Hibbing, J. R. 1994. Unfastening the Electoral Connection: Behavior of US Representatives when Reelection is No Longer a Factor. JOP 56: 214-227.

331 Hibbing, J. R. 1982. Voluntary Retirement from the US House: Who Quits. AJPS 26: 467-484.

332 -. 1986. Ambition in the House: Consequences of Higher Office Goals among US Representatives. AJPS 30: 651-665.

333 -. 1991. Contours of the Modern Congressional Career. APSR 85: 405-428.

334 Hodson, T., et al. 1995. Leaders and Limits: Changing Patterns of State Legislative Leadership under Term Limits. Spectrum 68 (3): 6-15.

335 Kernell, S. 1977. Toward Understanding 19th Century Congressional Careers. AJPS 21: 669-694.

336 Kiewiet, D. R.; Zeng, L. 1993. Congressional Career Decisions. APSR 87: 928-944.

337 Kim, C. L.; Patterson, S. C. 1988. Parliamentary Elite Integration in Six Nations. CP 20: 379-399

338 Laband, D. N.; Haughton, J. 1985. Toward an Economic Theory of Voluntary Resignation by Dictators. IRLE 5: 199-207.

339 Livingston, S.; Friedman, S. 1993. Reexamining Theories of Congressional Retirement. LSQ 18: 231-254.

340 Luttbeg, N. R. 1992. Legislative Careers in Six States. LSQ 17: 49-68.

341 Matthews, D. R. 1984. Legislative Recruitment and Legislative Careers. LSQ 9: 544-585.

342 McKelvey, R. D.; Riezman, R. 1992. Seniority in Legislatures. APSR 86: 951-965.

343 Moncrief, G. F. 1988. Dimensions of the Concept of Professionalism in State Legislatures. SALGR 20: 128-132.

344 -. 1994. Professionalism and Careerism in Canadian Provincial Assemblies. LSQ 19: 33-48.

345 Muller-Rommel, F. 1988. The Center of Government in West Germany: Changing Patterns under Fourteen Legislatures. EJPR 16: 171-190.

346 Nelson, G. 1977. Partisan Patterns of House Leadership Change. APSR 71: 918-939.

347 Nicholls, K. 1993. A Logit Model of Turnover in the Presidential Cabinet. CAP 20: 39-52.

348 Overby, L. M. 1993. Political Amateurism, Legislative Inexperience and Incumbency: Southern Republican Senators. Polity 25: 401-420.

349 Payne, J. L. 1982. Career Intentions and Electoral Performance of Members of the US House. LSQ 7: 93-99.

350 Rohde, D. W.; Shepsle, K. A. 1987. Leaders and Followers in the House: Woodrow Wilson's Congressional Government. CAP 14: 111-134.

351 Schansberg, D. E. 1994. Moving out of the House: Analysis of Congressional Quits. EI 32: 445-456.

352 Schroedel, J. R. 1994. Legislative Leadership over Time. PRQ 47: 439-466.

353 Sokolow, A. D. 1989. Legislators without Ambition: Why Small Town Citizens Seek Public Office. SALGR 21: 23-30.

354 Squire, P. 1993. Professionalism and Public Opinion of State Legislatures. JOP 55: 479-491.

355 Stewart, D. K.; Carty, R. K. 1993. Does Changing the Party Leader Provide an Electoral Boost? Canadian Provincial Parties. CJPS 26: 313-330.

356 Waldman, S. R. 1980. Majority Party Leadership in the House. PSCQ 95: 373-393.

357 West European Politics. 1991. Papers on European Prime Ministers. WEP 14 (2).

358 Wilson, R. K.; Jillson, C. C. 1989. Leadership Patterns in Continental Congress. LSQ 14: 5-38.

Legislative Behavior

359 Asher, H. B.; Weisberg, H. F. 1978. Voting Change in Congress: Dynamic Perspectives. AJPS 22: 391-425.

360 Bach, S. 1990. Suspension of the Rules, Order of Business and Development of Congressional Procedures. LSQ 15: 49-64.

361 Baron, D. P. 1994. A Sequential Choice Theory Perspective on Legislative Organization. LSQ 19: 267-296.

362 Baron, D. P.; Ferejohn, J. A. 1989. Bargaining in Legislatures. APSR 83: 1181-1206.

363 Berkman, M. B. 1994. State Legislators in Congress. AJPS 38: 1025-1055.

364 Bernstein, R. A. 1992. Determinants of Differences in Feelings toward Senators Representing the Same State. WPQ 45: 701-726.

365 Blydenberg, J. C. 1971. The Closed Rule and the Paradox of Voting. JOP 33: 57-71.

366 Bowler, S.; Farrell, D. M. 1993. Legislator Shirking and Voter Monitoring: Impacts of European Parliament Electoral Systems on Legislator-Voter Relationships. JCMS 31: 45-69.

367 Boynton, G. R.; Kim, C. L. 1991. Legislative Representation as Parallel Processing and Problem Solving. JTP 3: 437-462.

368 Browne, W. P. 1987. Social and Political Conditions of Issue Credibility: Legislative Agendas in the American States. Polity 20: 296-315.

369 Caldeira, G. A.; Clark, J. A.; Patterson, S. C. 1993. Political Respect in the Legislature. LSQ 18: 3-28.

370 Caldeira, G. A.; Patterson, S. C. 1987. Political Friendship in the Legislature. JOP 49: 953-975.

371 -. 1988. Contours of Friendship and Respect in the Legislature. APQ 16: 166-185.

372 Cavanagh, T. E. 1982. The Calculus of Representation: A Congressional Perspective. WPQ 35: 120-136.

373 -. 1982. Dispersion of Authority in the House. PSCQ 97: 623-638.

374 Chaffey, D. C. 1970. Institutionalization of State Legislatures. WPQ 23: 180-196.

375 Chesney, J. D. 1980. Impact of Analytic Ability on Congressional Behavior. PP 2: 38-56.

376 Clubok, A. B.; Berghorn, F. J.; Wilensky, N. 1969. Family Relationships, Congressional Recruitment and Political Modernization. JOP 31: 1035-1062.

377 Collie, M. P. 1988. Legislature and Distributive Policy Making in Formal Perspective. LSQ 13: 427-458.

378 Cooper, J.; Brady, D. W. 1981. Toward a Diachronic Analysis of Congress. APSR 75: 988-1006.

379 Cooper, J.; Young, C. D. 1989. Bill Introduction in the Nineteenth Century: A Study of Institutional Change. LSQ 14: 67-106.

380 Cover, A. D.; Brumberg, B. S. 1982. Impact of Congressional Mail on Constituent Opinion. APSR 76: 347-359.

381 Crain, W. M.; Goff, B. L. 1986. Televising Legislatures: An Economic Analysis. JOLE 29: 405-421.

382 Damgaard, E. 1980. The Function of Parliament in the Danish Political System. LSQ 5: 101-122.

383 Dilger, R. J.; Krause, G. A.; Moffett, R. R. 1995. State Legislative Professionalism and Gubernatorial Effectiveness. LSQ 20: 553-572.

384 Donald, L. E.; Farmsworth, D. L.; Fleming, J. S. 1978. Trends and Cycles in Legislative Productivity of the US Congress. QAQ 12: 19-44.

385 Engstrom, R. L.; O'Connor, P. F. 1980. Lawyer-Legislators and Support for State Legislative Reform. JOP 42: 267-276.

386 Eulau, H. 1987. The Congruence Model Revisited. LSQ 12: 171-214.

387 -. 1993. Congress as Research Arena. LSQ 18: 569-592.

388 Eulau, H.; Karps, P. 1977. The Puzzle of Representation: Specifying Components of Responsiveness. LSQ 2: 233-254.

389 European Journal of Political Research. 1986. Papers on Causes of Legislation. EJPR 14 (3).

390 Francis, W. L.; Weber, R. E. 1980. Legislative Issues in the States. LSQ 3: 407-421.

391 Franklin, C. H. 1993. Senate Incumbent Visibility over the Election Cycle. LSQ 18: 271-290.

392 Frantzich, S. E. 1979. Technological Innovation among Members of the House. Polity 12: 333-348.

393 Froman, L. A. 1968. Organization Theory and Explanation of Important Characteristics of Congress. APSR 62: 518-526.

394 Gilligan, T. W.; Krehbiel, K. 1994. Gains from Exchange Hypotheses of Legislative Organizations. LSQ 19: 181-214.

395 Goodsell, C. T. 1988. Architecture of Parliaments: Legislative Houses and Political Culture. BJPS 18: 287-302.

396 Greenberg, J.; Shepsle, K. A. 1987. The Effect of Electoral Rewards in Multiparty Competition with Entry. APSR 81: 525-537.

397 Greene, K. V.; Salavitabar, H. 1982. Senatorial Responsiveness, Characteristics of the Polity and the Political Cycle. PC 38: 263-270.

398 Grofman, B., et al. 1987. Stability and Centrality of Legislative Choice in the Spatial Context. APSR 81: 539-556.

399 Grofman, B.; Griffin, R.; Glazer, A. 1991. Is the Senate More Liberal than the House? LSQ 16: 281-296.

400 Gross, D. A. 1978. Representative Styles and Legislative Behavior. WPQ 31: 359-371.

401 Hibbing, J. R. 1988. Legislative Institutionalization with Illustrations from the British House of Commons. AJPS 32: 681-712.

402 Hill, J. S.; Williams, K. C. 1993. The Decline of Private Bills. AJPS 37: 1008-1031.

403 Hurley, P. A. 1982. Predicting Policy Change in the House: Longitudinal Analysis. BJPS 12: 375-384.

404 -. 1984. Electoral Change and Policy Consequences. APQ 12: 177-194.

405 Hurwitz, J. 1986. Issue Perception and Legislative Decision Making: Social Judgment Theory. APQ 14: 150-187.

406 -. 1988. Determinants of Legislative Cue Selection. SSQ 69: 212-223.

407 Jackson, J. E.; King, D. C. 1989. Public Goods, Private Interests and Representation. APSR 83: 1143-1164.

408 Jillson, C. C. 1988. Political Culture and the Pattern of Congressional Politics under the Articles of Confederation. Publius 18: 1-26.

409 Jillson, C. C.; Wilson, R. K. 1987. A Social Choice Model of Politics: Demise of the Continental Congress. LSQ 12: 5-32.

410 Johannes, J. R. 1980. The Distribution of Casework in the US Congress. LSQ 5: 517-544.

411 Johnson, L. K.; Gelles, E.; Kuzenski, J. C. 1992. Study of Congressional Investigations. CAP 19: 137-156.

412 Jones, B. D.; Baumgartner, F. R.; Talbert, J. C. 1993. Destruction of Issue Monopolies in Congress. APSR 87: 657-671.

413 Journal of Commonwealth and Comparative Politics. 1982. Papers on Parliamentary Reform. JCACP 20 (2).

414 Kalt, J. P.; Zupan, M. A. 1990. Apparent Ideological Behavior: Principal-Agent Slack in Political Institutions. JOLE 33: 103-131.

415 King, A. 1976. Modes of Executive-Legislative Relations: Great Britain, France and West Germany. LSQ 1: 37-65.

416 Korn, J. 1995. Legislative Veto and the Limits of Public Choice Analysis. PSCQ 109: 873-894.

417 Krehbiel, K. 1986. Unanimous Consent Agreements: Going Along in the Senate. JOP 48: 541-564.

418 -. 1988. Spatial Models of Legislative Choice. LSQ 13: 259-320.

419 -. 1995. Cosponsors and Wafflers. AJPS 39: 906-923.

420 Kuklinski, J. H. 1978. Representation and Elections: A Policy Analysis. APSR 78: 165-177.

421 Kuklinski, J. H.; Segura, G. M. 1995. Endogeneity, Exogeneity, Time and Space in Political Representation. LSQ 1995: 3-22.

422 Laband, D. N. 1988. Transactions Costs and Production in a Legislative Setting. PC 57: 183-186.

423 Lees, J. D. 1977. Legislatures and Oversight. LSQ 2: 193-208.

424 Legislative Studies Quarterly. 1982. Papers on Studies of Parliamentary History. LSQ 7 (2).

425 -. 1989. Papers on the Internal Operations of the Senate. LSQ 14 (3).

426 Levy, A. B.; Stoudinger, S. 1976. Sources of Voting Cues for the Congressional Black Caucus. JBS 7: 29-46.

427 Lott, J. R.; Bronars, S. G. 1993. Time Series Evidence on Shirking in the US House. PC 76: 125-150.

428 Lupia, A.; McCubbins, M. D. 1994. Who Controls? Information and the Structure of Legislative Decision Making. LSQ 19: 361-384.

429 Manley, J. F. 1973. The Conservative Coalition. ABS 17: 223-247.

430 Mayer, K. 1980. Legislative Influence: Toward Theory Development through Causal Analysis. LSQ 5: 563-585.

431 McCormick, J. M., Wittkopf, E. R. 1992. Effects of Party, Ideology and Issues on Congressional Foreign Policy Voting. APQ 20: 26-53.

432 McCrone, D. J.; Kuklinski, J. H. 1979. Delegate Theory of Representation. AJPS 23: 278-300.

433 McCubbins, M. D.; Schwartz, T. 1984. Congressional Oversight Overlooked. AJPS 28: 165-179.

434 McRae, T. 1983. Attitudes of Backbenchers to the Parliamentary System. Public Sector 6: 12-22.

435 Miller, M. C. 1993. Lawyers in Congress. CAP 20: 1-24.

436 Mishler, W. 1983. Scotching Nationalism in the British Parliament. LSQ 8: 5-28.

437 Mishler, W.; Hildreth, A. 1984. Legislatures and Political Stability. JOP 46: 25-59.

438 Moe, T. M. 1987. An Assessment of the Positive Theory of Congressional Dominance. LSQ 12: 475-520.

439 Mooney, C. Z 1994. Measuring State Legislative Professionalism. SALGR 26: 70-78.

440 -. 1995. Influences on State Legislative Professionalism. LSQ 20: 47-68.

441 Musolf, L. 1991. Congress, Policy Proposals and the Articulation of Values. POLCOM 8: 93-108.

442 Nye, M. A. 1993. Conservative Coalition Support in the House. LSQ 18: 255-270.

443 Obler, J. 1981. Legislatures and the Survival of Political Systems. PSCQ 96: 127-188.

444 Opello, W. C. 1986. Portugal's Parliament: An Organizational Analysis of Legislative Performance. LSQ 11: 291-320.

445 Oppenheimer, B. I. 1980. Policy Effects in House Reform: Decentralization and Capacity to Resolve Energy Issues. LSQ 5: 5-30.

446 Owens, J. R. 1986. Impact of Campaign Contributions on Legislative Outcomes in Congress. POLST 34: 285-295.

447 Panning, W. H. 1983. Formal Models of Legislative Processes. LSQ 8: 427-456.

448 Parker, G. R. 1980. Cycles in Congressional District Attention. JOP 42: 540-548.

449 -. 1980. Sources of Change in Congressional District Attentiveness. AJPS 24: 115-124.

450 -. 1985. Stylistic Change in the US Senate. JOP 47: 1190-1202.

451 -. 1989. Looking beyond Reelection: Revising Assumptions about Factors Motivating Congressional Behavior. PC 63: 237-252.

452 Parker, G. R.; Davidson, R. H. 1979. Why Do Americans Love Their Congressman So Much More than Their Congress? LSQ 4: 53-61.

453 Patterson, K. D.; Magleby, D. B. 1992. Trends: Public Support for Congress. POQ 56: 539-551.

454 Patterson, S. C. 1973. British House of Commons as a Focus for Research. BJPS 3: 363-381.

455 -. 1989. Understanding the British Parliament. POLST 37: 449-462.

456 Patterson, S. C.; Ripley, R. B.; Quinlan, S. V. 1992. Citizens' Orientations toward Legislatures. WPQ 45: 315-338.

457 Pedersen, M. N. 1984. Research on European Parliaments. LSQ 9: 505-529.

458 Piper, R. R. 1991. British Backbench Rebellion and Government Appointments. LSQ 16: 219-238.

459 Policy Studies Journal. 1977. Papers on Legislative Reform. PSJ 5 (4).

460 Political Quarterly. 1986. Papers on the Possibility of a Hung Parliament. PQ 57 (4).

461 Polsby, N. W. 1968. The Institutionalization of the House of Representatives. APSR 62: 144-168.

462 Polsby, N. W.; Gallaher, M.; Rundquist, B. S. 1969. Growth of the Seniority System in the US House. APSR 63: 787-807.

463 Potvin, M. 1994. Election of Civil Servants and Partisan Behaviour among Elected Representatives. IRAS 60: 423-446.

464 Rieselbach, L. N. 1992. Purposive Politicians Meet the Institutional Congress. LSQ 17: 95-111.

465 Sabatier, P. A.; Whiteman, D. 1985. Legislative Decision Making and Substantive Policy Information: Information Flow. LSQ 10: 395-421.

466 Salisbury, R. H. 1981. Congressional Staff Turnover and Ties-that-Bind. APSR 75: 381-396.

467 Salisbury, R. H.; Shepsle, K. A. 1981. US Congressmen as an Enterprise. LSQ 6: 559-576.

468 Scicchitano, M. J. 1981. Legislative Goals and Information Use. APQ 9: 89-102.

469 Shepsle, K. A. 1985. Prospects for Formal Models of Legislatures. LSQ 10: 5-20.

470 -. 1986. Positive Theory of Legislative Institutions: Enrichment of Social Choice and Spatial Models. PC 50: 135-184.

471 -. 1988. Representation and Goverance: The Great Legislative Trade Off. PSCQ 103: 461-484.

472 Shepsle, K. A.; Weingast, B. R. 1981. Structure Induced Equilibrium and Legislative Choice. PC 37: 503-520.

473 -. 1994. Positive Theories of Congressional Institutions. LSQ 19: 149-180.

474 Sinclair, B. D. 1983. Purposive Behavior in the US Congress. LSQ 8: 117-131.

475 Smith, R. A. 1984. Advocacy, Interpretation and Influence in the US Congress. APSR 78: 44-63.

476 Smith, S. S.; Flathman, M. 1989. Managing the Senate Floor: Complex Unanimous Consent Agreements. LSQ 14: 349-374.

477 Stewart, C. 1987. Does Structure Matter? Effects of Structural Change on Spending Decisions in the House. AJPS 31: 584-605.

478 Sullivan, J. L., et al. 1993. Dimensions of Cue-Taking in the House. JOP 55: 975-997.

479 Swanson, P. 1982. Influence of Recruitment on Structure of Power in the House. LSQ 7: 7-36.

480 Swift, E. K. 1987. The Electoral Connection Meets the Past: Lessons from Congressional History. PSCQ 102: 625-646.

481 Taagepera, R. 1972. Size of National Assemblies. SSR 1: 385-401.

482 Thompson, F. 1979. American Legislative Decision Making and the Size Principle. APSR 73: 1100-1108.

483 Thompson, M. S.; Silbey, J. H. 1984. Research on Nineteenth Century Legislatures. LSQ 9: 319-350.

484 Tucker, H. J. 1985. Legislative Logjams: A Comparative State Analysis. WPQ 38: 432-446.

485 Walker, J. L. 1977. Setting the Agenda in the US Senate. BJPS 8: 423-445.

486 Warren, R. S. 1984. Maximizing Models of Legislative Choice. PC 42: 287-294.

487 Weil, F. D. 1989. Sources and Structure of Legitimation in Western Democracies. ASR 54: 682-706.

488 Weingast, B. R. 1989. Political Institutions of Representative Government: Legislatures. JITE 145: 693-703.

489 Weingast, B. R.; Marshall, W. J. 1988. Industrial Organization of Congress: Why Legislatures Are Not Organized as Markets. JPE 96: 132-163.

490 Weissert, C. S. 1991. Determinants and Outcomes of State Legislative Effectiveness. SSQ 72: 797-806.

491 West, D. M. 1988. Activists and Economic Policy-making in Congress. AJPS 32: 662-680.

492 West European Politics 1990. Papers on Parliaments in Western Europe. WEP 13 (3).

493 Whitby, K. J.; Gilliam, F. D. 1991. A Longitudinal Analysis of Competing Explanations for the Transformation of Southern Congressional Politics. JOP 53: 504-518.

494 Wiggins, C. W. 1980. Executive Vetoes and Legislative Overrides in the American States. JOP 42: 1110-1117.

495 Wilcox, C.; Clausen, A. 1992. Profiling House Members: The Policy Dimensions Approach. CAP 19: 65-74.

496 Woolley, J. T.; LeLoup, L. T. 1989. Adequacy of the Electoral Motive in Explaining Legislative Attention to Monetary Policy. CP 21: 63-82.

497 Worthley, J. A.; Crane, E. G. 1976. Organizational Dimensions of State Legislatures. Midwest Review of Public Administration 10: 14-30.

498 Wright, G. C. 1989. Policy Voting in the Senate: Who Is Represented? LSQ 14: 465-487.

499 Wright, M. B. 1993. Shirking and Political Support in the US Senate. PC 76: 103-124.

500 Yarwood, D. L. 1970. Norm Observance and Legislative Integration: The Senate in 1850 and 1860. SSQ 51: 57-69.

501 Zupan, M. A. 1991. Local Benefit-Seeking in the Legislature: Congressional Staffing Decisions. EAP 3: 163-176.

Legislative Parties

502 Argersinger, P. H. 1992. Third Parties and the Institutionalization of Congress. JIDH 22: 655-690.

503 Berrington, H. 1968. Partisanship and Dissidence in the Nineteenth Century House of Commons. PARLA 21: 338-374.

504 Born, R. 1990. Surge and Decline, Negative Voting and the Midterm Loss Phenomenon. AJPS 34: 615-645.

505 Brady, D. W.; Bullock, C. S. 1980. Is There a Conservative Coalition in the House? JOP 42: 549-559.

506 Brady, D. W.; Cooper, J.; Hurley, P. A. 1979. Decline of Party in the House. LSQ 4: 381-408.

507 Brady, D. W.; Ettling, J. 1984. The Electoral Connection and the Decline of Partisanship in the House. CAP 11: 19-36.

508 Brand, J. 1989. Faction as Its Own Reward: Groups in British Parliament. PARLA 42: 148-164.

509 Burnstein, P. 1979. Electoral Competition and Changes in the Party Balance in the US Congress. SSR 8: 105-119.

510 Canon, D. T.; Sousa, D. J. 1992. Party System Change and Political Career Structures in Congress. LSQ 17: 347-364.

511 Clubb, J. M.; Traugott, S. A. 1977. Partisan Cleavage and Cohesion in the House. JIDH 7: 375-402.

512 Collie, M. P. 1988. Universalism and the Parties in the US House. AJPS 32: 865-883.

513 Copeland, G. W.; Overby, L. M. 1993. Legislative Socialization and Interbranch Rivalry: Consequences of Divided Party Government. CAP 20: 119-130.

514 Cox, G. W.; McCubbins, M. D. 1991. The Decline of Party Voting in Congress. LSQ 16: 547-570.

515 -. 1994. Party Government in the House. LSQ 19: 215-232.

516 Gehrlein, W. V.; Fishburn, P. C. 1986. Division of Power in Legislatures with Two Cohesive Subgroups. SCAW 3: 119-124.

517 Grierzynski, A.; Breaux, D. 1993. Money and the Party Vote in State House Elections. LSQ 18: 515-534.

518 Fishburn, P. C.; Gehrlein, W. V. 1984. Powers of Subgroups in Voting Bodies. SCAW 1: 85-95.

519 -. 1985. The Power of a Cohesive Subgroup within a Voting Body. SCAW 2: 197-206.

520 Hoadley, J. F. 1980. Emergence of Political Parties in Congress. APSR 74: 757-779.

521 Hurley, P. A.; Wilson, R. K. 1989. Partisan Voting Patterns in the Senate. LSQ 14: 225-250.

522 International Political Science Review. 1995. Papers on Party Government. IPSR 16 (2).

523 Kazee, T. A.; Thornberry, M. C. 1990. Congressional Recruitment and the American Party Organizations. WPQ 43: 61-80.

524 Kornberg, A.; Frasure, R. C. 1971. Policy Differences in British Parliamentary Parties. APSR 65: 694-703.

525 Leyden, K. M.; Borrelli, S. A. 1994. Party Contributions and Party Unity among US House Members. APQ 22: 421-452.

526 Norpoth, H. 1976. Explaining Party Cohesion in Congress: The Case of Shared Policy Attitudes. APSR 70: 1157-1171.

527 Patterson, S. C. 1989. Party Leadership in the US Senate. LSQ 14: 393-413.

528 Patterson, S. C.; Caldeira, G. A. 1988. Party Voting in the US Congress. BJPS 18: 111-132.

529 Poole, K. T.; Daniels, R. S. 1985. Ideology, Party and Voting in the US Congress. APSR 79: 373-399.

530 Shade, W., et al. 1973. Partisanship in the US Senate, 1869-1901. JIDH 4: 185-206.

531 Shaffer, B. D. 1977. Who Wins in the House: Effect of Declining Party Cohesion on Policy Outputs. SSQ 58: 121-128.

532 -. 1978. From Party Voting to Regional Fragmentation: The House. APQ 6: 125-146.

533 Shaffer, W. R. 1982. Party and Ideology in the House. WPQ 35: 92-106.

534 Sinnott, R. 1989. Locating Parties, Factions and Ministries in a Policy Space: Understanding the Party-Policy Link. EJPR 17: 689-705.

535 Strom, K. 1985. Party Goals and Government Performance in Parliamentary Democracies. APSR 79: 738-754.

536 Ward, D. S. 1993. The Continuing Search for Party Influence in Congress: Committees. LSQ 18: 211-230.

Margins and Turnover

537 Alford, J. R.; Hibbing, J. R. 1981. Increased Incumbency Advantage in the House. JOP 43: 1042-1061.

538 Ansolabehere, S.; David, B.; Fiorina, M. P. 1992. Vanishing Marginals and Electoral Responsiveness. BJPS 22: 21-38.

539 Bartlett, R. V. 1979. The Marginality Hypothesis: Electoral Insecurity, Self-Interest and Voting. APQ 7: 498-508.

540 Bauer, M.; Hibbing, J. R. 1989. Which Incumbents Lose in House Elections. AJPS 33: 262-271.

541 Beth, R. S. 1981. Incumbency Advantage and Incumbency Resources. CAP 9: 119-136.

542 Bienen, H.; van de Walle, N. 1992. A Proportional Hazard Model of Leadership Duration. JOP 53: 685-717.

543 Blair, D. K.; Henry, A. R. 1981. Family Factor in State Legislative Turnover. LSQ 6: 55-68.

544 Born, R. 1979. Generational Replacement and Growth of Incumbent Reelection Margins in the US House. APSR 73: 811-817.

545 Breaux, D. 1990. Specifying the Impact of Incumbency on State Legislative Elections. APQ 18: 270-286.

546 Brunk, G. G. 1982. Turnover and Voting Stability in the Senate. APQ 10: 363-373.

547 Brunk, G. G.; Minehart, T. 1984. Impact of Elite Turnover on Policy Formation. AJPS 28: 559-569.

548 Bullock, C. S. 1975. Redistricting and Congressional Stability. JOP 37: 569-575.

549 Bunce, V. 1976. Elite Succession, Petrification and Policy Innovation in Communist Systems. CPS 9: 3-42.

550 -. 1979. Leadership Succession and Policy Innovation in the Soviet Republics. CP 11: 379-402.

551 -. 1980. Changing Leaders and Changing Policies: Impact of Elite Succession on Budgetary Priorities in Democratic Countries. AJPS 24: 373-395.

552 -. 1980. The Succession Connection: Policy Cycles and Political Change in the Soviet Union and Eastern Europe. APSR 74: 966-977.

553 Bunce, V.; Roeder, P. G. 1986. Effects of Leadership Succession in the Soviet Union. APSR 80: 215-224.

554 Carey, J. 1994. Political Shirking and the Last Term Problem: Evidence for a Party Administered Pension System. PC 81: 1-22.

555 Cohen, J. E. 1984. Perceptions of Electoral Insecurity among Members Holding Safe Seats in State Legislatures. LSQ 9: 365-369.

556 Cohen, J. E.; Brunk, G. G. 1983. A Dynamic Test of the Marginality Hypothesis. PB 3: 293-307.

557 Collie, M. P. 1981. Incumbency, Electoral Safety and Electoral Turnover in the House. APSR 75: 119-131.

558 Cover, A. D. 1977. Incumbency in Congressional Elections. AJPS 21: 523-541.

559 Cox, G. W.; Morgenstern, S. 1993. The Increasing Advantage of Incumbency in the US States. LSQ 18: 495-514.

560 Cox, J.; Hager, G. L.; Lowery, D. 1993. Regime Change in Presidential and Congressional Budgeting. AJPS 37: 88-118.

561 Dick, A. R.; Lott, J. R. 1993. Reconciling Voters' Behavior with Legislative Term Limits. JPUBE 50: 1-14.

562 Donovan, T.; Snipp, J. R. 1994. Support for Legislative Term Limitations in California. JOP 56: 492-501.

563 Epstein, L. K.; Frankovic, K. A. 1982. Casework and Electoral Margins: Insurance is Prudent. Polity 14: 691-700.

564 Erikson, R. S. 1971. Advantage of Incumbency in Congressional Elections. Polity 3: 395-405.

565 -. 1976. Is There Such a Thing as a Safe Seat? Polity 9: 623-632.

566 Erickson, S. C. 1995. Entrenching of Incumbency: Reelections in the House, 1790-1994. CJ 14: 397-420.

567 Ferejohn, J. A. 1977. The Decline of Competition in Congressional Elections. APSR 71: 166-181.

568 Figlio, D. N. 1995. The Effect of Retirement on Political Shirking. PFQ 23: 226-241.

569 Fiorina, M. P. 1977. The Case of the Vanishing Marginals. APSR 71: 177-181.

570 Freeman, P. K. 1995. A Comparative Analysis of Speaker Career Patterns in US State Legislatures. LSQ 20: 365-376.

571 Garand, J. C. 1991. Electoral Marginality in State Legislative Elections. LSQ 16: 7-28.

572 Garand, J. C.; Gross, D. A. 1984. Changes in the Vote Margins for Congressional Candidates. APSR 78: 17-30.

573 Garand, J. C.; Wink, K.; Vincent, B. 1993. Changing Meanings of Electoral Marginality in House Elections. PRQ 46:27-49.

574 Gerber, E. R.; Lupia, A. 1995. Campaign Competition and Policy Responsiveness in Direct Legislation Elections. PB 17: 287-306.

575 Goidel, R. K.; Shields, T. G. 1994. Vanishing Marginals, the Bandwagon and the Mass Media. JOP 56: 802-810.

576 Haas, P. J., Wright, D. S. 1989. Administrative Turnover in State Governments. AAS 21: 265-277.

577 Hart, D. B.; Munger, M. C. 1989. Declining Electoral Competitiveness in the House: Impact of Improved Transportation. PC 61: 217-228.

578 Holbrook, T. M.; Tidmarch, C. M. 1993. Effects of Leadership Positions on Votes for Incumbents in State Legislative Elections. PRQ 46: 897-910.

579 Jacobson, G. C. 1987. The Marginals Never Vanished: Incumbency and Competition in the US House. AJPS 31: 126-141.

580 Johannes, J. R.; McAdams, J. C. 1981. Congressional Incumbency Effect. AJPS 25: 512-542.

581 Karp, J. A. 1995. Explaining Public Support for Legislative Term Limits. POQ 59: 373-391.

582 King, G.; Gelman, A. 1990. Estimating Incumbency Advantage without Bias. AJPS 34: 1142-1164.

583 -. 1991. Systemic Consequences of Incumbency Advantage in the US House. AJPS 35: 110-138.

584 King, J. D. 1994. Political Culture, Registration Laws and Voter Turnout among the American States. Publius 24 (4): 115-127.

585 Klier, T.; McPherson, M. 1991. Does Duration of Political Control Matter? Interstate Differences in Branch-Banking Laws. PC 70: 41-50.

586 Kostroski, W. 1978. Effect of Number of Terms on the Re-Election of Senators. JOP 40: 488-497.

587 Krashinsky, M.; Milne, W. J. 1988. Effect of Incumbency in 1984 Federal and 1985 Ontario Elections. CJPS 19: 337-343.

588 -. 1993. Effects of Incumbency in US Congressional Elections. LSQ 18: 321-344.

589 Kuklinski, J. H. 1977. District Competitiveness and Legislative Roll Call Behavior: The Marginality Hypothesis. AJPS 21: 627-638.

590 Li, W. L.; Ou-yang, H. 1991. Marxist vs. Confucian Effects on Elite Mobility: Turnover in the NPC Standing Committee. IAS 27: 57-77.

591 Mayhew, D. R. 1974. Congressional Elections: The Vanishing Marginals. Polity 6: 295-317.

592 Mondak, J. J.; McCurley, C. 1994. Cognitive Efficiency and the Congressional Vote: Coattail Voting. PRQ 47: 151-176.

593 Mondak, J. J. 1995. Term Limits and the Composition of the US House. PRQ 48: 701-750.

594 Nadeau, R.; Mendelsohn, M. 1994. Short-Term Popularity Boost Following Leadership Change in Great Britain. ES 13: 222-228.

595 Nelson, C.J. 1978 Effect of Incumbency on Voting in Congressional Elections. PSCQ 93: 665-678.

596 Norris, P.; Crewe, I. 1994. Did British Marginals Vanish? Proportionality and Exaggeration in British Electoral System. ES 13: 201-221.

597 Norton, P.; Wood, D. 1990. Constituency Service by MPs: Does It Contribute to a Personal Vote? PARLA 43: 196-208.

598 Opheim, C. 1994. Effect of US State Legislative Term Limits Revisited. LSQ 19: 49-60.

599 Parker, G. R. 1980. Advantage of Incumbency in House Elections. APQ 8: 449-464.

600 Payne, J. L. 1980. Personal Electoral Advantage of House Incumbents. APQ 8: 465-482.

601 Rausch, J. D. 1993. Testing Legislative Term Limits: San Mateo Board of County Supervisors as Laboratory. NCR 82: 149-156.

602 Reed, W. R.; Schansberg, D. E. 1992. Behavior of Congressional Tenure over Time. PC 73: 183-204.

603 -. 1994. Analysis of the Impact of Congressional Term Limits. EI 32: 79-91.

604 -. 1995. The House under Term Limits: What Would It Look Like? SSQ 76: 699-740.

605 Roeder, P. G. 1985. Do New Soviet Leaders Really Make a Difference? Rethinking the Succession Connection. APSR 79: 958-976.

606 Segura, G. M.; Nicholson, S. P. 1995. Sequential Choices and Partisan Transitions in US Senate Delegations. JOP 57: 86-100.

607 Shan, C. C.; Stonecash, J. M. 1994. Legislative Resources and Electoral Margins: New York Senate. LSQ 19: 79-94.

608 Shin, E. H.; Kim, I. K. 1985. Variations in the Duration of Reign of Monarchs. CPS 18: 104-122.

609 Shin, K. S.; Jackson, J. S. 1979. Membership Turnover in State Legislatures. LSQ 4: 95-104.

610 Southwell, P. L. 1995. Throwing the Rascals Out vs. Throwing in the Towel: Alienation, Support for Term Limits and Congressional Voting Behavior. SSQ 76: 741-748.

611 Sullivan, J. L.; Uslaner, E. M. 1978. Congressional Behavior and Electoral Marginality. AJPS 22: 536-553.

612 Tabarrok, A. A. 1994. A Survey, Critique and New Defense of Term Limits. CJ 14: 333-350.

613 Thompson, J. A.; Moncrief, G. F. 1993. Implications of Term Limits for Women and Minorities. SSQ 74: 300-309.

614 Tidmarch, C. M.; Londergan, E.; Sciortino, J. 1986. Interparty Competition in State Legislative Elections. LSQ 11: 353-374.

615 Weber, R. E.; Tucker, H. J.; Bruce, P. 1991. Vanishing Marginals in State Legislative Elections. LSQ 16: 29-48.

616 Westlye, M. C. 1983. Competitiveness of Senate Seats and Voting Behavior in Senate Elections. AJPS 27: 253-283.

617 Zupan, M. A. 1990. The Last Period Problem: Do Congressional Representatives Not Subject to a Reelection Constraint Alter Their Voting Behavior? PC 65: 167-180.

Roll Call Voting

618 Bax, F. R. 1981. A Method for Measuring Importance of Roll Calls in the House. PM 7: 81-94.

619 Bell, R. 1979. Mr. Madison's War and Long Term Congressional Voting Behavior. WAMQ 36: 373-395.

620 Bogue, A. G.; Marlaire, M. P. 1975. Of Mess and Men: The Bordinghouse and Congressional Voting. AJPS 19: 207-230.

621 Bond, J. R.; Fleisher, R. 1984. Presidential Popularity and Congressional Voting: Public Opinion as a Source of Influence in Congress. WPQ 37: 291-306.

622 Born, R. 1976. Cue-Taking within State Party Delegations in the US House. JOP 38: 71-94.

623 Borrelli, S. A.; Simmons, G. L. 1993. Congressional Responsiveness to Presidential Popularity. PB 15: 93-112.

624 Brams, S. J.; Fishburn, P. C. 1981. Reconstructing Voting Processes: 1976 House Majority Leader Election. PM 7: 95-108.

625 Bullock, C. S. 1995. Impact of Changing Racial Composition of Congressional Districts on Legislators' Roll Call Behavior. APQ 23: 141-158.

626 Bullock, C. S.; Brady, D. W. 1983. Party, Constituency and Roll Call Voting in the US Senate. LSQ 8: 29-44.

627 Burgin, E. 1994. Influences Shaping Members' Decision Making: Congressional Voting on the Persian Gulf War. PB 16: 319-342.

628 Coates, D. 1995. Measuring the Personal Vote of Members of Congress. PC 85: 227-248.

629 Coates, D.; Munger, M. C. 1995. Legislative Voting and the Economic Theory of Politics. SEJ 61: 861-872.

630 Collie, M. P. 1989. Electoral Patterns and Voting Alignments in the House. LSQ 14: 107-128.

631 Covington, C. R. 1988. Distribution of White House Social Invitations and Effects on Congressional Support. APQ 16: 243-265.

632 Covington, C. R.; Wrighton, J. M.; Kinney, R. 1995. A Presidency-Augmented Model of Presidential Success on House Roll Call Votes. AJPS 39: 1001-1024.

633 Cromwell, V. 1982. Mapping the Political World of 1861: A Multidimensional Analysis of House of Commons' Division Lists. LSQ 7: 281-297.

634 Davis, F. L. 1993. Balancing the Perspective on PAC Contributions: Impact on Roll Calls. APQ 21: 205-222.

635 Davis, M. L.; Porter, P. K. 1989. Test for Pure or Apparent Ideology in Congressional Voting. PC 60: 101-112.

636 Deckard, B. S. 1976. Political Upheaval and Congressional Voting. JOP 38: 326-345.

637 Dow, J. K.; Endersby, J. W. 1994. Campaign Contributions and Voting in the California Assembly. APQ 22: 334-353.

638 Elling, R. C. 1982. Ideological Change in the US Senate: Time and Electoral Responsiveness. LSQ 7: 75-92.

639 Fett, P. J. 1994. Presidential Legislative Priorities and Legislators' Voting Decisions. JOP 56: 502-512.

640 Fleisher, R. 1993. Explaining the Change in Roll Call Voting Behavior of Southern Democrats. JOP 55: 327-341.

641 -. 1993. PAC Contributions and Congressional Voting on National Defense. LSQ 18: 391-410.

642 Frendreis, J. P.; Waterman, R. W. 1985. PAC Contributions and Legislative Voting Behavior. SSQ 66: 401-412.

643 Glazer, A.; Robbins, M. 1985. How Elections Matter: A Study of US Senators. PC 46: 163-172.

644 Gross, D. A. 1979. Measuring Legislators' Policy Positions: Roll Call Votes and Preferences. APQ 7: 417-437.

645 Herrera, R.; Epperlein, T.; Smith, E. R. A. N. 1995. Stability of Congressional Roll-Call Indexes. PRQ 48: 403-416.

646 Heyck, T. W.; Klecka, W. 1973. British Radical MPs, 1874-1895. JIDH 4: 161-184.

647 Hibbing, J. R.; Marsh, D. 1987. Accounting for the Voting Patterns of British MPs on Free Votes. LSQ 12: 275-297.

648 Jackson, J. E. 1971. Statistical Models of Senate Roll Call Voting. APSR 65: 451-470.

649 Jones, B. D. 1974. Path Models of Congressional Voting. SSR 3: 243-260.

650 Katznelson, I.; Geiger, K.; Kryder, D. 1993. Limiting Liberalism: The Southern Veto in Congress. PSQ 108: 283-306.

651 Kenny, L. W.; Rush, M. 1990. Self-Interest and Senate Vote on Direct Elections. EAP 2: 291-302.

652 King, G. 1986. Significance of Roll Calls in Voting Bodies. SSR 15: 135-152.

653 Koford, K. J. 1989. Dimensions of Congressional Voting. APSR 83: 949-962.

654 -. 1991. On Dimensionalizing Roll Call Votes in the US Congress. APSR 85: 955-976.

655 Ladha, K. K. 1994. Coalitions in Congressional Voting. PC 78: 43-63.

656 Marin-Bosch, M. 1987. How Nations Vote in the General Assembly of the UN. IO 41: 705-724.

657 Martin, J. 1976. Presidential Elections and Administration Support among Congressmen. AJPS 20: 483-490.

658 McCrone, D. J. 1977. Identifying Voting Strategies from Roll Call Votes. LSQ 2: 177-192.

659 Nye, M. A. 1991. The US Senate and Civil Rights Roll Call Votes. WPQ 44: 971-987.

660 -. 1993. Changing Support for Civil Rights: House and Senate Voting. PRQ 46: 799-822.

661 Pattie, C. J.; Fieldhouse, E.; Johnston, R. J. 1994. Electoral Correlates and Consequences of Free Votes and Rebellions in the British House of Commons. BJPS 24: 359-380.

662 Poole, K. T. 1988. Recent Developments in Analytical Models of Voting in the US Congress. LSQ 13: 117-133.

663 Poole, K. T.; Daniels, R. S. 1985. Ideology, Party and Voting in Congress. APSR 79: 373-399.

664 Poole, K. T.; Rosenthal, H. 1985. Spatial Model for Roll Call Analysis. AJPS 29: 357-384.

665 -. 1991. Patterns of Congressional Voting. AJPS 35: 228-278.

666 Poole, K. T.; Rosenthal, H.; Koford, K. J. 1991. On Dimensionalizing Roll Call Votes in the US Congress. APSR 85: 955-978.

667 Poole, K. T.; Smith, R. A. 1994. A Spatial Analysis of Winning and Losing Motions in the Senate. PC 78: 23-42.

668 Pritchard, A. 1987. Deviations in Congressional Roll Call Voting Decisions. CAP 14: 135-150.

669 Rivers, D.; Rice, N. L. 1985. Public Opinion and Presidential Influence in Congress. AJPS 29: 183-196.

670 Schwartz, J. E.; Fenmore, B. 1977. Presidential Elections and Congressional Roll Call Behavior. LSQ 12: 409-422.

671 Segal, J. A.; Cameron, C. M.; Cover, A. D. 1992. A Spatial Model of Roll Call Voting in Supreme Court Confirmations. AJPS 36: 96-121.

672 Shaffer, W. R. 1991. Interparty Spatial Relationships in Norwegian Storting Roll Call Voting. SPS 14: 59-83.

673 Silbey, J. H. 1981. Congressional and State Legislative Roll Call Studies by US Historians. LSQ 6: 597-607.

674 Sinclair, B. D. 1976. Electoral Marginality and Party Loyalty in House Roll Call Voting. AJPS 20: 469-481.

675 -. 1977. Determinants of Aggregate Party Cohesion in the US House. LSQ 2: 155-176.

676 Smith, E. R. A. N.; Herrera, R.; Herrera, C. L. 1990. Measurement Characteristics of Congressional Roll Call Indexes. LSQ 15: 283-295.

677 Smith, S. S. 1981. Consistency and Ideological Structure of Senate Voting. AJPS 25: 780-795.

678 Stratmann, T. 1991. What Do Campaign Contributions Buy? Deciphering Causal Effects of Money and Votes. SEJ 57: 606-620.

679 Tamplin, V. L. 1987. Predicting Policy Choices of Individual Legislators. PRAPR 6: 241-274.

680 Tetlock, P. E. 1984. Cognitive Style and Political Belief Systems in the House of Commons. JPASP 46: 365-375.

681 Van Doren, P. M. 1990. Can We Learn the Causes of Congressional Decisions from Roll Call Data? LSQ 15: 311-340.

682 Vincent, J. E. 1978. Empirical Studies of Behavioral Patterns at the UN. PRR 7: 1-119.

683 Weisberg, H. F. 1972. Scaling Models for Legislative Roll Call Analysis. APSR 66: 1306-1315.

684 -. 1978. Evaluating Theories of Congressional Roll Call Voting. AJPS 22: 554-577.

685 Welch, W. P. 1982. Campaign Contributions and Legislative Voting: Milk Money and Dairy Price Supports. WPQ 30: 478-495.

686 Wilcox, C.; Clausen, A. 1991. Dimensionality of Roll Call Voting Reconsidered. LSQ 16: 393-406.

687 Wright, J. R. 1985. PACs, Contributions and Roll Calls: An Organizational Perspective. APSR 80: 567-588.

Vote Trading and Pork

688 Abler, D. G. 1989. Vote Trading on Farm Legislation in the US House. AJAE 71: 583-591.

689 American Political Science Review. 1975. Papers on Participation, Coalitions and Vote Trading. APSR 69: 908-928.

690 Baron, D. P. 1991. Majoritarian Incentives, Pork Barrel Programs and Procedural Control. AJPS 35: 57-90.

691 Bernholz, P. 1973. Logrolling, Arrow's Paradox and Cyclical Majorities. PC 15: 87-95.

692 -. 1977. Prisoner's Dilemma, Logrolling and Cyclical Group Preferences. PC 29: 73-84.

693 -. 1978. On the Stability of Logrolling Outcomes in Stochastic Games. PC 33: 65-82.

694 Crump, J. R. 1989. The Spatial Distribution of Military Spending in the US. GAC 3: 50-62.

695 Del Rossi, A. F. 1995. The Politics and Economics of Pork Barrel Spending: Federal Financing of Water Resources Development. PC 85: 285-306.

696 Enelow, J. M. 1980. On the Size of Vote Trades. PC 35: 197-203.

697 -. 1986. Stability of Logrolling. PC 51: 285-294.

698 Enelow, J. M.; Koehler, D. H. 1979. Vote Trading in a Legislative Context: Cooperative and Noncooperative Strategic Voting. PC 34: 157-175.

699 Evans, D. 1994. Use of Pork Barrel Projects to Build Policy Coalitions in the House of Representatives. AJPS 38: 894-917.

700 Haefele, E. T. 1970. Coalitions, Minority Representation and Vote-Trading Probabilities. PC 8:75-90.

701 Hird, J. A. 1991. Political Economy of Pork: Project Selection at the US Army Corps of Engineers. APSR 85: 429-456.

702 Kau, J. B.; Rubin, P. H. 1979. Self-Interest, Ideology and Logrolling in Congressional Voting. JOLE 22: 365-384.

703 Kiewiet, D. R.; McCubbins, M. D. 1985. Congressional Appropriations and the Electoral Connection. JOP 47: 59-82.

704 Koford, K. J. 1982. Centralized Vote Trading. PC 39: 245-268.

705 Lancaster, T. D.; Patterson, W. D. 1990. Comparative Pork Barrel Politics: Perceptions from the West German Bundestag. CPS 22: 458-477.

706 Levitt, S. D.; Snyder, J. M. 1995. Political Parties and the Distribution of Federal Outlays. AJPS 39: 958-980.

707 Lindsay, J. M. 1991. Testing the Parochial Hypothesis: Congress and the Strategic Defense Initiative. JOP 53: 860-876.

708 Meier, K. J.; Copeland, G. W. 1984. Congressional Decision Making and Federal Grants. APQ 12: 3-21.

709 Miller, N. R. 1977. Logrolling, Vote Trading and the Paradox of Voting. PC 30: 51-75.

710 Mueller, D. C.; Philpotts, G. C.; Vanek, J. 1972. Social Gains from Exchanging Votes. PC 13: 55-79.

711 Murphy, J. T. 1974. Political Parties and the Pork Barrel: Party Conflict and Cooperation in Public Works Committee. APSR 68: 169-185.

712 Oppenheimer, J. A. 1979. Outcomes of Logrolling in the Bargaining Set and Democratic Theory. PC 34: 419-434.

713 Owens, J. R.; Wade, L. L. 1984. Federal Spending in Congressional Districts. WPQ 37: 404-423.

714 Riker, W. H.; Brams, S. J. 1973. Paradox of Vote Trading. APSR 67: 1235-1247.

715 Savage, J. D. 1991. Saints and Cardinals in Appropriations Committees and the Fight against Distributive Politics. LSQ 16: 329-348.

716 Schwartz, T. 1977. Collective Choice, Separation of Issues and Vote Trading. APSR 71: 999-1010.

717 Shepsle, K. A.; Weingast, B. R. 1981. Political Preferences for Pork Barrel. AJPS 25: 96-111.

718 Stein, R. M.; Bickers, K. N. 1994. Congressional Elections and the Pork Barrel. JOP 56: 377-399.

719 Stratmann, T. 1995. Logrolling in the Congress. EI 33: 441-456.

720 Thompson, J. A.; Moncrief, G. F. 1988. Pursuing Pork in a State Legislature. LSQ 13: 393-402.

721 Tullock, G. 1970. A Simple Algebraic Logrolling Model. AER 60: 419-426.

722 Uslaner, E. M.; Davis, J. R. 1975. The Paradox of Vote Trading: Effects of Decision Rules and Voting Strategies on Externalities. APSR 69: 929-942.

723 Wilson, R. K. 1986. An Empirical Test of Preferences for the Political Pork Barrel: District Level Appropriations for River and Harbor Legislation. AJPS 30: 729-754.

MINORITY POLITICS

1 American Behavioral Scientist. 1995. Papers on Ethnicity. ABS 38 (3).
2 Aponte, R. 1991. Urban Hispanic Poverty. SOCP 38: 516-528.
3 Borjas, G. J. 1994. The Long Run Convergence of Ethnic Skill Differentials: Children and Grandchildren of Great Migration. ILRR 47: 553-573.
4 Brown, E. M. 1995. Bridging the Divide between Critical Race Theory and Mainstream Civil Rights Scholarship. YLJ 105: 513-548.
5 Cochran, D. C. 1995. Ethnic Diversity and Democratic Stability. PSCQ 110: 587-604.
6 Cotton, J. 1993. Color or Culture? Wage Differences. RBPE 21: 53-67.
7 Development 1992. Papers on Cultural Identity. Vol 1992 (4).
8 Ethnic and Racial Studies. 1979. Papers on Internal Colonization. EARS 2 (3).
9 -. 1985. Papers on Michael Banton's Racial and Ethnic Competition. EARS 8 (4).
10 -. 1985. Papers on Ethnicity and Race. EARS 8 (1), 1986 9 (3).
11 Finifter, A. W.; Finifter, B. M. 1995. Citizenship Change and Psychological Aftermath among American Migrants in Australia. CRSN 22: 1-22.
12 Fletcher Forum. 1992. Papers on Ethnic Identity and the Nation-State. FFWF 16 (2).
13 -. 1995. Papers on Minority Rights. FFWA 19 (1).
14 Gabriel, P. E.; Williams, D. R.; Schmitz, S. 1990. Relative Occupational Attainment of Young Blacks, Whites and Hispanics. SEJ 57: 35-46.
15 Grove, D. J. 1974. Differential Political and Economic Patterns of Ethnic and Race Relations. Race 15: 303-320.
16 -. 1978. Tests of the Ethnic Equalization Hypothesis. EARS 1: 175-195.
17 -. 1980. Effect of Economic Development and Growth on Ethnic Income. SICID 15: 22-36.
18 Harris, W. A. 1992. Ethnicity and Development. SAES 41: 225-230.
19 International Political Science Review. 1985. Papers on Ethnicity and Regionalism. IPSR 6 (2).
20 International Social Science Journal. 1987. Papers on Ethnic Phenomena. ISSJ 39 (1).
21 Kee, P. 1994. Native/Immigrant Employment Differences in the Netherlands: The Role of Assimilation and Discrimination. IRAE 8: 174-196.
22 Kerr, B.; Mladenka, K. R. 1994. Does Politics Matter? Time-Series Analysis of Minority Employment Patterns. AJPS 38: 918-943.
23 Liang, Z. 1994. On the Measurement of Naturalization. Demography 31: 525-548.
24 Shull, S. A.; Gleiber, D. W. 1995. Presidential Cycles in Civil Rights Policy. PSQ 25: 429-446.

25 Sidanius, J.; Pratto, F. 1993. Racism and Support of Free-Market Capitalism. PP 14: 381-402.
26 Smith, A. D. 1992. Chosen Peoples: Why Ethnic Groups Survive. EARS 15: 436-456.
27 Social Science Quarterly. 1977. Papers on Race, Ethnicity and Gender. SSQ 58 (3-4), 1978 59 (3), 1988 69 (4), and 1994 75 (1).
28 Society. 1990. Papers on Jewish-Americans. Vol 28 (1).
29 Sociological Perspectives. 1987. Papers on the Ethnic Economy. SP 30 (4).
30 Tienda, M.; Lii, D. T. 1987. Minority Concentration and Earnings Inequality. AJS 93: 141-165.
31 White, M. J. 1984. Racial and Ethnic Succession in Four Cities. UAQ 20: 165-184.
32 Zhou, M. 1993. Underemployment and Economic Disparities among Minority Groups. PRAPR 12: 139-157.

Affirmative Action

33 American Behavioral Scientist. 1984. Papers on Advancement after Affirmative Action. ABS 27 (3)
34 -. 1985. Papers on Affirmative Action. ABS 28 (6).
35 Annals. 1992. Papers on Affirmative Action. ANNALS 523.
36 Coate, S.; Loury, G. C. 1993. Will Affirmative Action Policies Eliminate Negative Sterotypes? AER 83: 1220-1240.
37 Donahue, J. J.; Heckman, J. J. 1991. Continuous vs. Episodic Change: Civil Rights Policy on the Economic Status of Blacks. JEL 29: 1603-1643.
38 Fletcher, J. F.; Chalmers, M. C. 1991. Attitudes of Canadians toward Affirmative Action. PB 13: 67-95.
39 Heckman, J. J.; Payner, B. S. 1989. Determining the Impact of Federal Antidiscrimination Policy on Economic Status of Blacks. AER 79: 138-177.
40 International Journal of Public Administration. 1995. Papers on Set-Asides, Minority Business Development and Public Contracting. Vol 18 (7).
41 Israel Yearbook on Human Rights. 1985. Papers on Discrimination and Affirmative Action. Vol 15.
42 Jackson, P. B.; Thoits, P. A.; Taylor, H. F. 1995. The Effects of Tokenism on America's Black Elite. SF 74: 543-558.
43 Kinder, D. R.; Sanders, L. M. 1990. White Opinion on Affirmative Action. SC 8: 73-103.
44 Kluegel, J. S.; Bobo, L. 1993. Opposition to Race-Targeting: Self-Interest, Stratification Ideology, or Racial Attitudes? ASR 58: 443-464.

45 Kluegel, J. S.; Smith, E. R. 1983. Affirmative Action Attitudes. SF 61: 797-824.
46 Leonard, J. S. 1990. The Impact of Affirmative Action Regulation and the Equal Employment Law on Black Employment. JEP 4: 47-63.
47 Lynch, F. R. 1984. The Politics of Affirmative Action Research. SI 54: 124-141.
48 Peterson, R. S. 1994. Role of Values in Predicting Fairness Judgments and Support for Affirmative Action. JSI 50: 95-116.
49 Public Administration. 1989. Papers on Implementing Equal Opportunity. PA 67 (1).
50 Public Personnel Management. 1978. Papers on Affirmative Action. PPM 7 (6) and 1981 10 (4).
51 Santoro, W. A. 1995. Black Politics and Employment Policies: Determinants of Local Government Affirmative Action. SSQ 76: 794-806.

Discrimination

52 Alternatives. 1994. Papers on Apartheid and World Order Studies. Vol 19 (2).
53 American Behavioral Scientist. 1995. Papers on Bell Curve and Scientific Racism. ABS 39 (1).
54 Annals. 1979. Papers on Race and Residence. ANNALS 441.
55 Ball-Rokeach, S. J.; Loges, W. E. 1994. Choosing Equality: Correspondence between Attitudes about Race and the Value of Equality. JSI 50: 9-18.
56 Banton, M. 1979. Two Theories of Racial Discrimination in Housing. EARS 2: 416-427.
57 Beck, E. M. 1980. Discrimination and White Economic Loss. SF 59: 148-168.
58 Beck, E. M.; Tolnay, S. E. 1990. Cotton and the Lynching of Blacks. ASR 55: 526-539.
59 Black, E. 1973. The Militant Segregationist Vote in the Post-Brown South. SSQ 54: 66-84.
60 Black, E.; Black, M. 1973. Demographic Basis of the Wallace Vote in Alabama. APQ 1: 279-304.
61 -. 1973. The Wallace Vote in Alabama. JOP 35: 730-736.
62 Black, M. 1978. Racial Composition and Support for Voting Rights in the South. SSQ 59: 435-450.
63 Bobo, L. 1983. Whites' Opposition to Busing. JPASP 45: 1196-1210.
64 Breit, W.; Horowitz, J. B. 1995. Discrimination and Diversity. PC 84: 63-76.
65 Bullock, C. S.; Campbell, B. A. 1984. Racist or Racial Voting in the 1981 Atlanta Municipal Election. UAQ 20: 149-164.
66 Burnstein, P. 1979. Public Opinion, Demonstrations and the Passage of Anti-Discrimination Legislation. POQ 43: 157-172.
67 Charles, M.; Grusky, D. B. 1995. Models for Describing the Underlying Structure of Sex Segregation. AJS 100: 931-971.
68 Comparative Studies in Society and History. 1986. Papers on Slavery. CSSH 28: 729-777.
69 Corzine, J.; Creech, J.; Corzine, L. 1983. Black Concentration and Lynchings. SF 61: 774-796.
70 Crosby, F. J.; Bromley, S.; Saxe, L. 1980. Studies of Black and White Discrimination and Prejudice. Psychological Bulletin 87: 546-563.
71 Dex, S. 1979. Theories of the Economics of Discrimination. EARS 2: 90-108.
72 Ellis, R. J.; Wildavsky, A. 1990. The Role of Abolitionists in the Civil War. CSSH 32: 89-116.
73 Emerson, M. O. 1994. Percent Black and Residential Segregation. SQ 35: 571-580.
74 Fishback, P. V. 1989. Can Competition among Employers Reduce Governmental Discrimination? JOLE 32: 311-328.
75 Galenson, D. W. 1981. Market Evaluation of Human Capital: Indentured Servitude. JPE 89: 446-467.
76 Gilens, M. 1995. Racial Attitudes and Opposition to Welfare. JOP 57: 994-1014.

77 Giles, M. W.; Cataldo, E. F.; Gatlin, D. S. 1975. White Flight and Percent Black: The Tipping Point. SSQ 56: 85-92.
78 Goebel, P. R.; Rosenberg, S. B. 1992. Analysis of Impact of Anti-Discrimination Legislation Based on Familial Status. PSCI 25: 161-174.
79 Hammond, J. L. 1977. Race and Electoral Mobilization: White Southerners. POQ 41: 13-27.
80 Henderson, C. W. 1993. Population Pressures and Political Repression. SSQ 74: 322-333.
81 Holt, T. 1976. On the Cross: Quantitative Methods in Reconstruction of Afro-American Experience. Journal of Negro History 61: 158-172.
82 Hormuth, S. E.; Stephan, W. G. 1981. Blaming the Victim: The "Holocaust." IJPE 4: 29-36.
83 Hwang, S.S.; Murcock, S.H. 1988. Population Size and Residential Segregation. SSQ 69: 818-834.
84 International Journal of Political Education 1981. Papers on Reactions to "Holocaust." IJPE 4 (1/2).
85 Inverarity, J. 1976. Populism and Lynching in Louisiana. ASR 41: 262-279.
86 Jackman, M. R. 1981. Education and Policy Commitment to Racial Integration. AJPS 25: 256-269.
87 Journal of Social Issues. 1982. Papers on Sexual Harassment. JSI 38 (4).
88 -. 1983. Papers on Racism and Women. JSI 39 (3).
89 -. 1985. Papers on Sexual Discrimination in Academia. JSI 41 (4).
90 Kadish, E. 1986. Discrimination in Employment: A Bibliography. LACP 49 (4): 211-235.
91 Kelly, W. R.; Snyder, D. 1980. Racial Violence and Socioeconomic Changes among Blacks. SF 58: 739-760.
92 Kinder, D. R.; Mendelberg, T. 1995. Political Impact of Prejudice among Desegregated Whites. JOP 57: 402-424.
93 Kinder, D. R.; Sears, D. O. 1981. Prejudice and Politics: Symbolic Racism vs. Racial Threats to the Good Life. JPASP 40: 414-431.
94 King, N. J. 1993. Postconviction Review of Jury Discrimination: Effects of Juror Race on Jury Decisions. MLR 92: 63-130.
95 Lawrence, G. H.; Kane, T. D. 1995. Military Service and Racial Attitudes of White Veterans. AFAS 22: 235-256.
96 Maier-Katkin, D.; Stemmler, S.; Stretesky, P. 1995. Immigration and Emergence of Right-Wing Violence in Unified Germany. CLASC 24: 1-18.
97 Manning, P.; Griffiths, W. S. 1988. Simulating Demography of African Slavery. JIDH 19: 177-202.
98 Margo, R. A. 1991. Segregated Schools and the Mobility Hypothesis: Local Government Discrimination. QJE 106: 61-73.
99 Mason, T. D. 1984. Individual Participation in Collective Racial Violence. APSR 78: 1040-1056.
100 Massey, D. S.; Denton, N. A. 1989. Hypersegregation in US Metropolitan Areas: Black and Hispanic Segregation along Five Dimensions. Demography 26: 373-391.
101 Massey, D. S.; Gross, A. B. 1991. Explaining Trends in Racial Segregation. UAQ 27: 13-35.
102 Massey, D. S.; Hajnal, Z. L. 1995. The Changing Geographical Structure of Black-White Segregation. SSQ 76: 527-542.
103 Massey, D. S.; Shibuya, K. 1995. The Effect of Spatially Concentrated Joblessness on the Well Being of African Americans. SSR 24: 352-366.
104 McConahay, J. B. 1982. Self-Interest vs. Racial Attitudes as Correlates of Anti-Busing Attitudes. JOP 44: 692-720.
105 McKinney, S.; Schnare, A. B. 1989. Trends in Residential Segregation. JUE 26: 269-280.
106 Merriman, W. R.; Parent, T. W. 1983. Sources of Citizen Attitudes toward Government Race Policy. Polity 16: 30-47.
107 Morgan, D.R.; Fitzgerald, M.B. 1979. Causal Perspective on School Segregation. SF 58: 329-335.

108 Myers, S. L.; Chan, T. 1995. Racial Discrimination in Housing Markets. SSQ 76: 543-561.

109 Naff, K. C. 1995. Perceptions of Discrimination. PSJ 23: 483-498.

110 Olzak, S. 1990. Political Context of Competition: Lynching and Urban Racial Violence. SF 69: 395-422.

111 O'Neill, D. J. 1987. American Ethnic Group Proportionality and Discrimination. PLS 17: 75-78.

112 Padgug, R. A. 1976. Problems in the Theory of Slavery and the Slave Society. SAS 40: 3-27.

113 Perry, H. L. 1991. Deracialization as an Analytical Construct in American Urban Politics. UAQ 27: 181-191.

114 Phillips, C. D. 1987. Exploring Relations among Forms of Social Control: Lynchings and Execution of Blacks in North Carolina. LASR 21: 361-374.

115 Policy and Politics. 1991. Papers on Racialization and Public Policy. PAP 19 (3).

116 Policy Studies Journal. 1978. Papers on Race and Gender. PSJ 7 (2).

117 Powers, D. A.; Ellison, C. G. 1995. Interracial Contact and Black Racial Attitudes: The Contact Hypothesis and Selectivity Bias. SF 74: 205-226.

118 Quillian, L. 1995. Prejudice as a Response to Perceived Group Threat: Population Composition and Anti-Immigrant and Racial Prejudice in Europe. ASR 60: 586-611.

119 Reed, J. S. 1980. The Contact Hypothesis Applied to the Sectional Beliefs and Attitudes of White Southerners. SF 59: 123-135.

120 Riga, P. J. 1981. The US Crisis over Slavery. AJJ 26: 80-111.

121 Ross, J. M.; Vanneman, R. D.; Pettigrew, T. F. 1976. Patterns of Support for George Wallace. JSI 32: 69-92.

122 Ross, M. H. 1995. Psychocultural Interpretation Theory and Peacemaking in Ethnic Conflicts. PP 16: 523-544.

123 Rossell, C. H. 1993. Using Multiple Criteria to Evaluate Public Policies: School Desegregation. APQ 21: 155-184.

124 Sigelman, L.; Welch, S. 1993. Contact Hypothesis Revisited: Black-White Interaction and Positive Racial Attitudes. SF 71: 781-796.

125 Smith, T. W. 1993. Actual Trends or Measurement Artifacts? A Review of Three Studies of Anti-Semitism. POQ 57: 380-393.

126 Sniderman, P. M., et al. 1991. The New Racism. AJPS 35: 423-447.

127 Sniderman, P. M.; Brody, R. A.; Kuklinski, J. H. 1984. Policy Reasoning and Political Values: Racial Equality. AJPS 28: 74-94.

128 Sniderman, P. M.; Tetlock, P. E. 1986. Symbolic Racism: Problems of Motive Attribution in Political Analysis. JSI 42: 129-150.

129 Solomos, J. 1986. Trends in the Political Analysis of Racism. POLST 34: 313-324.

130 Sould, S. 1992. Populism and Black Lynching in Georgia. SF 71: 431-450.

131 Stanfield, J. H. 1991. Racism in America and in Other Race-Centered Nation-States. IJCS 32: 243-260.

132 Steeh, C.; Schman, H. 1992. Did Racial Attitudes Change in the 1980s? AJS 98: 340-367.

133 Studlar, D. T. 1978. Policy Voting in Britain: Colored Immigration. APSR 72: 46-64.

134 Sunderland, G. 1993. Discrimination and Differentiation: Ethical and Biological Issue. JSPES 18: 455-466.

135 Tolnay, S. E.; et al. 1989. Black Lynching: The Power Threat Hypothesis. SF 67: 605-623.

136 Tolnay, S. E.; Beck, E. M. 1992. Racial Violence and Black Migration in the American South. ASR 57: 103-116.

137 Urban Affairs Quarterly. 1983. Papers on Race and Residential Segregation. UAQ 18 (3).

138 Wainscott, S. H.; Woodard, J. D. 1988. Second Thoughts on Second Generation Discrimination: School Resegregation in Southern States. APQ 16: 171-192.

139 Wald, K. D. 1980. Visible Empire: The Ku Klux Klan as an Electoral Movement. JIDH 10: 217-234.

140 Weigel, R. H.; Howes, P. W. 1985. Conceptions of Racial Prejudice: Symbolic Racism Reconsidered. JSI 41: 117-138.

141 Wilson, T. C. 1984. Urbanism and Racial Attitudes. UAQ 20: 201-210.

142 Wolfle, L. M.; Hodge, R. W. 1983. Racial Party Politics in Illinois, 1880-1924. SI 53: 33-60.

Election of Minorities

143 Alozie, N. O. 1992. Election of Asians to City Councils. SSQ 73: 90-100.

144 Alozie, N. O.; Manganaro, L. L. 1993. Black and Hispanic Council Representation: Does Council Size Matter? UAQ 29: 276-298.

145 Annals. 1978. Papers on Urban Black Politics. ANNALS 439.

146 Bledsoe, T.; Herring, M. 1990. Women in Pursuit of Political Office. APSR 84: 213-223.

147 Brace, K., et al. 1995. Minority Turnout and the Creation of Majority-Minority Districts. APQ 23: 190-203.

148 Brown, C.; Heighberger, N. R.; Shocket, P. A. 1993. Gender-Based Differences in Perceptions of Male and Female City Council Candidates. WAP 13: 1-18.

149 Browning, R. P.; Marshall, D. R.; Tabb, D. H. 1979. Minorities and Urban Electoral Change. UAQ 15: 206-228.

150 Bullock, C. S. 1984. Racial Crossover Voting and Election of Black Officials. JOP 46: 238-251.

151 Bullock, C. S.; MacManus, S. A. 1991. Municipal Electoral Structure and the Election of Councilwomen. JOP 53: 75-89.

152 Cain, B. E.; Kiewiet, D. R. 1984. Mexican-American Voting Behavior. SSQ 65: 315-327.

153 Carmines, E. G.; Huckfeldt, R. R.; McCurley, C. 1995. Mobilization, Counter-Mobilization, and the Politics of Race. PG 14: 601-620.

154 Citrin, J.; Green, D. P.; Sears, D. O. 1990. White Reactions to Black Candidates. POQ 54: 74-96.

155 Cole, L. 1974. Electing Blacks to Municipal Office: Structural and Social Determinants. UAQ 8: 17-39.

156 Darcy, R.; Choike, J. R. 1986. A Formal Analysis of Legislative Turnover: Women Candidates. AJPS 30: 237-255.

157 Darcy, R.; Hadley, C. D. 1988. Black Women in Politics. SSQ 69: 629-645.

158 Darcy, R.; Hadley, C. D.; Kirksey, J. F. 1993. Election Systems and Representation of Black Women. WAP 13: 73-90.

159 Davidson, C.; Korbel, G. 1981. At-Large Elections and Minority Group Representation. JOP 43: 982-1005.

160 de la Garza, R. O. 1974. Voting Patterns in Bicultural El Paso: Contextual Analysis of Chicano Behavior. Aztlan 5: 235-260.

161 Engstrom, R. L.: McDonald, M. 1981. The Election of Blacks to City Councils: Clarifying Impact of Electoral Arrangements on the Seats/Population Relationship. APSR 75: 344-354.

162 Engstrom, R. L.; Taebel, D. A.; Cole, R. L. 1989. Cumulative Voting as a Remedy for Minority Vote Dilution. JOLAP 5: 469-497.

163 Featherman, S. 1983. Ethnicity and Ethnic Candidates: Vote Advantages in Local Elections. Polity 15: 397-415.

164 Filer, J. E.; Kenny, L. W.; Morton, R. B. 1991. Voting Laws, Education Policy and Minority Turnout. JOLE 34: 371-393.

165 Garcia, J. A. 1976. Chicano Voting Patterns in School Board Elections: Bloc Voting and Internal Lines of Support for Chicano Candidates. Astibos Winter 1976/7: 1-14.

166 Gertzog, I.; Simard, M. M. 1981. Women and Hopeless Congressional Candidacies: Nomination Frequency. APQ 9: 449-466.

167 Grofman, B. 1991. Multivariate Methods and the Analysis of Racially Polarized Voting. SSQ 72: 826-833.

168 Guinier, L. 1991. Triumph of Tokenism: The Voting Rights Act and the Theory of Black Electoral Success. MLR 89: 1077-1154.

169 Guterbock, T. M.; London, B. 1983. Race, Political Orientation and Participation. ASR 48: 439-453.

170 Hero, R. E.; Tolbert, C. J. 1995. Latinos and Substantive Representation in the House of Representatives. AJPS 39: 640-653.

171 Herrick, R.; Welch, S. 1992. Impact of At-Large Elections on Representation of Black and White Women. NPSR 3: 62-74.

172 Kahn, K. F. 1994. Press Coverage of Women Candidates for Statewide Office. JOP 56: 154-173.

173 Latimer, M. K. 1979. Black Political Representation in Southern Cities. UAQ 15: 65-86.

174 Leeper, M. S. 1991. Impact of Prejudice on Female Candidates. APQ 19: 248-261.

175 Lieske, J. A.; Hillard, J. W. 1984. The Racial Factor in Urban Elections. WPQ 37: 545-563.

176 Lovensuck, J.; Norris, P. 1989. Selecting Women Candidates: Obstacles to Feminization of the House of Commons. EJPR 17: 533-562.

177 MacManus, S. A.; Bullock, C. S. 1989. Women on Southern City Councils. JPS 17: 32-49.

178 Matland, R. E. 1993. Institutional Variables Affecting Female Representation in National Legislatures: Norway. JOP 55: 737-755.

179 -. 1994. Putting Scandinavian Equality to Test: Experimental Evaluation of Gender Sterotyping of Political Candidates. BJPS 24: 273-292.

180 National Civic Review. 1995. Papers on the Voting Rights Act. NCR 84 (4).

181 Nechemias, C. 1987. Changes in Election of Women in State Legislative Seats. LSQ 12: 125-142.

182 O'Loughlin, J. 1982. Identification of Racial Gerrymandering. AAAG 72: 165-184.

183 Perkins, J.; Fowlkes, D. 1980. Opinion Representation vs. Social Representation: Or Why Women Can't Run as Women and Win. APSR 74: 92-103.

184 Pierce, P. A. 1989. Gender Role and Political Culture: The Electoral Connection. WAP 9: 21-46.

185 PS. 1983. Papers on Black Electoral Politics. PS 16 (3).

186 Publius. 1986. Papers on the Voting Rights Act. Vol 16 (4).

187 Radcliff, B.; Saiz, M. 1995. Race, Turnout and Public Policy in the States. PRQ 48: 775-794.

188 Rasmussen, J. 1981. Women Candidates in British By-Elections. POLST 29: 265-274.

189 Rule, W. 1981. Why Women Don't Run: The Critical Contextual Factors in Women's Legislative Recruitment. WPQ 34: 60-77.

190 -. 1990. Why More Women Are State Legislators. WPQ 43: 437-448.

191 Sapiro, V. 1981. When Are Interests Interesting? The Problem of Political Representation of Women. APSR 75: 701-716.

192 Sass, T. R.; Mehay, S. L. 1995. The Voting Rights Act, District Elections and the Success of Black Candidates in Municipal Elections. JOLE 38: 367-392.

193 Sheffield, J. F.; Hadley, C. D. 1984. Racial Voting in a Biracial City. APQ 12: 449-464.

194 Summers, M. E.; Klinkner, P. A. 1991. The Daniels Election in New Haven and Failure of the Deracialization Hypothesis. UAQ 27: 202-226.

195 Volgy, T. J.; Schwartz, J. E.; Gottlief, H. 1986. Female Representation and Quest for Resources: Female Activism and Electoral Success. SSQ 67: 156-168.

196 Welch, S. 1990. The Impact of At-Large Elections on the Representation of Blacks and Hispanics. JOP 10: 125-134.

197 Welch, S.; Hibbing, J. R. 1984. Hispanic Representation in the US Congress. SSQ 65: 328-335.

198 Welch, S.; Karnig, A. K. 1979. Correlates of Female Office Holding in City Politics. JOP 41: 478-491.

199 Welch, S.; Studlar, D. T. 1990. Multi-Member Districts and the Representation of Women. JOP 52: 391-412.

200 Wright, J. E. 1973. The Ethnocultural Model of Voting. ABS 16: 653-674.

Gender and Politics

201 Adler, M. A. 1994. Male-Female Power Differences at Work: A Comparison of Supervisors and Policymakers. SI 64: 37-55.

202 American Behavioral Scientist. 1982 Papers on Homosexuality. ABS 25 (4).

203 -. 1986. Papers on Gender Research. ABS 29 (3), 1986 29 (5), and 1987 31 (1).

204 -. 1994. Papers on Feminist Thought. ABS 37 (8).

205 American Journal of Sociology. 1987. Papers on Structured Inequality. AJS 93 (1).

206 American Politics Quarterly. 1977. Papers on Women and Politics. APQ 5 (3).

207 Andersen, K. 1975. Working Women and Political Participation. AJPS 19: 439-453.

208 Andersen, K.; Cook, E. A. 1985. Women, Work and Political Attitudes. AJPS 29: 605-625.

209 Annals. 1991. Papers on Feminism. ANNALS 515.

210 Baer, D. L. 1993. Political Parties: The Missing Variable in Women and Politics Research. PRQ 46: 547-576.

211 Banaszak, L. A.; Plutzer, E. 1993. Contextual Determinants of Feminist Attitudes. APSR 87: 147-157.

212 Barrett, E. J. 1995. Policy Priorities of African American Women in State Legislatures. LSQ 20: 223-248.

213 Baydas, M. M.; Meyer, R. L.; Aguilera-Alfred, N. 1994. Discrimination against Women in Formal Credit Markets. WD 22: 1073-1082.

214 Bennett, L. L. M.; Bennett, S. E. 1989. Enduring Gender Differences in Political Interest. APQ 17: 105-122.

215 Benze, J.; Declercq, E. 1985. Gender in Congressional and Statewide Elections. SSQ 66: 954-963.

216 Berman, D. R. 1993. Gender and Issue Voting: Policy Effects of Suffrage Expansion in Arizona. SSQ 74: 838-850.

217 Bernhardt, A.; Morris, M.; Handcock, M. S. 1995. Women's Gains or Men's Losses? The Shrinking Gender Gap in Earnings. AJS 101: 302-328.

218 Bock, W. W.; Beeghley, L.; Mixon, A. J. 1983. Religion, Socioeconomic Status and Sexual Morality: Reference Group Theory. SQ 24: 545-560.

219 Bourque, S. C.; Grossholtz, J. 1974. Political Science Looks at Female Participation. PAS 4: 225-266.

220 Calhoun, D. 1994. Separating Lesbian Theory from Feminist Theory. Ethics 104: 558-581.

221 Canadian Journal of Political and Social Theory. 1985. Papers on Feminism. CJPST 9 (1/2).

222 Caulfield, S. 1993. Women of Vice, Virtue and Rebellion: New Studies in Representation of the Female in Latin America. LARR 28: 163-174.

223 Clemens, E. S. 1992. Organizational Repertoires and Institutional Change: Women's Groups and the Transformation of US Politics, 1890-1920. AJS 98: 755-798.

224 Conover, P. J. 1988. Feminists and the Gender Gap. JOP 50: 985-1010.

225 Conover, P. J.; Sapiro, V. 1993. Gender, Feminist Consciousness and War. AJPS 37: 1079-1099.

226 Cook, E. A. 1993. Feminist Consciousness and Candidate Preference among American Women. PB 15: 227-246.

227 Costain, A. N.; Costain, W. D. 1985. Movements and Gatekeepers: Congressional Response to Women's Movement Issues. CAP 12: 21-42.

228 -. 1992. Political Strategies of Social Movements: Comparision of Women's and Environmental Movements. CAP 19: 1-28.

229 Costain, A. N.; Majstorovic, S. 1994. Congress, Social Movements and Public Opinion: Multiple Origins of Women's Rights. PRQ 47: 111-136.

230 Cotter, D. A., et al. 1995. Occupational Gender Segregation and Earnings Gap. SSR 24: 439-454.

231 Darcy, R.; Hadley, C. D. 1988. Black Women in Politics. SSQ 69: 629-645.

232 Dearden, J. 1974. Sex-Linked Differences in Political Behavior. SSI 13: 19-45.

233 Development. 1993. Papers on Women's Rights. Vol 1993 (4).

234 Dillingham, A. E.; Ferber, M. A.; Hamermesh, D. S. 1994. Gender Discrimination by Gender: Voting in a Professional Society. ILRR 47: 622-633.

235 Dolan, K.; Ford, L. E. 1995. Women in State Legislatures: Feminist Identify and Legislative Behaviors. APQ 23: 96-108.

236 Dworkin, R. 1979. Ideology Formation: Influences on Feminist Ideology. SQ 20: 345-358.

237 Ethics. 1989. Papers on Feminist Theory. Vol 99 (2).

238 Fine-Davis, M. 1989. Attitudes toward the Role of Women as Part of a Larger Belief System. PP 10: 287-308.

239 Firebaugh, G.; Chen, K. 1994. Vote Turnout of Nineteenth Amendment Women: Enduring Effect of Disenfranchisement. AJS 100: 972-996.

240 Flanagan, O. J.; Jackson, K. 1987. Justice, Care and Gender: The Kohlberg-Gilligan Debate Revisited. Ethics 97: 622-637.

241 Fletcher Forum. 1993. Papers on Gender in International Relations. FFWF 17 (2).

242 Folbre, N. 1993. Feminist Theories of Gender Bias in Economics. HPE 25: 167-184.

243 Fowlkes, D.; Perkins, J.; Rinehart, S. T. 1979. Gender Roles and Party Roles. APSR 73: 772-780.

244 Futures. 1989. Papers on Gender. Vol 21 (1).

245 Gladdie, R. E.; Bullock, C. S. 1995. Structure and Elite Influences on Female Candidates. SSQ 76: 749-762.

246 Golden, C. 1983. The Changing Role of Women: A Quantitative Approach. JIDH 13: 707-734.

247 Green, A. E. 1994. Geography of Changing Female Economic Activity. Regional Studies 28: 633-639.

248 Gruber, J. E. 1990. Methodological Problems and Policy Implications in Sexual Harassment Research. PRAPR 9: 235-254.

249 Gunderson, M. 1989. Male-Female Wage Differentials and Policy Responses. JEL 27: 46-117.

250 Gurin, P. 1985. Women's Gender Consciousness. POQ 49: 143-163.

251 Gwartney-Gibbs, P. A.; Lach, D. H. 1994. Gender and Workplace Dispute Resolution. LASR 28: 265-296.

252 Hansen, S. B.; Franz, L. M.; Netemeyer-Mays, M. 1976. Women's Political Participation and Policy Preferences. SSQ 56: 576-590.

253 Hayes, B. C. 1994. International Comparison of Gender Differences in Attitudes. IJPOR 6: 13-34.

254 Hayes, B. C.; Bean, C. S. 1993. Gender and Local Political Interest. POLST 41: 672-682.

255 Hernes, H. M. 1980. Support for the Women's Movement: A Diffusion Model. SPS 3: 265-273.

256 Hewitt, C. 1995. The Socioeconomic Position of Gay Men. AJEAS 54: 461-479.

257 Hill, D. B. 1981. Political Culture and Female Political Representation. JOP 43: 159-168.

258 Hirschmann, N. J. 1989. Freedom, Responsibility and Obligation: A Feminist Approach to Political Theory. APSR 83: 1227-1244.

259 Hochschild, A. R. 1973. Review of Sex Role Research. AJS 78: 1011-1029.

260 Human Rights Quarterly. 1981. Papers on Women and Human Rights. HRQ 3 (2).

261 Hyde, J. S. 1990. Meta-Analysis and the Psychology of Gender Differences. Signs 16: 55-73.

262 International Political Science Review. 1985. Papers on Women in Politics. IPSR 6 (3).

263 International Social Science Journal. 1983. Papers on Women in Politics and Social Movements. ISSJ 35 (4).

264 International Studies Notes. 1989. Papers on Women and Development. ISN 14 (3).

265 Jelen, T. G.; Thomas, S.; Wilcox, C. 1994. The Gender Gap in Comparative Perspective. EJPR 25: 171-186.

266 Jennings, M. K.; Farah, B. G. 1981. Social Roles and Political Resources: Men and Women in Party Elites. AJPS 25: 462-482.

267 Jones, E. B. 1991. Economics of Womens Suffrage. JLS 20: 423-437.

268 Journal of Criminal Law and Criminology. 1994. Papers on Gender and the Law. JCLAC 85 (1).

269 Journal of Law and Society. 1993. Papers on Feminist Theory and Legal Strategy. JLAS 20 (1).

270 Journal of Political Science. 1989. Papers on Women in Politics. JPS 17 (1/2).

271 Journal of Social Issues. 1978. Papers on the Gay Community. JSI 34 (3).

272 -. 1989. Papers on Comparable Worth. JSI 45 (4).

273 -. 1995. Papers on Gender Stereotyping, Sexual Harassment and the Law. JSI 51 (1).

274 Journal of State Government. 1987. Papers on Women as State Policy Makers. JSG 60 (5).

275 Kathlene, L. 1994. Power and Influence in State Legislative Policymaking: Interaction of Gender and Position in Committee Hearing Debates. APSR 88: 560-576.

276 Kelly, R. M.; Boutilierr, M. A. 1978. Mothers, Daughters and Socialization of Political Women. Sex Roles 4: 438-443.

277 Kincaid, D. 1978. A Positive Perspective on Widows in the US Congress. WPQ 31: 96-104.

278 Krauss, W. R. 1974. Political Implications of Gender Role. APSR 68: 1706-1723.

279 Law and Society Review. 1991. Papers on Gender and Sociolegal Studies. LASR 25 (2).

280 McDonagh, E. L. 1982. Differential Impact of Achieved and Derived Status upon the Political Participation of Women. AJPS 26: 280-297.

281 Mezey, S. G. 1978. Support for Women's Rights Policy: Local Politicians. APQ 6: 485-497.

282 -. 1981. Attitudinal Consistency among Political Elites: Support for the Equal Rights Amendment. APQ 9: 111-125.

283 Millennium. 1988. Papers on Women and International Relations. Vol 17 (3).

284 Newman, M. A. 1994. Gender and Lowi's Thesis: Implications for Career Advancement. PAR 54: 285-290.

285 Nice, D. C. 1986. State Opposition to the Equal Rights Amendment. SSQ 67: 315-328.

286 Orum, A., et al. 1974. Sex, Socialization and Politics. ASR 39: 197-209.

287 Paolino, P. 1995. Group-Salient Issues and Group Representation: Support for Women Candidates. AJPS 39: 294-313.

288 Peace Research Review. 1991. Papers on Women and Government. PRR 12 (2).

289 Pippa, N. 1985. The Gender Gap in Britain and America. PARLA 38: 192-201.

290 Policy and Politics. 1989. Papers on Gender, European Law and British Equal Opportunities Policies. PAP 17 (4).

291 Political Geography. 1990. Papers on Political Geography and Gender. PG 9 (4).

292 Political Science. 1993. Papers on Women and Politics in New Zealand. PSNZ 45 (1).

293 -. 1994. Papers on Feminism and Public Policy. PSCI 27 (2-3).

294 Politics and the Life Sciences. 1990. Papers on the Politics of Surrogate Contracts. PALS 8 (2).

295 PS. 1982. Papers on the Equal Rights Amendment. PS 15 (4).

296 Public Administration Review. 1993. Papers on Women in Public Management. PAR 53 (4).

297 Public Personnel Management. 1983. Papers on Comparable Worth. PPM 12 (4).

298 Ramsey, V. J.; Calvert, L. M. 1994. A Feminist Critique of Organizational Humanism. JABS 30: 83-107.

299 Randall, V. 1991. Feminism and Political Analysis. PANAL 39: 513-532.

300 Rapoport, R.; Stone, W. J.; Abramowitz, A. I. 1990. Sex and the Caucus Participant: Gender Gap and Presidential Nominations. AJPS 34: 725-740.

301 Review of Radical Political Economics. 1991. Papers on Women in the International Economy. RRPE 23 (3/4).

302 Rinehart, S. T. 1987. Research on Gender and Political Participation. CAP 14: 169 ff.

303 Saint-Germaine, M. A. 1989. Does Their Difference Make a Difference? Impact of Women on Public Policy in the Arizona Legislature. SSQ 70: 956-968.

304 Sapiro, V. 1982. Private Costs of Public Commitments or Public Costs of Private Commitments? Family Roles vs. Political Ambition. AJPS 26: 265-279.

305 Sapiro, V.; Farah, B. G. 1980. Political Ambition and Role Orientation among Female Partisan Elites. WAP 1: 13-35.

306 Scandinavian Political Studies. 1988. Papers on Feminism. SPS 11 (4).

307 Schlozman, K. L., et al. 1995. Gender and Citizen Participation. AJPS 39: 267-293.

308 Segal, M. W.; Hansen, A. F. 1992. Value Rationales in Policy Debates on Women in the Military: Congressional Testimony. SSQ 73: 296-309.

309 Shabad, G.; Andersen, K. 1979. Candidate Evaluation by Men and Women. POQ 43: 18-35.

310 Shapiro, R. Y.; Mahajan, H. 1986. Gender Differences in Policy Preferences. POQ 50: 42-61.

311 Sidanius, J.; Pratto, F.; Brieg, D. 1995. Group Dominance and the Political Psychology of Gender. PP 16: 381-397.

312 Signs. 1981. Papers on Feminist Theory. Vol 7 (1), 7 (3).

313 -. 1984. Papers on Lesbianism. Vol 9 (4) and 18 (4).

314 -. 1985. Papers on Female Communities. Vol 10 (4), and 14 (2).

315 -. 1987. Papers on Women and the Political Process. Vol 13 (1).

316 -. 1995. Papers on Feminisms. Vol 20 (4).

317 Singer, M. S. 1994. Mental Framing by Consequence Thinking: Its Effects on Judgements of Gender-Based Employment Selection. JEPSY 15: 149-172.

318 Social Policy. 1993. Papers on the Women's Movement. Vol 23 (4).

319 Social Research. 1983 Papers on Women's Morality. SR 50 (3).

320 Social Science Quarterly. 1976. Papers on Sex Stratification. SSQ 56 (4).

321 -. 1987. Papers on Sex Roles and Gender. SSQ 68: 102-156, and 74 (1).

322 Society. 1991. Papers on Sexual Harassment. Vol 28 (4).

323 -. 1993. Papers on Gays and the Military. Vol 31 (1).

324 Sociological Inquiry. 1986. Papers on Gender Roles. SI 56 (1).

325 Sociological Quarterly. 1995. Papers on Women, Work and Family. SQ 36 (2).

326 Songer, D. R.; Davis, S.; Haire, S. 1994. A Reappraisal of Diversification in Federal Courts: Gender Effects in the Courts of Appeals. JOP 56: 425-439.

327 Sorkin, A. L. 1973. On the Occupational Status of Women, 1870-1970. AJEAS 32: 235-244.

328 Spurr, S. J.; Sueyoski, G. T. 1994. Turnover and Promotion of Lawyers: Gender Differences. JHR 29: 813-842.

329 Thomas, S. 1989. Voting Patterns in the California Assembly: The Role of Gender. WAP 9: 43-56.

330 -. 1991. Impact of Women on State Legislative Policies. JOP 53: 958-976.

331 Thomas, S.; McCoy, C.; McBride, A. 1993. Deconstructing the Political Spectacle: Response to the Clarence Thomas / Anita Hill Sexual Harassment Hearings. AJPS 37: 699-720.

332 Thomas, S.; Welch, S. 1991. Impact of Gender on Activities and Priorities of State Legislators. WPQ 44: 445-456.

333 Togeby, L. 1994. The Gender Gap in Foreign Policy. JPR 31: 375-392.

334 Valentine, G. 1995. Geographies of Lesbian Landscapes. IJURR 19: 96-111.

335 Van der Ros, J. 1987. Class, Gender and Participatory Behavior. PP 8: 95-123.

336 Vega, A.; Firestone, J. M. 1995. Effects of Gender on Congressional Behavior and Substantive Representation of Women. LSQ 20: 213-222.

337 Volgy, T. J.; Volgy, S. S. 1974. Women and Politics: Political Correlates of Sex Role Acceptance. SSQ 55: 967-974.

338 Wassenberg, P. S. 1983. Gender Differences in Political Conceptualization. APQ 11: 181-203.

339 Welch, S. 1977. Women as Political Animals? A Test of Some Explanations for Male-Female Political Participation Differences. AJPS 21: 711-729.

340 -. 1978. Recruitment of Women to Office. WPQ 31: 372-381.

341 -. 1984. Are Women More Liberal than Men in the US Congress? LSQ 10: 125-134.

342 -. 1989. Congressional Nomination Procedures and the Representation of Women. CAP 16: 121-134.

343 Welch, S.; Sigelman, L. 1982. Changes in Public Attitudes toward Women in Politics. WPQ 39: 138-154.

344 -. 1989. A Black Gender Gap? SSQ 70: 120-123.

345 -. 1992. Gender Gap among Hispanics? The Comparison with Blacks and Anglos. WPQ 45: 181-199.

346 Wellington, A. J. 1994. Accounting for the Male-Female Wage Gap among Whites. ASR 59: 839-849.

347 Welch, S.; Hibbing, J. R. 1992. Financial Conditions, Gender and Voting in American Elections. JOP 54: 197-213.

348 West European Politics. 1985. Papers on Women and Politics in Western Europe. WEP 8 (4).

349 Western Political Quarterly. 1981. Papers on Women and Politics. WPQ 34 (1).

350 Wilcox, C. 1991. Causes and Consequences of Feminist Consciousness among Western European Women. CPS 23: 519-545.

351 With, D. 1986. Reinterpreting the Gender Gap. POQ 50: 316-330.

352 Wohlenberg, E. H. 1980. Correlates of Equal Rights Amendment Ratification. SSQ 60: 676-684.

353 Women and Poliitcs. 1985. Papers on Gender and Socialization to Power and Politics. WAP 5 (4).

354 -. 1986. Papers on Politics of Professionalism, Opportunity, Employment and Gender. WAP 6 (3).

355 -. 1987. Papers on Feminism and Approaches to Women and Politics Research. WAP 7 (3).

356 -. 1990. Papers on Women and the Constitution. WAP 10 (2).

357 -. 1991. Papers on International Perspectives of Women and Public Administration. WAP 11 (4).

358 World Development 1995. Papers on Gender and Macroeconomics. WD 23 (11).

359 Wright, G. 1991. Understanding the Gender Gap. JEL 29: 1153-1201.

Racial and Ethnic Politics

360 Aberbach, J. D.; Walker, J. L. 1970. Political Trust and Racial Ideology. APSR 64: 1199-1219.

361 Abramowitz, A. I. 1994. Issue Evolution Reconsidered: Racial Attitudes and Partisanship. AJPS 38: 1-24.

362 Acta Politica 1984. Papers on Consocialization-alism and Conflict Management in Belgium and the Netherlands. AC 19 (1).

363 Acuna, R. F. 1989. Current Research in Chicano Studies. Journal of American Ethnic History 8: 134-138.

364 American Behavioral Scientist. 1987. Papers on Methodological Innovations in Race Relations Research. ABS 30 (4).

365 American Journal of Sociology. 1974. Papers on Ethnicity and Race. AJS 80: 630-687.

366 Annals. 1978. Papers on Native Americans. ANNALS 436.

367 -. 1981. Papers on the US as a Multicultural Society. ANNALS 454.

368 -. 1993. Papers on Interminority Affairs. ANNALS 530.

369 Antunes, G.; Gaitz, C. M. 1975. Ethnicity and Participation. AJS 80: 1192-1211.

370 Ayers, I.; Waldfogel, J. 1994. A Market Test for Race Discrimination in Bail Setting. SLR 46: 987-1048.

371 Barrows, W. L. 1976. Ethnic Diversity and Political Instability in Africa. CPS 9: 139-170.

372 Bates, T.; Williams, D. L. 1993. Racial Politics: Does It Pay? SSQ 74: 507-522.

373 Bell, W.; Robinson, R. V., 1980. Cognitive Maps of Class and Racial Inequalities in England and the US. AJS 86: 320-349.

374 Black, E. 1971. Southern Governors and Political Change: Campaign Stances on Racial Segregation and Economic Development. JOP 33: 703-734.

375 Bobo, L. 1988. Attitudes toward the Black Political Movement. SPQ 51: 287-302.

376 Bobo, L.; Gilliam, F. D. 1990. Race, Sociopolitical Participation and Black Empowerment. APSR 84: 377-393.

377 Bonacich, E. 1972. A Theory of Ethnic Antagonism: The Split Labor Market. ASR 37: 547-559.

378 Borjas, G. J. 1994. The Long-Run Convergence of Ethnic Skill Differentials. ILRR 47: 553-573.

379 Bovasso, G. 1993. Self, Group and Public Interests Motivating Racial Politics. PP 14: 3-20.

380 Bowers, D. A.; Mitchell, C. R.; Webb, K. 1981. Modeling Bicommunal Conflict. Futures 13: 31-42, 115-127.

381 Boynton, G. R.; Kwon, W. H. 1978. An Analysis of Cosociational Democracy. LSQ 3: 11-26.

382 Buzan, B. C. 1980. Chicano Community Control, Political Cynicism and Validity of Political Trust Measures. WPQ 33: 108-119.

383 Cain, B. E.; Kiewiet, D. R.; Uhlaner, C. J. 1991. Acquisition of Partisanship by Latinos and Asian Americans. AJPS 35: 390-422.

384 California Law Review. 1994. Papers on Critical Race Theory. CLR 82 (4).

385 Carment, D. 1993. International Dimensions of Ethnic Conflict. JPR 30: 137-150.

386 Carment, D.; James, P. 1995. Internal Constraints and Interstate Ethnic Conflict: Irredentism. JCR 39: 82-109.

387 Carmines, E. G.; Stimson, J. A. 1982. Racial Issues and the Structure of Mass Belief Systems. JOP 44: 2-20.

388 Carsey, T. M. 1995. Contextual Effects of Race on White Voter Behavior. JOP 57: 221-228.

389 Cloutier, N. R. 1987. Who Gains from Racism? Impact of Racial Inequality on White Income Distribution. ROSE 45: 152-162.

390 Cohn, S.; Fossett, M. 1995. Why Racial Employment Inequality Is Greater in Northern Labor Markets. SF 74: 511-542.

391 Comer, J. C. 1978. Street Level Bureaucracy and Political Support: Mexican Americans. UAQ 14: 207-227.

392 Connor, W. 1973. Politics of Ethnonationalism. JIA 27: 1-21.

393 Cornacchia, E. J.; Nelson, D. C. 1992. Historical Differences in the Political Experiences of American Blacks and White Ethnics. EARS 15: 102-124.

394 Dawson, M. C.; Brown, R. E.; Allen, R. L. 1990. Racial Belief Systems, Religious Guidance and African-American Political Participation. NPSR 2: 22-44.

395 de la Garza, R. O. 1982. Chicano-Mexicano Relations: Framework for Research. SSQ 63: 115-130.

396 Dodoo, F. N. A.; Pinon, G. 1994. Earnings Differences among Mexican Origin Population in the US: Nativity and Citizenship Explanations. SP 37: 293-305.

397 Donahue, J. J.; Heckman, J. J. 1991. Continuous vs. Episodic Change: Impact of Civil Rights Policy on Economic Status. JEL 29: 1603-1643.

398 Dutter, L. E. 1990. Theoretical Perspectives on Ethnic Political Behavior in the Soviet Union. JCR 34: 311-334.

399 Eckert, W. A. 1976. Applicability of the Ethos Theory to Specific Ethnic Groups and the Prediction of Urban Political Forms. UAQ 11: 357-390.

400 Education and Urban Society. 1986. Papers on the Education of Minorities. EAUS 18 (4).

401 Eisinger, P. 1974. Racial Differences in Protest Participation. APSR 68: 592-607.

402 Elgie, R. A. 1980. Industrialization and Racial Inequality within the South. SSQ 61: 458-472.

403 Ellison, C. G.; Powers, D. A. 1994. The Contact Hypothesis and Racial Attitudes among Black Americans. SSQ 75: 385-400.

404 Engstrom, R. L.; Barrilleaux, C. J. 1991. Native Americans and Cumulative Voting. SSQ 72: 388-393.

405 Enloe, C. H. 1976. Ethnicity and Militarization: Factors Shaping Roles of Police in Third World Nations. SICID 11: 25-38.

406 Eschbach, K. 1993. Changing Identification among American Indians and Alaska Natives. Demography 30: 635-652.

407 Feagin, J. R. 1973. Intertribal Attitudes among Native American Youth. SSQ 54: 117-131.

408 Featherman, D. L.; Hauser, R. M. 1976. Changes in Socioeconomic Stratification of the Races. AJPS 82: 621-651.

409 Ford, R. T. 1994. Boundaries of Race: Political Geography in Legal Analysis. HLR 107: 1841-1922.

410 Foster, L. S. 1984. Voting Rights Act: Political Modernization and New Southern Politics. Southern Studies 23: 266-288.

411 Frisbie, W. P.; Neidert, L. 1977. Inequality and the Relative Size of Minority Populations. AJS 82: 1007-1030.

412 Garcia, F. C. 1973. Orientations of Mexican-American and Anglo Children toward the US Political Community. SSQ 53: 814-829.

413 -. 1981. Political Integration of Mexican Immigrants: Naturalization Process. IMR 15: 608-625.

414 -. 1981. Yo Soy Mexicano: Self-Identity and Sociodemographic Correlates. SSQ 62: 88-98.

415 -. 1982. Ethnicity and Chicanos: Measurement of Ethnic Identification, Identity and Consciousness. HJBR 4: 295-314.

416 -. 1987. Political Integration of Mexican Immigrants. IMR 21: 372-389.

417 Gibson, J. L. 1995. Political Freedom of African-Americans: Contextual Analysis of Racial Attitudes, Political Tolerance, and Individual Liberty. PG 14: 571-600.

418 Giles, M. W.; Buckner, M. A. 1993. David Duke and the Black Threat. JOP 55: 702-713.

419 Giles, M. W.; Hertz, K. 1994. Racial Threat and Partisan Identification. APSR 88: 317-326.

420 Gilliam, F. D.; Whitby, K. J. 1989. Race, Class and Attitudes toward Social Welfare Spending: Ethclass Interpretation. SSQ 70: 88-100.

421 Glaser, J. M. 1994. Back to the Black Belt: Racial Environment and White Racial Attitudes. JOP 56: 21-41.

422 Greely, A. M. 1975. A Model for Ethnic Political Socialization. AJPS 19: 187-206.

423 Grofman, B.; Handley, L. 1989. Black Representation: Making Sense of Electoral Geography at Different Levels of Government. LSQ 14: 265-280.

424 Grofman, B.; Migalski, M. 1988. Return of the Native: Supply Elasticity of the American Indian Population. PC 57: 85-88.

425 Guinier, L. 1991. Triumph of Tokenism: The Voting Rights Act and Theory of Black Electoral Success. MLR 89: 1077-1154.

426 Hadley, C. D. 1994. Blacks in Southern Politics: Agenda for Research. JOP 56: 585-600.

427 Harrison, B.; Gorham, L. 1992. Growing Inequality in Black Wages and Emergence of an African-American Middle Class. JPAAM 11: 235-253.

428 Herring, C. 1989. Convergence, Polarization, or What? Racially-Based Changes in Attitudes. SQ 30: 267-282.

429 Hispanic Journal of Behavioral Sciences 1991. Papers on Ethnic Identity. HJBS 13 (2).

430 Inglehart, R.; Woodward, M. 1967. Language Conflicts and Political Community. CSSH 10: 27-45.

431 International Journal of Comparative Sociology. 1979. Papers on Ethnic Conflict. IJCS 20 (1/2).

432 -. 1992. Papers on Ethnicity and Nationalism. IJCS 33 (1/2).

433 International Social Science Journal. 1992. Papers on Ethnic Conflict Resolution. ISSR 13 (4).

434 Jackman, M. R. 1977. Prejudice, Tolerance and Attitudes toward Ethnic Groups. SSR 6: 145-169.

435 Jackson, J. S. 1973. Alienation and Black Political Participation. AJPS 23: 755-771.

436 Jalali, R.; Lipset, S. M. 1992. Racial and Ethnic Conflicts. PSCQ 107: 585-606.

437 Jones, M. H. 1992. Political Science and the Black Political Experience. NPSR 3: 25-29.

438 Journal of Asian and African Studies 1985. Papers on Ethnic Identities and Prejudice. JAAS 20 (3/4).

439 Journal of Commonwealth and Comparative Politics. 1983. Papers on the Nationality Crisis in Canada. JCACP 21 (1).

440 Journal of Political Science. 1991. Papers on Ethnic Nationalism and International Relations. JPS 19.

441 Journal of Social Issues. 1987. Papers on Black Employment. JSI 43 (1).

442 Karnig, A. K.; McClain, P. D. 1985. The New South and Black Economic and Political Development. WPQ 38: 537-550.

443 Keiser, R. A. 1993. Explaining African-American Political Empowerment: Windy City Politics. UAQ 29: 84-116.

444 Killian, L. M. 1984. Organization, Rationality and Spontaneity in the Civil Rights Movement. ASR 49: 770-783.

445 Kinder, D. R.; Kiewiet, D. R. 1981. Prejudice and Politics: Symbolic Racism vs. Racial Threats to the Good Life. JPSP 40: 414-431.

446 Kinder, D. R.; Rhodebeck, L. A. 1982. Continuities in Support for Racial Equality. POQ 46: 195-215.

447 Kohfeld, C. W.; Sprague, J. 1995. Racial Context and Voting Behavior in One-Party Urban Political Systems. PG 14: 543-570.

448 Kosmin, B. A.; Keysar, A. 1995. Party Political Preferences of US Hispanics. EARS 18: 336-347.

449 Krepps, M. B.; Caves, R. E. Bureaucrats and Indians: Principal Agent Relations and Efficient Management of Tribal Forest Resources. JEBAO 24: 133-155.

450 Kuo, W. H. 1979. The Study of Asian Americans. SQ 20: 279-290.

451 Laitin, D. D. 1993. The Game Theory of Language Regimes. IPSR 14: 227-240.

452 -. 1994. Tower of Babel as a Coordination Game: Political Linguistics in Ghana. APSR 88: 622-634.

453 Lamare, J. 1982. Political Integration of Mexican American Children. IMR 16: 169-182.

454 Latino Studies Journal. 1991. Papers on the Latino-Hispanic Ethnic Identity. Vol 2 (3).

455 Lieberson, S.; Dalto, G.; Johnston, M. E. 1975. Course of Mother Tongue Diversity in Nations. AJS 81: 34-61.

456 Lieberson, S.; Hansen, L. K. 1974. National Development, Mother Tongue Diversity and Comparative Study of Nations. ASR 39: 523-541.

457 Lien, P. 1994. Ethnicity and Political Participation: Asian and Mexican Americans. PB 16: 237-264.

458 Londregan, J.; Bienen, H.; van de Walle, N. 1995. Ethnicity and Leadership Succession in Africa. ISQ 39: 1-26.

459 Lyon, J. M. 1994. Herder Syndrome: A Comparative Study of Cultural Nationalism. EARS 17: 224-237.

460 Mair, P. 1994. Correlates of Consensus Democracy and Puzzle of Dutch Politics. WEP 17: 97-123.

461 McClain, P. D. 1993. The Changing Dynamics of Urban Politics: Black and Hispanic Municipal Employment. JOP 55: 399-414.

462 McClain, P. D.; Karnig, A. K. 1990. Black and Hispanic Socioeconomic and Political Competition. APSR 84: 535-545.

463 McCleskey, C.; Merrill, B. 1973. Mexican American Political Behavior in Texas. SSQ 53: 785-798.

464 McLemore, L. B. 1972. Toward a Theory of Black Politics: Black and Ethnic Models Revisited. JBS 2: 323-331.

465 Meadwell, H. 1989. Ethnic Nationalism and Collective Choice Theory. CPS 22: 139-154.

466 Merelman, R. M. 1994. Racial Conflict and Cultural Politics in the US. JOP 56: 1-20.

467 Miller, A. H. 1971. Ethnicity and Political Behavior. WPQ 24: 483-500.

468 Miller, J. 1995. Why Was the Post-Communist Ethnic Revival So Vigorous? Australian Journal of Politics and History 41: 90-103.

469 Mitra, S. K. 1995. Rational Politics of Cultural Nationalism. BJPS 25: 57-78.

470 Murdock, M. M. 1983. Political Attachment among Native Americans and the National Political System. SSJ 20: 41-58.

471 Nagel, J. 1982. Political Mobilization of Native Americans. SSJ 19: 37-45.

472 -. 1993. Ethnic Nationalism: Politics, Ideology and the World Order. IJCS 34: 103-112.

473 -. 1995. American Indian Ethnic Renewal: Politics and the Resurgence of Identity. ASR 60: 947-965.

474 Nagel, J.; Olzak, S. 1982. Ethnic Mobilization. SOCP 30: 127-143.

475 Nair, K. S. 1983. Structural Pluralism and Ethnic Boundaries. EARS 6: 395-409.

476 Nakanishi, D. T. 1986. Asian American Politics: Agenda for Research. AMASJ 12: 1-27.

477 Nelson, D. C. 1979. Ethnicity and Socioeconomic Status as Sources of Participation: Ethnic Political Culture. APSR 73: 1024-1038.

478 Newman, S. 1991. Does Modernization Breed Ethnic Conflict? WP 43: 451-478.

479 -. 1992. Rise and Decline of Scottish National Party: Ethnic Politics in Post-Industrial Environment. EARS 15: 1-35.

480 Nielson, F. 1980. The Flemish Movement in Belgium after World War II. ASR 45: 76-94.

481 -. 1985. Toward a Theory of Ethnic Solidarity in Modern Societies. ASR 50: 133-149.

482 Olsen, M. C. 1970. Social and Political Participation of Blacks. ASR 35: 682-697.

483 Olzak, S. 1983. Ethnic Ties and Political Mobilization. AJS 89: 166-180.

484 Olzak, S.; Shanahan, S.; West, E. 1994. School Desegregation, Interracial Exposure and Antibusing Activity. AJS 100: 196-241.

485 O'Neill, J. 1990. The Role of Human Capital in Earnings Differences between Black and White Men. JEP 4 (4): 25-45.

486 Ortiz, I. D. 1980. Political Economy of Chicano Urban Politics. PLS 11: 41-54.

487 Pachon, H. P. 1987. Naturalization: Determinants and Process in the Hispanic Community. IMR 21: 299-310.

488 Padilla, A. M.; Lindholm, K. J. 1984. Hispanic Behavioral Science Research. HJPS 6: 13-32.

489 Padilla, Y. C. 1990. Social Science Theory on the Mexican-American Experience. SOCSER 64: 261-275.

490 Parenti, M. 1967. Ethnic Politics and Persistence of Ethnic Identification. APSR 61: 717-726.

491 Plural Societies. 1991. Papers on Regionalism, Minorities and Civil Society. PLS 21 (1/2).

492 Polinard, J.; Wrinkle, R. D.; de la Garza, R. O. 1984. Attitudes of Mexican Americans toward Irregular Mexican Immigration. IMR 18: 782-799.

493 Pool, J. 1970. National Development and Language Diversity. Sociologische Gids 17: 86-101.

494 Portes, A. 1984. The Rise of Ethnicity: Determinants of Ethnic Perceptions among Cuban Exiles in Miami. ASR 49: 383-397.

495 Portes, A.; Mozo, R. 1985. The Political Adaptation Process of Cubans and Other Ethnic Minorities. IMR 19: 35-63.

496 Publius 1977. Papers on Federalism and Ethnicity. Vol 7 (4).

497 -. 1988. Papers on Bicommunal Societies. Vol 18 (2).

498 Raden, D. 1994. Are Symbolic Racism and Traditional Prejudice Part of a Contemporary Authoritarian Attitude Syndrome? PB 16: 365-384.

499 Ragin, C. C. 1979. Ethnic Political Mobilization: Welsh Case. ASR 44: 619-635.

500 Reed, A. 1991. Race and Disruption of the New Deal Coalition. UAQ 27: 326-333.

501 Regional Politics and Policy. 1993. Papers on the Territorial Management of Ethnic Conflict. Vol 3 (1).

502 Ross, J. A. 1978. Test of Ethnicity and Economics as Contrasting Explanations of Collective Political Behavior. PLS 9: 69-82.

503 Ross, M. H. 1975. Political Alienation, Participation and Ethnicity. AJPS 19: 291-311.

504 Ryan, S. 1988. Explaining Ethnic Conflict: The Neglected International Dimension. RIS 14: 161-178.

505 Santiago, A. M.; Wilder, M. G. 1987. Residential Segregation and Links to Minority Poverty: Latinos. SOCP 38: 492-515.

506 Shull, S. A.; Gleiber, D. W. 1994. Testing a Dynamic Process of Policy Making in Civil Rights. SSI 31: 53-68.

507 Shultz, R. H. 1995. State Disintegration and Ethnic Conflict. ANNALS 541: 75-88.

508 Sigelman, C. K., et al. 1995. Understanding Racial Bias in Political Perceptions. AJPS 39: 243-265.

509 Signs. 1989. Papers on Race, Ethnicity and Class in Women's Lives. Vol 14 (4).

510 Smith, J. P.; Welch, F. R. 1989. Black Economic Progress after Myrdal. JEL 27: 519-564.

511 Smith, R. C. 1984. Black Appointed Officials: A Neglected Area of Research. JBS 14: 360-388.

512 Sniderman, P. M.; Tetlock, P. E. 1986. Reflections on American Racism. JSI 42: 173-187.

513 Snipp, C. M. 1986. The Changing Political and Economic Status of the American Indians. AJEAS 45: 145-157

514 Social Forces. 1990. Papers on Race and Ethnic Relations. SF 69 (1).

515 Social Science Quarterly. 1984. Papers on Mexican-American Experience. SSQ 65 (2).

516 -. 1984. Papers on Race and Ethnicity. SSQ 65: 112-180, and 71 (4).

517 Steiner, J. 1981. The Consociational Theory and Beyond. CP 13: 339-354.

518 Studlar, D. T. 1978. Policy Voting in Britain: Colored Immigration Issues. APSR 72: 46-64.

519 Thornton, R. 1981. Demographic Antecedents of a Revitalization Movement: Population Change, Population Size and the 1890 Ghost Dance. ASR 45: 88-96.

520 Turner, C. B.; Wilson, W. J. 1976. Dimensions of Racial Ideology: Urban Black Attitudes. JSI 32: 139-152.

521 Uhlaner, C. J.; Cain, B. E.; Kiewiet, D. R. 1989. Political Participation of Ethnic Minorities. PB 11: 195-231.

522 Urban Affairs Quarterly. 1984. Papers on Race in American Cities. UAQ 20 (2).

523 -. 1991. Papers on Deracialization in Politics. UAQ 27 (2).

524 Walton, H.; McLemore, L. B.; Gray, V. 1992. The Problem of Preconceived Perceptions in Black Urban Politics. NPSR 3: 217-229.

525 Wasserman, I. M. 1989. Prohibition and Ethnocultural Conflict: Missouri Prohibition Referendum of 1918. SSQ 70: 886-901.

526 Welch, S.; Conner, J. C.; Steinman, M. 1973. Political Participation among Mexican Americans. SSQ 53: 799-813.

527 Welch, S.; Foster, L. S. 1987. Class and Conservatism in the Black Community. APQ 15: 445-470.

528 Welch, S.; Sigelman, L. 1993. Politics of Hispanic Americans. SSQ 74: 76-94.

529 Wilson, E. J. 1985. Why Political Scientists Don't Study Black Politics, but Historians and Sociologists Do. PS 18: 600-607.

530 Wittberg, P. 1984. Effects of Local Authority on Neighborhood Attitudes: Comparison of Black and White Urbanities. UAQ 20: 185-200.

ORGANIZATIONAL BEHAVIOR

1 Aberbach, J. D.; Rockman, B. A. 1995. Political Views of US Senior Federal Executives. JOP 57: 838-852.
2 Administration and Society. 1975. Papers on Organizational Democracy. AAS 7 (1).
3 Administrative Science Quarterly. 1969. Papers on Experimental Organizations. ASQ 14 (2).
4 -. 1983. Papers on Organizational Culture. ASQ 28 (3).
5 -. 1992. Papers on Organizational Rewards. ASQ 37 (2).
6 American Journal of Sociology. 1988. Papers on Organizations and Institutions. AJS 94 (Sup).
7 Annals. 1977. Papers on Industrial Democracy. ANNALS 431.
8 -. 1983. Papers on Implementing Change in Government. ANNALS 466.
9 Aoki, M. 1990. Toward an Economic Model of the Japanese Firm. JEL 28: 1-27.
10 Arai, K. 1995. Organizational Loyalty. Hitotsubashi Journal of Economics 36: 21-32.
11 Ashford, S. J. 1988. Individual Strategies for Coping with Stress during Organizational Transitions. JABS 24: 19-36.
12 Baxter, V. 1989. The Process of Change in Public Organizations. SQ 30: 283-304.
13 Bendor, J. 1995. A Model of Muddling Through. APSR 89: 819-840.
14 Brudney, J. L.; Hebert, F. T. 1987. State Agencies and Their Environments. JOP 49: 186-206.
15 Cappelli, P. 1993. Are Skill Requirements Rising? Evidence from Production and Clerical Jobs. ILRR 46: 515-530.
16 Cohen, M. D.; March, J. G.; Olson, J. P. 1972. A Garbage Can Model of Organizational Choice. ASQ 17: 1-25.
17 Condrey, S. E. 1995. Reforming Human Resource Management Systems: Exploring the Importance of Organizational Trust. ARPA 25: 341-354.
18 Crystal, G. S. 1991. Why CEO Compensation Is so High. CMR 34: 9-29.
19 Dunseath, J.; Beehr, T. A.; King, D. 1995. The Job Stress-Social Support Buffering Hypothesis. RPPA 15: 60-83.
20 Ellis, R. J. 1991. Explaining Charismatic Leadership in Organizations. JTP 3: 305-320.
21 Gerber, E. R.; Jackson, J. E. 1993. Endogenous Preferences and the Study of Institutions. APSR 87: 639-656.
22 Gilboy, J. A. 1995. Regulatory and Administrative Agency Behavior: Accommodation, Amplification and Assimilation. LAP 17: 3-22.
23 Golembiewski, R. T. 1970. Planned Change in Organizational Style. ASQ 15: 79-83.
24 -. 1972. Building New Work Relationships. JABS 8: 135-148.
25 Golembiewski, R. T.; Munzenrider, R. F.; Carter, D. 1983. Phases of Progressive Burn-Out and Their Worksite Covariates. JABS 19: 461-482.
26 Gradstein, M.; Nitzan, S.; Paroush, J. 1990. Collective Decision Making and Limits on an Organization's Size. PC 66: 279-291.
27 Greve, H. R. 1995. Jumping Ship: Diffusion of Strategy Abandonment. AAS 40: 444-473.
28 Gul, F.; Lundholm, R. 1995. Endogenous Timing and Clustering of Agents' Decisions. JPE 103: 1039-1066.
29 Heimann, C. F. L. 1993. Understanding the Challenger Disaster: Organizational Structure and Design of Reliable Systems. APSR 87: 421-438.
30 Hougland, J. G. 1987. Criteria for Client Evaluation of Public Programs. SSQ 68: 386-394.
31 Hummon, N. P.; Doreian, P.; Teuter, K. 1975. A Structural Control Model of Organizational Change. ASR 40: 813-824.
32 International Political Science Review. 1984. Papers on Industrial Democracy. ISSJ 36 (2).
33 International Review of Administrative Sciences. 1995. Papers on Reengineering the Public Sector. IRAS 47 (3).
34 International Social Science Journal. 1977. Papers on the Study of International Organizations. ISSJ 29 (1).
35 Jos, P. H.; Tompkins, M. E. 1995. Administrative Practice and the Waning Promise of Professionalism for Public Administration. ARPA 25: 207-230.
36 Journal of Applied Behavioral Science. 1974. Papers on Organizational Development Theory. JABS 10 (4).
37 -. 1991. Papers on Organization Research Methods. JABS 27 (3).
38 -. 1991. Papers on Organizations. JABS 27 (4).
39 -. 1992. Papers on Intervention in Organizations. JABS 28 (1).
40 -. 1994. Papers on Authority and Organizations. JABS 30 (1).
41 -. 1995. Papers on Managing Diversity. JABS 31 (2).
42 Kaufmann, C. D. 1994. Psychological Explanations of Political Decision Making. ISQ 38: 557-586.
43 Keohane, R. O.; Martin, L. L. 1995. The Promise of Institutionalist Theory. IS 20: 5-93.
44 Khalil, E. L. 1995. Organizations vs. Institutions. JITE 151: 445-466.
45 Koelble, T. A. 1995. New Institutionalism in Political Science and Sociology. CP 27: 231-243.
46 Lahno, B. 1995. Trust, Reputation and Exit in Exchange Relationships. JCR 39: 495-510.

47 Lebovic, J. H. 1995. How Organizations Learn: US Government Estimates of Foreign Military Spending. AJPS 39: 835-863.

48 Le Grand, J. 1991. Theory of Government Failure. BJPS 21: 423-442.

49 Leifer, R. 1989. Understanding Organizational Transformation Using Dissipate Structure Model. HR 42: 899-916.

50 Lovaglia, M. J., et al. 1995. Negotiated Exchanges in Social Networks. SF 74: 123-156.

51 March, J. G.; Olson, J. P. 1984. New Institutionalism: Organizational Factors in Political Life. APSR 78: 734-749.

52 Masuch, M., Lepontin, P. 1989. Beyond Garbage Cans: An AI Model of Organizational Choice. ASQ 34: 38-67.

53 McGrath, P. 1994. Organizational Decline in Public Service. Administration 41: 362-384.

54 Moe, T. M. 1984. The New Economics of Organization. AJPS 28: 734-749.

55 -. 1991. Politics and the Theory of Organization. JOLEAO 7: 106-129.

56 Neary, H. M.; Winter, R. A. 1995. Output Shares in Bilateral Agency Contracts. JET 66: 609-614.

57 Ott, J. S.; Shafritz, J. M. 1994. Organizational Incompetence. PAR 54: 370-377.

58 Pacific Sociological Review. 1982. Papers on the Sociology of Organizations. PACSR 25 (2).

59 Public Administration. 1995. Papers on British Public Administration. PA 73 (1).

60 Public Administration Review. 1978. Papers on Governmental Productivity. PAR 38 (1).

61 Public Personnel Management. 1985. Papers on Governmental Productivity. PPM 14 (4).

62 Rainey, H. G.; Backoff, R. W.; Levine, C. H. 1976. Comparing Public and Private Organizations. PAR 36: 233-246.

63 Rothenberg, L. S. 1988. Organizational Maintenance and the Retention Decision in Groups. APSR 82: 1129-1152.

64 Scott, W. R. 1987. Adolescence of Institutional Theory. ASQ 32: 493-511.

65 Seiyama, K. 1986. Review of Mathematical Models of Formal Organizations. JMS 12: 71-96.

66 Skvoretz, J. 1984. Career Mobility as a Poisson Process: Career Dynamics in the Office of Comptroller of the Currency. SSR 13: 198-220.

67 Sociological Quarterly. 1977. Papers on Organizational Analysis. SQ 18 (1).

68 Spybey, T. 1984. Frames of Meaning: Rationality in Organizational Cultures. AS 27: 311-322.

69 Thompson, F. 1981. Utility Maximizing Behavior in Organized Anarchies. PC 36: 17-32.

70 Wallace, J. E. 1995. Organizational and Professional Commitment in Professional and Nonprofessional Organizations. ASQ 40: 228-255.

Administration

71 American Behavioral Scientist. 1994. Papers on Measuring Organizations. ABS 37 (7).

72 American Review of Public Administration. 1991. Papers on Outcome Assessment. ARPA 21 (3).

73 Annals. 1994. Papers on Dismissal. ANNALS 536.

74 Aucoin, P. 1990. Administrative Reform in Public Management. Governance 3: 115-137.

75 Baker, P. M., et al. 1988. Promotion Interest and Willingness to Sacrifice. JABS 24: 61-80.

76 Ballou, D.; Podgursky, M. 1993. Teachers' Attitudes toward Merit Pay. ILRR 47: 50-61.

77 Barth, E. 1994. Wages and Organizational Factors: Why Do Some Establishments Pay More? AS 37: 253-268.

78 Bawn, K. 1995. Political Control vs. Expertise: Congressional Choices about Administrative Procedures. APSR 89: 62-73.

79 Berman, E. M. 1994. Implementing Total Quality Management in State Governments. SALGR 26: 46-53.

80 Bozeman, B.; Ruscio, K. P. 1980. Administering Public Policy: A Bibliography. PSJ 9: 481-521.

81 Brehm, J.; Gates, S. 1993. Evaluating Models of Supervision on Police Behavior. AJPS 37: 555-581.

82 Daley, D. M. 1995. Pay for Performance and the Senior Executive Service: Attitudes about Success of Civil Service Reform. ARPA 25: 355-372.

83 De Groot, H. 1988. Decentralization Decisions in Bureaucracies as Principal-Agent Problem. JPUBE 36: 323-337.

84 Epstein, D.; O'Halloran, S. 1994. Administrative Procedures, Information and Agency Discretion. AJPS 38: 697-722.

85 Fox, F. V.; Ataw, B. M. 1979. The Trapped Administrator: Effects of Job Insecurity and Policy Resistance on Commitment to a Course of Action. ASQ 24: 449-471.

86 Gabris, G.T.; Mitchell, K. 1988. Impact of Merit Raise Scores on Employee Attitudes: Matthew Effect of Performance Appraisal. PPM 17: 369-386

87 Garen, J. E. 1994. Executive Compensation and Principal-Agent Theory. JPE 102: 1175-1199.

88 Golembiewski, R. T. 1977. Critique of Democratic Administration. APSR 71: 1488-1507.

89 -. 1978. Empirical Literature on Flexible Work Hours. Academy of Management Review 3: 837-853.

90 -. 1981. The Ideational Poverty of Two Modes of Coupling Democracy and Administration. IJPA 3: 1-65.

91 -. 1990. Positive and Practical Public Management. AAS 21: 493-500.

92 Grendstad, G.; Selle, P. 1995. Cultural Theory and the New Institutionalism. JTP 7: 5-28.

93 Industrial and Labor Relations Review 1983. Papers on Behavioral Research in Industrial Relations. ILRR 36 (3).

94 -. 1990. Papers on Compensation Policies. ILRR 43 (3).

95 Ingraham, P.; Ban, C. 1988. Politics and Merit: Can They Meet? RPPA 8: 7-19.

96 International Political Science Review. 1993. Papers on Public Administration and Political Change. IPSR 14 (4).

97 International Review of Administrative Sciences. 1986. Papers on Administrative Responsiveness. IRAS 52 (1).

98 -. 1986. Papers on Cultural Differences and Development Administration. IRAS 52 (4).

99 -. 1993. Papers on Public Sector Productivity. IRAS 59 (1).

100 Journal of Health and Human Resources Administration. 1984. Papers on Psychological Burnout. Vol 7 (Fall), 1986 9 (Summer), 1990 13 (1-2) and 1993 16 (Winter-Spring).

101 Journal of Social Issues. 1980. Papers on Public Productivity and Satisfaction. JSI 36 (4).

102 Journal of State Government. 1989. Papers on Governors as Managers. JSG 62 (4).

103 Kets de Vries, M. F. R. 1992. Motivating Role of Envy: Management Theory. AAS 24: 41-60.

104 Krauze, T.; Slomczynski, K. M. 1985. How Far to Meritocracy? SF 63: 623-642.

105 Lavigna, R. J. 1992. Predicting Job Performance from Background. PPM 21: 347-362.

106 Leiter, M. P.; Clark, D.; Durup, J. 1994. Distinct Models of Burnout and Commitment in the Military. JABS 30: 63-82.

107 Liou, K. T. 1994. Effect of Professional Orientation on Job Stress. RPPA 14: 52-63.

108 Lovrich, N. P. 1987. Merit Pay and Motivation in the Public Work Force. RPPA 7: 54-71.

109 Macey, J. R. 1992. Organizational Design and Political Control of Administrative Agencies. JOLEAO 8: 93-100.

110 McCubbins, M. D.; Noll, R. G.; Weingast, B. R. 1987. Administrative Procedures as Instruments of Political Control. JOLEAO 3: 243-274.

111 -. 1990. Positive and Normative Models of Due Process: An Integrative Approach to Administrative Procedures. JOLEAO 6: 307-330.

112 Noel, J. J. 1974. The Administrative Sector of Social Systems. SF 52: 549-558.

113 Nolan, P. D. 1979. Size and Administrative Intensity in Nations. ASR 44: 110-125.

114 Peters, B. G.; Hood, C. 1995. Erosion and Variety of Pay for High Public Office. Governance 8: 171-194.

115 Petersen, T. 1993. Economics of Organization: Principle-Agent Relationship. AS 36: 277-293.

116 Policy Studies Journal. 1980. Papers on Administrative Reform. PSJ 9 (8).

117 Policy Studies Review. 1986. Papers on Performance Management. PSR 6 (1).

118 Prewitt, L. B.; Phillips, J. D.; Yasin, K. 1991. Merit Pay in Academia. PPM 20: 409-418.

119 Public Administration and Development. 1993. Papers on Reforming Public Sector Management in Transitional Economies. PAAD 13 (4).

120 Public Administration Review. 1974. Papers on the Merit Principle. PAR 34 (5).

121 Review of Public Personnel Administration. 1986. Papers on Why Merit Plans Are Not Working. RPPA 7 (1).

122 -. 1988. Papers on Politics and Merit. RPPA 8 (2).

123 -. 1988. Papers on Civil Service. RPPA 8 (3).

124 -. 1990. Papers on Public Employee Attitudes and Motivations. RPPA 10 (3).

125 Ritzer, G. 1989. The Sociology of Work: A Metatheoretical Analysis. SF 67: 593-604.

126 Rotemberg, J. J. 1994. Human Relations in the Workplace. JPE 102: 684-717.

127 Rubin, H. J. 1989. Measures of Work Satisfaction among Economic Development Practitioners. SI 59: 165-189.

128 Schay, B. W. 1988. Effects of Performance Contingent Pay on Attitudes. PPM 17: 237-250.

129 Self, P. 1986. What's Gone Wrong with Public Administration. PAAD 6: 329-338.

130 Simpson, I. H. 1989. The Sociology of Work. SF 67: 563-581.

131 Sossin, L. 1993. Politics of Discretion: Toward a Critical Theory of Public Administration. CPA 36: 364-391.

132 State and Local Government Review. 1985. Papers on Stat Management Approaches. SALGR 17 (3).

133 Taylor, R. L.; Hunnicutt, G. G.; Keeffe, M. J. 1991. Merit Pay in Academia. RPPA 11: 50-65.

134 Thayer, F. C. 1987. Performance Appraisal and Merit Pay Systems: Disasters Multiply. RPPA 7: 36-53.

135 University of Chicago Law Review. 1990. Papers on Administering the Administrative State. UCLR 57 (2).

136 Wade, L. L. 1979. Public Administration, Public Choice and Pathos of Reform. ROP 41: 344-374.

137 Werlin, H. H. 1988. Theory of Political Elasticity: Clarifying Concepts in Micro-Macro Administration. AAS 20: 46-70.

138 Whicker, M. L.; Strickland, R. A.; Olshfski, D. 1993. Troublesome Cleft: Public Administration and Political Science. PAR 53: 531-541.

139 Wilson, P. A. 1994. Power, Politics and Other Reasons Why Senior Executives Leave Federal Government. PAR 54: 12-19.

140 Wise, L. R. 1988. Dimensions of Public Sector Pay Policies. RPPA 8: 61-83.

141 Yemin, E. 1993. Labour Relations in Public Service. International Labour Review 132: 469-490.

142 Zenger, T. R. 1992. Why Do Employers Only Reward Extreme Performance? Relationships among Performance, Pay and Turnover. ASQ 37: 198-219.

Bureaucratic Behavior

143 American Behavioral Scientist. 1979. Papers on Bureaucratic Maladies. ABS 22 (5).

144 Banks, J. S. 1989. Agency Budgets, Cost Information and Auditing. AJPS 33: 670-699.

145 Bendor, J. 1988. Formal Models of Bureaucracy. BJPS 18: 353-396.

146 Bendor, J.; Moe, T. M. 1985. Adaptive Model of Bureaucratic Politics. APSR 79: 755-774.

147 Bendor, J.; Taylor, S.; Van Gaalen, R. 1987. Politicians, Bureaucrats and Asymmetric Information. AJPS 31: 796-828.

148 Berg, B. 1984. Public Choice, Pluralism and Scarcity: Implications for Bureaucratic Behavior. AAS 16: 71-82.

149 Blais, A.; Dion, S. 1990. Are Bureaucrats Budget Maximizers? The Niskanen Model and Its Critics. Polity 22: 655-674.

150 Breton, A. 1995. Organizational Hierarchies and Bureaucracies. EJPE 11: 411-440.

151 Clarke, C. J. 1983. The End of Bureaucratization? Cross National Evidence. SSQ 64: 127-135.

152 Conybeare, J. A. C. 1984. Bureaucracy, Monopoly and Competition: The Budget Maximizing Model of Bureaucracy. AJPS 28: 479-502.

153 Eavey, C. L.; Miller, G. J. 1984. Bureaucratic Agenda Control. APSR 78: 719-733.

154 Education and Urban Society. 1981. Papers on Bureaucracy and Institutional Change. EAUS 13 (4).

155 Fantini, M. D. 1981. Effecting Change in Educational Bureaucracies. EAUS 13: 399-416.

156 Finlay, W., et al. 1995. Organizational Structure and Job Satisfaction: Do Bureaucratic Organizations Produce More Satisfied Employees? AAS 27: 427-449.

157 Frisbie, P. W. 1975. Measuring the Degree of Bureaucratization at the Societal Level. SF 54: 563-573.

158 Greene, K. V. 1984. Sequential Referenda and Bureaucratic Man. PC 43: 77-82.

159 Gryski, G. S.; DeCottis, A. R. 1981. Length of Service as an Influence on Federal Bureaucratic Attitudes and Behavior. JPS 9: 17-19.

160 Hamilton, G. G.; Biggart, N. W. 1985. Why People Obey: Theoretical Observations on Power and Obedience in Complex Organizations. SP 28: 3-28.

161 Hammond, T. H.; Miller, G. J. 1985. Social Choice Perspective on Expertise and Authority in Bureaucracy. AJPS 29: 1-28.

162 Headrick, T. E. 1992. Expert Policy Analysis and Bureaucratic Politics: Searching for Causes of the 1987 Stock Market Crash. LAP 14: 313-336.

163 Hill, L. B. 1991. Who Governs the American Administrative State? A Bureaucratic-Centered Image of Governance. JPART 1: 261-294.

164 Hitchcock, R. K.; Holm, J. D. 1993. Bureaucratic Domination in Hunter-Gatherer Societies. DAC 24: 305-338.

165 International Review of Administrative Sciences 1989. Papers on Administration without Bureaucratization. IRAS 55 (2).

166 Jenkins, B.; Gray, A. 1983. Bureaucratic Politics and Power. POLST 31: 177-193.

167 Journal of Applied Behavioral Science. 1980. Papers on Contemporary Bureaucracy. JABS 16 (3).

168 Kearney, R. C.; Sinha, C. 1988. Professionalism and Bureaucratic Responsiveness. PAR 48: 571-579.

169 Kim, P. S. 1994. Theoretical Overview of Representative Bureaucracy. IRAS 60: 385-398.

170 Laband, D. N. 1983. Federal Budget Cuts: Bureaucrats Trim the Meat, Not Fat. PC 41: 311-314.

171 Lewis, G. B. 1990. Comparing Attitudes of Bureaucrats and Ordinary People. PAR 50: 220-227.

172 McGuire, T. G. 1981. Budget-Maximizing Government Agencies. PC 36: 313-322.
173 McKee, M.; Wintrobe, R. 1993. Decline of Organizations and the Rise of Administrators: Parkinson's Law JPUBE 51: 309-327.
174 Meier, K. J. 1975. Representative Bureaucracy. APSR 69: 526-542.
175 Nachmias, D. 1984. Are Federal Bureaucrats Conservative? A Modest Test of a Popular Image. SSQ 65: 1080-1087.
176 Niskanen, W. A. 1975. Bureaucrats and Politicians. JOLE 18: 617-660.
177 Peters, B. G. 1979. Bureaucracy, Politics and Public Policy. CP 11: 339-358.
178 -. 1981. The Problem of Bureaucratic Government. JOP 43: 56-82.
179 Remmer, K. L.; Merkx, G. W. 1982. Bureaucratic Authoritarianism Revisited. LARR 17: 3-50.
180 Rhodes, E. 1994. Do Bureaucratic Politics Matter? Some Disconfirming Findings from the US Navy. WP 47: 1-41.
181 Rothschild-Whitt, J. 1979. Collectivist Organization: Alternative to Rational Bureaucratic Models. ASR 44: 509-527.
182 Rowat, D. C. 1990. Comparing Bureaucrats in Developed and Developing Countries. IRAS 56: 211-236.
183 Russett, B.; Monsen, R. J. 1975. Bureaucracy and Polyarchy as Predictors of Performance. CPS 8: 5-31.
184 Sabatier, P. A.; Loomis, J.; McCarthy, C. 1995. Hierarchical Controls, Professional Norms, Local Constituencies and Budget Maximization: US Forest Service. AJPS 39: 204-242.
185 Scholz, J. T.; Twombly, J.; Headrick, B. 1991. Street Level Political Controls over Federal Bureaucracy. APSR 85: 829-850.
186 Sigelman, L. 1972. Do Modern Bureaucracies Dominate Less Developed Politics? Imbalance Thesis. APSR 66: 525-528.
187 -. 1974. Bureaucratic Development and Dominance: Test of the Imbalance Thesis. WPQ 27: 303-313.
188 Sloan, J. W. 1978. US Policy Responses to the Mexican Revolution: The Bureaucratic Politics Model. JOLAS 10: 283-308.
189 Spiller, P. T.; Urbiztondo, S. 1994. Political Approaches vs. Career Civil Servants: Multiple Principals Theory of Political Bureaucracies. EJPE 10: 465-498.
190 Stanbury, W.; Thompson, F. 1995. Political Economy of Government Waste. PAR 55: 418-428.
191 Sutton, J. R. 1990. Bureaucrats and Entrepreneurs: Institutional Responses to Deviant Children in the US, 1890-1920s. AJS 95: 1367-1400.
192 Urban, M. E. 1984. Bureaucratic Ideology in the US and the Soviet Union. AAS 14: 139-174.
193 Villaume, A. C. 1978. Parkinson's Law and the US Bureau of Prisons. CC 2: 209-214.
194 Wood, B. D.; Waterman, R. W. 1991. Dynamics of Political Control of the Bureaucracy. APSR 85: 801-828.
195 -. 1993. The Dynamics of Political-Bureaucratic Adaption. AJPS 37: 497-528.

Crisis Decision Making

196 Allison, G. T. 1969. Conceptual Models of the Cuban Missile Crisis. APSR 63: 689-718.
197 American Behavioral Scientist. 1970. Papers on Behavior in Disasters. ABS 13 (3).
198 Banks, J. S. 1990. Equilibrium Behavior in Crisis Bargaining Games. AJPS 34: 599-614.
199 Bendor, J.; Hammond, T. H. 1992. Rethinking Allison's Models. APSR 86: 301-322.
200 Brecher, M. 1979. State Behavior in International Crisis. JCR 23: 446-480.
201 Brecher, M.; James, P. 1988. Patterns of Crisis Management. JCR 32: 426-456.
202 Cimbala, S. J. 1992. Behavioral Modification and the Cuban Missile Crisis: From Brinkmanship to Disaster Avoidance. AC 13: 252-284.
203 Contemporary Crises. 1990. Papers on Crisis Management. CC 14 (4).
204 European Journal of Political Research. 1984. Papers on the Management of Economic Crises. EJPR 12 (2).
205 Fearon, J. D. 1994. Signaling vs. Balance of Power and Interests: Test of a Crisis Bargaining Model. JCR 38: 236-269.
206 Fraser, N. M.; Hipel, K. W. 1982. Dynamic Modeling of the Cuban Missile Crisis. CMAPS 6: 1-18.
207 Glad, B. 1989. Personality, Political and Group Process Variables in Foreign Policy Decision Making: Carter and the Iranian Hostage Crisis. IPSR 10: 35-62.
208 Guttieri, K.; Wallace, M. D.; Suedfeld, P. 1995. The Integrative Complexity of American Decision Makers in Cuban Missile Crisis. JCR 39: 595-621.
209 Hart, P.; Rosenthal, U.; Kouzmin, A. 1993. Crisis Decision Making: Centralization Thesis Revisited. AAS 25: 12-46.
210 Hatzenbuehler, R. L.; Ivie, R. L. 1980. Justifying the War of 1812: A Model of Congressional Behavior in Early War Crises. SSH 4: 453-478.
211 James, P.; Harvey, F. 1992. Superpower Rivalry in International Crises. JOP 54: 25-53.
212 James, P.; Hristoulas, A. 1994. Domestic Politics and Foreign Policy: Evaluating a Model of Crisis Activity for the US. JOP 56: 327-348.
213 Jerusalem Journal. 1978. Papers on Crisis Behavior. JJ 3 (2/3).
214 Koopman, C.; Snyder, J.; Jervis, R. 1990. Theory Driven vs. Data Driven Assessment in a Crisis. JCR 34: 694-722.
215 Langlois, J. P. 1991. Rational Deterrence and Crisis Stability. AJPS 35: 801-832.
216 Leng, R. J. 1983. Coercive Bargaining in Recurrent Crises. JCR 27: 379-419.
217 Leng, R. J.; Walker, S. G. 1982. Comparing Two Studies of Crisis Bargaining. JCR 26: 571-591.
218 Mor, B. D. 1995. Crisis Initiation and Misperception. JTP 7: 351-358.
219 Morrow, J. D. 1989. Capabilities, Uncertainty and Resolve: Limited Information Model of Crisis Bargaining. APSR 33: 941-972.
220 Oneal, J. R. 1988. The Rationality of Decision Making during International Crises. Polity 20: 598-622.
221 Orbis. 1986. Papers on Crisis Decision Making. Vol 30 (1).
222 Powell, R. 1987. Crisis Bargaining, Escalation and MAD. APSR 81: 717-735.
223 -. 1989. Crisis Stability in the Nuclear Age. APSR 83: 61-76.
224 Public Administration Review. 1984. Papers on Emergency Management. PAR 45: Jan Special Issue.
225 Seeger, J. C. 1995. Crisis Research. ISN 20: 17-22.
226 Silver, A. 1971. Social and Ideological Bases of British Elite Reactions to Domestic Crisis in 1829-1832. PAS 1: 179-202.
227 Smith, S. 1980. Allison and the Cuban Missile Crisis: Bureaucratic Politics Model of Foreign Policy Decision Making. Millennium 9: 21-40.
228 Steiner, M. 1977. Elusive Essence of Decision: A Critical Comparison of Allison's and Snyder's Decision Making Approaches. ISQ 21: 389-422.
229 Stoll, R. J. 1983. A Computer Simulation of Government Behavior during Serious Disputes. SAG 14: 179-200.
230 Suedfeld, P.; Granatstein, J. L. 1995. Leader Complexity in Personal and Professional Crises: Concurrent and Retrospective Information Processing. PP 16: 509-522.

231 Verbeek, B. 1994. Do Individual and Group Beliefs Matter? British Decision Making during the
1956 Suez Crisis. CAC 29: 307-332.

Government Size

232 Abizadeh, S.; Basilevsky, A. 1990. Measuring the
Size of Government. PF 45: 353-377.

233 Abizadeh, S.; Yousefi, M. 1988. Empirical Reexamination of Wagner's Law. EL 26: 169-173.

234 -. 1988. Growth of Government Expenditure:
Canada. PFQ 16: 78-100.

235 Abrams, B. A.; Dougan, W. R. 1986. Effects of
Constitutional Restraints on Government Spending. PC 49: 101-116.

236 Afxentious, P. C. 1986. Wagner's Law: Cyprus. EN
2: 158-172.

237 American Behavioral Scientist. 1974. Papers on
the American Welfare State. ABS 17 (4).

238 Anderson, G. M.; Tollison, R. D. 1988. Legislative Monopoly and the Size of Government. SEJ
54: 529-545.

239 Bairam, E. I. 1995. Level of Aggression, Variable Elasticity and Wagner's Law. EL 48: 341-344.

240 Bartlett, B. 1994. How Excessive Government
Killed Ancient Rome. CJ 14: 287-304.

241 Bennett, J. T.; DiLorenzo, T. J. 1981. Underground Government: Subverting Constraints on
Public Sector Expansion. JSPES 6: 219-234.

242 Bernholz, P. 1986. Growth of Government, Economic Growth and Individual Freedom. JITE 142: 661-
683.

243 Berry, W. D.; Lowery, D. 1984. The Growing Cost
of Government. SSQ 65: 735-749.

244 -. 1984. Measurement of Government Size. JOP 46:
1193-1206.

245 -. 1987. Explaining Size of Public Sector:
Responsive and Excessive Government Interpretations. JOP 49: 401-440.

246 Bird, R. M. 1971. Wagner's Law of Expanding
State Activity. PF 26: 1-26.

247 Blais, A.; Blake, D.; Dion, S. 1993. Parties and
the Size of Government in Liberal Democracies.
AJPS 37: 40-62.

248 Borcherding, T. E. 1985. Causes of Government
Expenditure Growth. JPUBE 28: 359-382.

249 Bordo, M. D.; Landau, D. 1987. Growth of Government: A Protection Explanation. PC 53: 167-174.

250 Brosio, G.; Marchese, C. 1988. Growth of Government under Different Redistributive Rules. PFQ
16: 439-463.

251 Cameron, D. R. 1978. Expansion of Public Economy: Comparative Analysis. APSR 72: 1243-1261.

252 Castles, F. G. 1989. Big Governments in Weak
States: The Paradox of State Size. JCACP 27:
267-293.

253 Coughlin, P. J.; Mueller, D. C.; Murrell, P.
1990. Electoral Politics, Interest Groups and
the Size of Government. EI 28: 682-705.

254 Crain, W. M., et al. 1985. Legislative Specialization and Size of Government. PC 46: 311-316.

255 Crain, W. M.; Leonard, M. L. 1993. Right vs. the
Obligation to Vote: Effects on Government
Growth. EAP 5: 43-51.

256 Crain, W. M.; Tollison, R. D.; Kimenyi, M. S.
1985. Litigation, the Business Cycle and Government Growth. ZS 141: 435-443.

257 Dao, M. Q. 1994. The Determinants of the Size of
Government. JSEE 18: 1-14.

258 De Lorme, C.; Cartwright, P. A.; Kespohl, E.
1988. Effect of Temporal Aggregation on Wagner's
Law. PF 43: 373-387.

259 Diamond, J. 1977. Economic Testing of the Displacement Effect. Finanzarchiv 35: 398-404.

260 Dunleavy, P. 1985. Bureaucrats, Budgets and the
Growth of the State. BJPS 15: 299-328.

261 Feldman, A. M. 1985. A Model of Majority Voting
and Growth in Government. PC 46: 3-17.

262 Ferris, J. M. 1983. Demands for Public Spending:
An Attitudinal Approach. PC 40: 135-154.

263 Frantianni, M.; Spinelli, F. 1982. Growth of
Government in Italy. PC 20: 221-243.

264 Gandhi, V. P. 1971. Wagner's Law of Public
Expenditure. PF 26: 44-56.

265 Garand, J. C. 1988. Explaining Governmental
Growth in the US States. APSR 82: 837-852.

266 -. 1988. Measuring Government Growth in the
States. APQ 16: 405-424.

267 -. 1989. Measuring Government Size in States:
Models of Government Growth. SSQ 70: 487-496.

268 Greene, K. V.; Nelson, P. J. 1994. Legislative
Majorities and Alternative Theories of the Size
of Government. PF 49: 42-56.

269 Grossman, P. J. 1989. Federalism and the Size of
Government. SEJ 55: 580-593.

270 -. 1990. Government and Growth: Cross Sectional
Evidence. PC 65: 217-228.

271 Grossman, P. J.; West, E. G. 1994. Federalism
and the Growth of Government. PC 79: 19-32.

272 Hansen, S. B.; Cooper, P. 1980. State Revenue
Elasticity and Expenditure Growth. PSJ 9: 26-33.

273 Henrekson, M. 1993. Wagner's Law: A Spurious
Relationship? PF 48: 406-415.

274 Henrekson, M.; Lybeck, J. A. 1988. Explaining
the Growth of Government in Sweden: Disequilibrium Approach. PC 57: 213-232.

275 Higgs, R. 1985. Crisis, Bigger Government and
Ideological Change: The Ratchet Phenomenon. EEH
22: 1-28.

276 Inman, R. P. 1982. Economic Case for Limits to
Government. AER 72: 176-190.

277 Jones, J. D.; Joulfaian, D. 1991. Federal Government Expenditures and Revenues in the Early
Years of the American Republic. JOM 13: 133-155.

278 Joulfaian, D.; Marlow, M. L. 1990. Government
Size and Decentralization. SEJ 56: 1094-1102.

279 Journal of Public Economics. 1985. Papers on the
Growth of Government. JPUBE 38 (3).

280 Kamlet, M. S.; Mowery, D. C. 1983. Budgetary
Side Payments and Government Growth. AJPS 27:
636-664.

281 Karavitis, N. 1987. Causal Factors of Government
Expenditure Growth in Greece. AE 19: 789-807.

282 Kimenyi, M. S.; Shughart, W. F. 1989. Political
Successions and the Growth of Government. PC 62:
173-180.

283 Kristensen, O. P. 1982. Voter Attitudes and
Public Spending. EJPR 10: 35-52.

284 Larkey, P. D.; Stolp, C.; Winer, M. D. 1981.
Theorizing about the Growth of Government. JPP
1: 157-220.

285 Lee, D. R. 1989. The Impossibility of a Desirable Minimal State. PC 61: 277-284.

286 Lindbeck, A. 1985. Redistribution Policy and the
Expansion of Public Sector. JPUBE 28: 309-328.

287 Mahler, V. A. 1992. Measuring Public Sector Size
in Advanced Economy Countries. SIR 27: 311-325.

288 Mahler, V. A.; Katz, C. J. 1988. Social Benefits
in Advanced Capitalist Countries. CP 21: 37-52.

289 Mann, A. J. 1980. Wagner's Law: Mexico. NTJ 33:
189-201.

290 Marlow, M. L. 1988. Fiscal Decentralization and
Government Size. PC 56: 259-270.

291 Marlow, M. L.; Orzechowski, W. 1988. Controlling
Leviathan through Tax Reduction. PC 58: 237-246.

292 McKenzie, R. B. 1980. Economic Justification for
Government and Government Growth. Journal of
Social and Political Studies 5: 245-258.

293 Meltzer, A. H.; Richard, S. F. 1981. A Rational
Theory of Size of Government. JPE 89: 914-927.

294 -. 1983. Tests of a Rational Theory of the Size
of Government. PC 41: 403-426.

295 Mevorach, B. 1991. Government Policies: A Political Phillips Curve. JSPES 16: 77-106.

296 Miller, G. J.; Moe, T. M. 1983. Bureaucrats, Legislators and the Size of Government. APSR 77: 297-322.

297 Miranda, R. A. 1993. Post-Machine Regimes and the Growth of Government: A Fiscal History of Chicago. UAQ 28: 397-422.

298 Misiolek, W. S.; Elder, H. W. 1988. Tax Structure and Size of Government: Fiscal Illusion and Fiscal Stress. PC 57: 233-246.

299 Mitchell, J.; Feiock, R. C. 1988. Government Growth in the American States. SALGR 20: 51-58.

300 Mueller, D. C.; Murrell, P. 1986. Interest Groups and Size of Government. PC 48: 125-146.

301 Murrell, P. 1985. Size of Public Employment. JCE 9: 424-437.

302 Nelson, M. A. 1986. Voter Perceptions of Cost of Government: Local School Expenditures in Louisiana. PFQ 14: 46-68.

303 North, D. C. 1985. Growth of Government: Economic Historian's Perspective. JPUBE 28: 383-399.

304 Oh, C. H. 1995. System Size and Administrative Component in the American States: Economies of Scale Hypothesis. ARPA 25: 137-160.

305 Oxley, L. 1994. Cointegration, Causality and Wagner's Law. SJPE 41: 286-298.

306 Pathirane, L.; Blades, D. W. 1982. Defining and Measuring the Public Sector. RIW 28: 261-289.

307 Peltzman, S. 1980. Growth of Government. JOLE 23: 209-288.

308 Pennings, P. 1995. Impact of Parties and Unions on Welfare Statism. WEP 18: 1-17.

309 Proceedings. 1985. Papers on Controlling Federal Spending. PAPSC 35 (4).

310 Ram, R. 1987. Wagner's Hypothesis. REAS 69: 194-204.

311 Rasler, K. A.; Thompson, W. R. 1985. War Making and State Making: Governmental Expenditures. APSR 79: 491-507.

312 Reddy, K. N. 1988. Determinants of the Growth of Government Expenditure in India. IJPA 34: 211-226.

313 Rice, T. W. 1986. Determinants of Western European Government Growth. CPS 19: 233-258.

314 Rose, R. 1984. Programme Approach to the Growth of Government. BJPS 15: 1-28.

315 Sanders, A. 1988. Rationality, Self-Interest and Attitudes on Public Spending. SSQ 69: 311-324.

316 Scheetz, T. 1992. Evolution of Public Sector Expenditures: Argentine, Chile, Paraguay and Peru. JPR 29: 175-190.

317 Sigelman, L.; Whicker, M. L. 1988. The Growth of Government: Ineffectiveness of Voting and the Pervasive Political Malaise. SSQ 69: 299-310.

318 Steinmo, S. 1995. Why Is Government So Small in America? Governance 8: 303-334.

319 Szamuely, L. 1990. The Expansion of the Welfare State: International Comparison. AO 42: 183-195.

320 Tarschys, D. 1975. Growth of Public Expenditures. SPS 10: 9-31.

321 Tussing, A. D.; Henning, J. A. 1991. Measuring the Effect of Structural Change on Long-Term Public Expenditure Growth. PFQ 19: 393-411.

322 Wagner, R. E.; Weber, W. E. 1977. Wagner's Law, Fiscal Institutions and the Growth of Government. NTJ 30: 59-68.

323 West, E. G.; Winter, S. L. 1980. Optimal Fiscal Illusion and Size of Government. PC 35: 607-622.

Organizational Ecology

324 Amburgey, T. L.; Kelly, D.; Barnett, W. P. 1993. Dynamics of Organizational Change and Failure. ASQ 38: 51-73.

325 Barron, D. N.; West, E.; Hannan, M. T. 1994. Growth and Mortality of Credit Unions in New York City. AJS 100: 381-421.

326 Baum, J. A. C.; Singh, J. V. 1994. Organizational Niches and Dynamics of Organizational Mortality. AJS 100: 346-380.

327 Blau, P. M. 1970. A Formal Theory of Differentiation in Organizations. ASR 35: 201-218.

328 Bruderl, J.; Preisendorfer, P.; Ziegler, R. 1992. Survival Chances of Newly Founded Business Organizations. ASR 57: 227-242.

329 Carroll, G. R. 1983. A Stochastic Model of Organizational Mortality. SSR 12: 303-329.

330 Carroll, G. R.; Hannan, M. T. 1989. Density Delay in the Evolution of Organizational Populations. ASQ 34: 411-430.

331 -. 1989. Density Dependence in the Evolution of Populations of Newspaper Organizations. ASR 54: 524-548.

332 Carroll, G. R.; Harrison, J. R. 1994. On the Historical Efficiency of Competition between Organizational Populations. AJS 100: 720-749.

333 Carroll, G. R.; Swaminathan, A. 1991. Density Dependent Organizational Evolution in the Brewing Industry. AS 34: 155-176.

334 Casstevens, T. W. 1980. Birth and Death Processes of Governmental Bureaus. BS 25: 161-165.

335 Clarke, L.; Estes, C. L. 1991. Sociological and Economic Theories of Markets and Nonprofits: Home Health Organizations. AJS 97: 945-969.

336 Delacroix, J.; Swaminathan, A. 1991. Cosmetic, Speculative and Adaptive Change in the Wine Industry. ASQ 36: 631-661.

337 Donovan, B. L. 1995. Framing and Strategy: Explaining Differential Longevity in the Woman's Christian Temperance Union and the Anti-Saloon League. SI 65: 143-155.

338 Edwards, B.; Marullo, S. 1995. Organizational Mortality Declining Social Movement: Demise of Peace Movement Organizations. ASR 60: 908-927.

339 Freeman, J.; Boeker, W. 1984. Ecological Analysis of Business Strategy. CMR 26: 73-86.

340 Goldman, P. 1973. Size and Differentiation in Organizations. PSR 16: 89-106.

341 Halliday, T. C.; Powell, M. J.; Granfors, M. W. 1987. Minimalist Organizations: Bar Associations. ASR 52: 456-471.

342 -. 1993. Transformation of State Bar Associations from Market Dependence to State Reliance. ASR 58: 515-535.

343 Hannan, M. T.; Freeman, J. 1988. Ecology of Organizational Mortality: American Labor Unions. AJS 94: 25-52.

344 Haveman, H. A. 1993. Organizational Size and Change: Diversification in the Savings and Loan Industry. ASQ 38: 20-50.

345 -. 1995. Industry Dynamics, Turnover and Tenure Distributions. ASQ 40: 586-618.

346 Hodgson, G. M. 1994. Optimization and Evolution: Winter's Critique of Friedman Revisited. CJE 18: 413-430.

347 Hummon, N. P. 1971. A Mathematical Theory of Differentiation in Organizations. ASR 36: 297-303.

348 Langton, J. 1984. Ecological Theory of Bureaucracy: Josiah Wedgewood and British Pottery Industry. ASQ 29: 330-354.

349 Lazerson, M. H. 1988. Organizational Growth in Small Firms. ASR 53: 330-342.

350 Levinthal, D. 1991. Random Walks and Organizational Mortality. ASQ 36: 397-420.

351 Liebman, R. C.; Sutton, J. R.; Wuthnow, R. 1988. Sources of Denominationalism: Schisms in American Protestant Denominations. ASR 53: 343-352.

352 Lomi, A. 1995. Population Ecology of Organizational Founding. ASQ 40: 111-144.

353 Marquez, J. 1994. Life Expectancy of International Cartels. RIO 9: 331-341.

354 Mayhew, B. H., et al. 1972. System Size and Structural Differentiation: Harmonic Series Model of the Division of Labor. AJS 77: 750-765.

355 Mayhew, B. H.; Levinger, R. L. 1976. On the Emergence of Oligarchy in Human Interactions. AJS 81: 1017-1049.

356 Meyer, M. W. 1972. Size and the Structure of Organizations. ASR 37: 434-440.

357 Nielson, F.; Hannan, M. T. 1977. Expansion of National Education Systems: A Population Ecology Model. ASR 42: 479-490.

358 Peli, G., et al. 1994. Formalizing Organizational Ecology. ASR 59: 571-593.

359 Phillips-Patrick, F. J. 1991. Political Risk and Organizational Form. JOLE 34: 675-694.

360 Public Administration Review. 1974. Papers on Organizational Development. PAR 34 (2).

361 Rao, H.; Neilsen, E. H. 1992. Ecology of Agency Arrangements: The Mortality of S&L Associations. ASQ 37: 448-470.

362 Schaffer, M. E. 1989. Are Profit-Maximizers the Best Survivors? A Darwinian Model of Economic Natural Selection. JEBAO 12: 29-45.

363 Schulenburg, J. T. 1989. Women's Monastic Communities 500-1100 AD: Patterns of Expansion and Decline. Signs 14: 261-292.

364 Siegfried, J. J. 1994. National Collegiate Athletic Association: Cartel Behavior. Antitrust Bulletin 39: 599-609.

365 Somma, M. 1993. Theory Building in Political Ecology. SSI 32: 371-386.

366 Swaminathan, A. 1995. Proliferation of Specialist Organizations in American Wine Industry. ASQ 40: 653-680.

367 Tolbert, P. S.; Zucker, L. G. 1983. Institutional Sources of Change in the Formal Structure of Organizations: Diffusion of Civil Service Reform. ASQ 28: 22-39.

368 Torres, D. L. 1988. Professionalism, Variation and Organizational Survival. ASR 53: 380-394.

369 Wholey, D. R.; Christianson, J. B.; Sanchez, S. M. 1992. Organization Size and Failure among Health Maintenance Organizations. ASR 57: 829-842.

370 Young, R. C. 1988. Is Population Ecology a Useful Paradigm for the Study of Organizations? AJS 94: 1-24.

Voluntary Associations

371 Bagnoli, M.; Ben-David, S.; McKee, M. 1992. Voluntary Provision of Public Goods: The Multiple Unit Case. JPUBE 47: 85-106.

372 Baumgartner, F. R.; Walker, J. L. 1988. Survey Research and Membership in Voluntary Associations. AJPS 32: 908-928.

373 Curtis, J. E.; Grabb, E. G.; Baer, D. E. 1992. Voluntary Association Membership in Fifteen Countries. ASR 57: 139-152.

374 Frohlich, N., et al. 1975. Individual Contributions for Collective Goods. JCR 19: 310-329.

375 Heckathorn, D. D. 1993. Collective Action and Group Heterogeneity: Voluntary Provision vs. Selective Incentives. ASR 58: 329-350.

376 Hirschleifer, J. 1983. From Weakest Link to Best Shot: The Voluntary Provision of Public Goods. PC 41: 371-386.

377 Horton-Smith, D. 1972. Modernization and the Emergence of Voluntary Organizations. IJCS 13: 113-134.

378 Indian Journal of Public Administration. 1987. Papers on Voluntary Organizations. IJPA 33 (3).

379 International Journal of Comparative Sociology. 1980. Papers on Voluntary Associations and Development. IJCS 21 (3/4).

380 Kaufman, D. A. 1994. Welfare and the Private Provision of Public Goods When Altruism Increases. PFQ 22: 239-257.

381 Khanna, J.; Posnett, J.; Sandler, T. 1995. Charity Donations in the UK. JPUBE 56: 257-272.

382 McPherson, J. M. 1981. A Dynamic Model of Voluntary Affiliation. SF 59: 705-728.

383 -. 1983. Size of Voluntary Organizations. SF 61: 1044-1064.

384 Mestelman, S.; Fenny, D. 1988. Does Ideology Matter? Experimental Evidence on the Voluntary Provision of Public Goods. PC 57: 281-286.

385 Murnighan, J. K.; Kim, J. W.; Metzger, A. R. 1993. The Volunteer Dilemma. ASQ 38: 515-538.

386 Oliver, P. E. 1984. Active and Token Contributions to Local Collective Action. ASR 49: 601-610.

387 Politics and Society. 1992. Papers on Secondary Associations and Democracy. PAS 20 (4).

388 Popielarz, P. A.; McPherson, J. M. 1995. Niche Position, Niche Overlap and Duration of Voluntary Association Memberships. AJS 101: 698-720.

389 Recherche Sociale. 1976. Papers on Local Associations. RS 60 (Oct).

390 Saijo, T.; Nakamura, H. 1995. The Spite Dilemma in Voluntary Contribution Mechanism Experiments. JCR 39: 535-560.

391 Sciulli, D. 1986. Voluntaristic Action: Theoretical Foundations of Societal Constitutionalism. ASR 51: 743-766.

392 Siisiainen, M. 1992. Social Movements, Voluntary Associations and Cycles of Protest in Finland. SPS 15: 21-40.

393 Smith, D. H.; Baldwin, B. R. 1990. Voluntary Group Prevalence: Intercultural Understanding Groups (Sister City Programs). IJCS 31: 79-85.

394 Smith, T. W. 1990. Trends in Voluntary Group Membership. AJPS 34: 646-661.

395 Sundeen, R. A. 1988. Explaining Participation in Coproduction: Volunteers. SSQ 69: 547-568.

396 Vaillancourt, F. 1994. To Volunteer or Not. CANJE 27: 813-826.

397 Weesie, J. 1994. Incomplete Information and Timing in the Volunteer's Dilemma. JCR 38: 557-585.

398 Williams, J. A.; Babchuk, N.; Johnson, D. R. 1973. Voluntary Associations and Minority Status. ASR 38: 637-646.

399 Young, D. J. 1982. Voluntary Purchase of Public Goods. PC 38: 73-86.

400 Zech, C. E. 1982. Willingness to Assist as Volunteers in Provision of Local Public Goods: Firemen in German Cities. AJEAS 41: 303-314.

POLICY ANALYSIS

1 American Behavioral Scientist. 1994. Papers on Public Policy Making. ABS 38 (1).

2 Bickers, K. N.; Stein, R. M. 1994. A Portfolio Theory of Policy Subsystems. AAS 26: 158-184.

3 Brooks, J. E. 1985. Democratic Frustration in Anglo-American Politics: Inconsistency between Mass Public Opinion and Public Policy. WPQ 38: 250-261.

4 Burnstein, P. 1979. Necessary Conditions for Popular Control of Public Policy. Polity 23-37.

5 Cerny, P. G. 1989. Political Entropy and American Decline. Millennium 18: 47-64.

6 Comparative Political Studies. 1977. Papers on Policy Problems in Advanced Industrial Society. CPS 10 (3).

7 Cooper, S.; Cohn, E. 1994. Equity and Efficiency of State Lotteries. EOER 13: 355-362.

8 DeSantis, V. S.; Renner, T. 1994. Impact of Political Structures on Public Policies in US Counties. PAR 54: 291-302.

9 Doern, G. B. 1995. A Political-Institutional Framework for the Analysis of Competition Policy Institutions. Governance 8: 195-217.

10 Feick, J. 1992. Comparing Comparative Policy Studies. JPP 12: 257-285.

11 Gant, M. M. 1985. Irrelevance of Abstract Conceptualization for Public Policy Voting. Polity 18: 149-160.

12 Gilliatt, S. 1984. Public Policy Analysis and Conceptual Conservatism. PAP 12: 345-368.

13 Gillroy, J. M. 1992. The Ethical Poverty of Cost-Benefit Models. PSCI 25: 82-102.

14 Gordon, R. J. 1982. Price Inertia and Policy Ineffectivness in the US, 1890-1980. JPE 90: 1087-1117.

15 Government and Opposition. 1993. Papers on Interweaving Foreign and Domestic Policy Making. GAO 28 (2).

16 Griffin, R. C. 1995. On the Meaning of Economic Efficiency in Policy Analysis. LE 71: 1-15.

17 Heclo, H. 1972. Politics of Planning in France and Britain. CP 7: 285-298.

18 Hilgartner, S.; Bosk, C. L. 1988. The Rise and Fall of Social Problems: A Public Arenas Model. AJS 94: 53-78.

19 Hill, K. Q.; Hinton-Andersson, A. 1995. A Causal Analysis of Public Opinion-Public Policy Linkages. AJPS 39: 924-935.

20 Hill, K. Q.; Leighley, J. E.; Hinton-Andersson, A. 1995. Lower Class Mobility and Policy Linkage in the US States. AJPS 39: 75-86.

21 Hofferbert, R. I. 1966. Relation between Public Policy and Structural and Environmental Variables in American States. APSR 60: 73-82.

22 Hogan, J. B. 1972. Social Structure and Public Policy: Mexico and Canada. CP 4: 477-510.

23 Hubin, D. C. 1994. Moral Justification of Benefit-Cost Analysis. EAPHIL 10: 169-194.

24 International Political Science Review. 1986. Papers on Public Policy and Government Structures. IPSR 7 (1).

25 Jacobs, L. R. 1992. Recoil Effect: Public Opinion and Policymaking in the US and Britain. CP 24: 199-218.

26 Kaim-Caudle, P. 1993. Unintended Effects of Social Policy Measures. PSR 12: 102-113.

27 Kjellberg, F. 1977. Do Policies Really Determine Politics? And Eventually How? PSJ 5: 554-570.

28 MacRae, C. D. 1970. Social Science and the Sources of Policy: 1951-1970. PS 3: 294-310.

29 Mazmanian, D. A.; Sabatier, P. A. 1980. A Multivariate Model of Public Policy Making. AJPS 24: 439-468.

30 Monroe, A. D. 1979. Consistency between Public Preferences and Policy Decisions. APQ 7: 3-19.

31 Nadel, M. V. 1975. Private Governments and the Policy Making Process. JOP 37: 2-34.

32 Ostheimer, J. M.; Ritt, L. G. 1982. Abundance and American Democracy. JOP 44: 365-393.

33 Page, B. I.; Shapiro, R. Y. 1983. Effects of Public Opinion on Public Policy. APSR 77: 175-190.

34 Peters, B. G. 1972. Public Policy, Socioeconomic Conditions and the Political System. Polity 5: 277-284.

35 Peters, B. G.; Dougtie, J. C.; McCulloch, M. K. 1977. Types of Democratic Systems and Types of Public Policy. CP 9: 327-356.

36 Policy Sciences. 1976. Papers on Program and Policy Termination. PSCI 7 (2).

37 -. 1989. Papers on Policymaking in Developing Countries. PSCI 22 (3/4).

38 PS. 1994. Papers on Public Opinion and Policy. PS 27 (1).

39 Rausser, G. C.; Foster, W. E. 1990. Political Preference Functions and Public Policy Reform. AJAE 73: 641-652.

40 Reuter, P. 1986. Social Costs of the Demand for Quantification. JPAAM 5: 807-812.

41 Robey, J. S. 1982. Major Contributors to Public Policy Analysis. PSJ 10: 442-447.

42 Rose, R. 1973. Comparing Public Policy. EJPR 1: 67-93.

43 -. 1976. On the Priorities of Government. EJPR 4: 247-289.

44 Sacks, P. M. 1980. State Structure and the Asymmetric Society: Public Policy in Britain. CP 12: 349-376.

45 Sarangi, P. 1986. Determinants of Policy Change: A Cross National Analysis. EJPR 14: 23-44.
46 Schulman, P. 1975. Nonincremental Policy Making. APSR 69: 1354-1370.
47 Shapiro, R. Y.; Jacobs, L. R. 1989. Relationship between Public Opinion and Public Policy. PBA 2: 149-180.
48 Sharkansky, I. 1971. Economic Theories of Public Policy. MJPS 15: 722-740.
49 Smith, T. A. 1969. Toward a Comparative Theory of the Policy Process. CP 1: 498-515.
50 Stein, R. M. 1981. Allocation of Federal Aid Monies: Synthesis of Demand-Side and Supply-Side Explanations. APSR 75: 334-343.
51 Sternberg, E. 1989. Incremental vs. Methodological Policymaking in the Liberal State. AAS 21: 54-77.
52 Weiss, J. A.; Tschirhart, M. 1994. Public Information Campaigns as Policy Instruments. JPAAM 13: 82-119.
53 Wright, G. C.; Erikson, R. S.; McIver, J. P. 1987. Public Opinion and Policy Liberalism in the American States. AJPS 31: 980-1001.

Approaches

54 Alford, R.R.; Friedland, R. 1975. Political Participation and Public Policy. ANRS 1: 429-479.
55 American Behavioral Scientist. 1985. Papers on Collaborative Research and Policy. ABS 29 (2).
56 -. 1989. Papers on Action Research. ABS 32 (5).
57 Anderson, C. W. 1971. Comparative Policy Analysis: Design of Measures. CP 4: 117-131.
58 -. 1979. Place of Principles in Policy Analysis. APSR 73: 711-723.
59 Annals. 1977. Papers on Social Theory and Public Policy. ANNALS 434.
60 Athal, Y. 1983. Using the Social Sciences for Policy Formulation. ISSJ 35: 367-378.
61 Baehr, P. R. 1986. Think Tanks: Advising Government in Democratic Society. Futures 18: 389-400.
62 Baumgartner, F. R.; Jones, B. D. 1991. Agenda Dynamics and Policy Subsystems. JOP 53: 1044-1076.
63 Beghin, J. C. 1990. A Game-Theoretic Model of Endogenous Public Policies. AJAE 72: 138-148.
64 Behn, R. D. 1981. Policy Analysis and Policy Politics. POLAN 7: 199-226.
65 Boudon, R. 1983. Why Theories of Social Change Fail: Methodological Thoughts. POQ 47: 143-160.
66 Brewer, G. D. 1983. Some Costs and Consequences of Large Scale Social Systems Modeling. BS 28: 166-185.
67 Brock, D. W. 1987. The Role of Philosophers in Policy Making. Ethics 97: 786-791.
68 Brooks, H. 1984. Sponsorship and Social Science Research. Society 21: 81-83.
69 Brunk, G. G. 1989. Role of Statistical Heuristics in Public Policy Analysis. CJ 9: 165-189.
70 Bullard, J. B. 1991. Learning, Rational Expectations and Policy. FRBSTL 73 (1): 50-60.
71 Chinn, M. D. 1991. Beware of Econometricians Bearing Estimates: Policy Analysis in a Unit Root World. JPAAM 10: 546-567.
72 Cummings, S. 1984. Political Economy of Social Science Funding. SI 54: 154-170.
73 De Greene, K. B. 1994. Challenge to Policymaking of Large Scale Systems. JTP 6: 161-188.
74 DeLeon, P. 1986. The Trends in Policy Sciences Research. EJPR 14: 3-22.
75 Dowding, K. 1995. Critical Review of the Policy Network Approach. POLST 43: 136-158.
76 Drazen, A.; Masson, P. R. 1994. Credibility of Policies vs. Credibility of Policymakers. QJE 109: 735-754.
77 Durning, D.; Osuna, W. 1994. Policy Analysts' Roles and Value Orientations: Empirical Investigation Using Q Methodology. JPAAM 13: 629-657.
78 Dye, T. R. 1979. Politics vs Economics: Development of the Literature on Policy Determination. PSJ 7: 652-662.
79 Ethics. 1968. Papers on Philosophy and Public Policy. Ethics 79 (1), and 1987 97: 776-791.
80 European Journal of Political Research. 1992. Papers on Policy Networks. EJPR 21 (1/2).
81 Evans, J. S. B. T. 1982. Psychological Pitfalls in Forecasting. Futures 14: 258-265.
82 Finsterbusch, K.; Hamilton, M. R. 1978. Rationalization of Social Science Research in Policy Studies. IJCS 19: 88-106.
83 Funkhouser, G. R. 1984. Using Qualitative Historical Observations in Predicting the Future. Futures 16: 173-182.
84 Gormley, W. T. 1987. Institutional Policy Analysis. JPAAM 6: 153-169.
85 Gregory, R. 1989. Political Rationality or Incrementalism? Charles E. Lindbloom's Enduring Contribution to Public Policy. PAP 17: 139-154.
86 Halchmi, A. 1978. Spiral Model of Policymaking. JPS 5: 73-76.
87 Hale, D. 1988. Just What Is a Policy, Anyway? A Survey of Public Administration and Policy Texts. AAS 19: 423-452.
88 Hall, P. 1980. Great Planning Disasters: What Lessons Do They Hold? Futures 12: 45-50.
89 -. 1983. Policy Innovation and Structure of the State: Politics-Administration Nexus in France and Britain. ANNALS 466: 43-60.
90 Heclo, H. 1972. Policy Analysis. BJPS 2: 84-108.
91 Hedge, D. M.; Mok, J. W. 1987. Nature of Policy Studies: Content Analysis of Policy Journal Articles. PSJ 16: 49-62.
92 International Journal of Public Administration. 1995. Papers on Economic Modeling and Public Policy. IJPA 18 (1).
93 International Social Science Journal. 1990. Papers on Policy Actors. ISSJ 42 (1).
94 Jobert, B. 1989. Normative Frameworks of Public Policy. POLST 37: 376-386.
95 Journal of Business and Economic Statistics. 1995. Papers on Program and Policy Evaluation. JBAES 13 (2).
96 Journal of Theoretical Politics. 1990. Papers on Public Policy. JTP 2 (3).
97 Kartez, J. D. 1989. Rational Arguments and Irrational Audiences: Psychology, Planning and Public Judgment. JAPA 55: 445-456.
98 Klosterman, R. E. 1981. Economists' Case against Planning. JAPA 47: 361-367.
99 Knetsch, J. L. 1995. Assumptions, Behavioral Findings, and Policy Analysis. JPAAM 14: 68-78.
100 Kohfeld, C. W. 1981. Soft Data, Policy Process and Qualitative Dynamics. PM 7: 27-42.
101 Krenz, C.; Sax, G. 1986. What Quantitative Research Is and Why It Doesn't Work. ABS 30: 58-69.
102 Larkey, P. D.; Sproull, L. S. 1981. Models in Theory and Practice. PSCI 13: 233-246.
103 Leichter, H. M. 1977. Comparative Public Policy: Problems and Prospects. PSJ 5: 583-596.
104 Lewis-Beck, M. S. 1977. Relative Importance of Socioeconomic and Political Variables for Public Policy. APSR 71: 559-566.
105 Lowery, D.; Whitaker, G. P. 1994. Comparing Public Administration and Policy Analysis Approaches to Public Service Delivery. ARPA 24: 25-42.
106 Lowi, T. J. 1972. Four Systems of Policy, Politics and Choice. PAR 33: 298-310.
107 Mason, R. O.; Mitroff, I. I. 1980. Policy Analysis as Argument. PSJ 9: 579-584.
108 McClennen, E. F. 1983. Rational Choice and Public Policy. STAP 9: 335-379.

109 McGann, J. G. 1992. Academics to Ideologues: A Brief History of the Public Policy Research Industry. PS 25: 733-740.

110 McNown, R. 1986. Uses of Econometric Models: A Guide for Policy Makers. PSCI 19: 349-358.

111 Michalos, A. C. 1981. Facts, Values and Rational Decision Making. PSJ 9: 544-551.

112 Mucciaroni, G. 1992. The Garbage Can Model and the Study of Policy Making. Polity 24: 459-482.

113 Nelson, R. H. 1987. The Economics Profession and the Making of Public Policy. JEL 25: 49-91.

114 Peters, B. G. 1981. Comparative Public Policy: A Bibliography. PSR 1: 183-197.

115 Policy Sciences. 1975. Papers on Comparative Public Policy. PSCI 6 (4).

116 Policy Studies Journal. 1972. Papers on Political Science Policy Studies. PSJ 1 (1).

117 -. 1973. Papers on Policy Studies Methodology. PSJ 2 (2).

118 -. 1976. Papers on Administering Policy. PSJ 5 (1).

119 -. 1977. Papers on Models of Policy. PSJ 5 (3).

120 -. 1977. Papers on Comparative Public Policy. PSJ 5 (Special Issue).

121 -. 1979. Papers on Determinants of Public Policy. PSJ 7 (4).

122 Policy Studies Review. 1981. Papers on Anthropology and Public Policy. IPSR 1 (1).

123 -. 1984. Papers on Public Policy. PSR 4 (1).

124 Political Quarterly. 1983. Politics of Policy Analysis and the New Centralism. PQ 54: 335-337.

125 Proceedings American Philosophical Society. 1985. Papers on US Research Grants, 1933-1983. PAPS 129 (1).

126 PS. 1991. Papers on Theories of Policy Processes. Vol 24 (2).

127 Redman, D. A. 1994. Karl Popper's Theory of Science and Econometrics: The Rise and Decline of Social Engineering. JEI 28: 67-99.

128 Regan, P. M. 1986. Policy Analysis: The Limits of Empirical Analysis. Polity 18: 521-531.

129 Rushefsky, M. E. 1982. Technical Disputes: Why Experts Disagree. PSR 1: 676-685.

130 Sabatier, P. A. 1991. Political Science and Public Policy. PS 24: 144-146.

131 Schneider, A. L. 1986. Evaluation Research and Political Science: An Argument against the Division of Scholarly Labor. PSR 6: 222-235.

132 Schneider, A. L.; Ingram, H. 1990. Behavioral Assumptions of Policy Tools. JOP 52: 510-529.

133 Simeon, R. 1976. Studying Public Policy. CJPS 9: 548-580.

134 Sims, C. A. 1980. Macroeconomics and Reality. Econometrica 48: 1-48.

135 -. 1982. Policy Analysis with Economic Models. BPEA 1: 107-152.

136 -. 1986. Are Forecasting Models Usable for Policy Analysis? FRBM 10: 2-16.

137 Smith, G.; May, D. 1980. The Debate between Rationalist and Incrementalist Models of Decision Making. PAP 8: 147-162.

138 Social Science Quarterly. 1969. Papers on Planned Social Intervention. SSQ 50 (3).

139 -. 1982. Papers on the Zero Sum Society. SSQ 63: 360-380.

140 Society. 1977. Papers on the Policy Apparatus. Vol 14 (4).

141 Speckhard, R. A. 1982. Public Policy Studies: Coming to Terms with Reality. Polity 14: 501-517.

142 Springer, J. F. 1985. Policy Analysis and Organizational Decisions. AAS 16: 475-508.

143 Susman, G. I.; Evered, R. D. 1978. Assessment of Merits of Action Research. ASQ 23: 582-603.

144 Townsend, R. M. 1983. Forecasting the Forecasts of Others. JPE 91: 546-588.

145 Vickers, G. 1980. The Assumptions of Policy Analysis. PSJ 9: 552-558.

146 Walsh, C. 1987. Individual Irrationality and Public Policy: Merit-Demerit Policies. JPP 7: 103-134.

147 Watson, D. 1983. Philosophical Analysis and the Study of Social Policies. JSP 12: 491-514.

148 Weisbard, A. J. 1987. Role of Philosophers in the Public Policy Process. Ethics 97: 776-785.

149 Welle, P. G. 1990. Political Economy of Benefit-Cost Analysis. AEJ 18: 79-88.

150 West European Politics. 1980. Papers on Public Policy Comparisons: Scandinavia. WEP 3 (3).

151 Wright, G.; Ayton, P. 1986. The Psychology of Forecasting. Futures 18: 420-445.

Biopolitics

152 Alexander, R. D. 1974. Evolution of Social Behavior. Annual Review of Ecological Systems 5: 25-83.

153 Alvarze de Lorenzana, J. M.; Ward, L. M. 1987. On Evolutionary Systems. BS 32: 19-33.

154 Bechtel, W. 1982. Two Common Errors in Explaining Biological and Psychological Phenomena. POS 49: 549-574.

155 Beck, H. 1971. Minimal Requirements for a Biological Paradigm. BS 16: 442-456.

156 -. 1971. Neurocybernetic Foundations for a Theory of Biopolitics. CPS 3: 469-478.

157 -. 1975. Ethological Considerations on the Problem of Political Order. Political Anthropology 1: 109-135.

158 Behavioral Science. 1979. Papers on Sociobiology. BS 24 (1).

159 Campbell, D. T. 1975. On the Conflicts between Biological and Social Evolution and between Psychology and Moral Tradition. American Psychologist 30: 1103-1126.

160 Catton, W. R. 1994. Foundations of Human Ecology. SP 37: 75-96.

161 Charlesworth, W. R. 1982. Ontogeny of Political Behavior. ABS 25: 273-293.

162 Coleman, S. 1985. Human Brain, Social Conformity and Presidential Elections. JMS 11: 95-130.

163 Corning, P. A. 1971. Biological Bases of Behavior and Some Implications for Political Science. WP 23: 321-370.

164 -. 1973. Politics and the Evolutionary Process. Evolutionary Biology 7: 253-293.

165 Eysenck, H. J. 1980. Man as a Biosocial Animal. PP 2 43-61.

166 Haas, M. 1969. Biopolitics: Mortality Rates. BS 14: 257-280.

167 Halley, J. E. 1994. Sexual Orientation and the Politics of Biology. SLR 46: 503-568.

168 Hirschleifer, J. 1977. Economics from a Biological Viewpoint. JOLE 20: 1-52.

169 International Political Science Review. 1982. Papers on Biopolitics. IPSR 3 (1), and 8 (2).

170 Itzkoff, S. W. 1993. America's Unspoken Economic Dilemma: Falling Intelligence Levels. JSPES 18: 311-326.

171 Jaros, D. 1972. Biochemical Desocialization: Depressants and Political Behavior. MJPS 16: 1-28.

172 Kingsland, S. 1988. Evolution and Debates over Human Progress from Darwin to Sociobiology. PADR 14: 167-198.

173 Langton, J. 1979. Darwinism and the Sociocultural Evolution. AJS 85: 288-309.

174 Laponce, J. 1978. Relating Biological, Physical and Political Phenomena. SSI 17: 385-397.

175 Losco, J. 1985. Evolution, Consciousness and Political Thinking. PB 7: 223-247.

176 Magee, S. P. 1993. Bioeconomics and the Survival Model: Economic Lessons of Evolutionary Biology. PC 77: 114-132.

177 Masters, R. D. 1975. Politics as a Biological Phenomenon. SSI 14: 7-63.

178 -. 1982. Is Sociobiology Reactionary? Inclusive Fitness Theory. QRB 57: 275-292.

179 -. 1983. The Biological Nature of the State. WP 35: 161-193.

180 -. 1983. Evolutionary Biology, Political Theory and the State. JSBS 5: 439-450.

181 -. 1990. Evolutionary Biology and Political Theory. APSR 84: 195-212.

182 Means, R. 1967. Sociology, Biology and Analysis of Social Problems. SP 15: 200-212.

183 Miller, J. G. 1965. Living Systems. BS 10: 193-237, 337-379, 381-411.

184 Mokyr, J. 1991. Evolutionary Biology, Technological Change and Economic History. BER 43: 127-149.

185 Namboodiri, K. 1988. Ecological Demography. ASR 53: 619-633.

186 Peterson, S. A. 1976. Biopolitics. Journal of the History of Behavioral Sciences 12: 354-366.

187 -. 1983. Biological and Political Socialization: A Cognitive Link? PP 4: 265-288.

188 Peterson, S. A.; Somit, A. 1986. Biology and Politics: Ethology, Sociobiology and Evolution. PBA 1: 1-24.

189 Phillips, C. S. 1971. Revival of Cultural Evolution in Social Science Theory. JDA 5: 337-380.

190 Rasinski, K.A.; Tyler, T. R. 1986. Social Psychology and Political Behavior. PBA 1: 103-128.

191 Ross, M. H. 1981. When Does Ethnic Antagonism Displace Class Conflict? Sociobiological Hypothesis in Urban Africa. CUR 8: 5-28.

192 Rosser, J. B. 1992. Economic and Ecological Theories of Evolution. JEBAO 17: 195-215.

193 Sagan, E. 1992. Whatever Happened to Evolutionary Theory? SR 59: 739-758.

194 Shubert, G. 1983. Evolutionary Politics. WPQ 36: 175-193.

195 Social Research. 1969. Papers on Human Biology and Social Sciences. SR 36 (4).

196 Social Science Information. 1984. Papers on Biology and Social Life. SSI 23 (6).

197 Sociological Perspectives. 1994. Papers on Biological Theory in Sociology. SP 37 (3).

198 Somit, A. 1968. Biopolitics. BJPS 2: 209-238.

199 -. 1968. Toward More Biologically Oriented Political Science. MJPS 12: 550-567.

200 Stauffer, R. B. 1969. Biopolitics of Underdevelopment. CPS 2: 361-387.

201 Stephens, J. 1970. A More Biologically Oriented Political Science. MJPS 14: 687-707.

202 Teaching Political Science. 1989. Papers on Teaching about Intelligence. TPS 16 (2).

203 Watts, M. W.; Sumi, D. 1979. Studies in the Physiological Component of Aggression Related Attitudes. AJPS 23: 528-558.

204 White, E. 1981. Sociobiology, Neurobiology and Political Socialization. Micropolitics 1: 113-144.

205 -. 1982. Clouds, Clocks, Brains and Political Learning. Micropolitics 2: 279-309.

206 Wiegle, T. C. 1986. Psychophysiology and Politics. PBA 1: 25-44.

207 Willhoite, F. 1976. Primates and Political Authority. APSR 70: 1110-1126.

208 -. 1977. Evolution and Collective Intolerance. JOP 39: 367-384.

209 Women and Politics. 1983. Papers on Biopolitics and Gender. WAP 3 (2/3).

Evaluation and Utilization

210 Administrative Science Quarterly. 1983. Papers on the Utilization of Organizational Research. ASQ 28 (1 Pt 2).

211 Albaek, E. 1995. Utilization of Social Science in Public Policy Making. PSCI 28: 79-100.

212 American Behavioral Scientist. 1979. Papers on Utilization of Scientific and Social Science Information. ABS 22 (2), and 1987 30 (6).

213 -. 1983. Papers on the Use of Research by Government Commissions. ABS 26 (5).

214 Banks, J. S.; Clark, R. L. 1980. Evaluation Research and the Budget Cycle. PSJ 8: 1195-1202.

215 Berman, P. 1978. The Study of Macro and Micro Implementation. PUBP 26: 157-184.

216 Bowen, E. R. 1982. The Pressman-Wildavsky Paradox: Why Models Based on Probability Theory Can Predict Implementation Success. JPP 2: 1-22.

217 Bozeman, B. 1986. Credibility of Policy Analysis: Between Method and Use. PSJ 14: 519-539.

218 Buck, A., et al. 1993. Using the Delphi Process to Analyze Social Policy Implementation. PSCI 26: 271-288.

219 Bulmer, M. 1983. Does Social Science Contribute Effectively to the Work of Governmental Commissions. ABS 26: 643-668.

220 Cahill, A. G. 1991. Politics of Knowledge: Rise and Fall of Policy Analysis in State Legislatures. Journal of Management Science and Policy Analysis 8: 289-308.

221 Chen, H. T. 1988. Validity in Evaluation Research. PAP 16: 1-16.

222 Clarke, P. J. 1983. Performance Evaluation of Public Section Programmes. Administration 32: 294-311.

223 Clemen, R. T. 1989. Combining Forecasts: Review and Annotated Bibliography. IJF 5: 559-583.

224 Dery, D. 1984. Evaluation and Termination in the Policy Cycle. PSCI 17: 13-26.

225 Elmore, R. 1978. Organizational Models of Social Program Implementation. PUBP 26: 185-228.

226 Fox, C. J. 1987. Biases in Public Policy Implementation Evaluation. PSR 7: 128-141.

227 Greenburg, D. H.; Mandell, M. B. 1991. Research Utilization in Policymaking. JPAAM 10: 633-656.

228 Haveman, R. 1987. Policy Analysis and Evaluation Research after Twenty Years. PSJ 16: 191-218.

229 Hedrick, T. E. 1980. Interactions among Evaluation, Program Implementation and Policy. PSJ 8: 1203-1211.

230 Hennessy, M. 1982. The End of Methodology? Essay on Evaluation Research Methods. WPQ 35: 606-612.

231 Journal of Applied Behavioral Science. 1983. Papers on Uses of Behavioral Science JABS 19 (3)

232 Kash, D. E.; Ballard, S. C. 1987. Academic and Applied Policy Studies. ABS 30: 597-611.

233 Larson, R. C.; Berliner, L. 1983. On Evaluating Evaluations. PSCI 16: 147-164.

234 Lempert, R. 1989. Humility Is a Virtue: On the Publicization of Policy Relevant Research. LASR 23: 145-161.

235 Lincoln, Y. S.; Guba, E. E. 1986. Research, Evaluation and Policy Analysis. PSR 5: 546-565.

236 Matsushima, H. 1988. New Approach to the Implementation Problem. JET 45: 128-144.

237 McAdams, J. C. 1984. Anti-Policy Analysts. PSJ 13: 91-102.

238 Moulin, H. 1982. Non-Cooperative Implementation. MSS 3: 243-257.

239 Nelson, C. E., et al. 1987. The Utilization of Social Science Information by Policymakers. ABS 30: 569-577.

240 Patton, M. Q. 1980. Truth or Consequences in Evaluation. EAUS 13: 59-74.

241 Policy Analysis 1975. Papers on Policy Implementation. POLAN 1 (3).

242 Policy Sciences. 1988. Papers on Advocacy Coalitions. PSCI 21 (2/3).

243 -. 1995. Papers on Knowledge and Policy. PSCI 28 (1).

244 -. 1995. Papers on Policy Interpretation. PSCI 28 (2).

245 Policy Studies Journal. 1980. Papers on Analysis of Policy Impact. PSJ 8 (6).

246 -. 1980. Papers on Policy Implementation. PSJ 8 (4).

247 Pollard, W. E. 1987. Decision Making and the Use of Evaluation Research. ABS 30: 661-676.

248 Public Personnel Management. 1988. Papers on Performance Evaluation. PPM 17 (4).

249 Public Policy. 1980. Papers on Policy Evaluation and Implementation. Vol 8 (7).

250 Robinson, J. B. 1992. Risks, Predictions and Other Optical Illusions: Rethinking the Use of Science in Social Decision Making. PSCI 25: 237-254.

251 Sabatier, P. A.; Whiteman, D. 1985. Legislative Decision Making and Substantive Policy Information: Information Flow. LSQ 1: 395-421.

252 Schwartz, T. 1970. On the Possibility of Rational Policy Evaluation. TAD 1: 89-106.

253 Social Science Quarterly. 1976. Papers on Policy Evaluation and Policy Implementation. SSQ 57 (3).

254 Waterman, R. W.; Wood, B. D. 1992. What Do We Do with Applied Research? PS 25: 559-564.

255 Webber, D. J. 1987. Factors Influencing Legislator's Use of Policy Information and Implications for Promoting Greater Use. PSR 6: 666-676.

256 -. 1987. Legislators Use of Policy Information. ABS 30: 612-631.

257 Wittrock, B. 1982. Social Knowledge, Public Policy and Social Betterment: Review of Current Research on Knowledge Utilization in Policy Making. EJPR 10: 83-90.

Innovation and Diffusion

258 Administrative Sciences Quarterly. 1990. Papers on Innovation. ASQ 35 (1).

259 Ahonen, G. 1986. Do Policies Develop Like Scientific Paradigms? Safety and Health in Finland. EJPR 14: 305-320.

260 Allen, R.; Clark, J. 1981. State Policy Adoption and Innovation: Lobbying and Education. SALGR 13: 18-25.

261 Baltagi, B. H.; Griffin, J. M. 1988. A General Index of Technical Change. JPE 96: 20-41.

262 Benjamini, Y.; Gafni, A.; Maital, S. 1986. The Diffusion of Medical Technology: A Prisoner's Dilemma? SEPS 20: 69-74.

263 Berry, F. S. 1994. Sizing Up State Policy Innovation Research. PSJ 22: 442-456.

264 Berry, F. S.; Berry, W. D. 1990. State Lottery Adoptions as Policy Innovations. APSR 84: 395-415.

265 Brady, D. W.; Bullock, C. S.; Maisel, L. S. 1988. Electoral Antecedents of Policy Innovations. CPS 20: 395-422.

266 Brunk, G. G. 1988. Major Factors of American Inventive Activity. SSQ 69: 491-500.

267 Brunk, G. G.; Jason, G. J. 1981. Impact of Warfare on the Rate of Invention. Scientometrics 3: 437-455.

268 Burt, R. S. 1987. Social Contagion and Innovation: Cohesion vs. Structural Equivalence. AJS 92: 1287-1335.

269 Cambridge Journal of Economics. 1995. Papers on Technology and Innovation. CJE 19 (1).

270 Cheit, R. E. 1993. State Adoption of Model Insurance Codes. Publius 23: 49-70.

271 Craig, C. S.; Brown, L. A. 1978. Spatial Diffusion of Innovation. SAG 9: 29-52.

272 -. 1980. Simulating Spatial Diffusion of Innovation. SEPS 14: 167-180.

273 Cyr, A. B. 1983. A Crucial Regression Error in Research on Diffusion of State Policies. PM 9: 201-214.

274 DeBresson, C. 1989. Breeding Innovation Clusters: A Source of Development. WD 17: 1-16.

275 Deyle, R. E. 1994. Conflict, Uncertainty and the Role of Planning and Analysis in Public Policy Innovation. PSJ 22: 457-473.

276 Deyle, R. E.; Bretschneider, S. I. 1995. Spillovers of State Policy Innovations. JPAAM 14: 79-106.

277 Dosi, G. 1988. Sources, Procedures and Microeconomic Effects of Innovation. JEL 26: 1120-1130.

278 Downs, G. W.; Mohr, L. B. 1976. Conceptual Issues in Study of Innovation. ASQ 21: 700-714.

279 Feller, I. 1981. Public Sector Innovation as Conspicuous Production. POLAN 7: 1-20.

280 Feller, I.; Elmes, G.; Meyer, J. 1982. Spatial Aspects of Diffusion of Technological Innovations among American Municipal Governments. SEPS 16: 225-240.

281 Fisher, C. S.; Carroll, G. R. 1988. Telephone and Automobile Diffusion. AJS 93: 1153-1178.

282 Fliegal, F. C.; Kivlin, J. E. 1966. Attributes of Innovation as Factors of Diffusion. AJS 72: 235-248.

283 Forrester, J. W. 1981. Innovation and Economic Change. Futures 13: 323-331.

284 Frant, H.; Berry, F. S.; Berry, W. D. 1991. Specifying a Model of State Policy Innovation. APSR 85: 571-580.

285 Freeman, C. 1991. Innovation, Changes of Techno-Economic Paradigm and Biological Analogies in Economics. Revue Economique 42: 211-232.

286 Freeman, R. B. 1980. Indicators of the Impact of R&D on the Economy. Scientometrics 2: 375-385.

287 Frendreis, J. P. 1978. Innovation Characteristics as Correlates of Innovation Adoption in Cities. MRPA 12: 67-86.

288 Gatignon, H.; Eliashberg, J.; Robertson, T. S. 1989. Modeling Multinational Diffusion Patterns. Marketing Science 8: 231-247.

289 Gray, V. 1973. Innovation in the States: A Diffusion Study. APSA 67: 1174-1193.

290 -. 1975. Expenditures and Innovation as Dimensions of Progressivism. AJPS 18: 693-700.

291 Griliches, Z. 1990. Patent Statistics as Economic Indicators. JEL 28: 1661-1707.

292 Harisalo, R. 1982. Diffusion of Innovations in Finnish Municipal Administration. SPS 5:169-186.

293 Haynes, K. E.; Kumar, K. C.; Briggs, R. 1983. Regional Patterns in the Spatial Distribution of Public Policy Innovations. PG 2: 289-307.

294 Huff, D. L.; Lutz, J. M.; Srivastava, R. 1988. A Geographical Analysis of the Innovativeness of States. EG 64: 137-146.

295 Hynes, K. E.; Mahajan, V.; White, G. M. 1977. Innovation Diffusion. SEPS 11: 25-30.

296 International Social Science Journal. 1993. Papers on Innovation. ISSJ 45 (1).

297 Jackson, J. D.; Saurman, D. S.; Shughart, W. F. 1994. Legal Change in Transition and the Diffusion of State Lotteries. PC 80: 245-263.

298 Japp van Duijn, J. 1981. Fluctuations in Innovations over Time. Futures 13: 264-275.

299 Kamien, M. I.; Schwartz, N. L. 1975. Market Structure and Innovation. JEL 13: 1-37.

300 Kleinknecht, A. 1981. Observations on the Schumpeterian Swarming of Innovations. Futures 13: 293-307.

301 -. 1990. Are There Schumpeterian Waves of Innovations? CJE 14: 81-92.

302 Knoke, D. 1982. The Spread of Municipal Reforms. AJS 87: 1314-1339.

303 Knudsen, D. C., et al. 1994. Group Technology Adoption in the Midwest. GAC 25: 183-205.

304 Kobrin, S. J. 1985. Diffusion as an Explanation of Oil Nationalization. JCR 29: 3-32.

305 Kochanowski, P.; Hetzfeld, H. 1981. Often Overlooked Factors in Measuring Rate of Return to Government R&D Expenditures. POLAN 7: 153-167.

306 Lach, S.; Schankerman, M. 1989. Dynamics of R&D and Investment in the Scientific Sector. JPE 97: 880-904.

307 Lee, T.; Wilde, L. L. 1980. Market Structure and Innovation. QJE 94: 429-436.

308 Levine, C. H. 1985. Where Policy Comes From: Ideas, Innovations and Agenda Choices. PAR 45: 255-261.

309 Link, A. N. 1980. Firm Size and Efficient Entrepreneurial Activity: Reformulation of the Schumpeter Hypothesis. JPE 88: 771-782.

310 Lutz, J. M. 1987. Regional Leadership Patterns in Diffusion of Public Policies. APQ 15: 387-398.

311 Malerba, F.; Orsenigo, L. 1995. Schumpeterian Patterns of Innovation. CJE 19: 47-65.

312 Mansfield, E. 1980. Basic Research and Productivity Increase in Manufacturing. AER 70: 863-873.

313 McAdam, D.; Rucht, D. 1993. Cross National Diffusion of a Movement Idea. ANNALS 528: 56-74.

314 McLaughlin, R. 1982. Invention and Induction: Laudan, Simon and the Logic of Discovery. POS 49: 198-211.

315 Mensch, G.; Coutinho, C.; Kaasch, K. 1981. Changing Capital Values and Propensity to Innovate. Futures 13: 276-292.

316 Metcalfe, J. S. 1981. Impulse and Diffusion in Study of Technical Change. Futures 13: 347-359.

317 Midlarsky, M. I. 1970. Mathematical Models of Instability and a Theory of Diffusion. ISQ 14: 60-84.

318 Mohr, L. B. 1969. Determinants of Innovation in Organization. APSR 63: 111-126.

319 Morrill, R. L. 1968. Waves of Spatial Diffusion. JRS 8: 1-295.

320 Most, B. A.; Starr, H. 1990. Theoretical and Logical Issues in the Study of Diffusion. JTP 2: 391-412.

321 Nice, D. C. 1984. Teacher Competency Testing as a Policy Innovation. PSJ 13: 45-54.

322 Oakes, A. 1985. On Patents, R and D and the Stock Market Rate of Return. JPE 93: 390-409.

323 Parker, P. M. 1994. Aggregate Diffusion Forecasting Models in Marketing. IJF 10: 353-380.

324 Perry, J. L.; Danziger, J. N. 1980. Adoption of Innovations: Assessment of Computer Applications in Local Government. AAS 11: 461-492.

325 Policy and Politics 1985. Papers on Innovation in Economic Policy. PAP 13 (3).

326 Publius. 1985. Papers on Policy Diffusion in a Federal System. Vol 15 (4).

327 Rahmeyer, F. 1989. The Evolutionary Approach to Innovation Activity. JITE 145: 275-297.

328 Reed, S. R. 1983. Patterns of Diffusion in Japan and America. CPS 16: 215-234.

329 Ricerche Economiche. 1986. Papers on Innovation Diffusion. RE 40 (4).

330 Saracho, A. I.; Usategui, J. M. 1994. Innovation Diffusion Subsidies. EJPE 10: 357-372.

331 Savage, R. L. 1978. Policy Innovations as a Trait of the American States. JOP 40: 212-224.

332 -. 1985. Cases of Rapid Policy Diffusion. Publius 15: 111-126.

333 -. 1985. Diffusion, Research Traditions and Spread of Policy Innovations in Federal System. Publius 15 (Fall): 1-27.

334 Schiffel, D.; Kitti, C. 1978. Rates of Invention. Research Policy 7: 324-340.

335 Silverberg, G.; Dosi, G.; Orsenigo, L. 1988. Innovation, Diversity and Diffusion: A Self-Organization Model. EJ 98: 1032-1054.

336 Soderstrom, J., et al. 1985. Improving Technological Innovation through Laboratory-Industrial Cooperative R and D. PSR 5: 133-144.

337 Trajtenberg, M.; Yitzhaki, S. 1989. Diffusion of Innovations. JBAES 7: 35-47.

338 Van Duijn, J. J. 1981. Fluctuations in Innovations over Time. Futures 13: 264-274.

339 Walker, J. L. 1969. Diffusion of Innovations among the American States. APSR 63: 880-889.

340 -. 1973. Problems in Research and Diffusion of Policy Innovations. APSR 67: 1186-1191.

341 Wellhofer, E. S. 1989. Comparative Method and Study of Development, Diffusion and Social Change. CPS 22: 315-342.

342 World Development. 1992. Papers on the Diffusion of Information Technology. WD 20 (12).

343 Zhang, W. B. 1991. Multiregional Dynamics Based on Creativity and Knowledge Diffusion. ARS 25: 179-191.

344 Zhou, X. 1993. Occupational Power, State Capacities and Diffusion of Licensing in the States. ASR 58: 536-552.

POLITICAL COMMUNICATION

1 Abrahamsson, K. 1982. Knowledge Gaps, Bureaucracy and Citizen Participation: Alternative Communication Models. Communication 7: 75-102.

2 American Behavioral Scientist. 1974. Papers on Film and Politics in Developing Countries. ABS 17 (3).

3 -. 1979. Papers on Mass Media Uses. ABS 23 (1).

4 -. 1988. Papers on Media Culture. ABS 31 (2-3).

5 -. 1991. Papers on Media. ABS 35 (2).

6 -. 1993. Papers on Communication. ABS 37 (2).

7 Annuaire Suisse de Science Politique. 1982. Papers on the Media and Communication. ASSP 22.

8 Becker, J. D.; Preston, I. L. 1969. Media Use and Political Activity. JQ 46: 129-134.

9 Bennett, S. E. 1988. The Meaning of Political Ignorance Today. SSQ 69: 476-490.

10 -. 1989. Trends in American Political Information, 1967-1987. APQ 17: 422-435.

11 -. 1994. Persian Gulf War's Impact on American's Political Information. PB 16: 179-202.

12 Bond, J. R. 1985. Dimensions of Attention over Time. AJPS 29: 330-347.

13 Bennett, W. L. 1990. Toward a Theory of Press-State Relations in the US. JOC 40: 103-125.

14 Bergstrom, F. 1995. Information Input Overload. BS 40: 56-75.

15 Bimber, B. 1991. Information as a Factor in Congressional Politics. LSQ 16: 585-605.

16 Bormann, E. G.; et al. 1984. Rhetorical Visions of Committed Voters: Fantasy Theme Analysis of a Large Sample Survey. CSMC 1: 287-310.

17 Calloway, M. R.; Esser, J. K. 1984. Groupthink: Effects of Cohesiveness and Problem Solving Procedures on Group Decision Making. Social Behavior and Personality 12: 157-164.

18 Calloway, M. R.; Marriott, R. G.; Esser, J. K. 1985. Effects of Dominance on Group Decision Making: Stress Reduction Explanation of Groupthink. JPSP 49: 949-952.

19 Calvert, R. L. 1985. Value of Biased Information: Rational Choice Model of Political Advice. JOP 47: 530-555.

20 Choi, H. C.; Becker, S. L. 1987. Media Use, Issue / Image Discriminations and Voting. COMR 14: 267-291.

21 Corcoran, P. E. 1994. Presidential Concession Speeches. POLCOM 11: 109-132.

22 Courtright, J. A. 1978. Laboratory Investigation of Groupthink. COMM 45: 229-246.

23 Cox, R. C. 1995. Critical Theory and the Paradox of Discourse. ARPA 25: 1-20.

24 Craig, S. C.; Hurley, T. L. 1984. Political Rhetoric and the Structure of Political Opinion. WPQ 37: 632-640.

25 Dennis, J. 1986. Preadult Learning of Political Independence: Media and Family Communication. COMR 13: 401-433.

26 Development. 1990. Papers on Communication, Participation and Democracy. Vol 1990 (2).

27 Downing, J. D. 1990. US Media Discourse on South Africa. Discourse and Society 1: 39-60.

28 Dragoo, K.; Duits, M.; Haltom, W. 1993. Nagel-Erikson Hypothesis: Editorial Reactions to Church-State Cases. APQ 21: 368-378.

29 Duckworth, F. C. 1983. On the Influence of Debate on Public Opinion. POLST 31: 463-478.

30 European Journal of Communication. 1989. Papers on Eastern European Mass Media. Vol 4 (3).

31 Eveland, W. P.; McLeod, D. M.; Signorielli, N. 1995. Spiral of Silence during the Persian Gulf War. IJPOR 7: 91-109.

32 Fan, D. P. 1984. Mathematical Models for Impact of Information on Society. PM 10: 479-494.

33 -. 1985. Ideodynamics: Kinetics of the Evolution of Idea. JMS 11: 1-23.

34 Farace, V.; Donohew, L. 1965. Mass Communication in National Social Systems. JQ 42: 253-261.

35 Fischer, M. M.; Gopal, S. 1994. Artificial Neural Networks: Modeling Interregional Telecommunication Flows. JRS 34: 503-527.

36 Fisher, W. R. 1966. The Failure of Compromise in 1860-1861: A Rhetorical View. Speech Monographs 33: 364-371.

37 Flowers, M. L. 1977. Implications of the Janis Groupthink Hypothesis. JPSP 12: 888-896.

38 Foss, S. K. 1982. Evolution of Political Rhetoric. CSSJ 33: 367-378.

39 Galnoor, I. 1980. Political Communication and the Study of Politics. COMY 4: 99-112.

40 Gerbner, G., et al. 1984. Political Correlates of Television Viewing. POQ 48: 283-300.

41 Glynn, C. J.; McLeod, J. M. 1984. The Spiral of Silence. POQ 48: 731-740.

42 Goggin, M. L. 1984. The Ideological Context of Presidential Communications: Message Tailoring Hypothesis. APQ 12: 361-384.

43 Gottschalk, L. A.; Uliana, R.; Gilbert, R. 1988. Presidential Candidates and Cognitive Impairment Measured from Campaign Debates. PAR 48: 613-619.

44 Greenberg, S. R. 1970. Conversations as Units of Analysis in Personal Influence. JQ 52: 128-131.

45 Hahn, D. F.; Gohcher, R. M. 1972. Political Myth: Image and Issue. Today's Speech 20: 57-65.

46 Huckfeldt, R. R.; Sprague, J. 1987. Social Flow of Political Information. APSR 81: 1197-1216.

47 -. 1988. Choice, Social Structure and Political Information: Informational Coercion of Minorities. AJPS 32: 467-482.

48 International Political Science Review. 1986. Papers on Politics and the Media. IPSR 7 (4).

49 -. 1986. Papers on the Politics of New Communications. IPSR 7 (3).

50 Journal of International Affairs. 1993. Papers on Media in the Global System. JIA 47 (1).

51 Journal of Political Science. 1993. Papers on the Mass Media and Politics. JPS 21 (1).

52 Journal of Social Issues. 1986. Papers on Media Violence and Behavior. JSI 42 (3).

53 Katz, C.; Baldassare, M. 1994. Popularity in a Freefall: Measuring the Spiral of Silence at the End of the Bush Presidency. IJPOR 6: 1-12.

54 Krasner, S. D. 1991. Global Communications and National Power. WP 43: 336-366.

55 Lang, K.; Lang, G. E. 1983. New Rhetoric of Mass Communication Research. JOC 33: 128-140.

56 Lester, M. 1980. Newsworthiness: Interpretive Construction of Public Events. ASR 45: 984-994.

57 Longley, J.; Pruitt, D. G. 1980. Groupthink: A Critique of Janis's Theory. Review of Personality and Social Psychology 1: 74-93.

58 Manheim, J. B.; Lammers, W. W. 1981. The News Conference and Presidential Leadership in Public Opinion. PSQ 11: 177-188.

59 Mansfield, M. W.; Weaver, R. S. 1982. Political Communication Theory. COMY 5: 605-625.

60 McGraw, K. M.; Best, S.; Timpone, R. 1995. Impact of Elite Explanation and Polity Outcomes on Public Opinion. AJPS 39: 53-74.

61 McKelvey, R. D.; Ordeshook, P. C. 1986. Information, Electoral Equilibria and Democratic Ideal. JOP 48: 909-937.

62 Mueller, D. C.; Stratmann, T. 1994. Informative and Persuasive Campaigning. PC 81: 55-79.

63 Mutz, D. C. 1992. Mass Media and Depoliticization of Personal Experience. AJPS 36: 483-508.

64 -. 1994. Contextualizing Personal Experience: Role of Mass Media. JOP 56: 689-714.

65 Noelle-Neumann, E. 1974. Spiral of Silence. JOC 24: 43-51.

66 -. 1977. Methodological Applications of the Spiral of Silence Theory. POQ 41: 143-158.

67 -. 1983. Effects of Media on Mass Media Research. JOC 33: 157-165.

68 Pfau, M. 1989. Mass Media and American Politics. WPQ 42: 173-186.

69 -. 1993. Papers on Symbols and Politics. POLCOM 10 (2).

70 Political Quarterly. 1994. Papers on the British Broadcasting Corporation. PQ 65 (1).

71 Presidential Studies Quarterly. 1986. Papers on Media and the Presidency. PSQ 16 (1).

72 Price, V.; Zaller, J. 1993. Who Gets the News? Alternative Measures of News Reception and Their Implications for Research. POQ 57: 133-164.

73 Public Opinion Quarterly. 1973. Papers on Mass Communication Research. POQ 37 (4).

74 Rarick, D. L., et al. 1977. The Carter Persona: Analysis of Rhetorical Visions of Campaign 1976. QJS 63: 258-273.

75 Robinson, J. P.; Levy, M. R. 1986. Interpersonal Communication and News Comprehension. POQ 50: 160-175.

76 Sigelman, L.; Walkosz, B. J. 1992. Letters to the Editor as Public Opinion Thermometer: Martin Luther King Holiday in Arizona. SSQ 73: 938-946.

77 Sigman, S. J.; Fry, D. L. 1985. Differential Ideology and Language Use: Readers' Reconstruction and Descriptions of News Events. CSMC 2: 307-322.

78 Silverstein, B. 1987. Toward a Science of Propaganda PP 8: 49-60.

79 Society. 1977. Papers on TV Violence. Vol 14 (6)

80 Szecsko, T. 1986. Theses on the Democratization of Communication. IPSR 7: 435-442.

81 Taylor, G. 1982. Pluralist Ignorance and Spiral of Silence: A Formal Analysis. POQ 46: 311-335.

82 Tetlock, P. E. 1979. Identifying Victims of Groupthink from Public Statements of Decision Makers. JPSP 37: 1314-1324.

83 -. 1981. Pre to Post Election Shifts in Presidential Rhetoric. JPSP 41: 267-313.

84 -. 1984. Stability and Change in the Complexity of Senatorial Debate: Cognitive vs Rhetorical Style Hypotheses. JPSP 46: 979-990.

85 Tetlock, P. E., et al. 1992. Assessing Political Group Dynamics: Groupthink. APSP 63: 403-423.

86 Van Dijk, T. 1983. Discourse Analysis: The Structure of News. JOC 33: 20-43.

87 Walsh, J. F. 1986. Approach to Dyadic Communication in Social Movements. COMM 53: 1-15.

88 Weatherford, M. S. 1982. Interpersonal Networks and Political Behavior. AJPS 26: 117-143.

89 West European Politics. 1985. Papers on Broadcasting and Politics in Western Europe. WEP 8 (2).

90 -. 1986. Papers on the Communication Revolution in Western Europe. WEP 9 (4).

Agenda Setting

91 Adoni, H.; Mane, S. 1984. Media and the Social Construction of Reality. COMR 11: 323-340.

92 Behr, R. L.; Iyengar, S. 1985. Television News, Real World Cues and Changes in the Public Agenda. POQ 49: 38-57.

93 Bennett, W. L., et al. 1976. Images Construction of Political Issues: Amnesty. QJS 62: 109-126.

94 Carey, J. 1976. Setting Political Agenda: How Media Shape Campaigns. JOC 1976 (Spring): 50-57.

95 Christensen, S.; Daugaard Jensen, P. E. 1982. Communication and Political Agendas. Communication 7: 59-74.

96 Cohen, J. E. 1995. Presidential Rhetoric and the Public Agenda. AJPS 39: 87-107.

97 Cook, F. L., et al. 1983. Media and Agenda Setting: Effects on the Public, Interest Group Leaders, Policy Makers, Policy. POQ 47: 16-35.

98 Entman, R. M.; Rojecki, A. 1993. Freezing Out the Public: Elite and Media Framing of the US Anti-Nuclear Movement. POLCOM 10: 155-174.

99 Erbring, L.; Goldenberg, E. N.; Miller, A. H. 1980. Front Page News and Real World Cues: Agenda Setting by the Media. AJPS 24: 16-49.

100 Ghorpade, S. 1986. Agenda Setting: Advertising's Neglected Function. Journal of Advertising Research 26: 23-27.

101 Hill, D. B. 1985. Viewer Characteristics and Agenda Setting by News. POQ 49: 340-350.

102 Iyengar, S. 1979. Television News and Issue Salience: A Reexamination of the Agenda Setting Hypothesis. APQ 7: 395-416.

103 -. 1987. Television News and Citizens' Explanations of National Affairs. APSR 81: 815-831.

104 Kleinnijenhuis, J.; Rietberg, E. M. 1995. Parties, Media, Public and the Economy: Patterns of Societal Agenda-Setting. EJPR 28: 95-118.

105 Leff, D. R.; Protess, D. L.; Brooks, S. C. 1986. Crusading Journalism: Changing Public Attitudes and Policy Making Agendas. POQ 30: 300-315.

106 MacKuen, M. B. 1984. Exposure to Information, Belief Integration and Individual Responsiveness to Agenda Change. APSR 78: 372-391.

107 Manheim, J. B.; Albritton, R. B. 1984. Changing National Images: International Public Relations and Media Agenda Setting. APSR 78: 641-657.

108 McCombs, M. E.; Shaw, D. L. 1972. Agenda-Setting Function of the Mass Media. POQ 36: 176-187.

109 McLeod, J. M.; Becker, L. B.; Byrnes, J. E. 1974. Agenda Setting Function of Mass Media. COMR 1: 131-166.

110 Mead, T. D. 1994. Daily Newspaper as Political Agenda Setter: Metro Reform. SALGR 26: 27-37.

111 Spencer, J. W.; Triche, E. 1994. Media Construc-
    tions of Risk and Safety: Differential Framings
    of Hazard Events. SI 64: 199-213.
112 Wanta, W.; Hu, Y. 1994. Time-Lag Differences in
    Agenda Setting Process: Five News Media. IJPOR
    6: 225-240.
113 Weimann, G.; Brosius, H. B. 1994. Is There a Two
    Step Flow of Agenda Setting? IJPOR 6: 323-341.

Media Effects

114 Andison, F. S. 1977. TV Violence and Viewer
    Aggression. POQ 41: 314-331.
115 Ball-Rokeach, S. J.; Defleur, M. 1976. A Depend-
    ency Model of Media Effects. COMR 3: 3-21.
116 Baron, J. N.; Reiss, P. C. 1985. Aggregate
    Analyses of the Mass Media and Violent Behavior.
    ASR 50: 347-363.
117 Bartels, L. M. 1993. Messages Received: Politi-
    cal Impact of Media Exposure. APSR 87: 267-285.
118 Berry, C.; Clifford, B. R. 1987. Memory for
    Televised Information. Current Psychological
    Reviews 1: 171-192.
119 Bollen, K. A.; Phillips, D. P. 1982. Imitative
    Suicides: Effects of Television News Stories.
    ASR 47: 802-809.
120 Douglas, D. F.; Westley, B. H.; Chaffee, S. H.
    1970. Information Campaign that Changed Communi-
    ty Attitudes. JQ 47: 479-487.
121 Entman, R. M. 1989. How Media Affect What People
    Think: Information Processing. JOP 51: 347-370.
122 Erikson, R. S. 1976. Influence of Newspaper
    Endorsements in Presidential Elections. AJPS 20:
    207-234.
123 Feldman, S.; Sigelman, L. 1985. Political Impact
    of Prime Time Television: The Day After. JOP 47:
    566-578.
124 Funkhouse, G.; McCombs, M. E. 1971. The Rise and
    Fall of News Diffusion. POQ 50: 107-113.
125 Gantz, W.; Trenholm, S. 1979. Why People Pass on
    News: Motivations for Diffusion. JQ 56: 365-370.
126 Grush, J. E. 1976. Attitude Formation and Mere
    Exposure Phenomenon. JPSP 33: 281-290.
127 Hur, K. K. 1984. A Critical Analysis of News
    Flow Research. CSMC 1: 365-378.
128 Hurd, R. E.; Singletary, M. W. 1984. Newspaper
    Endorsement Influence on the 1980 Presidential
    Election Vote. JQ 61: 332-338.
129 Iyengar, S.; Lenart, R. 1989. Beyond Minimal
    Consequences: Survey of Media Political Effects.
    PBA 2: 21-38.
130 Iyengar, S.; Peters, M. D.; Kinder, D. R. 1982.
    Experimental Demonstrations of the Not so Mini-
    mal Consequences of Television News Programs.
    APSR 76: 848-858.
131 Koch, N. S. 1994. Effect of the New York Times
    on College Students' Political Information and
    Behavior. SSI 31: 29-38.
132 Lerner, R.; Rothman, S. 1989. Media, the Polity
    and Public Opinion. PBA 2: 39-76.
133 Manheim, J. B.; Albritton, R. B. 1986. Public
    Relations: The Failure of Public Information
    Campaigns. POLCOM 3: 265-292.
134 Mazur, A. 1982. Bomb Threats and the Mass Media:
    A Theory of Suggestion. ASR 47: 407-410.
135 Miller, A. H.; Goldenberg, E. N.; Erbring, L.
    1979. Impacts of Newspapers on Public Confi-
    dence. APSR 73: 67-84.
136 Mondak, J. J. 1995. Media Exposure and Political
    Discussion in US Elections. JOP 57: 62-85.
137 Mosley, P. 1984. Popularity Functions and Role
    of Media: The Popular Press. BJPS 14: 117-128.
138 Orbell, J. M. 1970. An Information Flow Theory
    of Community Influence. JOP 32: 322-338.
139 Page, B. I.; Shapiro, R. Y.; Dempsey, G. R.
    1987. What Moves Public Opinion? APSR 81: 23-43.
140 Phillips, D. P. 1980. Airplane Accidents, Murder
    and Mass Media. SF 58: 1001-1024.
141 -. 1981. Impact of Fictional Television Stories
    on US Adult Fatalities: Effect of the Mass Media
    on Violence. AJS 87: 1340-1359.
142 -. 1983. Impact of Mass Media Violence on US
    Homicides. ASR 48: 560-568.
143 Pfau, M. 1995. Papers on International News after
    the Cold War. POLCOM 12 (4).
144 Public Opinion Quarterly. 1980. Papers on Polls
    and the Media. POQ 44 (4).
145 Robinson, M. J. 1976. Public Affairs Television
    and Growth of Political Malaise: Selling the
    Pentagon. APSR 70: 409-432.
146 Schulz, N.; Weimann, J. 1989. Competition of
    Newspapers and Location of Political Parties. PC
    63: 125-147.
147 Sheley, J. F.; Ashkins, C. D. 1981. Crime, Crime
    News and Crime Views. POQ 45: 492-506.
148 Shields, T. G.; Goidel, R. K.; Tadlock, B. 1995.
    Impact of Media Exposure on Voting Decisions in
    Senate and House Elections. LSQ 20: 415-430.
149 Shoemaker, P. J. 1982. Perceived Legitimacy of
    Deviant Political Groups: Experiments on Media
    Effects. COMR 9: 249-286.
150 Smith, K. A. 1987. Effects of Newspaper Coverage
    on Community Issue Concerns and Local Government
    Evaluations. COMR 14: 379-395.
151 Stack, S. 1993. Effect of Modernization on
    Suicide in Finland. SP 36: 137-148.
152 Stone, P.; Brody, R. A. 1979. Modeling Opinion
    Responsiveness to Daily News: Lyndon Johnson.
    SSI 9: 95-122.
153 Tyler, T. R. 1980. Impact of Directly and Indi-
    rectly Experienced Events: Crime Related Judge-
    ments and Behaviors. JPSP 39: 13-28.
154 Ursprung, T. 1994. Use and Effect of Political
    Propaganda in Democracies. PC 78: 259-282.
155 Wagner, J. 1983. Media Do Make a Difference:
    Differential Impact of Mass Media on 1976 Presi-
    dential Race. AJPS 27: 407-430.
156 Watts, M. W.; Sumi, D. 1975. Desensitization of
    Children to Violence? Another Look at Televi-
    sion's Effects. ESOP 5: 1-24.
157 Zajonc, R. B. 1968. Attitudinal Effects of More
    Exposure. JPSP 9 (Supplement): 1-27.
158 Zimmer, T. 1983. Local News Exposure and Local
    Government Alienation. SSQ 64: 634-640.

News Coverage

159 Adams, W. C. 1987. Mass Media and Public Opinion
    about Foreign Affairs. POLCOM 4: 263-278.
160 Akinyemi, A. B. 1980. Religion and Foreign
    Affairs: Press Attitudes towards the Nigerian
    Civil War. JJIR 4: 56-81.
161 American Behavioral Scientist. 1989. Papers on
    Television News Research. ABS 33 (2).
162 Cancian, F. M.; Ross, B. L. 1981. Mass Media and
    the Women's Movement. JABS 17: 9-26.
163 Chester, E. W. 1991. Lyndon Baines Johnson: A
    Critical Evaluation of His Newspaper Obituaries.
    PSQ 21: 319-332.
164 Danielian, L. H.; Page, B. I. 1994. Interest
    Group Voices in TV News. AJPS 38: 1056-1078.
165 Entman, R. M. 1992. Blacks in News: Television,
    Racism and Cultural Change. JQ 69: 341-361.
166 Hacket, R. A. 1984. Bias and Objectivity in News
    Media Studies. CSMC 1: 229-259.
167 Hallin, D. C. 1984. Media, War in Vietnam and
    Political Support: Critique of the Thesis of an
    Oppositional Media. JOP 46: 2-24.
168 Hallin, D. C.; Mancini, P. 1984. Speaking of the
    President: Political Structure and Representa-
    tional Form in US and Italian Television News.
    Theory and Society 13: 839-859.

169 Haynie, S. L.; Dover, H. A. 1994. Prosecutorial Discretion and Press Coverage: The Decision to Try the Case. APQ 22: 370-381.

170 Kaid, L. L.; Boydston, J. 1987. Effectiveness of Negative Political Advertising. COMQ 35: 193-201.

171 Kaid, L. L.; Foote, J. 1985. How Network Television Coverage of President and Congress Compare. JQ 62: 59-65.

172 Kaid, L. L.; Towers, W. M.; Myers, S. L. 1981. Television Docudrama and Political Cynicism: Washington behind Closed Doors. SSQ 62: 161-168.

173 Kressel, N. J. 1987. Biased Judgments of Media Bias: The Arab-Israel Dispute. PP 8: 211-226.

174 Noyes, R. E.; Lichter, S. R.; Amundson, D. R. 1993. Was TV Election News Better? A Content Analysis of Campaign Coverage. JPS 21: 3-25.

175 Orman, J. 1984. Covering the American Presidency: Valenced Reporting in the Periodical Press. PSQ 14: 381-390.

176 Political Communication. 1993. Papers on Media and the Gulf War. POLCOM 10 (4).

177 Randall, D. M. 1987. Portrayal of Business Malfeasance in the Media. SSQ 68: 281-293.

178 Randall, D. M.; Lee-Sammons, L.; Hagner, P. R. 1988. Common vs Elite Crime Coverage in Network News. SSQ 69: 910-929.

179 Squire, P. 1988. Who Gets National News Coverage in the US Senate. APQ 16: 139-156.

180 Vallone, R. P.; Ross, L.; Lepper, M. R. 1985. Hostile Media Phenomenon: Biased Perception and Perceptions of Media Bias in Coverage of the Beirut Massacre. JPSP 49: 577-585.

Political Campaigns

181 American Politics Quarterly. 1991. Papers on the Media, Campaigns and Elections. APQ 19 (1).

182 Annals. 1976. Papers on Mass Media in Politics. ANNALS 427.

183 Ansolabehere, S.; Behr, R. L.; Iyengar, S. 1991. Mass Media and Elections. APQ 19: 109-139.

184 Bormann, E. G.; Koester, J.; Bennett, J. 1978. Political Cartoons and Salient Rhetorical Fantasies: 1976 Presidential Campaign. COMM 45: 317-329.

185 Brunk, G. G.; Fishkin, J. 1982. Media Coverage and Popularity of Presidential Candidates before National Nominating Conventions. COMR 9: 525-538.

186 Campbell, J. E.; Alford, J. R.; Henry, K. 1984. Television Markets and Congressional Elections. LSQ 9: 665-678.

187 Castle, D. S. 1991. Media Coverage of Presidential Primaries. APQ 19: 33-42.

188 Copeland, G. W.; Johnson-Cartee, K. 1990. Acceptance of Negative Political Advertising and Political Efficacy and Activity Levels. Southeastern Political Review 18: 415-427.

189 Counts, T. 1985. Effect of Endorsements on the Presidential Vote. JQ 62: 646-647.

190 Erickson, K. V.; Schmidt, W. V. 1982. Rhetoric and the Rose Garden Strategy. Southern Speech Communication Journal 47: 402-421.

191 Garramone, G. M. 1983. Issue vs. Image Orientation and Effects of Political Advertising. COMR 10: 59-76.

192 -. 1984. Voter Response to Negative Political Ads. JQ 61: 250-259.

193 -. 1985. Effects of Negative Political Advertising. JBEM 29: 147-159.

194 Garramone, G. M., et al. 1990. Effects of Negative Political Advertising on Political Process. JBEM 34: 299-311.

195 Husson, W., et al. 1988. An Interpersonal Communication Perspective on Images of Political Candidates. HCR 14: 397-421.

196 Jacobson, G. C.; Wolfinger, R. E. 1989. Information and Voting in California Senate Elections. LSQ 14: 509-530.

197 Just, M.; Crigler, A.; Wallach, L. 1990. What Viewers Learn from Spot Advertisements and Candidate Debates. JOC 40: 120-133.

198 Kahn, K. F. 1995. Characteristics of Press Coverage in Senate and Gubernatorial Elections. LSQ 20: 23-36.

199 Keeter, S. 1987. Television and Role of Candidate Personal Qualities in Voter Choice. POQ 51: 344-358.

200 Lodge, M.; Steenbergen, M. R.; Brau, S. 1995. Campaign Information and Dynamics of Candidate Evaluation. APSR 89: 309-326.

201 Martin, L. J. 1976. Recent Theories on Mass Media Potential in Political Campaigns. ANNALS 427: 125-133.

202 McBath, J. H.; Fisher, W. R. 1969. Persuasion in Presidential Campaign Communication. QJS 55: 17-25.

203 McLeod, J. M.; Glynn, C. J.; McDonald, D. C. 1983. Influence of Media Reliance on Voting Decisions. COMR 10: 37-58.

204 Meadow, R. G. 1985. Political Communications Research. JOC 35: 157-173.

205 Meadow, R. G.; Sigelman, L. 1982. Some Effects and Noneffects of Campaign Commercials. PB 4: 163-175.

206 Merritt, S. 1984. Negative Political Advertising. Journal of Advertising 13: 27-38.

207 Moore, D. W. 1987. Political Campaigns and the Knowledge-Gap Hypothesis. POQ 51: 186-200.

208 Pfau, M. 1987. Influence of Interparty Political Debates on Candidate Preference. COMR 14: 687-697.

209 Pfau, M.; Burgoon, M. 1988. Inoculation in Political Campaign Communication. HCR 15: 91-111.

210 Political Communication. 1991. Papers on Television and Election Campaigns. POLCOM 8 (3).

211 Prinz, T. S. 1995. Media Markets and Candidate Awareness in House Elections. POLCOM 12: 305-326.

212 Reed, W. R. 1989. Information in Political Markets. JOLEAO 5: 355-374.

213 Robinson, J. P. 1976. Interpersonal Influence in Election Campaigns: Two-Step Flow Hypothesis. POQ 40: 304-339.

214 Ross, M. H. 1992. Television News and Candidate Fortunes in Presidential Nomination Campaigns. APQ 20: 69-98.

215 Shelley, M. C.; Hwang, H. D. 1991. Mass Media and Public Opinion Polls in the 1988 Presidential Election. APQ 19: 59-79.

216 Sigelman, L.; Bullock, D. 1991. Presidential Campaign Coverage, 1885-1988. APQ 19: 5-32.

217 Siune, K. 1983. Mass Media and Election Campaigns: Theory and Analysis. Nordicom Review of Nordic Mass Communication Research 2: 17-27.

218 Sorauf, F. J. 1987. Campaign Money and the Press. PSCQ 102: 25-42.

219 Streitmatter, R. 1985. Impact of Presidential Popularity in News Coverage in Major Newspapers. JQ 62: 66-73.

220 West, D. M. 1994. Political Advertising and News Coverage in the 1992 California US Senate Campaigns. JOP 56: 1053-1075.

221 Woodward, J. D. 1993. Race for the Presidency: Coverage of Elections on Evening Television News Shows. JPS 21: 45-68.

222 Zaller, J. 1989. Bringing Converse Back In: Information Flow in Political Campaigns. PANAL 1: 181-234.

POLITICAL ECONOMY

1 Alesina, A.; Londregan, J.; Rosenthal, H. 1993. A Model of the Political Economy of the US. APSR 87: 12-33.
2 Alvarez, R. M.; Garrett, G.; Lange, P. 1991. Government Partisanship, Labor Organization and Macroeconomic Performance. APSR 85: 539-556.
3 Annals. 1972. Papers on Multinational Corporations. ANNALS 403.
4 Ayers, I. 1987. How Cartels Punish: A Structural Theory of Self-Enforcing Collusion. Columbia Law Review 87: 295-326.
5 Bachman, D. 1992. Effect of Political Risk on Forward Exchange Bias: Elections. JIMF 11: 208-219.
6 Barbalet, J. M. 1992. Class and Rationality: Olson's Critique of Marx. SAS 55 (Winter): 446-468.
7 Beck, N. 1982. Presidential Influence on the Federal Reserve. AJPS 26: 415-445.
8 Bornschier, V. 1980. Multinational Corporations and Economic Growth: Test of the Decapitalization Thesis. JDE 7: 191-210.
9 -. 1981. Dependent Industrialization in the World Economy. JCR 25: 371-400.
10 Brooker, R. G. 1983. Elections and Governmental Responsibility: Exploring a Normative Problem with Simulations. SAG 14: 139-154.
11 Carmichael, F. 1992. Multinational Enterprise and Strikes. SJPE 39: 52-68.
12 Comparative Studies in Society and History. 1979. Papers on Government in Preindustrial Economies. CSSH 21 (2).
13 Conybeare, J. A. C. 1980. International Organization and the Theory of Property Rights. IO 34: 307-334.
14 Crafton, S. M. 1980. Test of the Effect of Usury Laws. JOLE 23: 135-146.
15 Daedalus. 1987. Papers on Philanthropy, Patronage and Politics. Vol 116 (1).
16 DiLorenzo, T. J. 1983. Economic Competition and Political Competition. PC 40: 203-210.
17 Eichengreen, B. 1993. European Monetary Unification. JEL 31: 1321-1357.
18 Etudes Internationales. 1985. Papers on Multinationals. EINT 16 (2).
19 Faith, R. L.; Short, N. C. 1995. Bureaucratic Tenure and Economic Performance in Centrally Planned Economies. PC 83: 139-148.
20 Frantianni, M.; Von Hagen, J. 1990. Public Choice Aspects of European Monetary Unification. CJ 10: 389-411.
21 Hayes, B. C. 1995. Impact of Class on Political Attitudes. EJPR 27: 69-92.
22 Hodson, R.; Schervish, P. G.; Stryker, R. 1988. Class Interests and Class Factions in the Late Twentieth Century. Research in Politics and Society 3: 191-220.
23 Iida, K. 1993. The Political Economy of Exchange Rate Policy. JPP 13: 327-350.
24 International Studies Quarterly. 1972. Papers on Multinational Corporations. ISQ 16 (4).
25 Journal of Common Market Studies. 1987. Papers on Multinational Corporations and European Integration. JCMS 26 (2).
26 -. 1989. Papers on the European Monetary System. JCMS 27 (3) and JCMS 1990 28 (4).
27 Journal of International Affairs. 1989. Papers on International Political Economy. JIA 42 (1).
28 Kelley, J.; McAllister, I.; Mughan, A. 1985. The Decline of Class Revisited: Class and Party in England. APSR 79: 719-736.
29 Kent, S. A. 1983. Quaker Ethic and Fixed Price Policy: Max Weber and Beyond. SI 53: 16-32.
30 Kirkpatrick, G. 1994. Philosophical Foundations of Analytical Marxism. SAS 58: 34-52.
31 Kwon, G. H. 1995. The Declining Role of Western Powers in International Organizations: Exploring a New Model of UN Burden Sharing. JPP 15: 65-88.
32 Latin American Perspectives, 1993. Papers on Class Conflict in Latin America. LAPER 20 (2).
33 Laver, M. 1977. Intergovernmental Policy on Multinational Corporations. EJPR 5: 363-380.
34 Lockerbie, B. 1993. Economic Dissatisfaction and Political Alienation in Western Europe. EJPR 23: 281-294.
35 Loriaux, M. 1989. Comparative Political Economy as Comparative History. CP 21: 355-377.
36 Mauser, G. A.; Fitzsimmons, C. 1991. Effect of Election Polls on Foreign Exchange Rates: The 1988 Canadian Federal Election. POQ 55: 232-240.
37 Mehrling, P. G. 1986. Classical Model of the Class Struggle: Game-Theoretic Approach. JPE 94: 1280-1303.
38 Mingst, K. A.; Stauffer, R. E. 1979. Intervention Analysis of Political Disturbances, Market Shocks and Policy Initiatives in International Commodity Markets. IO 33: 105-118.
39 Mintz, A. 1988. Electoral Cycles and Defense Spending: Israel and the US. CPS 21: 368-381.
40 Mitchell, W. C. 1968. The New Political Economy. SR 68: 76-110.
41 Norpoth, H. 1987. Guns and Butter and Government Popularity in Britain. APSR 81: 949-959.
42 Nossal, K. R. 1980. Does the Electoral Cycle in the US Affect Relations with Canada? IJ 36: 208-227.

43 Przeworski, A.; Wallerstein, M. B. 1982. Structure of Class Conflict in Democratic Capitalist Societies. APSR 76: 215-238.

44 -. 1988. Structural Dependence of the State on Capital. APSR 82: 11-29.

45 Regional Science and Urban Economics. 1993. Papers on European Economic Integration. RSUE 23 (3).

46 Reiman, J. 1987. Exploitation, Force and Moral Assessment of Capitalism: Roemer and Cohen. PAPA 16: 3-41.

47 Review of Radical Political Economics. 1986. Papers on Empirical Studies of Marxian Crisis Theory. RRPE 18 (1/2).

48 Ringdal, K.; Hines, K. 1995. Patterns of Class Voting: Decline or Trendless Fluctuations? AS 38: 33-52.

49 Rosenberg, S. W. 1995. Against Neoclassical Political Economy: A Political Psychology Critique. PP 16: 99-136.

50 Skocpol, T. 1980. Political Responses to Capitalist Crisis: Neo-Marxist Theories of the State and the Case of the New Deal. PAS 10: 155-201.

51 Sociological Perspectives. 1992. Papers on the New Comparative International Political Economy. SP 35 (2).

52 Sunkel, O. 1973. Transnational Capitalism and National Disintegration in Latin America. Social and Economic Studies 22: 132-176.

53 Swedberg, R. 1986. The Critique of the Economy and Society Perspective. AS 29: 91-112.

54 Vanneman, R. D. 1980. US and British Perceptions of Class. AJS 85: 766-790.

55 Wright, E. O.; Martin, B. 1987. Transformation of the American Class Structure. AJS 93: 1-29.

Budgets

56 Alesina, A.; Perotti, R. 1995. Political Economy of Budget Deficits. IMFSP 42: 1-31.

57 Allen, C.; Vines, D. 1993. Should Clinton Cut the Budget or Is There a Paradox of Thrift? World Economy 16: 133-158.

58 Almond, S. 1965. Distribution between Capital Appropriations and Expenditures. Econometrica 30: 178-196.

59 Alt, J. E.; Lowry, R. C. 1994. Divided Government, Fiscal Institutions and Budget Deficits: Evidence from the States. APSR 88: 811-828.

60 Bails, D. G. 1990. Effectiveness of Tax-Expenditure Limitations. AJEAS 49: 223-238.

61 Barro, R. J. 1987. Government Spending, Interest Rates, Prices and Budget Deficits in the United Kingdom. JME 20: 221-247.

62 Berne, R.; Leanna, S. 1993. Cutback Budgeting: Long-Term Consequences. JPAAM 12: 664-684.

63 Berry, W. D. 1990. The Confusing Case of Budgetary Incrementalism. JOP 52: 167-196.

64 Berry, W. D.; Lowery, D. 1990. Understanding Budgetary Trade Offs. AJPS 34: 671-705.

65 Blejer, M. L.; Cheasty, A. 1991. Measurement of Fiscal Deficits. JEL 29: 1644-1678.

66 Bohn, H. 1995. Sustainability of Budget Deficits in a Stochastic Economy. JMCB 27: 257-271.

67 Brouthers, L. E.; Larson, J. S. 1988. Controlling Growth of Federal Spending: The 1974 Congressional Budget Reforms. ARPA 18: 419-428.

68 Bureaucrat. 1978. Papers on Zero Base Budgeting. Vol 7 (1).

69 Caiden, N. 1994. Budgeting in Historical and Comparative Perspective. PBAF 14: 44-57.

70 Campbell, B.; Ghysels, E. 1995. Federal Budget Projections: Bias and Efficiency. REAS 77: 17-31

71 Case, A. C.; Rosen, H. S.; Hines, J. R. 1993. Budget Spillovers and Fiscal Policy Interdependence. JPUBE 52: 285-307.

72 Castles, F. G. 1994. Is Expenditure Enough? On the Dependent Variable in Comparative Public Policy Analysis. JCACP 32: 349-363.

73 Cebula, R. J. 1988. Federal Government Budget Deficits and Interest Rates. PF 43: 337-348.

74 -. 1993. Analysis of Federal Budget Deficits and Interest Rates Directly Affecting Savings and Loans. SEJ 60: 28-35.

75 Cebula, R. J.; Belton, W. J. 1993. Government Budget Deficits and Interest Rates in the US. PF 48: 188-209.

76 Cebula, R. J.; Hung, C. 1992. Government Budget Deficits and Interest Rates. RISEC 39: 917-928.

77 Chester, E. 1977. Some Social and Economic Determinants of Non-Military Public Spending. PF 32: 176-185.

78 Chicoine, D. L.; Walzer, N.; Deller, S. C. 1989. Representative vs. Direct Democracy and Government Spending in a Median Voter Model. PF 44: 225-236.

79 Christ, C. F. 1979. Fiscal and Monetary Policies and Budget Restraint. AER 69: 526-538.

80 Clingermayer, J. C.; Wood, B. D. 1995. Disentangling Patterns of State Debt Financing. APSR 89: 109-120.

81 Coleman, K. M.; Wanat, J. 1975. Measuring Mexican Presidential Ideology through Budgets. LARR 10: 77-88.

82 Comiskey, M. 1993 Electoral Competition and Growth of Public Spending in Industrial Democracies. CPS 26: 350-374.

83 Croushore, D. D.; Koot, R. S.; Walker, D. A. 1990. Economic Stability and the Government Deficit. JPKE 12: 390-403.

84 Cukierman, A.; Meltzer, A. H. 1989. A Political Theory of Government Debt and Deficits. AER 79: 713-732.

85 Cullis, J. G.; Young, T. 1995. Detecting the Unseen Hand in Government: UK Budget Shares. AE 27: 251-258.

86 Dao, M. Q. 1995. The Determinants of Government Expenditures. OBES 57: 67-76.

87 Davis, O. A.; Dempster, M.; Wildavsky, A. 1966. A Theory of the Budgetary Process. APSR 60: 529-547.

88 Dearden, J. A.; Husted, T. A. 1990. Executive Budget Proposal, Executive Veto, Legislative Override and Uncertainty. PC 65: 1-19.

89 -. 1993. Do Governors Get What They Want? An Alternative Examination of the Line-Item Veto. PC 77: 707-724.

90 Dunleavy, P. 1985. Bureaucrats, Budgets and the Growth of the State. BJPS 15: 299-328.

91 Edin, P. A.; Ohlsson, H. 1991. Political Determinants of Budget Deficits. EER 35: 1597-1603.

92 Evans, P. 1987. Do Budget Deficits Raise Nominal Interest Rates? JME 20: 281-300.

93 Ferejohn, J. A.; Krehbiel, K. 1987. The Budget Process and the Size of the Budget. AJPS 31: 296-320.

94 Fischer, G. W.; Kamlet, M. S. 1984. Explaining Presidential Priorities: A Competing Aspiration Levels Model of Macrobudgetary Decision Making. APSR 78: 356-371.

95 Fisher, L. 1970. Politics of Impounded Funds. ASQ 15: 361-377.

96 Fuchs-Seliger, S. 1986. Rational Budgeters in the Theory of Social Choice. SCAW 3: 161-176.

97 Godwin, R. K.; Shepard, W. B. 1976. Political Processes and Public Expenditures. APSR 70: 1127-1135.

98 Goff, B. L. 1993. Evaluating Alternative Explanations of Federal Deficits. PC 75: 247-261.

99 Goldsmith, O. S. 1984. Simulations of State Government Fiscal Policy: Balanced Budget Multiplier. ARS 18: 57-65.

100 Habibi, N. 1994. Budgetary Policy and Political Liberty. WD 22: 579-586.

101 Hadjimatheou, G.; Tackie, A. 1992. Modelling Public Expenditure. IRAE 6: 65-92.

102 Hahm, S. D., et al. 1992. The Influence of the Gramm-Rudman-Hollings Act on Budgetary Outcomes. JPAAM 11: 207-234.

103 Hahm, S. D.; Kamlet, M. S.; Mowery, D. C. 1995. Influences on Deficit Spending in Industrial Democracies. JPP 15: 183 ff.

104 Hamilton, J. D.; Flavin, M. A. 1986. The Limitations of Government Borrowing. AEL 76: 808-819.

105 Horrigan, B. R. 1966. Determinants of the Public Debt of the US. EI 24: 11-23.

106 Jacobson, G. C. 1993. Deficit-Cutting Politics and Congressional Elections. PSQ 108: 375-402.

107 Jacoby, W. G. 1994. Public Attitudes toward Government Spending. AJPS 38: 336-361.

108 Jones, L. R.; McCaffery, J. L. 1994. Budgeting According to Wildavsky: A Bibliographical Essay. PBAF 14: 16-43.

109 Journal of Monetary Economics. 1987. Papers on Effects of Budget Deficits. JME 20 (2).

110 Kahn, J. 1993. Representing Government and Representing People: Budget Reform and Citizenship in New York City. JUH 19: 84-103.

111 Kamlet, M. S.; Mowery, D. C. 1987. Influences on Executive and Congressional Budgetary Priorities. APSR 81: 155-178.

112 Kamlet, M. S.; Mowery, D. C.; Su, T. T. 1987. An Analysis of Executive and Congressional Economic Forecasts. JPAAM 6: 365-384.

113 Kearns, P. S. 1994. State Budget Periodicity: Determinants and Effect on State Spending. JPAAM 13: 331-362.

114 Kiefer, D. M. 1988. A History of the US Federal Budget and Fiscal Policy. PF 43: 113-137.

115 Kobrak, P. 1993. Do Budget Deficits Matter? PSJ 21: 396-404.

116 Lanoue, D. J. 1991. Partisan Schemas and Economic Voting: Federal Budget Deficit and the 1988 Presidential Election. PB 13: 285-302.

117 Lindauer, D. L.; Velenchik, A. D. 1992. Government Spending in Developing Countries. World Bank Research Observer 7: 59-78.

118 Lloyd, R. E.; McGarrity, J. P. 1995. Analysis of the Senate Vote on Gramm-Rudman. PC 85: 81-90.

119 Manage, N.; Marlow, M. L. 1986. Causal Relationship between Federal Expenditures and Receipts. SEJ 52: 617-629.

120 Marlow, M. L. 1995. Influence of Special District Governments on Public Spending and Debt. AE 27: 569-573.

121 McMillin, W. D.; Beard, T. R. 1988. Do Budget Deficits Matter? JEAB 40: 295-308.

122 Muller, F. G.; Zimmermann, K. 1986. Determinants of Structural Changes in Public Budgets. EJPS 14: 481-498.

123 Musgrave, R. 1969. Cost-Benefit Analysis and the Theory of Public Finance. JEL 7: 797-806.

124 Natchez, P. B.; Bupp, I. C. 1973. Policy and Priority in Budget Process. APSR 67: 951-963.

125 Navin, J. C.; Navin, L. J. 1994. Evaluation of State Budget Stabilization Funds among Midwestern States. GAC 25: 445-466.

126 Newton, K. 1985. Why Local Budgets Grow. PA 12: 7-15.

127 Padgett, J. F. 1980. Bounded Rationality in Budgetary Research. APSR 74: 354-372.

128 Policy and Politics. 1984. Papers on Budgetary Decisionmaking. PAP 16 (4).

129 Policy Studies Journal. 1985. Papers on Responses to Budget Scarcity. PSJ 13: 471-562.

130 Poterba, J. M. 1994. State Responses to Fiscal Crises: Effects of Budgetary Institutions and Politics. JPE 102: 799-821.

131 -. 1995. Capital Budgets, Borrowing Rules and State Capital Spending. JPUBE 56: 165-187.

132 Public Budgeting and Finance. 1994. Papers on Aaron Wildavsky and Budgeting. PBAF 14 (1).

133 Ram, R. 1988. Causality between Government Revenue and Expenditure. PF 43: 261-270.

134 Rasinski, K. A. 1989. Effect of Question Wording on Public Support for Government Spending. POQ 53: 388-396.

135 Roubini, N. 1991. Economic and Political Determinants of Budget Deficits in Developing Countries. JIMF 10 (March Special Issue): S49-S72.

136 Roubini, N.; Sachs, J. 1989. Political and Economic Determinants of Budget Deficits in the Industrial Democracies. EER 33: 903-933.

137 Rubin, I. 1992. Budget Reform and Political Reform. PAR 52: 454-466.

138 Saunders, P. 1988. Explaining International Differences in Public Expenditures. PF 43: 271-291.

139 Schultze, C. L. 1992. Is There a Bias toward Excess in US Government Budgets or Deficits? JEP 6: 25-43.

140 Siermann, C. L. J.; De Haan, J. 1993. On Sustainability and Political Determinants of Government Debt in Developing Countries. RISEC 40: 81-92.

141 Speight, A. E. H., MacDonald, R. 1989. Does the Public Sector Obey the Rational Expectations-Permanent Income Hypothesis? Government Expenditures. AE 21: 1257-1266.

142 Stewart, C. 1988. Budget Reform as Strategic Legislative Action. JOP 50: 292-321.

143 Swank, D. H. 1988. Political Economy of Government Domestic Expenditure in Affluent Democracies. AJPS 32: 1120-1150.

144 Tabellini, G.; Alesina, A. 1990. Voting on the Budget Deficit. AER 80: 37-49.

145 Tanner, E.; Liu, P. 1994. Is the Budget Deficit Too Large? Further Evidence. EI 32: 511-518.

146 Teigen, R. L. 1980. Trends and Cycles in Composition of the Federal Budget. PSJ 9: 11-18.

147 Van Velthoven, B. C. J.; Van Winden, F. 1990. A Behavioral Model of Government Budget Deficits. PF 45: 128-161.

148 Waller, C. J. 1987. Deficit Financing and Role of the Central Bank: A Game Theoretic Approach. AEJ 15: 25-32.

149 Wanat, J. 1975. Bases of Budgetary Incrementalism. APSR 68: 1221-1228.

150 Whicker, M. L.; Moore, R. A. 1988. The Presidential Line Item Veto. PSQ 18: 143-156.

151 Wildavsky, A. 1985. A Cultural Theory of Expenditure Growth and (Un)balanced Budgets. JPUBE 28: 349-347.

152 Wlezien, C. 1994. The Politics of Impoundments. PRQ 47: 59-84.

Economics and Elections

153 Abramowitz, A. I.; Lanoue, D. J., Ramesh, S. 1988. Economic Conditions, Causal Attributions and Political Evaluations in the 1984 Presidential Election. JOP 50: 848-863.

154 Abrams, B. A. 1980. Influence of State-Level Economic Conditions on Presidential Elections. PC 35: 623-631.

155 Abrams, B. A.; Butkiewicz, J. L. 1995. The Influence of State Level Economic Conditions on the 1992 Presidential Election. PC 85: 1-10.

156 Alesina, A.; Cohen, G. D.; Roubini, N. 1992. Macroeconomic Policy and Elections in OECD Countries. EAP 4: 1-30.

157 Alt, J. E.; Chrystal, K. A. 1983. Criteria for Choosing Politico-Economic Model. EJPR 11: 115-123

158 Alvarez, R. M.; Nagler, J. 1995. Economics, Issues and Perot Candidacy. AJPS 39: 714-744.

159 Annett, A. M. 1993. Elections and Macroeconomic Outcomes in Ireland. EASR 25: 21-47.

160 Arcelus, F.; Meltzer, A. H. 1975. The Effect of Aggregate Economic Variables on Congressional Elections. APSR 69: 1232-1269.

161 Atesoglu, H. S.; Congleton, R. D. 1982. Economic Conditions and National Elections. APSR 76: 873-875.

162 Beck, N. 1982. Parties, Administrations and American Macroeconomic Outcomes. APSR 76: 83-93.

163 Bennett, R. W.; Wiseman, C. 1991. Economic Performance and Senate Elections. PC 69: 93-100.

164 Besley, T.; Case, A. C. 1995. Does Electoral Accountability Affect Economic Policy Choice? Gubernatorial Term Limits. QJE 110: 769-798.

165 Blood, D. J.; Phillips, P. C. B. 1995. Recession Headline News, Consumer Sentiment, the State of the Economy and Presidential Popularity. IJPOR 7: 2-22.

166 Bloom, H. S.; Price, H. D. 1975. Voter Response to Short Run Economic Conditions. APSR 69: 1240-1254.

167 Bowler, S.; Donovan, T. 1994. Economic Conditions and Voting on Ballot Propositions. APQ 22: 27-40.

168 Brophy-Baermann, M. 1994. Economics and Elections: Mexico. SSQ 75: 125-135.

169 Brown, W. W., Santoni, G. J. 1980. Economic Competition and Political Competition. PC 35: 27-36.

170 Carkoglu, A. 1995. Election Manifestos and Policy-Oriented Economic Voting. EJPR 27: 293-318.

171 Chappell, H. W. 1990. Economic Performance, Voting and Political Support. REAS 72: 313-320.

172 Chappell, H. W.; Keech, W. R. 1985. A New View of Political Accountability for Economic Performance. APSR 79: 10-27.

173 -. 1988. Employment Rate Consequences of Partisan Macroeconomic Policies. SEJ 55: 107-122.

174 Chressanthis, G. A.; Shaffer, S. D. 1993. Economic Performance and Senate Elections. PC 75: 263-277.

175 Chubb, J. E. 1988. Institutions, the Economy and Dynamics of State Elections. APSR 82: 133-154.

176 Claggett, W. 1983. Macro Economic Contractions, Socio-Welfare Programs and Congressional Election Outcomes. Polity 15: 429-438.

177 Clarke, H.D.; Stewart, M. C. 1994. Bankers Model of Presidential Approval. AJPS 38: 1104-1123.

178 -. 1995. Economic Evaluations, Prime Ministerial Approval and Governing Party Support. BJPS 25: 145-170.

179 Conover, P. J. 1985. Impact of Group Economic Interests on Political Evaluations. APQ 13: 139-166.

180 Conover, P. J.; Feldman, S. 1986. Emotional Reactions to the Economy. AJPS 30: 50-78.

181 Crain, W. M.; Deaton, T. H.; Tollison, R. D. 1978. Macroeconomic Determinants of the Vote in Presidential Elections. PFQ 6: 427-438.

182 Cuzan, A. G.; Bundrick, C. M. 1992. Selected Fiscal and Economic Effects on Presidential Elections. PSQ 22 (Winter): 127-134.

183 Cuzan, A. G.; Heggen, R. J. 1984. A Fiscal Model of Presidential Elections. PSQ 14: 98-108.

184 Erikson, R. S. 1989. Economic Conditions and the Presidential Vote. APSR 83: 567-576.

185 -. 1990. Economic Conditions and the Congressional Vote. AJPS 34: 373-405.

186 Fair, R. C. 1978. Effects of Economic Events on the Vote for President. REAS 60: 159-175.

187 Feldman, P.; Jondrow, J. 1984. Congressional Elections and Local Federal Spending. AJPS 28: 147-164.

188 Fenmore, B.; Volgy, T. J. 1978. Short Term Economic Change and Political Instability in Latin America. WPQ 31: 548-564.

189 Ferejohn, J. A. 1986. Incumbent Performance and Electoral Control. PC 50: 5-25.

190 Finkel, S. E.; Muller, E. N.; Seligson, M. A. 1989. Economic Crisis, Incumbent Performance and Regime Support. BJPS 19: 329-352.

191 Fiorina, M. P. 1978. Economic Retrospective Voting in National Elections. AJPS 22: 426-443.

192 Fiorina, M. P.; Shepsle, K. A. 1989. Is Negative Voting an Artifact? AJPS 33: 423-439.

193 Flanagan, S. C. 1980. Value Cleavages, Economic Cleavages and Japanese Voter. AJPS 24: 177-206.

194 Franz, G. 1986. Economic Aspirations, Well Being and Political Support in Recession and Boom: West Germany. EJPR 14: 97-112.

195 Frey, B. S.; Schneider, F. 1978. A Political-Economic Model of the UK. EJ 88: 243-253.

196 Galeotti, G.; Forcina, A. 1989. Political Loyalties and the Economy. REAS 71: 511-517.

197 Garrett, G.; Lange, P. 1989. Government Partisanship and Economic Performance: When and How Does Who Governs Matter? JOP 51: 676-698.

198 Goodhart, C. A. E.; Bhansali, R. J. 1970. Political Economy. POLST 18: 43-106.

199 Gough, P.; Brunk, G. G. 1983. State Level Economic Conditions and 1980 Presidential Election. PSQ 13: 62-69.

200 Haller, H. B.; Norpoth, H. 1994. Economic Expectations of US Voters. AJPS 38: 625-650.

201 Happy, J. R. 1989. Economic Preferences and Retrospective Voting in Canadian Federal Elections. CJPS 22: 377-387.

202 Harmel, R.; Robertson, J. D. 1986. Government Stability and Regime Support. JOP 48: 1029-1040.

203 Haynes, S. E. 1995. Electoral and Partisan Cycles between Economic Performance and Presidential Popularity. AE 27: 95-105.

204 Hibbing, J. R.; Alford, J. R. 1981. Electoral Impact of Economic Conditions. AJPS 25: 423-439.

205 Hibbs, D. A. 1977. Political Parties and Macroeconomic Policy. APSR 71: 1467-1487.

206 -. 1979. Mass Public and Macroeconomic Performance: Unemployment and Inflation. AJPS 23: 705-731.

207 -. 1984. Demand for Economic Outcomes: Macroeconomic Performance and Mass Political Support. JOP 44: 426-462.

208 -. 1985. Macro Economic Performance, Policy and Electoral Politics in Industrial Democracies. ISSJ 37: 63-74.

209 Hibbs, D. A.; Vasilatos, N. 1981. Economics and Politics in France: Economic Performance and Mass Political Support for Presidents. EJPR 9: 133-146.

210 -. 1982. Economic Outcomes and Political Support for British Governments among Occupational Classes. APSR 76: 259-281.

211 Holbrook, T. M. 1994. Campaigns, National Conditions and Presidential Elections. AJPS 38: 973-998.

212 Hudson, J. 1984. Prime Ministerial Popularity in the UK. POLST 32: 86-97.

213 Jonung, L.; Wodensjo, E. 1979. Effects of Unemployment, Inflation and Real Income on Government Popularity in Sweden. SJE 81: 343-353.

214 Kau, J. B.; Rubin, P. H. 1984. Economic and Ideological Factors in Congressional Voting. PC 44: 385-388.

215 Keech, W. R. 1982. Economic Outcomes and Political Support for British Governments among Occupational Classes. APSR 76: 259-284.

216 Kenney, P. J. 1983. Effect of State Economic Conditions on the Vote for Governor. SSQ 64: 154-162.

217 Kenski, H. C. 1979. Impact of Unemployment on Congressional Elections. APQ 7: 132-146.

218 Kiecolt, K. J. 1987. Group Consciousness and the Attribution of Blame for National Economic Problems. APQ 15: 203-222.

219 Kiewiet, D. R. 1981. Policy Oriented Voting in Response to Economic Issues. APSR 75: 448-459.

220 Kinder, D. R.; Kiewiet, D. R. 1979. Economic Discontent and Political Behavior: Personal Grievances and Collective Economic Judgments in Congressional Voting. AJPS 23: 495-527.

221 -. 1979. Sociotropic Politics. BJPS 11: 129-161.

222 Klorman, R. 1978. Trend in Personal Finances and the Vote. POQ 33: 31-48.

223 Kormenci, R. C.; Meguire, P. G. 1984. Cross Regime Evidence of Macroeconomic Rationality. JPE 92: 875-908.

224 Kornberg, A.; Clarke, H. D.; LeDuc, L. 1978. Correlates of Regime Support in Canada. BJPS 8: 199-216.

225 Kramer, G. H. 1971. Short Term Fluctuations in US Voting Behavior. APSR 65: 131-143.

226 -. 1983. Ecological Fallacy Revisited: Aggregate vs. Individual Level Findings on Economics and Elections and Sociotropic Voting. APSR 77: 92-111.

227 Kuechler, M. 1986. A Replication of Himmelweit's Consumer Model of Voting with German Election Data. EJPR 14: 81-96.

228 Kuklinski, J. H.; West, D. M. 1981. Economic Expectations and Voting Behavior in US House and Senate Elections. APSR 75: 436-447.

229 Leithner, C. 1993. Economic Conditions and the Vote. BJPS 23: 339-372.

230 Lepper, S. J. 1975. Voting Behavior and Aggregate Policy Targets. PC 18: 67-81.

231 Lewis, A. 1980. Attitudes to Public Expenditure and Their Relationship to Voting Preferences. POLST 28: 284-292.

232 Lewis, A.; Jackson, D. 1985. Voting Preferences and Attitudes to Public Expenditure. POLST 33: 457-466.

233 Lewis-Beck, M. S. 1980. Economic Conditions and Executive Popularity: French Experience. AJPS 24: 306-323.

234 -. 1983. Economics and the French Voter. POQ 47: 347-360.

235 -. 1985. Pocketbook Voting in US National Election Studies. AJPS 29: 348-356.

236 -. 1986. Economic Voting: Britain. AJPS 30: 315-346.

237 -. 1988. Economics and the American Vote. PB 10: 5-21.

238 Lewis-Beck, M. S.; Rice, T. W. 1985. Economic Conditions, Presidential Popularity and Voting in Mid-Term Elections. JOP 47: 2-30.

239 Leyden, K. M.; Borelli, S. A. 1995. The Effect of State Economic Conditions on Gubernatorial Elections: Does Unified Government Make a Difference? PRQ 48: 275-290.

240 Li, R. P. Y. 1976. Public Policy and Short-Term Fluctuations in US Voting Behavior. PM 3: 47-70.

241 Lockerbie, B. 1991. Prospective Economic Voting in US House Elections. LSQ 16: 239-262.

242 MacKuen, M. B. 1983. Political Drama, Economic Conditions and the Dynamics of Presidential Popularity. AJPS 27: 165-192.

243 MacKuen, M. B.; Erikson, R. S.; Stimson, J. A. 1992. Peasants or Bankers? American Electorate and the US Economy. APSR 86: 597-611.

244 Markus, G. B. 1990. Impact of Personal and National Economic Conditions on the Presidential Vote. AJPS 32: 137-154.

245 -. 1992. Impact of Personal and National Economic Conditions on Presidential Voting. AJPS 36: 829-834.

246 Meltzer, A. H.; Vellrach, M. 1975. Effects of Economic Policies on Vote for the Presidency. JOLE 18: 781-797.

247 Monroe, K. R. 1978. Economic Influences on Presidential Popularity. POQ 42: 360-370.

248 -. 1979. Inflation and Presidential Popularity. PSQ 9: 334-340.

249 -. 1981. Presidential Popularity: Almon Distributed Lag Model. PM 7: 43-70.

250 Nadeau, R.; Blais, A. 1993. Explaining Election Outcomes in Canada. CJPS 26: 775-790.

251 Nannestad, P.; Paldam, M. 1994. Vote-Popularity Function. PC 79: 213-246.

252 -. 1995. A Cross-Section Study of Economic Voting. EJPR 28: 33-62.

253 Niemi, R. G.; Stanley, H. W.; Vogel, R. 1995. State Economies and State Taxes: Do Voters Hold Governors Accountable? AJPS 39: 936-957.

254 Owens, J. R.; Olson, E. C. 1980. Economic Fluctuations and Congressional Elections. AJPS 24: 469-493.

255 Owens, J. R.; Wade, L. L. 1988. Economic Conditions and Constituency Voting in Great Britain. POLST 36: 30-51.

256 Pacek, A. C. 1994. Macroeconomic Conditions and Electoral Politics in East Central Europe. AJPS 38: 723-744.

257 Pacek, A. C.; Radcliff, B. 1995. Economic Voting and the Welfare State. JOP 57: 44-61.

258 Paldam, M. 1981. Survey of Theories and Findings on Vote and Popularity Functions. EJPR 9: 181-200.

259 Panzer, J.; Parades, R. D. 1991. Role of Economic Issues in Elections: 1988 Chilean Presidential Referendum. PC 71: 51-60.

260 Partin, R. W. 1995. Economic Conditions and Gubernatorial Elections: Is the State Executive Held Accountable? APQ 23: 81-95.

261 Pattie, C. J.; Johnston, R. J. 1995. Region, Economic Evaluations and Voting at the 1992 British General Election. EJPR 28: 1-32.

262 Peffley, M. 1984. Voter as Juror: Attributing Responsibility for Economic Conditions. PB 6: 275-294.

263 Peltzman, S. 1992. Voters as Fiscal Conservatives. QJE 107: 327-361.

264 Powell, G. B.; Whitten, G. D. 1993. A Cross National Analysis of Economic Voting. AJPS 37: 391-414.

265 Price, S.; Sanders, D. 1993. Modeling Government Popularity in Postwar Britain. AJPS 37: 317-334.

266 -. 1994. Economic Competence, Rational Expectations and Government Popularity in Post War Britain. MSESS 62: 296-312.

267 -. 1995. Economic Expectations and Voting Intentions in the UK. POLST 43: 451-471.

268 Radcliff, B. 1988. Aggregate Analysis and Economic Voting Revisited. JOP 50: 440-455.

269 -. 1992. Welfare State, Turnout and Economy. APSR 86: 444-456.

270 -. 1994. Economic Conditions and the Vote. PRQ 47: 721-732.

271 Reed, S. R.; Brunk, G. G. 1984. Test of Theories of Economically Motivated Voting: Japan. CP 17: 55-66.

272 Remmer, K. L. 1993. Political Economy of Elections in Latin America. APSR 87: 393-407.

273 Sanders, D.; Marsh, D.; Ward, H. 1993. Electoral Impact of Press Coverage of the British Economy. BJPS 23: 175-210.

274 Scarborough, E. 1991. Micro and Macro Analysis of Elections. EJPR 19: 361-398.

275 Scott, W. J.; Ropers, R. H. 1980. Unemployment and Political Partisanship. Sociological Focus 13: 359-368.

276 Shapiro, R. Y.; Conforto, M. 1980. Presidential Performance, the Economy and the Public's Evaluation of Economic Conditions. JOP 42: 49-81.

277 Sigelman, L. 1991. Jews and Pocketbook Voting. JOP 53: 977-992.

278 Sigelman, L.; Sigelman, C. K.; Bullock, D. 1991. Reconsidering Pocketbook Voting. PB 13: 129-150.

279 Sorensen, R. J. 1987. Macroeconomic Policy and Government Popularity in Norway. SPS 10: 301-322

280 Stein, R. M. 1990. Economic Voting for Governor and US Senate: Consequences of Federalism. JOP 52: 29-53.

281 Stigler, G. J. 1973. General Economic Conditions and National Elections. AER 63: 160-167.

282 Suzuki, M. 1991. Rationality of Economic Voting and the Macroeconomic Regime. AJPS 35: 624-642.

283 Swank, D. H. 1994. Partisan Views on the Economy. PC 81: 137-150.

284 Wade, L. L. 1989. The Influence of Sections and Periods on Economic Voting in Presidential Elections. PG 8: 271-288.

285 Weatherford, M. S. 1972. Economic Conditions and Electoral Outcomes: Class Differences in Political Response to Recession. AJPS 22: 917-938.

286 -. 1981. How Economic Events Affect Electoral Outcomes: A Model of Political Translation. Micropolitics 1: 269-294.

287 -. 1983. Economic Voting and the Symbolic Politics Argument. APSR 77: 158-174.

288 -. 1984. Economic Stagflation and Public Support for the Political System. BJPS 14: 187-205.

289 -. 1987. How Does Government Performance Influence Political Support? PB 9: 5-28.

290 Weisberg, H. F.; Smith, C. E. 1991. Influence of the Economy on Party Identification. JOP 53: 1077-1092.

291 Welch, S.; Foster, L. S. 1992. Impact of Economic Conditions on the Voting Behavior of Blacks. WPQ 45: 221-236.

292 Wilcox, C.; Allsop, D. 1991. Economics and Foreign Policy as Sources of Reagan Support. WPQ 44: 941-958.

293 Winder, R. C. 1992. Presidential Popularity and the Economy: Demographic Differences. JEBAO 18: 91-99.

Interest Groups

294 Abney, G.; Lauth, T. P. 1985. Interest Group Influence in City Policy Making. WPQ 38: 148-161.

295 Ainsworth, S. 1993. Regulating Lobbyists and Interest Group Influence. JOP 55: 41-56.

296 -. 1995. Electoral Strength and Emergence of Group Influence in the Late 1800s: Grand Army of the Republic. APQ 23: 319-338.

297 American Journal of Agricultural Economics. 1991. Papers on International Capital and Interest Groups. AJAE 73 (3).

298 Anderson, G. M.; Tollison, R. D. 1988. Democracy, Interest Groups and the Price of Votes. CJ 8: 53-70.

299 Anderson, K. 1995. Lobbying Incentives and the Pattern of Protection in Rich and Poor Countries. EDACC 43: 401-424.

300 Austen-Smith, D. 1987. Interest Groups, Campaign Contributions and Probabilistic Voting. PC 54: 123-140.

301 -. 1993. Information and Influence: Lobbying for Agendas and Votes. AJPS 37: 780-798.

302 Austen-Smith, D.; Wright, J. R. 1992. Competitive Lobbying for a Legislator's Vote. SCAW 9: 229-257.

303 Bacheller, J. M. 1977. Lobbyists and the Legislative Process: Environmental Constraints. APSR 71: 252-263.

304 Ball, R. 1995. Interest Groups, Influence and Welfare. EAP 7: 119-146.

305 Baumgartner, F. R.; Walker, J. L. 1989. Educational Policymaking and Interest Group Structure in France and the US. CP 21: 273-288.

306 Becker, G. S. 1993. Theory of Competition among Pressure Groups for Political Influence. QJE 98: 371-401.

307 Berry, J. M. 1978. On the Origins of Public Interest Groups. Polity 10: 379-397.

308 -. 1993. Citizen Groups and Changing Nature of Interest Groups in America. ANNALS 528: 30-41.

309 Brinig, M. F.; Holcombe, R. G.; Schwartzstein, L. 1993. The Regulation of Lobbyists. PC 77: 377-384.

310 Browne, C. 1989. Explanations of Interest Group Membership over Time. APQ 17: 32-53.

311 Browne, W. P. 1985. Variations in Behavior and Style of State Lobbyists and Interest Groups. JOP 47: 450-468.

312 -. 1990. Organized Interests and Issue Niches: A Search for Pluralism in a Policy Domain. JOP 52: 477-509.

313 Brace, P., et al. 1989. How Much Do Interest Groups Influence State Economic Growth. APSR 83: 1287-1308.

314 Brunk, G. G.; Wilson, L. A.; Hunter, K. 1991. Economic Innovation and Interest Groups. SSQ 72: 601-607.

315 Cameron, D. R. 1988. Distributional Coalitions and Sources of Economic Stagnation: Olson's Rise and Decline of Nations. IO 42: 561-603.

316 Castles, F. G. 1991. Democratic Politics, War and Catch Up: Olson's Thesis and Long Term Economic Growth. JTP 3: 5-36.

317 Chan, S. 1987. Growth with Equity: A Test of Olson's Theory for the Asian Pacific Rim Countries. JPR 24: 135-149.

318 Clingermayer, J. C.; Feiock, R. C. 1990. Adoption of Economic Development Policies in Large Cities: Economic, Interest Group and Institutional Explanations. PSJ 18: 539-552.

319 Cook, C. E. 1984. Participation in Public Interest Groups. APQ 12: 409-430.

320 Cummings, F. J.; Ruhter, W. E. 1980. Test of the Factor Supplier Pressure Group Hypothesis. PC 35: 257-266.

321 Davis, F. L.; Wurth, A. H. 1993. American Interest Group Research. POLST 41: 435-452.

322 Dawes, R. M., et al. 1986. Organizing Groups for Collective Action. APSR 80: 1171-1186.

323 Denzau, A. T.; Munger, M. C. 1986. Legislators and Interest Groups: How Unorganized Interests Get Represented. APSR 80: 89-106.

324 Edelman, S. A. 1992. Two Politicians, a PAC and How They Interact: Two Extensive Form Games. EAP 4: 289-305.

325 Education and Urban Society. 1981. Papers on Interest Groups. EAUS 13 (2).

326 Fischler, H. 1980. Monopolies, Market Interdependencies and the Logic of Collective Action: Mancur Olson's Group Therapy. PC 35: 191-196.

327 Forsythe, D. P.; Welch, S. 1983. Joining and Supporting Public Interest Groups. WPQ 36: 386-399.

328 Gais, T. L.; Peterson, M. A.; Walker, J. L. 1984. Interest Groups, Iron Triangles and Representative Institutions in American National Government. BJPS 14: 161-185.

329 Garand, J. C. 1992. Changing Patterns of Relative State Economic Growth over Time: Limitations on Cross Sectional Tests of Olson's Thesis. WPQ 45: 469-484.

330 Garson, G. D. 1975. On the Origins of Interest Group Theory. APSR 68: 1505-1509.

331 Goldsmith, A. A. 1986. Democracy, Political Stability and Economic Growth in Developing Countries: Olson's Theory of Distributional Coalitions. CPS 18: 517-531.

332 -. 1987. Does Political Stability Hinder Economic Development? Mancur Olson's Theory and the Third World. CP 19: 471-480.

333 Gopoian, J. D. 1984. What Makes PACs Tick? An Analysis of the Allocation Patterns of Economic Interest Groups. AJPS 28: 259-281.

334 Gormley, W. T. 1979. A Test of the Revolving Door Hypothesis at the FCC. AJPS 23: 665-683.

335 Gray, V.; Lowery, D. 1988. Interest Group Politics and Economic Growth in the US States. APSR 82: 109-131.

336 -. 1993. Diversity of State Interest Group Systems. PRQ 46: 81-98.

337 -. 1993. Stability and Change in State Interest Group Systems. SALGR 25: 87-96.

338 -. 1994. Interest Group Density and Diversity. IPSR 15: 5-14.

339 -. 1995. Demography of Interest Organization Communities. APQ 23: 3-32.

340 -. 1995. Interest Representation and Democratic Gridlock. LSQ 20: 531-552.

341 Greenwood, J.; Ronit, K. 1994. Interest Groups in the European Community. WEP 17: 31-52.

342 Grier, K. B.; Munger, M. C.; Roberts, B. E. 1994. Determinants of Industrial Political Activity. APSR 88: 911-926.

343 Hadley, C. D.; Barrilleaux, C. J. 1989. Questioning Interest Groups and PACS as Interchangeable Indicators. Policy 21: 598-605.

344 Hamm, K. E. 1986. Role of Subgovernments in US State Policy Making. LSQ 11: 321-352.

345 Hammack, D. C. 1981. Economic Interest Groups and Path Analysis: Approaches to the History of Power. JIDH 11: 695-704.

346 Hansen, J. M. 1985. Political Economy of Group Membership. APSR 79: 79-96.

347 Hayes, M. T. 1978. The Semi-Sovereign Pressure Group: A Critique. JOP 134-161.

348 Hoenack, S. A. 1989. Group Behavior and Economic Growth. SSQ 70: 744-767.

349 Hoyt, W. H.; Toma, E. F. 1989. State Mandates and Interest Group Lobbying. JPUBE 38: 199-213.

350 Hunter, K.; Wilson, L. A.; Brunk, G. G. 1991. Societal Complexity and Interest Group Lobbying. JOP 53: 488-503.

351 International Studies Quarterly. 1983. Papers on Olson's Rise and Decline of Nations. ISQ 27 (1).

352 Jackson, J. E.; Kingdon, J. W. 1992. Ideology, Interest Group Scores and Legislative Votes. AJPS 36: 805-823.

353 Jankowski, R. 1988. Preference Aggregation in Political Parties and Interest Groups: A Synthesis of Corporatist and Encompassing Organization Theory. AJPS 32: 105-125.

354 Kasza, G. J. 1993. Parties, Interest Groups and Administered Mass Organizations. CPS 26: 81-110.

355 Kennelly, B.; Murrell, P. 1991. Industry Characteristics and Interest Group Formation. PC 70: 21-40.

356 Kimenyi, M. S. 1989. Interest Groups: Transfer Seeking and Democratization: African Political Stability. AJEAS 48: 339-350.

357 Kindleberger, C. P. 1983. On the Rise and Decline of Nations. ISQ 26: 5-10.

358 King, D. C.; Walker, J. L. 1992. Provision of Benefits by Interest Groups. JOP 54: 394-426.

359 Knoke, D. 1985. Political Economies of Associations. Research in Political Science 1: 211-242.

360 -. 1988. Incentives in Collective Action Organizations. ASR 53: 311-329.

361 Krehbiel, K. 1994. Deference, Extremism and Interest Group Ratings. LSQ 19: 61-78.

362 Lessmann, S. 1989. Government, Interest Groups and Incrementalism. EJPR 17: 449-470.

363 Lowery, D.; Gray, V. 1994. Nationalization of State Interest Group System Density and Diversity. SSQ 75: 368-384.

364 -. 1995. Population Ecology of Gucci Gulch or the Natural Regulation of Interest Group Numbers. AJPS 39: 1-29.

365 Lowi, T. J. 1967. Interest Group Liberalism. APSR 61: 5-24.

366 Maitland, I. 1985. Interest Groups and Economic Growth Rates. JOP 47: 44-58.

367 Maloney, W. A.; Jordan, G.; McLaughlin, S. M. 1994. Interest Groups and Public Policy: Insider-Outsider Model Revisited. JPP 14: 17-38.

368 Matthews, T. 1990. Federalism and Interest Group Cohesion: Australia. Publius 20: 105-128.

369 McCallum, J.; Blais, A. 1987. Government, Special Interest Groups and Economic Growth. PC 54: 3-18.

370 McFarland, A. S. 1987. Interest Groups and Theories of Power in America. BJPS 17: 129-147.

371 -. 1991. Interest Groups and Political Time: Cycles in America. BJPS 21: 257-284.

372 Meier, K. J.; Copeland, G. W. 1983. Interest Groups and Public Policy. SSQ 64: 641-646.

373 Meier, K. J.; Van Lohuizen, J. R. 1978. Interest Groups in the Appropriations Process. SSQ 59: 482-495.

374 Meyer, D. S.; Imig, D. R. 1993. Political Opportunity and the Rise and Decline of Interest Group Sectors. SSJ 30: 253-270.

375 Micheletti, M. 1990. Toward Interest Inarticulation: Consequence of Corporatism for Interest Organizations. SPS 13: 255-276.

376 Miller, G. P. 1989. Public Choice at the Dawn of the Special Interest State: Butter and Margarine. CLR 77: 83-132.

377 Mitchell, J. M.; Mitchell, W. C. 1983. Truman's The Governmental Process: A Public Choice Perspective. Micropolitics 3: 67-87.

378 Mitchell, W. C.; Munger, M. C. 1991. Economic Models of Interest Groups. AJPS 35: 512-546.

379 Mixon, F. G. 1994. Constitutional and Economic Determinants of Lobbyist Activity in a Representative Democracy. RISEC 41: 1043-1051.

380 Mizruchi, M. S. 1989. Similarity of Political Behavior among Large American Corporations. AJS 95: 401-424.

381 Moe, T. M. 1980. A Calculus of Group Membership. AJPS 24: 593-632.

382 Munger, M. C. 1988. On the Political Participation of the Firm in the Electoral Process. PC 56: 295-298.

383 Murrell, P. 1984. An Examination of the Factors Affecting the Formation of Interest Groups. PC 43: 151-171.

384 Nardinelli, C.; Wallace, M. S.; Warner, J. T. 1987. Explaining Differences in State Growth: Catching Up vs. Olson. PC 52: 201-226.

385 Neustadt, A. 1990. Interest Group PACsmanship: Analysis of Campaign Contributions, Issue Visibility and Legislative Impact. SF 69: 549-564.

386 Neustadt, A.; Clawson, D. 1988. Corporate Political Groupings: Does Ideology Unify Business Political Behavior? ASR 53: 172-190.

387 Opheim, C. 1991. Explaining the Differences in State Lobbying Regulation. WPQ 44: 405-421.

388 Peterson, M. A. 1992. The Presidency and Organized Interests: White House Patterns of Interest Group Liaison. APSR 86: 612-625.

389 Peterson, P. E. 1990. The Rise and Fall of Special Interest Politics. PSCQ 105: 539-556.

390 Petracca, M. P. 1993. Tilling the Field of Interest Group Research. POPS 22: 61-69.

391 Policy Studies Journal. 1983. Papers on Interest Groups. PSJ 11 (4).

392 Poole, K. T. 1981. Dimensions of Interest Group Evaluation of the US Senate. AJPS 25: 49-67.

393 Richardson, J. 1995. Market for Political Activism: Interest Groups as a Challenge to Political Parties. WEP 18: 116-139.

394 Rothenberg, L. S. 1989. Why People Join Public Interest Groups. PC 60: 241-258.

395 Roy, W. G. 1981. Vesting of Interests and the Determinants of Political Power: American Industries. AJS 86: 1287-1310.

396 Sabatier, P. A.; McLaughlin, S. M. 1988. Belief Congruence of Governmental and Interest Group Elites with Their Constituencies. APQ 16: 61-98.

397 Salisbury, R. H. 1969. An Exchange Theory of Interest Groups. MJPS 13: 1-32.

398 Salisbury, R. H., et al. 1987. Who Works with Whom? Interest Group Alliances and Opposition. APSR 81: 1217-1234.

399 Salisbury, R. H.; Johnson, P. 1989. Who You Know vs What You Know: Uses of Government Experience for Washington Lobbyists. AJPS 33: 175-195.
400 Schneider, F.; Naumann, J. 1982. Interest Groups in Democracies: How Influential Are They? PC 38: 281-304.
401 Shaiko, R. G. 1986. Interest Group Research: Cultivating an Unsettled Plot. Polity 18: 720-732.
402 Smith, R. A. 1995. Interest Group Influence in the US Congress. LSQ 20: 89-139.
403 Snyder, J. M. 1992. Artificial Extremism in Interest Group Ratings. LSQ 17: 319-346.
404 Vries, J. 1983. Rise and Decline of Nations in Historical Perspective. ISQ 26: 11-16.
405 Walker, J. L. 1983. The Origins and Maintenance of Interest Groups in America. APSR 77: 390-406.
406 Waller, M. 1992. Groups, Interests and Political Aggregation in East Central Europe. JCS 8: 128-147.
407 Wallerstein, M. B. 1976. Terminating Entitlements: Veterans' Disability Benefits in the Depression. PSCI 7: 173-182.
408 Wiggins, C. W.; Hamm, K. E.; Bell, C. G. 1992. Interest Group and Party Influence Agents in the Legislative Process. JOP 54: 82-100.
409 Wirl, F. 1994. Dynamics of Lobbying: A Differential Game. PC 80: 307-323.
410 Wright, J. R. 1989. PAC Contributions, Lobbying and Representation. JOP 51: 713-729.

International Debt

411 Armendariz de Aghion, B. 1993. Analytical Issues in LDC Debt. WE 16: 467-482.
412 Berg, A.; Sachs, J. 1988. The Debt Crisis: Structural Explanations of Country Performance. JDE 29: 271-306.
413 Cato Journal. 1984. Papers on World Debt. CJ 4 (1).
414 Cepal Review. 1987. Papers on Latin American Debt. Vol 32 (Aug).
415 Cha, B. 1993. External Shocks and the Global Debt Crisis of LDCs. INTEJ 7: 49-60.
416 Chan, S. 1993. Relative Bargaining Power in International Debt. CMAPS 13: 29-60.
417 Development. 1989. Papers on Debt, Structural Adjustment and World Development. Vol 1989 (1).
418 Fry, M. J. 1989. Foreign Debt Instability. JIMF 8: 315-344.
419 Glasberg, D. S.; Ward, K. B. 1993. Foreign Debt and Economic Growth in the World System. SSQ 74: 703-720.
420 Hastings International and Comparative Law Review. 1989. Papers on the World Debt Crisis. Vol 12 (3).
421 Journal of Interamerican Studies and World Affairs. 1973. Papers on Latin American Foreign Investment. JIAS 15 (1).
422 Journal of International Affairs. 1984. Papers on Global Debt. JIA 38 (1).
423 Latin American Perspectives. 1989. Papers on Latin American Debt. LAPER 16 (1).
424 Li, C. A. 1992. Debt Arrears in Latin America: Do Political Variables Matter? JDS 28: 668-688.
425 New York University Journal. 1985. Papers on International Debt. NYUJ 17 (3).
426 PS. 1990. Papers on Latin American Debt. Vol 23 (3).
427 Snider, L. 1988. Political Strength, Economic Structure and the Debt Servicing Potential of Developing Countries. CPS 20: 455-487.
428 World Development. 1986. Papers on Balance of Payment Adjustments. WD 14 (8).

Political Business Cycle

429 Alesina, A.; Rosenthal, H. 1989. Partisan Cycles in Congressional Elections and the Macroeconomy. APSR 83: 373-398.
430 Alesina, A.; Sachs, J. 1988. Political Parties and Business Cycle in the US. JMCB 20: 63-82.
431 Allen, S. D. 1986. The Federal Reserve and the Electoral Cycle. JMCB 18: 88-94.
432 Allen, S. D.; McCrickard, D. L. 1991. Influence of Elections on Federal Reserve. EL 37: 51-55.
433 Allen, S. D.; Sulock, J. M.; Sabo, W. A. 1986. The Political Business Cycle. PFQ 14: 107-112.
434 Ames, B. 1980. The Political Expenditure Cycle in Latin America. PSJ 9: 40-47.
435 Beck, N. 1982. Does There Exist a Political Business Cycle? PC 38: 205-210.
436 -. 1982. Parties, Administrators and American Macroeconomic Outcomes. APSR 76: 83-93.
437 -. 1987. Elections and the Fed? Is There a Political Monetary Cycle. AJPS 31: 194-216.
438 -. 1991. The Fed and Political Business Cycle. CPI 9: 25-38.
439 Berry, W. D.; Lowery, D. 1989. Convergence and Divergence in Empirical Analyses of Fiscal Policy. APQ 17: 446-475.
440 Blais, A.; Nadeau, R. 1992. The Electoral Budget Cycle. PC 74: 389-404.
441 Bunce, V. 1980. Political Consumption Cycle. SS 32: 280-290.
442 Cato Journal. 1986. Papers on the Business Cycle. CJ 6 (2).
443 Chappell, H. W.; Keech, W. R. 1983. Welfare Consequences of the Six Year Presidential Term Evaluated in the Context of a Model of Political Economy. APSR 77: 75-91.
444 Chari, V. V.; Christiano, J.; Kehoe, P. J. 1994. Optimal Fiscal Policy in a Business Cycle Model. JPE 102: 617-652.
445 Davidson, L. S.; Frantianni, M.; Von Hagen, J. 1990. Testing for Political Business Cycles. JPM 12: 35-59.
446 -. 1992. Testing the Satisficing Version of the Political Business Cycle. PC 73: 21-36.
447 Detken, C.; Gartner, M. 1993. Are German Unions Rocking the Economy? Reappraisal of the Supply-Side Political Business Cycle. AE 25: 1345-1353.
448 Ellis, C. J.; Thoma, M. A. 1991. Causality in Political Business Cycles. CPI 9: 39-49.
449 -. 1993. Credibility and Political Business Cycles. JOM 15: 69-89.
450 Findlay, D. W. 1990. Political Business Cycle and Republican Administrators. PFQ 18: 328-338.
451 Frey, B. S.; Schneider, F. 1982. Political-Economic Models in Competition with Alternative Models. EJPR 10: 241-252.
452 Golden, D.; Poterba, J. M. 1980. Price of Popularity: The Political Business Cycle Reexamined. AJPS 24: 696-714.
453 Grier, K. B. 1987. Presidential Elections and Federal Reserve Policy. SEJ 54: 475-486.
454 -. 1989. A Political Monetary Cycle. AJPS 33: 376-389.
455 Hakes, D. R. 1988. Monetary Policy and Presidential Elections: A Nonpartisan Political Cycle. PC 57: 175-182.
456 Havrilesky, T. M. 1990. Public Choice Perspective on Cycle in Monetary Policy. CJ 9: 709-718.
457 -. 1994. Democracy, Elections and Macroeconomic Policy. EJPE 10: 85-110.
458 Haynes, S. E.; Stone, J. A. 1989. An Integrated Test for Electoral Cycles in the US Economy. REAS 71: 426-434.
459 -. 1990. Political Models of the Business Cycle Should Be Revived. EI 28: 442-465.
460 Hibbs, D. A. 1994. Partisan Model of Macroeconomic Cycles. EAP 6: 1-23.

461 Karnik, A. V. 1990. Elections and Government Expenditures: India. JQE 6: 203-212.

462 Keech, W. R. 1980. Elections and Macroeconomic Policy Optimization. APSR 24: 345-367.

463 Keech, W. R.; Pak, K. 1989. Electoral Cycles and Budgetary Growth in Veterans' Benefit Programs. AJPS 33: 901-911.

464 Keech, W. R.; Simon, C. P. 1985. Electoral and Welfare Consequences of Political Manipulation of the Economy. JEBAO 5: 177-202.

465 Lessmann, S. 1987. Incremental and Cyclical Developments in Public Expenditure in West Germany. EJPR 15: 241-252.

466 MacRae, C. D. 1977. A Political Model of the Business Cycle. JPE 85: 239-264.

467 May, A. M. 1987. Political Business Cycle: An Institutional Critique. JEI 21: 713-722.

468 Mayer, K. R. 1995. Electoral Cycles in Federal Government Prime Contract Awards. AJPS 39: 162-185.

469 McGavin, B. H. 1986. Political Business Cycle. QJBE 26: 36-49.

470 Meiselman, D. I. 1986. Is There a Political Monetary Cycle? CJ 6: 563-579.

471 Minford, P.; Peel, D. 1982. Political Theory of the Business Cycle. EER 17: 253-270.

472 Monroe, K. R. 1983. Political Manipulation of the Economy: A Closer Look at Political Business Cycles. PSQ 13: 37-49.

473 Mouritzen, P. E. 1989. Local Political Business Cycle. SPS 12: 37-56.

474 Nordhaus, W. D. 1975. Political Business Cycle. RES 42: 160-190.

475 -. 1989. Alternative Approaches to the Political Business Cycle. BPEA 1989 (2): 1-49.

476 Ortona, G. 1987. A Model of Political Business Cycle in a Soviet-Type Economy. EN 1: 107-118.

477 Pack, J. R. 1987. Political Policy Cycle: Presidential Effort vs Presidential Control. PC 54: 231-260.

478 Paldam, M. 1979. Is There an Electoral Cycle? SJE 81: 323-342.

479 Payne, J. L. 1991. Elections and Government Spending. PC 70: 71-82.

480 Richards, D. J. 1986. Unanticipated Money and the Political Business Cycle. JMCB 18: 447-457.

481 Rogoff, K. 1990. Equilibrium Political Business Cycles. AER 80: 21-36.

482 Rogoff, K.; Silbert, A. 1988. Elections and Macroeconomic Policy Cycles. RES 55: 1-16.

483 Rosenberg, J. 1992. Rationality and Political Business Cycle: Local Government. PC 73: 71-82.

484 Schneider, F. 1984. Public Attitudes toward Economic Conditions and Impact on Government Behavior. PB 6: 211-228.

485 Schultz, K. A. 1995. Politics of the Political Business Cycle. BJPS 25: 79-100.

486 Shugart, M. S. 1995. Electoral Cycle and Institutional Sources of Divided Presidential Government. APSR 89: 327-343.

487 Smyth, D. J.; Washburn, S. K.; Dua, P. 1989). Social Preferences, Inflation, Unemployment and the Political Business Cycle. SEJ 56: 336-348.

488 Smyth, D. J.; Woodfield, A. E. 1993. Inflation, Unemployment and Macroeconomic Policy in New Zealand. PC 75: 119-138.

489 Story, D. 1985. Policy Cycles in Mexican Presidential Politics. LARR 20: 139-162.

490 Strate, J.; Wolman, H.; Melchior, A. 1993. Are There Election Driven Tax and Expenditures Cycles for Urban Government? UAQ 28: 462-479.

491 Suzuki, M. 1992. Political Business Cycles in the Public Mind. APSR 86: 989-996.

492 -. 1994. Evolutionary Voter Sophistication and Political Business Cycles. PC 81: 241-262.

493 Van der Ploeg, F. 1989. Income, Unemployment, Inflation and State Spending in a Dynamic Political Economic Model. PC 60: 211-240.

494 Wasserman, I. M. 1983. Political Business Cycles, Presidential Elections and Suicide and Mortality Patterns. ASR 48: 711-720.

495 Weller, B. R. 1983. Political Business Cycle. SSQ 64: 398-403.

496 Williams, J. T. 1990. Political Manipulation of Macroeconomic Policy. APSR 84: 767-795.

497 Wolley, J. T. 1988. Partisan Manipulation of the Economy: Monetary Policy. JOP 50: 334-360.

498 Woolley, J. T.; LeLoup, L. T. 1989. Adequacy of the Electoral Motive in Explaining Legislative Attention to Monetary Policy. CP 22: 63-82.

Public and Private Goods

499 Andreoni, J. 1993. Test of the Public Goods Crowding-Out Hypothesis. AER 83: 1317-1327.

500 Aragon, Y.; Laffont, J. J.; Le Pottier, J. 1988. Testing the Democratic Hypothesis in the Provision of Local Public Goods. JPUBE 36: 139-151.

501 Bordignon, M. 1994. Consistent Conjectures and Private Provision of Public Goods. RE 48: 109-121.

502 Borukhov, E. 1972. Optimal Service Areas for Provision and Financing of Local Public Goods. PF 27: 267-281.

503 Breton, A. 1966. A Theory of Demand for Public Goods. Canadian Journal of Economics and Political Science 32: 455-467.

504 Cesario, F. J. 1976. Demand Curves for Public Facilities. ARS 10: 1-14.

505 Chamberlin, J. R. 1974. Provision of Collective Goods as a Function of Group Size. APSR 68: 707-716.

506 -. 1978. A Collective Goods Model of Pluralist Political Systems. PC 33: 97-114.

507 Conybeare, J. A. C. 1984. Public Goods, Prisoners' Dilemmas and the International Political Economy. ISQ 28: 5-22.

508 Cornes, R.; Sandler, T. 1994. Are Public Goods Myths? JTP 6: 369-388.

509 Craig, S. G.; Hsieh, E. W. T. 1994. Local Public Good Provision under Uncertainty: Monopoly Bureaus. JUE 36: 184-208.

510 Davis, O. A.; Whinston, A. B. 1967. The Distribution between Public and Private Goods. AER 57: 360-373.

511 DeBruin, G.P. 1985. Voting Procedures for Decision-Making on Public Goods. EJPR 13: 187-205.

512 Domberger, S.; Piggott, J. 1986. Privatization Policies and Public Enterprise. ECONR 62: 145-162.

513 Eastern European Economics. 1991. Papers on Privatization in Eastern Europe. Vol 30 (1).

514 Ellickson, B. 1973. A Generalization of the Pure Theory of Public Goods. AER 63: 417-432.

515 Feigenbaum, H. B.; Henig, J. R. 1994. Political Underpinnings of Privatization. WP 46: 185-208.

516 Firmin-Sellers, K. 1995. Politics of Property Rights. APSR 89: 867-881.

517 Fisher, J., et al. 1995. Heterogeneous Demand for Public Goods: The Voluntary Contributions Mechanism. PC 85: 249-266.

518 Frasca, R. R. 1980. Provision of a Public Good under Cournot Behavior. PC 35: 493-502.

519 Garratt, R.; Marshall, J. M. 1994. Public Finance of Private Goods: College Education. JPE 102: 566-582.

520 Gibson, B. B. 1980. Estimating Demand Elasticities for Public Goods. AER 70: 1069-1076.

521 Godwin, R. K.; Mitchell, R. C. 1982. Rational Models, Collective Goods and Nonelectoral Political Behavior. WPQ 35: 161-192.

522 Gradstein, M. 1992. Time Dynamics and Incomplete Information in Private Provision of Public Goods. JPE 100: 581-597.

523 -. 1994. Efficient Provision of a Discrete Public Good. IER 35: 877-897.

524 Gradstein, M.; Nitzan, S.; Slutsky, S. 1994. Uncertainty, Information and the Private Provision of Public Goods. EJPE 10: 449-464.

525 Hardin, R. 1971. Collective Action as an Agreeable N-Prisoners' Dilemma. BS 16: 472-481.

526 Head, J. G. 1970. Equity and Efficiency in Public Goods Supply. PF 25: 24-37.

527 Hewitt, D. 1985. Demand for National Public Goods. EI 23: 487-506.

528 Hovi, J. 1986. Binary Games as Models of Public Goods. SPS 4: 337-360.

529 Howlett, M.; Ramesh, M. 1993. Patterns of Policy Instrument Choice: Policy Styles, Policy Learning and Privatization Experience. PSR 12: 3-24.

530 International Review of Administrative Sciences 1988. Papers on Privatization. IRAS 54 (4) and 56 (1).

531 Isaac, R. M.; McCue, K. F.; Plott, C. R. 1985. Public Goods Provision in an Experimental Environment. JPUBE 26: 51-74.

532 Jackson, J. E.; King, D. C. 1989. Public Goods, Private Interests and Representation. APSR 83: 1143-1164.

533 Jones, P. R. 1993. Preferences for Private Goods: A Public Choice Critique of Political Process. POLST 41: 492-505.

534 Journal of Law and Society and Society. 1989. Papers on Thatcherism. JLAS 16 (1).

535 Journal of Policy Analysis and Management. 1987. Papers on Privatization. JPAAM 6 (4).

536 Kahneman, D.; Ritov, I. 1994. Determinants of Stated Willingness to Pay for Public Goods: The Headline Method. JORAU 9: 5-38.

537 Klein, D. B. 1990. Voluntary Provision of Public Goods? Turnpike Companies. EI 28: 788-812.

538 Kleindorfer, P. R.; Sertel, M. R. 1994. Auctioning the Provision of an Indivisible Public Good. JET 64: 20-34.

539 Laver, M. 1976. Exit, Voice and Loyalty Revisited: Strategic Production and Consumption of Public and Private Goods. BJPS 6: 463-482.

540 Law and Policy. 1991. Papers on Constitution Making and Privatization in Eastern Europe. LAP 13 (2).

541 Lesser, B. 1991. When Government Fails, Will the Market Do Better? Privatization / Market Liberalization Movement in Developing Countries. CJDS 12: 159-172.

542 Lowery, D.; et al. 1995. Empirical Evidence for Citizen Information and Local Market for Public Goods. APSR 89: 705-709.

543 Malkin, J.; Wildavsky, A. 1991. Why the Traditional Distinction between Public and Private Goods Should Be Abandoned. JTP 3: 355-378.

544 Marlow, M. L. 1991. Privatization and Government Size. PC 68: 273-276.

545 Marlowe, J. 1985. Private vs. Public Provision of Refuse Removal Service: Citizen Satisfaction. UAQ 20: 355-363.

546 Marsh, D. 1991. Privatization under Mrs. Thatcher. PA 69: 459-480.

547 McGuire, R. A.; Ohsfeldt, R. L.; Van Cott, T. N. 1990. More on Choice between Public and Private Production of a Publicly Funded Service. PC 66: 189-194.

548 Meerman, J. 1980. Are Public Goods Public Goods? PC 35: 45-58.

549 Moe, R. C. 1987. Exploring the Limits of Privatization. PAR 47: 453-460.

550 Morton, R. B. 1987. Group Majority Voting Model of Public Good Provision. SCAW 4: 117-131.

551 Nilson, S. S. 1981. Elections, Referendums and Public Goods. SPS 4: 1-18.

552 Nilsson, J. E. 1990. Private Funding of Public Investments: A Voluntary Funded Public Road. JOTEAP 24: 157-170.

553 Nowell, C.; Tinkler, S. 1994. The Influence of Gender on the Provision of a Public Good. JEBAO 25: 25-36.

554 Okuguchi, K. 1984. Utility Function, Group Size and Aggregate Provision of a Pure Public Good. PC 42: 247-246.

555 O'Reilly, T. 1995. Incentive Compatibility of Inferring Demand for Public Goods from Private Goods Demand. JPUBE 58: 309-317.

556 Papageorgiou, Y. Y. 1987. Spatial Public Goods. EPA 19: 331-352, 471-492.

557 Political Quarterly. 1984. Papers on Privatization. PQ 55 (2).

558 Political Science Quarterly. 1986. Papers on Promoting the Public Good. PSQ 101 (2).

559 Pommerehne, W. W.; Feld, L. P.; Hart, A. 1994. Voluntary Provision of a Public Good. Kyklos 47: 505-518.

560 Proceedings. 1987. Papers on Privatization. PAPSC 36 (3).

561 Provencher, B.; Burt, O. 1994. Private Property Rights Regime for the Commons: Groundwater. AJAE 76: 875-888.

562 Public Administration Review. 1987. Papers on Privatization. PAR 47: 453-484.

563 Quarterly Review of Economics and Finance. 1993. Papers on Privatization and Regulation in Latin America. QREF 33 (Special Issue).

564 -. 1994. Papers on Privatization, Deregulation and Property Rights. QREF 34 Special Issue.

565 Rongen, G. 1995. Efficiency in the Provision of Local Public Goods. EJPE 11: 253-264.

566 Ryan, M.; Ward, T. 1988. Privatizing Punishment. PQ 59: 86-90.

567 Saunders, P. 1995. Privatization, Share Ownership and Voting. BJPS 25: 131-136.

568 Schram, A. J. H. C. 1990. A Dynamic Model of Voter Behavior and the Demand for Public Goods among Social Groups in Great Britain. JPUBE 41: 147-182.

569 Schram, A. J. H. C.; Winden, F. 1989. Revealed Preferences for Public Goods: Voter Behavior. PC 60: 259-282.

570 Sell, J.; Wilson, R. K. 1991. Levels of Information and Contributions to Public Goods. SF 70: 107-124.

571 Snidal, D. 1979. Public Goods, Property Rights and Political Organizations. ISQ 23: 532-566.

572 Staaf, R. J. 1983. Privatization of Public Goods. PC 41: 435-440.

573 Stubbs, J. G.; Barnett, J. R. 1992. Geographically Uneven Development of Privatization. EPA 24: 1117-1135.

574 Talley, W. K. 1974. Optimality and Equality in the Provision of Public Goods by a Polycentric Political System. SEJ 41: 220-227.

575 Teske, P., et al. 1993. Establishing the Macro Foundations of Macro Theory: Information, Movers and Competitive Local Market for Public Goods. APSR 87: 702-716.

576 Thoreen, P. W. 1981. The Profitable Provision of Public Goods and Services. ABS 24: 573-598.

577 University of Pennsylvania Law Review. 1982. Papers on the Public-Private Distinction. UPLR 130 (6).

578 Urban Affairs Quarterly 1984. Papers on Coproduction. UAQ 19 (4).

579 Urban and Social Change Review. 1983. Papers on Privatization of Social Work. UASCR 16 (1-2).

580 West European Politics 1988. Papers on Privatization in Western Europe. WEP 11 (4).

581 William, A. 1966. Optimal Provision of Public Goods in a System of Local Government. JPE 74: 18-33.

582 World Development. 1989. Papers on Privatization. WD 17 (5).

Rent Seeking

583 Appelbaum, E.; Katz, E. 1986. Transfer Seeking and Avoidance: Social Costs of Rent Seeking. PC 48: 175-181.

584 -. 1987. Seeking Rents by Setting Rents: Political Economy of Rent Seeking. EJ 97: 685-699.

585 Beck, R.; Hoskins, C.; Connolly, J. M. 1992. Rent Extraction through Political Extortion. JLS 21: 217-224.

586 Buchanan, J. M.; Congleton, R. D. 1994. Incumbency Dilemma and Rent Extraction by Legislators. PC 79: 47-60.

587 Cato Journal 1986. Papers on the Transfer Society. CJ 6 (1).

588 Coate, S.; Morris, S. 1995. The Form of Transfers to Special Interests. JPE 103: 1210-1235.

589 Conybeare, J. A. C. 1982. The Rent Seeking State and Revenue Diversification. WP 35: 25-42.

590 Dixit, A.; Londregan, J. 1995. Redistributive Politics and Economic Efficiency. APSR 89: 856-866.

591 Durden, G. C. 1990. Effect of Rent Seeking on Family Income Levels. PC 67: 285-291.

592 Flowers, M. R. 1987. Rent Seeking and Rent Dissipation. CJ 7: 431-440.

593 Gelb, A.; Knight, J. B.; Sabot, R. H. 1991. Public Sector Employment, Rent Seeking and Economic Growth. EJ 101: 1186-1199.

594 Glazer, A. 1993. On the Incentives to Establish and Play Political Rent Seeking Games. PC 75: 139-148.

595 Gradstein, M. 1995. Intensity of Competition, Entry and Entry Deterrence in Rent Seeking Contests. EAP 7: 79-91.

596 Grampp, W. D. 1989. Rent Seeking in Arts Policy. PC 60: 113-121.

597 Hirschleifer, J. 1989. Conflict and Rent-Seeking Success Functions: Ratio vs. Difference Models of Relative Success. PC 63: 101-112.

598 Katz, E.; Rosenberg, J. 1989. Rent Seeking for Budgetary Allocation. PC 60: 133-144.

599 Krueger, A. O. 1975. Political Economy of the Rent Seeking Society. AER 64: 291-303.

600 Laband, D. N.; Sophocleus, J. P. 1988. Social Cost of Rent Seeking. PC 58: 269-276.

601 Lee, S. 1995. Endogenous Sharing Rules in Collective Group Rent Seeking. PC 85: 31-44.

602 Leininger, W. 1993. More Efficient Rent Seeking. PC 75: 43-62.

603 Linster, B. G. 1993. A Generalized Model of Rent Seeking Behavior. PC 77: 421-435.

604 -. 1993. Rent Seeking with Multiple Winners. PC 77: 437-444.

605 -. 1994. Cooperative Rent Seeking. PC 81: 23-34.

606 Lopez, R. A.; Pagoulatos, E. 1994. Rent Seeking and the Welfare Cost of Trade Barriers. PC 79: 149-160.

607 Mbaku, J. M. 1991. Military Expenditures and Bureaucratic Competition for Rents. PC 71: 19-32.

608 McCormick, R. E.; Tollison, R. D. 1979. Rent Seeking Competition in Political Parties. PC 33: 5-14.

609 Murphy, K. M.; Shleifer, A.; Vishny, R. W. 1993. Why Is Rent Seeking So Costly to Growth? AER 83: 409-414.

610 Nitzan, S. 1994. Modeling Rent Seeking Contests. EJPE 10: 41-60.

611 Perez-Castrillo, J. D.; Verdier, T. 1992. A General Analysis of Rent Seeking Games. PC 73: 335-350.

612 Rama, M. 1993. Rent Seeking and Economic Growth. JDE 42: 35-50.

613 Riaz, K.; Shogren, J. F.; Johnson, S. R. 1995. A General Model of Rent Seeking for Public Goods. PC 82: 243-260.

614 Scully, G. W. 1991. Rent Seeking in US Government Budgets. PC 70: 99-106.

615 Vedder, R.; Gallaway, L. E. 1991. War between the Rent Seekers. PC 68: 283-289.

616 Wiewel, W.; Persky, J.; Felsenstein, D. 1995. Are Subsidies Worth It? How to Calculate the Costs and Benefits of Business Incentives. GFR 11: 23-29.

617 Wyrick, T. L.; Arnold, R. A. 1989. Earmarking as a Deterrent to Rent Seeking. PC 60: 283-291.

POLITICAL GEOGRAPHY

1 Allen, P. M.; Sanglier, M. 1979. A Dynamic Model of Growth in a Central Place System. Geographical Analysis 11: 256-272.

2 Allen, P. R. B.: Rutledge, A. J. 1976. Annotated Bibliography of Mostly Obscure Articles on Human Territorial Behavior. SSI 15: 403-414.

3 Alperovich, G. 1993. Explanatory Model of City-Size Distribution. US 30: 1591-1601.

4 American Behavioral Scientist. 1978. Papers on Human Geography. ABS 22 (1).

5 Anderson, M. 1978. Renaissance of Territorial Minority in Western Europe. WEP 1: 128-143.

6 Annals of Regional Science. 1992 Papers on Geographic Information Systems. ARS 26 (1).

7 Archer, J. C., et al. 1989. The Geography of US Presidential Elections. SA 259 (1); 44-51.

8 Ashley, R. K. 1987. Geopolitics of Geopolitical Space: Toward a Critical Social Theory of International Politics. Alternatives 12: 403-434.

9 Barnes, T. J. 1987. Home Economicus, Physical Metaphors and Universal Models in Economic Geography. Canadian Geographer 31: 299-308.

10 -. 1990. Analytical Political Economy: Geographical Introduction. EPA 22: 993-1006.

11 Barnes, T. J.; Sheppard, E. 1992. Is There a Place for Rational Actor? Geographical Critique of the Rational Choice Paradigm. EG 68: 1-21.

12 Blum, U.; Dudley, L. 1991. Spatial Model of the State. JITE 147: 312-336.

13 Bogdanor, V.; Field, W. H. 1993. Core and Periphery in British Electoral Behaviour. ES 12: 203-224.

14 Books, J. W.; Prysby, C. L. 1988. Contextual Effects on Political Behavior. APQ 16: 211-238.

15 Borger, B. 1979. Urban Population Density Functions: Belgium. ARS 13: 15-24.

16 Clark, W. C. 1989. Human Ecology of Global Change. ISSJ 41: 315-346.

17 Clifford, P.; Sudbury, A. 1973. A Model for Spatial Conflict. Biometrika 60: 581-588.

18 Dacey, M. F. 1966. A County-Seat Model for the Areal Pattern of an Urban System. Geographical Review 56: 527-542.

19 Diskin, A.; Mishal, S. 1981. Spatial Models and Centrality of International Communities: Meetings between Arab Leaders. JCR 25: 655-676.

20 Goertz, G.; Diehl, P. F. 1984. A Territorial History of the International System. II 15: 81-93.

21 Gottman, J. 1982. The Basic Problem of Political Geography: Organization of Space and the Search for Stability. Tijdschrift voor Economische en Sociale Geografie 73: 340-349.

22 Gourevitch, P. A. 1979. Reemergence of Peripheral Nationalisms: Spatial Distribution of Political Leadership and Economic Growth. CSSH 21: 303-322.

23 Guillorel, H.; Levy, J. 1992. Space and Electoral Systems. PG 11: 205-238.

24 Hewitt, K. 1983. Place Annihilation: Area Bombing and Fate of Urban Places. AAAG 73: 257-284.

25 Hooks, F. 1994. Political, Economic and Military Influences on Geographic Space. ASR 59: 746-772.

26 International Political Science Review. 1980. Papers on Political Geography. IPSR 1 (4).

27 -. 1995. Papers on Communication and Political Geography. IPSR 16 (3).

28 Jakubs, J. F. 1981. A Distance Based Segregation Index. SEPS 15: 129-138.

29 Johnston, R. J. 1980. Political Geography without Politics. PIHG 4: 439-446.

30 -. 1982. The Changing Geography of Voting in US. TIBG 7: 187-204.

31 -. 1984. Marxist Political Economy, the State and Political Geography. PIHG 8: 473-492.

32 Johnston, R. J.; Pattie, C. J. 1995. People, Place and the Economic Theory of Voting. Politics 15: 9-18.

33 Keinath, W. 1985. The Spatial Component of Post-Industrial Society. EG 61: 223-240.

34 Laband, D. N. 1986. Private Interest in Public Redistribution: Public Choice View of Geographic Distribution of Federal Lands. PC 49: 117-126.

35 La Gory, M.; Nelson, J. 1978. An Ecological Analysis of Urban Growth. SQ 19: 590-603.

36 Levinson, D. M.; Kumar, A. 1994. The Rational Locator: Why Travel Times Have Remained Stable. JAPA 60: 319-332.

37 Logan, J. R. 1978. Growth, Politics and the Stratification of Places. AJS 84: 404-416.

38 Lowery, D.; Brunn, S. D.; Webster, G. R. 1988. The Spatial Impact of Reaganomics. GAC 19 (4): 49-67.

39 Mair, P.; McAllister, I. 1982. Territorial vs Class Appeal? Labour Parties of the British Isles Periphery. EJPR 10: 17-34.

40 Massey, D. S.; Denton, N. A. 1985. Spatial Assimilation as a Socioeconomic Outcome. ASR 50: 94-105.

41 Mayhew, B. H.; Levinger, R. L. 1976. Size and Density of Interaction in Human Aggregates. AJS 82: 86-110.

42 Morse, R. M. 1974. Trends and Patterns of Latin American Urbanization. CSSH 16: 416-447.

43 Muedeking, G. D.; Bahr, H. M. 1976. A Smallest Space Analysis of Skid Row Men's Behavior. PSR 19: 275-290.

44 Mulligan, G. F. 1984. Agglomeration and Central Place Theory. IRSR 9: 1-42.

45 O'Loughlin, J. 1986. Political Geography: Tilling the Fallow Field. PIHG 10: 69-83.

46 Pchelintsev, O. S. 1993. Regional Hierarchy under Threat: A Spatial Dimension of the Socio-Economic Crisis in the Former Soviet Union and Russia. IRSR 1993: 267-280.

47 Political Geography. 1987. Papers on Historical Studies of Geopolitics. PG 6 (2).

48 -. 1987. Papers on Place, Context and Voting. PG 6 (1).

49 -. 1988. Papers on Sectionalism in US Politics. PG 7 (2).

50 -. 1989. Papers on the Historical Study of Political Geography in Germany. PG 8 (4).

51 -. 1994. Papers on Spaces of Citizenship. PG 14 (2).

52 -. 1995. Papers on Contextual Models of Political Behavior. PG 14 (6/7).

53 Robertson, J. A. 1985. Geography of Competency. SR 52: 555-580.

54 Schellenberg, J. A. 1970. County Seat Wars. JCR 14: 345-352.

55 Schrodt, P. A. 1981. Conflict as a Determinant of Territory. BS 26: 37-50.

56 Shelley, F. M.; Archer, J. C. 1994. Political Geography of Contemporary Affairs: Presidential Election of 1992. PG 13: 137-160.

57 Smith, H. W. 1983. Estimated Crowding Capacity, Time and Territorial Markers. SI 53: 95-99.

58 Stephan, G. E.; McMullin, D. R. 1981. Historical Distribution of County Seats in the US: Time Minimization Theory. ASR 46: 907-917.

59 Stern, D. I. 1994. Historical Path-Dependence of the Urban Population Growth Density Gradient. ARS 28: 197-222.

60 Studies in Comparative International Development. 1987. Papers on the Geography of National and International Issues. SICID 22 (1-4) and 1988 23 (1-2).

61 Suh, S. H. 1987. On the Size Distribution of Cities: An Economic Interpretation of the Pareto Coefficient. EPA 19: 749-762.

62 Takayama, T. 1994. Thirty Years with Spatial and Intertemporal Economics. ARS 28: 305-322.

63 Taylor, P. J. 1982. A Materialist Framework for Political Geography. TIBG 7: 15-34.

64 Teller, L. N.; Vertefeuille, C. 1995. Understanding Spatial Inertia: Center of Gravity, Population Densities, Weber Problem and Gravity Potential. JRS 35: 155-164.

65 Thompson, W. R. 1981. Center-Periphery Interaction Patterns: Arab Visits. IO 35: 355-374.

66 Vasquez, J. A. 1995. Why Do Neighbors Fight? Proximity, Interaction, or Territoriality. JPR 32: 277-294.

67 Werf, B., Wije, C. 1991. The Spatial Structure of Large US Law Firms. GAC 22 (4): 157-174.

68 West European Politics. 1987. Papers on Territorial Politics of Western Europe. WEP 10 (4).

69 White, M. J. 1983. Measurement of Spatial Segregation. AJS 88: 1008-1018.

70 Winsberg, M. D. 1989. Income Polarization between the Central Cities and Suburbs of US Metropolises. AJEAS 48: 3-10.

71 Winslow, D. 1984. Political Geography of Deities: Space and the Pantheon in Sinhalese Buddhism. JASIAS 43: 273-292.

72 Woolstencroft, R. P. 1980. Electoral Geography. IPSR 1: 540-560.

73 Young, D. A. 1984. A Spatiotemporal Model of Civilization. BS 29: 111-126.

74 Young, O. R. 1994. Problem of Scale in Human-Environmental Relationships. JTP 6: 429-448.

Contagion and Neighborhoods

75 Alkperovich, G. 1980. Neighborhood Amenities and Impact on Density Gradients. ARS 14: 51-64.

76 Amburgey, T. L. 1986. Multivariate Point Process Models in Social Research. SSR 15: 190-227.

77 Aspin, L. T.; Hall, W. K. 1989. Friends and Neighbors Voting in Judicial Retention Elections. WPQ 42: 587-596.

78 Bardo, J. W. 1984. A Reexamination of the Neighborhood as Socio-Spatial Schema. SI 54: 346-358.

79 Beer, F. A. 1979. Epidemiology of Peace and War. JCR 23: 45-86.

80 Biddle, J. 1991. A Bandwagon Effect in Personalized License Plates? EI 29: 375-388.

81 Bodman, A. R. 1983. Neighborhood Effect. BJPS 13: 243-249.

82 Bowler, S.; Donovan, T.; Snipp, J. 1993. Local Sources of Information and Voter Choice in State Elections: Microlevel Foundations of Friends and Neighbors. APQ 21: 473-489.

83 Bremer, S. A. 1982. Contagiousness of Coercion: Spread of Serious International Disputes. II 9: 29-56.

84 Brunk, G. G.; Adams, J.; Ramesh, S. 1988. Contagion Based Voting. PG 7: 39-47.

85 Burbeck, S. L.; Raine, W. J.; Stark, M. J. A. 1978. Dynamics of Riot Growth: The Epidemiological Approach. JMS 6: 1-12.

86 Canon, B. C. 1978. Factionalism in the South. AJPS 22: 833-848.

87 Crane, J. 1991. Epidemic Theory of Ghettos and Neighborhood Effects on Dropping Out and Teenage Childbearing. AJS 96: 1226-1259.

88 Dubin, R. A. 1992. Spatial Autocorrelation and Neighborhood Quality. RSUE 22: 433-452.

89 Faber, J.; Houweling, H. W.; Siccama, J. G. 1984. Diffusion of War. JPR 21: 277-288.

90 Fitton, M. 1973. Neighbourhood and Voting. BJPS 3: 445-472.

91 Fried, M. 1982. Residential Attachment: Sources of Residential and Community Satisfaction. JSI 38: 107-120.

92 Garand, J. C. 1988. Localism and Regionalism in Presidential Elections: Is There a Home State or Regional Advantage? WPQ 41: 85-114.

93 Gilbert, C. P. 1991. Religion, Neighborhood Environments and Partisan Behavior: A Contextual Analysis. PG 10: 110-131.

94 Giles, M. W.; Dantico, M. K. 1982. Political Participation and Neighborhood Social Context Revisited. AJPS 26: 144-150.

95 Goswamy, M.; Kumar, A. 1990. Stochastic Model for Spread of Rumour. MSS 19: 23-36.

96 Gray, L. N.; Broembsen, M. H. 1974. On Simple Stochastic Diffusion Models. JMS 3: 231-244.

97 Hall, W. K.; Aspin, L. T. 1987. Friends and Neighbors Effect in Judicial Retention Elections. WPQ 40: 703-716.

98 Hamilton, J. D.; Hamilton, L. C. 1981. Models of Social Contagion. JMS 8: 133-160.

99 Huckfeldt, R. R. 1979. Political Participation and the Neighborhood Social Context. AJPS 23: 579-592.

100 -. 1983. Social Contexts, Social Networks and Urban Neighborhoods: Environmental Constraints on Friendship Choice. AJS 89: 651-669.

101 Huckfeldt, R. R.; Plutzer, E.; Sprague, J. 1993. Alternative Contexts of Political Behavior: Churches, Neighborhoods and Individuals. JOP 55: 365-381.

102 Huff, D. L.; Lutz, J. M. 1974. Contagion of Political Unrest in Independent Black Africa. EG 50: 352-367.

103 Jackson, P. 1991. Mapping Meanings: A Cultural Critique of Locality Studies. EPA 23: 215-228.

104 Knottnerus, J. D. 1988. Critique of Expectation States Theory: Theoretical Assumptions and Models of Social Contagion. SP 31: 420-445.

105 Kramer, D. C. 1990. Analysis of Friends and Neighbours Voting in a Geographically Split District. PG 9: 189-196.

106 Laponce, J. A. 1987. Assessing the Neighbour Effect on the Vote of Francophone Minorities in Canada. PG 6: 77-88.

107 Lewis-Beck, M. S.; Rice, T. W. 1983. Localism in Presidential Elections: Home State Advantage. AJPS 27: 548-556.

108 Massey, D. S. 1991. Political Place of Locality Studies. EPA 23: 267-281.

109 Midlarsky, M. I. 1978. Analyzing Diffusion and Contagion Effects: Urban Disorders of the 1960s. APSR 72: 996-1011.

110 Miller, D. L.; Mietus, K. J.; Mathers, R. A. 1978. Critical Examination of the Social Contagion Image of Collective Behavior: The Enfield Monster. SQ 19: 129-140.

111 Policy Studies Journal. 1987. Papers on Neighborhood Policy. PSJ 16 (2).

112 Political Geography. 1991. Papers on Contextual Models. PG 10 (2).

113 Prysby, C. L. 1976. Community Partisanship and Individual Voting Behavior: Methodological Problems of Contextual Analysis. PM 3: 183-198.

114 Przeworski, A. 1974. Contextual Models of Political Behavior. PM 1: 27-61.

115 Quah, D. 1993. Galton's Fallacy and Tests of the Convergence Hypothesis. SJE 95: 427-443.

116 Reynolds, D. R. 1969. Spatial Model for Analyzing Voting Behavior. AS 12: 122-131.

117 Rice, T. W.; Macht, A. A. 1987. Friends and Neighbors Voting in Statewide General Elections. AJPS 31: 448-452.

118 Ross, M. H.; Homer, E. 1976. Galton's Problem in Cross National Research. WP 29: 1-28.

119 Schwab, W. A. 1987. Three Ecological Models: Life Cycle, Arbitrage and Composition Models of Neighborhood Change. UAQ 23: 295-308.

120 Singer, B. 1984. Mathematical Models of Infectious Diseases. PADR 10: 347-366.

121 Social Research. 1988. Papers on Plagues. SR 55 (3).

122 Taibleson, M. H. 1976. Distinguishing between Contagion, Heterogeneity and Randomness in Stochastic Models. ASR 39: 877-880.

123 Todd, J. R.; Ellis, K. D. 1974. Analyzing Factional Patterns in State Politics: Texas. SSQ 55: 718-731.

124 Sociological Quarterly. 1990. Papers on Neighborhoods. SQ 31 (4).

125 Urban Affairs Quarterly. 1979. Papers on the Urban Neighborhood. UAQ 14 (3), and 1980 15 (4).

126 Warwick, P. 1978. Galton's Problem in Comparative Political Research. PM 5: 327-346.

127 Weinstein, M.; Ross, M. H. 1981. Galton's Problem and the Role of Theory. PM 7: 71-80.

128 Wright, G. C. 1977. Contextual Models of Electoral Behavior: Wallace Vote. APSR 71: 497-508.

129 Zimmer, T. A. 1983. Community and Communality in Voting Participation. SP 26: 185-200.

Location and Migration

130 American Behavioral Scientist. 1969. Papers on Migration. ABS 13 (1).

131 Annals. 1983. Papers on Refugees. ANNALS 467.

132 -. 1986. Papers on Transnational Migration. ANNALS 485.

133 -. 1986. Papers on Immigration. ANNALS 487, and 1994 534.

134 Bartik, T. J. 1988. Effects of Environmental Regulation on Business Location. GAC 19: 22-44.

135 -. 1993. Who Benefits from Local Job Growth? Migrants or Original Residents? REGS 27: 297-311.

136 Beaumont, J. R. 1981. Locational Allocation Problems in a Plain. SEPS 15: 217-230.

137 Beckmann, M. J. 1989. On the Shape and Size of Market Areas. ARS 23: 81-92.

138 Beguin, H.; Ipanga, T. 1991. Private vs Public Service Location Behaviour: Dentists. ARS 25: 115-130.

139 Bonvalet, C.; Carpenter, J.; White, P. 1995. Residential Mobility of Ethnic Minorities. US 32: 87-103.

140 Browne, D. L. 1981. Spatial Aspects of Post-1970 Work Force Migration in the US. GAC 12: 9-20.

141 Brunk, G. G. 1985. Congressional Rationality and Spatial Voting. PC 45: 3-17.

142 Campbell, B. C. 1989. Migration and Politics. JIDH 20: 263-269.

143 Campos, J. E. L.; Lien, D. 1995. Political Instability and Illegal Immigration. JPOPE 8: 23-33.

144 Carruthers, N. 1981. Location Choice When Price Is also a Decision Variable. ARS 15: 29-42.

145 Cebula, R. J. 1977. Migration Patterns and Local Government Policy toward Public Education. PC 32: 113-121.

146 Cebula, R. J.; Avery, K. L. 1983. Tiebout Hypothesis: Black Consumer-Voters. PC 41: 307-310.

147 Cebula, R. J.; Belton, W. J. 1994. Voting with One's Feet: Public Welfare and Migration of the American Indian. AJEAS 53: 273-280.

148 Clark, W. A. V.; Moore, E. G. 1982. Residential Mobility and Public Programs. JSI 38: 35-50.

149 Coexistence. 1991. Papers on the Emigre Experience. Vol 28 (2).

150 Davis, K. 1988. Social Science Approaches to International Migration. PADR 14: 245-261.

151 Deller, S. C.; Chicoine, D. L. 1988. Representative vs. Direct Democracy: Tiebout Test. PC 51: 69-72.

152 Development. 1993. Papers on Immigration and the International Division of Labor. Vol 1993 (1).

153 Economic Development and Cultural Change. 1982. Papers on Third World Migration and Urbanization. EDACC 30 (3).

154 Epple, D.; Zelenitz, A. 1981. Implications of Competition among Jurisdictions: Does Tiebout Need Politics? JPE 89: 1197-1217.

155 Epple, D.; Zelenitz, A.; Visscher, M. 1978. A Search for Testable Implications of the Tiebout Hypothesis. JPE 86: 405-426.

156 Ervin, D. J. 1987. Ecological Theory of Migration. SSQ 68: 866-876.

157 Espenshade, T. J.; Calhoun, C. A. 1993. An Analysis of Public Opinion toward Undocumented Immigration. PRAPR 12: 189-224.

158 Ethnic and Racial Studies. 1991. Papers on Migration and Migrants in France. EARS 14 (3).

159 Etudes Internationales. 1993. Papers on Migrations and Transnational Relations. EINT 24 (1).

160 European Journal of Political Research. 1988. Papers on Immigration. EJPR 16 (6).

161 Faist, R. 1995. Immigration, Integration and the Ethnicization of Politics: Germany. EJPR 25: 439-460.

162 Foreman-Peck, J. 1992. A Political Economy of International Migration, 1815-1914. MSESS 60: 359-376.

163 Freymeyer, R. H.; Ritchey, P. N. 1985. Spatial Distribution of Opportunities and Magnitude of Migration: Stouffer's Theory. SP 28: 419-440.

164 Graves, P. E.; Knapp, T. A. 1985. Hedonic Analysis in a Spatial Context: Theoretical Problems in Valuing Location-Specific Amenities. ECONR 61: 737-743.

165 Greenwood, M. J. 1985. Human Migration: Theory, Models and Empirical Studies. JRS 25: 521-544.

166 Harris, W. A. 1994. Theoretical Research on Migration. SCAW 11: 283-288.

167 Hattan, T. J.; Williamson, J. G. 1994. What Drove the Mass Migrations in the Nineteenth Century? PADR 20: 533-559.

168 Herzog, H. W.; Schlottman, A. M.; Boehm, T. P. 1993. Migration as Spatial Job-Search. REGS 27: 327-340.

169 International Journal. 1993. Papers on Migrants and Refugees. IJ 48 (2).

170 International Regional Science Review. 1988. Papers on Population Migration. IRSR 11 (3).

171 International Social Science Journal. 1984. Papers on Migration. ISSJ 36 (3).

172 Islam, M. N. 1989. Tiebout Hypothesis and Migration-Impact of Local Fiscal Policies. PF 44: 406-418.

173 Jenkins-Smith, H. C. 1991. Reflections on Research Strategy for the Study of Nuclear Waste Policy. PS 24: 157-166.

174 John, P.; Dowding, K.; Biggs, S. 1995. Residential Mobility in London: Behavioural Assumptions of the Tiebout Model. BJPS 25: 379-398.

175 Journal of International Affairs. 1993. Papers on Refugees and International Population Flows. JIA 47 (2).

176 Journal of Social Issues. 1982. Papers on Residential Mobility Theory. JSI 38 (3).

177 Kahley, W. J. 1990. Population Migration in the US. FRBA 76: 12-21.

178 Kasperson, R. E.; Golding, D.; Tuler, S. 1992 Social Distrust as a Factor in Siting Hazardous Facilities and Communicating Risks. JSI 48 (4): 161-187.

179 Kritz, M. M.; Nogle, J. M. 1994. Nativity Concentration and Internal Migration. Demography 31: 509-524.

180 Leitner, H. 1995. International Migration and the Politics of Admission and Exclusion in Postwar Europe. PG 14: 259-278.

181 Lober, D. J. 1995. Public Behavioral and Attitudinal Response to Siting a Waste Disposal Facility. PSJ 23: 499-518.

182 Lowery, D.; Lyons, W. E. 1989. The Impact of Jurisdictional Boundaries: Tiebout Model. JOP 51: 73-97.

183 Massey, D. S., et al. 1993. Theories of International Migration. PADR 19: 431-466.

184 -. 1994. International Migration Theory. PADR 20: 699-751.

185 McDowell, J. M.; Singell, L. D. 1993. An Assessment of Human Capital Content of International Migrants. REGS 27: 351-363.

186 Miezkowski, P.; Zodrow, G. R. 1989. Taxation and the Tiebout Model: Differential Effects of Head Taxes, Taxes on Land, Rents and Property Taxes. JEL 27: 1098-1146.

187 Mills, D. E. 1989. Is Zoning a Negative-Sum Game? Land Economics 65: 1-12.

188 Milne, W. J. 1993. Macroeconomic Influences on Migration. REGS 27: 365-373.

189 Milward, H. B.; Newman, H. H. 1989. State Incentive Packages and the Industrial Location Decision. EDQ 3: 203-222.

190 Moehring, H. B. 1988. Symbol vs. Substance in Legislative Activity: Illegal Immigration. PC 57: 287-294.

191 Morrison, A. R. 1993. What Drives Internal Migration in Guatemala? EDACC 41: 817-831.

192 Mumphrey, A. J.; Wolpert, J. 1973. Equity Considerations and Concessions in the Siting of Public Facilities. EG 49: 109-121.

193 Munley, V. G. 1982. Test of the Tiebout Hypothesis. PC 38: 211-217.

194 Newman, A. R. 1981. Test of the Okun-Richardson Model of Internal Migration. EDACC 29: 295-308.

195 Oates, W. E. 1981. On Local Finance and the Tiebout Model. AER Proceedings 71: 93-97.

196 Payne, B. A.; Olshansky, S. J.; Segel, T. E. 1987. Effects of Property Values of Proximity to a Site Contaminated with Radioactive Waste. NRJ 27: 579-590.

197 Percy, S. L.; Hawkins, B. W.; Maier, P. E. 1995. Revisiting Tiebout: Moving Rationales and Inter-jurisdictional Relocation. Publius 25: 1-18.

198 Peterson, P. E.; Rom, M. 1989. American Federalism, Welfare Policy and Residential Choices. APSR 83: 711-728.

199 Pines, D. 1991. Tiebout without Politics. RSUE 21: 469-490.

200 Plane, D. A. 1993. Demographic Influences on Migration. REGS 27: 375-383.

201 Pogodzinski, J. M.; Sass, T. R. 1990. Economic Theory of Zoning. Land Economics 66: 294-314.

202 -. 1991. Measuring Effects of Municipal Zoning Regulations. US 28: 597-621.

203 Porell, F. W. 1981. Spatial Impacts of Local Housing Programs: Turnover. JAPA 47: 59-69.

204 Proceedings. 1992. Papers on Immigration. PAPS 136 (2).

205 Recherche Sociale. 1980. Papers on Immigrant Workers. RS 73 (Jan).

206 -. 1981. Papers on Social Integration of Refugees from Southeast Asia. RS 77 (April-Sept).

207 Regional Studies. 1993. Papers on Migration. REGS 27 (4).

208 Richter, W. F. 1994. The Efficient Allocation of Local Public Factors in Tiebout's Tradition. RSUE 24: 323-340.

209 Romo, F. P.; Schwartz, M. 1995. Structural Embeddedness of Business Decisions: Migration of Manufacturing Plants. ASR 60: 874-908.

210 Rossi, P. H.; Shlay, A. B. 1982. Residential Mobility and Public Policy. JSI 38: 21-34.

211 Schneider, M. 1976. Migration, Ethnicity and Politics: Comparative State Analysis. JOP 38: 938-962.

212 -. 1989. Intermunicipal Competition, Budget Maximizing Bureaucrats and the Level of Suburban Competition. AJPS 33: 612-628.

213 Shelley, M. C.; Koven, S. G. 1993. Interstate Migration. PSJ 21: 243-270.

214 Shieh, Y. 1984. On the Space Curve and Industrial Location. ARS 18: 66-76.

215 Shumaker, S. A.; Stokols, D. 1982. Residential Mobility as Social Issue and Research Topic. JSI 38: 1-20.

216 Spectrum. 1994. Papers on Illegal Immigration. Vol 67 (1).

217 Teitz, M. B. 1968. Toward a Theory of Urban Public Facility Locations. Papers of the Regional Science Association 21: 35-51.

218 Tichenor, D. J. 1994. Politics of Immigration Reform in the US. Polity 26: 333-362.

219 Urban Anthropology. 1990. Papers on Immigrants in US Cities. Vol 19 (1-2).

220 West European Politics. 1994. Papers on the Politics of Immigration. WEP 17 (2).

221 Westerlund, O.; Wyzan, M. L. 1995. Household Migration and the Local Public Sector. REGS 29: 145-157.

222 Wilkie, M. E. 1977. Colonials, Marginals and Immigrants: Elite Stratification Theory. CSSH 19: 67-95.

223 Winter-Ebmer, R. 1994. Motivation for Migration and Economic Success. JEPSY 15: 269-284.

224 Zax, J. S. 1994. When Is a Move a Migration? RSUE 24: 341-360.

Political Culture and Region

225 Agnew, J. A. 1985. Spatial Variation in Political Expression: Scottish National Party. IPSR 6: 171-196.

226 -. 1988. The Myth of Regional Political-Economic Restructuring and Sectionalism in Contemporary American Politics. PG 7: 127-140.

227 Anderson, M. 1982. Political Problems of Frontier Regions. WEP 5: 1-17.

228 Archer, J. C. 1985. Some Geographical Aspects of the American Presidential Election of 1984. PG 4: 159-172.

229 -. 1988. Macrogeographical vs. Microgeographical Cleavages in American Presidential Elections. PG 7: 111-126.

230 Archer, J. C., et al. 1985. Counties, States, Sections and Parties in 1984 Presidential Election. PGEO 37: 279-287.

231 Auster, C. J. 1987. Melbin's Frontier Hypothesis: Outer Space Exploration. SI 57: 102-112.

232 Bensel, R. F. 1982. Sectional Stress and Ideology in the US House. Polity 14: 657-675.

233 Berman, D. R. 1988. Political Culture, Issues and the Electorate: The Progressive Era. WPQ 41: 169-180.

234 Bertsch, G. K.; Zaninovich, M. G. 1974. Factor Analytic Method of Identifying Different Political Cultures: Yugoslavia. CP 6: 219-244.

235 Bogdanor, V. 1977. Regionalism: Constitutional Aspects. PQ 48: 164-174.

236 Boyd, J. B. 1979. African Boundary Conflict. AFSR 22: 1-14.

237 Bradbury, J. 1985. Region and Industrial Restructuring Processes in the New Industrial Division of Labor. PIHG 9: 28-63.

238 Bueno de Mesquita, B. 1990. Pride of Place: The Origins of German Hegemony. WP 43: 28-52.

239 Bunker, S. G. 1984. Extraction, Unequal Exchange and Progressive Underdevelopment of an Extreme Periphery: Brazilian Amazon. AJS 89: 1017-1064.

240 Chilton, S. 1988. Defining Political Culture. WPQ 41: 419-446.

241 Clark, G. L. 1981. Factors Influencing Space-Time Lags of Regional Economic Adjustment. ARS 15: 1-14.

242 Coakley, J. 1982. National Territories and Cultural Frontiers: Conflicts of Principle in the Formation of States in Europe. WEP 5: 34-49.

243 Cox, K. R. 1969. Regions in Comparative Political Sociology. CPS 2: 68-98.

244 Crime, Law and Social Change. 1995. Papers on Immigration, Xenophobia and Right Wing Violence in Germany. CLASC 24 (1).

245 Deckard, B. S.; Stanley, J. 1974. Party Decomposition and Region: US House. WPQ 27: 249-264.

246 Elkins, D. J.; Simeon, R. 1979. What Does Political Culture Explain? CP 11: 127-146.

247 Erikson, R. S.; McIver, J. P.; Wright, G. C. 1987. State Political Culture and Public Opinion. APSR 81: 797-813.

248 Ersson, S.; Janda, K.; Lane, J. E. 1985. Ecology of Party Strength in Western Europe: A Regional Analysis. CPS 18: 170-205.

249 Fitzpatrick, J. L.; Hero, R. E. 1988. Political Culture and Political Characteristics of the American States. WPQ 41: 145-154.

250 Formisano, R. P. 1974. Deferential-Participant Politics: The Early Republic's Political Culture. APSR 68: 473-487.

251 Foster, C. R. 1982. Political Culture and Regional Ethnic Minorities. JOP 44: 560-568.

252 Gardette, X. 1980. Possible Reasons for the Present Regionalist Revival in France and Elsewhere. JAS 1: 9-13.

253 Geis, G. 1995. Is Germany's Xenophobia Qualitatively Different? CLASC 24: 65 ff.

254 Gerston, L. N.; Haas, P. J. 1993. Political Support for Regional Government in 1990s: Growing in the Suburbs? UAQ 29: 154-163.

255 Graber, R. B. 1988. Mathematical Interpretation of Circumscription Applied to Westward Expansion. ABS 31: 459-471.

256 Grimsson, O. R. 1978. Peripheries and Nationalism: The Faroes and Greenland. SPS 1: 315-327.

257 Hansen, N. 1977. Border Regions: A Critique of Spatial Theory. ARS 11: 1-14.

258 Hanson, R. L. 1980. Political Culture, Interparty Competition and Political Efficacy in the US. Publius 10: 17-36.

259 Hechter, M. 1973. Persistence of Regionalism in the British Isles. AJS 79: 319-342.

260 Herzik, E. B. 1985. Legal-Formal Structure of State Politics: A Cultural Explanation. WPQ 38: 413-423.

261 Hofferbert, R. I. 1968. Socioeconomic Dimensions of the American States. AJPS 12: 401-418.

262 Hunt, L. 1984. The Political Geography of Revolutionary France. JIDH 14: 535-560.

263 Hurlbert, J. S. 1989. The Southern Region: The Hypothesis of Cultural Distinctiveness. SQ 30: 245-266.

264 Hurrell, A. 1995. Explaining the Resurgence of Regionalism in World Politics. RIS 21: 331-358.

265 Inglehart, R. 1988. The Renaissance of Political Culture. APSR 82: 1203-1230.

266 International Journal. 1975. Papers on Regionalism. IJ 30 (4).

267 International Regional Science Review. 1995. Papers on the Future of Regional Science. IRSR 17 (3).

268 International Social Science Journal. 1987. Papers on Regional Science. ISSJ 39 (2).

269 Janda, K.; Gillies, R. 1983. How Well Does Region Explain Political Party Characteristics? PG 12: 179-203.

270 Janos, A. C. 1989. Politics of Backwardness in Continental Europe. WP 41: 325-358.

271 Jillson, C. C. 1988. Political Culture and the Pattern of Congressional Politics under the Articles of Confederation. Publius 18: 1-26.

272 Johnson, C. A. 1976. Political Culture in American States. AJPS 20: 491-510.

273 Johnston, R. J.; Pattie, C. J. 1990. Class, Attitudes and Retrospective Voting: Regional Variations in the 1983 General Election in Great Britain. EPA 22: 893-908.

274 Joslyn, R. A. 1980. Manifestations of Elazar's Political Subcultures: State Public Opinion and Content of Political Campaign Advertising. Publius 10: 37-58.

275 Jowitt, K. 1974. Organizational Approach to the Study of Political Culture in Marxist-Leninist Systems. APSR 68: 1171-1191.

276 Julnes, G.; Pindur, W. 1994. Determinants of Local Governmental Support for Alternative Forms of Regional Coordination. ARPA 24: 411-428.

277 Kincaid, J. 1980. Political Culture and Quality of Urban Life. Publius 10: 89-110.

278 -. 1980. Political Cultures in the American Compound Republic. Publius 10: 1-13.

279 Kinsey, L. S. 1976. National Political Integration and Disintegration: Quebec. CPS 9: 335-360.

280 Laitin, D. D.; Wildavsky, A. 1988. Political Culture and Political Preferences. APSR 82: 589-596.

281 Lawrence, R. Z. 1994. Regionalism. JJAIE 8: 365-387.

282 Lehman, E. W. 1972. Political Culture. SF 50: 361-370.

283 Lieske, J. A. 1993. Regional Subcultures of the US. JOP 55: 888-913.

284 Lowery, D.; Sigelman, L. 1982. Political Culture and State Public Policy. WPQ 10: 376-384.

285 Luke, T. W. 1989. Developing a Genealogy of the Political Culture Concept. History of Political Thought 10: 125-149.

286 Martis, K. C. 1988. Sectionalism and Congress. PG 7: 99-110.

287 McAllister, I.; Studlar, D. T. 1992. Region and Voting in Britain. AJPS 36: 168-199.

288 McCrone, D. J.; Bechhofer, F. 1993. The Scotland-England Divide: Politics and Locality in Britain. POLST 41: 96-107.

289 Meadwell, H. 1991. A Rational Choice Approach to Political Regionalism. CP 23: 401-422.

290 Mishler, W.; Mughan, A. 1978. Representing the Celtic Fringe: Devolution and Legislative Behavior in Scotland and Wales. LSQ 3: 377-408.

291 Moises, J. A. 1993. Elections, Political Parties and Political Culture in Brazil. JLATAS 25: 575-612.

292 Morgan, D. R.; England, R. E. 1987. Classifying the American States. SSQ 68: 405-417.

293 Morgan, D. R.; Hirlinger, M. W. 1989. Socioeconomic Dimensions of the American States. SSQ 70: 184-192.

294 Morgan, D. R.; Lyons, W. E. 1975. Socioeconomic Dimensions of American States. AJPS 19: 263-276.

295 Morgan, D. R.; Wilson, L. A. 1990. Diversity in the American States. Publius 20: 71-82.

296 Murauskas, G. T.; Archer, J. C.; Shelley, F. M. 1988. Metropolitan, Nonmetropolitan and Sectional Variations in Voting Behavior in Presidential Elections. WPQ 41: 63-84.

297 Naroff, J. L.; Madden, T. J. 1984. Using Discriminant Analysis to Predict Regional Shifts. GAC 14: 24-29.

298 Nesbitt-Larking, P. 1992. Methodological Notes on the Study of Political Culture. PP 13: 79-90.

299 Newman, S. 1994. Ethnoregional Parties. RPAP 4: 28-66.

300 Political Geography. 1995. Papers on Urban Regional Networks. PG 14 (4).

301 Publius. 1980. Papers on US Political Culture. Publius 10 (2) and 1991 21 (2).

302 Reisinger, W. M. 1995. Political Culture as Concept and Theory. IJPOR 7: 328-352.

303 Revista Mexicana. 1983. Papers on Regionalism in Mexico. RMCPS 28 (113/114).

304 Roeder, P. W. 1976. Classifying the American States. WPQ 29: 563-574.

305 Sayer, S. 1982. Economic Analysis of Frontier Regions. WEP 5: 64-80.

306 Schiltz, T. D.; Rainey, R. L. 1978. Geographical Distribution of Elazar's Political Subcultures. WPQ 31: 410-415.

307 Schrodt, P. A. 1981. Conflict as a Determinant of Territory. BS 26: 37-50.

308 Sharkansky, I. 1968. Regionalism, Economic Status and Public Politics in the American States. SSQ 49: 9-26.

309 -. 1969. The Utility of Elazar's Political Culture. Polity 2: 66-83.

310 Sharkansky, I.; Hofferbert, R. I. 1969. Dimensions of State Politics, Economics and Public Policy. APSR 63: 887-889.

311 Shefter, M. 1983. Regional Receptivity to Reform: Legacy of the Progressive Era. PSCQ 98: 459-484.

312 Shelley, F. M. 1988. Structure, Stability and Section in American Politics. PG 7: 153-160.

313 Shelley, F. M.; Archer, J. C. 1984. Political Habit, Political Culture and Electoral Mosaic of a Border Region. Geographical Perspectives 54: 7-20.

314 -. 1989. Sectionalism and Presidential Politics: Voting in Illinois, Indiana and Ohio. JIDH 20: 227-256.

315 Shields, J.; Weinberg, L. 1976. Reactive Violence and the American Frontier. WPQ 29: 86-101.

316 Smith, N. 1988. The Region is Dead! Long Live the Region. PG 7: 141-152.

317 Sniderman, P. M., et al. 1989. Political Culture and Double Standards: Attitudes toward Language Rights in the Canadian Charter of Rights and Freedoms. CJPS 22: 259-284.

318 Social Science Quarterly. 1968. Papers on Regionalism. SSQ 49: 9-38.

319 Starr, J.; Most, B. A. 1976. Substance and Study of Borders in International Relations Research. ISQ 20: 581-620.

320 Stern, L. N.; Dobson, D.; Scioli, F. P. 1973. Dimensions of Political Culture. CPS 5: 493-512.

321 Street, J. 1994. Political Culture from Civic Culture to Mass Culture. BJPS 24: 95-114.

322 Studies in Comparative Communism. 1983. Papers on Communist Political Culture. SCC 16 (1/2).

323 Swauger, J. 1980. Measuring Regional Agreement in Senate Voting. PGEO 32: 446-453.

324 Tagil, S. 1982. The Question of Border Regions in Western Europe. WEP 5: 18-33.

325 Tucker, H. J.; Herzik, E. B. 1986. The Problem of Region in American State Policy Research. SSQ 67: 84-97.

326 University of Chicago Law Review 1988. Selected Bibliography of Works on Political Culture. UCLR 55: 585-590.

327 Von Trotha, T. 1995. Political Culture, Xenophobia and Violence of the Radical Right in the Federal Republic of Germany. CLASC 24: 37-48.

328 West European Politics. 1982. Papers on Frontier Regions in Western Europe. WEP 5 (4).

329 Wildavsky, A. 1985. Change in Political Culture. Politics 20: 95-102.

330 -. 1988. Political Culture and Political Preferences. APSR 82: 593-596.

POLITICAL PARTIES

1 Anderson, C. J. 1995. Dynamics of Public Support for Coalition Governments. CPS 28: 350-383.
2 Beck, P. A.; Jennings, M. K. 1979. Political Periods and Political Participation. APSR 73: 737-750.
3 Bowler, S. 1990. Voter Perceptions and Party Strategies. CP 23: 61-83.
4 Bruce, J. M.; Clark, J. A.; Kessel, J. H. 1991. Advocacy Politics in Presidential Parties. APSR 85: 1089-1105.
5 Canovan, M. 1982. Two Strategies for the Study of Populism. POLST 30: 544-552.
6 Chappell, H.W.; Keech, W. R. 1986. Policy Motivation and Party Differences in Dynamic Spatial Model of Party Competition. APSR 80: 881-900.
7 Charlot, J. 1989. Political Parties: Towards a New Theoretical Synthesis. POLST 37: 352-361.
8 Coram, B. T. 1991. Why Political Parties Should Make Unbelievable Promises. PC 69: 101-106.
9 Cotter, C. P.; Bibby, J. F. 1980. Institutional Development of Parties and the Thesis of Party Decline. PSQ 95: 1-27.
10 Damgaard, E.; Svensson, P. 1989. Who Governs? Parties and Politics Denmark. EJPR 17: 731-745.
11 Eijk, C.; Oppenhuis, E. V. 1991. European Parties Performance in Electoral Competition. EJPR 19: 55-80.
12 European Journal of Political Research. 1992. Papers on Right Wing Parties. EJPR 22 (1).
13 Evans, G.; Heath, A.; Payne, C. 1991. Modelling Trends in Class-Party. ES 10: 99-117.
14 Evans, G.; Whitefield, S. 1993. Bases of Party Competition in Eastern Europe. BJPS 23: 521-548.
15 Farrell, D. M.; Wortmann, M. 1987. Party Strategies in the Electoral Market: Political Marketing. EJPR 15: 297-318.
16 Freeman, J. 1986. Political Culture of Democratic and Republican Parties. PSQ 101: 430-455.
17 Greenberg, J.; Shepsle, K. A. 1987. Effect of Electoral Rewards in Multiparty Competition with Entry. APSR 81: 525-537.
18 Harmel, R., et al. 1995. Performance, Leadership, Factions and Party Change. WEP 18: 1-33.
19 Herrera, R. 1995. Sources of Change in Democratic and Republican Parties. PRQ 48: 291-312.
20 Hill, K. Q.; Leighley, J. E. 1993. Party Ideology, Organization and Competitiveness as Mobilizing Forces. AJPS 37: 1158-1178.
21 Hofferbert, R. I.; Klingemann, H. D. 1990. Policy Impact of Party Programmes and Government Declarations in Germany. EJPR 18: 277-304.
22 Ingberman, D.; Villani, J. 1993. An Institutional Theory of Divided Government and Party Polarization. AJPS 37: 429-471.
23 Iversen, T. 1994. Logics of Electoral Politics: Spatial, Directional and Mobilization Effects. CPS 27: 155-189.
24 Katz, R. S. 1990. Party as Linkage: A Vestigal Function? EJPR 18: 143-161.
25 Konda, T. M.; Sigelman, L. 1987. Public Evaluations of American Parties. JOP 49: 814-829.
26 LeDuc, L. 1976. Semantic Differential Measures of British Party Strength. BJPS 61: 115-123.
27 Macey, J. R. 1990. Role of Democratic and Republican Parties as Organizers of Shadow Interest Groups. MLR 89: 1-29.
28 MacKuen, M. B.; Erikson, R. S.; Stimson, J. A. 1989. Macropartisanship. APSR 83: 1125-1142.
29 Mueller, E. H. 1977. Behavioral Correlates of Political Support. APSR 71: 454-467.
30 Mueller, E. H.; Jukam, T. O. 1977. On the Meaning of Political Support. APSR 71: 1561-1595.
31 Paddock, J. 1992. Inter-Party Ideological Differences in State Parties. WPQ 45: 751-760.
32 Peritore, N. P. 1988. Brazilian Communist Opinion: Q-Methodology of Parties. JDA 23: 105-135.
33 Rahn, W. M. 1993. Role of Partisan Sterotypes in Information Processing about Political Candidates. AJPS 37: 472-496.
34 Richardson, B. M. 1991. European Party Loyalties Revisited. APSR 85: 751-775.
35 Ritt, L. G. 1978. Socio-Economic Correlates of Party Reform. JPS 5: 92-96.
36 Rose, R.; Urwin, D. 1975. Social Cohesion, Political Parties and Strains in Regimes. CPS 2: 7-67.
37 Schlesinger, J. A. 1984. On the Theory of Party Organization. JOP 46: 369-400.
38 Silverman, L. 1985. Ideological Mediation of Party-Political Responses to Social Change. EJPR 13: 69-93.
39 Studies in Comparative Communism. 1988. Papers on USSR Local Party Organizations. SCC 21 (1).
40 Thomas, J. C. 1982. Ideological Change in Comparative Labor Parties. CPS 15: 223-240.
41 Webster, G. R. 1989. Partisanship in Presidential, Senatorial and Gubernatorial Elections. PG 8: 161-180.
42 Wellhofer, E. S. 1974. Political Parties as Communities of Fate: Tests with Argentine Party Elites. AJPS 18: 347-363.
43 -. 1979. Effectiveness of Party Organization. EJPR 7: 205-224.
44 -. 1990. Contradictions in Market Models of Politics: Party Strategies and Voter Linkages. EJPR 18: 9-28.
45 Wren, C. 1992. Political Parties and Government Behaviour. BER 44: 125-140.

Campaign Finance

46 Allen, M. P.; Broyles, P. 1991. Campaign Finance Reforms and Presidential Campaign Contributions of Wealthy Capitalist Families. SSQ 72: 738-750.

47 Annals. 1986. Papers on Campaign Finance Regulation. ANNALS 486.

48 Austen-Smith, D. 1987. Interest Groups, Campaign Contributions and Probabilistic Voting. PC 54: 123-139.

49 -. 1995. Campaign Contributions and Access. APSR 89: 566-581.

50 Banaian, K.; Luksetich, W. A. 1991. Campaign Spending in Congressional Elections. EI 29: 92-100.

51 Barbrook, A. T. 1987. Campaign Finance in American State Elections. CAR 2: 17-40.

52 Bender, B. 1988. Congressional Voting on Legislation Limiting Congressional Campaign Expenditures. JPE 96: 1005-1021.

53 Bennett, R. W.; Loucks, C. 1994. Savings and Loan and Finance Industry PAC Contributions to Incumbent Members of the House Banking Committee. PC 79: 83-104.

54 Brams, S. J.; Davis, M. D. 1973. Resource Allocation in Presidential Campaigning. Annals of the New York Academy of Sciences 219: 105-123.

55 Brody, C. J. 1983. Advertising Campaigns as Arms Races. SP 26: 323-340.

56 Chappell, H. W. 1994. Campaign Advertising and Political Ambiguity. PC 79: 281-304.

57 Clark, D.; Thomas, J. P. 1995. Probabilistic Voting, Campaign Contributions and Efficiency. AER 85: 254-259.

58 Columbia Law Review. 1994. Papers on Campaign Finance Reform. Vol 94 (4).

59 Fiorina, M. P. 1981. Some Problems in Studying the Effects of Resource Allocation in Congressional Elections. AJPS 25: 543-567.

60 Fisher, J. 1994. Why Do Companies Make Donations to Political Parties? POLST 42: 690-699.

61 Gelhorn, E., et al. 1995. Campaign Finance Enforcement: A Comparative View. JOLAP 11: 1-40.

62 Goddeeris, J. H. 1989. Modeling Interest Group Campaign Contributions. PFQ 17: 158-184.

63 Goidel, R. K.; Gross, D. A. 1994. A Systems Approach to Campaign Finance in House Elections. APQ 22: 125-153.

64 Grenzke, J. 1989. Candidate Attitudes and PAC Contributions. WPQ 42: 254-264.

65 Grier, K. B.; Munger, M. C. 1993. Comparing Interest Group PAC Contributions to House and Senate Incumbents. JOP 55: 615-643.

66 Grier, K. B.; Munger, M. C.; Torrent, G. M. 1990. Allocation Patterns of PAC Monies: Senate. PC 67: 111-128.

67 Hedges, R. B. 1984. Reasons for Political Involvement: Contributors to the 1972 Presidential Campaign. WPQ 37: 257-271.

68 Hersch, P. L.; McDougall, G. S. 1994. Campaign War Chests as a Barrier to Entry in Congressional Races. EI 32: 630-641.

69 Jacobson, G. C. 1978. Campaign Spending in Congressional Elections. APSR 72: 469-491.

70 -. 1990. Effects of Campaign Spending in House Elections. AJPS 34: 334-362.

71 Kenny, C. B.; McBurnett, M. 1994. An Individual Level Multiequation Model of Expenditure Effects in Contested House Elections. APSR 88: 699-710.

72 Krasno, J. S.; Green, D. P.; Cowden, J. A. 1994. Dynamics of Campaign Fundraising in House Elections. JOP 56: 459-474.

73 Levitt, S. D. 1994. Using Repeat Challengers to Estimate Effect of Campaign Spending on Election Outcomes in the US House. JPE 102: 777-798.

74 -. 1995. Congressional Campaign Finance Reform. JEP 9: 183-193.

75 Lohmann, S. 1995. Information, Access and Contributions: Signaling Model of Lobbying. PC 85: 267-284.

76 Lott, J. R. 1991. Does Additional Campaign Spending Really Hurt Incumbents? PC 72: 87-92.

77 Masters, M. F.; Keim, G. D. 1985. Determinants of PAC Contributions among Large Corporations. JOP 47: 1158-1173.

78 Mayer, K. R.; Wood, J. M. 1995. Impact of Public Financing on Electoral Competitiveness. LSQ 20: 69-88.

79 McAdams, J. C.; Johannes, J. R. 1987. Spending by House Challengers. AJPS 31: 457-484.

80 McBurnett, M.; Kenny, C. B. 1992. Dynamic Model of the Effect of Campaign Spending on Congressional Vote Choice. AJPS 36: 923-937.

81 McKeown, T. J. 1994. Epidemiology of Corporate PAC Formation. JEBAO 24: 153-168.

82 Moncrief, G. F. 1992. Increase in State Legislative Campaign Expenditures. WPQ 45: 521-538.

83 Morton, R.B.; Cameron, C. M. 1992. Elections and Theory of Campaign Contributions. EAP 4: 78-108.

84 Munger, M. C. 1989. A Simple Test of the Thesis that Committee Jurisdictions Shape Corporate PAC Contributions. PC 62: 181-186.

85 Mutz, D. C. 1995. Effects of Horse Race Coverage on Campaign Coffers: Strategic Contributing in Presidential Campaigns. JOP 57: 1015-1042.

86 Palda, F. 1992. Determinants of Campaign Spending: The Government Jackpot. EI 30: 627-638.

87 Regens, J. L.; Gaddie, R. E.; Elliott, E. 1994. Corporate PAC Contributions and Rent Provision in Senate Elections. SSQ 75: 152-165.

88 Rehbein, K. A. 1995. Foreign-Owned Firms' Campaign Contributions in the US. PSJ 23: 41-69.

89 Romer, T.; Snyder, J. M. 1994. The Dynamics of PAC Contributions. AJPS 38: 745-769.

90 Rosenthal, C. S. 1995. New Party or Campaign Bank Account? Explaining Rise of State Legislative Campaign Committees. LSQ 20: 249-268.

91 Schroedel, J. R. 1986. Campaign Contributions and Legislative Outcomes. WPQ 34: 371-389.

92 Smith, R. C. 1988. Financing Black Politics: Congressional Elections. RBPE 17 (1): 5-30.

93 Snyder, J. M. 1993. Market for Campaign Contributions: US Senate. EAP 5: 219-240.

94 Social Policy. 1995. Papers on Campaign Finance Reform. Vol 26 (1).

95 Stratmann, T. 1992. Are Contributors Rational? Political Action Committees. JPE 100: 647-664.

96 -. 1995. Campaign Contributions and Congressional Voting: Does Timing Matter? REAS 77: 127-136.

97 Su, T. T.; Neustadt, A.; Clawson, D. 1995. Business and the Conservative Shift: Corporate PAC Contributions. SSQ 76: 20-40.

98 Thielemann, G. S.; Dixon, D. R. 1994. Explaining Contributions. LSQ 19: 495-506.

99 Welch, W. P. 1981. Money and Votes: A Simultaneous Equation Model. PC 36: 209-234.

100 Wyrick, T. L. 1994. House Members as Residual Claimants: Campaign Spending. PC 79: 135-148.

Conventions and Nominations

101 Aldrich, J. H. 1980. A Dynamic Model of Presidential Nomination Campaigns. APSR 74: 651-669.

102 Bartels, L. M. 1985. Expectations and Preferences in Presidential Nominating Campaigns. APSR 79: 804-815.

103 -. 1987. Candidate Choice and Dynamics of the Presidential Nominating Process. AJPS 31: 1-32.

104 Beniger, J. R. 1976. Winning the Presidential Nomination: National Polls and State Primary Elections. POQ 40: 22-38.

105 Bochel, J.; Denver, D. 1983. Candidate Selection in the Labour Party. BJPS 13: 45-69.

106 Brams, S. J.; Garriga-Pico, J. E. 1975. Bandwagons in Coalition Formation: The Two-Thirds Rule. ABS 18: 472-496.

107 Budge, I.; Hofferbert, R. I. 1990. Mandates and Policy Outputs: US Party Platforms and Federal Expenditures. APSR 84: 111-131.

108 Budge, I.; Laver, M. 1986. Policy, Ideology and Party Distance: Election Programmes in Nineteen Democracies. LSQ 11: 607-618.

109 Congleton, R. D. 1989. Campaign Finances and Political Platforms. PC 62: 101-118.

110 Costain, A. N. 1978. Voting in American National Nominating Conventions. APQ 6: 95-120.

111 -. 1980. Changes in Role of Ideology in American National Nominating Conventions and among Party Identifiers. WPQ 33: 73-86.

112 Fine, T. S. 1994. Interest Groups and the Framing of the 1988 Democratic and Republican Party Platforms. Polity 26: 517-530.

113 Geer, J. G.; Shere, M. E. 1992. Party Competition and the Prisoner's Dilemma: An Argument for the Direct Primary. JOP 54: 741-761.

114 Goldstein, J. 1979. Candidate Popularity and Campaign Contributions in Pre-Nominating Stage. PSQ 9: 329-333.

115 Gurian, P. H. 1986. Resource Allocations Strategies in Presidential Nomination Campaigns. AJPS 30: 802-821.

116 -. 1993. Candidate Behavior in Presidential Nominating Campaigns. JOP 55: 115-139.

117 Gurian, P.H.; Haynes, A.A. 1993 Campaign Strategy in Presidential Primaries. AJPS 37: 335-341.

118 Heritage, J.; Greatbatch, D. 1986. Rhetoric and Response at Party Political Conferences. AJS 92: 110-157.

119 Herrnson, P. S.; Gimpel, J. G. 1995. District Conditions and Primary Divisiveness in Congressional Elections. PRQ 48: 117-134.

120 Kenney, P. J. 1992. A Model of Nomination Preferences. APQ 20: 267-286.

121 -. 1993. How Voters Form Impressions of Candidates's Issue Positions. PB 15: 265-288.

122 King, G., et al. 1993. Party Platforms and Government Spending. APSR 87: 744-750.

123 Lengle, J. L. 1980. Divisive Presidential Primaries and Electoral Prospects. APQ 8: 261-278.

124 McCann, J. A. 1995. Nomination Politics and Ideological Polarization: Attitudinal Effects of Campaign Involvement. JOP 57: 101-120.

125 McGregor, E. B. 1978. Uncertainty and National Nominating Coalitions. JOP 40: 1011-1043.

126 Monroe, A. D. 1983. American Party Platforms and Public Opinion. AJPS 27: 27-42.

127 Morton, R. B. 1993. Incomplete Information and Ideological Explanations of Platform Divergence. APSR 87: 382-391.

128 Nice, D. C. 1980. Ideological Stability and Change at Presidential Nominating Conventions. JOP 42: 847-853.

129 Nice, D. C.; Cohen, J. E. 1983. Ideological Consistency among State Party Delegations to the House, Senate and Conventions. SSQ 64: 871-881.

130 Roback, T. 1975. Delegates to the 1972 Republican National Convention. JOP 37: 436-468.

131 -. 1980. Motivation for Activism among Republican National Convention Delegates. JOP 42: 181-201.

132 Snyder, J. M. 1994. Safe Seats, Marginal Seats, and Party Platforms: Logic of Platform Differentiation. EAP 6: 201-213.

133 Soule, J.; McGrath, W. 1975. Presidential Nominating Conventions. AJPS 19: 501-517.

134 Stone, W. J.; Rapoport, R. B. 1994. Candidate Perception among Nomination Activists: Moderation Hypothesis. JOP 56: 1034-1052.

135 Stone, W. J.; Rapoport, R. B.; Atkeson, L. R. 1995. A Simulation Model of Presidential Nomination Choice. AJPS 39: 135-161.

136 Wielhouwer, P. W.; Lockerbie, B. 1994. Party Contacting and Political Participation. AJPS 38: 211-229.

General Elections

137 Abramowitz, A. I. 1988. Explaining Senate Election Outcomes. APSR 82: 385-403.

138 American Politics Quarterly. 1980. Papers on Congressional Elections. APQ 8 (4).

139 -. 1995. Papers on Redistricting. APQ 23 (2).

140 Balke, N. S. 1990. Rational Timing of Parliamentary Elections. PC 65: 201-216.

141 Banks, J. S.; Kiewiet, D. R. 1989. Patterns of Candidate Competition in Congressional Elections. AJPS 33: 997-1015.

142 Basehart, H. H.; Comer, J. 1995. Redistricting and Incumbent Reelection Success in Five State Legislatures. APQ 23: 241-253.

143 Bennett, S. E.; Bennett, L. L. M. 1989. Interest in Presidential Campaigns. Polity 22: 341-354.

144 Bond, J. R.; Covington, C. R.; Fleisher, R. 1985. Explaining Challenger Quality in Congressional Elections. JOP 41: 510-529.

145 Born, R. 1990. Shared Fortunes of Congress and Congressmen. JOP 52: 1233-1241.

146 -. 1991. Institutional and Election Forces on Congressional Incumbents. JOP 53: 764-799.

147 Brams, S. J.; Fishburn, P. C. 1983. Deducing Preferences and Choices in the 1980 Presidential Election. ES 1: 333-346.

148 Brown, C. 1988. Mass Dynamics of US Presidential Competitions, 1928-1936. APSR 82: 1153-1181.

149 Brown, R. D.; Woods, J. A. 1991. Toward a Model of Congressional Elections. JOP 53: 454-473.

150 Caldeira, G. A.; Patterson, S. C. 1982. Bringing Home Votes: Electoral Outcomes in State Legislative Races. PB 4: 33-67.

151 Campbell, J. E. 1985. Explaining Presidential Losses in Midterm Congressional Elections. JOP 47: 1140-1157.

152 -. 1992. Forecasting the Presidential Vote in the States. AJPS 36: 386-407.

153 Canon, D. T. 1993. Sacrificial Lambs or Strategic Politicians? Political Amateurs in US House Elections. AJPS 37: 1119-1141.

154 Chester, E. W. 1989. Is the All Politics Is Local Myth True? JSPES 14: 99-116.

155 Cohen, J. E.; Nice, D. C. 1982. Party Unity and Presidential Elections. PSQ 12: 317-329.

156 Conway, M. M. 1981. Political Participation in Midterm Congressional Elections. APQ 9: 221-244.

157 Cover, A. D. 1985. Surge and Decline in Congressional Elections. WPQ 38: 606-619.

158 -. 1986. Presidential Evaluations and Voting for Congress. AJPS 30: 786-801.

159 Cuzan, A. G. 1985. Expenditures and Votes: Downward Sloping Curves in US and Great Britain. PC 45: 19-34.

160 Davis, O. A.; Hinich, M. J.; Ordeshook, P. C. 1970. Mathematical Model of the Electoral Process. APSR 64: 426-448.

161 Enelow, J. M.; Munger, M. C. 1993. Elements of Candidate Reputation: Record and Credibility on Optimal Spatial Location. PC 77: 757-772.

162 Erikson, R. S. 1971. Electoral Impact of Congressional Roll Call Voting. APSR 65: 1018-1032.

163 -. 1988. The Puzzle of Midterm Loss. JOP 50: 1011-1029.

164 Field, W. H. 1994. Electoral Volatility and the Structure of Competition. WEP 17: 149-165.

165 Finkel, S. E. 1993. Reexamining the Minimal Effects Model in Recent Presidential Campaigns. JOP 55: 1-21.

166 Forsythe, R.; et al. 1993. Coordination in Multi-Candidate Elections. SCAW 10: 223-247.

167 Franklin, C. H. 1991. Eschewing Obfuscation? Campaigns and the Perception of Senate Incumbents. APSR 85: 1193-1214.

168 Fronbeck, B. E. 1984. Functional and Dramaturgical Themes of Presidential Campaigning. PSQ 14: 468-499.

169 Gant, M. M.; Davis, D. F. 1984. Negative Voter Support in Presidential Elections. WPQ 37: 272-290.

170 Garand, J. C.; Parent, T. W. 1991. Representation, Swing and Bias in Presidential Elections. AJPS 35: 1011-1031.

171 Goldenberg, E. N.; Traugott, M. W. 1980. Congressional Campaign Effects on Candidate Recognition and Evaluation. PB 2: 61-90.

172 -. 1981. Normal Vote Analysis of US Congressional Elections. LSQ 6: 247-258.

173 Gopoian, J. D. 1993. Compassion and Voting Behavior in Presidential Elections. Polity 24: 583-596.

174 -. 1993. Images and Issues in the 1988 Presidential Election. JOP 55: 151-166.

175 Granberg, D.; Brent, E. 1983. Preference Expectations Link in US Presidential Elections. JPSP 45: 477-491.

176 Gross, D. A.; Breaux, D. 1991. Historical Trends in US Senate Elections. APQ 19: 284-309.

177 Herrnson, P. S. 1986. Do Parties Make a Difference? Congressional Elections. JOP 48: 589-615.

178 -. 1989. National Party Decision Making, Strategies and Resource Distribution in Congressional Elections. WPQ 42: 301-324.

179 Hibbing, J.R.; Brandes, S.L. 1983. State Population and Success of Senators. AJPS 27: 808-819.

180 Hinckley, B. 1967. Interpreting House Midterm Elections: Toward a Measurement of the In-Party's Expected Loss of Seats. APSR 61: 694-700.

181 -. 1976. Issues, Information Costs and Congressional Elections. APQ 4: 131-152.

182 Holbrook, T. M. 1991. Presidential Elections in Time and Space. AJPS 35: 91-109.

183 Jacobson, G. C. 1989. Strategic Politicians and Dynamics of House Elections. APSR 83: 773-794.

184 Jacobson, G. C.; Kernell, S. 1990. National Forces in 1986 House Elections. LSQ 15: 65-88.

185 Journal of Law and Politics. 1992. Papers on Presidential Campaigns. JOLAP 8 (2).

186 Kenney, P. J.; Rice, T. W. 1986. Effect of Contextual Forces on Turnout in Congressional Elections. SSQ 67: 329-336.

187 Kenski, H. C.; Sigelman, L. 1993. Group Components of the 1988 Senate Vote. LSQ 18: 367-390.

188 Kernell, S. 1977. Presidential Popularity and Negative Voting: Alternative Explanation for the Midterm Congressional Decline. APSR 71: 44-66.

189 Krasno, J. S.; Green, D. P. 1988. Preempting Qualty Challengers in House Elections. JOP 50: 920-936.

190 Kritzer, H. M.; Eubank, R. B. 1979. Presidential Coattails Revisited. AJPS 23: 615-626.

191 Legislative Studies Quarterly. 1989. Papers on Senate Elections. LACP 14 (4).

192 Leithner, C. 1994. Stability and Change at Commonwealth Elections. AUSJPS 29: 460-483.

193 Levitin, T. E.; Miller, W. E. 1979. Ideological Interpretations of Presidential Elections. APSR 73: 751-771.

194 Levitt, S. D. 1994. Competing Explanations for the Midtern Gap in the US House. EAP 6: 25-37.

195 Lewis-Beck, M. S.; Rice, T. W. 1985. Are Senate Outcomes Predictable? PS 18: 745-753.

196 Lockerbie, B. 1992. Prospective Voting in Presidential Elections. APQ 20: 308-325.

197 Mann, T. E.; Wolfinger, R. E. 1980. Candidates and Parties in Congressional Elections. APSR 74: 617-632.

198 Marra, R. F.; Ostrom, C. W. 1989. Explaining Seat Change in the US House. AJPS 33: 541-569.

199 Martinez, M. D.; Delegal, T. 1990. Irrelevance of Negative Campaigns to Political Trust. POLCOM 7: 25-40.

200 Mattei, F.; Weisberg, H. F. 1994. Presidential Succession Effects in Voting. BJPS 24: 495-516.

201 Miller, A. H. 1990. Public Judgements of Senate and House Candidates. LSQ 15: 525-542.

202 Moore, D. W. 1987. Political Campaigns and the Knowledge Gap Hypothesis. POQ 51: 186-200.

203 Mughan, A. 1988. Comparing Mid-Term Popularity Functions. POLST 36: 704-710.

204 Nardulli, P. F. 1994. A Normal Vote Approach to Electoral Change. PB 16: 467-504.

205 Oppenheimer, B. I. 1989. Split Party Control of Congress. AJPS 33: 653-669.

206 Oppenheimer, B. I.; Stimson, J. A.; Waterman, R. W. 1986. Interpreting US Elections: The Exposure Thesis. LSQ 11: 227-247.

207 Packet, A.; Radcliff, B. 1995. Competitive Elections in Developing World. AJPS 39: 745-759.

208 Parker, G.R. 1981. Interpreting Candidate Awareness in Congressional Elections. LSQ 6: 219-233.

209 -. 1989. Role of Constituent Trust in Congressional Elections. POQ 53: 175-196.

210 Piereson, J. E. 1977. Sources of Success in Gubernatorial Elections. JOP 39: 939-958.

211 Political Communication. 1994. Papers on Strategic Communication Problems in Presidential Campaigns. POLCOM 11 (2).

212 Powell, L. W. 1989. Analyzing Misinformation: Perceptions of Congressional Candidates' Ideologies. AJPS 33: 272-293.

213 PS. 1989. Papers on Consultants. Vol 22 (1).

214 Rabinowitz, G.; Macdonald, S. E. 1986. The Power of the States in Presidential Elections. APSR 80: 65-87.

215 Ragsdale, L. 1994. Legislative Election Research. LSQ 19: 537-582.

216 Ragsdale, L.; Rusk, J. G. 1995. Candidates, Issues and Participation in Senate Elections. LSQ 20: 305-328.

217 Samuelson, L. 1987. Revealed Preference Phenomenon in Congressional Elections. PC 54: 141-170.

218 Scandinavian Political Studies. 1991. Papers on Election Campaigns. SPS 14 (3).

219 Serra, G.; Moon, D. 1994. Casework, Issue Positions and Voting in Congressional Elections. JOP 56: 200-213.

220 Shaffer, S.D.; Chressanthis, G.A. 1991. Accountability and Senate Elections. WPQ 44: 625-639.

221 Shamir, B. 1994. Ideological Position, Leaders' Charisma and Voting Preferences: Personal vs. Partisan Elections. PB 16: 265-287.

222 Sharp, S. A. 1994. A Statistical Study of Selective Candidate Withdrawal in a British General Election. ES 13: 122-131.

223 Shepsle, K. A. 1972. Strategy of Ambiguity: Uncertainty and Electoral Competition. APSR 66: 555-568.

224 Simon, D. M.; Ostrom, C. W.; Marra, R. F. 1991. The President, Referendum Voting and Subnational Elections in the US. APSR 85: 1177-1192.

225 Skaperdas, S.; Grofman, B. 1995. Modeling Negative Campaigning. APSR 89: 49-61.

226 Smyth, D. J.; Taylor, S. W. 1992. Why Do the Republicans Win the White House More Often than the Democrats? PSQ 22: 481-492.

227 Squire, P. 1992. Challenger Quality and Voting Behavior in Senate Elections. LSQ 17: 247-264.

228 -. 1995. Assessing the State of Congressional Elections Research. PRQ 48: 891-917.

229 -. 1995. Partisan Consequences of Congressional Redistricting. APQ 23: 229-240.

230 Squire, P.; Fastnow, C. 1994. Comparing Gubernatorial and Senatorial Elections. PRQ 47: 705-720

231 Stamm, K. R. 1987. Cognitive Strategies and Communication during a Presidential Campaign. COMR 14: 35-57.

232 Tufte, E. R. 1975. Determinants of the Outcome of Midterm Congressional Elections. APSR 69: 812-826.
233 Uslaner, E. M.; Conway, M. M. 1985. The Responsive Congressional Electorate: Watergate, Economy and Vote Choice in 1974. APSR 79: 788-803.
234 Wittman, D. 1983. Candidate Motivation: Alternate Theories. APSR 77: 142-147.
235 Wright, G. C.; Berkman, M. B. 1986. Candidates and Policy in Senate Elections. APSR 71: 497-508

Identification

236 Abramowitz, A. I.; McGlennon, J.; Rapoport, R. 1983. Party Activists in the US. IPSR 4: 13-20.
237 Abramson, P. R. 1976. Generational Change and the Decline of Party Identification in America. APSR 70: 469-478.
238 -. 1979. Party Identification: Life Cycle, Generational and Period Effects. AJPS 23: 78-96.
239 -. 1992. Of Time and Partisan Stability in Britain. BJPS 22: 381-395.
240 Abramson, P. R.; Ostrom, C. W. 1991. Macropartisanship. APSR 85: 181-192.
241 Allsop, D.; Weisberg, H.F. 1988 Measuring Change in Party Identification. AJPS 32: 996-1017.
242 Archer, K.; Ellis, F. 1994. The Opinion Structure of Activists: Reform Party of Canada. CJPS 27: 277-308.
243 Boree, O.; Katz, D. 1973. Party Identification and Its Motivational Base. SPS 8: 69-111.
244 Boynton, G. R.; Loewenberg, G. 1974. The Decay of Support for Monarchy and Hitler Regime in the Federal Republic of Germany. BJPS 4: 453-488.
245 Brown, C. 1982. The Nazi Vote. APSR 76: 285-302.
246 Browne, T. A. 1981. On Contextual Change and Partisan Attitudes. BJPS 11: 427-488.
247 Brustein, W.; Markovsky, B. 1989. The Rational Fascist: Party Membership. JPMS 17: 177-202.
248 Carmines, E. G.; Berkman, M. B. 1994. Paradox of Conservative Democrats. PB 16: 203-218.
249 Cassel, C. A. 1993. Converse's Theory of Party Support. JOP 55: 664-681.
250 Claggett, W. 1981. Partisan Acquisition vs. Partisan Intensity: Life Cycle, Generation and Period Effects. AJPS 25: 193-214.
251 Clarke, H. D., et al. 1985. Issue Volatility and Partisan Linkages. EJPR 13: 237-264.
252 Clarke, H. D.; Geigert, F. B.; Stewart, M. C. 1995. Domestic Political Beliefs of Southern Local Party Activists. PRQ 48: 151-168.
253 Clarke, H. D.; Kornberg, A. 1993. Public Attitudes toward Canada's Federal Political Parties. CJPS 26: 287-312.
254 Cotter, P. R. 1985. The Decline of Partisanship. APQ 13: 51-78.
255 Cox, G. W. 1986. Development of a Party Oriented Electorate in England. BJPS 16: 187-216.
256 Craig, S. C. 1988. The Decay of Mass Partisanship. Polity 20: 705-713.
257 Crewe, I.; Sarlvik, B.; Alt, J. E. 1977. Partisan Dealignment in Britain. BJPS 7: 129-190.
258 Dalton, R. J. 1984. Cognitive Mobilization and Partisan Dealignment. JOP 46: 264-284.
259 -. 1985. Political Parties and Representation: Supporters and Party Elites. CPS 18: 267-299.
260 Dobson, D.; Meeter, D. A. 1974. Alternative Markov Models for Describing Change in Party Identification. AJPS 18: 487-500.
261 Dreyer, E. C. 1973. Change in Stability and Party Identification. JOP 35: 712-722.
262 Eitzen, D. S.; Maranell, G. M. 1968. Political Party Affiliations of Professors. SF 47: 145-153
263 Evans, G. 1993. Class, Prospects and Life-Cycle: Explaining Association between Class Position and Political Preferences. AS 36: 263-276.
264 Feldman, S.; Zuckerman, A. S. 1982. Moving beyond Party Identification. CPS 15: 197-222.
265 Finifter, A. W.; Finifter, B. M. 1989. Party Identification and Political Adaption of American Migrants in Australia. JOP 51: 599-630.
266 Fiorina, M. P. 1976. Partisan Loyalty and the Six Component Model. PM 3: 7-18.
267 Franklin, C. H. 1984. Issue Preferences, Socialization and Evolution of Party Identification. AJPS 28: 459-478.
268 -. 1992. Measurement and Dynamics of Party Identification. PB 14: 297-310.
269 Franklin, C. H.; Jackson, J. E. 1983. Dynamics of Party Identification. APSR 77: 957-973.
270 Green, D. P.; Palmquist, B. 1994. How Stable is Party Identification? PB 16: 437-466.
271 Hadley, C. D. 1978. Teaching Political Scientists: Background and Politics. JPS 6: 51-66.
272 Hamilton, R. F.; Hargens, L. L. 1993. Politics of the Professors. SF 71: 603-628.
273 Harmel, R.; Gibson, R. K. 1995. Right-Libertarian Parties and the New Values. SPS 18: 97-118.
274 Haynes, S. E.; Jacobs, D. 1994. Macroeconomics, Economic Stratification and Partisanship: Shifts in Political Identification. AJS 100: 70-103.
275 Howell, S. E. 1980. The Behavioral Component of Changing Partisanship. APQ 8: 279-302.
276 -. 1981. Short Term Forces and Changing Partisanship. PB 3: 163-180.
277 Inglehart, R.; Hockstein, A. 1972. Alignment and Dealignment in France and US. CPS 5: 343-372.
278 International Political Science Review. 1983. Papers on Party Activists. IPSR 4 (1).
279 Johnston, R. 1992. Party Identification Measures in Anglo-American Democracies. AJPS 36: 542-559.
280 Katz, R. S. 1979. Dimensionality of Party Identification. CP 11: 147-164.
281 Katz, R. S.; Mair, P. 1992. Membership of Political Parties in Europe. EJPR 22: 329-345.
282 Krosnick, J. A. 1991. Stability of Party Preferences. AJPS 35: 547-576.
283 Lipset, S. M. 1982. Academic Mind at the Top: Political Behavior and Values of Faculty Elites. POQ 46: 143-168.
284 Lybeck, J. A. 1985. Is the Lipset-Rokkan Hypothesis Testable? SPS 8: 105-113.
285 Madden, P. 1987. Social Class Origins of Nazi Party Members. SSQ 68: 263-280.
286 Maggiotto, M. A.; Piereson, J. E. 1977. Partisan Identification and Electoral Choice: The Hostility Hypothesis. AJPS 21: 745-767.
287 Mair, P. 1989. Continuity, Change and the Vulnerability of Party. WEP 12: 169-187.
288 Markus, G. B. 1983. Dynamic Modeling of Cohort Change: Partisanship. AJPS 27: 717-739.
289 Meier, K. J. 1975. Party Identification and Vote Choice. WPQ 28: 496-505.
290 Miller, A. H.; Robbins, J. S. 1989. Who Did Vote for Hitler? Polity 21: 655-678.
291 Nadeau, R.; Stanley, H. W. 1993. Class Polarization and Partisanship among Southern Whites. AJPS 37: 900-919.
292 Niedermayer, O. 1986. Problems of Comparative Party Elites Research. EJPR 14: 253-259.
293 Norris, P.; Lovenduski, J. 1993. Supply-Side Explanations of Candidate Selection in Britain. BJPS 23: 373-408.
294 Palmer, H. D. 1995. Effects of Authoritarian and Libertarian Values on Conservative and Labour Party Support. EJPR 27: 273-292.
295 Parker, G. R. 1979. Trends in Party Preferences. APQ 7: 132-146.
296 Pierce, J. C. 1970. Party Identification and the Changing Role of Ideology. MJPS 14: 25-42.
297 Pierce, J.C.; Hagner, P. R. 1982. Conceptualization and Party Identification. AJPS 26: 377-387.
298 Pierre, J. 1986. Attitudes and Behaviour of Party Activists. EJPR 14: 465-479.

299 Political Behavior. 1992. Papers on Party Identification. PB 14 (3).

300 Pomper, G. M. 1977. Decline of Party in American Elections. PSQ 92: 21-42.

301 Reiter, H. L. 1989. Party Decline in the West. JTP 1: 325-348.

302 Rice, T. W. 1994. Partisan Change among Native White Southerners. APQ 22: 244-251.

303 Roettger, W. B.; Winebrenner, H. 1983. Voting Behavior of American Political Scientists. WPQ 36: 134-148.

304 Schmitt, H. 1989. On Party Attachment in Western Europe and the Utility of Eurobarometer Data. WEP 12: 122-139.

305 Selikar, O. 1980. Acquiring Partisan Preference in a Plural Society: Israel. PLS 11: 3-20.

306 Selle, P.; Svasand, L. 1991. Membership in Party Organizations and the Problem of the Decline of Parties. CPS 23: 459-477.

307 Shaffer, W. R. 1972. Partisan Loyalty and the Perceptions of Party, Candidates and Issues. WPQ 25: 424-433.

308 Shively, W. P. 1979. Development of Party Identification among Adults. APSR 73: 1039-1054.

309 St. Angelo, D.; Dobson, D. 1975. Party Identification and the Floating Vote. APSR 69: 481-490.

310 Turner, H. A.; Hetrick, C. C. 1972. Political Activities and Party Affiliations of American Political Scientists. WPQ 25: 361-374.

311 Wanat, J.; Burke, K. 1982. Estimating the Degree of Mobilization and Conversion in the 1890s: Nature of Electoral Change. APSR 76: 360-370.

312 Warneryd, K. 1994. Partisanship as Information. PC 80: 371-380.

313 Weisberg, H. F. 1980. Multidimensional Conceptualization of Party Identification. PB 2: 33-60.

314 Wellhofer, E. S. 1981. Political Incorporation of the Newly Enfranchised Voter: Organizational Encapsulation and Socialist Labor Party Development. WPQ 34: 399-414.

315 Whiteley, P. F., et al. 1994. Explaining Party Activism: Conservative Party. BJPS 24: 79-94.

316 Wittman, D. 1983. Candidate Motivation. APSR 77: 142-157.

317 Zipp, J. F. 1978. Left-Right Dimensions of Canadian Federal Party Identification. CJPS 11: 251-278.

Interparty Competition

318 Aistrup, J. A. 1993. State Legislative Party Competition: County Measure. PRQ 46: 433-446.

319 Austen-Smith, D. 1984. Two-Party Competition with Many Constituencies. MSS 7: 177-198.

320 Bonjean, C. M.; Lineberry, R. L. 1970. Urbanization-Party Competition. JOP 32: 305-321.

321 Brown, C. 1987. Voter Mobilization and Party Competition. ASR 52: 59-72.

322 Brown, R. D.; Wright, G. C. 1992. Elections and State Party Polarization. APQ 20: 411-426.

323 Budge, I. 1994. A New Spatial Theory of Party Competition. BJPS 24: 443-468.

324 Chappell, H. W. 1986. Policy Motivation and Party Differences in a Dynamic Spatial Model of Party Competition. APSR 80: 881-899.

325 Clarke, H. D.; Elliott, E.; Seldon, B. 1994. A Utility Function Analysis of Competing Models of Party Support. JTP 6: 289-306.

326 Darcy, R.; Choike, J. R. 1991. Party Competition in One Party Dominant System. JTP 3: 213-230.

327 Dunleavy, P.; Ward, H. 1981. Exogenous Voter Preferences and Parties with State Power: Economic Theories of Competition. BJPS 11: 351-380.

328 European Journal of Political Research 1990. Papers on Party Strategies and Party Voter Linkages. EJPR 18 (1).

329 Fiorina, M. P. 1977. An Outline for a Model of Party Choice. AJPS 21: 601-626.

330 Gibson, J. L., et al. 1983. Assessing Party Organizational Strength. AJPS 27: 193-222.

331 Gibson, J. L.; Frendreis, J. P.; Vertz, L. L. 1989. Changes in County Party Organizational Strength. AJPS 33: 67-90.

332 Green, D. P.; Palmquist, B. 1990. Of Artifacts and Partisan Instability. PM 9: 295-327.

333 Holbrook, T. M.; Van Dunk, E. 1993. Electoral Competition in the States. APSR 87: 955-962.

334 Huckfeldt, R. R.; Sprague, J. 1992. Political Parties and Mobilization. APSR 86: 70-86.

335 King, J. D. 1989. Interparty Competition in the American States. WPQ 42: 83-92.

336 Knutsen, O. 1988. The Impact of Structural and Ideological Party Cleavages in West European Democracies. BJPS 18: 323-352.

337 -. 1989. Cleavage Dimensions in Ten West European Countries. CPS 21: 495-533.

338 Kollman, K.; Miller, J. H.; Page, S. E. 1992. Adaptive Parties in Spatial Elections. APSR 86: 929-937.

339 Langton, K. P.; Rapoport, R. 1975. Social Structure, Social Context and Partisan Mobilization: Urban Workers in Chile. CPS 8: 318-344.

340 Macdonald, S. E.; Listhaug, O.; Rabinowitz, G. 1991. Issues and Party Support in Multiparty Systems. APSR 85: 1107-1131.

341 Mavrogordatos, G. T. 1987. Spatial Models of Party Competition. IPSR 8: 333-342.

342 Menahem, G. 1993. Social Cleavage, Political Division and Local Political Leadership Recruitment. JTP 5: 375-396.

343 Osborne, M. J. 1995. Spatial Models of Political Competition under Plurality Rule: Number of Candidates and the Positions. CANJE 28: 261-301.

344 Rabinowitz, G.; Macdonald, S. E.; Listhaug, O. 1991. Party Strategies in Multiparty Systems. CPS 24: 147-185.

345 Rae, D. W. 1995. Using District Magnitude to Regulate Party Competition. JEP 9: 65-75.

346 Ray, D.; Havick, J.J. 1981. Party Competition in State Legislative Elections. AJPS 25: 119-128.

347 Strom, K. 1990. Behavioral Theory of Competitive Political Parties. AJPS 34: 565-598.

348 Ware, A. 1989. Parties, Electoral Competition and Democracy. PARLA 42: 1-22.

349 Willeme, P.; De Pelsmacker, P. 1991. Determinants of Popularity of Parties in Flanders: A Market Share Approach. Cahiers Economiques de Bruxelles 131: 343-363.

Machines and Corruption

350 Alam, M. S. 1989. Corruption: The Political Economy of Underdevelopment. AJEAS 48: 441-456.

351 -. 1995. A Theory of Limits on Corruption. Kyklos 48: 419-435.

352 Alford, J. R., et al. 1994. The Political Cost of Congressional Malfeasance. JOP 56: 788-801.

353 Andvig, J. C. 1991. Economics of Corruption. Studi Economici 46: 57-94.

354 Antoci, A.; Sacco, P. L. 1995. Public Contracting Evolutionary Game with Corruption. ZN 61: 89-122.

355 Atkinson, M. M.; Mancuso, M. 1985. A Code of Conduct for Politicians? Elite Political Culture of Corruption in Canada. CJPS 18: 459-480.

356 Banducci, S. A.; Karp, J. A. 1994. Electoral Consequences of Scandal and Reapportionment in the 1992 House Elections. APQ 22: 3-26.

357 Banfield, E. C. 1975. Corruption as a Feature of Governmental Organization. JOLE 18: 587-616.

358 Barker, A. 1994. Political Scandals and Their Investigation Processes. CLASC 21: 337-374.

359 Basu, K.; Bhattacharya, S.; Mishra, A. 1992. Bribery and the Control of Corruption. JPUBE 48: 349-359.

360 Baum, D. 1991. Apparent Fraud in the 1861 Texas Secession Referendum. JIDH 22: 201-222.

361 Baum, D.; Miller, W. R. 1993. Ethnic Conflict and Machine Politics in San Antonio, 1892-1899. JUH 19: 63-84.

362 Benson, B. L. 1988. Corruption in Law Enforcement: Tragedy of the Commons Arising with Public Allocation Processes. IRLE 8: 73-84.

363 Boulay, H.; DiGaetano, A. 1985. Why Did Political Machines Disappear? JUH 12: 25-50.

364 Brown, M. C.; Halaby, C. N. 1987. Machine Politics in America, 1870-1945. JIDH 17: 587-612.

365 Clark, J. M. 1979. Moral Prerequisites of Political Support: Business Reactions to the Watergate Scandal. JPS 7: 40-64.

366 Clark, W. A. 1993. Crime and Punishment in Soviet Officialdom. EAS 45: 259-280.

367 Correa, H. 1985. Bureaucratic Corruption in Latin America and the US. SEPS 18: 63-79.

368 Cosson, J. 1988. Embezzlement of Business Funds by Simulated Swindles in Order to Create Clandestine Resources. CAR 3: 97-110.

369 Crime, Law and Social Change. 1993. Papers on Corruption and Reform. CLASC 19 (4) and 20 (4).

370 -. 1994. Papers on European Political Corruption. CLASC 22 (4).

371 -. 1995. Papers on Corruption. CLASC 23 (4).

372 DeLeon, P. 1989. Public Policy Implications of Systematic Political Corruption. CAR 4: 193-216.

373 Dey, H. K. 1989. Genesis and Spread of Economic Corruption. WD 17: 503-512.

374 Deysine, A. 1980. Political Corruption. EJPR 8: 447-462.

375 DiGaetano, A. 1988. Rise and Development of Urban Political Machines. UAQ 24: 242-267.

376 -. 1991. Origins of Urban Political Machines in the US. UAQ 26: 324-353.

377 -. 1991. Urban Political Reform: Did It Kill the Machine? JUH 18: 37-67.

378 Dimock, M. A.; Jacobson, G. C. 1995. House Bank Scandal's Impact on Voters. JOP 57: 1143-1159.

379 Dolan, K.; McKeown, B.; Carlson, J. M. 1988. Popular Conceptions of Corruption. CAR 3: 3-24.

380 Dudley, L.; Montmarquette, C. 1987. Bureaucratic Corruption as a Constraint on Voting Behavior. PC 55: 127-162.

381 Fackler, T.; Lin, T. 1995. Political Corruption and Presidential Elections. JOP 57: 971-993.

382 Feichtinger, G.; Wirl, F. 1994. Stability and Cyclicity of Corruption in Governments Subject to Popularity Constraints. MSS 28: 113-131.

383 Gardiner, J. A. 1986. Controlling Official Corruption and Fraud. CAR 1: 33-50.

384 Gardner, R. 1987. A Theory of the Spoils System. PC 54: 171-186.

385 Gillespie, K.; Okruhik, G. 1991. The Political Dimensions of Corruption Cleanups. CP 24: 77-96.

386 Goel, M. K.; Rich, D. P. 1989. On the Economic Incentive for Taking Bribes. PC 61: 269-276.

387 Goodman, M. 1975. Does Political Corruption Really Help Economic Development? Yucatan, Mexico. Polity 7: 143-162.

388 Gorta, A.; Forell, S. 1995. Linking Social Definitions of Corruption and Willingness to Take Action. CLASC 23: 315-344.

389 Grabosky, P. N. 1990. Citizen Co-Production and Corruption Control. CAR 5: 125-152.

390 Grimshaw, W. J. 1989. The Political Economy of Machine Politics. CAR 4: 15-38.

391 Gronbeck, B. E. 1978. The Theory of Political Corruption. QJS 70: 155-172.

392 Guterbock, T. M. 1979. Community Attachment and Machine Politics: Chicago. SSQ 60: 185-202.

393 Hope, K. R. 1987. Administrative Corruption and Administrative Reform. CAR 2: 127-148.

394 Huberts, L. W. J. C. 1994. Public Corruption and Fraud in the Netherlands. CLASC 22: 307-322.

395 Ichniowski, C.; Preston, A. 1989. Persistence of Organized Crime in New York City Construction. ILRR 42: 549-565.

396 Industrial and Labor Relations Review. 1989. Papers on Corruption in Union Management Relations. ILRR 42 (4).

397 Jacobson, G. C.; Dimock, M. A. 1994. Effects of Bank Overdrafts on the 1992 House Elections. AJPS 38: 601-624.

398 Johnston, M. 1983. Corruption and Political Culture in America. Publius 13: 19-39.

399 -. 1986. Political Consequences of Corruption. CP 18: 459-478.

400 -. 1986. Right and Wrong in American Politics: Conceptions of Corruption. Polity 18: 367-391.

401 Journal of Law and Politics. 1995. Papers on the Partisan Influences on Ethics Investigations. JOLAP 11 (3).

402 Kebschull, H. G. 1992. Political Corruption. PS 25: 705-708.

403 Kiser, E.; Tong, X. 1992. Determinants of Amount and Type of Corruption in State Fiscal Bureaucracies: Late Imperial China. CPS 25: 300-331.

404 Law and Contemporary Problems. 1978. Papers on the Criminal Liability of Government Officials. LACP 42 (1).

405 Maass, E. A. 1987. US Prosecution of State and Local Officials for Political Corruption. Publius 17: 179-184.

406 Malec, K. L.; Gardiner, J. A. 1987. Measurement Issues in Study of Official Corruption: Chicago. CAR 2: 267-278.

407 Marengo, F. D. 1988. Linkage between Corruption and Political Scandal. CAR 3: 65-80.

408 Mauro, P. 1995. Corruption and Growth. QJE 110: 681-712.

409 Maysfield, L. 1993. Voting Fraud in Early Twentieth-Century Pittsburgh. JIDH 24: 59-84.

410 Mbaku, J. M. 1992. Bureaucratic Corruption as Rent Seeking Behavior. KON 38: 247-265.

411 McCafferty, P. 1992. Style, Structure and Institutionalization of Machine Politics: Philadelphia. JIDH 22: 435-452.

412 Meier, K. J.; Holbrook, T. M. 1992. Political Corruption in the States. JOP 54: 135-155.

413 Michaels, J. W.; Miethe, T. D. 1989. Applying Theories of Deviance to Academic Cheating. SSQ 70: 870-885.

414 Miethe, T. D.; Rothschild, J. 1994. Whistleblowing and Control of Misconduct. SI 64: 322-347.

415 Mladenka, K. R. 1980. The Urban Bureaucracy and the Chicago Political Machine. APSR 74: 991-998.

416 Moodie, G. C. 1980. On Political Scandals and Corruption. GAO 15: 208-222.

417 Mookherjee, D.; Png, I. P. L. 1995. Corruptible Law Enforcers. EJ 105: 145-159.

418 Morgan, D. F. 1987. Varieties of Administrative Abuse: Ethics and Discretion. AAS 19: 267-284.

419 Mucciaroni, G. 1991. Defeat of Client Politics and Logic of Collective Action. PSJ 19: 474-494.

420 Myerson, R. B. 1993. Effectiveness of Electoral Systems for Reducing Government Corruption. GAEB 5: 118-132.

421 Nas, T. F.; Price, A. C.; Weber, C. T. 1986. A Policy Theory of Corruption. APSR 80: 107-120.

422 Nice, D. C. 1983. Political Corruption in the American States. APQ 11: 507-517.

423 Oberst, R. C.; Weilage, A. 1990. Quantitative Tests of Electoral Fraud: 1982 Sri Lankan Referendum. CAR 5: 49-62.

424 Parliamentary Affairs. 1995. Papers on the Politics of Sleaze. PARLA 48 (4).

425 Peters, J. G.; Welch, S. 1978. Political Corruption in America. APSR 72: 974-984.

426 -. 1978. Politics, Corruption and Political Culture: The State Legislature. APQ 6: 345-356.

427 -. 1980. Effects of Charges of Corruption on Voting Behavior in Congressional Elections. APSR 74: 697-708.

428 Radner, R. 1980. Collusive Behavior in Oligopolies with Long but Finite Lives. JET 22: 136-156.

429 Rasmusen, E.; Ramseyer, J. M. 1994. Cheap Bribes and the Corruption Ban: Coordination Game among Rational Legislators. PC 78: 305-327.

430 Rock, D. 1972. Machine Politics in Buenos Aires and the Argentine Radical Party. JOLAS 4: 233-256.

431 Rundquist, B. S.; Strom, G. S.; Petersen, J. G. 1977. Corrupt Politicians and Their Electoral Support. APSR 71: 954-963.

432 Schaffer, B. 1986. Access: A Theory of Corruption and Bureaucracy. PAAD 6: 357-376.

433 Scott, J. C. 1969. Corruption, Machine Politics and Political Change. APSR 63: 1142-1158.

434 Shogren, J. F. 1990. Optimal Subsidization of Baptists by Bootleggers. PC 67: 181-189.

435 Stewart, C. 1994. Correlates of Involvement in the House Bank Scandal. LSQ 19: 521-536.

436 Tager, M. 1988. Corruption and Party Machines in New York City. CAR 3: 25-40.

437 Thompson, V. M.; Thompson, E. A. 1993. Achieving Optimal Fines for Political Bribery. PC 77: 773-792.

438 Truelson, J. A. 1987. Blowing the Whistle on Systematic Corruption. CAR 2: 55-76.

Party Systems

439 Anderson, C. J. 1995. Party Systems and Dynamics of Government Support. EJPR 27: 93-118.

440 Annuaire Suisse de Science Politique. 1986. Papers on Swiss Parties and Movements. Vol 26.

441 Archer, K. 1989. Political Parties in Canada. CJPS 22: 389-400.

442 Betz, H. G. 1993. New Politics of Resentment: Radical Right-Wing Populist Parties in Western Europe. CP 25: 413-428.

443 Blondel, J. 1995. Systematic Analysis of Government-Party Relationships. IPSR 16: 145-168.

444 Carmines, E. G. 1991. Logic of Party Alignments. JTP 3: 65-85.

445 Chressanthis, G. A. 1990. Third Party Voting and the Rational Voter Model. PC 65: 189-193.

446 Chressanthis, G. A.; Stephen, D. S. 1993. Major-Party Failure and Third-Party Voting in Presidential Elections. SSQ 74: 264-273.

447 Clarke, H. D.; Suzuki, M. 1994. Partisan Dealignment and the Dynamics of Independence. BJPS 24: 57-78.

448 Collins, W.; Kleiner, A. F. 1985. Dynamics of Electoral Change in Two Party Systems. JMS 11: 77-94.

449 Communist and Post-Communist Studies. 1993. Papers on the Emergency of Pluralism in Eastern Europe. CAPCS 26 (4).

450 Comparative Political Studies. 1980. Papers on Measuring Party System Change. CPS 12 (4).

451 Cook, P. J. 1971. Robert Michels's Political Parties in Perspective. JOP 33: 773-796.

452 David, P. T. 1992. APSA Committee on Political Parties: Its Significance. POPS 21: 70-79.

453 Dennis, J. 1975. Trends in Public Support for the American Party System. BJPS 5: 187-230.

454 DeSart, J. A. 1995. Information Processing and Partisan Neutrality: The Party Decline Thesis. JOP 57: 776-795.

455 Dix, R. H. 1989. Cleavage Structures and Party Systems in Latin America. CP 22: 23-38.

456 -. 1992. Democratization and Institutionalization of Latin American Political Parties. CPS 24: 488-511.

457 Dwyre, D.; Stonecash, J. M. 1992. Changing State Party Organizations. APQ 20: 326-344.

458 Eliassen, K. A.; Svasand, L. 1975. Formation of Mass Political Organizations. SPS 10: 95-121.

459 Fukuda, S. I. 1992. Why Does a Two-Party System Exist? New Economic Explanation. EAP 4: 277-287.

460 Gold, H. J. 1995. Third Party Voting in Presidential Elections. PRQ 48: 751-774.

461 Harmel, R.; Janda, K. 1994. Integrated Theory of Party Goals and Party Change. JTP 6: 259-288.

462 Harmel, R.; Robertson, J. D. 1985. On the Study of New Parties. IPSR 4: 403-418.

463 Hazen, R. Y. 1995. Center Parties and Systemic Polarization. JTP 7: 421-446.

464 Herrnson, P. S. 1992. Why the US Does Not Have Responsible Parties. POPS 21: 91-99.

465 Herzog, H. 1987. Minor Parties. CP 19: 317-329.

466 Humes, B. D. 1990. Multi-Party Competition with Exit: Comment on Duverger's Law. PC 64: 229-238.

467 Inglehart, R.; Avram, H. 1972. Alignment and Dealignment of the Electorate in France and the US. CPS 5: 343-372.

468 International Political Science Review. 1985. Papers on New Political Parties. IPSR 6 (4).

469 Janda, K. 1983. Cross National Measures of Party Organizations and Organizational Theory. EJPR 11: 319-332.

470 Janda, K.; King, D. S. 1985. Formalizing and Testing Duverger's Theories of Political Parties. CPS 18: 139-169.

471 Jin, Y. 1995. Testing Political Party Institutionalization. JPMS 23: 43-64.

472 Journal of Theoretical Politics. 1989. Papers on Party Systems. JTP 1 (3).

473 Kames, D. H. 1989. Theory of American Political Party Development. JPMS 17: 263-290.

474 Kearny, E. N., Heineman, R. A. 1992. Scenario for a Centrist Revolt: Third Party Prospects. PSQ 22: 107-118.

475 Kim, J. O.; Ohn, M. G. 1992. Election Rules, Social Cleavage and Number of Political Parties: A Theory of Minor Party Persistence. SF 70: 575-600.

476 King, A. 1969. Political Parties in Western Democracies. Polity 2: 112-141.

477 Kirkpatrick, E. M. 1971. Toward a More Responsible Two Party System: Political Science, Policy Science, or Pseudo-Science? APSR 65: 965-990.

478 Klingemann, H. D.; Wattenberg, M. P. 1992. Decaying vs Developing Party Systems: Party Images in US and West Germany. BJPS 22: 131-150.

479 Koelble, T. A. 1989. Party Structures and Democracy: Michels, McKenzie and Duverger Revisited via Examples of German Green Party and British Social Democratic Party. CPS 22: 199-216.

480 Lagroye, J. 1989. Change and Permanence in Political Parties. POLST 37: 362-375.

481 Laver, M. 1989. Party Competition and Party System Change: Coalition Bargaining and Electoral Competition. JTP 1: 301-324.

482 LeDuc, L. 1985. Partisan Change and Development in Canada, Great Britain and US. CP 17: 379-398.

483 Lewis-Beck, M. S.; Squire, P. 1995. Presidential Ballot Access for Third Parties in the US. BJPS 25: 419-427.

484 Listhaug, O.; Macdonald, S. E.; Rabinowitz, G. 1990. Comparative Spatial Analysis of European Party Systems. SPS 13: 227-254.

485 Mair, P. 1989. Problem of Party System Change. JTP 1: 251-276.

486 May, J. D. 1973. Opinion Structure of Political Parties: Law of Curvilinear Disparity. POLST 21: 135-151.

487 McFaul, M. 1992. Russia's Emerging Political Parties. JOD 2: 25-40.

488 Mendilow, J. 1992. Public Party Funding and Party Transformation in Multiparty Systems. CPS 25: 90-117.

489 Meur, G.; Gassner, M.; Hubaut, X. 1985. A Mathematical Model for Political Bipolarization. EJPR 13: 409-420.

490 Miller, W. E. 1986. Party Identification and Political Belief Systems: Changes in Partisanship in the US. ES 5: 101-122.

491 Miller, W. L.; Mackie, M. 1973. The Electoral Cycle and the Asymmetry of Government and Opposition Popularity. POLST 21: 263-279.

492 Mishler, W.; Hoskin, M.; Fitzgerald, R. 1989. British Parties in the Balance: Long Term Trends in Labour and Conservative Support. BJPS 19: 211-236.

493 Mitchell, P. 1995. Party Competition in an Ethnic Dual Party System. EARS 18: 773-796.

494 Molinar, J. 1991. Counting the Number of Parties. APSR 85: 1383-1392.

495 Muller-Rommel, F. 1985. The Greens in Western Europe. IPSR 6: 483-499.

496 Nassmacher, K. H. 1989. Costs of Party Democracy in Canada. CAR 4: 217-244.

497 Nice, D. C. 1984. Polarization in the American Party System. PSQ 14: 109-116.

498 Ordeshook, P. C. 1970. Extensions to a Model of the Electoral Process and Implications for the Theory of Responsible Parties. MJPS 14: 43-70.

499 Ordeshook, P. C.; Shvetsova, O. V. 1994. Ethnic Heterogeneity, District Magnitude and the Number of Parties. AJPS 38: 100-123.

500 Owens, G. M. 1972. The Study of Political Parties in the Latin American Milieu. Journal of International and Comparative Studies 4: 78-109.

501 Peal, D. 1989. Politics of Populism: Germany and the American South in 1890s. CSSH 31: 340-362.

502 Pedersen, M. N. 1979. Dynamics of European Party Systems: Electoral Volatility. EJPR 7: 1-26.

503 Perspectives on Political Science. 1992. Papers on Responsible American Parties. POPS 21 (2).

504 Piereson, J. E. 1978. Issue Alignment and the American Party System. APQ 6: 275-308.

505 Poguntke, T. 1987. New Politics and Party Systems: A New Type of Party? WEP 10: 76-88.

506 Political Quarterly. 1987. Papers on Left of Center Realignment. PQ 58 (4).

507 Pomper, G. M. 1971. Toward a More Responsible Two Party System? What, Again? JOP 33: 916-940.

508 -. 1992. Concepts of Political Parties. JTP 4: 143-159.

509 Powell, G. B. 1981. Party Systems and Political System Performance: Participation, Stability and Violence. APSR 75: 861-879.

510 -. 1986. Extremist Parties and Political Turmoil. AJPS 30: 357-378.

511 Riker, W. H. 1976. Number of Political Parties: Duverger's Law. CP 9: 93-106.

512 -. 1982. Two-Party System and Duverger's Law: An Essay on the History of Political Science. APSR 76: 753-766.

513 Rohrschneider, R. 1994. How Iron Is the Iron Law of Oligarchy? Robert Michels and National Party Delegates in West European Democracies. EJPR 25: 207-238.

514 Rose, R. 1970. Persistence and Change in Western Party Systems. POLST 18: 287-319.

515 Salisbury, R. H.; MacKuen, M. B. 1981. On the Study of Party Realignment. JOP 43: 523-530.

516 Scarrow, H. A. 1986. Duverger's Law, Fusion and Decline of American Third Parties. WPQ 39: 634-647.

517 Shamir, M. 1984. Are Western Party Systems Frozen? CPS 17: 35-80.

518 Sigelman, L.; Yough, S. N. 1978. Left-Right Polarization in National Party Systems. CPS 11: 355-380.

519 Taagepera, R.; Grofman, B. 1985. Rethinking Duverger's Law: Predicting the Effective Number of Parties in Plurality and Proportional Representation Systems. EJPR 13: 341-352.

520 Taagepera, R.; Shugart, M. S. 1993. Predicting the Number of Parties: Duverger's Mechanical Effect. APSR 87: 455-464.

521 Taylor, M.; Valentine, H. 1971. Party Systems and Government Stability. APSR 65: 28-37.

522 Thomas, J. C. 1980. Policy Convergence among Political Parties and Societies in Developed Nations. WPQ 33: 233-246.

523 West European Politics. 1984. Papers on Party Politics in Western Europe. WEP 7 (4), and 1989 12 (4).

524 White, J. K. 1992. Responsible Party Government in America. POPS 21: 80-90.

525 Yearley, C. K. 1973. Provincial Party and Megalopolises: London, Paris and New York. CSSH 15: 51-88.

Realignments

526 Anderson, G. M.; Tollison, R. D. 1991. Congressional Influence and Patterns of New Deal Spending. JOLE 34: 161-175.

527 Brady, D. W. 1978. Critical Elections, Congressional Parties and Clusters of Policy Changes. BJPS 8: 79-100.

528 -. 1985. Reevaluation of Realignments in American Politics: The House. APSR 79: 28-49.

529 Brady, D. W.; Stewart, J. 1982. Congressional Party Realignment and Transformations of Public Policy. AJPS 26: 333-360.

530 Campbell, J. E. 1985. Sources of New Deal Realignment: Contributions of Conversion and Mobilization to Partisan Change. WPQ 38: 357-376.

531 Champagne, R. A. 1983. Conditions for Realignment in the US Senate. LSQ 8: 219-230.

532 Erickson, R. J.; Tedin, K. L. 1981. The 1928-1936 Partisan Realignments. APSR 75: 951-962.

533 Flanagan, S. C.; Dalton, R. J. 1984. Parties under Stress: Realignment and Dealignment in Advanced Industrial Societies. WEP 7: 7-23.

534 Geer, J. G. 1991. Critical Realignments and the Public Opinion Poll. JOP 53: 434-453.

535 Ginsberg, B. 1972. Critical Elections and the Substance of Party Conflict, 1844-1968. MJPS 16: 603-627.

536 Hagan, J. D. 1989. Domestic Political Regime Changes and Third World Voting Realignments in the United Nations. IO 43: 505-541.

537 Levine, M. V. 1976. Critical Realignment: Maryland. JOP 38: 292-325.

538 Macdonald, S. E.; Rabinowitz, G. 1987. Dynamics of Structural Realignment. APSR 81: 775-796.

539 Miller, W. L. 1971. Cross Voting and Dimensionality of Party Conflict in Britain during the Period of Realignment, 1918-1931. POLST 19: 456-461.

540 Nardulli, P. F. 1995. Critical Realignment, Electoral Behavior and Political Change. APSR 89: 10-22.

541 Rabinowitz, G.; Gurian, P. H.; Macdonald, S. E. 1984. Structure of Presidential Elections and the Process of Realignment. AJPS 28: 611-635.

542 Shortridge, R. M. 1976. Voter Realignment in the Midwest during the 1850s. APQ 4: 193-232.

543 Sinclair, B. D. 1977. Party Realignments and the Transformation of the Political Agenda: House. APSR 71: 940-953.

544 -. 1978. Policy Consequences of Party Realignment: Social Welfare Legislation in the House. AJPS 22: 56-82.

545 Tuchfarber, A. J., et al. 1995. Republican Tidal Wave of 1995: Hypotheses about Realignment, Restructuring and Rebellion. PS 28: 689-696.

546 Wanat, J.; Burke, K. 1982. Estimating the Degree of Mobilization and Conversion in the 1890s. APSR 76: 360-370.

POLITICAL SYSTEMS

1 Africa Today. 1995. Papers on the Politics of African Economic Integration. AT 42 (4).

2 Annals. 1978. Papers on the European Community. ANNALS 440.

3 Armour, L. 1992. Can Economic Systems Be Chosen? IJSE 19: 273-291.

4 Ayers, R. L. 1975. Political Regimes, Explanatory Variables and Public Policy in Latin America. JDA 10: 15-36.

5 Banks, A. S. 1972. Political Characteristics of Nation States. JOP 34: 246-257.

6 Bartlett, B. R. 1990. Capitalism in Africa. JDA 24: 327-349.

7 Berg-Schlosser, D. 1984. African Political Systems. CPS 17: 121-151.

8 Berg-Schlosser, D.; de Meur, G. 1995. Comparing Political Systems. EJPR 26: 193-219.

9 Brunk, G. G.; Caldeira, G. A.; Lewis-Beck, M. S. 1987. Capitalism, Socialism and Democracy. EJPR 15: 459-470.

10 Bueno de Mesquita, B.; Siverson, R. M.; Woller, G. 1992. War and the Fate of Regimes. APSR 86: 638-646.

11 Cahiers d'Etudes Africaines. 1982. Papers on African State Systems. CEA 22 (3/4).

12 Caporaso, J. A.; Pelowski, A. L. 1971. Economic and Political Integration in Europe. APSR 65: 418-433.

13 Civilizations. 1982. Papers on the Plural Societies of Black Africa. Vol 32/3 (2-1).

14 Coleman, K. M.; Davis, C. L. 1976. The Structural Context of Politics and Dimensions of Regime Performance: Political Efficacy. CPS 9: 189-206.

15 Collier, D. 1975. Timing of Economic Growth and Regime Characteristics in Latin America. CP 7: 331-360.

16 Cowhey, P. F.; Long, E. 1983. Theories of Regime Change: Hegemonic Decline or Surplus Capacity? IO 37: 157-188.

17 Cutch, R. M. 1993. Tolerating Economic Reform: Popular Support for Transition to a Free Market in the Former Soviet Union. APSR 87: 590-608.

18 Daedalus. 1993. Papers on Reconstructing Nations and States. Vol 122 (3).

19 -. 1995. Papers on the Future of the State. Vol 124 (2).

20 Dannehl, C. R.; Owens, J. R.; Gowth, A. J. 1994. Three-Variable Output Classification of Political Systems. Coexistence 31: 373 ff.

21 Dieli, R. F. 1977. Devaluation and Statism in Mexico. Interamerican Economic Affairs 30: 85-92.

22 Dix, R. H. 1982. The Breakdown of Authoritarian Regimes. WPQ 35: 554-573.

23 Easton, D. 1975. A Reassessment of the Concept of Political Support. BJPS 5: 435-457.

24 Eichenberg, R. C.; Dalton, R. J. 1993. Europeans and European Community: Public Support for European Integration. IO 47: 507-534.

25 European Journal of Political Research. 1993. Papers on Capitalism, Socialism and Democracy. EJPR 23 (2).

26 Gabel, M.; Palmer, H. D. 1995. Understanding Variation in Public Support for European Integration. EJPR 27: 3-20.

27 Gasiorowski, M. J. 1995. Economic Crisis and Political Regime Change. APSR 89: 882-897.

28 Government and Opposition. 1970. Papers on Anarchism. GAO 5 (4).

29 -. 1974. Papers on Sovereignty and Integration. GAO 9 (1).

30 Greif, A. 1994. Cultural Beliefs and the Organization of Society. JPE 102: 912-950.

31 Gurr, T. R. 1974. Persistence and Change in Political Systems 1800-1971. APSR 68: 1482-1504.

32 Haas, E. B. 1982. Words Can Hurt You or Who Said What to Whom about Regimes. IO 36: 207-244.

33 Hirschleifer, J. 1995. Anarchy and Its Breakdown. JPE 103: 26-52.

34 Hix, S. 1994. Approaches to the Study of the European Community. WEP 17: 1-30.

35 Hodgson, G. M. 1993. Theories of Economic Evolution: Taxonomy. MSESS 61: 125-143.

36 Huizenga, F. D. 1995. Regime Analysis. AAS 27: 361-378.

37 Journal of International Affairs. 1973. Papers on Multi-State Nations. JIA 27 (2).

38 -. 1981. Papers on Underground Economic Systems. JIA 35 (1).

39 Junne, G. 1992. Beyond Regime Theory. AP 27: 9-28.

40 King, D. Y. 1981. Regime Type and Performance: Authoritarian Rule, Semi-Capitalist Development and Rural Inequality in Asia. CPS 13: 477-504.

41 Krasner, S. D. 1982. Regimes and the Limits of Realism: Regimes as Autonomous Variables. IO 36: 497-510.

42 -. 1982. Structural Causes and Regime Consequences: Regimes as Intervening Variables. IO 36: 185-206.

43 -. 1984. Approaches to the State: Conceptions and Historical Dynamics. CP 16: 233-246.

44 Little, W. 1973. Electoral Aspects of Peronism, 1946-1954. JIAS 15: 267-284.

45 Nelson, R. R. 1995. Recent Evolutionary Theorizing about Economic Change. JEL 33: 48-90.

46 Nettl, J. P. 1968. The State as a Conceptual Variable. WP 20: 559-592.

47 Mitchell, R. B. 1994. Regime Design Matters: Oil Pollution and Treaty Compliance. IO 48: 425-458.

48 Mueller, E. N. 1970. Correlates and Consequences of Belief in Legitimacy of Regime Structures. MJPS 14: 392-412.

49 -. 1970. Representation of Citizens by Political Authorities: Consequences for Regime Support. APSR 64: 1149-1166.

50 Oneal, J. R. 1994. Affinity of Foreign Investors for Authoritarian Regimes. PRQ 47: 565-588.

51 Orbell, J. M.; Rutherford, B. M. 1973. Can Leviathan Make the Life of Man Less Solitary, Poor, Nasty, Brutish and Short? BJPS 3: 383-408. Comment BJPS 4: 245-249.

52 Paldam, M.; Skott, P. 1995. A Rational-Voter Explanation of Cost of Ruling. PC 83: 159-172.

53 Phillips, W. R.; Hall, D. R. 1970. Importance of Governmental Structure as a Taxonomic Scheme for Nations. CPS 3: 63-89.

54 Policy and Politics. 1990. Papers on European Central-Local Government Relations. PAP 18 (3).

55 Political Studies. 1995. Papers on Explaining State Structures. POLST 43 (1).

56 Res Publica. 1991. Papers on Constitutional Monarchy. RP 33 (1).

57 Rittberger, V.; Zurn, M. 1991. Regime Theory: Study of East-West Regimes. CAC 26: 165-184.

58 Rose, R.; Kavanagh, D. 1976. Monarchy in Contemporary Political Culture. CP 8: 548-576.

59 Schnytzer, A. 1994. An Economic Model of Regime Change: Freedom as Public Good. PC 79: 325-340.

60 Seligson, M. A.; Booth, J. A. 1993. Political Culture and Regime Type: Nicaragua and Costa Rica. JOP 55: 777-792.

61 Sloan, J. W.; Tedin, K. L. 1987. Consequences of Regime Type for Public Policy Outputs. CPS 20: 98-124.

62 Svalastoga, K. 1982. Integration, a Seven Nation Comparison. IJCS 23: 190-203.

63 Useem, B.; Useem, M. 1979. Government Legitimacy and Political Stability. SF 57: 840-852.

64 Vaubel, R. 1994. Political Economy of Centralization and European Community. PC 81: 151-190.

65 -. 1994. Public Choice Analysis of European Integration. EJPE 10: 227 ff.

66 Vayrynen, R. 1995. Bipolarity, Multipolarity and Domestic Political Systems. JPR 32: 361-371.

67 Weatherford, M. S. 1992. Measuring Political Legitimacy. APSR 86: 149-168.

68 Weil, F. D. 1989. Sources and Structure of Legitimation in Western Democracies. ASR 54: 682-706.

69 Weyland, K. 1995. Latin America's Four Political Models. JOD 6: 125-139.

70 White, J. W. 1981. Civil Attitudes, Political Participation and System Stability in Japan. CPS 14: 371-400.

71 Woldendorp, J. J. 1995. Neo-Corporatism as Strategy for Conflict Regulation. AP 30: 121-152.

Communism

72 Acta Oeconomica. 1992. Papers on Communist State Transitions to Market Economies. AO 44 (3/4).

73 Anderson, G. O.; Boettke, P. J. 1993. Perestroika and Public Choice: Economics of Autocratic Succession in Rent Seeking Society. PC 75: 101-118.

74 Bahry, D. 1980. Measuring Communist Priorities: Budgets, Investments and Problems of Equivalence. CPS 13: 267-292.

75 Bergesen, A. J. 1992. Communism's Collapse: A World System Explanation. JPMS 20: 133-152.

76 Daedalus. 1992. Papers on the End of Communism. Vol 121 (3).

77 Domanski, S.R. 1994. Why It Was So Easy to Break Communism and Why It Is So Difficult to Find Consensus. Eastern European Economics 32: 71-94.

78 Greene, T. H. 1971. Electorates of Nonruling Communist Parties. SCC 4: 68-103.

79 Journal of Communist Studies. 1990. Papers on Communism and Trade Unions in Europe. JCS 6 (4).

80 -. 1992. Papers on Communist Political Evolution. SCC 8 (1).

81 Journal of International Affairs. 1974. Papers on Communism and Detente. JIA 28 (2).

82 -. 1978. Papers on Leadership in the Communist States. JIA 32 (2).

83 Kautsky, J. H. 1973. Comparative Communism vs Comparative Politics. SCC 6: 135-170.

84 Lebowitz, M. A. 1994. Analytical Marxism and Marxian Theory of Crisis. CJE 18: 163-179.

85 Lowry, S. M. 1976. A Model for Predicting Succession in Communist Political Systems: Soviet Union. SCC 9: 145-151.

86 Marsh, R. M.; Parish, W. L. 1965. Modernization and Communism. ASR 30: 934-942.

87 Political Quarterly. 1991. Papers on Collapse of Communism. PQ 62 (1).

88 Poznanski, K. 1993. Communist Decay: The Role of Evolutionary Mechanisms. CAPCS 26: 3-24.

89 Raiklin, E. 1993. Disintegration of the Soviet Union. IJSE 20: 1-132.

90 Revue d'Etudes Comparatives Est-Ouest. 1992. Papers on the Transition of Central and Eastern Europe. RECEO 23 (4).

91 Rice, G. W. 1973. Electoral Prospects of Non-Ruling Communist Parties. AJPS 17: 611-621.

92 Science and Society. 1995. Papers on Leninism. SAS 59 (3).

93 Seidelman, R. 1984. Protest Theories and the Left in Power: Italian Cities under Communist Rule. WEP 7: 43-63.

94 Studies in Comparative Communism. 1971. Papers on East European Political Systems. SCC 4 (2).

95 -. 1973. Papers on Non-Ruling Communist States. SCC 6 (4).

96 -. 1978. Papers on European and Asian Communism. SCC 11 (4).

97 Studies in East European Thought 1993. Papers on Marxism and Socialism in Russia. Vol 45 (1/2).

98 White, S. 1983. What is a Communist System? SCC 16: 247-264.

99 World Development. 1987. Papers on the Socialist Economy of Cuba. WD 15 (1).

Democracy

100 Achen, C. H. Measuring Representation. AJPS 22: 475-510.

101 Alternatives. 1991. Papers on Democratization. Vol 16 (2).

102 American Behavior Scientist. 1992. Papers on Democracy. ABS 35 (4/5).

103 Anckar, D.; Anckar, C. 1995. Size, Insularity and Democracy. SPS 18: 211-230.

104 Apter, D. E. 1992. Democracy and Emancipatory Movements. DAC 3 (3): 139-173.

105 Armed Forces and Society. 1994. Papers on National Security and Democracy. AFAS 20 (3).

106 Azam, J. P. 1994. Democracy and Development. PC 1994: 293-305.

107 Beetham, D. 1993. Four Theorems about the Market and Democracy. EJPR 23: 187-202.

108 Berg-Schlosser, D.; De Meur, G. 1994. Conditions of Democracy in Interwar Europe: A Boolean Test. CP 26: 253-280.

109 Binford, M. B. 1983. Democratic Political Personality. PP 6: 663-684.

110 Bollen, K. A. 1980. Issues in Comparative Measurement of Political Democracy. ASR 45: 370-390.

111 -. 1983. World System Position, Dependency and Democracy. ASR 48: 468-479.

112 Bollen, K. A.; Granjean, B. 1981. Dimensions of Democracy. ASR 46: 651-659.

113 Brittan, S. 1975. Economic Contradictions of Democracy. BJPS 5: 129-159.

114 Buchanan, J. M. 1968. Democracy and Duopoly. AER 58: 322-331.

115 Burkhart, R. E.; Lewis-Beck, M. S. 1994. Comparative Democracy: Economic Development Thesis. APSR 88: 903-910.

116 Cachiers d'Etudes Africaines. 1995. Papers on the Decline of Democracy. CEA 35 (1).

117 Coleman, J.; Ferejohn, J. A. 1986. Democracy and Social Choice. Ethics 97: 6-25.

118 Dalton, R. J. 1994. Communists and Democrats: Democratic Attitudes in the Two Germanies. BJPS 24: 469-494.

119 Daniels, B. C. 1975. Democracy and Oligarchy in Connecticut Towns: General Assembly Officeholding. SSQ 56: 460-476.

120 Ethics. 1981. Papers on Representation. Ethics 91 (3).

121 Evans, G.; Whitefield, S. 1995. The Politics and Economics of Democratic Commitment: Democracy in Transition Societies. BJPS 25: 485-514.

122 Geddes, B. 1991. Game Theoretic Model of Reform in Latin American Democracies. APSR 85: 371-392.

123 Gedmin, J. 1993. The German Left and Democracy. WA 156: 46-51.

124 Gold, D. A.; Lo, C. Y. H.; Wright, E. O. 1975. Recent Developments in Marxist Theories of the Capitalist State. Monthly Review 2: 29-43.

125 Gottfried, P. 1991. Teaching Democratic Values. JSPES 16: 59-76.

126 Greven, M. T. 1995. Political Institutions and the Building of Democracy. EJPR 27: 463-476.

127 Gurr, T. R.; Jaggers, K.; Moore, W. H. 1990. The Growth of Democracy, Autocracy and State Power since 1900. SICID 25: 73-108.

128 Hampsher-Monk, I. 1980. Classical and Empirical Theories of Democracy. BJPS 10: 241-252.

129 Hewitt, C. J. 1977. Effect of Political Democracy and Social Democracy on Equality in Industrial Societies. ASR 42: 450-464.

130 Hurwitz, L. 1971. Index of Democratic Political Stability. CPS 4: 41-68.

131 -. 1972. Democratic Political Stability: Traditional Hypotheses Reexamined. CPS 4: 476-490.

132 International Political Science Review. 1991. Papers on Democracy. ISSJ 43 (2-3).

133 Jackman, R. W. 1972. Political Elites, Mass Publics and Support for Democratic Principles. JOP 34: 753-773.

134 -. 1973. Relation of Economic Development to Democratic Performance. AJPS 17: 611-621.

135 -. 1974. Political Democracy and Social Equality. ASR 39: 29-45.

136 Journal of International Affairs. 1985. Papers on the Dilemmas of Democracy. JIA 38 (2).

137 Kateb, G. 1991. Moral Distinctiveness of Representative Democracy. Ethics 91: 357-374.

138 Keman, H. 1993. Theoretical Approaches to Social Democracy. JTP 5: 291-317.

139 Landes, R. G.; Jabbra, J. G. 1981. Impact of Socio-Political Cleavages on Support for Democratic Orientations among Canadian Adolescents. Indian Political Science Review 15: 158-174.

140 Latin American Perspectives. 1988. Papers on Democratization and the Class Struggle in Latin America. LAPER 15 (3).

141 -. 1990. Papers on Post-Marxism, the Left and Democracy in Latin America. LAPER 17 (2).

142 Lijphart, A. 1968. Typologies of Democratic Systems. CPS 1: 3-44.

143 Lipset, S. M. 1969. Social Requisites of Democracy: Economic Development and Political Legitimacy. APSR 53: 69-105.

144 Loewenberg, G. 1970. Influence of Parliamentary Behavior on Regime Stability. CP 3: 177-200.

145 Manley, J. F. 1983. Neopluralism: Class Analysis of Pluralism. APSR 77: 368-383.

146 Mbachu, O. 1994. Democracy in Africa. Coexistence 31: 147-158.

147 Midlarsky, M. I. 1995. Environmental Influences on Democracy. JCR 39: 224-262.

148 Mishler, W.; Rose, R. 1994. Support for Parliaments and Regimes in Transition toward Democracy in Eastern Europe. LSQ 19: 5-32.

149 Muller, E. N. 1995. Economic Determinants of Democracy. ASR 60: 966-995.

150 Muller, E. N.; Seligson, M. A. 1994. Civic Culture and Democracy. APSR 88: 635-652.

151 Muller, E. N.; Seligson, M. A.; Turan, I. 1987. Education, Participation and Support for Democratic Norms. CP 20: 19-34.

152 O'Flaherty, B. 1990. Why Are There Democracies? Principal Agent Answer. EAP 2: 133-155.

153 Parliamentary Affairs. 1993. Papers on Building Democracy. PARLA 46 (4).

154 Peters, B. G.; Doughtie, J. C.; McCulloch, M. K. 1977. Types of Democratic Systems and Types of Public Policy. CP 9: 327-355.

155 Policy Sciences. 1993. Papers on Democracy and the Policy Sciences. PSCI 26 (3).

156 Political Science Quarterly. 1994. Papers on the Effectiveness of Presidential and Parliamentary Democracy? PSCQ 109 (3).

157 Political Studies. 1992. Papers on Prospects for Democracy. POLST 40 (Special Issue).

158 Przeworski, A. 1980. Social Democracy as Historical Phenomena. New Left Review 122: 27-58.

159 Rae, D. W. 1971. Democracy as a Property of Political Institutions. APSR 65: 111-119.

160 Remmer, K. L. 1995. New Theoretical Perspectives on Democratization. CP 28: 103-122.

161 Riley, J. M. 1985. On the Possibility of Liberal Democracy. APSR 79: 1135-1151.

162 Rubinson, R. B.; Quinlan, D. 1977. Democracy and Social Inequality. ASR 42: 611-622.

163 Sengupta, M. 1978. On a Concept of Representative Democracy. TAD 3: 249-262.

164 Sirowy, L.; Inkeles, A. 1990. Effects of Democracy on Growth and Inequality. SICID 25: 126-157

165 Sloan, J. W. 1989. Capabilities of Democratic Regimes in Latin America. LARR 24: 113-126.

166 Smith, A. K. 1969. Socioeconomic Development and Political Democracy. MJPS 13: 95-125.

167 Society. 1995. Papers on the Future of Liberal Democracy. Vol 32 (6).

168 Spectrum. 1993. Papers on Electronic Democracy. Vol 66 (2).

169 Starr, H. 1991. Democratic Dominoes. JCR 35: 356-381.

170 Studies in Comparative International Development. 1990. Papers on Measuring Democracy. SICID 25 (1).

171 Walker, J. L. 1966. Critique of Elitist Theory of Democracy. APSR 60: 285-295.

172 West European Politics. 1993. Papers on Social Democracy in Western Europe. WEP 16 (1).

173 -. 1995. Papers on the Crisis of Representation in Europe. WEP 18 (3).

174 Witman, D. 1989. Why Democracies Produce Efficient Results. JPE 97: 1395-1424.

175 World Development. 1993. Papers on Economic Liberalization and Democratization. WD 21 (8).

Federalism

176 Aranson, P. H. 1990. Federalism: The Reasons of Rules. CJ 10: 17-38.

177 Beer, S. H. 1978. Federalism, Nationalism and Democracy in America. APSR 72: 9-21.

178 Bell, C. R. 1989. Between Anarchy and Leviathan: The Design of Federal States. JPUBE 39: 207-221.

179 Bish, R. L. 1987. Federalism: A Market Economics Perspective. CJ 7: 377-396.

180 Breton, A. 1989. Growth of Competitive Governments. CANJE 22: 717-750.

181 Brunk, G. G.; Klemmack, D.; Roff, L. 1987. Do Citizens Care about Federalism? International Journal of Public Administration 9: 485-507.

182 Cato Journal. 1982. Papers on the New Federalism. CJ 2 (2).

183 -. 1990. Papers on Federalism and Economics. CJ 10 (1).

184 Dye, T. R. 1990. Policy Consequences of Intergovernmental Competition. CJ 10: 59-73.

185 Eichenberger, R. 1994. Benefits of Federalism and the Risk of Overcentralization. Kyklos 47: 403-420.

186 Etheredge, L. S. 1977. Optimal Federalism: Model of Psychological Dependence. PSCI 8: 161-171.

187 European Journal of Political Research. 1988. Papers on Intergovernmental Relations in Western Societies. EJPR 16 (4).

188 Futuribles. 1982. Papers on Decentralization. Vol 1982 (56).

189 Government and Opposition 1988. Papers on Imitating the Swiss Confederation. GAO 23 (1).

190 Grady, D. O. 1984. American Governors and State-Federal Relations: Attitudes and Activities. SG 57: 106-113.

191 Grant, D. S. 1995. Political Economy of Business Failures: Impact of Reagan's New Federalism. ASR 60: 851-873.

192 International Political Science Review. 1984. Papers on Pluralism and Federalism. IPSR 5 (4).

193 International Review of Administrative Science. 1987. Papers on Decentralization. IRAS 53 (4).

194 Mueller, D. C. 1971. Fiscal Federalism in a Constitutional Democracy. PUBP 19: 567-593.

195 Narang, A. S. 1991. Dynamics of Federalism in Canada. Journal of Constitutional and Parliamentary Studies 25: 164-186.

196 Nielsen, H. J. 1981. Size and Evaluation of Government: Danish Attitudes toward Politics at Multiple Levels of Government. EJPR 9: 47-60.

197 Ostrom, V. 1973. Can Federalism Make a Difference? Publius 3: 197-238.

198 PS. 1993. Papers on Federalism. PS 26 (2).

199 Public Administration Review 1970. Papers on Intergovernmental Relations. PAR 30 (3).

200 Publius. 1975. Papers on Intergovernmental Relations. Vol 5 (4).

201 -. 1978. Papers on Government Reorganization and the Federal System. Vol 8 (1).

202 -. 1984. Papers on Canadian Federalism. Vol 14 (1).

203 -. 1985. Papers on Federalism and Consociationalism. Vol 15 (2).

204 -. 1986. Papers on New Federalism. Vol 16 (1).

205 -. 1989. Papers on Federalism and Intergovernmental Relations in West Germany. Vol 19 (4).

206 -. 1992. Papers on Federalism and the Constitution. Vol 22 (1).

207 -. 1993. Papers on Federalism and Switzerland. Publius 23 (2).

208 -. 1993. Papers on Federal Preemption. Publius 23 (4).

209 Recherche Sociale. 1980. Papers on Decentralization. RS 75 (July-Oct).

210 Rose-Ackerman, S. 1981. Does Federalism Matter? Political Choice in a Federal Republic. JPE 89: 152-165.

211 Scheiber, H. N. 1978. American Federalism and the Diffusion of Power. University of Toledo Law Review 9: 619-680.

212 Schmidt, G. D. 1989. Political Variables and Governmental Decentralization in Peru. JIAS 31: 193-232.

213 Webber, D. J. 1989. Dimensions of Federalism in US Senate Voting. Publius 19 (Winter): 185-192.

214 Yoo, J. W.; Wright, D. S. 1993. Public Policy and Intergovernmental Relations: Effects of the Federalism Decade. PSJ 21: 687-699.

Imperialism

215 Anderson, J. L.; Lewit, T. 1992. A Contract with the Barbarians? Economics and the Fall of Rome. EEH 29: 99-115.

216 Boswell, T. 1989. Colonial Empires and the Capitalist World Economy: Colonization. ASR 54: 180-196.

217 Canadian Journal of Political and Social Theory. 1983. Papers on Beyond Dependency. CJPST 7 (1).

218 Caporaso, J. A. 1978. Dependence, Dependency and Power in the Global System. IO 32: 13-43.

219 Comparative Studies in Society and History. 1993. Papers on the Imperial State in the Middle Ages. CSSH 35 (3).

220 Daedalus. 1976. Papers on Edward Gibbon and the Decline and Fall of the Roman Empire. Vol 105 (3).

221 Duvall, R. 1978. Dependence and Dependencia Theory. IO 32: 51-78.

222 Eisenstadt, S. N. 1978. Sociological Aspects of Imperialism in the Ancient World. JJIR 3 (4): 94-106.

223 Fagen, R. R. 1977. Studying Latin American Politics: Dependencia Approach. LARR 12: 3-26.

224 Galtung, J. 1971. A Structural Theory of Imperialism. JPR 8: 81-117.

225 Gidengil, E. L. 1978. Centers and Peripheries: Galtung's Theory of Imperialism. JPR 15: 51-66.

226 Griffin, K.; Burley, J. 1985. Radical Analyses of Imperialism, the Third World and Transition to Socialism. JEL 23: 1089-1143.

227 Hills, J. 1994. Dependency Theory and Its Relevance Today: Telecommunications and Structural Power. RIS 20: 169-186.

228 Journal of Commonwealth and Comparative Politics. 1993. Papers on Decolonization. JCACP 31 (1).

229 Journal of Peace Research. 1980. Papers on Imperialism and Militarization. JPR 17 (2).

230 Latin American Perspectives. 1974. Papers on Imperialism and Dependence Theory. LAPER 1 (1), 1976 3 (1) 3 (4), 1977 4 (4), and 1979 6 (1).

231 Leonard, K. 1979. The Great Firm Theory of the Decline of the Mughal Empire. CSSH 21: 151-167.

232 Lewis, P. 1982. The Next Great Empire. Futures 14: 47-61.

233 Mack, A. 1974. Theories of Imperialism. JCR 18: 514-535.

234 Maoz, Z. 1984. Peace by Empire? Conflict Outcomes and International Stability. JPR 21: 227-241.

235 Modern Asian Studies. 1981. Papers on Imperialism, Nationalism and Change in Twentieth Century India. MAS 15 (3).

236 Morgan, I. 1982. Theories of Imperialism: Bibliography. JAS 6: 18-22.

237 Pelikan, J. 1982. Decline and Fall of Rome in Historical Paradigm. Daedalus 111: 85-92.

238 Science and Society. 1970. Papers on Imperialism and Neocolonialism. SAS 34 (1-2).

239 Smith, T. 1978. A Comparative Study of French and British Decolonization. CSSH 20: 70-102.

240 Strang, D. R. 1991. Global Patterns of Decolonization, 1500-1987. ISQ 35: 429-454.

241 Taagepera, R. 1978. Size and Duration of Empires. SSR 7: 108-127, 180-196.

242 Weede, E. 1978. US Support for Foreign Governments, or Domestic Disorder and Imperial Intervention. CPS 10: 497-528.

243 Williams, W. A. 1991. Empire as a Way of Life. Radical History Review 50: 71-102.

Military Regimes

244 Andreski, S. 1980. The Peaceful Disposition of Military Dictatorships. Journal of Strategic Studies 3: 3-10.

245 Eckhardt, W. 1971. Cross-Cultural Militarism. Journal of Contemporary Revolutions 3: 113-139.

246 Feit, E. 1973. Military Regimes in the Formation of Political Institutions. WP 25: 251-273.

247 Gregory, A. J. 1973. On Understanding Fascism. APSR 67: 1332-1347.

248 -. 1976. Fascism and Comparative Politics. CPS 9: 207-222.

249 Journal of Contemporary History. 1976. Papers on Fascism. JCH 11 (4) and 19 (4).

250 Laemmle, P. G. 1977. Epidemiology of Domestic Military Intervention. BS 22: 327-333.

251 Luckham, R. 1994. The Military, Militarization and Democratization in Africa. AFSR 37: 13-76.

252 McKinlay, R. D.; Cohan, A. S. 1975. Comparative Analysis of Political and Economic Performance of Military and Civilian Regimes. CP 8: 1-30.

253 -. 1976. The Economic Performance of Military Regimes. BJPS 6: 291-310.

254 -. 1976. Performance and Instability in Military and Nonmilitary Regimes. APSR 70: 850-864.

255 Nordlinger, E. A. 1970. Impact of Military Rule upon Economic and Social Change in Non-Western States. APSR 64: 1131-1148.

256 Putnam, R. D. 1967. Military Intervention in Latin American Politics. WP 20: 83-110.

257 Rejai, M.; Phillips, K. 1995. Military Leaders in Perspective. Coexistence 32: 137-148.

258 Remmer, K. L. 1978. Evaluating the Policy Impact of Military Regimes in Latin America. LARR 13: 39-54.

259 Sigelman, L. 1974. Military Size and Intervention: Feit's Hypothesis. JPMS 2: 95-100.

260 Wintrobe, R. 1990. Economic Theory of Dictatorship. APSR 84: 849-872.

261 World Affairs. 1987. Papers on Dictators. WA 149 (4).

Political Development

262 Ali, M. 1968. From Social Darwinism to Current Theories of Modernization. WP 20: 69-83.

263 Almond, G. A. 1965. Developmental Approach to Political Systems. WP 17: 183-214.

264 Banks, A. S. 1981. An Index of Socio-Economic Development. JOP 43: 390-411.

265 Ben-Dor, G. 1974. Corruption, Institutionalization and Political Development. CPS 7: 63-83.

266 -. 1975. Institutionalization and Political Development. CSSH 17: 309-325.

267 Bollen, K. A. 1979. Political Democracy and the Timing of Development. ASR 44: 572-587.

268 -. 1980. Issues in Measurement of Political Development. ASR 45: 370-390.

269 Bradshaw, Y. W.; Kaiser, P. J.; Ndegwa, S. N. 1995. African Development. AFSR 38: 39-66.

270 Collier, D.; Norden, D. L. 1992. Strategic Choice Models of Political Change in Latin America. CP 24: 229-243.

271 Comparative Studies in Society and History 1986. Papers on Development Theory. CSSH 28 (1).

272 Corning, P. A.; Hines, S. M. 1988. Political Development and Political Evolution. PALS 6: 141-155.

273 Crawford, B.; Lijphart, A. 1995. Explaining Political and Economic Change in Post-Communist Eastern Europe. CPS 28: 171-199.

274 Demerath, N. J.; Rhys, H. W. 1993. Religion and Ethnicity in Political and Economic Development. JUH 19: 26-62.

275 Development. 1992. Papers on Democracy, Participation and Development. Vol 1992 (3).

276 Eckstein, H. 1982. Political Development. WP 34: 451-486.

277 Gasiorowski, M. J. 1988. Economic Dependence and Political Democracy. CPS 20: 489-522.

278 Glahe, F.; Vorhies, F. 1989. Religion, Liberty and Economic Development. PC 62: 201-216.

279 Gonick, L. S.; Rosh, R. M. 1988. Structural Constraints of World Economy on Political Development. CPS 21: 171-199.

280 Grindle, M. S.; Thomas, J. W. 1989. Political Economy of Reform in Developing Countries. PSCI 22: 213-248.

281 Hill, K. Q. 1979. Political Institutionalization in Primitive Societies. BSR 14: 277-292.

282 Huntington, S. P. 1965. Political Development and Political Decay. WP 17: 386-430.

283 -. 1971. Modernization, Development and Politics. CP 3: 283-322.

284 International Social Science Journal. 1971. Papers on Nation Building. ISSJ 23 (3).

285 -. 1987. Papers on Transition Processes. ISSR 39 (4).

286 -. 1988. Papers on Modernity and Identity. ISSJ 40 (4).

287 McCrone, D. J.; Cnudde, C. F. 1967. Communications Theory of Democratic Political Development. APSR 61: 72-79.

288 Merkl, P. H. 1977. Study of European Political Development. WP 29: 462-475.

289 Migdal, J. S. 1974. Change among Individuals in the Process of Modernization. WP 26: 189-206.

290 Moaddel, M. 1994. Modernization and World-System Theories. ASR 59: 276-303.

291 Olson, M. 1968. Multivariate Analysis of National Political Development. ASR 33: 699-712.

292 -. 1993. Dictatorship, Democracy and Development. APSR 87: 567-576.

293 O'Shea, R. 1993. Multifaceted Modernization: Some Public Sector Hypotheses. IRAS 59: 99-114.

294 Pourgerami, A. 1988. Political Economy of Development: Development Democracy Growth Hypothesis. PC 58: 123-142.

295 Public Administration and Development. 1994. Papers on Developmental Institution Building. PAAD 14 (2).

296 Rhonda, R. 1978. Political Instability and Institutionalization in Developing Countries. Review of Public Data Use 6 (Jan): 38-44.

297 Rosenbaum, H. J.; Sederberg, P. C. 1971. The Occult and Political Development. CP 3: 561-574.

298 Rustow, D. A. 1968. Modernization and Comparative Politics. CP 1: 37-51.

299 Ruttan, V. W. 1991. What Happened to Political Development? EDACC 39: 265-292.

300 Sandbrook, R. 1975. Crisis in Political Development Theory. JDS 12: 163-185.

301 Shin, C. S.; Chey, M.; Kim, K. W. 1989. Support for Democracy in Korea: Douglas-Wildavsky Theory of Culture. CPS 22: 217-238.

302 Sigelman, L. 1974. Lerner's Model of Modernization. JDA 8: 525-536.

303 Stephens, J. D. 1989. Democratic Transition and Breakdown in Western Europe. AJS 94: 1019-1077.

304 Studies in Comparative International Development. 1983. Papers on Development Theory and Research. SICID 18 (4), and 1990 25 (2).

305 Takamori, H. 1973. Measuring Sociological Development. Developing Economies 11: 111-145.

306 Tantor, R. 1967. Political Development. MJPS 11: 145-172.

307 Taylor, C. L. 1972. Indicators of Political Development. JDS 8: 103-110.

308 Tipps, D. C. 1973. Modernization Theory and the Comparative Study of Societies. CSSH 15: 199-240.

309 Vanjanen, T. 1989. Democratization Related to Socioeconomic Variables. SPS 12: 95-128.

310 Venieris, Y. P.; Gupta, D. K. 1983. Sociopolitical and Economic Dimensions of Development. EDACC 31: 727-756.

311 Vorhies, F.; Glahe, F. 1988. Political Liberty and Social Development. PC 58: 45-72.

312 Wellhofer, E. S. 1989. Comparative Method and the Study of Development, Diffusion and Social Change. CPS 22: 315-342.

Socialism

313 Annals. 1990. Papers on Privatizing Socialism. ANNALS 507.

314 Coexistence. 1993. Papers on Socialism. Vol 30 (3).

315 Comparative Politics. 1978. Papers on the Policy Problems of Socialism. CP 11 (1).

316 Ethics. 1992. Papers on Markets and Equality under Capitalism and Socialism. Vol 102 (3).

317 Hardy, J. 1994. Transition to Where? IRAE 8: 335-340.

318 Hillman, A. Y. 1994. Transition from Socialism: Political Economy Perspective. EJPE 10: 191-226.

319 Jackman, R. W. 1980. Socialist Parties and Income Inequality in Western Industrial Societies. JOP 42: 135-149.

320 Journal of Contemporary History. 1976. Papers on Twentieth Century Socialism. JCH 11 (2/3).

321 Journal of Development Studies. 1988. Papers on Third World Socialist Economic Management. JDS 24 (4).

322 Lane, J. E. 1993. Twilight of the Scandinavian Model. POLST 41: 315-324.

323 -. 1995. Decline of the Swedish Model. Governance 8: 579-590.

324 Latin American Perspectives. 1988. Papers on the Transition to Socialism in Latin America. LAPER 15 (1).

325 Magagna, V. V. 1989. A Political Analysis of Class, Consumption and Socialism. Polity 21: 711-730.

326 Mesa-Lago, C. 1973. A Continuum Model to Compare Socialist Systems Globally. EDACC 21: 573-590.

327 Politics and Society. 1994. Papers on Rethinking Socialism. PAS 22 (4).

328 Revue d'Etudes Comparatives Est-Ouest. 1988. Papers on Developing Countries and Socialism. RECEO 19 (2).

329 Social Research. 1980. Papers on Socialism. SR 47 (1).

330 West European Politics. 1991. Papers on the Swedish Model. WEP 14 (3).

RELIGION AND POLITICS

1 American Behavioral Scientist. 1977. Papers on Contemporary Religion. ABS 20 (6).
2 –. 1986. Papers on Religion. ANNALS 483.
3 –. 1992. Papers on Political Islam. ANNALS 524.
4 Annals. 1970. Papers on US Religion. ANNALS 387, 1985 480, and 1993 527.
5 Bainbridge, W. S. 1995. Neural Network Models of Religious Belief. SP 38: 483-496.
6 Balch, R. W.; Farnsworth, G.; Wilkins, S. 1983. Reactions to Disconfirmed Prophecy in a Millennial Sect. SP 26: 137-158.
7 Berens, J. F. 1979. Religion and Revolution: Nationalism in America. CRSN 6: 233-245.
8 Choueiri, Y. M. 1993. Theoretical Paradigms of Islamic Movements. POLST 41: 108-116.
9 Dunn, C. W. 1986. Some Modest Proposals about an Immodest Subject. PS 19: 832-836.
10 Euben, R. 1995. Conflicting Assumptions about Human Behavior Held by Rational Actor Theory and Islamic Fundamentalism. PP 16: 157-178.
11 Heirich, M. 1977. Test of Widely Held Theories about Religious Conversion. AJS 83: 653-680
12 Jenkins, P.; Maier-Katkin, D. 1992. Satanism: Myth and Reality. CLASC 17: 53-75.
13 Journal of Interamerican Studies and World Affairs. 1979. Papers on the Catholic Church in Latin America. JIAS 21 (1).
14 Journal of Interdisciplinary History. 1993. Papers on Religion and History. JIDH 23 (3).
15 Kedourie, E. 1979. Religion and Politics: Arnold Toynbee and Martin Wight. BJPS 5: 6-14.
16 Khazanov, A. M. 1993. Muhammad and Jenghiz Khan: Religious Factor in Empire. CSSH 35: 461-179.
17 Law and Contemporary Problems. 1981. Papers on Religion. LACP 44 (2).
18 Levine, D. H. 1986. Religion and Politics in Historical Perspective. CP 19: 95-122.
19 McCormick, G. H. 1983. Dynamics of Doctrinal Change. Orbis 27: 266-273.
20 Medoff, M. H.; Skov, I. L. 1992. Religion and Behavior. JSE 21: 143-151.
21 Morgan, S. P. 1983. Religion and Morality: Are Religious People Nice People? SF 61: 683-692.
22 Newport, F. 1979. The Religious Switcher in the US. ASR 44: 528-552.
23 Political Quarterly. 1990. Papers on the Political Revival of Religion. PQ 61 (2).
24 Reichley, J. A. 1986. Democracy and Religion. PS 19: 801-806.
25 Riis, O. 1993. The Study of Religion in Modern Society. AS 36: 371-384.
26 Roele, M. 1993. Religious Behaviour as a Utility and Inclusive Fitness Optimizing Strategy. SSI 32: 387-426.

27 Shapiro, S. 1976. Morality in Religious Reformations. CSSH 18: 438-457.
28 Taub, D. E.; Nelson, L. D. 1993. Satanism in Contemporary America. SQ 34: 523-542.
29 Teaching Political Science. 1982. Papers on Religion and Politics. TPS 10 (1) and 11 (4).
30 Thompson, K. W. 1988. Religious Transformation of Politics and Political Transformation of Religion. ROP 50: 545-560.
31 Welch, K. W. 1981. Interpersonal Influence Model of Religious Commitment. SQ 22: 81-92.
32 Winslow, D. 1984. A Political Geography of Deities: Sinhalese Buddhism. JASIAS 43: 273-292.
33 Woodrum, E. 1985. Religious Belief Transformation. SI 55: 16-37.
34 Wuthnow, R. 1985. The Growth of Religious Reform Movements. ANNALS 480: 106-116.
35 Zaret, D. 1989. Religion and the Rise of Liberal Democratic Ideology in England. ASR 54: 163-179.
36 Zygmunt, J. F. 1972. When Prophecies Fail: A Theoretical Perspective. ABS 16: 245-268.

Churches

37 Allen, D. W. 1995. Order in the Church: Property Rights Approach. JEBAO 27: 97-117.
38 American Behavioral Scientist. 1974. Papers on the Church and Society. ABS 17 (6).
39 Beatty, K. M.; Walter, B. O. 1989. Group Theory of Religion and Politics. WPQ 42: 129-146.
40 Berger, P. L. 1984. The Sociological Study of Sectarianism. SR 51: 367-386.
41 Byrnes, T. A. 1993. The Politics of the American Catholic Hierarchy. PSQ 108: 497-514.
42 Comparative Studies in Society and History. 1976. Papers on Religion Renewal. CSSH 18 (4).
43 –. 1978. Papers on Religious Institutions. CSSH 20 (4).
44 Conflict. 1991. Papers on the Catholic Church. Vol 11 (4).
45 Dixon, D. E. 1995. New Protestantism in Latin America. CP 27: 479-492.
46 Ekelund, R. B.; Hebert, R. F.; Tollison, R. D. 1989. An Economic Model of the Medieval Church: Usury as Rent Seeking. JOLEAO 5: 307-331.
47 Gill, A. J. 1994. Religious Competition and Catholic Political Strategy in Latin America. AJPS 38: 403-425.
48 Glock, C. Y. 1993. Churches and Social Change in Twentieth Century America. ANNALS 527: 67-83.
49 Hadaway, C. K.; Marler, P. L.; Chaves, M. 1993. US Church Attendance. ASR 58: 741-752.

50 Liebman, R. C.; Sutton, J. R.; Wuthnow, R. 1988. Social Sources of Denominationalism: Schisms in Protestant Denominations. ASR 53: 343-352.

51 Stark, R.; Bainbridge, W. S. 1980. Interpersonal Bonds and Recruitment to Cults and Sects. AJS 85: 1376-1395.

52 Takayama, K.P.; Cannon, L.W. 1979. Formal Policy and Power in Protestant Denominations. SQ 20: 321-332.

53 Wald, K. D.; Owen, D. E.; Hill, S. S. 1988. Churches as Political Communities. APSR 82: 531-548.

54 -. 1990. Political Cohesion in Churches. JOP 52: 195-215.

55 Wallis, J. L. 1990. Modelling Churches as Collective Action Groups. IJSE 17: 59-72.

56 Waters, M. S.; Heath, W. C.; Watson, J. K. 1995. Positive Model of the Determination of Religious Affiliation. SSQ 76: 105-123.

57 Zaleski, P.; Zech, C. 1995. Optimal Size of a Religious Congregation. AJEAS 54: 439-460.

Economics and Society

58 American Journal of Comparative Law. 1987. Papers on Law and Religion. AJCL 35 (1).

59 Annals of Regional Science. 1994. Papers on Sustainable Resources and Religion. ARS 28 (1).

60 Ben-Yehuda, N. 1980. The European Witch Craze of the 14th to 17th Centuries. AJS 86: 1-31.

61 Bercovitch, S. 1982. Rhetoric as Authority: Puritanism and the Myth of America. SSI 21: 5-18

62 Blau, J.R.; Land, K.C.; Redding, K. 1992. Expansion of Religious Affiliation. SSR 21: 329-352.

63 Breault, K. D. 1986. Suicide in America: Durkheim's Theory of Religious and Family Integration. AJS 92: 628-656.

64 Clarke, P. B. 1979. Religious Factor in Developmental Process. Geneve-Afrique 17: 45-66.

65 Cole, W. A.; Hammond, P. E. 1974. Religious Pluralism, Legal Development and Societal Complexity: Civil Religion. JSSR 13: 177-189.

66 Davidson, J. D.; Pyle, R. E.; Reyes, D. V. 1995. Persistence and Change in the Protestant Establishment. SF 74: 157-176.

67 Dehejia, R.H.; Dehejia, V. H. 1993. Religion and Economic Activity in India. AJEAS 52: 145-154.

68 De Long, J. B. 1989. Protestant Ethic Revisited. FFWA 13: 229-242.

69 Dodson, M. 1993. Changing Spectrum of Religious Activism in Latin America. LAPER 20 (4): 61-74.

70 Dogan, M. 1995. Decline of Religious Beliefs in Western Europe. ISSJ 47: 405-418.

71 Ellison, C. G. 1992. Are Religious People Nice People? Black Americans. SF 71: 411-430.

72 Finke, R.; Iannaccone, L. R. 1993. Supply-Side Explanations for Religious Change. ANNALS 527: 27-39.

73 Gabennesch, H. 1988. When Promises Fail: Theory of Fluctuations in Suicide. SF 67: 129-145.

74 Gans, H. J. 1994. Symbolic Ethnicity and Symbolic Religiosity. EARS 17: 577-592.

75 Gilbert, C. P. 1991. Religion, Neighborhood Environments and Partisan Behavior. PG 10: 110-131

76 Girard, C. 1988. Church Membership and Suicide. AJS 93: 1471-1479.

77 Hammond, P. E.; Williams, K. R. 1976. Protestant Ethic Thesis. SF 54: 579-589.

78 Hoak, D. 1983. The Great European Witch Hunts. AJS 88: 1270-1274.

79 Holfield, E. B. 1983. Religion and Order in England and America. CSSH 25: 525-534.

80 Horsley, R. A. 1979. Social Roles of Accused in the European Witch Trials. JIDH 9: 689-716.

81 Hunter, J. D. 1987. Religious Elites in Advanced Industrial Society. CSSH 29: 360-374.

82 Journal of Asian Studies. 1993. Papers on Scripture and Society in Muslim Asia. JASIAS 52 (3).

83 Journal of Institutional and Theoretical Economics. 1994. Papers on the Economics of Religion. JITE 150 (4).

84 Journal of Social Issues. 1995. Papers on Religious Influences on Well Being. JSI 51: 13-32.

85 Lamb, M. L. 1992. Theology and Money: Rationality, Religion and Economics. ABS 35: 735-755.

86 Lazerwitz, B.; Harrison, M. I. 1979. American Jewish Denominations. ASR 44: 656-666.

87 Marshall, G. 1987. Which Way for the Sociology of Religion? CSSH 29: 375-380.

88 Messner, S. F. 1982. Societal Development, Social Equality and Homicide: The Durkheimian Model. SF 61: 225-240.

89 Nelson, H. M.; Whitt, H. P. 1972. Religion and the Migrant in the City: Holt's Cultural Shock Thesis. SF 50: 379-384.

90 Peek, C. W.; Curry, E. W.; Chalfant, H. P. 1985. Religiosity and Delinquency: Deviance Deterrence and Deviance Amplification. SSQ 66: 120-131.

91 Pescosolido, B. A.; Mendelsohn, R. 1986. Social Causation of Suicide. ASR 51: 80-100.

92 Pilarzyk, T. 1978. Conversion and Alternation Processes in Youth Culture: Religious Transformations. PSR 21: 379-406.

93 Pottenger, J. R. 1987. Mormonism and the American Industrial State. IJSE 14: 25-38.

94 Pryor, F. L. 1993. The Roman Catholic Church and the Economic System. JCE 17: 129-150.

95 Raines, J. P.; Jung, C. R. 1986. Knight on Religion and Ethics as Agents of Social Change. AJEAS 45: 429-440.

96 Reay, B. 1980. Social Origins of Early Quakerism. JIDH 11: 55-72.

97 Reese, L. A.; Brown, R. E. 1995. Effects of Religious Messages on Racial Identify and System Blame among African Americans. JOP 57: 24-43.

98 Roof, W. C. 1979. Socioeconomic Differentials among White Socioreligious Groups SF 58: 280-289

99 Simpson, M. E.; Conklin, G. H. 1989. Socioeconomic Development, Suicide and Religion: Durkheim's Theory. SF 67: 945-964.

100 Stone, D. M.; Potvin, R. H. 1986. Religion and Delinquency. SF 65: 87-105.

101 Tittle, C. R.; Welch, M. R. 1983. Religiosity and Deviance: Contingency Theory of Constraining Effects SF 61: 653-682.

102 Tole, L. A. 1993. Durkheim on Religion and Moral Community in Modernity. SI 63: 1-29.

103 Travis, R. 1990. Suicide in Cross Cultural Perspective. IJCS 31: 237-247.

104 Underhill, R. 1975. Economic and Political Antecedents of Monotheism. AJS 80: 841-861.

105 Veevers, J. E.; Cousineau, D. F. 1980. The Heathen Canadians: Demographic Correlates of Nonbelief. PACSR 23: 199-216.

106 Warner, R. S. 1993. The Sociological Study of Religion in the US. AJS 98: 1044-1093.

107 Waterman, A. M. C. 1987. Economists on the Relation between Political Economy and Christian Theology. IJSE 14: 46-68.

108 Wimberley, D. W. 1984. Socioeconomic Deprivation and Religious Salience. SQ 25: 223-238.

Policy Concerns

109 Beatty, K. M.; Walter, B. O. 1984. Religious Preferences and Practice: Political Tolerance. POQ 48: 318-329.

110 Bolton, S. C.; Ledbetter, C. 1983. Compulsory Bible Reading in Arkansas and Culture of Southern Fundamentalism. SSQ 64: 670-676.

111 Castles, F. G. 1994. Religion and Policy: Does Catholicism Make a Difference? EJPR 25: 19-40.

112 Driedger, L. 1974. Doctrinal Belief: Differential Perception of Social Issues. SQ 15: 66-80.

113 Drogus, C. A. 1995. Rise and Decline of Liberation Theology. CP 27: 465-478.

114 Elifson, K. W.; Hadaway, C. K. 1985. Prayer in Public Schools. POQ 49: 317-329.

115 Ellison, C.G.; Skerkat, D. E. 1993. Conservative Protestantism and Support for Corporal Punishment. ASR 58: 131-144.

116 Galston, W. A. 1986. Public Morality and Religion in the US. PS 19: 807-824.

117 Grasmick, H. G.; Bursik, R. J.; Cochran, J. K. 1991. Religiosity and Taxpayers' Inclinations to Cheat. SQ 32: 251-266.

118 Greeley, A. M. 1991. Religion and Attitudes toward AIDS Policy. SASR 45: 126-132.

119 Green, J. C.; Guth, J. L. 1991. Religion, Representatives and Roll Calls. LSQ 16: 571-584.

120 Guth, J. L., et al. 1995. Religious Beliefs and Environmental Policy. AJPS 39: 364-382.

121 Hand, C. M.; Van Liere, K. D. 1984. Religion, Mastery over Nature and Environmental Concerns. SF 63: 555-570.

122 Harrison, M. I.; Lazerwitz, B. 1982. Do Denominations Matter. AJS 88: 356-377.

123 Heath, W. C.; Waters, M. S.; Watson, J. K. 1995. Religion and Economic Welfare. JEBAO 27: 129-142

124 Hertel, B. R.; Hughes, M. 1987. Religious Affiliation, Attendance, and Support for Pro-Family Issues in US. SF 65: 858-882.

125 Hofrenning, D. J. B. 1995. Explaining Origins of Religious Interest Groups. SSJ 32: 35-48.

126 Hull, B.; Bold, F. 1995. Preaching Matters. JEBAO 27: 143-149.

127 Hunsberger, B. 1995. Religion and Prejudice: The Role of Religious Fundamentalism, Quest, and Right Wing Authoritarianism. JSI 51: 113-130.

128 Leege, D. C.; Welch, M. R.; Trozzolo, T. 1986. Religiosity, Church Social Teaching and Sociopolitical Attitudes. RRR 28: 118-128.

129 Munro, J. 1982. Religion, Age, Sex and Moral Issues: Some Relationships. PSNZ 34: 214-220.

130 Orbis. 1983. Papers on Religion and Foreign Policy. Vol 27 (3).

131 -. 1986. Papers on Liberation Theology. Vol 30 (3).

132 Peek, C. W.; Lowe, G. D.; Williams, L. S. 1991. Religious Fundamentalism and Sexism. SF 69: 1205-1222.

133 Pratt, H. J. 1972. Political Activism in the National Council of Churches. ROP 34: 323-341.

134 Studlar, D. T. 1978. Religion and White Racial Attitudes in Britain. EARS 1: 306-315.

135 Wald, K. D. 1992. Religious Elites and Public Opinion: Peace Pastoral. ROP 54: 112-143.

136 Wald, K.D.; Owen, D.E.; Hill, S.S. 1989 Evangelical Politics and Status Issues. JSSR 28: 1-16

Political Participation

137 Beatty, K. M.; Walter, B. O. 1988. Fundamentalists, Evangelicals and Politics. APQ 16: 43-60.

138 Brudney, J.L.; Copeland, G.W. 1984. Evangelicals as a Political Force: Reagan. SSQ 65: 1072-1079.

139 Buell, E.; Sigelman, L. 1985. Popular Support for the Moral Majority. SSQ 66: 426-434.

140 Cochran, C. E. 1988. Normative Dimensions of Religion and Politics. JPS 16: 14-23.

141 -. 1988. Political Science Confronts the Book. JOP 50: 219-234.

142 Comparative Studies in Society and History. 1983 Papers on Religion and Politics. CSSH 25 (2).

143 Daedalus. 1991. Papers on Religion. Vol 120 (3).

144 Fairbanks, J. D.; Burke, J. F. 1992. Religious Periodicals and Presidential Elections. PSQ 22: 89-106.

145 Friedman, M. 1980. Religion and Politics in Age of Pluralism: Ethnocultural. Publius 10: 45-76.

146 Green, J. C.; Guth, J. L.; Hill, K. A. 1993. The Christian Right in Congressional Campaigns. JOP 55: 80-91.

147 Guth, J. L., et al. 1988. Politics of Religion in America: Issues. APQ 16: 357-397.

148 Guth, J. L.; Green, J. C. 1986. Religion and Ideology among Contributors. APQ 14: 186-200.

149 Hertzke, A. D. 1988. American Religion and Politics. WPQ 41: 825-838.

150 Janda, K. 1989. Regional and Religious Support of Political Parties and Effects on Issue Positions. IPSR 10: 349-370.

151 Jelen, T. G. 1987. Effects of Religious Separation on Party Identification, Voting Behavior and Positions. Sociological Analysis 48: 30-45.

152 -. 1993. Political Consequences of Religious Group Attitudes. JOP 55: 178-190.

153 Johnson, E. D. 1984. Social Scientists Examine the New Religious Right. TPS 12: 4-11.

154 Journal of International Affairs. 1982. Papers on Religion and Politics. JIA 36 (2).

155 Journal of Political Science. 1988. Papers on Religion in American Politics. JPS 16 (1/2).

156 Kiecolt, K. J.; Nelson, H. M. 1988. Structuring of Political Attitudes among Liberal and Conservative Protestants. JSSR 27: 48-59.

157 -. 1991. Evangelicals and Party Realignment. SSQ 72: 552-569.

158 Knoke, D. 1974. Religious Involvement and Political Behavior. SQ 15: 51-65.

159 Lijphart, A. 1979. Religion vs Linguistic vs Class Voting. APSR 73: 442-461.

160 Macaluso, T. F.; Wanat, J. 1979. Voting Turnout and Religiosity. Polity 158-169.

161 McKeown, B.; Carlson, J. M. 1987. Influence of Religious Elites on Opinion. POLCOM 4: 93-102.

162 Miller, A. H.; Wattenberg, M. P. 1984. Religiosity and the 1980 Elections. POQ 48: 301-317.

163 Miller, W. E.; Raab, G. 1977. Religious Alignment at English Elections. POLST 25: 227-251.

164 Miller, W. E.; Southard, P. C. 1975. Confessional Attachment and Electoral Behavior in the Netherlands. EJPR 3: 219-258.

165 Morgan, D. R.; Meier, K. J. 1980. Politics and Morality: Referenda. SSQ 61: 144-148.

166 Olson, D. V. A.; Carroll, J. W. 1992. Religiously Based Politics: Religious Elites and the Public. SF 70: 765-786.

167 Orum, A. 1970. Religion and Rise of the Radical White: Wallace Support. SSQ 51: 674-688.

168 Patel, K.; Pilant, D.; Rose, G. 1982. Born-Again Christians in the Bible Belt: Religion, Politics and Ideology. APQ 10: 255-272.

169 Penning, J. M. 1988. Political Behavior of American Catholics. WPQ 41: 289-308.

170 Platt, G. M.; Williams, R. H. 1988. Religion, Ideology and Politics. Society 25: 38-45.

171 PS. 1995. Papers on Christian Right. PS 28 (1).

172 Reichley, J. A. 1986. Religion and American Politics. PSQ 101: 23-48.

173 Review of Politics. 1988. Papers on Religion and Politics. ROP 50 (4).

174 Social Research. 1992. Papers on Religion and Politics. SR 59 (1).

175 Tatalovich, R.; Daynes, B. W. 1981. Salience of Religion in Congressional Voting. JPS 8: 88-97.

176 West European Politics. 1982. Papers on Religion in Western European Politics. WEP 5 (2).

177 Wilcox, C. 1987. Popular Support for the Moral Majority. SSQ 68: 157-169.

178 -. 1987. Religious Orientations and Political Attitudes: New Christian Right. APQ 15: 274-296.

179 -. 1988. Political Action Committees of the New Christian Right. JSSR 27: 60-71.

180 Woodrum, E. 1988. Moral Conservatism in the 1984 Presidential Election. JSSR 27: 192-210.

SOCIAL CHOICE

1 Acta Sociologica 1993. Papers on Rational Choice. AS 36 (3).
2 Adams, J. 1990. Institutional Economics and Social Choice Economics: Commonalities and Conflicts. JEI 24: 845-859.
3 Aizerman, M. A. 1985. New Problems in the General Choice Theory. SCAW 2: 235-282.
4 American Behavioral Scientist. 1984. Papers on Methodological Individualism and Public Choice. ABS 28 (2).
5 -. 1994. Papers on Agency. ABS 37 (6).
6 Anbarci, N. 1995. Reference Functions and Balanced Concessions. CANJE 28: 675-682.
7 Arrow, K. J. 1977. Current Developments in the Theory of Social Choice. SR 44: 607-622.
8 Bandyopadhyay, T.; Sengupta, K. 1991. Revealed Preference Axioms. EJ 101: 202-213.
9 Baron, D. P. 1994. Electoral Competition with Informed and Uninformed Voters. APSR 88: 33-47.
10 Bernholz, P. 1993. Public Choice Theory: Items for a Research Agenda. PC 77: 29-37.
11 Bevir, M. 1994. Are There Perennial Problems in Political Theory? POLST 42: 662-675.
12 Binmore, K.; Samuelson, L.; Vaughan, R. 1995. Modeling Noisy Evolution. GAEB 11: 1-35.
13 Blair, D. H.; Pollack, R. A. 1983. Rational Collective Choice. SA 249: 88-95.
14 Blin, J. M.; Satterthwaite, M. A. 1978. Individual Decisions and Group Decisions: Fundamental Differences. JPUBE 10: 247-267.
15 Bonoit, J. P.; Kornhauser, L. A. 1994. Social Choice in a Representative Democracy. APSR 88: 185-192.
16 Bordley, R. F. 1985. Comparing Different Decision Rules. BS 30: 230-239.
17 Brams, S. J.; O'Leary, M. K. 1970. Axiomatic Model of Voting Bodies. APSR 64: 449-470.
18 Brooker, R. G. 1988. Truth as a Variable: Teaching Political Strategy. SAG 19: 43-58.
19 Brown, J. L.; Agnew, N. M. 1987. Feedback Bias from Ignoring the Outcome of Rejected Alternatives. BS 32: 34-41.
20 Camerer, C.; Loewenstein, G.; Weber, M. 1989. Curse of Knowledge in Economic Settings. JPE 97: 1232-1254.
21 Carling, A. H. 1987. The Schelling Diagram: On Binary Choice with Externalities. BS 32: 4-19.
22 Chamberlin, J. R. 1976. Diagrammatic Exposition of the Logic of Collective Action. PC 26: 59-74.
23 Chichilnisky, G. 1980. Social Choice and Topology of Spaces of Preferences. Advances in Mathematics 37: 165-176.
24 -. 1982. Structural Instability of Decisive Majority Rules. JMATHE 9: 207-221.
25 Chichilnisky, G.; Heal, G. 1983. Community Preferences and Social Choice. JMATHE 12: 33-61.
26 Colby, D. C. 1982. A Test of the Relative Efficacy of Political Tactics. AJPS 26: 751-753.
27 Coram, B. T. 1995. Social Democracy and Bargaining. CP 27: 215-230.
28 Cordato, R.; Gable, W. 1984. Lysander Spooner, Natural Rights and Public Choice ABS 28: 279-292
29 Cubitt, R. P. 1993. On the Possibility of Rational Dilemmas: Axiomatic Approach. EA 9: 1-23.
30 Cyert, R. M.; Simon, H. A. 1983. The Behavioral Approach: Emphasis on Economics. BS 28: 95-108.
31 Dasgupta, P.; Hammond, P.J.; Maskin, E. S. 1979. Social Choice Rules. RES 46: 181-216.
32 Debru, G. 1984. Economic Theory in the Mathematical Mode. SJE 86: 393-410.
33 Diskin, A.; Felsenthal, D. S. 1981. Experimental Examination of Samson's Dilemma CMAPS 5: 121-137
34 Dobbs, D. 1984. Public Choice and Political Rhetoric. ABS 28: 203-210.
35 Doignon, J. P.; Falmagne, J. D. 1984. Matching Relations and Dimensional Structure of Social Choices. MSS 7: 211-229.
36 Donaldson, D.; Roemer, J. E. 1987. Social Choice in Economic Environments with Dimensional Variation. SCAW 4: 253-276.
37 Donaldson, D.; Weymark, J. A. 1988. Social Choice in Economic Environments. JET 46: 291-308
38 Dowding, K. 1994. Compatibility of Behaviouralism, Rational Choice and the New Institutionalism. JTP 6: 105-118.
39 Downs, G. W.; Rocke, D. M. 1994. Principle Agent Problem Goes to War. AJPS 38: 362-380.
40 Elkin, S. L. 1982. Market and Politics in Liberal Democracy. Ethics 92: 720-732.
41 Feldman, S. 1982. Economic Self-Interest and Political Behavior. AJPS 26: 446-466.
42 Fiorina, M. P. 1975. Formal Models in Political Science. AJPS 19: 133-159.
43 Frohlich, N., et al. 1984. Beyond Economic Man. JCR 28: 3-24.
44 Fudenberg, D.; Levine, D. I.; Maskin, E. S. 1994. Folk Theorem with Imperfect Public Information. Econometrica 62: 997-1039.
45 Gillett, R. 1977. Collective Indecision. BS 22: 383-390.
46 Godwin, R. K.; Smith, W. B. 1979. Use of Commons Dilemma in Examining Allocation of Common Resources. WPQ 32: 265-277.
47 Goetze, D. 1994. Comparing Prisoner's Dilemma, Commons Dilemma and Public Goods Provision Designs in Experiments. JCR 38: 56-86.
48 Grafstein, R. 1987. Rational Choice and Social Choice. SSQ 68: 358-366.

49 -. 1992. Rational Choice. JOP 54: 259-268.
50 Grether, D. M.; Plott, C. R. 1979. Economic Theory of Choice and the Preference Reversal Phenomenon. AER 69: 623-638.
51 Grofman, B. 1985. Metapreferences and Reasons for Stability in Social Choice. TAD 19: 31-50.
52 Hackett, S.; Schlager, E.; Walker, J. 1994. Role of Communications in Resolving Commons Dilemmas. JEEM 27: 99-126.
53 Haefele, E. T. 1971. Utility Theory of Representative Government. AER 61: 350-367.
54 Hall, J. R. 1988. Types of Communal Groups, Rational Choice Theory and the Kanter Thesis. ASR 53: 679-692.
55 Hansson, B. 1973. The Independence Condition in the Theory of Social Choice. TAD 4: 25-49.
56 Harrison, E.; Seidl, C. 1994. Perceptional Inequality and Preferential Judgments: Distributional Axioms. PC 79: 61-82.
57 Harsanyi, J. C. 1969. Rational Choice Models of Political Behavior vs. Functionalist and Conformist Theories. WP 21: 513-538.
58 Hill, S. 1986. Lumpy Preference Structures. PSCI 19: 5-32.
59 Hillas, J. 1994. Sequential Equilibria and Stable Sets of Beliefs. JET 64: 78-102.
60 Hudson, J.; Jones, P. R. 1994. Testing for Self-Interest. JSE 23: 101-112.
61 Hylland, A.; Zeckhausen, R. 1979. Impossibility of Bayesian Group Decision Making with Separate Aggregation of Beliefs and Values. Econometrica 47: 1321-1336.
62 Journal of Law and Economics. 1975. Papers on the Economic Analysis of Politics. JOLE 18 (3).
63 Kelly, J. S. 1986. A series of notes on conjectures and unsolved problems in social choice. SCAW 3: 311-314; 1987 4: 63-67, 235-239; 1988 5: 81-85, 313-317; 1989 6: 71-76, 253-258, 311-335.
64 -. 1991. Social Choice Bibliography. SCAW 8: 97-169.
65 Kramer, G. H. 1977. Dynamical Model of Political Equilibrium. JET 16: 310-334.
66 Lane, S. 1983. Rationale for Government Intervention in Seller-Consumer Relationships. PSR 2: 419-428.
67 Laver, M. 1984. Politics of Inner Space: Tragedies of Three Commons. EJPR 12: 59-72.
68 Levine, M. E.; Plott, C. R. 1977. Agenda Influence and Its Implications. VLR 63: 561-604.
69 Lewin, L. 1988. Utilitarianism and Rational Choice. EJPR 16: 29-50.
70 McBride, M. E. 1990. Economic Approach to Political Behavior: Governors, Bureaucrats and Cost Commissions. PC 66: 117-136.
71 McKelvey, R. D. 1986. Covering, Dominance and Institution Free Properties of Social Choice. AJPS 30: 283-314.
72 McKelvey, R. D.; Ordeshook, P. C. 1983. Some Experimental Results that Fail to Support the Competitive Solution. PC 40: 281-292.
73 McLean, I. 1991 Rational Choice PSCQ 39: 496-512
74 McManus, M. 1982. Some Properties of Topological Social Choice Functions. RES 49: 447-460.
75 Miller, N. R. 1983. Pluralism and Social Choice. APSR 77: 734-747.
76 Moe, T. M. 1979. Scientific Status of Rational Models. AJPS 23: 215-243.
77 Monroe, K. R. 1995. Psychology and Rational Actor Theory. PP 16: 1-22.
78 Moulin, H. 1985 From Social Welfare Orderings to Acyclic Aggregation of Preferences. MSS 9: 1-17.
79 Mueller, D. 1976. Public Choice. JEL 14: 395-433
80 -. 1986. Rational Egoism vs. Adaptive Egoism as Fundamental Postulates for a Descriptive Theory of Human Behavior. PC 51: 3-23.
81 Myerson, R. B. 1983. Utilitarianism, Egalitarianism and the Timing Effect in Social Choice Problems. Econometrica 49: 883-897.
82 Nannestad, P. 1993. Reflections on the Status of Rational Choice Theory. SPS 16: 127-148.
83 Neal, P. 1988. Hobbes and Rational Choice Theory. WPQ 41: 635-652.
84 North, D. C. 1990. A Transaction Cost Theory of Politics. JTP 2: 355-368.
85 Nurmi, H. 1983. On Riker's Theory of Political Succession. SPS 6: 177-194.
86 -. 1984. Social Choice Theory and Democracy. EJPR 12: 325-334.
87 -. 1986. Mathematical Models of Elections and Relevance for Institutional Design ES 5: 167-182
88 Ostrom, E. 1991. Rational Choice Theory and Institutional Analysis. APSR 85: 237-243.
89 Oxley, L.; George, D. A. R. 1994. Linear Saddlepoint Dynamics on Their Head: The New Orthodoxy in Macrodynamics. EJPE 10: 389 ff.
90 Parks, C. D.; Vu, A. D. 1994. Social Dilemma Behavior of Individuals from Highly Industrial and Collectivist Cultures. JCR 38: 708-718.
91 Petracca, M. P. 1991. Rational Choice Approach to Politics: A Challenge to Democratic Theory. ROP 53: 289-319.
92 Plott, C. R. 1967. Notion of Equilibrium and Its Possibility under Majority Rule. AER 57: 787-806
93 -. 1976. Axiomatic Social Choice Theory: Overview. AJPS 20: 511-596.
94 Przeworski, A. 1985. Marxism and Rational Choice. PAS 14: 379-409.
95 Public Choice. 1993. Papers on Political Science and Public Choice. PC 77 (1) and 78 (1).
96 Quattrone, G. A.; Tversky, A. 1988. Contrasting Rational and Psychological Analyses of Political Choice. APSR 82: 719-736.
97 Rader, T. 1973. An Economic Approach to Social Choice. PC 15: 49-75.
98 Rapoport, A. 1988. Experiments with N-Person Social Traps. JCR 32: 457-488.
99 Richelson, J. T. 1975. Comparative Analysis of Social Choice Functions. BS 20: 331-337; 23: 38-44, 169-176; 24: 355; 26: 346-353.
100 -. 1975. A series of notes on the comparative analysis of social choice functions. BS 20: 331-337, 1978 23: 38-44, 169-176, 1990 35: 346-353.
101 -. 1978. Conditions of Social Choice Functions. PC 31: 79-110.
102 -. 1984. Social Choice and the Status Quo. PC 42: 225-234.
103 Riker, W. H. 1977. The Future of a Science of Politics. AMS 21: 11-39.
104 -. 1988. The Place of Political Science in Public Choice. PC 57: 247-258.
105 -. 1995. Political Psychology of Rational Choice Theory. PP 16: 23-44.
106 Robert, L. 1983. Problem of Value in the Constitution of Economic Thought. SR 50: 253-277.
107 Roberts, F. S. 1972. What if Utility Functions Do Not Exist? TAD 3: 126-139.
108 Romer, T.; Rosenthal, H. 1978. Political Resource Allocation, Controlled Agendas and the Status Quo. PC 33: 27-43.
109 -. 1983. A Constitution for Solving Asymmetric Externality Games. AJPS 27: 1-26.
110 Rowley, C. K. 1978. Liberalism and Collective Choice. MSESS 46: 224-251.
111 Salmon, P. 1994. Outrageous Arguments in Economics and Public Choice. EJPE 10: 409-426.
112 Samuelson, L. 1987. Revealed Preference Phenomenon in Congressional Elections. PC 54: 141-170.
113 Sandberg, I. W. 1978. Social Process Characterized by Weak Reciprocity. JOPS 3: 1-30.
114 Sandmo, A. 1990. Buchanan on Political Economy. JEL 28: 50-65.
115 Schellenberg, J. A. 1988. Test of Models for Solving the Bargaining Problem. BS 33: 81-96.
116 Schelling, T. C. 1973. Hockey Helmets, Concealed Weapons and Daylight Saving: Binary Choices with Externalities. JCR 17: 381-428.

117 Schneider, M.; Teske, P. 1992. Theory of Political Entrepreneur: Evidence from Local Government. APSR 86: 737-747.

118 Schoemaker, P. J. H. 1982. The Expected Utility Model. JEL 20: 529-563.

119 Schofield, N. J. 1980. Formal Political Theory. QAQ 14: 249-275.

120 Schulman, P. R. 1989. Logic of Organizational Irrationality. AAS 21: 31-53.

121 Schumacher, J. A. 1984. Model of a Human Being in Public Choice Theory. ABS 28: 211-232.

122 Sen, A. K. 1970. Impossibility of a Paretian Liberal. JPE 78: 152-157.

123 -. 1977. Social Choice. Econometrica 45: 53-89.

124 Sen, A. K.; Pattanaik, P. K. 1969. Necessary and Sufficient Conditions for Rational Choice under Majority Decision. JET 1: 178-202.

125 Sheffrin, S. M. 1980. Rational Expectations and Economic Models. ABS 23: 319-336.

126 Shepsle, K. A. 1979. Institutional Arrangements and Equilibrium in Multidimensional Voting Models. AJPS 23: 27-59.

127 -. 1989. Studying Institutions: Some Lessons from Rational Choice Approach. JTP 1: 131-148.

128 Shepsle, K. A.; Weingast, B. R. 1982. Institutionalized Majority Rule: A Social Choice Theory with Policy Implications. AER 72: 367-371.

129 -. 1984. Political Solutions to Market Problems. APSR 78: 417-434.

130 Slovik, P.; Fischhoff, B.; Lichtenstein, S. 1977. Behavioral Decision Theory. ARP 28: 1-39.

131 Smith, V. L. 1991. Rational Choice: The Contrast between Economics and Psychology. JPE 99: 877-897.

132 Sprumont, Y. 1995. Strategyproof Collective Choice in Economic and Political Environments. CANJE 28: 68-107.

133 Stewart, J. 1993. Rational Choice Theory, Public Policy and the Liberal State. PSCI 26: 317-330.

134 Stigler, G. J. 1972. Economic Competition and Political Competition. PC 13: 91-106.

135 Taylor, C. L. 1980. Formal Theory in Social Science. Inquiry 23: 139-144.

136 -. 1984. Social Choice Theory and the World in Which We Live. CJE 8: 189-196.

137 Taylor, M. 1968. Graph Theoretical Approaches to the Theory of Social Choice. PC 4: 35-48.

138 -. 1971. Mathematical Political Theory. BJPS 1: 339-382.

139 Tversky, A.; Kahneman, D. 1981. Framing of Decisions and the Psychology of Choice. Science 221: 453-458.

140 Von Briesen Raz, J. 1983. Probability Matching Behavior, Association and Rational Choice. BS 28: 35-52.

141 Ward, H. 1993. Game Theory and the Politics of the Global Commons. JCR 37: 203-235.

142 Weale, A. 1984. Social Choice vs. Populism? Riker's Political Theory. BJPS 14: 369-385.

143 Williamson, O. E.; Sargent, T. J. 1967. Social Choice: Probabilistic Approach. EJ 77: 797-813.

144 Wilson, R. B. 1972. Social Choice without the Pareto Principle. JET 5: 478-486.

145 Witt, U. 1992. The Endogenous Public Choice Theorist. PC 73: 117-134.

146 Wolf, C. 1979. A Theory of Non-Market Failures. PI 55: 114-133.

147 Wu, S. Z. 1983. Application of Pansystems Methodology to Economics. SE 3: 53-58; 4: 47-52, 117-124

148 Wu, S. Z.; Wu, X. M. 1985. Pansystems Investigation of Social Choice Problems. SE 5: 127-136.

149 Yilmaz, M. R. 1978. Multiattribute Utility Theory. TAD 9: 317-348.

150 Zechman, M. J. 1979. Dynamic Models of Voter's Decision Calculus: Incorporating Retrospective Considerations into Rational Choice Models of Individual Voting Behavior. PC 34: 297-315.

Coalitions

151 American Behavioral Scientist. 1975. Papers on Coalitions and Time. ABS 18 (4).

152 Austen-Smith, D. 1986. Legislative Coalitions and Electoral Equilibrium. PC 50: 185-220.

153 Austen-Smith, D.; Banks, J. S. 1988. Elections, Coalitions and Legislative Outcomes. APSR 82: 405-422.

154 Baker, P. M. 1981. Social Coalitions. ABS 24: 633-648.

155 Baron, D. P. 1989. A Noncooperative Theory of Legislative Coalitions. AJPS 33: 1048-1084.

156 -. 1991. Spatial Bargaining Theory of Government Formation. APSR 85: 137-164.

157 Baron, D. P.; Ferejohn, J. A. 1989. Bargaining in Legislatures. APSR 83: 1181-1206.

158 Biswas, T. 1994. Efficiency and Consistency in Group Decisions. PC 80: 23-34.

159 Brams, S. J.; Fishburn, P. C. 1995. When Is Size a Liability? Bargaining Power in Minimal Winning Coalitions. JTP 7: 301-316.

160 Browne, E. C. 1971. Coalition Formation in the European Context. CPS 3: 391-412.

161 Browne, E.C.; Feste, K.A. 1975. Qualitative Dimensions of Coalition Payoffs. ABS 18: 530-556.

162 Browne, E. C.; Franklin, M. N. 1973. Aspects of Coalition Payoffs. APSR 67: 453-469.

163 -. 1986. New Directions in Coalition Research. LSQ 11: 469-484.

164 Browne, E. C.; Rice, P. 1979. A Bargaining Theory of Coalition Formation. BJPS 9: 67-88.

165 Budge, I.; Herman, V. 1978. Coalitions and Government Formation. BJPS 8: 459-478.

166 Budge, I.; Laver, M. 1993. Policy Basis of Government Coalitions. BJPS 23: 499-520.

167 Chertkoff, J. M. 1975. Sequential Effects of Coalition Formation. ABS 18: 451-471.

168 Collie, M. P. 1988. Rise of Coalition Politics: Voting in the US House. LSQ 13: 321-342.

169 Colomer, J. M.; Martinez, F. 1995. Paradox of Coalition Trading. JTP 7: 41-64.

170 Daalder, H. 1986. Changing Procedures and Changing Strategies in Dutch Coalition Building. LSQ 11: 507-531.

171 Doron, G.; Sherman, M. 1995. Decision-Making Exposition of Coalition Politics: The Framer's Perspective of Size. JTP 7: 317-334.

172 Ferejohn, J. A. 1977. Decisive Coalitions in the Theory of Social Choice. JET 15: 301-306.

173 Foray, D. 1994. Users, Standards and the Economics of Coalitions and Committees. Information Economics and Policy 6: 269-293.

174 Franklin, M. N.; Mackie, T. T. 1984. Importance of Size and Ideology for Formation of Governing Coalitions. AJPS 28: 671-692.

175 Hammond, T. H.; Fraser, J. M. 1983. Baselines for Evaluating Explanations of Coalition Behavior in Congress. JOP 45: 635-674.

176 Hinckley, B. 1973. Coalitions in Congress: Size in a Series of Games. APQ 1: 339-360.

177 -. 1975. The Initially Strongest Player: Coalition Games and Presidential Nominations. ABS 18: 497-512.

178 Horowitz, J. K.; Just, R. E. 1995. Political Coalition Breaking and Sustainability of Policy Reform. JDE 47: 271-286.

179 Jenkins-Smith, H.C.; St. Clair, G. K.; Woods, B. 1991. Change in Policy Subsystems: Coalition Stability and Defection. AJPS 35: 851-880.

180 Kantor, S. E. 1995. Political Economy of Coalition Formation. EEH 32: 82-108.

181 Komorita, S. S. 1978. Evaluating Coalition Theories: Some Indices. JCR 22: 691-706.

182 Laver, M.; Shepsle, K. A. 1990. Government Coalitions and Interparty Politics. BJPS 20: 489-508.

183 Lieberman, B. 1975. Coalitions and Conflict Resolution. ABS 18: 557-581.

184 Maor, M. 1995. Inter-Party Determinants of Coalition Bargaining. JTP 7: 65-92.

185 Miller, A. H.; Wlezien, C.; Hildreth, A. 1991. A Reference Group Theory of Partisan Coalitions. JOP 53: 1134-1149.

186 Miller, C. E. 1979. Probabilistic Theories of Coalition Formation in Groups. BS 24: 259-268.

187 Mintz, A. 1995. The Noncompensatory Principle of Coalition Formation. JTP 7: 335-350.

188 Mo, J. 1994. Logic of Two-Level Games with Endogenous Domestic Coalitions. JCR 38: 402-422.

189 Murnighan, J. K. 1982. Evaluating Theoretical Predictions in the Social Sciences: Coalition Theories and Other Models. BS 27: 125-130.

190 Ordeshook, P. C.; Winer, M. D. 1980. Coalitions and Spatial Policy Outcomes. AJPS 24: 730-752.

191 Peleg, B. 1980. Theory of Coalition Formation in Committees. JMATHE 7: 115-134.

192 Poole, K. T.; Rosenthal, H. 1987. Congressional Coalition Patterns: Spatial Model. LSQ 12: 55-76

193 Reisinger, W. W. 1986. Assumptions in Theories of Coalition Performance. LSQ 11: 551-564.

194 Schlesinger, M. 1989. Legislative Governing Coalitions in Parliamentary Democracies: French Third Republic. CPS 22: 33-65.

195 Schofield, N. J. 1995. Coalition Politics: A Formal Model and Analysis. JTP 7: 245-282.

196 Taylor, M.; Laver, M. 1973. Government Coalitions in Western Europe. EJPR 1: 205-248.

197 Uslaner, E. M. 1975. A Contextual Model of Coalition Formation in Congress: Dimensions of Party and Political Time. ABS 18: 513-529.

198 Wood, S.; McLean, I. 1995. Recent Work in Game Theory and Coalition Theory. POLST 43: 703-717.

215 Kimber, R. 1981. Collective Action and the Fallacy of the Liberal Fallacy. WP 33: 178-196.

216 Laver, M. 1980. Political Solutions to the Collective Action Problem. POLST 28: 195-209.

217 Lipford, J. W. 1995. Group Size and Free-Rider Hypothesis: Churches. PC 83: 291-304.

218 Lott, J. R.; Davis, M. L. 1992. Review of the Political Shirking Literature. PC 74: 461-484.

219 Marwell, G.; Ames, R. E. 1980. Provision of Public Goods: Provision Points, Stakes, Experience and Free Rider Problem. AJS 85: 926-937.

220 -. 1981. Experiments on Provision of Public Goods. JPUBE 15: 295-310.

221 Miller, B. 1992. Collective Action and Rational Choice: Place, Community and Limits to Individual Self-Interest. EG 68: 22-42.

222 Miller, J. H.; Andreoni, J. 1991. Can Evolutionary Dynamics Explain Free Riding? EL 36: 9-15.

223 Moore, W. H. 1995. Rational Rebels: Overcoming the Free-Rider Problem. PRQ 48: 417-454.

224 Oliver, P. E.; Marwell, G. 1988. The Paradox of Group Size in Collective Action: A Theory of Critical Mass. ASR 53: 1-8.

225 Oliver, P. E.; Marwell, G.; Teixeira, R. 1985. A Theory of Critical Mass: Interdependence, Group Heterogeneity and the Production of Collective Action. AJS 91: 522-556.

226 Robertson, P. J.; Tang, S. Y. 1995. Role of Commitment in Collective Action. PAR 55: 67-80.

227 Schofield, N.J. 1975. Game Theoretic Analysis of Olson's Collective Action. JCR 19: 441-461.

228 Torsvik, G. 1994. When Groups Contribute to a Public Good: Importance of Institutional Framework for Collective Decisions. PC 80: 41-54.

229 Walker, H. A.; Togers, L.; Zelditch, M. 1988. Legitimacy and Collective Action. SF 67: 216-228

Collective Action

199 Andreoni, J.; McGuire, M. C. 1993. Identifying Free Riders: Algorithm for Determining Who Will Contribute to a Public Good. JPUBE 51: 447-454.

200 Arneson, R. J. 1982. Principle of Fairness and Free Rider Problems. Ethics 92: 616-633.

201 Becker, E.; Lindsay, C. M. 1994. Does the Government Free Ride? JOLE 37: 277-296.

202 Brace, P. 1988. Political Economy of Collective Action: The American States. Polity 20: 648-664.

203 Cerny, P. G. 1995. Globalization and Changing Logic of Collective Action. IO 49: 595-626.

204 Elster, J. 1985. Weakness of Will and Free Rider Problem. EAPHIL 1: 231-265

205 Goetze, D.; Galderisi, P. 1989. Explaining Collective Action. PC 62: 25-40.

206 Green, J., et al. 1976. Partial Equilibrium Approach to Free Rider. JPUBE 6: 375-394.

207 Gross, M. L. 1994. Jewish Rescue in Holland and France during the Second World War: Moral Cognition and Collective Action. SF 73: 463-496.

208 Hampton, J. 1987. Free-Rider Problems in Production of Collective Goods. EAPHIL 3: 245-273.

209 Huberman, B. A.; Glance, N. S. 1995. Dynamics of Collective Action. CE 8: 27-46.

210 Iannaccone, L. R. 1992. Reducing Free Riding in Collectives. JPE 100: 271-291.

211 Jankowski, R.; Brown, C. 1995. Political Success, Government Subsidization and Group Free Rider Problem. SSQ 76: 853-862.

212 Jones, P. R.; Cullis, J. G. 1993. Public Choice and Public Policy: Vulnerability of Economic Advice to Interpretation. PC 75: 63-78.

213 Journal of Theoretical Politics. 1992. Papers on Institutions and Common Resources. JTP 4 (3).

214 Kau, J. B.; Rubin, P. H. 1993. Ideology, Voting and Shirking. PC 76: 151-174.

Electoral Systems

230 Adams, J. D.; Kenny, L. W. 1986. Optimal Tenure of Elected Public Officials. JOLE 29: 303-328.

231 Amacher, R. C.; Boyes, W. J. 1978. Cycles in Senatorial Voting Behavior: Implications for the Optimal Frequency of Elections. PC 33: 5-14.

232 Amar, A. R. 1984. Choosing Representatives by Lottery Voting. YLJ 93: 1283-1308.

233 Ames, B. 1995. Strategy under Open-List Proportional Representation. AJPS 39: 406-433.

234 Bandelt, H. J.; Labbe, M. 1986. How Bad Can a Voting System Be? SCAW 3: 125-145.

235 Banzhaf, J. F. 1965. Weighted Voting Doesn't Work. Rutgers Law Review 19: 317-343.

236 -. 1968. Mathematical Analysis of the Electoral College. Villanova Law Review 14: 304-322.

237 -. 1968. Mathematical Analysis of Voting Power and Effective Representation. George Washington Law Review 36: 808-823.

238 -. 1976. Multimember Electoral Districts: Do They Violate One Man, One Vote YLJ 75: 1309-1388

239 Barrett, C. R.; Pattanaik, P. K. 1987. Aggregation of Probability Judgements. Econometrica 55: 1237-1241.

240 Bartholdi, J. J.; Tovey, C. A.; Trick, M. A. 1989. Voting Schemes for Which It Can Be Difficult to Tell Who Won. SCAW 6: 157-165.

241 Bawn, K. 1993. Logic of Institutional Preferences: German Electoral Law as a Social Choice Outcome. AJPS 37: 965-989.

242 Bensel, R. F.; Sanders, E. 1979. Effect of Electoral Rules on Voting Behavior: Electoral College and Shift Voting. PC 34: 609-638.

243 Blais, A. 1991. Debate over Electoral Systems. IPSR 12: 239-260.

244 Bordley, R. F. 1983. Pragmatic Method for Evaluating Election Schemes through Simulation. APSR 77: 123-141.

245 Brams, S. J.; Fishburn, P. C. 1978. Approval Voting. APSR 72: 831-847.

246 -. 1984. Proportional Representation in Variable-Size Legislatures. SCAW 1: 211-229.

247 -. 1988. Does Approval Voting Elect the Lowest Common Denominator? PS 21: 277-284.

248 Brandt, K. 1969. Voting Problems in Group Decisions. German Economic Review 7: 273-294.

249 Breton, A.; Galeotti, G. 1985. Is Proportional Representation Always the Best Electoral Rule? PF 40: 1-16.

250 Brischetto, R. 1995. Cumulative Voting as Alternative to Districting. NCR 84 (4): 347-354.

251 Budziszewski, J. 1986. A New Interpretation of Farquharson's Problem. PC 51: 129-140.

252 Bullock, C. S.; Gaddie, R. K. 1993. Changing from Multimember to Single-Member Districts: Partisan, Racial and Gender Consequences. SALGR 25: 155-163.

253 Campbell, D. E. 1977. Computational Criteria for Voting Systems. BJPS 7: 85-98.

254 Chamberlin, J. R.; Featherston, F. 1985. Selecting a Voting System. JOP 48: 347-369.

255 Collins, W. P. 1980. Political Behavior under the Unit Rule. APQ 8: 362-369.

256 Cox, G. W. 1987. Electoral Equilibrium under Alternative Voting Institutions. AJPS 31: 82-108.

257 -. 1990. Centripetal and Centrifugal Incentives in Electoral Systems. AJPS 34: 903-935.

258 -. 1994. Strategic Voting Equilibria under Single Nontransferable Vote. APSR 88: 608-621.

259 Cullis, J. G.; Jones, P. R.; Morrissey, O. 1991. Public Choice Perspectives on the Poll Tax. EJ 101: 600-614.

260 Curtice, J.; Steed, M. 1982. Electoral Choice and Production of Government: Changing Operation of Electoral System in the UK. BJPS 12: 249-298.

261 De Maio, G.; Muzzio, D. 1981. The 1980 Election and Approval Voting. PSQ 9: 341-363.

262 De Maio, G.; Muzzio, D.; Sharrard, G. 1983. Approval Voting. APQ 11: 365-174.

263 Dunleavy, P.; Margetts, H. 1995. Understanding the Dynamics of Electoral Reform. IPSR 16: 9-30.

264 Dyer, J. S.; Miles, R. E. 1976. Application of Collective Choice Theory to Selection of Trajectories for the Mariner / Saturn Project. Operations Research 24: 220-244.

265 Dyer, J. S.; Sarin, R. K. 1979. Group Preference Aggregation Rules Based on Strengths of Preference. MS 25: 822-832.

266 Estlund, D., et al. 1989. Democratic Theory and Public Interest: Condorcet and Rousseau Revisited. APSR 83: 1317-1342.

267 European Journal of Political Research. 1985. Papers on Electoral Systems. EJPR 13 (4).

268 Fain, J. R.; Dworkin, J. B. 1991. Voting Rules and Election Outcomes: When Does the True Majority Win? JLR 12: 247-260.

269 Felsenthal, D. S.; Machover, M. 1992. Should Condorcet's Voting Procedure Be Implemented? BS 37: 250-274.

270 -. 1995. Who Ought to Be Elected and Who Is Actually Elected? Empirical Investigation under Three Procedures. ES 14: 143-170.

271 Felsenthal, D. S.; Maoz, Z. 1988. A Comparative Analysis of Sincere and Sophisticated Voting under Plurality and Approval Procedures. BS 33: 116-130.

272 Felsenthal, D. S.; Maoz, Z.; Rapoport, A. 1986. Comparing Voting Systems in Elections: Approval-Plurality vs Selection-Plurality. SB 1: 41-53.

273 -. 1993. Evaluation of Six Voting Procedures: Do They Really Make Any Difference? BJPS 23: 1-28.

274 Fishburn, P. C. 1974. Simple Voting Systems and Majority Rule. BS 19: 166-176.

275 -. 1974. Social Choice Functions. SIAM Review 16: 63-90.

276 -. 1977. Models of Individual Preference and Choice. Synthese 36: 285-395.

277 -. 1983. Dimensions of Election Procedures: Analyses and Comparisons. TAD 15: 371-397.

278 Fishburn, P. C.; Brams, S. J. 1981. Approval Voting, Condorcet's Principle and Runoff Elections. PC 36: 89-114.

279 Fishburn, P. C.; Gehrlein, W. V. 1976. Analysis of Simple Two-Stage Voting Systems. BS 21: 1-12.

280 Gelman, A.; King, F. 1994. Enhancing Democracy through Redistricting. APSR 88: 541-559.

281 Gibbard, A. F. 1977. Manipulation of Voting Schemes that Mix Voting with Chance. Econometrica 45: 665-681.

282 Gillespie, C. C. 1972. Probability and Politics: Laplace, Condorcet and Turgot. PAPSC 116: 1-20.

283 Gillett, R. 1981. Asyptotic Likelihood of Agreement between Plurality and Condorcet Outcomes. BS 25: 23-88.

284 Gilligan, T. W.; Krehbiel, K. 1988. Complex Rules and Congressional Outcomes: Event Study of Energy Tax Legislation. JOP 50: 625-654.

285 Gilmour, J. B.; Rothstein, P. 1994. Term Limitation in Dynamic Model of Partisan Balance. AJPS 38: 770-796.

286 Goldburg, C. B. 1994. Accuracy of Game Theory Predictions for Political Behavior: Cumulative Voting in Illinois. JOP 56: 885-900.

287 Grofman, B. 1983. Measures of Bias and Proportionality in Seats-Votes Relationships. PM 9: 295-328.

288 Gryski, G. S.; Reed, B.; Elliott, E. 1990. Votes-Seats Relationship in State Legislative Elections. APQ 18: 141-157.

289 Hansen, P.; Thisse, J. F. 1981. Outcomes of Voting and Planning: Condorcet, Weber and Rawls. JPUBE 16: 1-15.

290 Hansen, S.; Palfrey, T. R.; Rosenthal, H. 1987. The Downsian Model of Electoral Participation: Formal Theory and Empirical Analysis of Constituency Size Effect. PC 52: 15-344.

291 Hill, I. D. 1988. Some Aspects of Elections: To Fill One Seat or Many. JRSS 151: 243-275.

292 International Political Science Review. 1995. Papers on Electoral Reform. IPSR 16 (1).

293 Jackman, S.; Vella, F. 1992. Electoral Redistricting and Endogenous Partisan Control. PANAL 3: 155-171.

294 Johnston, R. J. 1995. Conflict over Qualified Majority Voting in the European Union Council of Ministers: An Analysis of UK Negotiating Stance Using Power Indices. BJPS 25: 245-253.

295 Jones, M. P. 1995. Guide to the Electoral Systems of the Americas. ES 14: 5-22.

296 Joslyn, R. A. 1976. Impact of Decision Rules in Multicandidate Campaigns: 1972 Democratic Presidential Nomination. PC 25: 1-17.

297 Kiewiet, D. R. 1979. Approval Voting: The 1968 Election. Polity 12: 170-181.

298 King, G. 1989. Representation through Legislative Redistricting: A Stochastic Model. AJPS 33: 787-824.

299 King, G.; Browning, R. X. 1987. Democratic Representation and Partisan Bias in Congressional Elections. APSR 81: 1251-1273.

300 King, G.; Gelman, A. 1994. A Unified Method of Evaluating Electoral Systems and Redistricting Plans. AJPS 38: 514-554.

301 King, R. R. 1994. Experimental Investigation of Super Majority Voting Rules. JEBAO 25: 197-217.

302 Koford, K. J. 1982. Optimal Voting Rules under Uncertainty. PC 38: 149-165.

303 Landa, J. T. 1986. Political Economy of Swarming in Honeybees: Voting-with-the-Wings, Decision-Making Costs and Unanimity Rule. PC 51: 25-38.

304 Leech, D. 1992. Distribution of A Priori Voting Power: British Labour Party Conference and Electoral College. EJPR 21: 245-266.

305 Levenglick, A. 1975. Fair and Reasonable Election Systems. BS 20: 34-46.
306 Levin, J.; Nalebuff, B. 1995. An Introduction to Vote-Counting Schemes. JEP 9: 3-26.
307 Lijphart, A. 1990. Political Consequences of Electoral Laws. APSR 84: 481-496.
308 McKelvey, R. D.; Ordeshook, P. C. 1985. Sequential Elections with Limited Information. AJPS 29: 480-512.
309 McLean, I. 1988. Electoral Reform and Social Choice Theory. PQ 59: 63-71.
310 -. 1990. The Borda and Condorcet Principles: Three Medieval Applications. SCAW 7: 149-170.
311 Miller, N. R. 1977. Graph-Theoretical Approaches to the Study of Voting. AJPS 21: 769-803.
312 -. 1980. A New Solution Set for Tournaments and Majority Voting: Graph Theoretical Approaches to the Theory of Voting. AJPS 24: 68-96.
313 Moulin, H. 1982. Voting with Proportional Veto Power. Econometrica 50: 145-162.
314 Myerson, R. B. 1993. Incentives to Cultivate Favored Minorities under Alternative Electoral Systems. APSR 87: 856-869.
315 Niemi, R. G. 1983. An Exegesis of Farquharson's Theory of Voting. PC 40: 323-328.
316 Niemi, R. G.; Riker, W. H. 1976. The Choice of Voting Systems. SA 234: 21-27.
317 Niemi, R. G.; Winsky, L. R. 1992. Persistence of Partisan Redistricting Effects in Congressional Elections. JOP 54: 565-572.
318 Nitzan, S. 1981. Measures of Closeness to Unanimity and Their Implications. TAD 13: 129-138.
319 Nurmi, H. 1981. Properties of Voting Systems. SPS 4: 19-32.
320 -. 1983. Voting Procedures. BJPS 13: 181-208.
321 -. 1986. Mathematical Models of Elections and Their Relevance for Institutional Design. ES 5: 167-181.
322 -. 1992. Voting System Simulations. PC 73: 459-487.
323 Pattanaik, P. K. 1973. The Stability of Sincere Voting Situations. JET 6: 558-574.
324 Pedersen, W. 1993. The Majority Fallacy Reconsidered. AS 36: 343-356.
325 Policy Studies Journal. 1974. Papers on Electoral Reform. PSJ 2 (4).
326 -. 1980. Papers on Reapportionment. PSJ 9 (6).
327 Rapoport, A.; Felsenthal, D. S.; Maoz, Z. 1988. Seat Allocation in Proportional Representation Systems. TAD 24: 11-33.
328 Reader, S. A. 1994. Choosing a Population Basis to form Political Districts. HJLPP 17: 521-566.
329 Revista de Estudios Politicos. 1983. Papers on Spain's Electoral System. Vol 1983 (34).
330 Rosenthal, H. 1974. Game Theoretic Models of Bloc Voting under Proportional Representation. PC 18: 1-23.
331 Rush, M. E. 1992. Variability of Partisanship and Turnout: Gerrymandering Analysis and Representation Theory. APQ 20: 99-122.
332 Rusk, J. G. 1970. The Effect of the Australian Ballot Reform on Split Ticket Voting. APSR 64: 1220-1238.
333 Saari, D. G. 1990. The Borda Dictionary. SCAW 7: 279-317.
334 Segal, U.; Spivak, A. 1986. On the Single Membership Constituency and the Law of Large Numbers. PC 49: 183-190.
335 Sen, A. K. 1995. How to Judge Voting Schemes. JEP 9: 91-98.
336 Shamir, M. 1985. Changes in Electoral Systems as Interventions: Duverger's Hypothesis. EJPR 13: 1-10.
337 Steiner, H. G. 1986. Nonmeasurable Voting Bodies. International Journal of Mathematical Education in Science and Technology 17: 367-376.
338 Sunding, D. 1995. Social Choice by Majority Rule with Rational Participation. SCAW 12: 3-12.
339 Taagepera, R. 1973. Seats and Votes: Generalization of Cube Law of Elections. SSR 2: 257-276.
340 -. 1986. Reformulating the Cube Law for Proportional Representation Elections. APSR 80: 489-504.
341 Taylor, P. J. 1973. Implications of the Spatial Organization of Elections. TIBG 60: 121-136.
342 Texas Law Review. 1993. Papers on Regulating the Electoral Process. TLR 1993 (7).
343 Tufte, E. R. 1973. Relationship between Seats and Votes in Two Party Systems. APSR 67: 540-554.
344 Weber, R. J. 1995. Approval Voting. JEP 9: 39-49.
345 Wildgen, J. K.; Engstrom, R. L. 1980. Spatial Distribution of Partisan Support for Seats-Votes Relationship. LSQ 5: 423-436.
346 Widgren, M. 1994. Voting Power in the European Community Decision Making and Consequences of Two Different Enlargements. EER 38: 1153-1170.
347 Williams, K. C. 1994. Sequential Elections and Retrospective Voting. JTP 6: 239-255.
348 Williams, K. C., et al. 1976. Voter Decision Making in a Primary Election: Three Models of Choice. AJPS 20: 37-49.
349 Young, P. 1995. Optimal Voting Rules. JEP 9: 51-64.

Fuzzy Logic

350 Barrett, C. R.; Pattanaik, P. K. 1989. Fuzzy Sets, Preference and Choice. BER 41: 229-253.
351 Barrett, C. R.; Pattanaik, P. K.; Salles, M. 1986. The Structure of Fuzzy Social Welfare Functions. FUZZY 19: 1-10.
352 Biacino, L.; Simonelli, M. R. 1995. Fuzzy Common Knowledge. JME 24: 73-82.
353 Cioffi-Revilla, C. A. 1981. Fuzzy Sets and Models of International Relations. AJPS 25: 129-159.
354 Dale, A. I. 1980. Probability, Vague Statements and Fuzzy Sets. POS 46: 38-55.
355 Dimitrov, V. 1983. Group Choice under Fuzzy Information. FUZZY 9: 25-39.
356 Dutta, B. 1987. Fuzzy Preferences and Social Choice. MSS 13: 215-229.
357 Fedrizzi, M. 1986. Group Decisions and Consensus: Fuzzy Set Theory. RISEC 9: 53-61.
358 Fedrizzi, M.; Ostaiewicz, W. 1985. Group Decisions: Fuzzy Set Theory. RISEC 8: 21-37.
359 Harris, T. R.; Stoddard, S. W.; Bezdek, J. C. 1993. Application of Fuzzy-Set Clustering for Regional Typologies. GAC 24: 155-165.
360 Kim, J. B. 1983. Fuzzy Rational Choice Functions. FUZZY 10: 37-43.
361 Montero de Juan, J. F. 1987. Arrow's Theorem under Fuzzy Rationality. BS 32: 267-273.
362 -. 1987. Social Welfare Functions in a Fuzzy Environment. Kybernetes 16: 241-245.
363 Nijkamp, P. (13: 1979). Conflict Patterns and Compromise Solutions in Fuzzy Choice Theory. JPR 4: 67-90.
364 Nurmi, H. 1981. A Fuzzy Solution to a Majority Voting Game. FUZZY 5: 187-198.
365 -. 1981. Approaches to Collective Decision Making with Fuzzy Preference Relations. FUZZY 6: 249-259.
366 -. 1984. Probabilistic Voting: Fuzzy Interpretation and Extension. PM 10: 81-96.
367 Ok, E. A. 1995. Fuzzy Measurement of Income Inequality. SCAW 12: 111-136.
368 Sanjian, G. S. 1988. Fuzzy Set Theory and US Arms Transfers. AJPS 32: 1018-1046.
369 -. 1992. A Fuzzy Set Model of NATO Decision Making: Short Range Nuclear Forces in Europe. JPR 29: 271-286.

370 -. 1994. Competition, Multiple Objectives and Imprecision: Arms Trade Decision-Making as Fuzzy Multi-Criteria Game. JTP 6: 75-104.

371 -. 1995. A Fuzzy Systems Model of Arms Transfer Outcomes. CMAPS 14: 1-24.

372 Seitz, S. T. 1985. Fuzzy Modeling and Conflict Analysis. CMAPS 9: 53-67.

373 Spillman, B.; Spillman, R.; Bezdek, J. C. 1979. Coalition Formation in Decision Making Groups: Fuzzy Mathematics. Kybernetes 8: 203-211.

374 Tanino, T. 1984. Fuzzy Preference Orderings in Group Decision Making. FUZZY 12: 117-131.

375 Treadwell, W. A. 1995. The Fuzzy Set Theory Movement in the Social Sciences. PAR 55: 91-98.

376 Wayne, G. H. 1991. Possibility Theory and Fuzzy Sets: Energy and Environmental Policy Analysis. Journal of Energy and Development 17: 47-64.

377 Zahariev, S. 1987. Group Choice with Fuzzy Preference Relations. FUZZY 22: 203-213.

Game Theory and Simulations

378 Anselin, L. 1983. A Simulation Framework for Dynamics in Policy Space. CMAPS 7: 25-38.

379 Asilis, C. M. 1995. Equivalence of Time Consistency and Subgame Perfection in Stochastic Games. EER 39: 245-251.

380 Banks, J. S. 1989. Equilibrium Outcomes in Two Stage Amendment Procedures. AJPS 33: 25-43.

381 Banks, J. S.; Sobel, J. 1987. Equilibrium Selection in Signaling Games. Econometrica 55: 647-662.

382 Basu, K. 1987. Modeling Finitely Repeated Games with Uncertain Termination. EL 23: 147-151.

383 Battigalli, P. 1994. Structural Consistency and Strategic Independence in Extensive Games. RE 48: 347-376.

384 Bennet, E.; Zame, W. R. 1988. Bargaining in Cooperative Games. IJGT 17: 279-300.

385 Bigelow, B. E. 1978. Simulations in History. SAG 9: 209-220.

386 Bloomfield, R. 1994. Learning a Mixed Strategy Equilibrium in Laboratory. JEBAO 25: 411-436.

387 Brams, S. J. 1994. Game Theory and Literature. 7GAEB 6: 114-129.

388 Brams, S. J.; Doherty, A. E. 1993. Intransigence in Negotiations. JCR 37: 692-708.

389 Brams, S. J.; Hessel, M. P. 1984. Threat Power in Sequential Games. ISQ 28: 23-44.

390 Brams, S. J.; Wittman, D. 1981. Nonmyopic Equilibria in 2x2 Games. CMAPS 6: 39-62.

391 Brams, S. J.; Zagare, F. C. 1977. Deception in Simple Voting Games. SSR 6: 257-272.

392 Brandts, J.; MacLeod, W. B. 1995. Equilibrium Selection in Experimental Games with Recommended Play. GAEB 11: 36-63.

393 Butler, R. J.; Markulis, P. M.; Strang, D. R. 1988. Methods and Focus of Research on Simulation Gaming. SAG 19: 3-26.

394 Carlsen, F.; Haugen, K. 1994. Markov Perfect Equilibrium in Multi-Period Games between Sponsor and Bureau. PC 79: 257-280.

395 Cho, I. K.; Kreps, D. M. 1987. Signaling Games and Stable Equilibria. QJE 179-222.

396 Coleman, J. S. 1989. Simulation Games and Development of Social Theory. SAG 20: 144-164.

397 Cramton, P. 1984. Bargaining with Incomplete Information. RES 51: 579-593.

398 Crawford, V. P. 1995. Adaptive Dynamics in Coordination Games. Econometrica 63: 103-143.

399 Cripps, M. W.; Thomas, J. P. 1995. Reputation and Commitment in Two-Person Repeated Games without Discounting. Econometrica 63: 1401-1419.

400 Cunningham, J. B. 1984. Assumptions Underlying the Use of Different Types of Simulations. SAG 15: 213-234.

401 Demarzo, P. M. 1992. Coalitions, Leadership and Social Norms: The Power of Suggestion in Games. GAEB 4: 72-100.

402 Dittmer, L. 1981. Strategic Triangle: An Elementary Game Theoretical Analysis. WP 33: 485-515.

403 Dutter, L. E. 1981. Voter Preferences, Simple Electoral Games and Equilibria in Two-Candidate Contests. PC 37: 403-423.

404 Eavey, C. L.; Miller, G. J. 1984. Fairness in Majority Rule Games with Core. AJPS 28: 570-586.

405 Frohlich, N. 1992. An Impartial Reasoning Solution to the Prisoner's Dilemma. PC 74: 447-460.

406 Fudenberg, D.; Kreps, D. M. 1995. Learning in Extensive-Forms Games. GAEB 8: 20-55.

407 Fudenberg, D.; Levine, D. I. 1986. Limit Games and Limit Equilibria. JET 38: 261-279.

408 Fudenberg, D.; Maskin, E. S. 1986. Folk Theorem in Repeated Games. Econometrica 54: 533-554.

409 Fudenberg, D.; Tirole, J. 1983. Sequential Bargaining with Incomplete Information. RES 50: 221-247.

410 Gale, D. 1995. Dynamic Coordination Games. ET 5: 1-18.

411 Gale, J.; Binmore, K.; Samuelson, L. 1995. Learning to Be Imperfect: Ultimate Game. GAEB 8: 56-90.

412 Guth, W. 1991. Game Theory's Basic Question: Who Is a Player? JTP 3: 403-436.

413 Hackathorn, D. D. 1988. Collective Sanctions and the Creation of Prisoner's Dilemma Norms. AJS 94: 535-562.

414 Harsanyi, J. C. 1967. Games with Incomplete Information Played by Bayesian Players. MS 14: 159-182, 320-334, 486-502.

415 -. 1995. Equilibrium Selection for Games with Competing Information. GAEB 8: 91-122.

416 History of Political Economy. 1992. Papers on History of Game Theory. HPE 24 (Special Issue).

417 Ichiishi, T. 1990. Comparative Cooperative Game Theory. IJGT 10: 139-152.

418 Johnson, N. R.; Feinberg, W. E. 1977. A Computer Simulation of the Emergence of Consensus in Crowds. ASR 42: 505-521.

419 Journal of Applied Econometrics. 1993. Papers on Economic Inference. JAE 8 (Supplement).

420 Journal of Economic Theory. 1992. Papers on Evolutionary Game Theory. JET 57 (2).

421 Kim, H. 1995. Strongly Stable Core in Weighted Voting Games. PC 84: 77-90.

422 Kirchsteiger, G. 1994. Role of Envy in Ultimatum Games. JEBAO 25: 373-389.

423 Klein, D. B.; O'Flaherty, B. 1993. Game-Theoretic Rendering of Promises and Threats. JEBAO 21: 295-314.

424 Kreps, D. M.; Wilson, R. B. 1982. Sequential Equilibria. Econometrica 50: 863-894.

425 Laing, J. D.; Slotznick, B. 1995. On Collective Goods, Private Wealth, and the Core Solution of Simple Games with Sidepayments. PC 84: 49-62.

426 Le Breton, M. 1987. The Core of Voting Games. SCAW 4: 295-305.

427 Le Breton, M.; Salles, M. 1987. Generic Emptiness of the Local Core of Voting Games. SCAW 4: 287-294.

428 -. 1990. Stability Set of Voting Games. IJGT 19: 111-127.

429 Liebrand, W. B. G. 1983. The Classification of Social Dilemma Games. SAG 14: 123-138.

430 Li, S. 1994. Dynamic Stability and Learning Processes in 2x2 Games. EL 46: 105-111.

431 Leik, R. K.; Meeker, B. F. 1995. Computer Simulation for Exploring Theories: Interpersonal Cooperation and Conflict. SP 38: 463-482.

432 Lipman, B. L.; Seppi, D. J. 1995. Robust Inference in Communication Games with Partial Provability. JET 66: 370-405.

433 McKelvey, R. D.; Ordeshook, P. C. 1981. Experiments on the Core. JCR 25: 709-724.

434 McKelvey, R. D.; Ordeshook, P. C.; Winer, M. D. 1978. Competitive Solution for N-Person Games without Transferable Utility. APSR 72: 599-615.

435 McLeod, J. 1989. Computer Simulation. BS 34: 1-15.

436 Miller, N. R. 1977. Social Preference and Game Theory: Dilemmas of a Paretian Liberal. PC 30: 23-28.

437 Mo, J. 1995. Domestic Institutions and International Bargaining: Agent Veto in Two-Level Games. APSR 89: 914-924.

438 Murnighan, J. K.; Roth, A. E. 1983. Expecting Continued Play in Prisoner's Dilemma Games. JCR 27: 279-300.

439 Ohrenstein, R. A. 1989. Game Theory in the Talmud. IJSE 16: 57-67.

440 Olcina, G.; Urbano, A. 1994. Introspection and Equilibrium Selection in 2x2 Matrix Games. IJGT 23: 183-206.

441 Orbis. 1984. Papers on Political Gaming. Vol 27 (4).

442 Oswalt, I. 1993. Current Applications, Trends and Organizations in Military Simulation and Gaming. SAG 24: 153-189.

443 Parks, C. D.; Hulbert, L. G. 1995. High and Lower Trusters' Responses to Fear in a Payoff Matrix. JCR 39: 718-730.

444 Peleg, B. 1978. Representations of Simple Games by Social Choice Functions. IJGT 7: 81-94.

445 Pettit, P. 1985. Prisoner's Dilemma and Social Theory: Overview of Issues. Politics 20: 1-11.

446 Plott, C. R. 1967. Equilibrium and Its Possibility under Majority Rule. AER 57: 787-806.

447 Pratt, L. K.; Uhl, N. P.; Little, E. R. 1980. Evaluation of Games as a Function of Personality Type. SAG 11: 336-346.

448 Radzik, T. 1991. Saddle Point Theorems. IJGT 20: 23-32.

449 Rapoport, A. 1992. Game Theory Defined: What It Is and Is Not. RAS 4: 74-82.

450 Rationality and Society. 1992. Papers on Game Theory in the Social Sciences. RAS 4 (2).

451 Remus, W. E. 1981. Experimental Designs for Analyzing Data on Games. SAG 12: 3-14.

452 Riker, W.H. 1992. Entry of Game Theory into Political Science. HPE 24 (Spec Issue): 207-233.

453 Ritzberger, K. 1994. Theory of Normal Form Games from the Differentiable Viewpoint. IJGT 23: 207-236.

454 Ritzberger, K.; Weinbull, J. W. 1995. Evolutionary Selection in Normal-Form Games. Econometrica 63: 1371-1399.

455 Roth, A. E.; Erev, I. 1995. Learning in Extensive Form Games. GAEB 8: 164-212.

456 Rubinstein, A. 1979. Equilibrium in Supergames with the Overtaking Criterion. JET 21: 1-9.

457 Schmidt, C. 1990. Game Theory and Economics. Revue d'Economie Politique 100: 589-618.

458 Schofield, N. J. 1978. Instability of Simple Dynamic Games. REI 45: 575-594.

459 -. 1979. Instability of Simple Dynamic Games. RES 45: 575-594.

460 -. 1980. The Bargaining Set in Voting Games. BS 25: 120-129.

461 -. 1982. Bargaining Set Theory and Stability in Coalition Games. MSS 3: 9-31.

462 Schotter, A.; Schwodiauer, G. 1980. Economics and the Theory of Games. JEL 18: 479-527.

463 Schuermann, A. C.; Hommertzheim, D. L. 1983. Using Simulation Models in Demonstrating Statistical Applications. SAG 14: 47-62.

464 Schwartz, T. 1981. The Universal Instability Theorem. PC 37: 487-502.

465 Selton, R. 1975. A Re-Examination of the Perfectness Concept for Equilibrium Points in Extensive Games. IJGT 4: 25-55.

466 Sened, I. 1995. Equilibria in Weighted Voting Games with Sidepayments. JTP 7: 283-300.

467 Shogren, J. F.; Baik, K. H. 1992. Favorites and Underdogs: Strategic Behavior in an Experimental Contest. PC 74: 191-205.

468 Sieg, G.; Schulz, C. 1995. Evolutionary Dynamics in the Voting Game. PC 85: 157-172.

469 Simon, L. K.; Stinchcombe, M. B. 1995. Equilibrium Refinement for Infinite Normal-Forms Games. Econometrica 63: 1421-1443.

470 Simulation and Games. 1971. Papers on Computer Simulation. SAG 2 (1).

471 -. 1977. Papers on Human Growth Games. SAG 8 (1).

472 -. 1984. Papers on Games and Play. SAG 15 (1).

473 -. 1987. Papers on Business Gaming. SAG 18 (2).

474 -. 1993. Papers on Military Simulation. SAG 24 (2-3).

475 Sociological Perspectives. 1995. Papers on Computer Simulations and Sociological Theory. SP 38 (4).

476 Starbuck, W. H. 1983. The Computer Simulation of Human Behavior. BS 28: 154-165.

477 Stinchcombe, A. L. 1980. Is the Prisoner's Dilemma All of Sociology? Inquiry 23: 187-192.

478 Sutton, J. R. 1986. Non-Cooperative Bargaining Theory. RES 53: 709-724.

479 Swistak, P. 1992. What Games? Why Equilibria? Which Equilibria? Three Problems with Game Theory. RAS 4: 103-116.

480 Thiagarajan, S.; Stolovitch, H. D. 1979. Frame Games. SAG 10: 287-314.

481 Thorngate, W.; Carroll, B. 1987. Why the Best Person Rarely Wins: Embarrassing Facts about Contests. SAG 18: 299-320.

482 Ulph, A. 1987. Recent Advances in Oligopoly Theory from a Game Theory Perspective. JES 1: 149-172.

483 Wagner, R. H. 1983. The Theory of Games and the Problem of International Cooperation. APSR 77: 330-346.

484 Wang, M.; Hipel, K. W.; Fraser, N. M. 1988. Modeling Misperceptions. BS 33: 207-223.

485 Wildavsky, A. 1992. Indispensable Framework or Just Another Ideology? Prisoners' Dilemma as an Antihierarchical Game. RAS 4: 8-23.

486 Williams, R. H. 1980. Attitude Change and Simulation Games. SAG 11: 177-196.

487 Yano, M. 1990. A Local Theory of Cooperative Games. IJGT 19: 301-324.

Impossibility Theorems

488 Black, D. 1969. Arrow's Impossibility Theorem. JOLE 12: 227-248.

489 Blair, D. H.; Pollack, R. A. 1979. Collective Rationality and Dictatorship: Scope of the Arrow Theorem. JET 21: 186-194.

490 Blau, J. 1966. Direct Proof of Arrow's Theorem. Econometrica 34: 491-499.

491 Ferejohn, J. A.; Grether, D. M. 1977. Some New Impossibility Theorems. PC 30: 35-42.

492 Friedland, E. I.; Cimbala, S. J. 1973. Significance of Arrow's Theorem. TAD 4: 50-64.

493 Frohock, F. M. 1980. Rationality, Morality and Impossibility Theorems. APSR 74: 373-384.

494 Hardin, R. 1980. Infinite Regress and Arrow's Theorem. Ethics 90: 383-391.

495 Harsanyi, J. C. 1979. Bayesian Decision Theory: Rule Utilitarianism and Arrow's Impossibility Theorem. TAD 11: 289-318.

496 Hayden, G. M. 1995. Some Implications of Arrow's Theorem for Voting Rights. SLR 47: 295-318.

497 Holt, C. A. 1986. Preference Reversals and the Independence Axiom. AER 76: 508-513.

498 Johansen, L. 1969. Relevance of Kenneth Arrow's General Possibility Theorem to Economic Planning. Economics of Planning 9: 5-41.

499 Kirman, A. P.; Sondermann, D. 1972. Arrow's Theorem, Many Agents and Invisible Dictators. JET 5: 267-277.

500 Le Breton, M.; Uriarte, J. R. 1990. Robustness of Impossibility Result in Topological Approach to Social Choice. SCAW 7: 131-140.

501 MacKay, A. F. 1980. Impossibility and Infinity. Ethics 90: 367-382.

502 Packel, E. W. 1980. Impossibility Results in the Axiomatic Theory of Intertemporal Choice. PC 35: 219-228.

503 Riley, J. M. 1982. Arrow's Paradox and Infinite-Regress Arguments. Ethics 92: 670-672.

504 Ritz, Z. 1983. Restricted Domains, Arrow Social Choice Functions, Noncorruptible and Nonmanipulable Social Choice Correspondence: Private Alternatives. MSS 4: 155-179.

505 -. 1983. Restricted Domains, Arrow Social Choice Functions and Noncorruptible and Nonmanipulable Social Choice Correspondence: Private and Public Alternatives. JET 35: 1-18.

506 Schofield, N. J. 1984. General Relevance of the Impossibility Theorem in Smooth Social Choice. TAD 16: 21-44.

507 Sonsino, D. 1995. Impossibility of Speculation Theorems with Noisy Information. GAEB 8: 406-423.

508 Tanguiane, A. S. 1994. Arrow's Paradox and the Mathematical Theory of Democracy. SCAW 11: 1-82.

509 Tullock, G. 1967. The General Irrelevance of the General Impossibility Theorem. QJE 81: 256-270.

510 Van Til, R. H. 1978. Arrow's Impossibility Theorem. De Economist 126: 84-115.

511 Wilson, R. B. 1972. The Game Theoretic Structure of Arrow's General Possibility Theorem. JET 5: 14-20.

Median Voter

512 Barthelemy, J. P.; Monjardet, B. 1981. Median Procedure in Cluster Analysis and Social Choice Theory. MSS 1: 235-267.

513 Baumgardner, J. R. 1993. Tests of Median Voter and Political Support Maximization Models: Federal / State Welfare Programs. PFQ 21: 48-83.

514 Boyne, G. A. 1987. Median Voters, Political Systems and Public Policies. PC 53: 201-220.

515 Comanor, W. S. 1976. Median Vote Rule and the Theory of Political Choice. JPUBE 5: 169-178.

516 Farnham, P. G. 1987. Form of Government and the Median Voter. SSQ 68: 569-582.

517 Hansson, I.; Stuart, C. 1984. Voting Competitions with Interested Politicians: Platforms Do Not Converge to Preferences of the Median Voter. PC 44: 431-442.

518 Hinich, M. J. 1977. Equilibrium in Spatial Voting: Median Voting Result Is an Artifact. JET 16: 208-219.

519 Holcombe, R. G. 1980. An Empirical Test of the Median Voter Model. EI 18: 260-274.

520 -. 1989. Median Voter Model in Public Choice Theory. PC 61: 115-126.

521 Inman, R. P. 1978. Testing Political Economy's as if Proposition: Is the Median Income Voter Decisive? PC 33: 45-66.

522 Mathis, E. J.; Zech, C. E. 1986. Examination of the Relevance of the Median Voter Model. AJEAS 45: 403-412.

523 -. 1989. Median Voter Model Fails an Empirical Test. AJEAS 48: 79-88.

524 Murdock, J. C.; Sandler, T.; Hansen, L. 1991. An Econometric Technique for Comparing Median Voter and Oligarchy Choice Models of Collective Action: NATO Alliance. REAS 73: 624-631.

525 Rice, T. W. 1985. An Examination of the Median Voter Hypothesis. WPQ 38: 211-223.

526 Romer, T.; Rosenthal, H. 1979. Elusive Median Voter. JPUBE 12: 143-170

527 Rowley, C. K. 1984. Relevance of Median Voter Theorem. ZS 140: 104-126.

528 Sjoquist, D. L. 1981. A Median Voter Analysis of Variations in Property Taxes among Local Governments. PC 36: 273-286.

529 Turnbull, G. K.; Djoundourian, S. S. 1994. The Median Voter Hypothesis: Evidence from General Purpose Local Governments. PC 81: 223-240.

530 Turnbull, G. K.; Mitias, P. M. 1995. Which Median Voter? SEJ 62: 183-191.

531 Yinger, J. 1981. Capitalization and the Median Voter. AER Proceedings 71: 99-103.

Paradoxes

532 Bar-Hillel, M.; Margalit, A. 1988. How Vicious Are Cycles of Intransitive Choice? TAD 24: 119-145.

533 Beahrs, J. O. 1992. Paradoxical Effects in Political Systems. PP 13: 755-769.

534 Bell, B. C. 1978. What Happens When Majority Rule Breaks Down. PC 33: 121-126.

535 Benson, B. L.; Greenhut, M. L.; Holcombe, R. G. 1987. Interest Groups and the Antitrust Paradox. CJ 6: 801-807.

536 Bernholz, P. 1976. Liberalism, Logrolling and Cyclical Group Preferences. Kyklos 29: 26-37.

537 Breyer, F.; Gardner, R. 1980. The Liberal Paradox, Game Equilibrium and Gibbard Optimum. PC 35: 469-481.

538 Browne, E. C.; James, P.; Miller, M. 1991. Simulation of Local Intransitivities in Simple Voting Game under Majority Rule. BS 36: 148-156.

539 Candeal-Haro, J. C.; Indurain-Eraso, E. 1994. Moebius Strip and a Social Choice Paradox. EL 45: 407-412.

540 Carson, R. 1987. Voting Paradox and Possibility of a Social Welfare Function. EEJ 13: 281-291.

541 Chichilnisky, G. Heal, G. 1983. Conditions for Resolution of the Social Choice Paradox. JET 31: 68-87.

542 Cohen, L. R. 1979. Cycle Sets in Multi-Dimensional Voting Models. JET 22: 1-22.

543 Cohen, L. R.; Matthews, S. 1980. Constrained Plott Equilibria, Directional Equilibria and Global Cycling Sets. RES 47: 975-976.

544 DeMeyer, F.; Plott, C. R. 1970. Probability of a Cyclical Majority. Econometrica 38: 345-354.

545 Dobra, J. L. 1983. Empirical Studies of Voting Paradoxes. PC 41: 241-250.

546 Dobra. J. L.; Tullock, G. 1981. Empirical Measures of Voting Paradoxes. PC 36: 193-194.

547 Douglas J. 1984. How Actual Governments Cope with Paradoxes of Social Choice. CP 17: 67-84.

548 Fischer. D.; Schotter, A. 1978. Inevitability of the Paradox of Redistribution in the Allocation of Voting Weights. PC 33: 49-67.

549 Fishburn, P. C. 1974. Paradoxes of Voting. APSR 68: 537-548.

550 -. 1982. Monotonicity Paradoxes in Elections. Discrete Applied Mathematics 4: 119-134.

551 Gigliotti, G. A. 1988. Conflict between Naive and Sophisticated Choice as a Form of Liberal Paradox. TAD 24: 35-42.

552 Hansson, S. O. 1988. Rights and the Liberal Paradox. SCAW 5: 287-302.

553 Hirschleifer, J. 1991. The Paradox of Power. EAP 3: 177-200.

554 Hoenack, S. A. 1983. On the Stability of Legislative Outcomes. PC 41: 251-260.

555 Fine, B. J.; Fine, K. 1974. Social Choice and Individual Ranking. RES 41: 302-322, 459-475.

556 Fine, K. 1973. Conditions for the Existence of Cycles. Econometrica 41: 888-899.

557 Fishburn, P. C.; Gehrlein, W. V. 1980. Social Homogeneity and Condorcet's Paradox. PC 35: 403-419.

558 Gehrlein, W. V. 1983. Condorcet's Paradox. TAD 15: 161-197.

559 Gehrlein, W. V.; Fishburn, P. C. 1976. Probability of the Paradox of Voting. JET 13: 14-25.

560 Jones, B.; et al. 1995. Condorcet Winners and the Paradox of Voting: Probability Calculations for Weak Preference Orders. APSR 89: 137-146.

561 Kadish, M. R. 1983. Practice and Paradox: Social Choice Theory. Ethics 93: 681-694.

562 Kelsen, D. 1985. Liberal Paradox: A Generalization. SCAW 1: 245-250.

563 Leamer, E. E. 1980. Leontief Paradox. JPE 88: 495-503.

564 McCulloch, A. M. 1983. Voting Paradoxes and Primary Politics. PSQ 13: 575-588.

565 McKelvey, R. D. 1976. Intransitivities in Multidimensional Voting Models and Implications for Agenda Control. JET 12: 472-482.

566 -. 1979. General Conditions for Global Intransitivities in Formal Voting Models. Econometrica 47: 1085-1112.

567 McLean, I. 1995. The Independence of Irrelevant Alternatives before Arrow. MSS 30: 107-126.

568 Mitchell, D. W.; Trumbull, W. N. 1992. Frequency of Paradox in a Common N-Winner Voting Scheme. PC 73: 55-70.

569 Nicholson, M. B. 1965. Conditions for the Voting Paradox in Committee Decisions. Metroeconomica 7: 29-44.

570 Niemi, R. G.; Weisberg, H. F. 1968. Mathematical Solution for Probability of Paradox of Voting. BS 63: 488-497.

571 Niemi, R. G.; Wright, J. R. 1967. Voting Cycles and Structure of Individual Preferences. SCAW 4: 173-183.

572 Pressler, J. 1987. Rights and Social Choice: A Paretian Libertarian Paradox. EA 3: 1-22.

573 Rae, D. W.; Daudt, H. 1976. The Ostrogorski Paradox: Compound Majority Decisions. EJPR 4: 391-398.

574 Rapoport, A. 1984. The Expected Frequency and Mean Size of Paradox of New Members. TAD 17: 29-45.

575 Riker, W. H. 1980. Implications from the Disequilibrium of Majority Rule for the Study of Institutions. APSR 74: 432-446.

576 Rosenthal, R. W. 1981. Games of Perfect Information, Predatory Pricing and Chain Store Paradox. JET 25: 92-100.

577 Saari, D. G. 1987. Sources of Paradoxes from Social Choice and Probability. JET 41: 1-22.

578 -. 1989. A Dictionary for Voting Paradoxes. JET 48: 443-475.

579 Samuelson, P. A. 1977. St. Petersburg Paradoxes. JEL 15: 24-55.

580 Schofield, N. J. 1983. Generic Instability of Majority Rule. RES 50: 696-705.

581 Schwartz, T. 1994. Representation as Agency and the Pork Barrel Paradox. PC 78: 3-21.

582 -. 1995. Paradox of Representation. JOP 57: 309-323.

583 Selton, R. 1978. The Chain Store Paradox. TAD 9: 127-159.

584 Shelley, F. M. 1984. Notes on Ostrogorski's Paradox. TAD 17: 267-272.

585 Suzumura, K. 1980. Liberal Paradox and Voluntary Exchange of Rights Exercising. JET 22: 407-422.

586 Tsebelis, G. 1989. Abuse of Probability in Political Analysis: Robinson Crusoe Fallacy. APSR 83: 77-92.

587 Weiss, D. D. 1973. Wollheim's Paradox. PT 1: 154-170.

588 White, H. C. 1995. Social Networks Can Resolve Attitude Paradoxes in Economics and Psychology. JITE 151: 58-74.

Power

589 Aberbach, J. D. 1977. Power Consciousness. APSR 71: 1544-1560.

590 d'Aspremont, C.; Jacquemin, A.; Mertens, J. F. 1987. A Measure of Aggregate Power in Organizations. JET 43: 184-191.

591 Bardhan, P. 1991. The Concept of Power in Economics. EAP 3: 265-277.

592 Barry, B. 1980. Is It Better to Be Powerful or Lucky? POLST 28: 183-194, 338-352.

593 Brams, S. J. 1968. Measuring the Concentration of Power in Political Systems. APSR 62: 461-475.

594 Brams, S. J.; Affuso, P. J. 1976. Power and Size: A New Paradox. TAD 7: 29-56.

595 Burt, R. S. 1981. Comparative Power Structures in American Communities. SSR 10: 115-176.

596 Debnam, G. 1975. Nondecisions and Power. APSR 69: 899-907.

597 Holler, M. J. 1982. Forming Coalitions and Measuring Power. POLST 30: 262-271.

598 Kerbo, H. R.; Fave, L. R. D. 1979. The Empirical Side of the Power Elite Debate. SQ 20: 5-22.

599 Logan, J. R.; Zeitz, G. 1977. Mathematical Models in the Study of Power. AJS 83: 164-173.

600 Madsen, D. 1985. A Biochemical Property Related to Power-Seeking in Humans. APSR 79: 448-457.

601 Mitra, S. K. 1988. The Paradox of Power: Political Science as Morality Play. JCACP 26: 318-337.

602 Nurmi, H. 1978. Power and Support. MSSR 1: 5-24.

603 -. 1980. Game Theory and Power. ZN 40: 35-58.

604 Peng, Y. 1994. Intellectual Fads in Political Science: Political Socialization and Community Power Studies. PS 27: 100-108.

605 Rogowski, R. 1983. Structure, Growth and Power: Three Rationalist Accounts. IO 37: 713-738.

606 Skvoretz, J.; Willer, D. 1993. Exclusion and Power: Theories of Power in Exchange Networks. ASR 58: 801-818.

607 Tanaka, H. 1989. Power as Maximizing Behavior. BS 34: 199-206.

608 Wittman, D. 1976. Various Concepts of Power. BJPS 6: 449-462.

609 Yamagishi, T.; Gillmore, M. R.; Cook, K. S. 1987. Network Connections and Distribution of Power in Exchange Networks. AJS 93: 833-851.

Rationality

610 Agnew, N. M.; Brown, J. L. 1986. Bounded Rationality: Fallible Decisions in Unbounded Decision Space. BS 31: 148-161.

611 Aumann, R. J. 1995. Backward Induction and Common Knowledge of Rationality. GAEB 8: 6-19.

612 Binmore, K. 1987. Modeling Rational Players. EA 3: 179-214.

613 Elster, J. 1977. A Theory of Imperfect Rationality. SSI 16: 469-526.

614 -. 1993. Some Unsolved Problems in the Theory of Rational Behavior. AS 36: 179-190.

615 Ethics. 1985 Papers on Rationality and Morality. Vol 96 (1).

616 Forester, J. 1984. Bounded Rationality and the Politics of Muddling Through. PAR 44: 23-31.

617 Games and Economic Behavior. 1995. Papers on Rationality and Equilibrium in Strategic Interaction. GAEB 8 (1).

618 Goodin, R. E. 1979. Retrospective Rationality: Saving People from Their Former Selves. SSI 18: 967-990.

619 Grafstein, R. 1995. Rationality as Conditional Expected Utility Maximization. PP 16: 63-80.

620 Grether, D. M.; Plott, C. R. 1979. The Economic Theory of Choice and Preference Reversal Phenomenon. AER 69: 623-638.

621 Gustafsson, G.; Richardson, J. J. 1979. Concepts of Rationality and the Policy Process. EJPR 7: 415-436.

622 Hampton, J. 1994. Failure of Expected Utility Theory as Theory of Reason. EAPHIL 10: 195-242.

623 Hardin, R. 1984. Difficulties in the Notion of Economic Rationality. SSI 23: 453-467.

624 Harding, S. 1982. Is Gender a Variable in Conceptions of Rationality? Dialectica 36: 225-242.

625 Harless, D. W.; Cramerer, C. F. 1994. Predictive Utility of Generalized Expected Utility Theories. Econometrica 62: 1251-1289.

626 Harsanyi, J. C. 1966. A General Theory of Rational Behavior in Game Situations. Econometrica 34: 613-634.

627 -. 1975. Non-Linear Social Welfare Functions, or Do Welfare Economists Have a Special Exemption from Bayesian Rationality? TAD 6: 311-332.

628 -. 1983. Basic Moral Decisions and Alternative Concepts of Rationality. STAP 9: 231-244.

629 Hey, J. D.; Orme, C. 1994. Investigating Generalizations of Expected Utility Theory Using Experimental Data. Econometrica 62: 1291-1326.

630 Ivaldi, M. 1992. Survey Evidence on the Rationality of Expectations. JAE 7: 225-241.

631 Kantor, B. 1979. Rational Expectations and Economic Thought. JEL 17: 1422-1441.

632 Lensberg, T. 1987. Stability and Collective Rationality. Econometrica 55: 935-961.

633 Lipman, B. L. 1995. Information Processing and Bounded Rationality. CANJE 1: 42-67.

634 Margolis, H. 1981. New Model of Rational Choice. Ethics 91: 265-279.

635 McCormick, K. 1989. The Assumption of Rational Behavior in Economics. ROSE 47: 313-321.

636 McLean, I.; Orbell, J. M.; Dawes, R. M. 1991. What Should Rational Cognitive Misers Do? APSR 85: 1417-1420.

637 MacRae, D. 1973. Normative Assumptions in Public Choice. PC 16: 27-41.

638 Mendola, J. 1987. Gauthier's Morals by Agreement and Two Kinds of Rationality. Ethics 97: 765-775.

639 Moreh, J. 1988. Group Behavior and Rationality. SSI 27: 99-118.

640 Nelson, A. 1988. Economic Rationality and Morality. PAPA 17: 149-166.

641 Nilson, S. S. 1980. Rationality Depends on Situations. CAC 15: 47-50.

642 North, D. C. 1993. What Do We Mean by Rationality? PC 77: 159-162.

643 Ny, U. K. 1989. Individual Irrationality and Social Welfare. SCAW 6: 87-101.

644 Quiggen, J. 1987. Egoistic Rationality and Public Choice. ECONR 63 (March): 10-21.

645 Reny, P. J. 1995. Rational Behaviour in Extensive-Form Games. CANJE 28: 1-16.

646 Rorty, A. O. 1980. Self-Deception, Akrasia and Irrationality. SSI 6: 905-922.

647 Scandinavian Political Studies. 1992. Papers on Rationality and Institutions. SPS 15 (3).

648 Schotter, A.; Schwodiauer, G. 1980. Economics and the Theory of Games. JEL 18: 479-527.

649 Schwartz, T. 1972. Rationality and the Myth of the Maximum. Nous 6: 97-117.

650 Science and Society. 1993 Papers on Rationality. SAS 57 (4).

651 Sen, A. K. 1977. Critique of the Behavioral Foundations of Economic Theory. PPA 6: 317-344.

652 -. 1995. Rationality and Social Choice. AER 19: 139-154.

653 Shapiro, M. J. 1969. Rational Political Man: A Synthesis of Economic and Social-Psychological Perspectives. APSR 66: 1203-1225.

654 Simon, H. A. 1995. Rationality in Political Behavior. PP 16: 45-62.

655 Social Research. 1977. Papers on Rationality and Morality. SR 44 (4)

656 Sofianou, E. 1995. Post-Modernism and the Notion of Rationality in Economics. CJE 19: 373-389.

657 Sugden, R. 1985. Consistency Requirements in Choice Theory. Economica 52: 167-183.

658 Vickrey, W. S. 1977. Economic Rationality and Social Choice. SR 44: 691-707.

659 Wildavsky, A. 1994. Why Self-Interest Means Less Outside of a Social Context: Cultural Contributions Rational Choices. JTP 6: 131-160.

660 Zuckert, C. H. 1995. The Rationality of Rational Choice. PP 16: 179-198.

Risk and Uncertainty

661 Alvarez, R. M.; Franklin, C. H. 1994. Uncertainty and Political Perceptions. JOP 56: 671-688.

662 Anderson, E. 1988. Values, Risks and Market Norms. PAPA 17: 54-65.

663 Annals. 1979. Papers on Personal Risks and Societal Consequences. ANNALS 443.

664 Appelbaum, E.; Katz, E. 1981. Market Constraints as a Rationale for the Friedman-Savage Utility Function. JPE 89: 819-825.

665 Babcock, L., et al. 1995. Forming Beliefs about Adjudicated Outcomes: Perceptions of Risk and Reservation Values. IRLE 15: 289-303.

666 Bailey, M. J.; Olson, M.; Wonnacott, P. 1980. Marginal Utility of Income Does Not Increase: Borrowing, Lending and Friedman-Savage Gambles. AER 70: 372-379.

667 Bartels, L. M. 1986. Issue Voting under Uncertainty. AJPS 30: 709-728.

668 Bellante, D.; Link, A. N. 1981. Are Public Sector Workers More Risk Averse than Private Sector Workers? ILRR 34: 408-412.

669 Berger, L. A.; Hershey, J. C. 1994. Moral Hazard, Risk Seeking, and Free Riding. JORAU 9: 173-186.

670 Borner, S.; Brunetti, A.; Weber, B. 1995. Policy Reform and Institutional Uncertainty. Kyklos 48: 43-64.

671 Bowen, W. M. 1988. Tests of a Theory of Risk and Culture. RSP 18: 19-42.

672 Brod, D. 1992. Quantifying Uncertainty: Risk Analysis for Forecasting and Strategic Planning. GFR 8: 25-30.

673 Brunk, G. G. 1981. The Friedman-Savage Gambling Model. QJE 96: 341-348.

674 Chew, S. H.; Ho, J. L. 1994. Hope: The Attitude toward Timing of Uncertainty Resolution. JORAU 8: 267-297.

675 Cioffi-Revilla, C. A.; Starr, H. 1995. Opportunity, Willingness and Political Uncertainty: Theoretical Foundations of Politics. JTP 7: 447-476.

676 Cranor, C. F. 1990. Some Moral Issues in Risk Assessment. Ethics 101: 123-143.

677 Daedalus. 1990. Papers on Risk. Vol 119 (4).

678 Eoyang, C., et al. 1987. Risk Preferences in Military Decision Making. JPMS 15: 245-262.

679 Feldstein, M. S. 1969. Effects of Taxation on Risk Taking. JPE 77: 755-764.

680 Felsenthal, D. S. 1979. Group vs. Individual Gambling Behavior. BS 24: 334-345.

681 Ferejohn, J. A.; Noll, R. G. 1978. Uncertainty and Formal Theory of Political Campaigns. APSR 72: 492-505.

682 Fischhoff, B., et al. 1978. How Safe Is Safe? A Psychometric Study of Attitudes towards Technological Risks and Benefits. PSCI 9: 127-152.

683 Gemmill, G. 1992. Political Risk and Market Efficiency: British Stock and Options Markets in 1987 Election. Journal of Banking and Finance 16: 211-231.

684 Glazer, A.; Konrad, K. A. 1993. Evaluation of Risky Projects by Voters. JPUBE 52: 377-390.

685 Greene, K. V. 1973. Attitudes toward Risk and Relative Size of Public Sector. Finance Quarterly 1: 205-218.

686 Gregory, N. 1980. Relative Wealth and Risk Taking: Friedman-Savage Utility Function. JPE 88: 1226-1230.

687 Hadden, S. G.; Hazelton, J. 1980. Public Policy toward Risk. PSJ 9: 109-116.

688 Handa, J. C. 1971. A Theory of Risk Preference in Gambling. JPE 79: 1073-1083.

689 Journal of Social Issues. 1979. Papers on American Gambling. JSI 35 (3).

690 Joyce, K. M. 1979. Public Opinion and Politics of Gambling. JSI 35: 144-165.

691 Kahneman, D.; Tversky, A. 1979. Prospect Theory: Analysis of Decision Making under Risk. Econometrica 47: 262-291.

692 -. 1982. Psychology of Preference. SA 246: 160-173.

693 Kihlstrom, R. E.; Laffont, J. J. 1979. A General Equilibrium Entrepreneurial Theory of Firm Formation Based on Risk. JPE 87: 719-748.

694 Kirkpatrick, S. A., et al. 1978. Risks in Political Decision Making: Choice Shifts. ESOP 4: 55-92.

695 Lambert, P. J.; Weale, A. 1981. Equality, Risk Aversion and Contractarian Social Choice. TAD 13: 109-127.

696 Law and Policy 1989. Papers on Risk Behavior. LAP 11 (3).

697 Levy, H. 1994. Absolute and Relative Risk Aversion. JORAU 8: 289-307.

698 Lichtenstein, S.; Slovik, P. 1971. Reversal of Preferences between Bids and Choices in Gambling Decisions. Journal of Experimental Psychology 89: 46-55.

699 Loomes, G.; Segal, U. 1994. Observing Different Orders of Risk Aversion. JORAU 9: 239-256.

700 Machina, M. J. 1989. Dynamic Consistency and Non-Expected Utility Models of Choice with Uncertainty. JEL 27: 1622-1668.

701 Magnus, E. V. 1984. Preference, Rationality and Risk Taking. Ethics 94: 637-648.

702 Maskin, E. S. 1979. Decision Making under Ignorance with Implications for Social Choice. TAD 11: 319-337.

703 Masters, R.; Gibbs, M. 1989. Risk Taking Propensity of US Veterans. JPMS 17: 83-92.

704 Morrow, J. D. 1987. The Theoretical Basis of a Measure of National Risk Attitudes. ISQ 31: 423-438.

705 Munch, R. 1995. Political Regulation of Technological Risks. IJCS 36: 109-130.

706 Municipal Finance. 1971. Papers on Risk Management. MF 44 (1).

707 Page, B. I. 1976. Theory of Political Ambiguity. APSR 70: 742-753.

708 Panning, W. H. 1982. Uncertainty and Political Participation. PB 4: 69-81.

709 Paternoster, R., et al. 1983. Perceived Risk and Social Control: Do Sanctions Really Deter? LASR 17: 457-580.

710 Pauly, M.; Kunreuther, H., Vaupel, J. 1984. Public Protection against Misperceived Risks: Positive Political Economy. PC 43: 45-64.

711 Policy Studies Review. 1982. Papers on Public Policy toward Risk. PSR 1 (4).

712 Pryor, F. L. 1976. The Friedman-Savage Utility Function in Cross Cultural Perspective. JPE 84: 821-834.

713 Ravetz, J. 1994. The Economics as Elite Folk Science: Suppression of Uncertainty. JPKE 17: 165-184.

714 Renn, O.; et al. 1992. Social Amplification of Risk. JSI 48: 137-160.

715 Rushefsky, M. E. 1985. Assuming the Conclusions: Risk Assessment in the Development of Cancer Policy. PALS 4: 31-44.

716 Scarborough, G. I. 1988. Polarity, Power and Risk in International Disputes. JCR 32: 511-533.

717 Schoemaker, P. J. H. 1993. Determinants of Risk-Taking: Behavioral and Economic Views. JORAU 6: 49-73.

718 Semmel, A. K.; Minnix, D. 1978. Group Dynamics and Risk Taking. ESOP 4: 1-33.

719 Shepsle, K. A. 1972. The Strategy of Ambiguity: Uncertainty and Electoral Competition. APSR 66: 555-568.

720 Sienkiewicz, S. 1979. Impact of Uncertainty in Strategic Analysis. WP 32: 90-110.

721 Simon, J. D. 1985. Political Risk Forecasting. Futures 17: 132-148.

722 Sjoberg, L. 1979. Strength of Belief and Risk. PSCI 11: 39-57.

723 Smith, R. W.; Preston, F. W. 1984. Vocabularies of Motives for Gambling. SP 27: 325-348.

724 Society. 1989. Papers on Risk and Capitalism. Vol 27 (1).

725 Stevenson, L. 1988. Defense Policies and Evaluation of Risk. STAP 14: 215-235.

726 Tefft, S. K. 1990. Cognitive Perspectives on Risk Assessment and War Traps: Alternative to Functional Theory. JPMS 18: 57-78.

727 Tversky, A.; Kahneman, D. 1974. Judgement under Uncertainty: Heuristics. Science 185: 1124-1131.

728 Vaughan, E.; Seifert, M. 1992. Variability in the Framing of Risk Issues. JSI 48: 119-136.

729 Vertzberger, Y. Y. I. 1995. Rethinking and Reconceptualizing Risk in Foreign Policy Decision-Making. PP 16: 347-380.

730 Vinokur, A. 1971. Effects of Group Processes upon Individual and Group Decision Involving Risk. PSYB 76: 232-250.

731 Viscusi, W. K. 1993. The Value of Risks to Life and Health. JEL 31: 1912-1946.

732 Viscusi, W. K.; Magat, W. A.; Forrest, A. 1988. Altruistic and Private Valuations of Risk Reduction. JPAAM 7: 277-245.

733 Ward, H. 1989. Taking Risks to Gain Reassurance in Public Goods Games. JCR 33: 274-308.

734 Zojonc, R. B.; Wolosin, R. J.; Wolosin, M. A. 1972. Group Risk Taking under Various Group Decision Schemes. Journal of Experimental Social Psychology 8: 16-30.

Spatial Models

735 Aldrich, J. H. 1983. A Downsian Spatial Model with Party Activism. APSR 77: 974-990.

736 Austen-Smith, D. 1983. The Spatial Theory of Electoral Competition. EPC 1: 439-459.

737 -. 1987. Parties, Districts and the Spatial Theory of Elections. SCAW 4: 9-23.

738 Bartholdi, J. J.; Narasimhan, L. S.; Tovey, C. A. 1991. Recognizing Majority-Rule Equilibrium in Spatial Voting Games. SCAW 8: 183-197.

739 Bartolini, S.; Mair, P. 1990. Policy Competition, Spatial Distance and Electoral Instability. WEP 13: 1-16.

740 Campbell, D. E. 1994. A Foundation for Pareto Optimality in Spatial Models. EJPE 10: 441-448.

741 Davis, S. K. 1984. A Nonmetric Test of Spatial Theories of Elections. PM 10: 1-28.

742 Dutter, L. E. 1985. Spatial Preferences and Voter Choices in the Dutch Electorate. CPS 18: 251-263.

743 Enelow, J. M.; Hinich, M. J. 1982. Ideology, Issues and Spatial Theory of Elections. APSR 76: 493-501.

744 -. 1985. Estimating Parameters of a Spatial Model of Elections: 1980 Election. PM 11: 249-268.

745 -. 1989. A General Probabilistic Spatial Theory of Elections. PC 61: 101-114.

746 -. 1989. Location of American Presidential Candidates: Spatial Model of Elections. MCM 12: 461-470.
747 -. 1994. A Test of the Predictive Dimensions Model in Spatial Voting Theory. PC 78: 155-169.
748 Enelow, J. M., Hinich, M. J.; Mendell, N. R. 1986. Alternative Spatial Models of Elections. JOP 48: 675-693.
749 Gali, J. 1995. Expectations Driven Spatial Elections. RSUE 25: 1-20.
750 Glazer, A.; Grofman, B. 1988. Limitations of the Spatial Model? PC 58: 161-168.
751 Haynes, K. E.; Good, D. H.; Dignan, T. 1988. Discrete Spatial Choice and the Axiom of Independence from Irrelevant Alternatives. SEPS 22: 241-252.
752 Hinich, M. J.; Pollard, W. 1981. A New Approach to the Spatial Theory of Electoral Competition. AJPS 25: 323-341.
753 Hoyer, R. W.; Mayer, L. S. 1974. Comparing Strategies in a Spatial Model of Electoral Competition. AJPS 18: 501-523.
754 Krehbiel, K. 1988. Spatial Models of Legislative Choice. LSQ 13: 259-319.
755 Leonardi, G.; Papageorgiou, Y. Y. 1992. Conceptual Foundations of Spatial Choice Models. EPA 24: 1393-1408.
756 McKelvey, R. D. 1980. Ambiguity in Spatial Models of Policy Formation. PC 35: 385-402.
757 Merrill, S. 1994. A Probabilistic Model for the Spatial Distribution of Party Support in Multiparty Electorates. JASA 89: 1190-1197.
758 Miller, H. J.; Finco, M. V. 1995. Spatial Search and Spatial Competition. ARS 29: 67-110.
759 Myerson, R. B.; Weber, R. J. 1993. A Theory of Voting Equilibria. APSR 87: 102-114.
760 Owen, G. 1990. Stable Outcomes in Spatial Voting Games. MSS 19: 269-279.
761 Platt, G.; Poole, K. T.; Rosenthal, H. 1992. Directional and Euclidean Theories of Voting Behavior. LSQ 4: 561-572.
762 Poole, K. T.; Rosenthal, H. 1984. Presidential Elections: Spatial Analysis. AJPS 28: 282-312.
763 -. 1985. A Spatial Model for Legislative Roll Call Analysis. AJPS 29: 357-384.
764 Schofield, N. J.; Grofman, B.; Feld, S. L. 1988. Core and Stability of Group Choice in Spatial Voting Games. APSR 82: 195-211.
765 Shaffer, W. R. 1991. Interparty Spatial Relationships in Norwegian Storting Roll Calls. SPS 14: 59-63.
766 Shepsle, K. A. 1979. Institutional Arrangements and Equilibrium in Voting. AJPS 23: 27-59.
767 Williams, K. C. 1991. Advertising and Political Expenditures in a Spatial Election Game. SAG 22: 421-442.
768 -. 1994. Spatial Elections with Endorsements and Uninformed Voters. PC 80: 1-8.

Strategic Manipulation

769 Anbarci, N. 1993. Strategic Vote Manipulation in a Simple Democracy. JEBAO 20: 319-330.
770 Austen-Smith, D. 1992. Strategic Models of Talk in Political Decision Making. IPSR 13: 45-58.
771 Bjurulf, B. H.; Niemi, R. G. 1978. Strategic Voting in Scandinavian Parliaments. SPS 1: 5-22.
772 Brunk, G. G. 1990. Freshmen vs. Incumbents: Congressional Voting Patterns on Prohibition. Journal of American Studies 26: 235-242.
773 Calvert, R. L.; Fenno, R. F. 1994. Strategic and Sophisticated Voting in Senate. JOP 56: 349-376.
774 Campbell, J. E. 1979. Manipulation of Social Choice Rules by Strategic Nomination of Candidates. TAD 10: 247-263.
775 -. 1983. Ambiguity in the Issue Positions of Presidential Candidates. AJPS 27: 284-293.
776 Cohen, L. R.; Noll, R. G. 1991. Strategies for Voting and Abstaining. PB 13: 97-128.
777 Darcy, R. 1979. The Role of Ambiguity in Manipulating Voter Behavior. TAD 10: 265-279.
778 Denzau, A. T.; Riker, W. H.; Shepsle, K. A. 1985. Farquharson and Fenno: Sophisticated Voting and Home Style. APSR 79: 1117-1134.
779 Dutta, B. 1980. Strategic Voting in a Probabalistic Framework. Econometrica 48: 447-456.
780 Eckel, C.; Holt, C. A. 1989. Strategic Voting in Agenda-Controlled Committee Experiments. AER 79: 763-773.
781 Enelow, J. M. 1981. Saving Amendments, Killer Amendments and an Expected Utility Calculus of Sophisticated Voting. JOP 43: 1062-1089.
782 Enelow, J. M.; Koehler, D. H. 1979. Vote Trading in a Legislative Context: Cooperative and Noncooperative Strategic Voting. PC 34: 157-176.
783 Felsenthal, D. S.; Maoz, Z. 1988. Analysis of Sincere and Sophisticated Voting under Plurality and Approval Procedures. BS 33: 116-130.
784 Fishburn, P. C.; Brams, S. J. 1984. Manipulability of Voting by Sincere Truncation of Preferences. PC 44: 397-410.
785 Franklin, M. N.; Niemi, R. G.; Whitten, G. D. 1994. Tactical Voting. BJPS 24: 549-565.
786 Gibbard, A. F. 1973. Manipulation of Voting Schemes. Econometrica 41: 587-601.
787 Glazer, A.; et al. 1995. Strategic Vote Delay. LSQ 20: 37-46.
788 Hamm, K. E. 1982. Consistency between Committee and Floor Voting. LSQ 7: 473-490.
789 Heuer, R. 1981. Strategic Deception and Counter-Deception. ISQ 25: 294-327.
790 Kramer, G. H. 1972. Sophisticated Voting over Multidimensional Choice Spaces. JMS 2: 165-180.
791 Krehbiel, K.; Rivers, D. 1990. Sophisticated Voting in Congress. JOP 52: 548-578.
792 Levine, M. E.; Plott, C. R. 1977. Agenda Influence and Its Implications. VLR 63: 561-604.
793 Lublin, D. I. 1994. Strategic Politicians in US Senate Elections. JOP 56: 228-241.
794 Milesi-Ferretti, G. M.; Spolaore, E. 1994. How Cynical Can an Incumbent Be? Strategic Policy in Government Spending. JPUBE 55: 121-140.
795 Morton, S. 1988. Strategic Voting in Repeated Referenda. SCAW 5: 45-68.
796 Moulin, H. 1983. Strategic Aspects of Voting Procedures. Economie Appliquee 36: 711-719.
797 Nurmi, H. 1984. Strategic Properties of Methods of Group Decision Making. BS 29: 248-257.
798 Ordeshook, P. C.; Palfrey, T. R. 1989. Agendas, Strategic Voting and Signaling with Incomplete Information. AJPS 32: 441-466.
799 Ordeshook, P. C.; Schwartz, T. 1987. Agendas and Control of Political Outcomes. APSR 81: 179-199.
800 Pattanaik, P. K. 1976. Threats, Counterthreats and Strategic Voting. Econometrica 44: 91-103.
801 Plott, C. R.; Levine, M. E. 1978. Agenda Influence on Committee Decisions. AER 68: 146-160.
802 Robson, A. J. 1995. Evolution of Strategic Behavior. CANJE 28: 17-41.
803 Thomas, M. 1991. Issue Avoidance: The US Senate. PB 13: 1-20.
804 Tsebelis, G. 1995. Decision Making in Political Systems: Veto Players. BJPS 25: 289-326.
805 Uslaner, E. M. 1981. Logic of Defensive Issue Voting Strategies in Congressional Elections. APQ 9: 3-22.

SOCIAL POLICY

1 Afxentious, P. C. 1990. Basic Needs. CJDS 11: 241-257.
2 Bajgier, S. M.; Moskowitz, H. 1982. Interactive Model of Attitude and Risk-Benefit Formation Regarding Social Issues. PSCI 14: 257-278.
3 Dissent. 1991. Papers on Social Breakdown. Vol 38 (2).
4 Glenn, N. D. 1987. Social Trends in the US. POQ 51 Winter Supplement: S109-S126.
5 Heidenheimer, A. J. 1973. The Politics of Public Education, Health and Welfare. BJPS 3: 315-340.
6 Hersch, P. L.; McDougall, G. S. 1989 Do People Put Their Money Where Their Votes Are? Lottery Tickets. SEJ 56: 32-38.
7 Huber, E.; Stephens, J. D. 1993. Political Parties and Public Pensions. AS 36: 309-326.
8 Journal of Social Issues. 1991. Papers on Child Care Policy Research. JSI 47 (2).
9 Light, I. 1977. The Ethical Vice Industry. ASR 42: 464-478.
10 Moen, J. R. 1988. Trends in Retirement: American Men from 1860 to 1980. FRBA 73: 16-27.
11 Nice, D. C. 1988. State Deregulation of Intimate Rights. SSQ 69: 203-211.
12 Pratt, J.; Sparks, R. F. 1987. Critical Commentary on the Renaissance of Permissiveness as a Political Issue. CC 11: 3-24.
13 Rein, M. 1980. Methodology for Study of Interplay between Social Science and Social Policy. ISSJ 32: 361-370.
14 Rodgers, W. M.; Stuart, C. 1995. Efficiency of a Lottery as a Source of Public Revenue. PFQ 23: 242-254.
15 Ziegler, J. H.; Britton, C. R. 1981. Comparative Analysis of Socioeconomic Variations in Measuring the Quality of Life. SSQ 62: 303-312.

Abortion

16 Abramowitz, A. I. 1995. Its Abortion, Stupid: Voting in the 1992 Presidential Election. JOP 57: 176-186.
17 Alvarez, R. M.; Brehm, J. 1995. Ambivalence towards Abortion Policy. AJPS 39: 1055-1082.
18 American Politics Quarterly. 1993. Papers on the Politics of Abortion. APQ 21 (1).
19 Baker, R. K.; Epstein, L. K.; Forth, R. D. 1981. Social, Political and Religious Correlates of Attitudes on Abortion. APQ 9: 89-102.
20 Berkman, M. B.; O'Connor, R. E. 1993. Do Women Legislators Matter? Female Legislators and State Abortion Policy. APQ 21: 102-124.
21 Bond, J. R.; Johnson, C. A. 1982. Implementing a Permissive Policy: Hospital Abortion Services after Roe vs. Wade. AJPS 26: 1-24.
22 Brady, D. W.; Schwartz, E. P. 1995. Ideology and Interests in Congressional Voting: Politics of Abortion in the US Senate. PC 84: 25-48.
23 Casey, G. 1984. Intensive Analysis of a Single Issue: Attitudes on Abortion. PM 10: 97-124.
24 Conway, K. S.; Butler, M. R. 1992. Abortion Legislation as a Public Good. EI 30: 609-626.
25 Cook, E. A.; Jelen, T. G.; Wilcox, C. 1993. Generational Differences in Attitudes toward Abortion. APQ 21: 31-53.
26 -. 1993. State Political Cultures and Public Opinion about Abortion. PRQ 46: 771-782.
27 -. 1994. Issue Voting in Senate Elections: Abortion. CAP 21: 99-112.
28 Franklin, C. H.; Kosaki, L. C. 1989. The Supreme Court, Public Opinion and Abortion. APSR 83: 751-771.
29 Fried, A. 1988. Abortion Politics as Symbolic Politics: Belief Systems. SSQ 69: 137-154.
30 Gigliotti, G. A. 1980. Abortion and Women's Rights: Social Choice Formulation. AEJ 8: 83-88.
31 Goggin, M. L. 1993. Understanding the New Politics of Abortion. APQ 21: 4-30.
32 Gohmann, S. F.; Ohsfeldt, R. L. 1994. Voting in the House on Abortion Funding Issues. AJEAS 53: 455-474.
33 Gross, M. L. 1995. Participation in Abortion Politics. PRQ 48: 507-534.
34 Guth, J. L., et al. 1993. Sources of Antiabortion Attitudes: Religious Political Activists. APQ 21: 65-80.
35 Hansen, S. B. 1980. State Implementation of Supreme Court Decisions: Abortion Rates since Roe vs. Wade. JOP 42: 372-395.
36 Howell, S. E.; Sims, R. T. 1993. Abortion Attitudes and Louisiana Governor's Election. APQ 21: 54-64.
37 Jelen, T. G. 1984. Respect for Life, Sexual Morality and Abortion. RRR 25: 220-231.
38 -. 1988. Changes in the Attitudinal Correlates of Abortion. JSSR 27: 211-228.
39 Journal of Social Issues. 1992. Papers on Psychological Perspectives on Abortion. JSI 48 (3).
40 Kahane, L. H. 1994. The Political, Ideological and Economic Determinants of Abortion Position. AJEAS 53: 347-359.
41 Meier, K. J.; McFarlane, D. R. 1993. The Politics of Funding Abortion. APQ 21: 81-101.
42 Mooney, C. Z.; Lee, M. H. 1995. Legislative Morality in the States: Pre-Roe Abortion Regulation Reform. AJPS 39: 599-627.

43 Nevitte, N.; Brandon, W. P.; Davis, L. 1993. The American Abortion Controversy: Cross National Evidence. PALS 12: 19-30.

44 O'Connor, R. E.; Berkman, M. B. 1995. Religious Determinants of State Abortion Policy. SSQ 76: 447-459.

45 Owens, J. 1993. Abortion Politics as a Test Case of Feminist Political Theory: Is There a Specific Model for Women's Political Activity? PSNZ 45: 98-111.

46 Parliamentary Affairs. 1994. Papers on Abortion. PARLA 47 (2).

47 Patterson, M. J.; Hill, R. P.; Maloy, K. 1995. Abortion in America: Consumer-Behavior Perspective. JCON 21: 677-694.

48 Policy Studies Review. 1994. Papers on Abortion Policy. PSR 13 (1/2).

49 Powell-Griner, E.; Trent, K. 1987. Sociodemographic Determinants of Abortion. Demography 24: 553-561.

50 Sets, J. E.; Leik, R. K. 1993. Attitudes about Abortion and Varying Attitude Structure. SSR 22: 265-282.

51 Smith, K. B. 1994. Abortion Attitudes and Vote Choice in the 1984 and 1988 Presidential Elections. APQ 22: 354-369.

52 Spicer, D. N. 1994. World View and Abortion Beliefs. SI 64: 114-126.

53 Strickland, R. A.; Whicker, M. L. 1986. Banning Abortion: Senate Votes on a Bimodal Issue. WAP 6: 41-56.

54 -. 1992. Political and Socioeconomic Indicators of State Restrictiveness toward Abortion. PSJ 20: 598-627.

55 Tatalovich, R.; Schier, D. 1993. Persistence of Ideological Cleavage in Voting on Abortion Legislation in the House. APQ 21: 125-139.

56 Welch, M. R.; Leege, D. C.; Cavendish, J. C. 1995. Attitudes toward Abortion among US Catholics. SSQ 76: 142-157.

57 Wettstein, M. E. 1995. Impact of National Policy Change on Abortion Rates. SSQ 76: 607-618.

58 Wettstein, M. E.; Albritton, R. B. 1995. Effects of Public Opinion on Abortion Policies and Use in the American States. Publius 25: 91-106.

59 Wilcox, C. 1989. Political Action Committees and Abortion. WAP 9: 1-20.

60 Witt, S. L.; Moncrief, G. F. 1993. Religion and Roll Call Voting in Idaho: Abortion. APQ 21: 140-149.

Demography and Health

61 American Behavioral Scientist. 1985. Papers on Disability Policy. ABS 28 (3).

62 -. 1985. Papers on Mental Health Policy. ABS 28 (5) and 1987 30 (2).

63 -. 1989. Papers on Drug Abuse Debate. ABS 32 (3)

64 -. 1993. Papers on Health Reform. ABS 36 (6).

65 -. 1994. Papers on Health Policy. ABS 38 (2).

66 -. 1995. Papers on Aging. ABS 39 (2-3).

67 Annals. 1975. Papers on Drug Abuse. ANNALS 417, and 1992 521.

68 -. 1983. Papers on Health Policy. ANNALS 468.

69 -. 1986. Papers on Mental Health. ANNALS 484.

70 -. 1990. Papers on World Population. ANNALS 510.

71 Baveja, A., et al. 1993. Modeling Response of Drug Markets to Enforcement. SEPS 27: 73-90.

72 Boyer, G. R. 1989. Malthus Was Right after All: Poor Relief and Birth Rates in Southeastern England. JPE 97: 93-114.

73 Buchanan, R. J.; Ohsfeldt, R. L. 1993. Attitudes of State Legislators and State Medicaid Policies Related to AIDS. PSJ 21: 651-671.

74 Business Economics. 1993. Papers on Health Economics. BE 28 (2).

75 Button, J.; Rosenbaum, W. 1990. Gray Power, Gray Peril, or Gray Myth? Political Impact of Aging in Local Sunbelt Politics. SSQ 71: 25-38.

76 Coele, A. J.; Banister, J. 1994. Five Decades of Missing Females in China. Demography 31: 459-479.

77 Collison, M. 1994. Drug Offenders and Criminal Justice. CLASC 21: 49-72.

78 Cutler, N. E. 1977. Demography, Social-Psychology and Political Factors in Politics of Aging. APSR 71: 1011-1025.

79 Cutright, P.; Hout, M.; Johnson, D. R. 1976. Structural Determinants of Fertility in Latin America. ASR 41: 511-526.

80 Daedalus. 1986. Papers on Aging. Vol 115 (1).

81 -. 1994. Papers on Health Policy. Vol 123 (4).

82 Davis, C.; van den Oever, P. 1981. Age Relations and Public Policy in Advanced Industrial Societies. PADR 71: 1-18.

83 Diamond, J. 1994. Ecological Collapses of Past Civilizations. PAPS 138: 363-370.

84 Ferris, J. M.; Graddy, E. 1987. What Governs the Decision to Contract Out Local Hospital Service? Inquiry 24: 285-294.

85 Figlio, D. N. 1995. Effect of Drinking Age Laws and Alcohol Related Crashes. JPAAM 14: 555-566.

86 Goff, B.; Anderson, G. 1994. Political Economy of Prohibition. SSQ 75: 270-283.

87 Golley, F. B. 1988. Human Population from an Ecological Perspective. PADR 14: 199-212.

88 Grogan, C. M. 1994. Political-Economic Factors Influencing State Medicaid Policy. PRQ 47: 589-622.

89 Holmes, T. P. 1990. Self-Interest, Altruism and Health-Risk Reduction: An Economic Analysis of Voting Behavior. Land Economics 66: 140-149.

90 Iezzoni, L. I.; Shwartz, M.; Restuccia, J. 1991. Role of Severity Information in Health Policy Debates. Inquiry 28: 117-128.

91 Inquiry. 1989. Papers on Home Maintenance Organizations and Health Insurance. Inquiry 26 (3).

92 International Journal. Papers on Drug Policy. IJ 49 (1).

93 Johnson, P. 1986. Drinking, Temperance and the Construction of Identity in Nineteenth Century America. SSI 25: 521-530.

94 Journal of Interamerican Studies and World Affairs. 1988. Papers on Assessing the War on Drugs. JIAS 30 (2/3).

95 Journal of Political and Military Sociology. 1984. Papers on the Life Course and Generational Politics. JPMS 12 (1).

96 Journal of Social Issues. 1974. Papers on Population Policy. JSI 30 (4).

97 -. 1989. Papers on Mental Health Policy. JSI 45 (3).

98 Journal of State Government. 1991. Papers on the Crisis in Medical Care. JSG 64 (3).

99 Knott, J. H.; Weissert, C. S. 1995. Predicting Policy Targets through Institutional Structure: Primary Care Physicians. AAS 27: 3-25.

100 Kugler, J., et al. 1983. Political Determinants of Population Dynamics. CPS 16: 3-36.

101 Ladd, H. F. 1994. Fiscal Impacts of Local Population Growth. RSUE 24: 661-686.

102 Law and Contemporary Problems. 1986. Papers on Medical Malpractice. LACP 49 (2).

103 -. 1988. Papers on Antitrust and Health Care. LACP 51 (2).

104 -. 1991. Papers on Medical Malpractice. LACP 54 (1/2).

105 Law and Policy. 1994. Papers on the Socio-Legal Dynamics of AIDS. LAP 16 (3).

106 L'Etang, H. 1988. Effect of Drugs on Political Decisions. PALS 7: 12-17.

107 Livi-Bacci, M. 1994. Population Policies: Comparative Perspective. ISSJ 46: 317-330.

108 Loehman, E. T.; Park, S.; Boldt, D. 1994. Willingness to Pay for Gains and Losses in Visibility and Health. LE 70: 478-498.

109 Makela, K. 1983. The Uses of Alcohol and Their Cultural Regulation. AS 26: 21-32.

110 Martin, C. J. 1995. Sources of Firm Preference for National Health Reform. APSR 89: 898-913.

111 McCarthy, P. S.; Ziliak, J. 1990. Effect of MADD on Drinking-Driving Activities. AE 22: 1215-1227.

112 Meier, K. J.; Johnson, C. M. 1990. Regulating Alcohol and Its Deleterious Consequences. APQ 18: 404-429.

113 Mishler, W.; Campbell, D. B. 1978. Legislative Responsiveness to Public Health Care Needs in Canada. CP 10: 479-498.

114 New York University Journal. 1991. Papers on AIDS Policy. NYUJ 23 (4).

115 Overman, E. S.; Cahill, A. G. 1994. Information, Market Government and Health Policy. JPAAM 13: 435-453.

116 Pampel, F. C. 1994. Population Aging, Class Context, and Age Inequality in Public Spending. AJS 100: 153-195.

117 Pampel, F. C.; Williamson, J. B. 1985. Age Structure, Politics and Cross-National Patterns of Public Pension Expenditures. ASR 50: 782-798.

118 Perkins, M. K.; Gilbert, H. R. 1987. An Economic Analysis of Drug Control Policy. CAR 2: 41-54.

119 Peroff, K.; Podolak-Warren, M. 1979. Does Defense Cut Spending on Health? BJPS 9: 21-40.

120 Peterson, S. P.; Hoffer, G.; Millner, E. 1995. Are Drivers of Air-Bag-Equipped Cars More Aggressive? The Offsetting Behavior Hypothesis. JOLE 38: 251-264.

121 Policy Studies Journal. 1977. Papers on Population Policy. PSJ 6 (2).

122 -. 1980. Papers on Health Policy. PSJ 9 (2).

123 -. 1993. Papers on Disability Policy. PSJ 21 (4).

124 -. 1994. Papers on Disability. PSJ 22 (1, Part 2).

125 Politics and the Life Sciences. 1986. Papers on Politics and the Life Sciences. PALS 5 (1).

126 Population and Development Review. 1988. Papers on Population Policy. PADR 14 (Winter Sup).

127 Pritchett, L. H. 1994. Desired Fertility and the Impact of Population Policies. PADR 20: 1-56.

128 Proceedings. 1980. Papers on Regulation and Health Care Policy. PAPSC 33 (4).

129 Prskawetz, A.; Feichtinger, G. 1995. Endogenous Population Growth May Imply Chaos. JPOPE 8: 59-80.

130 PS. 1987. Papers on Health Care Policy. Vol 20 (2), and 1994 27 (2).

131 Reisman, D. A. 1994. Buchanan on Cost and Health. IJSE 21: 27-41.

132 Rhodebeck, L. A. 1993. Politics of Greed? Political Preferences among the Elderly. JOP 55: 342-364.

133 Russett, B., et al. 1981. Health and Population Patterns as Indicators of Income Inequality. EDACC 29: 759-779.

134 Sapolsky, H. 1969. The Floridation Controversy. POQ 33: 240-248.

135 Society. 1988. Papers on Surrogate Motherhood. Vol 25: 8-29.

136 Socio-Economic Planning Sciences. 1985. Papers on Health Care Policy for an Aging Population. SEPS 19 (4).

137 Sollars, D. L. 1992. Assumptions and Consequences of the War on Drugs. PSR 11: 26-39.

138 Sorenson, A. M.; Brownfield, D. 1989. Patterns of Adolescent Drug Use: Latent Structure Analysis. SSR 18: 271-290.

139 University of Pennsylvania Law Review 1992. Papers on Health Care Rationing. UPLR 140 (5).

140 Van Poppel, F.; De Beer, J. 1993. Measuring Effect of Changing Legislation on Frequency of Divorce: Netherlands. Demography 30: 425-441.

141 Wasserman, I. M. 1989. Effects of War and Alcohol Consumption on Suicide. SF 68: 513-530.

142 Weisbrod, B. A. 1991. Health Care Quadrilemma: Technological Change, Insurance, Quality of Care and Cost Containment. JEL 29: 523-552.

143 Winn, R. G.; Giacopassi, D. 1993. The Effect of Country-Level Alcohol Prohibition on Motor Vehicle Accidents. SSQ 74: 783-792.

144 Women and Politics. 1993. Papers on the Politics of Pregnancy. WAP 13 (3/4).

Education

145 Alwin, D. F. 1976. Assessing School Effects. Sociology of Education 49: 294-303.

146 Ambler, J. S. 1994. Who Benefits from Educational Choice? JPAAM 13: 454-476.

147 American Behavioral Scientist. 1989. Papers on Higher Education. ABS 32 (6), 1990 34 (2), and 1991 35 (1), 1995 38 (7).

148 Annals. 1983. Papers on Higher Education. ANNALS 35 (2).

149 -. 1987. Papers on Foreign Language Instruction. ANNALS 490, 1987 508, and 1994 532.

150 -. 1992. Papers on Literacy. ANNALS 520.

151 Anthony, K. 1981. An Economic Model of Teaching Effectiveness. AER 71: 1056-1059.

152 Ashraf, J. 1994. Differences in Returns to Education: Analysis by Race. AJEAS 53: 281-290.

153 Behrman, J. R.; Rosenzweig, M. R. 1994. Cross Country Data on Education and the Labor Force. JDE 44: 147-171.

154 Berger, M. C.; Toma, E. F. 1994. Variation in State Education Policies and Effects on Student Performance. JPAAM 13: 477-491.

155 Bolland, J. M.; Redfield, K. D. 1988. Limits to Citizen Participation in Local Education: Cognitive Interpretation. JOP 50: 1033-1046.

156 Burnell, B. S. 1991. Effect of School District Structure on Education Spending. PC 69: 253-264.

157 Cameron, K. 1978. Measuring Organizational Effectiveness in Institutions of Higher Education. ASQ 23: 604-629.

158 Card, D.; Kreuger, A. B. 1992. Does School Quality Matter? Returns to Education and Characteristics of Public Schools. JPE 100: 1-40.

159 Carmichael, H. L. 1988. Incentives in Academics: Why Is There Tenure? JPE 96: 453-472.

160 Castles, F. G. 1989. Explaining Public Education Expenditures in OECD Nations. EJPR 17: 431-448.

161 Cataldo, E. F.; Holm, J. E. 1983. Voting on School Finances. WPQ 36: 619-632.

162 Chesler, M.; Crawfoot, J.; Bryant, B. L. 1979. Organizational Context of School Discipline. EAUS 11: 496-510.

163 Clune, W. H. 1979. Evaluating School Discipline through Empirical Research. EAUS 11: 440-449.

164 Conway, S. C.; Camina, O. S. 1983. Public Funding of Private Education. JOL 9: 146-177.

165 Costrell, R. M. 1994. Simple Model of Educational Standards. AER 84: 956-971.

166 Creedy, J. 1994. Financing Higher Education: Public Choice and Social Welfare. FS 15: 87-108.

167 Daedalus. 1995. Papers on Inequality in Education. Vol 124 (4).

168 Denver, D.; Hands, G. 1990. Does Studying Politics Make a Difference? Political Knowledge, Attitudes and Perceptions of School Students. BJPS 20: 263-278.

169 Doring, H. 1992. Higher Education and Confidence in Institutions: The European Values Survey. WEP 15: 126-146.

170 Education and Urban Society. 1975. Papers on Educational Policy Research. EAUS 7 (3).

171 -. 1975. Papers on Urban Education. EAUS 7 (4), 1977 9 (4).

172 -. 1978. Papers on Bilingual Education. EAUS 10 (3).

173 -. 1979. Papers on Competency Testing. EAUS 12 (1).

174 -. 1979. Papers on the Politics of School Enrollment. EAUS 11 (3).

175 -. 1980. Papers on School Boards. EAUS 12 (4).

176 -. 1989. Papers on Size as an Educational Issue. EAUS 21 (2).

177 -. 1991. Papers on School Choice Plans. EAUS 23 (2).

178 Edwards, L. N. 1978. Analysis of Compulsory Schooling Legislation. JOLE 21: 203-222.

179 Ellinger, K.; Wright, D. E.; Hirlinger, M. W. 1995. School Revenue and Student Achievement in Oklahoma. SSJ 32: 299-308.

180 England, R. W. 1985. Public School Finance in the US. RRPE 17: 129-155.

181 Ethics. 1995. Papers on Citizenship, Democracy and Education. Vol 105 (3).

182 Evans, F. J. 1980. Toward a Theory of Academic Liberalism. JOP 42: 993-1030.

183 Frey, D. E. 1992. Can Privatizing Education Really Improve Achievement? EOER 11: 427-438.

184 Garcia-Penalosa, C. 1995. Paradox of Education or the Good Side of Inequality. OEP 47: 265-285.

185 Geneve-Afrique. 1990. Papers on Education and Development in Africa. Vol 28 (2).

186 Graham, A. E.; Husted, T. A. 1993. Understanding State Variations in SAT Scores. EOER 12: 197-202.

187 Hanushek, E. A. 1981. Throwing Money at Schools. JPAAM 1: 19-41.

188 -. 1986. Production and Efficiency in the Public Schools. JEL 24: 1141-1177.

189 Hepburn, M. A. 1980. Impact of the School Curriculum on the Political Knowledge of Students. TPS 7: 425-438.

190 Hoenack, S. A. 1994. Research Directions for the Economics of Education. Economics of Education Review 13: 147-162.

191 International Journal of Comparative Sociology. 1973. Papers on Higher Education in Developing Countries. IJCS 14 (3/4).

192 International Social Science Journal. 1985. Papers on the Science of Education. ISSJ 37 (2).

193 Jackman, M. R.; Muha, M. J. 1984. Education and Intergroup Attitudes: Moral Enlightenment, Superficial Democratic Commitment, or Ideological Refinement. ASR 49: 751-769.

194 Jones, B. M. 1980. Problem of Bias in Political Education. TPS 7: 407-424.

195 Jones, W. J. 1983. Can Evaluations Influence Programs: Compensatory Education. JPAAM 2: 174-183.

196 Journal of Education Finance. 1983. Papers on School Finance Reforms. Vol 8 (Spring).

197 Journal of Social, Political and Economic Studies. 1984. Papers on Private Education and Law. JSPES 9 (1).

198 Kang, J. M. 1993. Why the Rate of Return to Education Is Apparently Higher in LDCs than in Developed Countries. JESTUD 20: 32-36.

199 Kenny, L. W.; Schmidt, A. B. 1994. Decline in Number of School Districts in US. PC 79: 1-18.

200 Kowalewski, S. A.; Saindon, J. J. 1992. Spread of Literacy in a Latin American Peasant Society. CSSH 34: 110-140.

201 Lasson, K. 1990. Excesses in Pursuit of Truth and Tenure. HLR 103: 926-950.

202 Law and Contemporary Problems. 1990. Papers on Academic Freedom and Tenure. LACP 53 (3).

203 Lehnen, R. G. 1992. Constructing State Education Performance Indicators from ACT and SAT Scores. PSJ 20: 22-47.

204 Levy, D. 1979. Universities and Governments: The Comparative Politics of Higher Education. CP 12: 99-121.

205 Lima, A. K. 1981. An Economic Model of Teaching Effectiveness. AER 71: 1056-1059.

206 Lindsay, A. W.; Bailey, M. 1980. A Convex Polytope Technique for Analyzing the Performance of Universities. SEPS 14: 33-44.

207 Lott, J. R. 1987. Why Is Education Publicly Provided? CJ 7: 475-502.

208 Lynch, P. 1979. Public Policy and Competency Testing. EAUS 12: 65-80.

209 Manns, C. L.; March, J. G. 1978. Financial Adversity, Internal Competition and Curriculum Change in a University. ASQ 23: 541-552.

210 Martinez, V. J., et al. 1995. Consequences of School Choice. SSQ 76: 485-526.

211 McClure, R. H.; Wells, C. E. 1985. The Approximation of Utility Functions for Faculty Teaching Assignments. SEPS 19: 153-158.

212 McCormick, R. E.; Tinsley, M. 1987. Athletics vs Academics? SAT Scores. JPE 95: 1103-1116.

213 Meier, K. J.; Stewart, J. 1991. Cooperation and Conflict in Multiracial School Districts. JOP 53: 1123-1133.

214 Michaels, J. W.; Miethe, T. D. 1989. Academic Effort and College Grades. SF 68: 309-319.

215 Miller, T. 1981. Political and Mathematical Perspectives on Education Equity. APSR 75: 319-333.

216 Mintrom, M. 1993. Why Efforts to Equalize School Funding Have Failed. PRQ 46: 847-862.

217 Morgan, D. R.; Pelissero, J. P. 1989. Interstate Variation in Allocation of State Aid to Local Schools. Publius 19: 113-126.

218 Murray, C.; Herrnstein, R. J. 1992. What's Really behind the SAT Score Decline? PI 106 (Winter): 32-56.

219 Orloff, A. S.; Skocpol, T. 1984. Politics of Public Social Spending. ASR 49: 726-750.

220 -. 1984. Why Not Equal Protection? Politics of Public School Spending. ASR 49: 726-750.

221 Pelissero, J. P.; Morgan, D. R. 1987. State Aid to Public Schools. SSQ 68: 466-490.

222 Peltzman, S. 1993. Political Economy of Decline of American Public Education. JOLE 36: 331-384.

223 Policy Studies Journal. 1976. Papers on Education Policy Research. PSJ 4 (4).

224 -. 1981. Papers on Higher Education. PSJ 10 (1).

225 Policy Studies Review. 1983. Papers on Educating Handicapped Persons. PSR 2 (1).

226 Psacharopoulos, G. 1977. The Perverse Effects of Public Subsidization of Education, or How Equitable is Free Education? Comparative Education Review 21 (Feb): 69-90.

227 Public Choice. 1981. Papers on Collective Choice in Education. PC 36 (3).

228 Ralph, J. H.; Rubinson, R. 1980. Immigration and Expansion of Schooling in US. ASR 45: 943-954.

229 Ram, R. 1995. Public Educational Expenditures in the US. EOER 14: 53-61.

230 Riddle, P. 1993. Political Authority and University Formation, 1200-1800. SP 36: 45-63.

231 Rigney, D. 1991. Three Kinds of Anti-Intellectualism: Rethinking Hofstadter. SI 61: 434-451.

232 Ringer, F. K. 1977. Problems in the History of Higher Education. CSSH 19: 239-261.

233 Sakamoto, A.; Chen, M. D. 1991. Returns to Schooling by Establishment Size ASR 56: 765-771.

234 Sander, W. 1993. Expenditures and Student Achievement in Illinois. JPUBE 52: 403-416.

235 Shinn, D. C.; Van der Silk, J. R. 1988. School Reform Legislation in the American States. PSR 7: 537-562.

236 Smith, K. B. 1994. Policy, Markets and Bureaucracy: School Choice. JOP 56: 475-491.

237 Smith, K. B.; Meier, K. J. 1994. Politics, Bureaucrats and Schools. PAR 54: 551-558.

238 -. 1995. Politics and Quality of Education: Improving Student Performance. PRQ 48: 329-344.

239 -. 1995. Public Choice in Education: Markets and Demand for Quality Education. PRQ 48: 461-478.

240 Smith-Lovin, L.; Wilson, K. L. 1980. Educational Attainment and Measurement of Conceptual Variables. JABS 16: 547-565.
241 Sexton, E. A.; Highfill, J. R. 1993. Public Rates of Return on Investments in Higher Education. JSPES 18: 491-506.
242 Social Science Quarterly. 1974. Papers on Problems in Education. SSQ 55 (2).
243 Sonstelie, J. 1982. Welfare Cost of Free Public Schools. JPE 90: 794-808.
244 Steindl, F. G. 1990. University Admissions Requirements as Rent Seeking. PC 65: 273-280.
245 Teaching Political Science 1981. Papers on Social and Political Education. TPS 8 (3).
246 Tedin, K.L. 1994. Self-Interest, Symbolic Values and Equalization of Schools. JOP 56: 628-649.
247 Texas Law Review. 1988. Papers on Academic Freedom. TLR 66 (7).
248 Van Dyke, V. 1973. Equality and Discrimination in Education. ISQ 17: 375-404.
249 Verner, J. G. 1979. Environment, Political System and Educational Policy. CP 11: 165-188.
250 Wade, L. L.; Froth, A. J. 1989. Predicting Educational Outcomes by Political Regime. Coexistence 26: 147-160.
251 Walters, P. B.; Rubinson, R. 1983. Educational Expansion and Economic Output in US: Production Function Analysis. ASR 48: 480-493.
252 Ward, J. G. 1985. Predicting Fiscal Stress in Large City School Districts. Journal of Education Finance 11: 89-104.
253 Webb, F. R. 1989. The Debate on School District Size. EAUS 21: 140-153.
254 Weber, W. L.; Daneshvary, N. 1995. The Revenue-Expenditure Nexus: Local School Districts. QJBE 34: 25-41.
255 Weiher, G.R. 1988. Educational Reform Policy and Governmental Decentralization. APQ 16: 193-212.
256 West, E. G. 1985. The Real Costs of Tuition Tax Credits. PC 45: 61-70.

Poverty

257 Administration. 1988. Papers on Housing Policy. Vol 36 (4).
258 American Behavioral Scientist. 1991. Papers on Poverty. ABS 34 (4), and 1992 35 (3).
259 -. 1994. Papers on Homelessness. ABS 37 (3-4).
260 Annals. 1969. Papers on the War on Poverty. ANNALS 382.
261 -. 1983. Papers on Housing. ANNALS 465.
262 -. 1989. Papers on the Underclass. ANNALS 501.
263 Atkinson, A. B. 1991. Comparing Poverty Rates Internationally. WBER 5: 3-21.
264 Baker, S. G. 1994. Gender, Ethnicity and Homelessness. ABS 37: 476-504.
265 Bohanon, C. 1991. Economic Correlates of Homelessness. SSQ 72: 817-825.
266 Boni, F. G.; Seligson, M. A. 1973. Poverty and Federal Expenditures in Mexico. LARR 8: 105-110.
267 Borooah, V. K. 1991. Problems in the Measurement of Inequality of Poverty. IEJ 38: 12-38.
268 Calsyn, R. J.; Morse, G. A. 1991. Predicting Chronic Homelessness. UAQ 27: 155-164.
269 Casper, L. M.; McLanahan, S. S.; Garfinkel, I. 1994. The Gender-Poverty Gap. ASR 59: 594-605.
270 Cato Journal. 1985. Papers on Political Economy of Poverty. CJ 5 (1).
271 Eggers, M. L.; Massey, D. S. 1991. Structural Determinants of Urban Poverty. SSR 20: 217-240.
272 Emory Law Journal. 1983. Papers on Income Redistribution through Housing Regulation ELJ 32 (3).
273 Gaffikin, F.; Morrissey, M. 1994. Poverty in the 1980s: US and United Kingdom. PAP 22: 43-58.
274 Geisler, C. C. 1995. Land and Poverty in the US. LE 71: 16-34.

275 Giarratani, F.; Rogers, C. 1991. Some Spatial Aspects of Poverty in the US. PRAPR 10: 213-234.
276 Giles, C.; Webb, S. 1993. A Guide to Poverty Statistics. FS 14: 74-97.
277 Harpham, E. J.; Scotch, R. K. 1988. Rethinking the War on Poverty. WPQ 41: 193-207.
278 International Journal of Urban and Regional Research. 1986. Papers on Housing, Class and Marginality. Vol 10 (1).
279 -. 1993. Papers on Poverty and the Underclass. IJURR 17 (3).
280 Journal of the American Planning Association. 1987. Papers on Shelter Policy in Developing Countries. JAPA 53 (2).
281 Journal of Urban History. 1986. Papers on the Early Years of Public Housing. JUH 12 (4).
282 Massey, D. S.; Eggers, M. L. 1993. Concentration of Affluence and Poverty. UAQ 29: 299-315.
283 Massey, D. S.; Gross, A. B.; Shibuya, K. 1994. Migration, Segregation and Geographical Concentration of Poverty. ASR 59: 425-445.
284 Mohl, R. A. 1972. Poverty, Pauperism and Social Order in the Preindustrial American City, 1780-1840. SSQ 52: 934-948.
285 Moynihan, D. P. 1992. How the Great Society Destroyed the Family. PI 108 (Summer): 53-64.
286 Murray, C. 1985. Have the Poor Been Losing Ground? PSQ 100: 427-445.
287 Phelan, J., et al. 1995. Attitudes toward Homeless People. ASR 60: 126-140.
288 Policy and Politics. 1994. Papers on Housing Policy. PAP 22 (3).
289 Policy Studies Journal. 1979. Papers on Housing. PSJ 8 (2).
290 -. 1974. Papers on Poverty. PSJ 2 (3).
291 -. 1986. Papers on Rural Poverty. PSJ 15 (2).
292 Public Interest. 1986. Papers on Housing and the Homeless. PI 85 (Fall).
293 Rasmussen, D. W. 1994. Spatial Economic Development, Education and the New Poverty. IRSR 16: 107-118.
294 Ricketts, E. R.; Mincy, R. B. 1990. Growth of the Underclass. JHRES 25: 137-145.
295 Ricketts, E. R.; Sawhill, I. V. 1988. Defining and Measuring the Underclass. JPAAM 7: 316-325.
296 Ross, C.; Danziger, S.; Smolensky, E. 1987. Poverty in the US. Demography 24: 587-600.
297 Sawhill, I. V. 1988. Poverty in the US: Why Is It So Persistent? JEL 26: 1073-1119.
298 Schram, S. F.; Turbett, J. P.; Wilken, P. H. 1988. Child Poverty and Welfare Benefits: A Reassessment of the Claim that American Welfare Breeds Dependence. AJEAS 47: 409-422.
299 Shulman, S. 1990. Causes of Black Poverty. JEI 24: 995-1016.
300 Singh, V. P. 1991. Underclass in the US: Correlates of Economic Change. SI 61: 505-521.
301 Slesnick, D. T. 1993. Gaining Ground: Poverty in the Postwar US. JPE 101: 1-38.
302 Smith, P. K. 1993. Welfare as a Cause of Poverty. PC 75: 157-204.
303 Snow, D. A.; Anderson, L.; Koegel, P. 1994. Distorting Tendencies in Research on the Homeless. ABS 37: 461-475.
304 Urban and Social Change Review. 1984. Papers on Homelessness. UASCR 17 (1-2).
305 Wilkie, J. W. 1975. A Poverty Index for Mexico. LARR 10: 63-76.

State and Local

306 Annals. 1986. Papers on Industrial City. ANNALS 488.
307 -. 1995. Papers on Local Government. ANNALS 540.
308 Annals of Regional Science. 1988. Papers on Metropolitan Development. ARS 22 (3).

309 Beisel, N. 1990. Campaigns against Vice in Three American Cities, 1872-1892. ASR 55: 44-62.

310 Berch, N. 1992. Why Do Some States Play Federal Aid Game Better than Others? APQ 20: 366-377.

311 Bish, R. L. 1979. Public Choice Theory for Comparative Research on Urban Service Delivery. CUR 7: 18-26.

312 Booth, D. E. 1988. Urban Growth and Decline, Budgetary Incrementalism and Municipal Finances: Milwaukee, 1870-1977. EEH 25: 20-41.

313 Boyne, G. A. 1995. Population Size and Economies of Scale in Local Government. PAP 23: 213-222.

314 Brace, P. 1989. Isolating the Economies of States. APQ 17: 256-276.

315 -. 1991. Changing Context of State Political Economy. JOP 53: 297-317.

316 Brace, P.; Jewett, A. 1995. The State of State Politics Research. PRQ 48: 643-681.

317 Bryant, S. 1976. The Dimensions of Reformism in Urban Policy Analysis. UAQ 12: 117-124.

318 Cadwallader, M. 1991. Metropolitan Growth and Decline in the US. GAC 22: 1-16.

319 Camagni, R.; Diappi, L.; Leonardi, G. 1986. Urban Growth and Decline in Hierarchical System. RSUE 16: 145-160.

320 Capeci, J. 1994. Local Fiscal Policies, Default Risk and Municipal Borrowing Costs. JPUBE 53: 73-89.

321 Comparative Urban and Community Research. 1988. Papers on Power, Community and City. Vol 1 (1).

322 -. 1992. Papers on Global Restructuring and Urban Life. Vol 4.

323 Comparative Urban Research. 1979. Papers on Urban Political Economy. Vol 7 (1), and 1983 10 (1).

324 -. 1982. Papers on the Evolution of Urban Systems. CUR 9 (1).

325 -. 1983. Papers on Structuralist Urban Theory. CUR 9 (2).

326 -. 1985. Papers on Urbanization Research in Latin America. CUR 11 (1/2).

327 -. 1985. Papers on Urbanization in Africa. CUR 10 (2).

328 Congleton, R. D.; Bennett, R. W. 1995. On the Political Economy of State Highway Expenditures. PC 74: 1-24.

329 Corbett, M. 1979. Public Attitudes toward Community Service Needs. MRPA 12: 119-131.

330 Coulter, P. B. 1970. Comparative Community Politics and Public Policy. Polity 3: 22-43.

331 De Borger, B. et al. 1994. Explaining Differences in Productive Efficiency: Belgium Municipalities. PC 80: 339-358.

332 DiGaetano, A. 1994. Urban Governance in the Gilded Age: Political Culture, Social Control and Fiscal Ideology Theories. UAQ 30: 187-209.

333 Dowding, K., et al. 1995. Rational Choice and Community Power Structures. POLST 43: 265-277.

334 Downing, R. G. 1991. Urban County Fiscal Stress: Public Officials' Perceptions. UAQ 27: 314-325.

335 Duffy-Deno, K. T.; Dalenberg, D. R. 1990. Do Institutions Matter? NTJ 43: 207-215.

336 Edwards, J. T.; Galloway, T. D. 1981. Freedom and Equality: Political Ideology among City Planners and City Managers. UAQ 17: 173-194.

337 Environment and Planning A. 1991. Papers on Locality Studies. EPA 23 (2).

338 Erikson, R. S.; Wright, G. C.; McIver, J. P. 1989. Political Parties, Public Opinion and State Policy. APSR 83: 729-750.

339 Evans, H. E. 1992. A Virtuous Circle Model of Rural-Urban Development: Kenya. JDS 28: 640-667.

340 Feiock, R. C.; West, J.P. 1993. Competing Explanations for Policy: Recycling. PRQ 46: 399-420.

341 Fischer, C. S. 1995. The Subcultural Theory of Urbanism. AJS 101: 543-577.

342 Foster, K. A. 1993. Political Structure and Metropolitan Growth. PG 12: 523-548.

343 Friedrichs, J. 1993. A Theory of Urban Decline: Economic, Demographic and Political Elites. US 30: 907-917.

344 Garand, J. C.; Hendrick, R. M. 1991. Expenditure Tradeoffs in the States. WPQ 44: 915-940.

345 Garrard, J. A. 1977. History of Local Political Power. POLST 25: 252-273.

346 Gist, J. R.; Hill, R. C. 1981. Economics of Choice in the Allocation of Federal Grants. PC 36: 63-74.

347 Gold, S. D.; Erickson, B. M. 1989. State Aid to Local Governments. SALGR 21: 11-22.

348 Grady, D. O. 1991. Business Group Influence in State Development Policymaking. SALGR 23: 110-118.

349 Gray, V. 1976. Models of Comparative State Politics. AJPS 20: 235-256.

350 Grossman, P. J. 1990. Impact of Federal and State Grants on Local Government Spending: The Fiscal Illusion Hypothesis. PFQ 18: 313-327.

351 -. 1994. A Political Theory of Intergovernmental Grants. PC 78: 295-303.

352 Hansen, T. 1994. Local Elections and Local Government Performance. SPS 17: 1-30.

353 Hasnath, S. A.; Chatterjee, L. 1990. Public Construction in the US: Expenditure Patterns. ARS 24: 133-145.

354 Haughwout, A. F.; Richardson, C. J. 1987. Federal Grants to State and Local Government. PBAF 7: 12-23.

355 Heyndels, B.; Smolders, C. 1994. Fiscal Illusion at the Local Level: Flemish Municipalities. PC 80: 325-338.

356 Hogwood, B. W. 1995. Regional Administration in Britain. Publius 5: 267-291.

357 Holtz-Eakin, D.; Rosen, H. S. 1993. Municipal Construction Spending. EAP 5: 61-84.

358 Holtz-Eakin, D.; Rosen, H. S.; Filly, S. 1994. Intertemporal Analysis of State and Local Government Spending. JUE 35: 159-174.

359 Hoyt, W. H. 1990. Local Government Inefficiency and Tiebout Hypothesis: Does Competition among Municipalities Limit Government Inefficiency? SEJ 57: 481-496.

360 International Social Science Journal. 1988. Papers on the Local-Global Nexus. ISSJ 40 (3).

361 Jackson, R. A. 1992. Effects of Public Opinion and Political System Characteristics on State Policy Outputs. Publius 22: 31-46.

362 Jacobs, D. 1980. Dimensions of Inequality and Public Policy in the States. JOP 42: 291-306.

363 Jewell, M. E. 1982. The Neglected World of State Politics. JOP 44: 638-657.

364 John, P.; Cole, A. 1995. Models of Local Decision Making Networks. PAP 23: 303-312.

365 Journal of Social Issues. 1980. Papers on Psychological Perspectives on Cities. JSI 36 (2).

366 Journal of the American Planning Association. 1983. Papers on Planning the Development of Local Economies. JAPA 49 (3).

367 Journal of Urban History. 1987. Papers on Suburbanization. JUH 13 (3).

368 -. 1993. Papers on the Megalopolis. JUH 19 (2).

369 Kaplan, B. J. 1983. Metropolitics, Administrative Reform and Political Theory: The Greater New York City Charter of 1897. JUH 9: 165-194.

370 Kemp, K. A. 1978. Nationalization of the American States. APQ 6: 237-247.

371 Kemper, T. D. 1979. Social Psychological and Stratification Factors in the Decline of Municipal Services. SF 58: 422-442.

372 Klingman, D.; Lammers, W. W. 1984. Policy Liberalism Factor in State Politics. AJPS 28: 598-610

373 Lineberry, R. L.; Fowler, E. P. 1967. Reformism and Public Policies in Cities. APSR 61: 701-716.

374 Liner, G. H. 1994. Institutional Constraints, Annexation and Municipal Efficiency. PC 79: 305-324.

375 Lipshitz, G.; Raveh, A. 1994. Application of the Co-Plot Method in the Study of Socio-Economic Differences between Cities. US 31: 123-135.

376 Lowery, D.; Gray, V.; Hager, G. L. 1989. Public Opinion and Policy Change in the American States. APQ 17: 3-31.

377 Machin, H. 1978. Growing Hostility to Local Government Reform. WEP 1: 133-150.

378 MacManus, S. A. 1992. Floridians' Support for Proposition Three Limiting State Mandates on Local Government. SALGR 24: 103-112.

379 Marando, V. L.; Reeves, M. M. 1988. State Responsiveness and Local Government Reorganization. SSQ 69: 996-1004.

380 Marquette, J. F.; Hinckley, K. A. 1981. Competition, Control and Spurious Covariation: State Spending. AJPS 25: 362-375.

381 Meyer, F. A.; Baker, R. 1992. Overview of State Policy Problems. PSR 11: 75-80.

382 Meyer, W. B.; Brown, M. 1989. Locational Conflict in Nineteenth Century City. PG 8: 107-122.

383 Miranda, R. A.; Tunyavong, I. 1994. Patterned Inequality? Reexamining the Role of Distributive Politics in Urban Service Delivery. UAQ 29: 509-534.

384 Morgan, D. R.; Pelissero, J. P. 1980. Urban Policy: Does Political Structure Matter? APSR 74: 999-1006.

385 Mueller, K. J. 1987. Explaining Variance in State Assistance Programs in Local Communities. SALGR 19 (Fall): 101-107.

386 Nice, D. C. 1982. Party Ideology and Policy Outcomes in American States. SSQ 63: 556-565.

387 -. 1983. Representation in the States: Policy-making and Ideology. SSQ 64: 404-411.

388 -. 1984. Cooperation and Conformity among States. Polity 16: 494-505.

389 -. 1985. State Party Ideology and Policy Making. PSJ 13: 780-796.

390 Oechssler, J. 1994. City vs Firm Subsidy Game. RSUE 24: 391-407.

391 Ottensmann, J. R. 1981. The Spatial Dimension in the Planning of Social Services in Large Cities. JAPA 47: 167-174.

392 Pacific Sociological Review 1982. Papers on Research on Boom Towns. PACSR 25 (3).

393 Park, K. O. 1994. Expenditure Patterns and Interactions among Local Governments in Metropolitan Areas. UAQ 29: 535-564.

394 Patrick, T. M. 1980. Canonical Correlation: An Alternative Way to Look at Local Government Expenditures. GAC 11: 48-51.

395 Policy and Politics. 1976. Papers on Citizen Preferences and Urban Policy. PAP 4 (4).

396 -. 1977. Papers on British Urban Policy. PAP 5 (3).

397 Policy Studies Journal. 1975. Papers on Urban Policy. PSJ 3 (4).

398 -. 1981. Papers on Urban Service Distribution. PSJ 9 (7).

399 -. 1981. Papers on Urban Economic Crisis. PSJ 10 (2).

400 -. 1993. Papers on Local Government Policy. PSJ 21 (1).

401 Poterba, J. M. 1994. State Responses to Fiscal Crises. JPE 102: 799-821.

402 Public Personnel Management. 1983. Papers on the Community Development Grant Program. PPM 13 (3).

403 Publius. 1975. Papers on the Suburban Reshaping of American Politics. Vol 5 (1).

404 -. 1984. Papers on Urban Fiscal Stress. Vol 14 (2).

405 -. 1989. Papers on State Targeting. Vol 19 (2).

406 -. 1994. Papers on Interstate Relations. Vol 24 (4).

407 Raadschelders, J. C. N. 1994. Understanding the Development of Local Government: Dutch Case. AAS 25: 410-442.

408 Randall, R.; Wilson, C. 1989. Impact of Federally Imposed Stress upon Local Government and Nonprofit Organizations. AAS 21: 3-19

409 Regens, J. L.; Lauth, T. P. 1992. Trends in State Indebtedness. PAR 52: 157-161.

410 Regional Science and Urban Economics. 1991. Papers on Local Public Economics. RSUE 21 (3).

411 -. 1991. Papers on Urban Form. RSUE 21 (2).

412 -. 1995. Papers on Urban Land Use. RSUE 25 (4).

413 Revue Francaise d'Administration Publique. 1994. Papers on French Urban Politics. RFAD 71.

414 Robertson, K. A. 1995. Downtown Redevelopment Strategies. JAPA 61: 429-495.

415 Robey, J. S.; Jenkins, R. 1982. Economic Basis of State Policies. SSQ 63: 566-571.

416 Sass, T. R. 1991. Choice of Municipal Government Structure and Public Expenditures. PC 71: 71-87.

417 Schneider, M. 1986. Fragmentation and the Growth of Local Government. PC 48: 255-263.

418 Schwartz, H. M. 1994. Bureaucrats and State Reorganization. AAS 26: 48-77.

419 Schwartz, S. I.; Zorn, P. M. 1988. Critique of Quasiexperimental and Statistical Controls for Measuring Program Effects: Urban Growth Control. JPAAM 7: 491-505.

420 Sennett, R. 1990. American Cities: Grid Plan and the Protestant Ethic. ISSJ 42: 269-286.

421 Shkurti, W. J.; Winefordner, D. 1989. The Politics of State Revenue Forecasting in Ohio. IJF 5: 361-371.

422 Sigelman, L.; Smith, R. E. 1980. Consumer Legislation in the American States. SSQ 61: 58-70.

423 Simmie, J. 1986. Kondratiev Waves and the Future of British Cities. Futures 18: 787-794.

424 Social Science Quarterly. 1974. Papers on Measuring Urban Performance. SSQ 54 (4).

425 Sorensen, R. J. 1995. Demand for Local Government Goods: Impact of Parties, Committees, and Public Sector Politicians. EJPR 27: 119-141.

426 Stanford Journal of International Studies. 1978. Papers on Problems of Rapid Urban Growth. SJIS 13 (Spring).

427 Stein, R. M.; Hamm, K. E. 1994. Explaining State Aid Allocations. SSQ 75: 524-540.

428 Stern, D. I. Historical Path-Dependence of Urban Population Density Gradient. ARS 28: 197-222.

429 Stipak, B. 1977. Attitudes and Belief Systems Concerning Urban Services. POQ 41: 41-55.

430 Taylor, L. I. 1995. Allocative Inefficiency and Local Government. JUE 37: 201-211.

431 Thrift, N. J. 1985. British Urban and Regional Research. EPA 17: 7-24.

432 Titus, A. C. 1981. Local Governmental Expenditures and Political Attitudes. UAQ 16: 437-452.

433 Tobey, J. S.; Tajalli, H. 1988. Politics, Economics and Policy Responsiveness in the States. SALGR 20: 59-63.

434 Treyz, G. I. 1981. Predicting Economic Effects of State Policy Initiatives. GAC 12: 2-9.

435 Tucker, H. J. 1982. Use of Time in Cross Sectional State Policy Research. AJPS 26: 176-196.

436 Urban Affairs Quarterly. 1975. Papers on Urban Public Policy. UAQ 10 (4), and 1983 19 (1).

437 -. 1977. Papers on Urban Services. UAQ 12 (3).

438 -. 1982. Papers on Enterprise Zones. UAQ 18 (1).

439 -. 1983. Papers on Urban Theory. UAQ 19 (1).

440 -. 1983. Papers on Urban Transportation Policy. UAQ 19 (2).

441 -. 1984. Papers on Urban Citizenship. UAQ 20 (1).

442 -. 1985. Papers on the Urban Crisis. UAQ 20 (4).

443 Urban and Social Change Review. 1981. Papers on Neighborhood and Community. UASCR 14 (1).

444 Uslaner, E. M. 1978. Comparative State Policy Formation, Interparty Competition and Malapportionment: Key's Hypothesis. JOP 40: 409-432.

445 Wagner, R. E.; Weber, W. E. 1975. Competition, Monopoly and the Organization of Government in

Metropolitan Areas. JOLE 28: 661-684.

446 Walton, J. 1966. Community Power Structure. American Journal of Science 71: 430-438.

447 Wildasin, D. E.; Wilson, J. D. 1991. Theoretical Issues in Local Public Economics. RSUE 21: 317-332.

448 Wong, K. K. 1989. Policy Making in the American States. PSR 8: 527-547.

449 Wright, G. C.; Erikson, R. S.; McIver, J. P. 1987. Public Opinion and Policy Liberalism in the American States. AJPS 31: 980-1001.

450 Yagi, T. 1995. Deterioration of Public Capital and Optimal Policy of Local and Central Government. US 32: 123-134.

451 Yinger, J.; Ladd, H. F. 1989. Determinants of State Assistance to Central Cities. NTJ 42: 413-428.

Welfare

452 Acta Sociologica. 1982. Papers on the Informal Side of Welfare. AS 25 (1).

453 Amenta, E. 1991. Theories of the Welfare State and the American Experience. IJCS 32: 172-194.

454 American Behavioral Scientist. 1983. Papers on the Welfare State. ABS 26 (6).

455 Annals. 1985. Papers on the Welfare State. ANNALS 479.

456 Barr, N. 1992. Economic Theory and the Welfare State. JEL 30: 741-803.

457 Barrett, E. J.; Cook, F. L. 1991. Congressional Attitudes and Voting Behavior: Social Welfare. LSQ 16: 375-392.

458 Broach, G. T. 1973. Interparty Competition, State Welfare Policies and Nonlinear Regression. JOP 35: 737-743.

459 Brown, R. D. 1995. Party Cleavages and Welfare Effort in the American States. APSR 89: 23-33.

460 Carmines, E. G. 1974. Influence of State Legislatures on the Linkage between Interparty Competition and Welfare Policies. APSR 74: 1118-1124.

461 Cartoof, V. 1982. The Neglected Effects of AFDC Policies on Teenage Mothers. Child Welfare 61: 269-278.

462 Casetti, E.; Jones, J. P. 1987. Spatial Parameter Variation by Orthogonal Trend Surface Expansions: Welfare Participation. SSR 16: 285-300.

463 Castles, F. G.; McKinlay, R. D. 1979. Public Welfare, Scandinavia and the Futility of Sociological Approach to Politics. BJPS 9: 157-172.

464 -. 1979. Does Politics Matter? Welfare Commitment in Advanced Democratic States. EJPR 7: 169-186.

465 Cato Journal. 1983. Papers on Social Security. CJ 3 (2).

466 Clayton, J. L. 1976. Fiscal Limits of the Warfare-Welfare State: Defense and Welfare Spending in the US since 1900. WPQ 29: 364-383.

467 Cnudde, C. F.; McCrone, D. J. 1969. Party Competition and Welfare Policies in American States. APSR 63: 858-866.

468 Collier, D.; Messick, R. E. 1975. Prerequisites vs Diffusion: Alternative Explanations of Social Security Adoption. APSR 69: 1299-1315.

469 Cutright, P. 1965. Political Structure, Economic Development and National Social Security Programs. AJS 70: 539-555.

470 Danziger, S.; Haverman, R. H.; Plotnick, R. D. 1981. How Income Transfer Programs Affect Work, Savings and Income Distribution. JEL 19: 975-1028.

471 DeViney, S. 1983. Characteristics of the State and the Expansion of Public Social Expenditures. CSP 6: 151-173.

472 -. 1984. Political Economy of Public Pensions. JPMS 12: 295-310.

473 Emerson, M. O.; Van Buren, M. E. 1992. Conceptualizing Public Attitudes toward the Welfare State. SF 71: 503-510.

474 Ethics. 1990. Papers on the Welfare State. Vol 100 (3).

475 European Journal of Political Research. 1989. Papers on the Political Economy of Welfare. EJPR 17 (4).

476 Fawcett, H. 1995. Privatisation of Welfare: Impact of Parties on the Private / Public Mix in Pension Provisions. WEP 18: 150-169.

477 Feldman, S.; Zaller, J. 1992. Ideological Responses to the Welfare State. AJPS 36: 268-307.

478 Futuribles. 1985. Papers on Social Protection. Vol 1985 (2/3).

479 Gavin, G.; Molyneus, G.; DiVall, L. 1994. Public Attitudes toward Welfare Reform. Social Policy 25: 44-49.

480 Gottschalk, P. 1992. Intergenerational Transmission of Welfare Participation. JPAAM 11: 254-272.

481 Government and Opposition. 1985. Papers on the Welfare State. GAO 20 (3).

482 Griffin, L. J.; Devine, J. A.; Wallace, M. D. 1983. On the Economic and Political Determinants of Welfare Spending. PAS 12: 231.

483 Gusfield, J. 1979. Crisis of Theory in the Welfare State. PSR 22: 3-22.

484 Hanson, R. L. 1983. Content of Welfare Policy: States and Aid to Families with Dependent Children. JOP 45: 771-785.

485 Hasenfeld, Y.; Rafferty, J. A. 1989. Determinants of Public Attitudes toward Welfare State. SF 67: 1021-1048.

486 Hicks, A.; Misra, J. 1993. Political Resources and Growth of Welfare in Affluence Capitalist Democracies. AJS 99: 668-754.

487 Hicks, A.; Swank, D. H. 1984. On the Political Economy of Welfare Expansion. CPS 17: 81-120.

488 -. 1992. Politics, Institutions and Welfare Spending in Industrial Democracies. APSR 86: 658-674.

489 Hicks, A.; Swank, D. H.; Ambuhl, M. 1989. Welfare Expansion: Policy Routines and Mediation by Party, Class and Crisis. EJPR 17: 401-430.

490 Hinich, M. J.; Ordeshook, P. C. 1971. Social Welfare and Electoral Competition in Democratic Societies. PC 11: 73-88.

491 Hirschi, T.; Rank, M. R. 1991. Effect of Population Density on Welfare. SF 70: 225-235.

492 Isaac, L.; Kelly, W. R. 1982. Development Modernization and Political Class Struggle Theories of Welfare Expansion: AFDC. JPMS 10: 201-236.

493 Jennings, E. T. 1979. Competition, Constituencies and Welfare Policies in American States. APSR 73: 414-429.

494 Journal of Social Issues. 1980. Papers on Teenage Parenting. JSI 36 (1).

495 Journal of Social Policy. 1985. Papers on Income Transfer Policies. JSP 14 (3).

496 Judge, K.; Smith, J.; Taylor-Gooby, P. 1983. Public Opinion and the Privatization of Welfare. JSP 12: 469-490.

497 Kangas, O. E. 1995. Attitudes on Means-Tested Social Benefits in Finland. AS 38: 299-310.

498 Kelley, A. 1989. End to Incrementalism? Impact of Expenditure Restraint on Social Services Budgets. JSP 18: 187-210.

499 Letterie, J. W.; van Puyenbroek, R. A. G. 1985. Welfare: Interaction Effects of Collective Demands and Liberal Democracy. AP 20: 331-352.

500 Light, P. C. 1985. Social Security and Politics of Assumptions. PAR 45: 363-371.

501 Lindert, P. H. 1994. Rise of Social Spending. EEH 31: 1-37.

502 Mahler, V. A. 1990. Explaining the Growth of Social Benefits in Advanced Capitalist Countries. EPC 1990: 13-28.

503 Mahler, V. A.; Katz, C. J. 1988. Social Benefits in Advanced Capitalist Countries. CP 20: 37-51.

504 Martinez-Alier, J. 1991. Ecology and the Poor: A Neglected Dimension of Latin American History. JLATAS 23: 621-639.

505 Mebane, W. R. 1994. Fiscal Constraints and Electoral Manipulation in American Social Welfare. APSR 88: 77-94.

506 Miller, L. S. 1976. Structural Determinants of Welfare Effort. SOCSER 50 (March): 57-79.

507 Moffitt, R. 1983. Economic Model of the Welfare Stigma. AER 73: 1023-1035.

508 -. 1992. Incentive Effects of Welfare Policy. JEL 30: 1-61.

509 Mogull, R. G. 1990. Determinants of Federal Welfare Spending. PSQ 20: 355-371.

510 -. 1993. Determinants of States' Welfare Expenditures. JSE 22: 359-276.

511 Offe, C. 1987. Democracy against the Welfare State? PT 15: 501-537.

512 Olson, M. 1983. A Less Ideological Way of Deciding How Much Should be Given to the Poor. Daedalus 112: 217-236.

513 Pampel, F. C.; Williamson, J. B. 1988. Welfare Spending in Advanced Industrial Democracies. AJS 93: 1424-1456.

514 Peace Research Reviews. 1981. Papers on Hunger. PRR 8 (6).

515 Peters, B. G. 1972. Economic and Political Effects on Development of Social Expenditures. MJPS 16: 225-238.

516 Plotnick, R. D.; Winters, R. F. 1985. Theory of Income Redistribution. APSR 79: 458-473.

517 Policy and Politics. 1993. Papers on the Europeanization of Social Welfare. PAP 21 (2).

518 Politics and Society. 1988. Papers on the Welfare State. PAS 16 (4).

519 Pooler, J. 1983. Information Theoretic Methods of Labor Supply Responses to Transfer Programs. SEPS 17: 153-164.

520 Public Interest. 1974. Papers on the Great Society. PI 34 (Winter).

521 Public Policy. 1977. Papers on Income Maintenance. Vol 25 (1).

522 Ragin, C. C.; Bradshaw, Y. W. 1992. International Economic Dependence and Human Misery, 1938-1980. SP 35: 217-248.

523 Riley, J. M. 1986. Generalized Social Welfare Functions: Welfarism, Morality and Liberty. SCAW 3: 233-254.

524 Sander, W.; Giertz, J. F. 1986. Political Economy of State Welfare Benefits. PC 51: 209-219.

525 Scharpf, F. W. 1977. Public Organization and the Waning of the Welfare State. EJPR 5: 339-362.

526 Schram, S. F.; Turbett, J. P. 1983. Civil Disorder and the Welfare Explosion. ASR 48: 408-414.

527 Shah, P. J.; Smith, P. K. 1995. Do Welfare Benefits Cause the Welfare Caseload? PC 85: 91-106.

528 Shalev, M. 1983. The Social Democratic Model and Beyond: Research on the Welfare State. CSR 6: 315-352.

529 Shapiro, R. Y.; Young, J. T. 1989. Public Opinion and the Welfare State. PSCQ 104: 59-90.

530 Sharkansky, I. 1971. Resource Policy and Need Policy Linkages between Income and Welfare Benefits. MJPS 15: 722-740.

531 Sharp, E. B.; Maynard-Moody, S. 1991. Theories of the Local Welfare Role. AJPS 35: 934-950.

532 Shroder, M. 1995. Games the States Don't Play: Welfare Benefits and the Theory of Fiscal Federalism. REAS 77: 183-191.

533 Skocpol, T.; Amenta, E. 1986. States and Social Policies. ANRS 12: 131-157.

534 Skocpol, T.; Ikenberry, G. J. 1983. Political Formation of the Welfare State in Historical and Comparative Perspective. CSR 6: 87-148.

535 Smeeding, T. 1982. Anti-Poverty Effect of In Kind Transfers. PSJ 10: 499-522.

536 Society. 1986. Papers on Safety Nets and Welfare Ceilings. Vol 23 (2).

537 Stonecash, J. M.; Hayes, S. W. 1981. Welfare Policy in the American States. PSJ 9: 681-689.

538 Svallfors, S. 1995. The End of Class Politics? Structural Cleavages and Attitudes to Swedish Welfare Politics. AS 38: 53-74.

539 Taylor-Gooby, P. 1982. Two Cheers for the Welfare State: Public Opinion and Private Welfare. JPP 2: 319-346.

540 -. 1983. Moralism, Self-Interest and Attitudes to Welfare. PAP 11: 145-160.

541 Tompkins, G. L. 1975. A Causal Model of State Welfare Expenditures. JOP 37: 392-416.

542 Tweedie, J. 1994. A State Centered Model of Welfare Policymaking. AJPS 38: 651-672.

543 University of Chicago Law Review. 1992. Papers on the Bill of Rights and the Welfare State. UCLR 59 (1).

544 Urban and Social Change Review. 1972. Papers on Welfare Reform. UASCR 5 (2).

545 Van den Brink-Budgen, R. 1984. Freedom and the Welfare State. JSP 13: 21-40.

546 Wahl, A. M. 1994. Economic Development and Social Security in Mexico. IJCS 35: 59-81.

547 West, E. G. 1983. Marx's Hypothesis on the Length of the Working Day. JPE 91: 266-282.

548 Williamson, J. B. 1987. Social Security and Physical Quality of Life in Developing Nations. SIR 19: 205-228.

549 Williamson, J. B.; Pampel, F. C. 1986. Social Security and the Welfare State. IJCS 27: 15-30.

550 Williamson, J. B.; Weiss, J. E. 1979. Egalitarian Political Movements, Social Welfare Effort and Convergence Theory. CSR 2: 289-302.

551 Winegarden, C. R. 1973. Welfare Explosion: Determinants of AFDC. AJEAS 32: 245-256.

552 -. 1988. AFDC and Illegitimacy Ratios. AE 20: 1589-1601.

553 Wolf, D.; Greenberg, D. 1986. Dynamics of Welfare Fraud: Econometric Duration Model. JHRES 21: 437-455.

554 Wright, G. C. 1975. Interparty Competition and State Welfare Policy. JOP 37: 796-803.

TECHNOLOGY AND RESOURCES

1 Hendon, W. S. 1982. Accounting for Public Recreation Expenditures. AJEAS 41: 111-124.
2 Journal of the American Planning Association. 1982. Papers on Transportation Policy. JAPA 48 (3).
3 Journal of Theoretical Politics. 1994. Papers on Local Commons and Global Interdependence. JTP 6 (4).
4 Khator, R. 1993. Recycling: Policy Dilemma? PSJ 21: 210-226.
5 Klein, D. B.; Majewski, J. 1992. Economy, Community and Law: The Turnpike Movement in New York. LASR 26: 469-512.
6 Policy Studies Journal. 1977. Papers on Transportation Policy. PSJ 6 (1).

Agriculture and Rural Areas

7 Anderson, T. L.; Lueck, D. 1992. Land Tenure and Agricultural Productivity on Indian Reservations. JOLE 35: 427-454.
8 Annals. 1993. Papers on Rural America. ANNALS 529.
9 Balaam, D. W. 1984. The Political Economy of Farm Food Policy. CAP 10: 69-78.
10 Beghin, J. C.; Kherallah, M. 1994. Political Institutions and International Patterns of Agricultural Protection. REAS 76: 482-489.
11 Chicoine, D. L.; Deller, S. C.; Walzer, N. 1989. Size Efficiency of Rural Governments: Low Volume Rural Roads. Publius 19: 127-138.
12 Eckstein, Z. 1984. A Rational Expectations Model of Agricultural Supply. JPE 92: 1-19.
13 Etudes Internationales. 1982. Papers on Agricultural Politics in Industrial Nations. Vol 12 (1).
14 Green, G. P. 1987. Class and Class Interests in Agriculture: Support for New Deal Farm Programs among Tobacco Producers. SQ 28: 559-574.
15 Henry, G.; et al. 1993. Effects of Government Policies on the US Beef Cattle Industry. JPM 15: 117-139.
16 Hoffman, E.; Libecap, G. D. 1995. Failure of Government-Sponsored Cartels and Development of Federal Farm Policy. EI 33: 365-382.
17 International Organization. 1978. Papers on the Political Economy of Food. IO 32 (3).
18 International Regional Science Review. 1990. Papers on Location Analysis and Rural Economic Development. IPSR 13 (3) and 15 (1).
19 International Social Science Journal. 1969. Papers on Rural Politics. ISSJ 21 (2).
20 -. 1990. Papers on Peasantries. ISSJ 42 (2).
21 Journal of Development Studies. 1984. Papers on Development and Rural-Urban Divide. JDS 20 (3).
22 -. 1985. Papers on the Agrarian Question in Socialist Transitions. JDS 22 (1).
23 -. 1990. Papers on Rural Democratization. JDS 26 (3).
24 Journal of State Government. 1988. Papers on Rivitalizing Rural America. JSG 61 (1).
25 Khanna, J.; Huffman, W. E.; Sandler, T. 1994. Agricultural Research Expenditures: Public Goods Perspective. REAS 76: 267-277.
26 Lake, D. A. 1989. Export, Die, or Subsidize: The International Political Economy of American Agriculture. CSSH 31: 81-105.
27 Latin American Perspectives. 1982. Papers on Agriculture and Class in Latin America. LAPER 9 (3), 1987 14 (3), and 1988 15 (4).
28 Lewis-Beck, M. S. 1977. Agrarian Political Behavior in the US. AJPS 21: 543-566.
29 -. 1977. Explaining Peasant Conservatism: Western European Case. BJPS 7: 447-464.
30 Manig, W. 1979. The Spatial Dimensions of Rural Development: Size of Operational Areas of Farmers' Associations on Taiwan. AQ 3: 229-254.
31 Meier, K. J.; Wrinkle, R. D.; Polinard, J. L. 1995. Politics, Bureaucracy, and Agricultural Policy. APQ 23: 427-460.
32 Policy Studies Journal. 1978. Papers on Agriculture and Rural Policy. PSJ 6 (4), 1982 2 (1).
33 Praveen, J. 1994. The Short Run Tradeoff between Food Subsidies and Agricultural Production Subsidies. JDS 31: 265-278.
34 Proceedings. 1982. Papers on Food Policy and Farm Programs. PAPSC 34 (3).
35 Public Administration and Development. 1993. Papers on Managing Agricultural Research. PAAD 13 (3).
36 Publius. 1987. Papers on Rural Government. Vol 17 (4).
37 Rose-Ackerman, S.; Evenson, R. 1985. Political Economy of Agricultural Research and Extension. AJAE 67: 1-14.
38 Sexton, R. J. 1994. Noncooperative Game Theory: Agricultural Markets. Review of Marketing and Agricultural Economics 62: 183-200.
39 Swinnen, J.; Van der Zee, F. A. 1993. The Political Economy of Agricultural Policies. European Review of Agricultural Economics 20: 261-290.
40 Tuma, E. H. 1979. Agrarian Reform in Historical Perspective Revisited. CSSH 21: 3-29.
41 Variyam, J. N.; Jordon, J. L.; Epperson, J. E. 1990. Preferences of Citizens for Agricultural Policies. AJAE 72: 257-267.

42 Von Witzke, H. 1984. Poverty, Agriculture and Economic Development. European Review of Agricultural Economics 11: 439-453.

43 Welch, S.; Peters, J. G. 1983. Impact of Personal Finance on Congressional Voting on Agricultural Issues. JOP 45: 378-396.

Environment and Resources

44 American Behavioral Scientist. 1974. Papers on Politics of Energy and Environmental Policy. ABS 17 (5) and 1978 22 (2).

45 Annals of Regional Science. 1986. Papers on Environmental Conflict Analysis. ARS 20 (3).

46 -. 1987. Papers on Environmental Management. ARS 21 (2).

47 Bachmura, F. T. 1971. The Economics of Vanishing Species. NRJ 11: 657-673.

48 Bartik, T. J. 1988. Effects of Environmental Regulation on Business Location. GAC 19: 22-44.

49 Bernstein, R. A.; Horn, S. R. 1981. Explaining House Voting on Energy Policy. WPQ 34: 235-245.

50 Buttel, F. H.; Flinn, W. L. 1976. Environmental Politics. SQ 17: 477-490.

51 Calvert, J. W. 1979. Social and Ideological Bases of Support for Environmental Legislation. WPQ 32: 327-337.

52 Cato Journal. 1982. Papers on Land Use and Resource Development. CJ 2 (3).

53 -. 1982. Papers on Pollution. CJ 2 (1).

54 Cropper, M. L.; Oates, W. E. 1992. Environmental Economics. JEL 30: 675-740.

55 Development. 1990. Papers on Environmental Sustainability. Vol 1990 (2), and Vol 1992 (2).

56 Development and Change. 1994. Papers on Development and the Environment. DAC 25 (1).

57 Duval, R. D.; Froeneveld, L. 1987. Hidden Policies and Hypothesis Tests: Implications of Type II Errors for Environmental Regulation. AJPS 31: 423-447.

58 Energy Journal. 1991. Papers on Global Warming. Vol 12 (1).

59 Fernau, M. E.; Makofske, W. J.; South, D. W. 1993. Climate Change Uncertainties. Futures 25: 850-863.

60 Fischer, D. G. 1980. Climate and History. JIDH 10: 821-830.

61 Fortmann, L. 1990. Role of Professional Norms and Beliefs in the Agency-Client Relations of Natural Resource Bureaucracies. NRJ 30: 361-380.

62 Futures. 1982. Papers on Global Modeling. Vol 14 (2).

63 -. 1993. Papers on Knowledge Base of Futures Studies. Vol 25 (3).

64 -. 1994. Papers on Sustainability. Vol 26 (2).

65 Garner, R. 1993. The Animal Protection Movement in Britain. PARLA 46: 333-352.

66 Goldstein, W.; Mohnen, V. A. 1992. The Global Warming Debate. Futures 24: 37-53.

67 Hamilton, J. T. 1993. Politics and Social Costs: Estimating the Impact of Collective Action on Hazardous Waste Facilities. RJE 24: 101-125.

68 Hird, J. A. 1993. Congressional Voting on Superfund: Self-Interest or Ideology? PC 77: 333-358.

69 Horowitz, J. 1994. Preferences for Pesticide Regulation. Journal of Agricultural Economics 76: 396-406.

70 Howlett, M. 1994. Judicialization of Canadian Environmental Policy: The Canada-US Convergence Thesis. CJPS 27: 99-128.

71 Internasjonal Politikk. 1987. Papers on Politics of Oil. IP 1987 (5/6).

72 International Journal. 1989. Papers on the Greening of Politics. IJ 45 (1).

73 -. 1992. Papers on Environment and Development. IJ 47 (4).

74 -. 1995. Papers on Environmental Ethics and Changing International Order. IJ 71 (3).

75 International Political Science Review. 1993. Papers on Political Economy and Global Environment. IPSR 14 (1).

76 International Social Science Journal. 1982. Papers on Man in Ecosystems. ISSJ 34 (3).

77 -. 1986. Papers on Environmental Awareness. ISSJ 38 (3).

78 -. 1989. Papers on Sociosphere and Biosphere. ISSJ 41 (3).

79 -. 1991. Papers on Environmental Change. ISSJ 43 (4).

80 International Studies Notes. 1991. Papers on Global Environmental Change. ISN 16 (1).

81 Jackson, J. E. 1983. Measuring the Demand for Environmental Quality with Survey Data. JOP 45: 335-350.

82 Jaffe, A. B., et al. 1995. Environmental Regulation and the Competitiveness of US Manufacturing. JEL 33: 132-163.

83 Jones, C. O. 1972. A Bibliographical Essay on Politics and the Environment. APSR 66: 588-595.

84 Journal of International Affairs. 1991. Papers on Politics of Global Environment. JIA 44 (2).

85 Journal of Law and Society. 1991. Papers on Law, Policy and the Environment. JLAS 18 (1).

86 Journal of Political and Military Sociology. 1993. Papers on Politics and Environment. JPMS 21 (1).

87 Journal of Social Issues. 1980. Papers on Environmental Complexity and Policy Intervention. JSI 36 (2).

88 -. 1980. Papers on Environmental Stress. JSI 37 (1).

89 -. 1981. Papers on Energy Conservation. JSI 37 (2).

90 -. 1992. Papers on Environmental Hazards. JSI 48 (4).

91 -. 1994. Papers on Green Justice and Fairness in the Natural World. JSI 50 (3).

92 Keeter, S. 1984. Measurement of Public Opinion on Environmental Issues. PM 10: 267-292.

93 Langlois, R. N. 1982. Cost-Benefit Analysis, Environmentalism and Rights. CJ 2: 279-300.

94 Law and Contemporary Problems. 1991. Papers on Environmental Protection Agency. LACP 54 (4).

95 Law and Policy. 1993. Papers on Ozone Depletion and Climate Change. LAP 15 (1).

96 Lester, J. P., et al. 1983. Hazardous Wastes, Politics and Public Policy. WPQ 36: 257-285.

97 Millennium. 1990. Papers on Global Environmental Change and International Relations. Vol 19 (3).

98 Murrell, P.; Ryterman, R. 1991. Methodology for Testing Comparative Economic Theories: Environmental Policies. JCE 15: 582-601.

99 Namias, J. 1980. Severe Drought and Recent History. JIDH 10: 697-712.

100 Natural Resources Journal. Papers on Environmental Policy. NRJ 1971 11 (3), 1972 12 (2), 1975 15 (4), 1979 19 (1), 1981 21 (3), 1983 23 (3), 1988 28 (1), 1990 30 (2), 1992 32 (1), and 1993 33 (1).

101 -. 1976. Papers on Environmental Impact Statements. NRJ 16 (2).

102 -. 1989. Papers on Migratory Species. NRJ 29 (4).

103 -. 1989. Papers on Wilderness. NRJ 29 (1).

104 -. 1993. Papers on Wildlife Policy. NRJ 33 (4).

105 New York University Journal. 1988. Papers on Development and Environment. NYUJ 20 (3).

106 Pierce, J. C., et al. 1987. Environmental Policy Elites' Trust of Information Sources. ABS 30: 578-596.

107 Pierce, J. C.; Lovrich, N. P. 1980. Belief Systems Concerning Environment. PB 2: 259-283.

108 Policy and Politics. 1986. Papers on Environmental Policy and Politics. PAP 14 (1).

109 Policy Studies Journal. 1978. Papers on Energy Policy. PSJ 6 (1).

110 -. 1980. Papers on Environmental Policy. PSJ 9 (3), and 1982 11 (1).

111 Post, J. D. (13: 1979). Climatic Change and Historical Explanation. JIDH 10: 291-302.

112 Public Administration Review. 1975. Papers on the Energy Crunch. PAR 35 (4).

113 Rauscher, M. 1994. On Ecological Dumping. OEP 46 (Oct Sup): 822-840.

114 Regional Politics and Policy. 1994. Papers on Environmental Policy in Peripheral Regions. RPAP 4 (1).

115 Rhodes, T. C.; Wilson, P. N. 1995. The Political Economy of Environmental Conflict. LE 7: 106-121.

116 Rohrschneider, R. 1988. Citizens' Attitudes toward Environmental Issues. CPS 21: 347-367.

117 -. 1993. Environmental Belief Systems in Western Europe: A Hierarchical Model of Constraint. CPS 26: 3-29.

118 -. 1993. New Party vs Old Left Realignments: Environmental Attitudes, Party Policies and Partisan Affiliations in West Europe. JOP 55: 682-701.

119 Rose-Ackerman, S. 1977. Market Models for Water Pollution Controls. PUBP 25: 383-406.

120 Sears, D. O., et al. 1978. Political System Support and Public Response to Energy Crisis. AJPS 22: 56-82.

121 Seligman, C. 1989. Environmental Ethics. JSI 45: 169-184.

122 Skjaerseth, J. B. 1995. Fruitfulness of Various Models in the Study of International Environmental Politics. CAC 30: 155-178.

123 Smith, A. A.; Moote, M. A.; Schwalbe, C. R. 1993. An Analytical Survey of Federal Endangered Species Protection. NRJ 33: 1027-1076.

124 Smith, V. K.; Huang, J. C. 1995. Can Markets Value Air Quality? A Meta-Analysis of Hedonic Property Value Models. JPE 103: 209-227.

125 Social Theory and Practice. 1995. Papers on Environmentalism. STAP 21 (2).

126 Soroos, M. S. 1977. The Commons and Lifeboat as Guides for International Ecological Policy. ISQ 21: 647-674.

127 -. 1994. Global Change, Environmental Security, and the Prisoner's Dilemma. JPR 31: 317-332.

128 Swanson, T. M. 1994. Economics of Extinction. OEP 46 (Oct Sup): 800-821.

129 Templet, P. 1995. The Positive Relationship between Jobs, Environment and the Economy. Spectrum 68 (2): 37-50.

130 Van Liere, K. D.; Dunlap, R. E. 1980. Social Bases of Environmental Concern. POQ 44: 181-197.

131 Vries, J. 1980. Measuring the Impact of Climate on History. JIDH 10: 599-630.

132 West, C. T.; Lenze, D. G. 1994. Modeling Regional Impact of Natural Disaster and Recovery. IRSR 17: 121-150.

133 Weyant, J. P. 1980. Quantitative Models in Energy Policy. POLAN 6: 211-234.

134 Wood, B. D. 1988. Principals, Bureaucrats and Responsiveness in Clean Air Enforcement. APSR 82: 213-236.

135 World Development. 1992. Papers on Environmental Problems and Economic Calculations. WD 20 (4).

136 -. 1992. Papers on Environment and Development. WD 20 (4).

Science and Technology

137 Acs, Z. J.; Audretsch, D. B. 1988. Testing the Schumpeterian Hypothesis. EEJ 14: 129-140.

138 Aukutsionek, S. P. 1987. Theories of Cycles in Technical Progress. Matekon 23: 50-75.

139 Ayres, R. U. 1994. Toward a Non-Linear Dynamics of Technological Progress. JEBAO 24: 35-69.

140 Becker, G. 1984. Pietism and Science: Robert Merton's Hypothesis. AJS 89: 1065-1090.

141 Beveridge, A. A.; Rudell, F. 1988. Evaluation of Public Attitudes toward Science and Technology. POQ 52: 374-385.

142 Brannigan, A.; Wanner, R. A. 1983. Historical Distributions of Multiple Discoveries and Theories of Scientific Change. SSS 13: 417-435.

143 Brezis, E. S.; Krugman, P. R.; Tsiddon, D. 1993. Leapfrogging in International Competition: Cycles in National Technological Leadership. AER 83: 1211-1219.

144 Brickman, R. 1981. Comparative Political Analysis of Science and Technology. CP 13: 479-496.

145 Castro, B. 1968. Scientific Opportunities Foregone because of More Readily Available Federal Support for Research in Experimental than Theoretical Physics. JPE 76: 601-614.

146 Cohn, S. M. 1990. Political Economy of Nuclear Power. JEI 24: 781-811.

147 Cohn, S. V. 1986. Effects of Funding Changes upon the Rate of Knowledge Growth in Algebraic and Differential Topology. SSS 16: 23-60.

148 Cole, S.; Meyer, G. S. 1985. Little Science, Big Science Revisited. Scientometrics 7: 443-458.

149 Comanor, W. S.; Scherer, F. M. 1969. Patent Statistics as a Measure of Technical Change. JPE 77: 392-298.

150 Cornbilt, O. 1970. Factors Affecting Scientific Productivity: Latin America. ISSJ 22: 243-263.

151 Cottino, A. 1985. Science and Class Structure: The Alcohol Question in Italy. CC 9: 45-54.

152 de Solla Price, D. 1978. Ups and Downs in the Pulse of Science and Technology. SI 48: 162-171.

153 Del Sesto, S. L. 1980. Ideologies on Nuclear Power: Congressional Testimony. PUBP 27: 39-70.

154 -. 1983. Uses of Knowledge and Values in Technical Controversies: Nuclear Reactor Safety. SSS 13: 395-416.

155 Einsiedel, E. G. 1994. Mental Maps of Science. IJPOR 6: 35-44.

156 Elster, J. 1979. Risk, Uncertainty and Nuclear Power. SSI 18: 371-400.

157 Fisher, F. M.; Temin, P. 1973. Returns to Scale in Research and Development: What Does the Schumpeterian Hypothesis Imply? JPE 81: 56-70.

158 Fuchs, S. 1993. A Sociological Theory of Scientific Change. SF 71: 933-954.

159 Gamson, W. A.; Modigliani, A. 1989. Media Discourse and Public Opinion on Nuclear Power. AJS 95: 1-37.

160 Gillmor, G. S. 1986. Federal Funding and Knowledge Growth in Ionospheric Physics. SSS 16: 105-134.

161 Goddard, J. B. 1980. Technology Forecasting in a Spatial Context. Futures 12: 90-105.

162 Groothius, P. A.; Miller, G. 1994. Locating Hazardous Waste Facilities: Influence of NIMBY Beliefs. AJEAS 53: 335-346.

163 Harris, M. C.; Wynne, K. J. 1989. Explaining the Decline of Nuclear Power in the US. Journal of Energy and Development 14: 251-267.

164 Henry, M. S. 1981. Spatial and Temporal Economic Impact of Nuclear Energy Center. SEPS 15: 59-64.

165 Hufbauer, K. 1986. Federal Funding and Sudden Infant Death Research. SSS 16: 61-78.

166 Jacob, J. R. 1992. Political Economy of Science in Seventeenth Century England. SR 59: 505-532.

167 Jasper, J. M. 1988. The Political Life Cycle of Technological Controversies. SF 67: 357-377.

168 Kitschelt, H. 1986. Theories of Public Policy Making and Fast Breeder Reactor Development. IO 40: 65-104.

169 Kourany, J. 1982. Towards an Empirically Adequate Theory of Science. POS 49: 526-548.

170 Kuklinski, J. H.; Metlay, D. S.; Kay, W. D. 1982. Citizen Knowledge and Choice on the Complex Issue of Nuclear Energy. AJPS 26: 615-642.
171 Long, J. S.; McGinnis, R. 1981. Organizational Context and Scientific Productivity. ASR 46: 422-442.
172 Mandeville, T. 1983. Spatial Effects of Information Technology. Futures 15: 65-72.
173 Mayton, D. M.; Furnham, A. 1994. Value Underpinnings of Antinuclear Political Activism. JSI 50: 117-128.
174 Merton, R. K. 1988. Matthew Effect in Science. Isis 74: 600-623.
175 Natural Resources Journal. 1981. Papers on Nuclear Wastes. NRJ 21 (4).
176 Nelkin, D. 1981. Social and Political Dimensions of Nuclear Power: Three Mile Island. APSR 75: 132-145.
177 Policy Sciences. 1980. Papers on Technology Policy. PSCI 11 (3).
178 Policy Studies Journal. 1976. Papers on Science and Technology Policy. PSJ 5 (2).
179 Pollock, P. H.; Lilie, S. A.; Vittes, M. E. 1993. Hard Issues, Core Values and Vertical Constraint: Nuclear Power. BJPS 23: 29-50.
180 Rudig, W. 1987. Outcomes of Nuclear Technology Policy: Do Political Styles Make a Difference? JPP 7: 389-430.
181 Ruscio, K. P. 1987. Politics of Science and Technology. JOP 49: 277-281.

182 Sheldon, J. C. 1980. A Cybenetic Theory of the Physical Science Professions. Scientometrics 2: 147-167.
183 Shrum, W.; Wuthnow, R.; Buniger, J. 1985. Organization of Technology in Advanced Industrial Society: Technical Systems. SF 64: 46-63.
184 Simonton, D. K. 1978. Independent Discovery in Science and Technology. SSS 8: 521-532.
185 -. 1979. Multiple Discovery and Invention. JPSP 37: 1603-1616.
186 -. 1980. Techno-Scientific Activity and War. Scientometrics 2: 251-255.
187 Social Research. 1992. Papers on Science Policy. SR 59 (3).
188 Tatarewicz, J. N. 1986. The Federal Funding of Planetary Astronomy. SSS 16: 79-104.
189 Teaching Political Science. 1987. Papers on Teaching Science and Technology. TPS 14 (4).
190 Turner, S. P.; Chubin, D. E. 1976. Appraisal of Ortega, the Coles, and Science Policy: The Ecclesiastes Hypothesis. SSI 15: 657-662.
191 World Development. 1990. Papers on Science and Technology Policy Issues from the Periphery. WD 18 (11).
192 Yablonsky, A. I. 1980. On Fundamental Regularities in the Distribution of Scientific Productivity. Scientometrics 2: 3-34.

MISCELLANEOUS

1 Abbott, A. F.; Brady, G. L. 1991. Political Economy of Statutory Deadlines. CJ 10: 703-714.
2 Abelson, R. P., et al. 1982. Affective and Semantic Components in Political Person Perception. JPSP 42: 619-630.
3 Acta Sociologica. 1994. Papers on Social Networks. AS 37 (4).
4 Adams, R. D.; McCormick, K. 1992. Fashion Dynamics and Economic Theory of Clubs ROSE 50: 24-39.
5 Akerlof, G. A.; Dickens, W. T. 1982. Economic Consequences of Cognitive Dissonance. AER 72: 307-319.
6 Alba, R. D. 1981. Mathematical Approaches to the Study of Group Structure. ABS 24: 681-694.
7 Alchian, A. A.; Woodward, S. 1987. Reflections on the Theory of the Firm. Journal of Institutional and Theoretical Economics 143: 110-136.
8 Almond, G. A. 1988. Schools and Sects in Political Science. PS 21: 828-842.
9 Almond, G. A.; Powell, G. B. 1982. Evaluating Political Goods and Productivity. IPSR 3: 173-182.
10 Alt, J. E.; King, G. 1994. Transfers of Government Power: Time Dependence. CPS 27: 190-210.
11 American Behavioral Scientist. 1973. Papers on Models in Political History. ABS 16 (4).
12 -. 1978. Papers on Sports. ABS 21 (3).
13 -. 1981. Papers on Small Groups. ABS 24 (5).
14 -. 1983. Papers on Negotiation. ABS 27 (2).
15 -. 1990. Papers on Control Theory. ABS 34 (1).
16 -. 1992. Papers on Discourse Methods. ABS 36 (1)
17 -. 1992. Papers on Tourism. ABS 36 (2).
18 American Journal of Sociology 1995. Papers on Prediction in the Social Sciences. AJS 100 (6).
19 Anderson, J. W. 1981. The Methodology of Psychological Biography. JIDH 11: 455-476.
20 Andranovich, G. 1995. Applying Interest-Based Problem Solving to Challenges of Intergovernmental Collaboration. JABS 31: 429-474.
21 Annals. 1988. Papers on Anti-Americanism. ANNALS 497.
22 Annals of Regional Science. 1993. Papers on Knowledge Networks. ARS 27 (1).
23 Arnold, R. D. 1982. Overtilled and Undertilled Fields in American Politics. PSCQ 97: 91-104.
24 Australian Quarterly. 1995. Papers on Sports Politics. AQ 67 (1).
25 Axelrod, R.; Bennett, D. S. 1993. A Landscape Theory of Aggregation. BJPS 23: 211-234.
26 Ball, D. W. 1972. Olympic Games Competition: Structural Correlates of National Success. IJCS 13: 186-200.
27 Barley, S. R.; Meyer, G. W.; Gash, D. C. 1988. Cultures of Culture. ASQ 33: 24-60.

28 Baron, J. N.; Hannan, M. T. 1994. The Impact of Economics on Sociology. JEL 32: 1111-1146.
29 Bartholomew, D. J. 1985. Social Processes: Models and Methods. AJS 91: 683-686.
30 Bates, F. L.; Peacock, W. G. 1989. Conceptualizing Social Structure: Misuse of Classification in Structural Modeling. ASR 54: 565-577.
31 Beck, N.; Katz, J. N. 1995. What to Do and Not to Do with Time-Series Cross-Sectional Data in Comparative Politics. APSR 89: 634-647.
32 Bednar, R.L.; Kaul, T.J. 1979 Experimental Group Research: What Never Happened. JABS 15: 311-319.
33 Bergesen, A. J. 1977. Political Witch Hunts. ASR 42: 220-232.
34 Bernheim, B. D. 1994. A Theory of Conformity. JPE 102: 841-877.
35 Berntzen, E.; Selle, P. 1992. Values Count but Institutions Decide: Stein Rokkan in Comparative Political Sociology. SPS 15: 289-306.
36 Blaug, M. 1976. Empirical Status of Human Capital Theory. JEL 14: 827-855.
37 Bohren, O. 1990. Theory Development Processes in the Social Sciences: Stochastic Choice Theory. JEPSY 11: 1-34.
38 Boyne, G. A. 1985. Theory, Methodology and Results: Output Studies. BJPS 15: 473-515.
39 Brady, H. E.; Sniderman, P. M. 1985. Attitude Attribution: A Group Basis for Political Reasoning. APSR 79: 1061-1078.
40 Breton, A. 1993. Toward Presumption of Efficiency in Politics. PC 77: 43-65.
41 Brown, S. R. 1981. Political Implications of Ego Psychological and Object Relational Personality Theories. PP 3: 196-210.
42 Brown, S. R.; Thomas, D. B. 1986. Personality and Politics. PBA 1: 71-102.
43 Bryson, R. A.; Padoch, C. 1980. On the Climates of History. JIDH 10: 583-598.
44 Buchanan, J. M. 1965. Economic Theory of Clubs. Economica 29: 1-14.
45 Burbank, M. J. 1995. Psychological Basis of Contextual Effects. PG 14: 621-635.
46 Buroway, M. 1982. The Resurgence of Marxism in Comparative Sociology. AJS 88 (Sup): 1-29.
47 Bush, P. D. 1981. Radical Individualism vs. Institutionalism: Humanists and Behavioralists. AJEAS 40: 139-146.
48 Camerer, C.; Loewenstein, G.; Weber, M. 1989. The Curse of Knowledge in Economic Settings. JPE 97: 1232-1255.
49 Carroll, J. 1981. Role of Guilt in Formation of Society: England, 1350-1800. BJS 32: 459-503.
50 Chandrasekar, K. 1981. Productivity and Social Indicators. ANNALS 453: 153-168.

51 Chang, S. 1984. Do Disaster Areas Benefit from Disasters? GAC 15 (4): 24-31.

52 Clubb, J. M. 1981. History as a Social Science. ISSJ 33: 596-610.

53 Coats, A. W. 1989. Explanations in History and Economics. SR 56: 331-360.

54 Coleman, J. S. 1966. The Possibility of a Social Welfare Function. AER 56: 1105-1122.

55 Collins, R. 1981. On the Microfoundations of Macrosociology. AJS 86: 984-1014.

56 Congleton, R. D.; Sweetser, W. 1992. Political Deadlocks and Distributional Information. PC 73: 1-20.

57 Conway, M. M. 1989. Political Context of Political Behavior. JOP 51: 3-12.

58 Cook, I. E. 1991. Political Theorizing: Four Conceptions of the Nature of Theory. AUSJPS 26: 510-525.

59 Cook, T. E. 1980. Political Justifications: Use of Standards in Political Appeals. JOP 42: 511-539.

60 Crafts, N. F. R. 1987. Cliometrics. JAE 2: 171-192.

61 Cross, R. 1994. Falsification, Deductivism, Physics and Time Reversibility and Irreversibility in Economic Systems. JESTUD 21: 52-67.

62 Currie, G. 1980. Role of Normative Assumptions in Historical Explanation. POS 47: 456-473.

63 Dajani, M. S. 1984. Bibliography as Database. TPS 11: 100-105.

64 Daniel, C. 1984. Competition, Imperfect Competition and Dynamic Market Processes. AJEAS 43: 301-312.

65 Datta, L. E. 1982. The Politics of Qualitative Methods. ABS 26: 133-144.

66 Dearlove, J. 1995. Homo Sociologicus, Homo Economicus and the Political Science of the British State. EJPR 27: 477-506.

67 DeFelice, E. G. 1986. Causal Inference and Comparative Methods. CPS 19: 415-437.

68 De Long, J. B.; Lang, K. 1992. Are All Economic Hypotheses False? JPE 100: 1257-1272.

69 Dendrinos, D. S.; Sonis, M. 1993. Socio-Spatial Stocks and Antistocks: Logistic Map of Real Space. ARS 27: 297-314.

70 De Vany, A. S.; Saving, T. R. 1983. Economics of Quality. JPE 91: 979-1000.

71 Dex, S. 1985. The Use of Economists' Models in Sociology. EARS 8: 516-533.

72 Diesing, P. 1985. Hypothesis Testing and Data Interpretation: Milton Friedman. Research in the History of Economic Thought and Methodology 3: 61-89.

73 Di Renzo, G. J. 1981. Personality Typologies of Political Elites. Italian Journal of Psychology 8: 165-178.

74 Dominguez, J. I. 1995. Twenty-Five Years of Cuban Studies. Cuban Studies 25: 2-36.

75 Donovan, T. P. 1981. In Defense of History: A Comment upon Definition and Function. SSQ 62: 344-351.

76 Dore, M. H. I. 1988. Use of Mathematics in Social Explanation. SAS 52: 456-469.

77 Drakopoulos, D. A.; Torrance, T. S. 1994. Causality and Determinism in Economics. SJPE 41: 176-193.

78 Dryzek, J. S. 1986. The Progress of Political Science. JOP 48: 301-320.

79 Dryzek, J. S.; Leonard, S. T. 1988. History and Discipline in Political Science. APSR 82: 1245-1260.

80 Dyson, J. W.; Purkett, H. E. 1986. Review of Experimental Small Group Research. PBA 1: 71-102.

81 Dyzenhaus, D. 1992. Why Positivism is Authoritarianism. AJJ 37: 83-112.

82 Eckstein, H. 1988. Culturalist Theory of Political Change. APSR 82: 789-804.

83 Eells, E.; Sober, E. 1983. Probabilistic Causality and Question of Transitivity. POS 50: 35-57.

84 Efaw, F. 1994. Critical History of Methodological Individualism. Review of Radical Political Economics 26: 103-110.

85 Empey, L. T. 1984. How Is Social Order Possible? SP 27: 259-280.

86 Ennis, J. G. 1992. Social Organization of Sociological Knowledge: Intersection of Specialties. ASR 57: 259-265.

87 Epstein, L. G.; Hynes, J. A. 1983. Rate of Time Preference and Dynamic Economic Analysis. JPE 91: 611-635.

88 Eriksen, T. H. 1995. We and Us: Two Modes of Group Identification. JPR 32: 427-436.

89 Etheredge, L. 1979. Hardball Politics. PP 1: 3-26.

90 Ethics. 1986. Papers on Explanation and Justification in Social Theory. Vol 97 (1).

91 Etzioni, A. 1987. On Thoughtless Rationality (Rules of Thumb). Kyklos 40: 496-514.

92 Etzioni, A.; Diprete, T. A. 1979. Decline in Confidence in America. JABS 15: 520-526.

93 Eulau, H. 1976. Understanding of Political Life in America. SSQ 57: 112-153.

94 European Journal of Political Research. 1977. Papers on Political Generations. EJPR 5 (2).

95 -. 1983. Papers on Negotiation. EJPR 11 (2).

96 -. 1991. Papers on Political Science in Western Europe. EJPR 20 (3/4).

97 Fales, E. 1980. Uniqueness and Historical Laws. POS 47: 260-276.

98 Farnham, B. 1990. Political Cognition and Decision Making. PP 11: 83-111.

99 Farr, J. 1988. The History of Political Science. AJPS 32: 1175-1195.

100 Farr, J., et al. 1990. Can Political Science History Be Neutral? APSR 84: 587-610.

101 Faure, A. M. 1994. Some Methodological Problems in Comparative Politics. JTP 6: 307-322.

102 Fearon, J. D. 1991. Counterfactuals and Hypothesis Testing. WP 43: 169-198.

103 Finifter, A. W. 1974. The Friendship Group as a Protective Environment for Political Deviants. APSR 68: 607-625.

104 Firebaugh, G. 1980. Cross-National vs Historical Regression Models: Conditions of Equivalence in Comparative Research. CSR 3: 333-344.

105 Fisek, M. H.; Berger, J.; Norman, R. Z. 1991. Participation in Heterogeneous and Homogeneous Groups. AJS 97: 114-142.

106 Formisano, R. P. 1993. The New Political History and the Election of 1840. JIDH 23: 661-682.

107 Forsythe, R., et al. 1992. Anatomy of Experimental Political Stock Market. AER 82: 1142-1161.

108 Fraasen, B. C. 1980. Rational Belief and Probability Kinematics. POS 47: 165-187.

109 Freeman, L. C. 1992. The Sociological Concept of Group. AJS 98: 152-166.

110 Frendreis, J. P. 1983. Explanation of Variation and Detection of Covariation: Purpose of Comparative Analysis. CPS 16: 255-272.

111 Galasi, P. 1994. Individual Time Allocation: A Labour Supply Model. AO 46: 133-142.

112 Gareau, F. H. 1993. A Gramscian Analysis of Social Science Disciplines. ISSJ 45: 301-310.

113 Geddes, B. 1991. How the Cases You Choose Affect the Answers You Get: Selection Bias in Comparative Politics. PANAL 2: 131-150.

114 Gertler, M. S. 1988. Some Problems of Time in Economic Geography. EPA 20: 151-164.

115 Gilbert, A. 1987. Research on Latin America. Bulletin of Latin American Research 6: 197-208.

116 Glass, J. M. 1982. Schizophrenia and Language: Internal Structure of Political Reality. Ethics 92: 274-298.

117 Golembiewski, R. T. 1976. Measuring Change and Persistence in Human Affairs. JABS 12: 133-157.

118 -. 1981. Small Group Analysis in Political Behavior. Micropolitics 1: 295-319.

119 Good, I. J. 1983. Philosophy of Exploratory Data Analysis. POS 50: 283-295.

120 Goodin, R. E. 1981. Civil Religion and Political Witch Hunts. CP 14: 1-16.

121 Goodsell, C. T., et al. 1981. Bureaucracy Expresses Itself: How State Documents Address the Public. SSQ 62: 576-591.

122 Goodstein, L. D.; Dovico, M. 1979. Decline and Fall of the Small Group. JABS 15: 320-329.

123 Granberg, D.; Nanneman, T.; Kasmer, J. 1988. An Empirical Explanation of Two Theories of Political Perception. WPQ 41: 29-46.

124 Grandy, C. 1989. Can Government Be Trusted to Keep Its Part of a Social Contract? New Jersey and the Railroads, 1825-1888. JOLEAO 5: 249-269.

125 Greenstein, F.I. 1992. Can Personality and Politics Be Studied Systematically? PP 13: 105-128

126 Gregory, A. J. 1968. Political Science and the Uses of Functional Analysis. APSR 62: 425-439.

127 Grimes, A. R.; Kelly, W. J.; Rubin, P. H. 1974. Socioeconomic Model of National Olympic Performance. SSQ 55: 777-783.

128 Gundlach, E. 1994. Accounting for the Stock of Human Capital. WELTA 130: 350-374.

129 Gurin, P.; Miller, A.; Gurin, G. 1980. Stratum Identification and Consciousness. Journal of Social Psychology 40: 30-47.

130 Hall, J. R. 1988. Social Organization and Pathways to Commitment: Types of Communal Groups, Rational Choice Theory and the Kanter Thesis. ASR 53: 679-692.

131 Hall, P. A. 1994. Keynes in Political Science. History of Political Economy 26 (1).

132 Hamermesh, D. S.; Soss, N. M. 1974. An Economic Theory of Suicide. JPE 82: 83-98.

133 Hannan, M. T.; Carroll, G. R. 1981. Dynamics of Formal Political Structure: An Event History Analysis. ASR 46: 19-35.

134 Hardin, C. L.; Rosenberg, A. 1982. In Defense of Convergent Realism. POS 49: 604-615.

135 Havick, J. J. 1978. Approval of a Political Institution: Winners and Losers. JPS 6: 16-25.

136 Hayes, B. C.; Vean, C. S. 1993. Political Efficacy. EJPR 23: 261-280.

137 Hechter, M. 1984. When Actors Comply: Costs and the Production of Social Order. AS 27: 161-184.

138 Heilbroner, R. 1991. Economics as Universal Science. SR 58: 457-474.

139 Heiner, R. A. 1983. Origin of Predictable Behavior. AER 73: 560-59.

140 Herlihy, D. 1981. Numerical and Formal Analysis in European History. JIDH 12: 115-136.

141 Herrmann, R. K. 1988. The Empirical Challenge of the Cognitive Revolution: Strategy for Drawing Inferences about Perceptions. ISQ 32: 175-204.

142 Hindess, B. 1992. Power and Rationality: Western Concept of Political Community. Alternatives 17: 149-164.

143 Hobsbawm, E. J. 1981. Contribution of History to Social Science. ISSJ 33: 624-640.

144 Holcombe, R. G. 1980. Contractarian Model of the Decline in Classical Liberalism. PC 35: 277-286.

145 Hoover, K. D. 1990. Logic of Causal Inference: Econometrics and Conditional Analysis of Causation. EAPHIL 6: 207-234.

146 Howitt, P.; Wintrobe, R. 1995. Political Economy of Inaction. JPUBE 56: 329-353.

147 Huckfeldt, R. R. 1983. Social Context of Political Change. APSR 77: 929-944.

148 Hunt, J. P. 1985. Social Position, Political Consciousness and Political Behavior. JPMS 13: 75-82.

149 Hutter, J. L. 1972. Quantification in Political Science. MJPS 16: 313-323.

150 Hveem, H. 1970. Blame as International Behavior. JPR 1: 49-68.

151 Inoguchi, T. 1993. Japanese Politics in Transition: A Theoretical Review. GAO 28: 443-455.

152 International Journal. 1983. Papers on Ocean Politics. IJ 38 (3).

153 -. 1984. Papers on Polar Politics. IJ 39 (4).

154 -. 1988. Papers on Sports Politics. IJ 43 (4).

155 International Political Science Review. 1983. Papers on Political Clientelism. IPSR 4 (4).

156 -. 1983. Papers on Scarcity. IPSR 4 (3).

157 -. 1987. Papers on the Evolution of Political Science. IPSR 8 (1).

158 -. 1991. Papers on Politics of Art. IPSR 12 (1).

159 -. 1992. Papers on Applications of Political Theory in Politics. IPSR 13 (1).

160 International Review of Administrative Sciences. 1984. Papers on Ombudsmen. Vol 50 (3).

161 International Social Science Journal. 1981. Papers on Historiography. ISSJ 33 (4).

162 -. 1982. Papers on Images of World Society. ISSJ 34 (1).

163 -. 1982. Papers on Sports. ISSJ 34 (2).

164 -. 1983. Papers on the Political Aspects of Psychology. ISSJ 35 (2).

165 -. 1984. Papers on Epistemology. ISSJ 36 (4).

166 International Social Science Journal. 1986. Papers on Time and Society. ISSJ 38 (1).

167 -. 1987. Papers on Interdisciplinary Economic Analysis. ISSJ 39 (3).

168 -. 1988. Papers on Cognitive Science ISSJ 40 (1)

169 -. 1992. Papers on Historical Sociology. ISSJ 44 (3).

170 -. 1993. Papers on Political Sociology. ISSJ 45 (2).

171 International Studies Notes. 1985. Papers on Polar Politics. ISN 11 (3).

172 Jackman, R. W. 1985. Cross-National Statistical Research and the Study of Comparative Politics. AJPS 29: 161-182.

173 Jacobson, A. J. 1983. Democratic Participation and the Legal Structure of the Economy of Firms. SR 50: 803-850.

174 Jojima, K. 1991. Economics and Physics. IJSE 18: 1-288.

175 Journal of Applied Behavioral Science. 1975. Papers on Small Group Theory. JABS 11 (2), and 1979 15 (3).

176 -. 1976. Papers on Self-Help Groups. JABS 12 (3), 1993 29 (2).

177 -. 1989. Papers on Autobiography. JABS 25 (4).

178 -. 1993. Papers on Action Research. JABS 29 (4).

179 Journal of Area Studies. 1987. Papers on the Discipline of Area Studies. JAS 15 (Spring).

180 Journal of Contemporary History. 1973. Papers on Historians in Politics. JCH 8 (1).

181 -. 1991. Papers on Nationalism. JCH 26 (3/4).

182 Journal of Econometrics. 1988. Papers on Causality in Economics. JOE 39 (1/2).

183 Journal of Institutional and Theoretical Econometrics. 1994. Papers on State, New Institutional Economics, Bounded Rationality. JITE 150 (1).

184 Journal of Interdisciplinary History. 1981. Papers on the New History. JIDH 12 (1-2).

185 Journal of Political Science. 1990. Papers on Governments in-Exile. JPS 18.

186 -. 1992. Papers on Bibliography. JPS 20.

187 -. 1994. Papers on Political Outsiders. JPS 22: 1-92.

188 Journal of Public Policy. 1989. Papers on Signals for Steering Government. JPP 9 (3).

189 Journal of Social Issues. 1995. Papers on Obedience: The Milgram Experiments. JSI 51 (3).

190 Juster, F. T.; Stafford, F. P. 1991. Allocation of Time. JEL 29: 471-552.

191 Kalleberg, A. L. 1966. Logic of Comparison: The Comparative Study of Political Systems. WP 19: 69-82.

192 Kavanagh, D. 1991. Why Political Science Needs History. POLST 39: 479-495.

193 Kelley, H. H.; Michela, J. L. 1980. Attribution Theory. ARP 3: 457-501.

194 Kenney, P. J.; Rice, T. W. 1994. The Psychology of Political Momentum. PRQ 47: 923-938.

195 Kirkpatrick, S.A.; Davis, D.F.; Robertson, R. D. 1977. Decision Making in Small Groups. ABS 20: 33-64.

196 Kirn, M. E. 1977. Behavioralism, Post-Behavioralism and Philosophy of Science. ROP 39: 82-102.

197 Kiser, E.; Drass, K. A. 1987. Changes in the Core the World System and the Production of Utopian Literature. ASR 52: 286-293.

198 Klein, D. B. 1992. Promise Keeping: A Model of Credit Information Sharing. EAP 4: 117-136.

199 Knutsen, O. 1987. The Impact of Structural and Ideological Cleavages on West European Democracies. BJPS 18: 323-352.

200 Kohli, A., et al. 1995. The Role of Theory in Comparative Politics. WP 48: 1-49.

201 Kousser, J. M. 1990. Toward Total Political History: Rational Choice. JIDH 20: 521-560.

202 Krause, M. S. 1972. Festinger's Congitive Dissonance Theory. POS 39: 32-50.

203 Krosnick, J. A. 1990. Expertise and Political Psychology. SC 8: 1-8.

204 Kurth, J. R. 1979. Political Consequences of Product Cycle: Industrial History and Political Outcomes. IO 33: 1-34.

205 Ladd, E. C.; Lipset, S. M. 1974. American Political Science Community. TPS 2: 3-39; 3: 144-171.

206 Lamont, J. 1994. Pareto Efficiency, Egalitarianism and Difference Principles. STAP 20: 311-326.

207 Laslett, B. 1980. The Place of Theory in Quantitative Historical Research. ASR 45: 214-228.

208 Latin American Perspectives. 1986. Papers on Left-Wing Latin American Politics. LAPER 13 (2).

209 Law and Contemporary Problems. 1983. Papers on Law of the Sea. LACP 46 (2).

210 -. 1994. Papers on Accreditation. LACP 57 (4).

211 Lee, D. R. 1987. Tradeoff between Equality and Efficiency. PC 53: 149-166.

212 Legge, J. S. 1995. Explaining Jewish Liberalism in the US. SSQ 76: 124-141.

213 Leubsdorf, J. 1982. Three Models of Professional Reform. CORLR 67: 1021-1054.

214 Levine, N. 1974. Why Do Countries Win Olympic Medals? SASR 58: 353-360.

215 Lieberson, S. 1991. Small Ns and Big Conclusions: Reasoning in Comparative Studies Based on a Small Number of Cases. SF 70: 307-320.

216 Lijphart, A. 1971. Comparative Politics and the Comparative Method. APSR 65: 682-693.

217 -. 1975. Comparative Cases Strategy in Comparative Research. CPS 8: 158-177.

218 Lind, J. D. 1987. Exchange Processes in History: Integrating Micro and Macro Levels of Analysis. SQ 28: 223-246.

219 Line, M.; Roberts, S. 1976. Size, Growth and Composition of the Social Science Literature. ISSJ 28: 122-160.

220 Long, S. 1982. Irrational Political Beliefs: A Theory of Systemic Rejection. IJPE 5: 1-14.

221 Lowi, T. J. 1973. Politicization of Political Science. APQ 1: 43-72.

222 Mackenzie, W. J. M. 1971. The Political Science of Political Science. GAO 6: 277-302.

223 Manning, D.; Carlisle, Y. 1995. The Ideologies of Modern Politics. POLST 43: 482-496.

224 Margolis, J. 1980. The Trouble with Homunculus Theories. POS 47: 244-259.

225 Martin, M. W.; Sell, J. 1980. Marginal Utility of Information: Decision Making. SQ 21: 233-242.

226 Maserang, C. H. 1976. Factors Affecting Carrying Capacities of Nations. Journal of Anthropological Research 32: 255-275.

227 Mashkin, K. B.; Volgy, T. J. 1975. Socio-Political Attitudes and Musical Preferences. SSQ 56: 450-459.

228 Mayhew, B. H. 1973. System Size and Ruling Elites. ASR 38: 468-475.

229 McClosky, H.; Chong, D. 1985. Similarities and Differences between Radicals. BJPS 15: 329-363.

230 McCubbins, M. D. 1985. Politics of Flatland. PC 45: 45-60.

231 McGlen, N.; Rabushka, A. 1971. Polemics on Functional Analysis. MJPS 15: 133-147.

232 McGraw, K. M. 1990. Avoiding Blame: Political Excuses and Justifications. BJPS 20: 119-130.

233 -. 1991. Managing Blame: Effects of Political Accounts. APSR 85: 1133-1157.

234 McGraw, K. M.; Pinney, N. 1990. Effects of General and Domain Specific Expertise on Political Memory and Judgment Processes. SC 8: 9-30.

235 McHugo, G. J., et al. 1985. Emotional Reactions to Expressive Displays. JPSP 49: 1513-1529.

236 Mebane, W. R. 1991. Problems of Time and Causality in Survey Cross Sections. PANAL 2: 75-96.

237 Meckstroth, T. W. 1975. Most Different Systems and Most Similar Systems: Logic of Comparative Inquiry. CPS 8: 132-157.

238 Melanson, P. H.; King, L. R. 1971. Theory in Comparative Politics. CPS 4: 205-232.

239 Merelman, R. W. 1977. Moral Development and Radicalism. Youth and Society 9: 29-54.

240 Merrill, S. A. 1970. On the Logic of Comparative Analysis. CPS 3: 489-500.

241 Merton, R. K. 1995. The Thomas Theorem and the Matthew Effect. SF 74: 379-422.

242 Miles, I. 1991. Measuring the Future: Statistics and the Information Age. Futures 23: 915-934.

243 Millennium. 1985. Papers on Nationalism. Vol 14 (2).

244 -. 1995. Papers on Liberal Globalization. Vol 24 (3).

245 Miller, A. J. 1971. Consensus and Conflict in Functionalism: Implications for the Study of International Integration. CJPS 4: 178-190.

246 Miller, D. 1988. Ethical Significance of Nationality. Ethics 98: 647-662.

247 Mirowski, P. 1987. What Do Markets Do? Efficiency of the London Stock Market. EEH 24: 107-129.

248 -. 1989. Measurement without Theory Controversy. Economies et Societes 23: 65-87.

249 -. 1994. Social Network Analysis. AS 37: 329-344

250 Morse, S. J. 1980. National Identity from a Social Psychological Perspective. CRSN 7: 299-312.

251 Mullahy, J.; Sindelar, J. L. 1994. Do Drinkers Know When to Say When? EI 32: 383-394.

252 Muller, N. 1985. Real Structure Modeling. SSI 24: 603-624.

253 Municio, I. 1992. Ethnographic Approach to the Study of Institutional Change. ST 95: 113-138.

254 Myer, D. G.; Lamb, H. 1976. Group Polarization Phenomena. PSYB 83: 602-627.

255 Nalin, E.; Torstensson, J. 1995. Political Systems and Distortions. PC 84: 163-180.

256 Nandi, P. K. 1980. Sociology of Heckling. IJCS 21: 14-33.

257 National Civic Review. 1993. Papers on the Communitarian Debate. NCR 82 (3).

258 Nelson, J. S. 1980. Approaches, Opportunities and Priorities in Rhetoric of Political Inquiry. Social Epistemology 2: 21-42.

259 New York University Journal. 1992. Papers on Nationalism and Self-Determination. NYUJ 24 (4).

260 Noel, S. J. R. 1975. Canada and the American Question. JCACP 13: 87-110.

261 Noonan, J. T. 1988. Intellectual and Demographic History. Daedalus 117: 119-142.

262 Nowak, S. 1984. Schools and Working Methods in Social Science. ISSJ 36: 587-602.

263 Nurmi, H. 1993. Problems in the Theory of Institutional Design. JTP 5: 523-540.

264 Olneck, M. R.; Wolfe, B. L. 1978. Some Evidence on the Easterlin Hypothesis. JPE 86: 953-958.

265 Olson, M.; Bailey, M. J. 1981. Positive Time Preference. JPE 89: 1-25.

266 Perspectives on Political Science. 1994. Papers on Structural Realism. POPS 23 (2).

267 -. 1995. Papers on Revitalizing Political Socialization Research. POPS 24 (1).

268 -. 1995. Papers on Postmodernism. POPS 24 (2).

269 Petras, J.; Davenport, C. 1992. Prestigious Publications and Public Relevance: Vietnam War and Black Protest in ASR and APSR. CLASC 17: 107-122.

270 Phillips, D. C. 1987. Validity in Qualitative Research. EAUS 20: 9-24.

271 Pierson, C. 1984. New Theories of State and Civil Society. Sociology 18: 563-571.

272 Pitcher, B. L. 1981. Hawthorne Experiments: Evidence for a Learning Hypothesis. SF 60: 133-149.

273 Political Psychology. 1992. Papers on Prospect Theory. PP 13 (2).

274 -. 1993. Papers on Political Psychology. PP 14 (2).

275 Political Science 1980. Papers on Political Psychology. PSNZ 32 (1).

276 -. 1981. Papers on Political Sociology. PSNZ 33 (2).

277 Political Studies. 1976. Papers on Karl Marx. POLST 24 (1).

278 -. 1995. Papers on Explaining Change in British Politics. POLST 43 (4).

279 Political Theory. 1974. Papers on Quentin Skinner. PT 2 (3).

280 -. 1979. Papers on Jean-Paul Satre. PT 7 (2).

281 Politics and Society. 1990. Papers on Contested Exchange. PAS 18 (2).

282 -. 1990. Papers on Culture Politics. PAS 18 (4).

283 Politique Etrangere. 1986. Papers on the History of Political Science in France. PE 51 (1).

284 Poole, K. T.; Rosenthal, H. 1984. Polarization of American Politics. JOP 46: 1061-1079.

285 Pride, R. A. 1971. Pattern Analysis: Quantitative Historical Data. CPS 4: 361-372.

286 Proceedings American Philosophical Society. 1969. Papers on Cultural Anthropology. PAPSC 113 (5).

287 Prude, J. 1985. Trouble with Economic History. CSSH 27: 744-754.

288 PS. 1992. Papers on E. E. Schattschneider. Vol 25 (2).

289 Quddus, M.; Rashid, S. 1994. Overuse of Mathematics in Economics. EEJ 20: 251-265.

290 Rabinowitz, G. 1978. On the Nature of Political Issues. AJPS 22: 793-817.

291 Ragin, C. C.; Zaret, D. 1983. Theory and Method in Comparative Sociology. SF 61: 731-754.

292 Rapoport, R. B.; Stone, W. J. 1994. A Model for Disaggregating Political Change. PB 16: 505-532.

293 Recherche Sociale. 1975. Papers on Theories of Society. RS 53 (Jan).

294 Reid, D. M. 1984. Symbolism of Postage Stamps: A Source for the Historian. JCH 19: 223-250.

295 Reither, F. 1981. Thinking and Acting in Complex Situations: Experts' Behavior. SAG 12: 125-140.

296 Review of Politics. 1991. Papers on Leo Strauss. ROP 53 (1).

297 Revista Italiana di Scienza Politica. 1990. Papers on Comparative Method. Vol 20 (3).

298 Revista Mexicana. 1985. Papers on Elections, Parties and Reform in Mexico. RMCPS 31 (120).

299 -. 1989. Papers on the Crisis in Mexico's Study of Social Science. RMCPS 35 (135-137).

300 Revue Francaise d'Administration Publique. 1992. Papers on Ombudsmen. RFAP 1992 (64).

301 -. 1993. Papers on Administrating Culture. RFAP 1993 (65).

302 Revue Francaise de Science Politique. 1988. Papers on Political Anthropology. RFSP 38 (5).

303 Rhodes, J. K. 1971. Causality in Social Science. SI 41: 27-38.

304 Richins, M. L.; Rudmin, F. W. 1994. Materialism and Economic Psychology. JEPSY 15: 217-231.

305 Romanow, A. L. 1984. A Brownian Model for Decision Making. JMS 10: 1-28.

306 Rose, R. 1991. Comparing Forms of Comparative Analysis. POLST 39: 446-462.

307 Rosenau, P. M. 1988. Philosophy, Methodology and Research: Marxist Assumptions about Inquiry. CPS 20: 455-488.

308 Runciman, W. 1969. What is Structuralism? BJS 20: 253-265.

309 Samuelson, P. A. 1970. What Makes for a Beautiful Problem in Science? JPE 78: 1372-1377.

310 Sanderson, S. K. 1994. Evolutionary Materialism: Study of Social Evolution. SP 37: 47-74.

311 Sandler, T.; Tschirhart, J. T. 1980. The Economic Theory of Clubs. JEL 18: 1481-1521.

312 Sartori, G. 1970. Concept Misformation in Comparative Politics. APSR 64: 1033-1053.

313 -. 1991. Comparing and Miscomparing. JTP 3: 243-257.

314 Schwartz, B. 1978. Social Ecology of Time Barriers. SF 56: 1203-1220.

315 Science and Society. 1979. Papers on Marxist Political Economy. SAS 43 (3).

316 Seligman, A. 1988. Comparative Study of Utopias. IJCS 29: 1-12.

317 Sened, I. 1991. Contemporary Theory of Institutions. JTP 3: 379-402.

318 Seymour-Ure, C. 1982. Rumour and Politics. Politics 17: 1-9.

319 Shapiro, I. 1989. Gross Concepts in Political Argument. PT 17: 51-76.

320 Sheppard, B. H.; Hartwick, J.; Warshaw, P. R. 1988. Reasoned Action. JCON 15: 325-343.

321 Shrader, W. 1982. Demoralization in Modern Society. CC 6: 267-284.

322 Silverman, D.; Gubrium, J. F. 1994. Competing Strategies for Analyzing Contexts of Social Integration. SI 64: 179-198.

323 Simon, H. A. 1973. Structure of Ill Structured Problems. Artificial Intelligence 4: 181-201.

324 -. 1979. Fit, Finite and Universal Axiomatization of Theories. POS 46: 295-301.

325 Sims, C. A. 1981. What Kind of Science is Economics? JPE 89: 578-583.

326 Sirgy, M. J. 1990. Toward a Theory of Social Relations: Regression Analog. BS 35: 197-206.

327 Sjersted, F. 1979. Contradictions in Striving for Good Government. SSI 18: 945-966.

328 Sjoblom, G. 1977. Cumulative Problem in Political Science: Research Strategies. EJPR 5: 1-32.

329 Skinner, Q. 1969. Meaning and Understanding in History of Ideas. History and Theory 8: 3-53.

330 -. 1974. Some Problems in the Analysis of Political Thought and Action. PT 2: 277-303.

331 Skocpol, T.; Somers, M. 1980. Comparative History in Macrosocial Inquiry. CSSH 22: 174-197.

332 Sniderman, P. M., et al. 1991. Fallacy of Democratic Elitism: Elite Competition and Commitment to Civil Liberties. BJPS 21: 349-370.

333 Social Research 1975. Papers on Charisma, Legitimacy, Ideology and Weberian Themes. SR 42 (4).

334 -. 1976. Papers on Vico. SR 43 (3-4).

335 -. 1977. Papers on Hannah Arendt. SR 44 (1).

336 -. 1978. Papers on Ideological Bias in Psychology. SR 45 (3).

337 -. 1978. Papers on Karl Marx. SR 45 (4).

338 -. 1978. Papers on the Production of Culture. SR 45 (2)

339 -. 1980. Papers on Social History. SR 47 (3).

340 -. 1989. Papers on Explanation. SR 56 (2).

341 -. 1989. Papers on Philosophy and Politics. SR 56 (4) and 1990 57 (1).

342 -. 1991. Papers on Culture. SR 58 (2).

343 -. 1992. Papers on Frontiers of Social Inquiry. SR 59 (4).

344 -. 1993. Papers on Concept of Order. SR 60 (2).

345 -. 1995. Papers on Defining Boundaries of Social Inquiry. SR 62 (4).
346. Social Science Information. 1972. Papers on Social Stratification. SSI 11 (5).
347 -. 1983. Papers on National Identity, Miscegenation and Cultural Expression. SSI 22 (2).
348 Social Science Quarterly. 1972. Papers on Culture in the Social Sciences. SSQ 53 (2).
349 -. 1972. Papers on Theory Construction. SSQ 52: 815-851.
350 -. 1979. Papers on Thorstein Veblen. SSQ 60 (3).
351 -. 1983. Papers on Karl Marx. SSQ 64: 778-861.
352 -. 1987. Papers on Targeting Governmental Aid. SSQ 68 (3).
353 Social Theory and Practice. 1980. Papers on Dworkin. STAP 5 (3/4).
354 Society. 1980. Papers on Family Research Policy. Vol 17 (6).
355 -. 1983. Papers on Civil Defense. Vol 20 (6).
356 -. 1986. Papers on the Politicization of Scholarship. Vol 23 (3).
357 -. 1993. Papers on Polarizing US Culture. Society 30 (5).
358 Sociological Perspectives. 1991. Papers on Sociological Metatheorizing. SP 34 (3).
359 Somit, A.; Peterson, S. A.; Arwine, A. 1993. Birth Order and Political Behavior. IPSR 14: 149-160.
360 Spegele, R. D. 1980. Deconstruction Methodological Falsification in International Relations. APSR 74: 104-122.
361 Sproule-Jones, M. 1984. Methodological Individualism. ABS 28: 167-184.
362 Star, S. L.; Gerson, E. M. 1987. Management and Dynamics of Anomalies. SI 28: 147-170.
363 Statsvetenskaplig Tidskrift. 1980. Papers on the Economic Theory of Institutions. ST 1980 (5 Special Issue).
364 Stephens, J. 1973. Kuhnian Paradigm and Political Inquiry. AJPS 17: 467-488.
365 Stone, W. F. 1980. Myth of Left-Wing Authoritarianism. PP 2: 3-20.
366 Studlar, D. T.; Welch, S. 1987. Understanding the Iron Law of Andarchy. CPS 20: 174-191.
367 Sullivan, D. G.; Masters, R. D. 1988. Happy Warriors: Leaders' Facial Displays, Viewers' Emotions, Political Support. AJPS 32: 345-368.
368 Sum, L. T. 1990. Ethical Implications of Time in Economic Analysis. IJSE 17: 54-62.
369 Sun, L. 1992. Economics of the Golden Mean. IJSE 19: 47-59.
370 Svalastoga, K. 1976. Space, Population, Energy and Information. IJCS 17: 30-47.
371 Sylvan, D. A.; Goel, A.; Chandrasekaran, B. 1990. Political Decision Making from an Information Processing Perspective. AJPS 34: 74-123.
372 Taebel, D. A.; Elder, C. 1979. Does Individual Behavior Cause Systems, or Do Systems Cause Individual Behavior. UAQ 15: 229-235.
373 Tai, C. S.; Peterson, E. J.; Gurr, T. R. 1973. Sources of Anti-Americanism. JCR 17: 455-488.
374 Tetlock, P. E. 1981. Political Psychobiography. Micropolitics 1: 193-213.
375 -. 1983. Accountability and Complexity of Thought. JPASP 45: 74-83.
376 -. 1985. Accountability: Social Check on the Fundamental Attribution Error. SPQ 48: 227-236.
377 -. 1991. People as Politicians: Alternative Metaphor in Study of Judgement and Choice. Theory and Psychology 1: 85-104.
378 Tetlock, P. E.; Skitke, L.; Boettger, R. 1989. Coping with Accountability: Conformity, Complexity and Bolstering. JPASP 57: 632-641.
379 Teune, H.; Ostrowski, K. 1973. Political Systems as Residual Variables: Explaining Differences within Systems. CPS 6: 3-21.
380 Theory and Decision. 1979. Papers on Concept Formation and Theories. TAD 10 (1-4).

381 Thiagarajan, S.; Pasigna, A. L. 1985. Chain Gang: A Framework for Teaching Algorithms and Heuristics. SAG 16: 441-464.
382 Thomas, J. P.; McFadyen, R. G. 1995. Confidence Heuristic. JEPSY 16: 97-113.
383 Toby, J. 1994. Politics of Public Interest. PI 116 (Summer): 34-56.
384 Topolski, J. 1980. Application of the Marxist Theory to Historical Research. SR 47: 458-478.
385 Turner, R. J.; Wheaton, B.; Lloyd, D. A. 1995. Epidemiology of Social Stress. ASR 60: 104-125.
386 Tursky, B. M., et al. 1976. Evaluation of the Cognitive Component of Political Issues by Use of Classical Conditioning. JPSP 34: 865-873.
387 Tyler, T. R.; Caine, A. 1981. The Influence of Outcomes and Procedures on Satisfaction with Formal Leaders. JPASP 1: 281-292.
388 Tyler, T. R.; Rasinski, K. A. 1983. Explaining Political Events and Problems: Personal and Environmental Causality Micropolitics 2: 401-422
389 Uhlaner, C. J.; Grofman, B. 1986. Wish Fulfillment in 1980 Presidential Election PB 8: 101-129
390 University of Pennsylvania Law Review. 1991. Papers on Critiquing Normativity. UPLR 139 (4).
391 -. 1993. Papers on Blackmail. UPLR 141 (5).
392 Uriarte, J. R. 1987. Topological Structure of Continuous Preferences as a Space of Retractions and the Aggregation Problem. MSS 13: 259-272.
393 Uslaner, E. M. 1991. Comity in Context: Confrontation in Perspective. BJPS 21: 45-77.
394 Van Huyck, J. B.; Cook, J. P.; Battalio, R. C. 1994. Selection Dynamics, Asymptotic Stability and Adaptive Behavior. JPE 102: 975-1005.
395 Verba, S. 1967. Some Dilemmas in Comparative Research. WP 20: 111-127.
396 Wahlke, J. C. 1971. Policy Demand and System Support: Role of Represented. BJPS 1: 271-290.
397 -. 1979. Pre-Behavioralism in Political Science. APSR 73: 9-31.
398 Wangerin, P. T. 1993. Multidisciplinary Analysis of Persuasive Arguments. HJLPP 16: 195-240.
399 Wildavsky, A. 1987. Choosing Preferences by Constructing Institutions: A Cultural Theory of Preference Formation. APSR 81: 3-21.
400 -. 1989. If Institutions Have Consequences, Why Don't We Hear about Them from Moral Philosophers? APSR 83: 1343-1350.
401 Winter, D. G.; Carlson, L. A. 1988. Using Motive Scores in Psychobiographical Study: Richard Nixon. Journal of Personality 56: 75-103.
402 Woolf, S. 1989. Statistics and the Modern State. CSSH 31: 588-604.
403 World Affairs. 1987. Papers on Cultural Research Agenda for Latin American Politics. WA 150 (2).
404 World Development. 1993. Papers on Policies Involving Islands and Small States. WD 21 (2).
405 Wrong, D. 1993. The Present Condition of American Sociology. CSSH 35: 183-196.
406 Yale Law Journal. 1988. Papers on the Republican Civic Tradition. YLJ 97 (8).
407 Yang, B. 1992. The Economy and Suicide. AJEAS 51: 87-100.
408 Yin, R. K. 1981. The Case Study Crisis. ASQ 26: 58-65.
409 Yokoyama, A. 1991. An Economic Theory of Persuasion. PC 71: 101-115.
410 Zander, A. 1979. Study of Group Behavior during Four Decades. JABS 15: 272-282.
411 Zuckerman, A. S. 1982. New Approaches to Political Cleavage. CPS 15: 131-144.
412 -. 1989. Bases of Political Cohesion. CP 21: 473-495.
413 Zuckerman, H. 1978. Theory Choice and Problem Choice in Science. SI 48: 65-95.
414 Zwick, W. R.; Velicer, W. F. 1986. Comparison of Five Rules for Determining the Number of Components to Retain. PSYB 99: 432-442.

AUTHOR INDEX

Abbott, A., ET1
Abbott, A. F., XX1
Abdolali, N., IR408, IR735
Abel, R. L., LC1
Abelson, R. P., XX2
Aberbach, J. D., CP1, MP360, OB1, SC589
Abizadeh, S., OB232, OB233, OB234
Abler, D. G., LE688
Abney, G., PE294
Abowtiz, D. A., CP2
Abraham, K. G., EP411
Abrahamson, M., DP139
Abrahamsson, K., PC1
Abramowitz, A. I., CP185, CP186, MP300, MP361, PE153, PP137, PP236, SP16
Abrams, B. A., EP197, IR344, OB235, PE154, PE155
Abramson, P. R., AB309, AB338, AB368, CP103, LE312, PP237, PP238, PP239, PP240
Abuzadah, S., EP527
Achen, C. H., AB310, IR433, PS100
Acker, J. R., LC95, LC352
Acock, A., CP3
Acs, Z. J., TR137
Aczel, A. D., DP71
Adamany, D., LC388
Adams, J., IR461, PG84, SC2
Adams, J. D., LE1, SC230
Adams, P., AB239
Adams, R. D., XX4
Adams, W. C., PC159
Adelman, I., DP44
Adelstein, R. P., LC301
Ades, A., EP198
Adler, M. A., MP201
Adoni, H., PC91
Afatooni, A., DC1
Affuso, P. J., SC594
Afxentious, P. C., OB236, SP1
Agnew, J. A., CP187, IR1, PG225, PG226
Agnew, N. M., SC19, SC610
Aguilera-Alfred, N., MP213
Aguirre, B. E., DP1
Ahluwalia, M. S., EP155
Ahmed, S., EP792
Ahonen, G., PA259
Aiken, M. T., AB44
Ainsworth, S., LE313, PE295, PE296

Aistrup, J. A., PP318
Aivazian, V. A., EP547
Aiyagari, S. R., EP678
Aizerman, M. A., SC3
Ajzen, A., AB1
Akerlof, G. A., AB85, XX5
Akinyemi, A. B., PC160
Alam, M. S., EP199, PP350, PP351
Alba, R. D., XX6
Albaek, E., PA211
Albala-Bertrand, J. M., EP200
Albin, P. S., DP72
Albritton, R. B., PC107, PC133, SP58
Alcock, J. E., ET148
Alderson, A. S., EP481
Aldrich, J. H., CP103, CP104, CP188, CP295, IR857, LE101, LE202, LE312, PP101, SC735
Alesina, A., DP165, DP234, DP235, EP2, EP201, PE1, PE56, PE144, PE156, PE429, PE430
Aleskerov, F. T., CP189, CP190
Alexander, R. D., PA152
Alexandroff, A., IR834
Alford, J. R., EP619, LE537, PC186, PE204, PP352, PA54
Ali, M., PS262
Alker, H. R., IR2
Alkperovich, G., PG75
Allan, P., IR302
Allen, C., PE57
Allen, D. W., RP37
Allen, H. D., LC316
Allen, M. P., DC1, EP202, EP679, EP704, PP46
Allen, P. M., DP117, PG1
Allen, P. R. B., PG2
Allen, R., PA260
Allen, R. L., AB86, MP394
Allen, S. D., PE431, PE432, PE433
Allision, P. D., EP412
Allison, G. T., OB196
Allison, P. D., ET323
Allsop, D., AB302, IR830, PE292, PP241
Alm, J., EP680, EP681, EP682
Almond, G. A., PS263, XX8, XX9
Almond, S., PE58
Alozie, N. O., ET450, MP143, MP144
Alperovich, G., EP413, PG3
Alpert, G. P., LC508
Alschuler, L. R., EP203, EP204

Alt, J. E., EP156, IR3, IR218, PE59, PE157, PP257, XX10
Alvarez, R. M., CP188, CP191, EP59, PE2, PE158, SC661, SP17
Alvarze de Lorenzana, J. M., PA153
Alwin, D. F., SP145
Amacher, R. C., SC231
Amar, A. R., SC232
Amarcher, R., EP548
Amariglio, J., EP3
Amato, R., AB49
Amato, T., CP284
Ambler, J. S., SP146
Ambrosius, M. M., EP205, EP206
Ambuhl, M., SP489
Amburgey, T. L., OB324, PG76
Amdur, R., ET247
Amelung, T., EP793
Amenn, A., EP439
Amenta, E., SP453, SP533
Ames, B., PE434, SC233
Ames, R. E., SC219, SC220
Amos, O. M., DP166, DP167, DP168
Amundson, D. R., PC174
Amy, D. J., ET359
Anbarci, N., SC6, SC769
Anckar, C., PS103
Anckar, D., PS103
Andersen, K., AB187, AB339, MP207, MP208, MP309
Anderson, C. J., PP1, PP439
Anderson, C. W., IR609, PA57, PA58
Anderson, D. G., LE103
Anderson, E., SC662
Anderson, G., SP86
Anderson, G. M., IR610, OB238, PE298, PP526
Anderson, G. O., PS73
Anderson, J. E., EP685
Anderson, J. J., AB2
Anderson, J. L., PS215
Anderson, J. W., XX19
Anderson, K., PE299
Anderson, L., DC197, SP303
Anderson, M., PG5, PG227
Anderson, M. A., EP4
Anderson, P. A., IR4
Anderson, R. E., AB122
Anderson, S., EP550
Anderson, T., LC122
Anderson, T. L., TR7
Anderson, W., EP686

Anderton, C. H., IR259, IR260,
  IR261, IR293
Andison, F. S., PC114
Andjiga, N. G., LC96
Ando, H., CP193
Andranovich, G., XX20
Andreoni, J., ET149, ET150, LC302,
  PE499, SC199, SC222
Andreski, S., PS244
Andrews, D. W. K., EP153
Andvig, J. C., PP353
Anglin, R., EP207
Annett, A. M., PE159
Annez, P., IR377
Anselin, L., SC378
Ansolabehere, S., AB3, CP194, LE538,
  PC183
Antel, J., IR497
Antholis, W., IR774
Anthony, K., SP151
Antoci, A., PP354
Anton, J. J., IR9
Antunes, G., MP369
Aoki, M., OB9
Aponte, R., MP2
Appelbaum, E., PE583, PE584, SC664
Apter, D. E., PS104
Aracil, J., DP117
Arad, S., ET250
Aragon, Y., PE500
Arai, K., OB10
Aranson, P. H., LC98, PS176
Arbetman, M., EP320, IR106
Arce, C. C., CP57
Arce, D. G., EP61, ET324
Arce, M., EP61
Arcelus, F., PE160
Archer, D., LC353, LC354
Archer, J. C., CP76, EP687, PG7,
  PG56, PG228, PG229, PG230, PG296,
  PG313, PG314
Archer, K., PP242, PP441
Archibugi, D., IR10
Arendt, H., ET2
Argersinger, P. H., LE502
Arian, A., AB293
Arlen, J., EP688
Armendariz de Aghion, B., PE411
Armour, L., ET251, PS3
Arnhart, L., ET3
Arnold, B. L., LC2
Arnold, R. A., PE617
Arnold, R. D., XX23
Arrington, T. S., LC399
Arrow, K. J., ET252, ET253, SC7
Arshanapalli, G., DC336
Art, R., IR11, IR468
Artigiani, R., DC126
Arts, W., AB340
Arwine, A., XX359
Ascher, W., CP195
Ashenfeld, O., CP106
Ashenfelter, O., LC390
Asher, H. B., ET325, LE359
Ashford, S. J., OB11
Ashkins, C. D., PC147
Ashley, R. K., IR12, PG8
Ashraf, J., SP152
Asilis, C. M., SC379
Aspin, L. T., PG77, PG97
Ataw, B. M., OB85
Atesoglu, H. S., PE161
Atfeld, M., IR628
Athal, Y., PA60
Athanassakos, A., EP689
Atkeson, L. R., CP77, PP135
Atkins, B. M., LC3, LC391

Atkins, C. K., AB359
Atkinson, A. B., EP158, SP263
Atkinson, M. M., PP355
Attaran, M., EP62
Aucoin, P., OB74
Audretsch, D. B., TR137
Auerbach, K. D., IR345
Aukutsionek, S. P., TR138
Aumann, R. J., SC611
Austen-Smith, D., CP196, PE300,
  PE301, PE302, PP48, PP49, PP319,
  SC152, SC153, SC736, SC737, SC770
Auster, C. J., PG231
Austin, R. L., LC511
Avant, D. D., IR469
Avery, K. L., PG146
Avram, H., PP467
Axell, K., IR821
Axelrod, R., AB89, CP197, ET151,
  ET152, ET153, ET326, IR13, XX25
Ayers, I., MP370, PE4
Ayers, R. L., PS4
Ayres, R. U., TR139
Ayton, P., PA151
Azam, J. P., EP209, PS106
Azqueta, D., EP552

Baack, D., DP45
Baas, L. A., LE196
Babchuk, N., OB398
Babcock, L., SC665
Bach, S., LE204, LE360
Bacheller, J. M., PE303
Bachman, D., PE5
Bachman, J. G., IR470
Bachmura, F. T., TR47
Backhaus, J., LC99
Backoff, R. W., OB62
Backus, D. K., DP169
Badalamenti, A. F., DP2
Baehr, P. R., PA61
Baer, D., AB341
Baer, D. E., OB373
Baer, D. L., MP210
Baganha, M. I., PE210
Bagnoli, M., EP553, OB371
Bahni, B. S., EP498
Bahr, H. M., PG43
Bahry, D., PS74
Baik, K. H., SC467
Bailey, E. E., EP554
Bailey, M., SP206
Bailey, M. J., LC4, SC666, XX265
Bailey, W. C., LC355, LC356
Bails, D. G., PE60
Baily, M. N., EP63
Bain, E. G., ET394
Bain, P., DC313
Bainbridge, W. S., RP5, RP51
Bairam, E. I., OB239
Bajgier, S. M., SP2
Bak, P., DP140
Baker, J. R., LE323
Baker, M. H., LC479
Baker, P. L., DP73
Baker, P. M., OB75, SC154
Baker, R., SP381
Baker, R. K., SP19
Baker, S. G., SP264
Balaam, D. W., TR9
Balch, G. I., AB313
Balch, R. W., RP6
Baldassare, M., PC53
Baldwin, B. R., OB393
Baldwin, D. A., IR14
Baldwin, G. R., EP555
Baldwin, R., EP796, EP797, EP798
Balke, N. S., PP140

Ball, D. W., XX26
Ball, R., PE304
Ballard, S. C., PA232
Ballmer-Cao, T. H., EP422
Ballou, D., OB76
Ball-Rokeach, S. J., AB134, LC512,
  MP55, PC115
Baltagi, B. H., PA261
Ban, C., OB95
Banaian, K., PP50
Banaszak, L. A., MP211
Bandelt, H. J., SC234
Banducci, S. A., PP356
Bandyopadhyay, T., SC8
Banerjee, A. V., DP3
Banfield, E. C., PP357
Banister, J., SP76
Banks, A. S., DC3, DC4, EP211, PS5,
  PS264
Banks, D. L., ET200
Banks, J. S., OB144, OB198, PA214,
  PP141, SC153, SC380, SC381
Bankston, W. B., LC340
Banton, M., MP56
Banzhaf, J. F., SC235, SC236, SC237,
  SC238
Barbalet, J. M., PE6
Barbone, L., EP799
Barbrook, A. T., PP51
Bardes, B. A., AB225, AB279
Bardhan, P., SC591
Bardo, J. W., PG78
Bar-Hillel, M., SC532
Barkan, J. D., CP147
Barker, A., PP358
Barkey, K., DC127
Barley, S. R., XX27
Barlow, D. E., LC167
Barlow, M. H., LC167
Barlow, R., EP212
Barnes, T. J., PG9, PG10, PG11
Barnett, A., LC168, LC169
Barnett, J. R., PE573
Barnett, M., IR231
Barnett, W. P., OB324
Barnum, D. T., CP78
Baron, D. P., LE63, LE361, LE362,
  LE690, SC9, SC155, SC156, SC157
Baron, J. N., PC116, XX28
Baron, L., LC357
Barr, H., DP170
Barr, N., SP456
Barrett, C. R., SC239, SC350, SC351
Barrett, E. J., MP212, SP457
Barrilleaux, C. J., MP404, PE343
Barro, R. J., EP213, PE61
Barron, D. N., OB325
Barrow, D. J., LC476
Barrows, W. L., MP371
Barry, B., ET254, SC592
Barsade, S. G., ET161
Barsky, R. B., DP171
Bartels, L. M., IR471, LE104, LE276,
  PC117, PP102, PP103, SC667
Barthelemy, J. P., SC512
Bartholdi, J. J., ET154, SC240,
  SC738
Bartholomew, D. J., XX29
Barth, E., OB77
Bartik, T. J., PG134, PG135, TR48
Bartlett, B., OB240
Bartlett, B. R., PS6
Bartlett, R. V., LE539
Bartolini, S., SC739
Barton, A. H., AB90, AB91
Bartrip, P. W. J., EP556
Barzilai, G., IR613
Basehart, H. H., LE205, PP142

Basilevsky, A., OB232
Bassiouni, M. C., DC349
Basu, K., PP359, SC382
Batemarco, R., EP64
Bates, F. L., XX30
Bates, R. H., EP690
Bates, T., MP372
Batra, R., EP415, EP557
Battalio, R. C., XX394
Battigalli, P., SC383
Bauer, J. R., CP107
Bauer, M., LE540
Baum, D., DC170, PP360, PP361
Baum, D. N., EP214
Baum, J. A. C., OB326
Baum, L., LC5, LC392, LC393, LC394
Baumgardner, J. R., SC513
Baumgartner, F. R., LE3, LE412, OB372, PA62, PE305
Baumgartner, T., EP528
Baumol, W. J., DP74, DP75
Baveja, A., SP71
Bawn, K., OB78, SC241
Bax, F. R., LE618
Baxter, V., OB12
Baydas, M. M., MP213
Bayer, R. C., ET255
Beahrs, J. O., SC533
Bean, C. R., EP159, EP168
Bean, C. S., CP198, CP199, LE314, MP254
Beard, T. R., PE121
Bearman, P. S., IR472
Beatty, K. M., ET451, RP39, RP109, RP137
Beaumont, J. R., PG136
Bechhofer, F., PG288
Bechtel, W., PA154
Beck, E. M., DC260, MP57, MP58, MP136
Beck, F. D., EP263
Beck, H., PA155, PA156, PA157
Beck, N., DP236, EP65, PE7, PE162, PE435, PE436, PE437, PE438, XX31
Beck, P. A., CP4, CP5, CP200, DP237, EP691, PP2
Beck, R., PE585
Beck, W., EP680
Becker, E., SC201
Becker, G., TR140
Becker, G. S., PE306
Becker, J. D., PC8
Becker, L. B., PC109
Becker, S. L., PC20
Becker, W. E., ET361
Beckmann, M. J., PG137
Becquart-Leclercq, J., CP6
Bednar, R. L., XX32
Bee, R. H., LC234
Beeghley, L., MP218
Beehr, T. A., OB19
Beenstock, M., IR473
Beer, F. A., IR614, PG79
Beer, S. H., PS177
Beetham, D., PS107
Beghin, J. C., PA63, TR10
Beguin, H., PG138
Behn, R. D., PA64
Behr, R. L., PC92, PC183
Behrman, J. R., SP153
Beisel, N., SP309
Beittel, M., LC354
Beladi, H., EP415, EP557
Bell, B. C., SC534
Bell, C. G., PE408
Bell, C. R., PS178
Bell, D., EP416
Bell, J. B., DC350, DC351

Bell, R., CP7, ET362, LE619
Bell, W., MP373
Bellair, P. E., LC231
Bellante, D., SC668
Belman, C. L., DC261, EP417
Belton, W. J., PE75, PG147
Ben-David, S., OB371
Bender, B., PP52
Ben-Dor, G., PS265, PS266
Bendor, J., ET4, ET155, ET156, LE206, OB13, OB145, OB146, OB147, OB199
Benford, R. D., IR566
Benhabib, J., DP74, DP76
Beniger, J. R., PP104
Benjamin, C. M., IR380
Benjamin, J., IR615
Benjamin, R. W., IR15
Benjamini, Y., PA262
Benn, S. I., ET5
Bennet, E., SC384
Bennett, D. S., IR438, XX25
Bennett, J., PC184
Bennett, J. T., DC262, OB241
Bennett, L. L. M., MP214, PP143
Bennett, P. G., DC5, IR16
Bennett, R. R., LC170
Bennett, R. W., EP558, PE163, PP53, SP328
Bennett, S. E., AB92, AB93, AB226, CP108, MP214, PC9, PC10, PC11, PP143
Bennett, W. L., AB94, LE105, PC13, PC93
Bensel, R. F., PG232, SC242
Benseon, M., LC233
Benson, B. L., LC303, PP362, SC535
Benson, P. R., LC480
Ben-Yehuda, N., RP60
Benze, J., MP215
Berch, N., CP109, SP310
Bercovitch, J., IR17
Bercovitch, S., RP61
Berens, J. F., RP7
Beres, L. R., DC352
Berg, A., PE412
Berg, B., OB148
Berger, J., XX105
Berger, L. A., SC669
Berger, M. A., DC258
Berger, M. C., SP154
Berger, P. L., RP40
Berger, R. J., LC255
Bergesen, A. J., PS75, XX33
Berghorn, F. J., LE376
Bergman, M., DP172
Berg-Schlosser, D., PS7, PS8, PS108
Bergstrom, F., PC14
Bergstrom, T. C., ET118
Berk, R. A., LC304
Berkman, M. B., CP348, LE363, PP235, PP248, SP20, SP44
Berliner, L., PA233
Berman, D. R., EP215, MP216, PG233
Berman, E. M., ET363, OB79
Berman, P., PA215
Berndsen, R., DP4
Berne, R., PE62
Bernhardt, A., MP217
Bernheim, B. D., XX34
Bernholz, P., LE691, LE692, LE693, OB242, SC10, SC536
Bernick, E. L., ET327
Bernstein, R. A., LE364, TR49
Berntzen, E., XX35
Berrington, H., LE4, LE106, LE503
Berry, B. J. L., DP173
Berry, C., PC118

Berry, F. S., EP692, PA263, PA264, PA284
Berry, G., LE18
Berry, J. M., PE307, PE308
Berry, W. D., AB95, EP692, OB243, OB244, OB245, PA264, PA284, PE63, PE64, PE439
Berryman, A. A., DP47
Bersoff, D. M., ET298
Bertola, G., EP418
Bertsch, G. K., PG234
Besley, T., PE164
Best, J. J., LE64
Best, S., EP662, PC60
Beth, R. S., LE541
Bettenhausen, K., ET328
Betts, R. K., DC200
Betz, H. G., PP442
Beukel, E., IR567
Beveridge, A. A., TR141
Bevir, M., SC11
Beyerchen, A., DP5
Beyleveld, D., ET6
Bezdek, J. C., SC359, SC373
Bhagwati, J. N., EP800
Bhansali, R. J., PE198
Bhattacharya, D. K., EP6
Bhattacharya, S., PP359
Biacino, L., SC352
Bianco, W. T., LC305
Bibby, J. F., PP9
Bickers, K. N., DC54, LE718, PA2
Biddle, J., PG80
Bienen, H., LE542, MP458
Bigelow, B. E., SC385
Bigelow, J., DP48
Biggart, N. W., OB160
Biggs, S., PG174
Bikhchandani, S., DP6
Billingsley, K. R., AB233, AB234, AB235
Bimber, B., PC15
Binford, M. B., PS109
Bingham, R. D., EP216
Binmore, K., ET7, ET329, SC12, SC411, SC612
Birch, T. D., EP693
Bird, R. M., OB246
Bish, R. L., PS179, SP311
Bishop, G. F., AB314
Bishop, J. A., EP419
Bishop, J. H., EP66
Bishop, V. F., IR671
Biswas, T., SC158
Bjurulf, B. H., LE253, SC771
Black, D., LE207, SC488
Black, E., MP59, MP60, MP61, MP374
Black, J. H., CP201
Black, J. M., DC263
Black, M., AB275, IR116, MP60, MP61, MP62
Blackford, M. G., EP7
Blackley, P. R., EP694
Blades, D. W., OB306
Blair, D. H., SC13, SC489
Blair, D. K., LE543
Blair, D. W., LC171
Blais, A., CP202, OB149, OB247, PE250, PE369, PE440, SC243
Blake, D., OB247
Blake, F., AB137
Blanchard, W., ET256
Blank, R. M., EP160, EP420
Blau, J., SC490
Blau, J. R., LC244, RP62
Blau, P. M., OB327
Blaug, M., XX36
Blechman, B. M., IR474

Bledsoe, T., MP146
Blejer, M. L., PE65
Blin, J. M., SC14
Bloch, P. C., EP8
Block, C. R., LC172
Block, R. L., LC172, LC173
Blondel, J., PP443
Blood, D. J., PE165
Bloom, H. S., PE166
Bloomfield, R., SC386
Bloomquist, L. E., EP294
Blum, D. W., AB227
Blum, L., ET8
Blum, U., PG12
Blumstein, A., LC168, LC169, LC174,
    LC175
Blydenberg, J. C., LE365
Boadway, R., EP67, EP695, EP696
Bobbitt, P., LC6
Bobo, L., ET452, MP44, MP63, MP375,
    MP376
Bochel, J., PP105
Bock, W. W., MP218
Bodman, A. R., PG81
Boehm, C., ET119
Boehm, T. P., PG168
Boeker, W., OB339
Boettcher, W. A., IR18
Boettger, R., XX378
Boettke, P. J., PS73
Bogart, W. T., LE277
Bogdanor, V., PG13, PG235
Bogue, A. G., LE620
Bohanon, C., SP265
Bohman, G. M., AB228
Bohn, H., PE66
Bohnet, I., CP79
Bohren, O., XX37
Bohstedt, J., DC201
Boix, C., IR218
Bolce, L. H., DC238
Bold, F., RP126
Boldt, D., SP108
Bolland, J. M., AB160, SP155
Bollen, K. A., EP421, ET201, PC119,
    PS110, PS111, PS112, PS267, PS268
Bolton, S. C., RP110
Bonacich, E., ET9, MP377
Bond, D., ET257
Bond, J. R., LE107, LE208, LE621,
    PC12, PP144, SP21
Bonham, G. M., IR19
Boni, F. G., SP266
Bonin, J. P., ET157
Bonjean, C. M., PP320
Bonoit, J. P., SC15
Bonvalet, C., PG139
Books, J. W., CP203, PG14
Boor, M., LE108
Booth, A., DC98, DC99
Booth, D. E., SP312
Booth, J. A., PS60
Booth, W. J., ET365
Booth-Kewley, S., AB330
Borcherding, T. E., OB248
Bordignon, M., PE501
Bordley, R. F., LC176, SC16, SC244
Bordo, M. D., EP559, LC306, OB249
Boree, O., PP243
Borelli, S. A., LE152, PE239
Boren, L. C., DC83
Borger, B., PG15
Borgida, E., CP295, LE101
Borglin, A., ET258
Borjas, G. J., MP3, MP378
Bormann, E. G., PC16, PC184
Born, R., LE5, LE504, LE544, LE622,
    PP145, PP146

Borner, S., SC670
Bornschier, V., EP422, IR346, PE8,
    PE9
Borooah, V. K., SP267
Borrelli, S. A., AB273, LE525, LE623
Borukhov, E., PE502
Bosk, C. L., PA18
Boswell, T., PS216
Bouandel, Y., ET202
Boudon, R., PA65
Boulay, H., PP363
Bound, J., EP423
Bourque, S. C., MP219
Boutilierr, M. A., MP276
Bovasso, G., MP379
Bove, F. J., DP49
Bowen, D. R., DC128
Bowen, E. R., PA216
Bowen, T., LC395
Bowen, W. M., EP216, SC671
Bovenberg, A. L., EP424
Bowers, D. A., MP380
Bowers, W. J., LC349
Bowler, S., CP80, EP697, LE366,
    PE167, PG82, PP3
Bowles, P., EP68
Bowman, J. S., ET366
Boycko, M., EP52
Boyd, J. B., PG236
Boyd, R. L., EP425
Boyd, R. W., CP110
Boyd, S. R., LC155
Boydston, J., PC170
Boyer, G. R., SP72
Boyes, W. J., SC231
Boykin, M. L., AB205
Boyne, G. A., EP161, SC514, SP313,
    XX38
Boynton, G. R., LE6, LE209, LE278,
    LE367, MP381, PP244
Bozeman, B., OB80, PA217
Brace, K., MP147
Brace, P., LC396, LC397, LC432,
    LE109, LE110, PE313, SC202, SP314,
    SP315, SP316
Bradburn, N., AB390
Bradbury, J., PG237
Bradbury, K. L., CP81
Bradley, C. F., EP776
Bradley, M. D., EP358
Bradshaw, Y. W., EP217, EP218,
    PS269, SP522
Brady, D. W., LE319, LE378, LE505,
    LE506, LE507, LE626, PA265, PP527,
    PP528, PP529, SP22
Brady, F. N., ET367
Brady, G. L., XX1
Brady, H. E., AB3, AB4, CP8, CP167,
    XX39
Braithwaite, J., EP622, LC177, LC178
Brams, S. J., DP7, ET10, IR263,
    LE624, LE714, PP54, PP106, PP147,
    SC17, SC159, SC245, SC246, SC247,
    SC278, SC387, SC388, SC389, SC390,
    SC391, SC593, SC594, SC784
Brand, J., LE508
Brander, J. A., EP801, EP802
Brandes, S. L., PP179
Brandon, W. P., SP43
Brandt, K., SC248
Brandts, J., SC392
Brann, A. R., LC10
Brannigan, A., TR142
Brat, D. A., EP484
Brau, S., PC200
Brauer, D. A., EP426
Brawley, M. R., IR616
Breault, K. D., RP63

Breaux, D., LE517, LE545, PP176
Brecher, M., OB200, OB201
Bredow, W. V., IR475
Brehm, J., OB81, SP17
Brehmer, B., ET34
Breit, W., MP64
Bremer, S. A., IR617, IR618, IR619,
    PG83
Brennan, G., EP698, LE7
Brennan, P. G., LC203
Brennan, T. J., EP9
Brenner, M. J., EP69
Brenner, R., EP427
Brenner, S., LC398, LC399
Brent, E., PP175
Brent, E. E., LC481, LC482
Brereton, D., LC400
Bresnahan, T. F., EP219
Breton, A., DC202, OB150, PE503,
    PS180, SC249, XX40
Breton, R., DC202
Bretschneider, S. I., EP699, PA276
Breuning, M., CP296
Brewer, G. D., PA66
Breyer, F., EP428, SC537
Brezis, E. S., TR143
Brickman, R., TR144
Brieg, D., MP311
Brierly, A. B., EP70, EP220
Briggs, R., PA293
Brigham, J., LC7
Brignoli, H. P., DP174
Brill, A., ET472
Brilmayer, L., ET11
Brinig, M. F., PE309
Brint, S., AB96
Brischetto, R., SC250
Brito, D. L., IR292
Britt, C. L., LC179
Britt, D. W., LC483
Brittan, S., EP71, PS113
Britton, C. R., SP15
Broach, G. T., SP458
Brocheux, P., DC129
Brock, D. W., PA67
Brockett, C. D., DC6
Brod, D., SC672
Brodsky, D. M., CP82
Brody, A., DP238
Brody, C. J., PP55
Brody, R. A., AB5, AB6, AB229,
    CP204, CP205, ET94, IR760, LE132,
    MP127, PC152
Broembsen, M. H., PG96
Brokaw, A. J., CP83
Bromley, S., MP70
Bronars, S. G., DC264, LE427
Brook, R., ET259
Brooker, R. G., PE10, SC18
Brooks, C., AB342, EP10, EP25
Brooks, H., PA68
Brooks, J. E., PA3
Brooks, S. C., PC105
Broome, B. J., DC17, DC18
Brophy-Baermann, M., PE168
Brosio, G., OB250
Brosius, H. B., PC113
Brouthers, L. E., PE67
Brown, A., EP560, EP561
Brown, C., AB7, AB39, DP8, DP77,
    IR835, MP148, PP148, PP245, PP321,
    SC211
Brown, D. J., ET368
Brown, D. W., LC180, LC401
Brown, E. M., MP4
Brown, G. K., EP429
Brown, J. G., ET369
Brown, J. L., SC19, SC610

Brown, L. A., PA271, PA272
Brown, M., SP382
Brown, M. C., LC484, PP364
Brown, R. D., CP206, PP149, PP322,
    SP459
Brown, R. E., AB86, MP394, RP97
Brown, S. R., AB97, ET12, XX41, XX42
Brown, T. A., AB131, AB272
Brown, W., EP670
Brown, W. W., PE169
Browne, C., PE310
Browne, D. L., PG140
Browne, E. C., LE65, LE66, LE325,
    SC160, SC161, SC162, SC163, SC164,
    SC538
Browne, S. D., LE111
Browne, T. A., PP246
Browne, W. P., LE368, PE311, PE312
Brownfield, D., SP138
Browning, R. P., MP149
Browning, R. X., SC299
Brownsword, R., ET6
Broyles, P., PP46
Bruce, J. M., PP4
Bruce, P., LE615
Bruchey, S., EP221
Bruck, G., LE30
Bruderl, J., OB328
Brudney, J. L., OB14, RP138
Brumbeck, G. B., ET370
Brumberg, B. S., LE380
Brunetti, A., SC670
Brunk, G. G., AB290, AB291, AB292,
    AB298, CP111, ET333, ET371, LE546,
    LE547, LE556, PA69, PA266, PA267,
    PC185, PE199, PE271, PE314, PE350,
    PG84, PG141, PS9, PS181, SC673,
    SC772
Brunn, S. D., PG38
Brustein, W., IR708, PP247
Bryan, A. L., AB280
Bryant, B. L., SP162
Bryant, S., SP317
Bryson, R. A., XX43
Buchanan, J. M., CP229, EP72, LC100,
    LC101, LC102, PE586, PS114, XX44
Buchanan, R. J., SP73
Buck, A., PA218
Buckner, M. A., MP418
Bucovetsky, S., EP700
Budge, I., LE94, PP107, PP108,
    PP323, SC165, SC166
Budziszewski, J., SC251
Buechler, S. M., DC130
Buell, E., RP139
Bueno de Mesquita, B., IR219, IR228,
    IR251, IR264, IR367, IR568, IR620,
    IR621, IR622, IR623, IR624, IR625,
    IR628, IR627, IR628, IR629, IR630,
    IR631, IR632, IR685, IR705, PG238,
    PS10
Buhr, W., EP222
Bulkley, G., DC263
Bullard, J. B., DP78, PA70
Bullock, C. S., LE210, LE505, LE548,
    LE625, LE626, MP65, MP150, MP151,
    MP177, MP245, SC252
Bullock, D., AB8, PC216, PE278
Bulmer, M., PA219
Bulow, J., DP50
Bunce, V., LE549, LE550, LE551,
    LE552, LE553, PE441
Bundrick, C. M., PE182
Buniger, J., TR183
Bunker, S. G., PG239
Bupp, I. C., PE124
Burbank, M. J., XX45
Burbeck, S. L., PG85

Burdekin, R. C. K., EP73
Burgelman, R. A., EP11
Burgess, R., EP701
Burgin, E., LE627
Burgoon, M., PC209
Burk, J., IR477, IR478
Burke, J. F., RP144
Burke, J. P., LE112
Burke, K., PP311, PP546
Burke, W. L., LC8
Burkhart, R. E., PS115
Burklin, W. P., DP239
Burley, J., PS226
Burnell, B. S., SP156
Burnham, W. D., AB9
Burnovski, M., LC307
Burns, T. R., EP528
Burnside, C., DP175
Burnstein, P., IR633, LE509, MP66,
    PA4
Buroway, M., XX46
Burrow-Auffarth, K., CP50
Bursik, R. J., LC181, LC312, RP117
Burt, O., PE561
Burt, R. S., PA268, SC595
Burton, S. J., ET260
Burtt, S., ET373
Busch, M. L., EP843, ET158
Bush, P. D., XX47
Butkiewicz, J. L., PE155
Butler, A., DP78, DP79
Butler, C. A., ET154
Butler, J. S., IR479
Butler, M. R., SP24
Butler, R. J., SC393
Butler, S., ET159
Buttel, F. H., TR50
Button, J., EP702, SP75
Buzan, B., IR20, IR836
Buzan, B. C., MP382
Byers, J. D., DP240
Byrnes, J. E., PC109
Byrnes, T. A., RP41
Bystryn, M. N., DP241

Cable, S., CP9
Cadwallader, M., SP318
Cahan, S. F., EP562
Cahill, A. G., PA220, SP115
Caiden, N., PE69
Cain, B. E., MP152, MP383, MP521
Caine, A., XX387
Caldeira, G. A., LC182, LC402,
    LC403, LC404, LC405, LC406, LE369,
    LE370, LE371, LE528, PP150, PS9
Caldwell, M., LE36
Calhoun, C. A., PG157
Calhoun, D., MP220
Callaghan, K. J., LE113
Callahan, P., ET375
Callari, A., EP3
Callen, J. L., EP547
Calloway, M. R., PC17, PC18
Calsyn, R. J., SP268
Calvert, J. W., TR51
Calvert, L. M., MP298
Calvert, R. L., CP207, EP563, IR3,
    LE315, PC19, SC773
Calvin, L. D., EP754
Camagni, R., SP319
Camerer, C., SC20, XX48
Cameron, C. M., LC83, LC84, LC460,
    LE211, LE671, PP83
Cameron, D. R., OB251, PE315
Cameron, K., SP157
Cameron, S., EP703, LC358, LC359
Camina, O. S., SP164
Campbell, B., PE70

Campbell, B. A., MP65
Campbell, B. C., CP84, PG142
Campbell, D. B., SP113
Campbell, D. E., SC253, SC740
Campbell, D. T., PA159
Campbell, J. E., CP208, PC186,
    PP151, PP152, PP530, SC774, SC775
Campbell, J. L., EP679, EP704
Campbell, L. G., DC131, DC132
Campbell, S. H., IR743
Campbell, T. J., LC9
Campos, J. E. L., PG143
Camron, D. T., LE316
Canak, W. L., EP445
Cancian, F. M., PC162
Candeal-Haro, J. C., SC539
Cannizzo, C. A., IR368, IR634
Cannon, L. W., RP52
Cannon, M. W., IR635
Canon, B. C., EP564, LC5, LC408,
    LC409, PG86
Canon, D. T., LE510, PP153
Canova, F., DP176, DP177
Canovan, M., PP5
Canterbery, E. R., EP565
Canto, V. A., EP223
Cantor, D., LC183, LC188
Cantor, R. D., EP344
Capeci, J., SP320
Caporaso, J. A., EP224, PS12, PS218
Cappelli, P., OB15
Capron, H., CP112
Card, D., DC265, EP420, SP158
Carey, J., LE554, PC94
Carkoglu, A., PE170
Carleson, L., DP9
Carley, K., AB98
Carling, A. H., SC21
Carlino, G. A., EP225
Carlisle, Y., XX223
Carlsen, F., SC394
Carlsnaes, W., AB99, IR21
Carlson, J. M., PP379, RP161
Carlson, L. A., XX401
Carlson, L. J., IR369
Carment, D., ET377, IR370, MP385,
    MP386
Carmichael, F., PE11
Carmichael, H. L., SP159
Carmines, E. G., CP177, CP206,
    CP209, MP153, MP387, PP248, PP444,
    SP460
Carneiro, R. L., DP143
Carnevale, P. J., ET250
Carpenter, J., PG139
Carritte, J., EP226
Carro, J. L., LC10
Carroll, B., SC481
Carroll, C. D., EP430, EP431
Carroll, G. R., OB329, OB330, OB331,
    OB332, OB333, PA281, XX133
Carroll, J., XX49
Carroll, J. J., EP227, EP296, LC103
Carroll, J. W., RP166
Carruth, A., DC266
Carruthers, N., PG144
Carsey, T. M., MP388
Carson, C. S., EP432
Carson, R., AB100, SC540
Carter, D., OB25
Carter, G. L., DC203
Carter, H., IR480
Carter, R. G., LE280
Cartoof, V., SP461
Cartwright, P. A., OB258
Carty, R. K., LE355
Case, A. C., PE71, PE164
Casetti, E., EP450, SP462

Casey, G., SP23
Caspary, W. R., AB230, AB231, IR636
Casper, J. D., ET261, LC362, LC400
Casper, L. M., SP269
Cass, D., DP10
Cassel, C. A., AB101, CP113, CP210, PP249
Casstevens, H. T., LE68
Casstevens, T. W., LE67, LE68, OB334
Castle, D. S., PC187
Castles, F. G., AB102, OB252, PE72, PE316, RP111, SP160, SP463, SP464
Castro, B., TR145
Cataldo, E. F., MP77, SP161
Cattell, R. B., DP178
Catton, W. R., PA160
Caudill, S. B., EP567
Caulfield, S., MP222
Cava, A., ET363
Cavanagh, T. E., LE372, LE373
Cave, M., EP561
Cavendish, J. C., SP56
Caves, R. E., MP449
Cebula, R. J., DC267, LC124, PE73, PE74, PE75, PE76, PG145, PG146, PG147
Cederman, L. E., ET188
Cerny, P. G., IR371, PA5, SC203
Cesario, F. J., PE504
Cha, B., PE415
Chadwick, R. W., IR265
Chafetz, J. S., AB103
Chaffee, S. H., PC120
Chaffey, D. C., LE374
Chai, S. K., DC204
Chakravarty, S., EP229
Chalfant, H. P., RP90
Chalmers, D. A., DC7
Chalmers, M. C., MP38
Chamberlin, J. R., PE505, PE506, SC22, SC254
Chamblin, M. B., LC232
Champagne, R. A., PP531
Chan, S., EP433, PE317, PE416
Chan, T., MP108
Chandrasekar, K., XX50
Chandrasekaran, B., XX371
Chang, R., EP434
Chang, S., XX51
Chap, S., AB232
Chapman, B., LC11
Chappell, H. W., EP76, EP77, PE171, PE172, PE173, PE443, PP6, PP56, PP324
Chari, V. V., PE444
Charles, M., MP67
Charlesworth, W. R., PA161
Charlot, J., PP7
Chase, I., ET160
Chase-Dunn, C., EP230, IR346, IR837, IR838
Chatman, J. A., ET161
Chatterjee, B. B., ET13
Chatterjee, L., SP353
Chaves, M., RP49
Chayet, E. F., LC224
Cheasty, A., PE65
Cheit, R. E., PA270
Chen, C. H., EP231
Chen, H. T., PA221
Chen, K., DP140, MP239
Chen, M. D., SP233
Chen, P., DP80
Chenery, H. B., EP232
Chernotsky, H., EP315
Chertkoff, J. M., SC167
Chesler, M., SP162
Chesnais, J. C., LC360

Chesney, J. D., LE375
Chester, E., PE77
Chester, E. W., PC163, PP154
Chester, K. M., IR154
Chew, S. H., SC674
Chey, M., PS301
Chichilnisky, G., SC23, SC24, SC25, SC541
Chicoine, D. L., PE78, PG151, TR11
Chilton, R., LC184
Chilton, S., PG240
Chinn, D. L., EP233
Chinn, M. D., PA71
Chiorazzi, M., LC12
Chircios, T. G., LC167
Chirot, D., IR839
Chittick, W. O., AB233, AB234, AB235
Cho, I. K., SC395
Choi, H. C., PC20
Choike, J. R., MP156, PP326
Chong, D., ET162, XX229
Choptiany, L., ET262
Choucri, N., IR415
Choudhury, M. A., ET14
Choueiri, Y. M., RP8
Chowdhury, A. R., EP234
Chressanthis, G. A., PE174, PP220, PP445, PP446
Christ, C. F., PE79
Christensen, J. G., EP235
Christensen, S., PC95
Christerson, B., EP805
Christiano, J., PE444
Christiano, L. J., EP435
Christianson, J. B., OB369
Christie, D. J., IR569
Chrystal, K. A., PE157
Chu, C. Y. C., DP242
Chubb, J. E., PE175
Chubin, D. E., TR190
Chung, P., DC205
Chung, T. Y., LC13
Churchill, R. P., IR570
Cimbala, S. J., OB202, SC492
Cingranelli, D. L., ET203
Cioffi-Revilla, C. A., IR571, IR637, LE69, SC353, SC675
Citrin, J., AB294, CP10, CP11, CP12, EP706, LE114, MP154
Ciulla, J. B., ET378
Claggett, W., PE176, PP250
Clark, A., DC268
Clark, B., ET263
Clark, D., OB106, PP57
Clark, E., DC133
Clark, G. L., DC269, PG241
Clark, J., PA260
Clark, J. A., DP179, LE369, PP4
Clark, J. M., PP365
Clark, R. L., PA214
Clark, W. A., PP366
Clark, W. A. V., PG148
Clark, W. C., PG16
Clarke, C. J., OB151
Clarke, G. R. G., EP436
Clarke, H. D., AB343, AB344, CP3, PE177, PE178, PE224, PP251, PP252, PP253, PP325, PP447
Clarke, P. B., RP64
Clarke, P. J., PA222
Clarke, R. N., EP798
Clarke, S. E., EP236
Clarke, S. H., LC185
Claude, I. L., IR638
Clausen, A., LE495, LE686
Clawson, D., PE386, PP97
Clayton, J. L., SP466
Clemen, R. T., PA223

Clemens, E. S., MP223
Clifford, B. R., PC118
Clifford, P., PG17
Clingermayer, J. C., EP237, EP238, PE80, PE318
Clinton, R. L., LC106
Cloninger, D. O., LC186, LC187, LC485
Cloutier, E., DP34
Cloutier, N. R., MP389
Clubb, J. M., LE511, XX52
Clubok, A. B., LE376
Clucas, R. A., LE317
Clune, W. H., SP163
Cnudde, C. F., LE281, PS287, SP467
Coase, R. H., LC14
Coate, S., ET120, MP36, PE588
Coates, D., LE8, LE318, LE628, LE629
Coats, A. W., XX53
Cobb, L., DP52
Cobb, R. W., AB104
Cobb, S., IR481
Coburn, R. C., ET15
Cochran, C. E., RP140, RP141
Cochran, D. C., MP5
Cochran, J. K., RP117
Cochrane, J. H., DP11, DP180
Cockerham, W. C., IR482, IR483, IR484
Codrington, H., EP707
Coele, A. J., SP76
Cohan, A. S., PS252, PS253, PS254
Cohen, D., LC203
Cohen, G. D., PE156
Cohen, J., LC174
Cohen, J. E., CP114, EP568, LE70, LE115, LE555, LE556, PC96, PP129, PP155
Cohen, L. E., IR482, IR483, IR484, LC188, LC189, LC190, LC191, LC192, LC193, LC291, LC520
Cohen, L. R., SC542, SC543, SC776
Cohen, M. A., LC410
Cohen, M. D., OB16
Cohen, Y., DC106
Cohn, E., PA7
Cohn, S., DC270, DC271, EP239, MP390
Cohn, S. M., TR146
Cohn, S. V., TR147
Cohn, T., ET265
Coker, D. C., LE212
Colantuono, M. G., LC107
Colby, D. C., SC26
Cole, A., SP364
Cole, J. R. I., DC206
Cole, L., MP155
Cole, R. L., MP162
Cole, S., TR148
Cole, W. A., RP65
Coleman, J., PS117
Coleman, J. L., ET16, ET60, LC15
Coleman, J. S., SC396, XX54
Coleman, K. M., PE81, PS14
Coleman, S., PA162
Coll, J. C. M., ET169
Collie, M. P., LE213, LE377, LE512, LE557, LE630, SC168
Collier, D., EP240, PS15, PS270, SP468
Collier, K., LE116
Collier, R. B., EP240
Collins, D. G., EP13
Collins, J. J., LC194
Collins, R., XX55
Collins, W., PP448
Collins, W. P., SC255
Collison, M., SP77

Colomer, J. M., CP115, SC169
Comanor, W. S., SC515, TR149
Comer, J., PP142
Comer, J. C., MP391
Comiskey, M., PE82
Condrey, S. E., OB17
Conell, C., DC271
Conforto, M., PE276
Conge, P. J., CP13
Congleton, R. D., AB106, ET107,
    PE161, PE586, PP109, SP328, XX56
Conkin, J. G., LE9
Conklin, G. H., RP99
Conner, J. C., MP526
Connolly, J. M., PE585
Connor, W., MP392
Conover, P. J., AB107, AB108, AB109,
    AB121, AB168, AB346, CP14, CP15,
    CP212, EP78, IR782, LE182, MP224,
    MP225, PE179, PE180
Converse, P. E., AB10, AB11, AB110,
    AB315, CP271
Conway, K. S., SP24
Conway, M. M., PP156, PP233, XX57
Conway, S. C., SP164
Conybeare, J. A. C., EP806, EP807,
    EP808, IR220, IR221, IR485, IR639,
    IR640, OB152, PE13, PE507, PE589
Cook, B. B., LC411, LC412
Cook, C. E., PE319
Cook, E. A., MP208, MP226, SP25,
    SP26, SP27
Cook, F. L., PC97, SP457
Cook, I. E., XX58
Cook, J. P., XX394
Cook, K. S., SC609
Cook, P. J., PP451
Cook, T. E., AB347, XX59
Cooke, T. W., IR486
Cooley, T. F., LC304
Coombs, R. W., DP181
Cooper, J., LE214, LE319, LE320,
    LE378, LE379, LE506
Cooper, M. N., DC10
Cooper, P., OB272
Cooper, S., PA7
Cooter, R. D., LC19, LC108
Copeland, G. W., LE513, LE708,
    PC188, PE372, RP138
Copeland, M. A., ET266
Coram, B. T., IR268, PP8, SC27
Corbett, M., SP329
Corcoran, P. E., PC21
Cordato, R., SC28
Corfman, K. P., ET121
Cornacchia, E. J., MP393
Cornbilt, O., TR150
Cornell, S., LC109
Cornes, R., PE508
Corning, C. H., DC11
Corning, P. A., DC11, PA163, PA164,
    PS272
Cornwell, C., LC196
Cornwell, E., LC110
Correa, H., IR269, PP367
Corzine, J., MP69
Corzine, L., MP69
Cosson, J., PP368
Costain, A. N., MP227, MP288, MP229,
    PP110, PP111
Costain, W. D., MP227, MP288
Costrell, R. M., SP165
Cotter, C. P., PP9
Cotter, D. A., MP230
Cotter, P. R., PP254
Cottino, A., TR151
Cotton, J., MP6
Cotton, T. Y. C., IR641

Cottrell, A., DP243
Couclelis, H., DP144
Coughlin, C. C., EP571
Coughlin, P. J., CP213, CP214, OB253
Coughlin, R. M., AB111
Coulter, P. B., CP16, EP569, LC486,
    SP330
Counts, T., PC189
Courant, P. N., EP243, EP708
Courtright, J. A., PC22
Cousineau, D. F., RP105
Coutinho, C., PA315
Cover, A. D., LC460, LC461, LE380,
    LE558, LE671, PP157, PP158
Cover, J. P., LC361
Covington, C. R., LE117, LE631,
    LE632, PP144
Cowart, A. T., EP79, LC182
Cowden, J. A., PP72
Cowell, F. A., EP709
Cowhey, P. F., PS16
Cox, B., LC194
Cox, G. W., CP116, CP215, CP216,
    LE514, LE515, LE559, PP255, SC256,
    SC257, SC258
Cox, J., LE560
Cox, K. R., PG243
Cox, R., IR24, IR25
Cox, R. C., PC23
Crafton, S. M., PE14
Crafts, N. F. R., XX60
Craig, C. S., PA271, PA272
Craig, E., EP710
Craig, L. A., DP182
Craig, R. B., DC92
Craig, S. C., CP17, CP18, CP49,
    DC208, PC24, PP256
Craig, S. G., DP81, PE509
Crain, W. M., LE212, LE381, OB254,
    OB255, OB256, PE181
Craine, R., DP12
Cramerer, C. F., SC625
Cramton, P., SC397
Crandall, R. W., EP673
Crane, E. G., LE497
Crane, J., PG87
Cranor, C. F., SC676
Crawfoot, J., SP162
Crawford, B., PS273
Crawford, V. P., SC398
Creech, J., MP69, DC272, EP438,
    EP711, SP166
Cremer, M. E., ET142
Crenshaw, E. M., EP439, EP440, ET204
Crepaz, M., CP117
Crewe, I., CP15, LE596, PP257
Crigler, A., PC197
Cripps, M. W., SC399
Critchley, W. H., IR372
Croley, S. P., CP217
Cromwell, J., EP441
Cromwell, V., LE633
Cropper, M. L., EP570, TR54
Crosby, F. J., MP70
Cross, F. B., LC21
Cross, R., EP163, EP164, XX61
Croushore, D. D., PE83
Crowe, E. W., ET331
Crumm, E. M., IR26
Crump, J. R., IR488, LE694
Cruz, J. B., IR327
Crystal, G. S., OB18
Crystal, J., EP14
Cubitt, R. P., SC29
Cuddington, J. T., EP165
Cukierman, A., PE84
Cullen, J. B., DP45, ET110
Cullenberg, S., EP3

Cullis, J. G., PE85, SC212, SC259
Cullity, G., ET17
Cummings, F. J., PE320
Cummings, S., PA72
Cunningham, J. B., SC400
Cunningham, S. R., EP80
Currie, G., XX62
Currier, K. M., DP167
Curry, E. W., RP90
Curtice, J., SC260
Curtis, J. E., OB373
Cusack, T. R., EP166, IR373, IR528,
    IR840
Cutch, R. M., PS17
Cutler, N. E., AB236, SP78
Cutright, P., SP79, SP469
Cuzan, A. G., IR489, PE182, PE183,
    PP159
Cyert, R. M., SC30
Cyr, A. B., PA273

Daalder, H., SC170
Dacey, M. F., PG18
Dagenais, M. G., EP427
Dagger, R., ET18
D'Agostino, B., AB237
D'Aspremont, C., SC590
Dahl, R., CP19
Dajani, M. S., XX63
Dale, A. I., SC354
Dalenberg, D. R., SP335
Daley, D. M., OB82
Daley, J. M., ET419
Dalto, G., MP455
Dalton, R. J., AB112, PP258, PP259,
    PP533, PS24, PS118
Damgaard, E., LE72, LE382, PP10
Daneshvary, N., SP254
Daniel, C., XX64
Danielian, L. H., PC164
Daniels, B. C., PS119
Daniels, H., DP4
Daniels, R. S., LE529, LE663
Daniels, W. J., LC413
Dannehl, C. R., PS20
Dantico, M. K., PG94
Danziger, J. N., PA324
Danziger, S., EP442, SP296, SP470
Dao, M. Q., OB257, PE86
Darcy, R., MP156, MP157, MP158,
    MP231, PP326, SC777
Darrat, A. F., EP529
Dasgupta, P., SC31
Dasgupta, S., CP218
Datta, L. E., XX65
Daudt, H., SC573
Daugaard Jensen, P. E., PC95
Davenport, C., ET205, XX269
Davenport, M., IR347
David, B., LE538
David, H., DC209
David, P. T., PP452
David, S. R., IR222
Davidson, C., MP159
Davidson, J. D., RP66
Davidson, L. S., PE445, PE446
Davidson, R. H., LE215, LE216, LE452
Davis, C., SP82
Davis, C. L., PS14
Davis, D. F., CP238, EP400, IR556,
    PP169, XX195
Davis, D. W., ET453
Davis, F. L., LE634, PE321
Davis, J. R., LE722
Davis, K., PG150
Davis, L., EP15, SP43
Davis, M. D., IR263, PP54
Davis, M. L., LE217, LE635, SC218

Davis, O. A., PE87, PE510, PP160
Davis, S., MP326
Davis, S. K., SC741
Davis, W. W., IR642
Dawes, R. M., ET136, ET147, ET195, PE322, SC636
Dawson, M. C., AB86, MP394
Dawson, P. A., AB113
Day, R. H., DP76, DP145, DP183
Daynes, B. W., RP175
Dayton, E., ET163
De Beer, J., SP140
De Boef, S., CP219
De Borger, B., SP331
De Dreu, C. K. W., IR27
De Graaf, N. D., CP220
De Greene, K. B., DP13, DP14, DP146, DP184, DP185, PA73
De Groot, H., OB83
De Haan, J., EP81, EP712, PE140
De Haan, W., LC197
De Juan, A., EP682
De la Garza, R. O., AB348, MP160, MP395, MP492
De Long, J. B., RP68, XX68
De Lorme, C., DP17, OB258
De Maio, G., SC261, SC262
De Meur, G., ET267, PS8, PS108
De Pelsmacker, P., PP349
De Solla Price, D., TR152
De Vany, A. S., XX70
Deadman, D., LC262
Dean, W., DC107
Dearden, J., MP232
Dearden, J. A., PE88, PE89
Deardorff, A. V., EP809
Dearlove, J., XX66
Deaton, T. H., PE181
Debecker, A., DP116
Debnam, G., SC596
DeBresson, C., PA274
Debru, G., SC32
DeBruin, G. P., PE511
Dechert, W. D., DP82
Deckard, B. S., LE636, PG245
Decker, T.N., IR359
Declercq, E., MP215
DeCoster, G. P., DP83, DP84
DeCottis, A. R., OB159
Deeg, R., EP16
Deere, D. R., DC264
DeFelice, E. G., XX67
Defleur, M., PC115
DeGregorio, C., LE321
DeHaven-Smith, L., EP713
Dehejia, R. H., RP67
Dehejia, V. H., RP67
Dekker, P., AB12
Del Rossi, A. F., LE695
Del Sesto, S. L., TR153, TR154
Delacroix, J., EP244, OB336
Delaney, J. T., DC262, DC273
Delbeke, J., DP186
Delegal, T., PP199
DeLeon, P., PA74, PP372
DeLeon, R. E., EP82
Dellaportas, G., EP245
Deller, S. C., PE78, PG151, TR11
Delli Carpini, M. X., AB13, AB349, DC354
Delprato, D. J., DP159
Demarzo, P. M., SC401
Demerath, N. J., AB44, PS274
DeMeyer, F., SC544
Dempsey, G. R., PC139
Dempster, M., PE87
Demsetz, H., EP1
Demsetz, R. S., DC274

Dendrinos, D. S., DP85, XX69
Dennis, C., EP462
Dennis, J., AB350, PC25, PP453
Dent, D. W., AB238
Denters, B., CP20
Denton, F. H., DC12
Denton, N. A., MP100, PG40
Denton, T., IR643
Denver, D., AB114, PP105, SP168
Denzau, A. T., CP221, LC111, LE218, LE282, PE323, SC778
DeRouen, K. R., IR644
Dery, D., PA224
DeSantis, V. S., PA8
DeSart, J. A., PP454
DeSerpa, A. C., EP572
Dessler, D., IR645
Detken, C., DC275, PE447
Deudney, D. H., DC13
Deutsch, M., DC14, ET454
Deville, P., EP528
Devine, J. A., AB115, EP17, EP444, EP445, LC276, SP482
DeViney, S., SP471, SP472
Dex, S., MP71, XX71
Dey, H. K., PP373
Deyle, R. E., PA275, PA276
DeYoung, R., PE573
Deysine, A., PP374
Dia, A., IR809
Diamant, A., EP247
Diamond, G., IR470
Diamond, J., OB259, SP83
Diamond, L. J., EP270
Diamond, S. S., LC362
Diappi, L., SP319
Dickens, W. T., XX5
Dickerson, A. P., DC276
Dick, A. R., LC198, LE561
Diehl, P. F., EP397, IR271, IR272, IR273, IR274, IR275, IR374, IR383, IR384, IR385, IR389, IR490, IR646, IR647, PG20
Dieli, R. F., PS21
Diermeier, D., LE10
Diesing, P., XX72
Dietz, H. A., DC174
Dietz, T., DC214
DiGaetano, A., PP363, PP375, PP376, PP377, SP332
Dignan, T., SC751
Dilger, R. J., LE383
Dillingham, A. E., MP234
DiLorenzo, T. J., OB241, PE16
DiMento, J. F., EP574
Dimitrov, V., SC355
Dimock, M. A., PP378, PP397
Dion, D., ET152
Dion, S., OB149, OB247
DiPalma, G., AB14
Diprete, T. A., XX92
Di Renzo, G. J., XX73
Diskin, A., PG19, SC33
Dittmer, L., SC402
DiVall, L., SP479
Dix, R. H., DC138, PP455, PP456, PS22
Dixit, A., PE590
Dixon, C. F., LC513
Dixon, D. E., RP45
Dixon, D. R., PP98
Dixon, W. J., DC15, EP810, ET233, ET354, IR30, IR276, LC415, LE118
Djoundourian, S. S., SC529
Dobbs, D., SC34
Dobra, J. L., SC545, SC546
Dobson, D., PG320, PP260, PP309
Dockens, W. S., DP53

Dodd, L. C., LE219, LE220
Dodoo, F. N. A., MP396
Dodson, M., RP69
Doern, G. B., PA9
Doerpinghaus, H. I., EP586
Dogan, M., RP70
Doherty, A. E., SC388
Doignon, J. P., SC35
Dolan, K., MP235, PP379
Domanski, S. R., PS77
Domberger, S., PE512
Dometrius, N., LC414
Dominguez, J. I., CP21, XX74
Domke, W., IR107
Donabedian, B., ET364
Donaghy, K. P., IR277
Donahue, J. J., MP37, MP397
Donald, L. E., LE384
Donaldson, D., SC36, SC37
Donaldson, R. G., DP15
Donley, R. E., LE119
Donnelly, J., ET206, ET207, ET208
Donohew, L., PC34
Donovan, B. L., OB337
Donovan, J., EP811
Donovan, T., CP80, EP697, LE562, PE167, PG82
Donovan, T. P., XX75
Doppelt, G., ET19
Doran, C. F., IR648, IR649
Dore, M. H. I., XX76
Doreian, P., OB31
Dorfman, R., EP248
Doring, H., SP169
Dorn, R. M., LE47
Doron, G., SC171
Doshi, K., EP446
Dosi, G., PA277, PA335
Dos Santos, T., EP249
Doty, R. M., IR375
Dougan, W. R., AB116, OB235
Doughtie, J. C., PS154
Douglas, D. F., PC120
Douglas, J., SC547
Douglas, M., ET20
Dougtie, J. C., PA35
Dover, H. A., PC169
Dovico, M., XX122
Dow, J. K., LE637
Dowding, K., PA75, PG174, SC38, SP333
Downing, J. D., PC27
Downing, L. A., ET103
Downing, R. G., SP334
Downs, G. W., IR278, PA278, SC39
Dowrick, S., EP250
Doxey, M., IR31
Doyle, M. W., IR32
Dragoo, K., PC28
Drakopoulos, D. A., XX77
Dran, E. M., AB316
Draper, G. I. A. D., IR650
Drass, K. A., IR708, XX197
Drazen, A., PA76
Drexl, J., LC108
Dreyer, E. C., PP261
Dreze, J., EP168
Driedger, L., RP112
Driessen, P. A., LC22
Drogus, C. A., RP113
Druckman, D., DC16, DC17, DC18, DC277, IR33, IR476
Dryzek, J. S., EP447, XX78, XX79
Dua, P., EP543, PE487
Dubin, R. A., PG88
Dubois, P. L., CP222
Duch, R. M., ET462, ET463
Duckworth, F. C., PC29

Dudley, L., PG12, PP380
Duffy-Deno, K. T., SP335
Dugan, W. E., AB15
Duits, M., PC28
Duncan, A. K., EP251
Duncan, G. T., IR642
Dunham, R. G., LC508
Dunlap, R. E., TR130
Dunleavy, G. W., LE120
Dunleavy, P., LE322, OB260, PE90, PP327, SC263
Dunn, C. W., LC112, LE121, RP9
Dunn, J., DC139
Dunseath, J., OB19
Duong, D. V., DP147
Dupre, L., ET21
Durant, R. F., EP252
Durden, G. C., CP173, EP253, PE591
Durning, D., PA77
Durup, J., OB106
Dutt, N., AB343, AB344
Dutta, B., SC356, SC779
Dutter, L. E., MP398, SC403, SC742
Duval, R. D., IR809, TR57
Duvall, R., DC216, PS221
Dwivedi, O. P., ET381
Dworkin, J. B., SC268
Dworkin, R., ET268, MP236
Dwyre, D., PP457
Dye, T. R., EP254, EP691, EP714, LC113, PA78, PS184
Dyer, J. A., LC23
Dyer, J. S., SC264, SC265
Dyer, P. W., IR572
Dyson, J. W., XX80
Dyzenhaus, D., XX81

East, M. A., IR34
Easterlin, R. A., EP448
Easton, D., PS23
Easton, S. T., EP812, LE99
Eaton, A., DC270, DC315
Eaton, J., EP813
Eavey, C. L., ET276, ET277, OB153, SC404
Ebaugh, H. R. F., AB103
Eberwein, W. D., IR373, IR652
Eckberg, D. L., LC363
Eckel, C., SC780
Eckert, C. M., EP778
Eckert, W. A., MP399
Eckhardt, W., AB117, PS245
Eckstein, H., PS276, XX82
Eckstein, S., DC140
Eckstein, Z., EP255, TR12
Edelman, S. A., PE324
Edelstein, M., IR35
Eden, L., IR651
Ederington, L. H., EP83
Edin, P. A., PE91
Edinger, L., IR15, LE11
Edwards, B., OB338
Edwards, G. C., CP223, LE122, LE123
Edwards, J. E., AB317, AB330
Edwards, J. T., SP336
Edwards, L. N., SP178
Edwards, S., EP530, EP531, EP815
Eells, E., XX83
Efaw, F., XX84
Eggers, M. L., SP271, SP282
Ehrlich, I., LC308
Eichberger, J., LC114
Eichenbaum, M., DP175, EP435
Eichenberg, R. C., PS24
Eichenberger, R., EP86, PS185
Eichengreen, B., PE17
Eijk, C., PP11
Einsiedel, E. G., TR155

Eisenberg, T., LC390
Eisenstadt, S. N., DP16, PS222
Eisinger, P., EP256, MP401
Eisler, R., DP107
Eismeier, T. J., EP715
Eisner, M., AB351, DP244, DP245
Eitzen, D. S., PP262
Ekelund, R. B., DP17, RP46
Ekland-Olson, S., LC309
Elazar, D. J., DP246, LC115
Elder, C., XX372
Elder, H. W., OB298
Elder, R. E., LE134
Elgie, R. A., LE73, MP402
Eliashberg, J., PA288
Eliassen, K. A., PP458
Elifson, K. W., RP114
Elkin, S. L., EP576, LE124, SC40
Elkins, D. J., EP380, PG246
Elledge, B., EP253
Ellickson, B., PE514
Elling, R. C., LE638
Ellinger, K. P., SP179
Elliott, D., DP188
Elliott, E., DP29, PP87, PP325, SC288
Ellis, C. J., PE448, PE449
Ellis, F., PP242
Ellis, K. D., PG123
Ellis, R., ET269, ET270
Ellis, R. D., LC199
Ellis, R. J., MP72, OB20
Ellison, C. G., LC514, LC515, MP117, MP403, RP71, RP115
Elmes, G., PA280
Elmore, R., PA225
Elordi, C. A., EP55
Elrod, M. A., IR243
Elster, J., SC204, SC613, SC614, TR156
Ember, C. R., DC19
Ember, M., DC19
Emerson, M. O., MP73, SP473
Emmons, J., IR252
Empey, L. T., XX85
Enders, W., DC355
Endersby, J. W., LE221, LE637
Enelow, J. M., CP225, LE696, LE697, LE698, PP161, SC743, SC744, SC745, SC746, SC747, SC748, SC781, SC782
Engel, D. M., LC310
England, R. E., PG292
England, R. W., SP180
English, A., LC103
Engstrom, R. L., LE385, MP161, MP162, MP404, SC345
Enloe, C. H., MP405
Ennis, J. G., XX86
Entman, R. M., AB118, PC98, PC121, PC165
Eoyang, C., SC678
Epperlein, T., LE645
Epperson, C., ET417
Epperson, J. E., TR41
Epple, D., PG154, PG155
Epstein, D., OB84
Epstein, L., ET354, LC24, LC415, LC454
Epstein, L. G., XX87
Epstein, L. K., LE563, SP19
Erber, R., CP22
Erbring, L., PC99, PC135
Erev, I., SC455
Erfle, S., EP577
Ericksen, E. P., EP449
Erickson, B. M., SP347
Erickson, K. V., PC190
Erickson, M. L., LC338

Erickson, R. A., EP295
Erickson, R. J., PP532
Erickson, S. C., LE566
Eriksen, T. H., IR36, XX88
Erikson, R. S., AB222, AB318, AB319, CP118, LE283, LE284, LE564, LE565, PA53, PC122, PE184, PE185, PE243, PG247, PP28, PP162, PP163, SP338, SP449
Erlanger, H. S., LC516
Ershov, E. B., DP66
Ersson, S., EP325, PG248
Ervasti, H., EP84
Ervin, D. J., PG156
Eschbach, K., MP406
Eschet-Schwarz, A., LC116
Espenshade, T. J., PG157
Esser, J. K., PC17, PC18
Ester, P., AB12, AB352
Estes, C. L., OB335
Estlund, D., SC266
Etheredge, L., XX89
Etheredge, L. S., IR37, PS186
Ettling, J., LE507
Etzioni, A., EP716, XX91, XX92
Eubank, R. B., PP190
Euben, R., RP10
Eulau, H., LE222, LE386, LE387, LE388, XX93
Evans, A. S., DC27
Evans, C. L., LE232
Evans, D., LE699
Evans, F. J., SP182
Evans, G., AB139, PP13, PP14, PP263, PS121
Evans, H. E., SP339
Evans, J. S. B. T., PA81
Evans, L., EP869
Evans, M. D. R., DC220
Evans, P., EP257, PE92
Eveland, W. P., PC31
Evenson, R., TR37
Evered, R. D., PA143
Everett, K. D., DC210
Eysenck, H. J., PA165

Faber, J., IR225, IR376, IR654, PG89
Fackler, T., PP381
Fagen, R. R., PS223
Fagerberg, J., EP258
Fain, J. R., SC268
Faini, R., IR377
Fair, R. C., PE186
Fairbanks, J. D., LE125, RP144
Faist, R., PG161
Faith, R. L., CP229, PE19
Fales, E., XX97
Falk, B., DP189
Falmagne, J. D., SC35
Fan, C. C., EP450
Fan, D. P., PC32, PC33
Fantini, M. D., OB155
Farace, V., PC34
Farah, B. G., MP266, MP305
Fararo, T. J., DP54
Farber, H. S., DC279
Fardmanesh, M., EP340
Farley, J. E., IR655
Farmsworth, D. L., LE384
Farnham, B., XX98
Farnham, P. G., SC516
Farnsworth, G., RP6
Farnworth, M., LC286
Farr, J., XX99, XX100
Farrell, D. M., LE366, PP15
Farrington, D. P., LC168, LC169
Fastnow, C., PP230
Faure, A. M., XX101

Fave, L. R. D., SC598
Fawcett, H., SP476
Feagin, J. R., EP264, IR378, IR656, MP407, OB205, XX102
Feather, N. T., ET273
Featherman, D. L., MP408
Featherman, S., MP163
Featherston, F., SC254
Fedrizzi, M., SC357, SC358
Feeny, D., DC211
Feichtinger, G., PP382, SP129
Feick, J., PA10
Feierabend, I. K., DC21, DC22, DC141
Feierabend, R. L., DC21, DC22, DC141
Feig, D. G., LE223
Feigenbaum, H. B., PE515
Feinberg, W. E., DC212, SC418
Feiock, R. C., EP220, EP237, EP259, EP260, EP714, OB299, PE318, SP340
Feit, E., PS246
Feld, L. P., PE559
Feld, S. L., CP230, DP248, LE224, SC764
Feldman, A. M., EP19, OB261
Feldman, D., ET382, LC416
Feldman, P., PE187
Feldman, S., AB107, AB108, AB109, AB119, AB120, AB121, AB320, AB337, AB346, AB353, CP23, CP62, CP212, EP78, PC123, PE180, PP264, SC41, SP477
Feldstein, M. S., SC679
Felix, D., EP451
Feller, I., PA279, PA280
Fels, R., DP190
Felsenstein, D., PE616
Felsenthal, D. S., SC33, SC269, SC270, SC271, SC272, SC273, SC327, SC680, SC783
Felson, M., LC189, LC190
Felson, R. B., LC200, LC517
Fender, J., DP191
Fenifter, A. W., CP24
Fenmore, B., LE670, PE188
Fenn, P. T., EP556
Fenno, R. F., LE285, SC773
Fenny, D., OB384
Fenton, J., CP119, DP249
Fenwick, R., EP485
Ferber, M. A., MP234
Ferber, R., EP85
Ferejohn, J. A., CP120, CP121, CP207, CP231, LE14, LE279, LE362, LE567, PE93, PE189, PS117, SC157, SC172, SC491, SC681
Fernau, M. E., TR59
Ferrar, J. W., ET455
Ferrara, J., AB302, IR830
Ferris, J. M., EP20, OB262, SP84
Feshbach, S., IR447
Feste, K. A., SC161
Fett, P. J., LE639
Field, J. O., AB122
Field, W. H., PG13, PP164
Fieldhouse, E., LE661
Fields, G. S., EP452
Fields, J. M., AB321
Figlio, D. N., LE568, SP85
Filer, J. E., CP122, MP164
Filly, S., SP358
Finco, M. V., SC758
Findlay, D. W., PE450
Fine, B. J., SC555
Fine, K., SC555, SC556
Fine, T. S., PP112
Fine-Davis, M., MP238
Finifter, A. W., MP11, PP265, XX103
Finifter, B. M., MP11, PP265

Fink, E. C., LC119
Finke, R., RP72
Finkel, S. E., CP25, CP26, DC174, PE190, PP165
Finlay, W., OB156
Finn, J., IR657
Finsterbusch, K., PA82
Fiore, W., ET333
Fiorina, M. P., CP120, CP121, LE14, LE15, LE279, LE286, LE538, LE569, PE191, PE192, PP59, PP266, PP329, SC42
Fiorito, J., DC273
Firebaugh, G., EP262, EP263, MP239, XX104
Firestone, J. M., MP336
Firmin-Sellers, K., PE516
Fischer, B., EP532
Fischer, C. S., SP341
Fischer, D., IR280, SC548
Fischer, D. G., TR60
Fischer, F., ET383
Fischer, G. W., PE94
Fischer, M. M., PC35
Fischerkeller, M. P., AB247
Fischler, H., PE326
Fisek, M. H., XX105
Fishback, P. V., MP74
Fishbein, M., AB1, AB190
Fishburn, P. C., CP232, CP233, CP239, LE516, LE518, LE519, LE624, PP147, SC159, SC245, SC274, SC275, SC276, SC277, SC278, SC279, SC549, SC550, SC557, SC559, SC784
Fisher, B., ET261
Fisher, C. S., PA281
Fisher, D., DP182
Fisher, F. M., TR157
Fisher, J., PE517, PP60
Fisher, L., PE95
Fisher, R. C., EP717
Fisher, R. J., DC23
Fisher, S., LC201
Fisher, T. C. G., DC280
Fisher, W. R., PC36, PC202
Fishkin, J., ET30, ET384, PC185
Fiske, S., AB123, AB124
Fiske, S. T., DC70
Fitch, J. S., LC202
Fitton, M., PG90
Fitzgerald, M. B., MP107
Fitzgerald, R., PP492
Fitzpatrick, J. L., PG249
Fitzsimmons, C., PE36
Flanagan, O. J., MP240
Flanagan, S. C., AB354, AB355, AB356, PE193, PP533
Flanagan, T. J., LC203
Flanigan, W. H., DC24
Flathman, M., LE313, LE476
Flavin, M. A., PE104
Fleischmann, A., EP264, EP276
Fleisher, R., IR491, LE107, LE621, LE640, LE641, PP144
Fleishman, J. A., AB125, AB126, AB197
Fleitas, D., CP234
Fleming, J. S., LE384
Flemming, G. N., CP235
Fletcher, J. F., MP38
Fliegal, F. C., AB357, PA282
Flinn, W. L., TR50
Florkowski, F., DC281
Flowers, M. L., PC37
Flowers, M. R., EP580, PE592
Foff, R. W., DC25
Fogel, R. W., DP148

Fogelman, E., DC24
Folbre, N., MP242
Folger, R., LC510
Fong, G. R., EP265
Foote, J., PC171
Foray, D., SC173
Forcina, A., PE196
Ford, L. E., MP235
Ford, R. T., MP409
Forell, S., PP388
Foreman-Peck, J., PG162
Forester, J., SC616
Forkosch, M. D., ET31
Form, W. H., AB127
Formby, J. P., EP419, EP581
Formisano, R. P., PG250, XX106
Formuzis, P., EP718
Forrest, A., SC732
Forrester, J. P., EP384
Forrester, J. W., DP149, PA283
Forsythe, D. P., PE327
Forsythe, R., PP166, XX107
Forth, R. D., SP19
Fortmann, L., TR61
Foss, S. K., PC38
Fossett, M., MP390
Foster, C. R., PG251
Foster, K. A., SP342
Foster, L. S., MP410, MP527, PE291
Foster, W. E., PA39
Fowler, E. P., SP373
Fowler, L. L., CP236
Fowler, P. C., EP266
Fowler-Salamini, H., DC142
Fowlkes, D., MP183, MP243
Fox, C. J., PA226
Fox, D. J., IR299
Fox, F. V., OB85
Fraasen, B. C., XX108
Francis, W. L., LE225, LE323, LE390
Francisco, R. A., DC143, DC213
Franck, T. M., IR659
Francois, M. E., DC144
Francois, P., EP711
Frank, A. G., DP250
Frank, J. D., IR574
Frank, M. Z., DP86, DP87, DP88
Franke, H., LC204
Franklin, C. H., LE391, PP167, PP267, PP268, PP269, SC661, SP28
Franklin, M. N., CP85, CP237, SC162, SC163, SC174, SC785
Frankovic, K. A., LE563
Frant, H., PA284
Frantianni, M., OB263, PE20, PE445
Frantzich, S. E., LE324, LE392
Franz, G., PE194
Franz, L. M., MP252
Franz, M. G., EP740
Franzosi, R., DC282
Frasca, R. R., PE518
Fraser, E. E., ET210
Fraser, J., CP27
Fraser, J. M., SC175
Fraser, N. M., IR380, IR675, LE154, OB206, SC484
Frasure, R. C., LE524
Frederiksen, P. C., EP322
Freeman, G., AB239
Freeman, C., DP179, PA285
Freeman, J., OB339, OB343, PP16
Freeman, J. L., LC185
Freeman, J. R., AB95, IR46
Freeman, L. C., XX109
Freeman, P. K., LE226, LE303, LE570
Freeman, R. B., PA286
Frendreis, J. P., LE65, LE66, LE325, LE642, PA287, PP331, XX110

Freudenburg, W. R., IR633, LC25
Frey, B. S., CP79, CP86, EP86,
    EP816, PE195, PE451
Frey, H. J., SP183
Frey, R. S., DC214
Freymeyer, R. H., PG163
Fricks, S., IR406
Fried, A., SP29
Fried, C., ET274
Fried, M., PG91
Frieden, J. A., EP87
Friedland, E. I., SC492
Friedland, R., EP267, EP453, PA54
Friedman, G., DC283
Friedman, J., LC205, LC488
Friedman, M., EP88, RP145
Friedman, S., LE339
Friedman, XX72
Friedrichs, J., SP343
Friesema, H. P., LE289
Frisbie, P. W., OB157
Frisbie, W. P., MP411
Frischtak, C. K., DP219
Froeneveld, L., TR57
Frohlich, N., ET122, ET123, ET164,
    ET275, ET276, ET277, OB374, SC43,
    SC405
Frohock, F. M., SC493
Froman, L. A., LE393
Fronbeck, B. E., PP168
Frost, M., IR40
Froth, A. J., SP250
Fry, D. L., PC77
Fry, M. J., PE418
Fuchs, S., TR158
Fuchs-Seliger, S., PE96
Fudenberg, D., SC409, SC44, SC406,
    SC407, SC408
Fukao, K., DP192
Fukuda, S. I., PP459
Fullington, M. G., IR492
Funkhouse, G., PC124
Funkhouser, G. R., PA83
Funston, R., LC417
Furnham, A., DC284, TR173
Furobotin, E. G., EP268
Furuta, S., EP719

Gaarder, S. M., LE118
Gabel, M., PS26
Gabennesch, H., RP73
Gable, W., SC28
Gabriel, P. E., MP14
Gabris, G. T., OB86
Gaddie, R. E., CP300, PP87, IR771,
    SC252
Gaddis, J. L., IR42, IR381
Gaffikin, F., SP273
Gafni, A., PA262
Gagliani, G., EP454
Gais, T. L., PE328
Gaitz, C. M., MP369
Galanter, M., LC26
Galasi, P., XX111
Galderisi, P., SC205
Gale, D., SC410
Gale, J., SC411, SC749
Gale, J. R., CP83
Galenson, D. W., MP75
Galeotti, G., PE196, SC249
Gallaher, M., LE462
Gallaway, L. E., EP195, PE615
Gallhofer, I.N., IR43
Galloway, T. D., SP336
Galnoor, I., PC39
Galston, W. A., RP116
Galtung, J., IR44, PS224
Gamm, G., LE227

Gamson, W. A., TR159
Gandhi, V. P., OB264
Gannon, K., AB240
Gans, H. J., AB128, RP74
Gant, M. M., AB170, CP238, PA11,
    PP169
Gantz, W., PC125
Garand, J. C., EP288, LE571, LE572,
    LE573, OB265, OB266, OB267, PE329,
    PG92, PP170, SP344
Garcia, F. C., MP412, MP413, MP414,
    MP415, MP416
Garcia, J. A., MP165
Garcia-Penalosa, C., SP184
Gardette, X., PG252
Gardiner, J. A., PP383, PP406
Gardner, R., PP384, SC537
Gardner, S., IR553
Gareau, F. H., XX112
Garen, J. E., OB87
Garfinkel, I., SP269
Garner, R., TR65
Garramone, G. M., AB359, PC191,
    PC192, PC193, PC194
Garrard, J. A., SP345
Garratt, R., PE519
Garrett, G., EP59, EP90, EP93,
    EP326, PE2, PE197
Garriga-Pico, J. E., DP7, PP106
Garson, G. D., DC285, PE330
Garten, J. E., EP91
Gartner, M., DC275, DP251, PE447
Gartner, R., LC353, LC354, LC364
Gartrell, C. D., ET278
Garvie, D., EP582
Gash, D. C., XX27
Gasiorek, M., EP817
Gasiorowski, M. J., IR382, PS27,
    PS277
Gassholt, O., ET456
Gassner, M., PP489
Gates, S., OB81
Gatignon, H., PA288
Gatlin, D. S., MP77
Gaubatz, K. T., DP252
Gauthier, D. P., ET279
Gavin, G., SP479
Geddes, B., PS122, XX113
Gedmin, J., PS123
Geer, J. G., PP113, PP534
Geerken, M., LC207
Gehrlein, W. V., CP233, CP239,
    LE516, LE518, LE519, SC279, SC557,
    SC558, SC559
Geiger, K., LE650
Geigert, F. B., PP252
Geis, G., PG253
Geisler, C. C., SP274
Gelb, A., PE593
Gelhorn, E., PP61
Geller, D. P., EP315
Geller, D. S., DC26, IR575, IR660,
    IR661, IR662
Gelles, E., LE411
Gelman, A., AB322, LE582, LE583,
    SC280, SC300
Gelpi, C., IR438
Gely, R., LC117, LC418
Gemmill, G., SC683
Gencay, R., DP82, DP86
George, A. L., ET334, IR435, LE16,
    LE126
George, D., DC356
George, D. A. R., DP151, SC89
Gerber, E. R., LE574, OB21
Gerbner, G., PC40
Gerson, E. M., XX362
Gerston, L. N., PG254

Gertler, M. S., XX114
Gertzog, I., MP166
Geurts, P., CP20
Geva, N., IR740
Ghorpade, S., PC100
Ghysels, E., DP177, PE70
Giacopassi, D., SP143
Gianakis, G. A., LC489
Giarratani, F., SP275
Gibbard, A. F., ET280, ET335, SC281,
    SC786
Gibbs, J., ET32
Gibbs, M., SC703
Gibson, B. B., PE520
Gibson, H. E., EP92
Gibson, J. G., EP720
Gibson, J. L., ET457, ET458, ET459,
    ET460, ET461, ET462, LC404,
    LC405, LC419, LC420, LC421, LC422,
    MP417, PP330, PP331
Gibson, R. K., PP273
Gibson, W. A., EP812
Gick, M., AB129
Gidengil, E. L., PS225
Giertz, J. F., SP524
Gigliotti, G. A., SC551, SP30
Gilbert, A., XX115
Gilbert, C. P., PG93, RP75
Gilbert, H. R., SP118
Gilbert, R., PC43
Gilbert, R. J., EP583
Gilboy, J. A., OB22
Gilens, M., MP76
Giles, C., SP276
Giles, M. W., DC27, MP77, MP418,
    MP419, PG94
Gill, A. J., RP47
Gill, S., EP818
Gillespie, C. C., SC282
Gillespie, J. V., IR281, IR282
Gillespie, K., PP385
Gillespie, S., EP21
Gillett, R., SC45, SC283
Gilliam, F. D., LE493, MP376, MP420
Gilliatt, S., PA12
Gillies, R., PG269
Gilligan, M. J., EP93
Gilligan, T. W., EP584, LE17, LE228,
    LE394, SC284
Gilljam, M., AB16
Gillmor, G. S., TR160
Gillmore, M. R., SC609
Gillroy, J. M., PA13
Gills, B. K., DP250
Gilmore, C. G., DP89
Gilmour, J. B., SC285
Gilpin, R., EP819, IR663
Gimpel, J. G., PP119
Ginsberg, B., PP535
Gintis, H., ET263
Girard, C., RP76
Gist, J. R., SP346
Gitelson, A. R., LE195
Glad, B., AB241, OB207
Gladdie, R. E., MP245
Glahe, F., PS278, PS311
Glance, N. S., DP18, SC209
Glasberg, D. S., PE419
Glaser, J. M., MP421
Glass, D. P., LE127
Glass, J. M., XX116
Glazer, A., AB130, DC286, EP550,
    LE287, LE399, LE643, PE594, SC684,
    SC750, SC787
Gleiber, D. W., LE65, LE66, LE325,
    MP24, MP506
Glenn, N. D., SP4
Glick, H., LC27, LC423

Glismann, H. H., DP194
Glock, C. Y., RP48
Glynn, C. J., AB17, PC41, PC203
Gobalet, J. G., EP270
Gochman, C. S., IR664, IR665, IR666, IR715
Godard, J., DC287
Goddard, J. B., TR161
Goddeeris, J. H., PP62
Godwin, R. K., PE97, PE521, SC46
Goebel, P. R., MP78
Goel, A., XX371
Goel, M. K., PP386
Goel, R. K., EP271
Goerner, E. A., ET385
Goertz, G., IR383, IR384, IR385, IR490, IR647, IR826, PG20
Goertzel, T., IR493
Goetz, E. G., EP272
Goetz, M. L., EP721
Goetze, D., SC47, SC205
Goff, B., SP86
Goff, B. L., LE381, PE98
Goff, E. L., ET281
Goggin, M. L., PC42, SP31
Gohcher, R. M., PC45
Gohmann, S. F., SP32
Goidel, R. K., EP22, LE575, PC148, PP63
Gold, D. A., PS124
Gold, H. J., PP460
Gold, S. D., SP347
Goldberg, A. S., CP240, LE100
Goldburg, C. B., SC286
Golden, C., MP246
Golden, D., PE452
Golden, M., DC288
Goldenberg, E. N., PC99, PC135, PP171, PP172
Goldfeld, S. M., EP94
Goldgeier, J. M., IR843
Golding, D., PG178
Goldman, A. H., LC311
Goldman, A. I., ET386
Goldman, P., OB340
Goldman, S., LC424, LC425
Goldsmith, A. A., PE331, PE332, PE333
Goldsmith, A. H., EP4
Goldsmith, O. S., PE99
Goldstein, A., IR226
Goldstein, J., EP820, PP114
Goldstein, J. S., DP253, DP254, DP255, IR45, IR46
Goldstein, R. J., ET211, ET212
Goldstein, W., TR66
Goldstone, J. A., DC145
Golebiowska, E. A., ET464
Golembiewski, R. T., ET387, OB23, OB24, OB25, OB88, OB89, OB90, OB91, XX117, XX118
Golley, F. B., SP87
Gonick, L. S., PS279
Good, D. H., SC751
Good, I. J., XX119
Goodhart, C. A. E., PE198
Goodin, R. E., ET33, ET388, SC618, XX120
Goodman, A., EP455
Goodman, J. B., EP95
Goodman, J. S., LC110
Goodman, M., PP387
Goodsell, C. T., LE395, XX121
Goodstein, E., LE261
Goodstein, L. D., XX122
Goodstein, L. I., LC271
Gopal, S., PC35

Gopoian, J. D., CP241, PE333, PP173, PP174
Gordon, J. P. F., EP709
Gordon, J. W., ET389
Gordon, L. C., LC386
Gordon, R. J., EP533, PA14
Gordon, T. J., DP90, DP91
Gorham, L., MP427
Gormley, W. T., PA84, PE334
Gorr, W., EP699
Gorta, A., PP388
Goss, E. P., EP359
Goswamy, M., PG95
Gottfredson, M., LC214
Gottfried, P., PS125
Gottlief, H., MP195
Gottman, J., PG21
Gottschalk, L. A., PC43
Gottschalk, P., SP480
Gough, P., PE199
Gourevitch, P. A., AB242, PG22
Gove, W., LC207
Gowa, J., EP821, IR386
Gowth, A. J., PS20
Goyder, J., AB323
Grabb, E., AB341
Grabb, E. G., OB373
Grabendorff, W., IR667
Graber, R. B., PG255
Grabosky, P. N., PP389
Graddy, E., EP585, SP84
Gradstein, M., OB26, PE522, PE523, PE524, PE595
Grady, D. O., EP273, PS190, SP348
Grady, M. F., LC28
Graff, H. J., LC208
Grafstein, R., LC118, SC48, SC49, SC619
Graham, A. E., SP186
Graham, J. Q., LE326
Gramlich, E. M., EP23, EP708
Grampp, W. D., PE596
Granatstein, J. L., OB230
Granberg, D., AB16, AB131, AB324, PP175, XX123
Grandy, C., XX124
Granfors, M. W., OB341, OB342
Granger, C. W. J., DP19, DP20, DP104
Granjean, B., PS112
Grant, D. S., EP274, PS191
Grant, R., EP822
Grasmick, H. G., EP778, LC181, LC312, LC313, LC314, LC315, RP117
Grasso, P. G., EP456
Graves, P. E., PG164
Gray, A., OB166
Gray, L. N., PG96
Gray, V., EP275, MP524, PA289, PA290, PE335, PE336, PE337, PE338, PE339, PE340, PE363, PE364, SP349, SP376
Greatbatch, D., PP118
Greeley, A. M., RP118
Greely, A. M., MP422
Greenawalt, R. K., DC28
Green, A. M., MP247
Green, D. E., LC313, LC314
Green, D. P., AB18, AB132, EP706, ET466, LE114, MP154, PP72, PP189, PP270, PP332
Green, E. J., LE76
Green, F., EP457
Green, G. P., EP276, TR14
Green, J., SC206
Green, J. C., RP119, RP146, RP148
Green, J. M., DC298
Green, P., ET282
Green, P. A., LC316

Green, R. J., EP786
Green, S. L., EP534
Greenberg, C., DC215
Greenberg, D., LC317, SP553
Greenberg, J., LE396, PP17
Greenberg, M. S., LC266
Greenberg, S. R., PC44
Greenburg, D. H., PA227
Greene, J. P., CP242, DC146, LE44
Greene, K. V., LE397, OB158, OB268, SC685
Greene, T. H., PS78
Greenfield, L., AB133
Greenhut, M. L., SC535
Greenspan, D., DP91
Greenstein, F. I., LE112, XX125
Greenwood, C., IR668, IR669
Greenwood, J., PE341
Greenwood, M. J., PG165
Gregerson, H., DP92
Gregory, A. J., PS247, PS248, XX126
Gregory, N., SC686
Gregory, R., PA85
Greif, A., PS30
Grendstad, G., OB92
Grenzke, J., PP64
Grether, D. M., SC50, SC491, SC620
Greve, H. R., OB27
Greven, M. T., PS126
Grieco, J. M., ET165
Grier, K. B., EP277, LE128, LE288, PE342, PE453, PE454, PP65, PP66
Grierzynski, A., LE517
Griffin, J. M., PA261
Griffin, K., PS226
Griffin, K. N., LC426
Griffin, L. J., DC289, DC304, SP482
Griffin, R., LE18, LE399
Griffin, R. C., PA16
Griffith, D. E., IR542
Griffiths, W. S., MP97
Griliches, Z., PA291
Grimes, A. R., XX127
Grimes, P. W., EP170
Grimshaw, W. J., PP390
Grimsson, O. R., PG256
Grin, F., DP21
Grindle, M. S., PS280
Grofman, B., AB130, CP148, CP152, CP184, CP230, DC29, DP248, EP577, LE18, LE77, LE78, LE224, LE233, LE398, LE399, MP167, MP423, MP424, PP225, PP519, SC51, SC287, SC750, SC764, XX389
Grogan, C. M., SP88
Grogger, J., LC318
Gronbeck, B. E., PP391
Groom, A. J. R., IR387
Groot, F., DP282
Groot, W., DC290
Groothius, P. A., TR162
Groseclose, T., LE229
Gross, A. B., MP101, SP283
Gross, D. A., LE327, LE400, LE572, LE644, PP63, PP176
Gross, M. L., ET390, SC207, SP33
Grossholtz, J., MP219
Grossman, G. M., EP813
Grossman, H. I., DC147
Grossman, J. B., LC76
Grossman, M., LE178
Grossman, P. J., EP278, OB269, OB270, OB271, SP350, SP351
Grove, D. J., MP15, MP16, MP17
Groves, R. M., AB325
Groves, W. B., LC238
Grube, J. W., AB134
Gruber, J. E., MP248

Gruhl, J., LC85, LC427
Grumet, B. R., ET391
Grunberg, I., IR47
Grush, J. E., PC126
Grusky, D. B., MP67
Gryski, G. S., LC476, OB159, SC288
Guastello, S. J., DP55, DP56, DP57, DP58, DP59
Guba, E. E., PA235
Gubrium, J. F., XX322
Guesnerie, R., EP722
Guilford, J. P., AB19
Guillorel, H., PG23
Guilmartin, J. F., IR670
Guinier, L., MP168, MP425
Guiton, M. V., LE19
Gul, F., OB28
Gulalp, H., DP195
Gulati, R., IR227
Gulati, U. C., EP279
Gunderson, M., MP249
Gundlach, E., XX128
Gunn, E. M., ET392
Gupta, D. K., DC30, DC31, EP280, PS310
Gurian, P. H., PP115, PP116, PP117, PP541
Gurin, G., CP41, XX129
Gurin, P., CP41, MP250, XX129
Gurr, T. R., DC32, DC33, DC148, DC149, DC216, IR671, IR844, PS31, PS127, XX373
Gusfield, J., SP483
Gustafson, M., LE129
Gustafsson, G., SC621
Guterbock, T. M., MP169, PP392
Guth, J. L., RP119, RP120, RP146, RP147, RP148, SP34
Guth, W., SC412
Gutmann, A., ET393
Guttieri, K., OB208
Guuay, J. H., DP34
Guy, M. E., AB360
Gwartney-Gibbs, P. A., IR576, MP251
Gyimah-Brempong, K., LC209

Haas, E. B., ET166, PS32
Haas, J., DP231
Haas, K. C., LC428
Haas, M., IR48, PA166
Haas, P. J., LE576, PG254
Habibi, N., PE100
Hackathorn, D. D., SC413
Hacket, R. A., PC166
Hackett, S., SC52
Hadaway, C. K., RP49, RP114
Haddad, L., EP467
Hadden, S. G., SC687
Hadjiharalambous, S., CP241
Hadjimatheou, G., EP171, PE101
Hadley, C. D., MP157, MP158, MP193, MP231, MP426, PE343, PP271
Haeberle, S. H., LE230
Haefele, E. T., LE700, SC53
Hagafors, R., ET34
Hagan, J., LC2, LC319
Hagan, J. D., IR672, PP536
Hagen, E., EP458
Hager, G. L., LE130, LE560, SP376
Hagle, T. M., LC429
Hagner, P. R., AB135, PC178, PP297
Hahm, S. D., IR494, PE102, PE103
Hahn, D. F., LE131, PC45
Hahn, H., AB243
Haight, T., LE132
Haire, S., MP326
Hajnal, Z. L., MP102
Hakes, D. R., PE455

Hakim, S., LC205, LC488
Hakvoort, I., AB244
Halaby, C. N., PP364
Halchmi, A., PA86
Hale, D., EP723, PA87
Hale, M., LC285
Hall, D. R., PS53
Hall, J. R., SC54, XX130
Hall, M. G., LC396, LC430, LC431, LC432
Hall, P., PA88, PA89
Hall, P. A., XX131
Hall, R. L., LE231, LE232, LE233, LE234, LE328
Hall, T. D., IR837, IR838, IR839
Hall, W. K., PG77, PG97
Hallenberg, J., AB245
Haller, H. B., PE200
Halley, J. E., PA167
Halliday, F., IR49, IR673
Halliday, T. C., OB341, OB342
Halligan, M., DC238
Hallin, D. C., PC167, PC168
Halman, L., ET35
Haltiwanger, J., ET124
Haltom, W., AB136, PC28
Hamblin, R. L., DC64, IR283
Hamermesh, D. S., MP234, XX132
Hamill, R., AB137, AB167
Hamilton, G. G., OB160
Hamilton, H., ET101
Hamilton, J. D., DC357, PE104, PG98, TR67
Hamilton, L. C., DC357, PG98
Hamilton, M. R., PA82
Hamilton, R. F., PP272
Hamilton, V. L., ET36, ET283
Hamlin, A., LE7
Hamm, K. E., LE235, LE236, LE237, LE238, PE344, PE408, SC788, SP427
Hammack, D. C., PE345
Hammergren, L. A., EP281
Hammond, J., AB361
Hammond, J. L., MP79
Hammond, P. E., RP65, RP77
Hammond, P. J., SC31
Hammond, T. H., LC134, LE252, OB161, OB199, SC175
Hampsher-Monk, I., PS128
Hampton, A., DC34
Hampton, J., LC320, SC208, SC622
Hancke, B., DC291
Hand, C. M., RP121
Handa, J. C., SC688
Handberg, R., LC433
Handcock, M. S., MP217
Handley, L., MP423
Hands, G., AB114, SP168
Hanekom, S. X., ET394
Hanger, P. R., AB193
Hanley, C. P., IR569
Hanlon, J. J., LC506
Hannan, M. T., OB325, OB330, OB331, OB343, OB357, XX28, XX133
Hanneman, R. A., EP24
Hansen, A. F., MP308
Hansen, J. M., EP823, PE346
Hansen, L., SC524
Hansen, L. K., MP456
Hansen, N., PG257
Hansen, P., SC289
Hansen, S., SC290
Hansen, S. B., EP282, MP252, OB272, SP35
Hansen, T., SP352
Hansmann, H. B., LC365
Hanson, J. A., EP535
Hanson, R. L., PG258, SP484

Hanssen, J. I., EP724
Hansson, B., SC55
Hansson, I., SC517
Hansson, P., EP283, EP284
Hansson, P. A., DP93
Hansson, S. O., SC552
Hanushek, E. A., SP187, SP188
Happy, J. R., PE201
Haque, K. E., ET471
Hardin, C. L., XX134
Hardin, R., ET167, LC120, PE525, SC494, SC623
Harding, A., EP285
Harding, S., SC624
Hardy, J., PS317
Hare, P. G., EP286
Harff, B., ET213
Hargens, L. L., PP272
Hargrove, E. C., ET37
Harisalo, R., PA292
Harless, D. W., SC625
Harmel, R., PE202, PP18, PP273, PP461, PP462
Harpham, E. J., SP277
Harries, K., LC366
Harrington, J. E., ET168
Harrington, S. E., EP586
Harrington, W., EP587
Harriott, H. H., IR50
Harris, M. C., TR163
Harris, P., LC434
Harris, R., IR33
Harris, T. R., SC359
Harris, W. A., MP18, PG166
Harrison, A., DC292, DC293, DC294
Harrison, B., MP427
Harrison, B. T., IR674
Harrison, E., SC56
Harrison, G. W., EP588, EP589
Harrison, J. R., OB332
Harrison, M. I., RP86, RP122
Harsanyi, J. C., ET38, ET39, ET40, ET284, SC57, SC414, SC415, SC495, SC626, SC627, SC628
Hart, A., PE559
Hart, D. B., LE577
Hart, K. D., CP63
Hart, P., OB209
Hart, S., IR577
t'Hart, P., IR104
Hartley, T., IR495
Hartnagel, T. F., LC518
Hartwick, J., XX320
Hartwig, F., CP123, CP243
Harvey, F., IR436, IR578, OB211
Harvey, J. W., ET125
Hasenfeld, Y., SP485
Hashimoto, M., LC210
Haslett, D. W., ET214
Hasnath, S. A., SP353
Hastie, R., AB20
Hattan, T. J., PG167, EP459
Hatzenbuehler, R. L., OB210
Hauber, A. R., LC211
Haugen, K., SC394
Haughton, J., LE338
Haughwout, A. F., SP354
Hauser, R. M., MP408
Hausman, D. M., ET41, ET42
Haveman, H. A., OB344, OB345
Haveman, R., EP442, PA228
Haverman, R. H., SP470
Havick, J. J., PP346, XX135
Havrilesky, T. M., EP76, EP96, EP97, EP98, EP725, PE456, PE457
Hawkins, B. W., PG197
Hawrylyshyn, O., EP458
Hawthorne, M. R., EP726

Hay, A. M., CP253
Hayashi, F., ET126
Hayden, G. M., SC496
Hayduck, L. A., AB138
Hayes, B. C., MP253, MP254, PE21,
  XX136
Hayes, J. P., EP866
Hayes, M. N., LC121
Hayes, M. T., PE347
Hayes, S. W., SP537
Haynes, A. A., PP117
Haynes, D., EP252
Haynes, K. E., PA293, SC751
Haynes, S. E., PE203, PP274, PE458,
  PE459
Haynie, S. L., PC169
Hays, S. W., ET401
Hazelton, J., SC687
Hazelwood, L. A., DC35
Hazen, R. Y., PP463
Head, J. G., PE526
Headrick, B., LE143, OB185
Headrick, T. E., OB162
Heal, G., SC25, SC541
Healy, B., IR845
Heath, A., AB139, CP220, PP13
Heath, W. C., ET285, RP56, RP123
Hebert, F. T., ET336, OB14
Hebert, R. F., RP46
Hechter, M., DC150, PG259, XX137
Heckathorn, D. D., ET337, OB375
Heckman, J. J., MP37, MP39, MP397
Heclo, H., PA17, PA90
Hedge, D. M., EP590, EP591, PA91
Hedges, R. B., AB52, PP67
Hedley, R. A., AB362
Hedlund, R. D., LE226, LE237, LE278,
  LE289
Hedrick, T. E., PA229
Hedstrom, P., DC295
Heggen, R. J., PE183
Heidenheimer, A. J., SP5
Heighberger, N. R., MP148
Heilbroner, R., XX138
Heimann, C. F. L., OB29
Heineman, R. A., PP474
Heiner, R. A., XX139
Heinrichs, U., CP50
Heins, A. J., EP710
Heintz, P., IR846
Heirich, M., RP11
Heise, D. R., AB77
Hejka-Ekins, A., ET395
Helbing, D., AB21
Helburn, I. B., CP78
Heldrich, A., ET338
Hellemans, S., AB157
Heller, W. P., DP104
Helliwell, J. F., EP287
Hellman, D., LC251
Hellman, J. A., DC217
Helms, L. J., EP727
Helms, M. M., ET127
Helsley, R. W., ET128
Henderson, C. W., MP80
Henderson, T. A., LC490
Hendon, W. S., TR1
Hendrick, R. M., EP288, SP344
Henig, J. R., PE515
Henley, A., EP457
Hennessy, M., PA230
Henning, J. A., OB321
Henrekson, M., EP283, EP284, OB273,
  OB274
Henrikson, A. K., IR51
Henry, A. R., LE543
Henry, G., TR15
Henry, K., PC186

Henry, M. S., TR164
Henry, R. M., EP460
Hensel, P. R., IR388, IR389
Henshel, R. L., DP22
Hepburn, M. A., SP189
Heritage, J., PP118
Herlihy, D., XX140
Herman, V., LE91, SC165
Hermann, M. G., IR52, IR401
Hermkens, P., AB340
Hernes, H. M., MP255
Hernstein, J. A., CP244
Hero, R. E., MP170, PG249
Herrera, C. L., LE676
Herrera, R., AB140, LE645, LE676,
  PP19
Herrick, P. B., DC151
Herrick, R., LE290, LE329, LE330,
  MP171
Herring, C., MP428
Herring, M., MP146
Herrmann, D., AB246
Herrmann, R. K., AB247, XX141
Herrnson, P. S., PP119, PP177,
  PP178, PP464
Herrnstein, R. J., SP218
Herrup, C., LC212
Hersch, P. L., CP87, PP68, SP6
Hershey, J. C., SC669
Hertel, B. R., RP124
Hertz, K., MP419
Hertzke, A. D., RP149
Herzik, E. B., PG260, PG325
Herzog, H., PP465
Herzog, H. W., PG168
Herzon, F. D., AB141
Hesli, V. L., AB179
Hessel, M. P., SC389
Hessenius, C., CP28
Hester, P. G., CP71, DC104
Hetrick, C. C., PP310
Hetzfeld, H., PA305
Heuer, R., SC789
Hewitt, C., EP461, MP256
Hewitt, C. J., PS129
Hewitt, D., IR496, PE527
Hewitt, K., PG24
Hewlett, S. A., ET215
Hey, J. D., SC629
Heyck, T. W., LE646
Heyman, P. B., LC491
Heyndels, B., EP728, SP355
Heywood, J. S., EP172, EP417
Hibbing, J. R., EP729, LE330, LE331,
  LE332, LE333, LE401, LE537, LE540,
  LE647, MP197, MP347, PE204, PP179
Hibbs, D. A., DC296, DC297, EP462,
  EP730, PE205, PE206, PE207, PE208,
  PE209, PE210, PE460
Hickok, S., EP426
Hicks, A., DC318, EP289, EP290,
  IR527, SP486, SP487, SP488, SP489
Higgott, R., EP291
Higgs, R., LE291, OB275
Highfill, J. R., SP241
Hihn, J., DP44
Hijiya, J. A., ET129
Hildner, R. E., DC182
Hildreth, A., AB316, LE35, LE437,
  SC185
Hilgartner, S., PA18
Hill, D. B., MP257, PC101
Hill, I. D., SC291
Hill, J. K., EP536
Hill, J. S., LE402
Hill, K. A., IR53, RP146
Hill, K. Q., CP247, LE292, PA19,
  PA20, PP20, PS281

Hill, L. B., OB163
Hill, R. C., SP346
Hill, R. P., SP47
Hill, S., SC58
Hill, S. S., RP53, RP54, RP136
Hill, W. W., IR284
Hillard, J. W., MP175
Hillas, J., SC59
Hillman, A. Y., PS318
Hills, J., PS227
Himmelfard, G., ET43
Himmelstrand, U., AB142
Hinchman, L. P., ET216
Hinckley, B., CP245, LE109, LE110,
  LE160, LE239, PP180, PP181, SC176,
  SC177
Hinckley, K. A., SP380
Hinckley, R. H., AB248
Hindess, B., XX142
Hindus, M. S., LC213
Hines, J. R., PE71
Hines, K., PE48
Hines, S. M., PS272
Hinich, M. J., AB143, CP124, CP125,
  CP225, LE133, PP160, SC518, SC743,
  SC748, SC752, SP490
Hinton-Andersson, A., PA19, PA20
Hipel, K. W., IR675, LE154, OB206,
  SC484
Hirao, Y., IR285
Hirczy, W., CP126
Hird, J. A., LE701, TR68
Hirlinger, M. W., CP29, PG293, SP179
Hirsch, W.Z., DC298, EP85
Hirschi, T., LC214, SP491
Hirschleifer, J., ET169, ET170,
  OB376, PA168, PE597, PS33, SC553
Hirschman, A. O., EP292
Hirschmann, N. J., MP258
Hirshleifer, D., DP6
Hitchcock, J., ET44
Hitchcock, R. K., OB164
Hite, P. A., EP776
Hix, S., PS34
Ho, J. L., SC674
Hoadley, J. F., LE520
Hoak, D., RP78
Hobrook-Provow, T. M., AB144
Hobsbawm, E. J., XX143
Hochschild, A. R., MP259
Hocking, J., DC358
Hockstein, A., PP277
Hodder-Williams, R., LC436
Hodge, R. W., MP142
Hodgson, G. M., OB346, PS35
Hodson, R., PE22
Hodson, T., LC467, LE334
Hoekstra, V. J., LC437
Hoenack, S. A., LC367, PE348, SC554,
  SP190
Hoffer, G., SP120
Hofferbert, R. I., PA21, PG261,
  PG310, PP21, PP107
Hoffman, E., EP592, EP593, LE240,
  TR16
Hoffman, S., IR676
Hofley, J. R., LC386
Hofrenning, D. J. B., RP125
Hofstetter, C. R., CP245
Hogan, J. B., PA22
Hogan, J. M., IR579
Hogan, K. C., DP23
Hogan, T. D., EP537
Hoge, D. R., AB363
Hoge, J. L., AB363
Hoggart, K., EP99, EP731
Hogwood, B. W., SP356

Holbrook, T. M., CP246, LE20, LE578, PE211, PP182, PP333, PP412
Holcombe, R. G., LE21, PE309, SC519, SC520, SC535, XX144
Holfield, E. B., RP79
Hollander, H., ET171
Holler, M. J., SC597
Hollingsworth, J. R., EP24, EP293
Hollist, W. L., IR286, IR287
Holloway, S. K., IR847
Holm, H. H., IR848
Holm, J. D., AB145, OB164
Holm, J. E., SP161
Holmberg, S., AB324
Holmes, J. E., LE134
Holmes, T. P., SP89
Holsti, K. J., IR54
Holsti, O. R., AB249, AB250, AB251, AB252, AB253, AB254, AB255, AB256, AB257, AB258
Holt, C. A., SC497, SC780
Holt, R. T., DP60
Holt, T., MP81
Holtz-Eakin, D., SP357, SP358
Holyoak, K., AB129
Homer, E., PG118
Homer-Dixon, T. F., IR437
Hommertzheim, D. L., SC463
Hommes, C. H., DP121
Hood, C., OB114
Hook, S. W., EP825
Hooks, F., PG25
Hooks, G., EP294, IR677
Hoole, F. W., IR390
Hoover, D., DC36, DP24, ET226
Hoover, G. A., EP463
Hoover, K. D., EP100, XX145
Hope, K. R., PP393
Hopf, T., IR678
Horan, M. J., LC426
Horgan, J., DP152
Hormuth, S. E., MP82
Horn, S. R., TR49
Horowitz, J., TR69
Horowitz, J. B., MP64
Horowitz, J. K., SC178
Horrigan, B. R., PE105
Horsley, R. A., RP80
Horton-Smith, D., OB377
Hosek, J. R., IR497
Hoshino, E., IR348
Hoskin, M., PP492
Hoskins, C., PE585
Hossein-Zadeh, E., IR498
Hostetler, J. A., ET404
Hougland, J. G., OB30
House, L. L., IR207
House, R. J., LE135
Houston, R. A., LC30
Hout, M., EP25, SP79
Hout, W., IR849
Houweling, H. W., IR654, IR679, IR680, IR681, IR682, IR683, PG89
Hovi, J., ET172, PE528
Howard, R. E., ET45, ET208
Howe, E., ET46
Howe, R. E., ET286
Howell, S. E., AB146, PP275, PP276, SP36
Howes, P. W., MP140
Howitt, P., XX146
Howlett, M., PE529, TR70
Howsen, R. M., LC215, LC218
Hoyer, R. W., SC753
Hoyt, W. H., PE349, SP359
Hristoulas, A., OB212
Hsieh, E. W. T., PE509
Hu, Y., PC112

Huang, C., IR390, LE180
Huang, J. C., TR124
Huang, P. H., ET339
Huaraka, T., ET217
Hubaut, X., ET267, PP489
Hubbard, R. G., EP464
Huber, E., SP7
Huber, J. D., AB147, AB364
Huberman, B. A., DP18, SC209
Huberts, L. W. J. C., PP394
Hubin, D. C., PA23
Huckfeldt, R. R., AB22, DP94, MP153, PC46, PC47, PG99, PG100, PG101, PP334, XX147
Hudson, J., EP173, ET130, PE212, SC60
Hudson, W. E., EP296
Hufbauer, K., TR165
Huff, D. L., PA294, PG102
Huffman, W. E., TR25
Hughes, M., ET449, LC207, LC245, RP124
Huizenga, F. D., PS36
Hula, D. G., EP538
Hulbert, L. G., SC443
Hull, B., RP126
Humes, B. D., IR3, PP466
Hummon, N. P., OB31, OB347
Humphrey, C. R., EP295
Hundley, G., DC299
Hung, C., PE76
Hunnicutt, G. G., OB133
Hunsberger, B., RP127
Hunt, J. P., XX148
Hunt, L., PG262
Hunt, L. H., LC216
Hunt, R., LC492
Hunter, J. D., RP81
Hunter, J. E., IR288
Hunter, K., PE314, PE350
Hunter, S., AB200
Hunter, W. C., EP732
Hunter, W. J., EP733
Huntington, S. P., DC200, IR684, PS282, PS283
Hur, K. K., PC127
Hurd, R. E., PC128
Hurka, T., ET47
Hurlbert, J. S., PG263
Hurley, P. A., CP247, LE292, LE403, LE404, LE506, LE521
Hurley, T. L., PC24
Hurrell, A., PG264
Hurwitz, J., AB259, AB260, AB261, AB281, AB282, AB283, LE136, LE405, LE406
Hurwitz, L., PS130, PS131
Hussein, S. M., IR685
Husson, W., PC195
Husted, T. A., PE88, SP186
Hutchings, K., IR55
Hutchinson, J., EP164
Huth, P., IR438, IR439, IR440, IR441
Hutter, J. L., XX149
Hveem, H., XX150
Hwang, H. D., PC215
Hwang, S. S., MP83
Hyde, J. S., MP261
Hyde, M., EP296
Hyldtoft, O., EP594
Hylland, A., SC61
Hynes, E., LC321
Hynes, J. A., XX87
Hynes, K. E., PA295

Iannaccone, L. R., RP72, SC210
Ichiishi, T., SC417
Ichniowski, C., EP771, LC217, PP395

Ickes, B. W., DP196, DP197
Iezzoni, L. I., SP90
Ignagni, J., LC31
Iida, K., EP826, PE23
Ike, N., EP297
Ikenberry, G. J., EP827, SP534
Im, B. G., EP567
Imig, D. R., PE374
Imwalle, L. E., IR867
Inbar, E., IR613
Indurain-Eraso, E., SC539
Ingberman, D., PP22
Ingham, H., DC303
Ingham, M., DC303
Inglehart, R., AB148, AB338, AB365, AB366, AB367, AB368, MP430, PG265, PP277, PP467
Ingraham, P., CP59, OB95
Ingram, H., PA132
Inhaber, H., EP299
Inkeles, A., EP382, PS164
Inman, R. P., OB276, SC521
Innes de Neufville, J., ET220
Inoguchi, T., XX151
Intriligator, M. D., IR88, IR292
Inverarity, J., LC371, MP85
Ioannidis, C., EP27
Ipanga, T., PG138
Irsigler, F., DP199
Irwin, D. A., EP831
Irwin, G., CP249
Isaac, J., ET48
Isaac, L., SP492
Isaac, R. M., PE531
Isaac, W. L., DC304
Isard, W., IR89, IR293
Islam, M. N., PG172
Isserman, A. M., EP303
Itzkoff, S. W., PA170
Iusi Scarborough, G., IR228
Ivaldi, M., SC630
Iversen, T., LE80, PP23
Ivie, R. L., OB210
Iyengar, S., AB23, CP30, PC92, PC102, PC103, PC129, PC130, PC183

Jaamdar, S., LC263
Jaarsma, B., CP127
Jabbra, J. G., PS139
Jackman, M. R., ET467, ET468, MP86, MP434, SP193
Jackman, R. W., CP128, CP129, CP130, CP250, DC108, DC109, EP304, EP305, EP306, EP307, EP421, EP465, PS133, PS134, PS135, PS319, XX172
Jackman, S., SC293
Jackson, D., PE232
Jackson, J. D., PA297
Jackson, J. E., AB326, CP131, CP251, EP726, LE407, LE648, OB21, PE352, PE532, PP269, TR81
Jackson, J. S., LE609, MP435
Jackson, K., MP240
Jackson, M. W., ET398
Jackson, P., PG103
Jackson, P. B., MP42
Jackson, R. A., SP361
Jacob, H., LC493
Jacob, J. R., TR166
Jacobs, D., LC315, LC494, PP274, SP362
Jacobs, L. R., PA25, PA47
Jacobson, A. J., XX173
Jacobson, G. C., LE579, PC196, PE106, PP69, PP70, PP183, PP184, PP378, PP397
Jacoby, W. G., AB149, AB150, AB151, AB152, CP294, PE107

Jacquemin, A., SC590
Jaditz, T., DP95
Jaffe, A. B., TR82
Jaggers, K., PS127
Jahnige, T. P., LC425
Jakubs, J. F., PG28
Jalali, R., MP436
James, P., IR578, IR693, MP386,
    OB201, OB211, OB212, SC538
Janda, K., PG248, PG269, PP461,
    PP469, PP470, RP150
Jang, S. J., LC368
Jankowski, R., EP103, PE353, SC211
Jankowski, T. B., CP31
Janos, A. C., PG270
Janowitz, M., ET399
Japp van Duijn, J., PA298
Jarlov, C., AB24
Jaros, D., PA171
Jarrell, S. B., DC305, LC215, LC218
Jarsulic, M., DP25
Jas, R., DC306
Jason, G. J., PA267
Jasper, J. M., TR167
Jasso, G., ET289
Jehn, K. A., DC39
Jelen, T. G., MP265, RP151, RP152,
    SP25, SP26, SP27, SP37, SP38
Jenkins, A., IR320
Jenkins, B., OB166
Jenkins, J. C., DC154
Jenkins, P., RP12
Jenkins, R., SP415
Jenkins, W. R., CP243
Jenkins-Smith, H. C., PG173, SC179
Jennings, E. T., DC218, SP493
Jennings, M. K., AB25, AB52, AB153,
    AB154, AB370, AB371, CP4, CP5,
    IR502, MP266, PP2
Jentleson, B. W., AB262
Jeong, J. H., EP786
Jerison, M., EP722
Jervis, R., ET174, ET175, IR442,
    IR442, IR444, IR445, IR583, OB214
Jewell, M. E., CP252, LE293, SP363
Jewett, A., SP316
Jha, R., EP175
Jillson, C. C., LC122, LE358, LE408,
    LE409, PG271
Jin, Y., PP471
Job, B. L., AB95, DP60, LE162
Jobert, B., PA94
Johannes, J. R., LE410, LE580, PP79
Johansen, L., SC498
John, P., PG174, SP364
Johnson, C. A., PG272, SP21
Johnson, C. M., SP112
Johnson, D. R., OB398, SP79
Johnson, E. D., RP153
Johnson, G., EP423
Johnson, G. W., CP132
Johnson, J. T., IR694
Johnson, L. K., LE411
Johnson, M., ET400
Johnson, M. A., IR479
Johnson, M. P., AB69
Johnson, N. R., DC212, SC418
Johnson, P., PE399., SP93
Johnson, R. A., DP96
Johnson, S. R., PE613
Johnson, T. G., EP308
Johnson, T. H., DC110, DC115
Johnson, W., LC438
Johnson, W. A., AB341
Johnson-Cartee, K., PC188
Johnston, K., DC269
Johnston, M., PP398, PP399, PP400
Johnston, M. E., MP455

Johnston, R., PP279
Johnston, R. E., AB75, LC439
Johnston, R. J., CP253, CP254,
    LE661, PE261, PG29, PG30, PG31,
    PG32, PG273, PG294
Johnston, W., DP22
Jojima, K., XX174
Jondrow, J., PE187
Jones, B., SC560
Jones, B. D., EP309, LE412, LE649,
    PA62
Jones, B. M., SP194
Jones, C. C., CP288
Jones, C. I., EP310
Jones, C. O., TR83
Jones, D. C., ET157
Jones, D. L., IR310
Jones, E. B., DC307, MP267
Jones, G. W., LE322
Jones, J. D., OB277
Jones, J. P., SP462
Jones, L. R., PE108
Jones, M. H., MP437
Jones, M. P., SC295
Jones, P., ET290, IR294
Jones, P. R., ET130, PE533, SC60,
    SC212, SC259
Jones, R. C., AB26
Jones, T. R., LC25
Jones, W. J., SP195
Jones, W. T., ET49
Jonung, L., DP172, PE213
Jordan, G., PE367
Jordan, J. L., EP596, TR41
Jorgenson, D. W., EP734
Jorgerst, M. A., LE241
Jos, P. H., ET401, OB35
Josephy, N. H., DP71
Joslyn, R. A., PG274, SC296
Joulfaian, D., OB277, OB278
Jowitt, K., PG275
Joyce, K. M., SC690
Judd, C. M., AB27, AB47, AB155,
    AB185, CP34
Judge, K., SP496
Juhn, C., EP177
Jukam, T. O., CP45, DC58, PP30
Julnes, G., PG276
Jung, C., EP601
Jung, C. R., RP95
Junne, G., PS39
Just, M., PC197
Just, R. E., SC178
Juster, F. T., XX190

Kaasch, K., PA315
Kaase, M., CP255
Kabeer, N., AB28
Kacowicz, A. M., IR99
Kadish, E., MP90
Kadish, M. R., SC561
Kaempfer, W. H., EP562, EP833
Kafoglis, M. Z., LC124
Kagan, R. A., LC36, LC441
Kahane, L. H., SP40
Kahle, L. R., AB29
Kahley, W. J., PG177
Kahn, J., PE110
Kahn, K. F., MP172, PC198
Kahneman, D., ET52, PE536, SC139,
    SC691, SC692, SC727
Kaid, L. L., PC170, PC171, PC172
Kaim-Caudle, P., PA26
Kaiser, P. J., PS269
Kaizouji, T., DP98
Kalish, L., EP626
Kalleberg, A. L., ET53, XX191
Kallos, N., AB374

Kalof, L., DC214
Kalt, J. P., LC109, LE414
Kalton, G., AB333
Kames, D. H., PP473
Kamien, M. I., PA299
Kamlet, M. S., IR494, OB280, PE94,
    PE103, PE111, PE112
Kammler, H., IR507
Kanbur, R., EP467
Kanbur, S. M., EP468
Kane, T. D., MP95
Kane, T. J., LE297
Kang, J. M., SP198
Kangas, O. E., EP84, SP497
Kantor, B., SC631
Kantor, S. E., SC180
Kanwisher, N., AB264, IR399
Kaplan, B. J., SP369
Kaplowitz, N., AB265
Kapstein, E. B., IR100
Karapin, R. S., IR437
Karavitis, N., OB281
Karklins, R., DC43
Karmeshu, J. V. P., DC44
Karnig, A. K., MP198, MP442, MP462
Karnik, A. V., PE461
Karp, J. A., LE581, PP356
Karps, P., LE388
Karras, G., EP106
Karren, T., EP739
Kartez, J. D., PA97
Kaserman, D. L., EP567, EP602
Kash, D. E., PA232
Kaskarelis, I. A., DP202
Kasmer, J., XX123
Kasperson, R. E., PG178
Kasza, G. J., PE354
Kateb, G., PS137
Kathlene, L., MP275
Katz, C., PC53
Katz, C. J., EP740, OB288, SP503
Katz, D., PP243
Katz, E., PE583, PE584, PE598, SC664
Katz, H. C., DC310
Katz, J. N., XX31
Katz, N. H., IR400
Katz, R. S., PP24, PP280, PP281
Katznelson, I., LE650
Kau, J. B., EP107, EP108, LE702,
    PE214, SC214
Kaufman, D. A., OB380
Kaufman, J. L., ET46
Kaufman, R. R., EP315
Kaufmann, C. D., OB42
Kaufmann, P. J., ET341
Kaul, T. J., XX32
Kaun, D. E., ET54
Kautsky, J. H., DC155, PS83
Kautz, S., ET469
Kavanagh, D., PS58, XX192
Kaw, M., AB30
Kay, W. D., TR170
Kazee, T. A., LE523
Kazin, M., AB156
Kearney, R. C., OB168
Kearns, P. S., PE113
Kearny, E. N., PP474
Kebschull, H. G., PP402
Kedourie, E., RP15
Kee, P., MP21
Keech, W. R., EP77, PE172, PE173,
    PE215, PE443, PE462, PE463, PE464,
    PP6
Keeffe, M. J., OB133
Keeler, A., EP582
Keenan, D. C., DP99
Keenes, E., DP256, IR101
Keeter, S., AB13, PC199, TR92

Kegley, C. W., AB266, DC180, DP257, ET342, ET407, IR102, IR401, IR426
Kehoe, M. R., ET142
Kehoe, P. J., DP169, PE444
Keilany, Z., ET127
Keim, G. D., PP77
Keinath, W., PG33
Keiser, R. A., MP443
Kekes, J., ET55
Kelley, A., SP498
Kelley, H. H., XX193
Kelley, J., CP256, DC220, PE28
Kelley, R. C., CP257
Kelley, S., CP106, CP258
Kellser, R. C., LC317
Kelly, D., OB324
Kelly, J. S., SC63, SC64
Kelly, R. M., AB210, MP276
Kelly, W. J., XX127
Kelly, W. R., MP91, SP492
Kelman, S., LE297
Kelsen, D., SC562, DP100
Keman, H., EP109, PS138
Kemp, K. A., SP370
Kemper, T. D., SP371
Kende, I., IR402
Keniston, K., ET30
Kennamer, J. D., CP133
Kennelly, B., PE355
Kennen, G. F., ET403
Kenney, P. J., CP134, LE137, PE216, PP120, PP121, PP186, XX194
Kenny, C. B., AB31, PP71, PP80
Kenny, L. W., CP122, LE1, LE651, MP164, SC230, SP199
Kenski, H. C., LE294, PE217, PP187
Kenski, M. C., LE294
Kent, S. A., PE29
Keohane, R. O., ET153, IR103, IR851, OB43
Kephart, T., LE216
Kerbel, M. R., LE138
Kerbo, H. R., EP178, SC598
Keren, G., DC375
Kernell, S., LE335, PP184, PP188
Kerr, B., MP22
Kershaw, G., DC156
Kespohl, E., OB258
Kessel, J. H., CP245, PP4
Kets de Vries, M. F. R., OB103
Keysar, A., MP448
Khalaf, N. G., EP316
Khalil, E. L., DP27, ET131, OB44
Khan, H. A., IR348
Khanna, J., OB381, TR25
Khator, R., TR4
Khazanov, A. M., RP16
Kherallah, M., TR10
Kick, E. L., EP383
Kidd, R. F., LC74, LC224
Kidder, R. L., ET404
Kiecolt, K. J., AB32, PE218, RP156, RP157
Kiefer, D. M., PE114
Kiel, L. D., DP28, DP29
Kiewiet, D. R., LE139, LE336, LE703, MP152, MP383, MP445, MP521, PE219, PE220, PE221, PP141, SC297
Kihlstrom, R. E., SC693
Kilgour, D. M., IR446, IR701, IR833
Killian, L. M., MP444
Kim, C. K., IR523, LE337, LE367
Kim, H., DP173, SC421
Kim, H. M., DP173
Kim, I., LC303
Kim, I. K., LE608
Kim, J. B., SC360
Kim, J. O., PP475

Kim, J. W., IR269, OB385
Kim, K. W., PS301
Kim, P. S., OB169
Kim, W., IR702, IR703, IR704, IR705, IR706
Kimber, R., SC215
Kimenyi, M. S., OB256, OB282, PE356
Kincaid, D., MP277
Kincaid, J., PG277, PG278
Kinder, D. R., LE140, LE141, MP43, MP92, MP93, MP445, MP446, PC130, PE220, PE221
Kindleberger, C. P., PE357
King, A., EP110, LE415, PP476
King, D., OB19
King, D. C., LE242, LE407, PE358, PE532
King, D. S., PP470
King, D. Y., PS40
King, F., SC280
King, G., AB322, LC442, LE81, LE295, LE582, LE583, LE652, PP122, SC298, SC299, SC300, XX10
King, J., IR786
King, J. B., DP101
King, J. D., LE584, PP335
King, L. R., XX238
King, N. J., MP94
King, P., AB82
King, R. F., EP741
King, R. G., EP317
King, R. R., SC301
Kingdon, J. W., PE352
Kingsland, S., PA172
Kingston, J., IR275, IR374
Kinnard, D., IR508
Kinney, R., LE632
Kinsella, D., IR297
Kinsey, L. S., PG279
Kirby, A. M., IR707
Kirchgassner, G., CP135, CP259, SC422
Kirk, R. M., DC363
Kirkpatrick, E. M., PP477
Kirkpatrick, G., PE30
Kirkpatrick, S. A., AB267, SC694, XX195
Kirksey, J. F., MP158
Kirman, A. P., SC499
Kirn, M. E., XX196
Kiser, E., IR708, PP403, XX197
Kitschelt, H., AB157, TR168
Kitson, M., EP834
Kitti, C., PA334
Kivlin, J. E., PA282
Kjellberg, F., PA27
Klandermans, B., DC239
Klass, B., DC314
Kleck, G., LC225
Klecka, W., LE646
Kleiboer, M., IR104
Kleindorfer, P. R., PE538
Klein, D. B., PE537, SC423, TR5, XX198
Klein, R. A., IR510
Kleiner, A. F., PP448
Kleinknecht, A., PA300, PA301
Kleinnijenhuis, J., PC104
Klemmack, D., PS181
Klemperer, P., DP50
Klier, T., LE585
Kline, H. F., LE243
Kling, J. L., DP30
Klingberg, F. L., IR709
Klingel, D. M., AB29
Klingemann, H. D., PP21, PP478
Klingman, D., SP372
Klinkner, P. A., CP136, MP194

Klitgaard, R. E., ET56
Kloppenberg, J. T., ET405
Klorman, R., PE222
Klosko, G., ET57, ET406
Klosterman, R. E., PA98
Kluegel, J. S., LC191, MP44, MP45
Knack, S., CP137, CP138
Knapp, T. A., PG164
Knetsch, J. L., ET52, PA99
Knight, J. B., PE593
Knight, K., AB158, EP78, LE183
Knoke, D., AB33, CP260, CP261, PA302, PE359, PE360, RP158
Knopoff, L., DP153
Knott, J. H., SP99
Knottnerus, J. D., PG104
Know, W. E., AB378
Knudsen, D. C., PA303
Knutsen, O., AB375, PP336, PP237, XX199
Kobbervig, W., LC371
Kober, A., IR710
Kobrak, P., PE115
Kobrin, S. J., PA304
Kochanowski, P., PA305
Kocis, R. A., ET58
Kocs, S. A., IR711, LC37
Koegel, P., SP303
Koehler, D. H., LE698, SC782
Koelble, T. A., OB45, PP479
Koester, J., PC184
Koester, R. B., EP318
Koford, K. J., LE653, LE654, LE666, LE704, SC302
Kogane, Y., DP203
Kohfeld, C. W., LC323, MP447, PA100
Kohli, A., XX200
Kollman, K., PP338
Kollock, P., ET59
Kolodziej, E. A., DP258
Komesar, N. K., LC125
Komorita, S. S., SC181
Komura, C., EP835
Konda, T. M., AB71, PP25
Kondo, T., ET176
Kone, S. L., EP742
Konrad, K. A., SC684
Koopman, C., OB214
Koopmans, R., DC221
Koot, R. S., PE83
Kopala, P. S., CP71, DC104
Kopel, D. B., LC346
Korbel, G., MP159
Kormenci, R. C., EP318, PE223
Korn, J., LE416
Kornberg, A., AB344, LE524, PE224, PP253
Kornhauser, L. A., SC15
Korobov, V., EP52
Korper, S. H., DC18
Kosaki, L. C., SP28
Kosmin, B. A., MP448
Kosterman, R., IR447
Kostroski, W., LE586
Koubi, V., IR298
Kourany, J., TR169
Kousser, J. M., XX201
Kouzmin, A., OB209
Koven, S. G., PG213
Kowalewski, D., DC36, DC111, DC157, DC222, DP24, ET226
Kowalewski, S. A., SP200
Kposowa, A. J., EP180
Kramer, D. C., PG105

Kramer, G. H., DP31, PE225, PE226,
     SC365, SC790
Kramer, R. M., ET156
Krampen, G., CP35
Krane, D. A., DC366
Krashinsky, M., LE587, LE588
Krasner, S. D., EP836, PC54, PS41,
     PS42, PS43
Krasno, J. S., PP72, PP189
Kraus, J. S., ET60
Krause, G. A., EP111, EP603, LE383
Krause, M. S., XX202
Krauss, W. R., MP278
Krauze, T., OB104
Krebs, D., ET132
Krehbiel, K., LE228, LE244, LE245,
     LE246, LE247, LE394, LE417, LE418,
     LE419, PE93, PE361, SC284, SC754,
     SC791
Krell, G., IR509
Kreml, W. P., ET407
Krenz, C., PA101
Krepps, M. B., MP449
Kreps, D. M., ET177, SC395, SC406,
     SC424
Kress, K. J., ET61
Kressel, N. J., PC173
Kreuger, A. B., SP158
Kriesberg, L., IR510
Kriesky, J., DC315
Kristensen, O. P., EP743, OB283
Kritz, M. M., PG179
Kritzer, H. M., AB159, LC443, PP190
Krivo, L. J., LC379
Krohn, M. D., LC226, LC227
Krol, R., EP604
Krosnick, J. A., AB34, AB35, AB268,
     CP34, CP296, LE141, PP282, XX203
Krueger, A. O., PE599
Krugman, P. R., EP319, EP837, TR143
Krukones, M. G., LE142
Kruseman, J. L., CP112
Kryder, D., LE650
Kryshtanovskaya, O., AB301
Kubalkova, V., IR105
Kuechler, M., AB327, PE227
Kugler, J., EP320, IR106, IR107,
     IR299, IR403, IR448, IR759, IR852,
     SP100
Kuhn, K. U., EP665
Kukathas, C., ET227
Kukla, R. A., AB29
Kuklinski, J. H., AB160, ET470,
     LC444, LE296, LE420, LE421, LE432,
     LE589, MP127, PE228, TR170
Kulba, R. A., AB328
Kumar, A., PG36, PG95
Kumar, K. C., PA293
Kune, J. B., IR679
Kunreuther, H., SC710
Kuo, W. H., MP450
Kuper, L., IR712
Kurth, J. R., XX204
Kurz, M., ET133
Kushner, J., EP744
Kusi, N. K., EP321
Kuzenski, J. C., LE411
Kwon, G. H., PE31
Kwon, W. H., MP381
Kydland, F. E., DP169
Kyj, M. J., ET82
Kymlicka, W., ET228, ET408
Kyriazis, N., CP261

Laband, D. N., LE27, LE338, LE422,
     OB170, PE600, PG34
Labbe, M., SC234
Labys, W. C., DP83

Lach, D. H., IR576, MP251
Lach, S., PA306
La Civita, C. J., EP322
Lackey, D. P., IR585
Ladd, E. C., XX205
Ladd, H. F., SP101, SP451
Laden, A., ET294
Ladha, K. K., LE655
Laemmle, P. G., PS250
Laffey, E. S., DC158
Laffont, J. J., EP605, EP606, PE500,
     SC693
Lagon, M. P., AB269
La Gory, M., PG35
Lagroye, J., PP480
Lahno, B., OB46
Lai, K. S., DP204
Laing, J. D., LE248, SC425
Laitin, D. D., MP451, MP452, PG280
Lake, D. A., EP838, IR713, TR26
Lalman, D., IR264, IR367, IR404,
     IR629, IR630, IR631, IR685
Lamare, J., MP453
Lamb, H., XX254
Lamb, M. L., RP85
Lambelet, J. C., IR300, IR301, IR302
Lambert, P. J., SC695
Lambert, R. D., AB161
Lammers, W. W., PC58, SP372
Lamont, J., XX206
Lancaster, T. D., LE705
Land, K. C., LC183, LC190, LC191,
     LC520, RP62
Landa, J. T., SC303
Landau, D., EP112, EP323, LC306,
     OB249
Landau, S. F., DC45
Landes, D. S., DP154
Landes, R. G., PS139
Landes, W. M., LC38, LC445
Landsberger, H. A., DC159
Landsburg, S. E., AB376
Lane, D., LE28
Lane, F. C., EP324
Lane, J. E., EP325, PG248, PS322,
     PS323
Lane, R. E., ET295
Lane, S., SC66
Lang, G. E., PC55
Lang, K., PC55, XX68
Langan, P. A., LC194
Langbein, L. I., IR511
Lange, P., EP59, EP326, EP327, PE2,
     PE197
Langley, J., IR17
Langley, R. E., EP22
Langlois, J. P., IR449, OB215
Langlois, R. N., TR93
Langs, R. J., DP2
Langton, J., OB348, PA173
Langton, K. P., IR512, PP339
Lanning, S. G., EP31
Lanoue, D. J., LE143, PE116, PE153
Lanternari, V., AB162
Laponce, J., PA174
Laponce, J. A., CP262, CP263, PG106
Laqueur, W., DC364
Larkey, P. D., OB284, PA102
Larrain, J., AB163
Larrain, M., DP102
Larsen, E. R., DP103
Larsen, K. S., IR586
Larson, C. W., DP205
Larson, D. W., AB270, AB271
Larson, J. S., PE67
Larson, R. C., PA233
Lasher, E. L, LE297
Laslett, B., XX207

Lasley, J. R., LC495
Lasson, K., SP201
Latane, B., AB56, DP155
Latimer, M. K., MP173
LaTour, S., DC46
Lau, L. J., EP328
Lau, R. R., AB36, AB70, AB272, CP22
Lauderdale, P., LC371
Laurance, E. J., IR326
Lauth, T. P., PE294, SP409
Laver, M., LE82, LE92, LE94, PE33,
     PE539, PP108, PP481, SC67, SC166,
     SC182, SC196, SC216
Lavigna, R. J., OB105
Law, D., DC161, EP818
Lawrence, D. G., AB164
Lawrence, G. H., MP95
Lawrence, J. J., LC233
Lawrence, R. Z., EP469, PG281
Lawson, C., EP33
Lawson, C. W., EP839
Lazerson, M. H., OB349
Lazerwitz, B., RP86, RP122
Leamer, E. E., SC563
Leanna, S., PE62
Leatherman, J., DC47
Leathers, C. G., EP113, EP647
Leavitt, G. C., LC230
Le Breton, M., SC426, SC427, SC428,
     SC500
Lebovic, J. H., IR349, IR514, OB47
Lebow, R.N., IR450
Lebowitz, M. A., PS84
Ledbetter, C., RP110
LeDuc, L., CP88, PE224, PP26, PP482
Ledyard, J., CP264
Lee, D., IR515
Lee, D. R., EP72, EP114, OB285,
     XX211
Lee, J. R., IR714, LE146, LE147
Lee, J. W., EP213
Lee, M. H., SP42
Lee, R. D., DP242
Lee, S., PE601
Lee, T., PA307
Lee-Sammons, L., PC178
Leech, D., SC304
Leege, D. C., RP128, SP56
Leeper, M. S., MP174
Lees, J. D., LE423
Leff, C. S., LC344
Leff, D. R., PC105
Leff, M. H., LC344
Leftwich, A., EP329, EP330
Legge, J. S., XX212
Legler, J., EP15
Le Grand, J., OB48
Lehman, E. W., PG282
Lehmann, D., DC225
Lehmann, D. R., ET121
Lehnen, R. G., ET351, SP203
Leichter, H. M., PA103
Leifer, R., OB49
Leighley, J. E., PA20, PP20
Leik, R. K., SC429, SP50
Leininger, W., PE602
Leiser, D., AB377
Leiter, M. P., OB106
Leithner, C., PE229, PP192
Leitner, H., PG180
Leland, H. E., EP617
LeLoup, L. T., EP151, LE496, PE498
Lemarchand, R., IR516
Lembcke, J., DP206
Lempert, R., PA234
Lenart, R., PC129
Leng, R. J., IR664, IR715, IR716,
     OB216, OB217

Lengle, J. L., PP123
Lensberg, T., SC632
Lentz, B. F., LE27
Lenze, D. G., TR132
Leonard, J. S., MP46
Leonard, K., PS231
Leonard, M. L., OB255
Leonard, S. T., XX79
Leonardi, G., SC755, SP319
Leonardi, R., AB61
Lepgold, J., IR108
Lepontin, P., OB52
Le Pottier, J., PE500
Lepper, M. R., PC180
Lepper, S. J., PE230
Lerner, R., PC132
Lerter, M., AB123
LeSelva, S. V., DC95
Lesser, B., PE541
Lessmann, S., PE362, PE465
Lester, J. P., TR96
Lester, M., PC56
L'Etang, H., SP106
Letterie, J. W., SP499
Leubsdorf, J., XX213
Leung, S. F., LC324
Levenglick, A., SC305
Levin, J., SC306
Levin, M. A., EP747, LC446
Levine, C. H., DC325, OB62, PA308,
    RP18
Levine, D. I., SC44, SC407
Levine, M. E., SC68, SC792, SC801
Levine, M. V., PP537
Levine, N., XX214
Levine, P., IR303
Levinger, R. L., OB355, PG41
Levinson, D. M., PG36
Levinthal, D., OB350
Levitin, T. E., AB165, PP193
Levitt, S. D., LE706, PP73, PP74,
    PP194
Levy, A. B., LE426
Levy, D., AB377, SP204
Levy, F., EP470
Levy, H., SC697
Levy, J., PG23
Levy, J. S., IR109, IR231, IR717,
    IR718, IR719, IR720, IR721, IR722,
    IR723
Levy, M. R., PC75
Levy, S. G., DC48, DC49
Lewin, L., SC69
Lewis, A., PE231, PE232
Lewis, G. B., OB171
Lewis, K. A., EP197, IR344
Lewis, P., DC311, PS232
Lewis-Beck, M. S., CP265, DC162,
    DC226, EP618, EP619, PA104, PE233,
    PE234, PE235, PE236, PE237, PE238,
    PG107, PP195, PP483, PS9, PS115,
    TR28, TR29
Lewit, T., PS215
Ley, R. D., DP259
Leyden, K. M., LE525, PE239
Li, C. A., PE424
Li, J., EP845
Li, R., CP266
Li, R. P. Y., DC112, DP260, IR232,
    IR811, PE240
Li, S., SC431
Li, W. L., LE590
Lian, B., LE148
Liang, Z., MP23
Libecap, G. D., TR16
Licari, F., ET452
Lichbach, M. I., CP351, DC33, DC50,
    DC163, DC227, IR304, LC192, LC325

Lichtenstein, S., SC130, SC698
Lichter, S. R., PC174
Licklider, R., IR724
Lidz, V., LC54
Lieb, J., LC309
Lieberman, B., SC183
Lieberson, S., MP455, MP456, XX215
Liebman, R. C., OB351, RP50
Liebrand, W. B. G., SC430
Lien, D., PG143
Lien, D. H. D., EP690
Lien, P., MP457
Lieshout, R. H., IR233
Lieske, J. A., DC228, DC229, MP175,
    PG283
Light, I., SP9
Light, P. C., LE149, SP500
Lii, D. T., MP30
Lijphart, A., IR110, LE83, PS142,
    PS273, RP159, SC307, XX216, XX217
Lilie, S. A., TR179
Lim, D., EP331
Lima, A. K., SP205
Limongi, F., EP362
Lin, S. A. Y., EP214, EP332
Lin, T., PP381
Lincoln, Y. S., PA235
Lind, A. E., AB202
Lind, E. A., DC51
Lind, J. D., XX218
Lindauer, D. L., PE117
Lindbeck, A., EP34, OB286
Lindenberg, M., DP207
Lindert, P. H., EP471, SP501
Lindgren, J., LC496
Lindholm, K. J., MP488
Lindquist, D. P., CP65
Lindsay, A. W., SP206
Lindsay, C. M., SC201
Lindsay, J. M., IR517, LE150, LE151,
    LE707
Lindsay, P., AB378
Lindsey, L. B., EP748
Lindstrom, R., DC164
Line, M., XX219
Lineberry, R. L., PP320, SP373
Lineham, W. J., DC52
Liner, G. H., SP374
Link, A. N., EP107, PA309, SC668
Link, M. W., LC447
Linster, B. G., PE603, PE604, PE605
Linville, D., AB124
Liou, K. T., OB107
Lipford, J. W., SC217
Lipman, B. L., SC432, SC633
Lippert, E., IR518
Lipset, S. M., MP436, PP283, PS143,
    XX205
Lipshitz, G., SP375
Lipsky, M., DC230
Lipsky, W. E., DC165
Liska, A. E., LC231, LC232, LC233
Lissowski, G., ET296, ET297
Listhaug, O., AB166, AB180, CP95,
    CP270, PP340, PP344, PP484
Little, E. R., SC447
Little, G., SC20
Little, R., IR111, IR351, IR352,
    IR836
Little, W., PS44
Litz, R. A., EP620
Liu, J. H., DP155
Liu, P., PE145
Liu, T., DP104
Liu, Y. W., LC234
Livi-Bacci, M., SP107
Livingston, S., EP840, LE339
Lizotte, A., LC238

Lloyd, D. A., XX385
Lloyd, R. E., PE118
Lloyd-Jones, R., DP208
Lo, C. Y. H., PS124
Lober, D. J., PG181
Lockerbie, B., AB273, CP300, DC226,
    IR771, LE152, PE34, PE241, PP136,
    PP196
Lodge, M., AB55, AB137, AB167,
    AB168, CP267, CP268, PC200
Lodhi, A. Q., LC235
Loehman, E. T., SP108
Loewenberg, G., ET343, LE6, PP244,
    PS144, XX48
Lofdahl, C. L., EP400
Loftin, C., LC348, LC497
Logan, C. H., LC317, LC326
Logan, J. R., LC236, PG37, SC599
Loges, W. E., MP55
Lohmann, S., DP156, DP261, EP841,
    PP75
Lomi, A., OB352
London, B., EP333, MP169
Londregan, J., DC113, LE249, LE614,
    MP458, PE1, PE590
Long, E., PS16
Long, J. B., DP209
Long, J. S., TR171
Long, N. E., ET409, ET410
Long, S., XX220
Longley, J., PC57
Loomes, G., SC699
Loomis, J., OB184
Looney, R. E., EP334, EP335, EP472,
    IR519, IR520
Lopez, R. A., PE606
Lord, P. P., DC231
Lorenz, H. W., DP105, DP106
Loriaux, M., PE35
Losco, J., PA175
Lothian, J. R., EP842
Lott, J. R., LE427, LE561, PP76,
    SC218, SP207
Lotz, J. R., EP749
Loucks, C., EP558, PP53
Loury, G. C., MP36
Lovaglia, M. J., OB50
Lovell, G. W., IR725
Lovenduski, J., PP293
Lovensuck, J., MP176
Lovrich, N. P., OB108, TR107
Lowe, G. D., RP132
Lowenberg, A. D., EP833
Lowery, D., EP115, EP275, EP750,
    EP751, EP780, LE560, OB243, OB244,
    OB245, PA105, PE64, PE335, PE336,
    PE337, PE338, PE339, PE340, PE363,
    PE364, PE439, PE542, PG38, PG182,
    PG28, SP376
Lowi, T. J., PA106, PE365, XX221
Lowry, R. C., PE59
Lowry, S. M., PS85
Loye, D., DP107
Luban, D., ET230
Lublin, D. I., SC793
Lucas, R. E., EP35
Lucier, C., IR305
Luckenbill, D. F., LC345
Luckham, A. R., IR521
Luckham, R., PS251
Ludwig, J., AB333
Luebbert, G. M., IR313
Lueck, D., TR7
Luke, T. W., PG285
Luksetich, W. A., PP50
Lumsden, M., IR405
Lundholm, R., OB28
Lung, Y., DP157

Lupia, A., CP89, LE84, LE428, LE574
Luskin, R. C., AB37, AB38, AB160, CP113
Luterbacher, U., IR302, IR306, IR619, IR726
Luttbeg, N. R., AB169, AB170, LE340
Lutton, W., LC283
Lutz, C. H., IR725
Lutz, D. S., LC127, LC128
Lutz, J. M., PA294, PA310, PG102
Lux, T., DP32
Lybeck, J. A., OB274, PP284
Lynch, F. R., MP47
Lynch, J. P., LC237
Lynch, M. J., LC238
Lynch, P., SP208
Lynn-Jones, S. M., IR130
Lyon, J. M., MP459
Lyons, W. E., AB171, PG182, PG294

Maas, C. F., CP269
Maass, E. A., PP405
Mabry, R. H., LC171
Macaluso, T. F., RP160
Macaulay, H. M., EP624
Macaulay, S., LC55
MacCoun, R. J., LC56
MacDonald, R., PE141
Macdonald, S. E., AB62, AB166, CP270, CP293, PP214, PP340, PP344, PP484, PP538, PP541
Macey, J. R., OB109, PP27
MacGaffey, W., AB172
Machalek, R., LC193
MacHardy, K. J., DC166
Machin, H., SP377
Machina, M. J., SC700
Machover, M., SC269, SC270
Macht, A. A., PG117
Mack, A., PS233
MacKay, A. F., SC501
Mackenzie, W. J. M., XX222
Mackie, M., PP491
Mackie, T. T., SC174
MacKinnon, C., ET30
MacKuen, M. B., AB7, AB39, CP37, PC106, PE242, PE243, PP28, PP515
MacLaughlin, J., IR853
MacLeod, W. B., SC392
MacManus, S. A., MP151, MP177, SP378
MacPhee, C. R., EP853
MacRae, C. D., PA28, PE466
MacRae, D., SC637
Madden, P., PP285
Madden, T. J., PG297
Maddison, A., EP181
Madsen, D., SC600
Madsen, H. J., EP730
Magagna, V. V., PS325
Magat, W. A., SC732
Magee, S. P., PA176
Magenau, J., LC492
Maggiotto, M. A., AB274, AB305, AB306, AB307, CP17, CP18, PP286
Magleby, D. B., CP90, LE453
Magnus, E. V., SC701
Mahajan, A. K., DC44
Mahajan, H., MP310
Mahajan, V., PA295
Mahler, V. A., EP473, EP740, OB287, OB288, SP502, SP503
Mahon, J. E., EP336
Maier, P. E., PG197
Maier-Katkin, D., MP96, RP12
Mair, P., AB102, MP46, PG39, PP281, PP287, PP485, SC739
Maisel, L. S., PA265
Maisel, R., CP181

Maital, S., EP474, PA262
Maital, S. L., EP474
Maitland, I., PE366
Majeski, S. J., IR307, IR308, IR309, IR310, IR406, IR522, IR727
Majewski, J., TR5
Majstorovic, S., MP229
Majumdar, M., DP108
Makela, K., SP109
Makkai, T., EP622
Makofske, W. J., TR59
Malanchuk, O., AB182
Malec, K. L., PP406
Malerba, F., PA311
Malkin, J., PE543
Malnes, R., ET62
Maloney, W. A., PE367
Maloy, K., SP47
Maltzman, F., LE250
Maluwa, T., IR407
Mamalakis, M. J., EP337
Manage, N., PE119
Mancini, P., LC168
Mancuso, M., PP355
Mandel, E., DP210
Mandell, M. B., PA227
Mandeville, T., TR172
Mane, S., PC91
Maneval, H., IR523
Manganaro, L. L., MP144
Manheim, J. B., PC58, PC107, PC133
Manig, W., TR30
Manley, J. F., LE429, PS145
Mann, A. J., OB289
Mann, T. E., PP197
Manning, D., XX223
Manning, P., MP97
Manns, C. L., SP209
Mans, T. C., ET343
Mansfield, E., PA312
Mansfield, E. D., EP843, IR728, IR729, IR730
Mansfield, M. W., PC59
Manuelli, R., DP211
Manza, J., AB342, EP25
Maor, M., LE73, SC184
Maoz, Z., IR112, IR113, IR234, IR408, IR666, IR731, IR732, IR733, IR734, IR735, IR736, PS234, SC271, SC272, SC273, SC327, SC783
Mapel, D. R., ET63
Marando, V. L., SP379
Maranell, G. M., PP262
Maranto, R., DC365
March, J. G., OB16, OB51, SP209
Marche, G. W., LC373
Marchand, M., EP67, EP695
Marchese, C., OB250
Marchesini, R., LC186
Marchetti, C., DP262
Marcotte, D. E., EP182
Marcus, G. E., AB329, AB40, AB173, AB209, CP37, ET481
Marengo, F. D., PP407
Marenin, O., LC498
Margalit, A., SC532
Margetts, H., SC263
Marginson, P., EP670
Margo, R. A., MP98
Margolis, R. D., SC634
Margolis, J., XX224
Margolis, M., AB41, AB42, ET471
Marhuenda, F., EP752
Marin, D., EP338
Marin-Bosch, M., LE656
Mariotti, S., EP753
Markoff, J., DC167
Markovits, I., LC129

Markovsky, B., PP247
Marks, E., IR524
Marks, G., DC312, DP109
Marks, S. V., LE299
Markulis, P. M., SC393
Markus, G. B., AB43, AB315, CP271, IR502, PE244, PE245, PP288
Markus, L., DP60
Markusen, J. R., EP844
Marlaire, M. P., LE620
Marler, P. L., RP49
Marlin, M. R., EP339
Marlin-Bennett, R., IR114
Marlow, M. L., OB278, OB290, OB291, PE119, PE120, PE544
Marlowe, J., PE545
Marquette, J. F., CP38, SP380
Marquez, J., OB353
Marra, R. F., IR319, LE153, PP198, PP224
Marriott, R. G., PC18
Marsh, A., AB379
Marsh, D., LE647, PE273, PE546
Marsh, M., CP85
Marsh, R. M., PS86
Marshall, D. R., MP149
Marshall, G., RP87
Marshall, I. H., LC239
Marshall, J. M., PE519
Marshall, J. R., IR854
Marshall, W., EP584
Marshall, W. J., LE489
Martelli, M., DP42, DP284
Martin, A., EP36
Martin, B., PE55
Martin, C. J., SP110
Martin, J., AB139, LE657
Martin, J. M., LE85
Martin, L. J., PC201
Martin, L. L., EP215, IR115, OB43
Martin, M. W., ET64, XX225
Martin, P., EP116
Martin, R., EP340
Martinez, F., SC169
Martinez, M. D., PP199
Martinez, V. J., SP210
Martinez-Alier, J., SP504
Martis, K. C., PG286
Marullo, S., OB338
Marvasti, A., EP565
Marvick, E. W., LE19
Marwell, G., AB44, SC219, SC220, SC224, SC225
Marz, R., EP650
Maser, S. M., LC130
Maserang, C. H., XX226
Mashkin, K. B., XX227
Maskin, E. S., SC31, SC44, SC408, SC702
Mason, B., DC313
Mason, R., EP754
Mason, R. O., PA107
Mason, T. D., DC366, MP99
Massey, D. S., MP100, MP101, MP102, MP103, PG40, PG108, PG183, PG184, SP271, SP282, SP283
Masson, P. R., PA76
Masters, M. F., DC273, PP77
Masters, R., SC703
Masters, R. D., LE29, LE56, PA177, PA178, PA179, PA180, PA181, XX367
Masuch, M., OB52
Masumura, W. T., LC240
Mate, M., DC168
Matheny, A. R., EP671
Mathers, R. A., PG110
Mathis, E. J., SC522, SC523
Matland, R. E., MP178, LE179

Matsueda, R. L., LC519
Matsusaka, J. G., CP91, CP139,
  CP140, LE17
Matsushima, H., PA236
Mattei, F., PP200
Mattein, F., CP49
Matthews, D. R., LE341
Matthews, R. C. O., EP117
Matthews, S., SC543
Matthews, T., PE368
Mauro, P., PP408
Mauser, G. A., AB42, LC346, PE36
Mavrogordatos, G. T., PP341
Maxim, P. S., LC241
Maxwell, M., IR737
May, A. M., PE467
May, D., PA137
May, J. D., PP486
May, R. M., DP110, DP111
Mayer, K., LE430
Mayer, K. R., PE468, PP78
Mayer, L. S., SC753
Mayer, W., EP845, EP846
Mayer-Kress, G., IR323
Mayhall, S., IR817
Mayhew, B. H., OB354, OB355, PG41,
  XX228, LE591
Maynard-Moody, S., SP531
Mayo, J. W., EP602
Maysfield, L., PP409
Mayton, D. M., AB134, TR173
Mazlish, B., DC169
Mazmanian, D. A., PA29
Mazur, A., PC134
Mbachu, O., PS146
Mbaku, J. M., DC114, EP341, PE607,
  PP410
McAdam, D., PA313
McAdams, J. C., LE580, PA237, PP79
McAllister, I., AB380, CP256, LE298,
  PE28, PG39, PG287
McArthur, J., LE299
McBath, J. H., PC202
McBride, A., MP331
McBride, M. E., SC70
McBurnett, M., PP71, PP80
McCain, R. A., DP61
McCafferty, P., CP312, PP411
McCaffery, J. L., PE108
McCaffrey, D., DP112
McCall, P. L., LC513, LC515, LC520
McCallum, J., PE369
McCann, J. A., PP124
McCarthy, C., OB184
McCarthy, P. S., SP111
McClain, P. D., LC242, MP442, MP461,
  MP462
McCleary, W., EP755
McClelland, G. H., EP681
McClendon, J. A., DC314, DC315
McClennen, E. F., PA108
McCleskey, C., MP463
McClosky, H., AB14, ET472, XX229
McCluggage, V., LE222
McClure, R. H., SP211
McCollom, C. B., LC315
McCombs, M. E., AB45, AB82, PC108,
  PC124
McConahay, J. B., MP104
McConnell, K. E., CP92
McConnell, M. W., ET411
McConnell, S., DC316
McCormick, G. H., RP19
McCormick, J. M., AB275, AB308,
  ET232, IR116, IR117, IR587, LE431
McCormick, K., SC635, XX4
McCormick, R. E., CP272, PE608,
  SP212

McCoy, C., MP331
McCrary, P., DC170
McCraw, D. J., CP273
McCrickard, D. L., PE432
McCrohan, K. F., ET125
McCrone, D. J., LE281, LE432, LE658,
  PG288, PS287, SP467
McCubbins, M. D., CP215, CP274,
  EP563, EP623, LE139, LE428, LE433,
  LE514, LE515, LE703, OB110, OB111,
  XX230
McCue, K. F., PE531
McCulloch, A. M., SC564
McCulloch, M. K., PA35, PS154
McCurley, C., CP275, LE592, MP153
McDermott, M., AB174
McDonagh, E. L., CP276, LE300,
  LE301, MP280
McDonald, D. C., PC203
McDonald, I. M., DC272
McDonald, M., LE128, MP161
McDonogh, G. W., DC171
McDougal, S. L., LC180
McDougall, G. S., CP87, PP68, SP6
McDowall, D., LC245, LC246, LC347,
  LC348, LC497
McDowell, G. L., LC448
McDowell, J. M., PG185
McFadyen, R. G., XX382
McFarland, A. S., PE370, PE371
McFarland, S. G., LC374
McFarlane, D. R., SP41
McFaul, M., IR843, PP487
McGann, J. G., PA109
McGarrell, E. F., LC57
McGarrity, J. P., PE118
McGavin, B. H., PE469
McGee, M. C., AB175
McGillicuddy, N. B., DC100
McGinnis, H., EP342
McGinnis, M. D., ET178, IR235,
  IR311, IR341, IR409, IR432
McGinnis, R., TR171
McGlen, N., XX231
McGlennon, J., PP236
McGowan, P. J., DC110, DC115, EP343,
  IR236
McGranahan, D. A., EP475
McGrath, P., DC336, OB53
McGrath, W., PP133
McGraw, K. M., AB80, AB168, CP267,
  EP756, LE30, PC60, XX232, XX233,
  XX234
McGregor, E. B., PP125
McGregory, R. R., EP76
McGuire, C. B., IR605
McGuire, K. T., LC58, LC59
McGuire, M. C., ET65, SC199
McGuire, R. A., LC131, LC132, LC133,
  PE547
McGuire, T. G., OB172
McGuire, T. J., EP757
McHugo, G. J., XX235
McIver, J. P., AB222, PA53, PG247,
  SP338, SP449
McKay, D., LE31
McKee, M., EP553, EP589, OB173,
  OB371
McKelvey, R. D., CP231, LE251,
  LE342, PC61, SC71, SC72, SC308,
  SC433, SC434, SC565, SC566, SC756
McKenzie, R. B., CP272, EP624, ET66,
  OB292
McKeown, B., PP379, RP161
McKeown, T., IR108
McKeown, T. J., EP847, PP81
McKinlay, R. D., IR350, IR351, IR352,
  PS252, PS253, PS254, SP463, SP464

McKinney, S., MP105
McLanahan, S. S., SP269
McLauchlan, G., IR677
McLaughlin, R., PA314
McLaughlin, S. M., PE367, PE396
McLean, I., SC73, SC198, SC309,
  SC210, SC567, SC636
McLemore, L. B., MP464, MP524
McLemore, L. E., ET336
McLennan, B. N., EP344
McLeod, D. M., PC31
McLeod, J., SC435
McLeod, J. M., PC41, PC109, PC203
McMahon, C., ET412
McManus, M., SC74
McManus, W. S., LC375
McMillan, H., EP577
McMillin, W. D., EP118, PE121
McMullin, D. R., PG58
McMurray, C. D., LC451
McNair, E. S., EP345
McNiel, D. W., EP37
McNitt, A. D., ET231
McNown, R., PA110
McPhail, C., DC232, DC233
McPherson, J. M., OB382, OB383,
  OB388
McPherson, M., LE585
McPherson, M. S., ET42
McRae, T., LE434
McSwain, C. J., ET413
McVeigh, R., CP39
McWilliams, W. C., AB238
Mead, T. D., PC110
Meador, M., DC317
Meadow, R. G., PC204, PC205
Meadwell, H., MP465, PG289
Means, R., PA182
Mebane, W. R., SP505, XX236
Meckstroth, T. W., XX237
Medio, A., DP113
Medoff, M. H., RP20
Meeker, B. F., IR525, IR545, SC429
Meerman, J., PE548, IR357
Meernik, J., LC31
Meeter, D. A., CP249, PP260
Meguire, P. G., PE223
Mehay, S. L., EP346, MP192
Mehrling, P. G., PE37
Meier, K. J., CP277, LE708, OB174,
  PE372, PE373, PP289, PP412, RP165,
  SP41, SP112, SP213, SP237, SP238,
  SP239, TR31
Meier, R. F., LC338
Meiselman, D. I., PE470
Melanson, P. H., XX238
Melchior, A., PE490
Melese, F., IR312
Meleskie, M. F., LE154
Melko, M., IR410
Meltzer, A. H., OB293, OB294, PE84,
  PE160, PE246
Melvin, M. T., DP23
Menahem, G., PP342
Mendelberg, T., MP92
Mendell, N. R., SC748
Mendeloff, D., DC116
Mendelsohn, M., LE594
Mendelsohn, R., RP91
Mendilow, J., PP488
Mendola, J., ET67, SC638
Mendoza, J. L., DP1
Mensch, G., PA315
Menzel, D. C., ET414
Merelman, R. M., AB176, MP466, XX239
Merkl, P. H., PS288
Merkx, G. W., OB179
Merrifield, J., CP141, EP758

Merrill, B., MP463
Merrill, S., SC757
Merrill, S. A., XX240
Merriman, D., EP759
Merriman, W. R., MP106
Merritt, S., PC206
Mertens, J. F., SC590
Merton, R. K., TR174, XX241
Mesa-Lago, C., PS326
Messerschmidt, J., LC243
Messick, R. E., SP468
Messinger, S. L., LC304
Messner, S. F., LC236, LC244, LC278,
  LC368, LC376, LC499, LC521, RP88
Mestelman, S., OB384
Meszaros, J. W., LE32
Metcalfe, J. S., PA316
Metlay, D. S., TR170
Metz, R., DP199
Metz, T. E., CP83
Metzger, A. R., OB385
Meulemann, H., AB381
Meur, G., PP489
Mevorach, B., OB295
Meyer, C. K., ET333
Meyer, D. S., DC234, IR588, PE374
Meyer, F. A., SP381
Meyer, G. S., TR148
Meyer, G. W., XX27
Meyer, J., PA280
Meyer, M. W., OB356
Meyer, P. B., EP347
Meyer, R. L., MP213
Meyer, W. B., SP382
Mezey, M. L., LE33, LE34
Mezey, S. G., MP281, MP282
Miceli, M. P., ET415, ET416
Michaelis, P., EP625
Michaels, J. W., PP413, SP214
Michaels, R., EP626
Michalos, A. C., PA111
Michel, P., IR312
Michela, J. L., XX193
Micheletti, M., PE375
Micklewright, J., EP158
Middendorf, C., IR324
Middendorp, C. P., AB177
Middlestadt, S. E., AB190
Midford, P., EP848
Midlarsky, M. I., DC53, DC188,
  DC235, DC236, DC367, IR738, IR739,
  IR855, IR856, PA317, PG109, PS147
Miethe, T. D., LC245, LC246, PP413,
  PP414, SP214
Mietus, K. J., PG110
Miezkowski, P., PG186
Migalski, M., MP424
Migdal, J. S., PS289
Mikesell, J. L., EP760, LC247
Milbrath, L. W., AB178
Milburn, M. A., AB46, AB47, AB155,
  CP34
Miles, I., XX242
Miles, R. E., SC264
Milesi-Ferretti, G. M., SC794
Miller, A., XX129
Miller, A. H., AB179, AB180, AB181,
  AB182, CP40, CP41, CP278, DC238,
  MP467, PC99, PC135, PP201, PP290,
  RP162, SC185
Miller, A. J., XX245
Miller, B., IR121, SC221
Miller, C., DC170
Miller, C. E., SC186
Miller, D., ET68, XX246
Miller, D. L., PG110
Miller, E. N., CP26
Miller, E. S., EP627

Miller, G., TR162
Miller, G. J., ET69, LC134, LE252,
  OB153, OB161, OB296, SC404
Miller, G. P., PE376
Miller, H. J., SC758
Miller, J., MP468
Miller, J. A., DC182
Miller, J. G., ET298, PA183
Miller, J. H., ET150, PP338, SC222
Miller, J. L. L., DC64
Miller, L. S., SP506
Miller, M., SC538
Miller, M. C., LE435
Miller, N. R., LE709, SC75, SC311,
  SC212, SC436
Miller, R. A., CP130
Miller, T., SP215
Miller, W. E., AB165, AB181, CP142,
  PP193, PP490, RP163, RP164
Miller, W. L., PP491, PP539
Miller, W. R., PP361
Millner, E., SP120
Mills, D. E., PG187
Mills, E. S., EP225
Mills, T. C., DP33
Milne, W. J., LE587, LE588, PG188
Milner, C., EP348
Milner, H., EP849, ET179
Milstein, J. S., IR714
Milward, H. B., PG189
Mincy, R. B., SP294
Minehart, T., LE547
Miner, H., IR122
Miner, R. E., EP761
Minford, P., LC135, PE471
Mingst, K. A., PE38
Minnix, D., SC718
Minns, D. R., CP279
Mintrom, M., EP662., SP216
Mintz, A., EP349, IR526, IR527,
  IR740, PE39, SC187
Miranda, R. A., OB297, SP383
Mirande, A. M., CP42
Mirer, T., CP258
Miron, J. A., DP171
Mirowski, P., DP114, DP115, XX247,
  XX248, XX249
Mishal, S., PG19
Mishan, E. J., EP629
Mishler, W., LC449, LE35, LE436,
  LE437, PG290, PP492, PS148, SP113
Mishra, A., PP359
Mishra, B., EP581
Misiolek, W. S., OB298
Misra, A., DC318, SP486
Mitchell, C. R., IR741, MP380
Mitchell, D. W., DP83, DP84, SC568
Mitchell, E. J., DC172
Mitchell, G., IR605
Mitchell, G. E., CP143
Mitchell, J., OB299
Mitchell, J. M., PE377
Mitchell, K., OB86
Mitchell, M., LC377
Mitchell, N. J., ET232
Mitchell, P., PP493
Mitchell, R. B., PS47
Mitchell, R. C., PE378, PE521
Mitchell, W., LE123
Mitchell, W. C., LC136, PE40, PE377
Mitchell, W. F., EP183
Mitias, P. M., SC530
Mitra, S. K., MP469, SC601
Mitra, T., DP108
Mitroff, I. I., PA107
Mixon, A. J., MP218
Mixon, F. G., DC319, PE379
Mixon, J. W., EP513

Mizruchi, M. S., PE380
Mladenka, K. R., MP22, PP415
Mo, J., SC188, SC437
Moaddel, M., PS290
Modelski, G., DP263, DP264, DP265,
  IR123, IR742
Modigliani, A., AB276, TR159
Modis, T., DP116
Moe, R. C., PE549
Moe, T. M., EP630, EP631, LE36,
  LE206, LE438, OB54, OB55, OB146,
  OB296, PE381, SC76
Moehring, H. B., PG190
Moen, J. R., SP10
Moffett, R. R., LE383
Moffitt, R., SP507, SP508
Mofidi, A., EP762
Mogull, R. G., SP509, SP510
Mohl, R. A., SP284
Mohler, P. P., DP266
Mohnen, V. A., TR66
Mohr, L. B., PA278, PA318
Mohtadi, H., EP172
Moises, J. A., PG291
Mok, J. W., PA91
Mokyr, J., PA184
Moldovanu, B., ET180
Molinar, J., PP494
Moll, K. D., IR313
Molyneus, G., SP479
Moncrief, G. F., LE238, LE343,
  LE344, LE613, LE720, PP82, SP60
Mondak, J. J., AB184, CP275, CP280,
  CP281, LC450, LE155, LE592, LE593,
  PC136
Monjardet, B., SC512
Monroe, A. D., PA30, PP126
Monroe, K. R., ET134, ET135, ET417,
  PE247, PE248, PE249, PE472, SC77
Monsen, R. J., OB183
Montero de Juan, J. F., SC361, SC362
Montmarquette, C., EP427, PP380
Moodie, G. C., PP416
Moodie, D., LC327, PP417
Moon, B. E., DC15, EP810, ET233
Moon, D., CP44, CP144, CP282, PP219
Mooney, C. Z, LE439, LE440, SP42
Moore, D. W., IR124, PC207, PP202
Moore, E. G., PG148
Moore, G. H., DP212
Moore, M., EP632, LC60
Moore, M. K., LE329, LE330
Moore, R. A., PE150
Moore, W. H., DC164, PS127, SC223
Moore, W. J., DC320, DC321
Moote, M. A., TR123
Mor, B. D., OB218
Moran, M. J., EP668
Moreh, J., ET70, SC639
Morel, L., CP93
Morgan, D. F., PP418
Morgan, D. R, EP763, LC500, MP107,
  PG292, PG293, PG294, PG295, RP165,
  SP217, SP221, SP384
Morgan, I., PS236
Morgan, P. M., IR742
Morgan, S. P., RP21
Morgan, T. C., DC54, IR722, IR723,
  IR743
Morgenstern, S., CP216, LE559
Morikawa, T., ET181
Moritra, S., LC175
Morrill, R. L., PA319
Morris, M., MP217
Morris, S., PE588
Morris-Jones, W. H., LE37
Morrison, A. R., PG191
Morrison, C. C., DP213

Morrissey, M., SP273
Morrissey, O., SC259
Morrow, J. D., ET182, IR125, IR237,
  IR238, IR314, IR315, IR411, IR706,
  IR744, IR745, IR746, OB219, SC704
Morse, E. R., EP749
Morse, G. A., SP268
Morse, R. M., PG42
Morse, S. J., XX250
Morton, R. B., CP145, CP283, MP164,
  PE550, PP83, PP127
Morton, S., SC795
Mosekilde, E., DP117
Moses, L. N., EP633
Moskowitz, H., SP2
Mosley, P., IR353, PC137
Moss, R., DC368
Most, B. A., IR747, IR748, IR749,
  IR798, IR799, IR800, PA320, PG319
Moul, W. B., IR750, IR751
Moulen, J., LC96
Moulin, H., PA238, SC78, SC313,
  SC796
Mouritzen, P. E., PE473
Mowery, D. C., IR494, OB280, PE103,
  PE111, PE112
Moynihan, D. P., SP285
Mozo, R., MP495
Mucciaroni, G., PA112, PP419
Muedeking, G. D., PG43
Mueller, C. M., AB185
Mueller, D. C., LE38, LE710, OB253,
  OB300, PC62, PS194, SC79, SC80
Mueller, E. H., PP29, PP30, PS48,
  PS49
Mueller, J. E., AB277, AB278, CP94,
  ET473, LE156
Mueller, K. J., LE157, SP385
Mughan, A., CP199, CP237, PE28,
  PG290, PP203
Muha, M. J., SP193
Muhammad, M. E., IR752
Mukonoweshuro, E. G., DC55
Mulford, C. L., EP634
Mullahy, J., XX251
Mullen, J. K., EP350
Muller, E. N., CP45, DC174, DC175,
  EP38, EP476, EP477, PE190, PS149,
  PS150, PS151
Muller, F. G., PE122
Muller, N., XX252
Muller-Rommel, F., LE345, PP495
Mulligan, G. F., PG44
Mullins, W. A., AB186
Mulvey, G. C., DC322
Mumphrey, A. J., PG192
Muncaster, R. G., IR753
Munch, R., SC705
Munger, M. C., AB116, AB143, LE288,
  LE318, LE577, LE629, PE323, PE342,
  PE378, PE382, PP65, PP66, PP84,
  PP161
Municio, I., XX253
Munley, V. G., CP96, PG193
Munnell, A. H., EP119
Munro, J., ET71, RP129
Munzenrider, R. F., OB25
Murauskas, G. T., PG296
Murcock, S. H., MP83
Murdock, J. C., IR220, IR239, SC524
Murdock, M. M., MP470
Murnane, R. J., EP470
Murnighan, J. K., ET328, OB385,
  SC189, SC438
Murphy, H. S. K., DP62
Murphy, J. T., LE711
Murphy, J. W., DP63
Murphy, K. M., EP177, PE609

Murphy, L., DC311
Murphy, P., LC137
Murphy, P. R., ET418, ET419
Murphy, T. G., AB219
Murphy, W. F., LC468
Murray, A., EP351
Murray, C., SP218, SP286
Murray, H., IR510
Murrell, P., OB253, OB300, OB301,
  PE355, PE383, TR98
Murshed, S. M., IR354
Musgrave, R., PE123
Musgrove, P., EP478
Mushaben, J. M., DP267
Musolf, L., LE441
Musser, S. J., ET72
Mustafa, H., ET101
Mutz, D. C., AB48, PC63, PC64, PP85
Muzzio, D., SC261, SC262
Myatt, A., EP184
Myer, D. G., XX254
Myers, M. A., LC61
Myers, S. L., LC248, LC249, LC250,
  MP108, PC172
Myerson, R. B., PP420, SC81, SC314,
  SC759

Nachmias, D., CP46, OB175
Nadeau, R., AB49, CP284, DP34,
  LE594, PE250, PE440, PP291
Nadel, M. V., EP139, PA31
Naff, K. C., MP109
Nagel, J., EP479, LC328, MP471,
  MP472, MP473, MP474
Nagel, T., ET73
Nagin, D., LC329
Nagler, J., CP146, PE158
Nair, K. S., MP475
Nakamura, H., OB390
Nakanishi, D. T., MP476
Nalebuff, B., IR451, IR589, SC306
Nalin, E., XX255
Namboodiri, K., PA185
Namenwirth, J. Z., AB382
Namias, J., TR99
Nandi, P. K., XX256
Nanetti, R. Y., AB61
Nanneman, T., XX123
Nannestad, P., PE251, PE252, SC82
Narang, A. S., PS195
Narasimhan, L. S., SC738
Nardi, P. M., ET105
Nardin, T., ET420, IR754
Nardinelli, C., PE384
Nardulli, P. F., PP204, PP540
Naroff, J. L., LC251, PG297
Narud, H. M., LE86
Nas, T. F., PP421
Nash, A. E. K., LC62
Nash, J., LC330
Nassmacher, K. H., PP496
Natchez, P. B., PE124
Nathan, J. A., AB50
Naumann, J., PE400
Navin, J. C., PE125
Navin, L. J., PE125
Ndegwa, S. N., PS269
Neal, P., ET299, SC83
Near, J. P., ET415, ET416
Neary, H. M., OB56
Nechemias, C., MP181
Neckel, S., ET421
Needleman, C., LC252
Needleman, M. L., LC252
Neeler, M. C., CP285
Nefci, S. N., DP214
Neidert, L., MP411
Neilsen, E. H., OB361

Nelkin, D., TR176
Nell, E., EP39
Nelson, A., ET74, SC640
Nelson, C. E., PA239
Nelson, C. J., LE595
Nelson, D. C., MP393, MP477
Nelson, D. N., IR412
Nelson, G., LE346
Nelson, H. M., RP89, RP156, RP157
Nelson, J., PG35
Nelson, J. C., EP637
Nelson, J. F., LC253, LC254
Nelson, J. S., XX258
Nelson, L. D., RP28
Nelson, M. A., EP733, OB302
Nelson, P. J., OB268
Nelson, R. H., PA113
Nelson, R. R., EP120, PS45
Nelson, W. E., LC452
Nesbitt-Larking, P., PG298
Nesvold, B. A., DC141, IR609
Netemeyer-Mays, M., MP252
Nettl, J. P., PS46
Neubeck, K. J., EP506
Neufeld, M., IR126
Neuman, W. R., AB51
Neumann, I. B., IR36
Neumann, W. L., LC255
Neustadt, A., PE385, PE386, PP97
Nevitte, N., SP43
Newbery, D. M., EP583
Newlin, J. R., IR590
Newman, A. R., PG194
Newman, B. A., EP352
Newman, H. H., PG189
Newman, J., LE158
Newman, J. O., ET422, LC63
Newman, M. A., MP284
Newman, R. J., DC321
Newman, S., MP478, MP279, PG299
Newport, F., RP22
Newton, K., PE126
Neyman, A., ET183
Nguyen, D. T., EP250
Nice, D. C., LC138, LC378, LE159,
  MP285, PA321, PP128, PP129, PP155,
  PP422, PP497, SP11, SP386, SP387,
  SP388, SP389
Nicholls, K., LE347
Nicholson, M., IR741, IR755
Nicholson, M. B., SC569
Nicholson, S. P., LE606
Nickell, S. J., EP185
Nie, N. H., AB187, CP48
Niedermayer, O., PP292
Nielsen, F., EP480, EP481
Nielsen, H. J., PS196
Nielsen, K., DC60
Nielson, F., MP480, MP481, OB357
Niemi, R. G., AB25, AB49, AB52,
  AB188, AB371, CP49, CP147, CP284,
  LE253, PE253, SC315, SC316, SC317,
  SC570, SC571, SC771, SC785
Nieuwbeerta, P., CP220
Nigro, L. G., ET427
Nijkamp, P., DP118, DP119, DP215,
  SC363
Nilson, S. S., PE551, SC641
Nilsson, E. A., EP121
Nilsson, J. E., PE552
Nincic, M., IR413, IR528, LE160
Niou, E. M. S., IR128, IR240, IR414,
  IR756
Nisbett, R. E., AB53, ET145
Nishimura, K., DP120
Niskanen, W. A., OB176
Nitzan, S., OB26, PE524, PE610,
  SC318

Noel, A., EP638., IR355
Noel, J. J., OB112
Noel, S. J. R., XX260
Noelle-Neumann, E., AB54, PC65, PC66, PC67
Nogle, J. M., PG179
Nolan, P. D., OB113
Noll, R. G., OB110., SC681, SC776
Nollkaemper, A., IR129
Noonan, J. T., XX261
Norden, D. L., PS270
Nordhaus, W. D., PE474, PE475
Nordin, J. A., LE254
Nordlinger, E. A., PS255
Norman, R. Z., XX105
Norman, W., ET408
Norpoth, H., AB55, LC64, LE161, LE526, PE41, PE200
Norrander, B., CP148, CP286
Norris, P., LE596, MP176, PP293
Norstrom, T., LC256
North, D. C., EP40, OB303, SC84, SC642
North, R. C., IR415
Norton, B., DP216
Norton, D. A. G., EP852
Norton, P., LE597
Norway, PE279
Nossal, K. R., PE42
Notermans, T., EP166
Nowak, A., AB56, DP155
Nowak, S., XX262
Nowell, C., EP639, PE553
Nownes, A. J., CP149
Noyes, R. E., PC174
Nozicka, G. J., IR19
Nunn, C. Z., ET482
Nurmi, H., LE40, SC85, SC86, SC87, SC88, SC319, SC320, SC321, SC322, SC364, SC365, SC366, SC602, SC603, SC797, XX263
Nusse, H. E., DP121
Ny, U. K., SC643
Nye, J. S., IR103, IR130, IR591
Nye, M. A., LE442, LE659, LE660

Oakes, A., PA322
Oates, W. E., PG195, TR54
Oberst, R. C., PP423
Obler, J., ET423, LE443
O'Brien, K. M., DC323
O'Brien, M. J., DP99
O'Connor, K., LC454
O'Connor, P. F., LE385
O'Connor, R. E., ET75, SP20, SP44
Oechssler, J., SP390
Oegema, D., DC239
Ofer, G., EP353
Offe, C., SP511
O'Flaherty, B., PS152, SC423
Oguledo, V. I., EP853
Oh, C. H., OB304
O'Halloran, S., EP841, OB84
Ohlsson, H., PE91
Ohn, M. G., PP475
Ohrenstein, R. A., SC439
Ohsfeldt, R. L., LC132, LC133, PE547, SP32, SP73
Ok, E. A., SC367
O'Kane, R. H. T., DC117, DC118, DC119
Okrasa, W., ET297
Okruhik, G., PP385
Okuguchi, K., PE554
Olcina, G., SC440
Oldendick, R. W., AB225, AB279 AB314
O'Leary, B., LE322
O'Leary, M. K., SC17

Oleszek, W. J., LE216
Oliver, P. E., OB386, SC224, SC225
Olivera, J. H. G., EP354
O'Loughlin, J., IR757, IR758, MP182, PG45
O'Malley, P., LC257
Olneck, M. R., XX264
O'Neill, D. J., MP111
O'Neill, J., MP485
O'Neill, W., ET21
Olsen, M. C., MP482
Olsen, M. E., CP150
Olshansky, S. J., PG196
Olshfski, D., OB138
Olson, D. V. A., RP166
Olson, E. C., PE254
Olson, J. P., OB16, OB51
Olson, M., IR241, PS291, PS292, SC666, SP512, XX265
Olson, M. K., EP640
Olzak, S., MP110, MP474, MP483, MP484
Oneal, J. R., AB280, IR242, IR243, LE148, OB220, PS50
Onis, Z., EP355
Onuf, N. G., ET344
Opello, W. C., LE444
Opheim, C., LE598, PE387
Opotow, S., ET300
Opp, K. D., CP26, CP50, DC175, LC258
Oppenheimer, B. I., LE445, PP205, PP206
Oppenheimer, J. A., AB100, ET69, ET76, ET123, ET164, ET275, ET276, ET277, IR244, LE712
Oppenheimer, L., AB244
Oppenheim, F. E., ET234
Oppenhuis, E. V., PP11
Orbell, J. M., ET136, ET137, ET147, ET181, ET195, PC138, PS51, SC636
Ordeshook, P. C., CP125, CP305, IR128, IR240, IR414, IR756, LC305, LE133, LE251, PC61, PP160, PP498, PP499, SC72, SC190, SC308, SC433, SC434, SC798, SC799 SP490
O'Reilly, T., PE555
Oren, I., IR245, IR318
Organski, A. F. K., IR299, IR759, IR852
Orke, E. A., ET72
Orloff, A. S., SP219, SP220
Orman, J., PC175
Orme, C., SC629
Orme-Johnson, D. W., IR133
Ornstein, M. D., AB189
Orsenigo, L., PA311, PA335
Ortiz, I. D., MP486
Ortona, G., PE476
Ortuno-Ortin, I., EP752
Orum, A., MP286, RP167
Orzechowski, W., OB291
Osborne, M. J., PP343
O'Shea, R., PS293
Oseth, J. M., IR134
Oshima, H. T., EP482
Ostaiewicz, W., SC358
Ostheimer, J. M., PA32
Ostrom, C. W., IR135, IR319, IR530, IR857, LE153, LE162, LE163, LE164, LE185, PP198, PP224, PP240
Ostrom, E., SC88
Ostrom, V., ET77, LC140, PS197
Ostrowski, K., XX379
O'Sullivan, A., ET128
Osuna, W., PA77
Oswald, A., DC268
Oswald, S. L., DC334

Oswalt, I., SC442
Otaki, M., DP192
Otani, I., EP356
Ott, J. S., OB57
Ottati, V. C., AB57, AB190
Ottensmann, J. R., SP391
Ottensmeyer, E. J., EP295
Ougaard, M., IR136
Outram, D., DC176
Ou-yang, H., LE590
Overby, L. M., IR592, LC455, LE302, LE348, LE513
Overbye, E., CP151
Overgaard, P. B., DC370
Overman, E. S., SP115
Owen, D., ET424
Owen, D. E., RP53, RP54, RP136
Owen, G., CP152, SC760
Owens, G. M., PP500
Owens, J., SP45
Owens, J. E., EP122
Owens, J. R., LE446, LE713, PE254, PE255, PS20
Oxley, L., OB305, SC89
Oye, K. A., ET184

Pacek, A. C., CP153, PE256, PE257
Pacey, P. L., EP602
Pachon, H. P., MP487
Pack, J. R., EP765, PE477
Packard, N., DP122
Packel, E., CP231
Packel, E. W., LE14, LE240, SC502
Packet, A., PP207
Paddock, J., PP31
Padgett, J. F., PE127
Padgug, R. A., MP112
Padilla, A. M., MP488
Padilla, Y. C., MP489
Padoch, C., XX43
Page, B. I., CP204, CP287, CP288, IR171, IR760, LE41, PA33, PC139, PC164, SC707
Page, S. E., PP338
Pagoulatos, E., PE606
Pahre, R., ET185
Paige, J. M., DC240
Pak, K., PE463
Palda, F., IR356, PP86
Paldam, M., DC324, EP539, PE251, PE252, PE258, PE478, PS52
Palfrey, T. R., AB191, CP154, SC290, SC798
Palmer, H. D., PP294, PS26
Palmquist, B., PP270, PP332
Palmquist, M., AB98
Pammett, J. H., CP88, CP289
Pampel, F. C., SP116, SP117, SP513, SP549
Panitch, L., EP357
Panning, W. H., EP483, ET345, LE447, SC708
Panzer, J., PE259
Paolino, P., MP287
Papageorgiou, Y. Y., PE556, SC755
Parades, R. D., PE259
Parent, T. W., MP106, PP170
Parenti, M., MP490
Parish, W. L., PS86
Park, B., AB20
Park, H. S., ET235
Park, J. C., ET257
Park, K. O., SP393
Park, S., SP108
Park, W. G., EP484
Parker, G. R., LE42, LE255, LE448, LE449, LE450, LE451, LE452, LE599, PP208, PP209, PP295

Parker, P. M., PA323
Parker, R. N., EP485, LC381
Parker, S. L., AB58, LE42, LE255
Parks, C. D., SC90, SC443
Parks, R. P., CP221
Parnes, A. H., DC61
Paroush, J., OB26
Parsons, M. B., LC451
Parsons, R. W., AB91
Parsons, W., IR649
Partin, R. W., CP77, PE260
Pashigian, B. P., LC65
Pasigna, A. L., XX381
Pasta, S., LC296
Patchen, M., ET186
Patel, K., RP168
Paternoster, R., LC331, LC332, SC709
Pathirane, L., OB306
Patibandla, M., EP854
Patraeus, D. H., IR762
Patrick, T. M., SP394
Pattanaik, P. K., SC124, SC239,
   SC323, SC350, SC351, SC800
Patterson, K. D., LE453
Patterson, M. J., SP47
Patterson, S. C., LE278, LE337,
   LE369, LE370, LE371, LE454, LE455,
   LE456, LE527, LE528, PP150
Patterson, W. D., EP290, LE705
Pattie, C. J., CP254, LE661, PE261,
   PG32, PG273
Patton, M. Q., PA240
Paukert, F., EP486
Paul, T. V., IR763
Pauly, M., SC710
Pauly, P., DP204
Paust, J. J., DC177, ET236
Payne, B. A., PG196
Payne, C., PP13
Payne, J. L., CP73, EP540, LE256,
   LE349, LE600, PE479
Payner, B. S., MP39
Pchelintsev, O. S., PG46
Peacock, W. G., XX30
Peal, D., PP501
Pearson, F. S., IR766, IR767
Pearson, G., LC259
Pearson, W. M., LE43
Pedan, E. A., EP358
Pedersen, M. N., LE457, PP502
Pedersen, P. J., DC324
Pedersen, W., SC324
Peek, C. W., RP90, RP132
Peel, D., PE471
Peffley, M., AB259, AB260, AB261,
   AB281, AB282, AB283, LE136, PE262
Peled, D., EP678
Peleg, B., SC191, SC444
Peli, G., OB358
Pelikan, J., PS237
Pelissero, J. P., SP217, SP221,
   SP384
Pellikaan, H., AB336
Pelowski, A. L., PS12
Peltzman, S., EP641, OB307, PE263,
   SP222
Peng, Y., SC604
Penning, J. M., RP169
Pennings, P., OB308
Pepper, D., IR320
Percy, S. L., PG197
Peregoy, P. L., DP67
Perez, S. J., EP100
Perez-Castrillo, J. D., PE611
Peritore, N. P., PP32
Perkins, J., MP183, MP243
Perkins, L. P., LE257
Perkins, M. K., SP118

Perloff, R. M., CP51
Peroff, K., SP119
Perotti, R., EP201, PE56
Perry, C. S., EP642
Perry, H. L., MP113
Perry, J. L., PA324
Perry, J. S., DC325, ET425
Persky, J., PE616
Persson, T., EP766
Pescosolido, B. A., RP91
Pestieau, P., EP695
Peters, B. G., OB114, OB177, OB178,
   PA34, PA35, PA114, PS154, SP515
Peters, J. G., PP425, PP426, PP427,
   TR43
Peters, M. D., PC130
Petersen, J. G., PP431
Petersen, R., DC43
Petersen, T., OB115
Peterson, C. E., IR497
Peterson, E. J., XX373
Peterson, M. A., PE328, PE388
Peterson, P. E., LE44, PE389, PG198
Peterson, R. D., LC355, LC356, LC379
Peterson, R. S., MP48
Peterson, S. A., AB383, DC63, DC241,
   PA186, PA187, PA188, XX359
Peterson, S. P., SP120
Peterson, V. S., ET344
Pethig, R., LC114
Petracca, M. P., PE390, SC91
Petras, J., XX269
Petrocik, J. R., CP155, CP156
Pettersen, P. A., EP724
Pettigrew, T. F., MP121
Pettit, P., SC445
Pfau, M., PC68, PC69, PC143, PC208,
   PC209
Phares, D., EP767
Phelan, J., SP287
Phillips, C. D., MP114
Phillips, C. S., PA189
Phillips, D. C., XX270
Phillips, D. P., LC380, PC119,
   PC140, PC141, PC142
Phillips, J. D., OB118
Phillips, J. M., EP359
Phillips, K., PS257
Phillips, P. C. B., PE165
Phillips, W., DC12
Phillips, W. R., PS53
Phillips-Patrick, F. J., OB359
Philpotts, G. C., LE710
Piccigallo, P. R., DP268
Pierce, G. L., LC349
Pierce, J. C., AB59, AB135, AB192,
   AB193, LE220, PP296, PP297, TR106,
   TR107
Pierce, P. A., MP184
Pierce, R., CP95
Piereson, J. E., AB209, CP290,
   ET481, PP210, PP286, PP504
Pierre, J., PP298
Pierson, C., XX271
Piggott, J., PE512
Pilant, D., RP168
Pilarzyk, T., RP92
Pilat, D., EP56
Piliavin, I., LC333
Pindur, W., PG276
Pines, D., PG199
Pinney, N., XX234
Pinon, G., MP396
Pion-Berlin, D., IR532
Piore, M. J., EP186
Piper, R. R., LE458
Pippa, N., MP289
Pirog-Good, M. A., LC24

Pisano, V. S., DC371
Pitcher, B. L., DC64, XX272
Pizza, T., AB60
Plane, D. A., PG200
Platt, G., SC761
Platt, G. M., RP170
Plosser, C. I., DP209
Plotnick, R. D., EP442, SP470, SP516
Plott, C. R., EP41, EP643, ET78,
   PE531, SC50, SC68, SC92, SC93,
   SC446, SC544, SC620, SC792, SC801
Plous, S., IR321, IR595
Plutzer, E., MP211, PG101
Png, I. P. L., LC327, PP417
Podgursky, M., OB76
Podolak-Warren, M., SP119
Podrecca, E., EP360
Poe, S. C., AB144, ET237, IR357
Pogge, T. W., ET79
Pogodzinski, J. M., PG201, PG202
Pogue, T. F., EP768
Poguntke, T., PP505
Pol, E., DP64
Polinard, J., MP492
Polinard, J. L., TR31
Pollack, R. A., SC13, SC489
Pollard, W., SC752
Pollard, W. E., PA247
Pollins, B. M., EP855, EP856
Pollock, J. L., ET80
Pollock, P. H., TR179
Polsby, N. W., LE461, LE462
Pommerehne, W. W., PE559
Pomper, G. M., PP300, PP507, PP508
Pool, J., MP493
Poole, E. D., LC503
Poole, K. T., AB191, DC113, LE529,
   LE662, LE663, LE664, LE665, LE666,
   LE667, PE392, SC192, SC761, SC762,
   SC763, XX284
Pooler, J., SP519
Popielarz, P. A., OB388
Popper, F. J., DC178
Porell, F. W., PG203
Porter, P. K., LE635
Portes, A., MP494, MP495
Posen, B. R., IR536
Posner, R. A., EP645, EP646, C38,
   LC445
Posnett, J., OB381
Post, J. D., TR111
Poterba, J. M., PE130, PE131, PE452,
   SP401
Pottenger, J. R., RP93
Potvin, M., LE463
Potvin, R. H., RP100
Pourgeramin, A., PS294
Powell, C. A., IR380
Powell, G. B., AB364, CP48, CP157,
   PE264, PP509, PP510, XX9
Powell, L. W., CP291, PP212
Powell, M. J., OB341, OB342
Powell, R., IR146, IR147, IR597,
   IR598, OB222, OB223
Powell-Griner, E., SP49
Powers, D. A., MP117, MP403
Powlick, P. J., AB284, AB285
Poznanski, K., PS88
Pratt, H. J., RP133
Pratt, J., SP12
Pratt, L. K., SC447
Pratto, F., MP25, MP311
Praveen, J., TR33
Prebisch, R., EP126
Preisendorfer, P., OB328
Press, C., LC142
Pressler, J., SC572
Prest, W. A., LC30

Preston, A., EP771, LC217, PP395
Preston, F. W., SC723
Preston, I. L., PC8
Preston, L. M., ET53
Prewitt, K., CP48
Prewitt, L. B., OB118
Price, A. C., PP421
Price, B. L., DC82, IR424, IR746
Price, D. E., LE258
Price, E. O., DP168
Price, H. D., PE166
Price, H. E, DC373
Price, R., IR148
Price, S., PE265, PE266, PE267
Price, V., PC72
Pride, R. A., XX285
Prinz, T. S., PC211
Pritchard, A., LE668
Pritchett, L. H., SP127
Protess, D. L., PC105
Prothro, J. W., CP294
Provencher, B., PE561
Prskawetz, A., SP129
Prude, J., XX287
Pruitt, D. G., DC100, PC57
Pryor, F. L., RP94, SC712
Prysby, C. L., PG14, PG113
Przeworski, A., CP292, EP362, PE43,
    PE44, PG114, PS158, SC94
Psacharopoulos, G., SP226
Pugno, M., EP364
Puri, A., DP42, DP284, EP718
Purkett, H. E., XX80
Putnam, R. D., AB61, AB195, IR151,
    PS256
Putterman, L., ET157
Pyle, D., LC262
Pyle, R. E., RP66

Quah, D., PG115
Quandt, R. E., DP75, EP94
Quandt, W. B., IR152
Quarantelli, E. L., DP1
Quattrone, G. A., SC96
Quddus, M., XX289
Quester, A. O., IR486
Quiggen, J., SC644
Quigley, F., AB196
Quigley, J. M., LC365
Quillian, L., MP118
Quinlan, D., EP491, PS162
Quinlan, S. V., LE456
Quinn, D. P., EP365

Raab, G., RP163
Raack, R. C., DC120
Raadschelders, J. C. N., SP407
Rabin, M., ET301
Rabinowicz, G., AB62, AB166, CP270,
    CP293, CP294, PP214, PP340, PP344,
    PP484, PP538, PP541, XX290
Rabushka, A., XX231
Radcliff, B., CP153, CP159, CP160,
    MP187, PE257, PE268, PE269, PE270,
    PP207
Raden, D., MP498
Rader, T., SC97
Radice, H., EP128
Radner, R., PP428
Radzicki, M. J., DP158
Radzik, T., SC448
Rae, D. W., LC146, PP345, PS159,
    SC573
Rafferty, J. A., SP485
Ragin, C. C., EP244, MP499, SP522,
    XX291
Ragsdale, L., CP161, LE174, PP215,
    PP216

Rahav, G., LC263
Rahmeyer, F., PA327
Rahn, R. W., EP129
Rahn, W. M., CP295, CP296, PP33
Raiklin, E., PS89
Railton, P., ET81
Raine, W. J., PG85
Raines, J. P., EP647, RP95
Rainey, H. G., OB62
Rainey, R. L., PG306
Raj, B., EP487
Rajmaira, S., ET355
Ralph, J. H., SP228
Ram, R., EP271, EP366, OB310, PE133,
    SP229
Rama, M., PE612
Ramesh, M., PE529
Ramesh, S., PE153, PG84
Ramirez, C., AB296
Ramsey, R. W., DC179
Ramsey, V. J., MP298
Ramseyer, J. M., PP429
Randall, D. M., PC177, PC178
Randall, R., SP408
Randall, V., MP299
Rank, A. D., DC187
Rank, M. R., SP491
Rao, H., OB361
Raphael, T. D., IR153
Rapoport, A., SC98, SC272, SC273,
    SC327, SC449, SC574
Rapoport, D. C., DC374
Rapoport, R., MP300, PP236, PP339
Rapoport, R. B., PP134, PP135, XX292
Rarick, D. L., PC74
Rashid, S., XX289
Rasinski, K. A., AB78, AB80, AB390,
    CP297, ET302, ET303, PA190, PE134,
    XX388
Rasler, K. A., DC66, DP269, EP367,
    IR154, IR768, IR769, IR810, IR811,
    OB311
Rasmusen, E., PP429
Rasmusen, E. B., EP648, ET170
Rasmussen, D. W., LC303, SP293
Rasmussen, J., MP188
Rattinger, H., IR322
Raub, W., DC375
Rauma, D., LC304
Rausch, J. D., LE601
Rauscher, M., ET113
Rausser, G. C., PA39
Raveh, A., SP375
Ravetz, J., SC713
Rawls, J., ET304
Ray, B. A., LE259
Ray, D., CP298, PP346
Ray, E. J., EP858, EP368, IR770,
    IR824, IR858
Ray, J., LC334
Ray, M. A., EP170
Ray, R. D., DP159
Raymond, G. A., DC180, DP257, ET342
Reader, S. A., SC328
Reay, B., RP96
Rebelo, S., DP175, EP317
Reckers, P. M. J., EP774
Redding, K., RP62
Reddy, K. N., OB312
Redfield, K. D., SP155
Redman, D. A., PA127
Reed, A., MP500
Reed, B., SC288
Reed, C. G., EP812
Reed, J. S., LC522, MP119
Reed, M. D., LC232
Reed, S. R., PA328, PE271

Reed, W. R., CP299, LE602, LE603,
    LE604, PC212
Reese, L. A., EP369, EP370, RP97
Reeves, M. M., SP379
Regan, P. M., ET242, IR358, IR537,
    PA128
Regens, J. L., AB267, CP300, IR771,
    PP87, SP409
Reggiani, A., DP118
Regoli, R. M., LC503
Rehbein, K. A., PP88
Reichley, J. A., RP24, RP172
Reid, D. M., XX294
Reilly, B. J., ET82, ET83
Reilly, K. D., DP147
Reiman, J., PE46
Rein, M., EP166, SP13
Reinhardt, E. R., ET158
Reisinger, W. H., AB179, PG302,
    SC193
Reisman, D. A., SP131
Reiss, A. J., LC264
Reiss, P. C., PC116
Reiter, D., IR772
Reiter, H. L., PP301
Reither, F., XX295
Rejai, M., PS257
Remmer, K. L., OB179, PE272, PS160,
    PS258
Remus, W. E., SC451
Remy, R. C., AB50
Renn, O., SC714
Renner, T., PA8
Renshaw, E. F., EP542
Reny, P. J., SC645
RePass, D., AB63, AB64
Reshef, Y., DC327
Resnick, D., CP108, DP270
Ressler, R. W., DC319
Restuccia, J., SP90
Reuter, P., LC504, PA40
Reychler, L., DC67
Reyes, D. V., RP66
Reynolds, D. R., CP76, ET305, PG116
Reynolds, J. A. B., CP203
Reynolds, L. G., EP373
Reynolds, M. O., DC329
Rhee, B. K., EP430
Rhee, C., EP430
Rhine, S. L., CP162
Rhode, D. L., ET84
Rhodebeck, L. A., MP446, SP132
Rhodes, E., OB180
Rhodes, J. K., XX303
Rhodes, R., IR453
Rhodes, T. C., TR115
Rhodes, W. M., LC70
Rhonda, R., PS296
Rhys, H. W., PS274
Riaz, K., PE613
Rice, G. W., PS91
Rice, N. L., LE669
Rice, P., SC164
Rice, T. W., CP134, CP265, LE137,
    OB313, PE238, PG107, PG117, PP186,
    PP195, PP302, SC525, XX194
Rich, D. P., PP386
Rich, M. J., LC493
Richard, S. F., OB293, OB294
Richards, D., DP123, DP124, DP125
Richards, D. G., EP266
Richards, D. J., PE480
Richardson, B. M., CP302, CP303,
    PP34
Richardson, C. J., SP354
Richardson, J., PE393
Richardson, J. D., EP859
Richardson, J. J., SC621

Richardson, J. L., IR155
Richardson, L. E., LC147, LE303
Richardson, W. D., ET427
Richelson, J. T., SC99, SC100,
    SC101, SC102
Richins, M. L., XX304
Richter, J. G., IR419
Richter, S. G., EP130
Richter, W. F., PG208
Ricketts, E. R., SP294, SP295
Ricoeur, P., ET306
Riddle, P., SP230
Rieger, C., AB289
Rieselbach, L. N., LE464
Rietberg, E. M., PC104
Riezman, R., EP846, LE342
Riga, P. J., MP120
Riggle, E. D., AB57, CP304
Riggs, F. W., LE175
Riggs, L., EP784
Rigney, D., SP231
Riis, O., RP25
Riker, W. H., CP305, EP46, IR568,
    LC148, LE282, LE714, PP511, PP512,
    SC103, SC104, SC105, SC316, SC452,
    SC575, SC778
Riley, J. M., PS161, SC503, SP523
Rimmer, R., EP416
Rimmer, S., EP416
Rinehart, S. T., MP243, MP302
Ringdal, K., PE48
Ringelstein, A. C., LE176
Ringer, F. K., SP232
Ringquist, E. J., EP649
Ripley, B., IR156
Ripley, R. B., LE304, LE456
Risse-Kappen, T., AB286, IR157,
    IR420
Ritchey, P. N., PG163
Ritov, I., PE536
Ritt, L. G., PA32, PP35
Rittberger, V., PS57
Rittenberg, L., EP374
Ritz, Z., SC504, SC505
Ritzberger, K., SC453, SC454
Ritzer, G., OB125
Rivard, J. C., IR574
Rivers, D., CP306, LE246, LE669,
    SC791
Rizzo, M. J., LC71
Roach, B. L., ET416
Roark, S. J., EP774
Roback, T., PP130, PP131
Robbins, J. S., PP290
Robbins, M., LE287, LE643
Robert, L., SC106
Roberti, P., EP488
Roberts, B. E., LE213, PE342
Roberts, F. S., SC107
Roberts, J. C., IR114
Roberts, J. M., DP217
Roberts, M. L., EP776
Roberts, R. D., ET138
Roberts, S., XX219
Robertson, D., LC457
Robertson, J. A., PG53, LE88, LE89,
    LE90, PE202, PP462
Robertson, K. A., SP414
Robertson, P. J., SC226
Robertson, R. D., XX195
Robertson, T. S., PA288
Robey, J. S., PA41, SP415
Robins, R. S., DC151, LE47
Robinson, C. H., DC7
Robinson, J. B., DP160, PA250
Robinson, J. P., AB145, AB197, PC75,
    PC213
Robinson, M. J., PC145

Robinson, P. H., LC265
Robinson, R. V., MP373
Robinson, W. P., ET428
Robson, A. J., SC802
Rock, D., PP430
Rocke, D. M., IR278, SC39
Rockman, B. A., OB1
Rodgers, H. R., LC505
Rodgers, W. M., SP14
Rodriguez, F., EP777
Roeder, P. G., LE553, LE605
Roeder, P. W., PG304
Roele, M., RP26
Roemer, J. E., AB198, CP307, DC181,
    DP271, ET286, SC36
Roettger, W. B., PP303
Roff, L., PS181
Rogers, C., SP275
Rogoff, K., PE481, PE482
Rogowski, R., EP860, IR158, SC605
Rohde, D. W., ET346, LC458, LE177,
    LE312, LE350
Rohr, J. A., ET429
Rohrschneider, R., AB386, DC243,
    PP53, TR116, TR117, TR118
Rojecki, A., PC98
Rom, M., PG198
Romanow, A. L., XX305
Romer, C. D., DP218
Romer, T., CP96, CP308, PP89, SC108,
    SC109, SC526
Romero, D. W., CP309
Romo, F. P., PG209
Rongen, G., PE565
Ronit, K., PE341
Rood, R. M., IR236
Roof, W. C., RP98
Roper, R. T., LC72
Ropers, R. H., PE275
Rorty, A. O., SC646
Rosa, F. M., IR553
Rose, D. C., DC330
Rose, D. D., AB59
Rose, G., RP168
Rose, R., CP310, ET243, OB314, PA42,
    PA43, PP36, PP514, PS58, PS148,
    XX306
Rose-Ackerman, S., PS210, TR37,
    TR119
Rosecrance, R., DP272, IR834
Rosen, H. S., PE71, SP357, SP358
Rosen, R., LC36
Rosen, S., IR599, LC73
Rosenau, J. N., AB251, AB252, AB253,
    AB254, AB255, AB256, AB257, AB258
Rosenau, P. M., XX307
Rosenbaum, H. J., DC68, PS297
Rosenbaum, W., SP75
Rosenberg, A., XX134
Rosenberg, J., IR159, PE483, PE598
Rosenberg, N., DP219
Rosenberg, S. B., MP78
Rosenberg, S. W., AB65, AB199, CP55,
    CP311, CP312, PE49
Rosenblum, N. L., ET85
Rosendorff, B. P., LE211
Rosenfeld, P., AB330
Rosenfeld, R., LC174
Rosenstone, S. J., CP163, CP164
Rosenthal, A. S., LC280
Rosenthal, C. S., PP90
Rosenthal, H., CP96, CP154, CP308,
    DP234, LE664, LE665, LE666, PE1,
    PE429, SC108, SC192, SC290, SC330,
    SC526, SC761, SC762, SC763, XX284
Rosenthal, R. W., SC576
Rosenthal, U., OB209
Rosenzweig, M. R., SP153

Rosh, R. M., IR538, PS279
Roskamp, K. W., DP126
Ross, B. L., PC162
Ross, C., LE28, SP296
Ross, J. A., MP502
Ross, J. I., DC376
Ross, J. M., MP121
Ross, L., PC180
Ross, M. H., DC69, MP122, MP503,
    PA191, PC214, PG118, PG127
Ross, R. J. S., EP333
Ross, R. S., CP97
Ross, T. W., IR539
Rossana, R. J., EP489
Rossell, C. H., MP123
Rosser, J. B., DP127, PA192
Rossi, P. H., PG210
Rossum, R. A., ET430
Rotemberg, J. J., OB126
Roth, A. E., SC438, SC455
Roth, B. M., ET347
Rothenberg, L. S., OB63, PE394
Rothgeb, J. M., IR246
Rothman, S., PC132
Rothschild, J., PP414
Rothschild-Whitt, J., OB181
Rothstein, B., ET307
Rothstein, P., EP47, SC285
Rothstein, R. L., IR160
Roubini, N., DP235, PE135, PE136,
    PE156
Rouhana, N. M., DC70
Rourke, F., LE178
Rowat, D. C., OB182
Rowe, E. T., DC121
Rowland, C. K., EP650
Rowley, C. K., SC110, SC527
Rowthorn, R. E., EP131
Roy, W. G., PE395
Rozanski, J., EP861
Ruback, R. B., LC266
Rubin, H. J., OB127
Rubin, I., PE137
Rubin, J. Z., DC71
Rubin, P. H., EP108, EP651, LC4,
    LE702, PE214, SC214, XX127
Rubinfeld, D. L., CP165, EP23,
    EP708, LC19
Rubinson, R., SP228, SP251
Rubinson, R. B., EP375, EP490,
    EP491, IR346, PS162
Rubinstein, A., SC456
Rubison, R. M., IR282
Rucht, D., PA313
Rudell, F., TR141
Rudig, W., TR180
Rudmin, F. W., XX304
Ruggie, J. G., IR161
Ruhl, J. M., IR540
Ruhter, W. E., PE320
Ruiz-Castillo, J., EP492
Ruland, L. J., EP48
Rule, W., MP189, MP190
Rummel, R. J., DC72, DC73, DC74,
    DP65, IR162, IR163, IR164, IR165
Runciman, W., XX308
Runde, A. S., ET181
Rundquist, B. S., IR541, IR542,
    LE260, LE462, PP431
Ruscio, K. P., OB80, TR181
Rush, M., LE651
Rush, M. E., SC331
Rushefsky, M. E., PA129, SC715
Rushton, J. P., ET139
Rusk, J. G., AB331, CP56, CP161,
    CP342, PP216, SC332
Russell, C. A., DC182
Russell, G., IR166

Russett, B., AB287, EP493, EP494,
  IR167, IR421, IR439, IR440, IR441,
  IR495, IR543, IR544, IR600, IR736,
  IR773, IR774, IR859, IR860, OB183,
  SP133
Rustow, D. A., PS298
Rutherford, B. M., PS51
Rutledge, A. J., PG2
Ruttan, V. W., PS299
Ruzavin, G., DP161
Ryan, M., PE566
Ryan, S., MP504
Ryterman, R., TR98
Rytina, S., ET283
Rythina, J., AB127

Saari, D. G., DP35, DP128, SC333,
  SC577, SC578
Sabatier, P. A., AB200, LE465,
  OB184, PA29, PA130, PA251, PE396
Sabetti, F., LC149
Sabo, W. A., PE433
Sabol, W. J., LC250
Sabot, R. H., PE593
Sabucedo, J. M., CP57
Sacco, P. L., PP354
Sachs, J., DP220, EP371, PE136,
  PE412, PE430
Sack, F., LC267
Sacks, P. M., PA44
Saeed, K., EP49
Safra, Z., LC307
Sagan, E., PA193
Sagan, S. C., IR601
Sah, R. K., LC268
Sahr, R. C., AB66
Saijo, T., OB390
Sailer, L., DP92
Saindon, J. J., SP200
Saint-Germaine, M. A., MP303
Saiz, M., MP187
Sakamoto, A., SP233
Saks, M. J., LC74
Sakurai, M. M., IR422
Salamon, L. M., EP50
Salant, D. J., EP652
Salant, S. W., LE261
Salavitabar, H., LE397
Salisbury, B. R., CP313
Salisbury, R. H., LE466, LE467,
  PE397, PE398, PE399, PP515
Salkever, S. G., CP166
Salles, M., SC351, SC427
Salmon, P., SC111
Saltz, I. S., EP495
Salzberger, E. M., LC75
Sampson, R. J., DC75
Samuel, S. G. W., IR775
Samuels, W. J., ET308
Samuelson, L., ET329, PP217, SC12,
  SC112, SC411
Samuelson, P. A., SC579, XX309
Sanchez, I., EP682
Sanchez, S. M., OB369
Sandberg, I. W., SC113
Sandbrook, R., PS300
Sander, W., SP234, SP524
Sanders, A., OB315
Sanders, D., DC331, LE91, PE265,
  PE266, PE267, PE273
Sanders, D. L., EP774
Sanders, E., EP653, SC242
Sanders, J., EP267, EP453, ET36
Sanders, L. M., MP43
Sanders, L. T., LE43
Sanderson, S. K., XX310
Sandler, S., IR776

Sandler, T., DC355, IR220, IR221,
  IR239, IR247, IR640, OB381, PE508,
  SC524, TR25, XX311
Sandmo, A., SC114
Sanglier, M., EP202, PG1
Sanjian, G. S., SC368, SC369, SC370,
  SC371
Santerre, R. E., CP98
Santiago, A. M., MP505
Santiago, C. E., EP132, EP496
Santoni, G. J., PE169
Santoro, W. A., MP51
Saperstein, A. M., DP129, IR248,
  IR323, IR777
Sapiro, V., MP191, MP225, MP304,
  MP305
Sapolsky, H., SP134
Sapp, R., EP98
Sapsford, D., DC332
Saracho, A. I., PA330
Sarangi, P., PA45
Sarat, A., LC76, LC81
Sargent, T. J., DP211, DP221, SC143
Sarin, R. K., SC265
Saris, W. E., CP269, IR43, IR324
Sarlvik, B., CP333, PP257
Sartori, G., AB201, XX312, XX313
Sartorius, L. C., LC187
Sasaki, M., AB387
Sass, T. R., MP192, PG201, PG202,
  SP416
Satterthwaite, M. A., SC14
Saunders, P., EP497, PE138, PE567
Saurman, D. S., PA297
Savage, J. D., LE715
Savage, L., EP633
Savage, R. L., PA331, PA332, PA333
Saving, T. R., XX70
Sawhill, I. V., SP295, SP297
Sax, G., PA101
Saxe, L., MP70
Sayer, S., PG305
Sayers, C., DP95
Sayles, M. L., DC76
Sayrs, L. W., DP273, EP862, LE150
Scaff, L. A., CP58
Scarborough, E., PE274
Scarborough, G. I., IR219, SC716
Scarrow, H. A., PP516
Schaedel, R. P., DC244
Schaffer, B., PP432
Schaffer, M. E., OB362
Schahczenski, J. J., IR423
Schampel, J. H., IR778
Schankerman, M., PA306
Schansberg, D. E., LE351, LE602,
  LE603, LE604
Scharpf, F. W., SP525
Schay, B. W., OB128
Scheb, J. M., AB171, LC147, LC395
Scheetz, T., OB316
Scheiber, H. N., PS211
Scheide, J., EP376
Schellenberg, J. A., PG54, SC115
Schelling, T. C., ET431, SC116
Scheppele, K., LC77
Scherer, F. M., TR149
Schervish, P. G., PE22
Schier, D., SP55
Schiff, R. L., IR454
Schiffel, D., PA334
Schiltz, T. D., PG306
Schimmelpfennig, J., CP135
Schlager, E., SC52
Schleifer, S., AB332
Schlesinger, J. A., PP37
Schlesinger, M., SC194
Schlottman, A. M., PG168

Schlozman, K. L., CP8, CP167, MP307
Schmalbeck, R., LC78
Schman, H., MP132
Schmidt, A. B., CP283, SP199
Schmidt, C., SC457
Schmidt, D. E., DC333
Schmidt, G. D., PS212
Schmidt, W. V., PC190
Schmiegelow, H., IR168
Schmitt, D. R., ET187
Schmitt, H., PP304
Schmitz, S., MP14
Schnabel, C., DC266
Schnare, A. B., MP105
Schneider, A. L., DC77, PA131, PA132
Schneider, B. R., IR602
Schneider, F., PE195, PE400, PE451,
  PE484
Schneider, G., ET188
Schneider, M., EP372, LE48, PG112,
  PG211, SC117, SP417
Schneider, P., DC77, IR518
Schneider, S. K., CP59, ET348
Schneider, W., AB288
Schneier, E. V., ET349
Schnytzer, A., PS59
Schoemaker, P. J. H., SC118, SC717
Schofield, N. J., DP36, ET140, LE92,
  SC119, SC195, SC227, SC458, SC459,
  SC460, SC461, SC506, SC580, SC764
Scholing, E., EP377
Scholz, J. T., EP654, EP756, OB185
Schoolmaster, F. A., CP99
Schotter, A., SC462, SC548, SC648
Schoultz, L., AB67
Schousen, M. M., CP191
Schram, A. J. H. C., CP127, CP168,
  CP314, DP282, PE568, PE569
Schram, S. F., SP298, SP526
Schrodt, P. A., IR169, PG55, PG307
Schroedel, J. R., LE352, PP91
Schroeder, G. E., EP133
Schroeder, L. D., CP100
Schroeder, P. W., IR170
Schubert, G., AB68, LC459
Schuermann, A. C., SC463
Schuessler, R., ET189
Schulenburg, J. T., OB363
Schulman, H., AB69, AB321, IR779
Schulman, P., PA46
Schulman, P. R., SC120
Schulstad, P., EP655
Schultze, C. L., PE139
Schultz, K. A., PE485
Schultz, R. R., EP544
Schulz, C., SC468
Schulz, N., PC146
Schulze, W. D., EP681
Schumacher, J. A., SC121
Schuman, H., AB289, AB333
Schuster, M., DC281
Schwab, S. J., LC390
Schwab, W. A., PG119
Schwalbe, C. R., TR123
Schwartzstein, L., PE309
Schwartz, A. J., EP559
Schwartz, B., XX314
Schwartz, E. P., SP22
Schwartz, H. M., SP418
Schwartz, J. E., LE305, LE670, MP195
Schwartz, J. J., AB202
Schwartz, M., ET432, PG209
Schwartz, N. L., PA299
Schwartz, S. H., AB388
Schwartz, S. I., SP419
Schwartz, T., CP169, CP274, LE433,
  LE716, PA252, SC464, SC581, SC582,
  SC649, SC799

Schwartz-Shea, P., ET137
Schweitzer, R., EP98
Schweizer, U., LC150
Schweller, R. L., IR780
Schwenk, C. R., ET415
Schwodiauer, G., SC462, SC648
Scicchitano, M. J., EP591, LE468
Scioli, F. P., PG320
Sciortino, J., LE614
Sciulli, D., OB391
Scolnick, J., DC78
Scotch, R. K., SP277
Scott, C., DC334
Scott, J. C., DC183, PP433
Scott, W. J., EP778, PE275
Scott, W. R., OB64
Scully, G. W., EP134, EP378, PE614
Seale, J. L., EP511
Searing, D. D., AB202, CP15, LE11,
    LE49
Sears, D. O., AB70, AB272, CP315,
    MP93, MP154, TR120
Seater, J. J., EP489
Secrest, D., AB290, AB291, AB292,
    AB298, ET371
Sederberg, P. C., DC68, PS297
Seeger, J. C., OB225
Seegers, A., DC245
Segal, D. R., IR525, IR545
Segal, J. A., LC462, LC79, LC83,
    LC84, LC460, LC461, LE671
Segal, M. W., MP308
Segal, U., SC334, SC699
Segel, T. E., PG196
Segerston, P. S., ET87
Segura, G. M., LE421, LE606
Seidelman, R., PS93
Seidl, C., SC56
Seierstad, S., EP379
Seifert, M., SC728
Seitz, S. T., SC372
Seiyama, K., OB65
Seldon, B., PP325
Self, P., OB129
Seligman, A., XX316
Seligman, C., TR121
Seligson, M. A., AB261, CP60, DC58,
    DC197, PE190, PS60, PS150, PS151,
    SP266
Selikar, O., PP305
Sell, J., PE570, XX225
Selle, P., OB92, PP306, XX35
Sellers, C. G., DP274
Selton, R., SC465, SC583
Semmel, A. K., SC718
Sen, A. K., ET88, ET89, ET309,
    SC122, SC123, SC124, SC335, SC651,
    SC652
Sen, S., IR354
Sened, I., EP46, SC466, XX317
Sengupta, K., SC8
Sengupta, M., PS163
Sennett, R., SP420
Sephton, P., EP184
Seppi, D. J., SC432
Serra, G., CP44, LE306, PP219
Sertel, M. R., PE538
Sesardic, N., ET141
Sets, J. E., SP50
Setterfield, M., EP190
Sevon, G., AB377
Sewing-Thunich, F., IR523
Sexton, E. A., IR359, SP241
Sexton, R. J., ET190, TR38
Seymour-Ure, C., XX318
Sgontz, L. G., EP768
Shabad, G., MP309
Shabahang, H., IR343

Shabman, L., CP316
Shachar, R., LE50
Shade, W., LE530
Shaffer, B. D., LE531, LE532
Shaffer, R. A., EP178
Shaffer, S. D., CP170, PE174, PP220
Shaffer, W. R., LE179, LE533, LE672,
    PP307, SC765
Shafritz, J. M., OB57
Shah, P. J., SP527
Shaiko, R. G., PE401
Shalev, M., SP528
Shamir, B., PP221
Shamir, J., AB389
Shamir, M., AB293, AB389, ET474,
    PP517, SC336
Shan, C. C., LE607
Shanahan, S., MP484
Shapely, D., IR325
Shapiro, C. R., AB5, AB6, LE307
Shapiro, D. L., ET90
Shapiro, G., DC167
Shapiro, H., DC184
Shapiro, I., XX319
Shapiro, M., AB228, LC463, LC464
Shapiro, M. J., IR19, SC653
Shapiro, P., EP779
Shapiro, R. Y., EP36, IR171, PA33,
    PA47, PC139, PE276, SP529, MP310
Shapiro, S., RP27
Sharkansky, I., EP456, PA48, PG308,
    PG309, PG310, SP530
Sharp, E. B., CP101, EP380, SP531
Sharp, S. A., PP222
Sharpe, L. J., IR861
Sharrard, G., SC262
Shavell, S., LC269
Shaw, D. L., PC108
Shaw, T. M., IR172
Sheehan, R. S., LC80, LC449, LC466
Sheehey, E. J., EP381
Sheffield, J. F., MP193
Sheffrin, S. M., SC125
Shefter, M., PG311
Shehan, C., LC280
Sheldon, J. C., TR182
Sheley, J. F., LC270, LC276, LC506,
    PC147
Shell, K., DP10
Shelley, F. M., ET305, PG56, PG296,
    PG312, PG313, PG314, SC584
Shelley, M. C., PC215, PG213
Shepard, G. H., IR173
Shepard, W. B., PE97
Sheppard, B. H., XX320
Sheppard, E., PG11
Shepsle, K. A., LE82, LE227, LE247,
    LE262, LE263, LE282, LE350, LE396,
    LE467, LE469, LE470, LE471, LE472,
    LE473, LE717, PE192, PP17, PP223,
    SC126, SC127, SC128, SC129, SC182,
    SC719, SC766, SC778
Shere, M. E., PP113
Sherman, M., SC171
Shernock, S. K., DC79
Sherwin, R. G., IR326
Shibuya, K., MP103, SP283
Shieh, Y., PG214
Shields, J., PG315
Shields, T. G., LE180, LE575, PC148
Shihadeh, E. S., LC281
Shiller, R. J., EP52
Shin, C. S., PS301
Shin, E. H., LE608
Shin, K. S., LE609
Shinn, D. C., SP235
Shively, W. P., CP317, PP308
Shkurti, W. J., SP421

Shlay, A. B., PG210
Shleifer, A., PE609
Shocket, P. A., MP148
Shoemaker, P. J., PC149
Shogren, J. F., PE613, PP434, SC467
Short, N. C., PE19
Shorter, E., DC335
Shortridge, R. M., CP171, PP542
Shotland, R. L., LC271
Shrader, W., XX321
Shrader-Frechette, K., ET91
Shroder, M., SP532
Shrum, W., TR183
Shubert, G., PA194
Shugart, M. S., PE486, PP520
Shughart, W. F., OB282, PA297
Shull, S. A., MP24, MP506
Shulman, S., SP299
Shultz, R. H., IR781, MP507
Shumaker, S. A., PG215
Shvetsova, O. V., PP499
Shwartz, M., SP90
Siccama, J. G., IR654, IR680, IR681,
    IR682, IR683, PG89
Sidanius, J., LC377, MP25, MP311
Sieg, G., SC468
Siegfried, J. J., EP50, OB364
Sienkiewicz, S., SC720
Siermann, C. L. J., PE140
Sigel, R. S., CP61, DC80
Sigelman, C. K., LE51, LE184, MP508,
    PE278
Sigelman, L., AB71, AB72, AB319,
    AB349, CP62, CP172, DC81, EP751,
    EP780, IR470, IR782, LC414, LE51,
    LE181, LE182, LE183, LE184, MP124,
    MP343, MP344, MP345, MP528, OB186,
    OB187, OB317, PC76, PC123, PC205,
    PC216, PE277, PE278, PG284, PP25,
    PP187, PP518, PS259, PS302, RP139,
    SP422
Sigman, S. J., PC77
Sigmund, P. E., IR546
Signorielli, N., PC31
Siisiainen, M., OB392
Siklos, P. L., DP275
Silberman, J. I., CP173
Silbert, A., PE482
Silbey, J. H., LE483, LE673
Silbey, S., LC81
Silver, A., OB226
Silverberg, G., PA335
Silverman, D., XX322
Silverman, L., PP38
Silverstein, B., PC78
Simaan, M., IR327
Simard, M. M., MP166
Simeon, R., PA133, PG246
Simmie, J., SP423
Simon, C. P., PE464
Simon, D. M., LE52, LE153, LE163,
    LE164, LE177, LE185, PP224
Simon, D. O., EP781
Simon, H. A., SC30, SC654, XX323,
    XX324
Simon, J. D., SC721
Simon, L. K., SC469
Simmons, G. L., LE623
Simmons, R. T., ET137
Simonelli, M. R., SC352
Simonton, D. K., LE186, TR184,
    TR185, TR186
Simowitz, R., DC82, IR424, IR746
Simpson, I. H., OB130
Simpson, J., DC334
Simpson, M. E., DC81, RP99
Simpson, S. S., LC272

Sims, C. A., DP222, EP53, PA134, PA135, PA136, XX325
Sims, R. T., SP36
Sinclair, B. D., LC151, LE264, LE265, LE474, LE674, LE675, PP543, PP544
Sinclair, M. R., IR425
Sindelar, J. L., XX251
Singell, L. D., PG185
Singer, B., DP37, PG120
Singer, J. D., ET350, IR175, IR176, IR177, IR205, IR249, IR250, IR251, IR619, IR716, IR783, IR784, IR785, IR791, IR792, IR826, IR858
Singer, M. S., MP317
Singer, S. I., LC273
Singh, B., EP498
Singh, H., DC31
Singh, J. V., OB326
Singh, V. P., SP300
Singletary, M. W., PC128
Sinha, C., OB168
Sinnott, R., CP174, LE534
Sirgy, M. J., XX326
Sirowy, L., EP382, PS164
Sislin, J., IR328
Siune, K., PC217
Siverson, R. M., IR252, IR253, IR278, IR632, IR642, IR786, IR787, IR788, IR789, IR790, PS10
Sjersted, F., XX327
Sjoberg, A. F., ET92
Sjoberg, G., ET92
Sjoberg, L., SC722
Sjoblom, G., XX328
Sjoquist, D. L., CP100, SC528
Skalaban, A., EP656
Skaperdas, S., PP225
Skeels, J. W., DC336
Skerkat, D. E., RP115
Skhelsbaek, K., IR547
Skinner, D., LC251
Skinner, J., EP464
Skinner, Q., XX329, XX330
Skinner, R. A., IR426
Skipper, J. K., ET159
Skitke, L., XX378
Skjaerseth, J. B., TR122
Skocpol, T., DC185, IR862, PE50, SP219, SP220, SP533, SP534, XX331
Skogan, W. G., LC274
Skogh, G., LC335
Skolnick, J. H., EP657
Skott, P., PS52
Skov, I. L., RP20
Skvoretz, J., OB66, SC606
Slater, R. O., DC110
Slaughter, M. J., EP469
Sleet, D. A., DC22
Slemrod, J., EP494, EP499, EP500
Slesnick, D. T., SP301
Sloan, J. W., OB188, PS61, PS165
Slomczynski, K. M., OB104
Slotnik, B., LE248
Slottje, D. J., EP134, EP487
Slotznick, B., SC425
Slovik, P., SC130, SC698
Slutsky, S., PE524
Small, M., IR178, IR785, IR791, IR792
Smeeding, T., SP535
Smirnov, A. D., DP66
Smith, A., EP817, IR254
Smith, A. A., TR123
Smith, A. D., MP26
Smith, A. K., PS166
Smith, C. A., LE187
Smith, C. E., PE290

Smith, C. G., DC83
Smith, D. H., OB393
Smith, D. L., EP343, IR276
Smith, E. R., MP45
Smith, E. R. A. N., AB203, LE645, LE676
Smith, G., PA137
Smith, H. W., PG57
Smith, J., SP496
Smith, J. E., ET419
Smith, J. P., MP510
Smith, K. A., PC150
Smith, K. B., LE187, SP51, SP239, SP236, SP237, SP238
Smith, L. R. F., ET319
Smith, M. B. E., ET93
Smith, M. D., LC275, LC276, LC381
Smith, N., PG316
Smith, P. K., SP302, SP527
Smith, R., IR303
Smith, R. A., LE475, LE667, PE402
Smith, R. C., MP511, PP92
Smith, R. D., DP130
Smith, R. E., EP780, SP422
Smith, R. P., IR548
Smith, R. S., EP501
Smith, R. W., SC723
Smith, S., IR179, IR180, IR181, OB227
Smith, S. L., EP536
Smith, S. S., LE250, LE266, LE476, LE677
Smith, T., PS239
Smith, T. A., PA49
Smith, T. C., IR329
Smith, T. J., IR579
Smith, T. W., AB204, AB334, MP125, OB394
Smith, V. H., ET142
Smith, V. K., TR124
Smith, V. L., SC131
Smith, W. B., SC46
Smith, W. J., EP419
Smith-Lovin, L., SP240
Smoke, R., IR435
Smolders, C., EP728, SP355
Smolensky, E., EP502, SP296
Smolla, R. A., LC82
Smyth, D. J., EP118, EP543, PE487, PE488, PP226
Snidal, D., ET191, ET192, IR182, IR183, IR433, IR863, PE571
Snider, G. A., CP318
Snider, L., PE427
Sniderman, P. M., AB4, AB60, AB73, AB294, CP205, ET94, ET475, MP126, MP127, MP128, MP512, PG317, XX39, XX332
Snipp, C. M., MP513
Snipp, J., PG82
Snipp, J. R., LE562
Snow, D. A., SP303
Snyder, D., DC84, EP383, IR360, MP91
Snyder, G. H., IR184
Snyder, J., IR730, OB214
Snyder, J. M., LE249, LE267, LE706, PE403, PP89, PP93, PP132
Sobel, J., SC381
Sobel, R. S., LE21
Sober, E., XX83
Soderstrom, J., PA336
Soete, L., DP179
Sofer, S., IR187, IR794
Sofianou, E., SC656
Sokolow, A. D., LE353
Soldatos, G. T., LE53
Solingen, E., IR604
Sollars, D. L., SP137

Sollenberg, M., IR822
Solnick, L. M., EP346
Solomos, J., MP129
Solomou, S., DP223, EP834
Solow, R. M., EP192
Soltan, K. E., ET311
Somers, M., XX331
Somerville, J., IR795
Somit, A., AB383, LE188, PA188, PA198, PA199, XX359
Somma, M., OB365
Sondermann, D., SC499
Songer, D. R., CP320, LC83, LC84, LC465, LC466, LE268, MP326
Sonis, M., XX69
Sonsino, D., SC507
Sonstelie, J., EP779, SP243
Sophocleus, J. P., PE600
Sorauf, F. J., PC218
Sorensen, G., IR848
Sorensen, R. J., PE279, SP425
Sorenson, A. M., SP138
Soriano, L. J., DC88
Sorkin, A. L., MP327
Sorokin, G. L., IR255
Soroos, M. S., IR188, TR126, TR127
Soss, N. M., XX132
Sossin, L., OB131
Sould, S., MP130
Soule, J., PP133
Sousa, D. J., LE510
South, D. W., TR59
South, S. J., LC278, LC368
Southard, P. C., RP164
Southwell, P. L., CP175, LE610
Spangler, W. D., LE135
Sparks, R. F., LC279, SP12
Speckhard, R. A., PA141
Spector, B. I., IR189
Spegele, R. D., XX360
Speight, A. E. H., PE141
Spencer, B. J., EP801
Spencer, J. W., PC111
Spicer, D. N., SP52
Spiegel, U., LC488
Spiezio, K. E., DP276
Spilerman, S., DC249, DP37
Spiller, P. T., EP658, LC117, LC418, OB189
Spillman, B., SC373
Spillman, R., SC373
Spindler, C. J., EP384
Spinelli, F., OB263
Spitzer, M. L., EP592
Spitzer, R. J., LE189
Spivak, A., SC334
Spohn, C., LC85
Spolaore, E., SC794
Sprague, J., LC323, MP447, PC46, PC47, PG101, PP334
Sprague, T., DC31
Springer, J. F., PA142
Sproule-Jones, M., CP63, XX361
Sproull, L. S., PA102
Sprout, R. V. A., EP503
Sprumont, Y., SC132
Spurr, S. J., MP328
Spybey, T., OB68
Squire, P., AB335, LE354, PC179, PP227, PP228, PP229, PP230, PP483
Srinivasan, T. N., EP800
Srivastava, R., PA294
St. Angelo, D., PP309
St. Clair, G. K., SC179
St. John, C., EP784
St. Peter, L., ET482
Staaf, R. J., PE572
Staber, U., EP193

Stack, S., EP504, EP505, EP506, EP507, EP782, LC382, PC151
Staff, H., IR787
Staffin, P. D., DP38
Stafford, F. P., XX190
Stahl, D. O., EP863
Stambough, S. J., CP329
Stamm, K. R., PP231
Stanbury, W., OB190
Stanfield, J. H., MP131
Stanga, J. E., LC444
Stanley, H. W., PE253, PP291
Stanley, J., PG245
Stanley, T. D., DC305
Star, S. L., XX362
Starbuck, W. H., SC476
Stark, M. J. A., PG85
Stark, O., ET143, ET144
Stark, R., RP51
Starr, H., AB295, IR551, IR747, IR748, IR749, IR190, IR796, IR797, IR798, IR798, IR799, IR800, PA320, PS169, SC675, PG319
Starrels, J. M., LE54
Starrett, D. A., EP783
Stauffer, R. B., PA200
Stauffer, R. E., PE38
Stearns, M. L., LC87
Steed, M., SC260
Steed, R. P., AB205
Steeh, C., MP132
Steenbergen, M. R., AB57, PC200
Steffensmeier, D. J., LC280, LC281, LC282
Stegemann, K., EP864
Steger, W. P., LE150, LE151
Steiber, S. R., EP865, ET476
Stein, A. A., DC87, ET193, IR801, IR834, IR845
Stein, J. G., IR450
Stein, R. M., LE718, PA2, PA50, PE280, SP427
Steinbrunner, J., IR455
Steindl, F. G., SP244
Steiner, H. G., SC337
Steiner, J., ET351, MP517
Steiner, M., OB228
Steinman, M., MP526
Steinmo, S., OB318
Stekler, H. O., IR515
Stell, B. S., DC250
Stemmler, S., MP96
Stengos, T., DP86, DP87, DP88
Stenseth, N. C., DP47
Stephan, G. E., EP385, PG58
Stephan, W. G., MP82
Stephen, D. S., PP446
Stephens, G., DC339
Stephens, J., DP162, PA201, XX364
Stephens, J. D., DC340, PS303, SP7
Stephens, W. N., ET97
Stephenson, K., CP316
Stepick, A., EP386
Stern, L. W., ET341
Stern, D. I., PG59, SP428
Stern, L. N., PG320
Stern, N., EP387, EP701
Stern, P., IR552
Sternberg, E., PA51
Sternberg, R. J., DC88
Sternman, J. D., DP131, DP224
Steuenberg, B., EP659
Stevens, G., IR553
Stevenson, H. M., AB189
Stevenson, L., SC725
Stevenson, R. T., EP349
Stewart, C., LE477, PE142, PP435
Stewart, D. B., EP508

Stewart, D. K., LE355
Stewart, D. W., ET435
Stewart, J., PP529, SC133, SP213
Stewart, J. N., DP67
Stewart, M. B., DC292, DC294, DC295
Stewart, M. C., CP3, PE177, PE178, PP252
Stigler, G. J., EP135, EP509, EP660, PE281, SC134
Stimson, J. A., AB206, CP209, CP219, LE191, MP387, PE243, PP28, PP206
Stinchcombe, A. L., SC477
Stinchcombe, M. B., SC469
Stipak, B., SP429
Stockton, R. R., AB84
Stoddard, S. W., SC359
Stohl, M., ET245
Stoker, L., ET436, LE192
Stokes, D. E., CP321
Stokols, D., PG215
Stoll, R. J., IR190, IR330, IR427, IR802, IR864, OB229
Stolovitch, H. D., SC480
Stolp, C., OB284
Stolte, J. F., ET312
Stone, D. M., RP100
Stone, J. A., EP762, PE458, PE459
Stone, P., PC152
Stone, W. F., XX365
Stone, W. J., LE308, MP300, PP134, PP135, XX292
Stonecash, J. M., LE607, PP457, SP537
Storm, K., EP388
Story, D., EP389, PE489
Stoudinger, S., LE426
Stout, D. K., EP390
Stout, S., ET156
Stover, R. V., LC401
Straffin, P. D., IR263
Straits, B. C., CP176
Strang, D. R., PS240, SC393
Strasnick, S., ET98, ET99
Strate, J., PE490
Strate, J. M., CP31
Stratmann, T., LE678, LE719, PC62, PP95, PP96
Straus, M. A., LC357
Street, J., PG321
Streifel, C., LC281
Streitmatter, R., PC219
Stretesky, P., MP96
Strickland, D. A., AB75, LC158, OB138, SP53, SP54
Stroh, P., CP267, CP268
Strom, G. S., CP322, LE260, PP431
Strom, K., LE84, LE93, LE94, LE535, PP347
Stronge, W. B., EP544
Stroup, R. L., EP580, LC152
Struthers, J., CP323
Stryker, R., PE22
Stuart, C., LC335, SC517, SP14
Stuart, D., AB295
Stubbings, R. G., CP177
Stubbs, J. G., PE573
Studlar, D. T., AB380, MP133, MP199, MP518, PG287, RP134, XX366
Sturm, J. E., EP712
Su, T. T., PE112, PP97
Sudbury, A., PG17
Sudman, S., CP324
Suedfeld, P., AB296, DC187, LE58, OB208, OB230
Sueyoski, G. T., MP328
Suganami, H., IR803
Sugden, R., ET100, SC657
Suh, S. H., PG61

Sullivan, D. G., LE29, LE56, XX367
Sullivan, G., EP391
Sullivan, J. D., IR167
Sullivan, L. K., DC89
Sullivan, J. L., AB173, AB207, AB208, AB209, ET477, ET478, ET479, ET480, ET481, LE101, LE478, LE611
Sullivan, M., IR788
Sullivan, P. S., LC508
Sullivan, T., CP215, LE116, LE130, LE193, LE194
Sulock, J. M., PE433
Sum, L. T., XX368
Sumi, D., AB83, PA203, PC156
Summers, M. E., MP194
Sun, L., XX369
Sundeen, R. A., OB395
Sunderland, G., MP134
Sunding, D., SC338
Sunkel, O., PE52
Sussman, D., DC250
Sussman, G. I., PA143
Sussmann, H. J., DP68
Sutton, J. R., OB191, OB351, RP50, SC478
Suzuki, M., PE282, PE491, PE492, PP447
Suzuki, T., AB387
Suzumura, K., ET313, ET314, SC585
Svalastoga, K., DC90, PS62, XX370
Svallfors, S., SP538
Svasand, L., PP306, PP458
Svensson, L. G., ET315
Svensson, P., CP102, PP10
Svoboda, C. J., CP325
Svorny, S., EP604
Swaminathan, A., OB333, OB336, OB366
Swank, D. H., CP326, EP136, PE143, PE283, SP487, SP488, SP489
Swanson, B. E., EP398
Swanson, C., LC500
Swanson, P., LE479
Swanson, T. M., TR128
Swanson, W. R., LC110
Swauger, J., PG323
Swedberg, R., PE53
Sweetser, W., XX56
Swift, E. K., LE480
Swinnen, J., TR39
Swistak, P., ET296, SC479
Sykes, R. E., LC481, LC482
Sylan, D. J., IR727
Sylvan, D. A., IR361, XX371
Sylvia, R. D., ET101
Synder, G. H., IR256
Szalay, L. B., AB210
Szamrej, J., AB56
Szamuely, L., OB319
Szecsko, T., PC80
Szymanski, A., EP392

Taagepera, R., EP866, LE481, PP519, PP520, PS241, SC339, SC340
Tabarrok, A. A., LE612
Tabb, D. H., AB173, MP149
Tabellini, G., EP531, EP766, PE144
Taber, C. S., AB297, IR332
Tackie, A., PE101
Tadlock, B., PC148
Taebel, D. A., MP162, XX372
Tager, M., PP436
Taggart, W. A., AB15, LC336
Tagil, S., PG324
Taheri, J., EP194
Tai, C. S., XX373
Taibleson, M. H., PG122
Tainter, J. A., DP163
Taira, K., EP393

Tajalli, H., SP433
Takamori, H., PS305
Takayama, K. P., RP52
Takayama, T., PG62
Talbert, J. C., LE412
Talele, C. J., EP394
Talley, W. K., PE574
Tamashiro, H., AB290, AB291, AB292, AB298, ET371
Tamplin, V. L., LE679
Tanaka, H., SC607
Tanenhaus, J., LC468
Tang, S. Y., SC226
Tanguiane, A. S., SC508
Tanino, T., SC374
Tanner, E., PE145
Tanter, R., DC91, DC188
Tanton, J., LC283
Tantor, R., PS306
Tarascio, V. J., DP225, DP277
Tarrow, S., CP195, DC251
Tarschys, D., OB320
Tatalovich, R., LE195, RP175, SP55
Tatarewicz, J. N., TR188
Tate, C.N., ET237, LC433, LC469
Taub, D. E., RP28
Tauchen, G. E., EP510
Taylor, A., LE158
Taylor, C. L., PS307, SC135, SC136
Taylor, D. G., AB76
Taylor, G., LC505, PC81
Taylor, H. F., MP42
Taylor, I., LC284
Taylor, L., EP232, IR377
Taylor, L. I., SP430
Taylor, M., PP521, SC137, SC138, SC196
Taylor, P. J., PG63, SC341
Taylor, R. B., LC285, LC350
Taylor, R. L., OB133
Taylor, S., OB147
Taylor, S. W., PP226
Taylor-Gooby, P., SP496, SP539, SP540
Teachman, J., DC96
Tedin, K. L., PP532, PS61, SP246
Tefft, S. K., SC726
Teigen, R. L., PE146
Teitler, R. J., DC83
Teitz, M. B., PG217
Teixeira, R. J., SC225
Tejera, F., CP330
Telhami, S., AB268
Teller, L. N., PG64
Temchin, E. M., CP243
Temin, P., TR157
Templet, P., TR129
Tennefoss, M. R., IR253, IR789, IR790
Teogby, L., AB24
Terrell, L. M., IR555, IR805
Terrell, T. P., ET102
Teske, P., EP661, EP662, LE48, PE575, SC117
Tether, P., CP327
Tetlock, P. E., AB60, AB211, AB212, AB213, AB296, AB299, IR192, IR193, IR194, IR605, LE680, MP128, MP512, PC82, PC83, PC84, PC85, XX374, XX375, XX376, XX377, XX378
Teune, H., XX379
Teuter, K., OB31
Thachuk, K., LE58
Thagard, P., ET145
Thaler, R. H., AB79, ET52
Thaxton, R., DC189
Thayer, F. C., OB134
Theil, H., EP511

Theilmann, J., CP328
Therien, J. P., IR355
Thiagarajan, S., SC480
Thibaut, J., ET316
Thielemann, G. S., PP98
Thies, C. F., EP663
Thies, W., IR257
Thigpen, R. B., ET103
Thirlwall, A. P., EP141
Thisse, J. F., SC289
Thistle, P. D., EP581, LC361
Thoits, P. A., MP42
Thoma, M. A., PE448, PE449
Thomas, C. B., DC93
Thomas, D., AB72, ET438, LE196
Thomas, D. B., AB214, DC92, DC252, XX42
Thomas, D. R., EP512
Thomas, J. C., CP64, PP40, PP522
Thomas, J. P., PP57, SC399, XX382
Thomas, J. W., PS280
Thomas, L., AB77
Thomas, L. W., EP252
Thomas, M., SC803
Thomas, M. D., AB317
Thomas, N. C., DP270
Thomas, R., CP165
Thomas, R. E., DC93
Thomas, S., LE290, MP265, MP329, MP330, MP331, MP332
Thompson, C. R., LE95
Thompson, C. Y., LC340
Thompson, D. F., ET393, ET439, ET440
Thompson, E., CP82
Thompson, E. A., PP437
Thompson, F., CP178, LE482, OB69, OB190
Thompson, J. A., LE613, LE720
Thompson, J. L. P., DC253
Thompson, K. W., ET352, ET441, ET442, RP30
Thompson, M. S., LE483
Thompson, P., LC155
Thompson, R. S., EP27
Thompson, V. M., PP437
Thompson, W. R., DC112, DC122, DC123, DP226, DP269, DP278, EP367, EP867, IR154, IR232, IR562, IR768, IR806, IR807, IR808, IR809, IR810, IR811, OB311, PG65
Thomson, R. J., EP352
Thoreen, P. W., PE576
Thornberry, M. C., LE523
Thornberry, T. P., LC286
Thorngate, W., SC481
Thornton, M., DP17
Thornton, R., MP519
Thorson, G. R., CP329
Thorson, S. J., IR4
Thrift, N. J., SP431
Thurman, Q. C., EP784
Tichenor, D. J., PG218
Tideman, T. N., CP179
Tidmarch, C. M., LE578, LE614
Tiefenbach, H., EP403, EP517
Tienda, M., MP30
Tilly, C., DC84, DC254, DC335, LC235
Timberlake, M., DC102, EP257
Timmermann, V., EP377
Timpone, R., LE30, PC60
Tinkler, S., PE553
Tinsley, M., SP212
Tipps, D. C., PS308
Tirole, J., EP605, SC409
Tittle, C. R., LC287, LC483, RP101
Titus, A. C., SP432
Tobey, J. S., SP433
Toby, J., XX383

Toch, H., LC288
Todd, J. E., IR865, PG123
Togeby, L., ET456, MP333, SC229
Tolbert, C. J., MP170
Tolbert, P. S., OB367
Tole, L. A., RP102
Tollison, R. D., CP180, IR196, LE128, OB238, OB256, PE181, PE298, PE608, PP526, RP46
Tolnay, S. E., MP58, MP135, MP136
Toma, E. F., PE349, SP154
Tomkins, M. E., ET401
Tomlinson, R., IR847
Tompkins, G. L., SP541
Tompkins, M. E., OB35
Tong, X., PP403
Tonso, W. R., LC351
Toornvliet, L. G., LC211
Topel, R. H., EP177
Topolski, J., XX384
Tornell, A., EP395
Torrance, T. S., XX77
Torrent, G. M., PP66
Torres, D. L., OB368
Torres, J. F., EP396
Torstensson, J., XX255
Torsvik, G., SC228
Tourangeau, R., AB78, AB390
Tovey, C. A., SC240, SC738
Towers, W. M., PC172
Townsend, R. M., PA144
Townshend, C., DC94
Toye, J. F. J., EP785
Tracy, J. S., DC264
Trahan, E., EP542
Trainer, F. E., ET104
Trajtenberg, M., EP219, PA337
Trasnea, O., AB374
Traugott, M. W., PP171, PP172
Traugott, S. A., LE511
Travis, R., AB234, AB235, RP103
Treadwell, W. A., SC375
Trenholm, S., PC125
Trent, K., SP49
Treyz, G. I., SP434
Triche, E., PC111
Trick, M. A., ET154, ET194, SC240
Trilling, R. J., CP65
Trivers, R., ET146
Troden, S. G., IR197
Trozzolo, T., RP128
Trubek, D. M., LC88
Trubowitz, P., IR198
Truelson, J. A., PP438
Trumble, T., AB228
Trumbull, W. N., LC196, LC289, SC568
Tsakalotos, E., EP92, EP457
Tschirhart, J. T., EP639, XX311
Tschirhart, M., PA52
Tsebelis, G., IR199, LC305, LC337, SC586, SC804
Tshandu, Z., EP218
Tsiddon, D., TR143
Tsoutsoplides, C., IR362
Tsujimoto, R.N., ET105
Tu, P. N. V., DP39
Tuchfarber, A. J., PP545
Tuckel, P. S., CP181, CP330
Tucker, H. J., LE484, LE615, PG325, SP435
Tuckfarber, A. J., AB314
Tufte, E. R., PP232, SC343
Tuler, S., PG178
Tullock, G., CP182, CP331, EP277, LE721, SC509, SC546
Tuma, E. H., TR40
Tunkin, G. I., ET353
Tunyavong, I., SP383

Turan, I., PS151
Turbett, J. P., SP298, SP526
Turett, J. S., LE57
Turnbull, G. K., SC529, SC530
Turnbull, P. J., DC332, DC341
Turner, A. W., CP332
Turner, C. B., MP520
Turner, F. C., EP55
Turner, H. A., PP310
Turner, P. M., DP227
Turner, R. J., XX385
Turner, S. P., TR190
Tursky, B. M., XX386
Turunen-Red, A. H., EP863
Tushnet, M., LC89
Tussing, A. D., OB321
Tversky, A., AB79, SC96, SC139,
   SC691, SC692, SC727
Tweedie, J., SP542
Twombly, J., OB185
Tygart, C. E., LC383
Tyler, T. R., AB80, CP297, ET106,
   ET261, ET317, LC56, LC384, LC509,
   LC510, LE197, PA190, PC153, XX387,
   XX388
Tyszka, T., ET297

Uhl, N. P., SC447
Uhlaner, C. J., CP183, MP383, MP521,
   XX389
Uhlig, R., DP40
Ulen, T. S., EP664
Uliana, R., PC43
Ulmer, S. S., LC470, LC471
Ulph, A., SC482
Umbeck, J., LC156
Umez, B. N., CP66
Underhill, R., RP104
Ungar, S., IR333
Unnithan, N. P., LC385
Upton, G. J. G., CP333
Urban, M. E., OB192
Urbano, A., SC440
Urbiztondo, S., OB189
Uri, N. D., EP513
Uriarte, J. R., SC500, XX392
Ursprung, T., PC154
Urwin, D., PP36
Usategui, J. M., PA330
Useem, B., PS63
Useem, M., PS63
Usher, D., DP279
Uslaner, E. M., EP137, LE309, LE611,
   LE722, PP233, SC197, SC805, SP444,
   XX393
Utter, G. H., CP334, CP335

Vaillancourt, F., OB396
Valen, H., CP95
Valentine, G., MP334
Valentine, H., PP521
Valentino, N. A., CP352
Vallone, R. P., PC180
Van Ark, B., EP56
Van Buren, M. E., SP473
Van Cott, T. N., PE547
Van de Kragt, A. J. C., ET147, ET195
Van de Walle, N., LE542, MP458
Van den Berg, A., DC290
Van den Brink-Budgen, R., SP545
Van den Broek, A., CP67
Van den Oever, P., SP82
Van der Eijk, C., CP85, DP280, DP281
Van der Ploeg, F., PE493
Van der Ros, J., MP335
Van der Silk, J. R., SP235
Van der Veen, R. J., AB336
Van der Zee, F. A., TR39

Van Deth, J. W., CP336
Van Dijk, T., PC86
Van Doorn, L. J., CP269
Van Doren, P. M., LE277, LE681
Van Duijn, J. J., PA338
Van Dunk, E., PP333
Van Duyne, P. C., LC290
Van Dyke, V., ET108, SP248
Van Evera, S., IR812, IR813
Van Furstenberg, G. M., EP786
Van Gaalen, R., OB147
Van Geert, P., DP41
Van Ham, P., IR866
Van Hoose, D. D., EP138
Van Houweling, R. P., LE328
Van Huyck, J. B., XX394
Van Ijzendoorn, M. H., ET109
Van Lier, A., DP132
Van Liere, K. D., RP121, TR130
Van Lohuizen, J. R., PE373
Van Poppel, F., SP140
Van Puyenbroek, R. A. G., SP499
Van Raemdonck, D., EP397
Van Roon, G., DP228
Van Roozendaal, P., LE78, LE96
Van 't Hag, G. J., EP81
Van Til, R. H., SC510
Van Velthoven, B. C. J., EP787,
   PE147
Van Wijck, P., AB340
Van Winden, F., CP127, CP168, DP282,
   EP787, PE147
Van Witteloostuijn, A., DP132
Vanberg, V., ET107, LC102
Vanderleeuw, J. M., CP335
Vanek, J., LE710
Vanjanen, T., PS309
Vanneman, R. D., MP121, PE54
Variyam, J. N., TR41
Vasilatos, N., PE209, PE210
Vasquez, J., IR814, PG66
Vaubel, R., IR200, PS64, PS65
Vaughan, E., SC728
Vaughan, R., SC12
Vaughan, T. R., ET92
Vaughn, D., AB348
Vaupel, J., SC710
Vayrynen, R., DC47, IR334, IR815,
   PS66
Vean, C. S., XX136
Vedder, R., EP195, EP788, PE615
Vedlitz, A., AB81, CP68
Veerman, T. J., AB215
Veevers, J. E., RP105
Vega, A., MP336
Velasco, A., EP395
Velenchik, A. D., PE117
Velicer, W. F., XX414
Veljanovski, C. G., EP555
Vella, F., SC293
Vellrach, M., PE246
Venables, A. J., EP817, EP844
Vendrik, M. C. M., DP69
Venieris, Y. P., EP508, PS310
Verba, S., AB229, CP8, CP69, CP167,
   XX395
Verbeek, B., OB231
Verdier, D., EP868
Verdier, J. M., EP789
Verdier, T., PE611
Verner, J. G., SP249
Vernon, R., DC95
Vertefeuille, C., PG64
Vertzberger, Y. Y. I., IR201, SC729
Vertz, L. L., PP331
Verweij, M., IR202
Vescera, L., EP867
Viaene, J. M., EP48

Vickers, G., PA145
Vickers, J., EP665
Vickrey, W. S., SC658
Victor, B., ET110
Vila, B. J., LC291
Vilasuso, J., EP80
Villani, J., PP22
Villaume, A. C., OB193
Vincent, B., LE573
Vincent, J. E., LE682
Vines, D., PE57
Vinken, H., AB352
Vinokur, A., SC730
Viren, M., LC292
Virtanen, S., LE113
Viscusi, W. K., SC731, SC732
Vishny, R. W., PE609
Vishwakarma, K. P., DP229
Visscher, M., PG155
Visser, M., CP337
Vittes, M. E., TR179
Vlevis, G., LE253
Voevodsky, J., IR816
Vogel, D., EP139, ET443
Vogel, R., EP398, PE253
Vogler, D. J., LE269
Vogt, R., IR43
Volcansek, M. L., LC472
Volgy, S. S., MP337
Volgy, T. J., IR817, IR867, MP195,
   MP337, PE188, XX227
Von Briesen Raz, J., SC140
Von der Fehr, N. H. M., EP666
Von Hagen, J., PE20, PE445
Von Trotha, T., PG327
Von Witzke, H., TR42
Voos, P. B., DC261
Vorhies, F., PS278, PS311
Vree, J. K., DP133
Vries, J., PE404, TR131
Vries, M. S., ET196
Vroman, S. B., DC342
Vu, A. D., SC90
Vuchinich, S., DC96
Vural, A., IR770

Waddington, J., DC343
Wade, L. L., LE713, OB136, PE255,
   PE284, SP250
Wagner, J., AB216, PC155
Wagner, R. E., OB322, SP445
Wagner, R. H., ET197, IR203, IR428,
   IR456, IR457, IR606, IR818, IR819,
   SC483
Wahl, A. M., SP546
Wahlke, J. C., CP268, XX396, XX397
Wainscott, S. H., MP138
Wakeman, F., DC190
Walberg, H. J., EP399
Wald, K. D., MP139, RP53, RP54,
   RP135, RP136
Waldfogel, J., MP370
Waldman, M., ET124
Waldman, S. R., LE356
Waldron, J., AB391, LC77, LC92
Walker, D. A., PE83
Walker, H. A., SC229
Walker, J., SC52
Walker, J. L., LE485, MP360, OB372,
   PA339, PA340, PE305, PE328, PE358,
   PE405, PS171
Walker, S. G., AB217, AB218, AB219,
   AB300, IR204, OB217
Walker, T. G., ET354, LC415
Walkosz, B. J., LE51, PC76
Wallace, J. E., OB70
Wallace, M., EP274

Wallace, M. D., IR177, IR205, IR335, IR336, IR337, IR820, IR868, LE58, OB208, SP482
Wallace, M. S., EP686, PE384
Wallace, R., DP134
Wallach, L., PC197
Wallensteen, P., IR821, IR822
Waller, C. J., EP140, PE148
Waller, M., PE406
Wallerstein, I., DP230, IR869, IR870
Wallerstein, M. B., DC340, DC344, PE43, PE44, PE407
Wallis, J. L., RP55
Walsh, C., PA146
Walsh, E. J., CP9
Walsh, J. F., PC87
Walt, S. M., DC191, IR206
Walter, B. O., ET451, RP39, RP109, RP137
Walters, P. B., SP251
Walters, S. J. K., DC317
Walton, H., MP524
Walton, J., SP446
Waltz, K. N., IR823
Walzer, N., PE78, TR11
Wanat, J., LE198, PE81, PE149, PP311, PP546, RP160
Wang, K., IR824, IR675, SC484
Wang, S. W., EP790
Wang, T. Y., DC255, DC256
Wang, Y., LC293
Wangerin, P. T., XX398
Wann, J. J., ET190
Wanner, R. A., TR142
Wanta, W., AB82, PC112
Ward, D. S., LE536
Ward, H., PE273, PP327, SC141, SC733
Ward, J. G., SP252
Ward, K. B., PE419
Ward, L. M., PA153
Ward, M. D., EP400, ET355, IR207, IR338, IR556, IR707
Ward, T., PE566
Ware, A., PP348
Warf, B., PG67
Warland, R. H., CP9
Warman, F., EP141
Warner, B. D., LC484
Warner, J. T., EP686, PE384
Warner, R. S., RP106, LE486
Warneryd, K., PP312
Warr, M., ET318, LC294, LC338
Warshaw, P. R., XX320
Warwick, P., LE97, LE98, LE99, PG126
Washburn, S. K., PE487
Wassenberg, P. S., MP338
Wasserman, I. M., MP525, PE494, SP141
Wassmer, R. W., EP685
Wasylenko, M., EP227
Waterman, A. M. C., RP107
Waterman, H., CP70
Waterman, R. W., LE642, OB194, OB195, PA254, PP206
Waters, M. S., DC345, RP56, RP123
Watson, D., PA147
Watson, J., ET198
Watson, J. K., RP56, RP123
Watson, W. G., LC157
Wattenberg, M. P., AB182, CP278, CP338, PP478, RP162
Wattier, M. J., CP339
Watts, M. W., AB83, LC295, PA203, PC156
Waxman, L. M., ET466
Wayman, F. W., AB84, IR339, IR825, IR826, LE234
Wayne, G. H., SC376

Weakliem, D. L., CP340, CP341
Weale, A., SC142, SC695
Weart, S. R., IR827
Weatherford, M. S., PC88, PE285, PE286, PE287, PE288, PE289, PS67
Weaver, J. H., EP503
Weaver, R., IR225
Weaver, R. S., PC59
Webb, F. R., SP253
Webb, K., MP380
Webb, R. I., EP223
Webb, S., EP455, SP276
Webber, D. J., PA255, PA256, PS213
Weber, B., SC670
Weber, C. T., PP421
Weber, M., SC20, XX48
Weber, R., LC384
Weber, R. E., EP137, LC473, LE390, LE615
Weber, R. J., SC344, SC759
Weber, R. P., DP281, DP283, LE59
Weber, S., IR258
Weber, W. E., OB322, SP445
Weber, W. L., SP254
Webster, G. R., PG38, PP41
Webster, M., ET319
Webster, T. B. L., EP368
Weede, E., DC59, EP401, EP402, EP403, EP514, EP515, EP516, EP517, IR340, IR429, IR458, IR828, IR829, PS242
Weeks, J., EP518
Weesie, J., OB397
Weigel, G., ET444
Weigel, R. H., MP140
Weiher, G. R., SP255
Weil, D. N., EP431
Weil, F. D., EP519, LE487, PS68
Weilage, A., PP423
Weiler, W. C., LC367
Weiman, D., EP19
Weimann, G., PC113
Weimann, J., PC146
Weinberg, L., PG315
Weinblatt, J., LC205
Weinbull, J. W., SC454
Weiner, N. A., LC296
Weingast, B. R., EP142, EP563, EP584, EP667, EP668, ET356, IR208, LE247, LE263, LE270, LE472, LE483, LE488, LE489, LE717, OB110, SC128, SC129
Weinstein, M., PG127
Weisbard, A. J., PA148
Weisberg, H. F., CP184, CP342, LE359, LE683, LE684, PE290, PP200, PP241, PP313, SC570
Weisbrod, B. A., SP142
Weiss, D. D., SC587
Weiss, D. M., EP688
Weiss, H. J., CP343
Weiss, J. A., PA52
Weiss, J. E., SP550
Weissert, C. S., LE490, SP99
Welch, C. E., IR557
Welch, F. R., MP510
Welch, I., DP6
Welch, K. W., RP31
Welch, M. R., RP101, RP128, SP56
Welch, R., LE123
Welch, S., DC97, DC98, DC99, LC85, MP124, MP171, MP196, MP197, MP198, MP199, MP332, MP339, MP340, MP341, MP342, MP343, MP344, MP345, MP346, MP347, MP526, MP527, MP528, PE291, PE327, PP425, PP426, PP427, TR43, XX366
Welch, W. P., LE685, PP99

Welle, P. G., PA149
Weller, B. R., PE495
Wellford, C. F., LC297
Wellhofer, E. S., IR871, PA341, PP314, PP42, PP43, PP44, PP45, PS312
Wellington, A. J., MP346
Wells, C. E., SP211
Wells, G., EP869
Welsh, W. A., LE60
Welton, G., DC100
Wendt, A., IR209, IR210
Werlin, H. H., OB137
West, C. T., EP196, TR132
West, D. M., CP74, EP143, LE491, PC220, PE228
West, E., MP484, OB325
West, E. G., OB271, OB323, SP256, SP547
West, J., ET363
West, J. P., CP44, SP340
West, W., LE320
Westaway, T., EP348
Westbrook, S. D., IR558
Westcott, D. R., LC266
Westefield, L. P., LE271
Westerlund, O., PG221
Western, B., DC346
Westley, B. H., PC120
Westlye, M. C., LE616
Westphal, J. D., EP524
Wetstein, M. E., SP57, SP58
Wever, R. E., LE309
Weyant, J. P., TR133
Weyland, K., PS69
Weymark, J. A., SC37
Whaples, R., EP57
Wheaton, B., XX385
Wheeler, S., LC475
Whelan, B. J., CP174
Whicker, M. L., LC158, OB138, OB317, PE150, SP53, SP54
Whinston, A. B., PE510
Whitaker, G. P., PA105
Whitby, K. J., LE493, MP420
White, E., PA204, PA205
White, G., EP68
White, G. M., PA295
White, H., IR363
White, H. C., SC588
White, J. K., PP524
White, J. W., PS70
White, L. J., EP669
White, M. J., LC93, MP31, PG69
White, O. F., ET413
White, P., PG139
White, R. R., DC101
White, R. W., DP135
White, S., AB301, PS98
Whitefield, S., PP14, PS121
Whitehead, L., EP144, EP545
Whiteley, P. F., PP315
Whiteman, D., LE272, LE465, PA251
Whitfield, K., EP670
Whitt, H. P., LC385, LC386, RP89
Whitten, G. D., PE264, SC785
Wholey, D. R., OB369
Wiberg, H., IR559
Wickham-Crowley, T. P., DC192
Widgren, M., SC346
Wiegle, T. C., PA206
Wielhouwer, P. W., PP136
Wiesmeth, H., IR258
Wiewel, W., PE616
Wiggins, C. W., ET327, LE494, PE408
Wije, C., PG67

Wilcox, C., AB302, IR830, LE495, LE686, MP265, MP350, PE292, RP177, RP178, RP179, SP25, SP26, SP27, SP59
Wildasin, D. E., EP696, SP447
Wildavsky, A., MP72, PE87, PE151, PE543, PG280, PG329, PG330, SC485, SC659, XX399, XX400
Wilde, L. L., PA307
Wilder, M. G., MP505
Wildgen, J. K., SC345
Wilensky, N., LE376
Wiles, P., IR560
Wilhite, A., CP328
Wilken, P. H., SP298
Wilkenfeld, J., IR430, IR431
Wilkerson, J., LE273
Wilkie, J. W., SP305
Wilkie, M. E., PG222
Wilkins, M., EP145
Wilkins, S., RP6
Wilkinson, K. P., LC387
Willanueva, D., EP356
Willeme, P., PP349
Willemse, H. M., LC211
Willer, D., SC606
Willett, T. D., CP180, IR196
Willey, T., DP136
Willhoite, F., PA207, PA208
William, A., PE581
Williams, B. A., DC354, EP671
Williams, D. E., DC201
Williams, D. L., MP372
Williams, D. R., MP14
Williams, J. A., ET482, OB398
Williams, J. T., IR341, IR409, IR432, PE496
Williams, K. C., CP218, LE402, SC347, SC348, SC767, SC768
Williams, K. R., DC102, RP77
Williams, L. S., RP132
Williams, M., EP350
Williams, R. H., AB220, RP170, SC486
Williams, S. A., AB220
Williams, W. A., PS243
Williamson, J. B., SP117, SP513, SP548, SP549, SP550
Williamson, J. G., EP146, EP226, EP459, PG167
Williamson, O. E., SC143
Wilman, E. A., DP39
Wilson, B. M., ET190
Wilson, C., SP408
Wilson, E. J., MP529
Wilson, J. D., SP447
Wilson, J. M., IR337
Wilson, J. Q., ET111, ET112, ET445
Wilson, K., SP240
Wilson, L. A., PE314, PE350, PG295
Wilson, P. A., OB139
Wilson, P. N., TR115
Wilson, R. B., SC144, SC424, SC511
Wilson, R. K., LE274, LE358, LE409, LE521, LE723, PE570
Wilson, R. W., ET113, ET114, ET446
Wilson, S., IR561
Wilson, T. C., ET483, ET484, MP141
Wilson, T. D., AB53
Wilson, W. J., MP520
Wimberley, D. W., RP108
Winden, F., PE569
Winder, R. C., PE293
Windolf, P., DP231
Windt, T. O., LE199
Winebrenner, H., PP303
Wineforoner, D., SP421
Winegarden, C. R., SP551, SP552
Winer, M. D., OB284, SC190, SC434

Wink, K., LE573
Winkler, J. D., CP71
Winn, R. G., LC336, SP143
Winsberg, M. D., PG70
Winsky, L. R., SC317
Winslow, D., PG71, RP32
Winston, C., EP672, EP673
Winter, D. G., LE119, XX401
Winter, E., ET180
Winter, J. A., ET447
Winter, R. A., OB56
Winter, S. L., OB323
Winter-Ebmer, R., PG223
Winterford, D., IR520
Winters, L. A., EP870
Winters, R. F., EP742, SP516
Wintrobe, R., OB173, PS260, XX146
Wirl, F., LE61, PE409, PP382
Wise, L. R., ET425, OB140
Wiseman, C., PE163
With, D., MP351
Witman, D., PS174
Witt, S. L., SP60
Witt, U., DP164, SC145
Wittberg, P., MP530
Wittkopf, E. R. AB305, AB306, AB307, AB308, AB274, AB303, AB304, IR117, LE431
Wittman, D., EP520, ET320, IR342, IR831, PP234, PP316, SC390, SC608
Wittrock, B., PA257
Wlarwe, J., ET357
Wlezien, C., CP143, EP103, EP147, PE152, SC185
Wodensjo, E., PE213
Wohlenberg, E. H., MP352
Woldendorp, J. J., PS71
Wolf, C., SC146
Wolf, D., SP553
Wolf, P., LC298
Wolf, T. A., EP148
Wolf-Dieter, E., DC103
Wolfe, A., ET448
Wolfe, B. L., XX264
Wolff, E. N., EP149, EP521
Wolfinger, R. E., CP164, PC196, PP197
Wolfle, L. M., MP142
Wolfsfeld, G., CP72
Wolfson, M., DP42, DP284, IR343
Wolkoff, M. J., EP404, EP405
Woller, G., PS10
Wolley, J. T., PE497
Wolman, H., PE490
Wolosin, M. A., SC734
Wolosin, R. J., SC734
Wolpert, J., PG192
Wolpin, K. L., LC299
Wolters, J., CP259
Wong, K. K., SP448
Wonnacott, P., SC666
Woo, W. T., EP406
Wood, B. D., EP674, OB194, OB195, PA254, PE80, TR134
Wood, D., LE597
Wood, J. M., PP78
Wood, M., ET449
Wood, S., SC198
Woodard, J. D., MP138
Woodbury, N. R., IR563
Woodfield, A. E., PE488
Woodrum, E., ET115, RP33, RP180
Woods, B., SC179
Woods, J. A., PP149
Woods, R., DC257
Woodward, J. D., PC221
Woodward, M., MP430
Woodward, S., XX7

Woolf, S., XX402
Woolley, J. T., EP150, EP151, EP675, LE496, PE498
Woolstencroft, R. P., PG72
Worchel, P., DC104
Worthley, J. A., LE497
Wortmann, M., PP15
Woshinsky, D. H., CP73
Woycke, J., LE135
Wray, J. H., AB221
Wren, C., PP45
Wren, T. E., ET116
Wright, C. L., EP523
Wright, D. E., SP179
Wright, D. S., LE576, PS214
Wright, E. O., PE55, PS124
Wright, G., EP120, MP359, PA151
Wright, G. C., AB222, CP344, CP354, CP346, CP347, CP348, LE284, LE498, PA53, PG128, PG247, PP235, PP322, SP338, SP449, SP554
Wright, J. E., MP200
Wright, J. R., LC406, LC407, LE100, LE275, LE687, PE302, PE410, SC571
Wright, K. N., ET203
Wright, M., IR211
Wright, M. B., LE499
Wrighton, J. M., LE632
Wrinkle, R. D., MP492, TR31
Wrong, D., XX405
Wu, H. M., ET339
Wu, S., IR832
Wu, S. Z., SC147, SC148
Wu, X. M., SC148
Wurth, A. H., PE321
Wuthnow, R., OB351, RP34, RP50, TR183
Wyckoff, M. L., AB223, AB224
Wynne, K. J., TR163
Wyrick, T. L., PE617, PP100
Wyzan, M. L., PG221

Xhu, J. H., AB45

Yablonsky, A. I., TR192
Yaffe, M. D., IR212
Yagi, T., SP450
Yamagishi, T., SC609
Yang, B., XX407
Yaniv, G., EP791
Yano, M., DP120, SC487
Yao, D. A., IR9
Yarwood, D. L., LE500
Yasin, K., OB118
Ye, M. H., EP677
Yearley, C. K., PP525
Yeats, A., EP861
Yemin, E., OB141
Yeoward, S., EP164
Yezer, A. M. J., EP677
Yiannakis, D. E., LE310
Yilmaz, M. R., SC149
Yin, R. K., XX408
Yinger, J., SC531, SP451
Yitzhaki, S., PA337
Yoffie, D. B., EP849
Yokoyama, A., XX409
Yoo, J. W., PS214
Yost, D. S., IR213, IR608
Yough, S. N., PP518
Young, A., CP323
Young, C. D., LE379
Young, D. A., PG73
Young, D. J., OB399
Young, I. M., ET321
Young, J. T., SP529
Young, O. R., IR872, PG74
Young, P., SC349

Young, R. C., OB370
Young, T., PE85
Young, T. R., DP137, DP138
Yousefi, M., EP527, OB233, OB234
Yu, S. S., EP37
Yun, K. Y., EP734
Yunker, J. A., IR214

Zagare, F. C., IR446, IR448, IR460,
  IR833, SC391
Zagorin, P., DC193
Zahariev, S., SC377
Zahler, R. S., DP68
Zajac, E. J., EP524
Zajonc, R. B., PC157
Zald, M., DC258, EP58
Zaleski, P., RP57
Zaller, J., AB337, AB392, PC72,
  PC222, SP477
Zame, W. R., SC384
Zander, A., XX410
Zandvakili, S., EP525
Zaninovich, M. G., PG234
Zannaras, G., AB26
Zaret, D., RP35, XX291
Zarnowitz, V., DP232, DP233
Zaslavskii, A. I., DP43
Zax, J. S., PG224

Zech, C., RP57
Zech, C. E., OB400, SC522, SC523
Zechman, M. J., SC150
Zeckhausen, R., SC61
Zeckhauserk, R., IR241
Zeeman, E. C., DP70
Zegeye, A. A., EP526
Zeidenstein, H. G., LE200
Zeira, J., DP285
Zeitz, G., SC599
Zeldes, S. P., EP464
Zelditch, M., SC229
Zelenitz, A., PG154, PG155
Zelikow, P., IR215
Zelle, C., CP349
Zeng, L., LE336
Zenger, T. R., OB142
Zhang, W. B., PA343
Zhou, M., MP32
Zhou, X., PA344
Ziegler, J. H., SP15
Ziegler, R., OB328
Zielonka, J., ET117
Zilcha, I., EP255
Ziliak, J., SP111
Zimmer, T., PC158
Zimmer, T. A., PG129
Zimmer, U., IR840

Zimmermann, E., DC124
Zimmermann, K., PE122
Zimmerman, D., EP507
Zinnes, D. A., IR216, IR282, IR753,
  IR873
Zipp, J. F., CP350, PP317
Zivot, E., EP153
Zodrow, G. R., PG186
Zojonc, R. B., SC734
Zoll, R., IR518
Zorn, P. M., SP419
Zucker, L. G., OB367
Zuckerman, A. S., CP74, CP351,
  CP352, PP264, XX411, XX412
Zuckerman, E. W., CP352
Zuckerman, H., XX413
Zuckert, C. H., SC660
Zuckert, M., ET322
Zuk, G., LC476
Zuk, L. G., DP278, IR562, IR563
Zupan, M. A., CP353, CP354, EP648,
  LE201, LE311, LE414, LE501, LE617
Zurcher, L., LC309
Zurn, M., PS57
Zusman, P., LC159
Zwick, M., EP62
Zwick, W. R., XX414
Zygmunt, J. F., RP36

SUBJECT INDEX

Abolitionists, MP72
Abortion, SP16-60/Special Section
Absence of Memory, IR856
Absent Father Hypothesis, LE19
Absolutism, DC166
Abstention, CP125, CP239, CP317, SC776
Abundance, PA32
Academia, DC317, MP89, PA109
Academic Freedom, SP202, SP247
Academic Liberalism, SP182
Academics, SP159, SP212, SP214
Access, PP432
Accidents, DP154
Accommodation, OB22
Accountability, IR632, PP220, XX375, XX376, XX378
Accused, RP80
Action Research, CP35, PA56, PA143, XX178
Activism, CP9, CP70, ET75, PE393, RP133
Activists, EP143
ACT, SP203
Acyclic Aggregation, SC78
Ad Hoc Committees, LE269
Adaptation, MP495
Adaptive Behavior, XX394
Adaptive Change, OB336
Adaptive Egoism, SC80
Addiction, DP57
Address to the Nation, LE187
Adjudicated Outcomes, SC665
Adjudication, LC74, LC76
Administering Public Policy, OB80
Administration, OB71-142/Special Section, OB165, PE162, PE354, PE436
Administrative Abuse, PP418
Administrative Agencies, OB109
Administrative Ethics, ET427, ET435, ET440
Administrative Intensity, OB113
Administrative Procedures, EP612, OB78, OB110, OB111
Administrative Reform, OB74, OB116, SP369
Administrative Regimes, EP235
Administrative State, EP676, OB135, OB163
Administrative Turnover, LE576
Admirals, IR574
Adolescents, AB29

Advanced Industrial Societies, DC296, PA6
Adverse Selection Model, DC280
Advertising, CP194, PC191, PC197, PC220, PG274, PP55, PP56, SC767, also see Negative Advertising
Advice, PC19
Advising Government, PA61
Advocacy, DC196, LE475, PA242, PP4
Affiliation Referenda, DC315
Affirmative Action, MP33-51/ Special Section
Affluence, EP443, SP282
Africa, AB172, CP66, DC109, DC110, DC115, DC119, EP217, EP218, ET45 ET217, IR407, IR503, IR504, IR516, IR799, IR800, MP371, MP458, PE356, PG102, PG236, PS1, PS6, PS7, PS11, PS13, PS146, PS251, PS269, SP185, SP327
Afro-Americans, see Black Americans
Age Relations, SP82
Agencies, OB14
Agency, ET88, LC133, LE217, SC5, SC581
Agency Arrangements, OB361
Agency Behavior, OB22
Agency Budgets, OB144
Agency-Client Relations, TR61
Agency Contracts, OB56
Agency Decisions, OB28
Agency Discretion, EP563
Agenda, AB45, LE485
Agenda Control, LE206, PA308, SC565, SC780
Agenda Dynamics, PA62
Agenda Influence, SC68, SC792, SC801
Agenda Setting, PC91-113/Special Section, LC111, LC406
Agendas, PC94, PC95, SC108, SC799
Agent Veto, SC437
Agents, SC499
Agglomeration, PG44
Aggregate Data, CP249
Aggregate Production Function, EP118
Aggregation, EP489, PE406, SC239, XX25, XX392
Aggression, AB83, DC11, DC37, DC45, DC62, DC93, DC99, LC200, OB239, PA203

Aging, EP702, SP66, SP75, SP78, SP80, SP116, SP132, SP136
Agriculture, TR7-43/Special Section
Agrarian Political Behavior, TR13, TR28
Agrarian Question, TR22
Agrarian Reform, TR40
Agriculture Committee, LE209
Agricultural Exports, DP174
Agricultural Policy, TR31, TR39, TR41
Agricultural Protection, TR10
Agricultural Research, TR25, TR35, TR37
Ahistoricism, DC304
Aid to Families with Dependent Children, SP461, SP484, SP492, SP551, SP552
AIDS, RP118, SP73, SP105, SP114
Air Bags, SP120
Air Hijacking, DC360
Air Pollution, EP649, EP674
Air Quality, TR124, TR134
Airlines, EP560, EP621, EP633
Airplane Accidents, PC140
Akrasia, SC646
Alabama, MP60, MP61
Alaskan Natives, MP406
Alcohol, EP768, SP109, SP112, SP141, SP143, TR151
Algorithms, XX381
Alienated America, LC523
Alienation, AB180, CP1, CP11, CP12, CP20, CP24, CP46, CP175, ET81, IR558, LC480, LC523, LE610, MP435, MP503, PC158, PE34
Alignments, EP848, IR228
All Politics Is Local, PP154
All Volunteer Force, IR486
Alliances, IR217-258/Special Section, IR295, IR426, IR485, IR702, IR703, IR786, IR809, IR825, IR856
Alliance Formation, IR227, IR231, IR232, IR254, IR255, IR717
Allies, IR238
Allison, Graham, OB199, OB227, OB228
Allocations, IR826
Allocative Inefficiency, SP430
Almon Distributed Lag, PE249
Almond, Gabriel AB250

Almond-Lippmann Consensus, AB250
Alternation Processes, RP92
Alternative Defense, IR398
Alternative Dispute Resolution,
    DC65
Altruism, ET118-147/Special
    Section, ET195, OB380, SC732,
    SP89
Altruistic Fear, LC294
Altruistic Voting, ET128
Amateurism, LE348, PP153
Amazon, PG239
Ambiguity, LE41, PP56, PP223,
    SC707, SC719, SC775, SC777
Ambition, LE329, LE332, LE353,
    MP304, MP305
Amendments, CP99, LE204, SC781,
    SC380
American Cities, SP309
American Decline, EP91, PA5
American Leadership, EP131, EP146
American Party System, PP453,
    PP504
American Political Science Associ-
    ation Committee on Political
    Parties, PP452
American Political Science Review,
    XX269
American Politics, PC68, PG226,
    XX23, XX284
American Question, XX260
American Revolution, DC146
American Sociological Review,
    XX269
American States, see States
American Voter, AB41
American World Role, AB304, AB305
Amicus Curiae, LC407, LC466, LC454
Amnesty, PC93
Amplification, OB22
Analogical Transfer, AB129
Analogies, AB289
Analytic Ability, LE375
Analytical Marxism, PE30
Anarchy, ET140, ET153, ET158,
    ET165, ET184, IR122, IR147,
    IR190, IR240, IR414, OB69, PS28,
    PS33
Andarchy, XX366
Anglo-Hanse Trade War, EP807
Animal Protection Movement, TR65
Annexation, SP374
Anomalies, XX362
Anomie, AB340
Anthropology, EP12, PA122
Anti-Americanism, XX21, XX373
Antibusing, MP484
Antichaos, DP126
Antidiscrimination Policies, MP39,
    MP66, MP78
Antidumping Decisions, EP632
Anti-Federalists, LC448
Anti-Government Violence, DC204
Antigrowth Coalition, EP398
Antiheteroxy, LC295
Antihierarchical Games, SC485
Anti-Immigration, MP118
Anti-Incumbency, CP329
Anti-Intellectualism, SP231
Antinuclear Movement, IR588, PC98,
    TR173
Anti-Policy Analysts, PA237
Anti-Saloon League, OB337
Anti-Semitism, MP125
Antislavery Movement, LC452
Antistocks, XX69
Antistrike Laws, DC298
Antisystem Behavior, DC58

Antitrust, EP575, EP598, EP618,
    EP645, EP653, LC272, LC410,
    SP103
Antitrust Paradox, SC535
Antiwar Sentiments, IR779
Anxiety, CP37
Apaches, LC109
Apartheid, MP52
Appeasement, IR366
Applied History, IR201
Applied Research, ET92, PA232,
    PA254
Appointed Officials, MP511
Appointments, EP76
Appropriations, LE139, LE703, PE58
Appropriations Bills, LE204
Appropriations Committees, LE715
Appropriations Process, PE373
Approval-Plurality Voting, SC272
Approval Procedures, SC271, SC783
Approval Voting, SC245, SC247,
    SC261, SC262, SC278, SC297,
    SC344, also see Electoral
    Systems
Aptheker Thesis, DC184
Arab Leaders, PG19
Arab Visits, PG65
Arab-Israeli Conflict, IR599,
    PC173
Arbitrage, PG119
Architecture, LE395
Area Studies, XX179
Arendt, Hanna, XX335
Argentina, OB316, PP42, PP430
Argentine Radical Party, PP430
Argumentation, DC96, ET62, IR13,
    IR437, PA107, SC111, XX319,
    XX398
Aridity, PS147
Arima Models, DC227
Arizona, MP216, MP303, PC76
Arkansas, RP110
Armaments, IR272, IR291, IR336,
    IR509
Armed Conflict, IR650, IR653,
    IR822, also see War
Armed Forces and Society, IR478
Armed Force, IR694
Armies, IR472, IR533, IR516,
    IR536, IR539, also see Military
Arms, IR238, IR270, IR328
Arms Acquisition, IR330, IR332
Arms Control, DC13, IR266, IR267,
    IR270, IR276, IR289, IR298,
    IR303, IR315, IR317, IR325,
    IR331, IR339, IR565
Arms Control Verification, IR342
Arms Processes, IR286, IR287
Arms Production, EP334, EP472,
    IR520
Arms Races, IR259-343/Special
    Section, IR135, IR595, IR798,
    PP55
Arms Trade, IR262, IR296, IR303,
    SC370
Arms Transfers, IR265, IR297,
    IR326, SC368, SC371
Army Corps of Engineers, LE701
Army General Officers, IR508
Arrest Rates, LC281, LC310, LC317,
    LC326
Arrow, Kenneth, LE207
Arrow's Theorem, SC361, SC488,
    SC489, SC490, SC492, SC494,
    SC495, SC496, SC498, SC499,
    SC503, SC504, SC505, SC508,
    SC510, SC511, LE691

Articles of Confederation, LC145,
    LE408, PG271
Artificial Intelligence, IR4, OB52
Artificial Neural Networks, EP18,
    PC35
Art, AB133, DP61, XX158
Artistic Cycles, DP241
Arts Policy, PE596
Asian Americans, LC368, MP143,
    MP383, MP450, MP457, MP476
Asia, IR429, IR504, PE317, PS40,
    PS96, RP82
Assassination, DC48, DC350
Assault, LC243
Assimilation, MP21, OB22
Astronomy, TR188
Asymmetric Information, CP218,
    IR354
Asymmetric Society, PA44
Asymmetrically Informed Voters,
    CP218
Athletics, SP212
Atlanta, MP65
Attachment, MP470
Attack, IR775, IR832
Attack Advertising, CP194
Attention, AB68, PC12
Attentive Publics, LE278
Attitude Attribution, AB4, XX39
Attitude-Behavior Consistency,
    AB29
Attitude Change, AB7, AB31, AB39,
    AB220, SC486
Attitude Constraint, AB88, AB97,
    AB121, AB126, AB141, AB206,
    AB224, AB281, AB283, MP282,
    TR117
Attitude Formation, AB21
Attitude Paradoxes, SC588
Attitude Stability, AB61
Attitude Structure, AB47, AB125,
    AB187, AB353, SP50
Attitude Systems, AB155
Attitudes, AB1-392/Special
    Section, CP315, ET414, ET479,
    LE292, LE298, MP253, MP428
Attorney General, LC35
Attribution Theory, XX193
At-Large Elections, MP159, MP171,
    MP196
Auditing, OB144
Australia, CP198, CP199, EP698,
    LE87, LE158, LE314, PE368, PP265
Australian Ballot, SC332
Austria, DC166
Authoritarian Regimes, DC200, EP8,
    PS22, PS40, PS50
Authoritarianism, AB139, AB177,
    LE43, MP498, PP294, RP127,
    XX365, XX81
Authority, DC79, ET106, ET236,
    MP530, OB40, OB161, RP61, XX189
Autobiography, XX177
Autocracy, PS127
Autocratic Succession, PS73
Automation, DP181
Automobile Accidents, SP143
Automobiles, PA281
Axiomatic Theory, ET99
Axiomatization of Theories, XX324

B-1 Bomber, IR491
Backbenchers, LE241, LE434, LE458
Background Characteristics, OB105
Backwardness, PG270
Bail, MP370
Bail Risk, LC185
Bailouts, EP94

Balance of Payments, PE428
Balance of Power, DC13, IR236,
   IR170, IR234, IR418, IR428,
   IR750, IR756, IR819, IR834,
   IR845, IR855, IR864, IR873,
   OB205
Balance of Trade, EP792
Balance Theory, CP337
Balanced Budget Multiplier, PE99
Balancing, IR190
Balloons, DC332
Ballot Propositions, see Direct
   Democracy
Bandwagon Curve, DP38
Bandwagons, AB380, CP234, DP7,
   DP22, DP34, DP38, DP204, LE575,
   PG80, PP106
Bank Account Presidency, LE194
Bank Merger Regulations, EP573
Bankers, PE243
Bankers Model, PE177
Banking, EP559, EP603, EP626,
   LE585
Banking Committee, PP53
Banking Reform, EP656
Banking Regulation, EP596
Bankruptcy, EP32, LC93
Banton, Michael, MP9
Baptists, PP434
Bar Associations, OB341, OB342
Barbarians, PS215
Bargaining, CP78, DC265, DC277,
   DC278, DC279, DC310, DC325,
   DC345, ET121, ET143, IR456,
   LE92, LE193, LE362, OB205,
   OB216, OB217, OB219, OB222, SC6,
   SC27, SC115, SC157, SC164,
   SC384, SC397, SC409, SC437,
   SC478
Bargaining Legislation, DC345
Bargaining Power, PE416, SC159
Bargaining Set, LE712, SC460,
   SC461
Barristers, LC30
Bartley-Fox Gun Law, LC349
Basic Needs, DC15, ET233, SP1
Bayesian Inference, LC176, SC61,
   SC414, SC495, SC627
Beautiful Problems, XX309
Beef Cattle Industry, TR15
Behavioral Sciences, LC55, PA231
Behavioralism, SC30, SC38, XX47,
   XX196
Beirut Massacre, PC180
Belgium, CP54, MP362, MP480, PG15,
   SP331, SP355
Belief Aggregation, SC61
Belief Change, AB26
Belief Congruence, PE396
Belief Consensus, AB185
Belief Integration, PC106
Belief Sets, SC59
Belief Structure, AB169
Belief Systems, AB85-224/Special
   Section, AB232, AB251, AB270,
   AB271, AB294, AB298, AB346,
   IR208, LE680, MP238, MP387,
   MP394, PP490, SP29, SP429,
   TR107, TR117, XX108, XX220
Beliefs of American Leaders, AB255
Beliefs of the Public, AB321
Bell Curve, MP53
Beneficent Norms, ET323
Berlin, IR153
Bible, RP61, RP110
Bible Belt, RP168
Bibliography, XX63
Bicameralism, LE7

Bicommunal Conflict, MP380, MP497
Big Science, TR148
Bilingual Education, SP172
Bill Construction, LE260
Bill Introduction, LE379
Bill of Rights, LC119, LC141,
   SP543
Bimodal Issues, SP53
Binary Choice, SC21, SC116
Binary Games, LC96, PE528
Binding, LC433
Bioeconomics, PA176
Biological Analogies, PA285
Biological Systems, DP47
Biological Theory, PA197
Biology, PA167, PA195, PA196
Biopolitics, PA152-209/Special
   Section
Biosphere, TR78
Bipartisanship, IR117
Bipolar Systems, IR203, IR825,
   IR867, PP489, PS66
Birth Order, LE158, LE188, XX359
Birth Rates, SP72
Bishops' Peace Pastoral, RP135
Black Americans, AB86, DC238,
   ET453, ET466, LC379, PC165,
   PE291, PG146, PP92, RP71, RP97,
   also see Minority Politics
Black and White Thinking, AB241
Black Belt, CP261, MP421
Black Box Models, CP268
Black Concentration, MP69
Black Protest, XX269
Black Threat, MP418
Black-White Interactions, MP124
Black Women, MP88, MP157, MP158,
   MP212, MP231
Blackmail, LC269, XX391
Blame, PE218, XX150, XX232, XX233
Blaming the Victim, MP82
Bloc Concentration, IR427, IR864
Bloc Voting, MP165, SC330
Blue Collar Workers, EP162
Blue Laws, EP37
Bolstering, XX378
Bomb Threats, PC134
Bombings, LE4
Bond Ratings, EP83, EP581
Boolean Tests, PS108
Boom, PE194
Boom Towns, SP392
Bootleggers, PP434
Borda Principles, SC310, SC333
Border Effects, IR799
Border Regions, PG257, PG319,
   PG324
Bordinghouse, LE620
Born Again Christians, RP168
Borrowing, SC666
Boundaries, ET18, MP409
Boundaries of Inquiry, XX345
Boundary Conflict, PG236
Bounded Rationality, PE127, SC610,
   SC616, SC633, XX183
Boycotts, EP9
Brain, PA162
Brazil, EP328, PG239, PG291, PP32
Breakpoints, DP110
Brewing Industry, OB333
Bribery, EP658, PP359, PP386,
   PP429, PP437
Brinkmanship, IR589, IR597, OB202
Britain, see United Kingdom
British Broadcasting Corporation,
   PC70
British General Election of 1906,
   EP831

British Isles, see United Kingdom
British Sickness, EP71
British Stock Market, SC683
Broadcasting, PC89
Brownian Model, XX305
Bubbles, DP12, DP32, DP200
Buchanan, James, LC124, LC140,
   SC114
Buchanan-Tullock Model, LC124
Buddhism, PG71, RP32
Budget Cuts, OB170
Budget Cycle, PA214
Budget Maximizing Bureaucrats,
   OB149, OB152, OB172, OB184
Budget Side Payments, OB280
Budgets, PE56-152/Special Section,
   CP96, DP29, LC182, LE551, LE560,
   OB260, PE440, PE598, PE614,
   PS74, SP312
Buenos Aires, PP430
Bundestag, LE705
Burden Sharing, IR243
Bureau of Prisons, OB193
Bureaucratic Behavior, OB143-195/
   Special Section, AB232, CP127,
   EP247, EP613, EP624, EP659,
   IR11, OB158, OB227, PC1, PE90,
   PE607, PG212, PP415, PP432,
   SP418, TR31, TR134, XX121
Bureaucratic Adaption, OB195
Bureaucratic Authoritarianism,
   OB179
Bureaucratic Discretion, EP668
Bureaucratic Government, OB178
Bureaucratic Ideology, OB192
Bureaucratic Influences, EP111
Bureaucratic Maladies, OB143
Bureaucratic Morality, ET397,
   ET429
Bureaucratic Procedures, ET348
Bureaucratic Responsiveness, OB168
Bureaucratic Tenure, PE19
Bureaucratization, OB151, OB157,
   OB165
Bureaus, EP553, SC394
Burglary, LC188
Burnout, OB25, OB100, OB106
Bush, George, PC53
Business, ET378, PP97
Business Climate, EP227
Business Crime, LC290
Business Cycles, DP106, DP165,
   DP169, DP171, DP172, DP175,
   DP178, DP189, DP190, DP191,
   DP192, DP197, DP198, DP205,
   DP209, DP211, DP212, DP213,
   DP214, DP217, DP218, DP222,
   DP227, DP229, DP231, DP232,
   DP233, EP193, EP411, EP548,
   IR509, IR806, LC250, OB256,
   PE430, PE442, PE459, PE466,
   PE471
Business Ethics, ET368, ET443
Business Failures, PS191
Business Gaming, SC473
Business Group Influence, SP348
Business Incentives, PE616
Business Location, PG134, TR48
Business Malfeasance, PC177
Business Political Behavior,
   EP790, PE386
Business Principles, ET82
Business Strategy, OB339
Busing, MP63, MP104, MP484
Butter, PE376
Butterfly Catastrophe, DP57
By-Elections, MP188
Bystanders, LC271

Cabinet Duration, LE98
Cabinet Stability, LE62, LE65,
  LE66, LE78, LE81, LE93, LE99,
  LE325
Cabinets, LE62-100/Special
  Section, LE347
The Calculus of Consent, LC100,
  LC136, LC150
California, CP94, CP139, LC156,
  LC444, LE317, LE562, LE637,
  PC196
California Gold Rush, LC156
Campaign Advertising, see Adver-
  tising, and Negative Advertising
Campaign Coffers, PP68, PP85
Campaign Commercials, PC205
Campaign Committees, PP90
Campaign Communications, PC202,
  PC209
Campaign Coverage, PC174
Campaign Expenditures, PP52, PP82
Campaign Finance, PP46-100/Special
  Section, ET128, LE288, LE317,
  LE446, LE637, LE678, LE685,
  PC218, PE300, PE385, PP109,
  PP114
Campaign Finance Reform, PP46,
  PP58, PP74, PP94
Campaign News, PC174
Campaign Polls, AB322
Campaign Spending, PP50, PP69,
  PP70, PP73, PP76, PP80, PP86,
  PP100
Campaigns, PC181-222/Special
  Section, CP212, LE142, PC62,
  PC74, PC94, PP54, PP85, PP117,
  PP165, PP168, PP185, PP199,
  PP211, PP218, PP225, PP231,
  RP146, SC681
Canada, AB189, AB341, LE111,
  LE344, LE355, MP38, MP439,
  OB234, PA22, PE36, PE42, PE201,
  PE224, PE250, PG106, PG317,
  PP242, PP253, PP317, PP355,
  PP441, PP482, PP496, PS139,
  PS195, PS202, SP113, XX260
Canada-US Convergence Thesis, TR70
Canadian Charter of Rights, PG317
Cancer Policy, SC715
Candidate Awareness, PC211, PP208
Candidate Competition, PP141
Candidate Evaluations, AB57,
  CP184, CP212, CP236, CP268,
  CP271, CP294, CP295, CP296,
  CP304, CP309, CP342, CP345,
  MP309, PC200
Candidate Ideologies, PP212
Candidate Issue Positions, PP121
Candidate Motivation, PP234, PP316
Candidate Popularity, PP114
Candidate Preference Function,
  CP318
Candidate Presentation, CP311
Candidate Recognition, PP171
Candidate Reputation, PP161
Candidate Selection, PP105, PP293
Candidate Success, PP210
Candidate Withdrawal, PP222
Candidates, CP291, LE572, MP163,
  PC199, PP33, PP343, SC746, SC775
Cannon, Joe, LE319
Canonical Correlation, SP394
Capabilities, IR113, IR734, IR826
Capability Aggregation, IR237
Capability Concentration, IR661
Capability Distribution, IR634
Capacities, IR731

Capacity Concentration, IR729,
  IR825
Capacity Reconcentration, IR810
Capital, EP376, EP818, PA315,
  PE44, PE297
Capital Appropriations, PE58
Capital Budgets, PE131
Capital Flows, EP222, EP395
Capital Mobility, EP14, EP42,
  EP63, EP90, EP333
Capital Punishment, LC301, LC352,
  LC355, LC356, LC358, LC359,
  LC361, LC374, LC375, LC380,
  LC383
Capital Spending, PE131
Capital Taxation, EP766
Capitalism, EP12, EP333, ET112,
  IR509, IR862, MP25, PE46, PS6,
  PS9, PS25, PS124, PS316, SC724
Capitalist Crisis, PE50
Capitalist Development, DP195,
  DP210
Capitalist Societies, EP24
Capitalization, SC531
Capture, EP620, LE8
Care, MP240
Careerism, EP238, LE344
Careers, LE312-358/Special
  Section, LE570, LE510, OB66
Carrying Capacity, XX226
Cartels, EP31, OB353, OB364, PE4,
  TR16
Carter, Jimmy, LE179, LE196,
  OB207, PC74
Cartoons, PC184
Cascades, DP6, DP156
Case Selection, LC394
Case Studies, IR433, XX217, XX408
Casework, LE306, LE310, LE410,
  LE563, PP219
Casinos, LC205
Catastrophes, DP44-70/Special
  Section, DP157, DP215
Catastrophic Demand, IR560
Catching Up, EP250, EP284, PE384
Catholic Church, RP13, RP44, RP47,
  RP94
Catholic Hierarchy, RP41
Catholicism, DC318, RP111, RP169
Caucus Participants, MP300
Caucusing, CP286, DC100
Causal Analysis, IR269, LE430
Causal Inference, XX67, XX145
Causal Models, AB73, AB90
Causal Perceptions, AB200
Causal Reasoning, DP4
Causality, PS147, XX77, XX83,
  XX145, XX182, XX303
Celtic Fringe, PG290
Center of Gravity, PG64
Central America, DC6, DC160, DP207
Central Banks, EP68, EP73, EP81,
  EP95, EP140, PE148
Central Cities, PG70, SP451
Central Europe, PE256, PE406
Central-Local Relations, PS54
Central Place Theory, PG1, PG44
Centralism, PA124
Centralization, OB209, PS64
Centrally Planned Economies, DP196
Centrist Revolt, PP474
CEO Compensation, EP524, OB18
Certification Elections, DC281
Chain Gang, XX381
Chain Store Paradox, SC576, SC583
Challenger Disaster, OB29
Challenger Quality, PP144, PP227
Challengers, PP189

Chancellor Effect, LE32
The Changing American Voter, CP309
Chaos, DP71-138/Special Section,
  DP158, SP129
Chaotic Motion, DP105
Chaotic Tatonnement, DP98
Chaotic Time Series, DP90
Character, ET111, ET445, LE24
Character Coercion, LC345
Characteristic Function, IR422
Charismatic Leadership, OB20
Charisma, LE135, PP221, XX333
Charity, ET138, ET144, ET145,
  OB381
Cheating, ET413, PP413, RP117
Chemical Industry, EP609
Chemical Weapons, IR148
Cherwell, Lord, LE4
Chicago, MP443, OB297, PP392,
  PP406, PP415
Chicanos, MP160, MP165, MP363,
  MP382, MP395, MP415, MP486
Chicken Models, IR184
Chief Executives, LE101-201/
  Special Section
Chief Justices, LC439
Child Care, SP8
Child Poverty, SP298
Childbearing, PG87
Childhood, AB46, AB383
Children, ET101, MP412, MP453,
  OB191
Chile, CP21, OB316, PE259, PE294,
  PP339
China, AB183, CP43, DC161, DC173,
  DC189, DC190, DP242, EP231,
  IR46, LC293, PP403, SP76
Chinese Policy Debate, AB232
Choice Theory, SC3
Christian Right, RP146, RP171,
  RP178, RP179
Christian Theology, RP107
Christianity, ET405, IR577, RP168
Churches, RP37-57/Special Section,
  ET44, IR590, PG101, RP76, SC217
Church-State Relations, PC28
Cigarettes, EP703, EP759
Circumscription, PG255
Cities, CP101, MP31, MP173, PE318,
  PG61, RP89, SP284, SP306, SP355,
  SP373, SP382, SP390, SP391,
  SP420, SP423
Citizen Contacting, CP16, CP29,
  CP44, CP64, CP74, EP238
Citizen Groups, PE308
Citizen Information, PE542
Citizen Orientations, LE456
Citizen Participation, see Politi-
  cal Participation
Citizen-Police Encounters, LC510
Citizen Satisfaction, LC509, PE545
Citizenship, ET399, ET408, ET433,
  MP11, MP396, SP181
Citizenship Rights, EP58
City Councils, EP238, MP143,
  MP161, MP177, MP144, MP148
City Managers, SP336
City-Size Distribution, PG3
Civic Culture, PG321, PS150
Civic Tradition, XX406
Civic Virtue, EP756, ET373
Civil Conflict, DC32, DC40, DC216
Civil Defense, XX355
Civil Disobedience, DC252
Civil Disorder, DC98, DC232, IR482
Civil Liberties, ET225, ET238,
  LC408, LC469, XX332

Civil-Military Relations, IR499, IR454, IR504, IR521, IR540, IR554
Civil Procedure, LC43
Civil Religion, RP65, XX120
Civil Rights, ET204, LC147, LE659, LE660, MP4, MP24, MP37, MP397, MP506
Civil Rights Movement, AB44, MP444
Civil Servants, LE463
Civil Service, OB82, OB123, OB367
Civil Society, MP491, XX271
Civil War, DC180, IR472, MP72
Civil Wars, IR724
Civilian Regimes, PS252
Civilizations, DP16, PG73, IR684
Claims, ET472
Class, AB96, AB137, AB174, CP102, CP210, DC170, EP19, LC177, LC287, LC315, LC229, MP68, MP335, MP373, MP420, MP509, MP527, PE6, PE21, PE22, PE28, PE54, PE285, PG39, PP13, PP263, PS325, SP116, SP278, SP489, SP538, TR27, TR151
Class Conflict, DC220, PA191, PE32, PE37, PE43, PE55
Class Consciousness, CP340, EP10
Class Mobility, CP220, PA20
Class Polarization, PP291
Class Repression, LC498
Class Struggle, CP250, EP25, PS140, SP492
Class Voting, CP203, CP237, CP341, PE48, RP159
Classical Conditioning, XX386
Clausewitz, Karl von, DP5
Clearance Rates, LC187
Cleavage, DC8, XX411
Cleavage Dimensions, PP337
Cleavage Structures, PP455
Clergy, RP39
Client Evaluation, OB30
Client Politics, PP419
Clientelism, XX155
Climate, TR60, TR131
Climate Change, TR59, TR95, TR111
Clinton, Bill, PE57
Cliometrics, XX60
Closed Rule, LE365
Closeness, CP109, CP116, CP135, CP139, CP178, CP285
Closeness to Unanimity, SC318
Clubs, XX4, XX44, XX311
Clues, AB184
Cluster Analysis, AB125, SC512
Clustering, DP155
Coal Mining, DC271
Coalition Bargaining, PP481, SC184
Coalition Breaking, SC178
Coalition Formation, LE77, PP106, SC160, SC164, SC167, SC170, SC180, SC186, SC187, SC373
Coalition Governments, LE89, LE92, PP1
Coalition of Minorities, LE195
Coalition Payoffs, SC161, SC162
Coalition Performance, SC193
Coalition Stability, LE84, LE86
Coalition Trading, SC169
Coalitions, SC151-198/Special Section, DP7, EP337, ET319, ET347, IR157, LC399, LE72, LE77, LE82, LE97, LE100, LE655, LE689, LE699, LE700, PE315, PP125, SC152, SC155, SC401, SC461, SC597

Coase Theorem, EP547, EP552, EP565, EP572, EP589, EP666, EP592, EP593, EP601, EP635
Coattails, CP207, CP223, CP235, CP280, LE155, LE592
Code of Conduct for Politicians, PP355
Coercion, DC31, DC213, LC345, LC494
Coercive Bargaining, OB216
Coercive Power, IR27, IR781
Coerciveness of Government, DC22
Coexistence, IR835
Cognition, DP53, XX98
Cognitive Approaches, LC295
Cognitive Development, AB383, DC252
Cognitive Dissonance, XX5
Cognitive Frameworks, ET134
Cognitive Impairment, PC43
Cognitive Interpretation, SP155
Cognitive Maps, MP373
Cognitive Misers, ET136, SC636
Cognitive Mobilization, PP258
Cognitive Orientation, AB228
Cognitive Perceptions, AB299
Cognitive Perspectives, SC726
Cognitive Processes, AB78, CP244, IR19
Cognitive Revolution, XX141
Cognitive Science, ET386, XX168
Cognitive Sophistication, ET452
Cognitive Strategies, CP304, PP231
Cognitive Structure, AB170
Cognitive Style, AB19, AB211, AB212, LE680
Coherence Theories, ET61
Cohesion, DC87, XX412
Cohesiveness, PC17
Cohort Change, PP288
Cointegration, DC266, OB305
Cold War, AB230, AB270, AB278, IR25, IR35, IR42, IR74, IR102, IR157, IR246, IR419, IR420, IR567, IR651, IR870, LE118
Cold War Consensus, AB308
Collaboration, ET166, ET193, PA55
Collective Action, SC199-229/ Special Section, DC30, DC175, DC211, DC251, ET167, IR242, OB375, OB386, PE322, PE326, PG110, SC524, TR67
Collective Action Groups, PE360, RP55
Collective Bargaining, DC278, DC310, DC325
Collective Decision Making, CP189, ET313, LC96, OB26, SC110, SC132, SC365
Collective Economic Judgments, PE220
Collective Entities, ET108
Collective Goods, EP320, IR220, IR221, IR244, OB374, PE506, PE521, SC208, SC425
Collective Indecision, SC45
Collective Political Behavior, MP502
Collective Protests, CP71, DC76, DC104
Collective Rationality, CP26, LC11, SC489, SC632
Collective Sanctions, ET337, SC413
Collective Security, LC348
Collective Violence, DC40, DC64, DC84, DC199, DC285, DC339, IR394, LC235

Collectivist Cultures, SC90
Collectivist Organizations, OB181
College, AB81, PE519
Collusion, DP99, PE4, PP428
Colombia, DC179
Colombian National Congress, LE243
Colonialism, EP199, PS238
Colonials, PG222
Colonization, PS216
Colored Immigration, MP133, MP518
Combat, IR484
Combat Readiness, IR434
Comity, XX393
Commerce, EP126, EP856
Commitment, CP53, ET59, LE10, OB85, OB106, SC54, SC399, XX130
Committee Assignments, LE233, LE262, LE288
Committee Bias, LE233
Committee Capture, LE206
Committee Chairman, LE253, LE213
Committee Hearings, LE256, MP275
Committee Jurisdictions, LE242, PP84
Committee Membership Turnover, LE243
Committee Positions, LE265
Committee Power, LE246, LE263, LE266, LE267, LE270, LE273
Committee Size, LE225, LE272
Committee Systems, LE202, LE203, LE225, LE238, LE271
Committee Transfers, LE210
Committee Voting, LE240, LE275, SC788
Committees, LE202-275/Special Section, ET69, LE536, LE711, LE715, SC173, SC191, SC801
Commodity Markets, PE38
Commodity Policy, EP840
Common Law, LC71
Common Pool Resources, SC213
Commonwealth, PP192
Communal Groups, SC54, XX130
Communes, SC210
Communication Democratization, PC80
Communication Games, SC432
Communication Revolution, PC90
Communications, PC1, PC4, PC6, PC26, PC39, PC49, PC59, PC204, PG27, PS287
Communism, PS72-99/Special Section, CP195, PG322, PP32, PS118
Communist Collapse, PS75, PS87
Communist Countries, IR554
Communist Decay, PS88
Communist Electorates, CP195
Communist Foreign Trade, EP839
Communist Parties, PS91
Communist Priorities, PS74
Communist Systems, LE549, PS82, PS85
Communitarian Debate, XX257
Communities, ET18, ET374, LC229, PG129, SP321, SP443, XX142
Communities of Fate, PP42
Community Attachment, PP392
Community Development Grant Program, SP402
Community Influence, PC138
Community Mediation, DC100
Community Partisanship, PG113
Community Politics, SP330
Community Power Structures, SP333, SP446, SC604
Community Preferences, SC25

Community Satisfaction, PG91
Community Service, SP329
Community Structure, CP344
Comparable Worth, LC9, MP272,
  MP297
Comparative Analysis, CP289,
  XX110, XX240, XX306
Comparative Case Strategy, XX217
Comparative History, PE35, XX331
Comparative Inquiry, XX237
Comparative Legislative Studies,
  LE37
Comparative Method, PS312, XX67,
  XX216, XX297
Comparative Politics, PS83, XX31,
  XX101, XX113, XX172, XX200,
  XX216, XX238
Comparative Public Policy, PA10,
  PA57, PA103, PA114, PA115, PA120
Comparative Research, XX104,
  XX215, XX217, XX395
Comparing and Miscomparing, XX313
Compassion, PP173
Compensation Policies, OB18, OB94
Compensatory Education, SP195
Competence, CP275, CP281, PG53
Competency Testing, PA321, SP173,
  SP208
Competing Aspiration Levels Model,
  PE94
Competition, DP99, ET148, ET187,
  MP110, OB152, PP343, SC134,
  SP493, XX64
Competition among Jurisdictions,
  PG154
Competitive Governments, PS180
Competitive Solution, SC72
Competitiveness, PP20
Competitors, EP9
Complex Conflicts, DC5
Complex Dynamics, DP144, DP145,
  DP148
Complex Issues, TR170
Complex Rules, SC284
Complex Situations, XX295
Complex Societies, DP163
Complexity, DP139-164/Special
  Section, AB206, ET183, PE350,
  TR87, XX378
Complexity of Thought, XX375
Compliance, EP634, LC427
Composition Model, PG119
Compound Majority Decisions, SC573
Compound Republic, LC100
Compromise of 1860, PC36
Compromising Behavior, DC16
Comptroller of the Currency, OB66
Compulsory Schooling, EP255, SP178
Computer Applications, PA324
Computer Simulation, SC429, SC435,
  SC470, SC475, SC476
Concealed Weapons, SC116
Concentration, IR859
Concentration of Power, SC593
Concept Formation, XX380
Concept Misformation, XX312
Conceptual Conservatism, PA12
Conceptual Variables, SP240
Conceptualization, MP338
Concession Making, IR27
Concession Speeches, PC21
Concessions, SC6
Concordance, IR454
Condorcet, Marie-Jean, SC266,
  SC269, SC278, SC282, SC283,
  SC289, SC310, SC560
Condorcet's Paradox, SC557, SC558
Conferences, IR225

Confessional Attachment, RP164
Confidence Heuristic, XX382
Confirmation Votes, LC455
Conflict, DC1-378/Special Section,
  IR364-432/Special Section, DP42,
  DP284, EP862, ET73, ET186,
  ET196, ET393, IR88, IR275,
  IR609, IR670, IR667, IR715,
  IR758, LC76, LC494, LE182, PG55,
  PG307
Conflict Analysis, SC372
Conflict Helix, DP65
Conflict Intensity, DC42, DC70,
  DC71, EP61, IR121, IR391, IR416,
  IR525, MP362
Conflict of Interest, DC51
Conflict Outcomes, IR732
Conflict Reduction, DC14, DC17,
  DC46, DC47, DC67, DC88, IR397,
  IR400, IR404, IR417, LC76, SC183
Conflict Situations, DC80
Conformity, AB14, XX34, XX378
Conformist Theories, SC57
Confrontation, IR784, XX393
Confucianism, LE590
Congitive Dissonance, XX202
Congress, CP274, EP143, EP659,
  EP668, EP729, EP765, EP789,
  ET349, IR474, IR587, LC31, LE2,
  LE33, LE42, LE45, LE46, LE117,
  LE139, LE189, LE203, LE208,
  LE270, LE292, LE297, LE302,
  LE316, LE359, LE363, LE372,
  LE378, LE387, LE393, LE408,
  LE410, LE412, LE431, LE435,
  LE441, LE446, LE452, LE453,
  LE464, LE474, LE475, LE491,
  LE502, LE509, LE510, LE514,
  LE520, LE526, LE528, LE529,
  LE560, LE617, LE621, LE623,
  LE627, LE631, LE635, LE653,
  LE654, LE657, LE662, LE663,
  LE666, LE668, LE669, LE670,
  LE673, LE676, LE681, LE702,
  LE707, MP197, MP227, MP229,
  MP341, PC15, PC171, PE111,
  PE214, PG141, PG271, PG286,
  PP145, PP158, PP162, PP212,
  PP352, PP427, RP146, RP175,
  SC112, SC175, SC176, SC192,
  SC197, SC284, SC299, SP457,
  SC772, SC776, SC791, SC805, also
  see Legislatures
Congressional Black Caucus, LE426
Congressional Budget Reform, PE67
Congressional Candidates, CP291,
  LE572, MP166
Congressional Careers, LE312-358/
  Special Section
Congressional District Attention,
  LE448, LE449
Congressional Dominance, EP675,
  LE438
Congressional Elections, CP219,
  CP223, LE310, LE558, LE564,
  LE567, LE591, LE595, PE160,
  PE176, PE185, PE187, PE220,
  PE254, PE429, PP50, PP59, PP69,
  PP92, PP138, PP141, PP149,
  PP157, PP172, PP177, PP178,
  PP181, PP186, PP197, PP209,
  PP217, PP228, also see
  Elections, and Elections and
  Economics, and Election of
  Minorities, and Midtern
  Elections
Congressional History, LE480
Congressional Institutions, LE473

Congressional Investigations,
  LE411
Congressional Mail, LE380
Congressional Nomination Proce-
  dures, MP342
Congressional Norms, ET330, ET345,
  ET346, ET356
Congressional Oversight, LE211,
  LE433
Congressional Parties, PP527
Congressional Procedures, LE360
Congressional Recruitment, LE351,
  LE376, LE523
Congressional Stability, LE548
Congressional Staff, LE466, LE501
Congressional Tenure, LE602
Congressional Testimony, MP308,
  TR153
Congruence Model, LE386
Conjectures, SC63
Connecticut, PS119
Connecticut Compromise, LC122
Conquest, IR725
Conscience, LC312
Consciousness, PA175, XX148
Consensus, AB253, DC34, ET393,
  SC357
Consensus Democracy, MP460
Consequence Thinking, MP317
Consequentialism, ET81
Conservatism, AB87, AB103, AB107,
  AB117, AB156, AB204, CP262,
  EP724, MP527, PA12
Conservative Coalition, LE429,
  LE442, LE505
Conservative Democrats, PP248
Conservative Mobilization, EP724
Conservative Party, PP315
Conservative Shift, PP97
Consistency, LE677, SC158, SC657
Consocializationalism, MP362,
  MP517, PS203
Consolidated Government, LC448
Conspiracy of 1808, DC120
Constabulary Duty, IR545
Constituencies, LE276-311/Special
  Section, EP238, LC455, LC460,
  LE277, LE292, LE626, PE396,
  SP493
Constituency Attitudes, LE281,
  LE309
Constituency Benefits, LE280
Constituency Change, LE287
Constituency Differences, LE294
Constituency Influence, IR592,
  LE17, LE284, LE286, LE299,
  LE301, LE302
Constituency Opinion, LE276,
  LE283, LE289, LE291, LE297,
  LE304, LE307, LE311
Constituency-Representative
  Linkages, LE308
Constituency Service, LE279,
  LE295, LE303, LE597
Constituency Size Effect, SC290
Constituency Trust, PP209
Constitution Making, LC102, LC103,
  LC126, LC130, LC131
Constitutional Amendments, CP99,
  LC128, LC158
Constitutional Analysis, LC125
Constitutional Change, LC111
Constitutional Choice, LC113,
  LC146, LC149
Constitutional Convention of 1787,
  LC131, LC132
Constitutional Conventions, LC110,
  LC112, LC122, LC132

Constitutional Guarantees, LC99
Constitutional Law, LC82, LC153
Constitutional Monarchy, PS56
Constitutional Political Economy,
    LC120
Constitutional Reform, LC143
Constitutionalism, LC129, LC144
Constitutions, LC95-159/Special
    Section, ET427, IR467, LC7,
    LE124, LE252, MP356, OB391,
    PE540, PS206
Construction, PP395
Construction Spending, SP357
Constructive Model, ET93
Consumer Behavior Perspective,
    SP47
Consumer Conflict, EP139
Consumer Model of Voting, PE227
Consumer Protection Legislation,
    EP597, EP600, SP422
Consumer Relationships, SC66
Consumption, EP106, PS325
Consumption Function, EP478
Contact Hypothesis, MP117, MP119,
    MP124, MP403
Contacting, PP136
Contagion, PG75-129/Special
    Section, DC235, DC367, IR246,
    IR718, IR799, IR800, PA268
Contempt of Congress, LE124
Content Analysis, AB270, IR192,
    LE59, PA91
Contested Exchange, XX281
Contests, SC481
Contextual Effects, AB7, AB39,
    AB78, CP2, CP187, CP256, CP295,
    ET457, LC246, MP160, MP388,
    PG14, PG48, PG52, PG93, PG94,
    PG99, PG100, PG101, PG112,
    PG113, PG114, PP186, PP246,
    RP75, XX45
Continental Congress, LE358, LE409
Contingency Theory of Constraining
    Effects, RP101
Contra Aid, AB273
Contract Awards, PE468
Contractarian Model, LC77, SC695,
    XX144
Contracting Out, SP84
Contracts, LC45, LC156, MP40
Contributions, CP124, LE275, PP75,
    PP98
Contributors, PP95, RP148
Control Systems, AB237
Control Theory, XX15
Controlling Government, LC416
Controlling Individuals, LC308
Controversy, LE3
Conventions, PP101-136/Special
    Section
Convergence, EP250, MP428, PG115,
    SP550
Convergent Realism, XX134
Conversations, PC44
Converse, Philip, AB188, PC222,
    PP249
Conversion, PP311, PP530, PP546,
    RP92
Convex Polytope Technique, SP206
Cooperation, ET148-198/Special
    Section, DP261, EP9, EP654,
    EP855, EP863, IR29, IR45, IR121,
    IR183, IR208, IR278, IR295,
    IR309, IR376, IR406, LC159,
    LC491, LE698, LE711, SP213,
    SP388, SC429, SC483
Cooperative Game Theory, SC417,
    SC487

Cooperative Rent Seeking, PE605
Cooperative Strategic Voting,
    SC782
Cooperatives, ET157, ET190, EP193
Cooperators' Advantage, ET136
Coordination, ET193, SC410
Coordination Games, MP452, SC398,
    SC431
COPE, DC320
Coping, ET94
Co-Plots, SP375
Coproduction, OB395, PE578, PP389
Core, IR843, IR849, IR871, LC134,
    LE252, PG13, also see Peripher-
    ies
Core of a Game, SC421, SC425,
    SC426, SC427, SC433
Core Beliefs, AB120, AB353, TR179
Core Intervention, DC157
Core-Periphery Interactions, PG65
Corporal Punishment, RP115
Corporate Crime, LC324
Corporate Ethical Action, ET369
Corporations, PE380
Corporatism, EP235, EP240, EP242,
    EP275, EP281, EP289, EP300,
    EP357, EP457, PE353, PE375, PS71
Corporatist Model of Growth, EP290
Corrections Policy, LC261
Correlates of War, IR646, IR814
Correlation Exponent, DP104
Corruption, PP350-438/Special
    Section, PS265
Cosociational Democracy, MP381
Cosponsors, LE419
Cost Commissions, SC70
Cost Containment, SP142
Cost of Living, DC267
Cost-Benefit Analysis, EP522,
    EP555, LC71, PA13, PA23, PA149,
    PE123, TR93
Cotton, MP58
Cotton Ginning, ET190
Counterfactuals, XX102
Counterforce Strategies, IR606
Counterinsurgency Warfare, IR781
Counterintelligence, IR81
Countermajoritarian Institutions,
    LC449
Counter-Revolution, DC125
Counterthreats, SC800
Country Size, EP262, EP316, EP348,
    EP385, EP655, EP707, EP866,
    IR34, IR857
County Seats, PG18, PG54, PG58
County Supervisors, LE601
Coup Contagion Hypothesis, DC112
Coup Trap, DC113
Coupon Rationing, EP580
Coups d'Etat, DC106-124/Special
    Section, DC258, ET217, IR562
Cournot Behavior, PE518
Cournot Competition, DP132
Cournot-Nash Oligopoly, EP625
Court Directives, LC401
Court of Justice, LC405
Court Packing, LC117
Courts, CP274, LC33, LC66, LC70,
    LC76, LC397, LC400, LE45
Courts of Appeals, LC3, LC391,
    LC424, LC427, MP326
Covariance Structure Analysis, CP3
Covariation, XX110
Covert Policing, LC487
CPS Election Studies, AB315
Crash Theory, DP51
Crashes, DP32, DP50, DP51

Creativity, PA343
Credibility, IR446, IR571, PA76,
    PA217, PE449, PP161
Credit Information Sharing, XX198
Credit Markets, MP213
Crime, LC160-300/Special Section,
    ET283, LC70, LC302, LC305,
    LC316, LC319, LC328, LC333,
    LC337, LC338, LC349, LC383,
    LC400, LC485, LC488, LC493,
    LC497, LC500, LC520, PC147,
    PC153, PC178, PP366
Crime Control Ideology, LC203
Crime News, PC147
Crime Perceptions, LC176, PC147
Crime Rate, LC172, LC174, LC180,
    LC183, LC187, LC189, LC199,
    LC227, LC230, LC245, LC248,
    LC317, LC483
Crime Statistics, LC184, LC264
Crime Waves, LC272, LC284, LC479
Crime's Social Consequences, LC335
Criminal Behavior, LC1-523/Special
    Section
Criminal Careers, LC168, LC169
Criminal Justice, LC167, LC182,
    LC228, LC260, LC265, LC300,
    LC309, LC367, LC415
Criminal Liability of Officials,
    PP404
Crises, OB196-231/Special Section,
    IR153, IR257, IR449, IR665,
    SP489
Crisis Bargaining, OB205, OB217,
    OB219, OB222
Crisis Decision Making, OB196-231/
    Special Section
Crisis Escalation, IR440, IR575
Crisis Forecasting, IR131
Crisis Management, OB201, OB203,
    OB224
Crisis of Confidence, EP127
Critical Elections, LC417, PP527,
    PP534, PP535, also see Realign-
    ments
Critical Intervention, IR126
Critical Legal Studies, LC88,
    LC89, LC197, LC498
Critical Mass, SC224, SC225
Critical Morality, AB391
Critical Points, IR681
Critical Race Theory, MP4, MP384
Critical Theory, PC23
Cross National Research, AB327
Cross Pressure, LE117
Cross Sectional Analysis, SP435
Crossover Voting, MP150, PP539
Cross-Sector Effects, EP510
Crowding, DC97, DC98, DC99, LC218,
    PG57
Crowding-Out, PE499
Crowds, DC212, SC418
Crusades, IR610
Crusading Journalism, PC105
Cuba, CP21, DC162, PS99
Cuban Exiles, MP494, MP495
Cuban Missile Crisis, OB196,
    OB202, OB206, OB208, OB227
Cuban Revolution, DC140
Cube Law, SC339, SC340
Cue Taking, LE478, LE622
Cues, CP212, PC92
Cult of the Offensive, IR812
Cults, RP51, SC210
Cultural Anthropology, XX286
Cultural Beliefs, PS30
Cultural Change, DP6

Cultural Conformity, ET461
Cultural Differences, OB98
Cultural Distinctiveness, PG263
Cultural Expression, XX347
Cultural Frontiers, PG242
Cultural Identity, MP7
Cultural Nationalism, MP459, MP469
Cultural Politics, MP466
Cultural Rights, ET227
Cultural Shock, RP89
Cultural Theory of Expenditure
  Growth, PE151
Cultural Theory, IR202, OB92,
  XX399
Culture, AB210, DC9, ET20, ET298,
  ET449, IR120, IR639, PC4, PS301,
  SC659, XX282, XX301, XX338,
  XX342, XX348, XX357
Cultures of Culture, XX27
Cumulative Causation, EP394
Cumulative Voting, MP162, MP404,
  SC250, SC286
Curriculum Change, SP209
Curvilinear Disparity, PP486
Cusp Catastrophe, DP52, DP57, DP62
Customs, DP6
Cutback Budgeting, PE62
Cybenetic Theory, TR182
Cycle of Relative Power, IR649
Cycles, DP165-285/Special Section,
  IR768, PE146, PE490, SC556,
  TR143
Cycles in America, PE371
Cycles in Senatorial Voting, SC231
Cycles of Illegality, LC272
Cycles of Protest, OB392
Cyclical Fluctuations, DC316
Cyclical Irregularities, DP72
Cyclical Majorities, LE691, LE692,
  SC544
Cycling Sets, SC542, SC543
Cynicism, CP22, MP382, PC172
Cyprus, IR405, OB236

Darwin, Charles, OB362, PA172
Darwinism, ET3, PA173, PS262
Data, CP249
Data Interpretation, XX72
Daughters, MP276
The Day After, PC123
Daylight Savings Time, SC116
De Forest, Robert Weeks, ET129
Dead Dictators, DC200
Deadlines, XX1
Deadlocks, XX56
Deadly Force, LC496
Dealignment, CP349, PP257, PP258,
  PP277, PP447, PP467, PP533
Death, LE108
Death Penalty, LC352-397/Special
  Section
Death Squads, DC366
Debates, LE20, PC29, PC43, PC197,
  PC208
Debt, PE84, PE120, PE140, PE414,
  PE417, PE420, PE424, PE427, also
  see International Debt
Debt Financing, PE80
Decade of Neglect Controversy,
  IR500
Decapitalization Thesis, PE8
Decay, CP292, PS282
Deceit, ET90
Decentralization, DP45, OB83,
  OB278, PS188, PS193, PS209
Deception, EP620, EP651, ET10,
  SC789

Decision Making, CP189, CP230,
  CP244, DP123, ET37, ET351,
  ET363, IR19, LC503, LE16, PA137,
  PA247, SC365, SC369, SC374,
  SC691, SC770, SC797, XX305
Decision Making Costs, LE225
Decision Making Groups, ET328
Decision Making in Crises, OB196-
  231/Special Section
Decision Making Networks, SP364
Decision Markets, ET285
Decision Rules, EP370, LE722, SC16
Decision Theory, SC130
Decisions, SP106
Declaring War, CP300, IR615
Decline, see Economic Decline
Decline in Confidence, XX92
Decolonization, EP199, PS228,
  PS239, PS240
Deconstruction, MP331
Deconstruction Methodological
  Falsification, XX360
Deducing Majority Candidates,
  CP232
Deducing Preferences, PP147
Deep South, MP58, also see
  Southern United States
Default Risk, SP320
Defeat, PC21
Defectors, ET137
Defense, EP214, EP345, EP400,
  IR398, IR465, IR467, IR495,
  IR507, IR511, IR535, IR543,
  IR694, LE641, SP119, SP466
Defense Acquisition, IR534
Defense of Values by Armed Force,
  IR694
Defense Policies, SC725
Defense Procurement, IR9
Defense Spending, EP231, EP234,
  EP321, EP322, EP335, EP346,
  EP349, IR35, LE259, IR269,
  IR313, IR319, IR354, IR377,
  IR471, IR473, IR481, IR487,
  IR488, IR493, IR494, IR495,
  IR496, IR509, IR510, IR514,
  IR515, IR519, IR520, IR522,
  IR523, IR527, IR528, IR530,
  IR544, IR548, IR551, IR556,
  IR559, IR562, IR563, IR809,
  LE276, LE280, LE694, OB47, PE39,
  PE607
Defensive Issue Voting Strategies,
  SC805
Deference, LC102, LE10
Deferential-Participant Politics,
  PG250
Deficit Cutting Politics, PE106
Deficit Financing, PE148
Deficits, EP527, EP804, PE65,
  PE83, PE84, PE98, PE103, PE139
Degradation Rituals, LE105
Deindustrialization, DC303, EP60
Deities, PG71, RP32
Delegate Theory of Representation,
  LE432
Delegates, PP130
Delinquency, LC319, LC332, LC517,
  RP90, RP100
Delphi Process, PA218
Demand Curves, PE504
Demand Elasticities, PE520
Demobilization, DC217
Democracy, PS100-175/Special
  Section, AB364, CP84, CP108,
  DC80, EP209, EP287, EP382,
  EP421, EP461, EP476, EP491,
  EP515, ET291, ET305, ET411,

IR10, IR30, LE36, IR50, IR92,
  IR99, IR165, IR252, IR386,
  IR401, IR641, IR688, LE712,
  IR713, IR730, IR740, IR743,
  IR774, IR777, IR780, IR792,
  IR796, IR797, IR827, IR828,
  LC306, LC486, MP381, OB90, PA32,
  PC26, PE298, PE331, PP479, PS9,
  PS25, PS177, RP24, SC86, SC91,
  SP181, SC266, SP499, SP511,
  XX327
Democracy and War, IR829
Democracy's Golden Age, CP171
Democratic Administration, OB88
Democratic Attitudes, PS118
Democratic Commitment, PS121,
  SP193
Democratic Consensus, DC358
Democratic Hypothesis, PE500
Democratic Institutions, EP860
Democratic Norms, PS151
Democratic Orientations, PS139
Democratic Performance, PS134
Democratic Personality, PS109
Democratic Stability, MP5
Democratic Systems, PA35, PS142
Democratic Theories, AB329
Democratic Transitions, DP109,
  PS303
Democratic Values, AB386, PS125
Democratization, PE356, PP456,
  PS101, PS140, PS160, PS175,
  PS251, PS309
Democrats, PP226, PP248
Demographic History, XX261
Demography, SP61-144/Special
  Section
Demonstrations, MP66
Demoralization, XX321
Denial, AB46, AB215, LE382, PP10,
  PS196
Denominationalism, OB351, also see
  Protestantism
Density Delay, OB330
Density Dependence, OB331, OB333
Density Gradients, PG75
Density Interaction, PG41
Dentists, PG138
Dependence Theory, PS111, PS217,
  PS218, PS221, PS230, PS227, also
  see Economic Dependence
Dependencia, PS221, PS223
Dependency, DC255, IR849, IR850
Dependent Industrialization, PE9
Depressants, PA171
Deprivation, AB350, DC253
Deracialization, MP113, MP194,
  MP523
Deregulation, EP554, EP560, EP578,
  EP595, EP599, EP602, EP603,
  EP608, EP621, EP633, EP637,
  EP647, EP662, EP667, EP669,
  PE564, also see Regulation
Derivation Processes, CP296
Desegregation, MP123, MP484
Desertion, IR472
Desocialization, PA171
Detente, IR365, PS81
Determinant Sentencing, LC329
Determinism, XX77
Deterrence, IR433-460/Special
  Section, LC301-338/Special
  Section, EP654, IR255, IR299,
  IR403, IR460, IR575, IR589,
  IR601, IR607, IR781, LC356,
  LC361, LC371, LC374, LC375,
  LC380, LC485, OB215
Deterrence Failure, IR440

Detroit, LC347
Devaluation, PS21
Developing Economies, EP245, EP331
Developing World, PP207
Development, DP166, DP193, DP215,
    DP259, EP155, EP209, EP211,
    EP230, EP232, EP246, EP251,
    EP261, EP272, EP291, EP302,
    EP314, EP316, EP325, EP329,
    EP341, EP355, EP363, EP371,
    EP387, EP391, EP392, EP393,
    EP409, EP481, EP486, EP690,
    EP701, IR359, LC170, LC263,
    LC298, OB379, PA274, PA341,
    PE417, PS271, RP64, SP185,
    SP339, TR21, TR73, TR105, TR136,
    also see Economic Growth, and
    Industrial Policy, and Political
    Development
Development Administration, OB98
Development Aid, IR363
Development Democracy Growth
    Hypothhesis, PS294
Development Economics, EP228,
    EP229, EP394, EP407, also see
    Economic Growth
Development State, EP330
Deviance, LC258, LC295, PP413,
    RP101
Deviance Amplification, RP90
Deviance Deterrence, RP90
Deviant Children, OB191
Deviant Groups, PC149
Deviants, XX103
Devil's Staircase, DP103
Devolution, PG290
Devonshire, DC201
Demoralized Society, ET43
Depoliticizing of Political
    Theory, ET103
Diachronic Analysis, LE378
Dictatorship, LE338, PS260, PS261,
    PS292, SC489, SC499
Difference Maximizing, ET123
Difference Principles, XX206
Differences within Systems, XX379
Differentiable Viewpoint, SC453
Differential Game, IR312
Differential Topology, TR147
Differentiation, AB51, MP134,
    OB327, OB347, OB354
Difficult People, ET401
Diffuse Support, CP30
Diffusion, PA258-344/Special
    Section, DC64, DC201, DC235,
    DC271, IR654, IR747, IR787,
    MP255, OB27, OB367, PA326,
    PC124, PC125, PG89, PG96, PG109,
    PS312, SP468
Diffusion of Power, PS211
Dignity, ET206
Dimensional Variation, SC36
Dimensionality, LE686
Diminishing Utility, EP207
Diplomacy, EP856, ET442, IR151
Diplomatic History, IR178
Diplomatic Method, IR59
Direct Democracy, CP75-102/Special
    Section, AB243, DC315, EP702,
    EP760, LC116, MP525, OB158,
    PE78, PE167, PE259, PE551,
    PG151, PP224, PP360, PP423,
    RP165, SC795
Direct Elections, LE651
Direct Legislation, CP89, CP90,
    CP91
Direct Primaries, PP113
Direct Voting, EP663

Director's Law, EP509
Disability Policy, SP61, SP123,
    SP124
Disarmament, IR279, IR294, also
    see Arms Races
Disarmament Treaties, IR294
Disaster Avoidance, OB202
Disasters, ET348, OB197, OB202,
    PA88, XX51
Disciplinary Response, LC503
Discontent, CP17, CP45, DC208,
    DC54, EP479
Discourse, ET405
Discourse Analysis, PC86
Discourse Methodology, XX16
Discovery, TR184
Discretion, PP418
Discretionary Jurisdiction, LC392
Discrimination, MP52-142/Special
    Section, ET172, MP21, MP41,
    MP98, MP213, MP234, MP370, SP248
Discussion, CP79, PC136
Diseases, PG120
Disenfranchisement, MP239
Disequilibrium, OB274
Disequilibrium of Majority Rule,
    SC575
Disintegration, DC116, MP507,
    PG279
Dismissal, OB73
Displacement Effect, OB259
Dispute Escalation, IR112, IR427
Disputes, DC83
Dissent, DC36, DP24, ET226, ET229,
    ET389, LC325, LC391
Dissidence, LE503
Dissidents, DC31, DC205
Dissipate Structures, DC126, OB49
Dissociative Hypothesis, CP42
Distortions, XX255
Distribution, EP740
Distributional Axioms, SC56
Distributional Coalitions, EP402,
    PE315
Distributional Information, XX56
Distributive Injustice, AB340
Distributive Justice, ET270,
    ET274, ET277, ET279, ET297,
    ET311
Distributive Politics, EP142,
    LE377, LE715, SP383
Distributive Theory of Military
    Policy Making, IR542
District Council Economic
    Policies, EP99
District Judges, LC443
District Magnitude, PP345
Districts, SC328
Distrust, AB276, PG178
Disturbances, PE38
Diversity, OB41, PA335
Divided Government, EP841, LC143,
    LC147, LE5, LE15, LE31, LE513,
    PE59, PE486, PP22
Division Lists, LE633
Division of Labor, EP224, OB354,
    PG152
Division of Powers, LC108, LE516
Division of Scholarly Labor, PA131
Divorce, SP140
Docks, DC332
Doctrine, IR469, IR525
Domains, SC504, SC505
Domestic Audiences, IR378
Domestic Conflict, DC1-378/Special
    Section
Domestic Content Legislation,
    EP571

Domestic Crisis, OB226
Domestic Discontent, DC54
Domestic Disputes, IR766
Domestic Economic Policy, EP59-
    153/Special Section
Domestic Expenditures, EP136,
    PE143
Domestic Politics, AB242, IR151,
    IR776
Donagan-Aquinas Thesis, AB292
Double Standards, PG317
Douglas-Wildavsky Theory, PS301
Doves, AB229, AB237, AB276, AB287,
    IR421
Downs, Anthony, PP341
Downsian Model, CP277, SC290,
    SC735
Downward Sloping Curves, PP159
Dramaturgical Themes, PP168
Drinking, SP93
Drinking Age, SP85
Drinking and Driving, SP111, XX251
Dropping Out, PG87
Drought, TR99
Drug Addiction, DP57
Drug Offenders, SP77
Drug Policy, SP92, SP118
Drugs, EP640, SP63, SP67, SP71,
    SP94, SP106, SP137, SP138
Dualism, EP481
Due Process, ET203, OB111
Duke, David, MP418
Dulles, John Foster, AB249, AB295
Duopoly, PS114
Duration Dependence, IR639
Duration Model, SP553
Duration of Political Control,
    LE585
Duration of Reigns, LE608
Durkheim, Emile, LC227, RP63,
    RP88, RP99, RP102
Duty, ET423
Duverger's Law, PP466, PP470,
    PP479, PP511, PP512, PP516,
    PP519, PP520
Dworkin, Gerald, XX353
Dworkin's Rights Thesis, ET61
Dyadic Communication, PC87
Dyadic Systems, DP2
Dyads, IR330, IR367, IR630, IR429,
    IR617, IR662, IR778
Dynamic Processes, DP1-285/Special
    Section, PE522, SC378
Dynamic Economic Systems, DP4,
    DP43, DP97, XX87
Dynamic Games, DP36, SC458, SC459
Dynamic Market Processes, XX64
Dynamic Modeling, DP108, PP288
Dynamic Systems, DP29, DP96
Dynastic Cycle, DP155, DP242,
    DP279

Early American Republic, PG250
Earmarking, EP689, EP755, PE617
Earnings, EP180, EP416, ET289,
    also see Income
Earnings Inequality, EP470, MP30,
    MP485, also see Income
Earthquakes, DP153
Easterlin Hypothesis, LC241,
    LC281, XX264
Eastern Europe, CP224, CP226,
    DC309, EP286, IR412, LC129,
    LE552, PE513, PE540, PP14,
    PP449, PS90, PS94, PS148, PS273
East-West Confrontation, IR214
Ecclesiastes Hypothesis, TR190
Ecological Collapses, SP83

Ecological Demography, PA185
Ecological Dumping, TR113
Ecological Economics, ET14
Ecological Fallacy, PE226
Ecological Models, OB324-
    370/Special Section, DP53,
    DP119, LC193, LC291, LC293,
    LC434, PA160, PE364, PG16, PG35,
    PG119, PG156, PG248, SP504
Ecological Policy, TR126
Econometric Models, DP114, PA71,
    PA110
Economic Activity, RP67
Economic Advice, SC212
Economic Agendas, EP49
Economic Analysis, XX167
Economic Analysis of Crime and
    Law, LC11, LC19, LC90, LC92,
    LC93, LC196, LC289, LC292,
    LC303, LC335, SC62
Economic Aspirations, PE194
Economic Behavior, EP52
Economic Change, PA283, PE188
Economic Cleavages, PE193
Economic Competition, EP152, PE16,
    PE169
Economic Conditions, LC234, PE153,
    PE155, PE161, PE166, PE167,
    PE184, PE185, PE199, PE229,
    PE239, PE242, PE244, PE245,
    PE262, PE270, PE276, PE281,
    PE291, PE484, also see Elections
    and Economics
Economic Contradictions, PS113
Economic Crises, OB204, PE190,
    PS27
Economic Cycles, DP165-233/Special
    Section, IR815, LC167
Economic Data, DP95
Economic Decisions, LC469
Economic Decline, DP45, EP69,
    EP70, EP130, EP274, LC234, also
    see Productivity Growth Decline
Economic Dependence, EP230, EP244,
    EP249, EP257, EP263, EP315,
    EP343, EP368, EP375, EP391,
    EP392, EP403, IR639, PS277,
    SP522, also see Dependence
    Theory
Economic Deprivation, LC181
Economic Development, see Economic
    Growth
Economic Development Authorities,
    EP70
Economic Discontent, PE34, PE220
Economic Environments, SC37
Economic Evaluations, EP22, PE178,
    PE261, also see Economics and
    Elections
Economic Events, PE186, PE286
Economic Evolution, PS35
Economic Expectations, PE200,
    PE267
Economic Factors, LC215
Economic Flexibility, EP51
Economic Fluctuations, IR334
Economic Forecasts, EP78, PE112
Economic Geography, PG9, XX114
Economic Growth, EP197-410/Special
    Section, AB367, DP45, DP116,
    DP120, DP223, EP123, EP161,
    EP202, EP342, EP418, EP420,
    EP431, EP434, EP436, EP454,
    EP458, EP502, EP523, EP526,
    EP529, EP535, EP537, EP714,
    EP727, EP734, EP740, EP744,
    EP762, EP788, IR346, IR556,
    IR807, LC109, LC201, LC256,

LC385, LC386, MP17, MP18, MP264,
    MP374, OB127, OB242, OB270,
    OB349, PE8, PE313, PE316, PE317,
    PE318, PE329, PE332, PE335,
    PE348, PE366, PE369, PE384,
    PE419, PE593, PE609, PE612,
    PG22, PG35, PG135, PP387, PP408,
    PS15, PS115, PS134, PS164,
    PS278, SP293, SP319, SP348,
    SP366, SP419, SP426, SP469,
    SP546, TR18, TR42, also see
    Development, and Industrial
    Policy
Economic History, EP57, XX287
Economic Hypotheses, XX68
Economic Incentives, IR26
Economic Indicators, PA291
Economic Individualism, AB119
Economic Inequality, DC50, DC81
Economic Integration, EP102, PS1
Economic Issues, PE219
Economic Justice, ET251, ET303
Economic Justification for
    Government, OB292
Economic Liberalization, PS175
Economic Liberty, EP134, LC98
Economic Man, ET123, SC43
Economic Observations, EP861
Economic Openness, EP388
Economic Outcomes, PE207
Economic Output, SP251
Economic Performance, DC288, EP40,
    EP223, EP293, EP604, PE19,
    PE171, PE172, PE174, PE197
Economic Policy, EP1-872/Special
    Section, ET78, LE491, PA325,
    PE164, PE246
Economic Power, EP50
Economic Problems, PE218
Economic Psychology, XX304
Economic Rationality, ET74, SC623,
    SC658
Economic Reasoning, ET431
Economic Reform, DP66, EP90,
    EP133, PS17
Economic Revitalization, EP44
Economic Rights, ET45
Economic Sanctions, IR44, IR149
Economic Security, AB368
Economic Slowdown, EP117
Economic Socialization, AB372,
    AB377
Economic Stability, IR277, PE83
Economic Stagnation, PE315
Economic Statistics, EP21
Economic Strategies, EP36
Economic Structure, IR20
Economic Systems, DP19, EP13, PS3,
    PS38
Economic Theory, SC32, SC651, TR98
Economic Theories of Politics,
    SC1-805/Special Section, CP314,
    EP785, LE629
Economic Theories of Voting,
Economic Thought, ET266
Economic Time Series, DP189,
    DP214, DP221
Economic Values, EP55
Economic Voting, CP323, PE116,
    PE170, PE236, PE241, PE252,
    PE257, PE264, PE268, PE271,
    PE280, PE282, PE284, PE287
Economic Welfare, RP123
Economical Behavior, DP164
Economics, LC14, LC15, LC17, LC38,
    PA168, SC131, SC635, SC713,
    XX28, XX53, XX138, XX174, XX289,
    XX325

Economics and Elections, PC153-
    293/Special Section, LE161
Economies of Scale, OB304, SP313
Economies of States, SP314
Economists, LC42
Economists' Models, XX71
Economy, EP22, PE243, PE273, XX407
Economy and Society Perspective,
    PE53
Ecosystems, DP110, TR76
Editorials, PC28
Education, SP145-256/Special
    Section, AB93, AB150, CP68,
    CP129, DC209, DC278, EP214,
    EP328, EP506, EP711, ET452,
    ET456, ET468, MP86, MP164,
    MP400, OB155, OB357, PA260,
    PE519, SP5
Effective Support, CP65
Efficacy, AB313, CP3, CP18, CP25,
    CP27, CP30, CP49, CP72, CP60,
    CP62, PC188, PG258, PS14, XX136
Efficiency, CP86, ET314, PA16,
    SC158, XX40, XX211
Egalitarianism, ET123, SC81, XX206
Ego Psychological Theory of
    Personality, XX41
Egoism, SC80
Egoistic Rationality, SC644
El Paso, MP160
Elasticity, AB18, OB239
Elation, CP179
Elazar, Daniel, PG274, PG306,
    PG309
Election Calendars, CP114
Election Cycles, DP237, DP252,
    DP261, DP280, LE391
Election Experiments, CP248, CP262
Election Forecasts, CP156, CP225,
    CP242
Election Fraud, PP423
Election Frequency, SC231
Election Laws, see Electoral
    Systems
Election Manifestos, PE170
Election Margins, LE537-617/
    Special Section, CP139, LE286,
    LE292, LE509, LE577, LE674,
    PP78, PP333, PP481, SC9, SC752
Election Night Reporting, CP131
Election of 1840, XX106
Election of Minorities, MP143-
    200/Special Section
Election Polls, PE36
Election Programmes, PP108
Election Reform, SC263, SC292,
    SC309, SC325
Election Riots, DC222
Election Studies, AB315, CP347
Elections, PP137-235/Special
    Section, AB2, AB324, CP77,
    CP149, CP174, CP178, CP219,
    CP214, CP223, CP224, CP226,
    CP227, CP228, CP252, CP263,
    CP266, CP287, CP289, CP332,
    CP346, CP348, DC281, DC334,
    DP234, LC472, LE84, LE540,
    LE599, LE643, PC196, PE5, PE10,
    PE36, PE163, PE174, PE201,
    PE228, PE274, PE437, PE462, PG7,
    PG56, PG92, PG107, PG229, PG273,
    PG296, PP23, PP50, PP59, PP63,
    PP69, PP70, PP92, PP104, PP137,
    PP138, PP141, PP149, PP157,
    PP166, PP172, PP177, PP178,
    PP181, PP184, PP186, PP189,
    PP191, PP197, PP207, PP209,
    PP215, PP216, PP217, PP224,

PP227, PP228, PP230, PP381,
PP446, PP460, PP541, RP144,
RP162, SC87, SC112, SC153,
SC278, SC288, SC341, SC550,
SC741, SC737, SC743, SC744,
SC745, SC746, SC748, SC762,
SP352, XX298, also see Citizen
Participation, and Congressional
Elections, and Election of
Minorities, and Midterm
Elections, and Political Parties
Elections and Economics, PC153-
293/Special Section
Electoral Accountability, LE52,
PE164
Electoral Activities, CP148
Electoral Behavior, CP192, CP243,
CP256
Electoral Bias, PP170
Electoral Budget Cycle, PE440
Electoral Change, CP317, LE404,
PP311, PP448
Electoral Choice, CP282, CP306,
PP286
Electoral Coalitions, CP197
Electoral College, LE133, SC236,
SC242, SC304
Electoral Competitiveness, see
Election Margins
Electoral Connection, LE330,
LE480, LE507, MP184
Electoral Cycle, CP273, IR152,
IR563, LE53, PE39, PE42, PE431,
PE486, PP491
Electoral Districts, SC238
Electoral Equilibria, PC61, SC152,
SC256
Electoral Flows, CP352
Electoral Games, SC403
Electoral Geography, MP423, PG72
Electoral Insecurity, LE539,
LE555, also see Election Margins
Electoral Instability, SC739
Electoral Investment, CP215
Electoral Laws, SC241, SC307, also
see Electoral Systems
Electoral Market, PP15
Electoral Mobilization, MP79,
PP334
Electoral Motive, EP151, LE496,
PE498
Electoral Oscillation, CP155
Electoral Procedures, see
Electoral Systems
Electoral Process, PE382, PP160
Electoral Retribution, EP742
Electoral Rewards, PP17
Electoral Rules, SC242
Electoral Safety, LE557
Electoral Schemes, SC244
Electoral Strategy, SC233
Electoral Stress, EP115
Electoral Success, CP135, CP281
Electoral Swing, PP170
Electoral Systems, SC230-349/
Special Section, MP151, MP158,
PE511, PG23, PP420, SC786
Electoral Volatility, PP164, PP502
Electorate, CP351
Electronic Democracy, PS168
Elite Circulation, LE68
Elite Socialization, LE49
Elite Stratification, PG222
Elite Succession, see Turnover
Elites, AB61, AB112, AB140, AB154,
AB195, AB215, AB291, AB304,
AB305, AB348, ET462, ET474,
ET480, IR510, LC421, LE9, LE11,

LE12, LE25, LE28, LE54, LE298,
LE337, LE590, MP266, MP282,
MP305, OB226, PC60, PE396, PP42,
PP259, PP292, RP81, RP135,
RP161, RP166, SC598, SP343,
TR106, XX228, XX332
Elitist Theory, PS171
Emancipatory Movements, PS104
Embezzlement, PP368
Emergency Management, OB224
Emergent Social Phenomena, DP155
Emotional Reactions, LE174, XX235
Emotional Reactions to the
Economy, PE180
Emotions, AB40, AB49
Empathy, ET29, ET213
Empire, DC155, DC206, IR732,
PS216, PS232, PS234, PS241,
PS243, RP16
Empiricism, XX248
Employee Attitudes, OB86, OB128
Employment, EP154-196/Special
Section, DC307, EP429, MP21,
MP354, MP390, PE173
Encompassing Organization Theory,
PE353
End of the Cold War, IR25, IR42,
IR74, IR157
End of Wars, IR741
Endangered Species, TR123
Endogenous Timing, OB28
Endorsements, AB80, PC128, PC189
Enduring Rivalries, IR383, IR384
Enemies, AB247, AB263, AB265,
ET11, IR475
Energy, LE445, SC376, TR44
Energy Conservation, TR89
Energy Crisis, EP577, TR112, TR120
Energy Policy, LE196, TR49, TR109,
TR133
Energy Tax Legislation, SC284
Enfield Monster, PG110
Enforcement, LC187, LC327
Engel Curves, ET126
England, RP35, RP79, RP163, SP72,
TR166, XX49, also see United
Kingdom
Enlistees, IR486, IR497
Enterprise Zones, SP438
Enthusiasm, CP37
Entitlements, PE407
Entrepreneurial Activity, ET9,
OB191, PA309, SC693
Entropy, PA5
Entropy Maximization, CP253
Entry, CP33
Entry Deterrence, PE595
Environment, TR44-136/Special
Section, AB22, DP77, ET270,
IR520, LE294, RP120, RP121
Environmental Change, TR79, TR80,
TR97
Environmental Economics, EP552
Environmental Impact Statements,
TR101
Environmental Law, EP574
Environmental Movement, MP228
Environmental Policy, SC376
Environmental Protection Agency,
EP570, TR94
Environmental Regulation, PG134
Environmental Sustainability, TR55
Envy, EP19, OB103, SC422
Epidemiology, IR680, PG79, PG85,
PG87, PP81
Epistemology, ET409
Epochs, DP216
Equal Employment Law, MP46

Equal Opportunity, MP49, MP290
Equal Protection, SP220
Equal Rights Amendment, MP282,
MP285, MP295, MP352
Equality, ET260, ET269, ET272,
ET282, ET284, EP461, MP55,
PS129, PS135, PS316, SC695,
SP248, SP336
Equilibrium, CP125, CP221, DP31,
DP98, IR343, LE267, LE472, SC59,
SC65, SC92, SC126, SC392, SC403,
SC415, SC424, SC440, SC446,
SC456, SC465, SC466, SC469,
SC479, SC518, SC537, SC543,
SC738
Equilibrium Cycle, DP274
Equity, DP55, EP233, ET256, ET268,
ET314
Erikson Hypothesis, PC28
Error Correction Model, DC266
Error Variance, AB77
Escalation, IR253, IR271, IR274,
IR335, IR336, IR340, IR369,
IR375, IR438, IR589, IR683,
IR784, OB222
Essence of Decision, OB228
Essences, DP216
Establishment Violence, DC68
Ethclass Analysis, MP420
Ethical Analysis, ET382
Ethical Attitudes, EP774
Ethical Beliefs, AB298
Ethical Codes, ET437
Ethical Decision Making, ET363
Ethical Discourse, ET383
Ethical Guidance, ET413
Ethical Overlays, ET387
Ethical Political Behavior, ET417
Ethical Politics, ET434
Ethical Rules, ET118
Ethical Theory, ET26, ET367
Ethical Value Systems, ET72
Ethical Vice Industry, SP9
Ethical Voters, CP151, ET130
Ethical Work Climates, ET110
Ethics, ET1-484/Special Section,
AB339, CP151, EP41, IR166,
IR835, LC58, TR74, TR121
Ethics and Politics, ET398
Ethics Investigations, PP401
Ethics Laws, ET391
Ethnic Antagonism, MP377, PA191
Ethnic Boundaries, MP475
Ethnic Competition, MP9
Ethnic Conflict, IR370, MP122,
MP385, MP431, MP433, MP436,
MP386, MP478, MP501, MP504,
MP507, PP361
Ethnic Diversity, MP5, MP371
Ethnic Dual Party Systems, PP493
Ethnic Economy, MP29
Ethnic Equalization Hypothesis,
MP16
Ethnic Groups, ET467, MP26, MP399,
MP434
Ethnic Identity, MP12, MP415,
MP429, MP438, MP490
Ethnic Minorities, PG251
Ethnic Mobilization, MP474
Ethnic Model, MP464
Ethnic Nationalism, MP440, MP465,
MP472
Ethnic Perceptions, MP494
Ethnic Phenomena, MP20
Ethnic Political Culture, MP477
Ethnic Politics, MP360-530/Special
Section
Ethnic Relations, MP514

Ethnic Revival, MP468
Ethnic Skill Differentials, MP3,
    MP378
Ethnic Solidarity, MP481
Ethnic Succession, MP31
Ethnicity, IR830, LC495, MP1,
    MP10, MP19, MP27, MP163, MP365,
    MP369, MP393, MP405, MP432,
    MP457, MP458, MP467, MP477,
    MP496, MP502, MP503, MP509,
    MP516, PG211, PS274, RP74, SP264
Ethnicization, PG161
Ethnocentrism, AB162
Ethnocultural Conflict, MP525
Ethnocultural Model of Voting,
    MP200
Ethnographic Approach, XX253
Ethnonationalism, MP392
Ethnopolitical Conflict, IR844
Ethnoregional Parties, PG299
Ethology, PA188
Ethos Theory, MP399
Euclidean Theories, SC761
Euler Buckling, DP59
Eurobarometer, PP304
Europe, AB344, AB358, AB365, CP52,
    CP93, CP351, DC144, DC206,
    DC291, DP182, DP133 EP79, EP159,
    EP168, EP870, ET188, IR225,
    IR236, IR572, IR750, LE12, LE80,
    LE89, LE92, LE357, LE366, LE457,
    MP290, PE17, PE20, PE45, PG242,
    PG270, PP11, PP12, PP34, PP281,
    PP442, PP484, PS12, PS24, PS54,
    PS79, PS96, PS288, RP60, RP78,
    RP80, SC160, SC161, SC162,
    SP169, SP230, SC369, SP517,
    TR118, XX94, XX140
European Community, CP95, DC303,
    PE341, PS2, PS24, PS34, PS64,
    SC346
European Constitution, LC108
European Integration, ET188, PE25,
    PS24, PS26, PS65
European Monetary System, PE26
European Parliamentary Elections,
    CP174
European Party System, PP502
European State System, IR861
European Union, LC405
European Union Council of
    Ministers, SC294
Evaluating Theoretical Predic-
    tions, SC189
Evaluation, PA210-257/Special
    Section, PA95, PA131, SP195
Evaluation Research Methods, SP195
Evaluative Bias Heuristics, AB190
Evangelicals, RP136, RP137, RP138,
    RP157
Evasion, EP732
Event History Analysis, LE65,
    XX133
Events, AB282, XX388
Events Data, IR114
Evidence, LC29
Evil, IR699
Evolution, AB358, DP14, DP119,
    DC126, DP143, ET118, ET141,
    ET146, ET152, ET154, ET155,
    ET169, ET172, ET178, ET194,
    ET323, ET326, ET329, IR276,
    IR692, IR838, LC230, LC291,
    OB330, OB331, OB346, PA152,
    PA159, PA164, PA172, PA175,
    PA188, PA189, PA192, PA193,
    PA208, PA327, PC38, PS35, PS45,
    PS80, PS88, PP267, PS272, PP354,

SC12, SC420, SC454, SC802,
    SP324, XX157, XX310
Evolutionary Biology, PA176,
    PA180, PA181, PA184
Evolutionary Dynamics, SC222,
    SC468
Evolutionary Materialism, XX310
Evolutionary Politics, PA194
Evolutionary Systems, PA153
Exactions, EP746
Excessive Government, OB240, OB245
Exchange Analysis, LE178
Exchange Behavior, IR204
Exchange Bias, PE5
Exchange Hypotheses, LE394
Exchange Networks, SC606, SC609
Exchange Norms, ET341
Exchange Processes, XX218
Exchange Rates, see Foreign
    Exchange Rates
Exchange Relationships, OB46
Exchange Structures, ET59
Exchange Theory, PE397
Exchanges, OB50
Excise Tax, EP759
Exclusion, SC606
Exclusionary Rule, LC408
Excuses, XX232
Executions, LC355, LC366, LC382,
    MP114
Executive Compensation, OB87
Executive Popularity, PE233
Executive Veto, LE128
Executives, LE1-723/Special
    Section
Executive-Legislative Relations,
    LE44, LE415
Exit, EP11, ET107, ET137, OB46,
    PE539
Exit Polls, CP324
Expectation States Theory, PG104
Expectation-Disillusion Theory,
    LE183
Expectations, IR308
Expected Loss, PP180
Expected Utility, DC82, DC174,
    EP862, IR621, IR625, IR627,
    IR818, SC118, SC619, SC622,
    SC625, SC629
Expenditure Effects, PP71
Expenditure Growth, OB272
Expenditure Restraint, SP498
Expenditure Tradeoffs, SP344
Expenditures, EP444, EP717, PE72
Experimental Elections, CP248,
    CP262
Experimental Group Research, XX32
Experimental Organizations, OB3
Experimental Physics, TR145
Experiments, CP263
Expert Behavior, XX295
Expert Systems, AB297
Expertise, XX203, XX234
Explanation, DP4, XX53, XX76,
    XX90, XX340
Exploitation, EP392, PE46
Exploratory Data Analysis, XX119
Exponential Survival, LE69
Export-Led Growth Hypothesis,
    EP336, EP338
Export Subsidies, EP802
Exports, DP174, EP366, EP802, TR26
Exposure Thesis, PP206
Expressive Displays, XX235
Expressive Voting, DC286
Expropriative Crime, LC193, LC291
Extended Family, ET126

Extensive Form Games, PE324,
    SC406, SC455, SC645
External Capital, EP376
External Use of Force, DC54
Externalities, EP629, EP643,
    EP588, LE722
Externality Games, SC109
Extinction, TR47, TR128
Extortion, LC269, PE585
Extreme Performance, OB142
Extremist Parties, PP510

Facial Displays, LE56, XX367
Factions, LE508, LE534, PG86,
    PG123
Factor Supplier Pressure Group
    Hypothesis, PE320
Factory Fatalities, EP556
Facts, PA111
Faculty Elites, PP283
Fads, DP1, DP6, SC604
Fairness, CP297, ET52, ET250,
    ET256, ET258, ET267, ET281,
    ET294, ET299, ET301, ET304,
    ET315, ET316, ET317, LC152,
    MP48, SC200, SC404, TR91
Faithfully Representative Commit-
    tees, LE224
Falkland Islands War, IR659, IR675
Familial Status, MP78
Family, ET126, LE376, MP304, PC25,
    SP285, XX354
Family Values, AB339
Famine, DP242
Fantasy Theme Analysis, PC16
Farm and City, EP459
Farm Policy, LE688, TR14, TR16,
    TR34
Farmers' Associations, TR30
Faroe Islands, PG256
Farquharson, Robin, LE282, SC251,
    SC315, SC778
Fascism, PP247, PS248, PS249
Fashion, DP6, XX4
Fast Breeder Reactor, TR168
Favored Minorities, SC314
Favorite Sons, LE27
Favorites, SC467
Fear, LC294, SC443
Fear of Crime, LC206, LC285
Fear of Government, ET471
Federal Agencies, LC80
Federal Aid, PA50, SP310
Federal Communications Commission,
    EP564, EP568, PE334
Federal Courts, MP326
Federal Expenditures, PE119
Federal Grants, LE708, SP346,
    SP354
Federal Implementation, EP674
Federal Judiciary, LC476
Federal Lands, PG34
Federal Preemption, PS208
Federal Reserve, EP98, EP111, PE7,
    PE431, PE432, PE437, PE438,
    PE453
Federal Spending, EP694, LE706,
    LE713, OB309, PE67, PE187
Federal States, IR63, IR150,
    PS178, PS201
Federal Trade Commission, EP568
Federalism, PS176-214/Special
    Section, LC116, MP496, OB269,
    OB271, PE280, PE368, PG198,
    PS176, PS177, PS179, PS181,
    SP532
Feedback Bias, SC19, SC287
Feit's Hypothesis, PS259

Female Activism, MP195
Female Candidates, MP178, MP198,
  MP245, MP257
Female Communities, MP314
Female Economic Activity, MP247
Female Legislators, SP20
Female Political Activity, SP45
Feminism, MP204, MP209, MP211,
  MP220, MP221, MP224, MP235,
  MP236, MP237, MP258, MP269,
  MP293, MP299, MP306, MP312,
  MP316, MP355, SP45
Feminist Consciousness, MP225,
  MP226, MP350
Fenno, Richard, LE282, SC778
Fertility, SP79, SP127
Festinger, Leon, XX202
Fiery Chariot, LE106
Fifty Year Pulsation in Human
  Affairs, DP262
Films, PC2
Finance, EP87, EP811
Finance Industry, PP53
Financial Conditions, MP347
Financial Crises, DP176
Financial Deregulation, EP566
Financial Institutions, EP122
Financial Liberalization, EP92,
  EP141
Financial Markets, EP615, EP647
Financial Panics, DP17
Financial Services, EP75
Finland, OB392, PA259, PA292,
  PC151, SP497
Fiorina, Morris, LE5
Fire Service, DP134
Firearms, LC340, LC344, LC347
Firemen, OB400
Firm Diversification, DC330
Firm Size, PA309
Firms, OB9, OB349, PE382, SC693,
  XX173
First Elections, CP226, CP332
First Strike, IR606
Fiscal Behavior, IR348
Fiscal Conservatives, PE263
Fiscal Crises, PE130, SP401
Fiscal Decentralization, OB290
Fiscal Deficits, PE65
Fiscal Federalism, PS194, SP532
Fiscal Ideology, SP332
Fiscal Illusion, EP115, EP728,
  OB298, OB323, SP350, SP355
Fiscal Impact, CP272
Fiscal Institutions, PE59
Fiscal Model, PE183
Fiscal Policy, EP61, EP223, EP444,
  EP531, EP687, EP712, EP724,
  EP765, IR489, PE71, PE79, PE99,
  PE114, PE439, PE444, SP320
Fiscal Stress, OB298, SP252,
  SP334, SP404
Fiscal Variables, EP340
Fits of Morality, ET400
Flag Burning, LE297
Flanders, PP349
Flatland, XX230
Flatlaw, ET102
Flemish Movement, MP480
Flexible Work Hours, OB89
Floating Vote, CP349, PP309
Floor Behavior, LE268, LE270
Florida, EP702, SP378
Florida's Tax Amendment One, EP713
Floridation, SP134
Flow-of-Vote Estimates, CP187
Folk Ideologies, AB183
Folk Theorem, SC44, SC408

Folkways, ET349
Followership, LE23
Food, TR9, TR17, TR34
Force, DC54, ET342, IR762, LE162
Forecasting, AB219, PA81, PA83,
  DP90, DP91, DP93, PA136, PA151,
  PA223
Forecasting Bias, EP4, EP699
Forecasting the Forecasts of
  Others, PA144
Foreign Affairs, PC159, PC160
Foreign Affairs Images, IR60
Foreign Aid, IR344-363/Special
  Section, DC121
Foreign Debt, PE418, PE419
Foreign Economic Policy, EP825,
  EP830, IR69
Foreign Exchange Markets, DP23
Foreign Exchange Rates, DP71,
  DP204, EP14, EP48, PE23, PE36
Foreign Investment, EP5, EP54,
  EP145, EP218, EP305, EP333,
  IR346, PE421, PP88, PS50
Foreign Language Instruction,
  SP149
Foreign Ministers, IR123
Foreign Monopoly Rents, EP801
Foreign Policy, AB231, AB234,
  AB240, AB250, AB283, ET207,
  ET355, ET403, ET441, ET444, IR1,
  IR4, IR11, IR19, IR21, IR23,
  IR37, IR43, IR48, IR50, IR52,
  IR53, IR61, IR63, IR84, IR92,
  IR108, IR109, IR117, IR124,
  IR132, IR135, IR143, IR152,
  IR156, IR168, IR171, IR172,
  IR173, IR179, IR198, IR215,
  IR276, IR614, IR674, LE101,
  LE136, LE150, LE153, LE160,
  LE172, LE431, MP333, OB207,
  OB227, PE292, RP130
Foreign Policy Attitudes, AB225-
  308/Special Section
Foreign Policy Events, AB248
Foreign Policy Indicators, IR785
Foreign Policy Officials, AB271,
  AB284, AB285, IR51, IR154, IR201
Foreign Policy Rhetoric, IR193,
  IR204
Foreign Trade, EP839
Foreign Travel, LE185
Forest Service, OB184
Forests, MP449
Forgetfulness, LE50
Form of Government, SC516
Formal Models of Legislative
  Processes, LE447
Formal Political Structure, XX133
Formal Political Theory, SC42,
  SC119, SC135
Four Tigers, EP279
Fractals, DP91
Fragmentation, IR861
Frame Disputes, IR566
Frame Games, SC480
Frames of Meaning, OB68
Framing, ET149, MP317, OB337,
  PC98, PC111, SC139
France, CP6, DC84, DC127, DC167,
  DC335, EP638, LC235, LE3, LE29,
  LE73, LE326, LE415, PA17, PA89,
  PE209, PE233, PE234, PE305,
  PG158, PG252, PG262, PP277,
  PP467, PS239, SC194, SP413
Francophone Minorities, PG106
Franco-Italian Trade War, EP807
Fraud, PP360, PP383, PP394
Free Education, SP226

Free Market, PS17
Free Rider, CP168, ET17, IR226,
  SC199, SC200, SC204, SC206,
  SC208, SC210, SC211, SC217,
  SC219, SC223, SC669
Free Trade, EP795, EP821, EP831,
  EP837, EP849
Free Votes, LE647, LE661
Free Will, LC383
Freedom, ET19, ET234, ET243,
  ET461, LC152, MP258, OB242,
  PS59, SP336
Freight Carriers, ET419
French Revolution, DC169
Frenzies, DP50
Frequency of Paradox, SC568
Freshmen, LC395, SC772
Friedman, Milton, EP105, OB346
Friedman-Savage Utility Function,
  SC664, SC666, SC673, SC686,
  SC712
Friends and Neighbors Process
  PG75-129/Special Section
Friendship, LE371, PG100, XX103
Frontier Hypothesis, PG231
Frontiers, IR798, PG227, PG305,
  PG315, PG328
Frustration, CP349
Full Belly Thesis, ET45
Full Employment, EP171
Functional Analysis, DP162, LC265,
  XX126, XX231
Functional Conflict, IR371
Functionalism, SC57, SC726, XX245
Fundamental Attribution Error,
  XX376
Fundamentalism, RP110, RP137
Fusion Politics, PP516
Futures Studies, DP83, TR63, XX242
Fuzzy Information, SC352, SC355,
  SC366, SC367
Fuzzy Logic, SC350-377/Special
  Section
Fuzzy Mathematics, SC356, SC373,
  SC374
Fuzzy Modeling, SC363, SC364,
  SC372
Fuzzy Set Theory, SC350, SC353,
  SC354, SC357, SC358, SC359,
  SC368, SC369, SC375, SC376

Galton's Problem, PG115, PG118,
  PG126, PG127
Galtung's Theory, PS225
Gambling, EP657, LC205, LC504,
  SC673, SC680, SC688, SC689,
  SC690, SC698, SC723
Game Theory, SC378-487/Special
  Section, DC4, ET13, ET70, ET175,
  ET197, ET301, ET347, IR3, IR16,
  IR151, IR182, IR233, IR255,
  IR380, IR428, IR675, IR701,
  IR756, LC13, LC96, LC106, LC108,
  LC150, LC305, LC350, LE89,
  LE154, LE693, MP451, MP452,
  PE148, PE324, PE528, PP354,
  PS122, SC109, SC141, SC188,
  SC198, SC227, SC286, SC330,
  SC486, SC511, SC576, SC603,
  SC648, TR38
Gandhi, Mahatma, ET13, ET56
Garbage Can Model, OB16, OB52,
  PA112
Garrison State, LC202
Gatekeeping, AB133, LC392, LE218,
  MP227
Gauthier, David, ET25, ET67, SC638
Gays, MP202, MP256, MP271, MP323

Gender, MP201-359/Special Section, ET289, IR830, LC280, LC495, MP27, MP116, PA209, PE553, SC252, SP264, SC624
Gender Based Employment, MP317
Gender Bias, MP242
Gender Consciousness, MP250
Gender Differences, MP214, MP253, MP261, MP338
Gender Gap, MP217, MP224, MP265, MP289, MP300, MP333, MP344, MP345, MP351, MP359, SP269
Gender Power Differences, MP201
Gender Roles, MP243, MP278, MP324
Gender Segregation, MP67, MP230
Gender Sterotyping, MP179
Gender Stratification, MP320
Gender Wage Differentials, MP249
General Assembly, IR847, LE656, PS119
General Assistance Payments, LC199
General Fund Financing, EP689
General Purpose Technologies, EP219
General War, IR720
Generational Change, AB365, EP297, PP237
Generational Conflict, EP702
Generational Effects, AB289
Generational Politics, SP95
Generational Redistribution, EP428
Generational Replacement, LE544
Generational Rhythms, DP246
Generational Succession, AB112, AB236
Generational Transfer, AB153, LE27
Generations, AB252, IR830, PP238, PP250, XX94
Genocide, IR165, IR712
Geoculture, IR853
Geographic Information Systems, PG6
Geographical Factor, LC413
Geopolitical Space, IR12, PG8, PG25
Geography, XX114
Geography of Competency, PG53
Geography of International Conflicts, IR758
Geometric Lag, IR282
Geometry, DP122
Geopolitics, IR853, PG47
George, Alexander, LE165
Georgia, MP130
German Hegemony, PG238
Germany, AB381, AB386, CP255, DC120, DC266, DP267, EP56, IR475, IR523, LE4, LE6, LE32, LE345, LE415, LE705, MP96, OB400, PE194, PE227, PE447, PE465, PG50, PG161, PG238, PG244, PG253, PG327, PP21, PP244, PP247, PP478, PP479, PP501, PS118, PS205, PS123, SC241
Gerrymandering, MP182, SC331
Ghana, MP452
Ghettos, PG87
Ghost Dance, MP519
Gibbard Optimum, SC537
Gibbon, Edward, PS220
Gilligan, Carol, ET8
Gini Coefficients, EP233, EP512
Global Capitalism, EP333
Global Change, PG16
Global Commons, SC141
Global Communications, PC54
Global Conflict, IR390

Global Debt Crisis, see International Debt
Global Division of Labor, EP224
Global Environment, TR75
Global Finance, EP87
Global Governance, IR195
Global Hegemony, EP818
Global Modeling, TR62
Global Policy, IR76
Global Politics, DP263
Global Restructuring, SP322
Global System, PS218
Global Warming, TR58, TR66
Global Wars, IR807, IR808
Globalization, SC203, XX244
Golden Mean, XX369
Golden Rule, ET259
Goldwater, Barry, DP8
Golpes de Estado, DC107
Good Government, XX327
Good Life, MP445
Goodman Flow-of-Vote Estimates, CP187
Goodwin's Nonlinear Accelerator, DP105
Goverance, LE471
Government Aid, XX352
Government Borrowing, PE104
Government Bureaus, OB334
Government Coalitions, SC196
Government Collapse, LE88
Government Commissions, PA213, PA219
Government Cost, OB243, OB302
Government Debt, PE140
Government Decentralization, PS212, SP255
Government Declarations, PP21
Government Discrimination, MP74, MP98
Government Ethics, ET366, ET370, ET426, also see Public Ethics
Government Evaluation, PS196
Government Expenditures, EP786, OB277
Government Failure, EP113, OB48, PE541, SC146
Government Formation, LE63, SC156, SC165
Government Inefficiency, SP359
Government Intervention, ET213, SC66
Government Jackpot, PP86
Government Performance, LE535, PE289
Government Popularity, LE143, PE213, PE265, PE279
Government Power, XX10
Government Preferences, EP47
Government Productivity, OB60, OB61
Government Reorganization, PS201
Government Responsibility, PE10
Government Revenue, see Taxes
Government Size, OB232-323/Special Section, DC363, EP253, EP266, EP358, EP378, EP381, OB113, PE151, PE544
Government Spending, EP106, EP283, EP332, EP335, EP498, EP686, EP710, EP730, EP792, OB235, PE61, PE78, PE86, PE107, PE117, PE133, PE134, PE141, PE461, PE479, PP122, SC794, SP358
Government Spending Limits, EP114
Government Stability, PE202, PP521
Government Structures, PA24, PS53
Government Subsidization, SC211

Government Waste, OB190
The Governmental Process, PE377
Governments In-Exile, XX185
Governors, EP715, LE52, LE57, LE158, LE173, LE190, MP374, OB102, PE216, PE253, PE280, PS190, SC70
Grades, SP214
Gramm-Rudman-Hollings Act, IR494, PE102, PE118
Gramscian Analysis, IR24, XX112
Grand Army of the Republic, PE296
Granger Causality, CP66, EP173
Grants, SP350
Graph Theoretical Approaches, SC137, SC311, SC312
Graphical Argument Analysis, IR437
Grateful Electorate, LE310
Gravity Models, EP805, EP853
Gravity Potential, PG64
Gray Power, SP75, also see Aging
Great Britain, see United Kingdom
Great Crash, EP153
Great Firm Theory, PS231
Great Migration, MP3
Great Power Cooperation, IR45
Great Power War, IR703, IR704, IR718, IR719
Great Society, SP285, SP520, XX198
Greece, OB281
Greed, SP132
Green Justice, TR91
Green Party, PP479, PP495
Greening of Politics, TR72
Greenland, PG256
Gresham's Law, EP650
Gridlock, PE340
Gross Concepts, XX319
Gross National Product, DP180, EP432, EP435
Groundwater, PE561
Group Behavior, EP268, PE348, SC639, XX410
Group Beliefs, OB231
Group Consciousness, CP41, PE218
Group Decision Making, SC374, SC797
Group Decisions, SC14, SC248, SC357, SC358
Group Dominance, MP311
Group Economic Interests, PE179
Group Economic Outcomes, EP179
Group Heterogeneity, OB375
Group Identification, AB346, DC27, RP169, XX88
Group Influence, PE296
Group Integration, RP169
Group Membership, PE346, PE381
Group Polarization, XX254
Group Process Variables, OB207
Group Protest, DC195
Group Representation, MP287
Group Salient Issues, MP287
Group Size, DC75, PE554, SC217, SC224
Group Structure, XX6
Group Threat, MP118
Group Voting, LC112
Groups, AB350, CP183, PE406, XX105, XX109
Groupthink, PC17, PC18, PC22, PC37, PC57, PC82, PC85
Grove City, LC418
Growth Cycles, DP25, DP183
Growth Machines, EP285, EP372, EP398
Growth Management, EP252, EP260

Growth of Government, see Government Size
Growth Oriented Urban Alliances, EP264
Growth Pole Strategy, LC205
Growth Policy, see Economic Growth
Growth Rate, EP258, EP304, EP377, EP402
Growth Waves, DP226, EP867
Guatemala, PG191
Gubernatorial Effectiveness, LE383, CP246, CP325, PE239, PE260, PP20, PP41, PP210, PP230
Gubernatorial Powers, LE157
Guerrillas, DC128, DC131, DC182, DC131, DC352
Guilt, XX49
Gun Control, LC339-351/Special Section
Guns, LC341, LC348
Guns vs. Butter, IR526, PE41

Habits, DP69
Handicapped Persons, SP225
Happiness, AB390, EP448
Happy Warriors, XX367
Hard Issues, TR179
Hardball Politics, XX89
Hardship, DC84
Harlem, DC215
Harmonic Series Modeling, OB354
Harmony, ET404
Harsanyi Function, IR422
Harsanyi, John, ET7, ET285
Hart, Gary, LE192
Hawks, AB229, AB237, AB276, AB287, IR421
Hawley-Smoot Trade War, EP807
Hawthorne Effect, AB324
Hawthorne Experiments, XX272
Hayek's Cycle Theory, DP243
Hazard Events, PC111
Hazardous Waste, EP671, TR96
Hazardous Waste Facilities, PG178, TR67, TR162
Head Taxes, PG186
Headline Method, PE536
Headline News, PE165
Health, SP61-144/Special Section, PA259
Health Care Rationing, SP139
Health Insurance, SP91
Health Maintenance Organizations, OB369
Heat Waves, DP23
Hechter's Theory of Underdevelopment, EP239
Heckling, XX256
Hedonic Analysis, PG164, TR124
Hegemonic Decline, PS16
Hegemonic Logic, EP741
Hegemonic Shifts, DP250
Hegemonic Stability, IR3, IR47, IR863, IR866, IR867
Hegemonic War, IR663
Hegemony, EPB18, EP826, IR24, IR136, IR469, IR852, IR860
Herd Behavior, DP3, DP32
Herder Syndrome, MP459
Heresthetics, DC106, LC148
Heterogeneity, CP306, DC75, PG122, PP499, SC225
Heterogeneous Politicians, CP299
Heuristics, AB184, AB190, AB264, DP29, IR399, LC74, LE155, PA69, SC727, XX381, XX382
Hibbs, Douglass, DC331
Hidden Economy, EP6

Hierarchical Attitude Constraint, TR117
Hierarchical Economic Systems, DP135
Hierarchical Equilibrium Theory, IR739
Hierarchical Models, AB259, AB281, TR117
Hierarchical Needs, DP166
Hierarchical Systems, SP319
Hierarchical Theory, DP167
Hierarchical Voting, CP190
Hierarchies, OB349
Hierarchy, ET113, LC377
Higher Education, DP231, EP711, SP147, SP148, SP157, SP166, SP169, SP191, SP204, SP224, SP232, SP241
Highly Specialized Organizations, ET333
Highway Expenditures, SP328
Hill, Anita, MP331
Himmelweit's Model of Voting, PE227
Hispanics, MP2, MP14, MP100, MP144, MP196, MP197, MP345, MP448, MP461, MP462, MP487, MP488, MP528
Historians, XX180
Historical Analogies, AB289
Historical Explanations, XX62
Historical Laws, XX97
Historical Processes, DC304
Historical Research, XX384
Historical Sociology, XX169
Historical Theories, DC154
Historiography, XX161
History, IR201, XX11, XX43, XX52, XX53, XX75, XX100, XX106, XX140, XX143, XX184, XX192, XX201, XX207, XX218, XX287, XX331, XX339,
History of Ideas, XX329
Hitler, Adolf, PP244, PP290
Hobbes, Thomas, SC83
Hockey Helmets, SC116
Hofstadter, Richard, SP231
Holocaust, MP82, MP84
Holt's Cultural Shock Thesis, RP89
Holy War, IR752
Home Health Organizations, OB335
Home Maintenance Organizations, SP91
Home State Advantage, PG92, PG107
Home Style, LE30, LE282, SC778
Homelessness, SP259, SP264, SP265, SP268, SP287, SP292, SP303, SP304, also see Housing
Homeostat, LE209
Homicide, LC352-387/Special Section, LC499, LC521, PC142, RP88
Homo Economicus, XX66
Homo Sociologicus, XX66
Homo Sovieticus, EP52
Homosexuality, ET457, MP202
Homunculus Theories, XX224
Honeybees, SC303
Hope, SC674
Horse Race Coverage, PP85
Hospital Service, SP84
Hostages, DC375
Hostile Media Phenomenon, PC180
Hostility, ET341, IR176, PP286
House Bank Scandal, PP378, PP435
House Challengers, PP79
House Elections, LE540, LE599, PP63, PP70, PP184, PP189

House of Commons, AB212, ET331, LE120, LE241, LE322, LE401, LE454, LE503, LE633, LE661, LE680, MP176
House of Lords, LC457
House of Representatives, CP266, CP275, CP345, DP260, EP571, IR481, LE107, LE122, LE210, LE230, LE255, LE256, LE259, LE269, LE271, LE272, LE274, LE275, LE285, LE294, LE300, LE301, LE304, LE318, LE319, LE320, LE324, LE326, LE331, LE332, LE346, LE349, LE350, LE356, LE373, LE392, LE399, LE403, LE427, LE442, LE461, LE462, LE477, LE478, LE479, LE495, LE505, LE506, LE507, LE511, LE512, LE517, LE531, LE532, LE533, LE537, LE544, LE557, LE573, LE577, LE579, LE583, LE618, LE622, LE630, LE632, LE660, LE674, LE675, LE688, PE228, PE241, PG232, PG245, PP65, PP129, PP153, PP180, PP183, PP194, PP198, PP201, PP356, PP528, PP543, PP544, SC168, SP55, TR49
House Reform, LE445
Housing, MP56, PG203, SP257, SP261, SP272, SP278, SP288, SP289, SP292, also see Homelessness
Housing Markets, MP108
Housing Turnover Model, PG203
Huk Rebellion, DC172
Human Affairs, XX117
Human Agency, DP138
Human Beings, SC121
Human Capital, DP192, EP401, MP75, PG185, XX36, XX128
Human Dyadic Systems, DP2
Human Ecology, PA160, PG16
Human Geography, PG4
Human Growth Games, SC471
Human Nature, ET55
Human Progress, PA172
Human Relations, OB126
Human Resource Management Systems, OB17
Human Rights, ET199-246/Special Section, DC177, IR344, MP260
Human Rights Organizations, ET218
Humana, Charles, ET202
Humanism, MP298
Humanists, XX47
Humanitarian Intervention, ET207, IR669, IR686, IR690, IR698
Humanitarian Law of Armed Conflict, IR697
Humanitarianism, IR650
Human-Natural System Interactions, DP160
Hung Parliament, LE460
Hunger, SP514
Hunter-Gatherer Societies, OB164
Hypergames, DC4, IR675
Hypersegregation, MP100
Hypothesis Tests, TR57, XX102
Hysteresis, DP69, EP163, EP164, EP169, EP175, EP190

Iberoamerica, IR489
Icebergs, DC332
Idaho, SP60
Idealism, IR168
Ideas, EP840, IR157, IR453, PA308, XX329

Identity, PS286, SP93
Identity Formation, IR210
Ideodynamics, PC33
Ideograph, AB175
Ideological Bases, OB226
Ideological Bias, XX336
Ideological Change, LE638, PP40
Ideological Cleavages, SP55, XX199
Ideological Partisanship, EP365
Ideological Refinement, SP193
Ideological Voting, CP339
Ideology, AB85-224/Special
  Section, AB275, AB288, CP102,
  CP291, CP339, DC181, DC217,
  DC283, EP40, EP713, ET30, ET113,
  ET404, IR90, IR116, IR117,
  IR187, IR491, IR511, IR670,
  LC50, LC57, LC203, LC399, LC457,
  LC459, LC461, LC462, LE201,
  LE280, LE294, LE299, LE414,
  LE431, LE529, LE533, LE635,
  LE663, LE702, MP236, MP360,
  MP472, MP520, OB192, OB384,
  PA109, PC77, PE81, PE214, PE352,
  PE386, PG232, PP108, PP111,
  PP129, PP212, PP296, RP148,
  RP168, RP170, SC174, SC214,
  SC743, SP22, SP336, SP387,
  SP389, TR68, XX223, XX333
Ignorance, ET315, PC9, SC702
Ignorant Monopolist, DP164
Ill-Structured Problems, XX323
Illegal Behavior, LC313
Illegal Immigration, PG143, PG157,
  PG216
Illegal Sector of Capital, LC257
Illegitimacy, SP552
Illinois, MP142, PG314, SP234
Images, AB247, CP311, CP312, PC20,
  PP174, XX162
Imbalance Thesis, OB186, OB187
Imitation, PC140
Immigration, see Migration
Impasse Resolution, IR189
Imperfect Competition, EP844,
  EP859
Imperfect Detection, IR342
Imperfect Information, CP217
Imperfection, SC411
Imperial Intervention, PS242
Imperialism, PS215-243/Special
  Section
Impersonal Influence, AB48
Implementation, LC101, PA215,
  PA216, PA225, PA238, SC31
Implementation Problem, PA236
Import Barriers, EP799
Import Substituting Industrializa-
  tion, EP292
Impossibility Theorems, SC488-
  511/Special Section
Impoundments, PE95, PE152
Imprecision, SC370
Impression Driven Model, CP267
Imprisonment, LC175, LC328, LC336
In Kind Transfers, SP535
In Vitro Experiments, CP263
Inaction, XX146
Inapplicability Principle, DP130
Incapacitation, LC308
Incentive Pay, ET33
Incidence Analysis, EP717
Inclusive Fitness, PA178, RP26
Income, EP411-526/Special Section,
  DC56, DC260, EP255, EP334,
  EP391, MP389, PE213, PE493,
  PE591, PG70, SC666, SP133,
  SC367, SP470, SP516, SP521

Income Tax, EP704, EP714, EP718,
  EP791, see Taxation
Income Transfer Programs, EP442,
  SP470, SP495
Incomplete Enforcement, EP582
Incrementalism, LC463, PA51, PA85,
  PA137, PE63, PE149, PE362,
  PE465, SP312, SP498
Incumbency, CP216, CP275, CP281,
  CP328, CP329, LE295, LE537,
  LE541, LE320, LE348, LE391,
  LE540, LE541, LE544, LE545,
  LE557, LE558, LE559, LE564,
  LE566, LE579, LE582, LE583,
  LE587, LE588, LE595, LE599,
  LE600, PE189, PE190, PP146,
  PP167, SC772
Incumbency Advantage, CP216,
  CP328, LE580
Incumbency Dilemma, PE586
Indecision, SC45
Indentured Servitude, MP75
Independence Axiom, SC55, SC497
Independent Voting Behavior, CP257
Indeterminacy, DP94
India, OB312, PE461, PS235, RP67
Indiana, PG147, PG314
Indians, see Native Americas
Indifference Map, EP543
Indigenous Peoples, ET224
Indirect Taxes, EP695
Individual Behavior, XX372
Individual Decisions, SC14
Individual Differences Scaling,
  AB173
Individual Preferences, SC276
Individualism, XX47
Individualistic Rationalism, ET83
Induction, PA314, SC611
Industrial Aid, EP93
Industrial Change, EP298
Industrial Concentration, DC340,
  EP653
Industrial Conflict, DC296, DC332
Industrial Democracy, OB7, OB32
Industrial Development Groups,
  EP295
Industrial Development, EP480
Industrial Diversification, EP62
Industrial Growth, see Economic
  Growth
Industrial History, XX204
Industrial Location, PG189, PG214
Industrial Organization of
  Congress, LE489
Industrial Policy, EP197-410/
  Special Section, EP176, EP256,
  EP265, also see Economic Growth,
  and Development
Industrial Political Activity,
  PE342, also see Interest Groups
Industrial Relations, EP124,
  EP670, OB93
Industrial Revolution, DP208
Industrialization, EP89, EP211,
  EP224, LC201, MP402, PE9
Industry Characteristics, PE355
Industry Dynamics, OB345
Industry Structure, EP50, EP265
Ineffectiveness of Voting, OB317
Inequality, DC50, DC53, DC56,
  DC81, DC102, DC236, DC256,
  EP160, EP230, EP257, EP382,
  EP386, EP412, EP423, EP426,
  EP437, EP439, EP447, EP452,
  EP460, EP463, EP479, EP483,
  EP491, EP502, EP516, IR346,
  LC191, LC226, LC385, LC494,

MP411, PS40, PS162, PS164,
  PS319, SC56, SP133, SP184,
  SP362, SP383, also see Income
Inference, CP212, SC419, SC432,
  XX141
Infinite Regress, SC494, SC503
Infinity, SC501
Inflation, EP527-546/Special
  Section, DP178, DP278, PE173,
  EP718, IR551, LE88, PE206,
  PE213, PE248, PE487, PE488,
  PE493
Inflation Forecasts, EP536
Influence, EP50, IR328, LE116,
  LE475, PE301
Influential Behavior, CP279
Information, AB66, AB191, AB392,
  CP22, CP89, CP140, CP217, CP218,
  CP234, CP245, CP282, ET182,
  IR354, LE465, LE468, OB144,
  PC10, PC11, PC15, PC32, PC46,
  PC47, PC61, PC106, PC118, PC131,
  PC196, PC200, PC212, PE301,
  PE524, PP75, SC415, XX225, XX370
Information Age, XX242
Information Bias PC19
Information Campaigns, PC62, PC120
Information Cascades, DP6, DP156
Information Committees, LE228
Information Costs, PP181
Information Cycles, DP285
Information Effects, CP282
Information Flow, PA251, PC138,
  PC222
Information Overload, PC14
Information Processing, AB167,
  AB314, CP22, LC74, OB230, PC121,
  PP33, PP454, SC633, XX371
Information Sources, PG82, TR106
Information Technology, PA342,
  TR172
Information Theoretic Methods,
  SP519
Informational Paradox, LC301
Informed Citizen Problem, CP238
Inglehart, Ronald, AB355
Inherent Bad Faith Model, AB295
Initiation of Conflict, IR374
Injustice, AB80, ET51, ET293,
  ET300, also see Justice
Innovation PA258-344/Special
  Section, DP179, DP181, DP184,
  DP193, DP219, EP215, EP607,
  EP692, IR309, IR334, LC27,
  LE392, LE549, LE550, PA89,
  PA279, PA300, PA329, PA331,
  PA333, PA335, PA336, PA340,
  PE314
Innovation Clusters, DP223, PA274
Insider-Outsider Model, PE367
Instability, CP66, DC52, DC55,
  DC200, DP36, DP96, DP117, DP207,
  IR555, MP371, PA317, PE188,
  SC24, SC458, SC459, SC464, SC580
Institutional Analysis, DC363,
  SC88
Institutional Arrangements, SC126
Institutional Change, EP647,
  LC119, LE265, OB154, XX253
Institutional Confidence, SP169
Institutional Design, LC151, SC87,
  XX263
Institutional Economics, SC2,
  XX183
Institutional Logics, EP236
Institutional Politics, LE206
Institutional Rule Breaking, LC503
Institutional Strength, CP246

Institutional Structure, SP99
Institutional Support, LC405
Institutional Theory, OB64
Institutional Transfer, EP16
Institutional Values, ET422, LC63
Institutionalism, OB45, OB51,
  OB92, SC38, XX47
Institutionalist Theory, OB43
Institutionalization, LE374,
  LE401, LE461, PP471, PS265,
  PS266, PS281, PS296
Institutionalized Majority Rule,
  SC128
Institutionalized Presidency,
  LE144
Institutions, EP40, EP110, EP409,
  EP860, LC125, LC182, LE40, OB6,
  OB21, OB44, SC127, SC213, SC575,
  SC647, SP335, XX35, XX317,
  XX363, XX399, XX400
Insurance, LC23, SP142
Insurance Codes, PA270
Insurance Rate Classification,
  EP586
Insurrection, DC147, DC258
Integration, AB51, ET468, IR854,
  MP86, MP413, MP416, MP453,
  MP507, PG206, PG279, PS12, PS29,
  PS62
Integrative Complexity, AB296,
  IR153, IR193, IR194, OB208
Integrity, CP275, CP281, ET237
Intellectual Fads, SC604
Intelligence, IR5, IR81, IR131,
  IR134, PA170, PA202
Intense Minorities, AB16
Intentional Models, CP191
Interaction Density, PG41
Intercultural Understanding
  Groups, OB393
Interest Based Problem Solving,
  XX20
Interest Groups, PC294-410/Special
  Section, EP562, EP658, EP733,
  EP793, EP845, LC138, LC460,
  LC464, LC445, LC466, OB253,
  OB300, PC97, PC164, PE406,
  PE588, PP27, PP48, PP65, PP112,
  RP125, SC535
Interest Group Liberalism, PE365
Interest Group Ratings, PE352,
  PE361, PE403
Interest Group Systems, PE336
Interest Inarticulation, PE375
Interest Intermediation, EP300
Interest Rates, EP141, EP365,
  PE61, PE73, PE74, PE75, PE76,
  PE92
Interests, ET436
Intergovernmental Collaboration,
  XX20
Intergovernmental Competition,
  PS184
Intergovernmental Grants, SP351
Intergovernmental Organizations,
  IR177
Intergovernmental Relations,
  PS187, PS199, PS200, PS205
Intergroup Attitudes, SP193
Intergroup Conflict, DC23, DC49,
  DC75
Intergroup Relations, IR655
Interminority Affairs, MP368
Intermunicipal Competition, PG212
Internal Colonization, MP8, also
  see Migration
Internal Conflict, DC33
Internal Disorder, DC26

Internal Migration, PG179, PG191,
  also see Migration
Internal War, DC178, also see War
Internalization, LC313
International Alignment, IR426
International Atomic Energy
  Agency, IR580
International Communities, PG19,
  TR143
International Conflict, IR364-432/
  Special Section, DP42, DP284,
  IR30, IR424, IR621, IR627,
  IR630, IR639, IR652, IR733,
  IR735, IR745, IR758, LE182, also
  see War
International Cooperation, ET178,
  ET182, ET191, ET192, ET197,
  IR29, IR183, LC491
International Crises, IR153,
  IR257, IR449, IR665, OB211,
  OB200, OB220, also see Crises,
  and Crisis Decision Making
International Debt, PC411-428/
  Special Section, PE411, PE413,
  PE415, PE416, PE422, PE423,
  PE425, PE426
International Disputes, IR373,
  IR378, IR731, PG83, SC716
International Disturbances, IR71
International Economy, EP826,
  MP301
International Ethics, ET63, ET375,
  ET420
International Events, AB282
International Integration, XX245
International Investment Sanc-
  tions, EP833
International Law, ET353, IR653,
  IR668, LC32, LC37, LC440
International Market Access, EP872
International Mediation, IR17,
  IR97, IR104
International Negotiation, IR33,
  IR196
International News, PC143
International Organization, IR72,
  IR139, IR200, IR205, OB34, PE13,
  PE31
International Policy Cooperation,
  DP261, IR73
International Political Economy,
  EP816
International Political Interac-
  tions, EP855
International Public Relations,
  PC107
International Regimes, ET166
International Relations, IR1-873
  /Special Section, ET396, DP236,
  DP255, DP273, ET344, ET352,
  ET407, MP241, MP283, MP440, PG8,
  SC353, XX360
International Resolutions, ET353
International Role, AB238
International Rules, IR129
International Sanctions, IR31
International Security, IR20,
  IR130, IR396
International Stability, IR248,
  IR732, PS234
International Structures, IR234
International System, see World
  Systems
International Tensions, IR298
International Thought, IR211
International Violence, IR805
Internationalism, AB225, AB306

Interparty Competition, PP318-349/
  Special Section, EP388, LE614,
  PG258, PP6, PP14, PP113, PP481,
  SP444, SP458, SP460, SP467,
  SP554
Interparty Politics, SC182
Interparty Spatial Relationships,
  LE672
Interpersonal Communication, PC88,
  PC195
Interpersonal Generalization
  Theory, IR37, IR173
Interpersonal Influence, RP31
Interpersonal Responsibilities,
  ET298
Interpretation, LE475
Interpretation of Politicians,
  SC212
Interracial Contact, MP117, MP484
Interstate Commerce Act, EP584
Interstate Commerce Commission,
  EP637, EP664
Interstate Hostility Dynamics,
  IR753
Interstate Relations, SP406
Intertemporal Analysis, SP358
Intertemporal Choice, SC502
Intertribal Attitudes, MP407
Intervention, IR126, LC3, OB39,
  PS259
Intimate Behavior, SP11
Intolerance, ET453, ET458, ET459,
  ET461, ET462, ET463, ET474,
  ET479, PA208, also see Tolerance
Intractable Negotiations, IR189
Intragroup Conflict, DC39
Intranational Inequality, EP463
Intransigence, SC388
Intransitivities, SC538, SC565,
  SC566
Introspection, SC440
Inventive Activity, DP179, PA266,
  PA267, PA314, PA334, TR185
Inversionary Discourse, PS104
Investment, EP119, EP141, EP294,
  IR523, PS74
Investment Dependence, EP270
Involvement, AB24, AB27, CP51,
  CP67, PP67
Ionospheric Physics, TR160
Iowa, CP84
Iran, IR782
Iran-Contra Affair, AB6, ET379,
  LE124
Iranian Hostage Crisis, LE182,
  OB207
Ireland, PE159
Irish-Americans, MP5
Iron Law of Oligarchy, PP513
Iron Triangles, PE328
Irrational Audiences, PA97
Irrational Beliefs, XX220
Irrationality, PA97, PA146, SC643,
  SC646
Irredentism, MP386
Irrelevant Alternatives, SC567,
  SC751
Is Small Better, ET368
Islam, RP3, RP82
Islamic Fundamentalism, RP10
Islamic Movements, IR752, RP8
Islands, XX404
Isolationism, AB276, AB294, IR67,
  IR192
Israel, AB268, AB293, CP72, ET250,
  ET474, IR255, IR533, IR613,
  PC173, PE39, PP305
Issue-Attitude Agreement, LE292

Issue Avoidance, SC803
Issue Credibility, LE368
Issue Diversity, AB82
Issue Elasticity, AB75
Issue Evolution, MP361
Issue Linkage, IR196
Issue Monopolies, LE412
Issue Perception, LE405
Issue Positions, CP320
Issue Preferences, AB320, PP267
Issue Publics, AB34, AB268
Issue Salience, AB63, PC102
Issue Visibility, PE385
Issue Volatility, PP251
Issue Voting, AB62, CP209, CP247,
  CP270, CP293, LE101, SC667
Issues, AB64, AB114, CP294, CP320,
  SC743, XX290, XX386
Italy, AB61, DC371, LC149, LE69,
  OB263, PP247, PS93, TR151

J Curve, DC229, DC238
Janis, Irving, PC37, PC57
Janowitz, Morris, IR478
Japan, AB354, AB355, CP302, CP303,
  EP56, EP297, EP400, EP647,
  EP719, EP794, EP822, EP835,
  ET404, PA328, PE193, PE271,
  PS70, XX151
Japanese Firm, OB9
Jenghiz Khan, RP16
Jewish-Americans, MP28
Jewish Denominations, RP86
Jewish Liberalism, XX212
Jewish Rescue, SC207
Jews, PE277
Jihad, IR752
Job Absence, DP56
Job Insecurity, OB85
Job Performance, OB105
Job Satisfaction, OB156
Job Stability, EP182
Job Stress, OB19, OB107
Joblessness, MP103
Johnson, Lyndon, DP8, LE156,
  PC152, PC163
Joseph Effect, DP114
Judgement and Choice, XX377
Judgement Process, ET34
Judges, LC390, LC410, LC419, LC451
Judgment, AB20, AB133, IR55, IR145
Judgment Processes, XX234
Judicial Activism, CP136, LC448,
  LC473
Judicial Committee, LE257
Judicial Elections, LC426, LC472,
  PG77, PG97
Judicial Politics, LC388-476/
  Special Section
Judicial Process, LC66
Judicial Review, LC67, LC106,
  LC416, LC453
Judicialization of Politics, LC34
Jumping Ship, OB27
Juries, LC56, LC72
Jurimetric Analysis, LC457
Jurisdictional Boundaries, PG182
Jurors, CP137
Jury Decisions, MP94
Jury Discrimination, MP94
Just War, ET230, IR638, IR657
Justice, ET247-322/Special
  Section, EP693, IR355, LC162,
  MP240
Justifications, ET19, XX59, XX90,
  XX232
Juvenile Delinquency, LC220, LC241
Juvenile Law Reform, LC57

Kansas, CP87
Kanter Thesis, SC54, XX130
Kant, Immanuel, LC18
Kennedy, John F., AB295, LE179
Kenya, SP339
Keynesian Demand Management
  Policy, EP80
Keynesianism, IR527
Keynes, Maynard, XX131
Key, V. O., CP261, SP444
KGB, AB301
Killer Amendments, SC781
Kinetics, PC33
King, Martin Luther Holiday, ET450
Kissenger, Henry, AB295, AB300
Knowledge, CP320, EP663, EP840,
  IR105, PA220, PA257, PA343,
  SC20, SP168, SP189, TR170, XX22,
  XX48
Knowledge Gap Hypothesis, PC207,
  PP202
Knowledge Growth, TR147, TR160
Knowledge Hierarchies, EP840
Knowledge of Politics, AB13
Knowledge Utilization, PA257
Kohlberg, Lawrence, ET8, ET32,
  ET104, ET105, ET259, MP240
Kohlberg-Gilligan Debate, MP240
Kokn's Thesis, LC321
Kondratieff Waves, DP185, DP188,
  DP208, DP223, DP225, DP253,
  DP278, SP423
Korea, AB277, PS301
Ku Klux Klan, ET457, MP139
Kuhnian Paradigm, XX364
Kuznuts Curve, EP484
Kwangsi, DC158

Labor, EP189
Labor History, DC304
Labor Hoarding, DP175
Labor Market Transitions, EP158
Labor Organization, PE2
Labor Parties, PG39, PP40
Labor Relations, DC328
Labor Supply, DP69, SP519
Labor Violence, see Strikes
Laboratory Experiments, CP263, OB3
Labour Economics, DC322
Labour Party, PP105, PP492, SC304
Laffer Curve, EP64, EP72, EP722
Laisse Faire, AB139
Lakotas, LC109
Land, SP274
Land Inequality, DC6, DC57
Land Tenure, TR7
Land Use, TR52
Landscape Theory, XX25
Landslides, DP8
Language, DP41, MP430, MP452,
  XX116
Language Diversity, MP455, MP456,
  MP493
Language Regimes, MP451
Language Rights, PG317
Language Survival, DP21
Laplace, Jean, SC282
Last Term Problem, LE554, LE617
Latent Structure Analysis, SP138
Late-Deciding Voters, CP241
Latin America, CP36, CP285, DC92,
  DC107, DC151, DC182, DC192,
  DC207, DC224, DC231, DP44,
  DP174, EP14, EP55, EP203, EP204,
  EP281, EP292, EP312, EP336,
  EP368, EP386, EP389, EP396,
  EP451, EP532, EP535, EP546,
  EP777, EP811, EP814, IR388,

  IR492, IR505, IR513, IR520,
  IR540, IR546, IR667, IR842,
  LE60, MP222, PE32, PE52, PE188,
  PE272, PE414, PE421, PE423,
  PE424, PE426, PE434, PE563,
  PG42, PP367, PP455, PP456,
  PP500, PS4, PS15, PS122, PS140,
  PS141, PS165, PS223, PS256,
  PS258, PS270, PS324, RP13, RP45,
  RP47, RP69, SP79, SP200, SP326,
  SP504, TR27, TR150, XX115,
  XX208, XX403
Latin American Debt, see Interna-
  tional Debt
Latino-Hispanic Ethnic Identity,
  MP454
Latinos, MP170, MP383, MP505
Law, DC252, ET339, ET344, ET353,
  ET411, LC4, LC6, LC15, LC17,
  LC20, LC26, LC38, LC39, LC47,
  LC49, LC50, LC54, LC55, LC60,
  LC61, LC62, LC77, LC90, LC91,
  LC92, LC212, XX327
Law and Order, LC129, LC295
Law and Society, LC46, LC81
Law and Statistics, LC9
Law as Moral Judgment, ET6
Law as Rules of the Powerful, ET6
Law Enforcement, see Policing
Law Firms, LC36, LC86, PG67
Law Making, IR865
Law of Large Numbers, SC334
Law of the Sea, XX209
Law of War, IR754
Lawyer-Legislators, LE385
Lawyers, AB141, LC2, LC21, LC23,
  LC58, LC59, LC65, LC73, LE435,
  MP328
Leader Complexity, OB230
Leader Effectiveness, LE135
Leader Images, LE111
Leaders, LE312-358/Special
  Section, AB169, AB205, AB255,
  AB257, DC187, IR52, IR461,
  IR632, LE16, LE56, LE551, LE605,
  XX387
Leadership, DP226, DP265, LC102,
  LE19, LE22, LE23, LE24, LE26,
  LE39, LE47, LE60, LE55, LE80,
  LE166, LE315, LE316, OB20, PG22,
  PS82
Leadership Change, LE346, LE594
Leadership Duration, LE542
Leadership Effects, CP199
Leadership Patterns, PA310
Leadership Positions, LE578
Leadership Style, LE319
Leadership Succession, see
  Turnover
Learning, AB49, CP37, IR109, OB47,
  PA70
Learning Hypothesis, XX272
Left Corporatist Model of Growth,
  EP290
Left of Center Parties, CP153
Left Wing Authoritarianism, XX365,
  also see Authoritarianism
Left Wing Parties, EP540
Left Wing Politics, PS93, PS123,
  PS141, XX208
Left-Right Measurements, PP341
Left-Right Orientations, AB147
Left-Right Polarization, PP518
Left-Right Political Scales, AB102
Left-Right Semantics, AB157
Left-Right Thinking, AB161
Legal Culture, LC52, LC94
Legal Duties, ET16

Legal Ethics, LC58
Legal Justification, DC28
Legal Order, LC233
Legal Principles, IR659
Legal Procedures, ET317
Legal Profession, ET437
Legal Realism, ET422
Legal Reasoning, ET61, ET102
Legal Studies, LC1-523/Special
   Section, LC88, LC89, LC197
Legal Structure, XX173
Legality, IR483, LC129
Legislation, LE389
Legislative Activities, LE21
Legislative Agendas, LE368
Legislative Behavior, LE359-501/
   Special Section, AB118
Legislative Careers, LE312-358/
   Special Section
Legislative Choice, LE486
Legislative Coalitions, see
   Coalitions
Legislative Cues, LE406
Legislative Districting, CP216
Legislative Elections, CP196,
   PP215, PP346, also see Congres-
   sional Elections, and Elections,
   and Election of Minorities
Legislative Histories, LC10
Legislative Inexperience, LE348
Legislative Influence, LE430
Legislative Institutions, LE227,
   LE470
Legislative Integration, LE500
Legislative Issues, LE390
Legislative Leadership, LC467,
   LE334, LE352, also see Legisla-
   tive Careers
Legislative Logjams, LE484
Legislative Monopoly, OB238
Legislative Morality, SP42
Legislative Norms, ET325, ET327,
   ET331, ET336, ET343, also see
   Public Ethics
Legislative Organization, LE361,
   LE394
Legislative Overrides, LE494
Legislative Parties, LE502-536/
   Special Section, also see
   Political Parties
Legislative Process, PE408
Legislative Productivity, LE384,
   LE444
Legislative Professionalism, LE15,
   LE383, LE439, LE440
Legislative Recruitment, LE341
Legislative Reform, LE459
Legislative Socialization, LE513
Legislative Specialization, OB254
Legislative Structure, LE17
Legislative Vetos, LE416
Legislator Ideology, LE299
Legislatures, LE1-723/Special
   Section, LC451, LE202, LE456,
   LE469, LE483, LE488, OB296
Legitimacy, CP71, DC104, ET73,
   ET421, LC388, LC405, LC450,
   LC505, LE103, PC149, PS48, PS63,
   PS67, PS68, PS143, SC229, XX333
Legitimation, AB350, EP519, LE487
Legitimization of Violence, LC225
Leipzig, DP156
Leisure Activities, LC244
Lemons, EP617
Lending, SC666
Length of Service, OB159
Leninism, PS92
Leontief Paradox, SC563

Lerner's Model of Modernization,
   PS302
Lesbians, MP220, MP313, MP334
Less Developed Countries, EP112,
   EP377, IR348, PE411, PE415
Letters to the Editor, PC76
Levels of Analysis, AB148, CP346
Levels of Conceptualization,
   AB101, AB135, AB149, AB193,
   AB203
Levels of Identification, AB220
Leviathan, EP779, OB291, PS51
Liability, LC90
Libel, LC427
Liberal-Conservative Thinking,
   AB121, AB136, AB149, AB150,
   AB170, also see Ideology
Liberal Democracy, ET108, PS161,
   RP35, SC40
Liberal Economies, EP457
Liberal Fallacy, SC215
Liberal Institutionalism, ET165
Liberal Paradox, ET53, SC537,
   SC551, SC552, SC562, SC585
Liberalism, AB96, AB107, AB204,
   ET290, ET405, ET469, IR32,
   LC469, LE399, LE650, MP341,
   PA53, SC110, SC536, SP372,
   SP449, XX144, XX244
Liberalization, DC7
Liberation Theology, RP113, RP131
Libertarian Parties, PP273
Libertarianism, AB139, DC73, DC74,
   PP294
Liberty, ET89, ET100, EP134,
   ET201, LC98, MP417, PE100,
   PS278, PS311, SP523
License Plates, PG80
Licensing, EP617, PA344
Life Course, SP95
Life Cycle, PG119, PP238, PP250,
   PP263
Life Sciences, SP125
Lifeboat, TR126
Lijphart's Consensus Model, DC34
Limited Reciprocity, IR45
Limited Retaliation, IR598
Limited War, IR365
Lindbloom, Charles, PA85
Line Item Veto, LC155, PE89, PE150
Linguistic Voting, RP159
Linkage Organization, AB192
Linkage Salience, AB192
Lipset-Rokkan Hypothesis, PP284
Literacy, SP150, SP200
Literary Digest Poll, AB335
Litigation, ET341, LC24, LC40,
   LC59, LC80, LC83, OB256
Little Science, TR148
Living Systems, PA183
Living Wills, LC27
Lobbying Regulation, PE387, EP625,
   LE275, PA260, PE295, PE299,
   PE301, PE302, PE303, PE309,
   PE311, PE349, PE350, PE379,
   PE399, PE409, PE410, PP75, also
   see Interest Groups
Local Associations, OB389
Local Benefit-Seeking, LE501
Local Economic Growth, EP123,
   EP161, EP207, EP236, EP259,
   EP369, also see Economic Growth
Local Economies, EP295
Local Elections, MP163, SP352
Local Fiscal Policies, PG172
Local-Global Nexus, SP360
Local Government Reform, SP377,
   SP379

Local Governments, CP29, CP81,
   ET414, PA324, PC150, PE483,
   SC117, SP307, SP313, SP347,
   SP378, SP394, SP400, SP407,
   SP408, SP417, SP425, SP432,
   SP350, SP352
Local News, PC158
Local Party Organizations, PP39
Local Political Business Cycle,
   PE473
Local Political Interest, MP254
Local Political Power, SP345
Local Politics, SP306-451/Special
   Section
Local Public Economics, SP410,
   SP447
Local Public Goods, PE502
Local Schools, SP217
Localism, IR472, PG92
Locality Studies, PG103, PG108,
   PG288, PG337
Location, PG217, PP161, TR48
Location Analysis, TR18
Location Decisions, PG130-224/
   Special Section
Locational Conflict, SP382
Locational Logrolling, CP76
Location-Specific Amenities, PG164
Locus of Control, CP61
Logic of Collective Action, SC22
Logic of Comparison, XX191
Logic of Discovery, PA314
Logistic Growth, DP116
Logistic Map, XX69
Logit, LE347
Logrolling, CP76, LE691, LE692,
   LE693, LE697, LE702, LE709,
   LE712, LE719, LE721, SC536
London, PP525
Lone Wolf Questioning, LE256
Long Range Time Series, IR643
Long Waves, DP166, DP167, DP168,
   DP170, DP173, DP179, DP181,
   DP184, DP186, DP187, DP193,
   DP194, DP195, DP199, DP203,
   DP206, DP208, DP210, DP215,
   DP219, DP223, DP224, DP225,
   DP228, DP254, DP256, DP257,
   DP258, DP259, DP263, DP265,
   DP269, DP272, DP273, IR372,
   IR808
Losing Ground, SP286
Lotteries, LC247, PA7, PA264,
   PA297, SP6, SP14
Lottery Voting, SC232
Louisiana, MP85, OB302, SP36
Love, LE106
Low Intensity Conflict, IR134
Lowi, Theodore, MP284
Loyalty, IR476, LE212, OB10, PE539
Loyalty-Distance Model, CP333
Loyalty Filters, AB85
Luck, SC592
Lumpy Preference Structures, SC58
Lyapunov Exponent, DP82, DP112
Lying, ET54, ET358, ET413, ET428
Lynchings, MP58, MP69, MP85,
   MP110, MP114, MP130, MP135

Macrodynamics, SC89
Macroeconomic Contractions, PE176
Macroeconomic Cycles, PE460
Macroeconomic Geography, EP822
Macroeconomic Outcomes, PE162
Macroeconomic Performance, EP59,
   PE2, PE206, PE207, PE208, also
   see Economics and Elections

Macroeconomic Policy, PE156,
  PE173, PE205, PE279, PE457,
  PE488
Macroeconomic Policy Cycles, PE482
Macroeconomic Policy Optimization,
  PE462
Macroeconomic Rationality, PE223
Macroeconomics, EP2, EP39, EP53,
  EP103, EP144, PA134
Macropartisanship, PP240
Macropsychological Perspective,
  DP184
MADD, SP111
Madison, James, LE619
Maharishi Unified Field Theory,
  IR133, IR169
Major Power Rivalries, IR274
Major Wars, IR702
Majoritarian Incentives, LE690
Majority Fallacy, SC324
Majority Leader, LE624
Majority Rule, CP214, SC92, SC128,
  SC338, SC364, SC446, SC534,
  SC580
Majority Voting, SC294
Malapportionment, SP444
Malfeasance, PC177, PP352
Malpractice, LC28, SP102, SP104
Malthus, Thomas, SP72
Malvinas Islands War, IR659, IR675
Management Approaches, OB132
Managers, ET413
Managing the Economy, EP30
Mandates, PE349, SP378
Mandatory Voting Laws, CP126
Mandelbrot, Benoit, DP114, DP115
Manipulability of Voting, SC784
Manipulating Voter Preferences,
  CP312
Manipulation, SC786
Manufacturing, EP274, EP294, PA312
Maori, DC34
Marbury vs. Madison, LC106
Margarine, PE376
Marginal Utility of Income, SC666
Marginality, LE539, LE556, LE579,
  LE589, LE591, LE596, LE615,
  SP278
Marginalization, LC243
Marginals, PG222
Margins, see Election Margins
Mariner Project, SC264
Market Access, EP872
Market Areas, PG137
Market Constraints, SC664
Market Economies, PS72
Market Efficiency, SC683
Market Interdependencies, PE326
Market Justice, ET295
Market Liberalization, PE541
Market Models of Politics, PP44
Market Norms, SC662
Market Oriented Reform, EP148
Market Power, EP28
Market Problems, SC129
Market Share Approach, PP349
Market Shocks, PE38
Market Structure, PA299, PA307
Marketing, PP15
Markets, EP588, ET41, ET272,
  ET448, LE489, PS316, XX247
Markov Models, AB95, CP231, PP260
Markov Processes, DP37, DP273
Marx, Karl, PE6, SP547, XX277,
  XX337, XX351
Marxism, EP3, LC16, LC238, LE590,
  PE30, PS84, PS92, PS97, PS124,
  SC94, XX46, XX307, XX384

Marxist Crisis Theory, PE47, PS84
Marxist Long-Waves, DP216
Marxist Political Economy, AB115,
  PG31, XX315
Marxist-Leninist Systems, PG275
Maryland, PP537
Mass Armies, IR536
Mass Belief Systems, AB119
Mass Communication, AB359, PC30,
  PC34, PC55, PC73, also see
  Political Communication
Mass Media, DC349
Mass Migrations, PG167
Mass Movements, DC258
Mass Murder, IR165
Mass Organizations, PE354
Mass Political Action, CP26
Mass Political Organizations,
  PP458
Mass Preferences, AB18
Mass Violence, DC331
Massachusetts, CP81, LC213
Massive Retaliation, IR833
Mass-Elite Differences, LE298
Mastery over Nature, RP121
Matching Relations, SC35
Material Well-Being, AB340
Materialism, AB345, CP206, XX304,
  XX310
Mathematical Approaches, LC29,
  SC138, XX6, XX76, XX289
Matrix Games, SC440
Matthew Effect, OB886, TR174, XX241
Mau Maus, DC156
Mauritius, PC55
Maximin Principle, ET38
Maximization of Wealth as Justice,
  ET308
Maximizing Behavior, SC607
Maximum, SC649
Mayan Collapse, DP49
Mayas, IR725
Mayors, CP6
McKenzie's Theory, PP479
Meaning, XX329
Means-Testing, SP497
Measurement without Theory
  Controversy, XX248
Media, DC349, EP22, LE131, LE132,
  LE167, LE178, PC3, PC5, PC7,
  PC20, PC25, PC48, PC50, PC51,
  PC63, PC67, PC68, PC71, PC91,
  PC97, PC99, PC104, PC108, PC109,
  PC159, PC162, PC177, PC181,
  PC182, PC183, PC201, PC203,
  PC215, PC217, TR159
Media Bias, PC173, PC180
Media Coverage, DC333, EP577,
  MP172, PC187, PE273
Media Effects, PC114-158/Special
  Section
Media Exposure, PC117, PC136,
  PC148
Media Framing, PC98
Media Markets, PC211
Media Violence, PC52
Median Voter, SC512-531/Special
  Section, EP562, EP698, PE78
Mediation, DC100, IR17, IR97,
  IR104
Mediators, XX300
Medicaid, SP88
Medical Care, SP98
Medical Technology, PA262
Medieval Church, RP46
Medieval Popular Rebellions, DC168
Megalopolis, PP525, SP368

Melbin's Frontier Hypothesis,
  PG231
Members of Parliament, LE305,
  LE597, LE646, LE647
Membership Concentration, DC343
Membership Stability, LE205
Memory, AB20, IR856, XX234
Mental Economy, CP238
Mental Framing, MP317
Mental Health, AB328, SP62, SP69,
  SP97
Mental Maps, IR51, TR155
Mental Models, AB98
Mental Processes, AB53
Merchants of Death, IR560
Mere Exposure Phenomenon, PC126
Merit, OB76, OB82, OB86, OB95,
  OB104, OB108, OB118, OB120,
  OB121, OB122, OB128, OB133,
  OB134, OB142, PA146
Merton, Robert, TR140
Message Tailoring Hypothesis, PC42
Messianic Sanctions, DC374
Metaethics, ET12, ET24, ET64, ET82
Metagames, LE154
Metapreferences, SC51
Metatheory, IR209 OB125, XX358
Meteor Showers, DP23
Methodological Individualism, SC4,
  XX84, XX361
Methodology, DP133, PA230, XX38
Metropolitan Growth, SP308, SP318,
  SP342
Mexican Revolution, DC142, OB188
Mexican-Americans, MP152, MP391,
  MP396, MP414, MP412, MP413,
  MP416, MP453, MP457, MP463,
  MP489, MP492, MP395, MP515,
  MP526
Mexico, CP21, DC142, DC223, EP141,
  LE9, OB289, PA22, PE168, PE489,
  PG303, PP387, PS21, SP266,
  SP305, SP546, XX298, XX299
Miami, MP494
Mice and Men, DP144
Michels Model, PP451, PP479, PP513
Michigan Tax Limitation Amendment,
  EP753
Microeconomics, DP81
Middle Ages, PS219
Middle East, AB228, IR133, IR267
Midterm Elections, AB319, CP290,
  LE504, PE238, PP151, PP156,
  PP163, PP180, PP188, PP194,
  PP203, PP232, also see Congres-
  sional Elections
Midwest, CP171, PP542
Migration, PG130-224/Special
  Section, CP181, DC223, EP180,
  EP781, ET9, LC283, LC484, MP3,
  MP21, MP136, MP118, MP96, MP133,
  MP158, PP265, SP228, SP283
Migratory Species, TR102
Milgram Experiments, XX189
Militancy, DC314
Militarism, AB237, IR498, IR547,
  PS245
Militarization, IR462, IR537,
  IR538, MP405, PS229, PS251
Militarized Disputes, IR665,
  IR666, IR716, IR826
Military, IR461-563/Special
  Section, PS244-261/Special
  Section, EP401, ET371, IR762,
  MP323, OB106
Military Academies, IR461, IR553
Military Action, AB302, IR830
Military Aid, IR357, IR361

Military Alliances, IR220
Military Allocations, IR490
Military Buildups, IR275, IR374
Military Capacity, IR326
Military Commitments, IR412
Military Committee, LE259
Military Coups, DC114, DC116,
  DC122, DC123, also see Coups
  d'Etat
Military Culture, IR561
Military Decision Making, IR710,
  SC678
Military Deterrence, IR433-460/
  Special Section
Military Dictatorships, PS244
Military Disengagement from
  Politics, IR557
Military Doctrine, IR469
Military Efficiency, IR558
Military Effort, IR555
Military Equilibrium, IR343
Military Escalation, IR274
Military Establishments, IR461-
  563/Special Section, PS244-261/
  Special Section
Military Expenditures, see Defense
  Spending
Military Experience, AB267
Military Force, AB262, DP258,
  LE148
Military Governments, IR505
Military-Industrial Complex,
  IR333, IR481, IR541
Military Intervention, IR658,
  IR766, IR767, PS250, PS256
Military Issues, IR479
Military Keynesianism, IR527
Military Leaders, PS257
Military Manpower, IR466
Military Officers, IR524
Military Organization, IR480
Military Policy, AB276, IR468,
  IR474, IR536
Military Recruitment, IR539
Military Regimes, PS244-261/
  Special Section
Military Service, IR502, IR512,
  IR518, MP95
Military Simulation, SC442, SC474
Military Size, PS259
Military Sociology, IR531
Military Strategy, IR781
Military Technology, IR325
Military Tradition, IR540
Military Values, IR470
Milk, EP663
Millennial Sects, RP6
Miller-Stokes Data, LE283
Milwaukee, SP312
Mimicking Political Debate, MP43
Minimal Consequences, PC129
Minimal Effects Model, PP165
Minimal Information Elections,
  CP234
Minimal State, OB285
Minimal Winning Coalitions, SC159
Minimalist Organizations, OB341
Minimax Regret, CP134, CP202
Minimum Wage, EP108, EP132, EP174,
  EP429, EP496, EP510, EP513,
  LC210, LE246
Mining, EP642, IR512
Ministries, LE534
Minor Parties, PP465, PP475
Minority Cultures, ET228
Minority Districts, MP147
Minority Governments, LE73

Minority Politics, MP1-530/Special
  Section, LE613
Minority Representation, LE700
Minority Rights, MP13
Miranda Warning, LC465
Miscegenation, XX347
Misconduct, LC2
Misery, SP522
Misinformation, CP291, PP212
Mismanagement of Public Funds,
  EP235
Misperceived Risk, SC710
Misperceptions, IR457, SC484
Missing Females, SP76
Missouri, DC128
Mistrust, CP62
Mistrustful-Efficacious Hypothe-
  sis, CP27
Mobility, PG215
Mobility Hypothesis, MP98
Mobilization, CP9, CP21, CP38,
  CP39, CP62, CP283, CP292, DC207,
  DC217, MP153, MP410, MP471,
  MP483, MP499, PP20, PP311,
  PP530, PP546
Mobilization of Bias, LE234
Moderation Hypothesis, PP134
Modernity, ET204, PS286
Modernization, DC254, MP478,
  PC151, PS86, PS262, PS283,
  PS289, PS293, PS298, PS302,
  PS308
Modesty, ET97
Moebius Strip, SC539
Momentum, XX194
Monarchy, LE608, PP244, PS58
Monastic Communities, OB363
Monday Demonstrations, DP156
Monetarism, DP222
Monetary Analysis, EP88
Monetary Business Cycle, DP202
Monetary Cooperation, EP29
Monetary Policy, DP84, DP275,
  EP65, EP74, EP76, EP96, EP97,
  EP100, EP116, EP138, EP150,
  EP151, LE496, PE455, PE456,
  PE497, PE498
Monetary Regimes, EP725
Monetary System, PE26
Monetary Theory, EP105
Monetary Unification, PE17, PE20
Money, EP129
Money and Votes, PP99
Monopolies, OB152, PE326
Monopoly Rents, EP801
Monotheism, RP104
Monotonicity Paradoxes, SC550
Mood Theory, AB231
Moral Approaches, DC219, also see
  Ethics
Moral Argument, ET16
Moral Assessments, ET49
Moral Attitudes, ET115
Moral Basis of Politics, ET424,
  also see Public Ethics
Moral Behavior, ET113, ET176
Moral Character, ET84
Moral Code, ET39
Moral Cognition, SC207
Moral Community, ET83, RP102
Moral Conceptions, ET79
Moral Conflict, ET73, ET393
Moral Conservatism, RP180
Moral Considerations, ET2
Moral Convictions, ET411
Moral Decisions, SC628
Moral Decline, ET35

Moral Development, ET22, ET58,
  ET101, ET104, ET105, ET114,
  ET446, XX239
Moral Disagreement, ET5
Moral Duty, ET423
Moral Economy, DC129, ET365
Moral Education Theory of Punish-
  ment, LC320
Moral Efficiency, ET87
Moral Enlightenment, SP193
Moral Exclusion, ET51, ET293,
  ET300, ET454
Moral Hazard, SC669
Moral Issues, ET71, RP129
Moral Judgment, ET32, ET335
Moral Justifications, AB290
Moral Majority, RP139, RP177
Moral Mathematics, ET91
Moral Membership, ET85
Moral Obligation, ET65
Moral Panics, IR333, RP12
Moral Parochialism, ET18
Moral Philosophy, ET42
Moral Principles, ET384
Moral Reasoning, DC252, ET30,
  ET75, ET80, ET374, ET438
Moral Reform, ET449
Moral Responsibility, ET27, ET439
Moral Rights, ET108
Moral Stages, AB216
Moral Structures, ET99
Moral Theories, ET55
Moral Universals, ET119
Moral Values, ET44, ET388
Moralism, SP540
Morality, ET15, ET20, ET35, ET38,
  ET60, ET70, ET74, ET81, ET93,
  ET107, ET112, ET116, ET371,
  ET390, ET397, ET403, ET418,
  ET429, ET444, ET447, IR483,
  LC137, MP319, RP21, RP27, RP116,
  SC493, SC615, SC640, SC655,
  SP42, SP523, see Ethics
Morality of War, IR676
Moralizing, IR55
Morally Committed, LC314
Morals by Agreement, ET25, ET67,
  SC638
Morgenthau, Hans, IR186
Mormonism, RP93
Mortality, LC30, PE494
Mortality Rates, PA166
Most Different and Most Similar
  Systems, XX237
Mother Tongues, MP455, MP456
Mothers, MP276
Motive Attribution, MP128
Motive Scores, XX401
Motives, AB336
Motives of Public Officials, LE119
Movements, MP227, PP440, SP550
Muddling Through, OB13
Mughal Empire, PS231
Muhammad, RP16
Multicandidate Elections, PP166
Multicultural Society, MP367
Multidimensional Choice Spaces,
  SC790
Multilateral Assistance, IR345
Multilateral Cooperation, ET185
Multilateralism, IR28, IR65,
  IR115, IR161, IR224, IR345,
  IR851
Multimember Districts, CP216,
  MP199, SC238
Multinational Corporations, PE3,
  PE8, PE11, PE18, PE24, PE25,
  PE33

Multiparty Competition, PP466
Multiple Criteria, MP123
Multiple Discoveries, TR142, TR185
Multiple Equilibria, DP98
Multiple Indicators, AB313
Multiple Objectives, SC370
Multipolarity, PS66
Multistate Nations, PS37
Multistate System Endurance, IR840
Multivariate Point Process Models,
  PG76
Municipal Administration, PA292
Municipal Bond Proposals, CP76
Municipal Borrowing Costs, SP320
Municipal Charters, LC130
Municipal Efficiency, SP374
Municipal Elections, MP192
Municipal Employees, DC326, MP461
Municipal Finances, SP312
Municipal Government, PA280
Municipal Offices, MP155
Municipal Peace Actions, IR142
Municipal Reform, PA302
Municipal Services, SP371
Municipal Structure, SP416
Municipal Taxes, EP744
Murder, LC355, LC356, LC367, PC140
Music, XX227
Mutually Assured Destruction,
  OB222
Myopic Behavior, LE244
Myrdal, Gunner, MP510
Myth of America, RP61

Nagel-Erikson Hypothesis, PC28
Naive Empiricism, XX248
Nation Building, PS284
National Assemblies, LE481
National Attitudes, IR447
National Collegiate Athletic
  Association, OB364
National Council of Churches,
  RP133
National Disintegration, PE52
National Economy, EP87, EP128
National Election Studies, AB309,
  AB331
National Identity, LC123, XX250,
  XX347
National Integration, IR533
National Labor Relations Act,
  DC338
National Labor Relations Board,
  EP631
National Power, IR207
National Preferences, IR234
National Resources, EP378
National Security, PS105
National Self-Images, AB265
National Size, see Size of Country
National Territories, PG242
Nationalism, DC171, IR127, IR476,
  IR536, IR813, LE436, MP432,
  MP459, MP469, PG22, PG256,
  PS177, PS235, RP7, XX181, XX243,
  XX259
Nationality, ET68, XX246
Nationality Crisis, MP439
Nationalization, PA304
Nationalization of the American
  States, SP370
Nations, DP263, EP245, PG12, PS53
Native Americans, MP366, MP404,
  MP406, MP407, MP424, MP449,
  MP470, MP471, MP473, MP513,
  PG147, PG314, TR7
Nativity, MP396
Nativity Concentration, PG179

NATO, EP345, IR239, IR242, IR243,
  IR258, IR370, SC524
Natural Disasters, EP200, TR132
Natural Gas, EP636
Natural Rate of Unemployment,
  EP164, EP165, EP175
Natural Resources, TR44-136/
  Special Section, EP764
Natural Rights, SC28
Natural Selection, OB362
Naturalization, MP23, MP413, MP487
Naval Strategy Controversy, IR501
Navy, IR529, OB180
Nazis, PP245, PP285
Need Achievement, DC22
Negative Advertising, CP194,
  PC170, PC188, PC192, PC193,
  PC194, PC206, PP199, PP225
Negative Externalities, EP565
Negative-Sum Game, PG187
Negative Voting, LE504, PE192,
  PP169, PP188
Negativity Effects, AB36
Negligence, LC13, LC28
Negotiated Settlements, IR724
Negotiations, DC16, IR8, IR27,
  IR33, IR189, IR196, IR217,
  IR724, SC388, XX14, XX95
Neighborhoods, PG75-129/Special
  Section, LC164, LC181, PG125,
  RP75, SP443
Neoclassical Theory, EP280
Neocolonialism, PS238
Neocorporatism, EP247, PS71
Neoliberalism, EP355, IR128, IR147
Neo-Marxist Theories, PE50
Neopluralism, PS145
Neorealism, IR147, IR823
Netherlands, DP280, EP614, LC204,
  LC290, MP362, MP460, PP394,
  RP164, SC170, SC742, SP140,
  SP407
Network Connections, SC609
Neural Networks, DP147, DP229, RP5
Neurobiology, PA204
Neutral Principles, ET422
Neutralization, EP784
New Christian Right, RP179
New Class, AB96
New Deal, EP628, EP676, PE50,
  PP526, PP530, TR14
New Deal Coalition, MP500
New Federalism, PS182, PS191,
  PS204
New Haven, MP194
New History, XX184
New Institutionalism, OB45, OB92,
  SC38
New Jersey, XX124
New Justices, LC395
New Keynesian Economics, DP127
New Parties, PP59, PP468
New Political History, XX106
New Politics, AB342, PP505
New Protestantism, RP45
New Right, CP14
New South, MP410, MP442, also see
  Southern United States
New World Order, IR212, IR847,
  IR848, IR867
New York, LC57, LC203, LE607,
  PP525, TR5
New York City, DP134, LC217,
  PE110, PP395, PP436
New York City Charter, SP369
New York Times, PC131
New Zealand, CP273, DC34, LE314,
  MP292, PE488

News, PC99, PC125
News Comprehension, PC75
News Conferences, PC58
News Coverage, PC159-180/Special
  Section, PC220
News Diffusion, PC124
News Dynamics, PC159
News Flow, PC127
News Reception, PC72
Newspaper Endorsements, PC122
Newspapers, OB331, PC110, PC135,
  PC146, PC150
Newsworthiness, PC56
Nicaragua, AB290, DC160, PS60
Nice People, RP21, RP71
Nice Strategies, ET158
Niche Position, OB388
Nigeria, RP64
Nigerian Civil War, PC160
Nineteenth Amendment, LE300, MP239
Niskanen Model, OB149
Nixon, Richard, LE132, XX401
No Fault Insurance, LC23
Noah Effect, DP114
Noble Rebellion, DC166
Nominating Process, PP101-136/
  Special Section, CP286, MP300,
  MP342
Nomination, SC774
Nonalignment, IR80
Nonattitudes, AB10, AB55, AB59,
  AB72
Nonbeliefs, RP105
Noncompensatory Principle, SC187
Noncompliance, LC180
Nonconversion, DC239
Noncooperative Game Theory, TR38
Nondecisions, SC596
Nondurable Precautions, LC28
Nonelectoral Political Behavior,
  PE521
Nonequilibrium Solutions, LE14
Nonequilibrium Theory, DP107
Nongovernmental Organizations,
  EP408, IR195
Nonincremental Policy Making, PA46
Nonlinear Dependence, DP136
Nonlinear Dynamics, DP26, DP28,
  DP42, DP117, DP119, DP120,
  IR337, IR248, IR323, TR139
Nonlinear Instabilities, DP77
Nonlinear Time Series, DP20, DP33
Nonlinearity, DP5, DP78, DP102
Nonmarket Failures, SC146
Nonmeasurable Voting Bodies, SC337
Non-Nuclear Strategies, IR392
Nonparametric Regression, DP112
Nonprofit Organizations, ET125,
  OB335, SP408
Nontariff Barriers, EP809, EP843
Nonverbal Displays, LE29
Nonviolence, ET56, ET117
Nonvoting, CP108, CP161, CP175
Nonvoting Paradox, CP120, CP152,
  CP151
Normal Form Games, SC453, SC454
Normal Vote, LE254, PP172, PP204
Normative Assumptions, SC637
Normative Behavior, ET176
Normative Constraints, ET342,
  ET350, IR176
Normative Discourse, AB292
Normative Frameworks of Public
  Policy, PA94
Normative Principles, ET102
Normative Problem, PE10
Normative Tax Theory, EP693
Normative Theory, ET62, IR40

Normativity, XX390
Normlessness, AB67
Norms, ET323-357/Special Section,
   ET283, ET312, ET318, IR176,
   IR472, LC338, LE500, OB184,
   PS151, SC401, SC413, SC662, TR61
Norms of Distribution, ET347
North American Free Trade
   Agreement, EP824, EP871
North American Political Economy,
   EP828
North Carolina, MP114
Northern Ireland, DC101, DC253
North-South Issues, EP838, IR160,
   IR172
Norway, LE86, LE672, MP178, PE279,
   SC765
Not in My Backyard Beliefs, TR162
Nozick, Robert, ET103, ET253
Nuclear Disarmament, IR564, IR566,
   IR586
Nuclear Free Policy, IR593
Nuclear Freeze, IR579, IR587,
   IR590, IR592, LE302
Nuclear Learning, IR591
Nuclear Power, TR146, TR153,
   TR154, TR156, TR159, TR163,
   TR164, TR170, TR176, TR179
Nuclear Proliferation, IR581,
   IR582, IR602
Nuclear Restraint, IR604
Nuclear Safeguards, IR580
Nuclear Superpowers, IR567
Nuclear Technology, TR180
Nuclear Tests, IR331
Nuclear Threat, IR603
Nuclear War, EP493, EP494, EP499,
   EP500, IR569, IR576, IR584,
   IR596, IR594
Nuclear Waste, PG173, TR175
Nuclear Weapons, IR564-608/Special
   Section, IR320, IR595, SC369
Number of Candidates, PP343
Number of Cases, XX215
Number of Components to Retain,
   XX414
Number of Parties, PP520
Nygant vs. Board, LC414

Obedience, ET106, IR483, OB160,
   XX189
Obituaries, PC163
Object Relational Personality
   Theories, XX41
Obligation, CP334, DC252, ET57,
   ET65, ET399, ET406, ET438,
   ET448, MP258
Obligation to Vote, OB255
Occult, PS297
Occupational Classes, PE210, PE215
Occupational Interests, EP206
Occupational Power, PA344
Occupational Regulation, EP585
Ocean Politics, XX152
October War, AB228
Offense-Defense Balance, IR678
Offsetting Behavior Hypothesis,
   SP120
Ohio, PG314, SP421
Oil, PA304, TR71
Oil Depletion Allowance, LE208
Oil Pollution, PS47
Oil Prices, EP577
Oil-Price Shock, EP153
Okun-Richardson Model, PG194
Oligarchic Republics, IR827
Oligarchy, OB355, PS119
Oligarchy Choice Models, SC524

Oligopoly, EP813, PP428, SC482
Olson, Mancur, PE6, PE315, PE316,
   PE317, PE326, PE329, PE331,
   PE332, PE351, PE384, SC227
Olympic Games, XX26
Olympic Performance, XX127, XX214
Ombudsmen, XX160, XX300
On the Cross, MP81
One Issue at a Time Decision
   Making, CP230
One Issue at a Time Voting, CP225
One Man, One Vote Principle,
   CP274, SC238
One Party Dominant Systems, PP326
Ontario, LE587
Open Economies, EP832
Open Rule, LE270
Open Seats, CP235, LE155
Opening Statements, LC8
Operational Code, AB218, AB219,
   AB249, AB300, LE16
Opinion Dynamics, AB71
Opinion Formation, DP34
Opinion Leadership, AB72
Opinion Representation, MP183
Opinion Writing, LC439
Opportunity, MP354, PG163, SC675
Opportunity Costs, LE299
Opposition Popularity, PP491
Oppositional Media, PC167
Optimal Contingent Rules, LC135
Optimal Frequency of Elections,
   SC231
Optimal Punishment Theories, LC324
Optimal Spatial Location, PP161
Optimal Tenure, LE1, SC230
Optimization, OB346
Options Markets, SC683
Order, DP73, ET339, PA157, RP79,
   XX344
Order of Business, LE360
Order Parameters, DP155
Organization of Society, PS30
Organization of Economy, DP161
Organizational Behavior, OB1-400/
   Special Section, DP48, DP55,
   IR601, LE393, OB67, PA210,
   PE353, PE354, PP469
Organizational Change, DP48,
   LC438, OB31, OB324
Organizational Choice, OB16
Organizational Cohesion, DC123
Organizational Complexity, OB160
Organizational Culture, ET161,
   ET339, OB4, OB68
Organizational Decline, OB53
Organizational Democracy, OB2
Organizational Design, OB109
Organizational Development, OB36,
   OB360
Organizational Differentiation,
   OB340
Organizational Ecology, OB324-370/
   Special Section
Organizational Economics, DC204
Organizational Effectiveness,
   SP157
Organizational Encapsulation,
   PP314
Organizational Form, OB359
Organizational Founding, OB352
Organizational Hierarchies, OB150
Organizational Humanism, MP298
Organizational Incompetence, OB57
Organizational Irrationality,
   SC120
Organizational Maintenance, OB63

Organizational Mortality, OB326,
   OB329, OB338, OB343, OB350,
   OB368
Organizational Niches, OB326
Organizational Noncompliance,
   EP574
Organizational Politics, IR135
Organizational Populations, OB330
Organizational Resources, EP295
Organizational Size, OB344
Organizational Sociology, OB58
Organizational Style, OB23
Organizational Surveys, AB311,
   AB317
Organizational Transitions, OB11,
   OB49
Organizational Trust, OB17
Organized Crime, LC198, LC217,
   LC252, LC257, LC290, PP395
Organized Interests, PE388
Orientations, AB25, AB33
Ortega, TR190
Orthogonal Trend Surface Expan-
   sions, SP462
Ostracism, ET170
Ostrogorski Paradox, SC573, SC584
Others Welfare, ET121
Ottoman Empire, DC127, IR670
Outcome Assessment, OB72
Outer Space Exploration, PG231
Output Shares, OB56
Output Studies, XX38
Outrageous Arguments, SC111
Outside Agitators, DC212
Outsiders, XX187
Out-of-Character, LE184
Overcentralization, PS185
Overdrafts, PP397
Overrepresentation Hypothesis,
   LE208
Overseas Vote, CP327
Oversight, LE423
Overtilled and Undertilled Fields,
   XX23
Ownership, PS77
Ozone Depletion, TR95

Pacific Rim, PE317
Pacifism, DC67, IR713
Pair Interactions, AB21
Pakistan, IR318
Palestine, ET250
Panama Canal Treaties, AB275,
   IR116
Panics, DP15
Pansystems, SC147, SC148
Para Bellum Hypothesis, IR820
Paradigms, AB115, PA259
Paradox of Discourse, PC23
Paradox of Disintegration, DC116
Paradox of Leadership, LE51
Paradox of New Members, SC574
Paradox of Power, SC601
Paradox of Punishment, LC311
Paradox of Redistribution, SC548
Paradox of Representation, SC582
Paradox of State Size, OB252
Paradox of Thrift, PE57
Paradox of Vote Trading, LE714,
   LE722
Paradox of Voting, CP120, CP152,
   CP151, CP169, CP179, CP182,
   LE365, LE709, SC549, SC559,
   SC560, SC570
Paradoxes, SC532-588/Special
   Section, SC577, SC594
Paradoxical Conflict Outcome,
   IR734, IR770

Paradoxical Effects, SC533
Paraguay, OB316
Parallel Markets, EP410
Parallel Processing, LE367
Paramilitary Systems, DP134
Paratroopers, IR482, IR483
Paretian Liberal, SC122, SC436
Paretian Libertarian Paradox,
    SC572
Pareto Coefficient, PG61
Pareto Curve, EP485
Pareto Optimality, SC144, SC740,
    XX206
Parfit, Derek, ET23, ET91
Paris, PP525
Parity, IR338
Parking Tickets, LC498
Parkinson's Law, OB173, OB193
Parliamentary Architecture, LE395
Parliamentary Democracy, PS156
Parliamentary Election Timing,
    PP140
Parliamentary Reform, LE413
Parliaments, LE3, LE6, LE34, LE36,
    LE76, LE84, LE337, LE382, LE424,
    LE434, LE436, LE455, LE492,
    LE508, PS144, PS148, SC194
Parochial Hypothesis, LE707
Parochialism, IR517
Participation Modes, CP60
Particular Values, AB391
Parties, see Political Parties
Partisan Attitudes, PP246
Partisan Behavior, PG93, RP75
Partisan Bias, SC299
Partisan Change, PP302, PP482,
    PP530
Partisan Cleavage, LE511
Partisan Cycles, PE203, PE429
Partisan Instability, PP332
Partisan Intensity, PP250
Partisan Linkages, PP251
Partisan Manipulation of the
    Economy, PE497, also see
    Political Business Cycle
Partisan Stability, AB110
Partisan Sterotypes, PP33
Partisan Transitions, LE606
Partisanship, AB222, IR117, LE294,
    LE503, LE530, MP361, MP383,
    PE197, PE275, PP28, PP41, PP256,
    PP275, PP276, PP288, PP312,
    PP490, SC331
Party Activists, PP236, PP242,
    PP252, PP278, PP298, PP315,
    SC735, also see Pary Elites
Party Alignments, PP277, PP444,
    PP467, PP504
Party as Linkage, PP24
Party Attachment, PP304
Party Balance, LE509
Party Capacity Theory, LC3
Party Choice, PP329
Party Cleavages, SP459
Party Cohesion, LE526, LE531,
    LE675
Party Competition, see Interparty
    Competition
Party Conferences, SC304
Party Conflict, PP535, PP539
Party Contacting, PP136
Party Contributions, LE525
Party Cycles, DP234
Party Decision Making, PP178
Party Decline, LE507, PP9, PP254,
    PP301, PP306, PP454
Party Decomposition, PG245
Party Delegations, PP129

Party Differences, PP6
Party Discipline, ET331
Party Distance, PP108
Party Electoral Prospects, PP123
Party Elites, PP42, PP259, PP292
Party Failure, PP446
Party Goals, LE535, PP461
Party Government, LE75, LE515,
    LE522
Party Identification, PP236-317/
    Special Section, MP419, PE290,
    PP111, PP490, RP151
Party Ideology, PP20, PP31, SP386
Party Images, PP478
Party Influence, LE536
Party Leaders, LE13, LE271, LE314,
    LE355, LE356, LE527
Party Loyalties, CP288, LE674,
    PP34, PP266, PP307
Party Mobilization, PP339
Party Neutrality, PP454
Party Organization, LE523, PP37,
    PP43, PP177, PP331, PP457, PP469
Party Perceptions, PP307
Party Polarization, CP117, PP22,
    PP322
Party Preferences, PP282, PP295,
    PP305
Party Programmes, PP21
Party-Public Policy Linkage, LE534
Party Realignment, see Realign-
    ments
Party Reform, PP35
Party Stability, PP239
Party Strategies, PP3, PP15, PP44,
    PP328, PP344
Party Strength, PG248
Party Structures, PP479
Party Support, PP249, PP259, PP325
Party Systems, PP439-525/Special
    Section, CP211, LE510
Party Unity, LE525, PP155
Party-Voter Linkages, PP328
Party Voting, LE514, LE517, LE528,
    LE532
Past Decisions, LE61
Patents, PA291, PA322, TR149
Path Models, LE649, PE345
Patriotism, IR447, IR476, IR795
Patronage, PE15
Pattern Analysis, XX285
Pauperism, SP284
Pay, OB142
Peace, AB244, AB296, IR95, IR99,
    IR133, IR142, IR177, IR185,
    IR264, IR401, IR402, IR404,
    IR410, IR423, IR453, IR685,
    IR707, IR736, IR773, IR819,
    IR827, PG79, PS234
Peace Dividend, EP349, IR556
Peace Protests, DC234, DC250,
    DP267, IR96, IR588, OB338
Peace Research, EP862, IR7, IR89,
    IR91, IR94, IR138, IR141, IR175,
    IR387, IR400
Peace through Strength, IR420
Peaceful Settlements, IR30, IR407
Peacekeeping, IR68, IR379, IR545,
    IR686
Peacemaking, MP122
Peasant Agriculture, EP518
Peasant Conservatism, TR29
Peasant Movements, DC225, DC231,
    DC244
Peasant Politics, DC217
Peasant Rebellion, DC132, DC137,
    DC154, DC155, DC159, DC173,
    DC183, DC189

Peasant Societies, CP147, SP200
Peasant Strategies, DC219
Peasant Unrest, DC127
Peasants, DC129, DC154, DC163,
    DC185, DC197, DC211, PE243, TR20
Peloponnesian War, IR774
Penalties, LC338
Pendulum Hypotheses, IR809
Pensions, EP84, LE554, SP7, SP476
People as Politicians, XX377
People's Understanding of Poli-
    tics, AB199
Perceived Representativeness,
    CP350
Perceptions, AB17, AB99, AB214,
    AB265, IR705, SC56, SC661, XX123
Perceptual Dilemma, IR321
Perceptual Frameworks, AB95
Perestroika, DP66, PS73
Performance, OB142
Performance Evaluation, PA222,
    PA248
Performance Management, OB117
Period Effects, PP238, PP250
Periodical Press, PC175
Periods, PP2
Peripheral War, IR469
Peripheries, DC222, IR843, IR849,
    IR871, PG13, PG65, PS225, PG256,
    PG239, also see Core
Permanent Income Hypothesis, PE141
Permissiveness, SP12, SP21
Peronism, PS44
Perot, Ross, PE158
Persian Gulf War, AB58, AB302,
    IR498, IR613, IR673, IR700,
    IR737, IR830, LE58, LE627, PC11,
    PC31, PC176
Person Perception, XX2
Personal Attribute Models, LC433,
    LC469
Personal Concerns, CP205
Personal Development, ET413
Personal Experience, PC63, PC64
Personal Finances, PE222
Personal Grievances, PE220
Personal Influence, PC44
Personal Risks, SC663
Personal Savings, see Savings
Personal Vote, CP198, LE597, LE628
Personality, AB177, LC421, LE4,
    LE135, OB207, XX42, XX125
Personality Characteristics, IR52,
    IR154, IR461
Personality Concomitants, DC83
Personality Effects, IR37, IR173,
    IR192
Personality Typologies, XX73
Personalization, CP255
Persuasion, AB106, LE138, PC202,
    XX409
Persuasive Campaigning, PC62
Peru, DC131, DC174, IR512, OB316,
    PS212
Pesticide Regulation, EP570, TR69
Petrification, LE549
Petroleum, see Oil
Phase Changes, DP134
Philadelphia, PP411
Philadelphia System, DC13
Philanthropy, ET125, ET129, PE15
Philippines, CP193
Phillips Curve, EP538, OB295
Philosophers, PA67, PA148
Philosophical Argument, ET62
Philosophical Schools, XX262
Philosophy, PA79, PA147
Philosophy and Politics, XX341

Philosophy of Science, XX196
Phoenix Factor, EP320, IR106
Physical Science Professions,
   TR182
Physicians, SP99
Physics, TR145, XX174
Pietism, TR140
Pigou, Arthur, EP572
Pittsburgh, PP409
Place, PG48
Place Annihilation, PG24
Place Stratification, PG37
Plagues, PG121
Planned Economies, DP205
Planning, ET46, PA17, PA98
Platforms, PP107, PP109, PP112,
   PP122, PP126, PP127, PP132,
   SC517, see Conventions
Play, SC472
Plea Bargaining, LC48
Plural Societies, DC10, EP460,
   PS13
Pluralism, ET28, ET44, MP475,
   OB148, PE312, PE506, PP449,
   PS145, PS192, RP145, SC75
Pluralist Ignorance, PC81
Plurality of Value, ET63
Plurality, PP519
Plurality Rule, PP343
Plurality Voting, SC283, SC783
Plurilateralism, IR371
Pocketbook Voting, PE235, PE277,
   PE278
Poisson Processes, IR236, IR679,
   LC471, OB66
Poland, ET117
Polar Politics, XX153, XX171
Polarity, IR678, IR808, SC716
Polarity Principle, DC73
Polarization, DP155, MP428, PP463,
   XX284
Polarizing US Culture, XX357
Policing, LC477-510/Special
   Section, DC203, DC349, LC41,
   MP405, OB81, PP417, PP362
Policy, see Public Policy
Political Accounts, XX233
Political Action, CP17
Political Action Committees,
   LE634, LE641, LE642, LE687,
   PE324, PE333, PE343, PE385,
   PE410, PP53, PP64, PP65, PP66,
   PP77, PP81, PP84, PP87, PP89,
   PP95, PP97, RP179, SP59
Political Activists, SP34
Political Anthropology, XX302
Political Appeals, XX59
Political Argument, XX319
Political Behavior, DP259, PA161,
   PE380, PE521, XX57
Political Bibliography, XX186
Political Business Cycle, PE429-
   498/Special Section, DC275
Political Careers, LE312-358/
   Special Section, LE552, XX82,
   XX147, XX292
Political Communication, PC1-
   PC222/Special Section
Political Competition, PE16, PE169
Political Conferences, PP118
Political Consultants, PP213
Political Consumption Cycle, PE441
Political Control, EP563
Political Control of Bureaucracy,
   OB194
Political Culture, PG225-330/
   Special Section, ET269, LC459,
   LE395, LE408, LE584, MP184,

MP257, MP477, PP16, PP355,
   PP398, PP426, PS60, SP26,
   SP332
Political Cycles, DP235, DP239,
   DP244, DP247, DP251, DP268,
   DP270, DP271, LE50, LE397, PE455
Political Definitions, LC436
Political Development, PS262-312/
   Special Section, DC178, EP569,
   IR733, PS106, PS312, also see
   Development
Political Drama, PE242
Political Ecology, OB365, also see
   Organizational Ecology
Political-Economic Models, EP8,
   PE157, PE451
Political Economy, PE1-617/Special
   Section, EP125, EP638, LE89,
   PE1, PE35, PE40, PE49, PE27,
   PE51, PE198, PG10, PP350, PS294,
   SC114, SP315, SP323
Political Education, CP334, ET109,
   ET265, IR475, SP194, SP245
Political Elasticity, OB137
Political Entrepreneurs, LE48,
   SC117
Political Ethics, ET436
Political Evaluations, PE179
Political Events, XX388
Political Expenditure Cycle, PE434
Political Expenditures, SC767
Political Experiences, MP393
Political Expression, PG225
Political Friendship, LE370
Political Geography, PG1-PG330/
   Special Section, IR1, MP291,
   MP409, PG21, PG26, PG27, PG29,
   PG31, PG45, PG50, PG63, PG262,
   RP32
Political Goods, XX9
Political History, XX11
Political Identification, PP274
Political Independence, PC25
Political Institutions, CP128,
   XX135
Political Interest, MP214
Political Life, XX93
Political Life Cycle, TR167
Political Linguistics, MP452
Political Machines, PP350-448/
   Special Section, OB297
Political Malaise, OB317, PC145
Political Management, IR815
Political Manipulation of the
   Economy, PE464, PE472, PE496,
   also See Political Business
   Cycle
Political Markets, PC212
Political Modernization, LE376
Political Monetary Cycle, PE437,
   PE454, PE470
Political-Moral Disputes, LC409
Political Myth, PC45
Political Networks, CP352
Political Organizations, PE571
Political Orientation, MP169
Political Outcomes, SC799
Political Participation, CP1-354/
   Special Section, RP137-180/
   Special Section, EP505, LE689,
   MP169, MP207, MP252, MP280,
   MP302, MP307, MP335, MP339,
   MP369, MP394, MP435, MP457,
   MP477, MP482, MP521, MP526,
   PA54, PC1, PC26, PE382, PG94,
   PG99, PP2, PP136, PP509, PS70,
   PS151, PS275, SC708, SP155

Political Parties, LE502-536/
   Special Section, PP1-546/Special
   Section, CP102, CP153, EP99,
   EP156, EP344, EP388, EP465,
   EP505, EP527, EP540, LE17, LE96,
   LE195, LE626, LE663, MP210,
   MP266, MP305, OB247, OB308,
   PC146, PE162, PE353, PE354,
   PE393, PE408, PE430, PE608,
   PG39, PG269, PG299, RP150,
   SC197, SP338, SP476, XX298, also
   see Legislative Parties
Political Periods, CP4
Political Policy Cycle, PE477
Political Proximity, AB30
Political Psychology, AB160,
   EP125, EP280, LE165, PE49,
   SC105, XX203, XX274, XX275
Political Reasoning, AB4, AB60
Political Reliability, LE69
Political Science, CP336, IR737,
   LE37, OB138, PA130, PA131,
   PP512, SC104, SC452, SC601,
   SC604, XX8, XX38, XX78, XX79,
   XX96, XX99, XX157, XX221, XX222,
   XX283
Political Science History, XX100
Political Scientists, PP271,
   PP303, PP310, XX205
Political Shocks, IR385
Political Similarity, EP810
Political Socialization, AB383,
   PP250
Political Sociology, PG243, XX35,
   XX170, XX276
Political Spaces, AB11
Political Spectacle, MP331
Political Stock Market, XX107
Political Structure, AB50, DC26,
   IR701, PA8, SP342, SP384
Political Subcultures, PG306
Political Support, DC58
Political Systems, PS1-330/Special
   Section, LE443
Political Theorizing, XX58
Political Theory, EP723, ET103,
   ET240, MP258, PA181, SC11, XX159
Political Thinking, AB51, AB65
Political Thought, XX330
Political Translation, PE286
Political Turnover, see Turnover
Political Universe, AB9, AB15
Political World, AB109
Politicians, ET480
Politicians Records, PP161
Politicization of Scholarship,
   XX356
Politics, SP168, SP464
Politics-Administration Nexus,
   PA89
Politics and Morality, RP165
Politics as Moral Causes, ET432
Politics of Assumptions, SP500
Politics of Disorder, DC215
Politics of Ideas, EP840
Polity and Society, AB344
Poll Results, CP259
Poll Tax, EP720, SC259
Polls, AB312, AB380, CP324, PC144,
   PP104, see Surveys
Pollution, EP649, EP671, EP674,
   PS47, TR53
Polyarchy, OB183
Polycentric Political Systems,
   PE574
Polyethnic Society, DC55
Poor Relief, SP72
Popper, Karl, PA127

Popular Movements, CP43, DC190
Popular Participation, CP36
Popular Press, PC137
Popular Rebellions, DC168
Popularity, DP240, PC53
Popularity Functions, PC137, PE258
Population, PP179, SP70, SP87,
   SP96, SP107, SP121, SP126,
   SP127, XX370
Population Density, IR619, PG15,
   PG59, SP491
Population Density Gradient, SP428
Population Dynamics, DP85, DP242,
   SP100
Population Ecology, OB352, OB357,
   PE364
Population Growth, EP212, SP101,
   SP129
Population Heterogeneity, LC365
Population Size, ET47, MP83, SP313
Populism, MP85, MP130, PP5, PP501,
   SC142
Populist Parties, PP442
Pork Barrel Paradox, SC581
Pork Barrel Politics, LE688-723/
   Special Section
Pornography, ET449
Portfolio Measures, LC186
Portfolio Payoffs, LE92
Portfolio Theory, PA2
Portugal, LE444
Position Taking, LE179
Positivism, XX81
Posnerian Law, ET308
Possibility of Judgement, IR55
Postage Stamps, XX294
Postauthoritarian Elections, CP332
Postbehavioralism, XX196
Post-Cold War, IR371
Post-Communist Transitions, EP162
Post Hoc Ergo Propter, EP100
Postindustrism, AB365, PG33
Postliberal State, ET85
Post-Machine Regimes, OB297
Post-Marxism, PS141
Postmaterialism, AB338, AB342,
   AB345, AB366, CP117, CP206
Postmodernism, SC656, XX268
Pottery Industry, OB348
Poverty, SP257-305/Special
   Section, DC113, EP155, EP420,
   EP452, EP502, MP505, SP504,
   SP535, SP512, TR42, also see
   Income
Poverty Statistics, SP263, SP276,
   SP305
Power, SC589-609/Special Section,
   AB127, DC70, EP50, EP396, IR14,
   IR158, IR165, IR207, IR468,
   IR536, IR649, IR702, IR734,
   IR738, IR788, LC99, LC108,
   LE103, LE122, OB160, PE345,
   PE370, PE395, PS218, SC553,
   SC716, SP321, XX142
Power Concentration, DP124, IR858
Power Consciousness, SC589
Power Contenders, DC7
Power Cycle Theory, DP276
Power Differentials, IR662
Power Distributions, IR622, RP52
Power Dynamics, IR648
Power Elite, SC598
Power Indices, SC294, SC603
Power of Appointment, EP76
Power of Ideas, IR453
Power of Suggestion, SC401
Power Shifts, IR706
Power Structures, SC595

Power System Membership, IR660
Power Threat Hypothesis, MP135
Power Transition, IR661, IR681,
   IR682, IR683, IR704, IR815
Powerlessness, AB71
Praetorianism, DC111
Prayer in Public Schools, RP114
Preaching, RP126
Preadult Learning, PC25
Prebehavioralism, XX397
Precautionary Motives, EP464
Precedents, LC402, LC434
Predatory Pricing, SC576
Predator-Prey Model, DP39
Predictability, IR268, XX139
Prediction, XX18
Predictors of War, IR785
Preemptive Wars, IR772
Preference Aggregation, PE353
Preference Formation, XX399
Preference Functions, AB8, PA39
Preference Outliers, LE245
Preference Reversal, AB79, SC50,
   SC497, SC620, SC698
Preference Strength, SC265, SC722
Preferences, AB79, AB336, CP283,
   PG280, SC78, SC692, SC701, SP395
Preferential Judgments, SC56
Pregnancy, SP144
Preindustrial Economies, PE12
Prejudice, ET467, MP70, MP92,
   MP118, MP140, MP174, MP434,
   MP438, MP445, MP498, RP127
Premier's Departments, LE87
Prenegotiation, IR64
Preponderance, IR429
Presidency, AB6, AB165, AB171,
   AB322, CP193, CP223, CP242,
   CP251, CP265, CP266, CP297,
   CP315, CP321, DP260, EP76,
   EP789, LC148, LC442, LC460, LE2,
   LE9, LE33, LE36, LE45, LE46,
   LE52, LE64, LE108, LE110, LE116,
   LE119, LE129, LE134, LE135,
   LE141, LE144, LE146, LE148,
   LE150, LE152, LE155, LE162,
   LE164, LE167, LE168, LE170,
   LE172, LE174, LE176, LE177,
   LE184, LE189, LE191, LE193,
   LE196, LE197, LE200, LE201,
   LE280, LE347, LE560, LE621,
   LE657, LE670, PC71, PC128,
   PC155, PC168, PC171, PC175,
   PC184, PC189, PC202, PC215,
   PC221, PE7, PE81, PE116, PE150,
   PE153, PE154, PE181, PE182,
   PE183, PE184, PE186, PE199,
   PE209, PE238, PE242, PE244,
   PE245, PE246, PE248, PE276,
   PE284, PE293, PE388, PE453,
   PE455, PE477, PE489, PE494,
   PG228, PG230, PG314, PP4, PP41,
   PP46, PP67, PP143, PP147, PP148,
   PP151, PP152, PP155, PP169,
   PP170, PP173, PP174, PP175,
   PP182, PP193, PP196, PP214,
   PP224, RP144, RP180, SC746,
   SC762, SC775, XX389
Presidential Administration, EP630
Presidential Agenda, LE149
Presidential Approval, LE109,
   LE123, LE159, LE185
Presidential Campaigns, CP37,
   PC216, PP54, PP85, PP165, PP168,
   PP185, PP211, PP231
Presidential Candidates, AB40,
   AB182, LE101, LE127, LE160,
   PC43, PC185

Presidential Character, LE105,
   LE126, LE192
Presidential Coalitions, LE117
Presidential Coattails, CP208,
   CP329, PP190
Presidential Communications, PC42
Presidential Cycles, MP24
Presidential Elections, CP106,
   CP144, CP170, CP206, CP207,
   CP241, CP309, CP338, PA162,
   PC122, PG7, PG56, PG92, PG107,
   PG229, PG296, PP381, PP446,
   PP460, PP541, also see Elections
   and Elections and Economics, and
   Presidential Nominating
   Campaigns
Presidential Evaluations, PP158
Presidential Greatness, LE137,
   LE186
Presidential Influence, LE122,
   LE139, LE194, LE669
Presidential Leadership, LE114,
   LE121, LE125, PC58
Presidential Legislative Priori-
   ties, LE639
Presidential Legitimacy, LE103
Presidential Nominating Campaigns,
   LE104, MP300, PC214, PP101,
   PP102, PP103, PP104, PP115,
   PP116, PP135, SC177, SC296,
   also see Presidential
   Primaries
Presidential Performance, LE142
Presidential Personality, LE112,
   LE115
Presidential Persuasion, LE169
Presidential Popularity, CP265,
   CP290, LE107, LE132, LE147,
   LE153, LE156, LE161, LE163,
   LE183, LE195, LE198, LE623,
   PC219, PE165, PE177, PE203,
   PE247, PE249, PP188
Presidential Power, LE138, LE145
Presidential Primaries, CP188,
   CP339, PC187, PP117, PP123, also
   see Presidential Nominating
   Campaigns
Presidential Priorities, PE94
Presidential Prototypes, LE140
Presidential Rhetoric, LE199,
   PC83, PC96
Presidential Selection, PP114
Presidential Success, LE632
Presidential Succession, LE118,
   PP200
Presidential Support, LE136,
   LE181, LE182
Presidential Term, EP77, PE443
Presidential Values, LE187
Presidentialism, LE175
Press, PC218
Press Attitudes, PC160
Press Coverage, PC169, PC198
Press-State Relations, PC13
Pressman-Wildavsky Paradox, PA216
Pressure, IR763
Pressure Groups, PE306, PE347
Prestige, LC519, LE122
Prestigious Publications, XX269
Preventive War, IR756
Price Controls, EP663, EP677
Price Inertia, PA14
Price of Votes, PE298
Price Supports, LE685
Prices, DP220, DP254, PG144
Pricing of Crime, LC301
Pride of Place, PG238

Primaries, CP149, CP188, CP286, CP339, PP104, PP113, SC564, also see Elections, and Presidential Nominating Campaings
Primary Divisiveness, PP119
Prime Ministerial Popularity, PE178, PE212
Prime Ministers, LE67, LE106, LE120, LE143, LE158, LE188, LE322, LE357
Primitive Societies, PS281
Principal Agent Slack, LE414
Principal Agent Theory, EP658, LC84, MP449, OB83, OB87, OB115, PS152, SC39
Principled Organizational Dissent, ET389
Principles, AB114, ET53, PA58
Prior Beliefs, LC375
Priorities of Government, PA43
Prison, LC163, LC502, LC503
Prison Crowding, LC223, LC329
Prisoners' Dilemma, ET150, ET156, ET167, ET168, ET170, ET183, ET185, ET191, ET198, ET324, ET337, PE507, PE525, IR184, IR304, IR307, IR405, IR595, LE692, PA262, PP113, SC47, SC405, SC413, SC438, SC445, SC477, SC485, TR127
Private Accreditation, XX210
Private Bills, LE402
Private Consumption, EP106
Private Education, SP164, SP197
Private Goods, PC499-582/Special Section
Private Governments, PA31
Private Interests, EP827, LE407
Private Investment, IR35
Private Money, EP129
Private Roles, ET49
Private Sector, OB295, SC668
Privateering Wars, IR640
Privatizing Education, SP183
Privatizing Punishment, PE566
Privatization, PE512, PE513, PE515, PE529, PE530, PE535, PE540, PE541, PE544, PE546, PE549, PE557, PE560, PE562, PE563, PE564, PE567, PE573, PE579, PE580, PE582, SP84, SP183, SC476, SP496
Privileges, LC82
Probabilistic Preferences, CP233
Probabilistic Voting, EP845, PE300, PP48, PP57, SC366
Probability, SC354, SC577, SC586
Probability Choice Perspective, CP201
Probability Judgements, SC239
Probability Kinematics, XX108
Probability Matching Behavior, SC140
Problem Choice, XX413
Problem Solving Procedures, PC17
Problem Solving, XX20
Procedural Justice, ET261, ET305, ET316, ET317
Procedural Rules, LE251
Procedure, LE221, XX387
Process Theory, EP11
Procurement, IR9
Product Cycle, XX204
Production Function Analysis, EP220, SP251
Production of Government, SC260
Production, DP254
Productive Efficiency, SP331

Productivity Growth Decline, EP63, EP66, EP104, EP119, EP149, EP181, also see Economic Decline
Productivity, DC306, EP56, EP146, EP283, EP358, EP399, EP554, OB99, OB101, PA312, XX50
Professional Behavior, ET333, ET361
Professional Codes, ET364
Professional Deviance, LC2
Professional Ethics, ET1
Professional Ideologies, AB133
Professional Morality, ET64
Professional Practice, ET46
Professional Reform, XX213
Professional Values, ET362
Professionalism, DC210, LC490, LE321, LE343, LE344, LE354, MP354, OB35, OB70, OB107, OB168, OB368
Professionals, AB96
Professors, PP262, PP272
Profit, EP149, ET52
Program Effects, SP419
Program Implementation, PA229
Programme Approach, OB314
Progressive Ambition, LE312
Progressive Era, CP276, LE300, LE301, PG233, PG311
Progressive Taxation, EP711, EP718, EP752, EP776, also see Taxes
Progressivism, PA290
Prohibition, CP84, MP525, SC772, SP143, SP86
Projection, AB380
Proliferation, IR601
Promises, SC423
Promotion, OB75
Propaganda, IR6, PC154, PC78
Property Crime, LC190, LC234
Property Rights, EP1, EP46, EP133, PE13, PE516, PE561, PE564, PE571, RP37
Property Tax Abatements, EP685
Property Taxes, EP683, EP723, EP731, EP747, EP761, EP771, EP772, PG186, SC528
Property Values, LC251, PG196
Prophecy, RP6, RP36
Proportional Hazard Model, LE542
Proportional Representation, PP519, SC233, SC246, SC249, SC327, SC330
Proportional Veto Power, SC313
Proportionality, LE596, SC287
Proposed Spending, EP47
Proposition Thirteen, EP706, EP760, EP779
Proposition Three, SP378
Propositions, CP94
Prosecutions, LC502
Prosecutorial Discretion, PC169
Prospect Theory, IR18, SC691, XX273
Prospective Economic Voting, PE241
Prospective Voting, PP196
Protection, LC306, LC340, PE299
Protectionism, EP793, EP803, EP806, EP808, EP834, EP847, EP849, EP851, EP867
Protest Cycles, DC221, DC234
Protest Generation, AB370
Protest Groups, DC214
Protest Methods, DC250
Protest Participation, MP401
Protest Theories, PS93

Protestant Ethic, DC284, RP68, RP77, SP420
Protestantism, IR590, OB351, RP45, RP50, RP52, RP66, RP115, RP156
Protest, CP71, DC1, DC43, DC76, DC104, DC143, DC198, DC210, DC213, DC226, DC227, DC230, EP178, LC82, IR512, OB392
Proto-Modernity, ET204
Provability, SC432
Provincial Parties, PP525
Pro-Family Issues, RP124
Prudence, AB262, ET40, ET63
Psychoanalytic Perspectives, IR636
Psychobiography, XX19, XX374, XX401
Psychocultural Interpretation Theory, MP122
Psychodynamics, AB214
Psychological Analyses, SC96
Psychological Arousal, DC241
Psychological Phenomena, PA154
Psychological Pitfalls, PA81
Psychology, CP55, DP178, IR98, IR156, IR700, LC49, PA159, SC131, XX164, XX304, XX336
Psychology of Choice, SC139
Psychophysiology, DC63, PA206
Public Administration, ET366, ET367, ET383, ET395, ET409, ET410, MP296, MP357, OB35, OB59, OB96, OB129, OB131, OB136, OB138, PA87, PA105
Public Affairs Television, PC145
Public Agenda, AB45, PC92
Public Allocation Processes, PP362
Public Arena, PA18
Public Capital, SP450
Public Choice, S1-S805/Special Section, ET76, LC136, OB136, OB148, PE376
Public Cognition, AB123
Public Compensation, OB114
Public Confidence, EP754, PC135
Public Construction, SP353
Public Contracting, PP354
Public Debt, DP269, IR768, PE105
Public Education, PG145, SP160, SP222
Public Employment, EP166, OB124, OB301
Public Enterprise, EP312
Public Ethics, ET358-449/Special Section
Public Events, PC56
Public Expenditures, EP700, PE97, PE101, PE138, PE231, PE232, PE465, SP416
Public Facilities, PE504, PG192, PG217
Public Finance, EP723, EP785, PE123, PP78
Public Goods, PE499-582/Special Section, EP709, EP783, ET142, IR353, LE407, OB371, OB376, OB380, OB384, OB399, OB400, PE613, SC47, SC199, SC219, SC220, SC228, SC733
Public Information Campaigns, PA52, PC133
Public Interest, XX383
Public Interest Groups, PE307, PE319, PE327, PE394
Public Investment, EP119
Public Judgment, PA97
Public Law, LC68
Public Management, OB74, OB91
Public Morality, RP116

Public Office, LE353
Public Officials, ET439
Public Opinion, AB17, AB22, AB42,
  AB54, AB76, AB141, AB197, AB230,
  AB231, AB285, AB287, AB329,
  CP319, EP550, LC334, LC411,
  LC449, LE621, LE669, PA3, PA33,
  PA38, PA47, PC29, PC58, PC76,
  PC139, PC159, PG247, RP135,
  RP161, SC690, SP338, SP376,
  SP449, also see Surveys
Public Opinion Representations,
  AB48, AB284
Public Organizations, OB12, SP525
Public Party Funding, PP488
Public Pensions, EP226, SP117,
  SP472
Public Policy, AB189, CP32, CP274,
  EP109, EP110, EP247, EP309,
  ET111, ET382, ET384, ET445,
  OB177, PA1, PA3, PA4, PA11,
  PA12, PA15, PA19, PA21, PA22,
  PA29, PA31, PA33, PA34, PA35,
  PA37, PA41, PA48, PA49, PA51,
  PA54, PA59, PA69, PA85, PA96,
  PA104, PA108, PA100, PA112,
  PA113, PA121, PA123, PA126,
  PA130, PA133, PA141, PA146,
  PA211, PA226, PA257, PA293,
  PA310, PE344, PG173, PG310,
  PP108, PS4, PS61, RP111, SC212,
  SC514, SC756, SP99, SP208,
  SP330, SP338, SP340, SP361,
  SP362, SP376, SP381, SP386,
  SP387, SP389, SP415, SP433,
  SP434, SP449, SP489, TR96, also
  see Economic Policy, and Public
  Policy Analysis, and Social
  Policy
Public Policy Actors, PA93
Public Policy Administration,
  PA118
Public Policy Adoption, CP59,
  PA260
Public Policy Analysis, PA1-PA344/
  Special Section, PE305
Public Policy Analysis Approaches,
  PA54-151/Special Section
Public Policy Analysis Assump-
  tions, PA132, PA145
Public Policy Analysts Roles, PA77
Public Policy Apparatus, PA140
Public Policy Balancing Model, LE5
Public Policy Change, LE403, PA45,
  PP527
Public Policy Comparisons, PA150
Public Policy Competition, SC739
Public Policy Compliance, LE196
Public Policy Convergence, PP522
Public Policy Cooperation, EP656
Public Policy Cycle, LE552, PA224,
  PE489
Public Policy Determination, PA78
Public Policy Differentiation,
  CP307
Public Policy Dimensions, LE495
Public Policy Ethics, ET359, ET431
Public Policy Evaluation, PA245
Public Policy Experts, OB161,
  OB162
Public Policy Failure, AB6
Public Policy Formation, LE547,
  PA60
Public Policy Implementation,
  PA218, PA241, PA246, PA253, also
  see Implementation
Public Policy Ineffectivness, PA14
Public Policy Information, PA251

Public Policy Innovation, see
  Innovation
Public Policy Institutions, PA9
Public Policy Instrument Choice,
  PE529
Public Policy Interpretation,
  PA244
Public Policy Journal Articles,
  PA91
Public Policy Learning, PE529
Public Policy Making, MP506
Public Policy Moderation, LE286
Public Policy Networks, EP93,
  PA75, PA80
Public Policy Oriented Voting,
  PE219
Public Policy Politics, PA64
Public Policy Preferences, AB326,
  CP288, ET46, MP310
Public Policy Reasoning, AB73,
  MP127
Public Policy Reform, PA39
Public Policy Research Industry,
  PA109
Public Policy Resistance, OB85
Public Policy Responsiveness,
  LE574
Public Policy Space, LE534
Public Policy Statements, IR194
Public Policy Studies, PA74, PA82,
  PA91, PA116, PA117
Public Policy Styles, PE529
Public Policy Subsystems, PA2,
  PA62, SC179
Public Policy Targets, PE230
Public Policy Termination, PA36
Public Policy Textbooks, PA87
Public Policy Views, LE297
Public Policy Voting, CP204,
  LE498, MP133
Public Preferences, PA30
Public Programs, OB30, PG148
Public Relations, PC133
Public Relevance, XX269
Public Roads, PE552
Public Roles, ET49
Public Safety, LC264
Public Satisfaction, LC480
Public Schools, SP158, SP188,
  SP220, SP243
Public Sector, OB33, OB241
Public Sector Employment, PE593
Public Sector Innovation, PA279
Public Sector Management, OB119
Public Sector Pay, OB140
Public Sector Workers, SC668
Public Service, ET394, ET425
Public Service Delivery, PA105
Public Service Ethics, ET392
Public Service Location Behavior,
  PG138
Public Spending, EP20, EP23,
  EP743, OB262, OB283, OB315,
  PE77, PE82, PE120
Public Transfers, ET138
Public Utilities, EP581, EP652
Public Works, LE711
Publicization of Policy Research,
  PA234, see Utilization
Publicness, LE21
Public-Private Distinction, PE577
Punishment, LC160-300/Special
  Section, AB46, ET283, LC195,
  LC250, LC295, LC299, LC307,
  LC313, LC318, LC321, LC330,
  LC320, LC335, LC338, PE566, also
  see Deterrence
Puritanism, RP61

Purposive Models of Representative
  Behavior, LE269

Q Methodology, PA77, PP32
Quacks, EP617
Quakers, PE29, RP96
Qualified Majority Voting, SC294
Qualitative Dynamics, PA100
Qualitative Historical Observa-
  tions, PA83
Qualitative Methods, XX65
Qualitative Research, XX270
Quality, XX70
Quality of Life, AB379, EP451,
  IR492, SP15, SP548
Quality Standards, EP617
Quantification, XX149
Quantitative Historical Research,
  XX207
Quantitative Research, PA40, PA101
Quasi-Periodic Behavior, DP85,
  IR284
Quebec, PG279
Question Design, AB161, AB273,
  PE134, also see Surveys
Questionnaires, AB333
Questions, AB334
Queuing Theory, IR856

Race, MP360-530/Special Section,
  AB28, AB174, LC85, LC209, LC250,
  LC231, LC503, LC523, LE625,
  RP97, RP134, SC252, SP152
Race Relations, MP15, MP364
Race Targeting, MP44
Racial Attitudes, MP44, MP76,
  MP95, MP104, MP117, MP124,
  MP132, MP141, MP361, MP417,
  MP421
Racial Belief Systems, AB86, MP394
Racial Competition, MP9
Racial Conflict, MP466
Racial Context, MP447
Racial Crossover Voting, MP150
Racial Environment, MP421
Racial Equality, MP127, MP446
Racial Ideology, MP360, MP520
Racial Inequality, MP373, MP402
Racial Issues, MP387
Racial Policy, MP106
Racial Politics, MP360-530/Special
  Section
Racial Threat, MP419, MP445
Racial Violence, DC228, DC249,
  MP91, MP99, MP110, MP136
Racialization, MP115
Racism, ET466, IR699, MP25, MP53,
  MP88, MP126, MP129, MP131,
  MP389, MP512, PC165
Radical Members of Parliament,
  LE646
Radical Right, PG327, PP442
Radical Whites, RP167
Radicalism, XX239
Radicals, XX229
Radioactive Waste, PG196
Railroads, EP239, XX124
Rain, CP138
Rally Effect, AB5, AB58, AB200,
  AB280, LE113, LE147
Random Walk, DP180, DP204, DP240,
  OB350
Randomness, PG122
Ratchet Phenomenon, OB275
Rates of Return, DP88, EP149
Ratification Process, LC158
Rational Actors, ET134, RP10
Rational Altruists, ET147

Rational Arguments, PA97
Rational Behavior, SC614, SC635,
  SC645
Rational Bubbles, DP12
Rational Choice, SC1-SC805/Special
  Section, DP76, LC83, LC312,
  LC333, PA108, PG11
Rational Constraint, AB216
Rational Costs, CP115
Rational Decision Making, PA111
Rational Deterrence, IR436, IR607
Rational Dilemmas, SC29
Rational Egoism, SC80
Rational Expectations, PA70,
  PE141, SC125, SC631, TR12
Rational Fascists, PP247
Rational Frenzies, DP50
Rational Government, AB8
Rational Peasants, DC211
Rational Rebels, SC223
Rational Terrorists, DC365
Rationalism, PA137
Rationality, SC610-660/Special
  Section, AB116, AB232, CP26,
  CP100, CP111, CP123, CP158,
  CP166, CP177, CP238, CP277,
  CP316, DC129, EP405, ET60, ET67,
  ET74, ET83, ET107, ET145, ET176,
  ET195, ET282, ET345, ET356,
  IR311, IR457, OB68, OB220,
  OB315, PA85, PE6, PE282, PE483,
  PG141, RP85, SC489, SC493,
  SC611, SC613, SC615, SC630,
  SC632, SC701, XX91, XX142
Rationalization, CP296
Rawls, John, ET7, ET38, ET98,
  ET103, ET247, ET249, ET252,
  ET254, ET257, ET262, ET263,
  ET271, ET277, ET281, ET282,
  ET286, ET288, ET294, ET306,
  ET310, ET322, SC289
Rawls' Difference Principle, ET280
Rayburn, Sam, LE319
Reactive Linkage Model, IR530
Reactive Violence, PG315
Reagan Era, EP745
Reaganomics, AB66, PG38
Reagan, Ronald, AB6, AB241, LE110,
  LE159, LE276, PE292, RP138
Real Structure Modeling, XX252
Real World Cues, PC92
Realignment of the 1850s, DP148
Realignments, PP526-546/Special
  Section, DP249, LC388, PP462,
  RP157
Realism, ET175, IR70, IR100,
  IR128, IR168, IR212, XX116
Realpolitik, IR664
Reapportionment, PP356, SC326
Reason, AB199, ET39
Reasoned Action, XX320
Reasoning, XX39
Reasoning Chains, AB73
Reasoning Styles, AB240
Rebellion, see Revolution
Recession, PE165, PE194, PE285
Reciprocity, ET4, ET159, ET355,
  IR45, IR46, SC113
Recoil Effect, PA25
Reconstructing Nations, PS18
Reconstructing Voting Processes,
  LE624
Recreation, TR1
Recruitment, CP6, ET480, LE479,
  MP189, MP340, PP342
Recurrent Crises, OB216
Recurrent Militarized Disputes,
  IR388

Recycling, SP340, TR4
Red Scare, ET458
Redistribution, EP67, EP82, EP137,
  EP445, EP520, EP525, EP741,
  OB250, OB286, PE590, PG34,
  SP255, SP272
Redistricting, LC473, LE548,
  PP139, PP142, PP229, SC280,
  SC293, SC298, SC300, SC317
Reelection, LE330, LE451
Reelection Constraint, LE617
Reelection Margins, see Election
  Margins
Reference Functions, SC6
Reference Groups, MP218, SC185
Referenda, see Direct Democracy
Referral of Legislation, LE215
Referrals, LE216
Reform, OB136, PE137, PG311,
  PP369, PS122, PS280, XX298
Reform Party, PP242
Reformism, SP317, SP373
Refugees, PG131, PG169, PG175,
  PG206
Refuse Removal, PE545
Regime Change, LE560, PP536, PS16,
  PS27, PS59
Regime Characteristics, PS15
Regime Performance, PS14
Regime Repressiveness, DC56
Regime Stability, PS144
Regime Support, PE190, PE202,
  PE224, PS49
Regime Systems, PS254
Regime Theory, PS39, PS57
Regimes, EP362, EP863, ET166,
  ET191, ET193, IR408, IR519,
  IR616, IR632, IR735, IR866,
  IR872, LE608, PP36, PS4, PS10,
  PS32, PS36, PS40, PS41, PS42,
  PS47, also see Political Systems
Regional Administration, SP356
Regional Analysis, PG248
Regional Conflict, IR364
Regional Coordination, PG276
Regional Development, DP215,
  EP294, EP386
Regional Economic Policy, EP101
Regional Fragmentation, LE532
Regional Government, PG254
Regional Hierarchy, PG46
Regional Networks, PG300
Regional Powers, IR66
Regional Research, SP431
Regional Restructuring, PG226
Regional Rivalry, IR235
Regional Science, PG267, PG268
Regional Security, IR224
Regional Shifts, PG297
Regional Studies, DC142
Regionalist Revival, PG252
Regions, PG225-330/Special
  Section, LC513, LC515, MP19,
  MP491, PE261, PG92
Registration Laws, CP143, CP146,
  CP164, LE584
Registration Lists, CP137
Registration Reform, CP162
Regression, DP90, LC9, PA273,
  XX104
Regulation, EP547-677/Special
  Section, EP415, ET116, ET364,
  PE563, PG134, SP128, TR48, TR57,
  TR69, TR82
Regulatory Capture, EP606
Regulatory Constitutions, EP583
Regulatory Enforcement, EP620,
  EP654

Regulatory Federalism, EP591
Regulatory Institutions, EP605
Regulatory Policy Cycle, EP560
Regulatory Structure, EP623
Regulatory Threat Hypothesis,
  EP577
Rehabilitation, LC308
Reign Duration, LE608, see Regimes
Rejected Alternatives, SC19
Relative Deprivation, DC76, DC128,
  DC238, EP483
Relative Gratification, DC29
Relative Success, PE597
Relativism, ET15, ET420
Reliable Enemies, ET11
Reliable Systems, OB29
Religion Renewal, RP42
Religion, RP1-180/ Special
  Section, CP262, ET71, ET451,
  ET476, LC386, LE125, LE129,
  MP218, PC160, PS274, PS278,
  SP19, SP34, SP60
Religiosity, RP74, RP90, RP101,
  RP117, RP128, RP160, RP162
Religious Activism, RP69
Religious Affiliation, RP56, RP62,
  RP124
Religious Alignment, RP163
Religious Behaviour, RP26
Religious Belief Transformation,
  RP33
Religious Beliefs, RP5, RP70
Religious Change, RP72
Religious Commitment, RP31
Religious Competition, RP47
Religious Conversion, RP11
Religious Denominations, RP50,
  RP52, RP122, see Protestantism
Religious Doctrine, RP19, RP112
Religious Elites, RP81, RP135,
  RP161, RP166
Religious Fundamentalism, RP127,
  RP132
Religious Group Attitudes, RP152
Religious Guidance, MP394
Religious Institutions, RP43
Religious Interest Groups, RP125
Religious Involvement, RP158
Religious Messages, RP97
Religious Orientations, RP178
Religious Periodicals, RP144
Religious Pluralism, RP65
Religious Politics, RP166
Religious Reformations, RP27, RP34
Religious Right, RP153
Religious Salience, RP108
Religious Switchers, RP22
Religious Transformations, RP92
Remorse, CP179
Rent Dissipation, PE592
Rent Extraction, PE585
Rent Provision, PP87
Rent Seeking, PE583-617/Special
  Section, AB106, DC114, EP516,
  EP580, EP601, PG186, PP410,
  PS73, RP46, SP244
Rents, EP801
Repeated Referenda, SC795
Replication, AB328
Representation, AB194, LE367,
  LE388, LE407, LE421, LE471,
  PS49, PS100, PS120, SC331, SC581
Representative Bureaucracy, OB169,
  OB174
Representative Democracy, CP276,
  EP766, PS163, SC53
Representative Styles, LE400

Representative-Constituency
  Linkages, LE296
Repression, DC36, DC176, DP24,
  ET205, ET211, ET226, ET242,
  ET458, ET459, IR358, LC325, MP80
Repressive Regimes, IR356
Republican Administrators, PE450
Republican Civic Tradition, XX406
Republican Government, LC141
Republican National Convention,
  PP130
Republican Parties, PP16
Republican Thinking, LC139
Republican Tidal Wave, PP545
Republicanism, ET405
Republicans, CP138, PP226
Reputation, ET162, IR3, LE315,
  OB46, SC399
Research and Development, EP271,
  EP310, PA286, PA305, PA306,
  PA312, PA322, PA336, TR145,
  TR147, TR160, TR165, TR157,
  TR188
Research Grants, PA125
Resegregation, MP138
Resentment, PP442
Reservation Values, SC665
Residence, MP54
Residential Attachment, PG91
Residential Choices, PG198
Residential Mobility, PG139,
  PG148, PG174, PG176, PG210
Residential Segregation, MP105,
  MP137
Resignation, ET410
Resignation of Dictators, LE338
Resolve, IR113, IR731
Resource Allocation, PP59
Resource Development, TR52
Resource Model, CP8
Resources, TR44-136/Special
  Section
Respect, LE369, LE371
Response Instability, AB320
Response Set, AB161
Responsibilities, AB23, ET298,
  MP258
Responsible Parties, PP452, PP464,
  PP498, PP503, PP524
Responsible Two Party System,
  PP477, PP507
Responsiveness, LE388, OB97
Restricted Domains, SC504, SC505
Results, XX38
Retail Activity, EP37
Retaliation, EP817, IR598, IR833
Retention Decision, OB63
Retirement, LC429, LE320, LE324,
  LE328, LE331, LE339, LE568, SP10
Retrospective Considerations,
  SC150
Retrospective Rationality, SC618
Retrospective Voting, CP283,
  CP299, CP325, PE191, PE201,
  PG273, SC347
Revealed Preferences, AB28, AB337,
  PE569, PP217, SC8, SC112
Revenue Diversification, PE589
Revenue Elasticity, OB272
Revenue Forecasting, SP421
Revenue Maximizing Tax Rate, EP748
Revenue Seeking, EP800
Revenues, EP115, EP444, EP679,
  EP704, also see Taxes
Revitalization, MP519
Revolution, DC125-193/Special
  Section, DC148, DC149, DC151,
  DC174, DC190, DC193, DC245,

DC254, DC373, DP242, LC201,
  LE661, PG262, RP7, SC223
The Revolution Betrayed, DC134
Revolutionary Coalitions, ET319
Revolutionary Ideology, DC181
Revolutionary Leaders, DC187
Revolutionary Politics, DC189
Revolutionary Ritual, DC133
Revolutions of 1989, DC143
Revolving Door, EP568, EP652,
  PE334
Reward Structure, ET361
Rewards, OB5
Re-Election, LE586
Rhetoric, IR193, IR204, IR615,
  LE58, LE103, PC24, PC38, PP118,
  RP61, SC34
Rhetorical Style, PC84
Rhetorical Visions, PC16, PC74
Rhodesia, IR44
Richardson Models, IR265, IR304,
  IR311, IR327, IR330, IR798
Right and Wrong, ET400, PP400
Right-Privilege Distinction, LC82
Right to Die, LC423
Right to Work, DC319, DC267, EP170
Right Wing Parties, PP12
Right Wing Violence, MP96, PG244
Rights, EP58, ET18, ET45, ET64,
  ET88, ET93, ET201, ET209, ET214,
  ET221, ET314, ET399, ET472,
  LC11, LC82, SC552, SC572, SC585,
  TR93
Riker, William, SC85, SC142
Riot Commission Report, DC247
Riots, DC194-258/Special Section,
  PG109, PG85, SP526
The Rise and Decline of Nations,
  PE315, PE351, PE357, PE404
Risk, SC661-734/Special Section,
  EP468, EP518, ET270, IR622,
  IR705, LC25, LE100, OB359, PA250,
  PC111, PE5, PG178, SP2, SP89,
  TR156
Risk Analysis, SC672, SC676
Risk and Culture, SC671
Risk Aversion, EP94, SC668, SC693,
  SC695, SC697, SC699
Ritual, DC133
Rivalries, CP112, IR383, IR384,
  IR385
River and Harbor Legislation,
  LE723
Roads, TR11
Robbery, LC269
Robinson Crusoe Fallacy, SC586
Rodent Populations, DP144
Roe vs. Wade, SP21, SP35
Roemer, John, PE46
Rogowski's Model, EP848
Rokkan, Stein, XX35
Role of Government, EP55
Role Orientations, MP305
Role Theory, IR204
Roles, ET49
Roll Call Voting, LE618-687/
  Special Section, IR339, IR633,
  LC460, LE220, LE267, LE300,
  LE301, LE589, PG323, PP162,
  SC763, SC765, SP60
Roll Call Indexes, LE645
Roll Off, CP335
Roman Empire, OB240, PS215, PS220,
  PS237
Roosevelt, Franklin D., LC117,
  LE159
Rose Garden Strategy, PC190
Rostow, Walt, EP248

Rousseau, James, SC266
Rukeheim Hypothesis, LC230
Rule Choice, ET418, LC137
Rule of Law, ET385, XX327
Rule of the Virtuous, ET385
Rule Utilitarianism, ET40, SC495
Ruler Autonomy, IR708
Rules, ET37, ET260, IR129, LC71,
  LC120, SC284
Rules of Conduct, LE221
Rules of Method, LE221
Rules of Thumb, XX91
Ruling, PS52
Ruling Classes, LE25
Ruling Elites, XX228
Rumour, PG95, XX318
Runoff Elections, SC278
Rural Areas, TR7-43/Special
  Section
Russia, AB179, DC116, DC161,
  PP487, PS97, also see Soviet
  Union

Sacrifice, IR552
Saddle Point Theorems, SC89, SC448
Safe Seats, LE555, LE565
Safety, EP619, EP642, PA259, PC111
Safety Nets, SP536
Sales Tax, EP699
Salience, CP294
Samaritan's Dilemma, ET120
Samson's Dilemma, SC33
Samuelson Model, DP121
San Antonio, PP361
San Mateo, LE601
Sanctions, DC1, IR199, SC413,
  SC709
Satanism, RP12, RP28
Satellization, EP204
Satisfaction, OB101
Satisficing, PE446
Satisfied Powers, IR99
Satre, Jean Paul, XX280
Saturn Project, SC264
SAT, SP186, SP203, SP212, SP218
Savings, EP411-526/Special
  Section, EP696, IR360, SP470
Savings and Loans, EP558, EP669,
  OB344, OB361, PE74, PP53
Scale, PG74
Scale Economy, EP262
Scale Entropy, EP262
Scaling Models, LE683
Scandals, ET380, ET421, PP356,
  PP358, PP365, PP407, PP416
Scandinavia, PA150, SC771, SP463
Scandinavian Equality, MP179
Scarcity, OB148, XX156
Schelling Diagrams, SC21
Schema, AB86, AB89, AB124, AB129,
  AB160, AB167, AB168, AB182,
  AB271, PG78
Schisms, OB351
Schizophrenia, XX116
Schlesinger's Typology, LE329
School Aid, SP221
School Board Elections, CP165,
  MP165
School Boards, SP175
School Choice, SP177, SP210, SP236
School Curriculum, SP189
School Discipline, SP162, SP163
School Districts, SP156, SP199,
  SP213, SP253
School Effects, SP145
School Enrollment, SP174
School Finance, SP161, SP179,
  SP180, SP196, SP216

School Finance Elections, CP83, CP96, CP97
School Quality, SP158
Schools, EP702
Schumpeterian Waves, PA300, PA301, PA309, TR137, TR157
Science, TR137-192/Special Section, AB142, DP168, PA250, XX413
Scientific Change, TR142, TR158
Scientific Literacy, EP399
Scientific Opportunities Foregone, TR145
Scientific Productivity, TR150, TR171, TR192
Scotland, MP479, PG225, PG288, PG290
Scottish National Party, MP479
Search Behavior, CP218
Search for Love, LE106
Seasonal Cycles, DP171, DP177
Seat Allocation, SC327
Seat Change, CP208, PP198
Seats-Population Relationship, MP161
Seats-Votes Relationship, SC287, SC339, SC288, SC343, SC345
Secession, DC150, PP360
Secession Crisis, DC170
Second Image, AB242
Second Order Elections, CP174
Secondary Associations, OB387
Secretaries of State, IR82
Secrets, ET358
Sectarianism, RP40
Sectional Beliefs, MP119
Sectional Competition, EP653
Sectionalism, IR198, PG49, PG226, PG230, PG232, PG286, PE284, also see Regions
Sectoral Clashes, EP337
Sectoral Reallocation, EP402
Sects, RP51
Security, IR86, IR191, IR206, IR217, IR238, IR381, IR393, IR394, LE112, LE166
Security Communities, IR796
Security Dilemma, ET174, IR256
Security Policy, AB239, AB264, IR144, IR399
Security Regimes, IR444, IR591
Segmental Growth, EP385
Segregation, LC236, LC379, MP59, MP67, MP73, MP83, MP98, MP100, MP101, MP102, MP105, MP107, MP123, MP137, MP138, MP230, MP374, MP484, MP505, SP283
Segregation Index, PG28
Select Committees, LE241
Selection Bias, XX113
Selection Dynamics, XX394
Selection-Plurality Voting, SC272
Self-Deception, EP620, SC646
Self-Determination, XX259
Self-Esteem, AB294, LC421
Self-Help Groups, XX176
Self-Identification, AB108
Self-Interest, AB70, AB272, CP315, CP316, EP756, ET53, ET122, ET127, ET131, LE539, LE651, LE702, MP44, MP104, OB315, SC41, SC60, SC221, SC659, SP89, SP540
Self-Organization, DP140, DP147, DP153, DP157, DP158, DP161, PA335
Self-Regulation, EP559, ET116, ET364
Self-Reliance, ET94

Self-Selection Hypothesis, AB81
Selling the Pentagon, PC145
Semantic Differential, PP26
Semi-Capitalist Development, PS40
Senate, AB275, CP77, CP346, CP348, IR116, IR339, IR491, IR633, LC455, LC460, LE18, LE213, LE215, LE264, LE265, LE280, LE290, LE291, LE307, LE312, LE391, LE399, LE417, LE425, LE450, LE485, LE498, LE499, LE500, LE521, LE527, LE530, LE546, LE586, LE616, LE626, LE638, LE648, LE651, LE659, LE660, LE667, LE677, PC179, PC196, PE163, PE174, PE228, PE280, PE392, PG323, PP41, PP65, PP66, PP93, PP129, PP176, PP179, PP187, PP195, PP201, PP220, PP227, PP235, PP531, PS213, SC231, SC773, SC803, SP53, also see Congress
Senate Committees, LE258, also see Committees
Senate Delegations, LE606
Senate Elections, LE616, PP137, PP191, PP216, PP230, also see Elections
Senate Floor, LE476
Senate Incumbents, PP167
Senate Leadership, LE327, see Congressional Careers
Senate Responsiveness, LE397
Senate Speeches, PC84, IR192
Senior Federal Executives, OB82, OB139
Seniority System, LE217, LE342, LE462
Sentences, LC85, LC329, LC334
Separation of Powers, LC75
Sequential Choice Theory, LE361
Sequential Elections, SC308, SC347
Sequential Equilibria, SC59, SC424
Sequential Games, SC389
Sequential Referenda, OB158
Set-Asides, MP40
Severity, LC316
Severity Information, SP90
Sex Ratio, LC278
Sex Roles, MP259, MP321, MP337
Sexism, RP132
Sexual Discrimination, MP89
Sexual Harassment, MP87, MP248, MP273, MP322, MP331
Sexual Morality, MP218
Sexual Orientation, PA167
Shadow Interest Groups, PP27
Sharing Rules, PE601
Shelter Policy, SP280
Sheriff Departments, LC490
Shift Voting, SC242
Shift-Share Analysis, EP170, LC171
Shirking, IR511, LE366, LE427, LE499, LE554, LE568, SC214, SC218
Shocks, DP11
Show Trials, DC133
Sidepayments, SC425, SC466
Signaling, LE211, OB205, PP75, SC381, SC395, SC798, XX188
Significant Others, LC312
Silent Revolution, AB354, AB355, AB365, AB379
Simon-Homans Model, DP54
Simulations, SC378-487/Special Section, IR137, PE10, SC18, SC244
Simultaneous Equations, EP165

Sincere Truncation of Preferences, SC784
Sincere Voting, CP196, SC323
Single Issue Politics, CP307
Single Membership Constituency, SC334
Siouxs, LC109
Sister City Programs, OB393
Siting, PG181
Situation Model, PC27
Size, PG41, PS241, SC159, SC171, SC176, XX228
Size of Government, see Government Size
Size of Public Sector, SC685
Size Principle, LE482
Skid Row, PG43
Skill Requirements, OB15
Skinnerian Analysis, IR609, XX279
Slave Revolts, DC184
Slavery, LC452, MP68, MP97, MP112, MP120
Sleaze, PP424
Small Business, EP7, EP43
Small Groups, DC120, XX13, XX80, XX118, XX122, XX175, XX195
Small States, XX404
Small Town Citizens, LE353
Smallest Distance Hypothesis, CP269
Smallest Space Analysis, PG43
Smuggling, EP852
Snyder's Decision Making Approach, OB228
Social Advocacy, DC196
Social Attitudes, AB83, AB387
Social Background, LE11
Social Benefits, OB288, SP502, SP503
Social Breakdown, SP3
Social Change, AB328, CP38, DP137, EP528, LC189, LC245, LC391, PA65, PA341, PP38, PS312, RP48, RP95
Social Choice, SC1-805/Special Section, CP287, EP41, ET78, ET87, ET89, ET98, ET279, ET309, ET314, ET315, LC87, LE470
Social Choice Economics, SC2
Social Choice Functions, SC100, SC101, SC275
Social Choice Paradox, SC541
Social Cleavage, PP342
Social Coalitions, SC154
Social Cohesion, PP36
Social Conflict, DC9, DC41
Social Conformity, PA162
Social Consciousness, IR512
Social Consensus, ET283
Social Consumption Spending, EP17
Social Contagion, PA268
Social Context, CP2, CP256, PP339, SC659, also see Contextual Effects
Social Contract, EP627, XX124
Social Control, ET358, LC216, LC233, LC243, LC315, LC507, SC709, SC332
Social Costs, EP768, TR67
Social Darwinism, PS262
Social Dealignment, CP349
Social Decision Making, PA250
Social Democracy, EP461, PS138, PS158, PS172, SP528
Social Democratic Party, PP479
Social Development, EP352, PS311
Social Dilemmas, DP18, SC90, SC430
Social Disapproval, LC313

Social Dominance, LC377
Social Engineering, PA127
Social Equality, PS135, RP88
Social Equity, ET256
Social Evolution, PA159, XX310,
    also see Evolution
Social Exchange, ET171
Social Experimentation, EP85
Social Freedom, ET234
Social Groups, AB22
Social Hierarchy, LC377
Social History, XX339
Social Homogeneity, SC557
Social Indicators, XX50
Social Inequality, EP437, EP439,
    EP491, LC191, PS162
Social Inquiry, XX343
Social Insurance, EP678
Social Integration, ET133, XX322
Social Intervention, PA138
Social Investment, EP17
Social Judgment Theory, LE405
Social Justice, ET291, ET302,
    ET307
Social Learning, EP16, ET116,
    ET139
Social Life, PA196
Social Mobility, CP42
Social Mobilization, CP21, DC77,
    IR540
Social Movements, DC194-258/
    Special Section, AB185, ET449,
    MP228, MP263, OB338, OB392, PC87
Social Networks, IR376, OB50,
    PG100, SC588, XX3, XX249
Social Order, SP284, XX85, XX137
Social Osmosis, LC268
Social Policy, SC1-554/Special
    Section, EP84
Social Preferences, SC436
Social Pressure, CP168
Social Problems, AB90, PA18
Social Process, SC113, XX29
Social Protection, SP478
Social Psychology, PA190
Social Regulation, EP671
Social Relations, XX326
Social Relations of Production,
    EP121
Social Representation, MP183
Social Revolutions, LC201
Social Roles, AB328, MP266
Social Science, IR869, LC22, LC91,
    LC95, PA28, PA219, SC135, XX112,
    XX219, XX262
Social Science Funding, PA72
Social Science Research, PA82
Social Security, SP465, SP468,
    SP469, SP500, SP546, SP548,
    SP549
Social Sentiments, AB77
Social Services, SP391, SP498
Social Spending, SP219, SP501
Social Stratification, XX346
Social Strength, EP515
Social Stress, XX385
Social Structure, CP48, CP211,
    ET21, PP339
Social Studies of Law, LC1, LC22
Social Support Buffering
    Hypothesis, OB19
Social Systems, DP133, DP142
Social Theory, PA59, SC396, SC445,
    XX90
Social Traps, SC98
Social Trends, SP4
Social Values, AB384
Social Violence, DC177

Social Welfare, AB196, MP420,
    PE176, PP544, SC643, SP457,
    SP490, SP505
Social Welfare Orderings, SC78
Social Welfare Functions, EP38,
    SC351, SC362, SP523, SC540,
    SC627, XX54
Social Work, PE579
Socialism, PS313-330/Special
    Section, AB139, DP197, DP230,
    EP497, PS9, PS25, PS97, PS226
Socialist Countries, DP197, DP230,
    EP133
Socialist Economic Management,
    PS321
Socialist Labor Party, PP314
Socialist Parties, EP465, EP505,
    PS319
Socialist Transitions, TR22
Socialization, AB202, AB347,
    AB348, AB359, AB369, CP42, CP55,
    ET114, ET449, LC321, LE49,
    MP276, MP286, MP353, MP422,
    PA187, PA204, PP267, SC604,
    XX267
Societal Complexity, RP65
Societal Constitutionalism, OB391
Societal Development, RP88
Societal Organization, PS30
Societal Stress, IR555
Societal Well Being, RP84
Society, ET448, XX293
Sociobiology, DP73, DP178, PA158,
    PA172, PA178, PA188, PA191,
    PA204, also see Biopolitics
Sociocultural Evolution, PA173
Socioeconomic Conditions, PA34
Socioeconomic Crisis, PG46
Socioeconomic Deprivation, RP108
Socioeconomic Development, PS166,
    PS264, RP99
Socioeconomic Differences, SP375
Socioeconomic Stratification,
    MP408
Sociolegal Studies, LC53
Sociological Development, PS305
Sociological Knowledge, XX86
Sociological Metatheorizing, XX358
Sociological Theory, SC475
Sociology, CP55, LC47, MP47,
    SC477, XX28, XX55, XX71, XX405
Sociology of Law, LC54, LC93
Sociology of Organizations, OB58
Sociology of Politics, SP463
Sociology of Religion, RP87
Sociology of Work, OB125, OB130
Socio-Political Change, LC267
Socio-Political Cycles, DP234-285/
    Special Section
Socio-Political Instability, EP508
Socioreligious Groups, RP98
Sociosphere, TR78
Sociotechnical Change, DP184
Sociotechnical Systems, DP13,
    DP146
Sociotropic Politics, PE221, PE226
Socio-Spatial Schema, PG78
Socio-Spatial Stocks, XX69
Soft Data, PA100
Soldiers, IR506, IR525, IR545
Solid Waste, SP340
Sophisticated Behavior, LE218
Sophisticated Voting, LE282,
    SC271, SC551, SC773, SC778,
    SC781, SC783, SC790, SC791
Sophistication, AB32, AB37, AB38,
    CP270
Source Clues, AB184

Sources of Decay, CP292
South, see Southern United States
South Africa, EP833, IR53, PC27
South Carolina, LC213, LC382
Southeast Asia, PG206
Southern Africa, IR31
Southern Congressional Politics,
    LE493
Southern Congressional Veto, LE650
Southern Democrats, LE640
Southern Republican Senators,
    LE348
Southern United States, CP210,
    CP344, DC170, LC514, LC516,
    LC520, LC522, MP58, MP59, MP62,
    MP69, MP79, MP119, MP136, MP138,
    MP177, MP374, MP402, MP410,
    MP426, MP442, PG86, PG263,
    PP252, PP291, PP302, PP501,
    RP110
Sovereign Immunity, LC121
Sovereignty, DC13, IR208, PS29
Soviet-American Relations, ET334,
    IR341, IR563
Soviet Bloc, IR105
Soviet Foreign Policy, AB246
Soviet Officialdom, PP366
Soviet Union, AB227, AB245, AB260,
    AB263, AB282, EP353, ET334,
    ET463, IR46, IR194, IR269,
    IR319, IR412, IR567, LE28,
    LE118, LE550, LE552, LE553,
    LE605, MP398, OB192, PE476,
    PG46, PP39, PS17, PS85, PS89,
    also see Russia
Space, XX69, XX370
Space Curve, PG214
Space of Retractions, XX392
Spaces of Citizenship, PG51
Space-Time Lags, PG241
Spain, SC329
Spanish NATO Referendum, IR218
Spatial Analysis of Peace, IR707
Spatial Assimilation, PG40
Spatial Autocorrelation, PG88
Spatial Bargaining, SC156
Spatial Choice, SC751, SC755
Spatial Competition, SC758
Spatial Conflict, PG17
Spatial Context, LE398, also see
    Contextual Effects
Spatial Correlation Test for
    Chaos, DP125
Spatial Diffusion, DC295, PA319
Spatial Distance, SC739
Spatial Dynamics, DP118, DP119,
    DP144, DP157
Spatial Elections, PP338, SC749,
    SC767, SC768
Spatial Inertia, PG64
Spatial Job-Search, PG168
Spatial Models, SC735-768/Special
    Section, EP677, IR411, IR745,
    IR757, LC460, LE133, LE418,
    LE470, LE664, LE667, LE671,
    LE672, PG19, PP323, PP324,
    PP341, PP343, PP484, SC192,
    SC762
Spatial Organization of Elections,
    SC341
Spatial Parameter Variation, SP462
Spatial Policy Outcomes, SC190
Spatial Preferences, SC742
Spatial Public Goods, PE556
Spatial Search, SC758
Spatial Segregation, PG69
Spatial Theory, AB143
Spatial Variation, PG225

Spatial Voting, PG141, SC518, SC747
Spatial Voting Games, SC738, SC760, SC764
Spatiotemporal Model, PG73
Speaker of the House, LE317, LE319, LE570
Special District Governments, PE120
Special Interest Inefficiency, EP114
Special Interest Politics, PE389
Special Interest State, PE376
Special Interests, see Interest Groups
Special Rules, LC151
Specialist Organizations, OB366
Specialties, XX86
Speculation Theorems, SC507
Speeches from the Throne, LE59
Spending Decisions, LE477
Spending Policy, EP769
Spending Preferences, EP147
Spillovers, PE71
Spiral Model, AB247, DC144, PA86
Spiral of Silence, PC31, PC41, PC53, PC65, PC66, PC81
Spite Dilemma, OB390
Split Delegations, LE290
Split Labor Market, MP377
Split Party Control, PP205
Split Ticket Voting, CP191, LE5, SC332
Sponsors, EP553
Sponsorship, PA68
Spooner, Lysander, SC28
Sports, XX12, XX24, XX154, XX163
Sri Lanka, PP423
Stability, CP331, ET254, IR489, IR857, LE35, LE91, LE437, PE331, PE332, PE356, PP509, PS63, PS130, PS131, SC51, SC554, SC632
Stability Analysis, DP82
Stability of Punishment Hypothesis, LC304
Stability Set, SC428
Stabilization Policy, EP34, EP86, EP530, PE125
Stagflation, PE288
Stagnation, DP216, EP204, EP210
Standing Committees, LE222, LE227
Star Wars, IR290, IR316, IR323, LE707
Stare Decisis, LC463
State Aid, SP385, SP427
State Building, CP276
State Capacities, ET307, PA344
State Constitutions, LC97, LC154, also see Constitutions
State Department Country Reports, ET220
State Documents, XX121
State Economic Conditions, PE216
State Economic Development, EP206, EP273
State Efficacy, EP244
State Elections, PE175
State Enterprises, EP311
State Executives, LE43
State Farm, LC418
State Formation, PG242
State Indebtedness, SP409
State Intervention, EP218
State Legislative Communities, LE205
State Legislative Effectiveness, LE490

State Legislative Elections, CP252, LE545, LE571, LE615, PP346, SC288, also see Elections
State Legislative Policies, MP330
State Legislative Reform, LE385
State Legislators, LE323, LE363
State Legislatures, LE343, LE354, LE497, LE555, LE673, PA220
State Making, OB311
State Mandates, SP378
State of the World Message, IR785
State Owned Enterprises, EP33
State Party Delegations, LE622, PP129
State Party Ideology, SP389
State Political Economy, SP315
State Political Ideology, AB144
State Politics, SP306-451/Special Section, PG82, PG123, PG260, PG310
State Population, PP179
State Power, PS127
State Public Policy, PA284, SP338, SP361, SP381, SP415, SP434
State Reorganization, SP418
State Spending, PE113, SP380
State Strength, EP265
State Structures, PS55
State Supreme Courts, LC402, LC423, LC427, LC430, LC475
State Systems, PS11
Statescraft, ET381, IR166, IR657
The State, EP39, ET448, PS19, PS43, PS46, XX402
States (US), LE609, MP274, PA331, PG249, PG292, PG293, PG294, PG304, SP370, SP386, SP387, SP388
State-Sponsored Violence, IR640
Statism, DC209, PS21
Statistical Evidence, LC12, LC78
Statistical Heuristics, PA69
Statistical Inference, LC40
Statistics, XX242, XX402
Status, ET351, ET449
Status Inconsistency, IR817
Status Quo, SC102
Statutory Deadlines, XX1
Statutory Decisions, LC418
Stealing, ET413
Sterotypes, MP36, MP273
Stochastic Behavior, DP9
Stochastic Choice Theory, XX37
Stochastic Diffusion Models, PG96
Stochastic Games, LE693, SC379
Stochastic Models, OB329
Stock Indices, DP136
Stock Market Crash, OB162
Stock Market, EP27, PA322, SC683, XX107, XX247
Storting, LE672, SC765
Stragegic Voting, SC785
Strange Attractors, DP88, DP106
Stranger Violence, LC219
Strategic Analysis, SC720
Strategic Arms Voting, IR339
Strategic Behavior, LC37, SC467, SC802
Strategic Choice Models, PS270
Strategic Communication, PP211
Strategic Contributing, PP85
Strategic Culture, IR78
Strategic Decision Making, DP123
Strategic Defense Initiative, see Star Wars
Strategic Independence, SC383
Strategic Interaction, SC617

Strategic Manipulation, SC769-705/Special Section
Strategic Policy, DP264, IR39
Strategic Politicians, PP183, SC793
Strategic Significance, IR425
Strategic Studies, IR38, IR58
Strategic Threats, IR422
Strategic Triangle, SC402
Strategic Uncertainty, CP154
Strategic Vote Delay, SC787
Strategic Voting, LC430, LE698, SC771, SC779, SC780, SC782, SC795, SC798, SC800
Strategic Weapons Systems, IR517
Strategies, IR606
Strategy, IR41, IR387, LC119, OB337, SC18
Strategy Abandonment, OB27
Strategyproof Collective Choice, SC132
Stratification Ideology, MP44
Stratum Identification, XX129
Strauss, Leo, XX296
Street Level Bureaucracy, LC489, MP391
Stress, LC25, LC200, LE47, LE58, OB11, SP408
Stress Reduction, PC18
Strikes, DC259-347/Special Section, PE11
Strikes of 1877, DC339
Structural Blockage, EP244
Structural Break, EP487
Structural Change, LE477
Structural Cleavages, SP538
Structural Consistency, SC383
Structural Differentiation, IR371
Structural Ethics, ET21
Structural Modeling, XX30
Structural Realignment, PP538
Structural Realism, IR438, IR693, XX266
Structural Theory, CP352, DC154
Structuralism, XX308
Structuralist Urban Theory, SP325
Structure, LE477, OB356
Structure Induced Equilibria, LE267
Structure of the State, PA89
Structured Inequality, MP205
Student Achievement, SP179, SP234, SP238
Student Protests, DC63, DC92, DC241
Styles, TR180
St. Petersburg Paradox, SC579
Subcommittees, LE230, LE232, also see Committees
Subcultures, PG283, SP341
Subcultures of Violence, LC511-523/Special Section
Subgame Perfection, SC379
Subgovernments, LE208, PE344
Subgroups, LE518, LE519
Subjective Communicability, ET12
Subjective Culture, AB210
Subjective Powerlessness, AB71
Subnational Conflict, DC105
Subnational Elections, PP224
Subpresidential Voting, CP200
Subsidies, EP817, PE616, SP390, TR26, TR33
Substantive Representation, MP170
Suburban Competition, PG212
Suburbs, PG70, PG254, SP367, SP403
Succession, LE55, OB282, PS85, SC85

Succession Connection, LE552,
  LE605
Sudden Infant Death Syndrome,
  TR165
Suez Crisis, OB231
Suffrage, MP216, MP267
Suggestions, PC134, PC140
Suicide, IR854, LC360, LC385,
  LE108, PC119, PC151, PE494,
  RP63, RP73, RP76, RP91, RP99,
  RP103, SP141, XX132, XX407
Sunbelt, SP75
Sunspots, DP10, DP200
Super Majority Voting Rules, SC301
Superfund, TR68
Superpowers, IR62, IR276, IR409,
  IR432, IR458, OB211
Supervision, OB81
Supply Elasticity, MP424
Supply of Statistics, EP354
Supply-Side Economics, EP35
Supply-Side Explanations, PP293
Supply-Side Political Business
  Cycle, PE447
Supply-Side Religious Explana-
  tions, RP72
Support, CP30, DC239, LE56, PE190,
  PE194, PE202, PE215, PE224,
  PE289, PP29, PP30, PP365, PS23
Support for Congress, LE453
Support for Political Systems,
  PE288
Support Maximization Models, SC513
Supreme Court, ET354, LC10, LC58,
  LC59, LC64, LC69, LC79, LC80,
  LC84, LC95, LC117, LC147, LC352,
  LC388, LC394, LC395, LC398,
  LC399, LC403, LC404, LC406,
  LC407, LC409, LC412, LC413,
  LC415, LC417, LC418, LC429,
  LC433, LC434, LC436, LC437,
  LC441, LC442, LC444, LC447,
  LC449, LC450, LC454, LC456,
  LC458, LC461, LC462, LC466,
  LC468, LC471, SP28, SP35
Supreme Court Appointments, LC460,
  LC464
Supreme Court Confirmations, LE671
Supreme Court Decisions, LC31,
  LC414, LC427
Supreme Court Hypothesis, LC25
Supreme Court Justices, LC393,
  LC469
Supreme Court Review, LC470
Supreme Soviet, LE28
Surge and Decline, LE504, PP157
Surplus Value, LC238
Surprise Attacks, IR765
Surprise Literature, PS77
Surrogate Contracts, MP294
Surrogate Motherhood, SP135
Survey Data, TR801
Survey Research, LC7
Survey Research Center, AB309,
  AB318, AB318, AB331
Surveys, AB309-337/Special Section
Survival Model, PA176
Survival of Governments, LE91
Suspects, LC481
Suspension of the Rules, LE360
Sustainability, TR64
Sustainable Development, EP269
Sustainable Resources, RP59
Swallowtail Difference Equation,
  DP58
Swarming, SC303
Swarming of Innovations, PA300,
  also see Schumpeterian Waves

Sweden, DP172, OB274, PE213
Swedish Model, PS322, PS323, PS330
Swedish Welfare, SP538
Swindles, PP368
Switzerland, CP75, LC116, PP440,
  PS189, PS207
Symbolic Attitudes, AB35
Symbolic Ethnicity, RP74
Symbolic Interaction, LC481
Symbolic Politics, CP315, PE287,
  SP29
Symbolic Racism, MP93, MP128,
  MP140, MP445, MP498
Symbolic Religiosity, RP74
Symbolism, AB214
Symbols, PC69
System Interactions, DP160
System Performance, PP509
System Stability, PS70
System Support, XX396
Systematic Beliefs, AB326
Systemic Polarization, IR620
Systemic Rejection, XX220
Systemic Theories, IR683
Systems, XX372
Systems Analysis, DP162, DP141,
  DP159, LC425, PA66, PP63

Tactical Voting, SC785
Tactics, SC26
Taiping Rebellion, DC158
Taiwan, TR30
Talk, SC770
Talmud, SC439
Targeting, SP405
Tariffs, EP792-872/Special Section
Taste, AB376, DP61
Tatonnement, DP98
Tax Amnesties, EP680
Tax Breaks, EP729
Tax Burden, EP767
Tax Committees, LE208
Tax Competition, EP757
Tax Complexity, EP728
Tax Compliance, EP682, EP756,
  EP774
Tax Control, EP760
Tax Cycles, PE490
Tax Demand, EP733
Tax Elasticity, EP710
Tax Equality, EP763
Tax Evasion, EP709, EP716, EP754,
  EP784, EP791, RP117
Tax Fairness, EP716
Tax Incidence, EP557
Tax Innovation, EP692
Tax Progressivity, EP679, EP782
Tax Rates, EP350, EP700, EP749,
  EP790
Tax Reduction, OB291
Tax Referenda, EP702
Tax Reform, EP501, EP684, EP705,
  EP719, EP721, EP734, EP777,
  EP787, EP789
Tax Revolt, EP708, EP713, EP750,
  EP751, EP760, EP778, EP780, PE60
Tax Structure, EP743, OB298
Taxes, EP678-791/Special Section,
  DC299, EP254, EP115, EP318,
  EP365, EP424, EP444, EP525,
  EP823, ET125, LE208, PE133,
  PE253, PG186, SC259, SC528,
  SC679
Teachers, DC298, LC243, PP271
Teaching Assignments, SP211
Teaching Effectiveness, SP151,
  SP205
Technical Disputes, PA129

Technical Systems, TR183
Techno-Economic Transformations,
  DP173
Technological Adoption, PA303
Technological Change, DC327,
  PA261, PA316, SP142, also see
  Schumpeterian Waves
Technological Controversies, TR167
Technological Forecasting, TR161
Technological Innovation, see
  Innovation
Technological Leadership, EP120,
  TR143
Technological Progress, TR138,
  TR139, TR149
Technological Risk, LC25, SC682,
  SC705
Technological Transformation,
  EP482
Technology, TR137-192/Special
  Section, DP188, EP219, EP258,
  EP390, LC28, PA269
Techno-Scientific Activity, TR186
Teenage Mothers, PG87, SP461,
  SP494
Telecommunications, EP627, PC35,
  PS227
Telephone Rates, EP602
Telephones, PA281
Televised Speeches, LE185
Televising Legislatures, LE381
Television, PC114, PC174, PC118,
  PC123, PC141, PC156, PC165,
  PC171, PC199, PC210
Television Docudrama, PC172
Television Markets, PC186
Television Networks, PC46
Television News, PC92, PC101,
  PC102, PC103, PC119, PC130,
  PC161, PC164, PC214, PC221
Television Regulation, EP561
Television Viewing, PC40
Television Violence, PC79
Temperance, SP93
Temperature of Economic Systems,
  EP13
Temporal Aggregation, OB258
Tenure, SP159, SP201, SP202, SC230
Tenure Distributions, OB345
Term Limits, LE561, LE581, LE593,
  LE598, LE562, LE601, LE603,
  LE604, LE610, LE612, LE613,
  PE164, SC285
Termination, PA224
Termination of War, IR709
Terms of Trade, EP792
Territorial Change, IR647
Territorial Dimensions in
  Politics, IR871
Territorial Disputes, IR711
Territorial Management, MP501
Territorial Markers, PG57
Territorial Minorities, PG5
Territoriality, IR77, IR861, PG2,
  PG55, PG68, PG307
Terrorism, DC348-378/Special
  Section, IR403, IR640
Tertiary, EP257
Test Score Decline, EP66
Texas, CP99, LC155, MP463, PG123,
  PP360
Thatcher, Margaret, PE546
Thatcherism, CP254, PE534
Theft, LC256
Theology and Money, RP85
Theoretical Physics, TR145
Theorizing, IR55
Theory, XX38, XX58, XX207

Theory Acceptance, XX380
Theory Choice, XX413
Theory Construction, XX349, XX380
Theory of Justice, ET247, ET249,
   ET252, ET253, ET257, ET258,
   ET271, ET288, ET294, ET306,
   ET310, ET322
Theory of Value, ET86
Thermodynamic Model, DP27, EP13
Think Tanks, PA61
Thinking, ET2, PA175
Third Parties, LE502, PP445,
   PP460, PP474, PP483, PP516
Third Party Voting, PP446
Third Republic, SC194
Third World, DP283, EP263, EP305,
   EP334, EP335, EP373, EP391,
   EP439, EP472, EP495, EP838,
   IR222, IR231, IR297, IR519,
   IR520, IR538, MP405, PE332,
   PG153, PP536, PS226, PS321
Third World Foreign Policy, IR172
Third World Rivalries, IR297
Thomas, Clarence, LC455, LC456,
   MP331
Thomas Theorem, XX241
Thought Reform, DC133
Thoughtless Rationality, XX91
Thrasymmachos, ET344
Threat, DC27, DC70, IR228, IR694,
   LC269, LC399, MP118, SC389,
   SC423, SC800
Threat Hypothesis, DC102
Threat Perception, ET205
Three Mile Island, CP9, TR176
Thresholds, DP110, ET189
Throwing the Rascals Out, CP278,
   LE610
Ticket Splitting, CP200, CP353,
   CP354
Tiebout Hypothesis, CP98, EP788,
   PG146, PG147, PG151, PG154,
   PG155, PG172, PG174, PG182,
   PG186, PG193, PG195, PG197,
   PG199, PG208, SP359
Time, EP72, ET148, LC135, LC433,
   PE371, PG36, PG58, SC81, SC151,
   SC197, SP435, XX114, XX166,
   XX368
Time Allocation, XX111, XX190
Time and Frequency Domains, DP2
Time Barriers, XX314
Time Binding, LC433
Time Consistency, SC379
Time Dependence, XX10
Time Dynamics, PE522
Time Inconsistency, LC135
Time Minimization, PG58
Time Preference, XX87, XX265
Time Pressure, ET148, IR763
Time Reversibility, XX61
Time Series, DC304, DP20, DP30,
   DP33, DP87, DP122, IR643
Time Series Cross Sectional Data,
   XX31
Timing, EP536
Timing Effect, SC81
Timing of Domestic Choice, LE149
Tipping Point, MP77
Tips, ET159
Title VII, LC9
Tobacco Producers, TR14
Token Contributions, OB386
Tokenism, MP42, MP168, MP425
Tokyo Trade Round, EP827
Tolerance, ET450-484/Special
   Section, MP417, MP434, RP109
Tong, James, DC339

Topological Functions, SC23, SC74,
   SC500
Topological Structure, XX392
Tort Law, LC5
Total Political History, XX201
Total Quality Management, OB79
Tourism, EP26, XX17
Tournaments, SC312
Tower of Babel, MP452
Towns, PS119
Toynbee, Arnold, RP15
Trade, EP792-872/Special Section,
   EP90, EP469
Trade Balance, EP835
Trade Barriers, PE606
Trade Flows, EP805
Trade-GNP Ratio, EP866
Trade Liberalization, EP859
Trade Negotiations, EP798
Trade Patterns, EP810
Trade Policy, EP796, EP797, EP820,
   EP822, EP841, EP844, EP845,
   EP846, EP864, EP849
Trade Preferences, EP868
Trade Restrictions, EP858
Trade Sanctions, EP850
Trade Unions, DC263, DC272, DC291,
   DC311, DC341, DC343
Trade Wars, EP807
Trading Blocs, EP822
Traditional Values, AB357
Tragedy of the Commons, EP395,
   IR640, PE561, PP362, SC46, SC47,
   SC52, SC67, TR3, TR126
Transactions Costs, LC198, LE422,
   SC84
Transfer Policies, ET120, SP519
Transfer Seeking, PE356, PE583
Transfer Society, PE587
Transfers, PE588
Transition, PS285
Transition Societies, PS121
Transitivity, XX83
Transnational Capitalism, PE52
Transnational Coalitions, IR157
Transnational Economics, EP819
Transnational Regulation, EP579
Transportation, EP45, EP637,
   LE577, SP440, TR2, TR6
Trapped Administrators, OB85
Travel Times, PG36
Treasury Bill Rates, DP102
Treaties, IR225
Treaty Compliance, PS47
Trend Surface Analysis, DP49
Trial Court Elections, CP222
Trial Courts, LC51
Triple Alliance, IR221
Triple Entente, IR221
Trotsky, Leon, DC134, DC186
Trotskyism, DC186
Trucking, EP662
Truman, David, PE377
Truman, Harry, LE110, LE156
Trust, ET15, ET59, ET159, ET250,
   LE42, MP360, MP382, OB46, PP199,
   SC18
Trust in Government, CP10, CP22,
   CP23, CP40, CP60, CP85, LE114
Tuition Tax Credits, SP256
Tullock, Gordon, LC124, LC140
Turbulent Field Environment, DP13
Turmoil, PP510
Turning Points, DP30, DP229
Turnout, CP103-184/Special
   Section, LE584, MP147, MP164,
   MP187, MP239, PE269, PP186,
   RP160, SC331

Turnover, LE537-617/Special
   Section, CP328, LC429, LE67,
   LE347, LE576, LE590, LE609,
   MP156, MP458, OB142, OB345
Turnpikes, PE537, TR5
Two-Level Games, IR151, SC188,
   SC437
Two-Party Systems, PP319, PP448,
   PP459, also see Political
   Parties
Two Person Games, LC305
Two Presidents, LE151, LE171
Two-Stage Voting Systems, PP477,
   PP507, SC279
Two-Thirds Rule, DP7, PP106
Type II Errors, TR57
Tyrannicide, DC356

Ultimatum, SC422
Unanimity, SC318
Unanimity Rule, SC303
Unanimous Consent, LE248, LE313,
   LE417, LE476
Unanticipated Money, PE480
Unbelievable Promises, PP8
Uncertainty, SC661-734/Special
   Section, CP154, EP518, ET59,
   ET155, IR446, IR738, LE100,
   PA275, PE524, PP125, PP223,
   SC281, SC302, TR156
Uncertainty Resolution, SC674
Underclass, SP262, SP279, SP294,
   SP295, SP300
Underdevelopment, DC115, EP203,
   EP239, EP244, EP291, EP313,
   PA200, PG239, PP350
Underdog, AB380, CP234, LC470,
   SC467
Underemployment, MP32
Underground Economic Systems, PS38
Underground Government, EP758,
   OB241
Understanding, XX329
Unemployment, EP154-196/Special
   Section, AB343, EP429, EP540,
   EP543, LC179, LC183, LC226,
   LC262, LC276, LE88, PE206,
   PE213, PE217, PE275, PE487,
   PE488, PE493
Unemployment Compensation, EP158
Unequality, EP155
Unfairness, ET341
Unified Field Theory, IR169
Unified Government, PE239
Uniform Crime Report, LC207
Union Elections, DC334
Union-Nonunion Wage Gap, DC305
Union Shop, DC267
Unions, DC259-347/Special Section,
   EP59, EP107, EP172, OB308,
   OB343, PE447, PS79
Unit Roots, DP40, EP153, EP183,
   EP435, EP489, PA71
Unit Rule, SC255
Unit Solidarity, IR472
United Kingdom, AB376, AB379,
   AB380, CP199, CP203, CP237,
   CP254, CP256, CP284, CP340,
   DC302, DC313, DC332, DP202,
   DP208, EP6, ET48, EP171, EP416,
   EP614, EP739, EP870, ET400,
   IR352, LC284, LE143, LE305,
   LE415, LE454, LE458, LE524,
   MP133, MP188, MP290, MP289,
   MP373, OB226, PA17, PA25, PA44,
   PA89, PE28, PE31, PE41, PE54,
   PE61, PE195, PE210, PE212,
   PE215, PE236, PE255, PE265,

PE266, PG13, PG39, PG259, PG273,
   PG287, PG288, PP26, PP159,
   PP255, PP257, PP293, PP315,
   PP482, PP492, PS239, RP134,
   SC260, SP273, TR65, XX278
United Nations, IR10, IR31, IR57,
   IR140, IR195, IR686, IR847,
   IR865, LE656, LE682, PP536
Universal Instability Theorem,
   SC464
Universal Legislator, ET418, LC137
Universalism, ET69, ET96, LE512
Universals, ET36
Universities, IR464, SP204, SP206,
   SP230, SP244
Unorganized Interests, PE323
Unrest, DC22, DC61, PG102
Unseen Hand, PE85
Unsolved Problems, SC63
Unstable Systems, IR268
Upheaval, LE636
Urban Africa, PA191
Urban Citizenship, SP441
Urban Crisis, SP343, SP399, SP442
Urban Disorders, DC235
Urban Elections, MP149, MP175
Urban Form, SP411
Urban Government, PE490, SP332
Urban Growth, EP202, EP744, SP319,
   SP419, SP426, see Economic
   Growth
Urban Land Use, SP412
Urban Life, SP365
Urban Performance, SP424
Urban Policy, SP317, SP395, SP396,
   SP397, SP436
Urban Political Economy, SP323
Urban Political Systems, MP399,
   MP447
Urban Politics, LC446, LC484,
   MP113, MP145, MP486, MP524,
   SP413
Urban Poverty, SP271
Urban Redevelopment, SP414
Urban Reform, PC110, PP377
Urban Regimes, EP285
Urban Research, SP431
Urban Services, SP311, SP383,
   SP398, SP429, SP437
Urban Systems, SP324
Urban Theory, SP439
Urban Violence, LC242
Urbanization, EP386, ET483, LC235,
   MP141, PG42, PG153, SP326,
   SP327, SP341
Urbanization-Party Competition
   Hypothesis, PP320
Usury, PE14, RP46
Us, XX88
Utilitarianism, ET284, ET40,
   IR585, SC69, SC81, SC495
Utility, DC82, DC174, IR744,
   LC401, SC53, SC149
Utility Functions, AB3, ET163,
   PE554, SC107, SC664, SC666,
   SC673, SC686, SC712, SP211
Utilization of Policy Information,
   PA210-257/Special Section
Utopia, XX197, XX316

V Curve, DC29
Vague Statements, SC354
Validity, PA221, XX270
Value Change, AB343, AB354, AB368,
   AB381, AB382, AB385, IR553
Value Cleavages, PE193
Value Cycles, DP266
Value Differences, DC17, DC18

Value Dilemmas, LC492
Value Judgments, ET101
Value Orientations, AB375
Value Pluralism, AB213
Value Priorities, AB379
Value Rationales, MP308
Value Self-Confrontation, AB134
Value Terms, ET77
Value Trends, AB363
Values, AB338-392/Special Section,
   AB120, AB134, AB147, AB293,
   DC17, DC18, DP245, DP266, EP55,
   ET5, ET44, ET47, ET50, ET63,
   ET101, ET223, ET273, ET303,
   ET340, ET388, ET422, IR93,
   IR470, IR694, LC63, LC146, LC321,
   LC456, LC492, LC512, LE43,
   LE187, LE441, MP48, MP127,
   MP308, PA77, PA111, PP273,
   PP294, PS125, SC61, SC106,
   SC662, SP169, XX35
Vanishing Marginals, LE538, LE569,
   LE575
Vanishing Species, TR47
Veblen's Theory of Government
   Failure, EP113, EP647, XX350
Veil of Ignorance, ET315
Venezuela, CP21
Verbal Behavior, PC43
Verdict Correctness, LC72
Vertical Constraint, TR179
Vertical Trading, EP251
Veterans, SC703
Veterans Benefits, PE407, PE463
Veto Overrides, PE88
Veto Players, SC804
Vetoes, LE38, LE146, LE176, LE177,
   LE180, LE248, LE494, PE88
Vice, LC44, SP9, SP309
Vice President, CP338, LE20
Victim-Offender Dynamics, LC173,
   LC273
Victim Surveys, LC172
Victimization, LC191, LC194,
   LC221, LC224, LC237, LC246,
   LC253, LC254, LC266, LC279,
   LC294, LC364
Vietnam Generation, IR524
Vietnam War, AB229, AB243, AB251,
   AB272, AB277, AB300, IR506,
   IR508, IR633, IR674, IR714,
   IR760, IR761, IR793, IR804,
   LE112, PC167, XX269
Viewer Aggression, PC114
Vigilantism, DC68
La Violencia, DC179
Violence, DC6, DC12, DC24, DC28,
   DC29, DC38, DC40, DC45, DC53,
   DC56, DC57, DC59, DC60, DC64,
   DC66, DC68, DC69, DC73, DC74,
   DC77, DC79, DC81, DC83, DC84,
   DC85, DC86, DC89, DC90, DC94,
   DC95, DC101, DC141, DC177,
   DC199, DC204, DC236, DC253,
   DC256, DC285, DC331, DC351,
   DC363, DC367, IR394, IR805,
   LC173, LC200, LC202, LC225,
   LC231, LC235, LC236, LC275,
   LC341, LC385, LC478, LC512,
   LC520, LC522, MP96, PC52, PC79,
   PC114, PC116, PC141, PC142,
   PC156, PG244, PG327, PP509
Violent Attitudes, LC513, LC515
Violent Nations, IR671
Virtue, ET95, ET111, ET445
Virtuous Circle Model, SP339
Voice, DC287, PE539

Voluntary Associations, OB371-400/
   Special Section
Voluntary Contributions, PE517
Voluntary Cooperation, ET171
Voluntary Giving, ET142
Voluntary Provision, PE537
Volunteer Dilemma, OB385, OB397
Von Neumann-Morgenstern Decision
   Markets, ET285
Vote Counting Schemes, SC306, also
   see Electoral Systems
Vote Delay, SC787
Vote Manipulation, SC769
Vote-Popularity Function, PE251
Vote Price, PE298
Vote Selling, CP343
Vote Trading, LE688-723/Special
   Section, SC782
Voter Information, CP218
Voter Mobilization, PP321
Voter Registration Act, AB196
Voter Transition Models, CP249,
   CP253
Voting Behavior, CP185-354/Special
   Section, AB130, AB164, AB191,
   AB324, CP204, CP205, CP211,
   CP112, CP122, CP124, CP126,
   CP166, CP185, CP231, CP238,
   CP240, CP258, CP262, CP277,
   CP279, CP283, CP299, CP301,
   CP302, CP308, CP310, CP313,
   CP325, CP322, CP330, CP334,
   CP336, CP346, CP350, LC112,
   LC430, LE539, LE616, LE662,
   MP65, MP193, MP133, MP150,
   MP152, MP200, OB255, OB317,
   PC16, PC20, PC196, PE191, PE201,
   PE219, PE225, PE226, PE227,
   PE228, PE231, PE232, PE240,
   PE291, PE300, PE569, PG30,
   PG113, PG116, PG128, PG129,
   PP48, PP57, PP196, PP227, PP380,
   PP427, RP151, SC150, SC312,
   SC315, SC347, SC366, SC518,
   SC747
Voting Blocs, LC122, LC395
Voting Bodies, SC17
Voting Calculus, CP305
Voting Change, CP333, LE359
Voting Costs, CP115, CP272
Voting Cues, CP298
Voting Cycles, SC571
Voting Equilibria, SC759
Voting Fraud, PP409
Voting Games, SC391, SC421, SC426,
   SC427, SC428, SC460, SC466,
   SC468, SC738, SC760, SC764
Voting Institutions, SC256
Voting Market, CP221
Voting Paradoxes, SC545, SC546,
   SC540, SC549, SC564, SC569,
   SC578
Voting Power, SC237, SC304, SC346
Voting Procedures, SC269, SC273,
   SC320, SC796
Voting Rights, SC496
Voting Rights Act, MP168, MP180,
   MP186, MP192, MP410, MP425
Voting Rights Legislation, MP62
Voting Rules, SC301, also see
   Electoral Systems
Voting Stability, LE546
Voting Strategies, LE658, LE722
Voting Systems, see Electoral
   Systems
Voting with One's Feet, PG147,
   also see Tiebout Hypothesis
Voting with the Wings, SC303

Wackersdorf, LE61
Wafflers, LE419
Wage Bargaining, ET357
Wage Differences, MP6
Wage Gap, DC305, EP184, EP459,
    MP346
Wages, DP220, DP254, EP411, EP417,
    EP423, EP426, EP453, EP469,
    EP489, LC249, OB77, also see
    Income
Wagner's Law, OB233, OB236, OB239,
    OB246, OB258, OB264, OB273,
    OB289, OB305, OB322
Wales, MP499, PG290
Wallace, George, MP60, MP61,
    MP121, PG128, RP167
Wallerstein, Michael, EP324, IR862
War, IR609-833/Special Section,
    AB243, AB244, AB277, AB278,
    AB289, AB290, AB291, AB292,
    AB296, AB298, CP300, DC19, DC66,
    DC96, DC128, DC178, DC191, DP5,
    DP60, DP129, DP252, DP253,
    DP254, DP257, DP269, DP277,
    DP278, EP294, EP367, EP493,
    EP494, EP499, EP500, ET230,
    ET371, IR245, IR249, IR251,
    IR254, IR272, IR273, IR292,
    IR314, IR329, IR335, IR365,
    IR373, IR453, IR469, IR545,
    IR569, IR576, IR584, IR596,
    IR611, IR612, IR829, IR854,
    LC225, MP225, OB210, OB311,
    PA267, PE316, PG79, PG89, PS10,
    PS147, SC39, SP141, TR186
War Cues, IR614
War Cycles, DP253, DP277
War Diffusion, IR654, IR787, IR800
War Expectations, AB278
War Initiation, IR763
War Movies, IR537
War of 1812, OB210
War on Drugs, SP94, SP137
War on Poverty, SP260, SP277
War Participation, IR786
War Proneness, IR619, IR672
War Toys, IR537
War Trap, IR624, IR625, IR727,
    IR755, SC726
War Trauma, EP433
War Weariness Hypothesis, IR723
Warfare-Welfare State, SP466
Warrior Tradition, IR503
Werr's Power Function, LC176
Washington behind Closed Doors,
    PC172
Washington Community, LC58
Waste Disposal Facility, PG181
Water, CP99
Water Pollution, TR119
Water Resources Development, LE695
Watergate, LE102, PP233, PP365
Watergate Tapes, LE154
Weakness of Will, SC204
Wealth, EP19, EP449, EP471, EP518,
    EP521, LC99, SC425, SC686, also
    see Income
Weapons Technology, IR280
Weapons Testing, ET54

Weber, Max, PE29, SC289, XX333
Weber Problem, PG64
Weberian Hypothesis, ET447
Wedgewood, Josiah, OB348
Weighted Voting Systems, DP128,
    SC235, also see Electoral
    Systems
Welfare, SP452-554/Special
    Section, AB196, CP159, DC218,
    EP214, EP255, EP263, EP781,
    MP76, OB380, PE304, PG198, SP5,
    SP290, SP298, SP302
Welfare Benefits, SP527, SP530
Welfare Expansion, SP487, SP551
Welfare Fraud, SP553
Welfare Participation, SP480,
    SP491
Welfare Programs, SC513
Welfare State, CP159, EP58, EP402,
    EP445, ET423, IR355, OB292,
    OB308, OB319, PE257, PE269,
    SP453, SP454, SP455, SP456,
    SP466, SP473, SP474, SP477,
    SP481, SP483, SP485, SP511,
    SP518, SP525, SP528, SP529,
    SP534, SP539, SP543, SP545,
    SP549
Welfare Stigma, SP507
Well-Being, AB340
Western Europe, DC226, EP242,
    EP578, ET462, LC474, LE74, LE98,
    LE492, MP348, MP350, OB313,
    PC89, PC90, PE34, PE580, PG5,
    PG68, PG248, PG324, PG328,
    PP304, PP336, PP337, PP495,
    PP513, PP523, PS172, PS303,
    RP176, SC196, TR29, TR117, XX96,
    XX199
Westward Expansion, PG255
We, XX88
When Plans Fail, DC120
When Promises Fail, RP73
Whistleblowing, ET415, ET416,
    PP414, PP438
White Collar Crime, LC165, LC211
White Flight, MP77
White House, PE388, PP226
White House Social Invitations,
    LE631
Whites, RP167
Who Governs, PE197
Why the Best Person Rarely Wins,
    SC481
Widows in the US Congress, MP277
Wight, Martin, RP15
Wildavsky, Aaron, PE108, PE132,
    PS301
Wilderness, TR103
Wildlife, TR104
Wilson, Woodrow, ET444, LE350
Window of Vulnerability, IR437
Wine Industry, OB336
Wish Fulfillment, XX389
Witch Hunts, RP78, RP80, XX120,
    XX33
Wives, AB52
Wollheim's Paradox, SC587
Women, MP201-359/Special Section
    LC300, LE613, MP146, MP151,

MP171, MP174, MP177, MP183,
    MP222, MP346, MP356, MP357,
    MP509, SP76
Women and Politics Research, MP355
Women Candidates, MP156, MP172,
    MP176, MP287
Women in the Military, MP308
Women Legislators, SP20
Women's Christian Temperance
    Union, OB337
Women's Groups, MP223
Women's Involvement in Crime,
    LC278
Women's Morality, MP319
Women's Movement, MP227, MP255,
    MP318, PC162
Women's Rights, MP229, MP233,
    MP281, SP30
Work, EP442, EP610
Work Climates, ET110
Work Force Migration, PG140
Work Performance, DP57
Work Relationships, OB24
Work Satisfaction, OB127
Work Sociology, OB125, OB130
Work Stoppages, DC298
Work Values, AB362
Workers, PG205
Working Class, CP340, DP206, EP24
Working Day, SP547
Working Styles, LE321
Working Women, MP207
Workplace Dispute Resolution,
    MP251
World Capitalist System, IR862
World Economy, EP270, PS216
World Order, IR371, IR841, MP52,
    MP472
World Politics, IR32
World Regions, IR865
World Society, XX162
World Systems, IR834-873/Special
    Section, DC255, DP124, EP383,
    EP865, IR240, IR414, PS75,
    PS290, XX197
World Trade, EP829, also see Trade
World Values, AB378
World View, SP52
World War I, IR812
World War II, EP294, LC280
Writing to Congressmen, CP28
Wrongdoing, ET36

Xenophobia, PG244, PG253, PG327

Yes-No Voting, CP229
Young Voters, AB114
Youth Crime, LC210
Youth Culture, RP92
Youth Protests, DC209
Youth Violence, LC523
Yucatan, PP387
Yugoslavia, PG234
Yuppies, AB349, AB352, AB361

Zero Base Budgeting, PE68
Zero Sum Society, PA139
Zoning, PG187, PG201, PG202
Zurich, DP244

About the Compiler

GREGORY G. BRUNK has graduate degrees in political science, economics, and history. He has published over sixty articles in the social sciences and the humanities and half a dozen books, most recently co-authoring *Understanding Attitudes about War: Modeling Moral Judgments* (1996). One major focus of his current research is the relationship between complexity theory and nonlinear political dynamics.

ISBN 0-313-30259-6

HARDCOVER BAR CODE